PrincetonReview.com

D1309156

BEST 296
BUSINESS SCHOOLS

2009 EDITION

Nedda Gilbert
and the Staff
of The Princeton Review

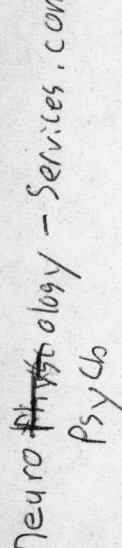

Neuro Physiology - Services.com
Psych

Random House, Inc.
New York

The Princeton Review, Inc.
2315 Broadway
New York, NY   10024
E-mail: bookeditor@review.com

ISBN: 978-0-375-42882-1

VP, Publisher: Robert Franek
Editor: Laura Braswell
Senior Production Editor: M. Tighe Wall
Executive Director, Print Production: Scott Harris
Account Manager: David Soto

Printed in the United States of America.

9 8 7 6 5 4 3 2 1

2009 Edition

ACKNOWLEDGMENTS

This book absolutely would not have been possible without the help of my husband, Paul. With each edition of this guide, his insights and support have been invaluable—this book continues to be as much his as it is mine. That said, I also need to thank my twelve-year-old daughter, Kaela, and her eight-year-old sister, Lexi, for enduring all the time I have spent immersed in this project.

A big thanks goes to Tom Meltzer and Anna Weinberg for their smart and savvy profile writing. The following people were also instrumental in the completion of this book: Scott Harris, M. Tighe Wall, Laura Braswell, David Soto, Ben Zelevansky, Jen Adams, Candace Pinson, Kristin O'Toole, Lana Kitto, and Seamus Mullarkey for putting all the pieces together; the sales staff at The Princeton Review, Josh Escott; Robert Franek and Young Shin, as well as Alicia Ernst and John Katzman, for giving me the chance to write this book; and to the folks at Random House, who helped this project reach fruition.

Thanks go to Kristin Hansen (Tuck '01) and Matt Camp (Tuck '02), and to Ramona Payne and all the folks at The Diversity Pipeline Alliance. I am also grateful for the unique insights provided by Cathy Crane-Moley, Stanford Graduate School of Business, Class of '92; Patricia Melnikoff and Chiara Perry, Harvard Business School, Class of '92; Caroline Grossman, University of Chicago Graduate School of Business, Class of '03; Sara Weiss, MIT Sloan School of Management, Class of '04; and Stephen Hazelton, MIT Sloan School of Management, Class of '05. Thanks are also due to the business school folks who went far out of their way to provide essential information. They continue to make this book relevant and vital.

Linda Baldwin, Director of Admissions, The Anderson School, UCLA

Derek Bolton, Assistant Dean and Director of Admissions, Stanford University School of Business

Eileen Chang, former Associate Director of Admissions, Harvard Business School

Allan Friedman, Director of Communications and Public Relations, University of Chicago

Wendy Hansen, Associate Director of Admissions, Stanford Business School

Stacey Kole, Deputy Dean for the full-time MBA Program and clinical professor of Economics, University of Chicago Graduate School of Business

Steven Lubrano, Assistant Dean and Director of the MBA Program, Tuck School of Business

Rose Martinelli, former Director of Admissions and Financial Aid, The Wharton School MBA Program

Jon McLaughlin, Assistant MBA Admissions Director, Sloan School of Management, MIT

Julia Min, Executive Director of MBA Admissions, UC—Berkeley, Haas School of Business

Jeanne Wilt, Assistant Dean of Admissions and Career Development, Michigan

Linda Meehan, Assistant Dean for Admissions, Columbia University

CONTENTS

INTRODUCTION

A RETURN TO OUR ROOTS

Over the past 14 years, The Princeton Review has annually published a guide to business schools. For the early editions of the guide, we collected opinion surveys from thousands of students at a select group of graduate business schools as well as school statistics from school administrators that include enrollment and demographic figures, tuition, and the average GMAT scores of entering students. We used the students' opinions to craft descriptive narratives of the schools they attended and reported the statistics in the sidebars of those narrative profiles.

For the 2001–2004 editions of this guide, we discontinued collecting opinion surveys from students and writing narrative descriptions of the schools; instead we focused solely on collecting and reporting school statistics. While we were able to report statistics for many more business schools in the new format (the last [2000] edition of the guide with narrative descriptions profiled only 80 schools, and the first edition of the statistics-only guide profiled 372 schools), we learned over the next few years that readers are interested in more than just school-reported statistics. They want to read what the experts—current graduate business school students—have to say about the experiences of today's graduate business student. They want from-the-horse's-mouth accounts of what's great (*and* what's not) at each school.

So in 2005 we decided to reintroduce the student survey-driven descriptive narrative, offering students a more intimate look at the inner workings of each school, and we've continued with this approach ever since.

We also brought back several top 10 lists that rank the profiled schools according to various metrics (more on the rankings later). You'll find these rankings on page 53.

Taken together, we believe that these candid student opinions, school statistics, and rankings provide a unique and helpful resource to help you decide what business schools to apply to. But let us stress that we hope that this book will not be the *only* resource you turn to when making this expensive (both in terms of time and treasure) decision to enter a graduate business program. Do additional research on the Internet and in newspapers, magazines, and other periodicals. Talk to Admissions Officers and current students at the programs that interest you. If at all possible, visit the campuses you are seriously considering. But treat the advice of all these resources (including ours) as you would treat advice from anyone regarding any situation: as input that reflects the values and opinions of others as you *form your own opinion*.

TWO TYPES OF ENTRIES

For each of the 445 business programs in this book, you will find one of two possible types of entries: a two-page profile with lots of descriptive text and statistics, or a straight statistical listing. Our descriptive profiles are driven primarily by 1) comments business students provide in response to open-ended questions on our student survey, and 2) our own statistical analysis of student responses to the many multiple-choice questions on the survey. While many business students complete a survey unsolicited by us at http://survey.review.com, in the vast majority of cases we rely on business school administrators to get the word out about our survey to their students. In the ideal scenario, the business school administration sends a Princeton Review-authored e-mail to all business students with an embedded link to our survey website (again, http://survey.review.com). If for some reason there are restrictions that prevent the administration from contacting the entire graduate business school student body on behalf of an outside party, they often help us find other ways to notify students of the fact that we are seeking their opinions, such as advertising in business student publications or posting on business student community websites. In almost all cases, when the administration is cooperative, we are able to collect opinions from a sufficient number of students to produce an accurate descriptive profile and ratings of its business school.

There is a group of business school administrators, however, that doesn't agree with us that current business school student opinions presented in descriptive profile and rankings formats are useful to prospective business school students. Administrators at the many AACSB-accredited business schools not appearing with two-page descriptive profiles are a part of this group. They either ignored our multiple attempts to contact them in order to request their assistance in notifying their students about our survey, or they simply refused to work with us at all. While we would like to be able to write a descriptive profile each of these many schools anyway, we won't do so with minimal business student opinion.

So if you are a prospective business school student and would like to read current business student opinion about schools that do not appear with a two-page descriptive profile, contact the schools and communicate this desire to them. (We include contact information in each of the business school data listings.) If you are a current business student at one of the many AACSB-accredited business schools without a two-page descriptive profile, please don't send us angry letters; instead, go to http://survey.review.com, complete a survey about your school, and tell all of your fellow students to do the same.

You will find statistics for business schools whose administrators were willing to report their school statistics to us but unwilling to allow us to survey their students under the school's name in the section of the book entitled "Business School Data Listings."

One more thing to note about the different entries: The majority of our various rankings lists are based wholly or partly on student feedback to our survey. Only one top 10 ranking, The Toughest to Get Into, is based on school-reported statistics alone. So while *any* of the 444 programs listed in the book may appear on that list, *only those schools with two-page descriptive profiles will appear on all other rankings lists.*

BUT SOME THINGS NEVER CHANGE

Admission to the business school of your choice, especially if your choice is among the most selective programs, will require your absolute best shot. One way to improve your chances is to make sure you apply to schools that are a good fit—and the comments provided by students in our descriptive profiles will provide more insight into the personality of each school than does its glossy view book.

In addition, you'll find plenty of useful information in Part I of this book on how to get in to business school and what to expect once you arrive. You'll find out what criteria are used to evaluate applicants and who decides your fate. You will also hear directly from admissions officers on what dooms an application and how to ace the interview. We've even interviewed deans at several of the top schools to share with you their take on recent events, including trends in business, b-school applications, recruitment, and placement.

Again, it is our hope that you will consult our profiles as a resource when choosing a list of schools that suit your academic and social needs, and that our advice is helpful to you during the application process. Good luck!

HOW WE PRODUCE THIS BOOK

In August 1999, we published *The Best 80 Business Schools, 2000 Edition*. By the time the 2001 edition of the guide was published, we had shifted our focus from student opinion-driven profiles of a select number of schools to more data-driven profiles of every graduate business school accredited by the AACSB. Although we continue to present readers with data from 444 accredited graduate b-school programs, we have reintroduced the student survey-based descriptive profile. In order to clarify our position, intent, and methodology, we've created a series of questions and answers regarding the collection of data and the production of our descriptive profiles.

How do we choose which b-schools to survey and profile? And why do some competitive schools have only a data listing?

Any business school that is AACSB-accredited and offers a Master of Business Administration degree may have a data listing included in the book, as long as that school provides us with a sufficient amount of school-specific data. In addition, this year we offered each of those accredited schools in which the primary language of instruction is English an opportunity to assist us in collecting online business student surveys.

Some schools were unable to solicit surveys from their students via e-mail due to restrictive privacy policies; others simply chose not to participate. Schools that declined to work with us to survey their students remain in the book, although they do not have a descriptive profile. A school with only a data listing does not suggest that the school is less competitive or compelling; we only separated these profile types into two sections for easier reference. If you're not sure where to find information on a school in which you're interested, you can refer to our alphabetical b-school listing in the back of the book.

There is no fee to be included in this book. If you're an administrator at an accredited business school and would like to have your school included, please send an e-mail to surveysupport@review.com.

What's the AACSB, and by what standards are schools accredited?

The AACSB stands for the Association to Advance Collegiate Schools of Business. In April 2003, the AACSB made some significant changes to its standards for accreditation. In fact, the actual number of standards went from 41 to 21. Some of the changes in accreditation included a shift from requiring a certain number of full-time faculty members with doctorates to a focus on teacher participation. Schools may employ more part-time faculty members if they are actively involved in the students' business education. The onus of both the development of a unique curriculum and the evaluation of the success of that curriculum will fall on each b-school, and schools will be reviewed by the association every five years instead of every ten. As a result of the changes in accreditation standards, a number of schools have been newly accredited or reaccredited.

How were the student surveys collected?

Back in Fall 2005, we contacted Admissions Officers at all accredited graduate b-schools and requested that they help us survey their students by distributing our Princeton Review–authored survey message to the student body via e-mail. The survey message explained the purpose of the survey and contained a link to our online business student survey. We had a phenomenal response from students—at least ten percent of full-time students responded at almost all institutions we surveyed; at many schools, we scored responses from as many as one-third or one-half of the student body—and nearly all students in a few cases.

The surveys are made up of 78 multiple-choice questions and 7 free-response questions, covering 5 sections: About Yourself, Students, Academics, Careers, and Quality of Life. Students may complete the secure online survey at any time and may save their survey responses, returning later, until the survey is complete and ready for submission. Students sign in to the online survey using their school-issued .edu e-mail address to ensure that their response is attributed to the correct school, and the respondent certifies before submission that he or she is indeed a current student enrolled in said program. In addition, an automated message is sent to this address once the student has submitted the survey, and they must click on a link in the e-mail message in order to validate their survey. We also offered a paper version of the survey to a few schools that were unable to e-mail their students regarding our online survey.

We use the resulting responses to craft descriptive profiles that are representative of the respondents' feelings toward the b-school they attend. Although well-written and/or humorous comments are especially appreciated, they would never be used unless they best stated what numerous students have told us.

What about the ranking lists and ratings?

When we decided to bring the student opinion-driven resources back into the fold, we updated our online survey and reconsidered all ranking lists. You will find that only a few of the rankings in this year's book resemble our b-school rankings of yesteryear. We've done our best to include only those topics most vital to success in business school, and we have added a few brand new lists that you will find timely and relevant.

We offer several ranking lists on a variety of considerations, from academic experience to career expectations, to the atmosphere for women and minority students. It must be noted, however, that none of these lists purport to rank the business schools by their overall quality. Nor should any combination of the categories we've chosen be construed as representing the raw ingredients for such a ranking. We have made no attempt to gauge the "prestige" of these schools, and we wonder whether we could accurately do so even if we tried. What we have done, however, is presented a number of lists using information from two very large databases—one of statistical information collected from business schools and another of subjective data gathered via our survey of 11,000 business students at 296 AACSB-accredited business schools. We do believe that there is a right business school for you, and that our rankings, when used in conjunction with our profile of each school, will help you select the best schools to apply to.

New to our rankings this year is our "Best Classroom Experience" list, based on students' answers to survey questions concerning their professors' teaching ability and recognition in the field, the integration of new business trends and practices into course offerings, and the level of student engagement in the classroom.

What do the schools have to say about all this?

Our contact at each school is kept abreast of the profile's status throughout the production process. After establishing a contact through whom we are able to reach online student respondents, we get to work writing our profiles and crunching the data. Once this information has been poured into profile pages, we send a copy of the school's profile to our contact via e-mail and snail mail. We request that the administrator review the data and comments included in the profile, and we invite their corrections to any inaccurate data, or text that may be misrepresentative of overall student opinion. With their suggestions in hand, we revisit survey responses and investigate any such claims of inaccuracy.

We are aware that a general distaste for rankings permeates the business school community, and that top schools have recently backed down from providing the data necessary for such calculations. We agree that overall rankings that purport to decide the "best" overall school are not so helpful to students, and that they may be tainted by the agendas of school administrators hoping to advance their schools' reputations, without taking the necessary measures to actually improve the quality of the school. This is why the meat of our book is the schools' descriptive profiles, which are meant to showcase each school's unique personality. The ranking lists are simply used as reference tools for students looking for a particular attribute in a prospective b-school. We don't claim to be the final word on what school has the best MBA program in the country—that's nearly impossible to determine. We simply relay the messages that the students at each school are sending us, and we are clear about how our rankings are determined.

HOW THIS BOOK IS ORGANIZED

This book is packed with information about business schools, and we want to make sure you know how to find what you're looking for. So here's a breakdown of how this book is organized.

Part I is comprised of several chapters that give you an idea of what to expect at business school and tell you how to put together a winning application.

Part II has our b-school ranking lists. Of the 11 lists, 7 are based entirely on student survey responses; 1 is based solely on institutionally reported data; and 4 are based on a combination of survey responses and statistical information. Along with each list, you will find information about which survey questions or statistical factors were used to calculate the rankings.

Part III contains profiles of all AACSB-accredited graduate schools with MBA programs divided into two sections: those with descriptive profiles based on student surveys, and those with only a statistical listing.

Part III-A: Business School Descriptive Profiles

Please see the sample descriptive profile below.

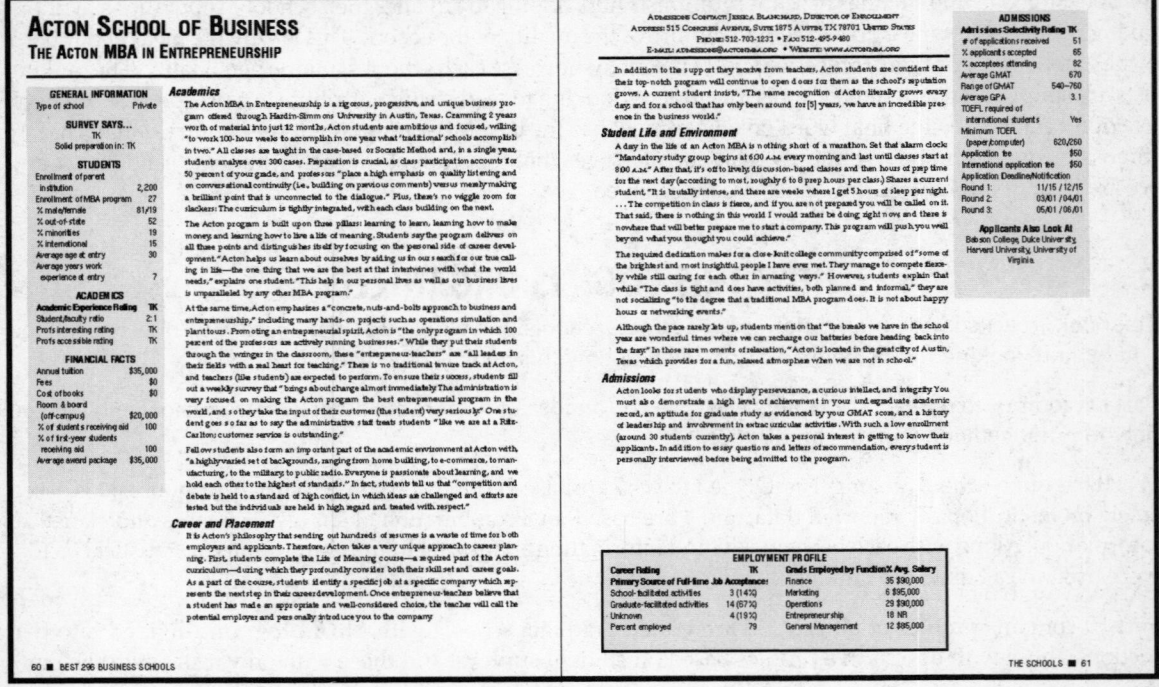

Each two-page spread is made up of eight major components. At the top of each page, you'll find the name of the business school, along with the name of an admissions contact and his or her address, phone number, fax number, if applicable, and e-mail address. This section also includes the b-school's website address. There are two sidebars (the narrow columns on the outer edge of each page) that contain information reported by the schools through the Business Data Set (BDS) and some student survey data as well. The Survey Says information reflects aspects of the school about which students feel the strongest; there are nine different possible results. We also offer an Employment Profile for each school, which is made up of statistical information from the BDS. The main body of the profile contains descriptive text discussing Academics, Placement and Recruiting, Student/Campus Life, and Admissions. Each description is based on student survey responses and may call upon statistical data where necessary.

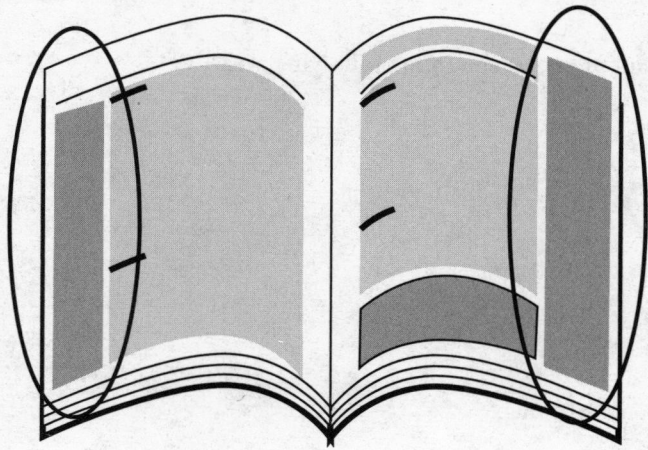

All information in the sidebars falls under the following categories: General Information, Academics, Financial Facts, and Admissions. Please note that not every category will appear for every school; in some cases the information is not reported or not applicable. These are the same data fields that are reported for those schools listed in Part III-B: Business School Data Listings, save for 4 of the 5 ratings, which appear only in the descriptive profiles.

Here is what each sidebar heading tells you.

General Information

Type of school

Public or private school

Affiliation

Any religious order with which the school is affiliated

Environment

Whether the campus is located in a metropolis, city, town, village, or rural setting

Academic Calendar

Whether the school schedule runs according to trimesters, semesters, quarters, or another calendar type like a 4-1-4 (4-month semester, 1-month interim term, 4-month semester)

Survey Says

Survey Says gives you an at-a-glance look at what students are most in agreement about at their school. You'll find up to six results per school. Three will reflect the top three subject areas as indicated by responses to the following question:

How well has your school prepared you in the following areas:

Marketing

Finance

Accounting

General management

Operations

Teamwork

Communication/Interpersonal skills

Presentation skills

Quantitative skills

Computer skills

Doing business in a global economy

Entrepreneurial studies

In addition, Survey Says may include (up to) three things from the following list that students were most in agreement about:

- Students like Hometown, State. Based on level of agreement with the statement, "I like the town where my school is located."

- Friendly students. Based on level of agreement with the statement, "Your business school classmates are friendly."

- Good social scene. Based on level of agreement with the statement, "Your business school classmates have active social lives."

- Good peer network. Based on level of agreement with the statement, "Your business school classmates are the type of people you want to network with after graduation."

- Cutting-edge classes. Based on responses to the question, "How well has your school integrated new business trends and practices into course offerings?"

- Helpful alumni. Based on responses to the question, "How helpful have alumni been in assisting you in your job search?"

- Happy students. Based on level of agreement with the statement, "Overall, I am happy here."

- Smart classrooms. Based on level of agreement with the statement, "Classroom facilities are equipped with computer/multimedia resources."

Students

Enrollment of parent institution

Total number of undergraduate and graduate students enrolled in parent institution program

Enrollment of MBA program

Total number of students enrolled in MBA programs at the business school, including both full- and part-time programs

"% male/female" through "% international"

Items based on demographic information about full-time b-school students as reported by the schools

Average age at entry

The average age of incoming first-year MBA students

Average years work experience at entry

The average years of work experience for incoming first-year MBA students

Academics

Academic Experience Rating

This rating measures the quality of the learning environment. Each school is given a score between 60 and 99. Factors taken into consideration include GMAT scores and undergraduate grades of enrolled students; percent accepted; percent enrolled; student/faculty ratio; and student survey questions pertaining to faculty, fellow students, and realization of academic expectations. This rating is intended to be used only to compare those schools within this edition of the book whose students completed our business student survey.

Please note that if a 60* Academic Experience Rating appears for any school, it means that the school didn't report all the rating's underlying data points by our deadline, so we were unable to calculate an accurate rating. In such cases, the reader is advised to follow up with the school about specific measures this rating takes into account.

Please also note that many foreign institutions use a grading system that is different from the standard U.S. GPA; as a result, we approximated their Admissions Selectivity and Academic Ratings, indicating this with a † following the rating.

Student/Faculty Ratio

The ratio of full-time graduate instructional faculty members to all enrolled MBA students

Professors Interesting Rating

Based on the answers given by students to the survey question, "Overall, how good are your professors as teachers?" Ratings fall between 60 and 99. This rating is intended to be used to compare those schools within this edition of the book whose students completed our business student survey.

Professors Accessible Rating

Based on the answers given by students to the survey question, "How accessible are your professors outside of the classroom?" Ratings fall between 60 and 99. This rating is intended to be used to compare those schools within this edition of the book whose students completed our business student survey.

% female faculty

Percent of graduate business faculty in the 2006–2007 academic year who were women

% minority faculty

Percent of graduate business faculty in the 2006–2007 academic year who were members of minority groups

Joint Degrees

A list of joint degrees offered by the business school. See Decoding Degrees on page 791 for the full name of each degree.

Prominent Alumni

School administrators may submit the name, title, and company of up to five prominent alumni.

Financial Facts

Please note that we rely on foreign institutions to convert financial figures into U.S. dollars. Please check with any foreign schools you are considering for up-to-date figures and conversion rates.

"Tuition (in-state/out-of-state)" and "Fees (in-state/out-of-state)"

In-state and out-of-state tuition and fees per academic year. At state-supported public schools, in-state tuition and fees are likely to be significantly lower than out-of-state expenses.

Books and supplies

Estimated cost of books and supplies for one academic year

Room and board

Cost of room and board on campus per academic year, and estimate of off-campus living expenses for this time period

"% of students receiving aid" through "% of students receiving grants"

Percent of students receiving aid, then specifically those receiving grants and loans. These numbers reflect the percentage of all enrolled MBA students that receive financial aid, regardless of whether or not they applied for financial aid or for specific aid types. Likewise, the second figure, "% of first year students receiving aid" takes into account all first-year MBA students, regardless of whether they applied for financial aid or specific aid types.

Average award package

For students who received financial aid, this is the average award amount.

Average grant

For students who received grants, this is the average amount of grant money awarded.

Average student loan debt

The average dollar amount of outstanding educational MBA loans per graduate (class of 2006) at the time of graduation

Admissions

Admissions Selectivity Rating

This rating measures the competitiveness of the school's admissions. Factors taken into consideration include the average GMAT score and undergraduate GPA of the first-year class, the percent of students accepted, and the percent of applicants who are accepted and ultimately enroll. No student survey data is used in this calculation. Ratings fall between 60 and 99. This rating is intended to be used to compare all schools within this edition of the book, regardless of whether their students completed our business student survey.

Please note that if a 60* Admissions Selectivity Rating appears for any school, it means that the school did not report all of the rating's underlying data points by our deadline, so we were unable to calculate an accurate rating. In such cases, the reader is advised to follow up with the school about specific measures this rating takes into account.

Please also note that many foreign institutions use a grading system that is different from the standard U.S. GPA; as a result, we approximated their Admissions Selectivity and Academic Ratings, indicating this with a † next to the rating.

of applications received

The total number of applications received for any and all MBA programs at the school

% applicants accepted

The percentage of applicants to which the school offered admission

% acceptees attending

Of those accepted students, the percentage of those who enrolled

Average GMAT

The average GMAT score for the first-year class

Average GPA

The average undergraduate GPA of the first year class, reported on a 4-point scale

TOEFL required of international applicants?

For those international students interested in applying, the b-school reports whether the Test of English as a Foreign Language (TOEFL) is required.

Minimum TOEFL (paper/computer)

The minimum TOEFL score necessary for consideration. We list acceptable scores for both the paper and computer versions of the test.

Application fee

The amount it costs to file an application with the school

"Application deadline" and "Regular notification"

This regular application deadline reflects the date by which all materials must be postmarked; the notification date tells you when you can expect to hear back.

International Application Fee

The amount it costs an international student to file an application with the school if it is different from the cost of the regular application.

"Early decision program" and "ED deadline/notification"

If a school offers an early decision option, we'll tell you when early decision apps are due to be postmarked, and when you'll be notified of the school's decision.

"Deferment available?" and "Maximum length of deferment"

Some schools allow accepted students to defer enrollment for a year or more, while others require students who postpone attendance to reapply.

Transfer students accepted?

Whether or not students are accepted from other MBA programs

Transfer Application Policy

Lets you know how transfer applications are reviewed and how many credits will be allowed to transfer from another program.

Non-fall admissions?

Some business schools may allow students to matriculate at the beginning of each semester, while for others, the invitation to attend stipulates that fall attendance is mandatory.

Need-blind admissions?

Whether or not the school considers applications without regard to the candidate's financial need

Applicants also look at

The school reports that students applying to their school are also known to apply to a short list of other schools.

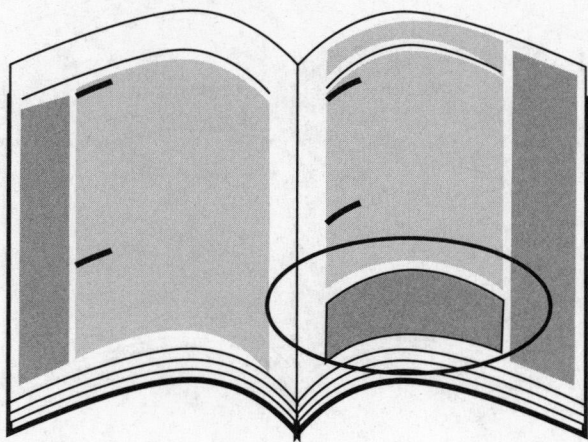

Career Rating

Taking into account both student survey responses and statistical data, this rating measures the confidence students have in their school's ability to lead them to fruitful employment opportunities, as well as the school's own record of having done so. Factors taken into consideration include statistics on the average starting salary and percent of students employed at graduation from the Business Data Set and comments from the student survey, assessing the efforts of the placement office, the quality of recruiting companies, level of preparation, and opportunities for off-campus projects, internships, and mentorships. Ratings fall between 60 and 99. This rating is intended to be used to compare only those schools within this edition of the book whose students completed our business student survey.

* Please note that if a 60* Career Rating appears for any school, it means that the school did not report all of the rating's underlying data points by our deadline, so we were unable to calculate an accurate rating. In such cases, the reader is advised to follow up with the school about the specific attributes this rating takes into account.

% grads employed within three months of graduation

This reflects the percentage of MBA grads who earned a job within three months of graduation.

Average starting salary

Average starting salary of all 2007 graduates

Grads employed by field %: avg. salary

Reflects the distribution of 2007 graduates across many different industries and the average starting salary for each field.

Top 5 employers hiring grads

Reflects the top five employers who hired 2007 job seeking full-time MBA graduates, and the number of students they hired.

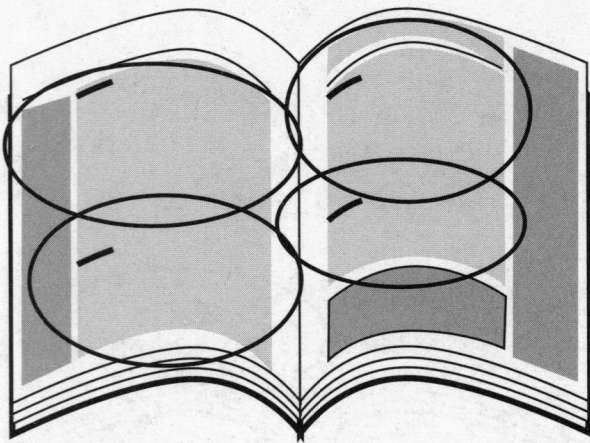

Each school's descriptive profile is made up of four sections which highlight those qualities that characterize the school as a unique institution. *Academics* covers students' opinions on the quality of professors, curriculum, special or noteworthy programs, the administration, and anything else academic in nature. *Career and Placement* deals with the school's efforts to secure internships and jobs for its current students and graduates; information about alumni assistance and popular recruiters of MBAs at the school may also be included. In *Student Life and Environment*, you'll find out how students balance work and play and whether they find it manageable to do so; often, you'll also find reviews of the school's facilities as well. Finally, the *Admissions* section describes what the Admissions Committee is looking for in potential students.

All quotes in these sections are taken from students' responses to our survey. We choose quotes that were consistent with the overall survey results.

Part III-B: Business School Data Listings

This section contains all of the statistical info that is presented in the sidebars of the descriptive profile. Each school in this section will include an Admissions Selectivity rating but will not include the other 3 ratings, the Survey Says section, or a descriptive profile.

Part IV: School Says

Part IV offers more detailed information about particular business schools authored by the schools themselves. The business schools included in this section pay a small fee for this space. These schools also have descriptive profiles or data listings in Part III.

Everything Else

Following Part IV, we offer a small section of profiles of b-schools who may pay a small fee for inclusion. Next is a section entitled *Decoding Degrees* that will help you make sense of the myriad degree abbreviations you'll see listed in the book. You'll then find the indexes—alphabetical by school name, and then by location. Finally, you'll have an opportunity to learn more about our author, Nedda Gilbert.

Enjoy and good luck!

PART I
ALL ABOUT BUSINESS SCHOOL

CHAPTER 1

THIS ISN'T YOUR FATHER'S (OR MOTHER'S) B-SCHOOL ANYMORE

THE NEW MBA CLASS: FEWER, YOUNGER, AND WORKING WHILE THEY LEARN

The MBA has always been seen as a golden passport, the trip ticket to romance and riches. The destination: career acceleration, power networks and recruiters, elite employers, and of course, generous paychecks.

But not everyone wants to make the trip. Several factors will always impact on the popularity of the MBA: 1) the state of the economy—interest in getting the MBA has generally waxed and waned with economic times; 2) trends and favorable or unfavorable press—in the 1980s, a rash of insider trading scandals in which MBAs were ensnared made the degree look smarmy and other graduate programs, notably law and medicine, look more appealing; 3) the immediacy of good professional opportunities—the collapse of the dot-com boom, followed by the severe retrenchment of traditional MBA destinations (such as investment banks and consulting firms) in a depressed economy, has left many current MBAs stranded; and 4) recruiter demand for newly minted MBAs—do employers see the skill sets of today's MBAs bringing measurable value to their companies?

B-SCHOOL: INTEREST AND APPLICATIONS ON UPSWING

After three straight years of declining applications, the numbers increased in 2006, and application volume continues to climb at many schools. Almost two-thirds of full-time MBA programs participating in the 2007 GMAC Application Trends Survey saw application levels rise in 2007. Part-time programs are still reporting an increase in volume. Among executive MBA programs, 63 percent saw applications increase, up from the previous year.

YOUNGER MINDS

Although growing applicant pools may make admission seem more competitive, there are now some unrecognized opportunities for candidates with less than the traditional two to four years of work experience to make a strong case for admittance.

Admissions officers at large benchmark schools such as Stanford say that this trend pre-dates the economic downturn. Derek Bolton, director of admissions at Stanford notes, "The pendulum has gone too far in one direction in terms of the number of younger candidates applying to b-school. It has not kept pace with the overall pace of applicants. We want more young applicants applying. The goal is to bring the average age down in the next couple of years."

"What's driving this is the willingness on the part of the b-schools to not be rigidly fixed on what's right for someone. We may not always be the best judge of when the best time is for a candidate to go to b-school," continues Bolton.

Wharton's former Director of Admissions Rose Martinelli observed "a shift in that we became more tuned in to when students are ready in their leadership, professional, and personal development. We see so many nontraditional students that we don't want to have rules on when they can apply. We don't want to miss out on fabulous applicants because they don't think they can get in."

"When the applicant pool continues to get older and older, then we're closing out younger applicants who are on a fast track." Martinelli continues, "Why should we wait? Why should they wait? We want to catch the human element in the application process."

This perspective continues to hold true. As University of Chicago's Stacey Kole sums up, "The pendulum had swung too far in terms of the type of student who should be admitted and when. Now schools are correcting that and experimenting, taking less experienced candidates. We believe that this experimentation is a good thing."

THE DRAW OF THE PART-TIME PROGRAM

Ironically, even as the economy appears to be in a slight upswing, many young adults are choosing to brave a newly robust job market over immersing themselves in the uncertainty—not to mention the high costs—of a graduate program in business or even law. Because part-time and executive education programs have not suffered the decline that full-time programs have, pundits say that the future of b-school may lie in programs that offer more flexible part-time opportunities, allowing students to get the degree without making a full-time commitment. In fact, Stacey Kole, Deputy Dean for the full-time MBA Program and Clinical Professor of Economics, University of Chicago Graduate School of Business states, "There is this tendency to think of the MBA as a full-time-only product. But schools like Chicago offer MBA programs in the evening, on weekends, and in executive program formats. For us, whether the student matriculates in our part-time or full-time program, the process is exactly the same. Ours is the same degree, only delivered in full-time, part-time, and weekend formats with different scheduling options. Chicago GSB offers individuals interested in an MBA considerable flexibility in how they pursue their education."

Kole continues, "Part-time and executive programs are now providing more of the outside-the-classroom, extracurricular experience that did not exist 10 years ago. For example, they are offering student-led clubs, speakers, and recruiter events that historically were the exclusive domain of full-time programs. This is one explanation for why part-time programs are looking like better substitutes for a full-time program."

There may be more to the story, too. Because they may be less likely to be in committed relationships or have families, younger students are more active, generous alumni, and b-schools can't afford to ignore the market that these younger students represent. Despite the heightened competition, candidates with less experience are increasingly being deemed worthy of a coveted b-school acceptance.

PAYBACK TIME

The MBA, particularly at the top schools, continues to pay out high dividends to grads. The salaries of 2007 alumni have risen against MBA 2006 salaries within every sector—from investment banking to the retail sector. Although salaries for U.S. alumni are still higher than those paid to their European counterparts, the gap is closing rapidly. That's a hefty return on investment. But the degree doesn't come with any promises. The world of business requires some risk, as many MBA wannabes found out several years go: You can enter a business school program at the height of the economy only to graduate when things are dismal. But you can also enter b-school at low tide then watch as the job market swells and employers are fighting over the newest and brightest MBA grads, including you.

FOREIGN MBA STUDENTS: THE NEW REALITY

Opportunities to study or work abroad during an MBA program are considered highly relevant. Likewise, international enrollment at U.S. business schools has always been a priority. At some schools, the percentage of foreign students has been sky-high, anywhere from 30 to 40 percent. Of course, that was before the new screening and tracking processes for international applicants went into effect.

Previously, our position was clear: International students represent a win-win proposition for both U.S. business schools and the foreign industries that send them here. American business schools prize the global perspective and diversity international students bring into the classroom and community; foreign businesses operating in a global economy desire expertise in U.S. business practices which are becoming the international standard.

Unfortunately, due to international security issues, this informal but critical partnership faces greater challenges. These have come primarily in the form of increased scrutiny. Foreign students must slog through tougher rules and procedures for obtaining and maintaining a visa under the United States Citizenship and Immigration Services (USCIS). And many foreign students feel that even if they are successful in obtaining a student visa, they will face an even tougher battle after they graduate: trying to get a work visa. That puts them back at square one. Though armed with an American MBA, they often find themselves looking for work in their home country—a scenario from which they may originally have wanted a professional out.

Foreign Students: Getting In

As of January 2003, U.S. institutions must comply with the Student and Exchange Visitor Information System, or SEVIS, which tracks foreign students and exchange visitors, as well as some foreign professors. While there is hope that SEVIS will prevent potential terrorists from slipping through the cracks, critics fear that the intensified scrutiny drives away many foreign applicants. The system causes major delays in obtaining a student visa and leaving or reentering the country. In addition, compliance with SEVIS requires the staff of international student offices to perform a great deal of data entry, detracting from the face-time advisors can spend with foreign students.

For the foreseeable future, students wishing to obtain a visa will not be able to escape the shadow of world events, but they should not be deterred. Most business schools stand firm on their commitment to foreign applicants throughout the entire process.

In fact, Don Martin, Director of Admissions at the University of Chicago notes that the number of international students enrolled at UChicago has remained constant. Martin says, "We have made no change in terms of our desire and commitment to enroll foreign students. This world will never go back to what it was before it became a global village. For the sake of diversity and the perspective international students bring to the table, or for understanding foreign business culture, we need to have people who represent that world in every sense."

Martin does agree that for foreign MBA students intending to study on American soil, "The journey of enrolling them is going to be more challenging. A part of that is tied into the changes the U.S. government has imposed on getting visas. Some applicants will need to take another year for the paperwork." But most notably, he sees different forces at play in the shrinking foreign MBA market, namely, the competition U.S. schools are feeling from business schools abroad. Martin continues, "The issue influencing more international business students away from U.S. business schools is the large amount of European, Australian, and Latin American business schools that heretofore I would not have thought would have had as much pull as they did. These business schools have become more visible and prominent. They are being ranked by the large news organizations and magazines. So I would say American business schools still want international students, but the ability to recruit and draw them here to us will be difficult against this new competition."

To those applying for a visa, Wharton's former Director of Admissions Rose Martinelli offers this advice: "Emphasize plans to return home, [not] plans to immigrate to the United States." If a visa is denied, many schools will defer admission and hold that student's spot until the visa is obtained. "It may take a little longer for students from some countries to get their visas. But decisions here are not made based on whether they got a visa or not. Decisions are made based on what they'll do at our school and on the contributions they'll make," sums up Martinelli.

Of course, all this is subject to change, perhaps even by the time of this book's publication. Non-U.S. citizens should visit the USCIS website (www.uscis.gov) for the latest information on student visas.

Foreign Students: Getting a Job

Just when a foreign student is ready to reap the rewards of his or her hard-won business degree, he or she hits another roadblock. And this one's a brick wall: an unforgiving and limited job market fueled not just by a new wartime security, but also a new nationalism.

Historically, foreign students have always had a tougher time than their American counterparts in trying to get that first job out of b-school. That's because of the hassle of sponsoring a foreigner on a visa, rigid immigration rules, and other cultural and relocation issues. Nonetheless, for grads of the top schools, there has always been a pot of gold waiting at the end of that long journey. That pot of gold has meant the opportunity to embark on an entirely new career and life—to be sponsored by a U.S. company, on U.S. soil, with post-MBA pay scales that supersede those of their home countries and launch them on a high-earnings career path.

Since September 11, the environment in the United States has changed, and the home-field advantage of American MBAs is even greater. Simply put, U.S. companies have been reluctant to offer a foreign MBA a plush job over an American MBA who is equally talented and qualified. The result is that foreign hires have been more limited to hard-to-fill positions, to employment in their locations abroad, or to positions in the student's home country. Many MBA recruiters won't even offer an international student an interview.

As for companies shrinking their foreign MBA hires down to bare bones, as we've said many times before, and Don Martin concurs, where you go to school matters. He explains, "Some companies have changed their hiring strategies. Fewer overall international students are being hired, but not at our school. Companies typically will drop down from their list of 10 schools they go to, to a much smaller number of programs. In a high percentage, we've remained on their lists. We are seeing 90 percent of our international students placed in internships and going on to full-time hires."

The result of the shrinking job market for most foreign students is that business schools have begun to cut back on the number of applicants admitted, and this has made it even tougher to get accepted. Many schools have begun to be upfront about the limited career opportunities on U.S. soil for foreigners. Indeed, this will soon be compounded by a reduction of more than 50 percent in the number of work visas the government issues annually to employees sponsored by their company.

But as the economy heats up and MBA hiring begins to rebound, it is possible that recruiters, particularly Wall Street and the top-flight consulting firms, will once again open their doors to whomever is most qualified, foreign or not. History, it should be remembered, shows us that the top jobs always go to the most capable applicants. This next cycle should be no different than the preceding cycles. Talent still rules.

In the meantime, buyers beware: An MBA is not the passport to riches it once was for foreign applicants. International students should think twice about the costs of pursuing a degree that may only deliver them back into the hands of their home countries saddled with the expense, but not the benefit, of an MBA education.

THE CONTINUING RELEVANCE OF BUSINESS SCHOOL

The MBA is such an attractive option because it *does* confer huge value on the recipient. Business schools know how to keep pace with the rapidly changing face of business. After all, that's *their* business, so you're never really out of the game. In fact, if you look at the nation's top business programs, you'll find exciting innovations in curriculum that reflect all that's new and relevant. This includes unique opportunities for teamwork, internships, and laboratory simulations that replicate real-world, real-time business scenarios.

The integration of these real-world experiences into the basics produces better-trained, more well-rounded managers, as graduates are more adept at discerning the correlation between principle and reality. Even so, programs and students in search of business knowledge that is more widely applicable and more relevant long-term has caused a strong return to fundamentals.

BACKPEDALING TO THE BASICS

Many top schools are reviving the old classics: It's back to basics. Both schools and students now have enough of a perspective to look back at the frenzy of the last business cycle and understand that enduring values are rooted in a solid foundation. Gone is the frothy demand for trendy courses on e-commerce and other hype-driven topics. Just four years ago, a class at Stanford on the principles of Internet marketing was oversubscribed. Last year, only a few people signed up for it.

So here's a sampler of the back-to-basics you'll get at b-school: An in-depth immersion in all of the key functional areas of an organization: marketing, management, sales, finance, operations, logistics, and so on. You'll look at these areas across dozens of industries and organizational types, from start-ups to Fortune 500 companies.

The renewed focus on basics doesn't mean that you'll find yourself shorted on current trends and events. Expect plenty of case study debate on corporate governance and the Enron debacle, and expect the themes of global perspective and technological competence to permeate many programs. You'll also find classes and seminars on leadership gaining popularity. "We're seeing a resurgence of leadership courses as students seek out professions and business models that are other-oriented," notes Stanford's Bolton. "This may be a new generation. But these are students who look at business as a positive force in the world, a more noble calling."

SURVIVOR POWER

Once you have your MBA, you can expect to hit the ground running. You'll start off your post b-school career with a load of contacts that you will periodically leverage over your career. Many graduates use the degree to embark on entirely new career paths than those that brought them to the school; consultants become bankers, entrepreneurs become consultants, marketers become financiers, and so on. The MBA has and will continue to be a terrific opportunity to reinvent oneself.

"An MBA is unlike any other professional degree because the breadth of knowledge poises you for a multitude of career choices," says Julia Min, Director of MBA Admissions for NYU Stern School of Business. "You can be an investment banker, yet two years from that point, segue into nonprofit work. You can move from banking to corporate finance, to a venture-capital proposition, to ultimately having an entrepreneurial experience. So it's a credential that allows you the flexibility to explore different industries; it's a long-term investment that will give you the tools to transition if you want to."

"What's wonderful about the MBA is that it provides fundamental skills that you can use whenever and wherever you need them," champions Martinelli. "I'm a cheerleader for the nontraditional because I feel the MBA is such a fundamental tool. It offers an ability to enter the business world and link passion with functionality."

"For example, for folks who want to go into public service or nonprofit, even the arts industry, they're very narrow fields. You need the passion and vision to be successful in them. But often credibility is undermined when you don't understand the business world's perspective," states Martinelli.

"You've got to know that industry if you're going to make it viable for the future. But you have to be able to know how to talk to the business world in order to get those investments to make it happen. And that's one of the reasons why an MBA is so valuable. It bestows credibility in the marketplace and helps us maintain these organizations in a world that doesn't often respect passion over the bottom line," she continues.

After a tough slog in 2002 and 2003, job prospects for recent MBA graduates are looking up. Hundreds of companies continue to visit and recruit from business school campuses, with today's MBA candidates receiving two job offers on average. Recruiters exist in a symbiotic relationship with business schools. Employers like to maintain a strong presence on campus—even during an economic downturn—so that they'll have their top picks of MBA talent when the good times return. Thus, MBA programs remain one of the most effective means to get oneself in front of recruiters and senior managers from the most desirable companies. And while that may not grant you "immunity" from an economy characterized by up and downs, it will absolutely improve your survivor power.

COMPETITION HAS EASED UP

With an economic recovery seemingly underway, the chance to dive into any number of secure, well-paying jobs will lure a percentage of professionals away from the MBA. After years of struggling through economic hardship, a decent paycheck from the pocket of a much improved labor market may seem the best bet. There's no doubt that risk-averse individuals would prefer the stability of a secure job to what might-be, could-be, or should-be two years down the road—even with an MBA in hand. This may keep the applicant pool smaller.

Additionally, the continued decrease in the number of foreign applicants, who at many schools comprised well over 20 percent of students, will keep applications down, too. Other factors include the fact that there are currently smaller percentages of people in the country who are in the typical age bracket of business school applicants. Lastly, the increased interest in part-time MBA programs may continue to drive the decline in full-time business school applications.

What does all of this mean? Basically this: If you have a handsome application and you plan on applying to the most competitive programs this year, you may find yourself met with welcoming arms.

AS THE SONG GOES...MONEY, MONEY, MONEY, MONEY...

But don't go buying the flashy car to go with that flashy degree quite yet. It needs to be said that, after several years of a slump, there could actually be a surge in this upcoming applicant pool that would correspond with improvements in the economy. Recruiters are once again storming the top business schools as hiring slowly returns to healthy levels. At programs like Chicago, Harvard, and Stanford, six-figure salaries and signing bonuses of $15,000-plus are still the norm. That's why it's important to remember that the MBA from the right school can deliver an immediate and hefty return on investment. According to the Graduate Management Admission Council Global MBA Graduate Survey of 2006, respondents reported an annual (mean) salary of $59,635 before entering business school and a (mean) salary of $92,000 in their first job out. This number is expected to continue to rise for the class of 2007. Amid a healthy recruiting environment built on strong employer confidence in the economy, the average new MBA with a job offer in hand will earn $92,360 during the first year of employment, up 4.2 percent from the $88,626 graduates in 2005 received. Moreover, two-thirds of job offers to MBAs in 2006 come with signing bonuses that average $17,603, up slightly from last year.

Another trend worth noting: Although applications are down overall at b-schools, that doesn't mean the quality of applicants has suffered. Notes Chicago's Kole, "Our applications are of high quality, and applicants appear to be quite focused with regard to why they seek an advanced degree. Whether they are career switchers or planning to resume their career path, those applicants who present a compelling story for why they want to be here leave a stronger impression with the admissions committee."

Top schools are always going to have people knocking at their doors. The possibility that business school applications in general could once again rise means you'll still want to be competitive. The long application process starts with developing a solid application strategy and applying to a diverse portfolio of schools.

Let Us Help You Decide

There are many factors to consider when deciding whether or not to pursue an MBA, and we'll help you make that decision in the following chapters. We'll also tell you a bit about each school in our profiles and prepare you to do further research on the schools on your list. We've worked hard to provide you with thorough information on every aspect of the MBA, but you don't have to take our word for it—see for yourself. Stanford's Bolton advises future applicants, "Start early. Visit as many schools as you can, because it's very hard to differentiate among programs from websites, books, and marketing materials. You need to get a feeling from walking down the halls."

After you decide to go, finding the right program can be extremely difficult. Bolton explains, "Applicants really have to dig beneath the programs they're looking at to determine what's going to make them happy. A lot of people wind up going to the wrong school. A lot of external factors contribute to that. People shouldn't worry about justifying the decision to others, but to themselves."

Making the Decision to Go

The next step for you may be b-school. Indeed, armed with an MBA you may journey far. But the success of your trip and the direction you take will depend on knowing exactly why you're going to b-school and just what you'll be getting out of it.

The most critical questions you need to ask yourself are the following: Do you really want a career in business? What do you want the MBA to do for you? Are you looking to gain credibility, accelerate your development, or move into a new job or industry? Perhaps you're looking to start your own business, in which case entrepreneurial study will be important.

Knowing what you want doesn't just affect your decision to go, it also affects your candidacy; admissions committees favor applicants who have clear goals and objectives. Moreover, once at school, students who know what they want make the most of their two years. If you're uncertain about your goals, opportunities for career development—such as networking, mentoring, student clubs, and recruiter events—are squandered.

You also need to find a school that fits your individual needs. Consider the personal and financial costs. This may be the single biggest investment of your life. How much salary will you forego by leaving the workforce? What will the tuition be? How will you pay for it? If you have a family, spouse, or significant other, how will getting your MBA affect them?

If you do have a spouse, you may choose a program that involves partners in campus life. If status is your top priority, you should simply choose the most prestigious school you can get into.

The MBA presents many opportunities but no guarantees. As with any opportunity, you must make the most of it. Whether you go to a first-tier school or to a part-time program close to home, you'll acquire the skills that can jump-start your career. But your success will have more to do with you than with the piece of paper your MBA is printed on.

Chapter 2

Blackberrys and Power Lunches: What Does an MBA Offer?

NUTS-AND-BOLTS BUSINESS SKILLS

Graduate business schools teach the applied science of business. The best business schools combine the latest academic theories with pragmatic concepts, hands-on experience, and real-world solutions.

B-schools also teach the analytical skills used to make complicated business decisions. You learn how to define the critical issues, apply analytical techniques, develop the criteria for decisions, and make decisions after evaluating their impact on other variables.

After two years, you're ready to market a box of cereal. Or prepare a valuation of the cereal company's worth. You'll speak the language of business. You'll know the tools of the trade. Your expertise will extend to many areas and industries. In short, you will have acquired the skills that open doors.

ACCESS TO RECRUITERS, ENTRÉE TO NEW FIELDS

Applicants tend to place great emphasis on "incoming" and "outgoing" statistics. First they ask, "Will I get in?" Then they ask, "Will I get a job?"

Obviously, the first is largely dependent on how selective the school is and the quality of your credentials. The latter question can almost assuredly be answered in the positive, "Yes, you will."

But the real question is: How many—and what kind—of offers will you receive? Again, that is dependent on the appeal of the school to recruiters (which is a readily available statistic you can get from each school) and the particular industry you elect to pursue. For example, investment banks and consulting firms are always going to come to the schools for formal recruiting periods, whereas more off-the-beaten-path choices will possibly require you to go off campus in search of opportunity.

It's Good to Be Wanted, It's Great to Be Paid

According to many top schools, recruiter appetite for new grads is up. The latest figures suggest a strong market for newly minted MBAs. This comes after several years of depressed interest in which the immediate economic value of the MBA was in question.

As we reported in Chapter 1, the average return on investment for business school grads in 2006 was an impressive 30 percent increase in annual salary. According to the Graduate Management Council, the before and after picture looks something like this: Average entering salary: roughly $59,635. Average first job out of school salary: $92,360. Presumably, starting salaries will continue to increase as the economy improves.

The majority of top grads receive a generous relocation package too. Indeed, if you were fortunate enough to have spent the summer between your first and second year at a consulting company, then you will, in all likelihood, also receive a "rebate" on your tuition. These companies often pick up a student's second-year tuition bill. The best package, however, goes to those MBA students who worked at the firm before b-school. These lucky capitalists often get their whole tuition paid for.

Getting the MBA for the Long Run

Although MBA hiring appears to be on an upswing, going to business school still requires you to take a bit of a gamble. Leaner years make business school a riskier proposition. The nation appears to be heading out of what has been a lingering recession, but economic factors are always unpredictable. Furthermore, the world has witnessed great political turmoil. All of these factors can quickly and negatively impact the job market for newly minted MBAs.

So as you make plans to go to b-school, you need to accept that there is some risk that the labor market won't greet you with open arms at graduation. Consider the plight of MBAs from just three years ago: when they entered b-school, the economy was roaring ahead. The immediate future looked exceptionally bright. Most MBAs probably thought that once they got in, they had it made, and they looked forward to generous starting salaries and bonuses. Few probably anticipated that tough times could hit so dramatically.

But that's just the point. Good times and bad times cycle in and out. Fortunately, it looks as though we are cycling into a good time. Many economic experts agree that the economy is looking up and the markets will continue to improve. This means traditional hirers of MBAs, such as the investment banks and consulting firms, may once again be wooing many a b-school grad. Still, it's hard to know when all of the recruiters who typically hire MBAs will feel comfortable again about bringing their hiring levels back up to what they were before the downturn.

The best way to consider the value of the degree is by focusing on its long-lasting benefits. "When people come here for their MBA, they talk about retooling for their life. They think about the long term and recognize that there are some short term hurdles," says Rose Martinelli, former director of admissions at the Wharton School. "Just out of business school, this is the very first job in a long career. This is really about building blocks and going for the long run. You may have to work harder to find a job now, but building your career is a lifelong process." The MBA gives you the tools, networking, and polish to meaningfully enhance your long-term prospects and earning potential.

"There is real opportunity here. The opportunity right now is to pursue your passion and perhaps not your wallet," continues Martinelli. "We're seeing more of an equalization in salary. Those high-paying jobs in finance, investment banking, and consulting are fewer and harder to find. So here you have an opportunity for a job with a true learning experience rather than one that just pays a lot. More people are going into nonprofit and government and making contributions back to the community."

Brand Power Counts

Of course, there is great variability with placement rates and starting salaries among schools. The MBA does not swap your tuition bill for a guarantee that you'll get rich quick. As we've noted, it is at the best schools—those that have the greatest prestige and global recognition—where the strongest recovery is taking place. It's brand power at work. Even in an uncertain economy, top schools will continue to produce in-demand MBAs for the marketplace.

Branded schools tend to have an extensive history with big recruiting companies because the schools are a steady source of exceptional talent. As the economy stabilizes and hiring creeps up again, recruiters are naturally going to orient themselves at the top-brand schools.

At the University of Chicago, Deputy Dean Stacey Kole notes: "Recruiting activity is up, in the order of 20 percent. Hiring activity has really skyrocketed. I think that companies are feeling more comfortable that the economy is in good shape and are resuming their pre-September 11 hiring patterns. We had thousands of interviews available for our grads."

At less prominent schools, the picture may not be quite as optimistic. It is important to consider placement rates and the list of companies that typically recruit on campus at any school you are considering.

GETTING A JOB

For most would-be MBAs, b-school represents a fresh beginning—either in their current profession or in an entirely different industry. Whatever promise the degree holds for you, it's wise to question what the return on your investment will be.

Several factors affect job placement and starting salary. School reputation and ties to industries and employers are important. At the top programs, the lists of recruiters read like a "Who's Who" of American companies. These schools not only attract the greatest volume of recruiters, but consistently get the attention of those companies considered to be "blue chip."

Not to be overlooked are lesser-known, regional schools that often have the strongest relationships with local employers and industries. Some b-schools (many of them state universities) are regarded by both academicians and employers as number one in their respective regions. In other words, as far as the local business community is concerned, these programs offer as much prestige and pull as a nationally ranked program.

Student clubs also play a big part in getting a job because they extend the recruiting efforts at many schools. They host a variety of events that allow you to meet leading business people, so that you can learn about their industries and their specific companies. Most important, these clubs are very effective at bringing in recruiters and other interested parties that do not recruit through traditional mainstream channels. For example, the high-tech, international, and entertainment student clubs provide career opportunities not available through the front door.

Your background and experiences also affect your success in securing a position. Important factors are academic specialization, academic standing, prior work experience, and intangibles such as your personal fit with the company. These days, what you did before b-school is particularly important; it helps establish credibility and gives you an edge in competing for a position in a specific field. For those using b-school to switch careers to a new industry, it's helpful if something on your resume ties your interest to the new profession. It's also smart to secure a summer job in the new area.

Finally, persistence and initiative are critical factors in the job search. Many fast tracks have been narrowed since the beginning of the decade. Increasingly, even at the best schools, finding a job requires off-campus recruiting efforts and ferreting out the hidden jobs.

A RETURN ON YOUR INVESTMENT

Not everyone measures their return on investment from business school with a dollar amount. (See the interview at the end of this chapter as one example.) We've heard many b-school grads explain that the fundamental skills, the network of people, and the proper environment in which to formulate their long-term career path were the most valuable things they wanted to get back from their MBA programs—in doing so, they considered the experience a success, regardless of their starting salary at graduation.

But for those who are anxious to start paying back those school loans, it's important to note that the industry in which you are hired can strongly affect your job prospects. Traditionally heavy hirers such as investment banking and consulting companies continue to lead the salary pack. Historically these sectors have offered the highest starting salaries and sign-on bonuses, with recruiters gravitating to the name-brand schools. At Chicago, Kole notes, "We saw tremendous activity in consulting, investment banking, investment management, and in leadership development programs. We are up in all of these areas, but most significantly in management consulting."

Also impacting your placement outlook is the geographic location of the school. Regional powerhouses such as Rutgers University in New Jersey may hold great sway at nearby, national employers such as Johnson & Johnson and Warner Lambert/Pfizer, providing graduates of those programs a unique competitive advantage. Although these companies reach out far and wide to recruit everywhere, a homegrown MBA may catch their attention and hold greater appeal.

As always, prioritize your criteria for school selection. Research who the top hirers are at any school you are considering. If you know what field you are interested in, look at how strong a particular business school's track record is in finding jobs for their graduates in that industry. To cement the relationships between school and recruiter, companies often foster a partnership with the school that includes sponsoring academic projects and internships, and hosting school club functions and informational cocktail hour events.

You may indeed be accepted at one of the nation's most prestigious schools, but if they lack real access to the type of industry you desire to work in, you are better off elsewhere.

FRIENDS WHO ARE GOING PLACES, ALUMNI WHO ARE ALREADY THERE

Most students say that the best part about b-school is meeting classmates with whom they share common goals and interests. Many students claim that the "single greatest resource is each other." Not surprisingly, with so many bright and ambitious people cocooned in one place, b-school can be the time of your life. It presents numerous professional and social opportunities. It can be where you find future customers, business partners, and mentors. It can also be where you establish lifelong friendships. After graduation, these classmates form an enduring network of contacts and professional resources.

Alumni are also an important part of the b-school experience. While professors teach business theory and practice, alumni provide insight into the real business world. When you're ready to interview, they can provide advice on how to get hired by the companies recruiting at your school. In some cases, they help you secure the interview and shepherd you through the hiring process.

B-schools love to boast about the influence of their alumni network. To be sure, some are very powerful, but this varies from institution to institution. At the very least, alumni will help you get your foot in the door. A resume sent to an alum at a given company, instead of to "Sir or Madam" in the personnel department, has a much better chance of being noticed and acted on.

After you graduate, the network continues to grow. Regional alumni clubs and alumni publications keep you plugged in to the network with class notes detailing who's doing what, where, and with whom.

Throughout your career, an active alumni relations department can give you continued support. Post-MBA executive education series, fund-raising events, and continued job placement efforts are all resources you can draw on for years to come.

CHAPTER 3

ADMISSIONS

PREPARING TO BE A SUCCESSFUL APPLICANT

GET GOOD GRADES

If you're still in school, concentrate on getting good grades. A high GPA says you've got not only brains but also discipline. It shows the Admissions Committee you have what you need to make it through the program. If you're applying directly from college or have limited job experience, your grades will matter even more. The Admissions Committee will have little else on which to evaluate you.

It's especially important that you do well in courses such as economics, statistics, and calculus. Success in these courses is more meaningful than success in classes like "Monday Night at the Movies" film appreciation. Of course, English is also important; b-schools want students who communicate well.

STRENGTHEN MATH SKILLS

Number-crunching is an inescapable part of b-school. If your work experience has failed to develop your quantitative skills, take an accounting or statistics course for credit at a local college or b-school. If you have a liberal arts background and did poorly in math, or got a low GMAT Math score, this is especially important. Getting a decent grade will go a long way toward convincing the Admissions Committee you can manage the quantitative challenges of the program.

WORK FOR A FEW YEARS—BUT NOT TOO MANY

Business schools have traditionally favored applicants who have worked full-time for several years. There are three primary reasons for this:

1. With experience comes maturity.

2. You're more likely to know what you want out of the program.

3. Your experience enables you to bring real-work perspectives to the classroom. Because business school is designed for you to learn from your classmates, each student's contribution is important.

Until recently, b-schools preferred to admit only those students with two to five years of work experience. The rationale was that at two years you have worked enough to be able to make a solid contribution, while beyond four or five, you might be too advanced in your career to appreciate the program fully. However, as we noted earlier in this book, there is a new trend among top schools toward admitting "younger" applicants—that is, candidates with limited work experience as well as those straight from college.

Depending on the schools to which you're applying and the strength of your resume of accomplishments, you may not need full-time, professional work experience. Of course, there's a catch: The younger you are, the harder you'll have to work to supply supporting evidence for your case as a qualified applicant. Be prepared to convince Admissions Committees that you've already done some incredible things, especially if you're hailing straight from college.

If you've targeted top-flight schools like Wharton, Columbia, or Stanford, applying fresh out of college is still a long shot. While your chances of gaining admission with little work experience have improved, your best shot is still to err on the conservative side and get a year or two of some professional experience under your belt.

If you're not interested in the big league or you plan on attending a local program, the number of years you should work before applying may vary. Research the admissions requirements at your target school. There's no doubt the MBA will jumpstart your career and have long-lasting effects on your business (and perhaps personal) outlook. If you're not ready to face the real world after college, plenty of solid b-schools will welcome you to another two years of academia.

There is one caveat to this advice, however. If your grades are weak, consider working at least three years before applying. The more professional success you have, the greater the likelihood that Admissions Committees will overlook your GPA.

Let Your Job Work for You

Many companies encourage employees to go to b-school. Some of these companies have close ties to a favored b-school and produce well-qualified applicants. If their employees are going to the kinds of schools you want to get into, these may be smart places to work.

Other companies, such as investment banks, feature training programs, at the end of which trainees go to b-school or leave the company. These programs hire undergraduates right out of school. They're known for producing solid, highly skilled applicants. Moreover, they're full of well-connected alumni who may write influential letters of recommendation.

Happily, the opposite tactic—working in an industry that generates few applicants—can be equally effective. Admissions Officers look for students from underrepresented professions. Applicants from biotechnology, health care, not-for-profit, and even the Peace Corps are viewed favorably.

One way to set yourself apart is to have had two entirely different professional experiences before business school. For example, if you worked in finance, your next job might be in a different field, like marketing. Supplementing quantitative work with qualitative experiences demonstrates versatility.

Finally, what you do in your job is important. Seek out opportunities to distinguish yourself. Even if your responsibilities are limited, exceed the expectations of the position. B-schools are looking for leaders.

March from the Military

A surprising number of b-school students hail from the military (although the armed forces probably had commanders in mind, not CEOs, when they designed their regimen). Military officers know how to be managers because they've held command positions. And they know how to lead a team under the most difficult of circumstances.

Because most have traveled all over the world, they also know how to work with people from different cultures. As a result, they're ideally suited to learn alongside students with diverse backgrounds and perspectives. B-schools with a global focus are particularly attracted to such experience.

The decision to enlist in the military is a very personal one. However, if you've thought of joining those few good men and women, this may be as effective a means of preparing for b-school as more traditional avenues.

CHECK OUT THOSE ESSAY QUESTIONS NOW

You're worried you don't have interesting stories to tell. Or you just don't know what to write. What do you do?

Ideally, several months before your application is due, you should read the essay questions and begin to think about your answers. Could you describe an ethical dilemma at work? Are you involved in anything outside the office (or classroom)? If not, now is the time to do something about it. While this may seem contrived, it's preferable to sitting down to write the application and finding you have to scrape for or, even worse, manufacture situations.

Use the essay questions as a framework for your personal and professional activities. Look back over your business calendar, and see if you can find some meaty experiences for the essays in your work life. Keep your eyes open for a situation that involves questionable ethics. If all you do is work, work, work, get involved in activities that round out your background. In other words, get a life.

Get involved in community-based activities. Some possibilities are being a big brother/big sister, tutoring in a literacy program, or initiating a recycling project. Demonstrating a concern for others looks good to Admissions Committees, and hey, it's good for your soul, too.

It's also important to seek out leadership experiences. B-schools are looking for individuals who can manage groups. Volunteer to chair a professional committee or run for an office in a club. It's a wide-open world; you can pick from any number of activities. The bottom line is this: The extracurriculars you select can show that you are mature, multifaceted, and appealing.

We don't mean to sound cynical. Obviously, the best applications do nothing more than describe your true, heartfelt interests and show off your sparkling personality. We're not suggesting you try to guess which activity will win the hearts of admissions directors and then mold yourself accordingly. Instead, think of projects and activities you care about, that maybe you haven't gotten around to acting on, and act on them now!

PICK YOUR RECOMMENDERS CAREFULLY

By the time you apply to business school, you shouldn't have to scramble for recommendations. Like the material for your essays, sources for recommendations should be considered long before the application is due.

How do you get great recommendations? Obviously, good work is a prerequisite. Whom you ask is equally important. Bosses who know you well will recommend you on both a personal and professional level. They can provide specific examples of your accomplishments, skills, and character. Additionally, they can convey a high level of interest in your candidacy.

There's also the issue of trust. B-school recommendations are made in confidence; you probably won't see exactly what's been written about you. Choose someone you can trust to deliver the kind of recommendation that will push you over the top. A casual acquaintance may fail you by writing an adequate, yet mostly humdrum letter.

Cultivate relationships that yield glowing recommendations. Former and current professors, employers, clients, and managers are all good choices. An equally impressive recommendation can come from someone who has observed you in a worthwhile extracurricular activity.

We said before you won't see *exactly* what's being written about you, but that doesn't mean you should just hand a blank piece of paper to your recommender. Left to their own devices, recommenders may create a portrait that leaves out your best features. You need to prep them on what to write. Remind them of those projects or activities in which you achieved some success. You might also discuss the total picture of yourself that you are trying to create. The recommendation should reinforce what you're saying about yourself in your essays.

About "big shot" recommendations: Don't bother. Getting some professional athlete who's a friend of your parent's to write you a recommendation will do you no good if he or she doesn't know you very well. Don't try to fudge your application; let people who really know you and your work tell the honest, believable, and impressive truth.

PREPARE FOR THE GRADUATE MANAGEMENT ADMISSION TEST (GMAT)

Most b-schools require you to take the GMAT. The GMAT is now a three-and-a-half-hour computer adaptive test (CAT) with multiple-choice Math and Verbal sections as well as an essay section. It's the kind of test you hate to take and schools love to require.

Why is the GMAT required? B-schools believe it measures your verbal and quantitative skills and predicts success in the MBA program. Some think this is a bunch of hooey, but most schools weigh your GMAT scores heavily in the admissions decision. If nothing else, it gives the school a quantitative tool to use to compare you with other applicants.

The test begins with the Analytical Writing Assessment (AWA) containing two essays questions. In the past, all questions that have appeared on the official GMAT have been drawn from a list of about 150 topics that appear in *The Official Guide to the GMAT* (published by the Educational Testing Service). Review that list and you'll have a pretty good idea of what to expect from the AWA. You will have 30 minutes to write each essay. By the way, you will be required to type your essay at the computer. Depending on how rusty your typing skills are, you may want to consider a bit of practice.

Next comes the multiple-choice section which has two parts: a 75-minute Math section and a 75-minute Verbal section. The Math section includes problem-solving questions (e.g., "Train A leaves Baltimore at 6:32 A.M. . . .") and data-sufficiency questions. Data-sufficiency questions require you to determine whether you have been given enough information to solve a particular math problem. The good news about these types of questions is that you don't actually have to solve the problem; the bad news is that these questions can be very tricky. The Verbal section tests reading skills (reading comprehension), grammar (sentence correction), and logic (critical reasoning).

For those unfamiliar with CAT exams, here's a brief overview of how they work: On multiple-choice sections, the computer starts by asking a question of medium difficulty. If you answer it correctly, the computer asks you a question that is slightly more difficult than the previous question. If you answer incorrectly, the computer asks a slightly easier question next. The test continues this way until you have answered enough questions that it can make an accurate (or so they say) assessment of your performance and assign you a score.

Most people feel they have no control over the GMAT. They dread it as the potential bomb in their application. Relax; you have more control than you think. You can take a test-preparation course to review the Math and Verbal material, learn test-taking strategies, and build your confidence. Test-prep courses can be highly effective. The Princeton Review offers what we think is the best GMAT course available. Even better, it offers two options for online preparation in addition to the traditional classroom course and one-on-one tutoring. Another option is to take a look at our book *Cracking the GMAT CAT*, which reviews all the subjects and covers all the tips you would learn in one of our courses.

How many times should you take the GMAT? More than once if you didn't ace it on the first try. But watch out: Multiple scores that fall in the same range make you look unprepared. Don't take the test more than once if you don't expect a decent increase, and don't even think of taking it the first time without serious preparation. Limiting your GMAT attempts to two is best. Three tries are okay if there were unusual circumstances. If you take it more than three times, the Admissions committee will think you have an unhealthy obsession. A final note: If you submit more than one score, most schools will take the highest.

If you don't have math courses on your college transcript or numbers-oriented work experience, it's especially important to get a solid score on the quantitative section. There's a lot of math between you and the MBA.

HOW THE ADMISSIONS CRITERIA ARE WEIGHTED

Although admissions requirements vary among business schools, most rely on the following criteria: GMAT score, college GPA, work experience, your essays, letters of recommendation (academic and/or professional), an interview with an admissions representative, and your extracurriculars. The first four are generally the most heavily weighted. The more competitive the school, the less room there is for weakness in any area. Any component out of sync, such as a weak GMAT score, is potentially harmful.

Happily, the admissions process at business school is one where great emphasis is placed on getting to know you as a person. The essay component is the element that allows the schools to do just that. Your essays can refute weaknesses, fill in gaps, and in general, charmingly persuade an admissions board you've got the right stuff. They are the single most important criteria in business school admissions.

But as we've just said, they're not the only criteria. All pieces of your application must come together to form a cohesive whole. It is the *entire application* that determines whether you win admission.

ANTICIPATE AND COORDINATE

The application process is very time-consuming, so anticipating what you need to accomplish within the admissions time frame is critical. To make the best use of our advice, you should first contact each of the programs on your personal list of schools. Their standards and criteria for admission may vary, and you'll need to follow their specific guidelines. Please note that the less competitive a school is, the more easily you may be able to breeze through (or completely omit) the rigorous requirements we identify as crucial in the application process for the top programs.

In addition, business school applicants are often overwhelmed by how much they have to do to complete not only one, but several applications. Proper management of the process is essential, since there are so many factors to coordinate in each application.

You'll have to prep for the GMAT, then actually take the test, round up some writers for your recommendations, follow up with those chosen to write recommendations, make sure the recommendations are mailed in on time, have your college transcript sent, and finally, write the essays. Of course, some schools require an interview as well. What makes all of this particularly challenging is that many applicants have to do all of this while balancing the demands of a full-time job.

We know that it takes a supreme force of will to complete even one application. As grad school applications go, a top business school's is pretty daunting. So if you don't stay focused on the details and deadlines, you may drop the ball.

There are many common and incredibly embarrassing mistakes you can avoid with prudent early planning. These include allowing your recommenders to miss the deadline, submitting an application full of typos and grammatical errors, sending one school an essay intended for another, or forgetting to change the school name when using the same essay for several applications. Applicants who wind up cramming for the GMAT or squeezing their essay writing into several all-nighters end up seriously shortchanging themselves.

APPLY EARLY

The best advice is to plan early and apply early. The former diminishes the likelihood of an accidental omission or a missed deadline. The latter increases your chances of acceptance.

The filing period ranges anywhere from six to eight months. The earlier you apply, the better your chances. There are a number of reasons for this:

First, there's plenty of space available early on. As the application deadline nears, spaces fill up. The majority of applicants don't apply until the later months because of procrastination or unavoidable delays. As the deadline draws close, the greatest number of applicants compete for the fewest number of spaces.

Second, in the beginning, Admissions Officers have little clue about how selective they can be. They haven't reviewed enough applications to determine the competitiveness of the pool. An early application may be judged more on its own merit than on how it stacks up against others. This is in your favor if the pool turns out to be unusually competitive. Above all, Admissions Officers like to lock their classes in early; they can't be certain they'll get their normal supply of applicants. Admissions decisions may be more generous at this time.

Third, by getting your application in early you're showing a strong interest. The Admissions Committee is likely to view you as someone keen on going to their school.

To be sure, some Admissions Officers report that the first batch of applications tend to be from candidates with strong qualifications, confident of acceptance. In this case, you might not be the very first one on line; but being closer to the front is still better than getting lost in the heap of last-minute hopefuls.

Of course, if applications are down that year at all b-schools or—thanks to a drop in its ranking—at the one to which you are applying, then filing later means you can benefit from admissions officers' desperate scramble to fill spaces. But this is risky business, especially since the rankings don't come out until the spring.

Conversely, if the school to which you are applying was recently ranked number one or two, applying early may make only a marginal difference. Swings in the rankings from year to year send school applications soaring and sagging. A newly crowned number-one or two school will be flooded with applications of a potential edge to be gained by filing earlier or later. Regardless from the beginning to the end of its filing period, do not put in your application until you are satisfied that it is the best you can make it. Once a school has passed on your application, it will not reconsider you until the following year.

ROUNDS VS. ROLLING ADMISSIONS

Applications are processed in one of two ways: rounds or rolling admissions. Schools that use rounds divide the filing period into three or so timed cycles. Applications are batched into the round in which they are received and reviewed in competition with others in that round. A list of a b-school's round dates can be obtained by contacting its Admissions Office if it employs this method. Applications to schools with rolling admissions are reviewed on an ongoing basis as they are received.

GMAT AND GPA

The GMAT and GPA are used in two ways. First, they're "success indicators" for the academic work you'll have to slog through if admitted—will you have the brainpower to succeed in the program? Second, they're used as benchmarks to compare each applicant to other applicants within the pool. At the more selective schools, you'll need a higher score and average to stay in the game.

Pearson VUE and the American College Testing Program (ACT) administer the GMAT. You'll need to register to take the exam by registering online at www.mba.com. Many applicants take the exam more than once to improve their scores. Test preparation is also an option for boosting your numbers—visit PrincetonReview.com for more information about The Princeton Review's GMAT courses.

Your college transcript is a major factor in the strength of your candidacy. Some schools focus more closely on the junior- and senior-year grades than the overall GPA, and most consider the reputation of your college and the difficulty of your course selections. A transcript loaded with offerings like "Environmental Appreciation" and "The Child in You" won't be valued as highly as one packed with calculus and history classes.

THE ESSAYS

Admissions committees consider the essays the clincher, the swing vote on the admit/deny issue. Essays offer the most substantive information about who you really are. The GMAT and GPA reveal little about you, only that you won't crash and burn. Your work history provides a record of performance and justifies your stated desire to study business. But the essays tie all the pieces of the application together and create a summary of your experiences, skills, background, and beliefs.

The essays do more than give answers to questions. They create thumbnail psychological profiles. Depending on how you answer a question or what you present, you reveal yourself in any number of ways—creative, witty, open-minded, articulate, mature, to name a few. On the other hand, your essay can also reveal a negative side, such as arrogance, sloppiness, or an inability to think and write clearly.

> **CHECK IT OUT:** Most top schools require multiple essays, and our popular book *Business School Essays that Made a Difference* lets you know how to ace them all. Including sample essays from successful applicants with comments from admissions officers on what worked and what didn't, *Business School Essays that Made a Difference* lets you know how to write the essays that will get you admitted. Pick it up at princetonreview.com/bookstore.

LETTERS OF RECOMMENDATION

Letters of recommendation function as a reality check. Admissions committees expect them to support and reinforce what they're seeing in the rest of your application. When the information doesn't match up with the picture you've painted, it makes you look bad. Because you won't see the recommendation (it's sent in "blind"), you won't even know there's a problem. This can mean the end of your candidacy.

That's why you need to take extreme care in selecting your references.

Scan each application for guidelines on choosing your references—business schools typically request an academic and a professional reference. The academic reference should be someone who can evaluate your performance in an academic environment. It's better to ask an instructor, teacher's aide, or mentor who knew you well than a famous professor who barely knew your name.

The same holds true for your professional reference. Seek out individuals who can evaluate your performance on many levels. The reference will be far more credible. Finding the right person to write your professional reference, however, can be trickier. You may not wish to reveal to your boss early on that you plan on leaving, and if the dynamics of your relationship are not ideal (hey, it happens once in a while), he or she might not make an appropriate reference. If this is the case, seek out a boss at a former job or someone who was your supervisor at your current job but has since moved to another organization. Avoid friends, colleagues, and clients as references unless the school explicitly says it's okay.

Advise your writers on themes and qualities you highlighted in your application. Suggest that they include real-life examples of your performance to illustrate their points. In other words, script the recommendation as best you can. Your boss, even if he or she is your biggest fan, may not know what your recommendation should include.

A great recommendation is rarely enough to save a weak application from doom. But it might push a borderline case over to the "admit" pile. Mediocre recommendations can be damaging; an application that is strong in all other areas now has a weakness, an inconsistency.

A final warning on this topic: Procrastination is common here. Micromanage your references so that each recommendation arrives on time! If need be, provide packaging for an overnight letter, have your reference seal it up, and then ship it out yourself.

The Interview

Not all business schools attach equal value to the interview. For some, it's an essential screening tool. For others, it's used to make a final decision on those caught somewhere between "admit" and "reject." Some schools may encourage, but not require, the interview. Others make it informative, with little connection to the admissions decision.

Like the letters of recommendation, an interview may serve as a reality check to reinforce the total picture. It may also be used to fill in the blanks, particularly in borderline cases.

If an interview is offered, take it. In person, you may be a more compelling candidate. You can use the interview to further address weaknesses or bring dull essays to life. Most importantly, you can display the kinds of qualities—enthusiasm, sense of humor, maturity—that can positively sway an admissions decision.

Act quickly to schedule your interview. Admissions Departments often lack the time and staff to interview every candidate who walks through their doors. You don't want your application decision delayed by several months (and placed in a more competitive round or pool) because your interview was scheduled late in the filing period.

A great interview can tip the scale in the "admit" direction. How do you know if it was great? You were calm and focused. You expressed yourself and your ideas clearly. Your interviewer invited you to go rock climbing with him or her the following weekend. (Okay, let's just say you developed a solid personal rapport with the interviewer.)

A mediocre interview may not have much impact, unless your application is hanging on by a thread. In such a case, the person you're talking to (harsh as it may seem) is probably looking for a reason not to admit you, rather than a reason to let you in. If you feel your application may be in that hazy, marginal area, try to be extra-inspired in your interview.

Approach this meeting as you would a job interview. Remember, you're being sized up as a person in all of your dimensions. Here are a few tips to use during the interview.

- Dress and act the part of a professional but avoid being stiff or acting like a stuffed shirt.

- Limit your use of business jargon. Interviewers often hear a lot of the same generic answers. They are more interested in you being your witty, charming, natural self.

- Be personable and talk about your passions, such as hobbies or a recent trip you've taken. The idea is to get the interviewer thinking of you as someone who will contribute greatly to the quality of campus life.

Highlight your achievements and excellence, even in something like gourmet cooking, but avoid stunts, such as pulling out a platter of peppercorn pate sautéed in anchovy sauce.

Chapter 4

Quotas, Recruitment, and Diversity

B-schools don't have to operate under quotas—governmental or otherwise. However, they probably try harder than most corporations to recruit diverse groups of people. Just as the modern business world has become global and multicultural, so too have b-schools. They must not only teach diversity in the classroom but also make it a reality in their campus population and, if possible, faculty.

Schools that have a diverse student body tend to be proud of it. They tout their success in profiles that demographically slice and dice the previous year's class by gender, race, and geographic and international residency. Prospective students can review this data and compare the diversity of the schools they've applied to.

However, such diversity doesn't come naturally from the demographics of the applicant pool. Admissions Committees have to work hard at it. In some cases, enrollment is encouraged with generous financial aid packages and scholarships.

While they don't have quotas per se, they do target groups for admission, seeking a demographic balance in many areas. Have they admitted enough women, minorities, foreign students, marketing strategists, and liberal arts majors? Are different parts of the country represented?

As we've said before, the best b-schools tend to attract top talent, students, and recruiters to their campus. Women and minorities are the most sought-after groups targeted for admission. So it's no surprise that programs that report higher-than-average female and minority enrollments tend to be among the very best.

AN INITIATIVE FOR MINORITIES

Some schools report higher minority enrollments than others, so our advice is consistent: You need to thoroughly research the program you've set your sights on. Consider your goals. Do you simply want to attend the most prestigious program? How will social factors impact your goals and experiences on campus?

Most business schools aspire to diversify their programs. It's the number of minorities applying to business school that has remained consistently low. An initiative of the Graduate Management Admissions Council called The Diversity Pipeline Alliance (DiversityPipeline.org) was formed to reverse this trend and increase the number of underrepresented minorities pursuing a business career. Much like the initiative for women, this organization plans a powerful marketing campaign with a pro-business career message for minority students from middle school to graduate school. It offers information on current opportunities for mentorships, internships, and financial assistance and provides an impressive roster of member organizations, services, and educational opportunities.

Minority enrollment at business schools is still quite low, so in all likelihood, you will not experience the dramatic upward shift in b-school demographics in the near future that initiatives like the Diversity Pipeline Alliance hope to influence. However, by recognizing the disparity between the minority presence in the U.S. and minority involvement in business education and practice, we are working toward a solution.

As you make up your mind about where you want to go for b-school, know that the scenario is positive and that new infrastructures exist to support your business career.

FEMALE APPEAL: BUSINESS SCHOOLS GET UP TO SPEED

If you've toured the campus and classrooms of a business school, you may have noticed something: On average, roughly 70 percent of any given MBA program's students are male. While this may make a nice pool of dating prospects for the women who are enrolled, it's not something business schools are happy with—far from it! In fact, it's something they are working to change as quickly as they can.

Beyond showing significantly higher application volume, MBA programs of all types are seeing female applications increase. About 64 percent of full-time MBA programs saw applications from women rise in 2006; the figure is 47 percent for part-time-programs and 50 percent for executive programs. While these numbers may not match the 50 percent male-to-female ratio of other graduate programs, closing the MBA gap is only a matter of time.

School Initiatives

How can we be sure that female enrollment will continue to increase? One reason is that getting women enthused about a career in business is a sky-high priority at business schools across the country these days. To wit, many business schools have launched their own women-only outreach and recruiting events. Columbia University hosts an annual "Women in Business" conference that brings together more than 700 alumnae, business leaders, students and prospective students to network and share ideas on achieving success in the marketplace. Linda Meehan, Assistant Dean for Admissions at Columbia Business School, knows that this outreach is working because "applicants walk away wowed by the extraordinary experience of being surrounded by so many intelligent, passionate and successful women." Events like these aim to dispel myths, discuss the perceived lack of role models, and help women make informed decisions.

Stanford's events, says Wendy Hansen, Associate Director of Admissions at the Stanford Business School, "focus on the educational experience, but also on the unique types of issues women have, such as: how does getting the MBA fit in with having a family or having a spouse? How do I make this experience fit in with my life?" Julia Min, Executive Director of Admissions at UC Berkeley's Haas School of Business, says attendees often find comfort in numbers. "Seeing such a large presence of women is empowering. They realize they're not in this alone, that there are other women around like them."

If all this sounds like good public relations, it is. Schools want to get the word out: MBAs offer women viable opportunities. But if the business schools are talking the talk, they're also walking the walk. There's nothing superficial about this campaign. Bit by bit, the MBA landscape for women is changing.

Opportunities begin even before the first day of class. At Stanford, admitted women are treated to one-on-one admit-lunches with female alumni. Once an admit gets to campus, they find MBA life is chock-full of student-run women and management programs, support groups, retreats, executive conferences, mentoring programs, and other dedicated resources for women only.

For many years now, most business programs have had an on-campus Partners Club for spouses and significant others—a benefit to both female and male students. Newcomers to the business-school scene include groups like The Parents Club and Biz Kids where students can find family-oriented classmates and activities. Columbia University's Mother's Network is an initiative that provides a formal support network for new, current and future b-school moms. Perhaps the most symbolic gesture of the increasing influence of women in business school is Stanford's provision of a private nursing room for MBA moms and their babies in its main classroom facility.

More Flexibility and Making it Work

Of course, there's still room for improvement. A continuing problem at business schools is a lack of course work and case study material featuring women leaders. Likewise, there is an absence of female professors on the academic front.

Apart from these lingering issues, business schools continue to tackle the particular challenges female students face. For many women, the late starting age can be a turn-off. But even here, there are new options and opportunities to consider.

If you are stressed out from trying to have it all and have written off getting an MBA, new early-initiative programs might make you pause and reconsider your decision. Harvard and Stanford have developed an early career track that aims to minimize the impact of the biological clock on a prospective applicant's decision to pursue an MBA. Other schools are likely to follow suit.

The early career track offers a solution that is as simple as it is practical: Admit women (and men) to the MBA program either straight out of college or with just a few years of work experience. Business schools hope that the option to attain their MBA early on in their careers will prompt more women to apply to their programs. With a bigger window to accomplish their professional goals, more women will turn to the MBA as a viable option that won't require them to sacrifice their personal lives.

Beginning a business career earlier eliminates the immediate problem of timing. But what happens down the road? While it helps to remove one timing issue, it can't indefinitely postpone the balancing act that shadows many women's careers. It's hard to rationalize the opportunity costs of the MBA knowing that the investment might be forsaken when tough choices have to be made.

Business schools blame misconceptions about the utility of the MBA for women's reticence on this front. They feel that many women underestimate the broad reach of the degree. The MBA is not just for hard-core careers like banking and finance, but is also useful in not-for-profit work, less high-stress industries such as consumer goods, and leadership positions in a wide range of fields.

Further, says Hansen, "There is a tremendous amount of flexibility in a general management degree. The MBA positions you much more effectively to make an impact wherever you fall at different points in your life. It gives you the tools and framework to apply those skills at different levels and in different intensities. For example, women can rise to a partner level or a senior leadership position and then scale back to a different role within the organization. They can also scale back to part-time work." In other words, the investment doesn't have to be forsaken; it might instead be redirected.

There's no doubt the return on investment (that's ROI in business speak) for the MBA is high. Six-figure salaries and sign-on bonuses that pay you back for the cost of your MBA tuition are hard to beat (and unlike medical, veterinary, and law school grads, you won't have malpractice premiums eating into your take-home pay). If you've thought business school might be right for you, keep investigating—you might be right.

WHERE ARE THE WOMEN IN MBA PROGRAMS?

Are you a professional woman in her mid-to-late twenties? Do you see graduate school in your future? During these tough times, you might envision yourself back on campus sooner rather than later. Downturns do tend to fuel grad school applications. After all, what better place to wait out the economy and avoid the gaping pit of joblessness?

Grad school can be a cure-all for many ills: It can jump-start or redirect a stubbornly off-track career; it can give you a place to hang out while you figure out what you want to be when you grow up (law school, a three-year degree, offers an even longer alternative); and it can transform your personal life as you vault into a new career. Even in uncertain times there is certainty in knowing that after two years in school you can emerge reborn as a professional with a spanking new identity, prescribed career track, and a solid alumni network.

Despite the huge appeal of graduate school, be it as an escape from bad times or as your true, chosen path, MBA programs have remained a problematic choice for many women. Female enrollment at law, medical, and veterinary schools now hovers at, or near, the 50 percent mark. So what's up with business schools? Why has female enrollment at business schools stagnated at about 30 percent?

Even during the best of times, business schools have struggled to attract women. Is this due to the unique challenges women face in building and sustaining their careers over a lifetime of choices, both professional and personal, or is there another reason? Clearly an MBA presents many opportunities, but, for women, will these opportunities upset their already delicate balancing acts?

THINKING OF FAMILY

Let's start with biology—as in biological clocks. Since a prerequisite for admission to many business programs is prior work experience, first-year business school students are typically a bit older than their law or med school counterparts. In fact, the average age for entering full-time MBA students is 28. This means that by the time graduation rolls around, MBA students are heading into their thirties—a prime time for marriage and children. For some women, that timing couldn't be worse.

Newly minted MBAs in their early thirties are just starting to reap the rewards of their business school investments by scoring brand new, mid-to-senior level jobs. With these jobs come ever-greater demands and time pressures. But, for many, the pressure to have a personal life is just as great. Those kinds of competing priorities are the very headaches women hope to avoid. Making matters worse, MBA jobs at the senior level can vault women into a culture that may still be dominated by old-school thinking (translation: men) and a culture that may be less tolerant of efforts to balance work commitments with family.

These dilemmas begin long before business school graduation. Again, because MBA students tend to be older, many women have to factor a partner or child into their graduate school decision, especially if it involves relinquishing a paycheck and/or relocation. Many of these women encounter a potential double standard: Husbands and boyfriends, especially those with careers, are often less willing to relocate on their female partner's behalf than vice versa.

NO URGENT MATTER

Another reason business school enrollment for women may be low is that an MBA is not a barrier to entry nor is it a requirement for success in business. In addition, it isn't a rite of passage in many fields that appeal to high numbers of women: marketing, publishing, fashion, and teaching. By contrast, notes Eileen Chang, former Associate Director of Admissions at the Harvard Business School, "If your objective is to be a lawyer or doctor, you simply can't practice without the requisite degree. Business school is fundamentally different because the career path is one where the MBA can put you on any number of tracks—be it banking, accounting, or management—but doesn't require a credential." Between the lack of a required degree for entering business and the late starting age to enter a program, some women perceive a high opportunity cost for the MBA.

FEAR OF MATH?

Why more women aren't pursuing an MBA is a question that business schools have been asking themselves for years. Some hard answers came in the form of a recent study by the University of Michigan's Business School Center for the Education of Women and the Catalyst Foundation. The following issues were identified as key deterrents to business school for women: the MBA is still seen as a male domain; there is a lack of support from employers; a lack of career opportunity and flexibility; a lack of access to powerful business networks and role models; and a perception that b-school is overloaded with math.

According to many schools, math fears are just that—fears. Harvard's Chang observes, "Maybe historically, math was considered a hurdle. But we see so many women who have strong skills coming from fields that are quantitative, such as banking and engineering, that I think the math fears are almost a myth. But this is a myth we want to work against. We want applicants to know they can handle the math."

Julia Min, Executive Director of Admissions at UC Berkeley's Haas School of Business, concurs, "The math phobia may be unfounded to a certain degree, and still it's a perception that has been long-lasting. Women [enter business school] and perform extremely well."

If you're frightened by math, you need to know that a business school education does require a basic command of the subject. "You do need to be comfortable with numbers," advises Wendy Hansen, Associate Director of Admissions at the Stanford Business School. "The strongest MBA programs are going to be rigorous in math. Knowing how to influence and lead an organization requires understanding the language of business, which includes accounting and finance."

Still, prospective MBAs with a math phobia need not panic; most programs will work with students who lack the necessary math background. "At Stanford, we have a pre-term program of courses before classes begin to get students up to speed," says Hansen, "We also encourage people to take quantitative courses before they come to our school to develop their skills."

If your math fears are not so easily assuaged, concerns about a persistent Old Boys Network might be. As Hansen notes, "Women may say, I don't see the masses of female role models doing what I want to do. That is going to change slowly. But it is going to change. We have to reach a point where those in school reach a place where they are out in the world having an impact."

OUR ADVICE

Look at the number of female MBA students attending your targeted school and evaluate whether you would feel comfortable there. Research the number and range of student organizations for women and speak with female MBAs about school life.

CHAPTER 5
MONEY MATTERS

HOW MUCH WILL IT COST?

THE TRUTH

To say that business school is an expensive endeavor is an understatement. In fact, to really gauge how expensive business school is, you need to look not only at your tuition costs and living expenses, but also at the opportunity cost of foregoing a salary for the length of your program. Think about it: You'll have a net outflow of money.

But keep in mind that, unlike law school or medical school, business school is just a two-year program. Once those two years are over, you can expect to reap the rewards of your increased market value. Unfortunately, business school differs from law school and medical school in a much less desirable way as well—there are serious limitations on the amount of money available through scholarships and grants. Most business school students will be limited to loans, and lots of them.

Try not to get too upset about borrowing the money for business school; think of it as an investment in yourself. But, like all investments, it should be carefully thought out and discussed with everyone (spouse, partner, etc.) concerned. This is especially important for those of you considering business school. You need a law degree to practice law, and a medical degree to practice medicine, but a business degree is not required to work in business. That said, certain professional opportunities may be tougher to pursue without an MBA on your resume.

THE COST OF B-SCHOOL

So get out some paper, a pencil, and a calculator, and figure out how much it will cost you to attend school. What should you include? Your opportunity cost (lost income) and your cost of attending b-school (tuition and fees). One more thing: For a more accurate assessment of your investment, you should figure taxes into the equation by dividing tuition cost by 0.65 (this assumes taxes of about 35 percent). Why? Because in order to pay tuition of $25,000, you would have to make a pre-tax income of about $38,500. If you are lucky enough to have a source of aid that does not require repayment, such as a grant, scholarship, or wealthy benefactor, subtract that amount from the cost of attending b-school.

For example, if you currently make $50,000 and plan to attend a business school that costs $25,000 per year, your investment would be approximately $177,000.

$(50,000 \times 2) + [(25,000 \times 2)/.65] = 177,000$

Now say you receive an annual grant of $5,000. Your investment would now be approximately $161,500.

$(50,000 \times 2) + [(20,000 \times 2)/.65] = 161,500$

How Long Will It Take You to Recoup Your Investment?

To estimate this figure, you first need to estimate your expected salary increase post-MBA. Check out the average starting salaries for graduates of the programs you are looking at and adjust upward/downward based on the industry you plan to enter. Subtract your current salary from your expected salary and you'll get your expected salary increase.

Once you complete the step above, divide your investment (tuition and fees plus lost income) by your expected salary increase, and then add 2 (the length of a full-time MBA program). If you are contemplating a one-year MBA program, just add 1.

Going back to the example above, if your pre-MBA salary is $50,000 and you expect to make $75,000 when you graduate, your expected salary increase is $25,000 (a 50 percent increase). Let's assume you did not receive a grant and that your investment will be about $177,000.

$(177,000/25,000) + 2 = 9.08$

It will take you approximately nine years to earn back your investment.

Keep in mind, these are approximations and don't take into account annual raises, inflation, and so on. But it is interesting, isn't it?

While business school is an expensive proposition, the financial rewards of having your MBA can be immensely lucrative as we discussed before. You won't be forced into bankruptcy if you finance it correctly. There are tried-and-true ways to reduce your initial costs, finance the costs on the horizon, and manage the debt you'll leave school with—all without selling your soul to the highest bidder.

Comparison Shopping

While cost shouldn't be the first thing on your mind when you are choosing a school, depending on your goals in getting an MBA, it might be fairly high on your list. Private schools aren't the only business schools. Many state schools have fantastic reputations. Regional schools may be more generous with financial aid. Tuition costs will vary widely between public and private schools, especially if you qualify as an in-state student. Keep in mind, however, that salary gains tend to be less dramatic at more regional schools.

HOW DO I FUND MY MBA?

The short answer: loans. Unless your company is underwriting your MBA, or you're able to pay your way in cash, you'll be financing your two years of business school through a portfolio of loans. Loans typically come in one of two forms: federal and private. Only a few of you will be lucky enough to qualify for, and get, grants and scholarships.

Anyone with reasonably good credit, regardless of financial need, can borrow money for business school. If you have financial need, you will probably be eligible for some type of financial aid if you meet the following basic qualifications:

- You are a United States citizen or a permanent U.S. resident.

- You are registered for Selective Service if you are a male, or you have documentation to prove that you are exempt.

- You are not in default on student loans already.

- You don't have a horrendous credit history.

International applicants to business school should take note: Most U.S. business schools will require all international students to pay in full or show proof that they will be able to pay the entire cost of the MBA prior to beginning the MBA program.

FEDERAL LOANS

The federal government funds federal loan programs. Federal loans are usually the "first resort" for borrowers because many are subsidized by the federal government and offer generous interest rates. Some do not begin charging you interest until after you complete your degree. Most federal loans are need-based, but some higher interest federal loans are available regardless of financial circumstances. Your business school's Financial Aid Office will determine what your need is, if any.

PRIVATE LOANS

Private loans are funded by banks, foundations, corporations, and other associations. A number of private loans are targeted to aid particular segments of the population. You may have to do some investigating to identify private loans for which you might qualify. As always, contact your law school's Financial Aid Office to learn more.

ALTERNATIVE SOURCES OF FUNDING

We've already mentioned these in one form or other, but they are worthy of a bit more attention.

The first alternative is sponsorship of your employer or educational reimbursement. Not all companies treat this the same way, but if you are able to get your employer to kick in a portion of the cost, you are better off than before. But beware, this benefit also comes with strings attached. Most companies that pay for your MBA will require a commitment of several years upon graduation. If you renege, you could be liable for the full cost of your education. Others will require that you attend business school part-time, which you may or may not want to do. Often, part-time students are ineligible to participate in on-campus recruiting efforts to the same extent as full-time students.

Educational reimbursement can come in another form as well. Some companies will provide sign-on bonuses to new MBAs that will cover the cost of a year's tuition. This is a fantastic development from the years of a robust economy, but it is by no means a guarantee during tougher times. Don't assume that you will have this option open to you just because it has been a common occurrence in past years.

The other "alternative" source of funding is a financial gift from family or another source. Either you have a resource that is willing and able to fund all or part of your MBA, or you don't. If you do, be thankful.

APPLYING FOR FINANCIAL AID

In order to become eligible for financial aid of any kind, you will need to complete the Free Application for Federal Student Aid, also known as the FAFSA. You complete and submit this form after January 1 of the year in which you plan to enter business school. You should aim to complete and submit this form as soon as possible after the first of the year to avoid any potential delays. The FAFSA is available from a school's Financial Aid Office. You can also download the form directly from the website of the U.S. Department of Education at FAFSA.ed.gov. A third option is to use the FAFSA Express software (also downloadable from the website) and transmit the application electronically.

It is important to note that the form requires information from your federal income tax returns. Plan to file your taxes early that year.

In addition to the FAFSA form, most schools will have their own financial aid form that you will be required to complete and submit. These often have their own deadlines, so it is wise to keep careful track of all the forms you must complete and all their respective deadlines. Yes, it's a lot of paperwork, but get over it. You'll be much happier when the tuition bill arrives.

LOAN SPECIFICS

GUIDE TO FEDERAL LOANS

Stafford Loans

Stafford loans require you to complete the FAFSA form in order to qualify. These are very desirable loans because they offer low-interest rates capped at 8.25 percent and are federally guaranteed. There is a limit to how much you can borrow in this program. The maximum amount per year you may borrow as a graduate student is $18,500; $10,000 of which must be unsubsidized loans. The maximum amount you may borrow in total is $138,500 (only $65,500 of this may be in subsidized loans). The aggregate amount includes any Stafford loans you may have from your undergraduate or other graduate studies.

Stafford loans come in two types: subsidized and unsubsidized. Subsidized loans are need-based as determined by your business school. They do not accrue interest while you are in school or in an authorized deferment period (such as the first six months after graduation). This cost is picked up by the government (hence the name "subsidized"). Repayment begins at that time. Unsubsidized loans are not need-based and do charge interest from the time of disbursement to the time of full repayment. You can pay the interest while you are in school or opt for capitalization, in which case the interest is added to the principal. You will pay more in the long run if you choose capitalization. Interest payments may be tax deductible, so be sure to check. The standard repayment period for both is 10 years.

You will pay a small origination and guarantee fee for each loan, but this is not an out-of-pocket expense. It is simply deducted from the loan amount. Some schools will allow you to borrow the money under the Stafford program directly from them, while others will require you to borrow from a bank. For more information on federal loans, call the Federal Student Aid Information Center at 800-433-3243.

Perkins Loans

Perkins loans are available to graduate students who demonstrate exceptional financial need. The financial aid office will determine your eligibility for a Perkins Loan. If you qualify for a Perkins Loan as part of your financial aid package, take it. The loans are made by the schools and are repaid to the schools, although the federal government provides a large portion of the funds. You can borrow up to $6,000 for each year of graduate study up to a total of $40,000 (this includes any money borrowed under this program during undergraduate study). The interest rates on this loan are low, usually 5 percent. There are no fees attached. The grace period is nine months upon graduation.

PRIVATE/COMMERCIAL LOANS

This is expensive territory. Not only are interest rates high, but terms are also quite different from those found with federal loans. You may not be able to defer payment of interest or principal until after graduation. Origination and guarantee fees are also much higher since these loans are unsecured. After all, banks and other specialized lenders exist to loan money to folks like you, and unlike the federal government, want to make money doing it. If you go this route, shop around diligently. Think of it as good practice for your post-MBA executive career.

Scholarships and Grants

The usual sources for this type of funding are alumni groups and civic organizations. This funding is limited, and actual awards tend to be small. Even if you benefited from generous scholarship funding as an undergraduate, it would be unwise to assume you'll have the same experience as a graduate student. But do investigate. You never know what's out there. Schools will frequently list any scholarships and grants that are available at the back of their financial aid catalog.

For more information

Find out more about your financing options for business school education at PrincetonReview.com.

Chapter 6
What B-School is Really Like

AN ACADEMIC PERSPECTIVE

The objective of all MBA programs is to prepare students for a professional career in business. One business school puts it this way:

Graduates should be all of the following:

1. Able to think and reason independently, creatively, and analytically.

2. Skilled in the use of quantitative techniques.

3. Literate in the use of software applications as management tools.

4. Knowledgeable about the world's management issues and problems.

5. Willing to work in and successfully cope with conditions of uncertainty, risk, and change.

6. Astute decision makers.

7. Ethically and socially responsible.

8. Able to manage in an increasingly global environment.

9. Proficient in utilizing technology as a mode of doing business.

Sound like a tall order? Possibly. But this level of expectation is what business school is all about.

Nearly all MBA programs feature a core curriculum that focuses on the major disciplines of business: finance, management, accounting, marketing, manufacturing, decision sciences, economics, and organizational behavior. Unless your school allows you to place out of them, these courses are mandatory. Core courses provide broad functional knowledge in one discipline. To illustrate, a core marketing course covers pricing, segmentation, communications, product-line planning, and implementation. Electives provide a narrow focus that deepen the area of study. For example, a marketing elective might be entirely devoted to pricing.

Students sometimes question the need for such a comprehensive core program, but the functional areas of a real business are not parallel lines. All departments of a business affect each other every day. For example, an MBA in a manufacturing job might be asked by a financial controller why the company's product has become unprofitable to produce. Without an understanding of how product costs are accounted for, this MBA wouldn't know how to respond to a critical and legitimate request.

At most schools, the first term or year is devoted to a rigid core curriculum. Some schools allow first-years to take core courses side by side with electives. Still others have come up with an entirely new way of covering the basics, integrating the core courses into one cross-functional learning experience, which may also include sessions on topics such as globalization, ethics, and managing diversity. Half-year to year-long courses are team-taught by professors who will see you through all disciplines.

TEACHING METHODOLOGY

Business schools employ two basic teaching methods: case study and lecture. Usually, they employ some combination of the two. The most popular is the case study approach. Students are presented with either real or hypothetical business scenarios and are asked to analyze them. This method provides concrete situations (rather than abstractions) that require mastery of a wide range of skills. Students often find case studies exciting because they can engage in spirited discussions about possible solutions to given business problems and because they get an opportunity to apply newly acquired business knowledge.

On the other hand, lecturing is a teaching method in which—you guessed it—the professor speaks to the class and the class listens. The efficacy of the lecture method depends entirely on the professor. If the professor is compelling, you'll probably get a lot out of the class. If the professor is boring, you probably won't listen, which isn't necessarily a big deal since many professors make their class notes available on computer disc or in the library.

THE CLASSROOM EXPERIENCE

Professors teaching case methodology often begin class with a "cold call." A randomly selected student opens the class with an analysis of the case and makes recommendations for solutions. The cold call forces you to be prepared and to think on your feet.

No doubt, a cold call can be intimidating. But unlike law school, b-school professors don't use the Socratic Method to torture you, testing your thinking with a pounding cross-examination. They're training managers, not trial lawyers. At worst, particularly if you're unprepared, a professor will abruptly dismiss your contribution.

Alternatively, professors ask for a volunteer to open a case, particularly someone who has had real industry experience with the issues. After the opening, the discussion is broadened to include the whole class. Everyone tries to get in a good comment, particularly if class participation counts heavily toward the grade. "Chip shots"—unenlightened, just-say-anything-to-get-credit comments—are common. So are "air hogs," students who go on and on because they like nothing more than to hear themselves pontificate.

Depending on the school, class discussions can degenerate into wars of ego rather than ideas. But for the most part, debates are kept constructive and civilized. Students are competitive, but not offensively so, and learn to make their points succinctly and persuasively.

A GLOSSARY OF INSIDER LINGO

B-school students, graduates, and professors—like most close-knit, somewhat solipsistic groups—seem to speak their own weird language. Here's a sampler of MBA jargon (with English translations):

Admissions Mistake: How each student perceives him or herself until getting first-year grades back from midterms.

Air Hogs: Students who monopolize classroom discussion and love to hear themselves speak.

B2B: "Business to Business"—a company that sells not to retail consumers, but to other enterprises. With the renewed focus on more traditional industries, this now stands for "Back to Basics."

B2C: "Business to Consumer"—a company that sells primarily to individual retail consumers. As with the above joke about B2B, business students occasionally say this really means "Back to Consulting."

Back of the Envelope: A quick analysis of numbers, as if scribbled on the back of an envelope.

Benchmarking: Comparing a company to others in the industry.

Burn Rate: Amount of cash a money-losing company consumes during a period of time.

Case Study Method: Popular teaching method that uses real-life business cases for analysis.

Cold Call: Unexpected, often dreaded request by the professor to open a case discussion.

Chip Shot: Vacant and often cheesy comments used not to truly benefit class discussion, but rather to get credit for participation.

Cycle Time: How fast you can turn something around.

Deliverable: Your end product.

Four Ps: Elements of a marketing strategy: Price, Promotion, Place, Product.

Fume Date: Date the company will run out of cash reserves.

Functional Areas: The basic disciplines of business (e.g., finance, marketing, R&D).

HP12-C: A calculator that works nothing like a regular one, used by finance types when they don't have Excel handy.

Lingo Bingo: A furtive game of Bingo whereby he who "wins" must work a decided upon, often trite phrase (see "chip shot") into the class discussion. For example: "I didn't actually read the case last night, but the protagonist is *two beers short of a six-pack*." The winner also earns a prize and the admiration of classmates.

Low Hanging Fruit: Tasks or goals that are easiest to achieve (consultant jargon).

Monitize: To turn an idea into a moneymaking scheme.

Net Net: End result.

Power Nap: Quick, intense, in-class recharge for the continually sleep-deprived.

Power Tool: Someone who does all the work and sits in the front row of the class with his or her hand up.

Pre-enrollment Courses: Commonly known as MBA summer camp—quantitative courses to get the numerically challenged up to speed.

Pro Forma: Financial presentation of hypothetical events, such as projected earnings.

Quant Jock: A numerical athlete who is happiest crunching numbers.

Rule of Three: You should not talk more than three times in any given class, but you should participate at least once over the course of three classes.

Run the Numbers: Analyze quantitatively.

Shrimp Boy: A student who comes to a corporate event just to scarf down the food.

Skydeck: Refers to the back row of the classroom, usually when it's amphitheater style.

Slice and Dice: Running all kinds of quantitative analysis on a set of numbers.

Soft Skills: Conflict resolution, teamwork, negotiation, oral and written communication.

Take-aways: The key points of a lecture or meeting that participants should remember.

The Five Forces: Michael Porter's model for analyzing the strategic attractiveness of an industry.

Three Cs: The primary forces considered in marketing: Customer, Competition, Company.

Value-Based Decision Making: Values and ethics as part of the practice of business.

YOUR FIRST YEAR

The first six months of b-school can be daunting. You're unfamiliar with the subjects. There's a tremendous amount of work to do. And when you least have the skills to do so, there's pressure to stay with the pack. All of this produces anxiety and a tendency to overprepare. Eventually, students learn shortcuts and settle into a routine, but until then, much of the first year is just plain tough. The programs usually pack more learning into the first term than they do into each of the remaining terms. For the schools to teach the core curriculum (which accounts for as much as 70 percent of learning) in a limited time, an intensive pace is considered necessary. Much of the second year will be spent on gaining proficiency in your area of expertise and on searching for a job.

The good news is that the schools recognize how tough the first year can be. During the early part of the program, they anchor students socially by placing them in small sections, sometimes called "cohorts." You take many or all of your classes with your section-mates. Sectioning encourages the formation of personal and working relationships and can help make a large program feel like a school within a school.

Because so much has to be accomplished in so little time, getting an MBA is like living in fast-forward. This is especially true of the job search. No sooner are you in the program than recruiters for summer jobs show up, which tends to divert students from their studies. First-years aggressively pursue summer positions, which are linked with the promise of a permanent job offer if the summer goes well. At some schools, the recruiting period begins as early as October, at others in January or February.

A DAY IN THE LIFE

MATT CAMP, FIRST YEAR
Tuck School of Business, Dartmouth College

7:00 A.M.: Get dressed. Out of the door by 7:45 A.M. to head to the campus dining hall for breakfast. If I have time, I'll grab the *Financial Times* and *The Wall Street Journal* and gloss over the front page. Today, I have an informal get-to-know-you-better meeting with a marketing professor over breakfast.

8:30 A.M.: Core class in Corporate Finance. Grab any seat in a tiered classroom set-up. I'm usually in the middle toward the side. If possible, the front row stays empty.

10:00 A.M.: Go to e-mail kiosk on campus and check messages. Hang out or do a quick run to the library to read more of the *Times*.

10:30 A.M.: Macroeconomics lecture/case study class. Again, no assigned seating. Expect cold calls on case. Cold calls are not terrifying. Professors are supportive, not out to embarrass you. Class discussion is lively, with a mix of people offering their views.

Noon: Back to the cafeteria. Tuck may be one of the few schools where everyone eats together at the same place. There isn't much in town, and you're tight on time, so it doesn't make sense to go back home or elsewhere. It's crowded, so I look for friends, but basically grab a seat anywhere at one of the large tables that seat six to seven. Professors, administrators, and students all eat at the same place. Food is above-average.

1:15 P.M.: Classes are over for the day. From this point, I begin to start homework; there's a lot of work to do. I can go to a study room on campus, but they get booked up pretty quickly for groups, so I head to the library. The majority of the people are doing work for tomorrow. It's rare to have someone working on a project that's due the following week. It's pretty much day-to-day.

4:00 P.M.: I head off to one of the scheduled sports I've signed up for. Today it's soccer, played about one mile from campus. I drive; friends hitch a ride with me. This is a big international scene, mostly men, but there's a small group of women too. It's definitely a game we play hard, but in a very congenial way.

6:00 P.M.: Head back to campus. I'm hungry. It's off to the dining hall again. Most first-years live in dorms, so home cooking is not an option. Almost all second-years live off-campus, so they head back for a home-cooked meal. Cafeteria is not crowded; I may eat alone.

7:00 P.M.: Head home for a quick shower and change. The night is just beginning.

7:30 P.M.: Meet with study group at school to flesh out rest of work that needs to be done in preparation for tomorrow's classes.

11:00 P.M.: Students and their wives/husbands or partners head out to play ice hockey at one of the two rinks here. Wives/husbands and partners play. There are different games going on for different skill levels. It's a lot of fun.

Midnight: Time to go and celebrate either a hard game or a sore butt, but everyone goes to get some wings and a beer. There are only two bars on campus, and they close at 1:00 A.M. so we head to one of them.

1:00 A.M.: After the bar closes, people head home.

1:15 A.M.: Exhausted, I go to bed. No TV. I've forgotten what that is.

YOUR SECOND YEAR

Relax, the second year is easier. By now, students know what's important and what's not. Second-years work more efficiently than first-years. Academic anxiety is no longer a factor. Having mastered the broad-based core curriculum, students now enjoy taking electives and developing an area of specialization.

Anxiety in the second year has more to do with the arduous task of finding a job. For some lucky students, a summer position has yielded a full-time offer. But even those students often go through the whole recruiting grind anyway because they don't want to cut off any opportunities prematurely.

Most MBAs leave school with a full-time offer. Sometimes it's their only offer. Sometimes it's not their dream job, which may be why most grads change jobs after just two years. One student summed up the whole two-year academic/recruiting process like this: "The first-year students collapse in the winter quarter because of on-campus recruiting. The second-years collapse academically in the first quarter of their second year because it's so competitive to get a good job. And when a second-year does get a job, he or she forgets about class entirely. That's why pass/fail was invented."

A DAY IN THE LIFE

KRISTIN HANSEN, SECOND-YEAR
Tuck School of Business, Dartmouth College

9:00 A.M.: Wake-up (my first class is at 10:30 A.M.) and finish work for Monday classes.

10:15 A.M.: Ride my bike to campus for 10:30 A.M. class.

10:30 A.M.: Head to International Economics class, an elective. I have only three classes this semester, my last. Prior to this I had four and a half classes each term. I front-loaded so I would have a light last semester. Grab a yogurt and juice on way in. Eat in class. We discuss a currency crisis case.

Noon: Head to study room to plug my personal computer into one of the many networked connections on campus to check e-mail. Finish work for next class.

1:00 P.M.: Grab a quick lunch in the dining hall. Will bring it to eat during class.

1:15 P.M.: Managerial Decision Making class, another elective. Today is the very last class that second-years will have at Tuck; we're off to graduation! Our professor brings in strawberries and champagne to celebrate. We all hang out and toast each other. This obviously doesn't happen everyday, but this is just the kind of thing a Tuck professor would do.

2:45 P.M.: I'm one of four Tuck social chairpersons, so I use this time to send e-mails to my co-chairs about the upcoming chili cook-off and farm party. Then I send a message to the school regarding other social events for the weekend. I get an e-mail from the New York office of CS First Boston, with whom I've accepted a job offer, with a calendar of the dates for my private client-services training.

3:00 P.M.: Go for a run, swim, or bike ride.

5:00 P.M.: Head home to shower and change. Usually I'd make dinner at home and eat, but tonight, I'm heading out to a social event. So I relax a bit and do an hour of preparation for the next day. On Monday, Tuesday, and Wednesday nights, the workload is heavier.

7:00 P.M.: Off to a Turkey Fry Dinner. This is a meal that will be prepared by my two economics professors. They donated this "dinner" for the charity student auction. Friends of mine bid on it and won. Each of eight bidders gets to bring a guest, and I'm one of the guests. The professors are hosting this at one of their homes. Basically, they're taking three large turkeys and fry-o-lating them.

8:30 P.M.: We all head out to an open mic night, led by the same two economics professors that hosted the Turkey Fry. It's held at a local bar. Anyone in the audience can get onstage and perform. I'm a member of the Tuck band, so I get up on stage with my acoustic guitar and play various folk and bluegrass songs. This is a great warm-up for the open mic night at Tuck.

10:45 P.M.: We head out for Pub Night in downtown Hanover.

1:00 A.M.: The bar closes, so we head to "The End Zone," one of the second-year houses close to campus. All the second-year houses are named; these are names that have been passed down from generation to generation. On a typical Thursday night at Tuck, a small number of students will stay out until 3:00 A.M. I'm usually one of them.

3:00 A.M.: I walk home. My house, called "Girls in the Hood," is just a ten-minute stroll away. I may grab a 3:00 A.M. snack. Then, I quickly fall asleep, exhausted.

Life Outside of Class

Business school is more than academics and a big-bucks job. A spirited community provides ample opportunity for social interaction, extracurricular activity, and career development.

Much of campus life revolves around student-run clubs. There are groups for just about every career interest and social need—from MBAs for a Greener America to the Small Business Club. There's even a group for significant others on most campuses. The clubs are a great way to meet classmates with similar interests and to get in on the social scene. They might have a reputation for throwing the best black-tie balls, pizza-and-keg events, and professional mixers. During orientation week, these clubs aggressively market themselves to first-years.

Various socially responsible projects are also popular on campus. An emphasis on volunteer work is part of the overall trend toward good citizenship. Perhaps to counter the greed of the 1980s, "giving back" is the b-school style of the moment. There is usually a wide range of options—from tutoring in an inner-city school to working in a soup kitchen to renovating public buildings.

Still another way to get involved is to work on a school committee. Here you might serve on a task force designed to improve student quality of life, 0r you might work in the admissions office and interview prospective students.

For those with more creative urges there are always the old standbys: extracurriculars such as the school paper, yearbook, or school play. At some schools, the latter is a dramatization of "b-school follies" and is a highlight of the year. Like the student clubs, these are a great way to get to know your fellow students.

Finally, you can play on intramural sports teams or attend the numerous informal get-togethers, dinner parties, and group trips. There are also plenty of regularly scheduled pub nights, just in case you thought your beer-guzzling days were over.

Most former MBA students say that going to b-school was the best decision they ever made. That's primarily because of nonacademic experiences. Make the most of your classes, but take the time to get involved and enjoy yourself.

PART II
SCHOOLS RANKED BY CATEGORY

On the following pages you will find eleven top 10 lists of business schools ranked according to various metrics. As we noted earlier, none of these lists purports to rank the business schools by their overall quality. Nor should any combination of the categories we've chosen be construed as representing the raw ingredients for such a ranking. We have made no attempt to gauge the "prestige" of these schools, and we wonder whether we could accurately do so even if we tried. What we have done, however, is presented a number of lists using information from two very large databases—one of statistical information collected from business schools, and another of subjective data gathered via our survey of 19,000 business students at 296 business schools.

Ten of the ranking lists are based partly or wholly on opinions collected through our business student survey. The only schools that may appear in these lists are the 296 business schools from which we were able to collect a sufficient number of student surveys to accurately represent the student experience in our various ratings and descriptive profiles.

One of the rankings, Toughest to Get Into, incorporates *only* admissions statistics reported to us by the business schools. Therefore, any business school appearing in this edition of the guide, whether we collected student surveys from it or not, may appear on this list.

Under the title of each list is an explanation of what criteria the ranking is based on. For explanations of many of the individual rankings components, turn to the "How This Book is Organized" section, on page 5.

It's worth repeating: There is no one best business school in America. There is a best business school for you. By using these rankings in conjunction with the descriptive profiles and data listings in subsequent sections of this book, we hope that you will begin to identify the attributes of a business school that are important to you, as well as those schools that can best help you to achieve your personal and professional goals.

Please note that in an effort to avoid comparing apples to oranges, we have not placed any international business schools on any of our rankings lists.

The top schools in each category appear in descending order.

TOUGHEST TO GET INTO

Based on the Admissions Selectivity Rating (see page 11 for explanation)

1. Stanford University
2. Harvard University
3. Columbia University
4. University of California—Berkeley
5. University of Pennsylvania
6. Massachusetts Institute of Technology
7. Yale University
8. New York University
9. University of Michigan—Ann Arbor
10. Dartmouth College

BEST CLASSROOM EXPERIENCE

Based on student assessment of professors' teaching abilities and recognition in their fields, the integration of new business trends and practices in the curricula, and the intellectual level of classmates' contributions in course discussions

1. Indiana University—Bloomington
2. Acton MBA in Entrepreneurship
3. Millsaps College
4. East Tennessee State University
5. Indiana University Southeast
6. Harvard University
7. Elon University
8. The University of Chicago
9. University of Virginia
10. Brigham Young University

BEST CAREER PROSPECTS

Based on the Career Rating (see page 13 for explanation)

1. Stanford University
2. Harvard University
3. University of Pennsylvania
4. University of California—Berkeley
5. University of Michigan—Ann Arbor
6. Dartmouth College
7. University of Virginia
8. Northwestern University
9. Cornell University
10. The University of Chicago

BEST PROFESSORS

Based on the Professors Interesting and Professors Accessible Ratings (see pages 9 and 10 for explanations)

1. University of Virginia
2. Indiana University—Bloomington
3. Acton MBA in Entrepreneurship
4. The College of William and Mary
5. Claremont Graduate University
6. The University of North Carolina at Chapel Hill
7. Harvard University
8. Penn State University
9. Washington University in St. Louis
10. Dartmouth College

MOST COMPETITIVE STUDENTS

BASED ON STUDENT ASSESSMENT OF HOW COMPETITIVE CLASSMATES ARE, HOW HEAVY THE WORKLOAD IS, AND THE PERCEIVED ACADEMIC PRESSURE

1. University of Pennsylvania
2. Vanderbilt University
3. Acton MBA in Entrepreneurship
4. Brigham Young University
5. Texas Southern University
6. Rutgers, The State University of New Jersey
7. Clemson University
8. Southern Methodist University
9. Howard University
10. University of Arkansas—Fayetteville

MOST FAMILY FRIENDLY

BASED ON STUDENT ASSESSMENT OF: HOW HAPPY MARRIED STUDENTS ARE, HOW MANY STUDENTS HAVE CHILDREN, HOW HELPFUL THE BUSINESS SCHOOL IS TO STUDENTS WITH CHILDREN, AND HOW MUCH THE SCHOOL DOES FOR THE SPOUSES OF STUDENTS

1. Brigham Young University
2. Dartmouth College
3. Indiana University—Bloomington
4. Harvard University
5. East Tennessee State University
6. University of Utah
7. University of Virginia
8. Northwestern University
9. The University of North Carolina at Chapel Hill
10. University of Houston—Victoria

BEST CAMPUS ENVIRONMENT

BASED ON STUDENT ASSESSMENT OF THE SAFETY, ATTRACTIVENESS AND LOCATION OF THE SCHOOL

1. University of California—Los Angeles
2. American University
3. The University of Iowa
4. Rice University
5. Stanford University
6. University of Virginia
7. University of Portland
8. University of Washington
9. Appalachian State University
10. Dartmouth College

BEST CAMPUS FACILITIES

BASED ON STUDENT ASSESSMENT OF THE QUALITY OF CLASSROOM, LIBRARY AND GYM FACILITIES

1. Bentley College
2. Baylor University
3. University of Alabama—Tuscaloosa
4. Indiana University—Bloomington
5. University of Virginia
6. Penn State University
7. Southern Methodist University
8. Harvard University
9. University of Georgia
10. University of California—Berkeley

BEST ADMINISTERED

BASED ON STUDENT ASSESSMENT OF HOW SMOOTHLY THE SCHOOL IS RUN, AND THE EASE WITH WHICH STUDENTS CAN GET INTO REQUIRED AND POPULAR COURSES

1. Harvard University
2. Vanderbilt University
3. University of Michigan—Ann Arbor
4. University of California—Berkeley
5. Northwestern University
6. Elon University
7. New York University
8. West Virginia University
9. Acton MBA in Entrepreneurship
10. Dartmouth College

GREATEST OPPORTUNITY FOR MINORITY STUDENTS

BASED ON THE PERCENT OF STUDENTS FROM MINORITIES, THE PERCENT OF FACULTY FROM MINORITIES, AND STUDENT ASSESSMENT OF RESOURCES FOR MINORITY STUDENTS, HOW SUPPORTIVE THE CULTURE IS OF MINORITY STUDENTS, AND WHETHER FELLOW STUDENTS ARE ETHNICALLY AND RACIALLY DIVERSE

1. Howard University
2. Barry University
3. Texas Southern University
4. University of Houston—Victoria
5. Delaware State University
6. Bowling Green State University
7. Texas A&M International University
8. The University of Texas at San Antonio
9. New Mexico State University
10. San Francisco State University

GREATEST OPPORTUNITY FOR WOMEN

BASED ON THE PERCENT OF STUDENTS WHO ARE FEMALE, THE PERCENT OF FACULTY WHO ARE FEMALE, AND STUDENT ASSESSMENT OF: RESOURCES FOR FEMALE STUDENTS, HOW SUPPORTIVE THE CULTURE IS OF FEMALE STUDENTS, WHETHER THE BUSINESS SCHOOL OFFERS COURSEWORK FOR WOMEN ENTREPRENEURS, AND WHETHER CASE STUDY MATERIALS FOR CLASSES PROPORTIONATELY REFLECT WOMEN IN BUSINESS

1. University of Massachusetts Amherst
2. Jacksonville State University
3. Mercer University—Atlanta
4. Western Carolina University
5. University of Tennessee—Chattanooga
6. George Washington University
7. University of California, Davis
8. St. Mary's University (TX)
9. State University of New York at Albany
10. Worcester Polytechnic Institute

PART III-A
BUSINESS SCHOOL
DESCRIPTIVE PROFILES

ACTON SCHOOL OF BUSINESS
THE ACTON MBA IN ENTREPRENEURSHIP

GENERAL INFORMATION

Type of school	Private

SURVEY SAYS...

Cutting edge classes
Solid preparation in:
Finance
Accounting
General management
Operations
Entrepreneurial studies

STUDENTS

Enrollment of parent institution	2,200
Enrollment of MBA program	27
% male/female	81/19
% out-of-state	52
% minorities	19
% international	15
Average age at entry	30
Average years work experience at entry	7

ACADEMICS

Academic Experience Rating	**99**
Student/faculty ratio	2:1
Profs interesting rating	99
Profs accessible rating	87

FINANCIAL FACTS

Annual tuition	$35,000
Fees	$0
Cost of books	$0
Room & board (off-campus)	$20,000
% of students receiving aid	100
% of first-year students receiving aid	100
Average award package	$35,000

Academics

The Acton MBA in Entrepreneurship is a rigorous, progressive, and unique business program offered through Hardin-Simmons University in Austin, Texas. Cramming 2 years worth of material into just 12 months, Acton students are ambitious and focused, willing "to work 100-hour weeks to accomplish in one year what 'traditional' schools accomplish in two." All classes are taught in the case-based or Socratic Method and, in a single year, students analyze over 300 cases. Preparation is crucial, as class participation accounts for 50 percent of your grade, and professors "place a high emphasis on quality listening and on conversational continuity (i.e., building on previous comments) versus merely making a brilliant point that is unconnected to the dialogue." Plus, there's no wiggle room for slackers: The curriculum is tightly integrated, with each class building on the next.

The Acton program is built upon three pillars: learning to learn, learning how to make money, and learning how to live a life of meaning. Students say the program delivers on all three points and distinguishes itself by focusing on the personal side of career development. "Acton helps us learn about ourselves by aiding us in our search for our true calling in life—the one thing that we are the best at that intertwines with what the world needs," explains one student. "This help in our personal lives as well as our business lives is unparalleled by any other MBA program."

At the same time, Acton emphasizes a "concrete, nuts-and-bolts approach to business and entrepreneurship," including many hands-on projects such as operations simulation and plant tours. Promoting an entrepreneurial spirit, Acton is "the only program in which 100 percent of the professors are actively running businesses." While they put their students through the wringer in the classroom, these "entrepreneur-teachers" are "all leaders in their fields with a real heart for teaching." There is no traditional tenure track at Acton, and teachers (like students) are expected to perform. To ensure their success, students fill out a weekly survey that "brings about change almost immediately. The administration is very focused on making the Acton program the best entrepreneurial program in the world, and so they take the input of their customer (the student) very seriously." One student goes so far as to say the administrative staff treats students "like we are at a Ritz-Carlton; customer service is outstanding."

Fellow students also form an important part of the academic environment at Acton with, "a highly varied set of backgrounds, ranging from home building, to e-commerce, to manufacturing, to the military, to public radio. Everyone is passionate about learning, and we hold each other to the highest of standards." In fact, students tell us that "competition and debate is held to a standard of high conflict, in which ideas are challenged and efforts are tested but the individuals are held in high regard and treated with respect."

Career and Placement

It is Acton's philosophy that sending out hundreds of resumes is a waste of time for both employers and applicants. Therefore, Acton takes a very unique approach to career planning. First, students complete the Life of Meaning course—a required part of the Acton curriculum—during which they profoundly consider both their skill set and career goals. As a part of the course, students identify a specific job at a specific company which represents the next step in their career development. Once entrepreneur-teachers believe that a student has made an appropriate and well-considered choice, the teacher will call the potential employer and personally introduce you to the company.

ADMISSIONS CONTACT: JESSICA BLANCHARD, DIRECTOR OF ENROLLMENT
ADDRESS: 515 CONGRESS AVENUE, SUITE 1875 AUSTIN, TX 78701 UNITED STATES
PHONE: 512-703-1231 • FAX: 512-495-9480
E-MAIL: ADMISSIONS@ACTONMBA.ORG • WEBSITE: WWW.ACTONMBA.ORG

In addition to the support they receive from teachers, Acton students are confident that their top-notch program will continue to open doors for them as the school's reputation grows. A current student insists, "The name recognition of Acton literally grows every day, and for a school that has only been around for [5] years, we have an incredible presence in the business world."

Student Life and Environment

A day in the life of an Acton MBA is nothing short of a marathon. Set that alarm clock: "Mandatory study group begins at 6:30 A.M. every morning and last until classes start at 8:00 A.M." After that, it's off to lively, discussion-based classes and then hours of prep time for the next day (according to most, roughly 6 to 8 prep hours per class.) Shares a current student, "It is brutally intense, and there are weeks where I get 5 hours of sleep per night. . . . The competition in class is fierce, and if you are not prepared you will be called on it. That said, there is nothing in this world I would rather be doing right now, and there is nowhere that will better prepare me to start a company. This program will push you well beyond what you thought you could achieve."

The required dedication makes for a close-knit college community comprised of "some of the brightest and most insightful people I have ever met. They manage to compete fiercely while still caring for each other in amazing ways." However, students explain that while "The class is tight and does have activities, both planned and informal," they are not socializing "to the degree that a traditional MBA program does. It is not about happy hours or networking events."

Although the pace rarely lets up, students mention that "the breaks we have in the school year are wonderful times where we can recharge our batteries before heading back into the fray." In those rare moments of relaxation, "Acton is located in the great city of Austin, Texas which provides for a fun, relaxed atmosphere when we are not in school."

Admissions

Acton looks for students who display perseverance, a curious intellect, and integrity. You must also demonstrate a high level of achievement in your undergraduate academic record, an aptitude for graduate study as evidenced by your GMAT score, and a history of leadership and involvement in extracurricular activities. With such a low enrollment (around 30 students currently), Acton takes a personal interest in getting to know their applicants. In addition to essay questions and letters of recommendation, every student is personally interviewed before being admitted to the program.

ADMISSIONS

Admissions Selectivity Rating	**89**
# of applications received	51
% applicants accepted	65
% acceptees attending	82
Average GMAT	670
Range of GMAT	540–760
Average GPA	3.1
TOEFL required of international students	Yes
Minimum TOEFL (paper/computer)	620/260
Application fee	$50
International application fee	$50
Application Deadline/Notification	
Round 1:	11/15 / 12/15
Round 2:	03/01 / 04/01
Round 3:	05/01 / 06/01

Applicants Also Look At
Babson College, Duke University, Harvard University, University of Virginia.

EMPLOYMENT PROFILE

Career Rating	89	Grads Employed by Function	% Avg. Salary
Primary Source of Full-time Job Acceptances		Finance	35 $90,000
School-facilitated activities	3 (14%)	Marketing	6 $95,000
Graduate-facilitated activities	14 (67%)	Operations	29 $90,000
Unknown	4 (19%)	Entrepreneurship	18 NR
Percent employed	79	General Management	12 $85,000

ALFRED UNIVERSITY
COLLEGE OF BUSINESS

Academics

If you're looking for an "intimate environment" for your MBA experience, Alfred University is well worth a look. This program serves a population of 17 graduate students. The result is a program with a "family atmosphere" where everyone is "really friendly and willing to help." As one student told us, "The greatest strength of Alfred University is its size. The classes are between 10 and 20 people, and the interaction is incredible. One really feels a part of the class discussions." The school is especially strong in entrepreneurial studies, an area abetted by the university's Center for Family Business and Entrepreneurial Leadership, a research center.

Professors at Alfred have the time to go the extra mile for students, and they "work hard to make sure you understand what they are teaching, but they also expect you to do your share of the work." Students also appreciate that "professors here are very diverse and have experiences [in other countries] ranging from Japan to Tunisia." With no crowd to fight, Alfred students have a better chance to shine (though keep in mind this also means there's no anonymity for anyone—"Show up to class prepared and hand your work in on time," advises one student). Another writes, "One professor liked a paper I wrote for his class. He offered to coauthor another paper with me and pursue getting it published. These opportunities are so valuable to me and something I would never have expected." And this sense of support and enterprise doesn't end in the classroom. As one student explains, "MBA students at Alfred receive great amounts of attention not only from faculty but also from business school staff. The Assistant Dean keeps a close eye on all of us to make sure we're getting everything we need: from bindings for term papers to a listening ear [for our] concerns."

Of course, a small school can only offer students so much. Some students find that there are "few academic options within the program," "too few courses," and "limited electives." Even so, they regard their MBA experience as extremely "positive." They approve of the school's "active learning" strategies, which emphasize teamwork, case studies, simulations, and field experience (usually gained through an internship). "As a result, I have found the program challenging, rewarding, and enriching," explains one student.

Career and Placement

All Alfred students receive career services through the Robert R. McComsey Career Development Center. The office provides one-on-one counseling sessions; workshops in interviewing, resume writing, and networking; a career library with online and conventional print resources; and annual job fairs. The school also boasts a 100 percent placement rate for its MBAs. Students point out, however, that Alfred's remote location complicates their search for jobs and internships. Many agree that "Alfred is a small community" and that "outside internships and projects are more difficult to obtain due to the university's rural location." However, over the past few years the administration had worked "to expand local, as well as international, opportunities with particular focus on MBA students," and as such, many find that the school currently "does very well in providing big city opportunities."

Prominent employers of Alfred MBAs include Alstom, AOL Communications, Avantt Consulting, Met Life/New England Financial, General Electric Company, Eli Lilly and Company, Citynet, Corning, Dresser Rand, Nestlé, NYSEG, Toro Energy, and Wal-Mart.

ADMISSIONS CONTACT: JEREMY SPENCER, DIRECTOR ADMISSIONS
ADDRESS: OFFICE OF GRADUATE ADMISSIONS, ALUMNI HALL, SAXON DRIVE ALFRED, NY 14802 US
PHONE: 800-541-9229 • FAX: 607-871-2198
E-MAIL: GRADINQUIRY@ALFRED.EDU • WEBSITE: BUSINESS.ALFRED.EDU/MBA.HTML

Student Life and Environment

Alfred, New York, is a quiet, rural town with few distractions, and accordingly, student life centers on campus. The university is a community of about 2,500 students, including 210 business undergrads and 17 MBAs, making it large enough to support all manner of activity. The "wide variety of clubs and organizations offer great opportunity for individual growth" and if you want a club "All you have to do is ask." One student explains, "Alfred's clubs and activities are astounding. Diverse clubs and organizations regularly attend student senate to discuss concerns that are circulating the student population."

Alfred's infrastructure includes "plenty of computers and good Internet bandwidth"; however, "The recreational facilities aren't the best, and the library needs help." Fortunately, a "large renovation and expansion project" is underway, which could be "the largest project for the university within the last few decades." The renovations are expected to "address shortcomings of the university, greatly enhance the campus, and benefit students." Also, while the "huge" dorms get glowing reviews, "Housing is really poor off campus."

Alfred's 16 Division III intercollegiate teams provide entertainment, as does the popular intramural sports program. The school's divisions of music, theater, and dance frequently hold performances. Alfred also has an active visual-arts community; it houses one of the best ceramic arts programs in the country. The "peaceful and safe" village of Alfred has a year-round population of 1,000 and surrounding towns are not much larger. These "secluded" surroundings lessen "the chances of distractions from studies," though when students need a break from the books, Rochester is only 80 miles away, with Buffalo only a little farther down the road—provided you have four-wheel drive in the winter.

Admissions

Applicants must provide the school with official copies of undergraduate transcripts, GMAT scores, TOEFL scores (for international students whose first language is not English), a personal statement, and letters of recommendation (preferably from former employers or professors). Previous work experience is not required, and an interview, while always recommended, is optional.

ADMISSIONS

Admissions Selectivity Rating	**74**
# of applications received	46
% applicants accepted	43
% acceptees attending	50
Average GMAT	483
Average GPA	3.16
TOEFL required of international students	Yes
Minimum TOEFL (paper/computer)	590/243
Application fee	$50
International application fee	$50
Deferment available	Yes
Maximum length of deferment	2 years
Transfer students accepted	Yes
Transfer application policy Transfer a maximum of 6 credit hours	
Non-fall admissions	Yes
Need-blind admissions	Yes

AMERICAN UNIVERSITY
KOGOD SCHOOL OF BUSINESS

GENERAL INFORMATION
Type of school	Private
Affiliation	Methodist
Environment	Metropolis
Academic calendar	Semester

SURVEY SAYS...
Students love Washington, DC
Cutting edge classes
Solid preparation in:
Accounting
Teamwork
Doing business in a global economy

STUDENTS
Enrollment of parent institution	9,136
Enrollment of MBA program	252
% male/female	64/36
% part-time	49
% minorities	3
% international	2
Average age at entry	28
Average years work experience at entry	4

ACADEMICS
Academic Experience Rating	**83**
Student/faculty ratio	23:1
Profs interesting rating	88
Profs accessible rating	97
% female faculty	35
% minority faculty	26

Joint Degrees
JD/MBA 4 years, MBA/MA in International Affairs 3 years, LLM/MBA 3 years.

Prominent Alumni
Marvin Shanken, Chairman, M. Shaken Communications; Loretta Sanchez, United States Congress; David Blumenthal, Senior Vice President and COO, Lion Brand Yarn Com.

FINANCIAL FACTS
Annual tuition	$28,266
Fees	$380
Room & board	$20,000
Average award package	$20,500

Academics

The "small and friendly" MBA program at American University's Kogod School of Business offers a "solid academic program" that, like its namesake (Robert P. Kogod, Charles E. Smith Co.), excels in the area of real estate. American's Washington, DC location situates it ideally to focus on international matters, and the school exploits that opportunity well, interjecting "an international perspective in class discussions that is second to none. Almost all classes integrate an international component."

Kogod's strengths extend far beyond real estate and international business, however. The school boasts a finance faculty that is "internationally recognized for their research. They are great instructors too." Students praise the commercial banking career track offered here and love the fact that the program "allows you to concentrate in two areas of expertise," which "lets you design your own MBA" and "is a great advantage in the job market." Kogod recently "created the first LLM/MBA in the country, which is an excellent way to combine international law studies and business."

Kogod's pedagogical approach embraces a mixture of case studies and theory, combined with plenty of group work that acts as good practice for the real world. Professors "have a great reputation and have done interesting research." They are also easy to contact because of an "open-door policy." Faculty members "bring a lot of academic and professional experience" to the program—another plus. "We have former investment bankers, former consultants, former CFOs, and lifelong academics," brags one student. Small class sizes "give Kogod an advantage over the other DC schools like Georgetown and GW. I know everyone by name, and that's a nice feeling." As a result, the program "feels like being in a big family. Everyone knows you and does their best to help you."

Kogod's DC address "creates many opportunities for networking, internships, etc." As one student puts it, "The DC location gives Kogod a huge advantage. There are so many more opportunities to pursue when you are in a big city. It also helps Kogod draw "international students from very diverse countries," enhancing in-class and networking experiences. Perhaps best of all, this is a school that "is in the middle of overhauling its curriculum" and is in construction on a new building that "will allow for more space to gather in study groups, do group projects, etc." One MBA professes, "I think there will be some great changes" in the school's near future.

Career and Placement

Career Services at Kogod "does a great job in involving alumni in school life. There are lots of networking opportunities . . . [and] lots of on-site visits with direct interactions with alumni, both young and more experienced." A Wall Street trip includes visits to "all the major financial institutions with alumni as tour guides and a session for Q & As and recruiting procedures and tips, concluded by an alumni networking dinner." Career Services Counselors also provide "constant information about new jobs/internship opportunities in the DC area and beyond."

Companies that have recently hired Kogod MBAs include: America Online, BearingPoint, Booz Allen Hamilton, Citigroup, Deloitte Touche Tohmatsu, Discovery Communications, Ernst & Young, ExxonMobil, Fannie Mae, Freddie Mac, The Gallup Organization, Goldman Sachs, IBM, Johnson & Johnson, JPMorgan, Lehman Brothers, Marriott International, MetLife, MSN, PricewaterhouseCoopers, Raytheon, U.S. Bank, the U.S. Government Accountability Office, the U.S. Securities and Exchange Commission, the U.S. Senate, and Unisys.

ADMISSIONS CONTACT: DAMON CALDWELL, SENIOR DIRECTOR FOR ENROLLMENT MANAGEMENT
ADDRESS: 4400 MASSACHUSETTS AVENUE NW WASHINGTON, DC 20016-8044 UNITED STATES
PHONE: 202-885-1913 • FAX: 202-885-1078
E-MAIL: KOGODMBA@AMERICAN.EDU • WEBSITE: WWW.KOGOD.AMERICAN.EDU

Student Life and Environment

The atmosphere in the Kogod MBA program "is low key, friendly, and accessible," with "a great learning environment. The students are all very friendly and socialize together regularly. The professors are very approachable and friendly, and have some impressive resumes. The academics are tough and the program is effective but not cutthroat." Kogod offers "many clubs and organizations in different fields," and students report that "involvement is highly encouraged."

Some here feel that "the program is not as social as others, and this is due in large part to the fact that the school is located in a relatively upscale neighborhood, and there are few restaurants or bars in the immediate area. Also, students tend to live all over Washington, DC," so "Getting large groups together can be difficult." Most agree that's a small trade-off for living "in one of the most exciting and fun cities in the country." As an added bonus, "There is so much work in DC that making $100K a year is almost automatic if you connect with the right government-related job."

Students here represent a variety of backgrounds. "I come from a military background," says one MBA, "and I really enjoy mingling and working with people from nonprofits, other government agencies, small companies, and large companies." The population includes a substantial international contingent.

Admissions

The Kogod Admissions Office requires the following from all applicants: a completed online application form; a personal statement of purpose in pursuing the MBA; a current resume; two letters of recommendation; an official transcript from all attended undergraduate and graduate institutions; and an official GMAT score report. International applicants whose first language is not English must also submit an official score report for other the TOEFL or the IELTS. An interview is required of all applicants.

ADMISSIONS

Admissions Selectivity Rating	**78**
# of applications received	411
% applicants accepted	54
% acceptees attending	30
Average GMAT	560
Range of GMAT	506–630
Average GPA	3.0
TOEFL required of international students	Yes
Minimum TOEFL (paper/computer)	600/100
Application fee	$75
International application fee	$75
Regular application deadline	Rolling
Regular notification	Rolling
Deferment available	Yes
Maximum length of deferment	1 year
Transfer students accepted	Yes
Transfer application policy	
They must meet the same requirements as a non-transfer student. Nine credits may be transferred into the program from an AACSB accredited MBA program	
Non-fall admissions	Yes
Need-blind admissions	Yes

Applicants Also Look At
George Mason University, Georgetown University, Johns Hopkins University, The George Washington University, University of Maryland—College Park.

EMPLOYMENT PROFILE

Career Rating	74
Primary Source of Full-time Job Acceptances	
School-facilitated activities	24 (51%)
Graduate-facilitated activities	23 (49%)
Average base starting salary	$74,884
Percent employed	97.8

Grads Employed by Function	% Avg. Salary
Finance	33 $70,133
Marketing	18 $74,500
MIS	4 $84,000
Operations	2 $46,000
Consulting	13 $82,000
General Management	11 $77,600
Other	15 $79,333

Top 5 Employers Hiring Grads
Deloitte, Bearing Point, Ernst & Young, IBM, KPMG

APPALACHIAN STATE UNIVERSITY
WALKER COLLEGE OF BUSINESS

GENERAL INFORMATION
Type of school	Public
Environment	Village
Academic calendar	Semester

SURVEY SAYS...
Students love Boone, NC
Smart classrooms
Solid preparation in:
Finance
Accounting
Quantitative skills

STUDENTS
Enrollment of parent institution	14,653
Enrollment of MBA program	22
% male/female	65/35
% out-of-state	12
% part-time	75
Average age at entry	26
Average years work experience at entry	4

ACADEMICS
Academic Experience Rating	**78**
Student/faculty ratio	20:1
Profs interesting rating	70
Profs accessible rating	81
% female faculty	20

FINANCIAL FACTS
Annual tuition (in-state/out-of-state)	$5,573/$16,574
Fees	$915
Cost of books	$1,200
Room & board (on/off-campus)	$4,082/$7,200
Average grant	$1,000

Academics

The nascent graduate business program at Appalachian State University's Walker College of Business offers a select few students "what is probably the most reasonably priced graduate program in the state—incredible bargain." At present, fewer than 20 students are enrolled in the program, which offers a conventional MBA, an MS in accounting, and graduate certificate programs in finance, human-resource management, and information systems. Housed in the same hall as the university's mainframe computer, the MBA program puts computers to good use, employing computer simulations and computer analysis as well as computer-aided instruction in the classroom.

First-year studies at Walker commence with MBA Enrichment, a required program that includes "orientation sessions, workshops, a team-building outdoor experience, and social time for students to get acquainted." The freshman curriculum is entirely prescribed and is designed to "provide students with a broad foundation of knowledge." Students must complete an internship or international experience between their first and second years. Second-year studies consist of five required courses and five electives. Instruction at Walker incorporates case study, group discussion, role playing, guest-led seminars, field projects, team projects, and individual presentations. Students tell us that the Walker approach consists of "lots of work: You have to read and study a lot, [and] you get to learn! With so many assignments and reading, we are turning ourselves into sources of knowledge."

MBAs tell us that faculty members "are very well prepared; they have both the academic and professional experience that makes their teaching valuable. Academic quality is one of the greatest strengths of the school." They warn, however, that the program has a few kinks to iron out. One student warns, "Organization and overall program direction are currently being reassessed and will be better defined and articulated by next year. Once the restructuring has had time to develop, the MBA program will be one of the best buys in the state for the money."

Career and Placement

ASU's MBA program is much too small to support its own Career Services Office; students must use the school's Career Development Center, which serves all ASU enrollees. The office offers a variety of career-prep classes in interviewing, resume writing, networking, cover letters, and job hunting. It also sponsors career fairs and provides online support including links to job boards and major-related resources.

Students recognize the limitations of their situation. They approvingly report, "The school has a good relationship with alumni and companies in nearby Charlotte, the second-largest financial mecca in the U.S.," but concede that that's not always enough. One student writes, "They need to do more to help students get internships and job positions. They do have departments and people that guide us and show us what steps we should take, but they should also have more agreements with some companies for sending students every year for internships." Companies most likely to hire Walker grads include Bank of America, BB&T, Duke Energy, IBM, Lowe's Companies, MDI, Murray Supply, North Carolina State University, Regeneron Pharmaceuticals, Rubbermaid Newell, Wachovia, and Wake Tech.

ADMISSIONS CONTACT: ANNA BASNIGHT, ADMISSIONS CONTACT
ADDRESS: ASU BOX 32068 BOONE, NC 28608-2068 UNITED STATES
PHONE: 828-262-2130 • FAX: 828-262-2709
E-MAIL: BASNIGHTAL@APPSTATE.EDU • WEBSITE: WWW.MBA.APPSTATE.EDU

Student Life and Environment

Unlike most MBA programs, Walker does not support much of an extracurricular scene; with its tiny student body, it can barely populate one club, let alone several. Accordingly, "most people pursue their own personal hobbies during their spare time. Being near the Blue Ridge Parkway and several ski slopes, a lot of people are involved in outdoor activities." As one student puts it, "If you like nature, long winters, and small, close-knit groups of friends, then you should look into ASU. And if you like skiing, you're golden."

On the other hand, "when you want to have some nightlife, there is almost none." That's because "[hometown] Boone is a very small town. It has several movie theaters, including one that is $1.50," but not much else to offer. As one student explains it, "This is a beautiful place, meant for studying." Fortunately, the university community at large (which numbers over 15,000 students) offers up many forms of diversion, including ASU's 18 intercollegiate athletic teams. The university houses several museums and is host to numerous performing-arts series.

When students crave a more urban environment, they road-trip to either Asheville or Winston-Salem; each is just under a two-hour drive from campus. Lexington, NC, is also only two hours away. It's not a huge city, but it is home to arguably the best barbecue in the state (and thus, from a Tar Heel perspective, the best barbecue in the world).

Admissions

Applications to the Walker MBA program are processed by the Admissions Office at the Cratis D. Williams Graduate School. Prospective students must submit GMAT scores, an undergraduate transcript, letters of recommendation, a resume (at least one year of work experience is required), and two essays. An interview is strongly recommended but not required. Applicants must have completed at least one undergraduate class in each of the following areas: calculus, microeconomics, and statistics (summer courses in these subjects are offered for applicants who do not meet this requirement). Students should arrive with a working knowledge of Microsoft Excel, Word, and PowerPoint.

The school uses a formula to set minimum admissions requirements. The formula is (GPA x 200) + GMAT = admissions score; GPA is tallied based only on the final 60 hours of undergraduate course work. An admissions score of at least 1050 is required but does not guarantee admission. Application materials must arrive no later than 3/1; admission is for the fall term only.

ADMISSIONS

Admissions Selectivity Rating	**90**
# of applications received	28
% applicants accepted	29
% acceptees attending	100
Average GMAT	540
Range of GMAT	470–700
Average GPA	3.4
TOEFL required of international students	Yes
Minimum TOEFL (paper/computer)	550/233
Application fee	$45
International application fee	$45
Regular application deadline	3/1
Regular notification	3/31
Deferment available	Yes
Maximum length of deferment	1 year
Transfer students accepted	Yes
Transfer application policy Up to six hours of graduate credit may be transferred for equivalent courses completed with at least grade of B.	
Non-fall admissions	Yes
Need-blind admissions	Yes

Applicants Also Look At

North Carolina State University, The University of North Carolina at Chapel Hill, The University of North Carolina at Greensboro, Western Carolina University.

Arizona State University
W.P. Carey School of Business

Academics

Students at Arizona State University's W.P. Carey School of Business say their school is "by far, the best b-school in the Southwest," boasting a range of progressive MBA programs, a strong foothold in the Phoenix business community, and a practical but fun approach to business education. A rising star in the business world, "The school is constantly striving to be recognized as one of the top business schools in the country by recruiting top faculty and remaining selective with student admission." As one student observes, "Each year we are getting more and more professors from distinguished b-schools. For the most part, the faculty is outstanding, and as you get into your specialization courses, they become recognized leaders in their fields." Academically, the school emphasizes case-based and team-oriented learning, maintaining a "good mix of lecture, cases, and project work in classes." ASU professors bring "current practical research, knowledge, and excellent teaching skills into the classroom." A current student attests, "I have taken away a tremendous amount of applicable information (both theoretical and practical) which I am able to apply to my job."

ASU offers a number of MBA options, including full-time and part-time programs, an online program, an executive MBA program, and the "Technology, Science, and Engineering MBA program, which has extremely challenging electives and several attractive certifications available." While the school is traditionally recognized for its excellence in Supply Chain Management and Sports Business, students reassure us that there is a "good variety of courses from all disciplines" at ASU, including many "creative offerings to meet emerging market trends." With a lockstep core program in the first year, ASU is characterized by "challenging course work with very high expectations from students." This intensity is balanced by a lively and fun academic environment, thanks to professors who are "professional and intelligent, but still know how to relate to students and bring humor into classes."

You won't have to worry about red tape and registration headaches at ASU. Unlike many public schools, "ASU's administration team takes many tasks off of the student's plate. They register students for classes, pick up their books and parking passes, and are easily accessible." The popular Dean Keim also draws his share of praises. A student relates, "We have brought in a relatively new dean who has created a culture of excellence and, to be honest, an environment of academic rigor beyond what I expected." An ideal learning environment, the "program is hosted in a high-tech facility, so it gives it a nice progressive feel. We're surrounded by clean rooms and technology labs."

Career and Placement

Students say "the Career Management Center is phenomenal, helping all students with every aspect of finding both an internship and a full-time position upon graduation." Working with the school's extensive alumni network and strong connections in the local business community, "The people in the Career Management Center sincerely want you to succeed, and they will do anything to get you the job/internship that you want."

Thanks to the "economic growth being experienced in Phoenix and the Southwest in general," as well as the school's great regional reputation, it's easy for students to land a plum position in Phoenix. "For supply-chain management students [in particular], the Career Management Center is superb. Recruiters are here nonstop throughout the year looking for both interns and full-time hires. From day one, it is made clear that it is the school's goal to get you a quality job." While Supply Chain students may receive the undivided attention of many recruiters, ASU students do well on the whole. "The class of 2007 had 100 percent

ADMISSIONS CONTACT: RUDY PINO, DIRECTOR, ADMISSIONS, W. P. CAREY MBA
ADDRESS: P.O. BOX 874906 TEMPE, AZ 85287-4906 UNITED STATES
PHONE: 480-965-3332 • FAX: 480-965-8569
E-MAIL: WPCAREYMBA@ASU.EDU • WEBSITE: WPCAREY.ASU.EDU/MBA

summer internship placement in 2006," and over 95 percent of last year's graduating class was employed within 3 months of graduation.

Student Life and Environment

Students at ASU are as warm and sunny as the desert itself. As one student explains, "Whether it be helping with homework, assisting with interview preparation, or just going out on a Thursday night, you know that somebody will be there for you." While the class size is growing annually, the ASU business program is still fairly community oriented. "On any given night off you will find many of us hanging out together socializing; we are an extremely close-knit community," says a current student. Part-timers admit that "being enrolled in a part-time program leads to little time for an active social life"; even so, these students "still make time for one another."

On campus, there are plenty of opportunities to get involved in the school community. When students need to burn off some stress they head to the intramural fields which are "filled every evening with soccer games, softball games—you name it." On top of that, "There is always something new and interesting happening, including study groups for classes, social events like skydiving and happy hours, networking events with alumni," and "opportunities to hear outstanding speakers (such as the Dutch ambassador to the U.S.)." Aside from school events, hometown Phoenix provides plenty of social and recreational opportunities, and "The weather and beautiful campus make getting up in the morning a lot easier."

Admissions

Admissions vary for the full-time; executive; and technology, science, and engineering programs. Applicants to all programs must submit a completed application form, undergraduate transcripts, and official GMAT scores. In the fall of 2007, full-time entering students had an average GMAT score of 675 and an average undergraduate GPA of 3.44. Students entering the evening program had an average GPA of 3.28 and an average GMAT score of 561. The school admits students who demonstrate a combination of strong academic credentials, leadership potential, work experience, and strong communication skills.

Prominent Alumni

Craig Weatherup, Former Chairman, The Pepsi Bottling Group; Steve Marriott, Vice President of Corp. Marketing, Marriott Hotels; Chris Cookson, President, Technologies, Sony Pictures; Peter Ruppe, VP & GM, Men's Training & Fitness, Nike; Jack Furst, Partner, Hicks, Muse, Tate & Furst, Inc.

FINANCIAL FACTS

Annual tuition (in-state/ out-of-state)	$6,228/$17,920
Fees	$10,000
Cost of books	$2,180
Room & board	$10,530
Average award package	$20,500
Average grant	$8,000
Average student loan debt	$39,000

ADMISSIONS

Admissions Selectivity Rating	**98**
# of applications received	545
% applicants accepted	32
% acceptees attending	50
Average GMAT	675
Range of GMAT	650–710
Average GPA	3.44
TOEFL required of international students	Yes
Minimum TOEFL (paper/computer)	600/250
Application fee	$65
International application fee	$80
Application Deadline/Notification	
Round 1:	10/19 / 12/14
Round 2:	12/21 / 2/22
Round 3:	2/1 / 4/4
Round 4:	4/4 / 5/16
Deferment available	Yes
Maximum length of deferment	1 year
Non-fall admissions	Yes
Need-blind admissions	Yes

Applicants Also Look At

The University of Texas at Austin, UCLA, Indiana University—Bloomington, University of Maryland, College Park, Michigan State University, University of Wisconsin—Madison, Washington University in St. Louis.

EMPLOYMENT PROFILE

Career Rating	87	Grads Employed by Function	% Avg. Salary
Primary Source of Full-time Job Acceptances		Finance	12 $84,857
School-facilitated activities	54 (70%)	Marketing	21 $81,312
Graduate-facilitated activities	22 (30%)	MIS	6 $86,666
Average base starting salary	$86,001	Operations	39 $88,867
Percent employed	97.4	Consulting	7 $87,860
		General Management	10 $78,166
		Other	5 NR

Top 5 Employers Hiring Grads
Raytheon, Quepasa, Chevron, Apple, Honeywell

AUBURN UNIVERSITY
COLLEGE OF BUSINESS

GENERAL INFORMATION
Type of school	Public
Environment	Town
Academic calendar	Semester

SURVEY SAYS...
Good social scene
Solid preparation in:
Marketing
Teamwork

STUDENTS
Enrollment of parent institution	23,547
Enrollment of business school	375
% male/female	65/35
% out-of-state	63
% part-time	80
% minorities	7
% international	32
Average age at entry	26
Average years work experience at entry	4.25

ACADEMICS
Academic Experience Rating	**86**
Student/faculty ratio	29:1
Profs interesting rating	94
Profs accessible rating	67
% female faculty	20
% minority faculty	5

Joint Degrees
Dual degree program with Industrial and Systems Engineering (2 1/2 years). Other dual-degree options available on case-by-case basis with approval of AU Graduate School.

Prominent Alumni
Mohamed Mansour, CEO, Mansour Group in Egypt; Joanne P. McCallie, Head Coach, Michigan State U. Women's Basketball; Wendell Starke, Past President of INVESCO.

Academics

Whether you're seeking a traditional on-campus MBA experience or the opportunity to earn your graduate degree from the comfort of your own home, Auburn University can accommodate you. The school offers three curriculum models: an on-campus MBA; the Graduate Outreach Program, which allows students to fulfill most of the obligations toward their degrees remotely (students must attend one five-day case analysis during their final fall semester, but otherwise never need to visit campus); and two Executive MBA programs (one a general EMBA, the other geared specifically to the needs of physicians), which require five one-week residencies over a two-year period, with the larger portion of instruction coming via Internet and DVD technologies. The distance program offers concentrations in finance, management information systems, technology management, marketing, and operations management. The full-time program offers all of these plus concentrations in agribusiness, economic development, economics, healthcare administration, human resources management, sports management, and supply chain management. The EMBA offers specializations in technology management and healthcare management.

Students in the on-campus program praise "the great sense of community" here, with "plenty of team building and leadership education. The "very team-based" approach to learning means "you will walk away with the ability to work effectively with anyone," especially "given the diversity of the classes in terms of ethnicity and academic background." Among the many academic disciplines covered here, students say that supply chain management, finance, and economics are standouts. Auburn professors "are really helpful" and "very approachable," but many feel that "some could foster more innovative teaching approaches." Administrators earn high marks for "knowing every random question about the program you can think up." As one MBA observes, "With such a small MBA class, the administration can provide plenty of attention."

Career and Placement

Auburn's Office of Student/Business Partnerships handles career counseling and recruitment services for MBAs. The office provides one-on-one counseling, seminars, workshops, and a career library; it also organizes career expos and on-campus recruiting events. Students see room for improvement, telling us the office "needs to actively create better business fairs and get names out to more companies... While it is good for many people if they want to stay local, it's hard to get your name out to specific companies and certainly ones that are out of the South" under current conditions. Employers most likely to hire Auburn MBAs include AmSouth Bank, Colonial Bank, Home Depot, Total Systems, and Wal-Mart; the school also maintains "working relationships" with such employers as Dell, Eli Lilly, Ernst & Young, KPMG, Rocky Mountain Clothing Company, and Trans Meridian Airlines. One in five graduates winds up in finance and accounting; operations and production, consulting, and MIS each claim about 17 percent of the graduating class.

Student Life and Environment

Auburn's MBA program draws "a great group from across the US and across the globe" with "a strong presence of diverse nationalities, including students from China, Thailand, India, Mali, Curacao, Guam, and Belgium." Some complain that too many students, both American and international, lack sufficient work experience, "which lessens their contributions in class," but they are otherwise satisfied with their peers. One tells us that "The Auburn MBA program has done a wonderful job at promoting cohesion among students. We feel like a family and are there to pull each other through. No matter what your views and characteristics are, you are accepted with an open mind."

Football occupies center stage in the life of the Auburn campus. "The football team brings about being part of something bigger than yourself," one student explains, while another simply observes that "The tailgating is the best." The surrounding town, though small, "is great for being social. Between the football games and the bars, we hang out a lot as an entire class. If anything, the social life sometimes gets in the way of school life because it's hard to turn down such a fun time." It's all business during the daytime, however, when most full-timers "come up to the student lounge in the business building to either do work or to socialize. It is a healthy environment that encourages fellowship." Part-timers are, of course, less engaged in campus life.

Admissions

All applicants to the Auburn MBA program must submit official transcripts for all post-secondary academic work, an official GMAT score report, three letters of recommendation, a completed application to the Graduate School (online only), and a completed application to the MBA program (paper only). Work experience and a personal interview are both encouraged, but neither is required. International students whose first language is not English must also submit TOEFL scores (minimum scores: 550 paper-and-pencil; 213 computer-based; 79 internet-based). Undergraduate-level competency in accounting, calculus, finance, macro- and microeconomics, management, marketing, and statistics are all prerequisites to starting the Auburn MBA program. Students lacking appropriate undergraduate credentials may purchase the corresponding courses on CD and must subsequently pass a competency exam in each course (administered by the university, by CLEP, or, for military candidates, through the DANTES system) prior to commencing work on the MBA. In an effort to boost the population of underrepresented students, Auburn makes recruiting trips to minority campuses.

FINANCIAL FACTS

Annual tuition (in-state/ out-of-state)	$5,250/$15,750
Fees	$430
Cost of books	$1,200
Room & board (off-campus)	$10,746
% of students receiving aid	95
% of first-year students receiving aid	81
% of students receiving grants	30
Average award package	$6,115
Average grant	$1,200
Average student loan debt	$14,665

ADMISSIONS

Admissions Selectivity Rating	**91**
# of applications received	131
% applicants accepted	45
% acceptees attending	61
Average GMAT	619
Range of GMAT	580–640
Average GPA	3.3
TOEFL required of international students	Yes
Minimum TOEFL (paper/computer)	550/213
Application fee	$25
International application fee	$50
Regular application deadline	3/1
Deferment available	Yes
Maximum length of deferment	1 year
Transfer students accepted	Yes
Transfer application policy AACSB schools only. Case-by-case basis and accepted in lieu of elective courses only. Limit of 12 credit hours.	
Need-blind admissions	Yes

EMPLOYMENT PROFILE

Career Rating	66	Grads Employed by Function	% Avg. Salary
Primary Source of Full-time Job Acceptances		Finance	21 $49,840
School-facilitated activities	15 (63%)	Marketing	12 $52,000
Graduate-facilitated activities	9 (38%)	MIS	17 $57,000
Average base starting salary	$56,488	Operations	17 $57,750
Percent employed	33	Consulting	17 $54,500
		General Management	12 $77,167
		Other	4 $42,000

AUBURN UNIVERSITY—MONTGOMERY
SCHOOL OF BUSINESS

GENERAL INFORMATION
Type of school	Public
Environment	City

SURVEY SAYS...
Friendly students
Solid preparation in:
Communication/interpersonal skills
Presentation skills
Quantitative skills

STUDENTS
Enrollment of business school	168
% male/female	50/50
% part-time	70
Average age at entry	28

ACADEMICS
Academic Experience Rating	**71**
Student/faculty ratio	20:1
Profs interesting rating	79
Profs accessible rating	78
% female faculty	25
% minority faculty	10

FINANCIAL FACTS
Cost of books	$1,500
% of students receiving aid	60
% of first-year students receiving aid	65
% of students receiving loans	45
% of students receiving grants	15
Average award package	$14,750
Average grant	$3,000

Academics

The AACSB-accredited MBA program at Auburn University Montgomery is "a great place to get your MBA at night," according to the program's locally based student body. Students here also appreciate the "affordable" tuition as well as the school's "reputation for academic excellence" and "instructors who bring real-life business experiences to the classroom" and "have connections in the business world." The program is designed for part-time students; in fact, any student wishing to exceed a course load of nine hours per semester must first receive approval from the dean of the School of Business.

The MBA program at AUM is divided into three parts. The first is called the Basic Program, consisting of 11 half-term courses covering business concepts typically taught at the undergraduate level (accounting, management, marketing, business law, microeconomics, macroeconomics, operations management, statistics, MIS, and finance). Students who can demonstrate sufficient background in these areas may petition to be exempted from some or all of these requirements. The second part of the program is the Business Core, a seven-course set of classes covering such integrative concepts as managerial applications of accounting information and synergistic organizational strategy (the latter is a capstone course), as well as such essential functions as marketing, data analysis, and managing personnel. The program concludes with either three or four electives, depending on whether the student chooses a General MBA or a specialization. Specializations are offered in accounting, contract management, economics, finance, global business management, information systems, management of information technology, management, and marketing. Students earning a GPA below 3.25 must pass comprehensive exams at the end of the program in order to graduate. The program must be finished within five years of starting.

AUM MBAs brag that "Professors are extremely knowledgeable, helpful, and outstanding in their areas," and that they also "understand that most of the evening students are fully employed and try to incorporate their day-to-day activities" into the curriculum. Most here "would like to see the use of more technology in the classroom" and complain that the school needs "all classrooms to be enabled with things like wireless internet access." Classrooms could also be improved by making them "resemble the real world, i.e. u-shaped seating"; at the very least, the school "needs to upgrade classroom furniture to make it feel less like a high school/junior high," students tell us.

Career and Placement

The Career Development Center (CDC) at AUM serves all university students and alumni. The office maintains a library of career-related material, including documents tracking salary and hiring trends around the region, state, country, and world. Career counseling services are available, as are job fairs and seminars and workshops in interviewing, job hunting, resume, and cover-letter writing. The office arranges internships and recruiting events for qualifying MBA students.

ADMISSIONS CONTACT: SHARON JONES, ADMISSION SPECIALIST
ADDRESS: P. O. BOX 244023 MONTGOMERY, AL 36124-4023 UNITED STATES
PHONE: 334-244-3623 • FAX: 334-244-3927
E-MAIL: VJONES1@MAIL.AUM.EDU • WEBSITE: WWW.AUM.EDU

ADMISSIONS

Admissions Selectivity Rating	**64**
# of applications received	68
% applicants accepted	100
% acceptees attending	100
Average GMAT	500
Average GPA	2.9
TOEFL required of international students	Yes
Minimum TOEFL	500
Application fee	$25
Regular application deadline	rolling
Regular notification	rolling
Non-fall admissions	Yes
Need-blind admissions	Yes

Student Life and Environment

AUM MBAs are "mostly working students between their mid-20s and mid-30s in age, with some being older." Most "work full-time and go to school at night" and, despite their busy schedules, find a way to remain "extremely focused on their class work and understanding of the material" while also being "extremely helpful, kind, open for conversation, and willing to do whatever it takes to see that everyone in class is successful." They "don't seem to have any specific clubs or organizations available to them, especially in the evening hours," but most agree that their extracurricular schedule wouldn't allow them time to participate.

Montgomery is a midsize southern city well known for its integral part in the civil rights movement. The population of the city is about evenly split between whites and blacks, with small Hispanic, Native American, and Asian populations accounting for a small minority. The city is home to the Alabama Shakespeare Festival, a year-round enterprise that mounts a dozen or more productions and attracts over 300,000 visitors annually. Another major attraction is the minor-league baseball Montgomery Biscuits, the AA affiliate of the Tampa Bay Devil Rays. And no Montgomery summer is complete without Jubilee CityFest, a three-day outdoor festival that in recent years has attracted such headlining musical acts as Taylor Swift, Erykah Badu, the Goo Goo Dolls, Ludacris, and Vince Gill.

Admissions

Applicants to the AUM MBA program must submit official transcripts for all previous post-secondary academic work, official GMAT score reports, and a completed application form. The screening committee may request an interview, typically in the case of borderline candidates; otherwise, interviews are not required. International applicants must meet all of the above requirements and must also provide certified English translations of any academic transcripts in a foreign language and a course-by-course evaluation of undergraduate work "by a recognized, expert service in the field of foreign credential evaluations and international admissions." Applicants whose first language is not English must submit TOEFL scores. Candidates may be admitted conditionally pending completion of prerequisite undergraduate-level classes in business.

EMPLOYMENT PROFILE	
Career Rating	62

AUGUSTA STATE UNIVERSITY
COLLEGE OF BUSINESS ADMINISTRATION

GENERAL INFORMATION
Type of school	Public
Environment	City
Academic calendar	Trimester

SURVEY SAYS...
Cutting edge classes
Solid preparation in:
General management
Presentation skills
Quantitative skills
Computer skills

STUDENTS
Enrollment of parent institution	6,333
Enrollment of business school	95
% male/female	60/40
% out-of-state	27
% part-time	67
% minorities	26
% international	14
Average age at entry	31
Average years work experience at entry	9

ACADEMICS
Academic Experience Rating	**82**
Student/faculty ratio	11:1
Profs interesting rating	81
Profs accessible rating	89
% female faculty	42

FINANCIAL FACTS
Annual tuition (in-state/out-of-state)	$2,520/$10,880
Fees	$273
Cost of books	$500
Room & board	$9,501

Academics

Convenience and cost are the two main reasons students cite for choosing the MBA program at Augusta State University. Many students here tell us that they attended the school as undergraduates and saw no reason to leave.

At ASU's MBA program, "Personal attention and career development are a given. Students have to actively work at not being known by the administration and faculty of the Business School." Service is key; despite its relatively small MBA enrollment, "ASU has a dedicated educational professional to usher graduate students through the program." One student notes, "The school is the perfect size. It is small enough to allow for more personal relations between the student and the teacher but is big enough to enjoy all the aspects of attending a college." A "low teacher/student ratio" and "professors who are approachable and willing to help students" are among the other perks of attending. ASU works hard to accommodate its students' schedules by offering "almost every needed subject in the program" during the fall and spring semesters.

MBAs at ASU must complete a 12-course sequence that includes 2 electives and 10 required courses in human resources management, marketing, finance, accounting, economics, production management, leadership, management information systems, business research methods, and an integrating course in strategic management. Students tell us that the school has traditionally been recognized for strengths for economics, finance, and accounting, as well as in "certain quantitative-based courses like market research." In addition, ASU has taken steps in order to better prepare the students for information-based knowledge. Those steps include "recently naming an information technology professor to chair the program."

Career and Placement

The ASU Career Center serves all undergraduates and graduate students at the university. Services are geared primarily toward undergraduates, in part because the school's graduate divisions are so small and in part because many graduate students—including many MBAs—attend while continuing in jobs they intend to keep post-graduation. The office sponsors an annual Career Fair and offers the standard battery of career services: job posting, counseling, mock interviews, on-campus recruiting, and more.

Student Life and Environment

Most ASU MBAs "work full-time during the day and attend classes at night," which means they have limited time to devote to extracurricular activities. Students tell us that "many professors acknowledge the average students' work/demand schedule and design their courses to allow students to catch up on the weekends." MBAs also appreciate how the small-school environment creates "the opportunity to get to know the students and faculty on a greater than superficial level," an opportunity students take advantage of by "congregating in a small centralized area of the building before classes." With so many chances to bond with peers and professors, it's no wonder students tell us that "the school feels like a family."

Full-time students—consisting primarily of international students and undergraduates proceeding directly from their BA program to the MBA—tell us that "there is an active campus life at ASU even though few students actually live on campus. There are so many groups to be involved with and [there are] always activities going on. The school spirit at ASU is so alive, and the students there really love their campus. Most of the MBA students are graduates of ASU, so I believe they feel the same as well." Clubs "are very active on campus." Phi Beta Lambda is one of the major ones for business students.

ADMISSIONS CONTACT: MIYOKO JACKSON, DEGREE PROGRAM SPECIALIST
ADDRESS: COLLEGE OF BUSINESS ADMINISTRATION MBA OFFICE, 2500 WALTON WAY AUGUSTA,
GA 30904-2200 UNITED STATES • PHONE: 706-737-1565 • FAX: 706-667-4064
E-MAIL: MBAINFO@AUG.EDU • WEBSITE: WWW.AUG.EDU/COBA/

MBAs tell us that the school has worked hard to beautify and improve this campus, which, they note, "was an arsenal during the Civil War. The school has done a great job of keeping that heritage intact" while simultaneously adding such assets as a " beautiful new student center" that "provides study areas, gym equipment, billiards, and a host of other activities for students that help to release school stress." Commuters warn that "parking is limited during morning hours, but afternoon and evening parking is very good."

The ASU student body is "broadly diverse in age, occupation, race, and educational background, but [they are] uniformly goal oriented, serious, and competitive, [while also] capable or working in a team environment." Students seem to appreciate this diversity. One student says, "I have come in contact with people from many different cultures, and it gives me a different outlook on business." Even though there are "so many international students," most "seem to be regular people with careers who have felt a need to improve themselves."

Admissions

Applicants to the Hull College of Business MBA program must submit all of the following: official transcripts for all undergraduate and graduate work; an official score report for the GMAT (test score can be no more than 5 years old); and a completed application form. In addition, international students whose first language is not English must submit an official score for the TOEFL and a financial responsibility statement. International transcripts must be submitted via Educational Credential Evaluators, Inc., a company that matches international course work to its American equivalent. The Admissions Committee looks for students with significant and diverse work experience, varied educational backgrounds, and sound academic achievement. Incoming students must be able to run word processing, spreadsheet, and database programs.

ADMISSIONS	
Admissions Selectivity Rating	**77**
# of applications received	38
% applicants accepted	84
% acceptees attending	88
Average GMAT	520
Range of GMAT	450–690
Average GPA	3.05
TOEFL required of international students	Yes
Minimum TOEFL (paper/computer)	550/213
Application fee	$30
International application fee	$30
Regular application deadline	Rolling
Regular notification	Rolling
Deferment available	Yes
Maximum length of deferment	1 year
Transfer students accepted	Yes
Transfer application policy Must meet regular MBA admission standards. Up to nine Semester credit hours may be accepted for transfer.	
Non-fall admissions	Yes

BABSON COLLEGE
F. W. OLIN GRADUATE SCHOOL OF BUSINESS

Academics

Students tell us that Babson College's F.W. Olin Graduate School of Business has "an excellent reputation for entrepreneurship," meaning that it "is 100 percent focused on the number-one trend in business today." Some, in fact, are convinced that this is "the best entrepreneurship program in the United States," and can point to top rankings in entrepreneurial business management and opportunity identification and assessment to back their opinions.

Babson's highly integrated curriculum "is incredibly rigorous. . . . None of the academic cases focuses on any one discipline. Instead, we look at a business case from many perspectives, just as a businessperson must in the 'real world.' A strategy problem is not simply a strategy problem. It has marketing, operational, organizational, and financial implications (among others) as well." One student adds, "Babson is known for developing the full thinker. The teaching methods and courses encourage creative thinking and idea generation. The professors and students, the clubs and the environment all weave together to support a balanced education focused on integrated business management from finances to leadership, both inside and outside of the classroom." This approach makes Babson "a good program for general management" as well as for entrepreneurship. Students also praise Babson's curriculum in technology management and tell us that "the school is making significant ground in areas that support entrepreneurship, such as the private equity and venture capital arenas."

Babson offers students a variety of program options. Full-time students may choose from a traditional 2-year program or an intensive 1-year program. Part-timers may choose from a traditional evening program and a fast-track, blended, partially online program. Students in all programs benefit from a faculty "as good as any business school in the world. Their rankings reflect this, and in my experience, their reputation is well deserved. The Babson faculty is comprised of many professors who left top-10 business schools to teach in a more innovative, leading-edge curriculum. They also tend to be leading practitioners within their fields."

Career and Placement

Babson's Center for Career Development "has made great progress in the last 2 years" and "has improved tremendously. It has taken a 'product management' approach, where the students are the product." One student notes, "The CCD has also gone way out of its way to get to know us. At the end of our first semester, the CCD had champagne and hors d'oeuvres for each BCAP group as we completed our final presentation. CCD has also undergone massive quantitative analysis of the market as it applies to Babson students. The results from this analysis and the new system have dramatically improved the internship/employment stats." Another adds, "While there are challenges in bringing in diverse employers, the companies visiting the school are of exceptional quality and provide real opportunities after graduation for those not starting their own businesses."

Employers who most frequently hire Babson MBAs include: Fidelity Investments, EMC Corporation, Adventis, Bose, Boston Scientific Corporation, IBM, Liberty Mutual Group, Merrill Lynch, Our Group, PricewaterhouseCoopers, Staples, Estee Lauder, General Electric Company, Deloitte Touche Tohmatsu, Proctor & Gamble, Morgan Stanley, and Dunkin' Brands.

Student Life and Environment

Babson offers graduate business students a modern campus at which "facilities are generally exceptionally well maintained." Students attend class in "modern classrooms" and

ADMISSIONS CONTACT: DENNIS NATIONS, DIRECTOR OF GRADUATE ADMISSIONS
ADDRESS: OLIN HALL BABSON PARK (WELLESLEY), MA 02457-0310 UNITED STATES
PHONE: 781-239-5591 • FAX: 781-239-4194
E-MAIL: MBAADMISSION@BABSON.EDU • WEBSITE: WWW.BABSON.EDU/MBA

"a clean and tidy environment, with wireless network access on most of the campus." The library "seems to have everything you need to do research and also offers free tutorials on important skills, such as b-plan writing, etc." As one student sums up, "Everything I need is at my fingertips, and all staff are very responsive. Computers, IT support, librarians, on-site cafes, on and on. It really is a privilege to attend here!" All that support is especially welcome given that "the course load is tough. We need to study long hours before class. It is overwhelming, and the idea of the school is to overwhelm students and make them learn things the hard way."

The Babson campus "is usually full of activity ranging from panel events, social gatherings, recruiting, to general student interaction." The "centralized structure of graduate activities lends itself to a high degree of interaction among MBA students," especially among full-time students, who also take advantage of "two campus bars—one graduate, one for undergrads—provide a nice outlet to unwind after class." One student in the 2-year full-time program describes the experience as "very social. In fact, I'm headed out in a few to see a fellow student's band play in Boston. There will be at least 20 other MBAs attending. Should be a blast! I love it here. Wish it was 3 years . . . ha!" The school works hard to acknowledge that students have lives beyond the classroom. One MBA reports, "Babson hosts a friends and family day with food and different activities. Babson also offers classes in which spouses can participate with very little cost. Movies are shown, and students and student's family are welcome."

Admissions

Applicants to Babson MBA programs must submit the following materials: official transcripts covering undergraduate work; an official GMAT score report; a resume or curriculum vitae (2 years of full-time post-undergraduate work experience is required); a completed application form; and personal essays. Candidates whose native language is other than English and who have not earned a degree in the United States, United Kingdom, Canada, Australia, or New Zealand must also submit: an official TOEFL iBT score report; and, official English translation and interpretation of all transcripts. Babson contacts all candidates to schedule an admissions interview.

FINANCIAL FACTS

Annual tuition	$38,500
Fees	$0
Cost of books	$2,384
Room & board	$14,704
% of students receiving aid	65
% of first-year students receiving aid	68
% of students receiving loans	47
% of students receiving grants	54
Average award package	$21,579
Average grant	$16,820
Average student loan debt	$69,146

ADMISSIONS

Admissions Selectivity Rating	86
# of applications received	566
% applicants accepted	57
% acceptees attending	49
Average GMAT	631
Range of GMAT	590–680
Average GPA	3.21
TOEFL required of international students	Yes
Minimum TOEFL (paper/computer)	600/250
Application fee	$100
International application fee	$100
Application Deadline/Notification	
Round 1:	11/15 / 1/15
Round 2:	1/15 / 3/30
Round 3:	3/15 / 04/30
Round 4:	04/15 / 05/15
Deferment available	Yes
Maximum length of deferment	1 year
Transfer students accepted	Yes
Transfer application policy We accept transfer credit from AACSB accredited programs into our Evening MBA program.	
Non-fall admissions	Yes
Need-blind admissions	Yes

EMPLOYMENT PROFILE

Career Rating	90	Grads Employed by Function	% Avg. Salary
Primary Source of Full-time Job Acceptances		Finance	25 $95,433
School-facilitated activities	57%	Human Resources	2 $107,500
Graduate-facilitated activities	43%	Marketing	14 $78,686
Percent employed	92	Operations	2 $64,667
		Consulting	13 $90,844
		Entrepreneurship	24 NR
		General Management	7 $92,222
		Other	13 $87,438

Top 5 Employers Hiring Grads
Fidelity Investments, Staples, Cigna, athenahealth, IBM

BARRY UNIVERSITY
ANDREAS SCHOOL OF BUSINESS

Academics

Besides offering all of the advantages of a small, private school, the Andreas School of Business at Barry University manages to offer a surprising number of custom-tailored options to meet the needs and goals of its student body. Part-timers, who make up about two-thirds of the student body here, can choose between evening classes (on both the main campus and several satellite campuses) or the Saturday MBA program. All MBA courses are taught by full-time faculty who hold terminal degrees. Full-time students can complete their program of study at the main campus. All students can opt for dual degrees in Human Resource Development, Nursing, Podiatry, and Sports Management: The last is an especially popular option, cited by a number of MBAs as their primary reason for choosing Barry. Besides a general MBA, Andreas also offers a full complement of areas of specialization, with options including accounting, finance, general business, international business, management, and marketing. Besides the MBA, the School of Business also offers a Master of Science in Accounting (MSA) and a Master of Science in Management (MSM).

All told, Barry provides choices that are typically available only at larger universities. Yet this program is relatively pint-size, to the great advantage of its MBAs. One such MBA explains, "Because the business school is small, you get the benefit of personalized attention. The administrators and class coordinators know your name, and professors can always make time for you to visit them." Another agrees, "No other school would give you such personal attention. Several of my classes have had fewer than 10 students, and the professor tailors the material to fit our schedules and individual ambitions. And because there's such close contact, it's easy to build relationships with professors. I even was able to collaborate with one professor on writing a business case that will appear in a textbook supplement."

Andreas classes "are designed to challenge students in several ways. One is the explanation of theories; others include the implementation of practical assignments or case studies." In keeping with the school's Catholic worldview, many courses "promote social responsibility." The school's religious affiliation also helps it attract international students, whose presence "truly prepares students for working with many different types of people in many different contexts."

Career and Placement

School of Business administrators and its Career Services Director maintain close working relationships with local, state, and national companies. One student in the past indicated, "While job placement efforts could certainly be improved, I, like most Barry MBAs, have a job already, so I'm not really worried about the post-graduation job hunt, and that might be why Barry doesn't bring more companies to campus and be more aggressive in job placement. But for those students who do need to find work after school, Barry isn't equipped to be the kind of resource they really need." Additionally, international students are among those who feel most strongly that these services must be improved. However, since then, the school has reported that during the 2005 school year the center increased its placement by 27.6 percent along with an accompanying wage increase. The Andreas School has also partnered with the following firms and companies: Burger King Corporation, Microsoft Latin America, Franklin Templeton, KPMG International, FBI, JM Family Enterprises, Robert Half International, Northwestern Mutual, Morgan Stanley, MTV Networks Latin America, Assurant, and Ryder.

ADMISSIONS CONTACT: JOSE J. POZA JR., ASSISTANT DEAN FOR MARKETING
ADDRESS: 11300 NE 2ND AVENUE MIAMI SHORES, FL 33161 UNITED STATES
PHONE: (305) 899-3535 • FAX: (305) 892-6412
E-MAIL: JPOZA@MAIL.BARRY.EDU • WEBSITE: WWW.BARRY.EDU/BUSINESS

Student Life and Environment

For MBA students, Barry is "mostly a commuter school, so most MBA students are on campus in the evenings or weekends. As a result, there is not much extracurricular life. Not that that's necessarily a bad thing; as one student observes, "Barry is tranquil and laid-back, the ideal place for a person who would get overwhelmed by a high-stress, backstabbing MBA program. The MBA school is also made for people already working full-time." The school offers "limited clubs" and didn't even have a graduate business association until students took the initiative to form one. Those who truly desire a higher level of involvement can find it here, though. One student explains, "I have made myself get involved. I am a former student-athlete, currently a residence assistant as well as a graduate assistant. So my life has been great here. There is potential for everyone if you look for it."

"There is a vast cultural diversity within the university" and the MBA program at Barry. "It is delightful to see the peace that exists among classmates." Students "are very willing to help one another. There are always study groups, and in every class all students have each others' phone numbers, e-mails, etc. so that we can discuss the class when we need to." One MBA notes, "Learning in a cohort group has been the number one reason my MBA experience at Barry has been so successful. We've bonded as classmates, collaborated on projects, and built friendships that will extend beyond our MBA studies. In general, Barry MBA students are culturally diverse, unfailingly nice, and, since most work full-time while going to school, eager to use their degree to move up the career ladder."

Barry is located in Miami Shores, a central location offering easy access to the entire Miami metropolitan area. The area surrounding the campus offers access to the beach, and plenty of shopping, dining, and housing.

Admissions

The Admissions Committee at Barry University School of Business looks closely at the following components of the application: undergraduate GPA; GMAT scores (in lieu of the GMAT, we also accept the GRE, LSAT, or the MCAT); quality of undergraduate curriculum; personal essay; resume; two letters of reference supporting the resume; and TOEFL scores (for non-native English speakers). The GMAT requirement may be waived for applicants with substantial managerial experience. All of the following are prerequisites to MBA study: 6 credit hours of introductory accounting; 6 credit hours of macro and microeconomics; 3 credit hours of algebra or precalculus; 3 credit hours of statistics; 3 credit hours of introductory computer skills; 3 credit hours of operations management; and 3 credit hours of marketing. Students may demonstrate competency in any of these areas through undergraduate work or through non-credit workshops offered by the Andreas School.

FINANCIAL FACTS

Annual tuition	$26,100
Cost of books	$1,500
Room & board	$13,000
% of students receiving aid	100
% of first-year students receiving aid	52
% of students receiving loans	41
% of students receiving grants	48
Average award package	$15,731
Average grant	$6,225

ADMISSIONS

Admissions Selectivity Rating	**80**
# of applications received	154
% applicants accepted	36
% acceptees attending	85
Average GMAT	469
Range of GMAT	400–640
Average GPA	3.0
TOEFL required of international students	Yes
Minimum TOEFL (paper/computer)	550/213
Application fee	$30
International application fee	$30
Regular application deadline	Rolling
Regular notification	Rolling
Deferment available	Yes
Maximum length of deferment	1 year
Transfer students accepted	Yes
Transfer application policy Up to six transfer credits	
Non-fall admissions	Yes

Applicants Also Look At

Florida Atlantic University, Florida International University, Nova Southeastern University, University of Miami.

EMPLOYMENT PROFILE

		Grads Employed by Function	% Avg. Salary
Career Rating	**61**		
Primary Source of Full-time Job Acceptances		Finance	32 NR
School-facilitated activities	22 (42%)	Human Resources	9 NR
Graduate-facilitated activities	3 (14%)	Marketing	9 NR
Unknown	32 (62%)	MIS	5 NR
Percent employed	9	Operations	9 NR
		General Management	18 NR
		Other	18 NR

BAYLOR UNIVERSITY
HANKAMER SCHOOL OF BUSINESS

Academics

A "Christian school with a strong emphasis on ethics," the Hankamer School of Business at Baylor University offers "high standards, a great reputation, and an intimate learning environment" to its small, full-time student population. Students tell us the program "strikes a perfect balance between holding students accountable for work and providing resources and mentoring for those who need a little extra assistance."

The Baylor MBA can be completed in 16 to 21 months, a plus for managers on the go. The curriculum is fully integrated "to tie everything together nicely" with a focus on "strong communication skills and management preparation." Study includes a series of 5-week, cross-disciplinary courses covering accounting, finance, statistics, marketing, information systems, and strategy; these classes are spread out over three semesters. The program also includes four semester-long core courses covering operations management, microeconomics, communications management, and organizational behavior. Students supplement the core with one elective during each of the three lockstep semesters. All students complete either a summer internship or a summer abroad as part of the program. The program also includes the Focus Firm practicum, a project in which students assess a real-life business problem and propose solutions. One MBA enjoyed the fact that "in the fall of 2006, students worked with executives at Hewlett-Packard to address core problems within the company."

The size of the program and the lockstep curriculum combine to create an "intimate environment where everyone knows everyone and we can build great relationships and friendships that I hope last a lifetime," says one MBA. Professors contribute to this environment; they "are readily available for one-on-one sessions during office hours and by appointment. . . . I am thoroughly impressed by the level of attention to detail that the staff and professors exert to provide us with a superb education," says a first-year student. The program also boasts "amazing facilities" and "an administration that works hard at making sure we have a great business school." Still another benefit of a Baylor MBA: "Great alumni networking in Texas to use for future jobs."

Career and Placement

Baylor employs two full-time career placement professionals to work exclusively with the school's approximately 90 MBA students as well as with alumni. Students tell us that "Career Services has picked up the pace a lot this year. You almost have to try to avoid them." Some still grumble that "placement rates for graduates are low" as are the "campus recruiting opportunities."

Employers who most frequently hire Baylor MBAs include: Accenture, Allergan, American Express, Annuity Board of the Southern Baptist Convention, Anadarko Petroleum, Bank One, Bearing Point, Capgemini, Comerica, Community Bank and Trust, ConocoPhillips Company, Countrywide, Deloitte Touche Tohmatsu, Echostar Communications, Ernst & Young, ExxonMobil, The Gallup Organization, Goldman Sachs, IBM, Intecap, the IRS, Johnson & Johnson, JPMorgan Chase, KPMG International, Kraft Foods, Merck, Perot Systems, PricewaterhouseCoopers, Protiviti, Q Investments, RSM McGladrey, Shell Oil, Southwest Airlines, Sprint, Steak 'n Shake Operations, UBS Financial Services, Verizon Wireless, Wal-Mart, and Zale Corporation.

Student Life and Environment

"The MBA class is very social" at Hankamer, where students "work hard together and play in our spare time." "Everyone in the MBA program is very close" "due to the small number of students in classes. Everyone knows everyone else" and "is willing and able

ADMISSIONS CONTACT: LAURIE WILSON, DIRECTOR, GRADUATE BUSINESS DEGREE PROGRAMS
ADDRESS: ONE BEAR PLACE #98013, 1311 S. 5TH STREET WACO, TX 76798-8013 UNITED STATES
PHONE: 254-710-3718 • FAX: 254-710-1066
E-MAIL: MBA_INFO@BAYLOR.EDU • WEBSITE: WWW.BAYLOR.EDU/MBA

to help one another and work together." "Almost all students work out in the student center after class, and there are always study groups and tutoring if you want to join them." Unsurprisingly, at this Christian university, "Religious resources are outstanding." Perhaps more surprising is the fact that "if a student wants a nightlife, that is also available." One student sums up, "School life is study hard and play hard. . . . We have an excellent wireless network through the entire campus. The health care facilities are top notch. Eateries are nice. Quality of life is good. Isn't life what we make of it anyway? We make it enjoyable here!"

Baylor's "easygoing" but "ambitious" MBAs "come from diverse backgrounds with different levels and backgrounds of experiences. Each of us has something excellent to contribute to our program. During team projects, we diligently engage in the activities to produce results. We respect one another," and "Each of us listens to our individual perspectives. We have learned and continue to learn to collaborate and build good relationships." Students tend to be "mostly recent undergraduates." The student body is ethnically diverse "in regards to international students."

Admissions

Those seeking admission to the Hankamer School must submit the following materials: a completed application (online application preferred); two letters of recommendation from individuals who know you professionally and can assess your skills and potential; official undergraduate transcripts (international students who attended a non-English-speaking school must provide professionally translated and interpreted academic records); a GMAT score report; a current resume; and personal essays detailing qualifications, experiences, and objectives in pursuing a Hankamer MBA. International students whose first language is not English must also submit a score report for the TOEFL (minimum score: 600, paper-based test; 250, computer-based test; or 100, Internet-based test). Hankamer processes applications on a rolling basis; candidates are notified of their admission status as soon as a decision is made.

ADMISSIONS

Admissions Selectivity Rating	**86**
# of applications received	126
% applicants accepted	53
% acceptees attending	66
Average GMAT	595
Range of GMAT	490–720
Average GPA	3.2
TOEFL required of international students	Yes
Minimum TOEFL (paper/computer)	600/250
Application fee	$50
International application fee	$50
Regular application deadline	6/15
Regular notification	rolling
Deferment available	Yes
Maximum length of deferment	1 year
Transfer students accepted	Yes
Transfer application policy	
Only 6 hrs may be transferred into the MBA program.	
Non-fall admissions	Yes
Need-blind admissions	Yes

Applicants Also Look At

Babson College, Rice University, Southern Methodist University, Texas A&M University—College Station, Texas Christian University, The University of Texas at Arlington, The University of Texas at Dallas.

EMPLOYMENT PROFILE

Career Rating	81	Grads Employed by Function	%	Avg. Salary
Percent employed	95	Finance	39	$59,808
		Marketing	5	$54,521
		MIS	5	NR
		Operations	28	$60,000
		General Management	11	$50,933
		Other	11	$60,000

BELLARMINE UNIVERSITY
W. FIELDING RUBEL SCHOOL OF BUSINESS

GENERAL INFORMATION

Type of school	Private
Affiliation	Roman Catholic

SURVEY SAYS...

Friendly students
Solid preparation in:
Teamwork
Communication/interpersonal skills
Presentation skills

STUDENTS

Enrollment of parent institution	3,001
Enrollment of business school	232
% male/female	56/44
% part-time	59
% minorities	7
% international	3
Average age at entry	26
Average years work experience at entry	5

ACADEMICS

Academic Experience Rating	**72**
Profs interesting rating	76
Profs accessible rating	72

Academics

If you think "team-based learning is the way to go," check out Bellarmine University's distinctive MBA program, which emphasizes collaboration, networking, and small, discussion-oriented classes. Bellarmine's program is cohort-based, which means students work with the same group of classmates throughout the MBA curriculum. A current student elaborates, "We are organized into groups at the beginning of the program and work together on each project throughout the entire program. We learn to work together as a team and work through our problems. It's an incredible experience." Another student writes, "Bellarmine's program is unique in that you learn and grow from your interaction with the other students. There is so much to learn from their experiences and insight that you aren't focused on solely what the professors are doing [and] saying, but pulling from what the class is sharing."

Given the school's focus on peer-to-peer interaction, Bellarmine professors are "more like facilitators" than lecturers. Small, discussion-based classes are a hallmark of the program, and the "teacher to student ratio is very low." You won't have to clamor to get your voice heard at Bellarmine; "small class sizes lead to more personal attention. Professors know and remember details of students from several years ago and keep up with many of them on a regular basis." A current student raves, "The faculty and staff are some of the best people I've met and should be commended for the job they do each and every day. They are all very dedicated to the success of the program." Bellarmine distinguishes itself further by teaching all material through case study and with a cross-disciplinary focus, rather than relying on traditional lecture, so Bellarmine graduates are trained to think in real-world scenarios. The result is a memorable and surprisingly exciting education. A student details, "Each class was a new experience. If I had to miss a class, I felt I would lose an important topic for discussion."

Another undeniable benefit to this small school is that there is "virtually no red tape" and "the administration is wonderful and could not make the admission and registration process any easier." Rather than getting the run-around, students say their "questions are answered promptly and accurately the first time asked." For working professionals, Bellarmine also offers weekend and weeknight MBA programs. A part-time student reports, "The layout of the program and the balance of classes is exactly what I needed to keep the stress level down and balance my work load. I wouldn't change anything about the experience; the faculty and staff have been amazing."

Career and Placement

As the only AACSB-accredited private school in Kentucky, Bellarmine students have a leg up in the local job market. On campus, the Bellarmine University Career Center serves students and alumni, offering resume preparation services, mock interviews, and an online job database. The Career Center also hosts campus recruiting and several career fairs.

Many of the school's part-time students plan to stay with their current employer after graduation, using the skills from their MBA to help move up the corporate ladder. To that end, the school is very successful. A current student enthuses, "I am easily able to complete tasks that I was incapable of before starting the MBA program. The program has improved my skills at work. I am now a candidate for one of the top positions within my company." For those who are looking to start their career after graduation, recent Bellarmine University graduates have taken jobs at AIG, Abercrombie and Fitch, Deloitte & Touche, Ernst and Young, GE Industrial, Sherwin Williams, U.S. Bank, Wells Fargo, and William M. Mercer Company.

ADMISSIONS CONTACT: LAURA RICHARDSON, DIRECTOR, MBA PROGRAM
ADDRESS: 2001 NEWBURG ROAD LOUISVILLE, KY 50205 UNITED STATES
PHONE: (502) 452-8258 • FAX: (502) 452-8013
E-MAIL: MBA@BELLARMINE.EDU • WEBSITE: WWW.BELLARMINE.EDU

Student Life and Environment

While they may study in the library from time to time, the Bellarmine business program caters to commuters and "no graduate students live on campus." Therefore, campus life is limited to class and study groups. Unfortunately, the school offers "a lot of activities for undergrads, but few for grad students—even fewer (if any) aimed at families." Still, students appreciate the school's convenient and peaceful location in Louisville's Highlands neighborhood, just a few minutes drive from downtown.

A local crowd, the school's student population is a nice mix of students who are "finishing up their undergrad" (the school allows business undergraduates to complete a BS and an MBA over five years though shared credits) as well as older, working students, some with families. While they are all in business school so as to promote their career, the vibe is "laid-back and friendly," as most of Bellarmine's levelheaded students are "very focused on balanced work/life and less about improving promotion chances at work."

Admissions

To apply to Bellarmine, students must submit undergraduate transcripts, GMAT scores, two letters of recommendation, and two personal essays describing their career goals and experience. As Bellarmine's program is largely interactive, students' qualitative skills are weighed alongside their quantitative abilities. While many MBA students have a professional and academic background in business or accounting, the campus also draws students from a range of areas, including non-profit and government organizations, health care, and humanities.

FINANCIAL FACTS

% of students receiving loans	34

ADMISSIONS

Admissions Selectivity Rating	**65**
# of applications received	88
% applicants accepted	95
% acceptees attending	90
Average GMAT	485
Range of GMAT	440–540
Average GPA	3.2
TOEFL required of international students	Yes
Minimum TOEFL (paper/computer)	550/213
Application fee	$25
International application fee	$25
Deferment available	Yes
Maximum length of deferment	5 years
Transfer students accepted	Yes
Transfer application policy Accept up to 12 graduate credits from an accedited University.	
Non-fall admissions	Yes

BELMONT UNIVERSITY
THE JACK C. MASSEY GRADUATE SCHOOL OF BUSINESS

Academics

The Jack C. Massey School of Business at Belmont University offers an academically rigorous program that is designed to meet the needs of nontraditional students. As one such student explains, "Belmont offers a flexible approach to taking classes—I could take classes [if] I needed that experience in my work." Most classes are offered in the evening, and students may elect to enroll in a full- or part-time program. Undergraduate courses in business areas such as accounting and economic analysis, along with competency in language and quantitative skills, are required to begin the graduate program. Belmont offers guidance on meeting or waiving these requirements where appropriate, including "the opportunity to take a year of prerequisite classes as part of the program," which helps students to prepare for the core.

The MBA program itself consists of 34 credit hours, 24 of which are taken up by required courses. These classes focus on the management aspects of technology, human resources, finance, and international business, and well as advanced skills in leadership, cost analysis, and entrepreneurship. With the 10 remaining credits, students may continue with a general business degree or pursue concentrations in accounting, finance, health care management, management of business processes and operations, or music business. Located in Nashville's West End, just blocks from Music Row and down the street from the classically oriented programs at Vanderbilt University's Blair School of Music, Belmont owns and operates the historic Studio B recording complex in conjunction with the Country Music Hall of Fame. "I chose Belmont because of its excellent music business program elective and because of its proximity to the music industry in Nashville," one student said. Opportunities for international study abound, with programs in Ireland, the Czech Republic, China, Chile, France, Germany, and Brazil.

All of the professors at Belmont "were top executives at one point in their careers." "The professors have business experience that I feel will create a richer learning experience," says one satisfied student. Described by students as "good, knowledgeable people who have a desire to teach," the professors at Belmont "are well educated and have impressive backgrounds in their fields." "I feel completely comfortable approaching the professors and am confident they are willing and eager to help me succeed," says one student. Students say the "administration is seamless," although they wish it were "more racially diverse." "Overall though, I think the school has a strong program," says one student, echoing the sentiments of his peers.

Career and Placement

Belmont employs a staff of advisors dedicated to meeting the needs of business students. At the university's Career Center, MBA students have access to a wide array of services including career planning, resume review, and alumni mentorship programs, as well as workshops on topics such as networking and salary negotiation. With many of Belmont's MBA graduates still living in middle Tennessee, both the school and currently-enrolled students find these alums to be the most useful resources in their job search. Students appreciate the "amount of contacts to the business world" that Belmont offers, but feel that "the school needs to improve its career services." Bridgestone/Firestone, Caterpillar, Hospital Corporation of America, Deloitte Touche Tohmatsu, and Ernst &Young are among the top firms that recruit at Belmont.

ADMISSIONS CONTACT: TONYA HOLLIN, ADMISSIONS ASSISTANT
ADDRESS: 1900 BELMONT BOULEVARD NASHVILLE, TN 37212 UNITED STATES
PHONE: 615-460-6480 • FAX: 615-460-6353
E-MAIL: MASSEYADMISSIONS@MAIL.BELMONT.EDU • WEBSITE: MASSEY.BELMONT.EDU

Student Life and Environment

Although the classes at Belmont take place in the evening, there is still a strong sense of community among students. As one student explains, "The main reason I went here is for the people." Students here are "very supportive and diverse. I have met a lot of great friends and contacts in the graduate school at Belmont." Many students are "young and recent graduates" and "don't have the level of contacts or job that would make them a good networking contact." While these students may not be "as mature or as settled" as some of the older students on campus, "Most are friendly and helpful." "Other [students] are older and have families" and can "provide knowledge from their career." Some students say their family situation could use some recognition from the university. "Because such a large population of students have children," students say it would be "extremely helpful if [the school] offered child care." Students have nothing but praise for their fellow students: "They are tomorrow's leaders. I look forward to working with each of them." "They are the type of people I would have chosen could I have hand-picked people to go to school with."

Admissions

To apply to the Jack C. Massey School of Business at Belmont, you'll need to submit your undergraduate transcript, GMAT scores, two references, a resume, and a one page statement of your career goals. At least 2 years of work experience is required, along with prior course work or competency in basic business subjects, quantitative skills, and communication skills. In 2006, the average GMAT score of the entering class was 503 and the average undergraduate GPA was 3.22. Students averaged about 6 and a half years of work experience.

ADMISSIONS

Admissions Selectivity Rating	**76**
# of applications received	49
% applicants accepted	73
% acceptees attending	75
Average GMAT	553
Range of GMAT	510–610
Average GPA	3.2
TOEFL required of international students	Yes
Minimum TOEFL (paper/computer)	550/213
Application fee	$50
International application fee	$50
Regular application deadline	7/1
Regular notification	7/1
Deferment available	Yes
Maximum length of deferment	1 year
Transfer students accepted	Yes
Transfer application policy May transfer up to 6 hours from an accredited university.	
Non-fall admissions	Yes
Need-blind admissions	Yes

Applicants Also Look At

Middle Tennessee State University, University of Tennessee, Vanderbilt University.

EMPLOYMENT PROFILE	
Career Rating	77

BENTLEY COLLEGE
THE ELKIN B. MCCALLUM GRADUATE SCHOOL OF BUSINESS

GENERAL INFORMATION

Type of school	Private
Environment	Town
Academic calendar	Semester

SURVEY SAYS...
Cutting edge classes
Smart classrooms
Solid preparation in:
Accounting
Computer skills

STUDENTS

Enrollment of parent institution	5,593
Enrollment of business school	606
% male/female	64/36
% out-of-state	8
% part-time	90
% minorities	3
% international	56
Average age at entry	26
Average years work experience at entry	4

ACADEMICS

Academic Experience Rating	**84**
Student/faculty ratio	10:1
Profs interesting rating	82
Profs accessible rating	81
% female faculty	32
% minority faculty	12

Joint Degrees
Dual Degrees are available.

Prominent Alumni
Joseph Antonellis, Vice Chairman, State Street Corporation; Ullas Naik, Managing Dir., GlobeSpan Capital Partners; Tosayee Ogbomo, Managing Dir., Goldman Sachs and Co.; Amy Hunter, VP, Boston Private Bank and Trust; Anthony P. DiBona, Executive VP, PTC.

Academics

With both "one of the most technologically advanced schools" in the country and "the ability to combine technology and people to create a phenomenal learning environment," The McCallum MBA program at Bentley College "has done a good job of creating a niche for itself in the Boston-area business-school environment." This predominantly part-time program boasts "amazing facilities" and strength in a number of technology-related and technology-assisted disciplines.

High-tech perks are what first catch prospective MBAs' attention here and for good reason. Bentley's resources include "an awesome trading center," a 3,500-square-foot facility complete with a trading floor with two Trans-Lux data walls, 60 work stations, an adjacent business suite, and a marketing center that features numerous state-of-the-art research and analysis labs. Bentley "blows other schools' facilities away," one student assures us. Also available are "top-notch centers to serve students in accounting, information technology, and cyberlaw; and a library that recently received a $16 million makeover. The library is "ideal for group projects, with its dozens of collaboration rooms, which can be reserved electronically and are equipped with LCD monitors, white boards, conference tables etc."

Bentley puts those facilities to excellent use in such diverse fields as marketing technology, finance, accounting, and information technology. In these areas especially, Bentley has an "excellent reputation that provides the best in career opportunities." The school also offers both an MS and a concentration in real estate management ("It offers Argus training for real estate"), and is "a leader in the field of human-computer interaction." Professors here "are presently involved in the Boston business community" and so transport "actual experience in the business world" to the classroom. "They bring creative approaches to challenge students in the classroom," although incoming students should also note that "most are hard-asses, but [the workload] really prepares you for the real world." Bentley "keeps the classes small, allowing for individual attention when needed." One student says, "I really didn't want any auditorium-style classes." Students also love the "flexibility in terms of scheduling, which makes it possible to take two courses a night after work if you need to." Ultimately, though, it's "Bentley's eagerness to set the bar for education in business/IT integration" that sets the school apart from the crowd.

Career and Placement

Bentley's Nathan R. Miller Center for Career Services (CCS) "is excellent" at serving the school's MBA students, who tell us that "everyone . . . is personally involved in helping you out." Counselors receive a strong assist from Bentley's solid "reputation among Boston-area employers." Students here benefit from the Career Management Series (CMS), a program designed to help them better position themselves in the battle for top jobs. CMS programs vary by area of concentration, meaning students receive plenty of field-specific assistance. The CSS provides lifetime service to alumni, another huge plus.

Top employers of Bentley MBAs include: Deloitte Touche Tohmatsu, Raytheon, Staples, State Street, Liberty Mutual, PepsiCo, PricewaterhouseCoopers, GE, Yankee Group, BearingPoint, Thermo Electron, Yahoo!, EMC, Fidelity, and Tyco.

ADMISSIONS CONTACT: SHARON HILL, DIRECTOR OF GRADUATE ADMISSIONS
ADDRESS: 175 FOREST STREET WALTHAM, MA 02452 UNITED STATES
PHONE: 781-891-2108 • FAX: 781-891-2464
E-MAIL: GRADADM@BENTLEY.EDU • WEBSITE: WWW.BENTLEY.EDU

Student Life and Environment

Full-time MBA students describe a full grad school experience, one buttressed by lots of group work, meetings, and events held by graduate student associations, and such on-campus amenities as numerous food options and "an excellent gym with flat-screen LCDs to watch while [working out] on the cardio machines." Students tell us that "there are tons of activities" in the Bentley community, but note that "it is also true that those activities and clubs are targeted to full-time students. For those who work 9 to 5, it is impossible to get involved in events." Full-timers and part-timers alike agree that "the campus is absolutely gorgeous, and it's great that it's completely wireless."

Full-time students also enjoy being a part of "a tight-knit group," which, in part, begins because they participate in a cohort program. "We spend a lot of time together, for better or worse. It's great for building tight bonds, but it's a little harder to meet people outside of that group." MBAs report that "students appear happy here. There is lots of mingling in between classes, and it appears people genuinely like meeting new people." One student adds, "The different backgrounds and experiences of my classmates really add a lot of value to class time."

Admissions

Applicants to the Bentley MBA program must submit all of the following materials to the Admissions Committee: a completed application form; official copies of all transcripts for all postsecondary academic work; an official GMAT score report; two letters of recommendation; three essays (topics detailed in application); and a resume. Applicants to the full-time, daytime MBA program or the MS plus MBA program must sit for an interview; interviews are optional for all other applicants. In addition to all of the above, international applicants must also submit an official score report for the TOEFL, IBT, or IELTS; an international student data form; a bank statement; and a letter detailing how the student intends to support him/herself while attending school. Bentley Admissions Officers pride themselves on personalizing the admissions process by looking at the whole person when making admissions decisions. Work experience is strongly preferred but not required.

FINANCIAL FACTS

Annual tuition	$23,664
Fees	$404
Cost of books	$1,375
Room & board	$12,865
% of students receiving aid	33
% of first-year students receiving aid	60
% of students receiving loans	22
% of students receiving grants	16
Average award package	$17,374
Average grant	$11,915
Average student loan debt	$21,276

ADMISSIONS

Admissions Selectivity Rating	**80**
# of applications received	388
% applicants accepted	75
% acceptees attending	62
Average GMAT	563
Range of GMAT	510–610
Average GPA	3.29
TOEFL required of international students	Yes
Minimum TOEFL (paper/computer)	600/250
Application fee	$50
International application fee	$50
Regular application deadline	3/1
Regular notification	Rolling
Application Deadline/Notification	
Round 1:	12/01 / 01/15
Round 2:	01/15 / 03/15
Round 3:	03/15 / 05/01
Early decision program?	Yes
ED Deadline/Notification	12/01 / 01/15
Deferment available	Yes
Maximum length of deferment	1 year
Non-fall admissions	Yes
Need-blind admissions	Yes

Applicants Also Look At

Babson College, Boston College, Boston University, Northeastern University.

EMPLOYMENT PROFILE

Career Rating	85	Grads Employed by Function	% Avg. Salary
Primary Source of Full-time Job Acceptances		Finance	33 $68,125
School-facilitated activities	8 (33%)	Marketing	17 $68,375
Graduate-facilitated activities	15 (63%)	MIS	21 $69,500
Unknown	1 (4%)	Operations	4 NR
Average base starting salary	$68,273	General Management	4 $26,000
Percent employed	92	Other	21 $77,500

Top 5 Employers Hiring Grads

Fidelity Investments; IBM; Deloitte Consulting; Boston Scientific; Raytheon

BERRY COLLEGE
CAMPBELL SCHOOL OF BUSINESS

Academics

The Campbell School of Business at Berry College offers a broad and contemporary business education in the context of a small, private school environment. Taking a whole-picture approach to learning, the program's stated mission is to "educate the head, heart, and hands" of future business leaders—a goal they achieve through a series of core courses in a range subject areas, including: analysis and problem solving, application of theory, technology, oral and written communication, global and political issues, demographic diversity, lifelong learning, and more. After completing the core course work, students must take at least three electives (or an equivalent of nine semester hours) and may also earn course credit through internship experiences.

Many students chose Berry because it "is small in size, and the teacher-to-student ratio is excellent." Indeed, the "community atmosphere on the campus" is one of the program's greatest strengths, and students say it's easy to receive plenty of "personal attention from the faculty." While they maintain a friendly and relaxed attitude, Campbell faculty promotes a high academic standard on campus. A current student raves, "We have some top-notch professors here who most definitely know their stuff and could rival Stanford professors any day of the week." Students admit, however, that there are a few drawbacks to attending a small school. Specifically, "Course offerings are slim" and do not always meet student needs.

The MBA program at the Campbell School of Business is designed for working professionals and managers in every business field, attracting students who are "goal oriented and are trying to better themselves in their current or future careers." In order to accommodate the special needs of students struggling to balance a career and an education, classes at Campbell meet 1 night a week. Furthermore, Berry professors are sensitive to the difficulties of keeping up with the work and school schedule, and they "take into consideration the outside responsibilities when it comes to assessing their students."

Campbell is an increasingly important presence in the North Georgia economic community, enjoying "great school recognition in the area." Playing an active role in the region and encouraging a sense of social consciousness in the student body, the school's involvement in the community goes beyond churning out talented business graduates. A current student explains, "Berry doesn't just try to trade cash for knowledge. It truly wants to change students for the better. The students here are very caring and go out of their way to make an impact in the community." Another adds, "Berry emphasizes the head, heart, and hands and abides by this with what the professors teach."

Career Placement

Campbell MBA students have access to the Berry College Career Development Center, through which they can work with professional career counselors and receive assistance looking for jobs and internships. The center provides job counseling and resume-preparation services, workshops, and online career search tools, as well as extensive materials on their website. Through the center, students can register for and attend a number of career fairs in the region, which draw major employers from the area. In February, the Career Development Center hosts the Employer Expo, a 2-day career fair held on the Berry campus.

DR. GARY WATERS, ASSOCIATE VICE PRESIDENT OF ENROLLMENT MANAGEMENT
ADDRESS: 2277 MARTHA BERRY HWY NW ROME, GA 30165-9987 UNITED STATES
PHONE: 706-236-2215 • FAX: 706-290-2178
E-MAIL: WWW.ADMISSIONS@BERRY.EDU • WEBSITE: CAMPBELL.BERRY.EDU

Student Life and Environment

Berry College's "peaceful and gorgeous" campus is one of the school's chief attractions. At 26,000 acres, these beautiful and green grounds are among the largest college campuses in the world. Graduate students may participate in all student activities at Berry, including movie nights, intramural sports, and cultural activities; however, MBA students admit that "there are no purely graduate focused resources."

Between school and career, Campbell students have plenty of responsibilities to keep them busy. Even so, most are "very outgoing, and many help out in the community with volunteer work." A great place to live, work, and study, Rome, Georgia is a small city that nonetheless offers plenty of entertainment options, such as art museums and parks as well as proximity to other Georgia cities. Students appreciate the town's pleasant culture, as well as its affordability. In fact, "Rent is fairly cheap" for those who wish to live off campus.

Admissions

To apply to Berry College Campbell School of Business, all prospective students must possess an undergraduate degree from an accredited college or university. Candidates must submit the graduate application form, an official transcript from all colleges and universities attended, official GMAT score, two letters of recommendation, an essay explaining their reasons for pursuing an MBA, and, for international applicants, a score of 550 or better on the TOEFL. Usually a GMAT score of at least 400 is required for entry to the program and an undergraduate GPA of at least 3.0. For all candidates, the school looks for students who display a promise of growth, seriousness of purpose, and a sense of responsibility. Undergraduate business majors with a grade point average of 3.0 or better may request permission from the Dean to be admitted to the postbaccalaureate MBA program.

ADMISSIONS

Admissions Selectivity Rating	**71**
# of applications received	10
% applicants accepted	80
% acceptees attending	75
Average GMAT	524
Average GPA	3.1
TOEFL required of international students	Yes
Minimum TOEFL (paper/computer)	550/213
Application fee	$25
International application fee	$30
Deferment available	Yes
Maximum length of deferment	one Semester
Transfer students accepted	Yes
Transfer application policy Maximum of three 3-Semester-hour courses, for a total of 9 Semester hours.	
Non-fall admissions	Yes

Applicants Also Look At
Kennesaw State University.

BIRMINGHAM-SOUTHERN COLLEGE

Academics

Birmingham-Southern College is a relative rarity in the graduate business world in that it is a tiny liberal arts school. It is so small, in fact, that business is the only area in which it offers any type of graduate instruction. The school is also unique in the degree it awards. Rather than offering a traditional MBA, the school offers a Master's of Arts in Public and Private Management (MPPM), a degree that stresses "a holistic approach to managerial leadership through a liberal arts curriculum." As one student puts it, the focus here is "more on leadership and management than on the numbers." The school also offers a 1-year certificate program in Public and Private Management for international students.

BSC has built a graduate business curriculum based on the themes of leadership, entrepreneurship, teamwork, ethics, critical analysis, business strategy, quantitative analysis, creativity, communication, and global perspectives. The incorporation of the school's strong liberal arts programs means that "Behavioral and political science professors have a place in the MPPM program," too, although some here feel that "the program places too much emphasis on those types of courses." All students must complete 16 three-credit classes, nine of which form the program's foundation requirements. Elective choices are limited, as are concentration options; students may currently concentrate only in public sector management, private sector management, or health care management. The program could improve by "increasing concentrations to include entrepreneurship, transportation/logistics, marketing, strategic management, corporate finance/controller, and IT/technology management," says one student. "I believe that by offering concentrations that are more specific, BSC can increase enrollment and provide a more individualized experience that could better serve the greater Birmingham area."

BSC's size may have some drawbacks, but it also ensures "small classes" and "personal attention" for each student in the program. The school's solid commitment to the program means also that a "dedicated administration" demonstrates a serious "interest in improving the program." Students agree the majority of "Professors are good communicators, experts in their fields, and appear to genuinely care about the students." "My overall academic experience is very good and appropriately challenging."

Career and Placement

BSC is primarily an undergraduate institution, and its Career Counseling Center is designed to provide placement and counseling services to undergraduates. Services here include self-assessments instruments; seminars and workshops in job search skills, resume writing, interviewing, and salary negotiation; mentoring and internship placement; and the administration of networking and recruiting events both on and off campus.

The school does not provide employment data for graduates of its MPPM program. Major employers in the Birmingham area include The University of Alabama at Birmingham, BellSouth, Baptist Health System, AmSouth Bank, American Cast Iron Pipe, Alabama Gas, BE&K, Alabama Power, Blue Cross and Blue Shield Association, Compass Bank, and federal, state, and local government.

Student Life and Environment

"Graduate students, for the most part, come to campus to attend classes at night and have jobs during the day" at Birmingham-Southern, meaning that most students attend part-time, taking two classes per semester to complete the program in 3 to 4 years. While on campus, students "frequently utilize the business school building, the cafeteria, the computer lab," and the library. One commuter students says, "I try to interact with fac-

ADMISSIONS CONTACT: BRENDA D. DURHAM, DIRECTOR OF MPPM ADMISSION
ADDRESS: 900 ARKADELPHIA ROAD, BOX 549052 BIRMINGHAM, AL 35254 UNITED STATES
PHONE: 205-226-4803 • FAX: 205-226-4843
E-MAIL: GRADUATE@BSC.EDU • WEBSITE: WWW.BSC.EDU/MPPM

ADMISSIONS	
Admissions Selectivity Rating	**60***
# of applications received	16
% applicants accepted	100
% acceptees attending	100
TOEFL required of international students	Yes
Application fee	$25
Deferment available	Yes
Maximum length of deferment	1 year
Non-fall admissions	Yes

ulty and staff whenever possible." Classes convene in the Marguerite Jones Harbert Building, built in 1987–1988. The complex includes computer labs, an auditorium, a conference center, and a behavioral science research center, which is utilized for the MPPM program.

The city of Birmingham is one of the major banking centers of the South, and its banks help feed the program's student body. The city is also the state's capital, and the government workforce also contributes to the population here. Birmingham-Southern is located on a wooded, 192-acre campus just three miles west of downtown Birmingham, making it both convenient and comfortable. The acreage means there's plenty of room for a baseball field, a softball field, a soccer field, tennis courts, an intramural field, and EcoScape, an art park that combines the work of local artists with a nature center. Mild winters help relieve the winter doldrums suffered by students' peers farther north. Spring and fall are reasonably mild, while summers can be oppressive.

BSC draws a "very diverse" student body "by race, gender, age, and economic background" to its MPPM program, meaning "Discussions are always interesting." "Classroom interaction is the best part of the MPPM program," offers one student. Most here have "white-collar careers, are married" and are in "their mid- to late 30s." They are typically "dedicated to work, school, and home." Some feel the program needs to tighten admissions requirements in order to push the program to the next level.

Admissions

Applicants to the Birmingham-Southern MPPM program must apply to the college's Office of Graduate Programs. The school requires applicants to submit a completed application, an essay discussing career goals and program objectives, a resume, two letters of recommendation, official transcripts for all postsecondary institutions attended, and any of the following entrance exams: the GMAT, the GRE, or the Miller Analogy Test (MAT). Applicants already holding advanced degrees are exempted from entrance exam requirements. Foreign students whose first language is not English must submit either an official TOEFL score report (minimum required score: 600, paper-based test; or 214, computer-based test) or comparable evidence of proficiency in written and spoken English. After initial review of applications, the school contacts potential candidates to schedule an entrance interview. BSC requires students to enter with at least 3 years of management experience.

BOSTON COLLEGE
CARROLL SCHOOL OF MANAGEMENT

Academics

The Carroll School of Management at Boston College enjoys a "great reputation with industry for producing graduates who can immediately produce" as well as a "strong reputation in finance" and several other disciplines. Add to the mix a "huge resource in our alumni network: BC alums are always eager to help fellow Eagles," and you understand why so many students here describe this as an "amazing program."

BC's marquee discipline is finance, but students are adamant that "BC is as strong a marketing school as it is a finance school" and that the school offers "a good marketing curriculum." Also, according to at least one student, "A hidden gem is Boston College's organizational studies focus. Holding many highly touted organizational behavior and organizational development professors, BC offers the opportunity for MBA students to take PhD-level classes in organization studies during the second year. The high quality of professors is recognized in the academic and business community." Throughout the MBA program, BC implements "an experiential curriculum." One student writes, "Not only does BC offer the MBA consulting project but also a business plan project during the second year and several investment management opportunities. It is extremely valuable to combine these opportunities with a traditional classroom education to provide an overall world-class experience." BC offers specializations in asset management, change leadership, competitive service delivery, corporate finance, entrepreneurial management, financial reporting and controls, global management, marketing informatics, and product and brand management. Students may also design their own fields of specialization.

BC "does a good job at teaching the hard technical skills as well as soft skills like communication and leadership." Prospective students should be aware that "the program has gone through some administrative changes in the past few years" and that "the program is changing," making it "feel a bit like an experiment right now." Students report that "the school has recently taken great effort to expand the curriculum and opportunities available to students, making it increasing more relevant to current business issues," and that the curriculum was completely overhauled for the Class of 2008. Students remain confident that, regardless of the changes, "BC is a school that is climbing in the rankings—small enough to have amazing faculty interaction—and will prepare me well for my intended career."

Career and Placement

BC's Office of Career Strategies "is unique in the time and effort spent working with every single student. We meet regularly with our career counselors. They are constantly working to coordinate events and seek increasingly more job opportunity for graduate management students." Still, some here complain that "on-campus recruiting is disappointing in terms of quality of employer and intern positions available" and that "there is little effort made to place students outside the Boston area." Fortunately, the alumni network is a "huge resource." One MBA explains, "Many of the big consulting or investment banking firms don't recruit on campus, but we have plenty of alumni at those firms. It's really up to the students to make the connections and ask for a lead."

Employers who most frequently hire BC MBAs include: Liberty Mutual, Staples, EMC Corporation, Boston Scientific Corporation, Fidelity Investments, Strategic Pricing Group, Gillette, Merrill Lynch, State Street Global Markets, UBS Warburg, and Wellington Management.

ADMISSIONS CONTACT: SHELLEY BURT, DIRECTOR OF GRADUATE ENROLLMENT
ADDRESS: FULTON HALL 315, 140 COMMONWEALTH AVENUE CHESTNUT HILL, MA 02467-3808 U.S.
PHONE: 617-552-3920 • FAX: 617-552-8078
E-MAIL: BCMBA@BC.EDU • WEBSITE: WWW.BC.EDU/MBA

Student Life and Environment

Life in the graduate management program at BC is "the best." One student explains, "BC is a very tight-knit community, and students spend a lot of time together both inside and outside of the classroom. Whether it's working in teams as part of the Diane Weiss Consulting Competition or having drinks at the weekly 'Thirsty Thursday' get-togethers, BC students form relationships that will last forever." Students remind us "not to forget the football games and the tailgate events organized by the GMA (Graduate Management Association)," or that "the strong nationally ranked athletics programs in football, basketball, and hockey create a wonderful bonding experience for students." One student sums up, "If you don't want to know your classmates, mingle with alumni, and study hard, Boston College is not the place for you."

Students also point out that "for such a small school there are a lot of clubs and activities for MBA students to partake in. Almost everyone is involved in some sort of activity, and many people belong to more than one club or organization," especially as students move through the program; first year "is hectic" enough that sometimes "School is the only thing that you seem to have time for," because "The academic workload is substantial. Fortunately, the camaraderie among students and the teamwork that takes place makes the experience worthwhile."

Admissions

Applicants to the MBA program at Boston College must submit the following materials to the school: a completed application; a current resume and a separate employment history; two personal essays (students may submit a third optional essay); two letters of recommendation, an official transcript from each degree-granting undergraduate and graduate program attended; and an official GMAT score report. International applicants who attended a non-English language institution must have their transcripts translated and interpreted by a professional service. International students whose first language is not English must submit an official TOEFL score report unless they received their undergraduate degrees from an institution at which the language of instruction is English. BC strongly encourages applicants to apply online.

Prominent Alumni

John Fisher, President & CEO, Saucony; Norman Chambers, President & COO of NCIS Building Systems, Inc.; Paul LaCamera, President & GM, WCVB-TV, Channel 5; Alexis Sarkissian, CEO Vivid Collection; Ronald Logue, Chairman & CEO, State Street Corporation.

FINANCIAL FACTS

Annual tuition	$31,528
Fees	$150
Cost of books	$1,500
Room & board	$17,047
% of students receiving aid	79
% of students receiving loans	59
% of students receiving grants	64
Average award package	$30,889
Average grant	$18,692
Average student loan debt	$50,059

ADMISSIONS

Admissions Selectivity Rating	**92**
# of applications received	754
% applicants accepted	38
% acceptees attending	36
Average GMAT	651
Range of GMAT	610–690
Average GPA	3.4
TOEFL required of international students	Yes
Minimum TOEFL (paper/computer)	600/250
Application fee	$100
International application fee	$100
Application Deadline/Notification	
Round 1:	11/15 / 1/15
Round 2:	1/15 / 3/15
Round 3:	3/15 / 5/01
Transfer students accepted	Yes
Transfer application policy	
4 courses are accepted (with a grade of B or higher) from other AACSB MBA Programs.	
Need-blind admissions	Yes

Applicants Also Look At

Babson College, Boston University, Columbia University, Georgetown University, Harvard University, Massachusetts Institute of Technology, New York University.

EMPLOYMENT PROFILE

Career Rating	86	Grads Employed by Function	% Avg. Salary
Primary Source of Full-time Job Acceptances		Finance	24 $84,700
School-facilitated activities	37 (59%)	Human Resources	1 NR
Graduate-facilitated activities	26 (41%)	Marketing	14 $81,577
Average base starting salary	$87,468	MIS	1 NR
Percent employed	99	Operations	3 $75,500
		Consulting	8 $100,250
		General Management	7 $80,815
		Other	6 $111,000

Top 5 Employers Hiring Grads
Duff & Phelps; Johnson & Johnson; KPMG; State Street / State Street Global Markets; General Electric

BOSTON UNIVERSITY
SCHOOL OF MANAGEMENT

Academics

The Boston University School of Management boasts a number of first-rate programs, including a number of specialized MBA programs to suit the needs of the especially ambitious. Students praise the school and love the direction in which the program is headed, telling us that "the Dean of the school is a powerhouse of influence for our community and is continuously upgrading the facilities and the resources available to students and alumni."

BU excels in finance, marketing, and strategy departments, "all of which have renowned professors teaching MBA students in them. Many formerly taught at the Harvard Business School." Students also approve of the Health Sector Management program, which "excels in putting students in contact with leading health companies and service providers. Boston is a great place for both world-class hospital systems and a burgeoning biotechnology community. For students interested in the health sector, it's a great program that is continuing to evolve." BU's MBA in Public and Nonprofit Management is "extremely strong, teaching not only the management skills necessary for public and nonprofit organizations, but the benefit and skills necessary for the management of for-profit social enterprise companies." An MS/MBA in information systems offers "a great technology program in a city that is a hotbed for innovation."

The SMG's faculty is "passionate about what they teach and are available to answer questions outside of class. In addition, professors collaborate with each other to make sure students develop completely. For example, just recently our marketing professor spoke with our data analysis professor about a common shortcoming that arose in our marketing presentations." BU also offers its MBA Program "a strong and developing alumni network. BU has a large Executive MBA program, as well as part-time MBA students who are all integrated into the business environment of Boston and prove to be extremely useful in career efforts."

Career and Placement

Students report a much-improved Career Center at BU: "they are doing a great job and have shown great improvement in the past [few] years." Students also tell us that "there is now an extremely strong pharma presence recruiting at BU. Phizer, Eli Lilly, and Bristol Meyers all are recruiting heavily from BU." Some still see room for improvement; one such student writes, "Many of the companies that come to campus to recruit are local. Although some big names that have national or even global presence do recruit here, it is a challenge to find a job if you are looking in a specific area that is not Boston."

Top employers of BU MBAs include: BearingPoint, Medtronic, Citigroup, IBM Corporation, Ernst & Young, Fidelity Investments, IDC, Intel, Raytheon, Colgate Palmolive, EMC Corporation, HSBC, JPMorgan Chase, L'Oréal, and Reebok.

Student Life and Environment

Life at BU "is busy," writes one full-time student. "Although we're only in class for an average of 3 hours per day, I spend an average of 8 hours on campus, working individually or within my groups in between classes, meeting with professors, etc. Weekends (Fridays through Sunday) are days to read, work on individual assignments, and meet with groups." The workload isn't overwhelming, though; "The School of Management does an excellent job of maintaining a rigorous academic environment while still concentrating on creating a career network that will enable you to succeed after school." Beyond the classroom, students enjoy various club activities and school events. "Organized groups constantly make their presence known through on-campus speakers and events, and most do a good job of mixing social and academic pursuits." One student notes, "The school facilities are excellent, and membership to a great fitness center comes with your tuition: weights, cardio, pool, basketball court, and climbing wall."

Only about 40 percent of MBAs here attend full-time, about 30 percent of whom are international students (students from India and China are especially well represented, according to student response). Students also tell us that "classmates include a good mix of younger and older students, ranging in backgrounds from acting to engineering. They are gregarious, nerdy, competitive, and entertaining." There is a sense among some, however, that "there is somewhat too little work experience from members of our class" (even though the average full-time student enters the program with 4-plus years of work experience).

Those who have the time to socialize (part-timers typically include a number of students with full-time jobs, leaving them little spare time) extol the school's "exciting location near nightlife and Fenway Park. Parking is pretty good, with metered spots close to the school." There is also a parking garage located directly under the school itself. Social life "is extensive and highly important. Boston nightlife is omnipresent and enjoyed to the nth degree. This city allows for adventure right outside of the classroom and the students take advantage of it intensely."

Admissions

Applicants to the BU MBA program must submit the following materials: a completed application; a current resume; personal essays, in response to application questions; two letters of recommendation; official copies of transcripts for all undergraduate and graduate work; and an official GMAT score report. Interviews are required for some applicants and are scheduled at the request of the school. In addition to the above materials, international students must also submit an official score report for the TOEFL or IELTS (students whose first language is other than English only; minimum TOEFL score of 250 on paper-based exam, 250 on the old computer-based exam; minimum IELTS score of 7 across each band); a financial declaration; copies of all current visa or I-20 documentation; and a copy of the initial passport page.

FINANCIAL FACTS

Annual tuition	$34,930
Fees	$440
Cost of books	$1,436
Room & board (off-campus)	$11,305
% of students receiving aid	97
% of first-year students receiving aid	90
% of students receiving loans	57
% of students receiving grants	85
Average award package	$29,039
Average grant	$20,533

ADMISSIONS

Admissions Selectivity Rating	93
# of applications received	1,725
% applicants accepted	43
% acceptees attending	51
Average GMAT	668
Range of GMAT	600–730
Average GPA	3.4
TOEFL required of international students	Yes
Minimum TOEFL (paper/computer)	600/250
Application fee	$125
Regular application deadline	3/15
Regular notification	5/1
Application Deadline/Notification	
Round 1:	11/15 / 01/01
Round 2:	01/15 / 03/01
Round 3:	03/15 / 05/01
Transfer students accepted	Yes
Transfer application policy Classes must be AACSB-accredited.	
Need-blind admissions	Yes

Applicants Also Look At

Harvard University, Massachusetts Institute of Technology, New York University, University of California—Berkeley, Yale University.

EMPLOYMENT PROFILE

Career Rating	87	Grads Employed by Function	% Avg. Salary
Primary Source of Full-time Job Acceptances		Finance	24 $83,000
School-facilitated activities	55 (60%)	Marketing	16 $84,091
Graduate-facilitated activities	12 (13%)	MIS	5 $89,000
Unknown	25 (27%)	Operations	3 $80,000
Percent employed	95	Consulting	12 $91,762
		General Management	3 $77,000
		Other	1 NR

Top 5 Employers Hiring Grads
Fidelity Investments; Bank of America; State Street Bank; EMC; AT&T

BOWLING GREEN STATE UNIVERSITY
COLLEGE OF BUSINESS ADMINISTRATION

GENERAL INFORMATION
Type of school	Public
Environment	Town
Academic calendar	Semester

SURVEY SAYS...
Solid preparation in:
Accounting

STUDENTS
Enrollment of parent institution	21,132
Enrollment of business school	95
% male/female	58/42
% out-of-state	1
% part-time	42
% minorities	55
% international	47
Average age at entry	26
Average years work experience at entry	5

ACADEMICS
Academic Experience Rating	**85**
Profs interesting rating	83
Profs accessible rating	87
% female faculty	28
% minority faculty	38

Joint Degrees
MBA with Graduate Certificate in Organizational Change, 18 months.

FINANCIAL FACTS
Annual tuition	$15,252
Fees (in-state/ out-of-state)	$1,672/$12,634
Cost of books	$1,500
Room & board (off-campus)	$6,000
% of students receiving aid	100
% of first-year students receiving aid	100
% of students receiving loans	35
% of students receiving grants	100
Average award package	$16,880
Average grant	$13,015
Average student loan debt	$16,310

Academics

Looking for a "quality education" with "high standards" that keep "student success as a primary goal"—all while offering an MBA degree that can be completed in 14 months? For those hoping to fast-track their business careers, the MBA program at the College of Business Administration at Bowling Green State University provides an excellent (and speedy) opportunity for students, even if they didn't get their undergraduate degree in business. And for only one additional semester's work, a specialization in accounting, finance, or management information systems can be added.

"The workload is heavy, and the classes are demanding," students tell us. However this is bolstered by the "very supportive" professors. One student explains, "When I started BGSU, I thought it would be a piece of cake for me. But I soon realized that the professors were serious about their work and expectations and settled for nothing but the best." Despite the rigors of the curriculum, most students find the program manageable thanks to the fact that "everyone seems willing to help each other out." Even those without prior business degrees or experience note that this collegial atmosphere and the "professors' accessibility outside the classroom and readiness to assist in learning were of great importance to my success in BGSU MBA program."

Students agree that the majority of professors "are very knowledgeable and willing to help." "Some are outstanding, while some are just okay," explains one student. "Two out of every three classes . . . were great," adds another; however, "It seemed like each semester we had one professor that wasn't the best." The curriculum puts a heavy emphasis on group projects and teamwork, which functions to help students make "a connection between theory and practice and help to develop skills."

The College of Business' full-time program features "a leadership assessment and development component consisting of a series of workshops" that "lead students through an ongoing process of reflection and self-discovery so that each obtains a better understanding of his or herself in relation to a desired management career." Students find the workshops helpful in their career development, especially the "Professional Development Sessions on Fridays," where they meet and interact "with industry leaders . . . in a professional and mentorship atmosphere."

Career and Placement

To assist BGSU students in their job searches, the College of Business offers "a series of co-curricular professional development seminars, covering topics such as oral presentation and report writing, team facilitation, effective negotiations, career planning, and organizational politics." Some report though that "career opportunities for MBAs are not well organized" and that students are "mostly on their own" in the job hunt. In particular, international students find it "very tough to find a job."

Recent employers of BGSU MBAs include American Express, American Greetings, Ernst & Young, Marathon Ashland, National City Corporation, Nationwide Insurance, Owens Corning, Plante & Moran, Progressive Insurance, and State Farm Insurance. The school reports that over half its graduates find their first job outside the United States.

ADMISSIONS CONTACT: SHEILA K. IRVING, DIRECTOR, GRADUATE STUDIES IN BUSINESS
ADDRESS: 369 BUSINESS ADMINISTRATION BUILDING BOWLING GREEN, OH 43403 UNITED STATES
PHONE: 419-372-2488 • FAX: 419-372-2875
E-MAIL: MBA-INFO@BGSU.EDU • WEBSITE: WWW.BGSUMBA.COM

Student Life and Environment

Students at BGSU agree that the student body is a "very diverse group from almost every continent" that consists of "very intelligent, committed, and dedicated" individuals. Statistics state that for the school at large, while "90 percent" of students are from Ohio, a whopping 55 countries are represented on campus. Additionally, about one-third of the MBAs are international students. The school also notes that "across all programs, students range in age from 22 to 52, with an average of 29. The average work experience of full-time, part-time, and executive students is 3, 6, and 10 years, respectively, but work experience is not required of full-time or part-time students."

On a campus of over 19,000 students, the College of Business facility is home to "a smaller community of professors, business students, and equipment where it is extremely easy to locate resources. Classrooms and a computer lab are located on the main floor, and professors and more computer labs are located upstairs. At BGSU, time is not wasted locating resources." MBAs also appreciate the "high standards" of "the school's programs" and "extracurricular activities" that "provide a well-rounded educational experience." They also tell us that "there are many diverse clubs and activities," such as The Business Club that "has social activities ranging from guest speakers to having beers at the local bar. Sometimes we even invite our professors."

While no one would mistake Bowling Green for a megalopolis, students find this "quiet" and "friendly" town charming and completely lacking in "distractions." "The university is the city for the most part," says one student. Others extol the "low prices" and "very cheap places to live off campus." But, "More than anything, it's safe." BGSU's location provides "easy access to Chicago, Cleveland, and Detroit." But if you crave "a large city," Toledo is "only 15 to 20 [minutes] away." But be sure to bundle up as "The weather may be a bit harsh during winter."

Admissions

The College of Business Administration at BGSU doesn't require applicants to have business experience for admission as "the full-time program is designed for students who will be new to their chosen fields." That said, prior work experience is a factor when it comes to securing an assistantship. Applicants must submit two official transcripts from each college attended, GMAT scores, a current resume, three letters of recommendation, and a personal statement; interviews are optional and can be conducted in person or by telephone. International students must also provide the school with TOEFL scores if their native language is not English.

ADMISSIONS

Admissions Selectivity Rating	**84**
# of applications received	135
% applicants accepted	49
% acceptees attending	77
Average GMAT	550
Range of GMAT	400–650
Average GPA	3.27
TOEFL required of international students	Yes
Minimum TOEFL (paper/computer)	550/213
Application fee	$30
International application fee	$30
Regular application deadline	Rolling
Regular notification	Rolling
Deferment available	Yes
Maximum length of deferment	1 year
Transfer students accepted	Yes
Transfer application policy	Limited to a maximum of six graduate credit hours of transfer credit from AACSB accredited institutions.
Non-fall admissions	Yes
Need-blind admissions	Yes

BRANDEIS UNIVERSITY
BRANDEIS INTERNATIONAL BUSINESS SCHOOL

GENERAL INFORMATION

Type of school	Private
Environment	Town
Academic calendar	Semester

SURVEY SAYS...
Cutting edge classes
Solid preparation in:
Finance
Teamwork
Quantitative skills
Doing business in a global economy

STUDENTS

Enrollment of parent institution	4,397
Enrollment of MBA program	350
% male/female	58/42
% part-time	15
% minorities	9
% international	72
Average age at entry	28
Average years work experience at entry	4

ACADEMICS

Academic Experience Rating	**89**
Student/faculty ratio	8:1
Profs interesting rating	88
Profs accessible rating	96
% female faculty	43
% minority faculty	33

Prominent Alumni
Juan Buendia, Partner, SBC Brinson;
Udaibir Das, Deputy Chief,
International Monetary Fund;
Caroline Faivet, President, Swatch
Group US; Amy Kessler, Managing
Director, Bear Stearns; Nikolay
Vassilev, Minister of the Economy,
Bulgaria.

Academics

While many MBA programs offer a few international business classes, at the International Business School (IBS) at Brandeis University, "globalization and economic interdependence is at the core of the program." Renowned for its finance and economics departments, IBS students receive a "well-rounded global business education with great quantitative skills." Professors are "widely known in their fields and have both academic and professional experiences," and classes are a "good mixture between case study method and lecture based method." Outside the classroom, "the MBA program requires all students to have spent time working abroad before they can graduate" and basic proficiency in a language other than English is also required. A truly international environment, the school's academic focus is reflected in its students, who hail from "different backgrounds and more than 50 countries." Says a current student, "I learned a lot about different cultures and enjoyed different perspectives which prepared me for a career in a multinational environment."

In addition to the IBS, Brandeis's Heller School for Social Policy and Management operates the Heller MBA in Non-Profit Management. This distinctive program has a unique "focus on 'managing for a social mission,'" which combines the rigors of a traditional MBA program with an emphasis on mission-based organizations and companies." In addition to coursework in finance and accounting, organizational and operations management, and social justice, students incorporate practical experience through case studies and consulting projects. Students can tailor this 16-month program through elective coursework, including "courses at other Boston area schools for subjects that are not offered at Heller."

Students in both Brandeis business programs say the academic experience is "outstanding." Professors are "leaders in their field, and many have come from industry, so have vast experience which they are very eager to share with students." Fortunately, "the school has a good faculty/student ratio that facilitates easy access and personal touch with professors and staff." Plus, the "small class sizes also give you the opportunity to participate in class discussions more often, which highly contributes to your communication skills and self-confidence." "The curriculum can be very demanding and intense," requiring "endless projects, homework, and exams." Even so, the academic experience is rewarding and enjoyable. A student adds, "Class is challenging, but professors get us laughing and thinking at the same time."

Career and Placement

The IBS Career Center helps students through every step of the job search process, offering career counseling, mock interviews, resume and cover letter preparation, campus career fairs, and an updated list of open positions. If you want individualized career assistance, you're in luck; "at IBS you definitely enjoy personal attention from the career services." Two-thirds of Brandeis students take jobs in the United States after graduation. However, for those who'd like to work abroad, "this relatively young school makes itself visible to employers throughout the globe." In recent years, Brandeis students went on to jobs at Citibank, Morgan Stanley, Nomura Research, Rice Group, Standard and Poor's, Smith Barney, United Airlines, and UBS Warburg. Twenty-five percent of students took jobs in international banking and 20 percent in asset management.

Heller MBA candidates also benefit from extensive professional support through the Heller School's Career Services office. About 77 percent of Heller MBA graduates take jobs at non-profit organizations, such as AIDS Action Committee or Environmental

ADMISSIONS CONTACT: CHRISTOPHER STORER, ASSISTANT DIRECTOR
ADDRESS: 415 SOUTH STREET, MS 032 WALTHAM, MA 02454 UNITED STATES
PHONE: (781) 736-2252 • FAX: (781) 736-2263 • E-MAIL: ADMISSION@LEMBERG.BRANDEIS.EDU
WEBSITE: WWW.BRANDEIS.EDU/GLOBAL

Defense, with another 17 percent taking positions in the public sector. Of the three percent of Heller graduates who take a job in a for-profit company, many choose a position that relates to their socially minded degree.

Student Life and Environment

Diversity is the name of the game at Brandeis's progressive business programs, which attract students "from a range of backgrounds. One may have worked as a physician in India, the other in air traffic control." A student adds, "Not only are there students from 60 different countries, but the unique environment fosters camaraderie between the different ethnic groups and nationalities. There is no such thing as the "American crowd" and "international crowd". It's just one big cluster of people from all corners of the globe." On campus, Brandeis offers "a great deal of activities and events so that everyone, regardless of their interests, is represented. In addition to the events run by our Student Services office, we have a number of clubs, some more professionally focused such as the Marketing Club [and the] International Business Women Club, and others that are more activity focused, such as the Golf Club or the Soccer Club." Socially, students gather for "golf Saturdays, karaoke nights, international night, ice skating, bowling nights, pot luck dinners, semi-formal and formal dances, and many other events at the university scale and also around the Boston area." At the end of the school day, "a bunch of us will often go out and grab a beer together in downtown Waltham."

What's more, with Boston just 30 minutes away, "students can take the free school shuttle to downtown areas" where they can "enjoy the memorable Bostonian experience."

Admissions

Typical Brandeis MBA students are between 24 and 28 years old and had an undergraduate GPA of about 3.3. The school looks for GMAT scores in the 600s, and requires at least two years of professional work experience before entering the program. In addition to test scores and official undergraduate transcripts, students must submit three letters of recommendation and a current resume.

FINANCIAL FACTS

Annual tuition	$31,532
Cost of books	$12,000
Room & board	
(on/off-campus)	$5,500/$9,000
% of students receiving aid	80
% of first-year students receiving aid	80
% of students receiving loans	50
% of students receiving grants	84
Average grant	$15,166
Average student loan debt	$23,000

ADMISSIONS

Admissions Selectivity Rating	89
# of applications received	584
% applicants accepted	42
% acceptees attending	72
Average GMAT	600
Range of GMAT	500–710
Average GPA	3.3
TOEFL required of international students	Yes
Minimum TOEFL (paper/computer) 600/250	
Application fee	$55
International application fee	$55
Regular application deadline	2/15
Regular notification	3/15
Early decision program?	Yes
ED Deadline/Notification	12/15 / 1/15
Deferment available	Yes
Maximum length of deferment	2 years
Need-blind admissions	Yes

Applicants Also Look At

Babson College, Boston College, Georgetown University, Harvard University, Massachusetts Institute of Technology, New York University, Thunderbird.

EMPLOYMENT PROFILE			
Career Rating	77	Grads Employed by Function	% Avg. Salary
		Finance	54 NR
		Consulting	13 NR
		Global Management	25 NR
		Non-profit	8: NR

BRIGHAM YOUNG UNIVERSITY
MARRIOTT SCHOOL OF MANAGEMENT

GENERAL INFORMATION
Type of school	Private
Affiliation	Church of Jesus Christ
	of Latter-day Saints
Environment	City
Academic calendar	2 Semester

SURVEY SAYS...
Friendly students
Good peer network
Happy students
Solid preparation in:
Finance
Teamwork

STUDENTS
Enrollment of parent	
institution	34,174
Enrollment of	
business school	305
% male/female	85/15
% out-of-state	34
% minorities	9
% international	19
Average age at entry	29
Average years work	
experience at entry	3.5

ACADEMICS
Academic Experience Rating	**97**
Profs interesting rating	92
Profs accessible rating	89
% female faculty	16
% minority faculty	1

Joint Degrees
MBA/JD 4 years, MBA/MS IPD
Program with Engineering
Department 3 years, MAcc/JD 4
years, MPA/JD 4 years.

Prominent Alumni
Andrea Thomas, Senior VP, Private
Brands, Wal-mart; D. Fraser
Bullock, Founder/Managing Director,
Sorenson Capital; Robert Parsons,
Executive VP & CFO, Exclusive
Resorts; David W. Checketts, Chair,
Sports Capital Partners; Bill P.
Benac Sr., Senior VP & CFO,
American Rail Car Industries.

Academics

Brigham Young University, the educational Mecca of the Church of Jesus Christ of Latter-Day Saints (commonly referred to as 'the Mormon Church'), "is truly a hidden gem," according to its students, who point out that "BYU consistently ranks near the top of the nation in return on investment." That distinction results from a combination of factors: low tuition, excellent quality of instruction, and an "incomparable alumni network," which collectively produce in the nation's number two percentage increase in salary for graduates, according to The Financial Times.

Unsurprisingly (given its church affiliation), "BYU stresses ethics in business," a fact that appeals to the school's predominantly LDS student body. One student points out the program's "emphasis on social change and corporate social responsibility. Many of the students have lived or worked in third world countries and have a strong desire to give back and improve the world around them." Students also love that the BYU MBA is "a smaller program that enables students to have working relationships with faculty and opportunities to do more than in larger programs," but "is large enough to have a good network while small enough for the network to have a family-like feel. We are a very tight-knit group in the BYU MBA program," especially important since "much of the coursework is done in groups" here.

BYU "has a fantastic reputation for accounting, corporate finance, and human resources," and "the marketing program has also grown to become a strength" and is now fastest growing and high-profile majors" on campus, with its "students getting internships and job offers at top CPG, technology, and retail companies." The school's organizational behavior and human resources program "is superior," with recruitment "beginning one month into class. There are many excellent companies who come to campus in October...Excellent companies came and left here empty-handed because students had so many options. Also, it's an HR track in an MBA program, which exposes us to both HR and business, and companies really value that." BYU professors "typically had experience teaching at Harvard, Stanford or Wharton, where they earned awards for their teaching quality. I believe they chose BYU for the same reason that I did: The culture can't be duplicated elsewhere."

Career and Placement

Career services at Marriott are provided by the Steven and Georgia White Business Career Center, which school materials describe as "the focal point for the school's placement, internship, and field study efforts." Facilities include a reference library, interview rooms, a large presentation room, 20 interview rooms, and an eRecruiting system. School materials identify nearly 100 companies that recruit at the Marriott School. Students praise the "top-notch career placement people" and the "committed and talented alumni network."

School promotional materials list the following recruiting companies that visit the BYU campus: 3M, American Express, Amgen, Bain & Company, BMW, Caterpillar, Centex, Cisco, Citigroup, DaimlerChrysler, Dell, Deutsche Bank, Eli Lilly, FedEx, Ford Motor Company, General Electric, Goldman Sachs, Honeywell, JP Morgan, Lockheed Martin, Nike, NBC, PepsiCo, Rolex, Union Pacific, Vanguard Group, Wal-Mart, and Zions Bank. About one-quarter of BYU MBAs enter the finance and accounting sector; about one in six takes a job in human resources. Students tell us, "We are starting to compete in the private equity and venture capital field really well."

ADMISSIONS CONTACT: YVETTE ANDERSON, MBA PROGRAM ADMISSION COORDINATOR
ADDRESS: 635 TNRB PROVO, UT 84602 UNITED STATES
PHONE: 801-422-3500 • FAX: 801-422-0513
E-MAIL: MBA@BYU.EDU • WEBSITE: MARRIOTTSCHOOL.BYU.EDU/MBA

Student Life and Environment

BYU's commitment to its MBA program can be seen in the facilities upgrades currently under way. Students report that the Tanner Building, home to the MBA program, "is undergoing an extensive expansion that will increase its size by approximately 30 percent with new state-of-the-art classrooms and facilities." Students are pleased both with the upgrade and the way in which the addition "speaks to the school's recognition of weaknesses and their promptness with finding solutions."

Life on the BYU campus presents "many opportunities to socialize and network with other classmates. For example, one of our fellow students is a chocolate expert, so we are having a gourmet chocolate tasting event. In addition, almost every week there is a cultural awareness mixer or an opportunity to hear from well-known guest speakers. So far, we've heard from the CEO of Citigroup, the whistleblower from Enron, and many more very recognizable business leaders." Extracurricular life also includes "a plethora of opportunities to enter case competitions. Local companies partner with the school to sponsor web analytics competition, business plan competition, social change competition, and venture capital competition." Students' spouses and families receive excellent support at BYU; writes one MBA, "The Spouses Association takes care of the needs of spouses, creates babysitting and playgroups, organizes dinners to be brought to families after childbirth."

Admissions

A completed application to the Marriott MBA program includes an application form, personal essays, an official GMAT score report, official transcripts for all post-secondary academic work, three letters of recommendation (one academic, two professional), an honor code commitment form, and a personal statement of intent. An interview is required; the school contacts applicants who have cleared initial screening to set up an interview appointment. International students must submit all of the above and must also provide financial disclosure forms and, if appropriate, TOEFL scores. Full-time post-undergraduate professional experience is highly recommended but not required; those lacking such experience are expected to demonstrate other outstanding qualifications through testing, undergraduate work, etc. Personal attributes are also considered. While students need not belong to the Church of Jesus Christ of Latter-Day Saints, "an understanding of and a commitment to support the church's mission are necessary."

FINANCIAL FACTS

Annual tuition	$8,700
Fees	$0
Cost of books	$1,760
Room & board	$6,460
% of students receiving aid	85
% of first-year students receiving aid	89
% of students receiving loans	33
% of students receiving grants	80
Average award package	$7,889
Average grant	$5,641
Average student loan debt	$21,888

ADMISSIONS

Admissions Selectivity Rating	91
# of applications received	423
% applicants accepted	53
% acceptees attending	70
Average GMAT	661
Range of GMAT	640–690
Average GPA	3.5
TOEFL required of international students	Yes
Minimum TOEFL (paper/computer)	590/240
Application fee	$50
International application fee	$50
Application Deadline/Notification	
Round 1:	12/01 / 02/01
Round 2:	01/15 / 03/15
Round 3:	03/01 / 05/01
Round 4:	05/01 / 07/01
Early decision program?	Yes
ED Deadline/ Notification	1/15 / 03/15
Deferment available	Yes
Maximum length of deferment	2 years
Transfer students accepted	Yes
Transfer application policy	
15 credit hours of approved graduate-level courses.	
Need-blind admissions	Yes

Applicants Also Look At

Arizona State University, Harvard University, Stanford University, University of Pennsylvania, University of Utah, Utah State University, Weber State University.

EMPLOYMENT PROFILE

Career Rating	85	Grads Employed by Function	% Avg. Salary
Primary Source of Full-time Job Acceptances		Finance	30 $85,863
School-facilitated activities	45 (49%)	Human Resources	15 $79,812
Graduate-facilitated activities	33 (36%)	Marketing	16 $80,893
Unknown	14 (15%)	Operations	8 $74,852
Average base starting salary	$81,834	Consulting	3 $80,167
Percent employed	98	General Management	18 $75,133
		Other	10 $92,933

Top 5 Employers Hiring Grads

Microsoft; Ford; Honeywell; WiPro Technologies; American Express; Bank of America; DaimlerChrysler; Ensign Group, Hewlett-Packard, Johnson & Johnson; Nestle, City Group, Exxon-Mobil, General Electric

BROCK UNIVERSITY
FACULTY OF BUSINESS

Academics

Ontario's Brock University enjoys "a good reputation for business and accounting" among students and area businesses. As one student puts it, "Overall, considering the fact that the MBA program is new, the administration has done a great job. They have accomplished AACSB accreditation within a few short years and are making excellent hiring decisions for professors."

Brock's chief asset, students tell us, is its small classes, which "help encourage a lot of discussion with teachers and students. The teachers here are eager to hear your insight on situations while still educating you on how to take your thinking to the next level." Students also love the "great facilities that provide easy wireless Internet access" and the "many computers on campus," and they appreciate the "great opportunities to become involved with the school. This school provides anyone interested in becoming an active and contributing member of university society the chance to get involved." Prospective students should note that the workload here can be quite heavy, as one student explains: "As I've always heard about MBA programs anywhere, it's not rocket science, but the volume [of work] may kill you!"

The Brock MBA includes a sequence of required courses and an option for specialization in one of four "streams": accounting, finance, human resource management, and marketing. Students may also opt for a general MBA. Students may choose to replace up to three of their specialization courses with independent research projects; such projects are subject to the approval of the dean and the MBA Committee.

Career and Placement

The Faculty of Business at Brock University maintains a Business Center Development Office to serve all undergraduates and graduates enrolled at the faculty. The office manages the Graduate Recruitment Program for MBA students; through this program, students have access to employer information sessions and on-campus interviews. A Career Expo in the fall brings employers to campus for recruiting purposes. The office also offers resume review, interviewing and job search workshops, online job search tools, and assistance with international job placement. While Brock's website claims that the school boasts "the highest employment rate of any university in Ontario," students counter that "there are not a lot of companies recruiting from our program due to lack of knowledge about it." But students expect that career and placement issues will sort themselves out as the school sends more MBAs into the business world to "help other Brock students as they enter their careers."

Student Life and Environment

Brock University is located in St. Catharines, a mere 12 miles from Niagara Falls and just 70 miles from Toronto. Students call the location "a great strength," pointing out that St. Catharines is "a great city that is near Toronto and the States. It is very safe and the rent is super cheap. There are tons of bars to party at and everyone in St. Catharines just wants to have a good time. That can really make a difference when you are stressed out from working too much and you need a break." "Great weather" and "a nice campus" that is "not too big so that it is comfortable for newcomers" complete the picture. Students accustomed to more cosmopolitan locales claim, however, that St. Catharines is "a small town with not a lot to offer in terms of extracurriculars."

Most of Brock's MBAs are younger full-time students with little professional experience. They "are interested in school but also enjoy hanging out together. There are lots of great people to get to know and you become close friends." As one student observes, "Due to the fact that this program has relatively younger students, participation in activities is very high. The students have to participate because if we don't do it, there is not a large student body behind us to carry us." Brock does its part to facilitate extracurricular life: "The school provides opportunities to get involved with athletics and clubs," notes one MBA. One such exciting opportunity is the Corporate Social Responsibility Center, which "will match students to projects in the nonprofit sector. This will help students with connecting to opportunities off campus."

Admissions

Admission to the MBA program at Brock is based on five main criteria. The quality of one's undergraduate education is most important; Brock seeks students with at least a 3.0 undergraduate GPA. A minimum GMAT score of 550 is required, as are three letters of recommendation from professors and/or supervisors at work; a personal statement; and, as the Brock website states, a "resume detailing the applicant's education and career to date." Applications are assessed holistically; strength in one area may be sufficient to compensate for weaknesses elsewhere, according to the school's website. Professional experience, though preferred, is not required. Those whose first language is not English must demonstrate English proficiency through the TOEFL (minimum score 575, or 230 on the TOEFL (CBE), or 4.5 on the TWE).

ADMISSIONS

Admissions Selectivity Rating	**85**
# of applications received	99
% applicants accepted	64
% acceptees attending	29
Average GMAT	600
Range of GMAT	550–700
Average GPA	3.4
TOEFL required of international students	Yes
Minimum TOEFL (paper/computer)	620/260
Application fee	$100
International application fee	$100
Deferment available	Yes
Maximum length of deferment	1 year
Transfer students accepted	Yes
Transfer application policy Up to ten courses of advanced standing plus two courses of transfer credit	
Non-fall admissions	Yes
Need-blind admissions	Yes

Applicants Also Look At
McMaster University, Wilfrid Laurier University (Canada).

EMPLOYMENT PROFILE

Career Rating	83	Grads Employed by Function	%	Avg. Salary
Primary Source of Full-time Job Acceptances		Finance	26	$54,000
Unknown	28 (100%)	Human Resources	11	$50,000
Percent employed	97	Marketing	7	$66,000
		MIS	4	$45,000
		Consulting	4	$61,000
		General Management	4	$95,000
		Other	40	NR

BRYANT UNIVERSITY
GRADUATE SCHOOL OF BUSINESS

GENERAL INFORMATION

Type of school	Private
Environment	Town
Academic calendar	Semester

SURVEY SAYS...

Cutting edge classes
Solid preparation in:
General management
Teamwork
Communication/interpersonal skills

STUDENTS

Enrollment of parent institution	3,651
Enrollment of business school	298
% male/female	66/34
% part-time	100
Average age at entry	28
Average years work experience at entry	6

ACADEMICS

Academic Experience Rating	**81**
Student/faculty ratio	20:1
Profs interesting rating	83
Profs accessible rating	87
% female faculty	27
% minority faculty	20

Prominent Alumni

David M. Beirne, Gen. Partner, Benchmark Capital Partners; William J. Conaty, Sr. VP, General Electric; Robert P. Mead, President, Tyco Engineered Products & Services; Thomas Taylor, President & CEO, Amica Insurance; Kristian P. Moor, Exec. VP, Domestic General Insurance.

FINANCIAL FACTS

Room & board	$10,000
Average award package	$13,640
Average grant	$16,235
Average student loan debt	$21,683

Academics

Students choose Bryant University's MBA program for the school's "reputation of being a top business school in the area" and for its "amazing facilities." In January 2006, the school gave students another reason to select Bryant: a revamped program that allows part-time students to enjoy the same benefits of cohort learning that full-time students enjoy. Under this new system, part-time students are grouped in cohorts of 30 to 35 with whom they move through the program (which they typically complete in 2 years). Each student is also assigned to a study team for the length of the program. Teams are constructed by administrators to provide the widest possible range of life and career experiences to the study group.

The MBA at Bryant consists of two preparatory courses in economics and statistics; eight core in accounting, computer information systems, finance, management, marketing, and operations; and four electives offered in a wide range of disciplines. "The academics are far from stressful but keep a steady pace." Students praise the program's "very educational methods of teaching: case study, group learning, and projects" and tell us that they do "plenty of presentations to prepare us for the business world." Even more importantly, the program focuses on "practical applications of theories and concepts." Students also enjoy the extent of the curriculum, describing it as "very oriented toward the overall business world. I have friends attending other business schools, and they are not getting the breadth of information that we are getting."

Bryant faculty typically "have been in the actual workforce and have an understanding of how the ideas that they are teaching apply to the real world," yet don't lack for academic credentials. "Many of the relevant writings were written by our professors," points out one student. Students find the faculty "dedicated and passionate as a whole."

Career and Placement

The Amica Center for Career Education serves the undergraduate students, graduate students, and alumni of Bryant University. The office provides counseling services, assessment instruments, and workshops on resume writing, interviewing, and job-search skills. The center maintains a career services library and facilitates contact with alumni through the school's Alumni Career Network. Students wish that the school would "improve in the number and diversity of on-campus recruiting companies, for example, companies based outside of Rhode Island."

Student Life and Environment

Bryant University is a "tight-knit, small school" where "people genuinely care about the community and each other." Explains one part time student in the MBA program, "I wasn't expecting to become as connected to Bryant as I was to my undergraduate university. They have made me feel like part of the community very well here." Students praise the "attractive" campus for both its beauty ("There is a fountain and a bridge in the middle of campus.") and its convenience. One student reports, "Parking is convenient and close to the classrooms. All of the classes are in one building, which reduces walking from building to building in inclement weather. The library is huge and offers unparalleled resources."

While "The Graduate Student Council is very active in getting graduate participation at all school sporting events," this is still largely a program of overcommitted part-time students, people managing not only an academic career but also full-time jobs and, often, family obligations. While students enjoy a strong esprit de corps—one reinforced by the school's recent switchover to cohort-based learning—they do not have much time to bond outside their classrooms and study groups.

ADMISSIONS CONTACT: KRISTOPHER SULLIVAN, ASSISTANT DEAN OF THE GRADUATE SCHOOL
ADDRESS: 1150 DOUGLAS PIKE SMITHFIELD, RI 02917-1284 UNITED STATES
PHONE: 401-232-6230 • FAX: 401-232-6494
E-MAIL: GRADPROG@BRYANT.EDU • WEBSITE: WWW.BRYANT.EDU

Bryant is located just outside the city of Providence. The location provides access not only to Rhode Island's biggest city but also to Boston, just an hour's drive to the north. The city of Providence offers a wide selection of great dining and entertainment options; it is also one of the nation's leaders in jewelry design and manufacturing. Major employers include the Bank of America, Verizon, and Blue Cross and Blue Shield Association.

Bryant MBAs "have diverse backgrounds. There is a wide dispersion of ages and social status. There are students who are married with children, newlyweds, single, and just out of undergrad. The wide diversity of experience and lifestyles has made the program interesting." The cohort system means that "moving through the program with the same group enables you to make lasting friendships with your colleagues."

Admissions

Applicants to graduate programs at Bryant University must provide the Admissions Department with the following materials: a completed application form; a personal statement of objectives (no less than 500 words long); a current resume; one letter of recommendation from a professional who can evaluate your skills and potential; official transcripts for all previous undergraduate and graduate work (regardless of whether it resulted in a degree); and an official GMAT score report. In addition to the above, international students must also provide a statement of finances, professional translation and interpretation of any foreign language transcripts, and, for those whose first language is not English and who did not earn an undergraduate degree from an English-speaking institution, an official TOEFL score report.

ADMISSIONS

Admissions Selectivity Rating	**81**
# of applications received	106
% applicants accepted	64
% acceptees attending	69
Average GMAT	579
Range of GMAT	530–630
Average GPA	3.2
TOEFL required of international students	Yes
Minimum TOEFL (paper/computer)	580/237
Application fee	$80
International application fee	$80
Regular application deadline	7/1
Regular notification	Rolling
Deferment available	Yes
Maximum length of deferment	1 year
Transfer students accepted	Yes
Transfer application policy Transfer credits are limited to two courses from an AACSB-International accredited master's program.	
Non-fall admissions	Yes
Need-blind admissions	Yes

Applicants Also Look At
Babson College, Bentley College, Suffolk University, University of Rhode Island.

BUTLER UNIVERSITY
COLLEGE OF BUSINESS ADMINISTRATION

Academics

At Butler, an MBA student may major in finance, international business, leadership, or marketing. There is also a combined program leading to both a Doctor of Pharmacy and an MBA. All students must take a core curriculum, which begins with what's known as a Gateway Experience, a day-long immersion in the activities of a local business followed by an evening of analysis by the students. Students "love how this school works with local businesses to enhance experiential learning and to also provide a sort of 'symbiotic' relationship." The students "help the businesses by offering solutions to their current problems, and they also help us learn by providing us with actual business problems." That practical exercise gets students thinking about scenarios that will show up in future courses such as ethics, financial management, managerial finance, and related subjects, which account for about half the credits needed for the degree. The students then move into areas of specialization and finish things off with what's known as a Capstone Experience, which is somewhat of an extended version of the Gateway Experience they encountered at the beginning of the program. It addresses more complex issues and allows the student to make good use of the knowledge gained during the program.

"Flexibility" is a definite key word when in comes to describing the MBA program at Butler. "It is not a lockstep program, meaning that if I missed a class, I would not have to wait an entire year to retake it," one student explains. "The approach that the school takes at understanding that the part-time MBA students have lives outside of the classroom" is a strength of the program, students say, and "I travel frequently for my job, and I have yet to encounter a professor who has not attempted to help ensure I would be caught up when I return," adds another. Classes are offered on evenings and weekends, and though some students would like to see the schedule of classes expanded, they uniformly praise the quality of teaching that goes on in them. "The professors at Butler are excellent. They make themselves available to their students and truly enjoy interaction in the classroom," and "Professors have demonstrated mastery of their subject as well as an ability to relate theory of a subject to real-world situations," students say.

Throughout the program students find that the emphasis is on "high-quality and high-value, in-class lessons, and great real-world learning." Many courses are taught by professors in conjunction with business leaders, and the case studies and problems students work on in class are most often real-world business issues. "Incorporation of practical business cases and scenarios in conjunction with the course work" is a hallmark of the program, as are "up-to-date, relevant [classroom] activities and problems" and "small class size, so that one can really get to know the other students and the professors."

Career and Placement

Most of Butler's MBA students are employed while completing the degree. Some students feel that "since almost all students are already working full-time, there is little emphasis on new career opportunities," remarking that Career Services seem to be geared toward undergraduates. However, being located in Indianapolis, a city ranked in the "Top 10 Best Places for Business and Careers" in a ranking of the 200 largest metropolitan areas in the United States by *Forbes*, helps with prospects. "There are thousands of top companies right in our backyard," students point out. "Many local companies have allowed students to participate in hands-on business simulations, and prominent business leaders have come to campus to speak and network." Butler's "regional reputation with business and community leaders and the number of very successful alumni working in the region" are also strong points for those who are job hunting.

ADMISSIONS CONTACT: STEPHANIE JUDGE, DIRECTOR OF MARKETING
ADDRESS: COLLEGE OF BUSINESS ADMINISTRATION, 4600 SUNSET AVENUE INDIANAPOLIS,
IN 46208-3485 U.S. • PHONE: 317-940-9221 • FAX: 317-940-9455
E-MAIL: MBA@BUTLER.EDU • WEBSITE: WWW.BUTTERMBA.COM

Eli Lilly and Company, Roche, First Indiana Bank, Regions Bank, Firestone, and the NCAA are among those who employ Butler's MBA graduates.

Student Life and Environment

MBA students love Butler's small-school atmosphere and personal touch. "Butler is a beautiful campus. Although I live off campus, I am always surprised by how many students are around participating in various on-campus activities," notes one student. "My classes include students from different ethnic, cultural, social, and religious backgrounds. This leads to great discussions on the wide varieties of experiences we have had in our careers." "Everyone on campus is engaging and helpful. Because of the small campus and class size, you get to know a number of peers, professors and administration well," others say. Students find the workload moderate, the administration responsive, and their fellow students friendly and focused. Noting that "the school is small enough to have a personal touch," "You can easily get the help and support that you need." Some would like better child care support and more opportunities to involve spouses in their academic lives, but they like the attention both faculty and staff pay to the needs of working students with families. "Most are busy with careers just like I am, but that gives us common ground to support each other in balancing work, school, and life," one student says.

Admissions

The Admissions Committee for the MBA program at Butler weighs an applicant's undergraduate GPA, GMAT score, letters of recommendation, and work experience most heavily. Though most students are from the Midwest, residency is not a factor that Butler, a private institution, takes into account, and it also does not consider a student's extracurricular activities. In 2007 the average GPA of admitted students was 3.32/4.0, and their GMAT score ranged from 500–690. Most students had 5 or more years of work experience.

ADMISSIONS	
Admissions Selectivity Rating	**73**
# of applications received	76
% applicants accepted	60
% acceptees attending	78
Average GMAT	550
Range of GMAT	500–690
Average GPA	3.3
TOEFL required of international students	Yes
Minimum TOEFL (paper/computer)	550/213
Application fee	$0
Regular application deadline	7/15
Regular notification	8/10
Deferment available	Yes
Maximum length of deferment	1 year
Transfer students accepted	Yes
Transfer application policy Up to 9 credit hours, pending approval.	
Non-fall admissions	Yes

Applicants Also Look At
Indiana University—Purdue University Indianapolis, Indiana University at Bloomington.

CALIFORNIA POLYTECHNIC STATE UNIVERSITY—SAN LUIS OBISPO
ORFALEA COLLEGE OF BUSINESS

GENERAL INFORMATION
Type of school	Public
Environment	Town
Academic calendar	Quarter

SURVEY SAYS...
Students love San Luis Obispo, CA
Good social scene
Good peer network
Solid preparation in:
Teamwork
Communication/interpersonal skills
Presentation skills

STUDENTS
Enrollment of parent institution	19,777
Enrollment of business school	119
% male/female	69/31
% out-of-state	23
% part-time	15
% minorities	7
% international	5
Average age at entry	26
Average years work experience at entry	3

ACADEMICS
Academic Experience Rating	**70**
Student/faculty ratio	25:1
Profs interesting rating	62
Profs accessible rating	82
% female faculty	20
% minority faculty	15

Joint Degrees
MBA/MS (Engineering Management), MBA/MS (Computer Science), MBA/MS (Electrical Engineering), MBA/MS (Mechanical Engineering), MBA/MS (Industrial and Technical Studies), MBA/MS (Industrial Engineering), MBA/MS (Civil and Environmental Engineering), MBA/Master of Public Policy, MBA/MS (Economics). Generally take 2 years to complete.

Academics

Students praise "the focus on career preparation" in the MBA program at California Polytechnic State University's Orfalea College of Business, telling us that "Orfalea has a hands-on approach. It's not as theoretical as some programs; here, you take on real-world challenges. Companies that recruit here frequently comment that they prefer Cal Poly grads because they 'hit the ground running' after being hired." Students also greatly appreciate the reasonable tuition; one writes, "This place is a great deal in terms of bang for your buck. If I had gone someplace else, I'd be in debt for decades." The school is an exceptionally good deal for students in the accelerated Track 1 full-time MBA; they complete the program in 1 year, saving the additional tuition, expenses, and fees that some in the Track 2 program (one year full-time plus additional part-time study) incur.

In either program, students pursue "a learn-by-doing policy adhered to throughout the college." One student reports, "In the upcoming quarter, I will be involved in a team competing against teams from other schools in making important business decisions for a simulated company in a simulated market. Not only will this help me learn what types of decisions and information I will encounter in the real world, it also gives me a great add-on for my resume and subject to talk about during interviews." A mentoring program provides another great add-on; it "allows students to 'hook up' with a mentor prominent in the business world (mine is the vice president of a large chain of banks) starting from the second week of classes." Yet another perk of the program is a two-and-a-half week trip to China (mandatory for Track 1, encouraged for Track 2), which some here feel is the "most informative" part of the program.

Orfalea's faculty is "well prepared and knowledgeable" with professors who "emphasize the importance of teamwork." Small class sizes "really allow students to get to know one another and create a friendly atmosphere conducive to creating strong bonds." On the downside, students complain that "the short time period of the program leaves out room for some electives that would be beneficial or exciting to take" and that "most of the teachers focus too heavily on grades. The school will improve when more focus is on learning and less on grades. The design does not encourage risk taking so students select easier classes." Nearly 20 percent of Orfalea MBAs pursue dual-degree programs, taking second degrees in such areas as engineering, architecture, and public policy.

Career and Placement

Orfalea's Career Placement Services "do a great job of preparing students for the recruiting process and following through with companies to ensure that they continue to recruit Cal Poly grads." The school has strong "connections to Bay Area companies." The small size of the program, however, may affect recruitment activities somewhat; one student says, "Since this is a technical school, the majority of employers are seeking engineers or related fields. It's difficult for someone with a non-technical background (like a degree in management) to find a range of employers at the job fair."

Orfalea MBAs most often work for: Northrup Grumman, Raytheon, Rantec, General Dynamics, Sun MicroSystems, Deloitte Touche Tohmatsu, Qualcomm, IBM, Agilent Technology, Amgen, Lawrence Livermore Labs, Pacific Gas & Electric, USDA, Department of Veterans Affairs, KPMG International, Pratt & Whitney, Morgan Stanley, Boston Scientific Corporation, PricewaterhouseCoopers, Sandia National Lab, Lam Research, Columbia Sportswear, and Adelaida Cellars.

ADMISSIONS CONTACT: CHRIS CARR, ASSOCIATE DEAN OF GRADUATE PROGRAMS
ADDRESS: 1 GRAND AVENUE, OCOB SAN LUIS OBISPO, CA 93407 UNITED STATES
PHONE: 805-756-2637 • FAX: 805-756-0110
E-MAIL: MBA@CALPOLY.EDU • WEBSITE: WWW.MBA.CALPOLY.EDU

Student Life and Environment

San Luis Obispo is "primarily an undergrad campus," but grad students find ways to get in on the action. They're "very social; everyone wants to be involved with each other and with the events taking place. There are speakers every week, and the attendance is fairly good." The fact that "the program is relatively small" means "Everyone gets to know each other well. This is not like a commuter school."

The town of San Luis Obispo "is a great place loaded with clubs and situated in a great location for all manner of activities. Public transit is free for students. Because the town is so attractive, there is often less activity on campus than you would see at other schools, but the student population is 50 percent of the city, so almost any place becomes a gathering place for students." Students arriving from big cities may find that the leisurely pace of life here requires some adjustment.

Orfalea students "come from a variety of different backgrounds but are all very motivated to further their careers. The attitude at the school is more of camaraderie and cooperation than competition." The population "is very young compared to other grad schools, but most students have at least a few . . . years of experience."

Admissions

The Admissions Office at the Orfalea College of Business consider all of the following components of a student's application: GMAT score (middle 80 percent of student body scores between 540 and 680); TOEFL score (where applicable); two official copies of undergraduate transcript (the middle 80 percent of student body earns between 2.9 and 3.7); two letters of recommendation; a personal statement; and a resume. Prior work experience, while preferred, is not required. Prospective dual-degree candidates must apply to, and be accepted to, each program separately. All international applicants must provide statements of purpose and financial responsibility, a spouse/dependent declaration, and a signed health insurance contract; they must also submit to an educational background check.

Prominent Alumni

Robert Rowell, President, Golden State Warriors; Linda Ozawa Olds, Founder, Jamba Juice; Bill Swanson, Chairman & CEO, Raytheon Company; Burt Rutan, President, Scaled Composites, designer SpaceShipOne; Gary Bloom, CEO, Veritas.

FINANCIAL FACTS

Annual tuition (in-state/ out-of-state)	$3,756/$16,179
Fees	$1,995
Cost of books	$1,566
Room & board (on/off-campus)	$8,745/$8,793
% of students receiving aid	45
% of first-year students receiving aid	25
% of students receiving loans	45
% of students receiving grants	5
Average award package	$11,634
Average grant	$2,176

ADMISSIONS

Admissions Selectivity Rating	90
# of applications received	243
% applicants accepted	59
% acceptees attending	84
Average GMAT	615
Range of GMAT	580–750
Average GPA	3.3
TOEFL required of international students	Yes
Minimum TOEFL (paper/computer)	550/213
Application fee	$55
International application fee	$55
Regular application deadline	7/1
Regular notification	rolling
Transfer students accepted	Yes
Transfer application policy Maximum of 8 unit transfer	
Need-blind admissions	Yes

Applicants Also Look At

Arizona State University, California State University—Sacramento, San Diego State University, University of California—Davis, University of California—Irvine, University of California—Los Angeles, University of California—Berkeley.

EMPLOYMENT PROFILE	
Career Rating	86
Percent employed	100

CALIFORNIA STATE POLYTECHNIC UNIVERSITY—POMONA
COLLEGE OF BUSINESS ADMINISTRATION

GENERAL INFORMATION
Type of school	Public
Environment	City
Academic calendar	Quarter

SURVEY SAYS...
Helfpul alumni
Happy students
Solid preparation in:
Teamwork
Communication/interpersonal skills
Presentation skills
Quantitative skills

STUDENTS
Enrollment of parent institution	19,800
Enrollment of business school	350
% male/female	55/45
% minorities	20
% international	18
Average age at entry	32
Average years work experience at entry	10

ACADEMICS
Academic Experience Rating	**85**
Student/faculty ratio	15:1
Profs interesting rating	78
Profs accessible rating	67

FINANCIAL FACTS
Annual tuition (in-state/out-of-state)	$4,420/$6,100
Cost of books	$3,000
Room & board (on/off-campus)	$5,000/$8,000
Average grant	$18,500
Average student loan debt	$12,000

Academics

Cal Poly Pomona offers a number of intriguing MBA options to its predominantly part-time student body. Like nearly all business schools, Cal Poly Pomona offers a general MBA, but unlike many schools, Cal Poly Pomona offers required courses for the degree both on campus and "off campus at a variety of locations throughout Southern California," through its Professional MBA (PMBA) program. For students with precisely defined goals, Cal Poly Pomona offers the Career MBA, through which students may specialize in one of 11 predefined areas or design a custom emphasis of their own. Finally, Cal Poly Pomona offers the only MSBA in Information Systems Auditing in the United States.

Cal Poly Pomona stresses a "learn-by-doing teaching/learning style" that students appreciate. The approach "forces students to work in groups and deal with teamwork while polishing presentation skills. This is very valuable." Students also appreciate the fact that Cal Poly "has decent technology and wireless access. I like the fact the school can keep up with technology." Cal Poly Pomona's MBA program "offers a high-quality, well-structured education with challenging courses, and students definitely learn a lot." The faculty "brings real business experiences and problems to the table. They are still active in the business world—not a bunch of stuffy academics with outdated information and notes." As one student sums up, "The overall experience here has been exceptional, especially considering the fact that it is a state school! The administration bends over backward for the students to fix any problems students or faculty may have. Professors are all top-quality and have a definite interest in seeing the students learn."

PMBA students at remote sites are particularly impressed with the level of service they receive. One PMBA student writes, "I live in a remote area, and the school provides instructors to teach not online but in person. The experience is perfect and quite rewarding." Faculty members "are very helpful and accessible despite the fact that classes are off campus."

Career and Placement

Career services for MBAs here are provided by the Cal Poly Pomona Career Center (CPPCC), a central office serving all undergraduate and graduate students at the university. The CPPCC provides all standard counseling and placement services. Many students do not even use the service; they already have jobs that they hope to advance in by earning a graduate degree. Those who do visit the office wish that it would "focus on providing more internships, part-time jobs, and full-time job opportunities."

Student Life and Environment

Cal Poly Pomona "is a commuter campus" for MBAs, who largely agree that "campus life is for undergrads who don't work. There is little time for working adults to enjoy campus life, but there is no shortage of clubs and organizations to join for those who want to." When students here get together outside of class, it is to complete required group projects, not to pound some brews or organize a lecture series. Cal Poly Pomona's MBAs appreciate the fact that "the campus is also continually improving its facilities and growing to become more modern and state-of-the-art every year."

ADMISSIONS CONTACT: ANYONE, ADMINISTRATIVE COORDINATOR
ADDRESS: 3801 WEST TEMPLE AVE. POMONA, CA 91768 UNITED STATES
PHONE: 909-869-3210 • FAX: 909-869-4529
E-MAIL: ADMISSIONS@CSUPOMONA.EDU • WEBSITE: WWW.CSUPOMONA.EDU/~MBA

Those who take classes at one of the school's satellite sites report that "classrooms are rented by the university at our site; thus, there are few student activities or resources here. There is no need for us to travel to the main campus, so we don't. The online services are excellent and that makes dealing with the university easy. And even though I am not at the main campus, I do have access to all main campus services and resources if I ever decide to travel there."

The MBA student body is "extremely diverse in terms of age, ethnicity, undergrad majors, and experience levels. Most are commuters who work full-time, come to class, and can't wait to get home after class is over. Most have very busy lives and do not network too strongly within this campus. It's a good group, but career- and family-minded, not socially minded." A substantial number are "enginerds" who "are broadening their intellect by going to b-school."

Admissions

Cal Poly Pomona operates on a quarterly academic schedule; the school accepts MBA applications for each quarter. All of the following components of the application are carefully considered: complete postsecondary academic record as reflected in official transcripts; GMAT scores (must be no more than five years old); two letters of recommendation from current or former employers; and a resume. Applicants who attended an undergraduate institution at which English is not the primary language of instruction must provide official TOEFL scores. Applicants must meet the following criteria to be considered for admission: an overall undergraduate GPA of at least 3.0; a minimum GMAT score of 450; and, if required, TOEFL scores of at least 580 on the paper-and-pencil test or 237 on the computer-based test. Meeting minimum requirements does not guarantee admission to the program.

ADMISSIONS	
Admissions Selectivity Rating	**87**
# of applications received	163
% applicants accepted	30
% acceptees attending	59
Average GMAT	540
Range of GMAT	450–720
Average GPA	3.2
TOEFL required of international students	Yes
Minimum TOEFL (paper/computer)	580/237
Application fee	$55
International application fee	$55
Regular application deadline	rolling
Regular notification	rolling
Deferment available	Yes
Maximum length of deferment	1–2 quarters
Transfer students accepted	Yes
Transfer application policy Maximum of 3 transferrable classes (13 Units)	
Non-fall admissions	Yes
Need-blind admissions	Yes

EMPLOYMENT PROFILE	
Career Rating	77

CALIFORNIA STATE UNIVERSITY—CHICO
COLLEGE OF BUSINESS

Academics

With a "unique combination of excellent and caring professors, a well-run program, and a great environment," the College of Business at California State University—Chico well serves the needs of its part-time and full-time MBA student populations. Students tout the school's convenient location, strong regional reputation, and affordable tuition in citing their reasons for choosing the school.

The Chico MBA requires students to complete 30 credit hours of graduate-level courses. The core curriculum consumes 21 credit hours; the remaining nine are devoted to electives. Students may take all their electives in one discipline to earn a degree with a concentration in accounting, finance, human resources, management information systems, marketing, or supply chain management; or, they may take electives in a variety of disciplines to earn a general management degree. Students lacking undergraduate coursework in business and management may be required to complete up to 27 credit hours of foundation coursework prior to commencing the MBA. Students can complete the MBA program in 18 months by attending on a full-time basis; all students must complete the program within five years of commencing. A Professional MBA (PMBA) program is also available. PMBA classes meet on Saturdays only; students complete the PMBA in 24 months.

Students here appreciate the program's emphasis on group projects. One tells us: "Nearly every class has teamwork. This truly prepares you for the real working world" and helps students develop "people and presentation skills and good verbal and written communication skills." They also approve of the curriculum's focus on "developing practical skills that make graduates effective," calling the Chico MBA "a great hands-on education system." Professors here "are caring and have both practical and academic knowledge" and "are willing to back up students in regard to group-related problems. There is a great support system in this MBA program." On the downside, some here feel that "the program could be improved by making it more rigorous, or at least by requiring a higher level of commitment from the students."

Career and Placement

MBA career-planning activities at Cal State Chico are handled by the office of Career Planning and Placement, which, according to the school's website, "engages in various recruitment, retention, graduation, and placement activities to support its diverse student population." About one in five Chico MBAs works in government after receiving the MBA; one in ten is employed in the financial services sector. Operations and production, consulting, and finance and accounting each claim about 20 percent of Chico MBAs. Students report that the MBA program "does a great job of placing graduates in jobs." Top employers of Chico MBAs include Accenture, Bearing Point, Capgemini, Chevron, Deloitte & Touche, Ernst & Young, IBM, KPMG, and SAP.

ADMISSIONS CONTACT: KENDYL DUNIVAN, PROGRAM ANALYST
ADDRESS: GRADUATE BUSINESS PROGRAMS, GLENN HALL, ROOM 121 CHICO, CA 95929-0041 U.S.
PHONE: 530-898-4425 • FAX: 530-898-5889
E-MAIL: KDUNIVAN@CSUCHICO.EDU • WEBSITE: WWW.CSUCHICO.EDU/COB/CURRENT/GRAD

Student Life and Environment

Cal State Chico is situated on a "charming campus in a great town with a huge park." Chico itself is "a wonderful community with enough diversity to make it interesting, but small enough to make the lifestyle warm and comfortable." The combined result of these factors is "a friendly environment" for MBAs. One student speculates the Chico "has more entrepreneurs per capita than any other US city, which means a creative and business-supportive environment." Top employers in the area include Enloe Medical Center, the county and city governments, the university, TriCounty Banks, Sierra Nevada Brewery, and SunGard Bi-Tech.

The Cal State Chico campus offers "quite a bit of activities and performances," but few MBAs have the time for such diversions. As one explains, "Generally, MBA classes are during evenings, so there's really not much time for us to be involved in. During the daytime, there's quite a bit of things going on, but for us who hold full-time jobs, we don't really have time and energy for it."

Chico attracts a youngish student body; reports one MBA, "Most of my fellow students are younger and unmarried. They are friendly and nice to work with but only half have work experience that adds value to the program." The "team-oriented" program requires students to be "cooperative and friendly," and most here are "wonderful and hardworking, although there are a few slackers." Students note "a large disparity between the international students, students who came directly from their undergraduate studies, and those students who have been working for several years."

Admissions

Applicants may be admitted to the Chico MBA program under the 'Conditionally Classified' status if they (1) have earned a satisfactory undergraduate GPA (at least 2.75 for the final 60 semester hours of undergraduate work or comparable grades in a more recently undertaken graduate program); (2) have received acceptable GMAT scores (at least 50th percentile in math and verbal portions); and (3) have demonstrated aptitude in business and management through academic and/or career achievement. Applicants must provide the Admissions Committee with official transcripts for all undergraduate and graduate work; an official score report for the GMAT; letters of recommendation; a personal statement of purpose; and a resume. Two years of work experience is recommended but not required. Students advance from "Conditionally Classified" status to "Classified Status" once they have completed (or placed out of) the non-degree "common body of knowledge" prerequisites to the MBA program. Finally, students are reclassified as degree candidates once they have successfully completed at least nine credit hours toward the MBA degree.

FINANCIAL FACTS

Annual tuition	
(in-state/out-of-state)	$0/$3,051
Fees	$4,278
Cost of books	$1,386
Room & board	
(off-campus)	$8,876
% of students receiving aid	24
% of first-year students	
receiving aid	9
% of students receiving loans	21
% of students receiving grants	21
Average award package	$6,277
Average grant	$1,550

ADMISSIONS

Admissions Selectivity Rating	74
# of applications received	119
% applicants accepted	72
% acceptees attending	66
Average GMAT	518
Range of GMAT	360–650
Average GPA	3.0
TOEFL required of	
international students	Yes
Minimum TOEFL	
(paper/computer)	550/213
Application fee	$55
International application fee	$55
Regular application deadline	rolling
Regular notification	rolling
Deferment available	Yes
Maximum length of	
deferment	1 year
Transfer students accepted	Yes
Transfer application policy	
Must meet our admissions criteria and transfer work must be from an AACSB accredited school.	
Non-fall admissions	Yes
Need-blind admissions	Yes

Applicants Also Look At
California State University—Sacramento, San Francisco State University.

EMPLOYMENT PROFILE

Career Rating	79	Grads Employed by Function	% Avg. Salary
		Finance	22 NR
		Marketing	11 NR
		MIS	11 NR
		Operations	22 NR
		Consulting	23 NR
		Other	11 NR

Top 5 Employers Hiring Grads
Chevron; Bearing Poin; Capgemini; IBM; Deloitte & Touche

CALIFORNIA STATE UNIVERSITY—EAST BAY
COLLEGE OF BUSINESS AND ECONOMICS

Academics

The MBA program at California State University—East Bay offers its busy student body an excellent assortment of specializations to choose from: 14 to be exact, including options in accounting, business economics, various computer-related areas, entrepreneurship, management, e-business, international business, information technology management, marketing management, finance, human resources management, operations and materials management, strategic management taxation, and supply chain management. Most classes here meet in the evenings, making them convenient for a student body comprised mainly of full-time workers.

The CSUEB MBA track includes foundation courses, which can be waived for students who earned undergraduate degrees in business; proficiency requirements in mathematics and statistics; 12 credits in core courses; four credits in international requirements, fulfilled by a course in international business or international economics; a five-credit capstone experience, consisting of either an entrepreneurship practicum or a seminar in strategic management; and course work sufficient to complete an MBA Option (what many schools call a "specialization" or "concentration"). In total, 45 quarter credits are required toward the MBA here.

In all programs, students appreciate the fact that "professors are very sympathetic to family and work issues." They report that "the professors are great in supply chain management," using "case studies that are oriented on real-life situations," and that "the accounting program is superb." Most of all, they love the low cost of attending. Some worry, however, that "the state is reducing its financial support of CSU, and that's caused a reduction in the number of classes offered. This is not a positive trend."

Career and Placement

CSUEB MBAs receive career guidance from the university's Career Development Center (CDC). Individual counseling is available to help students develop a personalized career plan. The school maintains an online resume database, as well as a website with numerous helpful links for MBAs. "Proximity to Silicon Valley" is also a boon to students. Since "this MBA program is catered to working professionals," many students are already involved in a career track.

Student Life and Environment

Those who get involved with campus life at CSUEB tell us that "life at school is dramatically enhanced when participating in campus organizations." Clubs such as the new MBA Association and the Operations Management Society, for example, "bring in speakers from top companies to address us, and good speakers from outside are sometimes invited to classes to talk about relevant topics." Few here, however, have the time or inclination to pursue such life-enhancing experiences. "This is a commuter school, and there's not too much life on campus," sums up one typical student.

Business school facilities, students tell us, need improvement, but the new Valley Business Technology Center was recently completed. Students appreciate the day-care facility and "a good library full of helpful librarians." "Nice weather and an outstanding view over the bay" also make difficult days a little less stressful.

Nearly half the MBA student population at CSUEB is international, which creates a student body that is "not only from diverse employments, but also from diverse cultures, representing ideas and business methods from all over the world. Everyone shares experiences and everyone is very easy to talk to."

ADMISSIONS CONTACT: DR. DORIS DUNCAN, DIRECTOR OF MBA PROGRAMS
ADDRESS: 25800 CARLES BEE BOULEVARD HAYWARD, CA 94542 UNITED STATES
PHONE: 510-885-2419 • FAX: 510-885-2176
E-MAIL: DORIS.DUNCAN@CSUEASTBAY.EDU • WEBSITE: CBEGRAD.CSUEASTBAY.EDU

Admissions

Applications to all graduate business programs at CSUEB are evaluated on the basis of academic transcripts for all undergraduate and post-undergraduate work, and GMAT scores. As the school's website states, "Admission is automatic for applicants with (1) a minimum 1050 'Index Score' and (2) minimum twentieth percentile GMAT Verbal and Quantitative scores. [Index Score = (Upper Division GPA x 200) + Total GMAT]." Students must demonstrate writing proficiency prior to enrolling in graduate-level courses; this can be achieved with a score of "clear competency" on the university's Writing Skills Test (WST) or a score of at least 4.5 on the GMAT essay. International students must prove proficiency in English in one of a few ways: by earning a TOEFL (Test of English as a Foreign Language) score of at least 550 (paper-based test) or 213 (computer-based test); by earning an IELTS (International English Language Testing System) score of at least 7.0; or by submitting an official transcript verifying receipt of a bachelor's degree from "a U.S. college or university or an international college or university where English is the principal language of instruction."

Average grant	$11,478
Average student loan debt	$25,626

ADMISSIONS

Admissions Selectivity Rating	**75**
# of applications received	234
% applicants accepted	78
% acceptees attending	65
Average GMAT	539
Range of GMAT	400–630
Average GPA	3.23
TOEFL required of international students	Yes
Minimum TOEFL (paper/computer)	550/213
Application fee	$55
International application fee	$55
Regular application deadline	5/31
Regular notification	6/30
Transfer students accepted	Yes
Transfer application policy With approval one may transfer up to 13 units.	
Non-fall admissions	Yes

Applicants Also Look At

California State University—Sacramento, San Francisco State University, San José State University, University of California—Davis, University of California—Berkeley.

CALIFORNIA STATE UNIVERSITY—FRESNO
CRAIG SCHOOL OF BUSINESS

GENERAL INFORMATION

Type of school	Public
Academic calendar	Semester

SURVEY SAYS...
Solid preparation in:
General management
Teamwork
Communication/interpersonal skills
Presentation skills
Entrepreneurial studies

STUDENTS

Enrollment of parent institution	21,000
Enrollment of business school	129
% male/female	75/25
% out-of-state	15
% part-time	100
% minorities	30
% international	20
Average age at entry	26
Average years work experience at entry	4

ACADEMICS

Academic Experience Rating	**81**
Student/faculty ratio	6:1
Profs interesting rating	74
Profs accessible rating	64
% female faculty	33
% minority faculty	6

Prominent Alumni
Ryan Turner, CEO, Chemicals; Jeff Booey, Plant Manager, Glass Manufacturing; Martin Bergman, Operations Manager, Glass Manufacturing.

FINANCIAL FACTS

Annual tuition (in-state/ out-of-state)	$1,811/$6,102
Cost of books	$650
Room & board (off-campus)	$10,700
Average grant	$3,000
Average student loan debt	$20,000

Academics

The MBA program at California State University—Fresno's Craig School of Business is designed with the working student in mind. All weekday classes here meet just once a week, from 6:00 P.M. to 8:45 P.M. Saturday morning classes (usually scheduled from 9:00 A.M. to 11:45 A.M.) are also available.

The Craig MBA consists of 11 classes and a final project. The curriculum commences with six core courses covering such fundamental areas as leadership, MIS, finance, accounting, marketing, and ethics. Students then complete three electives. Electives may be used to create a specialization in agribusiness, entrepreneurship, finance, human resource management, MIS, or marketing; or, students may choose to graduate with a General Management degree. The program concludes with a capstone class in Business Policy and Strategy and a culminating project or thesis.

Up to five introductory foundation courses that do not count toward the graduate degree may be required of some entering students. Students who have earned an undergraduate degree in business from an AACSB-accredited institution within the last seven years generally do not have to take these courses. Those not meeting these criteria may be able to place out of some or all of the introductory courses through examination.

Students identify entrepreneurship and courses dealing with globalization as the program's strengths. Those studying MIS, however, warn that "there currently are not enough professors to offer all of the courses, making it difficult to complete the degree." MBAs here appreciate the fact that the Craig School "has made a point to invest itself into the community for the sake of the community, as well as for the sake of the students. Fresno State feels like a hub of the community, and it's exciting to be affiliated with it." Professors here "are typically passionate about their subject matter, which leads to interesting classes, even when the material isn't what I'd like to be studying (accounting, for example)."

Career and Placement

Career and placement services for Craig MBAs are limited. The school does not have a dedicated Career Services Office; rather, a single Career Services Office serves all undergraduate and graduate students at the university. The office provides a number of recruiting events and other support services, but few are designed to serve the unique needs of MBAs. An MBA Student Association offers additional services, organizing events that "connect MBA students with alumni, faculty, and local community, and business leaders" in order to "build a professional network and lay the foundation for friendships that will last a lifetime." Most Craig students are part-time students with full-time jobs (many attend at their employers' expense), and for them the dearth of career services is not a major drawback.

Student Life and Environment

It's all business (pun intended!) on the Craig MBA campus, as one student expresses: "Extracurricular activities coincide with class times," making participation difficult. While "there are a number of activities available for undergraduate students, it's hard to make these available for graduate students who are busy with work throughout the day."

However, the Craig school is in the process of upgrading its facilities, and many here believe that the "facilities will be amazing in a few years." The library is being remodeled and the university has recently opened a 15,000-seat entertainment and sports center (Savemart Center), the largest of those facilities in California's Central Valley. This

ADMISSIONS CONTACT: DR. RAFAEL SOLIS, DIRECTOR OF GRADUATE PROGRAMS
ADDRESS: 5245 NORTH BACKER AVENUE FRESNO, CA 93740 UNITED STATES
PHONE: 559-278-2107 • FAX: 559-278-2572
E-MAIL: MBAINFO@CSUFRESNO.EDU • WEBSITE: WWW.CRAIG.CSUFRESNO.EDU/MBA

venue is used for a variety of sports events ranging from basketball to ice hockey. It has also hosted musical, drama, and dance shows. Hopefully, this new recreation center will cater to graduate students' hectic schedules and provide them with multiple extracurricular options.

The Craig student body "represents a varied mix of industries, allowing for a 'cross-section' view of industries in general" during class discussions and group projects. Many foreign students attend, and "though there are times when language barriers exist, our lives are expanded by their presence." MBAs here report that "although we are so different in terms of age, ethnic background, and work experience, we are all here, going through the same courses and moaning about the same tough professors. There's a feeling of 'We're in this together.'"

Admissions

Admission to the Craig MBA program is determined primarily by the applicant's undergraduate grade point average (GPA) during the final two years of undergraduate work, and GMAT scores. The average admitted student arrives with a GPA of 3.4 and a GMAT score of 566. The quality of undergraduate institution and curriculum pursued are considered when evaluating GPA. Work experience, personal statement, and two letters of recommendation (from employers, professors, or professional peers) also figure into the admissions decision. Because the GMAT score is a major factor in admissions, the admissions office strongly encourages all candidates to prepare for the exam for at least six to eight weeks. International students must have a minimum TOEFL score of 550 (paper-based test) or 213 (computer-based test) to be considered.

ADMISSIONS

Admissions Selectivity Rating	**80**
# of applications received	99
% applicants accepted	63
% acceptees attending	47
Average GMAT	580
Range of GMAT	550–690
Average GPA	3.4
TOEFL required of international students	Yes
Minimum TOEFL (paper/computer)	550/213
Application fee	$55
International application fee	$55
Regular application deadline	3/1
Regular notification	Rolling
Deferment available	Yes
Maximum length of deferment	1 year
Transfer students accepted	Yes
Transfer application policy	All foundation courses may be waived through prior coursework. Up to 9 units of credit may be transferred.
Non-fall admissions	Yes
Need-blind admissions	Yes

Applicants Also Look At

California Polytechnic State University—San Luis Obispo, Santa Clara University, University of California—Davis.

CALIFORNIA STATE UNIVERSITY—FULLERTON
MIHAYLO COLLEGE OF BUSINESS AND ECONOMICS

Academics

California State University—Fullerton offers a part-time MBA program featuring "flexible schedules," a "location in the vibrant Orange County economy," and a "low tuition that allows me to pay for my education without going into a large degree of debt." In this last regard it differs from its neighbor and competitor UCLA. Students here feel that, despite the difference in price, both schools share "the prestige of being a major source of a highly educated workforce in California."

MBA students at Cal Fullerton must complete between 11 and 15 courses, depending on their academic background in business disciplines. Ten core courses cover fundamental principles; some cover basics (e.g., financial accounting, microeconomics) and others take an interdisciplinary approach (e.g., legal and ethical environment in business, management information in the corporate environment). Students with undergraduate degrees in business or extensive professional experience may be able to place out of some core courses. Students may devote four courses to developing a concentration (five if they chose international business). Concentrations are available in accounting, economics, e-commerce, entrepreneurship, finance, information systems, international business, management, management science, and marketing. A general degree is also available.

Students praise the school's "teaching philosophy, which is underpinned with both practical and theoretical applications" and love "the amount of attention that is given to each student." "It's great that each professor has not only learned my name, but has gotten to know me individually in the classroom," one student says, "I feel that most all professors are very receptive to providing assistance and guidance related to students' professional work experience and are happy to support positive opportunities for students." Some here feel that the program could be more challenging, telling us that "building more rigor in would help." Others, while noting, "The workload is not overly heavy," tell us that they "feel as though we are learning quite a lot."

Career and Placement

Cal State Fullerton Career Planning and Placement Center provides career services to MBAs at both the Fullerton and Irvine campus locations. Services include walk-in counseling, interview tips, resume review, and job databases. Students may continue to utilize these facilities for up to one year after they graduate for a $25 fee. While some here report that there are "a lot of career events organized," others complain that "due to the lack of institutional funding and a small administrative staff, students are not provided enough opportunity to network among local professionals and entities." Employers who most frequently hire Cal Fullerton MBAs include Ernst and Young, LLP, KPMG, The Home Depot, Mercury Insurance, Pacific Life, and Target.

ADMISSIONS CONTACT: PRE-ADMISSION ADVISOR, PRE-ADMISSION ADVISOR
ADDRESS: PO BOX 6848 FULLERTON, CA 92834-6848 UNITED STATES
PHONE: 714-278-3622 • FAX: 714-278-7101
E-MAIL: MBA@FULLERTON.EDU • WEBSITE: BUSINESS.FULLERTON.EDU/GRADUATEPROGRAMS

Student Life and Environment

"CSUF is a commuter school" with "small class sizes that provide a sense of community in the program," but most here "usually just go to class and go home." Those who can stick around for extracurriculars will find a "very diverse" campus life among "over 37,000" other students, "which makes for a very busy campus." There are plenty of business-related activities, including "15 clubs and organizations…and job fairs with what feels like countless employers looking to hire students," but these are targeted almost exclusively to the undergraduate population. The MBA program does do a good job of "supporting a lot of students from abroad."

Fullerton nurtures a campus culture that is "relaxed yet serious enough to get to work when necessary." "Buildings are located close enough to each other so that students from other schools can talk to each other," one student says. While MBAs have complained in the past about classroom resources, a new facility scheduled to go online in the fall of 2008 should address those concerns.

Most students here are "full-time working professionals who contribute greatly to the program. They have a great deal of work experience, are very competitive, and provide great insights during class discussions." They're an older group who are "very outspoken," but whose professional experience justifies their being so. The student body also includes "a good portion of foreign exchange students."

Admissions

Cal State Fullerton requires the following of all applicants to its MBA program: an "acceptable bachelor's degree from an appropriately accredited institution," with a minimum GPA of 2.5 for the final two years of undergraduate work; two sets of transcripts for all undergraduate and graduate academic work; GMAT scores reflecting placement in the top 50 percent on the verbal, analytical, and quantitative sections of the exam; a completed background sheet that includes a summary of academic and professional experience and a personal statement of purpose; up to three letters of recommendation from employers or professors; and demonstrated proficiency in calculus, statistical analysis, and introductory-level computer programming. International students whose first language is not English must score a minimum 570 on the TOEFL paper-and-pencil exam, 230 on the computer-based exam, or 88 on the iBT. Applications are accepted for the fall and spring semesters and are processed on a rolling basis. Programs can fill prior to the application deadline, so applying as early as possible is highly recommended.

ADMISSIONS

Admissions Selectivity Rating	**86**
# of applications received	764
% applicants accepted	47
% acceptees attending	60
Average GMAT	540
Range of GMAT	400–770
Average GPA	3.3
TOEFL required of international students	Yes
Minimum TOEFL (paper/computer)	570/230
Application fee	$55
International application fee	$55
Regular application deadline	6/15
Regular notification	Rolling
Transfer students accepted	Yes
Transfer application policy Students may transfer in up to 9 units.	
Non-fall admissions	Yes
Need-blind admissions	Yes

EMPLOYMENT PROFILE	
Career Rating	**74**
Average base starting salary	$65,000–$70,000

CALIFORNIA STATE UNIVERSITY—LONG BEACH
COLLEGE OF BUSINESS ADMINISTRATION

GENERAL INFORMATION
Type of school	Public
Environment	City
Academic calendar	Semester

SURVEY SAYS...
Solid preparation in:
Marketing
Accounting
General management

STUDENTS
Enrollment of parent institution	36,800
Enrollment of business school	369
% male/female	58/42
% out-of-state	1
% part-time	70
% minorities	15
% international	30
Average age at entry	29
Average years work experience at entry	5

ACADEMICS
Academic Experience Rating	**85**
Student/faculty ratio	25:1
Profs interesting rating	89
Profs accessible rating	73

Joint Degrees
The MFA/MBA 3 years.

FINANCIAL FACTS
Annual tuition	$8,136
Fees (in-state/ out-of-state)	$4,000/$10,202

Academics

For practically minded business students, CSU Long Beach offers three affordable and efficient MBA options: the Fully Employed MBA, the Self-Paced Evening MBA, and the one-year Accelerated MBA. Catering to working adults in the Southern California region, these "focused, fast-paced, and competitive" programs are specially designed to help students balance professional and personal commitments while pursuing their educations. To that end, the programs are highly successful, offering a convenient and user-friendly educational experience. A current student explains, "The ease and inclusiveness of the school are exemplary. Every professor or administrator is highly accessible, and I have no problems at all getting into needed classes." Another adds, "The FEMBA program is specifically targeted to busy professionals, holding classes exclusively on Saturdays. The program administration goes out of their way to make sure we are getting everything we need." Indeed, CSU Long Beach runs smoothly from top to bottom, and "there is good communication with the administration to make suggestions for changes and improvement."

Like administrators, CSU faculty is "closely connected with [the students], and they are extremely helpful." Bringing both real-world and academic expertise to the classroom, "professors are well-versed and have a strong command of the subjects they teach." In addition, the diversity of the "required coursework gives a balanced exposure to different business areas." Interaction is highly encouraged and "student-driven class activities" form the backbone of the educational experience. In fact, be prepared for "as many as three to five major group projects per semester." As a result, your classmates at CSULB will also be your teachers. Drawing a range of students from the region, graduate students at CSU are "very diverse in work experience, culture, backgrounds, and motivation." What's more, the school boasts "a large percentage of international students that are able to contribute a lot of different perspectives to the program. With the move towards a global business world, making these connections during the program are a big bonus." Most importantly, when it comes to group work, "all of the students that survived the program are smart, creative, team players, and committed to doing the best that they can each and every quarter."

Career and Placement

Students at the College of Business Administration are served by the MBA Career Management Services, which maintains an MBA job board and hosts on-campus recruiting events in a variety of business disciplines. The services also maintains contact with the school's alumni and maintains an up-to-date online job database for MBA students. In addition, students may choose to attend special workshops and seminars to assist in career development, or participate in one of the many large, campus-wide career fairs hosted by CSULB's Career Development Center. Many big companies have visited campus in recent years, including Alaska Airlines, Accountants Incorporated, American Capital Group, California National Bank, CVS/Carmark Pharmacy, First Investors, Kelly Scientific Resources, Ameriprise Financial, Boeing, Northrop Grumman, and Comerica Bank, among others.

ADMISSIONS CONTACT: MARINA FREEMAN, GRADUATE PROGRAMS ADMISSIONS MANAGER
ADDRESS: 1250 BELLFLOWER BOULEVARD LONG BEACH, CA 90840-8501 UNITED STATES
PHONE: 562-985-5565 • FAX: 562-985-5590
E-MAIL: MBA@CSULB.EDU • WEBSITE: WWW.CSULB.EDU/COLLEGES/CBA/MBA

Student Life and Environment

A safe, cooperative, and pleasant campus atmosphere creates an appealing backdrop for CSULB's MBA programs. A current student explains, "The campus is very casual, and the students are very nice and friendly. It is like a second home, and I feel comfortable and safe in the environment." Since CSULB's graduate programs are designed for working adults, it's no surprise that "most students are part time, working during the day and coming to school at night. The majority of MBA students are only on campus three to six hours per week." However, those who would like to augment their coursework with a bit of extracurricular stimulation should not despair: "There are opportunities to participate in seminars and other social events with the MBA Association" and "there's a strong nucleus, which mingles off-campus throughout the semester." No matter what your background, you'll feel at home at this large public school community, which draws students who "range from open-minded thinkers to engineers who like to think by the rules."

Admissions

Admissions criteria vary at CSU, depending on the program to which you are applying. In recent years, students entering the full-time, accelerated MBA had an average GMAT score of 520, an average GPA of 3.2, and an average age of 26. Evening MBA and Fully-Employed MBA candidates entered with a GMAT score of 555 and 536, respectively.

ADMISSIONS

Admissions Selectivity Rating	**83**
# of applications received	320
% applicants accepted	50
% acceptees attending	168
Average GMAT	555
Range of GMAT	751–670
Average GPA	3.2
TOEFL required of international students	Yes
Minimum TOEFL (paper/computer)	550/213
Application fee	$55
International application fee	$55
Regular application deadline	3/30
Regular notification	Rolling
Deferment available	Yes
Maximum length of deferment	One semester
Transfer students accepted	Yes
Transfer application policy Must meet our admissions criteria	
Non-fall admissions	Yes
Need-blind admissions	Yes

Applicants Also Look At

California State University—Fullerton, California State University—Los Angeles, Pepperdine University, University of California—Irvine.

CALIFORNIA STATE UNIVERSITY—NORTHRIDGE
COLLEGE OF BUSINESS AND ECONOMICS

Academics

"California State University—Northridge's greatest strengths are its diverse student population, its understanding of the educational needs of the surrounding community, and its commitment to students' educations," MBAs in this "affordable" Los Angeles graduate program tell us. Students, predominantly full-time employees attending the school in evenings in order to improve their promotability, appreciate that the program is "inexpensive and designed to get you through your degree quickly." They also benefit from the fact that "CSUN has a great reputation for producing great MBA graduates. The school is well respected in the area as well as [in] the defense industry."

CSUN's MBA program offers electives in accounting, economics, entertainment, finance, information systems, international business, management, and marketing. MBAs enjoy "an open work environment" in which "fellow students are not extremely competitive, which creates a good learning environment." They also respect how the program's leaders are "driven to expand the curriculum to be state-of-the-art while also adding value to the degree by recognizing alums' and students' accomplishment on a regular basis. There is a passion for business at this school that I did not expect." This passion permeates the classroom, where "teachers are friendly and excited about what they do," although students warn: "The quality of the professors has a wide variety. Some are great, extremely effective, and impactful; others are not engaging, don't seem interested in teaching, and are not effective."

CSUN stresses a "relevant curriculum" through such innovations as its entertainment industry concentration. The program is "self-directed," meaning that students have some flexibility in sequencing their coursework. While students agree: "For the money, it can't be beat," they also recognize some shortcomings inherent to state funding. One wishes that "the state would stop cutting the budget so much." Others concede that the program "lacks some of the extras that private and better-funded schools enjoy" and yearn for such perks as "an option to travel abroad as a cumulating experience project—many of us work for multinational companies" and "more extensive use of online collaborative learning in a global business-related framework."

Career and Placement

The Career Center at California State University—Northridge serves the entire undergraduate and graduate student population. Counselors there offer workshops in interviewing, resume writing, and job search strategies. The office arranges on-campus interviews and alumni meet-and-greets, and it also maintains a database of job listings. Students tell us: "There are monthly speakers from the community who are business leaders. They are informative about what to expect in future job pursuits." Professors, likewise, can be a useful source of job leads and advice. Otherwise, the school is largely absent from counseling and placement activities, focusing its efforts on undergraduates. The vast majority of MBAs here are not actively looking to leave their current employers, so the school's lack of career resources is not a major inconvenience to them.

ADMISSIONS CONTACT: OSCAR W. DESHIELDS, JR., PH.D., DIRECTOR OF GRADUATE PROGRAMS
ADDRESS: 18111 NORDHOFF STREET NORTHRIDGE, CA 91330-8380 UNITED STATES
PHONE: 818-677-2467 • FAX: 818-677-3188 • E-MAIL: MBA@CSUN.EDU
WEBSITE: CSUN.EDU/MBA

FINANCIAL FACTS

Fees	$3,618
Cost of books	$1,300
Room & board	$9,328

ADMISSIONS

Admissions Selectivity Rating	**90**
# of applications received	249
% applicants accepted	27
% acceptees attending	70
Average GMAT	560
Range of GMAT	460–690
Average GPA	3.3
TOEFL required of international students	Yes
Minimum TOEFL (paper/computer)	550/213
Application fee	$55
International application fee	$55
Regular application deadline	5/1
Regular notification	rolling
Deferment available	Yes
Maximum length of deferment	1 Semester
Transfer students accepted	Yes
Transfer application policy	9 units max transfer credit
Non-fall admissions	Yes
Need-blind admissions	Yes

Applicants Also Look At

California State University—Long Beach, California State University—Los Angeles, Pepperdine University, University of California—Los Angeles.

Student Life and Environment

"CSUN is a commuter school, so many people live outside campus" and "don't spend much time here." A typical student describes the routine: "I attend class twice per week for lectures and communicate via conference calls or weekend meetings with fellow students. It's a fairly typical commuter college experience." Even those who only visit for classes appreciate the campus's "easy access to cafes and restaurants for when you don't have time to stop for dinner" and recognize that "the campus has made good efforts to make space available in the library and other buildings for students to meet when they are required to do group work." Those who choose to immerse themselves in campus life tell us that the experience is "exceptional. The school has a tremendous amount of student-related activities and accommodations. As an alumnus of CSUN's undergraduate program, I am very proud to be a member of the community."

CSUN MBAs are "inquisitive and genuine for the most part, and looking for new career paths or networking opportunities. Many intend to continue working where they are after graduation." They tend to be "laid-back and open-minded—i.e., not brutally competitive—which is perfect for the mid-career person looking to enhance his skill set." They are also "very encouraging to each other. We have study groups and are always willing to help each other. Everyone has different backgrounds, and we're able to learn from each others' experiences."

Admissions

Admission to the CSUN MBA program is competitive. Applicants are expected to have achieved a minimum GPA of 3.0 during their final two years (60 semester credits/90 quarter credits) of undergraduate work and to reach at least the 50th percentile rank on all sections of the GMAT. A minimum of one of year post-undergraduate professional experience is acceptable, although three to five years is the preferred length. Applicants whose native language is not English must earn a minimum score of 213 on the computer-based TOEFL. CSUP expects all incoming MBA candidates to have completed a battery of prerequisite business and management courses at the undergraduate level; those who have not must first complete the Fundamentals of Business Administration Certificate program offered through the College of Extended Learning.

CALIFORNIA STATE UNIVERSITY—SAN BERNARDINO
COLLEGE OF BUSINESS AND PUBLIC ADMINISTRATION

GENERAL INFORMATION

Type of school	Public
Environment	City
Academic calendar	Quarter

SURVEY SAYS...

Happy students
Solid preparation in:
Accounting
Presentation skills
Quantitative skills
Computer skills

STUDENTS

Enrollment of parent institution	17,066
Enrollment of business school	325
% male/female	60/40
% out-of-state	1
% part-time	44
% minorities	21
% international	38
Average age at entry	28
Average years work experience at entry	4

ACADEMICS

Academic Experience Rating	**76**
Student/faculty ratio	20:1
Profs interesting rating	83
Profs accessible rating	70
% female faculty	1
% minority faculty	1

Joint Degrees

MBA/PhD Information Science.

Prominent Alumni

Yuzo Tobisaka, President, Mitsubishi Corp.; Larry Sharp, CEO, Arrowhead Credit Union; Dr. GnanaDev, Medical Director of Surgery, Arrowhead Hospital; Yusef Akcayoglu, President, TAV Constuction Dubai/Turkey.

Academics

Students tell us that the College of Business and Public Administration at California State University—San Bernardino offers "a good mix of practical and theoretical business applications and concepts" in a program that delivers in a variety of disciplines, all "at a very good price." According to those we surveyed, the program is the perfect size, "small enough that you can build relationships with the professors and administration, but also big enough to give students some independence and freedom to do things on their own."

Entrepreneurship leads the pack here; the MBA entrepreneurship program was ranked among the nation's top four by Entrepreneur magazine in 2006. The program is well supported by the CBPA's Inland Empire Center for Entrepreneurship, a research center that promotes entrepreneurship in the surrounding area. Operations management is also reportedly strong. Students here may pursue either a part-time or full-time MBA with one of eight concentrations: accounting, entrepreneurship, finance, information assurance and security, mgmt, information management, management, marketing, and operations management/supply chain management. While a few feel that "it would be nice if the school had a general MBA option, rather than having to select a major," most see no problem with the current system.

San Bernardino operates on a quarterly schedule, meaning that the term flies by quickly. The curricular emphasis "is practical and exposes you to real-world experiences." One student offers this example: "For my MBA project, l did a marketing plan for a company in Palm Springs called Crystal Pure drinking water. They manufacture water-purifying machines, and from the plan we developed they realized $1.6 million in sales within six months. Their websites had many hits from customers around the world. Professors "are seasoned in their fields of study and provide real-world application for what we learn. We don't just read about business, we create it, and we grow it."

Career and Placement

The Career Development Center at CSUSB serves all students at the university, undergraduate and graduate. Counselors there offer workshops in interviewing, resume writing, and job search strategies. The office arranges on-campus interviews and alumni meet-and-greets, and it also maintains a database of job listings. Some students wish that the school "would build stronger relationships with local companies," while others note that "there really isn't a demand for MBA graduates in San Bernardino County." However, many agree, "The teachers are always there to help when you need them . . . and are very willing to help in getting jobs or career advice," and faculty "bring their students in touch with prospective employers outside the classroom."

Employers likely to hire CSUSB MBAs include Arrowhead Credit Union, GE Transportation, Enterprise Rent-a-Car, American Express Financial, ESRI, Internal Revenue Service, the Central Intelligence Agency, Target, Arthur Anderson, FEMA, Wells Fargo, and almost all the regional accounting firms, banks, and credit unions.

ADMISSIONS CONTACT: BETH A. FLYNN, DIRECTOR OF MBA PROGRAM
ADDRESS: 5500 UNIVERSITY PARKWAY SAN BERNARDINO, CA 92407 UNITED STATES
PHONE: 909-537-5703 • FAX: 909-537-7582
E-MAIL: MBA@CSUSB.EDU • WEBSITE: CBPA.CSUSB.EDU/MBA

Student Life and Environment

The CSUSB MBA program "has students from all over the world who make class discussions interesting and make one grow an appreciation of different cultures." MBAs here "are encouraged to do research and be involved in community activities," and the school offers "leadership development programs and faculty research seminars where students are also invited. This prepares students for future leadership roles in society." The degree to which students can take advantage of these opportunities varies; a sizeable portion of the student body is part time, typically pursuing a degree in addition to full-time employment.

The CSUSB campus "provides the latest technology for the students and an extremely comfortable setting." All students enjoy "plenty of places to relax and the scenery (the campus recently received an excellence award for its facilities management)." A recently completed student union includes "a new cutting-edge recreational sports facility," and students tell us, "The Fullerton Art Museum is also a great leisure escape." Conveniently, "Everything is within walking distance, and you get to know familiar faces because the campus is not as large as other CSUs."

Admissions

Applicants to the CSUSB MBA program must first apply for admission to the university, which requires a baccalaureate with a GPA of at least 2.5 for the final two years of undergraduate work. Students clearing this hurdle may then apply for admission to the MBA program. Applicants must submit two sets of official transcripts for all post-secondary academic work; an official GMAT score report; and a personal statement. Three letters of recommendation are recommended but are technically optional. International students must additionally provide an Affidavit of Financial Support and TOEFL scores (minimum score 550 paper, 213 computer, 79 Internet). The minimum requirement for admission to the program is a formula score of 1050 under the formula ((undergraduate GPA ? 200) + GMAT score), with a minimum GMAT score of 470 and a minimum GPA of 2.5. No student may begin MBA work without having earned at least a C grade in the following undergraduate courses or their equivalent at another accredited institution: financial accounting I and II; microeconomics; macroeconomics; business finance; corporate finance; information management; business law; management and organization behavior; expository writing for administration; strategic management; marketing principles; business statistics; and principles of supply chain management.

FINANCIAL FACTS

Annual tuition	
(in-state/out-of-state)	$0/$9,000
Fees	$4,500
Cost of books	$1,800
Room & board	
(on/off-campus)	$9,000/$12,000
% of students receiving aid	61
% of first-year students	
receiving aid	60
% of students receiving loans	61
% of students receiving grants	5
Average award package	$12,917
Average grant	$1,000
Average student loan debt	$25,834

ADMISSIONS

Admissions Selectivity Rating	73
# of applications received	264
% applicants accepted	72
% acceptees attending	64
Average GMAT	527
Range of GMAT	470–760
Average GPA	3.1
TOEFL required of	
international students	Yes
Minimum TOEFL	
(paper/computer)	550/213
Application fee	$55
International application fee	$55
Regular application deadline	7/1
Regular notification	9/1
Application Deadline/Notification	
Round 1:	04/01 / 05/01
Round 2:	06/01 / 07/01
Round 3:	07/01 / 08/01
Round 4:	08/01 / 09/01
Early decision program?	Yes
ED Deadline/Notification	0
	2/01 / 06/01
Deferment available	Yes
Maximum length of	
deferment	1 year
Transfer students accepted	Yes
Transfer application policy	
Three graduate courses may be	
transferred into the MBA program	
from approved U.S. Universities.	
Non-fall admissions	Yes
Need-blind admissions	Yes

Applicants Also Look At

California State Polytechnic University—Pomona, California State University—Fullerton, California State University—Los Angeles, University of California—Riverside.

EMPLOYMENT PROFILE	
Career Rating	63

CARNEGIE MELLON UNIVERSITY
TEPPER SCHOOL OF BUSINESS

Academics

Tepper's MBA program attracts workhorses and future IT and science industry leaders with a "heavily quantitative" emphasis. The program's 20 distinct tracks and concentrations include biotechnology, technology leadership, wealth and asset management, and quantitative analysis. As a result, "Students are just as likely to be able to calculate a discounted cash flow as to identify optimal supply chain quantities and overstock levels" by the time they graduate. But "The program's greatest strength goes deeper than that"; so-called "hard skills" make Tepper students "excellent analytical thinkers."

The Tepper year consists of four mini-semesters, which means that first-year students are straddled with 10 full courses before winter break. Students say that this "grueling" schedule "prepares you extremely well for your internship and beyond." The "class load lightens up" for second-years, and "Students are able to really focus their learning in areas where they are most interested." "This takes the form of corporate-sponsored projects (GM, Bosch, Equitable Resources, Caterpillar), entrepreneurship, and independent academic study with faculty," as well as elective courses that must satisfy distributional requirements in economics, "quant," IT, organizational behavior, strategy, and a concentration of one's choice. The one required second-year course is called Management Game, a team business simulation in which students can draw on a board of real corporate leaders, negotiate labor contracts with real labor leaders, and compete with students from international business schools. "The rigor of our course work is tough but appropriate," says one student. "After going through this, I am fearless about entering the business world." Students would like to see "more detailed courses regarding the markets and where they are going" and "additional courses in foreign languages." For the most part, Tepper's faculty and "attentive" administration "could not be better."

Career and Placement

Tepper has "very strong ties with top management consulting firms," and "The Career Office is good for the traditional areas: finance, consulting, and ops." Indeed, more than half of the Class of 2006 works in finance and consulting alone, with median first-year salaries of $95,000 and $110,000 respectively. (To keep the momentum going, the Career Office recently hired "industry-specific Career Counselors" for these two sectors.) An additional third of 2006 grads work in manufacturing (median salary: $85,100) and technology (median salary: $90,000). Fewer than one percent work in the nonprofit/government arena.

Recruitment comes in many forms, including the credit-bearing kind. Sometimes "large firms come in and literally 'open call' their problems/projects." Faculty also "quietly select" star pupils "to assist them with major consulting projects." One student reports, "For my last mini-semester, I am working on two projects. I will be making just about the same amount over the next 2 months as I will be making over the next 4 months with my permanent employer."

Students would like to see the Career Center diversify, and some progress has been made in the arena. Over the past few years, the career center has continued "working to woo" high-tech California and Silicon Forest firms, and Tepper now hosts "interviews for financial firms . . . en masse" at its "New York campus." In any event, "I think that getting employers to Pittsburgh is no longer an issue," says one student. "The school had a record number of companies recruiting on campus this year." The Career Opportunities Center could further "improve by attracting firms that look for well-rounded employees with quantitative skills instead of [just] for quants."

ADMISSIONS CONTACT: LAURIE STEWART, EXECUTIVE DIRECTOR OF MASTERS ADMISSIONS
ADDRESS: TEPPER SCHOOL OF BUSINESS, 5000 FORBES AVENUE PITTSBURGH, PA 15213 U.S.
PHONE: 412-268-2272 • FAX: 412-268-4209
E-MAIL: MBA-ADMISSIONS@ANDREW.CMU.EDU • WEBSITE: WWW.TEPPER.CMU.EDU

Student Life and Environment

Tepper students describe one another as "team-oriented problem-solvers who work until a task is 100 percent complete." The "atmosphere is obviously competitive but amicable." During the recruitment season, students pull together; someone "who has completed his interview will oftentimes share the questions he received with fellow applicants who are still waiting for their turn. This type of support is amazing." The same is true for exam time, when "Classmates have circulated their self-prepared study guides prior to exams, helping everyone cut down on their prep time." The downside to this team spirit, says one student, is "a lot of cheating."

Typical Tepper students are "bright people who have been extremely successful in their past careers," and are fairly "homogeneous in terms of educational background and pre-MBA experience, targeting a fairly narrow set of post-MBA careers," many of which require the hard skills that Tepper hones. A full 70 percent of the class of 2008 holds undergraduate degrees in engineering, IT, and the sciences; an additional quarter studied economics, accounting, and business. On the other hand, nearly 30 percent of Tepper's approximately 300 students are international, and another tenth are of color. "I thought I knew diversity. . . . "At Tepper, I was awestruck," says one student.

Students like cheap, leafy Pittsburgh. "This area of town is very much centered around the schools," offering a "somewhat laid-back feeling" and plenty of "comfortable, close housing." This means that "most people live close to campus and spend a lot of time there, which fosters a good community." Students maintain "a very active social life." "There is a weekly bar night out, and about twice a month the school sponsors beer and food on Friday night. That is called B**RS and is a great time to hang out with faculty, the PhDs, and fellow MBAs." Because there are events that also include spouses and families, "there is an activity and a social life no matter what stage in life you are" in.

Admissions

Tepper's most recent application required two long essays on professional goals and contribution to the school's diversity. Applicants then answered three out of five short questions about professional background and personal character, with the option to include an additional essay.

Like many schools, Tepper staggers its admission deadlines, with unofficial preference going to early-round applicants. International students must apply no later than March. However, unlike at many schools, rolling admission is available after April for domestic candidates. Most successful applicants have undergraduate GPAs above 3.0 and GMAT scores above 700.

Prominent Alumni

David A. Tepper, CEO & Founder, Appaloosa Management; David Coulter, Managing Director & Sr. Adv., Warburg Pincus LLC; Lewis Hay III, President & CEO, FPL; Yoshiaki Fujimori, President & CEO, GE Consumer Finance; Pamela Zilly, Sr. Managing Dir., The Blackstone Group.

FINANCIAL FACTS

Annual tuition	$45,250
Fees	$394
Cost of books	$1,300
Room & board	$13,500
% of students receiving aid	74
% of students receiving grants	74
Average award package	$33,000
Average grant	$12,827

ADMISSIONS

Admissions Selectivity Rating	96
# of applications received	1,331
% applicants accepted	30
% acceptees attending	46
Average GMAT	696
Average GPA	3.3
TOEFL required of international students	Yes
Minimum TOEFL (paper/computer)	600/100
Application fee	$100
International application fee	$100
Application Deadline/Notification	
Round 1:	10/29 / 12/21
Round 2:	1/7 / 3/11
Round 3:	3/10 / 4/30
Round 4:	4/28 / 6/2
Need-blind admissions	Yes

Applicants Also Look At

Cornell University, Duke University, Massachusetts Institute of Technology, New York University, University of Chicago, University of Michigan, University of Virginia.

EMPLOYMENT PROFILE

Career Rating	95	Grads Employed by Function	%	Avg. Salary
Primary Source of Full-time Job Acceptances		Finance	44	$92,426
School-facilitated activities	93 (72%)	Marketing	15	$90,411
Graduate-facilitated activities	34 (26%)	MIS	2	$84,750
Unknown	2 (2%)	Operations	5	$101,667
Average base starting salary	$97,394	Consulting	22	$112,918
Percent employed	95	General Management	10	$91,669
		Other	2	$120,000

Top 5 Employers Hiring Grads
Booz-Allen Hamilton; Deloitte; A.T. Kearney; Constellation Energy Group; Merck

CASE WESTERN RESERVE UNIVERSITY
WEATHERHEAD SCHOOL OF MANAGEMENT

GENERAL INFORMATION

Type of school	Private
Environment	Metropolis
Academic calendar	Semester

SURVEY SAYS...
Happy students
Smart classrooms
Solid preparation in:
Teamwork
Communication/interpersonal skills

STUDENTS

Enrollment of parent institution	10,163
Enrollment of business school	565
% male/female	69/31
% part-time	71
% minorities	9
% international	49
Average age at entry	27
Average years work experience at entry	3.4

ACADEMICS

Academic Experience Rating	**81**
Student/faculty ratio	9:1
Profs interesting rating	77
Profs accessible rating	83
% female faculty	21
% minority faculty	2

Joint Degrees
MBA/JD 4 years, MD/MBA 5 years, MS in Nursing/MBA 2.5 years, Master in nonprofit organizations/JD 4 years, Master in Nonprofit/MA 2.5 years, MBA/MS in Social Administration 2.5 years, MBA/Master of International Management 2.5 years, Master of Accountancy/MBA 2 years, MBA/Master of Public Health 2.5 years.

Prominent Alumni
John Breen, CEO (ret.) Sherwin Williams; Clayton Deutsch, Managing Partner, McKinsey & Co., Chicago; David Daberko, Chairman and CEO, National City Bank; John Neff, CEO (ret.) Vanguard Fund; Joseph Sabatini, Managing Director, JP Morgan.

Academics

Offering the "top organizational behavior program in the world," the Weatherhead School of Management at Case Western University is widely regarded as "one of the country's top graduate business programs," ensuring "brand equity in a Weatherhead degree" to all who succeed here. Students tell us that Weatherhead also excels in entrepreneurship and management information systems and that its finance program "is underrated." "I've been very impressed with it," says one student. A stellar regional reputation makes Case the ideal choice for those who "want to live and work in Ohio."

Weatherhead offers a conventional 2-year, full-time MBA, a "well-regarded" 11-month accelerated MBA, and a part-time program with great flexibility that allows students to work toward their degree at a pace that works for them. All programs include the Leadership Assessment and Development (LEAD) course, a distinctive program feature designed to help students develop long-term career goals and strategies. The Weatherhead MBA also incorporates a Strategic Issues and Applications (SIA) integrative capstone course that centers on case studies and group projects.

Not satisfied to rest on its laurels, Weatherhead is currently in a period of transformation. Students tell us that the "Administration is currently working on focusing our programs to differentiate us" and warn that "some people who came here for a specific reason that is not in the 'plan' anymore may feel they were offered something that wasn't available." A revolving door within the administration further underscores the transition. As far as deans go, one student reports, "We're on something like our fifth one in 4 years" (in reality, it's more like four deans in eight years). Some tell us that "the biggest issue is with the turnover of deans in the School of Management and some faculty leaving because of this." Things are looking up here, though; as one student puts it, "While the school has gone through a lot of change in the last few years, the new staff and administration are remarkably more accessible, transparent, capable, and inclusive in their current roles, as well as in the strategic plan for the school in the future."

Career and Placement

The Career Development Center (CDC) at Case has "a brand-new staff, and students have already been placed for full-time jobs or internships with top companies. . . . For students who haven't found a job, the CDC provides resume reviews; recorded mock interviews with staff, faculty, and alumni professionals who volunteer their time; online mock interviews; Career Fridays, which bring in speakers to give seminars on anything from case interviewing to negotiating a job offer; free access to career websites; access for students to our alumni database; feedback on actual interviews; and a library of career-related books and practice manuals for students to borrow."

Employers who frequently hire Weatherhead MBAs include: Johnson & Johnson, American Greetings, Progressive, Bristol West, Emerson Electric, PNC Bank, Ohio Savings, General Electric Company, Deloitte Touche Tohmatsu, Eaton, Ernst & Young, McKinsey & Company, National City Corporation, Key Corporation, and IBM.

Student Life and Environment

"There is a real sense of community here" among Weatherhead full-timers, who tell us that they "get to know the professors, staff, and students all very well. Many professors go on a first-name basis with students and will attend social events the school has put on." Extracurricular events include "the 'Pull up a Chair' event, which takes place once a month and is put on by professors. There have been ping-pong tournaments, a business fashion show sponsored by Talbots, and a billiards contest." Clubs including the

Entrepreneurship Venture Association, the Marketing Club, Net Impact, and the Weatherhead Wine Society are all active and allow for outside-the-classroom interaction. Weatherhead is located "in the heart of Cleveland's cultural center," within a couple of blocks of the Botanical Gardens, Severance Hall ("home of the world-renowned Cleveland Orchestra"), Cleveland Museum of Art, The Museum of Natural History, and the Children's Museum.

"There are three types of students at Weatherhead," students tell us: "Engineering/foreign students who typically lack real-world substance; young professionals who maintain work/home/school; and family/parents types who put more energy into their home life, but still contribute with their business expertise." Weatherhead's full-time student body "is about 40 percent international students which makes for an enormous amount of different ideas and backgrounds," says one student. "Each and every one of them brings a lot of experience, creativity, dedication, and ideas to the table." Many tend to be on the youngish side, however, with little in the way of professional background; some American students also find that the shaky English skills of some international students can be a barrier to communication.

Admissions

Applicants to Weatherhead MBA programs must submit the following materials to the Admissions Office: a completed application form; official copies of transcripts for every undergraduate or graduate program attended; an official GMAT score report; two letters of recommendation; a current resume; and essay responses to three questions provided as part of the application package. International students whose transcripts are not in English must have their transcripts translated and interpreted by a professional service. Students whose first language is not English must also submit an official score report for the TOEFL. All international applicants must submit a statement of financial responsibility. The school requires an interview for admission. Weatherhead prefers candidates to submit their applications online. Hard-copy applications may take longer to process, the school warns.

FINANCIAL FACTS

Annual tuition	$33,650
Fees	$3,332
Cost of books	$1,830
Room & board (on/off-campus)	$0/$16,791
% of students receiving aid	95
% of first-year students receiving aid	95
% of students receiving loans	35
% of students receiving grants	90
Average award package	$20,414
Average grant	$14,322
Average student loan debt	$51,674

ADMISSIONS

Admissions Selectivity Rating	**85**
# of applications received	286
% applicants accepted	67
% acceptees attending	48
Average GMAT	611
Range of GMAT	560–660
Average GPA	3.2
TOEFL required of international students	Yes
Minimum TOEFL (paper/computer)	600/250
Application fee	$50
International application fee	$50
Regular application deadline	3/1
Regular notification	4/15
Application Deadline/Notification	
Round 1:	12/1 / 01/31
Round 2:	01/15 / 03/1
Round 3:	03/01 / 04/15
Round 4:	03/1 / 06/01
Transfer students accepted	Yes
Transfer application policy	
Maximum number of transferable credits is 6 Semester hours from an AASCB-accredited program.	
Non-fall admissions	Yes
Need-blind admissions	Yes

Applicants Also Look At

Carnegie Mellon, The Ohio State University, University of Notre Dame, University of Pittsburgh, University of Rochester, Vanderbilt University, Washington University in St. Louis.

EMPLOYMENT PROFILE

Career Rating	**83**	**Top 5 Employers Hiring Grads**
Primary Source of Full-time Job Acceptances		IBM; American Greetings; Eaton;
School-facilitated activities	13 (32%)	Progressive; National City
Graduate-facilitated activities	9 (23%)	
Unknown	18 (45%)	
Percent employed	73	

CATHOLIC UNIVERSITY OF LEUVEN/GHENT UNIVERSITY
VLERICK LEUVEN GHENT MANAGEMENT SCHOOL

GENERAL INFORMATION

Type of school	Public

SURVEY SAYS...

Students love Leuven, VB
Solid preparation in:
Operations
Doing business in a global economy
Entrepreneurial studies

STUDENTS

Enrollment of parent institution	30,000
Enrollment of business school	250
% male/female	60/40
% out-of-state	90
% part-time	80
% international	90
Average age at entry	32
Average years work experience at entry	7

ACADEMICS

Academic Experience Rating	**92**
Student/faculty ratio	4:1
Profs interesting rating	80
Profs accessible rating	62
% female faculty	25
% minority faculty	100

Prominent Alumni

Frank Meysman, CEO, Sara Lee;
Roger Chua, COO, Banking; Bill
Bygrave, Professor/Author; Lutgart
Van Den Berghe, Corporate
Governance; Sophie Manigart,
Entrepreneurial Finance.

Academics

Executive development programs are huge at Vlerick Leuven Ghent: The Belgian business school hosts over 3,000 managers in its open-enrollment seminars and company-specific programs, but the school is also home to a growing MBA program, one whose stature around the world is growing. The school currently offers a full-time English language MBA at its Leuven campus, a part-time Dutch language MBA at its Ghent campus, and a part-time English language MBA at both campuses. The full-time general MBA can be completed in one year, as can master's degrees in marketing and financial management; an MBA in financial services takes two years to complete. In total, about 250 students pursue MBAs at VLG.

Vlerick Leuven Ghent was founded in 1953 by Professor Andre Vlerick; over the years it has developed associations with Ghent University and the Katholieke Universiteit Leuven, and today it serves as the autonomous management school of these prestigious universities, the two largest in Belgium. Association with these two more established schools provides a solid research base; the school's autonomy allows it to "build strong ties with the business community" and "enables it to respond to the development needs of this community in an optimal way," according to the school's brochure. As one student observes, "The fact that the school is backed up by two recognized universities is apparent. It benefits greatly from its location and the support and research of its two parent universities."

MBA programs at Vlerick Leuven Ghent maintain "a strong international focus" derived not only from the curriculum but also from the student body. One student writes, "The basic strength of this program is the dual academic-practical approach. On the one hand, the academic orientation of the professors builds a solid knowledge foundation, while on the other, the experiences of the rest of the multicultural group enrich the whole educational experience." Students tell us that "professors and academics show a lot of respect for the audience, are extremely knowledgeable, and have in many cases extensive personal activity in the fields of management they are covering." MBAs here especially enjoy "the specialization seminars in entrepreneurship and doing business in Europe." Many students feel, however, that "the international MBA could use more international faculty. Most teachers are from Belgium." Students also report that "the workload is extremely heavy," but add that the benefits of the program—good value in a major economic center of the European Union—outweigh any shortfalls.

Career and Placement

The Career Services Office (CSO) at Vlerick Leuven Ghent organizes regular career events on campus; the office also coordinates multi-campus events and online recruiting. In an effort to keep pace with the internationalization of the school's curriculum and student body, the CSO has spent the last few years developing business contacts throughout the world to supplement its already strong base of Belgian businesses. The CSO also offers counseling services and advice on resume writing, interviewing, searching for jobs, and salary negotiation. According to the school's website, "The intention [of the CSO's efforts] is to develop a career management program that throughout the entire year will operate as an integral part of the various courses, with presentations, interactive workshops, and networking events." The office also plans to develop "a lifelong career guidance program, whereby alumni of Vlerick Leuven Ghent Management School will become even more deeply involved in activities organized by the CSO." Students tell us these efforts are working, praising the "great alumni network."

Student Life and Environment

Full-time students at Vlerick Leuven Ghent experience a nonstop academic grind. One student reports, "Life in school starts every day (including exams period, studying for the exams, most of weekends) at 9:00 P.M. and ends at 12:00 A.M. After that, individual work at home is usually required. In this frame, the quality of life can't be good. But then again, this is a commitment well known before the enrollment, so its consistency is remarkable. I personally face time problems and issues with domestic tasks (laundry, house cleaning, nutrition). I skipped visiting my home country at Christmas to catch up with the material I needed to know . . . and this is the situation that I face [at] Easter." Some here manage to squeeze in some free time; they describe "an excellent lifestyle in the very small and safe student town of Leuven, with lots of social, sports, and cultural activities." One student notes, "Belgium is a beer-drinker's paradise. Need I say more?"

Students "represent every continent, which makes participating in the group a very interesting learning experience." They are "active social animals and real team players, and students are very much diversified in professional and academic experience and competencies."

Admissions

Admission to the Vlerick Leuven Ghent Management School requires an undergraduate degree from an institution "recognized by the relevant authorities of the home country." Work experience "is beneficial but not required." Other admissions requirements depend on the method of application; students may choose the "distance procedure" or the "on-campus assessment procedure." Both require a completed application, a resume, a copy of one's passport, and official copies of all postsecondary transcripts and diplomas. The distance procedure requires, in addition, an official GMAT score report, an official TOEFL score report (students whose native language is English are exempted from this requirement), two letters of recommendation, and a personal statement. On-campus assessment "requires your attendance at one of [the school's] in-house admission tests, which consist of an analytical test, a written comprehension test, and two personal interviews (a motivation interview and a management potential/knowledge interview)."

FINANCIAL FACTS

Annual tuition	$25,000
Cost of books	$0
Room & board	$12,000
% of students receiving aid	10
% of first-year students receiving aid	10
% of students receiving grants	10
Average student loan debt	$12,500

ADMISSIONS

Admissions Selectivity Rating	93
# of applications received	300
% applicants accepted	34
% acceptees attending	53
Average GMAT	636
Range of GMAT	600–680
Average GPA	3.5
TOEFL required of international students	Yes
Minimum TOEFL (computer)	255
Application fee	$50
International application fee	$50
Regular application deadline	6/30
Regular notification	7/14
Application Deadline/Notification	
Round 1:	01/22 / 02/01
Round 2:	03/24 / 04/01
Round 3:	06/30 / 07/14
Deferment available	Yes
Maximum length of deferment	1 year
Need-blind admissions	Yes

Applicants Also Look At

Bocconi University, Cranfield University, ESADE, HEC School of Management—Paris, IMD (International Institute for Management Development), INSEAD, RSM Erasmus University.

EMPLOYMENT PROFILE

Career Rating	85	Grads Employed by Function	% Avg. Salary
Primary Source of Full-time Job Acceptances		Finance	15 $120,000
School-facilitated activities	25 (45%)	Marketing	10 $120,000
Graduate-facilitated activities	15 (30%)	Strategic Planning	5 $120,000
Unknown	14 (25%)	Consulting	15 $120,000
Percent employed	90	Entrepreneurship	20 $120,000
		General Management	10 $120,000
		Venture Capital	5 $120,000
		Internet/New Media	5 $120,000
		Non-profit	5 $120,000

Top 5 Employers Hiring Grads

Bechtel; Inbev; Belgacom; ING Bank; US Foreign Service

CHAPMAN UNIVERSITY
THE GEORGE L. ARGYROS SCHOOL OF BUSINESS AND ECONOMICS

GENERAL INFORMATION
Type of school	Private
Affiliation	Disciples of Christ
Environment	Metropolis
Academic calendar	Semester

SURVEY SAYS...
Students love Orange, CA
Happy students
Smart classrooms
Solid preparation in:
Accounting

STUDENTS
Enrollment of parent institution	5,908
Enrollment of business school	196
% male/female	62/38
% out-of-state	13
% part-time	59
% minorities	9
% international	19
Average age at entry	25
Average years work experience at entry	2

ACADEMICS
Academic Experience Rating	**87**
Student/faculty ratio	22:1
Profs interesting rating	88
Profs accessible rating	79
% female faculty	25
% minority faculty	22

Joint Degrees
JD/MBA 4 years, MBA/MFA.

Prominent Alumni
The Honorable George Argyros, CEO, Arnel and Affiliates; The Honorable Coretta Sanchez, Member of US Congress; David Bonior, Former Member of US Congress; Steve Lavin, Sports Analyst; Michael Bell, Tony Award Nominee.

Academics

Armed with "a great reputation," an "outstanding entrepreneurial program," and "a great location right in the middle of Orange County, which makes it relatively easy for commuters to get to and makes plenty of entertainment and activities available to people on campus," Chapman University has a lot to offer the predominantly part-time student body in its MBA program. Some students will even go so far to project that Chapman will one day "be one of the best b-schools in the nation" and that they "are a part of something that is going to be very special."

Chapman's evening MBA program—which can be completed on either a part-time or full-time basis—loads students up with core requirements; 33 of the 52 credits necessary for graduation are devoted to the core here. "Small class sizes and excellent resources" complement "a very personal program" that allows students to "interact with the faculty in a better way." Full-time students also love the program's 15-month duration, which, while sometimes imposing a challenging pace, is "very good" at delivering a quick return on time invested. The school adds that "Students in the Argyros School of Business and Economics can take advantage of the classes, seminars, and scholarly opportunities afforded by our research centers: The Ralph W. Leatherby Center for Entrepreneurship and Ethics, The Walter Schmidt Center for International Business, and the A. Gary Anderson Center for Economic Research." Chapman also offers an Executive MBA program.

Chapman currently offers electives in accounting, business economics, corporate governance, entrepreneurship, environmental economics, finance, human resources, international business, management, marketing, sales, and taxation. Students report: "Entrepreneurship is currently strong and growing. It offers many opportunities for students and most of all accepts any suggestions for further expansion." Students also brag: "The school has great connections and sponsors within the community. This leads to outstanding opportunities for networking as well as learning from standout professionals not employed by the university."

Career and Placement

Chapman's MBA Career Management Center is "fast becoming a first-rate resource for emerging business leaders seeking a leg up on the job market," students report, telling us that "direct access to career counseling, alumni job referrals, and 20/20 interviews have vaulted the program to a new level." Furthermore, "The online portal provides job listings for full-time, part-time, and internship opportunities, as well as subscription access to Vault's career search resources." This service is further strengthened by "an increasing focus on networking" and a "great director and terrific staff that do a lot to communicate the availability of resources." "The business school as a whole is recognizing networking as key to the success of the schools reputation, which ties directly to the success of its students," a student notes. Students generally agree that "Chapman's career management services are a vital link for students in their pursuit of greater career opportunities" and that the office is "one of the strongest parts of the program."

ADMISSIONS CONTACT: DEBRA GONDA, ASSOCIATE DIRECTOR
ADDRESS: BECKMAN HALL, ONE UNIVERSITY DR. ORANGE, CA 92866 UNITED STATES
PHONE: 714-997-6745 • FAX: 714-997-6757
E-MAIL: GONDA@CHAPMAN.EDU • WEBSITE: WWW.CHAPMAN.EDU/ARGYROS

Student Life and Environment

Among the highlights of the Chapman MBA program are the Distinguished Speaker series and Dinner for 8 programs, both of which provide exposure to high-powered business figures and networking opportunities. As one student explains, "Tonight the Dinner for 8 is being hosted by billionaire and former ambassador George Agyros. We have had various executives of multi-billion dollar companies speak at the Distinguished Speaker series, including the CEO of Allergan, David Pyott. Their talks were inspiring and delivered in an intimate venue." More networking opportunities present themselves because "there are many alumni that are very involved with the program and willing to give back to current MBAs." "Whether they are asked to host a dinner or be a distinguished speaker, alumni are able and willing to help if given the opportunity."

Chapman MBAs enjoy a friendly environment in which they "rarely have issues finding someone to answer questions or help solve problems." "Chapman is what a University should be: a place that shapes people into outstanding business professionals." Students tend to be "on the young side" with quite a few "fresh out of undergrad" but also a good crowd of "hard-working professionals with great insights." Together these two groups create "a combination that results in a great balance."

Admissions

The admissions office factors "academic performance, leadership ability, work experience, and communication skills" into each of it decisions. The school requires a minimum GPA of 2.5 for the applicants' final two years' worth of undergraduate credits (either the final 60 semester credits or the final 90 quarter credits). All applications must include an official GMAT score report, sealed copies of official transcripts for all post-secondary academic work, two letters of recommendation "from individuals familiar with the applicant's academic or professional abilities," and a completed application with a personal statement "explaining why the applicant is interested in pursuing a graduate degree at Chapman." Two years of business-related work experience is preferred. International applicants "whose native language is not English must submit results of the Test of English as a Foreign Language (TOEFL) or International English Language Testing System (IELTS). TOEFL scores must be a minimum of 550 (paper-based), 213 (computer-based), or 80 (Internet-based) and must have been taken within two years of the date of application for admission to Chapman."

FINANCIAL FACTS

Annual tuition	$23,270
Cost of books	$3,000
Room & board	
(on/off-campus)	$9,900/$12,500
% of students receiving aid	77
% of first-year students	
receiving aid	55
% of students receiving loans	24
% of students receiving grants	14
Average award package	$19,529
Average grant	$15,000
Average student loan debt	$19,600

ADMISSIONS

Admissions Selectivity Rating	82
# of applications received	91
% applicants accepted	55
% acceptees attending	56
Average GMAT	570
Range of GMAT	528–620
Average GPA	3.3
TOEFL required of	
international students	Yes
Minimum TOEFL	
(paper/computer)	550/216
Application fee	$50
International application fee	$50
Regular application deadline	7/1
Regular notification	rolling
Deferment available	Yes
Maximum length of	
deferment	1 year
Transfer students accepted	Yes
Transfer application policy	
Transfer up to six units of course work	
Non-fall admissions	Yes
Need-blind admissions	Yes

Applicants Also Look At

California State University—Fullerton, Pepperdine University, University of California—Irvine, University of Southern California.

EMPLOYMENT PROFILE	
Career Rating	63
Percent employed	11

THE CHINESE UNIVERSITY OF HONG KONG
FACULTY OF BUSINESS ADMINISTRATION

GENERAL INFORMATION
Type of school   Public

SURVEY SAYS...
Friendly students
Good social scene
Good peer network
Smart classrooms

STUDENTS
Enrollment of parent
  institution   18,642
Enrollment of
  business school   366
% male/female   64/36
% part-time   81
% international   77
Average age at entry   28
Average years work
  experience at entry   5

ACADEMICS
Academic Experience Rating   **76**
Profs interesting rating   65
Profs accessible rating   82
% female faculty   21

Joint Degrees
JD/MBA 3–5 years.

Prominent Alumni
Mr. Lawrence Yee, Managing Director, GC, Dun & Bradstreet (HK) Ltd.; Mr. Henry Yan, Managing Director, UBS AG; Mr. Antony Hung, Manaing Director, Merrill Lynch (Asia Pacific) Ltd; Mr. Jackson Cheung, Cheif Executive, Societe Generale Asia Ltd.; Ms. Lau, Bing Ying, Managing Director, Kimberly-Clark (HK) Ltd.

Academics

In 1966, The Chinese University of Hong Kong became the first school in China to offer a full-time MBA program. Today, the university boasts one of the most reputable business schools in Asia and the Pacific, attracting students for its "international recognition, good academic reputation, and diverse teacher and student pools." A great entryway for those seeking a professional position in Hong Kong, the school boasts a "strong alumni network" in the city and an excellent reputation in the region. In particular, the school is touted for its programs in finance and marketing, with a special emphasis on Chinese business. Through lecture, case studies, group work, directed research, and discussion, classes are a balance of "individual and group efforts that cultivate teamwork among students that is important for business." Group work is particularly gratifying at CUMBA, where students comprise "a very diverse group from just about every continent. Their combined work experience and life experiences has really contributed to the program."

Maintaining a working relationship with various universities in mainland China and Taiwan, the school's "administration is very dedicated and efficient." The school attracts faculty from all over the world, and the current teaching staff includes professors from Australia, Hong Kong, Europe, New Zealand, mainland China, Southeast Asia, Taiwan, and the United States. Despite their varied origins, CUMBA faculty are deeply engaged in the Hong Kong business culture. A student attests, "Teaching staff are actively involved in the business community in areas of research and consulting. So there are lots of firsthand findings and . . . information [on] local business trends." On the whole, students appreciate the school's progressive outlook, saying professors "stay abreast of the real-life market and keep up to date with their own knowledge."

While Cantonese is the dominant language spoken in Hong Kong, courses at CUMBA are taught in English, with the exception of a few elective courses whose unique nature demands instruction in Chinese. The 54-unit curriculum consists of required core course work, followed by electives. Through electives, students have the option to pursue a concentration in one of three areas: China business, finance, or marketing. The full-time curriculum can be completed in 16 months of study, including internships. Without an internship, the program can be completed as quickly as 12 months. Either way, the program is intense, with a "busy workload and no breaks in between terms." In addition to the traditional MBA programs offered through the school, students may choose to pursue a joint-degree with partner universities in Mainland China or the HEC School of Management in France or the University of Texas at Austin.

Career and Placement

As part of the MBA experience, students at The Chinese University of Hong Kong are expected to develop career goals and design a plan of action to meet those goal. The Career Planning and Development Centre facilitates students looking for summer internship placements, as well as students looking for permanent positions after graduation. The center also hosts an executive development series on presentation, communication, and project management, and a series of career talks and interview workshops.

The school has strong ties in the Hong Kong business community, as well as a large regional alumni network. In recent years, the following companies have recruited CUMBA graduates: Cathay Pacific Airways, Citibank, NA, Deloitte Touche Tohmatsu, Esso HK, Goldman Sachs (Asia), Hang Seng Bank, IBM China/HK, Kimberly-Clark (Hong Kong), KPMG International, Merrill Lynch (Asia), Morgan Stanley, Nestlé HK, PARKnSHOP, Procter & Gamble (HK), The Bank of East Asia, and The Boston Consulting

Mr. Lawrence Chan, Adm Director, Marketing & Student Recruiting
Address: Rm. G01, Leung Kau Kui Building, CUHK Shatin, NT, Hong Kong
Phone: 011-852-2609-7783 • Fax: 011-852-2603-6289
E-mail: cumba@cuhk.edu.hk • Website: www.cuhk.edu.hk/mba

Group. In 2006, 59 percent of graduating students took positions in Hong Kong (42 percent of whom where not originally from Hong Kong), and another 35 percent accepted positions elsewhere in China. The majority of students took positions in banking and finance.

Student Life and Environment

CUMBA boasts a "beautiful campus" environment, and both part-time and full-time students take classes in the school's MBA Town Centre, a modern and spacious 900-square-meter facility located in the school's central campus. In addition to the extensive computer facilities available via the larger university, MBA students have access to over 100 microcomputers in the Town Centre, connected via LAN network. MBA students have the option of living on campus in the graduate residence halls; they also have access to the school's sports facilities, including three indoor gyms and an Olympic-sized swimming pool.

One of the major attractions of CUMBA is its diverse student population, who bring experience "from a variety of professions and cultures." Totally student run, the MBA Student's Association sponsors a broad range of social and professional events, including executive seminars, company visits, and study tours to mainland China. The school also sponsors various social and recreational events, such as charity and fund-raising activities and sports teams, although some students say "Campus life is not adapted to international students at all." Even part-timers enjoy a sense of community. One says, "I am a part-time student. Fellow students usually have dinner gatherings after school."

Admissions

To be considered for admission to CUMBA, prospective students must hold an undergraduate degree (with at least a B average), have at least 3 yeas of relevant work experience post-graduation, and submit current GMAT scores. The average GMAT score for accepted applicants changes every year; however, the class average usually hovers between 620–640. Interviews are required for all short-listed applicants, either in person or via telephone, as determined by the selection committee.

FINANCIAL FACTS

Annual tuition	$30,460
Cost of books	$11,500
Room & board	
(on/off-campus)	$3,000/$20,500
% of students receiving grants	69
Average grant	$6,793

ADMISSIONS

Admissions Selectivity Rating	**89**
# of applications received	838
% applicants accepted	56
% acceptees attending	75
Average GMAT	626
Average GPA	3.3
Application fee	$25
International application fee	$25
Regular application deadline	3/31
Regular notification	6/15
Early decision program?	Yes
ED Deadline/	
Notification	12/15 / 02/28
Deferment available	Yes
Maximum length of	
deferment	1 year
Need-blind admissions	Yes

EMPLOYMENT PROFILE

Career Rating	66	Grads Employed by Function	% Avg. Salary
Primary Source of Full-time Job Acceptances		Finance	48 NR
School-facilitated activities	1 (3%)	Human Resources	2 NR
Graduate-facilitated activities	19 (45%)	Marketing	12 NR
Unknown	22 (52%)	Strategic Planning	2 NR
Percent employed	21	Consulting	7 NR
		Entrepreneurship	10 NR
		General Management	17 NR
		Other	2 NR

Top 5 Employers Hiring Grads
Fortis Bank; JP Morgan; Goldman Sachs; 3M China

THE CITADEL
SCHOOL OF BUSINESS ADMINISTRATION

GENERAL INFORMATION
Type of school	Public
Environment	City
Academic calendar	Semester

SURVEY SAYS...
Students love Charleston, SC
Friendly students
Good peer network
Cutting edge classes
Solid preparation in:
Accounting

STUDENTS
Enrollment of parent institution	3,283
Enrollment of business school	251
% male/female	74/26
% out-of-state	16
% part-time	88
% minorities	3
Average age at entry	26

ACADEMICS
Academic Experience Rating	**72**
Student/faculty ratio	10:1
Profs interesting rating	85
Profs accessible rating	78
% female faculty	17

Joint Degrees
PharmD/MBA 4 years, MBA/Health Care Administration 2–6 years, MBA/Sports Management, MBA/International Business, MD/MBA.

Academics

The Military College of South Carolina, The Citadel operates undergraduate programs for a corps of 2,000 cadets, while simultaneously offering a range of graduate programs to 1,000 civilians in the evenings. The school's MBA program, offered through the School of Business Administration, "is accredited by the AACSB International and has an outstanding reputation for the quality of its academics." In addition to its reputation, the "low faculty to student ratio," small class sizes, and convenient evening class schedule attract a wide range of Charleston professionals to this well-recognized program. Academically, the school blends tried-and-true academic theory with practical know-how, maintaining "a good mix of some older, tenured professors, but also some new professors coming in to mix things up." Whether young or old, "the professors are all experienced professionals that are capable of lending a wide range of practical knowledge to the lessons they teach." With an excellent faculty to student ratio, "classes involve discussion and interaction," which helps to bring "theoretical and real life experiences" together in an effective manner.

By all accounts, the "School of Business office goes out of their way to answer questions, assist in admissions, class registration, and financial aid." A current student attests, "The staff is very helpful. They go out of their way to help in any way they possibly can, even if it is not their particular job." Recently, The Citadel's School of Business Administration has been busy overhauling the MBA curriculum. The recently refurbished program has a reduced number of pre-requisites and electives, and simultaneously introduces a substantial emphasis on leadership within the curriculum. Today, the MBA curriculum consists of fourteen required courses and two elective courses. Students may also take additional coursework to satisfy the requirements for a certificate in health care administration, or sports management, or continue working towards one of two joint-degree programs: PharmD/MBA or MD/MBA. One unique co-curricular offering at The Citadel is the Mentor Association, which matches business students with leaders in the local business community. Students who choose to participate in this program will be matched with a powerful business leader based on common interest and career path. Current mentors include executives at companies like Corning, Xerox, Oracle Corporation, Philip Morris, Ernst & Young, Kimberly Clark Corporation, IBM, and Wachovia Bank.

Career and Placement

The Citadel's Career Services center maintains an online job and resume database for current students and alumni. The center also has working relationships with several online job boards, which give students a wide breadth of places to begin their job hunt. In addition, the center organizes several annual career fairs, which are open to the entire school community. In recent years, the following firms have recruited students at The Citadel's career fairs: AT&T, ArborOne Financial, Computer Sciences Corporation, Elliott Davis LLC, Mass Mutual Financial Group, MetLife, and Deloitte Consulting. Students admit that "there is not as much big business in the city, therefore there is not much big-time job opportunity here." However, they are quick to point out that "the administration does the best they can at getting us totally prepared for big business."

In addition to the efforts of the Career Services team, "The Citadel's rich tradition allows its students to draw on enthusiastic alumni for guidance and support." In fact, many students feel that the school's "career network is the biggest strength" of the program, as a Citadel degree places them among the school's loyal and extensive alumni network.

ADMISSIONS CONTACT: KATHY JONES, DIRECTOR OF BUSINESS SCHOOL OPERATIONS
ADDRESS: 171 MOULTRIE STREET CHARLESTON, SC 29409 UNITED STATES
PHONE: 843-953-5257 • FAX: 843-953-6764
E-MAIL: MBADIRECTOR@CITADEL.EDU • WEBSITE: CITADEL.EDU/CSBA

Student Life and Environment

Given The Citadel's distinct identity as a military college, graduate students admit, "the Graduate School has a noticeable stigma of being ancillary to the corps of cadets." While they recognize the school's long-standing history and reputation, many feel the administration should "place more emphasis on graduate school (the new president has been much better about this)." While they aren't in the limelight, the business school nonetheless creates a nice, insular community, attracting "friendly and engaging" students from "a multitude of cultures and backgrounds." In the academic arena, "the student body is easy-going and willing to participate in class and group projects. Overall, the experience is one of learning and social gathering."

All students commute to campus from across Charleston and "because school is taught at night, there is little opportunity to mingle outside of the classroom." Nonetheless, students reassure us that "most people are extremely busy but they are happy to meet for a burger or beer." In addition, the school hosts an MBA Association, a social and networking group for graduate business students.

Admissions

Admission to the Citadel's MBA program is based on a student's scholastic aptitude and capacity for graduate study. To apply, students must submit official GMAT scores, undergraduate transcripts, two personal essays, a resume, two letters of recommendation, and, for international students, a TOEFL score. In addition, a personal interview with the Director of Business School Operations or the Director of External Programs may be required.

FINANCIAL FACTS

Annual tuition (in-state/ out-of-state)	$5,040/$9,054
Fees	$30
Room & board (on-campus)	$0

ADMISSIONS

Admissions Selectivity Rating 60*

Average GMAT	496
Range of GMAT	435–560
TOEFL required of international students	Yes
Minimum TOEFL (paper/computer)	550/213
Application fee	$30
Regular application deadline	7/20
Regular notification	7/20
Deferment available	Yes
Maximum length of deferment	1 year
Transfer students accepted	Yes
Transfer application policy A maximum of six hours credit for graduate courses from an accredited institution.	
Non-fall admissions	Yes
Need-blind admissions	Yes

Applicants Also Look At
Clemson University, Lander University.

EMPLOYMENT PROFILE	
Career Rating	62

CITY UNIVERSITY OF NEW YORK—BARUCH COLLEGE
ZICKLIN SCHOOL OF BUSINESS

GENERAL INFORMATION
Type of school	Public
Environment	Metropolis
Academic calendar	Semester

SURVEY SAYS...
Students love New York, NY
Smart classrooms
Solid preparation in:
Doing business in a global economy

STUDENTS
Enrollment of parent institution	16,524
Enrollment of business school	1,592
% male/female	57/43
% out-of-state	32
% part-time	85
% minorities	11
% international	44
Average age at entry	28
Average years work experience at entry	5.6

ACADEMICS
Academic Experience Rating	**67**
Student/faculty ratio	35:1
Profs interesting rating	66
Profs accessible rating	81
% female faculty	23
% minority faculty	5

Joint Degrees
JD/MBA 4.5 years.

Prominent Alumni
Larry Zicklin, Former Managing Partner, Neuberger Berman; Marcel Legrand, Sr. Vice President, Monster.com; JoAnn Ryan, President, ConEdison Solutions; William Newman, Founder & Chairman New Plan Excel Realty Trust; Hugh Panero, President & CEO, XM Satellite Radio.

Academics

"Baruch is the third-ranked MBA program in New York City, but the tuition is only one-third of NYU or Columbia," students at Baruch's Zicklin School of Business say, spurring many to compare a Zicklin MBA to a value stock and to describe it as "a hidden gem among MBA programs." Accounting and finance are Zicklin's strongest areas; the New York location and the presence of an on-campus simulated trading floor mean finance is also a plus discipline.

Full-time MBA students at Zicklin who participate in an honors program "have a small cohort group within a huge university (Baruch College) and an even larger university system (CUNY), so we get the best of both worlds." Perks include "personalized assistance from full-time honors staff, priority registration for classes, private study areas, numerous career panels and opportunities to meet with executives on campus, and the best professors on campus. Top that, Columbia!" Part-time students may choose between the cohort-based Accelerated Part-Time MBA program, which delivers a degree in just more than 2 years, and the Flex-Time MBA program, a more traditional part-time program in which students schedule evening classes around their typically heavy work schedules.

No matter what program students pursue, they discover that "Zicklin really leverages its New York City location well. We get some great speakers on campus and organize 'treks' to companies." The faculty draws from the city's high-powered business community; one student reports, "Some of the professors are great, and they have real-world experience, e.g., a trader is currently teaching a finance class, and even though his assignments are very long (I've already put [in] 30-plus hours on this project) I am learning a lot." Another adds, "I respect the fact that many professors are current or former executives in their respective fields. This lends an air of authenticity to the lessons and allows you to learn real-life applications, not just about what's written in a textbook." Finally, students appreciate how "Baruch is working hard to promote this school in New York City and on a more national level. This is important because it will draw more companies to recruit here and will continue to attract high-quality students. Baruch is increasing its efforts to get more alumni involved with the school and works hard to increase its presence within the business community in New York."

Career and Placement

Zicklin's Graduate Career Management Center offers business graduate students a broad range of online career development and job search tools, including self assessments and a variety of job boards. The office also schedules regular corporate presentation and information sessions and alumni events and holds regular career management workshops.

Employers who most frequently hire Zicklin graduates include: Citigroup, Colgate-Palmolive, Deloitte Touche Tohmatsu, Goldman Sachs, KPMG International, Lehman Brothers, Ernst & Young, and PricewaterhouseCoopers.

Student Life and Environment

Full-time MBAs report a deluxe graduate school experience at Baruch, telling us that "each day is packed with a wide variety of panels, speakers, and other club activities. There are numerous corporate-sponsored competitions in a variety of fields. . . . The area for the graduate students is nice, with all necessary technology and space to study." Baruch has "fantastic gym and swimming pool facilities, and the campus is very compact, and everything is reachable within minutes." Part-time students are less involved with campus life, but not completely shut out. One student writes, "Baruch has some events tailored specifically for grad students, such as the GSA Social, an event where students can meet each other, hang out, and enjoy great food from this Italian restaurant. It's definitely worth going [to], even if only for 1 hour after class."

Students note that "technology, in terms of classroom facilities, is great, especially the simulated trading floor and other career development centers," but warn that "when it comes to administrative duties, the technology is not very integrated. We have some portals that are school specific and others for the statewide requirements. At the beginning of school it was difficult to handle all of the different usernames and passwords to the different sites."

Like the population of its hometown, Zicklin's student body "is diverse and rich in experiences, be it travel, life or work experience. It really makes your classmates interesting." Zicklin has "a lot of international students. There are more than 70 different countries represented at Baruch."

Admissions

All applicants to Zicklin MBA and MS programs must have an accredited bachelor's degree or its international equivalent (official transcripts for all postsecondary academic work required) and must submit an official score report for the GMAT. Students whose first language is not English and who have not graduated from a U.S. undergraduate or graduate school must also submit an official score report for the TOEFL/TWE. Applications must also include a complete application form (hard copy or online), a current resume, two letters of recommendation (at least one should be from a current employer), and an essay describing career goals and explaining why a master's degree in business is important in achieving those goals. In addition to the above, international applicants must also submit translated copies of all transcripts and letters of recommendation; in some cases, applicants may be required to have transcripts evaluated by an independent evaluating agency such as World Educational Services. International applicants must also obtain an F-1 or J-1 visa and must submit a Declaration and Certification of Finances and an Affidavit of Support.

FINANCIAL FACTS

Annual tuition (in-state/ out-of-state)	$8,800/$17,100
Fees	$238
Cost of books	$1,200
Room & board (off-campus)	$20,000
% of students receiving aid	80
% of first-year students receiving aid	95
% of students receiving loans	19
% of students receiving grants	60
Average award package	$9,200
Average grant	$4,100
Average student loan debt	$30,000

ADMISSIONS

Admissions Selectivity Rating	79
# of applications received	1,066
% applicants accepted	67
% acceptees attending	57
Average GMAT	579
Range of GMAT	530–620
Average GPA	3.2
TOEFL required of international students	Yes
Minimum TOEFL (paper/computer)	590/243
Application fee	$125
International application fee	$125
Regular application deadline	4/30
Regular notification	6/15
Deferment available	Yes
Maximum length of deferment	1 year
Transfer students accepted	Yes
Transfer application policy Up to 12 credits from an AACSB-accredited institution may be transferred.	
Non-fall admissions	Yes
Need-blind admissions	Yes

Applicants Also Look At
Columbia University; Fordham University; Hofstra University; New York University; Pace University; Rutgers, The State University of New Jersey; St. John's University.

EMPLOYMENT PROFILE

Career Rating	83	Grads Employed by Function	% Avg. Salary
Primary Source of Full-time Job Acceptances		Finance	65 $71,907
School-facilitated activities	15 (60%)	Marketing	26 $63,746
Graduate-facilitated activities	8 (32%)	Consulting	4 NR
Unknown	2 (8%)	Other	5 NR
Average base starting salary	$71,299	**Top 5 Employers Hiring Grads**	
Percent employed	83	Ernst & Young; Deloitte; KPMG; Grant Thornton; Lehman Brothers	

CLAREMONT GRADUATE UNIVERSITY
THE PETER F. DRUCKER AND MASATOSHI ITO GRADUATE SCHOOL OF MANAGEMENT

Academics

The Peter F. Drucker and Matatoshi Ito Graduate School of Management at Claremont, known as just "Drucker" for short, finds its basic philosophy in business scholar Peter Drucker's focus on the knowledge economy and in his interest in the management of people and ideas. Flowing from that is an emphasis also on values and ethics as a basis for management and economic decisions. A recently implemented and now-required seminar called the Drucker Difference introduces all beginning MBA students to how the school approaches this—not only through courses in business policy and ethics but also how it plays out in the study of topics including economics and finance.

Students at Drucker are required to complete 32 credits of core courses, comprising slightly more than half of the 60 required for the MBA. That core includes classes in marketing, finance, and operations, as well as advanced study in strategy, and a course in morality and leadership. Students may continue with a general business orientation, select a concentration from Drucker's offerings (in strategy, finance, leadership. marketing, and global business), or choose from topics in the university's other graduate schools and obtain dual majors in fields such as biosciences and cultural management. Drucker also offers an executive MBA program and courses leading to the PhD in business. MBA Students can explore opportunities to study in England, Japan, the Netherlands, and other countries.

Small classes, high standards, and the focus on values are important to students in the program. "Drucker's reputation for ethical responsibility toward the notion of business" was an attraction for many in choosing the school in the first place, and "The intimate environment, which lends itself to a great deal of interaction with the faculty and other students," is another oft-cited strength. "Drucker School professors challenge you to use your whole brain and are always accessible outside of class," students agree . "I get to interact with them rather than a TA," one says. "Course work is extremely relevant and insightful." Professors with professional and academic experience "relate lessons learned into the course work."

The administration earns praise as well. When students hit a snag, "They are there to remedy the problem within the day, a couple of hours actually. Response times are amazing, compared to my undergrad state school," says one student. This supports an academic atmosphere that is "the industry leader in values-centered management training and multidimensional strategic thinking," students say. Here, there is an "emphasis on ethical management" and "on teamwork."

Career and Placement

Nearly three-quarters of Drucker's students attend full-time, and opinion on how helpful the school's Career Center is to both full- and part-time students is mixed. "Career services—although improving—could be more of [a] resource, and the school should arrange for, incorporate, partner, administer, and mandate internships as part of the MBA curriculum," one student reports. "We have our own representative [at the career center] now, which will really change things," another counters. Assisting students with "relationships with employers and networking" is an area that could use a boost, students agree. Ernst & Young, Southern California Edison, Western Asset Management, and Northrup Grumman are among companies that often recruit Drucker graduates.

ADMISSIONS CONTACT: BRANDON TUCK, RECRUITING & ADMISSIONS
ADDRESS: 1021 NORTH DARTMOUTH AVENUE CLAREMONT, CA 91711 UNITED STATES
PHONE: 909-607-7811 • FAX: 909-607-9104
E-MAIL: DRUCKER@CGU.EDU • WEBSITE: WWW.DRUCKER.CGU.EDU

Student Life and Environment

"We are very serious, so most of my time spent on campus is in a study room or with a study group" one student says, summing up the "intrinsically driven" but "not competitive" atmosphere that many find at Drucker. "My fellow students show a genuine interest in my success both at school and in life. We help each other through difficult times at school and in our personal lives," adds another. Many students at this school—where "Everyone knows one another by name"—come from international backgrounds, "which I think is terrific," one student notes. "The exchange and learning between people from different business and cultural background[s] has taught me quite a lot." Students agree that diversity is a benefit, but at the same time add that the school "needs more local students" and "should offer a better variety of electives during the 7:00 to10:00 P.M. time frame for students who work full-time." Those who live on campus find that "student housing is a major deficiency, especially for married students." Still, students generally agree that "Claremont is a great place to live. Weather is ideal, mountains are scenic" and the "excellent main street" is within walking distance.

Admissions

In keeping with the school's overall philosophy, the Admissions Office is committed to looking at the whole person when evaluating applicants for admission. GMAT scores are required, as are undergraduate transcripts, three letters of recommendation and a personal statement responding to questions regarding the contributions a student could make to the school's community and how the student has resolved an ethical dilemma that he or she has faced. For the executive MBA program, GMAT scores are not required; instead the school asks for at least 10 years of work experience along with a personal interview. Drucker generally accepts about half of those who apply for the MBA program. In 2007, those students had an average GMAT score of 635, a GPA of 3.18, and averaged 4 years of work experience.

FINANCIAL FACTS

Annual tuition	$42,488
Fees	$250
Cost of books	$1,500
Room & board	
(on/off-campus)	$12,000/$13,000
% of students receiving aid	67
% of first-year students	
receiving aid	65
% of students receiving loans	70
% of students receiving grants	50
Average award package	$15,000
Average grant	$6,800
Average student loan debt	$42,686

ADMISSIONS

Admissions Selectivity Rating	87
# of applications received	181
% applicants accepted	53
% acceptees attending	43
Average GMAT	635
Range of GMAT	570–700
Average GPA	3.18
TOEFL required of	
international students	Yes
Minimum TOEFL	
(paper/computer)	600/250
Application fee	$60
International application fee	$60
Application Deadline/Notification	
Round 1:	11/15 / 02/01
Round 2:	02/01 / 04/01
Round 3:	04/01 / 05/15
Round 4:	05/15 / 06/15
Deferment available	Yes
Maximum length of	
deferment	1 year
Transfer students accepted	Yes
Transfer application policy	
The maximum number of transferable credits is 10 units.	
Non-fall admissions	Yes
Need-blind admissions	Yes

Applicants Also Look At

Pepperdine University, University of California—Irvine, University of California—Los Angeles, University of Southern California.

EMPLOYMENT PROFILE

Career Rating	84	Grads Employed by Function	%	Avg. Salary
Primary Source of Full-time Job Acceptances		Finance	22	$67,875
School-facilitated activities	7 (39%)	Human Resources	11	$49,000
Graduate-facilitated activities	8 (44%)	Marketing	28	$77,800
Unknown	3 (17%)	MIS	5	$62,000
Average base starting salary	$70,361	Operations	6	$95,000
Percent employed	82	Consulting	17	$63,333
		General Management	11	$80,500

CLARK UNIVERSITY
GRADUATE SCHOOL OF MANAGEMENT

Academics

A small graduate business program strong in finance (so strong, in fact, that it offers both an MBA with a finance concentration and a Master of Science in Finance), the Graduate School of Management at Clark University offers students "a smaller community" in which they "get to know teachers personally." Clark also excels in international and global studies, an area of study that benefits greatly from the international perspectives of a "diverse student population," of whom nearly three-quarters originate from outside the U.S.

The Clark MBA "is designed to build an excellent foundation in business fundamentals and the critical management judgment needed to analyze complex situations, to plan strategic actions, and to lead people effectively" through a core curriculum of 7- and 14-week classes. Students appreciate the system's flexibility, although some feel that "there are some 7-week courses that should really be a 14-week courses (example: Quantitative Techniques for Derivatives Evaluation), and there are some 14-week classes which should really be 7-week courses (example: CEO Leadership)." Through their choice of electives, students may concentrate in accounting, finance, global business, international development, community, and environment, information systems, or marketing, or they may pursue an MBA in general management without an area of concentration.

The Clark curriculum places a lot of emphasis on "team creation," with students doing "a lot of quality work as a team." One student writes, "The classes are challenging, very interactive, and they give us plenty of opportunity to practice skills, critical decision-making, and business interactions." Professors here "are accessible for concerns or guidance" and are "extremely accommodating and willing to take the time to make sure that we all succeed." Clark's administration is "organized yet flexible."

Career and Placement

The Stevenish Career Management Center at Clark's GSOM provides a range of services, including individual advising, resume and cover letter assistance, online and hard-copy job listings, workshops, internship placement, alumni networking events, alumni professional seminars, career fairs, and on-campus recruiting events. The office also maintains a full career library. Some students still wish it would do more, telling us that "the school definitely needs to improve the career center, helping students to get more jobs and internships." They say that although the center "has gone through significant change [for the better], it still needs to work harder at getting students into the working world."

Employers who hire Clark MBAs include: Analog Devices, Anheuser-Busch, ARAMCO, Bloomberg, LP, Comcast, Dell, Deutsche Bank, EMC, Fallon Healthcare System, the Federal Reserve Bank, Fidelity Investments, General Dynamics, Hewlett-Packard, KPMG International, Lucent Technologies, Public Consulting Group, Staples, Waters Corporation, the World Bank, and the Worcester Art Museum.

Student Life and Environment

At Clark "There are plenty of activities and quality entertainment offered all week long and on weekends." That's why "You are never bored unless you choose to be." Student groups organize numerous events, including international dinners, ski trips, and parties. According to one MBA, "Life is filled with diversity, from the discussions in class to the activities at a social event. Faculty and staff have a very good relationship with students and are very helpful."

In an effort to improve campus safety, the school provides escorts to students who need to go shopping or otherwise travel within one mile of campus between 4:00 P.M. and 4:00 A.M. Students with cars may find themselves making the 1-hour drive to Boston on nights when they want some big-city entertainment.

Clark's student body includes a large international contingent that "draws heavily from China, India, and Taiwan." "Most of us come from diverse backgrounds," says one student. "I am part of a minority of students who hail from South America. I enjoy working in teams with students from India, the Middle East, and Southeast Asia. It has been a great opportunity to get to know their cultures." One student describes her fellow classmates as "interesting, well traveled, sophisticated, and charming." As a group, though, "There is often a lack of experience" from the professional world before they enter the program.

Admissions

Clark offers applicants an unusual option; the school accepts either the GMAT or the GRE. A 5-year BA/MBA program for Clark undergraduates is available. Clark requires the following of applicants: a completed admissions application; a personal essay; a current resume; two letters of recommendation; and official transcripts from all undergraduate and graduate programs previously attended. Interviews are optional. International applicants must submit all of the above as well as an official score report for the TOEFL (if their native language is other than English) and proof of the financial means to support oneself while attending the program.

FINANCIAL FACTS

Annual tuition	$22,260
Fees	$1,050
Cost of books	$800
Room & board	
(on/off-campus)	$8,400/$9,500
% of students receiving grants	40
Average award package	$10,000
Average grant	$8,000

ADMISSIONS

Admissions Selectivity Rating	86
# of applications received	262
% applicants accepted	65
% acceptees attending	46
Average GMAT	518
Range of GMAT	450–600
Average GPA	3.2
TOEFL required of international students	Yes
Minimum TOEFL (paper/computer)	550/213
Application fee	$50
International application fee	$50
Regular application deadline	6/1
Regular notification	Rolling
Deferment available	Yes
Maximum length of deferment	1 year
Transfer students accepted	Yes
Transfer application policy	

A maximum of two courses may be transferred into the program. Courses must have been taken at an AACSB accredited school.

Non-fall admissions	Yes
Need-blind admissions	Yes

Applicants Also Look At

Bentley College, Brandeis University, Northeastern University, Suffolk University, University of Massachusetts—Amherst, Worcester Polytechnic Institute.

EMPLOYMENT PROFILE

Career Rating	69	Grads Employed by Function	% Avg. Salary
Primary Source of Full-time Job Acceptances		Finance	22 $43,300
School-facilitated activities	2 (17%)	Marketing	50 $95,000
Graduate-facilitated activities	4 (33%)	MIS	6 $55,000
Unknown	6 (50%)	Operations	5 $45,000
Percent employed	58	Consulting	6 $39,000
		General Management	6 $55,000
		Internet/New Media	5 $50,000

CLARKSON UNIVERSITY
SCHOOL OF BUSINESS

GENERAL INFORMATION
Type of school	Private
Environment	Village

SURVEY SAYS...
Cutting edge classes
Smart classrooms
Solid preparation in:
General management
Operations
Teamwork
Doing business in a global economy

STUDENTS
Enrollment of parent institution	2,949
Enrollment of business school	52
% male/female	65/35
% out-of-state	21
% part-time	12
% minorities	2
% international	15
Average age at entry	24
Average years work experience at entry	2

ACADEMICS
Academic Experience Rating	**65**
Student/faculty ratio	3:1
Profs interesting rating	74
Profs accessible rating	80
% female faculty	29
% minority faculty	5

Joint Degrees
MBA/ME Engineering 2 years.

Prominent Alumni
William Harlow, VP Corporate Development; Paul Hoeft, President and CEO; Elizabeth Fessenden, President, Flexible Packaging; David Fisher, President; Vickie Cole, President and CEO.

Academics

Clarkson University is best known for its fine engineering programs, so it should come as no surprise that the focus at Clarkson University School of Business is on developing business acumen in engineers. Students recognize what makes their school special, telling us, "Clarkson's academic record is outstanding. It is a competitive engineering school with a growing business program." The curriculum stresses that students approach problem-solving creatively to "focus on the big picture." As one student explains, "Life at Clarkson is academically strenuous but a balance of mind, body, and spirit is encouraged by the business school." Clarkson's history as a "technical school" comes in handy for those students interested in the business side of engineering since "Many technical companies are attracted to the school" and the campus has "strong industry connections" and a "good reputation in the technology world."

Clarkson MBAs are anxious to get their degrees and move on, and the school's accelerated 1-year program suits their needs perfectly. One MBA writes, "After four years of undergrad I don't mind a little extra work load to have a master's in one year." Students agree that "the workload is intense" and places "a strong stress on the team-based experience." All this hard work pays off in the end, though, as students feel that "the group-work emphasis will help in future employment" and "The fast pace and large workload proves [their] ability to work under pressure." Despite this "challenging" atmosphere, students get a break from their studies during the *Globalization and Ethics Week* where corporate executives and alumni speak on various topics.

Clarkson MBAs note that the school's "small size does not sacrifice the quality of most professors." "They are always available and put in every effort to assist students," says one student. Another enthuses, "Professors are incredibly concerned with student progress. They are very accessible outside the classroom and more than willing to start up conversations in the middle of a hallway with any student." However, "They will not tell you the way to succeed. All they will do is guide you in your search to find success." In this way, "The faculty at Clarkson treat their students as equals," which MBAs appreciate.

Career and Placement

Clarkson MBAs receive career services from the Graduate Career Services Office and the university's Career Center, which serves all students at the university. The center schedules career fairs each semester, puts students in contact with Clarkson's alumni network, and provides students with access to the online job database MonsterTrak. MBAs give the office mixed reviews. Some wish it would "attract a more diverse pool of job recruiters in relation to the interests of the students in the program." "They could try to get more business related type firms," adds a student. However, others praise the "many helpful resources such as e-recruiting" that are provided.

Clarkson MBAs most frequently find work with IBM, Accenture, Lockheed Martin, GE, Cooper Industries, Frito-Lay, HSBC, Knowledge Systems and Research, Texas Instruments, and Whiting Turner. While the majority of graduates remain in the Northeast, students are placed throughout the country.

ADMISSIONS CONTACT: JOSHUA LAFAVE, ASSOCIATE DIRECTOR, GRADUATE BUSINESS PROGRAMS
ADDRESS: 8 CLARKSON AVE., CU BOX 5770 POTSDAM, NY 13699 UNITED STATES
PHONE: 315-268-6613 • FAX: 315-268-3810
E-MAIL: BUSGRAD@CLARKSON.EDU • WEBSITE: WWW.CLARKSON.EDU/MBA

Student Life and Environment

The majority of Clarkson's student body is full-time, and they report a predictable rhythm to their school days. "You are generally on campus from 8:00 A.M. until 6:00 or 7:00 P.M. There is a lot of work and a lot of meetings to attend with group members," explains one student. As it's a business school, the prevailing mood is businesslike. Students "treat each day as if it were a work day" by dressing "business casual" and acting in "a professional manner." The business school facility follows suit with its "multiple computer labs," "student lounges," and "Learning Development Labs."

Potsdam, of course, is hardly a bustling metropolis. The closest large city is Ottawa, which lies approximately 90 miles and one international border to the north. One student simply states, "It's pretty cold, unless it's summer then it's pretty hot." With "only about three bars in town which are shared with a local SUNY school," students find "not much raucous" about the social scene, saying "It's pretty ho-hum." "Unless you skate or enjoy winter sports, there isn't much else in Potsdam to do," says one student.

Some students, however, manage to see the glass as half full instead of half empty. "A vast diversity of sports, intramurals, and clubs allow students to keep busy outside of class and to socialize with their peers," explains one student. A "majority" of Clarkson students are "involved in an activity of one sort or another." Another adds that the school provides for a "fun environment." Fortunately for all, Clarkson's accelerated 1-year program keeps most students too busy to worry about what type of fun they are, or are not, missing. Students work hard all week long and through much of the weekend as well. One MBA explains, "Weekends are spent doing work all day long. You go out with friends one night a week on the weekend; that's about it."

Admissions

The admissions department at Clarkson University requires that applicants submit an undergraduate transcript, GMAT or GRE scores, TOEFL scores (if necessary), and a Test of Spoken English (TSE) (for international students whose native language is not English; the TSE can be administered via telephone), a detailed resume, two one-page personal essays, and three letters of reference. Awards of merit-based scholarships are determined during the admissions process; no separate application is required. Those requiring foundation course work prior to commencing their MBAs "may enroll in the courses at Clarkson during the summer Business Concepts Program before entering the advanced MBA program. For students doing graduate work at another university, they may be allowed to transfer in nine credit hours of graduate work."

FINANCIAL FACTS

Annual tuition	$33,215
Fees	$215
Cost of books	$2,000
Room & board	$7,000
% of students receiving aid	85
% of first-year students receiving aid	85
% of students receiving loans	75
% of students receiving grants	85
Average award package	$26,715
Average grant	$6,500
Average student loan debt	$34,930

ADMISSIONS

Admissions Selectivity Rating	**74**
# of applications received	136
% applicants accepted	74
% acceptees attending	46
Average GMAT	550
Range of GMAT	510–595
Average GPA	3.3
TOEFL required of international students	Yes
Minimum TOEFL (paper/computer)	600/250
Application fee	$25
International application fee	$35
Regular application deadline	rolling
Regular notification	rolling
Deferment available	Yes
Maximum length of deferment	1 year
Transfer students accepted	Yes
Transfer application policy Students may transfer up to 9 credit hours of graduate work from another AACSB accredited institution.	
Non-fall admissions	Yes
Need-blind admissions	Yes

Applicants Also Look At

Rensselaer Polytechnic Institute, Rochester Institute of Technology, State University of New York at Binghamton, Syracuse University, University of Rochester.

EMPLOYMENT PROFILE

Career Rating	79	Grads Employed by Function	% Avg. Salary
Primary Source of Full-time Job Acceptances		Finance	2 $45,000
School-facilitated activities	18 (51%)	Marketing	3 $50,050
Graduate-facilitated activities	13 (37%)	MIS	3 $62,500
Unknown	14 (12%)	Operations	19 $57,800
Percent employed	90	Consulting	7 $63,000

Top 5 Employers Hiring Grads
IBM; Lockheed-Martin; Stanley Works; Central Hudson; Crane

CLEMSON UNIVERSITY
COLLEGE OF BUSINESS AND BEHAVIORAL SCIENCE

GENERAL INFORMATION
Type of school	Public
Environment	Village

SURVEY SAYS...
Happy students
Smart classrooms
Solid preparation in:
Communication/interpersonal skills
Quantitative skills

STUDENTS
Enrollment of parent institution	17,585
Enrollment of business school	178
% male/female	64/36
% out-of-state	53
% part-time	67
% minorities	4
% international	29
Average age at entry	28
Average years work experience at entry	4.7

ACADEMICS
Academic Experience Rating	**77**
Student/faculty ratio	4:1
Profs interesting rating	75
Profs accessible rating	68

Joint Degrees
MBA/Master in International Management.

Prominent Alumni
J. Strom Thurmond, U.S. Senator (died 2003); Kristie A. Kenney, U.S. Ambassador to the Philippines; Robert H. Brooks, President, Naturally Fresh Foods; Nancy Humphries O'Dell, Access Hollywood co-anchor; Mark Richardson, President, Carolina Panthers.

Academics

Native South Carolinians seeking the MBA will have a hard time beating the ratio of value to quality that they'll find at Clemson University. Thanks to lower in-state tuition costs, Palmetto State residents can earn a highly regarded business degree for a small fraction of what their peers elsewhere in the country spend. Beautiful weather and first-rate intercollegiate football further sweeten the deal.

Approximately 30 full-time students enter Clemson's MBA program each year; full-timers make up a little less than half the student body. The program, students warn, "moves quickly. We complete 62 graduate-level credits in 21 months." One student explains, "I recommend the program to anyone who is confident that they can keep up with a heavy workload through effective time-management and teamwork skills." The first year is devoted entirely to foundation courses, some taught in a "highly intensive, highly rigorous seven-week format." The second year allows students to choose special-izations in one of four designated tracks (innovation and entrepreneurial leadership, supply chain and information management, real estate and marketing management). Double degrees are not uncommon here; one student in our survey was earning an MBA in tandem with an MS in Parks, Recreation, and Tourism Management, while several oth-ers noted that "Clemson is strong in engineering and research, so it's a good place for engineers and scientists seeking business education." Students in all areas praise "the reputation of the professors and the school's reputation throughout the Southeast."

Part-time classes meet in the evening at the University Center of Greenville; the program is open only to those with at least two years of work experience. The program consists of five core courses (some or all of which can be waived based on prior academic work or passing a proficiency exam), eight required advanced courses, and three electives. The program offers more flexibility than does the full-time program but also provides fewer opportunities for teamwork and group projects. Participants appreciate the fact that "classes only meet one night per week, which makes it easier on family life." They also tell us that "some professors are fantastic, and others are not so hot. Overall, though, the good outweighs the bad."

Career and Placement

Clemson MBAs benefit from the Office of MBA Career Development, which "assists students and their career development." The office offers career placement support including one-on-one professional coaching, personalized placement assistance as well as a range of self-assessment instruments, job-search counseling, interviewing and resume-writing workshops, seminars, and online job databases. Students praise the value of alumni connections but also feel that the office "needs help with national job-placement services. Clemson is very well connected within the state but not so much out-side of the state."

Companies most likely to recruit Clemson MBAs include Accenture, BB&T, Coca-Cola, Datastream Systems Inc., Deloitte Touche Tohmatsu, Duke Power Co., Hewlett-Packard, Hitachi, Lexmark International, Michelin North America, Milliken, PricewaterhouseCoopers, Procter & Gamble, Schlumberger, Sonoco, Trane Co., and Wachovia.

Student Life and Environment

"The greatest strength of Clemson University is the 'Clemson Family,'" and MBAs here agree. "The network of alumni and friends is outstanding. Every graduate is more than willing to lend a hand to a fellow Tiger." Community spirit runs especially high during football season, which "is very fun. Enthusiasm generated by the interest in football leads to better community involvement in . . . the university." The surrounding town of Clemson "is dedicated to the university. There is a small downtown area with plenty of bars/restaurants, nearby mountains/lakes, and plenty of other social activities for students to partake in." As one student sums up, "Clemson University is a special place. There are plenty of opportunities for intramural sports, nightlife, guest lectures and speeches, university events, and cultural events."

Clemson MBAs tend to be "laid-back people keeping very rigorous schedules. Small-town life helps because there aren't too many distractions." They are "very supportive of one another. We aid each other through study sessions, workshops, and other methods to ensure that everyone understands the material." One full-time MBA points out, "The other students are truly what make this program excellent. I have built so many friendships that I know I will take with me into the business world. We often take trips together, including spring break, study abroad, professional seminars, etc. Working so closely over the past few years in the classroom has really helped us to become tightly knit and great friends outside of the classroom."

Admissions

Applicants to the MBA program at Clemson must submit a current resume (two years of work experience are required for the Career Accelerator curriculum; work experience is preferred, but not required, for the Career Launch curriculum); one official transcripts representing all undergraduate work (an overall GPA of at least 3.0 in a non-business major is preferred); two letters of recommendation; a one- to two-page personal statement (required of applicants to the Career Launch MBA); phone interview and an official GMAT score report (score of at least 580 preferred for applicants to the full-time program). Non-native English speakers applying to the full-time program must submit TOEFL scores.

FINANCIAL FACTS

Annual tuition (in-state/ out-of-state)	$7,282/$14,570
Cost of books	$1,700
Room & board	$11,480
% of students receiving aid	64
% of first-year students receiving aid	70
% of students receiving loans	26
Average award package	$8,601

ADMISSIONS

Admissions Selectivity Rating	82
# of applications received	122
% applicants accepted	67
% acceptees attending	56
Average GMAT	595
Range of GMAT	540–650
Average GPA	3.4
TOEFL required of international students	Yes
Minimum TOEFL (paper/computer)	580/237
Application fee	$55
International application fee	$55
Regular application deadline	6/15
Regular notification	6/30
Deferment available	Yes
Maximum length of deferment	1 year
Transfer students accepted	Yes
Transfer application policy Can transfer a maximum of 12 Semester hours of acceptable coursework.	
Non-fall admissions	Yes
Need-blind admissions	Yes

Applicants Also Look At
Auburn University, University of South Carolina.

EMPLOYMENT PROFILE			
Career Rating	**78**	**Grads Employed by Function**	**% Avg. Salary**
Primary Source of Full-time Job Acceptances		Human Resources	7 NR
School-facilitated activities	5 (38%)	Marketing	29 $75,665
Graduate-facilitated activities	5 (38%)	Operations	14 $60,000
Unknown	3 (24%)	Consulting	14 $75,000
Percent employed	76	General Management	29 NR
		Non-profit	7: NR

Top 5 Employers Hiring Grads
Resurgent Capital Services; General Electric; Lockheed Martin; America Online; Schneider Electric

THE COLLEGE OF WILLIAM & MARY
THE MASON SCHOOL OF BUSINESS

GENERAL INFORMATION
Type of school	Public
Environment	Village
Academic calendar	Semester

SURVEY SAYS...
Friendly students
Solid preparation in:
Finance
Teamwork
Communication/interpersonal skills
Presentation skills
Quantitative skills

STUDENTS
Enrollment of parent institution	7,500
Enrollment of business school	304
% male/female	72/28
% out-of-state	24
% part-time	57
% minorities	6
% international	35
Average age at entry	26
Average years work experience at entry	3.5

ACADEMICS
Academic Experience Rating	**85**
Student/faculty ratio	2:1
Profs interesting rating	95
Profs accessible rating	98
% female faculty	18
% minority faculty	21

Joint Degrees
MBA/JD 4 years, MBA/MPP 3 years, MGM w/ Thunderbird 2.5 years.

Prominent Alumni
C. Michael Petters, CEO, Northrop Grumman Newport News; Mr. Gary M. Pfeiffer, CFO, E.I. DuPont de Nemours, Inc.; Mr. Daniel J. Ludeman, President & CEO, Wachovia Securities; Mr. C. Larry Pope, President & COO, Smithfield Foods; James "Buck" McCabe, CFO, Chick-fil-A.

Academics

Students speak highly of the curriculum at the College of William & Mary 's Mason School of Business, but for most it's "the intangibles, particularly the Executive Partners network, Career Acceleration Modules, and Field Consultancy Programs" that elevate this program and have MBAs declaring it "absolutely wonderful." Mason offers three MBA options, one full-time and two part-time. Part-time options include the flex MBA, a nine-semester sequence consisting of 3-hour, once-weekly classes; and the executive MBA, with classes meeting on alternate weekends.

Full-timers rave about the school's Executive Partners network, "a mentorship program for students under the auspice of our Leadership Class" that takes advantage of "Williamsburg's dozens of retired C-level executives who tire of golf and are looking to participate. Those men and women are a huge resource," as they "hold more knowledge than you can access in your time with them (luckily they respond to e-mails and take phone calls as well). They volunteer to come help us and genuinely care about how we do. They are worth their weight in gold."

Mason's Career Acceleration Modes in entrepreneurship, investments and financial services, corporate finance, B2B Marketing, B2C Marketing, and Enterprise Engineering combine training and field projects for companies such as Philip Morris, DuPont, and Hamilton Beach. Field Consultancy Programs puts second-year students to work consulting for the likes of Cox Communications, Sprint, and Blue Cross and Blue Shield Association. Students tell us that both experiences are invaluable.

Mason also shines in the less glamorous task of teaching the MBA curriculum. Professors "are absolutely amazing. They will blow you away with their across-the-board commitment to helping the students completely understand the material." The curriculum itself "puts a strong emphasis on teamwork, leaving no doubt that we will come out extremely well prepared to deal with others both in and out of the workforce." Mason's current facility "is a bit outdated, but we're expecting a brand new state-of-the-art facility in 2009. It would definitely improve the classroom atmosphere and study rooms." One student points out that "prospective students should look at the trajectory of a program. With the expansion of the program and the new building on its way, William & Mary is well on its way to establishing itself as a top-notch MBA program that can reasonably compare itself to Fuqua and Darden."

Career and Placement

Students tell us that recruiting is on the upswing at the Mason School, although "due to the size of the school, there are only certain companies willing to come to campus to recruit." There is, however, a select group that comes here, and it is growing over time. The Executive Partners network has been a recruiting boon, "grooming students to find positions within current recruiting firms and attracting distant companies to campus once they see what students at this little school can do." Students also point out that "when a student decides to pursue an alternative career or company, the Career Services Office is very helpful in developing strategies for that student."

Top employers of Mason MBAs include: Google, Kelloggs, Limited Brands, McKesson, Johnson & Johnson, North Highland Consulting, Chatham Financial, Bearingpoint, Wachovia Securities, Booz Allen Hamilton, Legg Mason, Vanguard, HSBC, Bank of America, IBM, Perot Systems, and Smithfield.

ADMISSIONS CONTACT: KATHY WILLIAMS PATTISON, DIRECTOR, MBA ADMISSIONS
ADDRESS: PO BOX 8795, BLOW HALL, OFFICE 254 WILLIAMSBURG, VA 23187 UNITED STATES
PHONE: 757-221-2900 • FAX: 757-221-2958
E-MAIL: ADMISSIONS@MASON.WM.EDU • WEBSITE: MASON.WM.EDU/MASON

Student Life and Environment

For full-time students at Mason, "The first half of the day is spent in classroom. In the second half, a student ends up partly completing team assignments and partly completing individual assignments." Team projects "create the opportunity to interact with other students" and develop "a great deal of camaraderie, but it is an intense 2 years full of self-improvement and demanding course work." Many students "spend evenings studying late, usually past midnight."

Even so, students do find time to socialize. The opportunities in town are limited, as Williamsburg offers only "a small-town environment. If that's what you want, you will love it here. It is beautiful and safe and loaded with historical activities. Big city it is not. Williamsburg is great, and it is very community based. You will get to know your classmates very well. It is easy to feel very comfortable." Students see an upside to the challenges Williamsburg presents. One student writes, "There are only three bars, and that forces students in the b-school and law school to excel socially. Any large town has a big enough nightlife to seem exciting. We make ours exciting—city social scenes are cake after having fun in such a small environment."

Admissions

Applicants to the full-time, flex, and executive MBA programs must submit official academic transcripts for all undergraduate and graduate work; an official GMAT score report; letters of recommendation; personal essays; and a resume. International applicants whose first language is not English must submit official score reports for either the TOEFL or the IELTS.

FINANCIAL FACTS

Annual tuition (in-state/ out-of-state)	$16,140/$27,930
Fees (in-state/ out-of-state)	$5,260/$5,470
Cost of books	$1,500
Room & board	$15,349
% of students receiving aid	74
% of first-year students receiving aid	70
% of students receiving loans	44
% of students receiving grants	34
Average award package	$18,650
Average grant	$14,080
Average student loan debt	$37,743

ADMISSIONS

Admissions Selectivity Rating	**81**
# of applications received	303
% applicants accepted	59
% acceptees attending	45
Average GMAT	613
Range of GMAT	540–690
TOEFL required of international students	Yes
Minimum TOEFL (paper/computer)	600/250
Application fee	$100
International application fee	$100
Regular application deadline	4/1
Regular notification	5/1
Need-blind admissions	Yes

Applicants Also Look At

Pennsylvania State University, University of Virginia, Vanderbilt University, Wake Forest University.

EMPLOYMENT PROFILE

Career Rating	85	Grads Employed by Function	% Avg. Salary
Primary Source of Full-time Job Acceptances		Finance/Accounting	33 $80,456
School-facilitated activities	23 (59%)	Marketing/Sales	14 $64,500
Graduate-facilitated activities	13 (33%)	Operations/Production	6 NR
Unknown	3 (8%)	Consulting	33 $75,090
Average base starting salary	$76,297	General Management	11 $89,200
Percent employed	83	MIS	3 NR

Top 5 Employers Hiring Grads

Wachovia/Wachovia Securities; IBM/IBM Consulting Services; Bearingpoint; Perot Systems; Google

COLORADO STATE UNIVERSITY
COLLEGE OF BUSINESS

Academics

A distance-learning leader, Colorado State University has consistently endeavored to deliver one of the best distance-learning MBAs in the country. Its efforts seem to have paid off. Students in the program agree that "the CSU School of Business is an innovator in distance-learning techniques; it has worked the kinks out both academically and operationally." The school also offers a part-time evening MBA program. Both the evening and the distance-learning MBA are "comprehensive lockstep programs" that are identical in content.

Here's how the CSU MBA works: Part-time MBAs attend classes on campus two evenings for 21 months, and the distance MBA can be completed in the same period of time or extended for up to four years. Classes are taped, burned to DVD, and sent to students in the distance-learning program. Distance learners tell us that their program "seems less 'distancy' because of the recorded lectures on DVD and the fact that we have the identical pace and curriculum as the on-campus students." Students in both programs keep in touch with their professors and each other through a communications software product that allows professors to post assignments and students to complete projects in a virtual meeting space. One student writes, "The program requires extensive use of work teams in a virtual environment, which is 100 percent what a graduate will likely experience in today's business world, because most coworkers will be located in another building, state, time zone, or country."

Whether they complete the program on campus or at home, students enjoy a curriculum that "is not just theory, but very heavy on application. What is taught has immediate applications at my job," comments one working student. CSU professors "are tough and require a heavy workload," but they are also "understanding of the demands on part-time students" and can be "flexible with emergencies." They "teach cutting-edge theory and practice" and are informed by their own experience in the business world. "All professors have worked or are currently working in the industry they are teaching us about. The adjunct professors are also well qualified and put a tremendous amount of time into the students." Accounting, economics, and finance are reportedly the faculty's strongest areas. Perhaps the greatest drawback of the program is that it offers only a general MBA. One student explains, "The school does not offer electives, only core courses." Nearly all students here agree that CSU's strengths far outweigh its weaknesses, however; sums up one MBA, "The school is very ambitious and works hard to create a program that really serves the business students. It is an outstanding program."

Career and Placement

The part-time nature of CSU's MBA program is designed for working professionals, who comprise the vast majority of the student body. The school maintains a College of Business Career Liaison to coordinate activities between the College of Business and the university's Career Center, but the responsibilities of this office are primarily aimed at serving undergraduates. This doesn't have much of an impact on MBAs, however, since most CSU MBAs already have good jobs with such powerhouses as Agilent, Argen, Celestica, Colgate-Palmolive, ConAgra, FedEx, Hewlett-Packard, Honeywell, MCI WorldCom, National Textiles, Parson Group, Siemens, Sun Microsystems, UPS, and Wells Fargo Bank.

ADMISSIONS CONTACT: RACHEL STOLL, GRADUATE ADMISSIONS COORDINATOR
ADDRESS: 164 ROCKWELL HALL, 1270 CAMPUS DELIVERY FORT COLLINS, CO 80523-1270 U.S.
PHONE: 970-491-3704 • FAX: 970-491-3481
E-MAIL: RACHEL.STOLL@COLOSTATE.EDU • WEBSITE: WWW.BIZ.COLOSTATE.EDU/MBA

Student Life and Environment

Nestled in the foothills of the Rockies "with a beautiful view," Colorado State University "is a thriving, vibrant community" of 24,000 students, 1,550 faculty, and numerous administrators and employees. The school offers "great access to many academic and social venues, and a pleasant campus atmosphere that supports learning." Taking advantage of these proves "a little tough for older students. Within the MBA program, people are juggling so many balls that they hardly have time to partake." Those who can manage a few free moments enjoy and appreciate the "strong clubs and activities [and] plenty of intramural sports." Many distance students "never visit the campus at all," however.

Among the on-campus student body, "work experiences vary from vet students to engineers in high-tech companies to nurses and general mangers at *Fortune* 100 companies." One MBA writes, "There are even some students who work for not-for-profit firms, which adds yet another level of interest to class discussions and the overall quality of the program at Colorado State University." One student notes, however, that "the program does attract a lot of professional engineers. I wish there were more variety in terms of work experience." A solid mix of international MBAs includes "students from Asia, Latin America, and Canada." Distance learners come "from all types of backgrounds and from all over the place." The average age of students is around 35, and the typical CSU student has about 10 to 15 years of work experience.

Admissions

CSU admits on-campus MBAs in the fall only; distance learners are admitted for either the fall or the spring semester. All applicants must submit a completed application form, a resume, a cover letter, an official GMAT score report, two copies of official transcripts for all postsecondary academic work, and three recommendations. Applicants whose native language is not English must also submit an official TOEFL score report. According to the school's website, CSU looks to "select a richly diverse set of students with various undergraduate degrees and professional experiences. Additional requirements include a minimum of four years post-undergraduate professional work experience, previous academic performance, GMAT scores, work experience, and recommendations are some of the factors considered. In addition, the applicant's personal cover letter should reflect carefully considered reasons for pursuing a business degree at the master's level." Applicants with GPAs below 3.0 must include a letter explaining the circumstances under which they received such grades.

ADMISSIONS

Admissions Selectivity Rating	**79**
# of applications received	206
% applicants accepted	86
% acceptees attending	84
Average GMAT	620
Range of GMAT	530–650
Average GPA	3.2
TOEFL required of international students	Yes
Minimum TOEFL (paper/computer)	565/227
Application fee	$50
International application fee	$50
Regular application deadline	5/1
Regular notification	6/1
Deferment available	Yes
Maximum length of deferment	1 year
Non-fall admissions	Yes
Need-blind admissions	Yes

Applicants Also Look At

Arizona State University, Florida State University.

COLUMBIA UNIVERSITY
COLUMBIA BUSINESS SCHOOL

Academics

When it comes to business education, Columbia University has an almost unfair advantage over its competitors: its New York City address. Students here tout "the only great business school in New York City, which gives it a huge advantage over the Harvards and Stanfords of the world" because "whether or not you want to stay here, access to New York City is an unmatched experience that cannot be overstated: The connections made, the speakers we get, the opportunities to visit company offices, are incredible." As one student looking to get into the media and entertainment industry puts it, "New York city location gives access to real world in whatever field one desires…there are so many alums and industry experts in my desired area that Columbia Business School connects me with."

Columbia excels in finance—a natural fit for a b-school in a world finance capital—as well as in related fields like accounting and economics. One student immersed in all three assures us that "The faculty in these departments are outstanding and widely recognized outside of the school. I've had Fed officials, C-level finance managers and well-known investment managers teaching my electives." But these disciplines are just the tip of the iceberg; Columbia also offers outstanding programs in social enterprise and development, real estate, marketing (featuring another NYC touch: a focus on luxury goods), entrepreneurship, and management. There's "a great international focus" throughout the "very analytical" curriculum, which includes "a well-rounded core curriculum and amazing electives across all disciplines."

Columbia's location means "many opportunities for part-time internships as well as networking events. These off-campus opportunities are equivalent to taking several extra classes" and "are an invaluable resource for learning about industries and a great addition to material covered in class." It also means that the school can supplement its "globally respected" full-time faculty with "many adjunct professors who are leaders in their industry and are well positioned to incorporate real-world issues." Students warn, "The workload intensity doesn't seem to abate during the second year" as it does in other top programs; coupled with recruiting activities, this makes for "a schedule that can be overwhelming for even the most robotic among us." They also complain that CU's facilities are "old and cramped" but add that plans for a new building are in the works.

Career and Placement

The Career Management Center at Columbia benefits from a tremendous parlay: a top-flight business school located in the financial capital of the world. The office helps students coordinate internship and employment searches and also provides "a range of complementary resources…ranging from intimate workshops on interviewing and presentation skills to a five-part course on different aspects of the job," according to the school's website. The CSO also draws from the region's many business leaders for lectures, seminars, and panel discussions. The school reports: "Hundreds of employers actively recruit at Columbia Business School each year, conducting thousands of on-campus interviews and numerous corporate presentations. Columbia also receives thousands of job postings for off-campus full-time and intern positions." Students add, "Recruiting opportunities and alumni are the greatest strengths of the program. Recruiting is very intense because recruiters are all over you the minute you step in the door. This lasts until you succumb to one of them and take your resume off the market by accepting an offer."

Nearly half the class of 2007 landed in the finance sector; one-fifth of the class found work in consulting (average starting salary $113,824). Top employers include: McKinsey

& Company, Citi, Goldman Sachs & Co., Deutsche Bank, Booz Allen Hamilton, JP Morgan, Merrill Lynch, Lehman Brothers, Morgan Stanley, Boston Consulting Group.

Student Life and Environment

Columbia MBAs are organized into 'clusters,' groups of "65 or so students with whom you take most of your classes." Students love the system, saying, "It's unbelievable and builds everlasting and close-knit relationships among students." One student tells us: "Most of your social life takes place with your cluster. They become your new family. However, it is completely OK to have your own life outside of school and no one judges you for not attending every event. But, if you want to do nothing but socialize with classmates, there is something you could be doing every night of the week." And not just on campus; there's "great balance given the location" that "allows you to have your own life outside of school." Restaurants, bars, clubs, all manner of entertainment, museums, parks, and just about anything else you can imagine is a subway ride away.

Campus life is quite robust; students "have to balance the myriad activities and events taking place at and around campus. On a given day, one might have to choose between studying, listening to a Wall Street CEO speak on campus, attending one of a number of recruiting presentations, attending a club meeting, or hitting the bars with classmates. Overall, though, I'd rather have too many choices than none at all, and some of the choices are remarkable. I've crossed both Jim Cramer and John Mack (Morgan Stanley CEO) in the bathroom on campus." The program is home to more than "[90] student-run clubs and associations."

Admissions

The Admissions Department at Columbia notes, "Columbia Business School selects applicants from varied business and other backgrounds who have the potential to become successful global leaders. Their common denominators are a record of achievement, demonstrated leadership and the ability to work as members of a team." The school also reports: "By design, efforts are made to admit students who add different perspectives to the learning experience. In this way, students are continually learning from the diverse professional experiences and cultural/geographical backgrounds of their classmates. Columbia Business School has also maintained, through a concerted strategic effort, one of the highest enrollments of women and underrepresented minorities among top business schools. The Office of Admissions, in conjunction with the School's Black Business Students Association, Hispanic Business Association, and African American Alumni Association, sponsors information sessions and receptions for prospective students. Fellowships are also available for minority students." Admission to the program is extremely competitive.

FINANCIAL FACTS

Annual tuition	$43,436
Fees	$1,986
Cost of books	$900
Room & board	$18,900

ADMISSIONS

Admissions Selectivity Rating	99
# of applications received	5,623
% applicants accepted	16
% acceptees attending	77
Average GMAT	707
Range of GMAT	660–760
Average GPA	3.4
TOEFL required of international students	Yes
Application fee	$250
International application fee	$250
Regular application deadline	4/22
Regular notification	Rolling
Early decision program?	Yes
ED Deadline/Notification September entry	10/8 / 12/30
Non-fall admissions	Yes
Need-blind admissions	Yes

Applicants Also Look At

Harvard University, Stanford University, University of Pennsylvania.

EMPLOYMENT PROFILE

Career Rating	96	Grads Employed by Function	%	Avg. Salary
Primary Source of Full-time Job Acceptances		Finance	54	$105,700
School-facilitated activities	299 (52%)	Marketing	7	$92,438
Graduate-facilitated activities	79 (14%)	Operations	1	$117,500
Unknown	194 (34%)	Consulting	27	$113,824
Average base starting salary	$107,265	General Management	3	$123,000
Percent employed	93	Other	8	$107,280

Top 5 Employers Hiring Grads
McKinsey & Company; Citi; Goldman Sachs; Deutsche Bank; Booz Allen Hamilton

CONCORDIA UNIVERSITY
JOHN MOLSON SCHOOL OF BUSINESS

GENERAL INFORMATION
Type of school	Public
Academic calendar	Trimester

SURVEY SAYS...
Students love Montreal, QC
Good peer network
Solid preparation in:
Marketing
Teamwork

STUDENTS
Enrollment of parent institution	44,533
Enrollment of business school	450
% male/female	17/83
% out-of-state	54
% part-time	41
% international	37
Average age at entry	29
Average years work experience at entry	6

ACADEMICS
Academic Experience Rating	**87**
Student/faculty ratio	12:1
Profs interesting rating	83
Profs accessible rating	68
% female faculty	26

Prominent Alumni
Irving Teitelbaum, Founder, Chairman and CEO, La Senza; Keith Conklin, President and CEO, Nestle Canada; Alice Keung, Senior Vice President of Information Technology; Lawrence Bloomberg, Former COO, National Bank; Jean-Yves Monette, Executive President & CEO Van Houtte Café.

Academics

The John Molson School of Business MBA program "is steeped in pragmatism," students tell us. "This isn't a theoretical program. You come out of the JMSB able to apply the stuff you learned in the workplace" because "whenever possible, we learn by doing." As one student explains, "I could have gone to another business school in Montreal that has a better brand name, but I felt at John Molson I would be able to learn more everyday tools that I can apply in the real world, and not just a bunch of models that don't fit the real world." "Strong ties with the business community and great alumni" add further value to a JMSB MBA.

Finance and marketing are the strongest areas here, students tell us. Executive MBA students report that the EMBA-only aviation management program is also good. Molson professors are "leaders in their respective fields" who are "knowledgeable...and for the most part, do an excellent job communicating this knowledge in a passionate way." The administration is "quite friendly and helpful for day-to-day questions," though "there are bureaucratic issues within the school (such as the lack of a standard grading scale)." "Overall, though," one student says, "it's pretty good."

One of the high points of the school's academic year is the John Molson MBA Case Competition, held on campus and billed as "the only truly global case competition in the world." JMSB students are extremely passionate about this event. The Concordia Small Business Consulting Bureau offers students another opportunity to flex their business muscles while helping local businesses fine-tune their business plans and reach new consumers. The school offers a co-op option to all full-time students; the school's big-city setting strengthens this option considerably.

Career and Placement

In the past students have reported problems with career services at Concordia, but those seem to be a thing of the past "as new management of the Career Management Services Center arrived last year and is putting together many initiatives to make graduate students have a much better chance of connecting with employers and take charge of their job search." The office has also "worked hard to foster cooperation between career placement and the co-op program," exploiting previously underutilized synergies. The center provides the standard complement of career counseling, guest lectures, mock interviews, job postings, and seminars in networking, resume writing, and salary negotiation.

Employers who most frequently hire Molson MBAs include Royal Bank, Bombardier, Deloitte Consulting, CIBC, Hasbro, Deutsche Bank, ICAO, Lafarge North America, IMS Health, and CN. Approximately one-third of Concordia MBAs take jobs in consulting; about one-quarter wind up in marketing and sales.

ADMISSIONS CONTACT: D'ARCY RYAN, DIRECTOR, ADMINISTRATIVE & ACADEMIC SERVICES
ADDRESS: 1455 DE MAISONNEUVE BLVD. WEST, GM 710 MONTREAL, QC H3G 1M8 CANADA
PHONE: 514-848-2727 • FAX: 514-848-2816
E-MAIL: E_LOBO@JMSB.CONCORDIA.CA • WEBSITE: WWW.JOHNMOLSON.CONCORDIA.CA

Student Life and Environment

"There are many student-run clubs and thus activities abound" for Concordia MBAs, "making it extremely easy to participate beyond the regular classroom…and bond outside of school." Organizations provide "various initiatives going on throughout the year," including "a social event every Thursday, and some sort of dinner or big social networking event about twice per semester." Students engage in "some charity events as well: hockey, poker tournaments, and fundraising for Breast Cancer and Make-a-Wish Foundation." One student opines that Concordia provides "a great environment not only in which to learn but also to network."

The vibe at Concordia is "very informal and open." "Students come and go from the lounge to their classes and openly share their insights or talents to assist others," a student explains. "It's a very team-oriented atmosphere, and not as cutthroat as I thought it would be." Students happily report that "a new building for the John Molson School of Business will be open in 2009 and the student social spaces will be more generous." Many are "especially excited about it being a green building, the first building in the world whose heat and power will be generated by solar panels."

Molson students are "a diverse lot," "with a good number of international students as well as a varied range of work experience backgrounds." About half "work full time and study part time while still taking an impressive course load." "The full-time students are extremely involved in student life, even more so than the part-time students, running events and case competitions and doing extremely well at it," one student says. "The networking opportunities are amazing and you finish your business school with a large extended network of friends that have bonded with you through many shared experiences beyond the classroom." As another student puts it, "The social experience at the JMSB is phenomenal. I have made friends for life."

Admissions

Concordia admissions officers seek students with "real-world work experience, strong academic backgrounds, clear career objectives, and a commitment to excellence." Applicants must meet the following minimum requirements: undergraduate GPA of 3.0; two years of full-time work experience; a GMAT score of 600; and, for international students who have not previously completed an undergraduate degree in English or French, a TOEFL score of 600 (paper-based), 250 (computerized), or an IELTS score of at least 7.0. Career/leadership potential, level of maturity, communication skills, and how closely the student's goals match those of the program are also weighed. Complete applications include a personal essay, a resume, official undergraduate transcripts, three letters of recommendation, and test scores. Applications are processed on a rolling basis, a method that favors those applying early.

FINANCIAL FACTS

Annual tuition (in-state/ out-of-state)	$1,668/$12,000
Fees (in-state/ out-of-state)	$945/$1,000
Cost of books	$3,992
Room & board (on/off-campus)	$4,842/$10,688
% of students receiving aid	28
% of first-year students receiving aid	32
Average award package	$9,000
Average grant	$8,111

ADMISSIONS

Admissions Selectivity Rating	88
# of applications received	458
% applicants accepted	43
% acceptees attending	55
Average GMAT	616
Range of GMAT	620–690
Average GPA	3.0
TOEFL required of international students	Yes
Minimum TOEFL (paper/computer)	600/250
Application fee	$64
International application fee	$64
Regular application deadline	Rolling
Regular notification	Rolling
Application Deadline	
Round 1:	June
Round 2:	Oct
Round 3:	Feb
Early decision program?	Yes
Deferment available	Yes
Maximum length of deferment	1 year
Transfer students accepted	Yes
Transfer application policy Applicants may be eligible for advanced standing.	
Non-fall admissions	Yes
Need-blind admissions	Yes

Applicants Also Look At

HEC Montreal, McGill University, Queen's University, University of Toronto, York University.

EMPLOYMENT PROFILE

Career Rating	76	Grads Employed by Function	% Avg. Salary
		Finance	14 NR
		Marketing	24 NR
		Operations	21 NR
		Consulting	34 NR
		General Management	3 NR

Top 5 Employers Hiring Grads
Bombardier; Deloitte Consulting

CORNELL UNIVERSITY
JOHNSON GRADUATE SCHOOL OF MANAGEMENT

GENERAL INFORMATION

Type of school	Private
Environment	Town
Academic calendar	Semester

SURVEY SAYS...

Friendly students
Good peer network
Helpful alumni
Smart classrooms
Solid preparation in:
Finance
Accounting

STUDENTS

Enrollment of parent institution	20,638
Enrollment of business school	267
% male/female	72/28
% minorities	22
% international	26
Average age at entry	27
Average years work experience at entry	5

ACADEMICS

Academic Experience Rating	**95**
Profs interesting rating	85
Profs accessible rating	98
% female faculty	34
% minority faculty	34

Joint Degrees

MBA/MILR, MBA/MEng, MBA/MA
Asian Studies, JD/MBA 4 years,
MBA/MPS-RE, MD/MBA 5 years.

Prominent Alumni

Jim Morgan, Chairman of Applied
Materials; Dan Hesse, President and
CEO, Nextel Corp.; Nancy
Schlichtina, CEO, Henry Ford Health
Systems; H. Fisk Johnson,
Chairman of S.C. Johnson and Son;
Warren Staley, Chairman and CEO
of Cargill Incorporated.

Academics

Students praise the "variety of MBA programs and areas of study" at Cornell University's Johnson Graduate School of Management, where an Accelerated MBA and Executive MBA program complement the traditional 2-year MBA. They also praise the availability of "specialized courses during the first year." The first year consists of eight required courses (Microeconomics for Management, Financial Accounting, Marketing Management, Statistics for Management, Managerial Finance, and Strategy, Managing Operations, and Managing and Leading in Organizations) and a choice of electives or participation in the Immersion Learning program. Eighty percent of students choose to participate in this "well-structured" practicum, which "provides great preparation" to "career switchers" and internship-seekers. Second year students choose an all-elective program. This system, says one student, "allowed me to become a real expert in the field I have selected." Among other strong specializations is the Asset Management track, bolstered by a student-run trading floor with a "$14-million-dollar hedge fund," and an investment studio in the Parker Center for Investment Research. Students also reserve high praise for the Center for Sustainable Global Enterprise, which gives students "amazing access to [top] companies" and schools them in "the strategic advantages a focus on sustainability can offer to innovative private enterprise." Johnson also offers 23 international business courses and study abroad opportunities in numerous countries.

Students say that Johnson's "world-class faculty" is "very accessible." ("I have gotten rides to school by my professors who see me waiting for the bus," says one student.) They also appreciate that the academics allow for more of a work-life balance than at some other schools ("There are no regular courses on Fridays . . . which makes it easier to take short vacations or just relax"). In addition, "The school encourages pursuits outside Johnson," "from cooking classes at the Hotel School to athletic classes (such as sailing on the lake)."

Career and Placement

Johnson alumni "pull us into the top firms," says one MBA candidate. Another affirms, "Cornellians can call any other Cornellian anywhere in the world and we help each other." Where "others care about the consequences of helping, we just do it." In addition, "Our career center is awesome. They really help students find relevant jobs." The top employers of Johnson graduates are American Express, Citigroup, General Electric Company, Deloitte Touche Tohmatsu, JP Morgan, Amgen, Bear Stearns, Deutsche Bank, Johnson & Johnson. The average starting salary is $98,600, with international students reporting slightly lower salaries than domestic students. Ninety percent of the last graduating class received offers before commencement.

Student Life and Environment

Students say Cornell deserves its reputation as "the 'nice' business school," where "Students get ties out of their locker to help classmates make a great impression at I-banking and consulting corporate briefings." In other words, Cornell students will "gladly help a struggling classmate out anytime." "We hunt as a pack," says one MBA candidate of his "bright and collaborative" peers. As if to underscore the "collegial" climate, Johnson students don't hesitate to praise one other. "My classmates are bright, motivated, genuine people who are all about results," says one student. "People here don't talk about themselves all the time like a lot of business types—they just get the job done." Another adds that Johnson students are "some of the smartest students amongst all schools, but the difference is that Johnson students won't tell you how smart they are." "Students, especial-

ADMISSIONS CONTACT: MR. RANDALL SAWYER, DIRECTOR, ADMISSIONS AND FINANCIAL AID
ADDRESS: 111 SAGE HALL ITHACA, NEW YORK 14853, NY 14853 UNITED STATES
PHONE: 607-255-4526 • FAX: 607-255-0065
E-MAIL: MBA@JOHNSON.CORNELL.EDU • WEBSITE: WWW.JOHNSON.CORNELL.EDU

ly those in the Sustainable Enterprise program, are extremely intelligent nontraditional thinkers and intent on exploring ways new ways of doing business."

Hometown Ithaca is famous for its "beautiful scenery" and "outdoor activities such as cliff climbing, yachting, and hiking." It's also isolated and cold, qualities that foster intimacy among the small student body. "At the Johnson School, it is always 70 degrees and bright . . . in the atrium," jokes one student, a place where "We have frequent social hours." Students are extremely active in nearly 70 organized teams and clubs ("Spouses/partners are welcome and encouraged to join these organizations"), and spend their scanty free time winding down together. "On weekends, there is usually one big social event at night where the majority of the school will gather, and the rest of the weekend is typically spent with smaller groups of friends at a variety of locales." "Whether it's the indoor soccer club playing at 11:00 P.M. on a Sunday night, or the whole lot of us crowding the Palms (a local bar) on Thursday nights, you will always find a group of us out doing something enjoyable." One student warns, "If you enjoy going to dive bars and getting drunk with classmates this is the place for you. If you seek international conversation about global events over wine, look elsewhere."

Admissions

The Johnson application is online only and includes three 400-word essays (two mandatory, one optional). Mandatory topics cover professional achievement and career goals, and the optional essay may be used to detail extenuating circumstances or provide additional bolstering information. Johnson initially reviews applicants through a two-reader system; those who make the cut receive an interview, and only disputed files go to committee. As with other systems, this simply means that it pays to present an extremely strong case for admission. Last year's entering class reported an average GPA of 3.3, average GMAT score of 680, and 5 years of work experience.

FINANCIAL FACTS

Annual tuition	$44,950
Fees	$1,550
Cost of books	$1,100
Room & board	$10,750
% of students receiving aid	78
% of students receiving loans	66
% of students receiving grants	40
Average award package	$48,212
Average student loan debt	$73,800

ADMISSIONS

Admissions Selectivity Rating	96
# of applications received	2,177
% applicants accepted	25
% acceptees attending	49
Average GMAT	680
Range of GMAT	480–770
Average GPA	3.27
TOEFL required of international students	Yes
Minimum TOEFL (paper/computer)	600/250
Application fee	$200
International application fee	$200
Regular application deadline	
Regular notification	
Application Deadline/Notification	
Round 1:	10/10 / 12/7
Round 2:	11/14 / 1/11
Round 3:	1/9 / 3/5
Round 4:	3/19 / 4/30
Non-fall admissions	Yes
Need-blind admissions	Yes

Applicants Also Look At

Columbia University, Dartmouth College, Harvard University, Northwestern University, University of Michigan, University of Pennsylvania.

EMPLOYMENT PROFILE

Career Rating	96	Grads Employed by Function	% Avg. Salary
Primary Source of Full-time Job Acceptances		Finance	23 $95,700
School-facilitated activities	172 (64%)	Marketing	22 $93,600
Graduate-facilitated activities	95 (36%)	Consulting	18 $112,600
Average base starting salary	$98,600	General Management	11 $92,500
Percent employed	95	Other	4 $98,500

Top 5 Employers Hiring Grads
Citi; General Electric; Deloitte Consulting LLP; JP Morgan; McKinsey & Company

DARTMOUTH COLLEGE
TUCK SCHOOL OF BUSINESS

GENERAL INFORMATION

Type of school	Private
Environment	Village
Academic calendar	Quarters

SURVEY SAYS...

Good social scene
Good peer network
Helpful alumni
Solid preparation in:
General management
Teamwork

STUDENTS

Enrollment of parent institution	5,700
Enrollment of business school	500
% male/female	66/34
% minorities	16
% international	35
Average age at entry	28
Average years work experience at entry	5

ACADEMICS

Academic Experience Rating	**98**
Student/faculty ratio	9:1
Profs interesting rating	88
Profs accessible rating	99
% female faculty	23
% minority faculty	15

Joint Degrees

MBA/MALD, MBA/MPA, MBA/MSEL, MBA/MA, MD/MBA, MPH/MBA, MEM/MBA.

Prominent Alumni

Steven Roth, Chairman and CEO, Vornado Realty Trust; Elyse Allan, President & CEO, General Electric Canada; Roger McNamee, Co-Founder & Advisory Director, Elevation Partners; Thomas McInerney, Chairman and CEO, ING Insurance Americas; Debi Brooks, Co-Founder, Michael J. Fox Foundation.

Academics

There is no rest for the weary at Tuck, where the "intensive academic core for first-years is accelerated and rigorous." During the elongated (32-week) school year, students take 16 courses, only one of which is elective. One of these is Tuck's trademark First-Year Project, a course in which student teams develop new business ventures or act as consultants in existing ventures, and in which grades rest on the final presentation and other outcomes. This method reflects Tuck's emphasis on "academic deliverables, such as group papers, projects, and presentations." The second year consists of 12 elective courses, which may reflect well-rounded interests or a specialization. For example, Tuck recommends that a student interested in nonprofit and sustainability management take Corporate Social Responsibility, Entrepreneurship in the Social Sector I and II, Ethics in Action, the Tuck Global Consultancy international field study, and Strategic Responses to Market Failure. One student reports, "I feel completely prepared to take on my career post-Tuck. The school does a fantastic job of working students hard in the first year, teaching them the core fundamentals of business, and letting them craft their own paths during the second year." One student notes, "Tuck could update its core curriculum and case study assignments to reflect the current business environment, i.e., more standard courses to better understand the private-market investment climate, corporate ethics, digital media/entertainment, and emerging economies."

Tuck operates through "full immersion." Students "do a lot of work in study groups, which are assigned and required for first-years." Mandatory team rotation forces each student to work closely with a wide swath of his or her peers during the first year. The small class size and isolated location reinforces class cohesiveness and fosters intimacy between MBA students and Tuck faculty and staff. Professors host social "gatherings at their homes and get involved with student organizations." "I have had lunches, dinners, or drinks with the majority of my professors," reports one second-year, "and I am treated with a respect that goes beyond [typical] teacher-student interactions." Administrators are "the nicest people on Earth." Some have even been known to "come in on a Sunday evening and bring food and coffee for us when we have exams." The overall "quality" of faculty and administration alike is "extraordinary."

Career and Placement

Tuck is "very focused on helping students land the jobs they came here to get." "The Career Development Office works tirelessly on behalf of students," though this benefit is most useful for students pursuing "traditional career paths (i.e., consulting, finance, general management)." However, "students interested in other opportunities (i.e., marketing, retail) may need to do more work outside the Career Development Office." Dartmouth is a magnet for recruiters, and "one of the best parts of Tuck is that visiting executives spend meaningful time with us. They don't stop by on their way to another meeting; rather, they have lunch and/or dinner with us, hold individual office hours, and make an effort to share their experiences with members of the class." Recruitment is Northeast focused, but the career office "is continually trying to reach out to West Coast firms"—the ones who often "recruit locally at Stanford and UCLA"—"and does a couple of treks for students interested in returning to the West." The tides may be turning; one student reports seeing "Google, Microsoft, and PG&E on campus this year," a possible "indication that a more diverse lineup of firms [is] coming to Tuck."

Students seeking jobs in "nontraditional" vocations and regions will have better luck with Tuck's extremely strong, supportive alumni network. One student told this story of success: "I e-mailed a Tuck alum who is a managing director at a bulge-bracket investment bank in London, and he called me 5 minutes later to talk. He arranged a personal office visit...and

ADMISSIONS CONTACT: DAWNA CLARKE, DIRECTOR OF ADMISSIONS
ADDRESS: 100 TUCK HALL HANOVER, NH 03755 UNITED STATES
PHONE: 603-646-3162 • FAX: 603-646-1441
E-MAIL: TUCK.ADMISSIONS@DARTMOUTH.EDU • WEBSITE: WWW.TUCK.DARTMOUTH.EDU

actually talked HR into sending me straight to second round interviews, because the firm's London office didn't recruit on campus...all because I put 'Tuck' in the subject line."

Tuck's most recent graduating class reports a median total annual compensation of $160,000. Top employers includeMcKinsey's & Company; Lehmen Brothers; Bain & Company; Boston Consulting Group; and Oliver Nyman.

Student Life and Environment

Students call posh, pretty Hanover "the quintessential small, New England, Ivy League town," "within a short drive of many great ski resorts" and far removed "from the hustle and bustle of a big city." Unlike many schools, most first-years live on campus. Couples and families live in the Dartmouth-owned Sachem Village housing complex or elsewhere off-campus. The environment is extremely "intimate" and "supportive." Tuckies consider their school very family-friendly, telling us that partners are an integral part of the social scene, and note that "classmates who have children while at Tuck" are surrounded by a "phenomenal support network." Tuck is very inclusive of gay and lesbian students and partners.

The isolated location and clustered housing contribute to "a great deal of school spirit" and "strong camaraderie" in a "work-hard, play-hard environment." "Tuck students really transplant their lives to be here...we make friends quickly here and socialize a lot with our classmates." Students belong to more than 60 clubs, teams, and publications, and attend numerous social functions every week. "The end of the week is typically characterized by social mixers (Tuck Tails), small group dinners...and the occasional full-blown party (winter and spring formals, Tuck Vegas, beach party)." Students report that "sports are very much a part of life at Tuck."

No one gripes about the intimacy, which results in great friendships and means close business ties in the future. "I have had a substantive conversation with each of my 240 classmates and will feel very comfortable calling any of them after graduation for career advice and/or business counsel," reports one Tuckie. Feelings seem to differ when it comes to partying, however. Many students are happy that "ice hockey and beer pong are just as much a part of the Tuck experience as Decision Science and Global Economics," while others aren't wild about "re-living [their] college frat-house experience." The class of 2009 is 36 percent international and an additional 16 percent of color, but students would like to see "more Africans and African Americans" in their class.

Admissions

Like many other schools, Tuck wants to know that you love it for what it is, not only for what it can do for you; show that you have researched the school thoroughly. The class of 2009 reports an average GPA of 3.5 and GMAT score of 713.

FINANCIAL FACTS

Annual tuition	$40,650
Fees	$275
Cost of books	$3,025
Room & board (on/off-campus)	$9,725/$11,030
% of students receiving aid	78
% of first-year students receiving aid	79
% of students receiving loans	87
% of students receiving grants	54
Average award package	$50,428
Average grant	$15,372
Average student loan debt	$90,078

ADMISSIONS

Admissions Selectivity Rating	98
# of applications received	2,584
% applicants accepted	19
% acceptees attending	51
Average GMAT	713
Range of GMAT	660–760
Average GPA	3.46
TOEFL required of international students	Yes
Application fee	$220
International application fee	$220
Application Deadline/Notification	
Round 1:	10/10 / 12/14
Round 2:	11/14 / 2/8
Round 3:	1/9 / 3/21
Round 4:	4/2 / 5/16
Early decision program?	Yes
ED Deadline/ Notification	10/10 / 12/14
Deferment available	Yes
Maximum length of deferment	case by case basis
Need-blind admissions	Yes

Applicants Also Look At

Columbia University, Harvard University, Northwestern University, Stanford University, University of Pennsylvania.

EMPLOYMENT PROFILE

Career Rating		98	Grads Employed by Function	% Avg. Salary
Average base starting salary		$107,406	Finance	39 $103,716
Percent employed		96	Marketing	8 $93,934
			Operations	1 NR
			Consulting	36 $115,699
			General Management	8 $107,687
			Other	8 $101,820

Top 5 Employers Hiring Grads

McKinsey & Company; Lehman Brothers; Bain & Company; Boston Consulting Group; Oliver Wyman

DELAWARE STATE UNIVERSITY
COLLEGE OF BUSINESS

GENERAL INFORMATION

Type of school	Public

SURVEY SAYS...

Good peer network
Solid preparation in:
Accounting
Operations
Teamwork
Communication/interpersonal skills
Presentation skills
Quantitative skills
Computer skills
Doing business in a global economy
Entrepreneurial studies

STUDENTS

Enrollment of parent institution	0
Enrollment of MBA program	82
% male/female	38/62
% out-of-state	34
% part-time	15
% minorities	71
% international	33
Average age at entry	26
Average years work experience at entry	2

ACADEMICS

Academic Experience Rating	**61**
Profs interesting rating	61
Profs accessible rating	82
% female faculty	10
% minority faculty	80

Academics

Most of the students enrolled in the MBA program at Delaware State University's College of Business choose the program for its "convenient location" and for its attention to the needs of the "working professionals and aspiring managers" who attend here (classes are held exclusively during evening hours and weekends). The school describes its MBA as "an accelerated program geared towards working adults" that can be completed in 18 months by those taking two courses per eight-week term and in just 12 months by those taking three courses per term. Even those shouldering a lighter workload can complete the program in two years by attending at least one summer session.

The DSU MBA program is designed to promote integrative learning in a functional context so that students can build important managerial and organizational skills. The program requires students to complete 21 credit hours of core courses, one capstone course, and nine credit hours of electives, which can be used to pursue a concentration in a single subject. Students lacking corresponding undergraduate coursework may be required to take some or all of 18 credit hours in foundation courses. Foundation courses cover the following subjects: accounting, economics, finance, management information systems, marketing, and quantitative methods. Students may attempt to place out of any of these courses by passing a comprehensive exam, developed by the College of Business faculty, in the subject.

DSU's required core courses cover advanced economics, marketing management, business law and ethics, financial management, organizational leadership and behavior, operations analysis and management, and information and technology management. The capstone course is entitled Applied Strategic Management. Electives are offered in finance, information systems, and general management; concentrations are available in finance and information systems. Students may also participate in a case project in order to fulfill one of their elective requirements. According to the school's website, the case project "tests the student's strategic thinking and analytic skills" by requiring students either to (1) assess a company's income statement, balance sheet, annual reports, and other such documentation and provide recommendations; (2) manage an investment portfolio; or, (3) analyze "a series of general management cases that cover a broad range of strategic issues facing companies."

In order to graduate, students must earn a minimum grade point average of 3.0 with no more than six credit hours with a grade of C. Students who receive a grade of D or F during a course will be dismissed from the program; the school has procedures in place for students to appeal dismissal and/or academic probation. Students are required to complete the program in no more than five years.

Career and Placement

According to the school's website, the DSU Career Services office provides "technological and practical resources to provide students with the talent to conduct job searches, to become proficient in effective interviewing and presentation, and understanding the fit between their competencies and occupational requirements. Students also gain marketable experience through on- and off-campus collegiate activities, campus and community service, research projects, cooperative education, and internships to prepare them to manage their careers pre- and post-graduation." The service is designed primarily for the benefit of undergraduates, although graduate students and recent alumni may also utilize it.

ADMISSIONS CONTACT: KISHOR SHETH, DIRECTOR OF MBA PROGRAM
ADDRESS: DELAWARE STATE UNIVERSITY, MBA OFFICE, 1200 NORTH DUPONT HIGHWAY DOVER,
DE 19901 UNITED STATES • PHONE: 302-857-6906 • FAX: 302-857-6945
E-MAIL: KCSHETH@DESU.EDU • WEBSITE: DESU.EDU

Student Life and Environment

Students in the DSU MBA program form "a very culturally and ethnically diverse" group. Most are "hard-working students with full time jobs" and "many have families to support," but there are also "some fresh college grads" in the mix. These "dedicated and helpful" students contribute to an intellectually challenging atmosphere."

DSU is located in Dover, the state capital. The state government and the United States Air Force are among the area's top employers; others include Playtex, Procter & Gamble, and General Mills, all of which have manufacturing facilities in or around Dover. The city is conveniently located, with fairly easy access to Philadelphia, Washington DC, and Baltimore.

Admissions

Applicants to the Delaware State MBA program must submit the following documentation to the Admissions Committee: a completed application; official transcripts for all previous undergraduate and graduate work; an official score report for the GMAT; two letters of recommendation from individuals capable of assessing the candidate's ability to succeed in a graduate business program; a resume; and, a personal statement of career objectives and personal philosophy. In order to earn unconditional admission, applicants must have completed all foundations courses at the undergraduate level, and they must show an undergraduate GPA of at least 2.75, a minimum GMAT score of 400, and earn a score of at least 975 under the formula [(undergraduate GPA ? 200) + GMAT score]. Applicants failing to meet these requirements may be admitted conditionally if they have an undergraduate GPA of at least 2.5 and a minimum GMAT score of 400; or, have an undergraduate GPA of at least 3.0 or an upper-division GPA of at least 3.25; or, meet all requirements except for the foundations requirement. Students admitted conditionally will have their status changed to 'unconditional admission' once they have completed three MBA-level courses with a grade of at least B; they must submit a satisfactory GMAT score before being allowed to register for a fourth MBA-level course. Applicants with significant work experience (at least five years) in management may apply for admission as non-traditional students; the school may waive GPA and GMAT requirements for such applicants.

FINANCIAL FACTS

Annual tuition (in-state/ out-of-state)	$10,320/$22,860
Fees	$525
Cost of books	$1,500
Room & board (on/off-campus)	$10,380/$7,320

ADMISSIONS

Admissions Selectivity Rating	**62**
# of applications received	91
% applicants accepted	90
% acceptees attending	100
Average GMAT	400
Range of GMAT	350–660
Average GPA	2.75
TOEFL required of international students	Yes
Application fee	$40
International application fee	$40
Deferment available	Yes
Maximum length of deferment	1 year
Transfer students accepted	Yes
Transfer application policy	Credits may be transferred at the discretion of the MBA Director
Non-fall admissions	Yes

Applicants Also Look At
University of Delaware.

DREXEL UNIVERSITY
BENNETT S. LEBOW COLLEGE OF BUSINESS

GENERAL INFORMATION
Type of school	Private

SURVEY SAYS...
Students love Philadelphia, PA
Smart classrooms
Solid preparation in:
Accounting

STUDENTS
Enrollment of parent institution	18,466
Enrollment of business school	784
% male/female	56/44
% out-of-state	60
% part-time	71
% minorities	17
% international	57
Average age at entry	34
Average years work experience at entry	7.5

ACADEMICS
Academic Experience Rating	**80**
Student/faculty ratio	26:1
Profs interesting rating	74
Profs accessible rating	85
% female faculty	33
% minority faculty	30

Joint Degrees
MD/MBA, MBA/MS in Television Management, JD/MBA.

Prominent Alumni
Raj Gupta, Chairman & CEO, Rohm & Haas; Nicholas DeBenedictis, Chairman, AquaAmerica; Gary Bernstein, Vice President, IBM; Elaine M. Garzarelli, Frm Exec VP Lehman Bros., Pres Garzarelli Capitol; Dominic J. Frederico, Chairman, President and CEO, Assured Guaranty.

Academics

Drexel University is "a top-ranking engineering school," so it should come as no surprise that its LeBow College of Business "has a great reputation for running a hands-on applied program" with "a solid focus on technology." The school's "applied learning philosophy" drives a co-op program "that's one of the best in the country, allowing students to graduate with relevant work experience in their field of study."

LeBow works hard to meet students' needs, offering "a tremendous diversity in the number of programs. There is a program available to meet your individual needs based on your personal and professional lives." These include a 1-year and a 2-year full-time MBA (the former is "the only 1-year program in Philadelphia and includes an international trip in the spring term to provide hands-on international learning"); a 2-year evening cohort MBA (called the LEAD MBA, for LeBow Evening Accelerated Drexel MBA, this program "is very convenient for working professionals, with all classes held on the same 2 nights of the week throughout the program and all classes scheduled by the school"); a more traditional part-time professional MBA; and an online part-time MBA called MBA Anywhere, "which is flexible enough to fit your work schedule, yet has three campus residencies as well, allowing interaction with fellow students." In addition, LeBow also offers an executive MBA and several corporate on-site programs.

Many of the programs offer a broad range of choices in area of concentration (the 1-year program does not offer concentration, only a general MBA). Techie disciplines such as MIS do well here; students also extol offerings in entrepreneurship (the Baiada Center for Entrepreneurship is known as one of the school's many assets), health care systems, and financial management. LeBow also offers a concentration in operations management with a focus on supply chain management. In all disciplines, Drexel professors "are active in research and publishing and are always willing to answer questions about classwork" and are "demanding but fair" in the classroom. "Many are Wharton professors who have simply transferred across the street," students tell us.

Career and Placement

The LeBow Career Services Office is "great with one-on-one sessions and tries hard to be extremely helpful." One MBA writes, "I have found the office very helpful in providing pointers to enhance my resume as well as in providing contact information for companies of interest." Even so, many students feel that "the office could do a better job of bringing recruiters on campus to recruit those of us with 5-plus years of work experience. It seems that the majority of the recruiters that come on campus are primarily recruiting those individuals that have little to no work experience."

Employers most likely to hire LeBow MBAs include: Deloitte Touche Tohmatsu, Guardian, Lockheed Martin, PricewaterhouseCoopers, Citizens Bank, Siemens, Merck, SAP, Rohm & Haas, and Vanguard.

Student Life and Environment

Drexel's location "is excellent, because Philadelphia is a big city with lots of opportunities. Proximity to other big cities like New York City, Baltimore, and Washington, DC is another advantage." University City, the neighborhood in which Drexel is located, provides "lots of great shops and restaurants. Philadelphia has numerous museums, a wide variety of restaurants, theaters, etc. Students have the opportunity to explore the city because downtown is so close."

Full-time students enjoy a full slate of extracurricular activities, telling us that The MBA Association is "the greatest asset of the school." "The association has networking events, organizes social outings in Philadelphia, finds professional networking opportunities for fellow students, establishes [and] administers clubs, holds weekly happy hours, liaises between the students and the administration, organizes field trips, and has many other events. Registration into the association is not mandatory, but by the end of the first quarter most students are signed on, because of how the association makes life at Drexel more enjoyable." One student reports that "there seems to be a buzz on campus about the increased student activity in clubs." Part-time students don't participate as heavily outside the classroom since "A lot of activities organized by student groups often conflict with evening class schedules." Those in the LEAD MBA program tell us they "meet twice a week for classes and try to connect via e-mail daily to give each other tips and words of wisdom. Drexel always has a spread of food and drinks for us when we arrive, which is great! After a long day at work and a 3-plus-hour class on finance, it's nice to have a sweet snack to keep you going." LeBow's facilities include "a new business building with a number of computers, a Starbucks, and classrooms that are laid out well for discussions and presentations."

Admissions

Admissions requirements vary by program at LeBow. According to the school's website, LeBow "is interested in well-rounded applicants who have a consistent record of significant achievement and outstanding potential for future success in a variety of areas." Applicants must provide the Admissions Committee with official copies of all college and university transcripts; GMAT scores; letters of recommendation; a personal statement; and a resume. An interview is optional and typically occurs only if the school requests one. Students whose first language is not English and who do not hold an academic degree from a U.S. institution must also submit an official score report for the TOEFL.

FINANCIAL FACTS

Annual tuition	$50,100
Fees	$800
Cost of books	$1,200
Room & board	
(off-campus)	$15,000
% of students receiving grants	64
Average grant	$15,500

ADMISSIONS

Admissions Selectivity Rating	**92**
# of applications received	718
% applicants accepted	50
% acceptees attending	64
Average GMAT	610
Range of GMAT	540–660
Average GPA	3.21
TOEFL required of	
international students	Yes
Minimum TOEFL	
(paper/computer)	600/250
Application fee	$50
International application fee	$50
Regular application deadline	8/24
Regular notification	Rolling
Early decision program?	Yes
ED Deadline/Notification	
Summer: 10/01 and 12/01 / 01/01	
Deferment available	Yes
Maximum length of	
deferment	12 months
Transfer students accepted	Yes
Transfer application policy	
Completed application and all supporting materials to be reviewed by Admissions Committee.	
Non-fall admissions	Yes
Need-blind admissions	Yes

Applicants Also Look At
Temple University, University of Pennsylvania, Villanova University.

EMPLOYMENT PROFILE

Career Rating	69	Grads Employed by Function	%	Avg. Salary
Primary Source of Full-time Job Acceptances		Finance	42	$66,144
Average base starting salary	$61,021	Human Resources	3	$0
Percent employed	23	Marketing	31	$52,833
		MIS	5	$0
		Operations	3	$0
		Consulting	5	$0
		General Management	8	$0
		Other	3	$0

Top 5 Employers Hiring Grads
Deloitte & Touche; Bank of America; TIAA Cref; PriceWaterhouseCoopers; Campbell Soup Company

DUKE UNIVERSITY
THE FUQUA SCHOOL OF BUSINESS

Academics

Student involvement—not just in academics, but in all facets of extracurricular life—is a hallmark of the MBA program at Duke's Fuqua School of Business. Students here use the term "Team Fuqua" to sum up the collaborative spirit that binds MBAs, professors, and administration. "A strong focus on leadership" is fostered by the school's Center on Leadership and Ethics and "Coach K [Duke basketball coach Mike Krzyzewski, to the uninitiated] takes an active role in this organization and provides an excellent link to real-world leadership."

Fuqua terms are "rapid-paced," lasting only six weeks (classes meet in two two-hour sessions weekly). The curriculum "emphasizes leadership and communication skills," with outstanding offerings in marketing, finance, and health management. Students describe the program as "well-balanced, with strengths in many areas," and boast that it "allows [them] to explore many different options." One MBA student says that the professors are "leaders in their fields. They are engaged in the class, and they are highly passionate about their subjects. It's hard to imagine a professor making basic accounting enjoyable, but my professor has me loving the class because of his energy and passion."

Students and administrators are also on the same team at Duke. "Fuqua is exceptionally responsive to student feedback, and any issue is resolved quickly." For example, "Duke University has made a specific point in the last two years to get its top professors back into teaching core courses after some weakness two years ago in student reviews of core classes. They have been successful, and it has made the core course offerings very strong." Duke MBAs are deeply involved in nearly all aspects of managing the program, which they describe as "almost completely student-run. Almost any event you attend—whether career, speaker, social, or otherwise—is devised, organized, and marketed by students."

Duke also offers three Executive MBA options: an MBA Weekend Program that meets alternate weekends in Durham; an MBA Global Program that combines distance learning and international in-classroom residencies; and the MBA Cross Continent Program that combines week-long international residencies and distance learning. The Global Program requires a minimum of 10 years of professional experience; the Cross Continent Program is designed for less experienced managers.

Career and Placement

Students agree that Fuqua's Career Management Center "has recently taken a huge step forward." The hiring of a new director and additional staff has resulted in improved services and enhanced communication between the CMC and students. "Career counselors are extremely dedicated and have even been known to come in on the weekends to help students/clubs," students tell us. The CMC also boasts "a new online tool that makes the job application and research process a lot simpler and more user-friendly." As a bonus, alumni are "phenomenally loyal. Alums bend over backward to help students find jobs and offer career wisdom."

Employers most likely to hire Fuqua MBAs include Johnson & Johnson, IBM, American Express Company, McKinsey & Company, Kraft Foods, Citigroup, Deloitte Consulting, Bank of America, Bear Sterns, DuPont, and Eli Lilly & Company.

ADMISSIONS CONTACT: LIZ HARGROVE RILEY, ASSISTANT DEAN AND DIRECTOR OF ADMISSIONS
ADDRESS: 1 TOWERVIEW DRIVE DURHAM, NC 27708-0104 UNITED STATES
PHONE: 919-660-7705 • FAX: 919-681-8026
E-MAIL: ADMISSIONS-INFO@FUQUA.DUKE.EDU • WEBSITE: WWW.FUQUA.DUKE.EDU

Student Life and Environment

Duke offers "excellent health care and leadership resources." The Team Fuqua spirit pervades all aspects of life at Duke, including extracurricular activities. On Fuqua Fridays, the school "provides free food, beer, and wine to all Fuqua students, faculty, and their families." One happy student writes, "It's great to see everyone outside of the classroom, and to meet people's wives, husbands, and kids." MBAs also enjoy "regular cultural events," such as "two International Food Festivals each year, International Week, Asian Festival, Latin American/South American events, and events with European business leaders." Students "arrange an annual MBA Games event at which many top-tier business schools compete." The school uses the "monies raised to help the North Carolina Special Olympics athletes to compete." Despite their busy schedules, students also find time to collaborate on FuquaVision, an *SNL*-like parody of life at Fuqua produced "at least once per term. The films are a riot and really show the initiative of students here."

Basketball fanatics could hardly find a happier home, nor could golf enthusiasts; the Duke course is the best of many excellent local facilities available to Duke students. Students point out that "the weather here is great, and the area is outstanding for families." Hometown Durham, although small, "has tons of great restaurants and more to do than most people think." It also offers easy access to Raleigh and Chapel Hill; together the three cities form North Carolina's Triangle region, which offers a decent (if sprawling) approximation of urban amenities. One student sums up, "With 800 like-minded classmates around, a great climate, awesome natural resources, and (Chapel Hill's) Franklin Street only a short drive away, there is plenty to do. The culture and people are great, and school will suck up any ounce of time you give it."

Admissions

Applicants to the Fuqua MBA program must provide the Admissions Department with a one-page business resume, three essays (describe your work experience; describe your career goals; explain what you will contribute to the Fuqua Program), official GMAT scores, official transcripts for all postsecondary academic work, and two recommendations. An interview, though not required, is "strongly encouraged." International students must also provide official TOEFL scores if English is not their first language. To promote recruitment of underrepresented students, Duke conducts MBA Workshops for Minority Applicants, participates in "aggressive minority scholarship programs with partners, including the Toigo Foundation," and hosts the Leadership Education and Development (LEAD) Summer Business Institute. The Weekend Executive MBA prefers at least five years of professional experience; the Global Executive MBA requires a minimum of 10 years' professional experience; the Cross Continent Executive MBA requires three to nine years' experience.

FINANCIAL FACTS

Annual tuition	$41,670
Fees	$3,993
Cost of books	$3,640
Room & board (off-campus)	$13,900
% of students receiving aid	74
% of first-year students receiving aid	75
% of students receiving loans	65
% of students receiving grants	40
Average award package	$48,217
Average grant	$14,977
Average student loan debt	$82,155

ADMISSIONS

Admissions Selectivity Rating	95
# of applications received	2,955
Average GMAT	690
Range of GMAT	650–720
Average GPA	3.4
TOEFL required of international students	Yes
Application fee	$185
International application fee	$185
Application Deadline/Notification	
Round 1:	11/1 / 1/18
Round 2:	1/3 / 3/7
Round 3:	3/3 / 4/21
Deferment available	Yes
Maximum length of deferment	conditional
Need-blind admissions	Yes

EMPLOYMENT PROFILE

Career Rating	96	Grads Employed by Function	%	Avg. Salary
Primary Source of Full-time Job Acceptances		Finance	33	$96,546
School-facilitated activities	229 (72%)	Marketing	26	$91,993
Graduate-facilitated activities	88 (28%)	Operations	3	$95,875
Average base starting salary	$98,510	Consulting	22	$114,507
Percent employed	87	General Management	15	$91,084
		Other	1	$98,333

Top 5 Employers Hiring Grads

Johnson & Johnson; Citigroup; Bank of America; McKinsey & Company; Deloitte Consulting

DUQUESNE UNIVERSITY
JOHN F. DONAHUE GRADUATE SCHOOL OF BUSINESS

Academics

With the introduction of a new sustainability-focused MBA program, a growing reputation, and an unwavering emphasis on ethical approaches to business principles, students at the Donahue Graduate School of Business say "it is a truly exciting time at Duquesne University." Duquesne offers an evening MBA program for working professionals, dual degree programs, and several master's programs, as well as their flagship offering: "a new 11-month full-time program, focusing primarily in sustainability." While the school has maintained a solid regional reputation for many years, a student observes, "Since launching the MBA Sustainability program, I have noticed an unstoppable momentum. Students, faculty, and administration are relentlessly involved in new research, case competitions, and program development." In addition to the academic energy the new program has produced, students say adding sustainability to the MBA is "perfect for the student looking for a career edge," as very few graduate business programs offer the highly specialized training they receive at Duquesne. On a broader scale, business courses throughout the curriculum "emphasize both the subject areas and the ethical and sustainability considerations. This holistic combination produces balanced individuals who learn to solve problems while protecting the rights of others and the environment." In addition, students can add depth to their MBA through one of ten established concentrations (including business ethics, environmental management, marketing, and taxation) or top off the experience with international business skills through a semester abroad at one of the school's partner universities in France, Colombia, Mexico, Japan, China, Belgium, or Germany.

In addition to its innovative curricular offerings, Duquesne distinguishes itself through its "genuine interest in the success of their students." Duquesne professors "like to teach and are skilled instructors." A current student shares, "With rare exception, all of my professors are wonderful teachers who take the time to explain material." In particular, students appreciate the fact that "particular professors are brought in straight from the work world and know their field inside and out." What's more, at this small school, students benefit from ample interaction with faculty. For example, "students form close relationships with faculty and often begin joint research projects out of the classroom. This research is usually published where the student is recognized as primary, secondary, or joint author."

When it comes to the workload, "Tests are killer but the papers are manageable." However, students also remind us that "this is not a heavy quant school, and there is a heavy emphasis on the soft skills in the business world." To that end, teamwork is heavily emphasized and "the MBA students come from a variety of backgrounds, bringing many perspectives to classroom discussions. This enhances the learning experience by broadening our perspectives and encouraging us to contribute to the discussions." In addition to excellence, convenience is key to a Duquesne education; the program allows undergraduate business majors to waive a large percentage of required courses, and the "program that is set up to make education accessible by conducting classes in several locations around the city of Pittsburgh."

Career and Placement

The Duquesne University Career Services Center provides career services to undergraduate students, graduate students, and alumni. Through DuqConnection, students can post their resumes, register for career fairs, and view current job openings online. On campus, the center hosts two major career fairs each year. In addition, the Career Services Center maintains contact with other universities, which sponsor more career fairs or job-related forums, giving student access to a range of career opportunities in the greater region. Recently, the following employers recruited Duquesne graduates: Allegheny Energy, American Eagle Outfitters, Bayer, Deloitte, Ernst & Young, GlaxoSmithKline, Highmark, Intel, PricewaterhouseCoopers, Roadway Express, and Verizon Wireless.

With a largely regional reputation, "Duquesne University is well known and respected in Western Pennsylvania, but loses some credibility outside of the state." As a result, some feel the school should "allocate more resources to assisting students with finding employment nationally and internationally."

Student Life and Environment

According to its students, Duquesne graduate business programs attract a group of "intelligent people who sincerely care about their academic and professional careers." The overall "atmosphere is friendly and supportive," and students "work on projects outside of school, have started clubs, and socialize regularly. I believe that some of us will stay in close contact long down the road." A current student adds, "My cohorts spend a lot of time together, eating, studying, and going out on the drink. We have our own computer lab. It is similar to an office setting where work and chatter coexist."

Duquesne's "beautiful" campus is "located in the heart of Downtown Pittsburgh," an affordable, big city that also boasts a respectable business community. In addition to overhauling the curriculum, students are proud to report that "there are long-range plans for new construction of LEED Certified buildings, not to mention the retrofitting of current buildings." Of the many facilities available to graduate students on the Duquesne campus, "the new fitness center is a definite selling point." On the downside, "parking is terrible, which is funny considering the campus is mostly commuters."

Admissions

Applicants to Duquesne are evaluated based on their undergraduate transcripts, letters of recommendation, autobiographical statement, GMAT scores, and work experience. Generally speaking, a minimum GMAT score of 550 is required for admission to the program. Students with more than ten years of high-level business experience may be able to waive the GMAT requirement.

FINANCIAL FACTS

Annual tuition	$20,989
Fees	$1,998
Cost of books	$2,500
Room & board (on-campus)	$8,546
% of students receiving aid	70
% of first-year students receiving aid	70
% of students receiving grants	13
Average grant	$15,000

ADMISSIONS

Admissions Selectivity Rating	**70**
# of applications received	124
% applicants accepted	81
% acceptees attending	65
Average GMAT	520
Average GPA	3.1
TOEFL required of international students	Yes
Minimum TOEFL (paper/computer)	550/213
Regular application deadline	5/1
Regular notification	6/1
Deferment available	Yes
Maximum length of deferment	1 year
Transfer students accepted	Yes
Transfer application policy	

The Donahue School will accept up to 15 transfer credits from an accredited college or university.

Non-fall admissions	Yes
Need-blind admissions	Yes

Applicants Also Look At
University of Pittsburgh.

EMPLOYMENT PROFILE	
Career Rating	74

EAST CAROLINA UNIVERSITY
COLLEGE OF BUSINESS

GENERAL INFORMATION
Type of school	Public
Environment	Town
Academic calendar	Semester

SURVEY SAYS...
Friendly students
Good social scene
Solid preparation in:
Teamwork
Communication/interpersonal skills
Quantitative skills
Computer skills

STUDENTS
Enrollment of parent institution	34,351
Enrollment of business school	621
% part-time	68

ACADEMICS
Academic Experience Rating	**82**
Student/faculty ratio	20:1
Profs interesting rating	87
Profs accessible rating	83
% female faculty	24
% minority faculty	5

Joint Degrees
MD/MBA 1 year.

FINANCIAL FACTS
Annual tuition (in-state/ out-of-state)	$5,779/$16,095
Cost of books	$500

Academics

East Carolina University is a medium-sized public school that offers a fully accredited MBA program both online and on campus. Academically, the MBA curriculum is designed to provide a "solid foundation in business fundamentals across the board." Students are required to complete a series of breadth classes in seven business areas, and later, may tailor their education through elective coursework in areas like finance, health care, and supply chain management. A current student attests, "I am an aspiring entrepreneur and I chose this institution for its comprehensive curriculum to build a solid, broad business foundation. I feel I chose well." In addition to coursework, "there are numerous opportunities available to become involved with department-related projects and academic groups," or to augment your experience (while lowering the tuition price) through graduate assistantships. Students can also add international experience to the MBA through one of two summer exchange programs in China and Australia.

Despite the school's low in-state tuition, East Carolina University isn't besieged by the bureaucratic hassles that plague other public institutions. Led by an administrative staff that is "very accessible and willing to lend a helping hand," students assure us that "when the university becomes aware of an improvement needed, they are quick to respond." In fact, "if you are an on-campus student, you get the opportunity to know the school's administrators on a first name basis. They are very accessible and want to help." In addition to the administrative support, students are guided in their academic career through an assigned advisor, "who is always available and always has the answers you need." Experts in the business school experience, "all of the advisors and staff for the MBA program have received an MBA from ECU; therefore they know how the courses are and how the curriculum is set up first hand."

If you are planning to pursue a degree part time, be aware that "the homework and class work is very demanding and time-consuming," which can be particularly challenging for those who are balancing a full life outside of school. A first-year student writes, "So far, I have been very stressed out adapting to the MBA program, but the program has enough flexibility to allow me time to get adjusted to the course load." For extremely busy professionals, East Carolina University also gives students the "ability to complete the entire MBA online," or the opportunity to complete the degree through a combination of online and campus classes. Fortunately, "the distance education program is well run" and online students benefit from the same quality academic programs you'll find on campus. A student attests, "Every professor I have had treats online students exactly as they treat their on-campus students and holds us to the same standards."

ADMISSIONS CONTACT: LEN RHODES, ASSISTANT DEAN FOR GRADUATE PROGRAMS
ADDRESS: 3203 BATE BUILDING GREENVILLE, NC 27858-4353 UNITED STATES
PHONE: 252-328-6970 • FAX: 252-328-2106
E-MAIL: GRADBUS@ECU.EDU • WEBSITE: WWW.BUSINESS.ECU.EDU

Career and Placement

Through ECU's Career Services office, students can get highly individualized counseling services and participate in a range of career development activities. Students particularly appreciate the fact that the team at Career Services "know you by name and remember speaking with you. They are quick to respond to any questions or concerns you might have." A current student adds, "They go through your entire resume and help you tweak it until it is just right, and they even hold regular mock-interviews with actual company personnel."

Career Services also maintains a monthly schedule of campus recruiting events, campus interviews, and corporate speakers. Companies that visited campus in the past year include Credit-Suisse, CIA, Wachovia Bank, Sherwin Williams, FMI, Coyote Logistics, Lowes, Vanguard, Northwestern Mutual, and BB&T Bank.

Student Life and Environment

Boasting a pleasant campus environment with a touch of Southern charm, ECU "has a great atmosphere from small-town North Carolina. Everyone at the university is friendly and always willing to help." Within the business school, "the graduate student body is professional and everyone seems genuinely eager to learn." While the school draws a predominantly local crowd, you'll still feel at home, even if you aren't from the area. A current MBA attests, "My fellow students are very helpful. I am not from North Carolina and many of them are very eager to show me around and help me out." Located in the small city of Greenville, the school's "on-campus facilities such as gym, theater, auditorium are good to excellent, and offer opportunities for staying healthy and active."

The Graduate Business Association (GBA), the largest graduate student group on the ECU campus, "is well run and is a good association for socializing." Both the business school and the GBA host various recreational and career-development events throughout the year. Even an online student shares, "I get tons of emails about everything going on all the time, so I never feel in the dark." While they are well apprised of the many things they are missing, part-time and online students say they rarely participate in campus life. Explains one, "Keeping up with your familial obligations and job plus school leaves almost no time for anything else."

Admissions

East Carolina University admits students using an admission index number, which is calculated using a student's standardized test scores and undergraduate GPA. To be eligible for the program, students must hold an undergraduate degree in any subject. Students in the most recent graduating class had an average undergraduate GPA of 3.15 and an average GMAT score of 505.

ADMISSIONS	
Admissions Selectivity Rating	**71**
# of applications received	236
% applicants accepted	76
% acceptees attending	82
Average GMAT	500
Average GPA	3.13
TOEFL required of international students	Yes
Minimum TOEFL (paper/computer)	550/213
Application fee	$60
International application fee	$60
Regular application deadline	Rolling
Regular notification	Rolling
Deferment available	Yes
Maximum length of deferment	1 year
Transfer students accepted	Yes
Transfer application policy Maximum of 9 Semester credit hours from AACSB accredited institution accepted.	
Non-fall admissions	Yes
Need-blind admissions	Yes

EAST TENNESSEE STATE UNIVERSITY
COLLEGE OF BUSINESS AND TECHNOLOGY

Academics

There aren't many choices at the College of Business and Technology at East Tennessee State University—the small program maintains only three business and four technology departments (accounting, economics/finance—urban studies, management/marketing)—but for those who are interested in a general-purpose business degree, ETSU delivers. In addition to the traditional MBA, the school also offers an MAcc (master's of accounting), an MPA (master's of public administration), and a graduate certificate in business administration for "those who seek a basic understanding of business administration but who may not be able to make the commitment of time, effort, and money required to seek a master's degree."

MBAs at ETSU feel that "the administration and faculty here are very student-oriented. Most have set times when they are available outside of class; others excel and really go the extra mile both in class presentation and in their availability to those students that require extra instruction." Professors are regarded as "very knowledgeable in their fields, and many of them are widely recognized as great scholars." One student writes, "Most of them have a work background that can lead to some very good discussions in class, and [the professors present] the applications of the concepts in the real world through their stories." Faculty members are also "easy to work with and understanding about personal matters that can arise."

Students say "We are like a family at ETSU. You go through the same classes with pretty much the same group of students. We are all interested in each other's success. There is low competition." Most students agree that the school does "a very good job of getting the student prepared with the knowledge that is needed in the workplace, but there is just so much that can be taught in the classroom setting." Many students have full-time jobs, and say "true learning from the classroom is applied to the jobs that are obtained after school." But balancing work and school responsibilities can leave some students feeling overextended. One student warns: "Most likely you have one or two people who do not participate in group [projects], leaving the workload for the other two or three people. Those individuals who do not participate always get the same grade." Across the board, students love that "the school is large enough to offer remote-learning facilities, and classes are generally available at convenient times for working adults." Most of all, however, students appreciate that professors "show a major interest in students' ability to understand the work."

Career and Placement

The Career Placement and Internship Services Office at East Tennessee University serves the school's entire undergraduate and graduate student body. The office hosts recruitment visits from various companies, sponsors and participates in career fairs, maintains online job boards and resume books, and offers counseling in interview skills, job search, career match, and resume writing. In the spring of 2004, on-campus recruiters included New York Life, Norfolk Southern, Wachovia, and Wells Fargo. Students are aware that "Johnson City is a small town, which limits the amount of recruiting that is done on campus." Even so, many "believe that [the] school could improve by really showing students what is available out there and helping them find jobs when they get done. It is there right now [at the Career Placement and Internship Services Office], but a student really has to push to find it."

Student Life and Environment

East Tennessee State University is located in Johnson City, a small Appalachian city close to both the North Carolina and Virginia borders. The surrounding area, dubbed the

ADMISSIONS CONTACT: DR. MARTHA POINTER, DIRECTOR OF GRADUATE STUDIES
ADDRESS: PO BOX 70699 JOHNSON CITY, TN 37614 UNITED STATES
PHONE: 423-439-5314 • FAX: 423-439-5274
E-MAIL: BUSINESS@BUSINESS.ETSU.EDU • WEBSITE: WWW.ETSU.EDU/CBAT

Tri-Cities region, also includes Bristol and Kingsport; the charming town of Abingdon, Virginia, is also not too far afield. The area is an outdoor enthusiast's paradise, offering plenty of opportunities for hiking, climbing, skiing, and nature walks. The Tri-Cities area is a rising force in the health care industry, with a developing biotech industry that could bring big players to the region.

With 11,000 students (about 2,000 of whom are graduate students), the ETSU campus has the population to support a busy social scene. MBAs report, "There is a very good social scene, with Thursday nights being the night that most students go out to the clubs. There are not a lot of clubs in the area, but there are many places that one can go and have a beer if they so choose." Students try to find time to support their men's basketball team, the ETSU Bucs, which in the 2003–2004 year won its second consecutive trip to "the Big Dance" (that's the NCAA Tournament to the uninitiated).

ETSU has expanded in recent years, adding several new buildings, including a fitness center (students love the "new, fully equipped athletic facility"). Not all MBAs take the time to enjoy the ETSU campus, however; they note that "the school is a high commuter school. This leads to a low participation level in on-campus clubs" and other activities. Those who do participate recommend the school's several national honor societies. One student touts "the university organization called 'President's Pride.' Through this organization, I am able to socialize with other students, faculty, administrators, and [members of the] community by volunteering for university/community functions."

Through its Adult, Commuter, and Transfer Services (ACTS) Office, ETSU assists its many nontraditional students in adapting to student life. ACTS staff advise students on the nuts and bolts of registration, direct them to the campus's various tutoring services, and help parents find child-care services. This last one can be a problem for MBAs, who typically attend evening classes. One such student comments, "I have a 15-month-old, and I have tried to get some type of care for my child so I can study or attend group meetings, and I have had no luck. This has been the most frustrating part of my school experience."

Admissions

Applications to the College of Business and Technology at East Tennessee State University are considered on a rolling basis. Applicants must submit the following to the Graduate Admissions Office: official copies of transcripts for all undergraduate and graduate work, standardized test scores (GMAT for the MBA or MAcc, GRE for the MPA), TOEFL scores (where applicable; minimum score 550), a personal statement, letters of recommendation, and a resume. Applicants to the MPA program must have a minimum undergraduate GPA of 3.0. All applicants are presumed to be competent with computers and math literate through calculus.

FINANCIAL FACTS

Annual tuition (in-state/ out-of-state)	$5,446/$15,722
Fees	$1,100
Cost of books	$1,000
Room & board (on/off-campus)	$5,000/$6,000
% of students receiving aid	25
% of first-year students receiving aid	25
% of students receiving grants	25
Average award package	$6,000
Average grant	$6,000
Average student loan debt	$10,000

ADMISSIONS

Admissions Selectivity Rating	75
# of applications received	70
% applicants accepted	77
% acceptees attending	85
Average GMAT	535
Range of GMAT	450–700
Average GPA	3.3
TOEFL required of international students	Yes
Minimum TOEFL (paper/computer)	550/213
Application fee	$25
International application fee	$35
Regular application deadline	6/1
Regular notification	rolling
Deferment available	Yes
Maximum length of deferment	1 year
Transfer students accepted	Yes
Transfer application policy Up to 9 approved hours MAY be accepted.	
Non-fall admissions	Yes
Need-blind admissions	Yes

Applicants Also Look At

University of Tennessee, Virginia Tech.

EMPLOYMENT PROFILE

Career Rating	70	Grads Employed by Function	%	Avg. Salary
		Human Resources	10	$30,000
		Marketing	10	$38,000
		Entrepreneurship	10	$35,000
		General Management	50	$30,000

Top 5 Employers Hiring Grads
Eastman Chemical

EASTERN MICHIGAN UNIVERSITY
COLLEGE OF BUSINESS

GENERAL INFORMATION

Type of school	Public
Environment	City
Academic calendar	Semester

SURVEY SAYS...
Solid preparation in:
General management
Teamwork
Communication/interpersonal skills
Presentation skills
Computer skills

STUDENTS

Enrollment of parent institution	22,848
Enrollment of business school	288
% male/female	65/35
% out-of-state	27
% part-time	59
% minorities	34
% international	57
Average age at entry	28
Average years work experience at entry	4

ACADEMICS

Academic Experience Rating	**71**
Student/faculty ratio	23:1
Profs interesting rating	71
Profs accessible rating	80
% female faculty	33
% minority faculty	32

Joint Degrees
BBA/MSA (Accounting) 5 years,
BBA/MSA (Accounting Information
Systems) 5 years.

Prominent Alumni
Jan Bertsch, VP Sales & Marketing
Finace, Chrysler Group; Keith
Moore, CEO, ITVNet; Joseph
Chrzanowski, Executive
Director/GM; Robert Skandalaris,
Chairman & CEO, Noble
International; Michael Procida,
Executive Director of HR/Ford.

Academics

The MBA program at Eastern Michigan University offers its students "world-class opportunities" complemented by a "small-school feel" and "affordability." EMU emphasizes broad business perspectives through training in hard and soft skill competencies such as leadership and accounting. Students appreciate the curriculum's focus on teaching basic business principles but wish courses would "truly get down to the nitty gritty." The "diversity of international students within the MBA program" brings international perspectives to the classroom. Many students are drawn to EMU because of its "very accessible" evening program which allows students to "work full-time and commute to school for class in the evenings." The core curriculum includes courses in areas such as business communication, quantitative analysis, supply chain management, financial management, and management. Upon completion of the core, students may pursue degrees in general business or specialize in a number of areas including e-business, entrepreneurship, enterprise business intelligence, finance, human resource management, internal auditing, international business, marketing, nonprofit management, and supply chain management.

Students who have undergraduate degrees in business may qualify for an accelerated program, which contributes to the "younger crowd" on campus "who have come right from undergrad." Students say that "the university highly encourages and promotes global/cultural awareness. We have fabulous courses and academic programs abroad courses to enrich student experiences." They also appreciate "the flexibility of the program. Students can either go part-time or full-time depending on their job responsibilities." Describing their "outstanding" professors as "mentors who have a deep investment in seeing us succeed," students appreciate that their professors' teaching skills are complemented by real work experience. "The professors are well-rounded people," and "Most of them worked in the business world before they began teaching." "They are really concerned about [us] doing well," another student observes. Some students would like to see changes, though. "Still too many lectures," says one. "They need to expand on their course offerings. There is a pretty good mix of MBA specializations, but most are general business basics." Another student noted that the school "needs to be more hands-on and get students active in their education."

Student opinion of the administration is mostly positive. As one student explains, "I feel that the faculty and administration is supportive in every way. In addition, they provide one-on-one networking opportunities, advice, [and] mentoring." Another student points out that "advisors and administrators [are] very helpful, knowledgeable, and accessible," and appreciates that "when you need to speak with someone regarding an important issue, it can be handled that day." The "biggest problems [are] with financial aid."

Career and Placement

Eastern Michigan is located in Ypsilanti, ten minutes from the academic hub of Ann Arbor in one direction, and 25 minutes to the metropolis of Detroit in the other. That adds up to a great location for job hunting, and is especially convenient for those students at EMU who are already employed while attending classes. The university's Career Center is available to help graduate students in the College of Business, but most MBA students seem to rely on personal networking, existing job contacts, and student clubs and organizations for employment leads. "I work full-time and commute to school for class in the evenings. I am usually on campus to attend class, conduct research, or meet with a project team" points out one such student. Another adds, "I really enjoy the clubs, connections, special events, and networking opportunities" available on EMU's campus. "Small classes provide great opportunity to make friends and [build a] professional network," says another. Ford Motor Company, Google, Ernst & Young, Target, Comerica Bank, Chase Bank, Proctor & Gamble, and Borders Group are among those who recruit on campus.

Student Life and Environment

Most of Eastern Michigan's classes take place at night and on weekends, which poses some challenges for its student community. "EMU is a commuter school, so it doesn't have the social activities that other business schools may have. I wish there were more social events for business school graduate students," says one. Another student described his peers as "real, honest—not superficial." They are "goal oriented and hard-working. Academics are the first priority for most." As to the student body itself, "Eastern Michigan's students are very diverse. I am Caucasian and I am the minority in almost all of my classes," one says. Another student describes his fellow students as "very open to new experiences; diverse from all areas of the globe, which is special for a smaller business school; hardworking." As a commuter school with night classes, several students wish to see security and safety on campus improved, though others agree with the student who says, "It is located in a great area, 10 minutes from Ann Arbor and 25 minutes from Detroit. Social activities are abundant due to the location of University of Michigan, Wayne State University, and the City of Detroit."

Admissions

GMAT scores, a one-page personal statement describing your plans and goals, and GPA rank, along with TOEFL scores for non-native speakers of English, are required for admission to Eastern Michigan's MBA program. The minimum GMAT score required is 450 and the minimum GPA accepted is 2.5/4.0. In 2006, the average GMAT score was 470, and the average GPA of students accepted into the MBA program was 3.0. Eastern Michigan generally accepts about 60 percent of those who apply to the MBA course, and on average, students have 4 years of work experience.

FINANCIAL FACTS

Annual tuition (in-state/ out-of-state)	$6,714/$13,226
Fees	$1,674
Cost of books	$1,000
Room & board	$8,870
% of students receiving aid	40
% of first-year students receiving aid	9
% of students receiving loans	32
% of students receiving grants	8
Average award package	$11,034
Average grant	$4,509

ADMISSIONS

Admissions Selectivity Rating	71
# of applications received	268
% applicants accepted	52
% acceptees attending	49
Average GMAT	451
Range of GMAT	450–530
Average GPA	3.1
TOEFL required of international students	Yes
Minimum TOEFL (paper/computer)	550/213
Application fee	$35
International application fee	$35
Regular application deadline	5/15
Regular notification	6/15
Application Deadline/Notification	
Round 1:	05/15 / NR
Round 2:	10/15 / NR
Round 3:	03/15 / NR
Round 4:	04/15 / NR
Deferment available	Yes
Maximum length of deferment	1 year
Transfer students accepted	Yes
Transfer application policy	
6 credits may be accepted for the core and 6 credits for electives upon approval.	
Non-fall admissions	Yes
Need-blind admissions	Yes

Applicants Also Look At

Central Michigan University, Michigan State University, Oakland University, University of Michigan, University of Michigan—Dearborn, Wayne State University, Western Michigan University.

EMPLOYMENT PROFILE

Career Rating	60*	Grads Employed by Function	%	Avg. Salary
		Finance	9	$44,500
		Human Resources	8	$40,400
		Marketing	15	$61,500
		MIS	8	$44,500
		Operations	16	$52,600
		Consulting	7	$49,600
		General Management	18	$57,500
		Other	1	$50,000

Top 5 Employers Hiring Grads
Ford Motor Company; Price Waterhouse Coopers, LLP; Comerica; Creative Solutions; Thomson Tax and Accounting

EASTERN WASHINGTON UNIVERSITY
COLLEGE OF BUSINESS AND PUBLIC ADMINISTRATION

Academics

For the "mostly working students who take night classes" pursuing MBAs at Eastern Washington University, the College of Business and Public Administration appeals on a number of levels: It's relatively inexpensive, it is close to home, and the extremely diligent can complete their graduate degrees here in one year. "Small classes" and "professors who are friendly, great communicators, and easy to reach with questions" further bolster the school's attractiveness.

Entrepreneurship is among the standout disciplines at EWU, in part due to the presence of the school's active Center for Entrepreneurial Studies. Students also speak highly of the program's courses in healthcare administration. Because the business facility also houses the school's Public Administration program, EWU students have a unique opportunity to combine an MBA with an MPA.

The EWU MBA consists of 49 credit hours. Core courses constitute 33 hours of required work; electives take up the remaining 16 hours. Foundation courses can add up to an additional 32 hours of required coursework; many or all of these courses may be waived for students with relatively recent undergraduate business degrees. Because EWU operates on a quarterly academic calendar, students who place out of foundation courses may complete the program in one year by taking 10+ credits per semester. Students love the convenience of evening scheduling and praise their professors for their flexibility. One reports that they "are willing to tailor work to what individuals need. I'm working on a tailor-made project, and I will have a business plan and start up when done." Expanded distance-learning options are on students' short wish lists.

Career and Placement

The Office of Career Services provides counseling and placement services for the entire EWU student body. The office organizes occasional career fairs and posts notices for other career fairs held in the area. In addition, the office hosts on-campus interviews and other recruitment events and maintains an online placement files service, which provides students' resumes, letters of recommendation, and other documents to prospective employers. Most of Career Services' efforts are directed at the school's substantial undergraduate population. Students tout the program's "strong alumni connections," which can be helpful to those in the program seeking post-degree employment.

ADMISSIONS CONTACT: CYNTHIA PARKER, PROGRAM COORDINATOR
ADDRESS: 668 NORTH RIVERPOINT BLVD., SUITE A SPOKANE, WA 99202-1677 UNITED STATES
PHONE: 509-358-2248 • FAX: 509-358-2267
E-MAIL: CPARKER@MAIL.EWU.EDU • WEBSITE: WWW.EWU.EDU/MBA

Student Life and Environment

The smallish, predominantly part-time MBA program at EWU is a mix of working professionals, EWU undergraduates continuing directly through to their MBAs, and a 20 percent international population made up largely of Asian students. Collectively, they are "very helpful and cooperative, and good at working in teams," and are typically "smart, hard-working, going places, no-silver-spoon kids" who constitute a "very diverse group ethnically, age-wise, and in terms of previous experience."

The size and part-time nature of the program is not conducive to a cohesive student community. Students don't even get to tap into the culture of EWU's main campus because the MBA program is located on a satellite campus in downtown Spokane, 20 miles from the main campus. While the location stunts extracurricular life, it does have the advantage of convenience for those students who work in the downtown area. Most students don't have much time for bonding and after-class fun anyway. A typical student explains his situation: "I work full-time at an executive level job. I am able to juggle my work and school load, but there is not a lot of time for much else."

Classes convene at the Riverpoint Higher Education Park, located on the banks of the Spokane River. The facility is home to EWU's College of Business and Public Administration, a boon to those seeking a dual degree in those two fields. Riverpoint houses a 200-seat auditorium and a number of state-of-the-art classrooms.

Admissions

Eastern Washington University requires all the following materials from applicants to its MBA program: two copies of the completed application for admission to a graduate program; two copies of official transcripts for all post-secondary academic work; and an official GMAT score report no more than five years old. The MBA program director reserves the right to require additional information. International applicants whose first language is not English must provide all of the above materials as well as an official TOEFL score report (students must score 580 for admission to the MBA program. EWU requires a minimum undergraduate GPA of 3.0 during the final 90 quarter hours or 60 semester hours of undergraduate work and a minimum GMAT score of 450. The school's website notes: "All students who graduate from the MBA program should have some practical work experience. The majority of students accepted into the program are working professionals and meet this requirement. For those students who enter the program lacking professional work experience, an internship should be part of the student's MBA program. Up to four (4) four credits earned while in an internship may be used for MBA elective credit."

FINANCIAL FACTS

Annual tuition (in-state/ out-of-state)	$6,465/$11,850
Fees	$105
Cost of books	$1,500
Room & board (on/off-campus)	$6,900/$12,000
% of students receiving aid	25
% of first-year students receiving aid	25
% of students receiving loans	20
% of students receiving grants	5

ADMISSIONS

Admissions Selectivity Rating	**65**
# of applications received	90
% applicants accepted	99
% acceptees attending	83
Average GMAT	511
Range of GMAT	430–690
Average GPA	3.3
TOEFL required of international students	Yes
Minimum TOEFL (paper/computer)	580/237
Application fee	$100
International application fee	$100
Regular application deadline	1/1
Regular notification	1/1
Deferment available	Yes
Maximum length of deferment	1 year
Transfer students accepted	Yes
Transfer application policy We will accept up to 12 transfer credits.	
Non-fall admissions	Yes
Need-blind admissions	Yes

ELON UNIVERSITY
MARTHA AND SPENCER LOVE SCHOOL OF BUSINESS

GENERAL INFORMATION
Type of school   Private
Affiliation   United Church of Christ
Academic calendar   Trimester

SURVEY SAYS...
Good peer network
Solid preparation in:
Communication/interpersonal skills
Presentation skills
Doing business in a global economy

STUDENTS
Enrollment of parent institution	5,456
Enrollment of business school	150
% male/female	100/0
% part-time	100
Average age at entry	32
Average years work experience at entry	8

ACADEMICS
Academic Experience Rating	**85**
Student/faculty ratio	24:1
Profs interesting rating	98
Profs accessible rating	79
% female faculty	30
% minority faculty	13

Prominent Alumni
Christina Baker, Executive VP and CFO, Capital Bank; Steven Casey, Founder & Board Secretary, Expression Analysis; Allan Davis, CEO, AllFab Solutions; Kathleen Galbraith, Chief Mktg. & Bus. Dev. Officer, Durham Reg. Hosp.; Bernadette Spong, CFO, Rex Hospital.

Academics

The MBA program at Elon University is "a program on the rise," students tell us, citing "excellent facilities and a brand-new business school building" among the factors driving its ascent. A "globally-focused curriculum, which is important in today's economy" and a relatively low cost of attending (as compared to area competitors Wake Forest, Duke, and UNC—Chapel Hill) also draw area business hopefuls to the school.

Elon works hard to optimize its MBA experience. Students tell us that "the administration of the program is as close as you can get to flawless" and that the school is "very well run, more like a business serving it customers well as opposed to a bureaucratic organization." "There are regular opportunities to provide feedback on courses and unmet needs to the program administrator and he will listen," one student says. The school also does a great job of soliciting "a strong corporate and alumni support system that allows for the latest technology and educational methods to be utilized." As a result, the Love School has a new three-story home that includes a state-of-the-art finance center streaming real-time data from global financial markets, a 240-seat multimedia wireless theater, and plenty of study, conference, and classroom space.

The Elon MBA is a small program, making it difficult to avoid substandard teachers—fortunately, "Only about two or three of our thirteen teachers belong in the 'not so good' category...while everyone else is excellent," one student notes. However, this intimate environment can also result in a "lack of choices for electives." A student explains, "Most are management-related and it is difficult for someone to find financial- and economic-focused electives to meet a particular career focus." In the plus column, "Most all the professors have worked in the fields that they teach in, so they have real-world experiences." Students also appreciate that "the MBA program is an experiential program in that each class requires some outside activities pertaining to the course."

Career and Placement

Career placement services are provided by Elon's Career Development office, which serves all students in the university. Services offered to MBAs include a battery of self-assessment tools, faculty advising, and seminars with area business leaders (through the Legends of Business program, students have met with and learned from Jerry D. Neal, co-founder of RF Micro Devices; Thomas J. Murrin, former Westinghouse exec and former Deputy Secretary at the US Commerce Department; Leslie M. "Bud" Baker, Jr., former Chair/President/CEO of Wachovia; and J Richard Munro, former Chair and CEO of Time, Inc.) Students tell us, "The MBA faculty goes above and beyond by assisting graduate students with support in areas such as educational mapping as well as with registration and career services." Even so, most here agree that "Career Services is not the best at Elon" and that "more corporate recruiting on campus would add much to a program that is already wonderful."

Elon MBAs work for some of the area's top employers, including Banner Pharmacaps, Ciba Specialty Chemicals, Cisco Systems, Duke Health Systems, GE, GKN Automotive, IBM, LabCorp, Sony Ericsson, UNC Hospitals, Underwriters Laboratories, and Wachovia.

ADMISSIONS CONTACT: ARTHUR W. FADDE, DIRECTOR OF GRADUATE ADMISSIONS
ADDRESS: 2750 CAMPUS BOX ELON, NC 27244 UNITED STATES
PHONE: (800) 334-8448 EXT. 3 • FAX: (336) 278-7699
E-MAIL: ELONMBA@ELON.EDU • WEBSITE: WWW.ELON.EDU/MBA

Student Life and Environment

Elon is "very big about building community among the MBA students" through "activities such as midterm pizza nights, golf outings, and social events such as football games, basketball games, and local theater trips." However, "Due to the nature of a part-time graduate program, many students are not involved in the life of the school." Some do embrace extracurricular fun, telling us, "We frequently have social gatherings on weekends and before classes so that the students have opportunities to decompress." The MBA Student-Alumni Association is active, bringing in "guest lecturers who are excellent."

The "beautiful" Elon campus is "moderately sized but has a strong community feel." "The buildings and landscaping are gorgeous and MBA students have access to all of the same gym, dining, and event resources as undergraduates," one student explains. The school's small hometown (also called Elon) "grew up around the school and blends with the campus." The larger city of Greensboro is close by, with Winston-Salem and Durham about an hour's drive away, and Raleigh and Charlotte just a little further down the line.

Elon's student body is "a mixture of people very experienced in the business world (bankers, lawyers, senior leaders in their organizations) and a lower percentage of folks who are not very experienced." They tend to be "very helpful and all with a good sense of humor." "They're never too serious but always willing to do what is necessary to complete project work or other course assignments," one student says. "Most classmates are people that I would network with and hopefully develop friendships with."

Admissions

The Elon MBA requires a minimum of two years' professional experience of all applicants. A completed application must include three letters of recommendation (two from work supervisors), official transcripts from all post-secondary schools attended, and GMAT scores. An interview is recommended but not required. Students whose native language is not English must also submit TOEFL scores (minimum 550 written, 213 computer); those who graduated from non-English programs overseas must have their transcripts translated and the grades interpreted by a professional service. Applicants must exceed a formula score of 1000 under the formula [(undergraduate GPA ? 200) + GMAT score], and must also have a minimum GMAT score of 470 and a minimum GPA of 2.7. Undergraduate classes in financial accounting, finance, microeconomics, and statistics are prerequisites to enrollment in the MBA program. Students may begin in August or January; applications are assessed on a rolling basis.

FINANCIAL FACTS

Annual tuition	$24,076
Average award package	$10,709
Average grant	$5,133
Average student loan debt	$18,523

ADMISSIONS

Admissions Selectivity Rating	**77**
# of applications received	96
% applicants accepted	74
% acceptees attending	86
Average GMAT	523
Range of GMAT	480–570
Average GPA	3.02
Minimum TOEFL (paper/computer)	550/213
Application fee	$50
International application fee	$50
Regular application deadline	Rolling
Regular notification	Rolling
Deferment available	Yes
Maximum length of deferment	1 year
Transfer students accepted	Yes
Transfer application policy A student may transfer up to 9 Semester hours of credit from another AACSB accredited school.	
Non-fall admissions	Yes
Need-blind admissions	Yes

Applicants Also Look At

North Carolina State University, The University of North Carolina at Greensboro, Wake Forest University.

EMORY UNIVERSITY
GOIZUETA BUSINESS SCHOOL

Academics

With a "great reputation," a "great location" in one of the fastest growing cities in one of the "fastest growing regions in the United States," and the "familial atmosphere" of "a small school with an extremely close-knit community," the Goizueta Business School at Emory University has a large stockpile of assets with which to justify its consistently high national ranking. Goizueta offers a traditional 2-year full-time MBA, an accelerated 1-year MBA, and a part-time evening MBA and Executive MBA.

Nearly everyone here agrees that "the focus on leadership and communications" within the Goizueta curriculum is a tremendous asset and is one of the program's chief drawing cards. "In addition to teaching the basic skills necessary for a career in business, the school is good at fine-tuning students' presentation, leadership, and interpersonal skills," explains one student. MBAs here also tout "one of the top marketing programs in the country." The core curriculum here offers "a mixture of soft and analytical skills" that "develop the needed business skills" in future managers, students report. Students in all disciplines benefit from "the small size" of the program coupled with its "large resources (Emory has a very large endowment)."

Goizueta is "a place full of passionate people," from students on up to the administration. The program's small size means "that everybody knows everybody on a first-name basis, and that includes students, faculty, administrators, Admissions, Career Management, and the Dean. . . . That also means that the students and faculty alike are super approachable and always willing to talk, guide, and discuss. That has been my biggest source of learning at school." Students here enjoy "a high level of involvement in the planning of the program and the strategy of the school," working closely with an administration that is "incredibly responsive to student ideas and requests. If you have an idea, they will help you achieve it. The atmosphere is one of high motivation in a very supportive environment."

Career and Placement

There is some dissatisfaction among students with the Goizueta Career Management Center, and many students complain about the number of companies visiting campus to recruit. "I think that any problems with the career center stem from the size of the school," explains one student. "A school that only graduates about 200 a year just isn't going to attract a ton of companies." Students report that "no one in the administration or student body is complacent" about recruitment. In fact, they feel that "everyone is working diligently to improve the situation." A few even find the office "extremely effective. Any student who makes the effort to seek out assistance is sure to receive answers and support as well as unsolicited follow-ups. Also, various professors and alumni have offered connections or have otherwise offered assistance," helping to mitigate whatever problems exist. "The school has had 100-percent placement for summer internships for as long as I've been here," says one impressed student.

Employers who most frequently hire Emory MBAs include: Adjoined Consulting, A.T. Kearney, Bank of America Securities, Bright House, CHEP International, Deloitte Touche Tohmatsu, Delta Air Lines, Earthlink, Goldman Sachs, The Home Depot, IBM, ING, JPMorgan Chase, Kurt Salmon & Associates, Lehman Brothers, Navigant Consulting, PricewaterhouseCoopers, Sun Trust Bank, UPS, Wachovia, and Zyman Marketing Group.

ADMISSIONS CONTACT: JULIE R. BAREFOOT, ASSOCIATE DEAN AND DIRECTOR OF MBA ADMISSIONS
ADDRESS: 1300 CLIFTON ROAD ATLANTA, GA 30322 UNITED STATES
PHONE: 404-727-6311 • FAX: 404-727-4612
E-MAIL: ADMISSIONS@BUS.EMORY.EDU • WEBSITE: WWW.GOIZUETA.EMORY.EDU

FINANCIAL FACTS

Annual tuition	$39,000
Fees	$476
Cost of books	$2,000
Room & board	$16,810

ADMISSIONS

Admissions Selectivity Rating 95

# of applications received	1,017
% applicants accepted	37
% acceptees attending	48
Average GMAT	685
Range of GMAT	670–740
Average GPA	3.34
TOEFL required of international students	Yes
Minimum TOEFL (paper/computer)	600/100
Application fee	$150
International application fee	$150
Regular application deadline	3/1
Regular notification	rolling
Deferment available	Limited
Maximum length of deferment	1 year
Need-blind admissions	Yes

Applicants Also Look At

Duke University, New York University, Northwestern University, The University of North Carolina at Chapel Hill, University of Michigan, University of Pennsylvania, University of Virginia.

Student Life and Environment

"There is definitely a work-hard, play-hard mentality at Goizueta," where students enjoy "plenty of opportunities to socialize." Favorites include International Potluck—"a great event hosted by the school to learn about other cultures;" "coffee and bagels as a school each Wednesday morning," and "Kegs in the Courtyard and Late Night" on Thursdays. These events "are actively looked forward to by the whole student community." Students tell us that "everyone spends most of first year on campus involved in classes, clubs, social events, recruiting events. There is always something to do. Second year gives you more of an opportunity to create your own schedule. Some people choose to stay actively involved, while others pursue directed study projects, international exchanges, family life, etc." Students appreciate that "spouses are heavily integrated into all campus and off-campus social events."

MBAs at Goizueta "are assigned to sections at the beginning of the year, which become tight groups," but "with only 350 students" in the program, "Everyone knows each other." The school works hard to promote unity. "We have had events like a Halloween Ball and Section Feud (trivia contest)," reports one student, "The Program Office also has a semester-ending town hall meeting to discuss how the year is going and what changes need to be implemented for improvements."

Admissions

Applicants to the Goizueta MBA program must submit the following materials: a completed online application; official transcripts for all undergraduate and graduate schools attended; an official GMAT score report; two letters of recommendation; essays; resume; personal interview. An interview, while not required, is "strongly recommended." International students whose first language is not English must also submit official score reports for either the TOEFL or the IELTS. Candidates for the 1-year program must have an undergraduate degree in a business-related discipline, engineering, or a strong quantitative background and "solid business experience."

EMPLOYMENT PROFILE

Career Rating	91	Grads Employed by Function	% Avg. Salary
Primary Source of Full-time Job Acceptances		Finance	28.5 $92,256
School-facilitated activities	77 (55%)	Marketing	22.9 $86,796
Graduate-facilitated activities	63 (45%)	Operations	2.8 $86,750
Average base starting salary	$93,059	Consulting	25 $103,545
Percent employed	89	General Management	11.8 $93,642
		Other	7 $50,000

Top 5 Employers Hiring Grads

ATKearney; Bank of America; Citigroup; Deloitte Consulting; Ernst & Young.

ESADE Business School

Academics

A tiny, diverse, bilingual MBA program, located in the world-class city of Barcelona, ESADE will appeal to students who want to develop managerial and leadership skills in the context of a highly international environment. Academically, the school "provides a combination of case analysis and theory," complimented by an overarching "emphasis on developing interpersonal skills." "Marketing and finance are two strong fields here at ESADE" and themes in corporate responsibility are woven throughout the curriculum. Classes are taught in both English and Spanish (students may choose to take classes in one language, or a combination), and many students take advantage of their ESADE education as an opportunity to improve their language skills. For those who are already fluent in Spanish and English, the school also offers German or French courses.

While the school's appealing Barcelona location is a major attraction for many students, be forewarned that ESADE's MBA program is highly demanding. While completing core coursework, you are more likely to spend your time in the library than at Barcelona's bars and clubs. Fortunately, the "work load dropped to more manageable levels during the second half of the program, during the electives." Despite the rigors of the program, you won't fall through the cracks at this small school. With a low enrollment, especially in the full-time programs, "the school pays attention to the individual." In addition, "because of the relatively small size of the school, administration is efficient and flexible." At the moment, ESADE's administrators are working overtime, as they "transition from a small, boutique school to a European leader." A student explains, "They are now one of the top ranked European schools and are doing the best they can to act like one."

Drawing faculty from 13 different countries, including Argentina, Chile, India, Italy, and the United States, ESADE "professors are without exception passionate and knowledgeable about their subjects. All encourage active participation by the students." A current student attests, "The academic experience has been great, as teachers are very good in general and the environment in class with my classmates is rewarding." On that note, many ESADE students say their classmates are an indispensable part of the MBA experience, which emphasizes "building up relationships and getting exposed to different cultures." Despite the school's patently international environment, some feel "ESADE should strengthen its link with emerging countries, namely, China [and] India."

Career and Placement

ESADE's Career Services staff operates the comprehensive Career Management Programme (CMP), designed to help students advance in their professional goals, both during their studies and after graduation. Through the CMP, students have access to various career development workshops and seminars, through which they learn to assess their strengths, identify markets, interview successfully, and negotiate a job offer. Career Services also hosts a number of campus recruiting events, including MBA Career Week (mostly focused on consulting and financial positions), International Career Day, MBA Career Forum, and various corporate presentations. The school maintains contact with hundreds of companies in numerous countries. A current student writes, "I was impressed by the portfolio of companies that come to interview on campus."

ADMISSIONS CONTACT: ROSALIA GALAN, ADMISSIONS OFFICER
ADDRESS: AV. D'ESPLUGUES, 92-96 BARCELONA, 08034 SPAIN
PHONE: 011-34-934-952-088 • FAX: 011-34-934-953-828
E-MAIL: MBA@ESADE.EDU • WEBSITE: WWW.ESADE.EDU

In 2006, the ESADE student body represented 31 different countries. Within this diverse group, 45 percent of students found jobs in Spain, and 23 percent in other Western European countries (40 percent of ESADE candidates took jobs in countries of which they were not nationals, which is a good sign for students who would like to use their ESADE education as a jumping-off point for an international career.) Marketing and sales positions were the most popular, drawing almost 30 percent of graduates, followed by finance, which drew 22 percent of the graduating class.

Student Life and Environment

International diversity is the cornerstone of the ESADE experience, as the school draws its small student body from "more than 30 nationalities." On the whole, ESADE's serious students are "driven to play a role as future international leaders in their respective fields." However, the environment is distinctly cooperative, not cutthroat. A student shares, "The teamwork orientation the school prides itself on can be felt anytime, right from the group work through the cafeteria."

Obviously, the school environment is enhanced by the fact that ESADE is "located in Barcelona, one of the nicest European cities." However, be forewarned that "the heavy workload gets in the way" of enjoying cultural and recreational activities, especially during the core curriculum. Even so, "Spain puts a premium on living well" and students manage to balance work and play throughout their ESADE education. A current student reassures us, "Despite the tough academic requirements of the school, most students do enjoy a very active social live outside of pure academia." Another adds, "The first year you practically live in school [and] there is great pressure, but there is always time for social activities."

Admissions

ESADE's admissions requirements vary by program. To be admitted to ESADE's 18-month MBA program, students must demonstrate intellectual ability through strong undergraduate performance and competitive test scores, and should have at least two years of relevant, full-time work experience before beginning the program. To be admitted to the one-year MBA program at ESADE, prospective students must hold an undergraduate degree in business, economics, engineering, or an equivalent field. In addition, one-year students must have at least five years of relevant professional experience before beginning the program.

FINANCIAL FACTS

Annual tuition	$41,325
Cost of books	$435
Room & board	$17,400
% of first-year students receiving aid	40
Average grant	$18,474

ADMISSIONS

Admissions Selectivity Rating	86
% acceptees attending	65
Average GMAT	640
Range of GMAT	610–720
TOEFL required of international students	Yes
Minimum TOEFL (paper/computer)	600/250
Application fee	$125
International application fee	$125
Regular application deadline	6/30
Regular notification	6/30
Deferment available	Yes
Maximum length of deferment	1 year
Non-fall admissions	Yes
Need-blind admissions	Yes

EMPLOYMENT PROFILE

Career Rating	85	Grads Employed by Function	% Avg. Salary
		Finance	16 NR
		Marketing	23 NR
		Consulting	23 NR
		General Management	34 NR
		Other	3 NR
		Non-profit	1: NR

ESSEC BUSINESS SCHOOL
THE ESSEC MBA PROGRAM

Academics

If you're looking for a "flexible" MBA at "a major player on the international level among European business schools" and one of "the top business schools in France," ESSEC is a school you should consider. After completing seven management fundamentals courses, ESSEC MBAs fashion their own curricula, choosing from more than "200 electives" each semester. Students love the freedom, telling us that "each quarter, we can basically chose to take classes at ESSEC Business School in Paris or Singapore, do an internship with a company in France or abroad, or go on an exchange program abroad with one of ESSEC MBA's 80 academic partners," whose ranks include many prestigious names in the United States and around the world. The school's administration "does a great job of managing this 'a la carte' system," allowing students to "choose almost any courses we want in order to create our specialization and formation."

Because ESSEC believes that students should make "a constant connection between work and the classroom," all students must have at least 18 months of validated professional experience prior to graduation. These internships are easy to find thanks to ESSEC's "great relationship with the business world." The school "has strong links with international finance and consulting companies;" and a campus in Singapore means that opportunities to intern in Southeast Asia are constantly developing. ESSEC's practical philosophy permeates the classroom as well; here "Courses are not just theory. We have a lot of business cases given by corporate partners, and we have a lot of work every week to prepare other business cases in groups (teamwork is very important here)." Throughout the program, there is a "prominent international dimension" bolstered by "the school's ever-increasing partnerships overseas."

The faculty includes "outstanding professors recognized in their fields of specialization, people who publish a lot. They help us get most prepared for our chosen profession and they are also very available and most willing to give us useful insights." Part-time faculty are drawn from "top-notch businesswomen and men and successful entrepreneurs. In any case, they always have a great experience and very useful insights to share."

Career and Placement

Students report that "ESSEC is the best passport to great job opportunities in France and worldwide. The school administration and students are really eager to keep in very close contact with firms. There is a constant exchange between the academic, student and business world. Companies are often involved in student projects too." The school's "excellent relations with European businesses" help students procure the internships required to complete their MBAs. While ESSEC's connections are strongest in France, "Many foreign companies also recruit (largely for their French subsidies), such as the consulting companies McKinsey, BCG, etc. ESSEC is part of their main target schools for recruiting."

Employers most likely to hire ESSEC MBAs include: PricewaterhouseCoopers, L'Oréal, Renault, Societe Generale, Deloitte Touche Tohmatsu, Danone, Michelin, BNP Paribas, Capgemini, Accenture, EDF-GDF, Pinault Printemps Redoute, Procter & Gamble, Deutsche Bank, 3 Suisses International, Pfizer, LVMH, Ernst & Young, Boston Consulting Group, A.T. Kearney, SC Johnson, and Bain.

Student Life and Environment

ESSEC encourages students to participate in extracurricular life, and students respond, forming "about 80 different clubs" that encompass not only business activities but also "theater, a choir, painting, photography, sports, and social groups." The area surrounding ESSEC, Cergy Pontoise, is "an ugly Parisian suburb" located "about an hour from the

Mrs. Marie-Noelle Koebel, Dean for Admissions and Academic Affairs
Address: Avenue Bernard Hirsch, B.P. 50105 Cergy-Pontoise, 95021 France
Phone: 011-33-1-3443-3259 • Fax: 011-33-1-3443-3260
E-mail: demars@essec.fr • Website: www.essec.edu

FINANCIAL FACTS	
Annual tuition (EU)	$38,315
Annual tuition (Non-EU)	$53,641
Cost of books	$765

center of the city by commuter train." Some describe it as "a modern city with very good amenities, including an artificial lake for sailing or rowing and other water sports, a nearby skating rink, and very good town libraries." Others tell us that "living in Cergy can be a little bit disappointing for those who would prefer the dense atmosphere of Paris to ESSEC school life." Local housing "is pretty easy to find" and "not too expensive."

ESSEC is "undergoing immense changes," students tell us, reporting that "buildings are being built, and new professors are being recruited at an international level. The school is going global and will become internationally known very soon." Some here tell us that "you can stay all day long at ESSEC, and there's always something to do and somewhere to go." Even those who complain that "facilities here could improve" acknowledge that "that is exactly what the school is doing. The current development program aims to double the space available and to upgrade facilities."

Admissions

Students are admitted to ESSEC either as traditional MBAs (this is the way international students enter the program), French MBAs, or as "grande école" students (French students who have attended 1 or 2 years of postsecondary school and are now ready for intensive, focused study in a discipline such as business). Students applying to the traditional MBA program must provide the school with an official GMAT or TAGE-MAGE score report, official transcripts for all postsecondary academic work, an interview, and a resume. Applicants must be under the age of 32; 1 or 2 years of professional experience is highly recommended. French MBA students follow the "Admission sur Tirste" admissions path. "Grande école" applicants must meet a variety of requirements, including completion of preparatory undergraduate business classes and completion of at least one 6-month internship.

ADMISSIONS	
Admissions Selectivity Rating	**99**
# of applications received	4,571
% applicants accepted	13.5
% acceptees attending	89
Average GMAT	674
TOEFL required of international students	Yes
Minimum TOEFL (paper/computer)	600/250
Application fee	$245
International application fee	$245
Application Deadline/Notification	
Round 1:	10/08 / 12/03
Round 2:	02/25 / 04/07
Round 3:	04/30 / 06/13
Early decision program?	Yes
Deferment available	Yes
Maximum length of deferment	1 year
Need-blind admissions	Yes

EMPLOYMENT PROFILE			
Career Rating		87	
Primary Source of Full-time Job Acceptances		**Grads Employed by Function**	**% Avg. Salary**
School-facilitated activities	121 (40%)	Finance	33 $62,649
Graduate-facilitated activities	9 (3%)	Human Resources	2 $47,668
Percent employed	94	Marketing	22 $49,919
		Operations	1 NR
		Strategic Planning	1 $50,387
		Consulting	26 $57,205
		General Management	5 $49,035
		Internet/New Media	3 $46,302

FAIRFIELD UNIVERSITY
CHARLES F. DOLAN SCHOOL OF BUSINESS

GENERAL INFORMATION
Type of school	Private
Affiliation	Roman Catholic/Jesuit
Environment	Town
Academic calendar	Semester

SURVEY SAYS...
Students love Fairfield, CT
Cutting edge classes
Solid preparation in:
Finance
Accounting

STUDENTS
Enrollment of	
business school	134
Average age at entry	29
Average years work	
experience at entry	4

ACADEMICS
Academic Experience Rating	**88**
Student/faculty ratio	23:1
Profs interesting rating	79
Profs accessible rating	75
% female faculty	36
% minority faculty	2

Prominent Alumni
Dr. E. Gerald Corrigan, Managing Director, Goldman, Sachs & Co.; Robert Murphy, Jr., Senior VP, The Walt Disney Company Foundation; Christopher McCormick, President & CEO, LL Bean, Inc.; Dr. Francis Tedesco, President, Medical College of Georgia.

Academics

The Dolan School of Business at Fairfield University excels in finance, a strength that dovetails nicely with the school's proximity to America's financial center, New York City. Students report that "the placement of the school in relation to key industries/businesses is a particular strength" and that "the ties with well-placed alumni are invaluable." Location also allows Dolan to draw its faculty from a powerful pool. One MBA notes, "Most all professors are either published authors or business owners (e.g., fund managers and investment advisors). This is very beneficial as they teach us in the real-world scenarios."

"Jesuit traditions and philosophies" aren't just slogans here; students pick Fairfield "for its strong commitment to Jesuit ideals." Jesuit values include an emphasis on teaching, and here students "work with professors outside of class regarding personal business situations, and all are more than willing to speak and help where they can." Professors are "flexible and accommodating;" two valuable traits in serving a working-professional part-time student body. One student observes that they "want to create a comfort level for their students, knowing that will make them most successful in school. Fairfield's teachers also are thick-skinned when students challenge them in class discussions. They encourage such open-minded dialogue; the instructors are not like some of the other high-and-mighty professors who insist their way of thinking is the only way."

Part-timers here enjoy "flexible night schedules and course terms," as the school offers a variety of seven- and fourteen-week terms as well as mini-term options. "This program is tailored for working students," MBAs here agree. Resources are solid; "The school is as technologically advanced as could be expected, and is more so than some of other colleges in the area and neighboring states." Students' wish list includes "more online hybrid classes. For those of us with a long commute to school after work, online hybrids are helpful because I still get classroom interaction, but without the commute every week."

Career and Placement

The Dolan MBA program is a small, predominantly part-time program in which most students already have careers. In fact, a number of students actually attend at their employers' expense. This situation creates a relatively small demand for career services within the program, so students seeking such services must use the Career Planning Center that serves the entire university. The Dolan Graduate Business Association, run by students, is probably the most aggressive advocate for career services within the program. Professors and alumni are also regarded as valuable resources for those seeking internships or careers. Most students wish that the school would "bring a greater diversity of businesses to career fairs." "Right now every business is in the financial arena, I would like to see them expand beyond those borders," one student says.

Employers most likely to hire Dolan MBAs include General Electric, People's Bank, American Skandia, United Technologies, Pitney Bowes, The Common Fund, Bayer Corporation, UBS Warburg, Gartner, Unilever, and Pfizer.

DR. DANA A. WILKIE, ASSISTANT DEAN/DIRECTOR OF GRADUATE PROGRAMS
ADDRESS: 1073 NORTH BENSON ROAD FAIRFIELD, CT 06824 UNITED STATES
PHONE: 203-254-4000 • FAX: 203-254-4029
E-MAIL: GRADADMIS@MAIL.FAIRFIELD.EDU • WEBSITE: WWW.FAIRFIELD.EDU/MBA

Student Life and Environment

"There is little to no interaction outside of class," Fairfield MBAs report, explaining that "Since most students are working professionals, most are preoccupied outside of the MBA program." However, "This doesn't detract from the educational experience." Students note that "there have been many attempts to create extracurricular activities, but with little response from the graduate student population…. In practice, most part-time, fully employed students are too busy to take part in such activities." Still, some believe that "if there were more networking opportunities for students," they "would feel better situated when searching for jobs." "The only activities for graduate students occur one night, during class time, at the beginning of each semester," one student says. On the other hand, another points out, "there have been many attempts by faculty and staff to listen to students and respond to their needs, but in practice, most part time, fully employed students are too busy to take part in such activities."

The Fairfield campus is "dynamic in that it's like an oasis." "It has a rural, small-school feel in a major metropolitan area. Major NYC-area and Fairfield County companies such as IBM, GE, and Pepsi, as well as many media, publishing, and financial companies are all within a 60- to 90-minute drive of the campus, allowing for students to land opportunities at a major company without having to move far."

Admissions

Applications may be submitted to Dolan via mail or the internet. Applications are processed on a rolling basis, and students may commence the program in any term. The Admissions Committee considers applicants' post-secondary academic records, GMAT scores, two letters of recommendation, and resume or other self-evaluation of work experience. In general, applicants are expected to have achieved a minimum undergraduate GPA of 3.00 and a score of at least 500 on the GMAT. International students from non-English speaking countries must submit TOEFL scores (a minimum score of 550 paper and pencil, 75 to 80 computer-based, is required). Applicants to the MS program in Accounting and Taxation must meet all the above criteria and must also provide a Statement of Certification from their accounting department faculty and a letter of recommendation from either a former employer or a faculty member outside the discipline of accounting. This program is only open to students who hold, or are in the process of earning, an undergraduate degree in accounting. All entering students in all programs must demonstrate proficiency in microeconomics, macroeconomics, calculus, and statistics. Successful completion of undergraduate work in these areas is the most common way of demonstrating proficiency.

FINANCIAL FACTS

Annual tuition	$22,680
Fees	$100
Cost of books	$1,000
Average grant	$5,000

ADMISSIONS

Admissions Selectivity Rating	**85**
# of applications received	75
% applicants accepted	43
% acceptees attending	94
Average GMAT	523
Range of GMAT	500–650
Average GPA	3.23
TOEFL required of international students	Yes
Minimum TOEFL (paper/computer)	550/213
Application fee	$55
International application fee	$55
Regular application deadline	rolling
Regular notification	rolling
Deferment available	Yes
Maximum length of deferment	1 year
Transfer students accepted	Yes
Transfer application policy	6 credits or Jesuit University Transfer Program
Non-fall admissions	Yes

Applicants Also Look At

Quinnipiac University, Sacred Heart University, University of Connecticut, University of Hartford.

FAIRLEIGH DICKINSON UNIVERSITY
SILBERMAN COLLEGE OF BUSINESS

Academics

Most of the MBA offerings from Fairleigh Dickinson University are available at both of the school's campuses: the College at Florham campus, located in Madison, and the Metropolitan campus, located in Teaneck. A few specialized programs are available at the Metropolitan campus only; these include the full-time one-year Global Business Management MBA program.

Students appreciate the convenience of the two campuses—although students must enroll at one campus, they are free to take classes at either—and the "flexibility of the program to accommodate working schedules," an important factor for the schools' 463-plus part-time students, most of whom work full-time. Students also appreciate the fact that FDU offers a "well-rounded program" with a "breadth of concentrations." The school offers concentrations in entrepreneurial studies, finance, human resource management, international business, management, management with concentrations in: corporate communications, global business (1-year program), and information systems, marketing, pharmaceutical management, executive MBA programs in management and health and life sciences management, and also MS programs in accounting and taxation. Those in a hurry to finish their degrees especially appreciate the five-week- long Saturday classes. One student explains, "The workload is heavy given the short time period, but without taking some of these classes, I would probably only take one class per semester, and it would have taken me a lot longer to complete the program."

FDU MBAs tell us that the regularly-reviewed "classwork here is fine and moderately challenging." Students enjoy a "good rapport among students" and great professors, especially "the adjuncts who bring a great deal of real-life experience to the classroom." One first-year student says, "I have taken five courses so far. Out of these classes, three of the professors I would rate as top-shelf. I was challenged intellectually and gained a lot from these classes. The other two were introductory classes, yet the professors were always accessible and passionate about their subject. There are definitely some hidden treasures in the faculty." In the past, students have complained that "convoluted processes and unhelpful individuals" have marred their dealings with the school; however, a new administration has been instituted throughout the past two years, and is striving to make things more student centered. Some also feel that "the school needs to upgrade some of the classrooms"; it is currently in the process of examining its facilities to make technological upgrades.

Career and Placement

Each of FDU's campuses maintains its own Career Development Center. Both offices offer self-assessment tools, one-on-one counseling, libraries, resume critiquing, interview and job-search seminars, job listings, on-campus recruitment interviews, co-op and internship services, and career fairs. Past on-campus recruiters have included Advanced Technology Group, Ameriprise Financial, AXA Advisors, the Drug Enforcement Agency, First Investors, Northwest Mutual, ProFinance, Wachovia, and the World Savings Bank, CitiGroup, Deloitte Touche Tohmatsu, KPMG International, Colgate Palmolive, and PricewaterhouseCoopers.

Student Life and Environment

Most of FDU's full-time MBAs (as well as many part-time students) attend the Metropolitan campus in Teaneck, not far from the George Washington Bridge, thus providing easy access to New York City. The program is housed in Dickinson Hall, which offers three microcomputer laboratories, an auditorium, classrooms, and office space. The wooded campus straddles the Hackensack River.

ADMISSIONS CONTACT: SUSAN BROOMAN, DIRECTOR OF GRADUATE RECRUITMENT & MARKETING
ADDRESS: 1000 RIVER ROAD, T-KB1-01 TEANECK, NJ 07666 UNITED STATES
PHONE: 201-692-2554 • FAX: 201-692-2560
E-MAIL: GRAD@FDU.EDU • WEBSITE: WWW.FDU.EDU

FDU's College at Florham campus in Madison attracts mostly part-time students. The campus was landscaped by famed architect Frederick Law Olmstead; unfortunately for most MBAs, it's often dark here when they arrive and leave, making it more difficult to appreciate the surrounding beauty. Not that students would have much time to take in their environment anyway, since "most of the MBA students also work full-time. They don't have time for involvement with the school outside the classroom."

At both sites, FDU attracts "a very mixed conglomerate of people" that includes "lots of foreign students." These "intelligent, hardworking, and dedicated" MBAs don't socialize much, but "you meet a lot of people anyway because there are a lot of group assignments." Students are "competitive, but in a friendly way." A considerable number are just starting out in their careers; writes one student who isn't, "I am a mid-career manager and am older than most of the students. However, I do not feel out of place. All of my classes have been great, and the diversity of experiences has resulted in great learning sessions."

Admissions

Applicants to the FDU MBA program must apply to a specific campus; after being admitted, students are permitted to register for classes at either campus. Applications are processed on a rolling basis, with the exception of a few of specialized programs. All applications must include official transcripts for all academic work completed after high school, an official GMAT score report, and a completed application form. Certain programs also require interviews and letters of recommendation; check with the school to learn whether your desired program is included. Students who have not completed all prerequisite courses for the MBA may be admitted conditionally; they may enroll in undergraduate business classes on a nondegree basis in order to qualify for the MBA program. International students whose native language is not English and who have not completed undergraduate degrees in an English-language institution must take the TOEFL and achieve a satisfactory score.

FINANCIAL FACTS

Annual tuition	$16,074
Fees	$608
Cost of books	$2,000
Room & board	$13,598
% of students receiving aid	65
% of students receiving loans	37
% of students receiving grants	17
Average award package	$3,500
Average grant	$5,100

ADMISSIONS

Admissions Selectivity Rating	**84**
# of applications received	632
% applicants accepted	322
Average GMAT	485
Average GPA	3.5
TOEFL required of international students	Yes
Minimum TOEFL (paper/ computer/Internet)	550/213/79
Application fee	$40
International application fee	$40
Regular application deadline	rolling
Regular notification	rolling
Deferment available	Yes
Transfer students accepted	Yes
Transfer application policy Core courses can be waived by meeting FDU waiver policy. 6 graduate level credits can be transferred from other AACSB schools.	
Non-fall admissions	Yes
Need-blind admissions	Yes

EMPLOYMENT PROFILE		
Career Rating	60*	**Top 5 Employers Hiring Grads**
		Deloitte; Price Waterhouse; KPMG; Rothstein Kass; Merrill Lynch

FAYETTEVILLE STATE UNIVERSITY
SCHOOL OF BUSINESS AND ECONOMICS MBA PROGRAM

Academics

The School of Business and Economics at Fayetteville State University, a campus of the University of North Carolina system, offers both on-site and online MBA courses to both full-time and part-time students. Undergraduates pursuing a three-two BA/MBA and international students fill out the full-time population; the remaining majority of students are part-timers who typically work full-time while earning a graduate degree. The latter are well served by UNCFSU's "flexible curriculum" and by the school's partnerships with large local employers, including the US Army at Fort Bragg and the Cape Fear Valley Health System (the school offers an MBA in healthcare, with "classes right on the hospital campus," one participant reports). The school is accredited by the AACSB International.

The UNCFSU MBA is open to all students with undergraduate degrees, including those with no background in business; such students must complete up to 18 credit hours of non-degree foundation courses covering accounting, statistics, finance, microeconomics, macroeconomics, management, communication, and marketing. Students with previous coursework or extensive experience in these areas may place out of some or all foundation courses. The degree-applicable MBA curriculum consists of 24 credit hours of core curriculum and 12 credit hours of electives. Students may take all electives in a single area to develop a concentration in accounting, finance, healthcare, international business, management, project management, or marketing, or they may mix and match electives to earn an MBA in general business. The school offers a fairly even mix of onsite and online classes, with the former more likely to outnumber the latter slightly in any given semester.

Students praise the "high quality of instructors and the friendly atmosphere offering students opportunities to grow intellectually. Many are "very impressed with the technology used in the classrooms and available for the students, particularly the offsite access to several software programs and library resources." Convenience and a developing local reputation seem to be the chief selling points among current students; they like how they can get a relatively inexpensive MBA "with the convenience of taking some classes online, which cuts down on added expenses" and also that the school "has greatly improved the community perception that it is doing a good job with our young people."

Career and Placement

Placement and career counseling services are provided by the Office of Advisement and Career Services Center at UNCFSU. The office serves all undergraduates, graduates, and recent alumni "in their preparation for securing meaningful employment." Services include workshops, symposia, classroom presentations, career exploration seminars, and job fairs. A Career Resource Library "offers materials and information regarding careers, the job search process, and company literature as well as graduate schools and fellowship programs." Access to online job search tools allows students to utilize a broad range of local, national, and international job-search engines.

Student Life and Environment

UNCFSU serves a student body that consists mostly of "focused working professionals" (their rank include "doctors, accountants, bankers, and soldiers") with some undergraduates (in the three-two program) and international students in the mix. "Students in the program are extremely friendly and willing to share their experiences and collaborate with studies," one student here informs us. "Most have families, though some don't."

As at most part-time programs serving working students, extracurricular life here is minimal. Some bemoan the dearth of activities, student associations and groups, and "speakers from large businesses and corporations visiting the campus," but many wouldn't notice the difference even if all these activities arrived tomorrow. They're simply too busy with work, school, and life to make time for extracurricular activities. An international student from Romania tells us that the environment is hospitable to foreign students, saying: "It felt like home from the first day of school. Everybody is friendly and helpful and the instructors are always trying to push the students' limits towards higher achievements that will prepare them better for the job market."

Admissions

Degree-seeking applicants to UNCFSU must provide the Admissions Committee with the following materials: a completed application form; official transcripts for all undergraduate and graduate institutions attended (international students must have their transcripts evaluated by an approved agency such as the World Education Service); an official score report for the GMAT; and two letters of recommendation. Students whose native language is not English must submit an official score report for the Test of English as a Foreign Language (TOEFL). International applicants must complete a different application form and must provide proof of their ability to support themselves financially while attending the institution. Degree-seeking applicants must earn a formula score of at least 950 under the formula [(undergraduate GPA 200) + GMAT score], with a minimum GMAT score of 375. Those failing to meet the above requirements but who have a minimum GPA of 2.5 or a GMAT score of at least 450 may be admitted under the Professional Development status, and may later be reclassified as degree-seeking students. Current undergraduates who have carried a GPA of at least 3.0 for the trailing 60 credit hours and earn a formula score of at least 1000 are eligible for the three-two BA/MBA degree program.

FINANCIAL FACTS
Annual tuition (in-state/ out-of-state)	$2,118/$11,708
Fees	$1,218
Cost of books	$400
Room & board (on-campus)	$6,000
% of students receiving grants	3

ADMISSIONS
Admissions Selectivity Rating	**64**
# of applications received	150
% applicants accepted	80
% acceptees attending	90
Average GMAT	470
Range of GMAT	410–500
Average GPA	3.2
TOEFL required of international students	Yes
Minimum TOEFL (paper/computer)	550/213
Application fee	$25
International application fee	$25
Regular application deadline	7/15
Deferment available	Yes
Maximum length of deferment	one year
Transfer students accepted	Yes
Transfer application policy Up to six credit hours could be transferred from an AACSB accredited program.	
Non-fall admissions	Yes

Applicants Also Look At
The University of North Carolina at Pembroke, Campbell University, University of North Carolina at Wilmington, North Carolina Central University.

FLORIDA ATLANTIC UNIVERSITY
COLLEGE OF BUSINESS

GENERAL INFORMATION
Type of school   Public
Environment   City
Academic calendar   Semesters

SURVEY SAYS...
Solid preparation in:
Communication/interpersonal skills
Presentation skills

STUDENTS
Enrollment of parent
  institution   26,525
Enrollment of
  business school   548
% male/female   57/43
% out-of-state   13
% part-time   65
% minorities   27
% international   17
Average age at entry   30
Average years work
  experience at entry   6.5

ACADEMICS
Academic Experience Rating   82
Student/faculty ratio   14:1
Profs interesting rating   94
Profs accessible rating   72
% female faculty   30

Academics

The Barry Kaye School of Business at Florida Atlantic University "offers some interesting and unique programs," including a well-regarded MBA in sport management, an environmental MBA, a master's in forensic accounting, and distance learning options "with no obligation to physically attend classes," which makes for an especially appealing feature to the many busy professionals earning degrees here. Students especially appreciate how online courses counter "FAU's habit of scheduling all courses at the same time" by making it possible to "take a mix of online and onsite courses to get through the program much faster."

FAU's sport management program "has a great reputation" and capitalizes on a strong local industry in order to allow students "to learn from industry professionals" and serve career-boosting internships. Likewise, FAU's graduate communications program is "intense and extensive. You must be certified in speaking and writing to graduate from this program. They give you all the tools you need to be a success and require you to do the work you need to get yourself to the level expected." Students also praise the accounting program, saying it's "just excellent—the courses offered, course content, instructors. It is a very demanding program (much more demanding than the MBA)." Students in the MBA program concur, telling us, "The academics aren't overly demanding, since the university recognizes that many of its master's students also are employed full-time, but it is important to be able to balance everything."

The FAU curriculum features "a strong focus on presentations and group work." Some approve, while others believe "there's too much focus on this. Most of the people here are career professionals and work on teams daily. Sometimes, the stress of meeting with members for assignments can be a bit overwhelming," especially when team members live in different cities. Classes include "free-flowing and wide-ranging discussions. Professors consider alternative points of view and create an environment to foster open and honest discussion." As at many large schools, "Going through the administration can be complicated. Persistence is key."

Career and Placement

FAU's College of Business houses the Career Resources and Alumni Relations Center to provide undergraduates and graduate business students with "invaluable guidance with interviewing skills, resume preparation, locating employment opportunities and locating internships." The office also compiles student resumes on a CD-ROM to be distributed to South Florida businesses. Graduate students have exclusive access to the Job Connection, an internet-based notification system that alerts them to job postings that match their qualifications. FAU participates in a statewide job fair held in the autumn, and "the school offers an online job board and hosts two large job fairs during the school year," but some complain that "there is a noticeable absence of top-tier companies recruiting graduates" at these events.

TIFFANY NICHOLSON, ASSOCIATE DIRECTOR OF ACADEMIC SUPPORT SERVICES
ADDRESS: 132 FLEMING WEST, 777 GLADES ROAD BOCA RATON, FL 33431 UNITED STATES
PHONE: 561-297-2786 • FAX: 561-297-1315
E-MAIL: MBA@FAU.EDU • WEBSITE: WWW.BUSINESS.FAU.EDU

Student Life and Environment

FAU MBAs are typically "employed full-time during the day so the involvement in campus activities is low; however, everyone is very friendly, and once we get to know each other we do mingle outside of the classroom (at least the students in our twenties). There are lots of activities available if you choose to take part, especially athletic events."

The FAU campus provides "a supportive environment" with "state-of-the-art technology" and plenty of "sun and palm trees." The campus is "growing as FAU is becoming a top-tier school in Florida. More buildings are being built, and they make the campus a beautiful place to be." Hometown Boca is "a fantastic location. It's close to the beach and close to Miami and Fort Lauderdale," providing plenty of opportunities for internships and career networking.

Students here "come from many walks of life" and "are all employed in various fields." "We have doctors, lawyers, entrepreneurs, professors, CPAs, etc.," one student explains. "You name it, we have it! Each of them is a professional in their own right and is seeking to enhance their knowledge base." All these commitments mean that students are "always on the run" and that "not too many have spare time to get together and study." However, when time allows, the program attendees' "diverse nationalities and backgrounds lead to great discussions." "About 90 percent of my classmates in my global culture class were not born in the United States. It's a great multicultural mix."

Admissions

Admission to a FAU MBA program requires the following: an undergraduate degree with a GPA of at least 3.0 (on a four-point scale) for the final 60 semester hours of undergraduate course work from an accredited institution; and, a score of at least 500 on the GMAT, earned within the previous five years. In addition to the above qualifications, international students whose first language is not English must also submit official score reports indicating a score of at least 600 on the TOEFL and at least 250 on the Test of Spoken English (TSE). All international applicants must submit Certification of Financial Responsibility and must provide translation and accredited evaluation of their undergraduate transcripts (the latter is necessary only if a grading system other than the American system was used at the degree-granting institution). Letters of recommendation, a resume, an interview, and a personal statement are optional for all applicants. After undergraduate record and standardized test scores, work history is the most important factor in admissions decisions.

FINANCIAL FACTS

Annual tuition (in-state/ out-of-state)	$4,410/$16,434
Cost of books	$1,100
Room & board (on/off-campus)	$9,000/$12,000

ADMISSIONS

Admissions Selectivity Rating	**81**
# of applications received	359
% applicants accepted	55
% acceptees attending	73
Average GMAT	540
Range of GMAT	510–580
Average GPA	3.3
TOEFL required of international students	Yes
Minimum TOEFL (paper/computer)	600/250
Application fee	$30
International application fee	$30
Regular application deadline	7/1
Regular notification	Rolling
Deferment available	Yes
Maximum length of deferment	up to 1 year
Transfer students accepted	Yes
Transfer application policy We allow the transfer of up to 6 Semester credit hours from an AACSB accredited graduate program. Credits must be no more than 7 years old.	
Non-fall admissions	Yes
Need-blind admissions	Yes

Applicants Also Look At

Florida Gulf Coast University, Florida International University, Florida State University, University of Central Florida, University of Florida, University of South Florida.

EMPLOYMENT PROFILE	
Career Rating	73

FLORIDA GULF COAST UNIVERSITY
LUTGERT COLLEGE OF BUSINESS

GENERAL INFORMATION

Type of school	Public
Academic calendar	Semester

SURVEY SAYS...
Solid preparation in:
General management
Operations
Teamwork
Doing business in a global economy

STUDENTS

Enrollment of parent institution	9,358
Enrollment of business school	151
% male/female	54/46
% out-of-state	2
% part-time	68
% minorities	10
% international	21
Average age at entry	29

ACADEMICS

Academic Experience Rating	**83**
Student/faculty ratio	3:1
Profs interesting rating	90
Profs accessible rating	78
% female faculty	29
% minority faculty	13

FINANCIAL FACTS

Annual tuition (in-state/ out-of-state)	$4,542/$19,449
Fees (in-state/ out-of-state)	$1,297/$1,946
Cost of books	$950
Room & board (on-campus)	$8,267
% of students receiving aid	58
% of first-year students receiving aid	35
% of students receiving loans	13
% of students receiving grants	46
Average award package	$6,990
Average grant	$3,305
Average student loan debt	$12,504

Academics

The Lutgert College of Business at Florida Gulf Coast University offers both a full-time and a part-time MBA program as well as an Executive MBA, an MS in accounting and taxation, and an MS in computer information systems. The school offers a broad range of MBA courses online to facilitate distance learning. Location and cost are among the top reasons cited for attending; students also appreciate that "the College of Business, both undergrad and graduate, is very well established in the local community."

The FGCU MBA "emphasizes the application of analytical, technical, and behavioral tools to solve organizational problems" with "a focus on teamwork and team building so that students frequently work closely together." The program consists of 24 hours of foundation courses, 21 hours of core courses, and 9 hours of concentration courses; students with solid business backgrounds or college transcripts deep in business courses may have some or all of the foundation courses waived. Concentrations are offered in general management, interdisciplinary studies, finance, information systems, or marketing. Students approve, telling us that the school has "a tremendous faculty and staff backed with a tremendous amount of intelligence." "A majority of the faculty holds PhDs and frequently publish articles and books as well," a student explains. Finance is particularly strong, as "a majority of the professors come from companies and institutions such as Gillette and the Federal Reserve. These professors hold advanced degrees from schools like Wharton and Harvard." The program itself, says one MBA, "offers a globally aligned business education through a quality Master's program. FGCU is integrated with schools in Germany and elsewhere abroad." A student population in which "multiple nationalities, ethnic groups, and minorities are represented" amplifies this international focus.

Lutgert opened in 1997, and students see its newcomer status as a plus. One explains: "Being a newer school, it has jumped headfirst into solving the web-based education and capitalizing on using the Internet to advance the teachers' ability to manage classroom assignments, work, and lessons. They are light-years ahead of most schools that may appear larger and more experienced but have failed to grasp the integration of solid web-based education." The school's novelty also pays dividends in "the modernity of its infrastructure," which includes "a great, clean, small campus" with a "great library with plenty of quiet areas and an abundance of resources and references."

Career and Placement

All career services at Florida Gulf Coast University are provided by the school's Career Development Services office, which assists undergraduates and graduate students in all areas. The office sponsors a variety of events throughout the year, including workshops, seminars, on-campus recruiting visits, and a career fair. Participants in the school's Spring 2008 Career Expo included Alliance Financial, Ameriprise, Colonial Life, Gartner, Northwestern Mutual, Orion Bank, Primerica Financial Services, and Wells Fargo. Students would like to see "a stronger showing of large international companies in recruiting season." Because the school is relatively new—FGCU welcomed its first students in 1997—its alumni network is small, but growing.

Student Life and Environment

Most FGCU MBAs have little time for campus life. Quite a few, in fact, rarely visit campus at all since the school also serves a sizeable distance-learning population. Even those who attend classes in person typically work full time. Many have family obligations too, leaving little (make that "no") time for extracurriculars. International students, who attend full time, are one exception to the rule. The other includes some students who have proceeded directly from undergraduate study to the MBA program. (While a number of these attend part time while working, others attend on a full-time basis.) Students tend to be "resourceful, smart, and innovative." One informs us that "this region of Florida breeds entrepreneurs, and the Florida Gulf Coast University MBA program caters to that audience. We receive a quality education for learning how to start, maintain and operate, and capitalize on all our resources to make a business successful."

The FGCU campus is located 15 minutes from the Gulf of Mexico, in a small city with great weather and a laid-back vibe. Students agree that the quality of life in the area is high. As one student puts it, "It's 76 degrees on March 11. Any other questions?" Top-area employers include Lee Memorial Hospital, SWFL Regional Medical Center, the government, local colleges and universities, and real estate and resort developers. The area is growing quickly, creating opportunities for both managers and entrepreneurs. The university is growing as well, with lots of new facilities developing all the time.

Admissions

Admission to the MBA program at FGCU is based on a combination of undergraduate GPA and GMAT scores. To be considered, applicants much have either a minimum GPA of 3.0 for their final 60 credit hours of undergraduate work or a minimum GMAT score of 500; and a formula score of at least 1050 under the formula [(undergraduate GPA 200) + GMAT score], with a minimum GMAT score of at least 400. International students whose first language is not English must also submit TOEFL scores (minimum 550 written, 213 computerized, 79 internet-based). Students may apply for admission to either the fall or spring semester. Students may complete a maximum of nine credit hours of graduate level courses before gaining official admission to the program.

ADMISSIONS	
Admissions Selectivity Rating	**72**
# of applications received	102
% applicants accepted	75
% acceptees attending	65
Range of GMAT	383–600
Average GPA	3.02
TOEFL required of international students	Yes
Minimum TOEFL (paper/computer)	550/213
Application fee	$30
International application fee	$30
Regular application deadline	6/2
Regular notification	7/2
Deferment available	Yes
Maximum length of deferment	1 Semester
Transfer students accepted	Yes
Transfer application policy 6 Credits maybe transfered of approved graduate level course work from a regionally accredited institution.	
Non-fall admissions	Yes
Need-blind admissions	Yes

FLORIDA INTERNATIONAL UNIVERSITY
ALVIN H. CHAPMAN GRADUATE SCHOOL OF BUSINESS

GENERAL INFORMATION
Type of school   Public
Environment   Metropolis

SURVEY SAYS...
Cutting edge classes
Solid preparation in:
Operations
Teamwork
Doing business in a global economy

STUDENTS
% male/female   54/46
% part-time   88
% international   19
Average age at entry   30
Average years work
    experience at entry   6

ACADEMICS
Academic Experience Rating   93
Student/faculty ratio   10:1
Profs interesting rating   79
Profs accessible rating   84
% minority faculty   46

Joint Degrees
MBA/Master of Science in Finance,
MBA/Master of Science in
Management Information Systems,
MBA/MSIRE, MBA/MSHRM, MIB.

Prominent Alumni
Carlos Alvarez, Mayor, Miami Dade
County; Juan Figuereo, VP, Mergers
and Aquisitions, Wal-Mart Stores,
Inc.; Ana Lopez-Vazquez, CEO
Baptist Health Enterprises; Dennis
Klinger, VP & Chief Info. Off.,
Florida Power & Light Com.; Carlos
Migoya, Regional Pres., Wachovia
Bank, N.A..

Academics

As its name suggests, Florida International University fixes a steady gaze on global commerce through its Chapman Graduate School of Business. This is especially true for students in FIU's 1-year, full-time International MBA program, but each of the school's varied alternatives stresses international business in its curriculum, with a particular focus on Latin America and the Caribbean (two regions whose populations are well represented in the Miami area). FIU also emphasizes entrepreneurial studies and the development of technological know-how throughout its curriculum. "Overall, a business school student should expect to leave with a very thorough understanding of how changes in business units, companies, industries, and the greater economic ecosystem impact each other," one student says.

In addition to its International MBA program, FIU also offers a 20-month executive MBA featuring an integrated curriculum taught "in cohort format, two classes per quarter" and including a global business trip that provides networking opportunities with corporate leaders abroad; a 20-month professional MBA, with classes also held on Saturdays; a flexible evening MBA, which allows students to choose the number of classes they take per semester while also allowing for a concentration in entrepreneurship, marketing, international business, finance, human resource management, or management information systems; and a downtown MBA, a concentrated 18-month program designed for busy professionals who want to study on a convenient schedule at a convenient location.

With all these choices, it is no wonder that students praise the convenience of obtaining an FIU MBA. They also love the relatively low cost of tuition, which, coupled with the "quality of the program," means a great return on investment. Students are uniform in their admiration for an "outstanding faculty" that "is clearly in tune with the theory and practice in their respective fields. They are well versed in international business and rely heavily on current events to stimulate class discussions and case studies, and they do a great job of incorporating advanced technologies into the program." While some here wish the school would "expand the areas of concentration to encompass such disciplines as corporate accounting," most would agree that "this school's strong emphasis on global business is much needed" when a student goes out into the business world.

Career and Placement

Chapman's Career Management Services office provides graduate students and alumni with counseling and placement assistance. The office works closely with the university's Career Services office to coordinate career fairs, on-campus interviews, and other career-related events. Students tell us that FIU's alumni network is large and very helpful.

Top employers of FIU MBAs (including currently employed students attending one of the part time programs) include: American Airlines, Anteon Corporation, Bajaj-Allianz, Bank of America, BAP Developers, Bayview Financial, Caterpillar, CIA, C.R. Bard, Deloitte Touche Tohmatsu, Enterprise Risk Management, Filesx, Florida International University, Google, Halliburton, Humana, Interstate Container, ITESM USA, Johnson & Johnson, Microsoft Licensing, Morrison, Brown, Argiz & Farra LLP, Mr. Sake, Novartis, OBM International, Oracle, Paetec, PricewaterhouseCoopers, Proctor & Gamble, Protivity, Sears Holding Corporation, Smith Hanley, The NBA, The Seminole Tribe, TracFone Wireless, United Motors of America, Wachovia, Weston Financials, Whirlpool Corporation.

ADMISSIONS CONTACT: PRISCILLA FERREIRA, SENIOR MANAGER, GRADUATE RECRUITING
ADDRESS: 11200 S. W. 8TH STREET - CBC 200 MIAMI, FL 33199 UNITED STATES
PHONE: 305-348-3880 • FAX: 305-348-7204
E-MAIL: CHAPMAN@FIU.EDU • WEBSITE: BUSINESS.FIU.EDU

Student Life and Environment

Full-time students extol FIU's campus life, telling us that "the Student Government Association at FIU involves all its students, including graduate students, and it's a great environment to learn excellent communication and interpersonal skills." Part-timers, however, tell us that they "are not really involved in any type of campus-life organizations or events." Full-timers and part-timers alike agree that academic life "fosters a very collegial environment. This works very well to create an atmosphere of learning."

FIU's student body "represents a truly international class, with students coming from many different countries. It is great experience to be a part of such a student body." Students include "businesspeople with different industrial backgrounds, different cultures, and with a lot of experience in their respective industries." The programs "have people from both corporate American and from the public sector, and they bring different strengths to the table." They are typically "amicable and are always putting maximum effort," making them "great people to be friends with."

Admissions

Admissions requirements to FIU's MBA programs vary somewhat from program to program. As a general rule, students with the best combination of grade point average (GPA), applicable test scores, and pertinent work experience who also meet specific program requirements will have the first opportunity to enter the programs, according to the school's website. Applicants to the school's popular International MBA program must submit the following materials: an official copy of an undergraduate transcript, with a GPA of at least 3.0 in upper-division course work strongly preferred; official proof of undergraduate degree; a current resume; a personal statement; and an official GMAT or GRE score report. In addition to the above documents, international students whose primary language is not English must also provide an official score report for the TOEFL (minimum score: 550, paper-based test; 213, computer-based test) or the IELTS (minimum score: 6.3 overall). They must also submit their transcripts to a translation agency, to be forwarded to FIU, and they must provide the following documents: Declaration of Certification of Finances (DCF); a bank letter; a sponsor letter if applicable; and an F-1 transfer if they already have an F-1 Visa.

FINANCIAL FACTS

Annual tuition (in-state/ out-of-state)	$29,500/$34,500
Cost of books	$2,000
Room & board (on/off-campus)	$10,000/$13,000
Average award package	$21,080
Average grant	$5,000
Average student loan debt	$40,000

ADMISSIONS

Admissions Selectivity Rating	92
# of applications received	1,275
% applicants accepted	45
% acceptees attending	74
Average GMAT	548
Range of GMAT	523–600
Average GPA	3.19
TOEFL required of international students	Yes
Minimum TOEFL (paper/computer)	550/213
Application fee	$30
International application fee	$30
Regular application deadline	Rolling
Regular notification	Rolling
Deferment available	Yes
Maximum length of deferment	1 year
Transfer students accepted	Yes
Transfer application policy A student may receive permission to transfer up to six Semester hours of graduate credit towards his or her degree program.	
Non-fall admissions	Yes
Need-blind admissions	Yes

EMPLOYMENT PROFILE

Career Rating	72	Grads Employed by Function	%	Avg. Salary
Primary Source of Full-time Job Acceptances		Finance	50	$82,250
School-facilitated activities	4 (50%)	Marketing	25	$53,750
Graduate-facilitated activities	4 (50%)	Operations	13	$70,000
Average base starting salary	$69,313	General Management	12	$48,000
Percent employed	25			

FLORIDA STATE UNIVERSITY
COLLEGE OF BUSINESS

Academics

The College of Business at Florida State University offers a variety of options to suit the diverse needs of its MBA student body. Students straight out of college and anxious to earn a graduate degree typically find their way to the school's one-year full-time MBA program. Busy professionals can choose between an on-campus part-time program and an online program with "an asynchronous, totally web-based curriculum." The super-ambitious can pursue joint degrees in business and law or business and social work. In all programs, the reasonable tuition ("It's a prestigious school at a great value," writes one student) and "the growing reputation of the business school" are compelling factors in bringing students aboard.

Florida's full-time MBA is a cohort-based lockstep curriculum, with students remaining in the same work group throughout the twelve-month program. Students in the program may concentrate in finance or marketing and supply chain management, or they may earn a general MBA. Part-time students complete the same core courses and study with the same professors as do their full-time counterparts; however, they are not divided into cohorts and they cannot pursue a concentration. The online MBA can be completed in its entirety remotely. Again, students complete the same core courses with the same professors as do other FSU MBAs. The online MBA allows for concentrations in real estate and analysis or hospital administration. Students may also complete a general MBA.

FSU faculty members receive strong grades overall. Students tell us, "The professors in the business department are amazing. They are very congenial and well spoken. They are helpful at all times. Most teachers are older and contain a strong sense of experience. They know how to teach a class that is entertaining, interactive, and fun." Some warn that "There are quite a few professors here with heavy accents that may take a little concentration to understand," but even they concede that "their willingness to help you outside the classroom and brilliance far outweigh this drawback." Teachers also "do a very good job of keeping class interesting by incorporating technology, group assignments, etc."

Career and Placement

Because FSU's MBA program is small and largely part time, the school does not maintain a separate career services office for graduate students in business. It does, however, sponsor an MBA Internship Program in which "carefully structured project work" allows both students and employers to "realize the benefits of this program." The school also offers coaching and career-related resources in order to help students plan their job search and marketing of their skills. The school hosts semiannual MBA Networking Night events and on-campus and videoconference interviews. It also provides students access to a host of job-posting resources. Students report, "Our career center is great about creating internship opportunities. However, as far as full-time positions after graduation, the focus is more on undergrads. There are few recruiters that come specifically for MBAs." In the plus column, "Networking seems to be one of the biggest strengths of Florida State. Through the College of Business, my sorority, and all the amazing staff, the opportunities are endless."

Employers most likely to hire FSU MBAs include BB&T, CSX, Harris, JP Morgan, Protiviti, and Wachovia Bank.

ADMISSIONS CONTACT: LISA BEVERLY, ADMISSIONS DIRECTOR
ADDRESS: GRADUATE PROGRAMS, COLLEGE OF BUSINESS, FSU TALLAHASSEE, FL 32306-1110 U.S.
PHONE: 850-644-6458 • FAX: 850-644-0588
E-MAIL: GRADPROG@COB.FSU.EDU • WEBSITE: WWW.COB.FSU.EDU/GRAD

Student Life and Environment

Full-timers at FSU basically get to extend their college years by one, albeit with a heavier workload. Students tell us: "Life is relaxed and challenging. We have a lot of work but ample time to complete it. Everyone wants to have a good time, but it's about priorities. If you go to class, you will succeed." Campus life offers "the perfect balance of challenging schoolwork, amazing social groups, and fun nightlife," and "the School of Dance and Music puts on (sometimes free) performances for the community. FSU energizes Tallahassee," a city that is "a great place to be" although "it is a small town and can get boring quick." One student suggests "picking up a hobby that you can do around town in all the parks and woods—Frisbee, mountain biking, kayaking, football, whatever—just stay involved in a physical activity."

Part-time students engage mostly in class and study groups. One observes: "It's nice being able to see the same people semester after semester. That gives us all a sense of warmth when we get into new classes. Life here is pretty busy, people running around trying to get things done on time...not much different from in the real world." Part-timers regard themselves as "more adaptable and friendly" than their full-time peers, whom they regard as "still a bit immature."

Admissions

The Admissions Office at Florida State University requires all of the following from applicants to its MBA program: two official copies of transcripts for all post-secondary academic work; an official GMAT score report; three letters of recommendation from former professors and/or employers; a current resume; a personal statement; and a Florida Residency affidavit, if appropriate. Students must have proficiency working with PCs. International students whose first language is not English must also submit an official score report for the TOEFL (minimum score: 600 paper-based test, 250 computer-based test, or 100 Internet-based test). All test scores must be no more than five years old. The school lists the following programs designed to increase recruitment of underrepresented and disadvantaged students: the FAMU Feeder Program, FAMU Graduate & Professional Days, GradQuest, MBA Advantage, Minority Student Orientation Program, Leslie Wilson Assistantships, the Delores Auzenne Minority Fellowship, and the University Fellowship.

FINANCIAL FACTS

Annual tuition (in-state/ out-of-state)	$9,600/$36,153
Cost of books	$5,750
Room & board (on/off-campus)	$13,000/$15,000
% of students receiving aid	29
% of first-year students receiving aid	29
% of students receiving grants	29
Average award package	$10,000
Average grant	$2,500

ADMISSIONS

Admissions Selectivity Rating	87
# of applications received	546
% applicants accepted	55
% acceptees attending	72
Average GMAT	558
Range of GMAT	500–610
Average GPA	3.35
TOEFL required of international students	Yes
Minimum TOEFL (paper/computer)	600/250
Application fee	$30
International application fee	$30
Regular application deadline	2/1
Regular notification	rolling
Deferment available	Yes
Maximum length of deferment	1 year
Transfer students accepted	Yes
Transfer application policy Transfer applicants must complete the same application process as all other applicants.	
Non-fall admissions	Yes
Need-blind admissions	Yes

Applicants Also Look At
University of Central Florida, University of Florida, University of South Florida.

EMPLOYMENT PROFILE

Career Rating	60*	Top 5 Employers Hiring Grads
		Wachovia Bank; U.S. Staffing; CSX Corporation; Harris; Avaya

FORDHAM UNIVERSITY
GRADUATE SCHOOL OF BUSINESS ADMINISTRATION

GENERAL INFORMATION

Type of school	Private
Affiliation	Roman Catholic/Jesuit
Environment	Metropolis
Academic calendar	Trimester

SURVEY SAYS...

Students love New York, NY
Friendly students
Good peer network
Happy students
Solid preparation in:
Teamwork

STUDENTS

Enrollment of parent institution	15,771
Enrollment of business school	1,548
% male/female	61/39
% part-time	76
% minorities	7
% international	13
Average age at entry	28
Average years work experience at entry	5.5

ACADEMICS

Academic Experience Rating	**83**
Student/faculty ratio	8:1
Profs interesting rating	81
Profs accessible rating	70
% female faculty	26

Joint Degrees

JD/MBA, MBA/MIM.

Prominent Alumni

Nemir Kidar, Founder/President, Investcorp Bank; James N. Fernandez, EVP, Tiffany and Company; Patricia Fili Kurshel, EVP, Time Warner; Frank Petrilli, President, CEO, TDWaterhouse.

Academics

With top-dog competitors like Columbia University and NYU just a short subway ride away from its Manhattan campus, Fordham's Graduate School of Business Administration has quite a crowd to elbow its way through in order to get the attention it deserves. The school faces a "catch-22": Located anywhere else in the country, Fordham's program would be much better known and much more highly regarded. But at the same time, if it were located anywhere else it couldn't piggyback on the world's business center or the faculties of its competitors, from which it sometimes draws adjunct professors.

Students at Fordham recognize that they have a good thing going, and they have faith that the rest of the world will soon catch on. The school already has a solid reputation in accounting and tax. Its finance department enjoys "a strong reputation on Wall Street," and for good reason: "Professors in Finance are like the drill sergeants in the Marines. They make you work, and they make you think. It is all very practical. They touch on theory here and there, but mostly help you to understand why you need to know this, and then you learn it inside and out. They are also very open to questions. They never force you to just accept that this is the way it is done." Fordham also boasts "the only communications and media management concentration in New York City," a program that sets students up for careers with the city's many broadcast giants.

Fordham caters to part-time students with a "great, flexible schedule" that "allows students to switch between full- and part-time attendance just by taking more or fewer classes. Other schools require you to withdraw and reapply; you don't have to go through that process here." Students who live or work in Westchester County may wish to take advantage of the program's satellite campus in Tarrytown, at which all required courses and select electives are offered. The many full-time employed students here appreciate these conveniences. As one student explains, "The greatest strength of the school is the flexibility it offers. It has core courses and a minimum number of credits to be taken, but you can choose which core courses you want to start with and with what professors. You can also take some elective courses in the first year. It allows you to do internships outside of the summer months because you can regulate your class hours yourself, and there are many evening classes."

Career and Placement

The Fordham MBA Career Services Office provides placement and counseling to the school's business graduate students. The office benefits greatly from the school's location in a world finance center; one student observes, "Although not a Top 10 school—yet—Fordham still attracts some of the top 200 businesses located in the New York metro area to recruit for employment." Even so, students are aware that their student body is at best the third choice of most big recruiters in New York. One MBA writes, "Honestly, campus recruitment is difficult. Top companies do not invest enough money in recruiting the very talented, best, and brightest students at Fordham." The perception that "career services and a larger, better-equipped staff for career services are needed" does not help matters though the school is enhancing career services and training for students. On a positive note, "the school is currently getting more involved with the alumni," which should improve networking opportunities. Full-timers also benefit from their interactions with part-time students, "most of whom work for prestigious companies in New York City. Networking with the part-time students can lead to jobs and internships."

ADMISSIONS CONTACT: CYNTHIA PEREZ, DIRECTOR OF ADMISSIONS AND FINANCIAL AID
ADDRESS: 33 WEST 60TH STREET, 4TH FLOOR NEW YORK, NY 10023 UNITED STATES
PHONE: 212-636-6200 • FAX: 212-636-7076
E-MAIL: ADMISSIONSGB@FORDHAM.EDU • WEBSITE: WWW.BNET.FORDHAM.EDU

Student Life and Environment

Life in Fordham's MBA program "is very social, with Thursday happy hours every week where you can meet full-time and part-time students and network. There are also many opportunities to join clubs and actively participate in the many activities arranged by the different clubs. You don't have time to do everything!" The school's Lincoln Center location means that fine dining and upscale shopping are just outside the school's doors. One student notes, "We're in the heart of New York City, just off of Central Park at Lincoln Center. It's a great place to enjoy the spring and summer weather. Catching up in Central Park on a Wi-Fi-enabled computer is definitely one of the perks."

About the only criticism of Fordham's facilities is that MBAs feel a little crowded out by other students. One MBA observes, "They need to separate the graduate business school from the other graduate schools located on the campus. The law school feels separate, but the business school shares many resources with both undergraduate and other graduate programs. A graduate business lounge and special study areas within the library that facilitate discussion groups would really help."

Admissions

Admission to the Fordham MBA program is competitive. Applicants must submit all of the following materials: a completed application, either hard copy or online; copies of all postsecondary transcripts; an official GMAT score report; two letters of recommendation, preferably from current supervisors, managers, clients, and/or coworkers; a personal statement of length 500 to 1,000 words; and a current resume. International applicants whose first language is not English must also submit an official TOEFL score report. Interviews are not required, but can be granted at the applicant's request. Interview availability is limited; those wishing to interview are encouraged to make their request early in the admissions process. The median GMAT score among admitted students is 600 in the full-time program, 575 in the part-time program.

FINANCIAL FACTS

Annual tuition	$32,775
Fees	$340
Cost of books	$1,080
Average grant	$4,500

ADMISSIONS

Admissions Selectivity Rating	82
# of applications received	1,131
% applicants accepted	63
% acceptees attending	57
Average GMAT	595
Range of GMAT	540–670
Average GPA	3.18
TOEFL required of international students	Yes
Minimum TOEFL (paper/computer)	600/250
Application fee	$65
International application fee	$65
Regular application deadline	6/1
Regular notification	Rolling
Deferment available	Yes
Maximum length of deferment	1 year
Transfer students accepted	Yes
Transfer application policy ACCSB Accredited school; Prerequisite and Core Courses can be waived based on course work taken at other institution.	
Non-fall admissions	Yes
Need-blind admissions	Yes

Applicants Also Look At

Boston University; City University of New York—Baruch College; Columbia University; New York University; Pace University; Rutgers, The State University of New Jersey; St. John's University.

EMPLOYMENT PROFILE

Career Rating	83	Grads Employed by Function	%	Avg. Salary
Primary Source of Full-time Job Acceptances		Finance	63	$79,545
School-facilitated activities	11 (32%)	Marketing	17	$80,250
Graduate-facilitated activities	24 (68%)	MIS	8	$73,333
		Operations	3	$85,000
		Consulting	3	$90,000
		Other	6	$104,250

Top 5 Employers Hiring Grads
Ernst & Young; GE Captial; Duff & Phelps; Citigroup; Church & Dwight

Francis Marion University

School of Business

Academics

The School of Business at South Carolina's Francis Marion University offers a "convenient" MBA program "scheduled in the evening to accommodate working students." Since FMU is a state school, it does so at a price that doesn't break the bank.

This small school—one of the smallest state universities to earn AACSB accreditation, according to the university view book—affords "plenty of good one-on-one time with teachers" to its almost exclusively part-time student body. FMU offers both a general MBA and an MBA with a concentration in Health Management. The former is designed to serve the general business population of the Pee Dee region and beyond; the latter is directed toward individuals currently employed in the health care field and/or those with backgrounds in health care. The Health Management Degree is delivered to FMU students through online classes and resources.

All FMU MBAs must complete courses in accounting for management control, managerial economics, financial theory and applications, management science and statistics, marketing, and finance. Students in the general MBA program must also complete classes in financial accounting, information systems, international business, production management, entrepreneurship, and strategic management. Students pursuing a health concentration must also complete classes in health policy, health economics, health care delivery systems, financial management for health care organizations, and health law and risk management. Students in health management may also take three hours of elective course work. At the conclusion of the program, students must pass comprehensive final examinations covering 10 of 12 functions.

MBAs tell us that the program meets their needs, although some feel that "there is too much busywork" and others complain that "some classes are too easy, more suitable to undergraduates than MBAs." One student suggests, "Tailor the program to the real jobs graduates will get." Many also feel that "the school needs to offer more and a wider variety of MBA classes." Most, however, tell us that the convenience and cost of the degree are strong positives.

Career and Placement

FMU's MBA program is too small to support career services dedicated exclusively to its students. MBAs receive career assistance from the university's Office of Career Development, which serves undergraduates and graduates in all divisions. Students here also benefit from an active Alumni Association, whose newest chapter is the MBA Alumni Chapter.

ADMISSIONS CONTACT: BEN KYER, DIRECTOR
ADDRESS: BOX 100547 FLORENCE, SC 29501-0547 UNITED STATES
PHONE: 843-661-1436 • FAX: 843-661-1432
E-MAIL: ALPHA1@FMARION.EDU • WEBSITE: ALPHA1.FMARION.EDU/~MBA

ADMISSIONS	
Admissions Selectivity Rating	**62**
# of applications received	33
% applicants accepted	85
% acceptees attending	93
Average GMAT	400
Average GPA	3.0
TOEFL required of international students	Yes
Minimum TOEFL (paper/computer)	550/213
Application fee	$25
Regular application deadline	Rolling
Regular notification	Rolling
Deferment available	Yes

Student Life and Environment

Life in the FMU MBA program "can be hectic," especially toward the end of the semester. "It seems like all projects and exams are due at the same time," writes one student. Most students are "intelligent and hardworking . . . professional adults trying to obtain a common goal" while juggling careers and family obligations along with their academic responsibilities. As a result, few participate in extracurricular activities.

To enhance campus life, FMU hosts regular artists and lecture series. The school also houses an art gallery that displays student and faculty work as well as traveling exhibitions, film series, a planetarium and observatory, concerts, and festivals. FMU's Patriots compete in Division II of the NCAA. Popular spectator sports include basketball, soccer, men's baseball, women's softball, and women's volleyball.

FMU is located just outside of Florence, SC, a city of 33,000 that offers movie theaters, malls, restaurants, a symphony orchestra, and professional hockey (the Pee Dee Pride skate in the East Coast Hockey League). The city is located at the intersections of I-95 and I-20, making travel in all four cardinal directions a snap. Columbia, Charleston, Myrtle Beach, and Fayetteville, NC, are all within 100 miles.

Admissions

Applicants to the FMU MBA program must submit a completed application; official transcripts for all postsecondary academic work, in a sealed envelope addressed to the applicant from the awarding school; official GMAT scores; two letters of recommendation; and a personal statement of purpose. All materials must be delivered to the school in a single envelope or package. In addition, international applicants must submit official TOEFL scores and a Confidential Financial Statement form demonstrating their ability to pay all expenses related to an FMU MBA. All successful applicants meet the following minimum guidelines: a score greater than 950 under the formula [(undergraduate GPA × 200) + GMAT score] or a score greater than 1000 under the formula [(GPA for final 60 hours of undergraduates work × 200) + GMAT score]. Applicants with non-business undergraduate degrees are generally required to complete the business foundation sequence prior to beginning work on their MBA. The sequence is an 18-hour, 8-course curriculum covering the basics of accounting, economics, statistics, business law, management, information systems, finance, and marketing. Students with undergraduate business degrees typically have this requirement waived.

THE GEORGE WASHINGTON UNIVERSITY
SCHOOL OF BUSINESS

GENERAL INFORMATION

Type of school	Private
Environment	Metropolis
Academic calendar	Semester

SURVEY SAYS...

Students love Washington, DC
Good social scene
Good peer network
Solid preparation in:
Teamwork
Presentation skills
Doing business in a global economy

STUDENTS

Enrollment of parent institution	25,078
Enrollment of business school	3,930
% male/female	60/40
% out-of-state	80
% part-time	63
% minorities	15
% international	40
Average age at entry	29
Average years work experience at entry	5

ACADEMICS

Academic Experience Rating	**91**
Student/faculty ratio	25:1
Profs interesting rating	80
Profs accessible rating	95
% female faculty	27
% minority faculty	10

Joint Degrees

MBA/JD 4 years, MBA/MA (International Affairs), MBA/MS (Finance).

Prominent Alumni

Colin Powell, MBA, Former US Secretary of State; Henry Duques, BBA & MBA, Former President & CEO, First Data Corp.; Edward M. Liddy, MBA, Chairman & CEO, Allstate Insurance; Michael Enzi, BBA, US Senator; Clarence B. Rogers, Jr., MBA, Chairman, President & CEO, Equifax, Inc.

Academics

For many aspiring business school students, The George Washington University School of Business is simply too good to pass up. First, there's hometown Washington, DC, with its international flavor and job opportunities in "all three sectors," not to mention the school's "tremendous" diversity of academic options. In addition to a popular program in international business, GW offers concentration options in environmental management, management science, tourism and hospitality, and an "increasingly popular" real estate and urban development specialization. Joint-degrees with the law school and Elliott School of International Affairs provide another powerful draw.

"Teamwork during the first year is a priority," and entering MBA students are challenged by the cohort-oriented core curriculum emphasizing principles in general management. Second-year students have the opportunity to select a specialization and choose from a broad set of electives whose "breadth and depth" are universally appreciated. This means that prospective GW students should anticipate exposure to a wide variety of courses, such as Energy Management, Management of the Acute Care Hospital, Sports Law, and Business Representation and Lobbying, many of which would not even be available at most b-schools. Second-year students also complete a capstone course, Business Strategy, which deals with the developing world and culminates in a lengthy team report on environmental strategic management.

Students say that professors at GW "are feast or famine," noting that "a few are spectacular" and "always accessible," while others appear not to "care about their students or classes and are much more concerned with their own work." Luckily, "The small size of the program results in individual attention from the faculty and administration." While some students take a dim view of the administration ("Politics rule the place, and it is hard to get [the] proper attention the full-time MBA program deserves"), they also appreciate some of its upsides, such as "supportive" funding of "academic extracurricular activities such as business case competitions." Students also love the "much-needed and appreciated" "new business building" on campus, which "drastically improved the quality of facilities and technology for teaching the MBA program."

Career and Placement

The F. David Fowler Career Center "was totally revamped" recently, and most students are ecstatic about the changes. "The school hired professional consultants, and they are absolutely fantastic!" says one student. "I can't say enough about the advisors or the resources they provide!" Another student is disappointed that there is now only "one Career Center for business school undergrads and grads," and says that "faculty in specific departments" and "connections with alumni" are "much more helpful in sharing opportunities."

Fortunately, "Employers love GW and GW students," and "Many GW grads are working in the field in DC." While nearly half of grads go into consulting and finance, GW is also something of a feeder school for the public sector, sending 9 percent of its graduates into government positions. More than a tenth accept positions in the nonprofit sector. Top recruiters on campus include BearingPoint, Deloitte Consulting, Friedman Billings Ramsey, Johnson & Johnson, Jones Lang LaSalle, KPMG, Merrill Lynch Capital, Pfizer, U.S. Government agencies, Wells Fargo, World Bank.

Student Life and Environment

You "can't beat" GW's "ideal location" in downtown DC, which gives students "access to all the resources of the greater Washington, DC area. This includes cultural events like plays and concerts, speakers, and social events." The school's location also provides an "outstanding environment to get internship or work at international organizations, NGOs, government, or other outstanding firms." The school's "very diverse" community includes "many international and minority students," who represent "a wealth of culture [and] ideas." The first-year curriculum's cohort setup "fosters a sense of unity" among GW students, who call their peers "driven, motivated," and "always willing to help one another." "I loved the feeling of community at GW," says one student. Another student concurs: "It is small enough so I am known or recognized by program faculty and students, but large enough that everyone doesn't know everyone else's business." "Students and alumni are extremely involved and helpful in academic and club events," and students appreciate that they "are able to be very entrepreneurial in starting clubs and hosting panels." On "Thursday night, we have IPOs (informal public outings) [in which] people from school gather for drinks and a good time." Students complain, however, that the MBA Association "must keep in mind [that] some students can't afford $10 beers and $20 cover charges for IPOs."

Admissions

Recently admitted MBA students at The George Washington University had an average GMAT score of 625 and 5 years of full-time work experience. As at most b-schools, applicants straight out of college face tough obstacles when it comes to the admissions process and to fitting in among their peers, but some do overcome these obstacles. GW does not accept 3-year degrees; to be accepted, grads of such programs must earn 2-year master's degrees.

By offering some merit scholarships and endowed scholarships for which international students are eligible, GW flouts the b-school convention of bleeding students dry financially. Many students, both domestic and international, cited generous scholarships as a deciding factor in their choice of GW.

FINANCIAL FACTS

Annual tuition	$31,320
Fees	$30
Cost of books	$2,530
Room & board	$16,380
% of students receiving aid	40
% of first-year students receiving aid	57
% of students receiving loans	50
% of students receiving grants	40
Average award package	$25,000
Average grant	$10,000
Average student loan debt	$40,655

ADMISSIONS

Admissions Selectivity Rating	96
# of applications received	919
% applicants accepted	55
% acceptees attending	54
Average GMAT	618
Range of GMAT	570–710
Average GPA	3.26
TOEFL required of international students	Yes
Minimum TOEFL (paper/computer)	600/250
Application fee	$60
International application fee	$60
Regular application deadline	5/1
Regular notification	Rolling
Deferment available	Yes
Maximum length of deferment	1 year
Transfer students accepted	Yes
Transfer application policy	Standard Application Procedures
Non-fall admissions	Yes
Need-blind admissions	Yes

Applicants Also Look At

Boston College, Boston University, Georgetown University, New York University, Thunderbird, University of Maryland—College Park, Vanderbilt University.

EMPLOYMENT PROFILE

Career Rating	82	Grads Employed by Function	%	Avg. Salary
Average base starting salary	$74,137	Finance	36	$77,063
Percent employed	87	Human Resources	2	NR
		Marketing	24	$69,300
		Operations	6	$69,547
		Consulting	19	$72,111
		General Management	2	NR
		Other	11	$71,000

GEORGETOWN UNIVERSITY
MCDONOUGH SCHOOL OF BUSINESS

GENERAL INFORMATION

Type of school	Private
Affiliation	Roman Catholic-Jesuit
Environment	Metropolis
Academic calendar	Module

SURVEY SAYS...

Students love Washington, DC
Friendly students
Good peer network
Helpful alumni
Solid preparation in:
Doing business in a global economy

STUDENTS

Enrollment of parent institution	13,652
Enrollment of business school	470
% male/female	64/36
% minorities	10
% international	30
Average age at entry	28
Average years work experience at entry	5.2

ACADEMICS

Academic Experience Rating	**91**
Student/faculty ratio	7:1
Profs interesting rating	84
Profs accessible rating	95
% female faculty	32
% minority faculty	16

Joint Degrees

MBA/MSFS 3 years, MBA/MA (Physics) 3 years, MBA/JD 4 years, MBA/MPP 3 years, MBA/MD 5 years, MBA/PhD (Physics) 5 years.

Academics

Offering "a diverse global environment in the world's greatest capital city," the McDonough School of Business at Georgetown University offers an MBA with a strong international focus bolstered by "its international enrollment" and the second-year Global Integrative Experience, a course that culminates in a mandatory 9-day, international consulting experience. The school's location in the nation's capital—a magnet for diplomats and international business reps—further enhances the school's global scope.

McDonough's "innovative curriculum" capitalizes on the university's many strengths by "integrating other elements of the Georgetown University, such as the Public Policy Institute and the School of Foreign Service," thereby exploiting an advantage to "merge public and private interests to create well-rounded, business-minded individuals." The MBA program also benefits from "access to Georgetown University-related activities, such as speakers and workshops," and a "highly responsive alumni" who are "very receptive to networking with MBA students."

McDonough's full-time program operates on a modular calendar, a system many here wish the school would abandon. Students tell us that "five classes crammed into 6-week modules is too much," not allowing students "to delve into course material." The school is responding by moving to a 7-week module with 4 classes. Students who would love to see an upgrade to facilities will not have to wait much longer; "a gorgeous brand-new building in the center of campus" will be dedicated to the business school in 2009. The school introduced a part-time evening program during the 2006–2007 academic year.

MBAs at Georgetown benefit from "small class sizes" because it "encourages a great deal of interaction." Also, students appreciate "a faculty that is very dedicated to teaching, which is clearly distinct from many schools that are more research focused." While international business is McDonough's greatest strength, it isn't its only standout discipline; students laud the "strong management" offerings and note that the school is "a hidden gem for investment banks." Students also appreciate the school's Jesuit underpinnings, which stress ethics, immersion in the liberal arts and philosophy, and the importance of community service.

Career and Placement

McDonough students have complained about career services in the past, but many now emphatically tell us that "there has been considerable improvement" in this area, and "Whereas there was a time when the Career Management Center could have stepped up its efforts, this is no longer the case." The addition of a new Dean and a new Director of Career Management sparked the transformation; today, "Career Management is very dedicated. The office is extremely helpful in providing advice and consultation. Furthermore, the quality of the companies and the job opportunities that are made available to students are outstanding."

Employers who most frequently hire McDonough graduates include: Citigroup, Booz Allen Hamilton, Credit Suisse, Merrill Lynch, AES, America Online, Lehman Brothers, International Finance Corporation (IFC), 3M, American Express Company, Avaya, Bank of New York, Deloitte Touche Tohmatsu, Ford Motor Company, and JPMorgan Chase.

Student Life and Environment

"The workload is intense" at McDonough, with the module system rushing classes along to the point that "it can interfere with the internship/job search. Even so, students who are driven find ways to make it work." Because full-timers attend classes in four separate cohorts, "There isn't much opportunity for you to interact with the three-fourths of the class not in your own cohort," but the "Significant amounts of group work help foster teamwork skills and force people to deal with uncomfortable or unfamiliar situations within their cohorts." Students do get to interact with folks outside their cohorts through "a decent number of clubs and social activities."

Georgetown University is a hub of political and intellectual activity; its many schools host "lectures and activities . . . that are extremely interesting. There are many opportunities to attend lectures with prominent speakers, such as Kofi Anan, [the] President of Afghanistan, etc., who are visiting town." Washington, DC offers even greater diversions, with "many cultural outlets that are unique to DC such as restaurants, nightlife, a great zoo, and museums."

McDonough MBAs enjoy a "highly cooperative environment. Classmates are not at all competitive." The student body "is extremely diverse in both background and professional experience. Even a student without a strong business/financial background would feel comfortable studying here." Part-time evening students "tend to have full-time jobs. Many are married and have kids; they have absolutely no time to socialize."

Admissions

McDonough students report that "the admission process is smooth here because Georgetown likes to meet individually with each student." Applicants must submit all of the following materials: an application form (online application is preferred); a resume; a personal statement of affiliations, community contributions, and personal interests; three required essays; official transcripts for all postsecondary academic work; two evaluations, preferably from professional supervisors; and an official GMAT score report. Interviews are encouraged but are conducted only at the invitation of the school after December 15. International students must submit official score reports for the TOEFL or IELTS in addition to the above materials. McDonough requires a minimum of 2 years of post-collegiate professional experience (and prefers 3 or more) prior to admission.

FINANCIAL FACTS

Annual tuition	$35,328
Fees	$2,303
Cost of books	$2,134
Room & board	$13,000
% of students receiving aid	76
% of first-year students receiving aid	38
% of students receiving loans	80
% of students receiving grants	26
Average award package	$45,000
Average grant	$12,000
Average student loan debt	$58,000

ADMISSIONS

Admissions Selectivity Rating	92
# of applications received	1,515
% applicants accepted	41
% acceptees attending	36
Average GMAT	665
Range of GMAT	620–720
Average GPA	3.2
TOEFL required of international students	Yes
Minimum TOEFL (paper/computer)	600/250
Application fee	$175
International application fee	$175
Regular application deadline	2/8
Regular notification	3/28
Application Deadline/Notification	
Round 1:	11/30 / 01/25
Round 2:	02/08 / 03/28
Round 3:	04/25 / 05/30
Need-blind admissions	Yes

EMPLOYMENT PROFILE

Career Rating	90	Grads Employed by Function	%	Avg. Salary
Primary Source of Full-time Job Acceptances		Finance	43	$91,089
School-facilitated activities	109 (67%)	Human Resources	1	NR
Graduate-facilitated activities	53 (33%)	Marketing	19	$82,576
Unknown	32	Operations	2	$84,333
Average base starting salary	$87,985	Consulting	24	$90,185
Percent employed	89	General Management	6	$91,055
		Other	3	$60,000

GEORGIA INSTITUTE OF TECHNOLOGY
COLLEGE OF MANAGEMENT

GENERAL INFORMATION
Type of school	Public
Environment	Metropolis
Academic calendar	Semester

SURVEY SAYS...
Students love Atlanta, GA
Friendly students
Happy students
Smart classrooms
Solid preparation in:
Operations
Quantitative skills

STUDENTS
Enrollment of parent institution	18,000
Enrollment of business school	214
% male/female	71/29
% out-of-state	45
% part-time	30
% minorities	23
% international	27
Average age at entry	27
Average years work experience at entry	3.2

ACADEMICS
Academic Experience Rating	**91**
Profs interesting rating	80
Profs accessible rating	88
% female faculty	21

Joint Degrees
Any Masters or PhD degree at
Georgia Tech.

Prominent Alumni
David C. Garrett, JR, Retired
Chairman and CEO, Delta Airlines;
Jack Guynn, President and CEO—
retired, Federal Reserve Bank of
Atlanta; Tom A. Fanning, Executive
Vice President, CFO, The Southern
Co.

Academics

As part of a university that is home to one of the best-known engineering schools in the United States, it's not surprising that the MBA program at Georgia Institute of Technology focuses on the quantitative aspects of business. During the first year of the program, students are required to take core courses in areas such as accounting and management, while the second year is taken up with concentrations within the business school or from other areas of the university. Full-time students participate in an internship between the first and second years of the program. Fifty-four credits are required for the MBA, with concentrations available in accounting, finance, information technology management, marketing, organizational behavior, operations management, strategic management within the business school. Dual-degree programs with any other subjects offered by the university is a popular option. Georgia Tech also offers an Executive MBA in Management of Technology, Global Executive MBA, Master of Science in Quantitative and Computational Finance, and courses leading to the PhD in Business. Institutes of Entrepreneurship, New Venture Development, and International Business allow for advanced study in those areas, and students may study abroad in Argentina, Brazil, China, Colombia, Denmark, France, Germany, Japan, Mexico, Netherlands, South Korea, Spain, and Turkey.

In Fall 2007, Georgia Tech began offering an evening MBA program for the first time. It is expected to take 3 years to complete rather than the full-time program's 2 years, with students attending classes 2 nights a week. Course offerings and admissions standards are expected to be similar to those of the full-time day program.

Students are drawn to the emphasis on technology, and to the costs at Tech, which arelower than some comparable business schools in the South. "Georgia Tech's MBA program has the same quality as higher-ranked programs, and with a much better return on investment," students say. The school, which is "known for technology," offers "one of the best entrepreneurship opportunities in the country," with "strong operations and IT management programs," they add. The quality of teaching is generally well regarded, too, as is the administration. "The administration is student focused, the professors challenge you, and the academic experience helps because it mirrors the real business experience" at Georgia Tech. "Extremely knowledgeable and very helpful," professors make themselves available to all students. "I have sat down with professors I have never taken a class from to solicit their feedback on industry projects," one student tells us.

Career and Placement

The Jones Career Center offers MBA career-guide materials, job-bank databases, and participation in a nationwide interviewing consortium with 15 other business schools, as well as career fairs and assistance targeted to international students.

Atlanta's big-city locale is a plus for students in their job search, as are the "amazing" career services offered at the business school. "The location in the heart of Atlanta can't be beat in terms of access to companies," one student points out. Meanwhile, the staff at the Career Center "get outstanding companies to come to the school and really work to get you in front of any company you are pursing," another adds. "They will help you tremendously," one student sums up. Among the companies recruiting at Georgia Tech are Bank of America, BearingPoint, BellSouth, Delta Airlines, Microsoft, Siemens, Turner Broadcasting System, and The Home Depot.

Student Life and Environment

Most of Georgia Tech's MBA students have academic and professional backgrounds in engineering, the hard sciences, and business. Women outnumber the men in this program. While there are areas for improvement, students appreciate their classmates who "are fun, friendly, smart, and insightful. The size of the class makes it possible to really get to know them," and overall they are "supportive. I have learned just as much from my classmates as I have from my classes," says one student. Many would like to see better "alumni relations, [and more] domestic student geographical diversity" along with "better inclusion of spouses and children into school activities." As one student puts it, "I've heard some fellow students comment that it's not quite as family friendly as they might like since the majority of the students don't have kids (although many are married)," but at least students have taken it upon themselves to plan more activities that include significant others. Most students agree that there's a great camaraderie here. "Every student adds value, and no one is admitted just to improve numbers," says one satisfied student. "The learning occurs in and out of the classroom," and "It feels like we are a team, not competing against each other, but challenging ourselves to be better," says another. One sums up: "My classmates are open, personable people who truly try to help one another out. I feel as though our class is building the strong network that will last for years to come."

Admissions

GMAT scores, undergraduate GPA, work experience, and the results of a personal interview are factors than weigh most heavily with those who evaluate applicants for Georgia Tech's MBA program. Personal essays and recommendations are also important, with extracurricular activities carrying less weight. A class in business calculus is a required prerequisite for enrollment, and familiarity with probability theory is suggested as well. A TOEFL score of 600/250/100 is required of those whose first language is not English. In 2006, the average GMAT score of those admitted was 665, with a range of 550 to 760, and the average GPA was 3.41. Georgia Tech generally accepts around 40 percent of those who apply. Enrolling students average 3 and half years of work experience, with many coming from engineering backgrounds.

FINANCIAL FACTS

Annual tuition (in-state/ out-of-state)	$7,218/$28,870
Fees	$1,146
Cost of books	$1,400
Room & board	$12,000
% of students receiving grants	30
Average grant	$6,000
Average student loan debt	$16,000

ADMISSIONS

Admissions Selectivity Rating	**95**
# of applications received	269
% applicants accepted	40
% acceptees attending	70
Average GMAT	665
Range of GMAT	610–710
Average GPA	3.4
TOEFL required of international students	Yes
Minimum TOEFL (paper/computer)	600/250
Application fee	$50
International application fee	$50
Regular application deadline	3/15
Regular notification	Rolling
Deferment available	Yes
Maximum length of deferment	1 year
Need-blind admissions	Yes

Applicants Also Look At

Carnegie Mellon, Emory University, Indiana University—Bloomington, Purdue University, The University of North Carolina at Chapel Hill, University of Maryland—College Park, Vanderbilt University.

EMPLOYMENT PROFILE

Career Rating	93	Grads Employed by Function	%	Avg. Salary
Primary Source of Full-time Job Acceptances		Finance	11	$64,500
School-facilitated activities	58%	Human Resources	1	NR
Graduate-facilitated activities	27%	Marketing	9	$77,000
Unknown	15%	MIS	1	NR
Percent employed	98	Operations	17	$79,888
		Consulting	44	$83,695
		General Management	7	$87,750
		Other	5	$86,343

GEORGIA SOUTHERN UNIVERSITY
COLLEGE OF BUSINESS ADMINISTRATION

Academics

A "hidden gem" in the peach state, Georgia Southern University's small, AACSB-accredited business school offers "affordability and amicability" to a largely local population. At Georgia Southern, students can pursue an MBA degree in general management, or customize the program through a specialization in one of three areas: health services, information systems, and international business. Georgia Southern offers their part-time, evening MBA programs at their Statesboro and Savannah campuses, as well as a part-time, distance learning MBA at the Coastal Community College campus in Brunswick, GA. The school also operates an AASCB-accredited, Web MBA program, which can be completed over the course of five semesters, and MAcc degrees, with an optional concentration in forensic accounting. The "reasonable tuition" is a feature of any graduate program so, no matter what or how you choose to study, "considering the high quality of instruction, the overall cost of attending is a steal."

In the classroom, practical applications of business principles are duly emphasized, and "professors often use current events to explain business concepts." A current student writes, "The professors are detail-oriented and the instruction that they provide can be taken away from academia and applied to the real world." With a total enrollment of fewer than 300 students in the graduate programs, Georgia Southern's "greatest strengths are smaller class sizes and the availability of faculty to students outside of class." In this friendly atmosphere, "professors gave us their cell phone numbers and home numbers to help with accessibility. They were always willing to help with questions, even at home in their personal time." In addition to the faculty, "the administration is approachable" and "very sensitive and supporting of its student body."

Georgia Southern allows senior business majors in the undergraduate school to begin their work towards an MBA before they have received their undergraduate degree. Because MBA courses are taught in the evenings, these students can take undergraduate courses during the day and attend graduate-level courses at night. As a result, there is a smattering of fifth-year seniors in the MBA program; however, most students "are employed full time with several years [of] work experience." Catering to working students, "we have a diverse population and our instructors understand that most of us work or have other situations." On the whole, the academic atmosphere is stimulating and collegial, with students who are "very competitive, sharp, and goal-oriented individuals looking to advance their careers by pursuing graduate education."

Career and Placement

The Georgia Southern University Career Services Department hosts a number of university-wide events and services, and also maintains a satellite office in the business school. The department's comprehensive student services include career assessment, mock interviews, and recruiting events and career fairs, and the department will assist business students with internship and co-op placements, as well as professional placements. However, for younger students who are getting their feet wet in the business world, many feel that "more resources should be established to link business students with job opportunities," including "stronger encouragement of internships and mentoring opportunities (maybe even build it into the curriculum)."

The Career Services Department hosts several career fairs and campus recruiting events, which are open to the entire undergraduate college and graduate students. Employers who recently visited campus include AT&T, Babies R Us/Toys R US, Bank of Eastman, Enterprise Rent-a-Car, GEICO, IBM, John Deere, Mary Kay, McKesson, MetroPower, Pet Smart, Sherwin Williams, Target Stores, Verizon Wireless, and Wells Fargo Financial.

ADMISSIONS CONTACT: DR. MICHAEL MCDONALD, GRADUATE PROGRAM DIRECTOR
ADDRESS: P. O. BOX 8050 STATESBORO, GA 30460-8050 UNITED STATES
PHONE: 912-681-5767 • FAX: 912-486-7480
E-MAIL: GRADSCHOOL@GEORGIASOUTHERN.EDU • WEBSITE: COBA.GEORGIASOUTHERN.EDU/MBA

Student Life and Environment

Georgia Southern University is a vivacious and "beautiful" campus environment, which offers a full range of student clubs, activities, and resources. However, a large majority of business students take classes at satellite campuses, or only arrive at GSU in the evenings. Others don't come to campus at all, as they are enrolled in the school's online MBA program. Therefore, a large percentage of MBA students don't have much opportunity to participate in campus activities. A current student explains, "Unfortunately, because all graduate classes are only offered at night, graduate students don't have much opportunity to join and be active in student organizations that hold their meetings during the times we are in class (6:30–9:15)."

Students who join the MBA program directly after undergrad are more likely to take advantage of the campus environment. A fifth-year senior explains, "I live on campus in a suite-style residence hall that is only 5-10 minutes (walking) from the business building, which makes my life extremely convenient." For younger students (and those who wish to participate), "the school sponsors many activities and events. We have great athletic events such as football, baseball, and basketball."

Admissions

Students are admitted to Georgia Southern University based on an admissions index, calculated by combining their undergraduate GPA and standardized test scores. A minimum GMAT score of 430 is required for admission. Students who have not taken the GMAT may be provisionally admitted if their undergraduate GPA was 3.25 or higher; these students will be expected to submit acceptable GMAT scores before they finish their third course at the business school.

FINANCIAL FACTS

Annual tuition (in-state/ out-of-state)	$3,516/$14,060
Fees	$1,124
Cost of books	$1,200
Room & board (on/off-campus)	$6,860/$2,760
% of students receiving aid	83
% of first-year students receiving aid	90
% of students receiving loans	52
% of students receiving grants	62
Average award package	$10,905
Average grant	$5,385

ADMISSIONS

Admissions Selectivity Rating	70
# of applications received	115
% applicants accepted	79
% acceptees attending	71
Average GMAT	505
Range of GMAT	458–550
Average GPA	3.17
TOEFL required of international students	Yes
Minimum TOEFL (paper/computer)	530/213
Application fee	$50
International application fee	$50
Regular application deadline	6/1
Regular notification	7/1
Application Deadline/Notification	
Round 1:	03/01 / 04/01
Round 2:	10/01 / 11/01
Round 3:	03/15 / 04/01
Deferment available	Yes
Maximum length of deferment	1 year
Transfer students accepted	Yes
Transfer application policy	
No more than 6 Semester hours of graduate credit may be transferred.	
Non-fall admissions	Yes
Need-blind admissions	Yes

Applicants Also Look At

Georgia State University, Kennesaw State University, University of Georgia.

GEORGIA STATE UNIVERSITY
J. MACK ROBINSON COLLEGE OF BUSINESS

GENERAL INFORMATION
Type of school	Public
Environment	Metropolis
Academic calendar	Semester

SURVEY SAYS...
Solid preparation in:
Doing business in a global economy

STUDENTS
Enrollment of parent institution	27,137
Enrollment of business school	1,209
% male/female	61/39
% part-time	55
% minorities	23
% international	15
Average age at entry	28
Average years work experience at entry	5

ACADEMICS
Academic Experience Rating	**88**
Student/faculty ratio	25:1
Profs interesting rating	84
Profs accessible rating	93
% female faculty	32
% minority faculty	23

Joint Degrees
MBA/JD, MBA/MHA (Health Administration) 2.8–5 years.

Prominent Alumni
James E. Copeland, Deloitte & Touche; A.W. Bill Dahlberg, Chairman of Mirant; Kenneth Lewis, Chairman & CEO, Bank of America; Richard H. Lenny, Former Chairman, Hershey Foods; Mackey McDonald, Chairman, VF Corp.

Academics

Candidates interested in earning an MBA at Georgia State have the option of enrolling either part time or full time, with program completion ranging from twelve months to five years. The expansive curriculum offers a number of concentrations including actuarial science, entrepreneurship, marketing, business economics, operations management, personal financial planning and risk management. Students can also pursue joint degrees in law and health administration. Applicants looking to study international business should investigate the Global Partners MBA (GPMBA), a full-time, 14-month program spanning four continents. Students study in Atlanta, Rio de Janeiro, and Paris and attend a two-week business tour of China.

While you can no doubt find the occasional dissenter, many students at Georgia State are rather impressed with their b-school education. The vast majority of professors are "personable," "caring," and really "work to help you understand the material." Most bring years of business experience into the classroom and make a concerted effort to "stay up to date with the latest trends in their field." Additionally, instructors are adept at "facilitating discussions...using case studies," often illustrating concepts within a practical framework. Students also laud their "engaging" professors for fostering a classroom environment that makes one "eager to learn more about the business world."

Moreover, students appreciate that "the curriculum is really geared for working professionals so you can apply your learning [in] real time." Many extol the "flexibility of the part-time programs" noting they "really try to cater to people who work full time." Most classes are "very focused on teamwork and group projects." There is also "a primary emphasis on application of ideas and techniques and a lesser concentration on theory."

Many students applaud the administration, noting the "friendly, helpful, and polite" staff ensures everything runs "very smoothly." One first-year student does offer this final piece of advice: "The Financial Aid staff is a bit overextended, due to the size of the school, but if you start efforts early, it works fine."

Career and Placement

Though some students wish career services would "promote networking outside of the classroom that is convenient for working professionals," Robinson's Career Management Center for Graduate Students does provide a variety of services. MBA candidates have access to the Robinson Career Connection, an online database where students can upload resumes, search for jobs and internships, and register for campus events. Furthermore, Robinson offers exceptional training in interview preparation. Students can take advantage of both mock interviews as well as InterviewStream, an online video system that they can access from the comfort of their home. Additionally, resources like the Executive Coaching Program present eligible students with the chance to meet, one-on-one, with business professionals. All of these opportunities help to ensure that Georgia State students meet their career goals and aspirations.

In the 2007–2008 academic year, the top ten recruiters of Georgia State MBAs were Deloitte Consulting; Hewitt Associate; KPMG, LLP; UNUM Corporation; Ernst & Young, LLP; Tauber & Balser, PC; Coca-Cola Enterprises Inc.; Towers Perrin; Frazier & Deeter, LLC; and Wachovia Securities Financial Network.

ADMISSIONS CONTACT: DIANE FENNIG, DIRECTOR, GRADUATE STUDENT SERVICES
ADDRESS: SUITE 625, 35 BROAD STREET ATLANTA, GA 30302-3988 UNITED STATES
PHONE: 404-463-7130 • FAX: 404-463-7162
E-MAIL: MASTERSADMISSIONS@GSU.EDU • WEBSITE: ROBINSON.GSU.EDU

Student Life and Environment

The Georgia State student body is comprised of "driven, currently working professionals, with high expectations." Many are "very independent and focused on their area of interest." Since the "majority of students work full time," there's a dearth of "socializing outside of class." Despite limited fraternizing, "there is a wonderful camaraderie amongst MBA students." Indeed, a number are quick to characterize their peers as "friendly," "helpful," and "articulate" as well as "willing to [both] share their experiences and learn from the experiences of others." Additionally, the majority "reach [out] to other students [to] form networking circles." Also of importance, Georgia State manages to attract an applicant pool that offers "varied backgrounds," both in terms of industry and geography. This greatly benefits students as they are privy to "additional global perspectives from classmates."

A multi-campus school, "the environment changes with locale." While "two of the campuses are dedicated to the business school," those students who "desire the traditional collegiate atmosphere" should look into attending the main campus. Regardless of where you enroll, Georgia State students have the bustling city of Atlanta at their fingertips. Offering a variety of fine dining and entertainment, Atlanta is also home to top companies such as Turner Broadcasting, Coca Cola, Bell South, and The Home Depot—perfect for the ambitious MBA candidate.

Admissions

Applicants to GSU MBA programs must submit all of the following materials to the Office of Admissions: official copies of transcripts for all postsecondary academic work; an official GMAT score report; a resume (at least two years of full-time professional experience is preferred); and two personal essays. Letters of recommendation are not required but are considered for those candidates who submit them. International students must submit, in addition to the above materials, evidence of sufficient financial resources to fund their MBA studies; an independent evaluation of all academic transcripts for work completed abroad; and, for students whose first language is not English, an official score report for the TOEFL. International students are required to carry a full-time course load.

FINANCIAL FACTS

Annual tuition (in-state/ out-of-state)	$7,868/$28,532
Fees	$988
Cost of books	$1,200
Room & board	$11,160
% of students receiving aid	27
% of first-year students receiving aid	31
% of students receiving loans	26
% of students receiving grants	1
Average award package	$16,876
Average grant	$7,766
Average student loan debt	$13,652

ADMISSIONS

Admissions Selectivity Rating	86
# of applications received	401
% applicants accepted	58
% acceptees attending	74
Average GMAT	602
Range of GMAT	560–640
Average GPA	3.37
TOEFL required of international students	Yes
Minimum TOEFL (paper/computer)	610/255
Application fee	$50
International application fee	$50
Regular application deadline	4/1
Regular notification	6/15
Deferment available	Yes
Maximum length of deferment	two Semesters
Non-fall admissions	Yes
Need-blind admissions	Yes

Applicants Also Look At

City University of New York—Baruch College, Clark Atlanta University, Emory University, Georgia Institute of Technology, Kennesaw State University, Mercer University—Atlanta, University of Georgia.

GONZAGA UNIVERSITY
GRADUATE SCHOOL OF BUSINESS

Academics

Jesuit-run Gonzaga University is "ethics-based, family-oriented, and strives to produce people ready for the real world and its challenges, both professionally and socially," all of which appeal to the MBA students in its Graduate School of Business. A "great reputation in the business community," especially for its "great accounting program," and an "awesome flexible curriculum structure" that "is designed with working individuals in mind (with evening and online classes)" also draw area business grads to the program.

Gonzaga's MBA curriculum consists of 22 credits in core courses (11 two-credit classes) and 11 credits in electives, through which students may develop a concentration if they wish. Students who did not major in business as undergraduates are typically required to complete a series of foundation requirements prior to beginning work on their MBA. Students report that the curriculum is "broad and covers many aspects of the modern business environment, with opportunities to specialize in finance, economics, accounting, etc." Professors "integrate course material throughout the program" and "rarely present contradicting information" as "the material in the program is well planned." Students also appreciate that the program "has a very good grasp on current trends in the business world and effectively integrates those trends into the class curriculum." Some, however, wish for "more updated technology and computer labs," while others believe the program would benefit from "more course-end teamwork projects." "Students need to have more opportunities to simulate complex projects and the teamwork needed to solve them," one student notes.

Gonzaga's "small size and interactive environment…offers a plethora of opportunities for students looking to expand their horizons." "For those who are entrepreneurial, the Hogan Center offers hands-on experience, as do other business classes such as business consulting, which enables students to try their hand at consulting for a real local business." Gonzaga introduced a new healthcare management concentration in 2007, of which one student says, "There are some bumps, but overall, it is excellent."

Career and Placement

The Gonzaga Career Center and the School of Business Administration staff and faculty provide career counseling and placement services to MBAs here, including: Career 301 Seminars covering self-assessment, career planning, resume writing, and conducting a successful job search; mock interviews and interview critiques; on-campus recruiting and interviewing; a career-resources library; alumni events; and internship placement assistance. Students complain, "Gonzaga's only weak point is connecting students to careers after graduation…. Due to the small size of both the city of Spokane and of the university, not a lot of major companies recruit at Gonzaga, and a lot more legwork is needed on behalf of the student to find his or her post-graduation path than at some other major universities. Thus, the MBA program may best benefit those who already know where they want to go after they graduate."

Employers of Gonzaga business graduates include Avista, Bank of America, Boeing, Deloitte, Ernst & Young, Honeywell, Itron, KPMG, Microsoft, Price Waterhouse, and Starbucks. Fifty percent of Gonzaga MBAs go into finance and accounting.

Student Life and Environment

Gonzaga's MBA candidates include "everything from recent college graduates to ex-military officers to professionals who have families and full-time jobs." Many feel that the population includes too many students "who have just got their bachelor's degree with no work experience and have no valuable input to conversations or the academic environment. The school really needs experienced professionals." Students tend to be "friendly and hardworking," down-to-earth, not stuck on themselves, and "real," and, according to one of those ex-military officers, "very energetic and willing to take risks, similar to those that I had taken in life. I like how open-minded they are to the ideas presented and the materials."

Students are "fairly isolated from the campus in that our classes start at the end of the traditional day and our building is on one edge of the campus. The great thing, though, is our building is amazing, has everything we need in one place, and the lounge has a fantastic view of a lake beneath and downtown in the distance." Evening classes "allow working professionals to attend classes." One student notes, "I cannot say enough about the flexibility and responsiveness of the MBA program team. From professors to the administrative staff, this experience has been outstanding."

Those who choose to engage in campus life tell us that it is "full of opportunities to get involved in fun activities and helpful charities. The basketball games are free for students and are full of excitement" and, as an added bonus, revenue "generated by the basketball team is used to improve the school and the school's reputation." Local charities "love the help from grad students and rely on them for help in creating business plans, conducting market research, and planning marketing activities." Hometown Spokane is "a small town in eastern Washington, cold during the winter, and not all that exciting compared to Seattle, which is four hours away."

Admissions

Applicants to the MBA program at Gonzaga must submit two official copies of all postsecondary academic transcripts, official GMAT scores (minimum score of 500 required), resume, two letters of recommendation, and a complete application (which includes three short essays). International students must also submit official TOEFL scores (if English is not their first language) and a financial declaration form. An interview may be required of some international applicants. Work experience is not required, "although the majority of students who enter the program have four or five years prior work experience."

FINANCIAL FACTS

Annual tuition	$12,780
Cost of books	$600
Room & board	$4,500
% of students receiving aid	90
% of first-year students receiving aid	90
% of students receiving loans	50
% of students receiving grants	50
Average award package	$14,000
Average grant	$2,000
Average student loan debt	$12,000

ADMISSIONS

Admissions Selectivity Rating	**79**
# of applications received	114
% applicants accepted	74
% acceptees attending	90
Average GMAT	572
Range of GMAT	500–610
Average GPA	3.4
TOEFL required of international students	Yes
Minimum TOEFL (paper/computer)	570/230
Application fee	$50
International application fee	$50
Regular application deadline	Rolling
Regular notification	Rolling
Deferment available	Yes
Maximum length of deferment	4 years
Transfer students accepted	Yes
Transfer application policy	
Up to 6 credits can be transferred in from non-Jesuit MBA programs.	
Non-fall admissions	Yes
Need-blind admissions	Yes

Applicants Also Look At
Eastern Washington University, Seattle University, University of Portland, University of Washington, Washington State University.

EMPLOYMENT PROFILE

Career Rating	77	Grads Employed by Function	% Avg. Salary
Primary Source of Full-time Job Acceptances		Finance	50 NR
School-facilitated activities	50%	Human Resources	5 NR
Graduate-facilitated activities	50%	Marketing	10 NR
		Strategic Planning	5 NR
		Consulting	5 NR
		Entrepreneurship	5 NR
		General Management	5 NR
		Venture Capital	5 NR
		Other	5 NR
		Non-profit	5: NR

GRAND VALLEY STATE UNIVERSITY
SEIDMAN COLLEGE OF BUSINESS

GENERAL INFORMATION
Type of school	Public
Environment	Metropolis
Academic calendar	Semester

SURVEY SAYS...
Cutting edge classes
Solid preparation in:
Accounting
General management

STUDENTS
Enrollment of parent institution	23,295
Enrollment of business school	266
% part-time	88
Average age at entry	31
Average years work experience at entry	9

ACADEMICS
Academic Experience Rating	**78**
Student/faculty ratio	25:1
Profs interesting rating	91
Profs accessible rating	78
% female faculty	14
% minority faculty	28

Joint Degrees
MSN/MBA (Nursing) 4 years.

FINANCIAL FACTS
Annual tuition (in-state/ out-of-state)	$5,850/$10,800
Fees	$90
Cost of books	$1,500
Room & board (on/off-campus)	$6,500/$5,000

Academics

With an "excellent technology infrastructure"—the DeVos Center, which houses the business program, opened in 2000—"beautiful grounds and buildings," and "a strong program that is well-recognized within the region," Grand Valley State University provides an affordable graduate experience to its predominantly working-professional student body. As one student puts it, "Grand Valley offers an excellent value for a very good MBA program."

GVSU's Seidman College offers an MBA as well as Master's of Science degrees in taxation and accounting. Students who pursue the 33-credit MBA program part time typically complete the program in two years. The curriculum includes three electives; students may graduate with a concentration in a specific discipline by choosing all three electives from that discipline. A degree with an emphasis on innovation and technology management is available as well; it requires the completion of a fourth elective, lengthening the program to 36 credits.

Students praise GVSU for providing "small classroom size" that "seems to be very helpful when it comes to getting the help needed." The "high caliber" faculty is "very astute, visionary, shrewd, capable, and highly qualified," ensuring that students are "both challenged and adequately supported." Administrators "put themselves in the shoes of the students and give 100 percent effort to ensure that our education experience at GVSU is fruitful and worthwhile." Overall, students perceive "excellent customer service here" and appreciate that the school is "located in an economically growing area," providing access to business connections both during and after the program.

Career and Placement

The school reports that "The Seidman MBA is a program primarily for working professionals, as opposed to a full-time MBA program. Most students are employed when they begin their MBA studies and remain employed by the same firms when they graduate." Students add, however, that "there is a trend for more and more full-time students...There are also career fairs every semester where companies from around Michigan and the nation will come to talk with graduates and upcoming graduates. As more full-timers enter the program, more of these companies will come to the fairs." A central career services office serves undergraduates and graduates; one student who attended GVSU as an undergraduate tells us that "I have not had much experience with the career placement services at the graduate level; undergraduate career services are good."

Student Life and Environment

The DeVos Center, home to the Seidman College of Business, offers "a variety of places to eat as well as a bookstore and tuition payment center," all of which make the hectic lives of GVSU's part-time students a little bit easier. One student happily reports: "I very rarely have to leave the campus to accomplish all of my tasks. This is extremely pleasing to a student juggling family, work, and school." The school "is making a concerted effort to create study space on campus," which students also appreciate.

The atmosphere within the Seidman MBA program is "easygoing but professional." Most students visit campus only when necessary, and the school works hard to accommodate them. As one explains, "I like that I get all the information I need for class via BlackBoard or through the Library's class reserve system. That makes it much easier for me as a part-time student."

ADMISSIONS CONTACT: CLAUDIA BAJEMA, GRADUATE BUSINESS PROGRAMS DIRECTOR
ADDRESS: 401 W. FULTON GRAND RAPIDS, MI 49504 UNITED STATES
PHONE: 616-331-7400 • FAX: 616-331-7389
E-MAIL: GO2GVMBA@GVSU.EDU • WEBSITE: WWW.GVSU.EDU/BUSINESS

Hometown Grand Rapids is a substantial city with a metropolitan area population of nearly three quarters of a million, making it the second-largest city in Michigan. Grand Rapids has been one of the nation's furniture capitals for more than a century. Manufacturing still provides a solid base for the local economy, although shipping and the health industry also claim substantial workforces. GVSU students tell us, "The restaurants and the cultural venues in Grand Rapids are beyond compare when you look at cities of this size."

GVSU students tend to be "very busy, task-oriented, serious with their studies, and very focused in their lives." They are "mostly professionals" although there are some students fresh out of college in the mix. They tend to be "fairly young," "most are married, and some have children." Most are "friendly with good people skills," making them excellent partners for team projects.

Admissions

The GSVU Admissions Committee applies the following formula: [(undergraduate GPA for final 60 hours of coursework + 200) + GMAT score. Applicants scoring above 1100 with a GMAT score of at least 500 are admitted to the program. Applicants scoring 1100 with a GMAT score between 450 and 490 are reviewed by the admissions committee "for predictive indicators of success with respect to quantitative and qualitative GMAT scores and grades earned in courses deemed to be relevant to graduate curriculum." Some such applicants may be admitted conditionally pending successful completion of background courses. The committee may make the same recommendation to applicants who score at least 500 on the GMAT but do not earn an 1100 formula score. Applicants whose first language is not English are required to score at least 550 on the TOEFL.

ADMISSIONS

Admissions Selectivity Rating	**76**
# of applications received	146
% applicants accepted	82
% acceptees attending	85
Average GMAT	566
Range of GMAT	520–680
Average GPA	3.3
TOEFL required of international students	Yes
Minimum TOEFL (paper/computer)	550/213
Application fee	$30
International application fee	$30
Regular application deadline	12/1
Regular notification	rolling
Deferment available	Yes
Maximum length of deferment	1 year
Transfer students accepted	Yes
Transfer application policy Students may transfer up to 9 credits.	
Non-fall admissions	Yes
Need-blind admissions	Yes

Applicants Also Look At

Western Michigan University.

HARVARD UNIVERSITY
HARVARD BUSINESS SCHOOL

Academics

A "tried-and-true General Management focus with no concentrations or majors and no published GPAs," a "pedagogical approach that relies strongly on the case method," and most of all "a reputation as the best business program in the country" make Harvard Business School one of the top prizes in the MBA admissions sweepstakes. Applicants lucky enough to gain admission here rarely decide to go elsewhere.

The school's full-time-only program is relatively large; approximately 900 students enter the program each year. Students tell us, "Despite its large size, the school feels surprisingly small" thanks to a combination of factors. First is an administration that "could be a role model for any enterprise. This place is very well run." Second is the subdivision of classes into smaller sections of 90 students, who together attack approximately 500 case studies during their two years here. Finally, there's a faculty that "is obviously committed to excelling at teaching and developing relationships with the students. Each faculty member loves being here, regardless of whether they are a superstar or not, and that makes a difference. Faculty guide discussion well and enliven the classroom."

The case method predominates at Harvard; explains one student, "I sit in my section of 90 students every day and debate business topics. My section mates come from all walks of life and all of them are incredibly successful. I prepare my 13 cases per week so that I can contribute to this environment." Students love the approach, although they point out that "the case method is not as great for quantitative courses such as finance." Numerous field-study classes supplement the program, especially during the second year, which is devoted to elective study. School-wide initiatives—combinations of interdisciplinary classes, field study, contests, and club work—encourage research and provide added focus in the areas of social enterprise, entrepreneurship, global issues, and leadership.

Ultimately, though, HBS' strength resides in the quality of its instructors. One student notes, "HBS is one of the few schools where a large part of the professor's evaluation is based on classroom teaching. The professors at HBS are wonderful teachers and take great interest in their students." As one first-year puts it, "If first semester is representative of the whole experience, I'll be a happy grad. My accounting professor managed to make accounting my favorite class (seems unimaginable!), and I'll definitely take whatever he teaches during the second year of elective courses."

Career and Placement

Harvard Business School hardly needs a Career Development Center, any more than Rolls Royce needs salesmen to move its cars. The school maintains a robust career services office all the same, providing a full range of counseling and internship- and career-placement services, with more than 40 career coaches seen by more than 80% of the class. There are more than 800 recruiting events on campus each year; of those, 400 focus on full-time employment and the other 400 focus on summer internships. Nearly half of all MBAs remain on the East Coast after graduation, about a third of whom take jobs in New York City. Nineteen percent find international placements; 9% of the class work in Europe and 6% work in Asia.

Student Life and Environment

Life at HBS "is as hectic as you want it to be." One student writes, "My life is pretty much moving along at breakneck speed. I wouldn't want it any other way because the school offers an incredible amount and array of activities, from volunteer consulting to running conferences." Because Harvard University is a magnet for innovative and prestigious thinkers in all disciplines, "This place is like a candy store for a five-year-old; you want to eat a lot more than what's good for you. You can spend all your time on studies, lectures from academics/politicians from all over the world, visiting business leaders, conferences, sports, or the nightlife. A 60-hour day would be appropriate."

Students generally manage to find the time to enjoy "a very social and outgoing environment" at HBS. One married student writes, "Most weekends my husband and I have a choice: the 'college scene' where we can hit up the Harvard or Central Square bars with the singles, or the 'married scene' where we have dinner, play goofy board games, and drink with our 'couple friends.' Either can be a great escape from the other, and both are always a lot of fun!" Close relationships are easy to forge here, as "the section system means you have 89 close friends in the program, which makes learning and being here fun. It also means in the business world there will always be 89 incredibly smart, connected people who will go to bat for me no matter what."

The population of this program is, unsurprisingly, exceptional. As one MBA explains, "The quality of people here is unlike anything I've experienced. For the first time in my adult life, I'm surrounded by people whose interests and abilities fascinate and inspire me. All religions, nationalities, cultures, and sexual orientations exist here, happily, and together. I think Boston cultivates this kind of 'meshing of all thoughts' in such a way that everyone is comfortable, and everyone learns. The city and the school are both comfortable in their own skins, and the students take on that characteristic here."

Admissions

Applicants to Harvard Business School must submit a "complete HBS application portfolio, including personal essays, academics transcripts, and three letters of recommendation." In addition, students must provide scores from the GMAT, and applicants from non-English-speaking countries must submit scores for either the TOEFL or the IELTS (scores must be no more than two years old). Applications must be submitted online. Academic ability, leadership experience, and unique personal characteristics all figure prominently into the admissions decision. The school's viewbook notes that "because our MBA curriculum is fast-paced and rigorously analytical, we strongly encourage all applicants to complete introductory courses in quantitative subjects such as accounting, finance, and economics before coming to HBS. For some candidates, we may make admission contingent upon their completing such courses before they enroll." Good luck!

FINANCIAL FACTS

Annual tuition	$43,800
Fees	$7,100
% of students receiving aid	70
% of first-year students receiving aid	70
% of students receiving loans	65
% of students receiving grants	51
Average award package	$55,673
Average grant	$22,000
Average student loan debt	$77,550

ADMISSIONS

Admissions Selectivity Rating	99
# of applications received	7,424
% applicants accepted	14
% acceptees attending	88
Average GMAT	713
TOEFL required of international students	Yes
Minimum TOEFL (paper/computer)	630/267
Application fee	$235
International application fee	$235
Application Deadline/Notification	
Round 1:	10/15 / 1/21
Round 2:	1/6 / 4/2
Round 3:	3/11 / 5/12
Need-blind admissions	Yes

EMPLOYMENT PROFILE

Career Rating	99	Grads Employed by Function	% Avg. Salary
Primary Source of Full-time Job Acceptances		Finance	45 $123,288
Average base starting salary	$115,665	Marketing	11 $100802
Percent employed	99.7	Consulting	22 $115,533
		General Management	11 $111,276
		Other	2 $93,834

HEC MONTREAL
MBA PROGRAM

GENERAL INFORMATION
Type of school   Public

SURVEY SAYS...
Students love Montreal, QC
Solid preparation in:
General management
Doing business in a global economy

STUDENTS
Enrollment of parent institution	12,100
Enrollment of business school	430
% male/female	67/33
% part-time	60
% international	55
Average age at entry	31
Average years work experience at entry	7

ACADEMICS
Academic Experience Rating	86
Student/faculty ratio	7:1
Profs interesting rating	86
Profs accessible rating	74
% female faculty	26

Prominent Alumni
Mr. Louis Couillard, President, Pfizer France; Mr. Thierry Vandal, President, Hydro-Quebec; Mr. Jianwei Zhang, President, Bombardier China; Mr. Luc Sicotte, President, Canderel; Mr. Yannis Mallat, President and CEO, Ubisoft.

Academics

HEC Montreal (Hautes Études Commerciales) offers "a strong MBA program based on practical issues" that emphasizes "a case-based teaching style" and has "real consulting opportunities incorporated into the curriculum." That, along with the school's "strong network in Quebec and excellent reputation," has made HEC Montreal one of the world's top MBA programs outside the United States. Students here may pursue an intensive one-year program in English or French or a three-year part-time program in French. All programs are housed in a "state-of-the-art facility" with "great libraries and study rooms."

HEC Montreal's one-year program starts with two phases of core courses, followed by a specialization period and a concluding two-course sequence in corporate responsibility. The entire program evinces "a team focus," as "every person has to work in teams that are assigned and specially designed." "The whole program is very community- and network-oriented" and thus "forces students to realize how important it is to rely on others and to help team members in order to increase results and efficiency." Classes are delivered in six-week increments, which students describe as "very challenging." "It forces students and teachers to prepare more, and to be ready for every class," one student explains. Students appreciate how the program provides "so many resources invested to ensure the satisfaction of the student body," including "great programs like Campus Abroad," a three-week international program that includes company tours and meetings with business leaders.

Part-timers here enjoy "a good flexible program that support full-time work and MBA courses using the same quality teachers that full-timers get." Students in all programs laud the curriculum's "strong emphasis on durable growth and business ethics. The curriculum is planted on solid foundations. We're definitely not going to be Master Bulls**t Artists." They also appreciate how "HEC is extremely well connected and well regarded by Quebec's business community." "Several professors act as consultants for Canadian or international companies that have operations in Quebec," a student says. "Also, there are regular meetings and presentations at school with business leaders, making the whole program very 'real world.' No stale academic courses here!"

Career and Placement

The HEC Montreal Career Management Services team provides career and placement services to MBAs here. Services include online job search, with international listings and email notification of appropriate postings; workshops and consulting services; CareerLeader, a self-assessment and career-management program; the Vault online career library; mentoring; mock interviews; recruitment events, including career days and on-campus interviewing; and information sessions. Students praise the "exceptional efforts made by career services for job placement" here.

Companies that recruit on campus include Accenture, Air Canada, Bell Canada, Bombardier, CIBC World Markets, Cirque du Soleil, Deloitte, Emirates National Oil Company, Ernst & Young, GE Commercial Finance, IBM, Johnson & Johnson, L'Oreal, Matrox, McKinsey, Merck Frosst, Pratt & Whitney, Procter and Gamble, RBC Financial Group, Scotiabank, TD Financial Group, Toyota, and UPS.

Student Life and Environment

The HEC campus is "a vibrant environment with people from all over the place" with "excellent resources at our disposal such as libraries, classrooms, and technology." As one student puts it, "Our school is just amazing: The design of it is sharp, they keep it real clean, and we have access to many facilities on campus: gym, bank machine, lounges. The food at the cafeteria is really good. We have access to a bunch of activities from dance classes to any organized sport activities (climbing, soccer, running club, volley-ball, swimming). We are located next to restaurants, coffee shop, a subway entrance, all kind of stores and a lot of them are open 24/7." "The campus and buildings are beautiful and safe." The school is "located in the center of town," which "provides help for lodging and activities that are smartly connected to the school."

HEC's one-year programs are "very intensive," so "students spend a lot of time with each other" and "life is very hectic." Classes generally run from early morning to late afternoon, after which students participate in team projects and assignment discussion, "then go home and prepare for the next class." All that cooperation promotes bonding, creating "a tight-knit community that enjoys many group activities, including weekly happy hours." Clubs and associations "encourage and generate a nice social life inside and around the school." "The MBA students' association is particularly good, even if it's difficult to connect full-time and part-time students."

Admissions

Admission to the MBA program at HEC Montreal is competitive; the school reports that it is "unable to accept all eligible candidates who apply" because class space is limited. Admissions decisions are based on academic record, professional experience (three years minimum required), standardized test scores (TAGE-MAGE or GMAT), letters of recommendation, and candidates' career objectives. Applicants must provide the school with official transcripts for all post-secondary academic work, a curriculum vitae, and an official score report for standardized tests. The application includes supplementary questions, to be answered in essay form. Interviews are granted at the request of the admissions office only. Applicants to the English-language full-time intensive program must demonstrate English proficiency via testing (TOEFL, IELTS, or HEC's own HECTOPE) if their native language is not English. Non-native French speakers applying to the French-only program must complete the Test de français international (an ETS-administered exam). Applicants who are not citizens of Canada must obtain a certificat d'acceptation du Québec (C.A.Q.) and a document attesting to their right to reside in Canada (Student Authorization or Ministerial Permit). The school recommends that accepted students apply for these documents as soon as they receive confirmation of their admission to the program.

FINANCIAL FACTS

Annual tuition (in-state/ out-of-state)	$6,200/$24,000
Cost of books	$2,250
Room & board (off-campus)	$15,500
Average grant	$6,800

ADMISSIONS

Admissions Selectivity Rating	78
# of applications received	412
% applicants accepted	62
% acceptees attending	67
Average GMAT	600
Range of GMAT	540–680
TOEFL required of international students	Yes
Minimum TOEFL (paper/computer)	600/250
Application fee	$75
International application fee	$75
Regular application deadline	3/15
International application deadline	2/1
Regular notification	4/1
Deferment available	Yes
Maximum length of deferment	1 year
Need-blind admissions	Yes

EMPLOYMENT PROFILE

Career Rating		81	Grads Employed by Function	%	Avg. Salary
Primary Source of Full-time Job Acceptances			Finance	29	$66,000
School-facilitated activities		30%	Marketing	20	$67,000
Graduate-facilitated activities		50%	MIS	7	$65,200
Unknown		20%	Operations	4	$62,800
Percent employed		69	Consulting	17	$72,150
			General Management	11	$71,400
			Other	12	$78,000

Top 5 Employers Hiring Grads
RBC Financial Group; Bombardier; TD Bank Financial Group; Deloitte; SAP Canada

HEC School of Management—Paris
HEC MBA Program

Academics

Located just outside Paris, HEC School of Management attracts students for its superb setting, international focus, and "reputation and for being among Europe's top 10 business schools." Offering MBA and graduate business programs in a combination of both French and English, as well as an English-only program, the HEC MBA begins with a comprehensive core curriculum, including essential business coursework in marketing, business economics, corporate finance, and statistics. There is a "strong focus on ethics/corporate governance and sustainability" within the program, as well as an incredibly international perspective. Of particular note are the "opportunities to learn French and work in France for non-native speakers." In fact, "the school offers French language courses as a part of curriculum," and requires that all students (even those who are already bilingual) take a language course while pursuing their MBA. In addition to promoting language skills, the school generally excels in the "development of managerial soft skills and of team work."

Balancing efficiency with rigor, HEC's MBA is "a two-year program condensed into 16 months, so there is a high workload." Drawing faculty from the European business community, "professors are generally good with a few brilliant lecturers." A student in the bilingual section shares, "I am very lucky to have French professors that are very well known in their respective fields in France and internationally." Partially state run, the school's French administration is often described as "bureaucratic" and not particularly efficient. At the same time, students appreciate the fact that the school helps them "adjust into the French system, like [assisting with] residence permits." Its European location means HEC is strategically placed between numerous economic powerhouses, and just a short ride to Paris and the many important corporations there.

Your classmates are an essential part of the learning experience at HEC, which draws a truly "international student body with participants from over 40 countries." When the program begins, students are divided into "work groups," designed to maximize diversity in terms of country of origin, multicultural background, and professional experience. Fortunately, "the work groups are effective and encourage collaboration rather than elitist competition." On top of that, professors generally "promote discussion so we learn from each other" in class.

Career and Placement

The HEC career services department offers a range of career development workshops, as well as conferences and seminars in both French and English. Keep in mind that the majority of opportunities for HEC graduates are in Paris, which is great for those who want to work in Europe, but also means that it can be "difficult for non-French-speaking participants to get good jobs." In particular, students note that "there are no MBA-specific events organized until April, and even then only 15–20 companies attend." However, students note that the school's 25,000 "alumni are a good resource" for finding jobs in France and internationally. In fact, 88 percent of students had jobs within three months of graduation, with an average salary of ?47,000 for graduates who stay in France, and ?69,000 for graduates who take jobs in other countries. Sixty-six percent of graduates take positions in the Paris region.

ADMISSIONS CONTACT: ISABELLE COTA, DIRECTOR OF ADMISSIONS AND DEVELOPMENT
ADDRESS: 1 RUE DE LA LIBERATION JOUY-EN-JOSAS CEDEX, 78351 FRANCE
PHONE: 011 33 (0)139 67 95 46 • FAX: 011 33 (0)139 67 74 65
E-MAIL: ADMISSIONMBA@HEC.FR • WEBSITE: WWW.MBA.HEC.EDU

FINANCIAL FACTS

Annual tuition	$62,506
Cost of books	$1,651
Room & board	
(on/off-campus)	$18,714/$23,714
% of students receiving aid	70
Average award package	$42,500
Average grant	$9,750

ADMISSIONS

Admissions Selectivity Rating	**97**
# of applications received	1,825
% applicants accepted	19
% acceptees attending	54
Average GMAT	660
Range of GMAT	600–770
Average GPA	3.7
TOEFL required of	
international students	Yes
Minimum TOEFL	
(paper/computer)	600/250
Application fee	$200
International application fee	$200
Regular application deadline	5/26
Regular notification	7/4
Deferment available	Yes
Maximum length of	
deferment	1 year
Non-fall admissions	Yes
Need-blind admissions	Yes

Applicants Also Look At
IMD(International Institute for Management Development), INSEAD, London Business School, New York University.

Student Life and Environment

With students from 40 countries and a range of professional backgrounds, HEC is characterized by its diversity. A current student shares, "I really like my fellow students; this is a truly international school so we have a great variety of nationalities and business experiences from all over the world." Student life is rewarding and active, as "there are many clubs and most of the students live on campus, especially during the core phase." In addition to the day-to-day pleasures of student life, "Cultural Weeks (Japan Week, Latin America Week) and parties on holidays such as Diwali are a strong part of the culture of the school, and a highlight in the calendar as most of the students attend the events."

The school's pretty campus is set "up a hill in a tiny town in the Paris suburbs," from which "it takes an hour to get to Paris by public transportation." There are few attractions in the surrounding community; however, students appreciate the fact that "you do not have many distractions so you can dedicate more time to studying." Fortunately, "the outdoor sports facilities and the location of the school are lovely—huge grounds, and it's great to go for walks." With a world-class city just a stone's throw away, it's not surprising that "many people go to Paris for weekend, and enjoy the cultural and entertainment life there."

Admissions

HEC admissions process is somewhat lengthy. First, each candidate is evaluated based on their standardized test scores and undergraduate performance, as well as quantitative factors as evidenced in their personal recommendations and work experience. After candidates have passed the first stage of review, they must arrange for two in-person interviews with HEC alumni, HEC professors, French Embassy representatives, or other HEC community members. Each of these interviews begins with a 10-minute presentation by the MBA candidate, followed by a question-and-answer session. Last year's entering class had an average GMAT score of 660, with a range between 600 and 750.

EMPLOYMENT PROFILE

Career Rating	81	Grads Employed by Function	% Avg. Salary
Primary Source of Full-time Job Acceptances		Finance	29 $118,494
School-facilitated activities	58 (40%)	Marketing	20 $100,116
Graduate-facilitated activities	62 (43%)	MIS	2 NR
Unknown	24 (17%)	Operations	1 NR
Average base starting salary	$114,172	Consulting	22 $114,438
Percent employed	74	General Management	7 $116,193
		Other	19 NR
		Top 5 Employers Hiring Grads	
		BNP Paribas; Citigroup; LVMH; Johnson & Johnson; Lehman Brothers	

HHL—Leipzig Graduate School of Management

Academics

HHL—Leipzig Graduate School of Management offers German and international business students an appealing mix of a well-established name and modern innovation. Founded in 1898, HHL is the oldest business school in Germany, and its students benefit from its deserved reputation as a solid training ground for European managers. The MBA program, however, is relatively new, having only graduated its first class in 2001. Because the program is still in its nascent stages, students tell us, "It is striving to achieve more in the global ranking, so they really make an effort, as opposed to many established schools that expect their reputation to work for them." Since the program runs its course in a scant 15 months, it also appeals to the cost-conscious and to those in a hurry to climb the corporate ladder of success.

The HHL curriculum is divided into three categories. Core courses cover the basics in management; this segment of the program is particularly well-suited to the German students "whose prior academic training was not focused on business but rather was in the natural sciences, humanities, or social sciences" and whom the Admissions Office targets. Specialization courses in accounting, finance, marketing, business organization, and strategy allow students to hone a particular skill set. Students tell us that specializations in finance, marketing, and strategy "are the tops, especially finance and marketing with very well-known professors who publish a lot in their field and are on boards of corporations." Application courses in such areas as entrepreneurship, innovation management, and corporate-government relations keep students abreast of contemporary issues in the business world.

HHL professors "can be contacted almost 24 hours a day," and "those who are comfortable with English can even be fun in classes." Internships, study abroad, and independent study options are all available. A high-quality education at a reasonable price is cited by students as one of the main reasons they chose the school.

Career and Placement

HHL MBAs report with satisfaction that "one of the big strengths of this program is its excellent contact to companies. Almost all top companies in consulting, banking, and industry come for presentation and recruiting. Companies react surprisingly positively when saying that you are from our school." One student comments, "Concerning placement, there is a huge database of direct contact people. Rather than applying over a 'website' one can contact people or alumni. This helps to stay away from the crowd that applies over recruiting websites of companies."

According to HHL, the school "has a record of placing graduates with prominent international firms—including BASF, Bayer, BCG, Bertelsmann, BDO, Booz Allen Hamilton, Boston Consulting Group, Daimler, Deutsche Bank, E.ON, Ernst & Young, Ford, Henkel, Johnson & Johnson, Kirch-Gruppe, KPMG International, McKinsey & Company, Nestlé, PricewaterhouseCoopers, Procter & Gamble, Siemens, Tui, and Volkswagen—as well as with many German 'Mittelstand' companies." Other companies that recruit on campus include A.T. Kearney, Accenture, Allianz AG, BMW, Citibank, FairAd, Goldman Sachs, Horváth & Partner, Lufthansa Cargo, OnVista, Porsche, Sachsen Bank, and Wellington.

ADMISSIONS CONTACT: PETRA SPANKA, EXECUTIVE DIRECTOR
ADDRESS: JAHNALLEE 59 LEIPZIG, 04109 GERMANY
PHONE: +49341- 9851734 • FAX: 01149341- 9851 731
E-MAIL: PETRA.SPANKA@HHL.DE • WEBSITE: WWW.HHL.DE

Student Life and Environment

An accelerated academic schedule at HHL means that "life is somewhat focused on the courses. There is a lot of pre-work and post-work to do for almost all courses. Most courses integrate a high amount of applied case studies and group work. In some weeks/months the balance of studying and doing other things is bad (i.e., a lot of studying)." One student notes, "Classes in finance are especially tough, but teach a lot that you need later in respective jobs." Even so, there is some time leftover to socialize. One MBA writes, "The school organizes a lot of parties and integrates in social-life staff (i.e., professors) and students. The professors and students are almost on a friendship level and they help the students where they can."

Many students were attracted to the school because it represents "a somewhat wild mixture of nations, ages, and backgrounds," with about one third hailing from Germany and the rest "from different countries in Asia, South and North America, Europe, etc. Also, they have different working experiences; some of them are businessmen, some are engineers. Some worked for law firms, some served in the Navy as IT engineers." What they all share in common is that they "are ready to help, ready to work, and ready to party." As one student observes, "They are very interesting and challenging to work with. I can't imagine better fellow students!"

Leipzig is "a great town [with] a long academic record [and] many sports facilities," students tell us. Bach and Schumann put this ancient trade center on the musical map, and their traditions are carried on today in the city's many concert halls, theaters, cafés and cabarets, jazz clubs, and discos. The city is conveniently located for travel to and from Berlin, Dresden, and Weimar, as well as to major Czech and Polish cities.

Admissions

All applicants to HHL's MBA program must submit GMAT scores (according to the school, students with scores of at least 650 "are more likely to be offered admission than applicants with lower scores"), proof of undergraduate degree and transcripts, two recommendations, a resume, and a completed application. Non-native English speakers must also submit proof of English proficiency. HHL accepts TOEFL scores to fulfill this requirement. The admissions committee convenes once a month to consider all completed applications, at which point it decides either to accept, reject, or wait-list each candidate.

FINANCIAL FACTS

Annual tuition	$28,350
Cost of books	$100
Room & board (off-campus)	$7,500
% of students receiving aid	20
% of first-year students receiving aid	15
Average grant	$150,000

ADMISSIONS

Admissions Selectivity Rating	**88**
# of applications received	130
% applicants accepted	54
% acceptees attending	64
Average GMAT	610
Range of GMAT	550–780
Average GPA	3.5
TOEFL required of international students	Yes
Minimum TOEFL (paper/computer)	600/250
Application fee	$0
International application fee	$0
Regular application deadline	6/1
Regular notification	6/14
Application Deadline/Notification	
Round 1:	04/01 / 04/14
Round 2:	05/01 / 05/14
Round 3:	06/01 / 06/14
Deferment available	Yes
Maximum length of deferment	1 year
Transfer students accepted	Yes
Transfer application policy Coursework and examinations in an economic degree program at another university or college of equal status.	
Need-blind admissions	Yes

EMPLOYMENT PROFILE

Career Rating	81	Grads Employed by Function	% Avg. Salary
Primary Source of Full-time Job Acceptances		Accounting	6 NR
School-facilitated activities	24 (40%)	Finance	6 NR
Graduate-facilitated activities	18	Human Resources	5 NR
Unknown	18	Marketing	12 NR
Percent employed	95	MIS	5 NR
		Operations	12 NR
		Consulting	12 NR
		Communications	10 NR
		Entrepreneurship	5 NR
		General Management	12 NR
		Global Management	5 NR
		Other	5 NR
		Internet/New Media	6 NR

HOFSTRA UNIVERSITY
FRANK G. ZARB SCHOOL OF BUSINESS

GENERAL INFORMATION
Type of school	Private
Environment	City
Academic calendar	4/1/4

SURVEY SAYS...
Smart classrooms
Solid preparation in:
Finance
Teamwork
Computer skills

STUDENTS
Enrollment of parent institution	12,490
Enrollment of business school	537
% male/female	65/35
% out-of-state	4
% part-time	70
% minorities	15
% international	30
Average age at entry	28
Average years work experience at entry	5

ACADEMICS
Academic Experience Rating	**76**
Student/faculty ratio	10:1
Profs interesting rating	80
Profs accessible rating	89
% female faculty	19
% minority faculty	24

Joint Degrees
JD/MBA 4 years, BBA/MBA 5 years, BBA/MS 5 years

Prominent Alumni
Patrick Purcell, President and Publisher, Boston Herald and Herald; James Campbell, President and CEO, GE Consumer and Industrial; Ellen Deutsch, SVP & Chief Growth Officer, The Hain Celestial Group; Bruce Gordon, CFO & SVP, Walt Disney Internet Group; Kathy Marinello, CEO of Ceridian Corp.

Academics

Hofstra is "the school with the best academic reputation on Long Island," an ideal location (bucolic, close to NYC, and near most students' homes and jobs) for the vast majority of its students. Excellent professors and technological resources round out the picture. "My academic experience so far has been very pleasurable," reports one Zarb student. "Professors treat you like a customer, doing their best to meet [and] satisfy your needs [and] concerns. The campus is beautifully maintained, and the university has devoted a lot of resources to improvement [and] expansion of infrastructure and technology on campus." "The business school is making an effort to stay abreast of industry trends, inviting industry leaders as guest speakers, [and] maintaining technologically up-to-date classrooms." Moreover, "The campus is mostly wireless, and every classroom is equipped with SMART Board and AV." To top it off, "The administration is accessible and friendly. They work with each student one-on-one and have the best interests of the student in mind."

Zarb's MBA students must ascend five academic stepping-stones to earn the 48-credit degree. Residency workshops (noncredit classes on such topics as library resources, calculus, and statistics), core competency courses (survey economics, business, and ethics classes), and the advanced core (set courses in accounting, business computer information systems, finance, international business, management, marketing, and quality management) make up the bulk of the program. Well-prepared students can place out of a limited number of courses in these three areas, but those longing for electives must simply console themselves with the quality of teaching within the requirements. "The professors are very engaging and dynamic. I don't find myself getting bored in class but really interested, and [I'm] learning new ideas," says one student. Another adds, "There are no strict lectures, and students always offer comments, ideas, and opinions. Debates have even formed from time to time. Class is quite stimulating." A five-course concentration allows students considerably more freedom in pursuing their passions—from finance to health services management to international business to sports management. One finance major says, "I learned a great deal about finance . . . and business management overall. My professors were great. Most had industry experience and were up to date with current industry trends." The final component is an integrative capstone revolving around teamwork and management simulation.

Zarb's 2.5-year MBA curriculum is broad, deep, and somewhat flexible, allowing students to place out of a limited number of classes and focus on their passions. But Zarb doesn't offer the guidance to match. Students gripe that requirements "aren't clear" and recommend that school administrators "help students choose better classes and inform students about certain classes not offered in the next semester so students can choose other classes."

Career and Placement

The "excellent career center" connects MBAs with jobs in what students call "quality companies in the areas of investment banking, private equity, and institutional finance." Nearly all students take jobs in the Northeast, and the finance and accounting industries account for more than half of students' first jobs post-graduation. Top employers are Integrated Business Systems, Citigroup, Goldman Sachs, Canon USA, Deloitte Touche Tohmatsu, GE, Ernst & Young, Cablevision, Protiviti, BDO Seidman, MSC Direct, Computer Associates, Hain Celestial, Marcum and Kliegman LLP, and ADP.

ADMISSIONS CONTACT: CAROL DRUMMER, DEAN FOR GRADUATE ADMISSIONS
ADDRESS: 126 HOFSTRA UNIVERSITY, 105 MEMORIAL HALL HEMPSTEAD, NY 11549
PHONE: 800-463-7672 • FAX: 516-463-4664
E-MAIL: GRADSTUDENT@HOFSTRA.EDU • WEBSITE: WWW.HOFSTRA.EDU/BUSINESS

Student Life and Environment

"Hofstra is mostly a commuter school," explains one Zarb student. "The problem is that it could be more than that, but it doesn't try." But other students see it differently. "[Students] are very involved in clubs and activities," declares one student. Students enjoy "home sporting events [and] drama productions." "The campus is vibrant and beautiful. It feels like a second home to me." Suburban Hempstead is "close to NYC" near the Long Island Railroad which makes for an easy commute into the city, but quiet enough to "allow [students] to concentrate on studying."

Students describe one another as "hardworking, driven"—indeed, most "are working full-time while attending classes"—"cooperative," and "very friendly." Though they "tend to be single and in the early stages of their careers," Zarb students do "represent a wide range in ages" and backgrounds, and, as a result, they "bring different opinions" and "life/work experience" "to each [classroom] discussion." Nearly half of the "very diverse" student body is female, and the full-time cohort is one-fourth international and one-fourth students of color. The vast majority "are already employed full-time," most "in the particular field they would like to be in." As a result of having concrete goals, students are very "motivated" and "focused on their education."

Admissions

Hofstra "has a good reputation, and its entrance requirement is not as high as some other top-tier schools in the city," says one student happily, although another student sees this more as a cause for gripes: "The school could be more selective in who it accepts and, thus, raise some of the academic standards." Indeed, Zarb's 78 percent acceptance rate paints a rosy picture for determined applicants who may not have stellar academic credentials or extensive work experience. The average entering student reports a 3.14 GPA, 521 GMAT, and 5 years of work experience.

FINANCIAL FACTS

Annual tuition	$14,760
Fees	$970
Cost of books	$1,000
Room & board (on/off-campus)	$10,400/$11,760
% of students receiving aid	55
% of first-year students receiving aid	53
% of students receiving loans	39
% of students receiving grants	34
Average award package	$18,203
Average grant	$9,164

ADMISSIONS

Admissions Selectivity Rating	70
# of applications received	306
% applicants accepted	78
% acceptees attending	52
Average GMAT	521
Range of GMAT	470–560
Average GPA	3.14
TOEFL required of international students	Yes
Application fee	$60
International application fee	$60
Regular application deadline	Rolling
Regular notification	Rolling
Deferment available	Yes
Maximum length of deferment	1 year
Transfer students accepted	Yes
Transfer application policy	Number of transferable credits is limited to a maximum of 9 credits.
Non-fall admissions	Yes
Need-blind admissions	Yes

Applicants Also Look At

City University of New York—Baruch College, New York University, Pace University, St. John's University.

EMPLOYMENT PROFILE

Career Rating	80	**Grads Employed by Function**	**%**	**Avg. Salary**
Primary Source of Full-time Job Acceptances		Finance	58	$64,571
School-facilitated activities	8 (33%)	Marketing	13	$64,333
Graduate-facilitated activities	9 (38%)	MIS	13	$88,333
Unknown	7 (29%)	Operations	8	$60,000
Average base starting salary	$68,000	Consulting	8	$75,000
Percent employed	76	**Top 5 Employers Hiring Grads**		
		Citigroup; Openlink; Deloitte; Deutsche Bank; Nokia		

HONG KONG U. OF SCIENCE AND TECHNOLOGY
HKUST BUSINESS SCHOOL

Academics

For students looking to begin a career in Hong Kong or on the Asian continent, The Hong Kong University of Science and Technology operates one of the region's most well respected MBA programs, spearheaded by the "best faculty in Asia." Located in a prominent "financial hub," HKUST students benefit from the unique "opportunity to live in Hong Kong and study Asian Business in an environment unparalleled anywhere else across the continent." In addition to the exceptional contacts and experience that the school's location inherently supplies, "the program provides well-rounded foundational coursework across a spectrum of business topics." On top of required classes, "elective offerings are diverse and interesting," comprising more than 40 percent of the MBA curriculum. Many students point out the strength of the school's "world renowned finance department," saying the program boasts "a very competitive environment, especially in more quantitatively oriented courses."

Despite HKUST's strength in quantitative fields, the well-balanced academic program includes "abundant soft skills training." In the classroom, professors focus on "developing critical and problem-solving skills using business cases and real-world questions, in addition to teamwork." On that note, group work and class discussions are also emphasized throughout the curriculum, with good results. With over 20 nations represented within a full-time MBA class of just 70 students, "the group discussions in class are enriched by such a varied mix of cultures and experiences."

Attracting a team of business experts from across the world, "HKUST has a good mix of professors who are former industry practitioners with many years of experience, as well as brilliant researchers who are on the cutting edge of what the future is going to bring." A current student enthuses, "Hong Kong is a unique place where many academic superstars want to teach. Currently there are three visiting faculty professors who are absolute experts in their fields." In the lecture hall, these expert teachers excel at "combining theory with real-life examples and making their lectures relevant and practice-oriented." When it come to the administration, students say the program is "well organized," and headed by a friendly and helpful staff. If you have a question or concern, "the MBA office representatives are always available, even during their lunch break."

Career and Placement

The HKUST Career Services Office offers individual counseling, group workshops, a well-stocked career library, and a packed calendar of networking events and alumni activities. A current student enthuses, "The Career Office has been exceptional in providing advisory services for existing students, and in creating opportunities for students to network with existing business entities for future career placements."

The school's stellar reputation in Asia puts HKUST graduates in the running for top jobs in the region. In 2007, about two-thirds of the graduating class took jobs in Hong Kong, while another 10 percent went to mainland China. Despite their regional renown, students worry that the school's "reputation is undervalued in comparison to its quality. It is hardly known in the USA or Europe." At the same time, students are quick to point out that many US business schools operate exchange programs with HKUST, which is helping to promote the school's name internationally.

Currently, HKUST graduates who took jobs in Hong Kong reported an average annual salary of HK$560,154 (or US$72,000), and 45 percent of graduates received salaries that were three times higher than their pre-MBA wages. A partial list of employers recruiting at HKUST includes ACNielsen, AIA Hong Kong, Asian Development Bank, Bank of

China, Morgan Stanley, Nortel, PepsiCo, Philips, Royal Bank of Scotland, Star Group Ltd, and Woodward Consulting.

Student Life and Environment

HKUST's challenging curriculum demands a lot of time and energy. As a result, "a great deal of the day is taken up by team meetings, preparing for presentations, and doing homework." Fortunately, the campus atmosphere is pleasant and inclusive, and "the common rooms and the MBA lounge [are] a sort of a big living room for the MBA community." Boasting an idyllic location in one of Hong Kong's quieter neighborhoods, "HKUST has arguably the best campus views in the world. The school is built into a mountain overlooking the South China Sea providing stunning views all around. It has a National Geographic feel to it." In addition, the campus "recreational facilities are excellent," including "multiple pools, gyms, tennis courts, [and] soccer fields."

Social and academic life is vibrant at HKUST. After class, "the school organizes a wide variety of networking, alumni and business leader events for students to attend, to grow their business contacts and to broaden their outlook in business in Asia." In addition, students get together to blow off steam, planning "trips to various places in Hong Kong for fun," or "socializing and partying" with their classmates.

Admissions

To apply to the HKUST MBA program, students must possess an undergraduate degree and have at least one year of professional work experience. The current HKUST business student had a GMAT score between 550-700, a TOEFL score of 600 or above, and three to five years of work experience before entering the program.

FINANCIAL FACTS

Annual tuition	$41,000
Cost of books	$1,300
Room & board	
(on/off-campus)	$4,600/$6,200

ADMISSIONS

Admissions Selectivity Rating	60*
Range of GMAT	560–720
Minimum TOEFL	
(paper/computer)	600/250
Application fee	$64
International application fee	$64
Regular application deadline	3/15
Regular notification	5/31
Application Deadline/Notification	
Round 1:	12/15 / 02/29
Round 2:	03/15 / 05/31
Deferment available	Yes
Maximum length of	
deferment	1 year

EMPLOYMENT PROFILE				
Career Rating	81	Grads Employed by Function	%	Avg. Salary
Percent employed	95	Finance	29	NR
		Marketing	9	NR
		Strategic Planning	24	NR
		Consulting	12	NR
		General Management	14	NR
		Other	12	NR

HOWARD UNIVERSITY
SCHOOL OF BUSINESS

GENERAL INFORMATION
Type of school	Private
Environment	Metropolis
Academic calendar	Semester

SURVEY SAYS...
Good social scene
Good peer network
Cutting edge classes
Solid preparation in:
Teamwork
Communication/interpersonal skills
Presentation skills

STUDENTS
Enrollment of parent institution	11,433
Enrollment of business school	131
% male/female	51/49
% out-of-state	73
% part-time	24
% minorities	70
% international	30
Average age at entry	27
Average years work experience at entry	3

ACADEMICS
Academic Experience Rating	**78**
Student/faculty ratio	3:1
Profs interesting rating	73
Profs accessible rating	84
% female faculty	30
% minority faculty	88

Joint Degrees
JD/MBA 4 years, MD/MBA 5 years, PharmD/MBA 5 years, BBA/MBA (Accounting) 5 years, BSE/MBA (Engineering) 5.5–6 years.

Prominent Alumni
Marianne Becton, Dir., Public Pol./Strategic Alliance, Verizon; Kerry L. Nelson, Sr. VP, Nonprofit Foundations, Northern Trust; Rodney E. Thomas, CEO, Thomas & Herbert Consulting, LLC.

Academics

Students who want "a school with great recruitment" that will challenge them academically turn to Howard University, one of the nation's most prestigious Historically Black institutions. With a full-time day program, an accelerated part-time program, and a conventional part-time program, Howard has options to accommodate a wide range of students.

The entire MBA program is relatively small, with the majority of students enrolled full-time. The size of the program nurtures "a positive and supportive atmosphere." Students appreciate the "support and mentoring that is actively given by the administration. . . . They really do root for the success of their students." They help students in other ways as well. One MBA tells us that one of the university's strengths lies in the "availability of financial aid. Howard University has a legacy of being benevolent, which is followed diligently by the School of Business."

Students praise Howard for its "good supply chain management program," for its entrepreneurship program, and for offering a combined JD/MBA. Concentrations are available in entrepreneurship, finance, human resources management, information systems, international business, marketing, and supply chain management. Professors here "have this zeal" that is "refreshing." They also employ "some very up-to-date teaching styles." Students mention that their professors "all seem to not only have working knowledge of how the business world operates, but also seem genuinely passionate the subject matters they teach." The academics are "challenging" but students believe that means they will be "helpful in the workplace."

MBAs here warn that the full-time program is still ironing out some kinks. "I have seen steady progress; however, additional full-time staff is needed to move the full-time day program to the next level," says one MBA. "The next few years will determine the commitment from the university in regards to the MBA program." They also feel that "Howard could stand to improve on having better technological facilities." Fortunately, the administration "seems actively involved in ensuring that its students are well prepared for the world of management," suggesting that the program's shortcomings will soon be addressed.

Career and Placement

Students tell us that "the biggest strength of the school is the networking aspect of the curriculum. No one can say that Howard is not a highly visible program, especially when it comes to recruiting minorities." Indeed, many choose to attend Howard "because of the number and quality of companies recruiting MBAs from Howard University." With "several career fairs and numerous companies that come to interview and hire" the students, Howard works hard to provide each student with ample recruitment opportunities.

Employers that frequently hire Howard MBAs include: Citigroup, Dell, Clark Construction, Deloitte Touche Tohmatsu, Eaton Corporation, Ernst & Young, IBM, Intel, KPMG International, MetLife, Merrill Lynch, Microsoft, PricewaterhouseCoopers, Sprint, SunTrust, Stockamp and Associates, Tyco, United Technologies Corporation, Accenture, Bank of America, Honeywell, ING, Johnson & Johnson, Procter & Gamble, Roche Pharmaceuticals, American Express, AT&T, Booz Allen Hamilton, Capital One, Cisco Systems, FedEx, Freddie Mac, Jones Lang LaSalle, Lockheed Martin, Meadwestraco, and Standard & Poors.

ADMISSIONS CONTACT: MBA ADMISSIONS, OFFICE OF GRADUATE PROGRAMS
ADDRESS: 2600 SIXTH STREET, NW, SUITE 236 WASHINGTON, DC 20059 UNITED STATES
PHONE: 202-806-1725 • FAX: 202-986-4435
E-MAIL: MBA_BSCHOOL@HOWARD.EDU • WEBSITE: WWW.BSCHOOL.HOWARD.EDU

Student Life and Environment

Life at Howard "is a balancing act between getting all the course work [done] and networking with the companies that often visit our campus." Fortunately, "the school ensures that there is no lack of support or resources, thus making it possible for us to take advantage of all there is to be offered." Students also try to make time for the "many activities Howard has to offer. Our Graduate Business Student Council (GBSC) sponsors a variety of events such as happy hours, ice skating, and clothes drives." They "attempt to keep students active in the community while offering them a social environment to express themselves on the weekend." Then, of course, there's Washington DC, a vibrant metropolis with opportunities on both the career and extracurricular fronts.

Howard's academically demanding MBA program is undoubtedly "time consuming. Some of the professors really want us to get into depth about the subject matter," says one MBA. "Many of our classes require group projects," which is "one of the challenges at Howard, especially with such a diverse mix of students. The students look out for each other, though. There are informal study groups and networks to help." That looking out doesn't end in the classroom. At Howard, students "interact with each other like family and care about each other like family. This relationship makes studying and even partying together easy and fun." Facilities "are somewhat adequate for what needs to be done." Students "have [their] own computer lab and lounge where we meet and socialize between classes. The lab is where we spend most our day studying, having group meetings, or just taking care of things before we head home for the evening."

Admissions

Applicants to the Howard MBA program must submit the following materials to the Admissions Office: a completed application form; an up-to-date resume; an official score report for the GMAT (taken no more than 5 years before date of application); official transcripts for all undergraduate and graduate course work; three completed evaluation and recommendation forms, completed by at least one academic and one professional supervisor (the school encourages students to submit letters of recommendation in addition to these forms); a personal statement describing the applicant's abilities, experiences, and goals in pursuing the MBA; and proof of at least 1 year of significant post-collegiate professional or managerial experience. Applicants must have completed advanced college algebra and/or calculus in order to be admitted. International applicants must submit all of the above plus a Statement of Financial Resources. International students who attended a non-English speaking undergraduate institution must have their transcripts translated and interpreted by a professional service. They must also submit an official score report for the TOEFL.

FINANCIAL FACTS

Annual tuition	$16,175
Fees	$805
Cost of books	$2,400
Room & board (on/off-campus)	$16,000/$19,600
% of students receiving aid	88
% of first-year students receiving aid	88
% of students receiving loans	59
% of students receiving grants	53
Average award package	$22,243
Average grant	$16,388
Average student loan debt	$37,834

ADMISSIONS

Admissions Selectivity Rating	79
# of applications received	169
% applicants accepted	49
% acceptees attending	63
Average GMAT	530
Range of GMAT	480–570
Average GPA	3.17
TOEFL required of international students	Yes
Minimum TOEFL (paper/computer)	550/213
Application fee	$65
International application fee	$65
Regular application deadline	4/1
Regular notification	5/1
Application Deadline/Notification	
Round 1:	11/15 / 01/01
Round 2:	02/01 / 03/01
Round 3:	04/01 / 05/01
Round 4:	05/15 / 06/01
Early decision program?	Yes
ED Deadline/ Notification	11/15 / 01/01
Deferment available	Yes
Maximum length of deferment	2 Semesters
Transfer students accepted	Yes
Transfer application policy Can transfer a maximum of 6.0 credit hours from an AACSB-accredited Graduate Business Program.	
Non-fall admissions	Yes
Need-blind admissions	Yes

Applicants Also Look At

American University, Clark Atlanta University, George Mason University, Georgetown University, The George Washington University, University of Maryland—College Park.

EMPLOYMENT PROFILE

Career Rating	91	Grads Employed by Function% Avg. Salary	
Primary Source of Full-time Job Acceptances		Finance	30 $85,889
School-facilitated activities	23 (72%)	Human Resources	3 $80,000
Graduate-facilitated activities	9 (28%)	Marketing	23 $84,000
Percent employed	86	Operations	27 $75,186
		Consulting	7 $87,500
		General Management	3 $85,000
		Other	7 $84,000

Top 5 Employers Hiring Grads
Dell; Tyco; Intel; IBM; UTC

IAE UNIVERSIDAD AUSTRAL
MANAGEMENT AND BUSINESS SCHOOL

Academics

Future MBAs choose IAE Universidad Austral's intensive one-year program because of the school's "excellent reputation in Argentina and throughout Latin America" as well as for the speed with which it delivers results. The bilingual program (classes are taught in Spanish and English), which runs from January to December, has been honed over time to provide a quality education to its students. As the school's website states, the one-year MBA program "is the result of the 25-year experience IAE has acquired in providing part-time Executive MBA programs and the contributions of many years of delivering full-time programs supplied by the Harvard Business School and the IESE of Barcelona."

IAE's "intensive" program is "a one-year hardworking MBA. The schedule runs from 9:00 A.M. to 6:00 P.M., with only a two-hour break in the middle of the day (from 12:30 P.M. to 2.30 P.M.) for sports and eating." The program begins with a month-long "leveling course," during which students are reacquainted with fundamental quantitative skills in statistics, mathematics, and accounting. The second module of the program consists of an extensive core curriculum that focuses on three areas: "technical skills in marketing, finance, etc.; critical thinking skills that teach you new ways to approach both professional problems and personal problems; and teamwork skills." During the third module, students choose from a selection of electives. The fourth and fifth modules of the program are devoted to interdisciplinary analysis of business problems, fieldwork, networking, and developing management skills.

Students speak highly of the program, reporting that "professors are all very good. Most of them have PhDs, and they have a lot of patience. They always are able to help you inside and outside the class." The program runs smoothly, and this ease is especially important given the amount of work piled on students; no one here has time to wade through bureaucratic red tape. As one MBA notes, "The administration provides exceptional service. It is well prepared for the needs of its classmates: Everything we need is available for us." And perhaps most important, "IAE has very good contacts with businesses in Latin America, and a very important aspect is that it provides us with internal and external mentors."

Career and Placement

The Career Services Department at IAE works with students and companies to facilitate recruitment and placement. Students report, however, that "the department is underdeveloped, especially in the international job market." The alumni network, on the other hand, "is unbelievable," according to students; one reports, "I could speak to many important executives from the best companies of my country because they were alumni." Employers who have worked with IAE include Alto Parana SA, Arthur D. Little, Banco Galicia, Belise & Asociados, Bodegas Lagarde, CCBA SA, Citibank NA, Fiat Argentina, Ford Argentina, GE Capital Cia, Global Praxis, Hart Casares, Johnson & Johnson Medical SA, KPMG Consultores, Kraft Food Argentina, McKinsey & Company, Nestlé Argentina SA, Novartis Argentina SA, Sade Skanska Ingeniería y Construcciones SA, and The Walt Disney Company.

ADDRESS: CASILLA DE CORREO N°49 - MARIANO ACOSTA S/N° Y RUTA NAC. 8 PILAR - BS.AS, 1629
ARGENTINA
PHONE: 011 54.2322.48.1000 • FAX: 011 54.2322.48.1050
E-MAIL: FFRAGUEIRO@IAE.EDU.AR • WEBSITE: WWW.IAE.EDU.AR/WEB2005_ENG/HOME/HOME

Student Life and Environment

IAE's campus "is located in Pilar, 50 kilometers from the capital" of Argentina, in a beautiful setting "with a lot of trees, grass, and greenery everywhere." Despite the bucolic setting, "you can find everything near the campus: a mall, restaurants, supermarkets, movies, gas stations, etc." Campus facilities include areas where students "can play soccer, tennis, and rugby during the two-hour lunch break." Big-city life isn't too far off, as "the campus is one hour away from Buenos Aires." Students note, however, that "since IAE's program is a one-year MBA, the workload is so heavy that there is very little time to do activities outside the classroom." Classes convene from 9:00 A.M. to 6:00 P.M.; most students "study until 9:00 P.M., then have some dinner with friends," and then call it a day.

About 70 percent of IAE's students are Argentine; the remaining students come from other parts of Latin America, Europe, and the United States. Students are drawn from all sectors: marketing, banking, consulting, engineering, services, and even agriculture are represented here. About half the students consider themselves "young entrepreneurs," and nearly as many see themselves as "young, socially oriented professionals." Students generally "have great senses of humor, don't hesitate to help one another, and enjoy hanging out, drinking beer and wine, and watching movies."

Admissions

Applicants to the full-time MBA program at IAE must have at least three years of postundergraduate work experience. The admissions department requires all of the following materials: official transcripts for all postsecondary academic work; an official GMAT score report (minimum acceptable score 550; IAE also offers its own skills exam which can be taken in lieu of the GMAT); a resume; personal essays; letters of recommendation; a completed application form; and, for students whose first language is not English, a minimum TOEFL score of 570 (paper-based test) or 230 (computer-based test). The admissions committee uses the above materials to screen candidates. Those deemed possible candidates for the program must undergo an admissions interview with an IAE professor and members of both the admissions and career management departments.

FINANCIAL FACTS	
Annual tuition	$17,000

ADMISSIONS	
Admissions Selectivity Rating	**84**
# of applications received	111
% applicants accepted	57
% acceptees attending	76
Average GMAT	618
TOEFL required of international students	Yes
Minimum TOEFL (computer)	230

EMPLOYMENT PROFILE		
Career Rating	**71**	**Grads Employed by Function% Avg. Salary**
		Accounting	2 NR
		Finance	4 NR
		Human Resources	4 NR
		Marketing	13 NR
		Operations	6 NR
		Consulting	11 NR
		Communications	2 NR
		Entrepreneurship	2 NR
		Non-profit	6: NR

ILLINOIS INSTITUTE OF TECHNOLOGY
STUART GRADUATE SCHOOL OF BUSINESS

Academics

The Stuart Graduate School of Business at Chicago's Illinois Institute of Technology recognizes the diverse needs of its student body and works hard to accommodate them all. Those looking to expedite their MBAs, for example, can enroll in the school's full-time program; about one-third of the students here do just that. Those who want to pursue their degrees contemporaneously with their careers have a number of part-time options, including the lockstep "two-year part-time fast-track MBA" (offered at the school's Rice Campus in Wheaton) and the "customizable world-class MBA." Classes are scheduled during weekdays, evenings, and weekends for the convenience of all of Stuart's constituencies. All MBA programs consist of a minimum of 16 classes; specialization is available in all but the fast-track program and requires an additional four classes.

IIT is a world-class research institution, and, not surprisingly, Stuart MBAs benefit from the presence of the high-powered academics here. Three research centers—the Center for Financial Markets, the Chicago Geospatial Exchange, and the Center for Sustainable Enterprise—offer unique options to adventurous MBAs. There is even an optional specialization in sustainable enterprise that trains students "to identify, develop, communicate, and help implement practical and equitable business strategies that advance the ecological sustainability of the Chicago area while fostering current and future economic viability." Stuart was recently ranked among the world's leaders in incorporating environmental management.

Many here, however, prefer more traditional fare. Stuart MBAs laud the school's entrepreneurship program as well as offerings in finance and marketing. Some extol the advantages conferred by the presence of a health care concentration, and quite a few full-timers take advantage of dual-degree programs in law or public administration. Throughout the curriculum, students praise "the use of technology and real-life examples, and the application of business problems." Stuart professors "are always willing to help and provide out-of-the-classroom tutorials and further explanations," plus "their experience and techniques are outstanding." Similarly, administrators "are extremely helpful and go out of their way to get to know each student personally and help anyone." With IIT's small cohorts, "there is no crowding in the libraries, computer labs, etc. And, we get to learn a lot from group discussions." For many, though, "the school's greatest strength is its strategic location. It is because of its location that we are able to get internships and other opportunities to work." About the only weakness here, students tell us, is that "the school's image needs to be improved. The rankings need improvement and people need to know about IIT a lot more."

Career and Placement

The Office of Career Services at the Stuart MBA program provides students with one-on-one career counseling, workshops in interviewing and resume preparation, and research on companies and opportunities appropriate to each student's goals. A self-assessment, conducted as students enter the program, helps the office tailor its services to the individual needs of each MBA. The university at large conducts career fairs through its Career Development Center.

Employers who most frequently hire Stuart MBAs include Bank One, Northern Trust, Bank of America, ABN-Amro, Lucent Technologies, JPMorgan, Navistar, Johnson & Johnson, Capitol One, Vankampen, US EPA, Reuters, Cantor Fitzgerald, McLagan Partners, Motorola, Inc., and Akamal Trading. About half of all Stuart MBAs remain in the Midwest after graduation; most of the rest head to one of the two coasts.

ADMISSIONS CONTACT: BRIAN JANSEN, DIRECTOR OF ADMISSIONS
ADDRESS: 565 W. ADAMS STREET CHICAGO, IL 60661 UNITED STATES
PHONE: 312-906-6567 • FAX: 312-906-6549
E-MAIL: ADMISSIONS@STUART.IIT.EDU • WEBSITE: WWW.STUART.IIT.EDU

Student Life and Environment

IIT's main MBA programs are located "in a separate building in downtown Chicago. That building houses law and business school students only, so there isn't much activity there really, just serious-looking students walking to and fro. The main campus has more life, and there is a free shuttle to transport you between campuses. I appreciate the peace and quiet of our building, though. It's very easy to find a nook to study in without constant interference," remarks one student. MBAs participate in "lots of study groups. We also have socials every Wednesday, and students often go out into town in small groups." Despite these opportunities, many here feel that they "need more organizations, activities, a bigger career center, and more seminars and activities with others outside the school (i.e. businesses, other universities, etc.)."

The student body includes many who have considerable work experience, as well as "a lot of diversity in terms of nationality and occupation." One student observes, "The diverse population aids in creating a learning experience unlike any other. Students learn as much (if not more) outside the classroom than in the classroom, just by interacting with everyone around them." When they can find the time, students love to take advantage of "the world's biggest financial city," which also offers plenty in the way of culture, entertainment, fine dining, and nightlife. Again, it comes back to location. "Stuart is located near the Chicago loop in the midst of big-name business companies, allowing for excellent networking and job opportunities. It's also very close to public transportation."

Admissions

The IIT Stuart Graduate School of Business requires applicants to submit GMAT scores, official undergraduate transcripts for all schools attended, two letters of recommendation from people "who can attest to your academic or professional qualifications," two required essays (personal statement and career goals) with the option to submit additional essays (describe a difficult challenge you have faced, describe your ideal company), and a resume. International students must also submit TOEFL scores no more than two years old. Undergraduate transcripts in languages other than English must be accompanied by an English translation.

FINANCIAL FACTS

Annual tuition	$24,332
Fees	$960
Cost of books	$890
Room & board (on/off-campus)	$10,750/$13,860
% of students receiving aid	86
% of first-year students receiving aid	81
% of students receiving loans	11
% of students receiving grants	49
Average award package	$5,468
Average grant	$3,172
Average student loan debt	$61,800

ADMISSIONS

Admissions Selectivity Rating	**73**
# of applications received	222
% applicants accepted	70
% acceptees attending	21
Average GMAT	565
Range of GMAT	510–600
Average GPA	3.0
TOEFL required of international students	Yes
Minimum TOEFL (paper/computer)	550/213
Application fee	$75
International application fee	$75
Regular application deadline	8/15
Regular notification	Rolling
Deferment available	Yes
Maximum length of deferment	1 year
Transfer students accepted	Yes
Transfer application policy May transfer up to 4 core courses and 2 elective courses.	
Non-fall admissions	Yes
Need-blind admissions	Yes

EMPLOYMENT PROFILE

Career Rating	86	Grads Employed by Function	% Avg. Salary
Primary Source of Full-time Job Acceptances		Finance	22 $68,000
School-facilitated activities	3 (13%)	Marketing	22 $94,333
Graduate-facilitated activities	5 (21%)	MIS	11 NR
Unknown	16 (66%)	Operations	11 $55,000
Percent employed	80	Consulting	6 $53,500
		General Management	17 $52,000
		Other	11 $64,500

Top 5 Employers Hiring Grads
Intel; Bank of America; Morningstar; Fidelity; Johnson and Johnson

ILLINOIS STATE UNIVERSITY
COLLEGE OF BUSINESS

Academics

With a new $30 million College of Business building that students describe as "state-of-the-art" and "absolutely amazing," the College of Business at Illinois State University is clearly making a big investment in the future of undergraduate and graduate business studies. The school's MBA program is tailored toward the needs of part-time students: Classes convene once a week, always starting at 6:00 P.M. About one-quarter of the student body attends full-time, typically taking three classes per semester. Part-time students usually enroll in one or two classes per semester.

With a total of 200 students, the MBA program at ISU is small enough to allow "individualized attention from professors." Students praise the "big university resources with a small classroom focus" here. One MBA writes, "Although the atmosphere is challenging, the professors are available to assist students outside of class periods, and I believe they are personally vested in the success of their students. I believe I am getting the quality of education one would only expect to find at nationally known private colleges." The size of the program has its drawbacks as well: Several students in our survey complained that "electives are few and far between. Almost all electives are only offered every two years." To clarify, of the 23 MBA electives offerings, 8 are offered every year and 15 are offered every other year.

The ISU curriculum is divided into three segments: foundation work, core courses, and electives. Seven foundation courses cover the material typically covered in an undergraduate business program; students with undergraduate business degrees typically are allowed to forego all of these classes. Nine core courses and three electives must be completed by all MBAs. Students may use their electives to develop an area of concentration in accounting, finance, international business, management, marketing, or fine arts administration. The arts program is relatively unique, helping the school draw students from outside the immediate region.

Career and Placement

Illinois State University's career services include resume and job posting through eRecruiting. Other services are provided by the Career Center, which serves the entire undergraduate and graduate population of the university. Students report that the university's "affiliation with such local companies as State Farm, Caterpillar, Mitsubishi, and Country Companies" translates into "great internship opportunities." Students also feel that "getting more diversity in corporate recruiters from different areas of business other than finance and insurance to appeal to a broader MBA group" should be a major priority of the MBA program. The school reports that 94 percent of its MBAs are employed at the time of their graduation.

ADMISSIONS CONTACT: SJ CHANG, ASSOCIATE DEAN FOR MBA AND UNDERGRADUATE PROGRAMS
ADDRESS: CAMPUS BOX 5570, MBA PROGRAM NORMAL, IL 61790-5570 UNITED STATES
PHONE: 309-438-8388 • FAX: 309-438-7255
E-MAIL: ISUMBA@EXCHANGE.COB.ILSTU.EDU • WEBSITE: WWW.MBA.ILSTU.EDU

Student Life and Environment

"You are able to become as involved as you would like" in the MBA program at ISU. Students report that "various activities take place on campus, and it is up to each student to get involved. Clubs, events, sports, and plays are just a few of the options that students have to choose from." Students enjoy "a great social network with the MBAs. We all have a lot of classes together as it is a relatively small group. We build homecoming floats and meet for drinks regularly. There seems to be a very good balance between learning, getting our work done, and sharing our experience."

Not everyone gets involved, of course. Many of the students here are part-time students with full-time jobs, and many just want to fulfill their academic obligations and get home. One student explains: "School life is spent with three-hour classes per week for each course. Group meetings for projects, research, case studies, and homework assignments: This is very much the pattern for 90 percent of the courses." While "the workload can be tough," most here agree that "the homework load is fair, and expectations are fair. The culture is typically Midwestern, with values of accountability for oneself and helping out others. This starts with the professors and is imparted to the students."

While the school reports that the average work experience of full-time MBA students is 2.59 years, some of our survey respondents find their full-time peers' lack of work experience troubling. As one puts it, "I have noticed a tremendous difference between those students [with little work experience] and the ones with careers. It can be very frustrating to work with full-time students because they do not exert as much effort or have strong time-management or leadership skills." They also "cannot speak from experience or relate real-life stories to the class." Large local companies such as State Farm, Country Companies, and Mitsubishi contribute many students to the part-time program.

Admissions

Applicants to the ISU MBA program must submit applications to both the graduate college of the university and the MBA program. To receive priority in the admissions process, applications should be received February 1; applications for spring entry are due by September 1. All applications must include two official copies of transcripts for all academic work completed beyond high school; GMAT scores; a resume; two personal essays; and two letters of reference. GPA for the final 60 credit hours of undergraduate work and GMAT scores are the primary determining factors in the admissions decision. In recent years, successful applicants have posted an average GPA of 3.4 and an average GMAT score of 545. International students whose first language is not English must submit TOEFL scores. A minimum score of 600 on the paper-and-pencil test or 250 on the computer-based test is required. Work experience is considered "beneficial" and is "strongly encouraged," but is not required.

FINANCIAL FACTS

Annual tuition (in-state/ out-of-state)	$4,656/$9,696
Fees	$1,366
Cost of books	$1,025
Room & board (on/off-campus)	$6,148/$6,455
% of students receiving aid	94
% of first-year students receiving aid	89
% of students receiving loans	53
% of students receiving grants	95
Average award package	$14,150
Average grant	$7,096
Average student loan debt	$20,439

ADMISSIONS

Admissions Selectivity Rating	**71**
# of applications received	71
% applicants accepted	83
% acceptees attending	68
Average GMAT	524
Range of GMAT	500–580
Average GPA	3.47
TOEFL required of international students	Yes
Minimum TOEFL (paper/computer)	600/250
Application fee	$40
International application fee	$40
Regular application deadline	
Regular notification	
Early decision program?	Yes
ED Deadline/ Notification	02/01 / 02/15
Deferment available	Yes
Maximum length of deferment	1 year
Transfer students accepted	Yes
Transfer application policy must be in good academic standing and complete all regular application requirements, maximum 9 hours transfer credit accepted	
Non-fall admissions	Yes
Need-blind admissions	Yes

Applicants Also Look At

Bradley University, Northern Illinois University, University of Illinois at Urbana-Champaign.

EMPLOYMENT PROFILE

Career Rating	**77**

IMD INTERNATIONAL
INTERNATIONAL INSTITUTE FOR MANAGEMENT DEVELOPMENT

GENERAL INFORMATION

Type of school	Private

SURVEY SAYS...

Friendly students
Good peer network
Solid preparation in:
General management
Teamwork
Communication/interpersonal skills
Doing business in a global economy
Entrepreneurial studies

STUDENTS

Enrollment of parent institution	8,000
Enrollment of business school	90
% male/female	78/22
% international	98
Average age at entry	31
Average years work experience at entry	7

ACADEMICS

Academic Experience Rating	**99**
Student/faculty ratio	2:1
Profs interesting rating	85
Profs accessible rating	76
% female faculty	8

Prominent Alumni

Mr KY Lee, Chairman, BenQ Corporation; Mr Kjeld Kristiansen, President, LEGO Group; Mr Juergen Fischer, President of Commercial Operations Group, Hilton I; Mr Bo Risberg, CEO, Hilti, AG; Mr Mark Cornell, CEO, Champagne Krug SA.

Academics

Within a stone's throw of Lake Geneva's shores, the International Institute for Management Development in Lausanne, Switzerland, specializes in "leadership development with top professors and exceptional facilities." The unique aspect of this program is its emphasis on real world learning which is supported through its "excellent faculty" who are not tenured, but rather work on a contract basis, meaning that they are effectively coming straight to the classroom from the boardroom. The school prides itself on being "a global meeting place" and this is evidenced by mix of nationalities and ages of its students and professors. "It's probably the smallest business school in the world," one student notes, "with only 90 students a year." Thanks to this "small class," students "can always enjoy one-on-one relations" with their "professors, career officers, and other resources." "The professors are often leaders or respected academics in their fields who are open to class discussion," one student says.

Many here appreciate the "opportunity for hands-on learning, with the start-up and consulting projects, in addition to the emphasis on leadership and opportunities for personal development." In line with IMD's global outlook comes an emphasis on real world experience. "Applied learning" and "problem-based learning" reign supreme here. Be forewarned though, the workload ain't light. "The most important skill to survive here is to prioritize the heavy workload," a student advises. Part of this time management involves working together and most students at IMD are pleased to find a "very collaborative work environment." "The workload is such that it is not possible to do everything, so students tend to divide up work." Any idea what this kind of teamwork might allow? If you were thinking something along the lines of "diversity," you're right. Most students here have already been part of the workforce, with around "seven to eight years of experience," and represent "41 nationalities from all over the world." Where else could you find out about everything from "the banana business to elevators [in places as disparate] as Zimbabwe and Mauritius"? All this makes for "an intensive but life-changing year!"

For the most part, "Everything runs like Swiss clockwork." "We get very attentive staff which sorts out everything from mobile phones to setting up bank accounts," one student explains. The "friendly and helpful" staff "cooperate positively" with students. "I'm glad the campus is good because I spent 100 hours a week there," one student explains. "Part of how we managed it is due to how helpful everyone is down there." But into every MBA, a little rain must fall. Students wouldn't mind seeing the school "market itself" and "increase brand awareness among the general public" so that it would "be better known outside of Europe." As one student explains, "It has a great reputation among those who know it, but as it's a small school, it isn't well recognized in the US, for instance."

Career and Placement

After an "extremely busy first six months," IMD students settle into the second half of the year, where "project work is mixed with classes and recruiting." A huge part of this time involves working with career services to find a job. Many here note that since there is such a small number of students, their "career search is very individualistic and you can go for something off the usual track." IMD's career services center takes a personal approach to finding its students jobs by having them work with career coaches who help them "to better define [their] career goals" through surveys, "individual career strategy sessions," and workshops that cover everything from "networking" to "negotiating salary." Most impressive is the school's "class marketing," wherein IMD distributes short profiles of its MBA students "available for employment to over 5,000 companies and managers worldwide." The school also sends out a "résumé portfolio" to "over 250 organizations" that includes a "one-page résumé for each participant." This, in combination with ever-present "company presentations and on-campus recruiting," makes for happily employed students. "It allowed me to make a huge career leap to another level," one student says.

Student Life and Environment

You can thank the Romans for Lausanne. They originally founded it as a military camp but it went through many, many more incarnations and occupants until it reached its present state as one of the most beautiful locales in all of Europe. With over 15 museums, film and music festivals, several universities, nearby vineyards, and a massive focus on all things related to sports (which comes as no surprise considering the International Olympic Committee's headquarters is located here), there's no shortage of things to see or do regardless of the season. That said, for IMD students, "The heavy workload sometimes hampers social activities." A common complaint here is that the school "could improve its efforts to set aside time for more networking in a social environment." More often that not—and when time allows—students take things into their own hands and "go out of their way to organize social events or trips away." "Ninety percent of my time was spent on work, although there were different clubs or parties to attend almost every weekend," one undeterred student says. Another student sums up his experience, "IMD is a particular school and program in some senses. Since it doesn't belong to a university, its campus is smaller than the average and, therefore, it doesn't have on-campus housing....Overall, life at IMD has been spectacular both for me and my family. Lausanne is a lovely town, the campus is well-located...and people are friendly and competent and the support for families and spouses is fantastic." Others note, "The sports facilities could be improved." However, one thing that gets a unanimous vote of confidence is the "fantastic lunch buffet" and "amazing dessert table."

Admissions

In considering applicants for the MBA program, IMD requires its students to have a bachelor's degree or equivalent from an accredited institution, GMAT score, a minimum of three years full-time work experience (although they stress that the average among current students is seven years), and near-fluency in English (the TOEFL is not required, but considering your year at IMD will involve writing and speaking in English, your language skills had better be up to snuff). If you're unsure of where you stand, these good people have set up a MBA Assessment Form on their website (www.imd.ch/programs/mba/Assess-your-chances.cfm) where you can enter your stats and get a clear idea of whether you're a likely candidate for admission.

FINANCIAL FACTS

Annual tuition	$52,839
Fees	$19,586
Cost of books	$0
Room & board	
(off-campus)	$11,843
% of students receiving aid	30
% of students receiving loans	23
% of students receiving grants	11
Average award package	$37,898
Average grant	$25,964

ADMISSIONS

Admissions Selectivity Rating	97
# of applications received	425
% applicants accepted	26
% acceptees attending	82
Average GMAT	671
Range of GMAT	640–730
Application fee	$319
International application fee	$319
Regular application deadline	9/1
Regular notification	Rolling
Application Deadline/Notification	
Round 1:	04/01 / roll
Round 2:	06/01 / roll
Round 3:	08/01 / roll
Round 4:	09/01 / roll
Non-fall admissions	Yes
Need-blind admissions	Yes

Applicants Also Look At
Columbia University, Harvard University, INSEAD, London Business School, Stanford University, University of Oxford, University of Pennsylvania.

EMPLOYMENT PROFILE

Career Rating	94	Grads Employed by Function	% Avg. Salary
Primary Source of Full-time Job Acceptances		Finance	11 NR
School-facilitated activities	56 (77%)	Human Resources	3 NR
Graduate-facilitated activities	17 (23%)	Marketing	34 NR
Average base starting salary	$130,000	Operations	5 NR
Percent employed	93	Consulting	25 NR
		General Management	22 NR

Top 5 Employers Hiring Grads
McKinsey & Co; AstraZenica; BCG; Danaher; Dupont

INDIANA STATE UNIVERSITY
COLLEGE OF BUSINESS

Academics

Mainly geared toward students early in their business careers, the MBA program at Indiana State University offers graduate-level preparation to aspiring managers and business professionals. "You get a lot of value for the money" at ISU, where small class sizes and public-school tuition combine to deliver plenty of bang for your buck. With fewer than 100 students in the MBA program, the school offers a friendly and caring environment in which to study. Students repeatedly report that the "faculty is very knowledgeable," but also "very friendly, always willing to help, and very supportive." The school's administration also earns praise for its accessibility. The result is a school community in which "everyone works together to achieve a common goal: allowing us to get our MBA in an excellent environment. The whole school—including the dean—recognizes the MBAs and appreciates what they do for the school."

The Indiana State MBA consists of 33 semester units (plus foundational course work for students who did not study business as an undergraduate), which can be completed in one year and four months of full-time study. Students wishing to continue to work while they earn their MBAs may also choose to study part-time. Part-time students tell us that the school's small and intimate environment is particularly beneficial for them, as "the small size of the university and of the MBA program is advantageous in getting to know fellow students, even if one works full-time." Through core course work and electives, the program emphasizes strategic thinking, problem-solving skills, organizational change, international business, and group dynamics.

The program's emphasis on critical thinking means that "students come out of school without the idea that they already know everything. Students are more than willing to learn and can think outside the box." But students also have plenty of access to hands-on projects: Business students have the opportunity to assist faculty in real-world research projects through programs such as the Small Business Development Center (SBDC), which provides business planning assistance to start-up companies, and through consulting services to existing small businesses. In addition, the school offers excellent Graduate Assistantship programs, which cover the cost of tuition and give participants the opportunity to "work with faculty on a daily basis."

Career and Placement

In 2004, the College of Business opened the Career Experience Center (CEC), where students can research positions using the Sycamore CareerLink electronic database, attend career-building workshops, and prepare for interviews. A premier institution in the tri-state area, students at Indiana State University say their school "provides opportunities in the region which otherwise would not exist;" however, they also point out that the school could provide more internship and job fairs to improve the career development opportunities available to students.

ADMISSIONS CONTACT: DALE VARBLE, DIRECTOR, MBA PROGRAM
ADDRESS: INDIANA STATE UNIVERSITY, 800 SYCAMORE STREET TERRE HAUTE, IN 47809-BUS U.S.
PHONE: 812-237-2002 • FAX: 812-237-8720
E-MAIL: MBA@INDSTATE.EDU • WEBSITE: WEB.INDSTATE.EDU/SCHBUS/MBA

Student Life and Environment

Like many business schools, ISU tends to attract two types of students: recent graduates and older, returning students, "many of whom are part-time." Not surprisingly, part-time students tend to limit their campus activities to class and have little interest in extracurricular socializing. The full-time students tend to be more social. As many have recently graduated from college, they share a general camaraderie and sense of campus culture. In fact, many of the full-time students "live in the same housing, so they have gotten to know each other well." Moreover, the faculty and staff help to promote unity and spirit amongst the MBA population: For example, a second-year student tells us, "I am VP of our MBA Association and try to plan social events in which the faculty participates. We have had decent turnout considering the fact that professors do have lives outside of ISU." Campus culture in general is welcoming, and "students are generally very friendly with one another and accepting of new students from varied backgrounds."

For those looking for a typically collegiate experience, the ISU campus is home to over 10,000 students. The active college community provides a wide variety of clubs, organizations, and activities for interested students, so "there is plenty to do as long as students make an attempt to get involved in student organizations such as fraternities, sororities, or any other social club." The school's "many international students" provide the student body with a diversity of backgrounds and experiences. The school's location in downtown Terre Haute, Indiana, also provides students with plenty of off-campus opportunities to amuse themselves.

Admissions

In considering applicants for the MBA program, Indiana State University considers the following criteria: acceptance to the School of Graduate Studies; successful completion of undergraduate degree; GPA of at least 2.5; basic computing skills; GMAT scores; and prerequisite competency. Prerequisite course work for the program includes micro- and macroeconomics, financial and managerial accounting, finance, principles of marketing, principles of management, management science, and statistics. Potential students must display a GMAT-GPA admissions index of 1050 or higher (the admissions index numbers are calculated by multiplying GPA by 200 and adding GMAT scores). However, the school states that "applicants with an index between 950 and 1050, or whose grade point average is less than 2.5 on a 4-point scale, will be considered on a case-by-case basis."

FINANCIAL FACTS

Annual tuition (in-state/ out-of-state)	$4,410/$8,760
Fees	$78
Cost of books	$900
Room & board	$7,800
% of students receiving aid	30
% of first-year students receiving aid	30
% of students receiving grants	30
Average award package	$12,210
Average grant	$6,210

ADMISSIONS

Admissions Selectivity Rating	**81**
# of applications received	11
% applicants accepted	36
Average GMAT	510
Range of GMAT	430–750
Average GPA	3.04
TOEFL required of international students	Yes
Minimum TOEFL (paper/computer)	550/213
Application fee	$35
International application fee	$35
Regular application deadline	rolling
Regular notification	rolling
Deferment available	Yes
Maximum length of deferment	2 years
Transfer students accepted	Yes
Transfer application policy Will accept 6 credit hours from AACSB accredited Universities.	
Non-fall admissions	Yes

Applicants Also Look At

Ball State University, Illinois State University, Indiana University—Kokomo, Indiana University—Purdue University Indianapolis, McMaster University, Purdue University, The University of Texas at Austin.

EMPLOYMENT PROFILE			
Career Rating	**60***	**Grads Employed by Function**	**% Avg. Salary**
		Human Resources	10 NR
		Marketing	10 NR
		MIS	10 NR
		General Management	30 NR

INDIANA UNIVERSITY—BLOOMINGTON
KELLEY SCHOOL OF BUSINESS

GENERAL INFORMATION
Type of school	Public
Environment	Town
Academic calendar	Semester

SURVEY SAYS...
Good peer network
Happy students
Smart classrooms
Solid preparation in:
Marketing
Quantitative skills

STUDENTS
Enrollment of parent institution	37,351
Enrollment of business school	780
% male/female	73/27
% out-of-state	85
% part-time	41
% minorities	12
% international	41
Average age at entry	28
Average years work experience at entry	5

ACADEMICS
Academic Experience Rating	**97**
Student/faculty ratio	26:1
Profs interesting rating	98
Profs accessible rating	99
% female faculty	25
% minority faculty	15

Joint Degrees
MBA/JD 4 years, MBA/MA (area studies) 3 years, MBA/MA (Telecommunications) 3 years, MBA/JD 3 years.

Prominent Alumni
John T. Chambers, President and CEO, Cisco Systems, Inc.; Phillip Francis, Chairman & CEO, PETsMART, Inc.; Jeff M. Fettig, Chairman and CEO, Whirlpool Corporation; Hideo Ito, Chairman, CEO Toshiba; Bradley Alford, President & CEO, Nestle Brands Co.

Academics

Not many top 20 MBA programs earn accolades for their "down-to-earth culture," but the Kelley School of Business at Indiana University—Bloomington isn't just any top-20 MBA program. Maybe it's the school's distance from the nation's economic epicenters, or maybe it's just the confidence that comes from having "a phenomenal faculty" and a highly innovative, highly respected curriculum, but whatever the reason, students here leave the program with not only a first-rate education but also a singularly warm and fuzzy feeling about the school and their experiences there.

The Kelley MBA commences with a 15-week integrated core curriculum "consisting of eight subjects taught by eight faculty. It's an amazing learning experience." Students tell us that "the core is frustrating, challenging, and fun all at the same time. The integrated curriculum helps students make connections between business functions." It helps that "core faculty are excellent teachers although most also have extensive research backgrounds." The core and a leadership/professional/career development module consume most of the first semester; the second allows students to begin major and elective work, enhanced by industry-focused, week-long 'academies' that provide concentrated exposure to a business sector through guest speakers, seminars, field trips, and case competitions. Many students make key business contacts through their academy experiences; one student reports, "Everyone in the Investment Management Academy got their jobs through alumni, who took special interest in helping us succeed at their companies."

Students tell us that it's difficult to find a weak discipline here; Indiana "is strong across all core disciplines," providing a "great all-around business education covering marketing, operations, finance, and entrepreneurship." But it's the friendly and supportive atmosphere that impresses students most; they report glowingly of "faculty who are always willing to help students outside of class, for career searches, school projects, internships and even full-time work issues." One MBA sums up, "The greatest strength of the school is the collaborative environment fostered by the administration, faculty, and students. I truly feel like people try to help each other as much as possible."

Career and Placement

Top b-schools rarely have recruiting woes, and although Indiana isn't exactly a hop, skip, and jump from Wall Street, Kelley has little trouble attracting top recruiters to campus. One student reports, "There are approximately 100 companies that come to recruit 200 MBA grads. For finance majors, there are substantially more jobs than students." Indiana's famously loyal alumni network is also helpful when it comes time to find a job.

Not content with being merely excellent, the school works hard to broaden its recruiting profile. Students tell us that "over the past several years, many new companies have started to recruit on campus. Because Kelley is so strong in marketing, finance, and general management, most of the companies had a focus in one of those areas. Recently, the Career Placement Center has renewed its focus on consulting, investment banking, and investment management firms."

Top recruiters of Kelley MBAs include: Cummins, Target, Kraft Foods, Eli Lilly and Company, 3M Company, Ford Motor Company, Procter & Gamble, Intel, General Electric Company, Banc of America Securities, Guidant Corporaton, IBM, Microsoft, Northwest Airlines, PricewaterhouseCoopers.

ADMISSIONS CONTACT: JAMES HOLMEN, DIRECTOR OF ADMISSIONS AND FINANCIAL AID
ADDRESS: 1275 EAST TENTH STREET, SUITE 2010 BLOOMINGTON, IN 47405-1703 UNITED STATES
PHONE: 812-855-8006 • FAX: 812-855-9039
E-MAIL: MBAOFFICE@INDIANA.EDU • WEBSITE: WWW.KELLEY.INDIANA.EDU/MBA

Student Life and Environment

The Kelley program is quite labor intensive, especially during the first semester of first year. One first-semester student says, "If I am not preparing for the next day's classes, I am working with my team on a deliverable or . . . participating in mock interviews." The school's excellent facilities, which include breakout rooms and "a great student lounge where students mingle and work," provide a study-friendly environment. When students have free time, they "hit a rotation of four or five bars, tailgate during football season, and, of course, participate in school-sponsored activities," as well as join professional and social groups. Because most students live within five miles of campus, "You will often run into fellow students at the grocery store, out at restaurants, or at the mall. Life here is pleasant, uncrowded, and affordable." Even jaded urbanites find Bloomington agreeable as well as "surprisingly forward-thinking and modern. There are new and high-end apartments opening up . . . within walking distance to downtown Bloomington, making the school car-optional (in the right locations)." Students with significant others happily report that "a Partners Club supports current students' family members and partners. It's been a tremendously positive experience for my wife and me," writes one student.

Kelley students enjoy "great school spirit" in "a very collaborative environment. Students are not competitive. We have student-led review sessions and feel that we have achieved a goal when our colleagues succeed." They are the type of "very driven, hard-working, extremely bright people" you would expect to find at a top program. More than a third are "are from the Midwest and plan on staying in the Midwest. Perhaps for this reason, they don't have the egos you may find at other business schools (perhaps in bigger cities)."

Admissions

The Kelley MBA program is highly selective. The Admissions Office considers all the following factors: academic record, including cumulative grade point average, area of concentration, balance of electives, and trend of grades; GMAT scores; work experience (2 or more years strongly recommended); evidence of leadership ability; two letters of reference; and personal essays. Successful applicants need not have majored in business as undergraduates but should understand algebra and statistics and have some facility with spreadsheets. Calculus is important for some majors. Kelley has four separate application deadlines, with separate screening for each batch of applicants. In general, your chances are better if you apply early; however, it is better to wait for a later deadline if doing so will improve your application. Those seeking merit scholarships should try to apply by the January 15 deadline.

FINANCIAL FACTS

Annual tuition (in-state/ out-of-state)	$16,796/$33,414
Fees	$1,438
Cost of books	$1,900
Room & board	$8,750
% of students receiving aid	95
% of first-year students receiving aid	95
% of students receiving loans	90
% of students receiving grants	60
Average award package	$28,550
Average grant	$15,500
Average student loan debt	$36,000

ADMISSIONS

Admissions Selectivity Rating	**94**
# of applications received	1,227
% applicants accepted	34
% acceptees attending	56
Average GMAT	656
Range of GMAT	610–700
Average GPA	3.37
TOEFL required of international students	Yes
Minimum TOEFL (paper/computer)	600/250
Application fee	$75
International application fee	$75
Regular application deadline	3/1
Regular notification	4/30
Application Deadline/Notification	
Round 1:	11/15 / 02/01
Round 2:	01/15 / 03/30
Round 3:	03/01 / 04/30
Round 4:	04/15 / 05/30
Deferment available	Yes
Maximum length of deferment	1 year
Need-blind admissions	Yes

Applicants Also Look At

Purdue University, The University of North Carolina at Chapel Hill, The University of Texas at Austin, University of Michigan, Vanderbilt University, Washington University in St. Louis.

EMPLOYMENT PROFILE	
Career Rating	92
Primary Source of Full-time Job Acceptances	
School-facilitated activities	130 (77%)
Graduate-facilitated activities	38 (22%)
Average base starting salary	$88,644
Percent employed	90

INDIANA UNIVERSITY—KOKOMO
SCHOOL OF BUSINESS

GENERAL INFORMATION
Type of school	Public
Environment	Village
Academic calendar	Semester

SURVEY SAYS...
Cutting edge classes
Solid preparation in:
Accounting
General management
Operations
Communication/interpersonal skills
Quantitative skills
Computer skills

STUDENTS
Enrollment of parent institution	2,635
Enrollment of business school	112
% male/female	45/55
% part-time	84
% minorities	11
% international	1
Average age at entry	37
Average years work experience at entry	8

ACADEMICS
Academic Experience Rating	**75**
Student/faculty ratio	7:1
Profs interesting rating	77
Profs accessible rating	80
% female faculty	40
% minority faculty	35

Academics

The School of Business at Indiana University—Kokomo capably serves area professionals seeking to advance their careers through an MBA degree. Students here praise the program's "excellent reputation" with area employers as well as its "convenient location" and small class sizes that "make for an intimate setting. Students are people, not numbers here." A public school that is one of only a dozen AACSB-accredited MBA programs in the state of Indiana, Kokomo provides a compelling option to businesspeople seeking an affordable career advancement opportunity in and around this city of 50,000.

IU Kokomo's program is "attuned to the regional industry base" of north-central Indiana but is also flexible enough to "foster effective management of resources in diverse organizational units and settings," according to the school's promotional material. Because nearly all its students work full time, the program offers flexible scheduling. All required classes are held during the week in the evening hours; electives are offered either during the day or in the evenings. Classes are alternately offered in 8- and 16-week formats, accommodating both those in a hurry to complete course work and those who wish to learn at a (somewhat) less frantic pace. Except for a capstone course, classes may be taken in any order, another accommodation to the convenience of IU's busy students. Such convenience comes with a tradeoff, however, making it impossible for the school to fully integrate the curriculum. Some here feel that "the program should add an integrated case study that encompasses at least two courses per semester," an impossibility under the current system.

Part-time students typically complete Kokomo's 30-credit MBA program in four years. The program is small, facilitating student-teacher interaction, and fortunately professors here "are very approachable and show genuine interest in the students' academic and professional success." The downside of the school's size is that it limits options. Some students complain that some courses are not offered frequently enough.

Career and Placement

IU Kokomo does not aggressively promote its career services for MBA students. Because most students in the program "are employed full time in positions of responsibility," few actually require placement services or career counseling, and those who do generally rely on the assistance of their professors. MBAs may take advantage of the university's Office of Career Services, which maintains job boards, a Career Library and Resource Center, and online career-related databases. The program also features an MBA Association that works to schedule networking and recruitment events for current graduate students.

Student Life and Environment

IUK attracts a student body that is "diverse in gender, race, and age," with "lots of women and minorities" filling out the ranks. MBAs here tend to be "working adults looking to improve their skill sets." They have "multiple demands on their time" in addition to school, including careers and, quite often, family obligations. Some are friendly, but others "tend to stick together with fellow students from the same employer" and are "not always welcoming to outsiders."

ADMISSIONS CONTACT: LINDA FICHT, ASSISTANT DEAN AND MBA DIRECTOR
ADDRESS: PO BOX 9003 KOKOMO, IN 46904-9003 UNITED STATES
PHONE: 765-455-9465 • FAX: 765-455-9348
E-MAIL: LFICHT@IUK.EDU • WEBSITE: WWW.IUK.EDU/MBA

IUK is "strictly a commuter campus" where students "come in, go to class, and leave." It is worth highlighting the efforts of the MBA Association (MBAA), which organizes social and intellectual events for those students who do spend time on campus. The school invites business leaders as part of its distinguished lecture series, enabling students to learn from some of the business world's top players. Some here feel that "the safety of students attending night classes is an issue. I never see security at night and the lighting could be better." Statistics indicate that the city of Kokomo has a below average rate of such common crimes as assault, robbery, and automobile theft. Top employers in Kokomo include Delphi Electronics & Safety, Howard Regional Health, Saint Joseph Hospital, Haynes International, Meijer, and the university.

Admissions

Admission to the MBA program at IU Kokomo requires a bachelor's degree from an accredited college or university (business major not required); a completed application to the program; a personal statement of career goals; and official transcripts for all post-secondary academic work. Most applicants must also submit GMAT scores; those already holding graduate degrees from accredited institutions, however, are exempted from this requirement. A formula score of at least 1,000 under the formula [(undergraduate GPA + 200) + GMAT score] is required of all applicants who submit GMAT scores. Successful completion of undergraduate-level courses in calculus, statistics, and composition and a background in microcomputer applications are prerequisites to beginning the MBA program; these courses can be completed after admission to the program, however. Some qualified applicants may be denied admission due to space and resource constraints; admissions decisions are made on a rolling basis, so it pays to apply as early as possible. International applicants must meet the aforementioned requirements and must also submit TOEFL scores (minimum score 550). The M.B.A. program admits students for fall, spring, and summer semesters. IU Kokomo accepts students with deficiencies in their business education background; such students are required to complete up to 18 credit hours of foundation courses in business.

FINANCIAL FACTS

Annual tuition (in-state/ out-of-state)	$7,593/$17,064
Fees	$456
Cost of books	$850

ADMISSIONS

Admissions Selectivity Rating	**74**
# of applications received	22
% applicants accepted	100
% acceptees attending	82
Average GMAT	506
Average GPA	3.0
TOEFL required of international students	Yes
Minimum TOEFL (paper/computer)	550/213
Application fee	$40
International application fee	$60
Regular application deadline	8/1
Regular notification	rolling
Deferment available	Yes
Transfer students accepted	Yes
Transfer application policy 6 credits from AACSB accredited schools.	
Non-fall admissions	Yes
Need-blind admissions	Yes

Applicants Also Look At

Indiana University—Bloomington, Purdue University.

INDIANA UNIVERSITY OF PENNSYLVANIA
EBERLY COLLEGE OF BUSINESS AND INFORMATION TECHNOLOGY

Academics

"Affordable and away from the hustle and bustle of the city," the Eberly College of Business and Information Technology at Indiana University of Pennsylvania

offers a "high-quality education at a very affordable price." Thanks to the school's numerous partnerships with overseas schools, Eberly also provides "international exposure" and is "a great fit for international students, since it offers a diverse academic program and environment with the opportunity to interact with students from different parts of the world," as well as EMBA programs at several urban locations in greater Pittsburgh.

Students appreciate that "IUP's MBA program is large enough to be widely recognized by employers yet small enough to allow for many one-on-one learning experiences." Professors here "are diverse in background, culture, and work experience" and "have a handle on the real world." "One of my management professors serves as an external consultant for the World Bank and the United Nations, and it has been a pleasure to interact with her and participate in her class," reports one MBA. My marketing professor has been an advisor/consultant of the government of the former Czechoslovakia Republic during the country's transition from state-owned and planned to a market economy. I was impressed by his vast experience and passion for teaching marketing." IUP's "tough but helpful" instructors bring "a myriad of global, real-world experiences" to the classroom. Sure, they "expect a lot from you, but that is a good thing. The environment is very focused on helping you succeed." Students also appreciate the program's "top-notch" technological capabilities that include "multiple computer labs, computers, projectors, and document readers in every classroom, campus wide Wi-Fi, and the availability of almost any software program you might encounter in the workforce."

Students see their program as "strongly geared toward manufacturing." Some feel the program "could benefit from introducing more service-industry scenarios and case studies," while others would like to see "more concentrations like entrepreneurship, supply chain management, and statistics." Those days may not be that far off if the "growing popularity of IUP" leads to an expansion of the program. Currently the school offers concentrations only in accounting, finance, human resource management, international business, entrepreneurship and supply chain management, and marketing.

Career and Placement

IUP's Career Development Center provides counseling and placement services to the university's undergraduates, graduate students, and alumni. Assistance in resume writing, interviewing, and job-hunting skills is available. The office maintains an extensive library, provides hard-copy and online job postings, and organizes recruiting events both on and off campus. Students wish the office would "get more recruiters to come onto campus so the students would not have to travel off campus for interviews."

Companies recruiting on the IUP campus include: Alcoa, American Express, Bristol-Myers Squibb Company, Champion International, CIGNA, DuPont Company, Eddie Bauer, EDS, ExxonMobil, Federated Investors, General Motors, Georgia Pacific, IBM, JC Penney, K-Mart, BNY Mellon, PepsiCo, PNC Bank, Sony Electronics, Sun Microsystems, Wal-Mart, The Walt Disney Company, Westinghouse, Bayer, Kennametal, Naval Audit, Army Audit, 84 Lumber, Enterprise Bank, Enterprise Rent-A-Car, and Medrad. Public accounting firms including Deloitte Touche Tohmatsu; Ernst & Young; PricewaterhouseCoopers; KPMG International; recruit on campus.

Student Life and Environment

IUP is located in Indiana, Pennsylvania, "a very attractive town with a very friendly atmosphere" that, for many, makes it "the perfect atmosphere to explore business at a comfortable pace to understand the basics before being thrown into a very rapid workforce. This town and school give the students an opportunity to learn at their own pace." While many appreciate that the "pretty" school is isolated "from many of the dangers city campuses must deal with," some bemoan the fact that "there are not too many attractions around," even if it does have a "very nice environment for study." Some see the remote location as an impediment to increased on-campus job recruiting.

Campus life includes "many clubs that one could get involved in" as well as lots of events, meetings, and projects, to the point that "there isn't much time for anything else." Explains one student, "IUP encourages students to network with one another and to become involved to get the most out of our graduate school experience. I know I will be leaving this program with a group of people located all around the world that I will be able to contact throughout my career."

IUP's MBA program is home to "an extremely diverse population of international students with a wide array of real-world knowledge that allow for an eye-opening education, especially in the international field of business." Most are young, as "Older students attend classes at a satellite location."

Admissions

All students in the MBA program at IUP must have completed an undergraduate degree at an accredited college or university with a grade point average of at least 2.6. The school requires official transcripts from all postsecondary schools attended, an official GMAT score report (minimum score of 450 required), two letters of recommendation from professors (for those completing undergraduate study) or from employers/supervisors (for those with at least 4 years of professional experience), a completed resume, and a one-page personal statement of goals in pursuing an MBA. In addition to the above, international students must also submit a Foreign Student Financial Affidavit. Those who attended undergraduate institutions at which English is not the primary language must have their transcripts translated and interpreted by a professional service. International students whose first language is not English must submit an official TOEFL score report (minimum score of 200 on the computer-based test, 533 on the paper-based test).

FINANCIAL FACTS

Annual tuition (in-state/ out-of-state)	$6,214/$9,944
Fees	$734
Cost of books	$1,000
Room & board	$5,442
% of students receiving aid	51
% of first-year students receiving aid	31
Average award package	$8,100
Average grant	$8,100

ADMISSIONS

Admissions Selectivity Rating	**74**
# of applications received	258
% applicants accepted	77
% acceptees attending	77
Average GMAT	532
Range of GMAT	450–620
TOEFL required of international students	Yes
Minimum TOEFL (paper/computer)	550/213
Application fee	$30
International application fee	$30
Regular application deadline	7/30
Regular notification	Rolling
Deferment available	Yes
Maximum length of deferment	1 year
Transfer students accepted	Yes
Transfer application policy Written request for transfer required of transfer applicants. Maximum of six credits transfer.	
Non-fall admissions	Yes
Need-blind admissions	Yes

Applicants Also Look At

Clarion University, Duquesne University, Penn State University, University of Pittsburgh, West Virginia University.

EMPLOYMENT PROFILE

Career Rating	74	Grads Employed by Function% Avg. Salary	
Primary Source of Full-time Job Acceptances		Other	73 $51,211
Percent employed	72		

INDIANA UNIVERSITY—SOUTH BEND
SCHOOL OF BUSINESS AND ECONOMICS

GENERAL INFORMATION
Type of school	Public
Academic calendar	Semester

SURVEY SAYS...
Friendly students
Cutting edge classes
Happy students
Smart classrooms
Solid preparation in:
Finance

STUDENTS
Enrollment of parent institution	7,459
Enrollment of business school	1,200
Average age at entry	26

ACADEMICS
Academic Experience Rating	**62**
Student/faculty ratio	17:1
Profs interesting rating	72
Profs accessible rating	65
% female faculty	15
% minority faculty	33

Academics

The School of Business and Economics at Indiana University—South Bend gears its MBA program toward the needs of the part-time student. Here, "classes meet once a week in the evening, making it easy to attend school and work full-time." Most classes begin at 7:00 P.M., accommodating students who have to travel some distance after work in order to get to class. MBA students here typically take two classes in each of the fall and spring semesters and one class during each summer session; this allows most students who hold business undergraduate degrees to complete the program in just two years.

Phase I of the IU South Bend MBA covers skills prerequisite to advanced business study. Classes in economics, financial accounting, financial management, marketing, mathematics, organizational behavior, and statistics cover material typically covered in undergraduate business programs. Students with undergraduate business degrees typically place out of these courses; other students may place out by passing a competency examination in each field. Phase II consists of seven core courses in buyer behavior, international business, legal and ethical issues in business, management information systems, managerial price theory, production management, and strategic financial management. Phase III covers advanced subjects and allows for students to take two electives. Phase IV consists entirely of a capstone course. Students must pass a final comprehensive exam in order to receive their degrees.

Students here praise the "excellent MIS/MIT offerings" and the "small classes with friendly, approachable professors" who "have a wealth of experiences in the business world. The whole experience is very student-centered here." A "great library and facilities" and "strength in the high-technology area" help students handle the heavy burden of the program, and international students enjoy "strong support in housing, counseling, etc." Many here, however, feel that "the program needs to allow for specialization" and wish that "the school could offer more choices for specific strategic business classes and project management classes."

Career and Placement

The Career Services Office at IU South Bend serves the entire student and alumni population of the school. The office is primarily dedicated to undergraduates, although its services are also available to MBAs. The office provides the standard complement of job-search services, skills seminars, personal assessments, and one-on-one counseling. The following is a partial list of employers who attended IUSB's spring job fair in 2008: First Source Bank, AM General, Ave Maria Press, Bankers Life and Casualty Company, Becker Professional Review, Cintas, Citigroup, Craighead, Lange and Hough, Crowe Chizek and Company, Fastenal, Fastsigns, JPMorgan Chase, John Hancock Financial Network, Lippert Components Inc., Menards, Northwestern Mutual Finance Network, Peoplelink Staffing Solutions, Productivity Management, Inc., SCORE, Spyglass Search, and the Teachers Credit Union.

ADMISSIONS CONTACT: SHARON PETERSON, GRADUATE BUSINESS RECORDS REPRESENTATIVE
ADDRESS: 1700 MISHAWAKA AVENUE, P O BOX 7111 SOUTH BEND, IN 46634-7111 UNITED STATES
PHONE: 574-520-4138 • FAX: 574-520-4866
E-MAIL: GRADBUS@IUSB.EDU • WEBSITE: WWW.IUSB.EDU/~BUSE/GRAD

Student Life and Environment

The IU South Bend MBA program caters to part-time students, the majority of whom are "full-time employed, mostly with children, working to improve their situation." Full-time students "tend to be international students" representing "a wide mix of nationalities from Africa, Asia, the Americas, etc." This "mostly friendly and helpful" population includes individuals from "a wide range of ages, from the 20s to the 50s." Students note that "all the diversity in the student body helps us see things from different perspectives."

Don't expect to pal around with your classmates here, though, as "going to class at night and working all day leaves little time for socializing during the week." IU South Bend MBA students "have mostly a commuter attitude. They only spend time on campus to attend class."

IU South Bend is a midsize state university with an undergraduate population of approximately 6,400 and a graduate population of about 1,100. South Bend is a substantial city, with a population of over 100,000. Major employers in the metropolitan area include IU South Bend, the University of Notre Dame, Memorial Hospital, St. Joseph Regional Medical Center, ADP, AG Edwards, Bosch, Coachman Industries, FedEx, Honeywell, Liberty Mutual, and State Farm. The advertising, aviation, biotechnology, engineering, finance, and nonprofit sectors all have a strong presence in the region. South Bend's location offers relatively easy access to Indianapolis, Chicago, Detroit and Cleveland.

Admissions

The MBA program at Indiana University—South Bend requires applicants to submit all of the following: a completed application and data sheet, available online; official transcripts for all postsecondary academic work; two letters of recommendation (recommendation form available online); a personal statement describing one's background, outlining one's goals in the program, and recounting an experience that led to personal growth; and an official score report for the GMAT. International students whose native language is not English must submit all of the above as well as an official score report for the TOEFL; minimum required score for consideration is 550 (paper-based test) or 213 (computer-based test). Applications are accepted for admission commencing with the Fall, Spring, or Summer semesters. IU South Bend admits students at two levels: Full Admission and Probationary Admission. Full Admission requires a minimum GMAT score of 450 and an undergraduate business degree from an AACSB-accredited school with a minimum GPA of 2.75. Probationary Admission is granted to applicants "whose GPA does not quite meet minimum standards." All students must maintain an in-program GPA of at least 2.75 in order to remain in the program, and to graduate from the program.

FINANCIAL FACTS

Annual tuition (in-state/ out-of-state)	$4,050/$9,720
Cost of books	$700
Room & board (on/off-campus)	$5,000/$8,000

ADMISSIONS

Admissions Selectivity Rating	**62**
# of applications received	59
% applicants accepted	100
% acceptees attending	32
Average GMAT	498
Range of GMAT	440–650
Average GPA	2.96
TOEFL required of international students	Yes
Minimum TOEFL (paper/computer)	550/213
Application fee	$45
International application fee	$55
Regular application deadline	7/1
Regular notification	rolling
Deferment available	Yes
Maximum length of deferment	1 year
Non-fall admissions	Yes

Applicants Also Look At
University of Notre Dame, Western Michigan University.

INDIANA UNIVERSITY—SOUTHEAST
SCHOOL OF BUSINESS

GENERAL INFORMATION

Type of school	Public
Environment	Village
Academic calendar	Semester

SURVEY SAYS...

Cutting edge classes
Solid preparation in:
Operations
Computer skills

STUDENTS

Enrollment of parent institution	6,164
Enrollment of business school	238
% part-time	99
Average age at entry	29
Average years work experience at entry	6

ACADEMICS

Academic Experience Rating	**90**
Student/faculty ratio	15:1
Profs interesting rating	94
Profs accessible rating	79
% female faculty	26
% minority faculty	26

Joint Degrees

Dual MBA/MSSF 3–4 years.

Academics

Area business grads choose Indiana University Southeast because "it offers the best combination of cost and quality of education while still being close to home." "IU brand recognition" sways many who recognize that the school "offers the big-name IU degree" along with "an administration that runs like a small college." Flexibility is another major factor; the school fashions its schedule to accommodate its almost-entirely part-time student body and offers two convenient locations; one on the IUS main campus in New Albany, the other a Graduate Center in downtown Jeffersonville that students say "makes things easier, because we don't have to go to campus at night and walk from the back of the parking lot because all the students going to class during the day have taken all the spots."

IUS offers a general MBA and a Master's of Science in Strategic Finance (MSSF), each requiring 36 credit hours; students may earn a combined MBA/MSSF by completing 51 credit hours. The 36-hour programs consist of 30 hours of required classes and six hours of electives; students report that the required courses "build on and contribute to the understanding of concepts taught. I always find myself relating back to other classes I have taken." Academics are "demanding." As one student puts it, "The program takes a hard line on academics. There's no 'pay your fee, get your C' at this school."

MBAs are most impressed with the faculty at IUS, whom they describe as "knowledgeable and caring," "wonderful and very accessible outside of class." The strength of the faculty contributes substantially to the program's "quality reputation in the region with area professionals." That's an impressive accomplishment given the price of attending; as one student observes, "The cost of this program was so low that I was concerned about its quality, but after looking into their reputation with colleagues that attended this and other local schools, I feel I made the right choice." Of course, that low price tag means the school has to skimp in some areas; students wish there were "more classrooms with computers instead of old desks that are hard to squeeze into" and complain that "the library, bookstore, and other campus services close down very early, making the campus less accessible to night MBA students."

Career and Placement

IUS' Office of Career Services and Placement receives middling marks from MBAs. Some describe the office as "extremely helpful," but many more declare the office "practically nonexistent...IU Southeast MBAs are largely left on their own. Sometimes e-mails come telling you of opportunities, but that's about it." Fortunately, "Most students are currently employed in companies with growth potential" and so are not on the job market. According to one student, "Most local opportunities are in financial services, insurance, healthcare. GE, YUM, and Papa John's, and smaller companies have opportunities available, and if someone is willing to move there is more available." Attendees at a recent business and industry job fair included AFLAC, AT&T, Cox Radio, Enterprise, FedEx, Kelly Services, Kroger, Northwestern Mutual Financial, Target, and Zappos.

Student Life and Environment

IUS is "mainly a commuter campus" for MBAs, although the school "has made strides to change the perception by working on construction of dorms. I still suspect that most MBA professionals will continue living off campus." That's because most MBAs are "balancing work with class and coursework" as well as family obligations; they're not the 'live on campus' type. The school works to accommodate their needs; writes one, "The child care center on campus is very inviting. My kids love to go there and will miss it when I graduate." On the downside, "The school shuts down at about 6 p.m., which means night students have trouble getting to necessary services before they close."

The part-time environment is not especially conducive to extracurricular activities, and indeed "many attempts have been made to generate interest in clubs for MBA students, but those events are overwhelmingly poorly attended." All the same, students tell us that "there are clubs and activities for MBAs to get involved with if they desire and opportunities to network. If someone does not get involved, it's most likely the person either does not get to know fellow class members or chooses not to get involved. As a person goes through program, he/she meets more people and networks better."

The IUS student body "ranges from recent graduates to people who have been working for 25+ years and are interested in furthering their careers by moving into managing in their field." It's a "friendly, supportive" group who make "good team members" and "bring a diverse work background to the learning experience." While "gender and age group diversity are great," the school is still "much more white" than it might be, although "the diversity of ethnic groups is improving."

Admissions

Completed applications to the IUS MBA program must include an official GMAT score report, official copies of all undergraduate transcripts, and a resume. The school uses the following formula to evaluate candidates: [(undergraduate GPA × 200) + GMAT score], IUS looks for candidates with a formula score of at least 1050, with GMAT scores of at least 470. The school also considers work experience. Students with undergraduate degrees in business are likely to place out of some or all of the school's eight foundation courses in business; all other admitted students must complete these foundation courses before beginning work on the actual MBA.

ADMISSIONS

Admissions Selectivity Rating	81
# of applications received	91
% applicants accepted	66
% acceptees attending	100
Average GMAT	561
Range of GMAT	513–623
Average GPA	3.2
TOEFL required of international students	Yes
Minimum TOEFL (paper/computer)	550/213
Application fee	$35
International application fee	$55
Regular application deadline	rolling
Regular notification	rolling
Deferment available	Yes
Transfer students accepted	Yes
Transfer application policy Students may transfer a maximum of 6 graduate credit hours from another AACSB-accredited MBA program.	
Non-fall admissions	Yes
Need-blind admissions	Yes

Applicants Also Look At
Bellarmine University, University of Louisville.

EMPLOYMENT PROFILE

Career Rating	60*	Grads Employed by Function	%	Avg. Salary
		Finance	35	$87,450
		Marketing	34	$84,407
		MIS	1	$105,000
		Operations	4	$87,500
		Consulting	11	$100,875
		General Management	7	$87,500
		Other	4	$97,000
		Top 5 Employers Hiring Grads		
		Johnson & Johnson	7	
		Cummins	6	
		General Electric	5	
		Eaton	4	
		Citigroup	4	

INSEAD

GENERAL INFORMATION

Type of school	Private

SURVEY SAYS...

Good social scene
Good peer network
Solid preparation in:
General management
Doing business in a global economy
Entrepreneurial studies

STUDENTS

Enrollment of business school	887
% male/female	76/24
% international	89
Average age at entry	29
Average years work experience at entry	5

ACADEMICS

Academic Experience Rating	**74**
Student/faculty ratio	7:1
Profs interesting rating	98
Profs accessible rating	77
% female faculty	15

Prominent Alumni

Lindsay Owen-Jones, CEO, L'Oreal; Helen Alexander, CEO, The Economist Group; Patrick Cescau, CEO, Unilever; Paul Jr. Desmarais, CEO, Power Corp. Canada.

Academics

INSEAD brands itself as "the business school for the world," and it can provide hard facts to support its claim. Students tell us the program is "is incredibly international, unrivaled by any other school," with a broad international student population and campuses in both France and Singapore. One student observes: "My fellow students come from 70 countries. My study group is an epitome of globalization: a Mexican investment banker, a Taiwanese accountant, a French Navy officer, an American diplomat, and a Bulgarian marketer, all exchanging knowledge in INSEAD. How much better could it be?" Further driving the point home is the fact that INSEAD is "the only prestigious MBA program that requires three languages upon exit."

Students, grateful for a program that "is not only US-centric," love the international focus at INSEAD. They also appreciate the fact that it's a 10-month program that "gives quicker return on investment" than longer, more expensive MBA programs. INSEAD has "a strong reputation in consulting and general management" that translates into "placement success with top-tier consulting firms." The school also offers "exceptional private equity and investment courses (private equity, realizing entrepreneurial potential, leveraged buyouts, etc.)." Perhaps the school's greatest strength, though, is the quality of its student body; one MBA tells us, "The work experience of all candidates is extremely high, which creates in-depth, dynamic discussions and learning in the classroom." Another adds: "At this point, any question I have about any country or industry can be solved by simply asking the right classmate."

As in most accelerated programs, "academics are extremely challenging" at INSEAD, especially "for someone completely new to business or on topics for which you have no knowledge. " However, "At the same time there is a stress toward making sure that students understand the basics and all that is necessary for business. What's more, other students who have had experience or who studied business in undergrad are always open to help and encourage each other." The large size of the program, coupled with the speed at which it is completed, "sometimes makes it feel as though you are passing through an MBA factory, which has been doing things the same way for a long time." Even so, "The administration is generally prompt and receptive, especially with regards to clubs, network and career activities," and is also very efficient. For example, "Many people change their minds during the year about which campus they want to be in for the next period, and the school is very good at trying to understand every situation and to accommodate their desires."

Career and Placement

INSEAD maintains Career Management Services (CMS) offices on both its French and Singaporean campuses. The offices promote students to employers around the globe while providing MBAs with one-on-one counseling and coaching, job search strategies, and on-campus recruiting events. Some students complain that CMS counselors are "used to a specific way of working and don't think outside the box. The focus is all on consulting, finance, and maybe a little industry." Others say, "Career Services is doing a good job, but there is room for improvement, as the school has a lot to offer on the job market." Nearly all agree that the school's substantial alumni network is "very helpful and intent on seeing current graduates succeed."

Employers most likely to hire INSEAD MBAs include McKinsey & Company; American Express; Booz Allen Hamilton; General Electric; Eli Lilly; Barclays Capital; Citigroup; Johnson & Johnson; Bain & Company; A.T. Kearney; Honeywell; Philip Morris; and Royal Dutch Shell. Nearly 40 percent of INSEAD MBAS wind up in consulting functions; one in five goes into finance and accounting.

Student Life and Environment

"The INSEAD year is a very intense period," students tell us, noting, "As there are classes every day, we have to study just like in high school and more or less all the time. There is a lot of group work...But, we all understand the quality of the people around us and the need for social interaction," and most here find time for fun.

INSEAD's Fontainebleau campus "is extremely dynamic. There's always something going on, but at the same time depends on the intake. At the end of the day, activities are driven by students. Sometimes, the one-year nature of the program makes keeping activities and clubs continuous a bit challenging." Weekends often feature "fantastic parties at chateaus in the French countryside. The school even provides shuttle buses. Can you beat that?" The Singapore campus "is superb" and "quite relaxed because of the setting."

Admissions

INSEAD has two intake points, in September and January. Students may apply to begin the program at either time; application is online only. All applicants must provide a personal profile, resume, five personal essays (with a sixth optional essay), two recommendations attesting to leadership potential and management capacity, a photograph, a statement of integrity, an official GMAT score report (the school recommends a score in at least the 70th percentile in both the verbal and quantitative sections), and official transcripts for all post-secondary academic work. In addition, all students must enter the program with proficiency in English and a second language. Non-native English speakers may submit results from the TOEFL, TOEIC, CPE, or IELTS; English speakers must provide certification of a second language. A third commercially useful language (sorry, no Latin!) is required to graduate; while language instruction is available through INSEAD, the intensity of the MBA program is such that the school recommends students get a start on their third language before the program begins. The applicant's choice of campus is not taken into account in the admission decision; however, placement at one's campus of choice is not fully guaranteed.

FINANCIAL FACTS

Annual tuition	$63,400
Cost of books	$1,500
Room & board (off-campus)	$28,500
% of first-year students receiving aid	50
Average grant	$15,000

ADMISSIONS

Admissions Selectivity Rating	**60***
Average GMAT	702
Range of GMAT	620–790
Average GPA	4.0
TOEFL required of international students	Yes
Minimum TOEFL (paper/computer)	620/260
Application fee	$250
Regular application deadline	3/23
Regular notification	6/24
Application Deadline/Notification	
Round 1:	03/23 / 06/24
Round 2:	05/18 / 09/09
Round 3:	06/29 / 10/14
Non-fall admissions	Yes
Need-blind admissions	Yes

EMPLOYMENT PROFILE			
Career Rating	**90**	**Grads Employed by Function**	**% Avg. Salary**
Percent employed	80	Finance	14 $124,212
Average base starting salary	$106,043	Marketing	7 $117,802
		Operations	2 $106,946
		Strategic Planning	10 $113,031
		Consulting	43 $123,987
		General Management	9 $116,706
		Other	3 $104,114

IONA COLLEGE
HAGAN SCHOOL OF BUSINESS

GENERAL INFORMATION
Type of school	Private
Affiliation	Roman Catholic
Environment	City
Academic calendar	Trimester

SURVEY SAYS...
Cutting edge classes
Solid preparation in:
Presentation skills

STUDENTS
Enrollment of parent institution	4,323
Enrollment of business school	311
% male/female	57/43
% out-of-state	10
% part-time	81
% minorities	23
% international	10
Average age at entry	28
Average years work experience at entry	3

ACADEMICS
Academic Experience Rating	**68**
Student/faculty ratio	6:1
Profs interesting rating	72
Profs accessible rating	81
% female faculty	20
% minority faculty	5

Prominent Alumni
Alfred F. Kelly, Jr., President, American Express Company; Robert Greifeld, President, NASDAQ; Randel A Falco, Chairman & CEO, AOL; Philip Maisano, Vice Chair & CIO, The Dreyfus Corporation.; Catherine R. Kinney, President and Co-COO of NYSE Group Inc.

Academics

The Hagan School of Business at Iona College enjoys "a solid reputation in New York." That, and "the flexibility of the program"—it "offers many distance learning and hybrid courses so that you can take lecture classes with your peers, or web-based classes on your own time"—appeal to the predominantly part-time student body here. Hagan also fits the needs of those in a hurry to complete their degrees; explains one MBA, "The classes are on a trimester basis, meaning the overall length of the program is shorter, allowing you to graduate faster." Students tell us that "the trimester schedule of classes seems to be designed with working individuals in mind."

Hagan has a relatively small graduate business program, creating a "small-school setting that allows a sense of community amongst the students and the teachers." Students may attend classes on the main campus in New Rochelle or at the Rockland Graduate Center in Pearl River. Online classes are available. The school also offers onsite MBA at Wyeth Ayert Pharmaceutical offices. Regardless of the option, Iona works hard to accommodate working students and their employers. One student writes, "The cooperation between the school and the company in which I was an employee was great. The school facilitated many factors for the students including parking, general access, registering, paying, and having small classes. They also provide classes through distance learning."

Iona professors "are savvy in all areas and tend to be knowledgeable and available when needed." They are demanding, but they "are great as long as you do the work and pay attention to what they are talking about." Students appreciate that "it seems like [professors] are all very involved in their fields, consulting or running their own businesses, [which] allows them to stay current and apply real experience to academic theory." Iona offers concentrations in finance, human resource management, information systems, management, marketing, and public accounting. The school also offers certificate programs in international business and e-commerce, business continuity and risk management, sports and entertainment studies, and general accounting.

Career and Placement

The Gerri Ripp Center for Career Development handles counseling and placement services for all Iona students and alumni. Students tell us that "Iona has several career guidance and placement programs and several academic and community social justice programs in the Catholic tradition. Iona is one of the most respected colleges in the greater New York metropolitan region." Even so, many here feel the office needs to improve its game. One student says, "Career services are important to many MBA students who are looking to leave their current employer after completing the MBA program. There are limited resources in the area of career services for these individuals, however."

Student Life and Environment

"There is life constantly on campus" at Iona's main campus in New Rochelle, MBAs tell us. "Even after 5:00 [P.M.], which could be considered off peak, there are always students milling about. We frequently get together after classes to meet and talk. Many graduate students belong to clubs and athletic teams, which brings a strong sense of community." One student adds, "It's fast paced because everyone is involved in something, from clubs to athletics to on-campus jobs. It's a very friendly environment and not too small or not too big." Students at the satellite campuses tell us that "the majority of clubs, activities, etc., occur at the New Rochelle campus." These students "pretty much attend class and then go home. Students do not hang out at the Rockland Graduate Center. Most go to their classes and then go home to their families. However, everyone is friendly, and you do get to know your classmates."

Iona MBAs are a mixed group. On the New Rochelle campus, "Many are young, fresh from getting their undergraduate degree." In fact, some are recent graduates of Iona, taking advantage of course waivers to speed through their MBAs. However, "There are also many who are older, with children, trying to balance their school, career, and life. It is a diverse group in terms of ethnicity, experiences, and personality." A number of Iona's full-timers are international students who "are able to give international insight into the very globally focused business courses."

Admissions

Applicants to the Hagan MBA program must submit the following materials: a completed Hagan School of Business application form, along with a $50 application fee; copies of official transcripts from each undergraduate and graduate institution attended; two letters of recommendation; and an official score report for the GMAT reflecting a score no more than 5 years old (the GMAT requirement may be waived for applicants with at least 7 years of post-undergraduate professional experience). International applicants must submit all of the materials listed above, as well as an official score report for the TOEFL, WES, and cash support affidavit. Transcripts in languages other than English must be translated and interpreted by an approved service. Applications are processed on a rolling basis and are valid for 1 full year from the day they are received by the school. Applicants may request an interview, which the school recommends but does not require.

FINANCIAL FACTS

Annual tuition	$19,224
Fees	$150
% of students receiving aid	72
% of first-year students receiving aid	74
% of students receiving loans	55
% of students receiving grants	43
Average award package	$18,574
Average grant	$2,553
Average student loan debt	$17,463

ADMISSIONS

Admissions Selectivity Rating	**64**
# of applications received	128
% applicants accepted	84
% acceptees attending	77
Average GMAT	450
Range of GMAT	300–600
Average GPA	3.25
TOEFL required of international students	Yes
Minimum TOEFL (paper/computer)	550/213
Application fee	$50
International application fee	$50
Regular application deadline	rolling
Regular notification	rolling
Deferment available	Yes
Maximum length of deferment	1 year
Transfer students accepted	Yes
Transfer application policy	Max of 6 upper-level credits accepted.
Non-fall admissions	Yes
Need-blind admissions	Yes

Applicants Also Look At

Fordham University, Pace University.

ITHACA COLLEGE
SCHOOL OF BUSINESS

Academics

MBA students in Ithaca College's small graduate program may choose between two programs: an MBA in business administration and an MBA in professional accountancy. Both degrees require 35 credit hours and can be completed by full-time students in 12 months—and this is the selling point of the program. As one student explains, "A 1-year program offered me a faster track to my post-MBA life."

The curriculum for Ithaca's Business Administration MBA starts with function-level analysis of firms. Once students have mastered the workings of an individual business, the focus grows wider to encompass entire industries, finally concluding with a project in which students analyze an industry of their choice and assess individual firms within that industry. Classes emphasize "a balance between building technical and interpersonal skills," and students praise professors for their "hands-on teaching philosophy." "The faculty is always willing to bend over backwards to meet students' academic and professional needs," says one student. "While the professors remain rather rigid in their expectations of students, most will work tirelessly with students to ensure they succeed." Another student notes, "The school does a good job offering elective courses that are in line with students' career aspirations. Since the program is small, faculty surveys students prior to each semester. The result is a course offering that honestly reflects the interests of students. I see this adaptability as Ithaca's greatest strength because it can help overcome the obstacles often associated with a smaller business school."

Ithaca's Professional Accountancy MBA primarily functions as the culmination of a 5-year undergraduate/graduate program for students in the college's undergraduate accounting program, although candidates from other schools can gain admission. Most here agree that although "many students that graduated from Ithaca as undergrads" are now part of the MBA program, there are also "older" or "married" students in attendance.

The curriculum includes a thorough review of principles of business administration as well as advanced instruction in financial accounting and reporting, managerial and cost accounting, auditing, taxation, and principles of business law. Students in both programs are full of praise for the school. "Overall, I think the school is really starting to take off. Ithaca worked hard to receive AACSB accreditation, [and] since that happened the school has retained high standards for both students and faculty." Another adds, "Tuition is high, but you can definitely see where the money went. Everything from the smart boards in the classrooms—which help make articulating difficult accounting concepts much easier—to the trading room is state-of-the-art."

Students note that the 1-year duration of the program helps offset the relatively high cost of attending. That said, while it had been a "little pricey" in the past, "Prices have come down." They also appreciate the fact that the business school administration "welcome(s) comments and suggestions from the grad students on what could help better the program. If you have any problems, they do their best to help you solve the issues." The future's looking good here, so bring your shades.

ADDRESS: OFFICE OF GRADUATE STUDIES, ITHACA COLLEGE, 101 TERRACE CONCOURSE ITHACA, NY 14850-7020 UNITED STATES
PHONE: (607) 274-3527 • FAX: (607) 274-1263
E-MAIL: MBA@ITHACA.EDU • WEBSITE: WWW.ITHACA.EDU/BUSINESS/MBA

Career and Placement

The Ithaca College Career Services Office provides self-assessment inventories, e-Recruiting tools, one-on-one advising, mock interviews, workshops, a library, and on-campus recruiting. The school also hosts a graduate school job fair and other special recruiting events. Though despite all this, some students find that "Ithaca could do a better job attracting recruiters from upper-tier businesses." While they appreciate the "many local recruiters on campus" and "ample alumni network and mentoring program," some still find a dearth of businesses at which they're "trying to get [their] foot in the door."

Employers who recruit on the Ithaca campus include Lockheed-Martin, Merrill Lynch, PricewaterhouseCoopers, Ernst & Young, Deloitte & Touche Tomastu, KPMG International, and an active alumni recruiting network.

Student Life and Environment

MBA students at Ithaca College enjoy "a great community atmosphere" at a school that "is just the right size, so that you can go anywhere and know somebody, and meet somebody new." One student writes, "All students are easygoing and approachable. The small size of the program means that many people have identical course schedules. This makes for a tight-knit group of students and strong, long-lasting friendships."

The demands of the program keep MBA students "pretty detached from the rest of the campus. You never deal with grad students from any of the other programs (unless they happen to take a business elective)." However, "Students work hard and play hard" when their schedule allows. "Most weekends I find myself in one or more bars or restaurants eating and drinking with classmates," says one student. Ultimately, "Life at Ithaca is good."

Admissions

Applicants to Ithaca's MBA program must have completed either a bachelor's program in business or accounting, or a bachelor's program in any field along with having taken Ithaca's Pre-MBA Modules. Post-undergraduate work experience is not required; in fact, many students enter the program immediately after completing work on their bachelor's degree. Successful applicants typically have "an undergraduate GPA of 3.0 or higher and a minimum GMAT score of 500." All applications must include official undergraduate transcripts, official GMAT scores, and two letters of recommendation in addition to the essay. Merit-based academic scholarships are also available from the program.

FINANCIAL FACTS

Annual tuition	$23,400
Cost of books	$1,500
% of students receiving aid	29
% of first-year students receiving aid	35
% of students receiving grants	29
Average grant	$4,875

ADMISSIONS

Admissions Selectivity Rating	**70**
# of applications received	32
% applicants accepted	88
% acceptees attending	86
Average GMAT	526
Range of GMAT	490–550
Average GPA	3.21
TOEFL required of international students	Yes
Minimum TOEFL (paper/computer)	550/213
Application fee	$40
International application fee	$40
Regular application deadline	6/1
Regular notification	6/20
Deferment available	Yes
Transfer students accepted	Yes
Transfer application policy Transfer credits from AACSB-accredited institutions accepted on case-by-case basis.	
Non-fall admissions	Yes
Need-blind admissions	Yes

Applicants Also Look At

State University of New York at Binghamton, Syracuse University.

JACKSONVILLE STATE UNIVERSITY
COLLEGE OF COMMERCE AND BUSINESS ADMINISTRATION

Academics

The College of Commerce and Business Administration at Jacksonville State University offers a small, predominantly part-time AACSB-accredited MBA program that students praise for its convenience, affordability, and "personalized attention." The school serves the city of Jacksonville and the eastern Alabama region.

JSU offers both full-time and part-time MBA tracks. JSU's undergraduate program generally provides the majority of full-time students, as most continue directly from their bachelor's degree on to earn their master's. The part-time program is the almost-exclusive domain of area residents "who are working full-time and trying to get ahead in their careers by getting an MBA."

A sequence of foundation courses makes the JSU MBA available to everyone, even students with no previous academic experience in business. The eight-course foundation track covers business organization and administration; statistics; principles of financial accounting; macroeconomics; business; finance; business law and ethics; operations and technology; and marketing. Students with undergraduate course work in these areas may place out of the courses and begin immediately on degree-related course work, which consists of 10 courses: seven required courses, one organization class chosen from a group of three, one international business class chosen from a group of three, and an elective. Students may choose to pursue a concentration in accounting, which requires an additional six hours of course work.

All candidates for a master's degree at JSU must pass comprehensive oral examinations at the end of their program, which some here find stressful and unnecessary. "I do not agree with the oral exams policy. If instructors believe that a student knows the material and that student makes the grade on exams and projects, that should be sufficient," writes one student. Otherwise, students generally express satisfaction with the program, praising the school's administration ("It has a good vision and is focused") and the "well-read, detail-oriented, and dedicated" professors who "have good experience in the fields in which they teach." While most here applaud the school's efforts to provide distance-education options, they also anxiously await the day when the school works the bugs out of the system. One MBA warns, "The school often puts too many students in the distance-learning classes. Also, we lose 20 minutes on average per class due to technical difficulties."

Career and Placement

JSU's Office of Career Placement Services is oriented primarily toward serving the school's undergraduate programs, although it also offers services to graduate students and alumni. The office coordinates career fairs, referrals, on-campus job interviews, and job listings. It also maintains a reference room, conducts mock interviews, and offers workshops in resume writing. Students can sign up for an e-mail service that notifies them whenever new jobs are posted with the school. Individual career counseling is offered through the Office of Counseling and Career Services.

ADMISSIONS CONTACT: DR. JEAN PUGLIESE, ASSOCIATE DEAN
ADDRESS: 700 PELHAM ROAD N JACKSONVILLE, AL 36265 UNITED STATES
PHONE: 256-782-5329 • FAX: 256-782-5321
E-MAIL: PUGLIESE@JSU.EDU • WEBSITE: WWW.JSU.EDU

Student Life and Environment

Students describe their peers as "academically curious, energized, competitive, and sociable." While "there are a lot of activities from student organizations Monday to Thursday" available to MBAs on the FSU campus, most students are "way too busy balancing personal lives (jobs, spouses, kids, volunteer work, church) and school to worry about clubs!" Once Friday rolls around, "most residents go home, and the campus is a ghost town on weekends." The school could "improve school spirit and attendance at school activities" but so many students only have time to be on campus for class that the point might be moot.

JSU is the largest employer in Jacksonville, an eastern Alabama town of approximately 8,000. Other major employers in the area include the Anniston Army Depot, the Regional Medical Center, and a number of manufacturing and distribution concerns. Jacksonville is less than 100 miles from Atlanta and Birmingham.

Admissions

Applicants to the JSU MBA program must meet one of the following minimum requirements to be considered for unconditional admission: a score of at least 950 under the formula [(undergraduate GPA × 200) + GMAT score]; or a score of at least 1000 under the formula [(undergraduate GPA for final 64 hours of course work taken toward undergraduate degree × 200) + GMAT score]. Scores of 850 (entire undergraduate GPA) or 900 (final 64 hours) are sufficient to qualify students for conditional admission. Students admitted conditionally must earn a GPA of at least 3.0 for their first 12 hours of graduate course work and must complete the course work within a time frame established by the Graduate Committee. All applicants must first seek admission to the College of Graduate Studies; only after gaining admission to the college are they admitted to a particular program. Applicants must then provide the college of Graduate Studies with official copies of all postsecondary academic transcripts and three Graduate Reference forms completed by people who can assess the applicant's potential for success in the MBA program. Applicants whose native language is not English must provide an official TOEFL score report.

FINANCIAL FACTS

Annual tuition (in-state/ out-of-state)	$4,050/$8,100
Cost of books	$1,500
Room & board (on/off-campus)	$2,500/$8,500
Average grant	$1,000

ADMISSIONS

Admissions Selectivity Rating	**72**
# of applications received	25
% applicants accepted	72
% acceptees attending	83
Average GMAT	484
Range of GMAT	400–690
Average GPA	3.27
TOEFL required of international students	Yes
Minimum TOEFL (paper/computer)	500/173
Application fee	$20
International application fee	$20
Transfer students accepted	Yes
Transfer application policy 6 hrs. of approved courses.	
Non-fall admissions	Yes
Need-blind admissions	Yes

JOHN CARROLL UNIVERSITY
THE BOLER SCHOOL OF BUSINESS

GENERAL INFORMATION
Type of school	Private
Affiliation	Roman Catholic/Jesuit
Environment	Metropolis
Academic calendar	Semesters

SURVEY SAYS...
Good peer network
Cutting edge classes
Solid preparation in:
Marketing
General management

STUDENTS
Enrollment of parent institution	3,766
Enrollment of business school	177
% male/female	52/48
% out-of-state	14
% part-time	63
Average age at entry	25
Average years work experience at entry	3

ACADEMICS
Academic Experience Rating	**73**
Student/faculty ratio	17:1
Profs interesting rating	88
Profs accessible rating	71
% female faculty	12
% minority faculty	1

Joint Degrees
Communications Management 2–3 years, Nonprofit Adminstration 2–3 years.

Academics

The Boler School of Business at John Carroll University features programs "designed for students who want to move into positions of leadership in organizations and want an in-depth knowledge of business and leadership skills that will help them achieve their goals." Many students note, "JCU does seem to cater towards accounting students more than any other area." However, others add: "Although accountancy is an important program, it is by no means the only strong concentration in the MBA. Many classes build off of accounting, as having to deal with budgets is typically found in all types of jobs, not just accounting." All in all, praise is widespread, particularly when it comes to the "erudite" and "dedicated" professors. Strangely enough, students at Boler tend to be fonder of the adjunct faculty than the tenured professors. As one student explains, "Professors are top-notch, and many are adjunct who are currently in the business world and can bring current situations and trends to the table, whereas some tenured faculty have been out of the business world (or never in it to start with) for a while and may not be as current with today's business experience as students would like." That said, despite this "unique opportunity to learn real applications," some find that "part-time professors tend not to invest as much into the development of their students."

Another thing students appreciate at Boler is the program's willingness to work around their schedules. The school states that "Our program is flexible for students who are working full-time and may want to take one class in some semesters, two classes in some semesters or may need to take a semester off from classes based on work or family demands. At the same time, our program can be completed on a full-time basis for those students who are taking a break from work." Part of this involves allowing undergraduate students who majored in business to take three courses per term in order to graduate in one year. Many JCU accounting undergrads proceed directly to Boler's accountancy program, which in turn accounts for why so many undergrad alumni are current grad students. "I went here as an undergrad and the fifth-year program was hard to pass up," one student says. Some wouldn't mind seeing a "little more in the way of resources for women," "more selection offered for electives," and "improving" financial aid.

Career and Placement

The search for a job starts at home with Boler students—literally. "The greatest strength of John Carroll is its dedicated professors and great location within the Cleveland area," one student explains. "Many companies like to recruit at John Carroll due to the abundance of great candidates." Strong alumni ties are bolstered by a career center that schedules interviews, organizes job fairs that draw a substantial number of companies to campus, offers help with resumes, and provides "career coaches" that aid students in "making sense of their own career path." "Our graduates get jobs," one student says. "Each year over 90 percent of our Boler School of Business graduates receive job offers in their chosen field of interest or have been accepted into graduate school." 'Nuff said.

GAYLE BRUNO-GANNON, ASSISTANT TO THE DEAN, GRADUATE BUSINESS PROGRAMS
ADDRESS: 20700 NORTH PARK BOULEVARD, NONE UNIVERSITY HEIGHTS, OH 44118-4581 U.S.
PHONE: 216-397-1970 • FAX: 216-397-1833
E-MAIL: GGANNON@JCU.EDU • WEBSITE: WWW.JCU.EDU/BOLER/GRADS

Student Life and Environment

While most might love to say "Hello, Cleveland!" every night, the truth of the matter is that "The MBA program is mostly comprised of part-time students who are not interested in joining clubs or becoming involved in on-campus activities." Or, to take the word of a blunter student, "I want to get my studies completed and move on. No interest in reliving undergraduate." Though it could be a question of the chicken-and-the-egg in terms of whether the large percentage of commuters affects how vibrant the social life is, many here bemoan the lack of student life while acknowledging that they would be too busy to partake if there were any. That said, most happily find themselves in classes surrounded by "very articulate, intelligent, friendly, and interesting" students. "The people that I have met are very down to earth, classy individuals," one student explains. "They are very intelligent, and have a desire to be there working. There is a wide variety of races, religions, as well as married and single people. Overall, the classmates I have had are ones I can resonate with." "Most are right out of undergrad so not as experienced, but yet still are able to contribute to discussions based upon past work or internship experience." The atmosphere is "competitive without being overly intense." Ultimately, while you may only "say hi when passing each other," when the chips are down and the stress-levels high, students "support each other."

Admissions

In JCU's own words, the MBA program is "open to individuals who have earned a bachelor's degree from an accredited university and who show high promise of success in graduate business study." Applicants to the program should submit official transcripts from all or any colleges attended, GMAT scores, one letter of recommendation, a resume, and need to complete both an application form (available on the school's website) and an essay entitled "Graduate Business Education: Enabling Me to Achieve My Personal Goals and Become a Leader." International students must also provide TOEFL scores, appropriate financial documentation, and, when applicable, an English translation of all documents submitted in a language other than English. The program also has a rolling enrollment, meaning that you can enter at the beginning of the spring, summer, or fall semesters.

FINANCIAL FACTS

Annual tuition	$14,274
Fees	$0
Cost of books	$1,200
% of students receiving aid	48
% of first-year students receiving aid	54
% of students receiving loans	44
% of students receiving grants	8
Average award package	$17,239
Average grant	$2,400
Average student loan debt	$10,322

ADMISSIONS

Admissions Selectivity Rating	**78**
# of applications received	50
% applicants accepted	98
% acceptees attending	65
Average GMAT	558
Range of GMAT	500–610
Average GPA	3.16
TOEFL required of international students	Yes
Minimum TOEFL (paper/computer)	550/215
Application fee	$25
International application fee	$35
Regular application deadline	rolling
Regular notification	rolling
Deferment available	Yes
Maximum length of deferment	1 year
Transfer students accepted	Yes
Transfer application policy	
Applicants from members of the Network of MBA Programs at Jesuit Universities and Colleges, will have all MBA credits transferred and on a case-by-case basis.	
Non-fall admissions	Yes
Need-blind admissions	Yes

Applicants Also Look At

Case Western Reserve University, Cleveland State University.

KENNESAW STATE UNIVERSITY
MICHAEL J. COLES COLLEGE OF BUSINESS

GENERAL INFORMATION

Type of school	Public
Environment	Town
Academic calendar	Semester

SURVEY SAYS...

Cutting-edge classes
Helpful alumni
Happy students
Solid preparation in:
Accounting
Communication/interpersonal skills
Computer skills

STUDENTS

Enrollment of parent institution	20,118
Enrollment of business school	819
% male/female	100/0
% part-time	100
Average age at entry	35
Average years work experience at entry	9

ACADEMICS

Academic Experience Rating	**89**
Student/faculty ratio	6:1
Profs interesting rating	84
Profs accessible rating	83
% female faculty	35
% minority faculty	20

Prominent Alumni

Chris Sapsis, Airline Pilot/Transportation; Marco Horn, PhD Student/Education; Bob Wise, Director/Information Systems; Rosalind King, System Support Manager; Clinton Rowe, President/IT.

Academics

Great teaching is a trademark of the Coles College of Business, which offers flexible degree programs for working professionals in a friendly, student-oriented atmosphere. The school's talented professors are "supportive and enthusiastic to teach, and show an amazing sense of sympathy to their students. They are also very knowledgeable in their fields and are prepared to teach above and beyond what is required." Academics have a practical focus, and professors make a point of incorporating their professional experience into classroom discussions. In fact, "most of the professors are practicing professionals or have had many years of experience in their fields. The research and articles written by these professors is impressive." A current student writes, "Many of the classes have directly overlapped with functions performed in my current role at work and have enabled me to immediately add value to my company."

Kennesaw offers a MAcc degree and several MBA options, of which the most popular is the Coles MBA. This flexible, part-time degree is offered at the school's Kennesaw campus, at Cobb Galleria, and in Dalton, as well as online. Designed for working adults, the Coles MBA offers courses once a week or on the weekends, as well as "mini-mesters" three times a year. The program can be completed in just 18 months, though this remarkably flexible school allows students up to six years to complete their degree. Students appreciate the "great class scheduling for full-time workers;" however, they also note that class availability isn't consistent. While "all classes are offered at least once a year," "some semesters the elective course offerings are a little thin."

Exhibiting a genuine interest in teaching, "professors are available and genuinely care about the success of their students." Likewise, when it comes to the school's staff and directors, "the administration is very helpful and accessible all the way up to the dean of the business school." In fact, "MBA students are treated like customers of the university" and the administrative staff "arrive[s] at work everyday with the intent to serve the students." In this and other ways, students at Coles are given the respect, support, and service a professional adult would expect from their business school. A current student explains, "The greatest strength of my school is the independent yet supportive atmosphere. Students get to make their own decisions but can receive help in any way they need it."

Career and Placement

Coles is the "largest business school in Georgia," which gives it a commanding presence in the region, as well as an extensive alumni network. In addition, the school works hard to maintain a "connection with the local business community," which helps serve students while they are pursuing their degree and afterwards.

Students in the business school are served by the "great career services team" at KSU's Career Services Center, which offers interview prep, cover letter and resume review, one-on-one counseling, and access to several online job boards. The center also organizes campus career expos and career fairs throughout the year. A current student shares, "I would like to stress how much KSU tries to get employers on campus. They have career fairs in both spring and fall. They even have a separate event just for the accounting firms."

ADMISSIONS CONTACT: DAVID BAUGHER, DIRECTOR OF ADMISSIONS
ADDRESS: 1000 CHASTAIN ROAD, #0132 KENNESAW, GA 30144 UNITED STATES
PHONE: 770-423-6087 • FAX: 770-423-6141
E-MAIL: KSUGRAD@KENNESAW.EDU • WEBSITE: WWW.COLESMBA.COM

Student Life and Environment

Kennesaw State's campus has a laid-back, collegiate feel, with great facilities and plenty of resources for both undergraduate and graduate students. At the business school and the larger university, "student life around campus during the warmer months is very upbeat and you can find students lounging outside in the warm weather all of the time." A current student adds, "There are innumerable resources for students: the library, computer labs, special tutoring labs, clubs, groups, free extracurricular classes….The campus is secure, beautiful and very student-friendly." For those who live on campus, "housing is awesome and the gym facilities make you want to work out." An added advantage is the surrounding community, which "is very nice and is one of the safest in the country." In addition, "Atlanta is close enough to take advantage of the big city activities but far enough to avoid the big city problems."

Despite the appealing atmosphere at Kennesaw, most graduate students don't get too involved in the school community. A current student explains, "The undergraduate life seems very active from what I can tell, and the graduate students interact a great deal. However, because it is a commuter school, graduate activities are not as well attended. Additionally, many events take place during the daytime when those who work cannot attend." While it doesn't foster a strong campus atmosphere, the diverse locations and flexible schedule of the graduate business programs attract "students of all ages, with families and without. I believe the youngest I have met was 24 and the oldest around [their] 50s." In addition, "KSU seems to have a very large international student body. I have met students from all over the world, and it seems that nearly 50 percent of my classmates have foreign accents."

Admissions

Admissions to Coles is based on a student's undergraduate performance, standardized test scores, and professional experience. In addition to undergraduate transcripts, GMAT scores, and a resume, students may choose to send letters of recommendation for consideration, though they are not required.

FINANCIAL FACTS
Average student loan debt $20,500

ADMISSIONS
Admissions Selectivity Rating	**83**
# of applications received	242
% applicants accepted	55
% acceptees attending	83
Average GMAT	550
Range of GMAT	500–710
Average GPA	3.39
TOEFL required of	
international students	Yes
Minimum TOEFL	
(paper/computer)	550/213
Application fee	$50
International application fee	$50
Regular application deadline	8/1
Regular notification	
Deferment available	Yes
Maximum length of	
deferment	1 year
Transfer students accepted	Yes
Transfer application policy	
Transfer credit from AACSB	
International accredited universi-	
ties is possible. Limits and restric-	
tions apply.	
Non-fall admissions	Yes
Need-blind admissions	Yes

Applicants Also Look At
Georgia State University, University of Georgia.

KENT STATE UNIVERSITY
THE COLLEGE OF BUSINESS ADMINISTRATION AND GRADUATE SCHOOL OF MANAGEMENT

Academics

An affordable and efficient place to get a graduate business degree, students choose Kent State for its flexible class schedules, respected faculty, and "excellent reputation in Northeast Ohio and beyond." Operating at Kent State's main campus, the Stark campus, and at a satellite campus in Lorain, the Graduate School of Management offers full-time and part-time MBA programs, as well as a MAcc degree and MS degrees in accounting and financial engineering. Throughout the curriculum and through co-curricular activities, Kent State emphasizes teamwork, ethical leadership, creative problem solving, applications of technology, and global perspectives. To support these educational goals, "the professors at Kent have extensive international business experience and a good grasp on what is driving the global marketplace." They are also active professionals, who offer real-world insights in the classroom. A current MBA candidate explains, "I have always admired that my professors worked for 20-plus years in their field before teaching. I appreciate learning from experienced individuals, not just people who learned how to teach." While they aren't career educators, Kent State professors are nonetheless highly dedicated instructors who "have a genuine interest in giving students the tools they need to succeed."

The MBA begins with a set of foundation courses, which may be waived for students who hold an undergraduate degree in business, followed by a set of core courses. After completing the core, students have the opportunity to tailor their education through one of six concentrations in finance, marketing, human resource management, management information systems, international business, or accounting. Some students would like to see "more flexibility in what courses are required as part of the core curriculum." However, on the whole, they say the academic program is well balanced and effective. A student writes, "It provides a very clear picture of the business world and also challenges students to go deeper into the issues. The combination of general business and specific skills was nearly perfect in my opinion."

Full-time students can complete the MBA coursework in anywhere between 15 months and two years. Professional MBA students usually need about two and a half years to finish their degree, though the school allows up to six. Students warn us, however, that given the school's extensive foundational requirements, "as a non-business undergraduate... there's no way to realistically graduate in two years." For students who choose to pursue an MBA on a part-time basis, students reassure us that "in general, coursework isn't especially rigorous, except for final projects." Keep in mind, however, that the "workload can vary considerably by course and professor," so you may find some semesters are a bit more challenging than other. If you need a little extra help to get by, "most professors are very good, [and] advisors are accessible and helpful."

ADMISSIONS CONTACT: LOUISE DITCHEY, DIRECTOR, MASTER'S PROGRAMS
ADDRESS: P.O. BOX 5190 KENT, OH 44242-0001 UNITED STATES
PHONE: 330-672-2282 • FAX: 330-672-7303
E-MAIL: GRADBUS@KENT.EDU • WEBSITE: BUSINESS.KENT.EDU/GRAD

Career and Placement

The Career Services Center and Employment at Kent State offers resume writing and interview coaching, an alumni job hotline, campus interviews, and updated vacancy listings. The center also hosts a number of campus career fairs and recruiting events, which bring over 500 employers to campus annually. Many students, however, come to Kent State because it has a good reputation at their current company, and they hope to use the degree as a springboard towards a better position. These students aren't looking for a new position, per se; however, they do feel Kent State will help them advance in their professional goals. A current student enthuses, "The MBA program has made me feel like I am able to move up a couple levels and eventually take that coveted top spot at CEO."

In 2005, the average starting salary for graduates of the full-time program was $49,085, and the starting salary for students in the part-time program was $66,333, with 2.8 average job offers received per student. Thirty-six percent of students took jobs in the manufacturing industry while another 20 percent went into financial services.

Student Life and Environment

Through the graduate school as well as the larger university, there are "many opportunities to be involved in extracurricular activities" at Kent State. Clubs and organizations targeted at graduate business students include the Graduate Management Association, a social and career development group, as well as a number of organizations offered through the larger university, such as Graduate Student Senate. With an enrollment of just 100 students in the full-time program, students "know each other well and work together. We take part in associations and share experiences." On the flip side, many students in the Professional MBA "come for class and leave right away afterward;" not surprisingly, they feel they "don't have much time for life at school," as work, home life, and homework keep them sufficiently busy. While they may not get together outside of class, the mix of older and younger students creates an excellent academic atmosphere. A student explains, "Kent benefits greatly from the many outstanding businesses that encourage employees to pursue an MBA. This real-world experience is a nice complement to the younger students' enthusiasm and technological savvy."

Admissions

There is no stated minimum GPA or GMAT score to be accepted to Kent State's MBA program. However, in recent years, the mean undergraduate GPA for students in the full-time program was 3.2–3.4, and the mean GPA for part-time Professional MBA students was 3.0–3.1. Roughly 80 percent of applicants are accepted to the programs each year.

FINANCIAL FACTS

Annual tuition (in-state/ out-of-state)	$8,968/$15,980
Fees	$0
Cost of books	$1,200
Room & board (on/off-campus)	$8,690/$8,000
% of students receiving aid	40
% of first-year students receiving aid	17
Average award package	$15,668

ADMISSIONS

Admissions Selectivity Rating	69
# of applications received	93
% applicants accepted	83
% acceptees attending	49
Average GMAT	520
Range of GMAT	470–570
Average GPA	3.36
TOEFL required of international students	Yes
Minimum TOEFL (paper/computer)	550/213
Application fee	$30
International application fee	$30
Regular application deadline	4/1
Regular notification	4/15
Deferment available	Yes
Maximum length of deferment	1 year
Transfer students accepted	Yes
Transfer application policy 12 credit hours from an AASCB accredited program.	
Non-fall admissions	Yes
Need-blind admissions	Yes

Applicants Also Look At

Case Western Reserve University, Cleveland State University, John Carroll University, The Ohio State University, The University of Akron, Youngstown State University.

EMPLOYMENT PROFILE

Career Rating	71	Grads Employed by Function	% Avg. Salary
Primary Source of Full-time Job Acceptances		Finance	33 $50,987
School-facilitated activities	6 (50%)	Human Resources	8 $32,500
Graduate-facilitated activities	3 (25%)	Marketing	25 $50,833
		MIS	16 $48,000
		Other	16 $47,500

Top 5 Employers Hiring Grads
Ernst and Young; Nationwide Insurance; Nasa Glenn Research Cente; Hill, Barth & King, LLC; RDL Architects

LAMAR UNIVERSITY
COLLEGE OF BUSINESS

Academics

The MBA program at Lamar University's College of Business serves a predominantly local population drawn to the school by "convenience, affordability, and the reputation of the program." Small class sizes providing a "personal" feel, and lots of "access to professors" creates "opportunities for individuals to get involved and shine." Two of Lamar's greatest assets are its "faculty-to-student ratio and the individualized attention that the school provides," one student writes.

Lamar offers a Cohort MBA, a full-time evening program that includes several experiential learning opportunities. The program is intense; classes meet 4 nights a week, and the curriculum goes pretty much nonstop for 16 months, but those who tough it out are rewarded with an MBA earned in a relatively short time for relatively little money. Cohort MBA participants must have earned an undergraduate degree in business. The school also offers a traditional MBA, which also meets in the evenings, but it allows for part-time attendance. The traditional MBA program is open to all college graduates; those who lack the requisite academic business background must complete a series of leveling courses before commencing the MBA proper.

Both programs earn praise for "being convenient to professionals in the area and working to meet the needs of the students." University staffers "make a point to know each student personally" and the administration "is very accommodating. Schedules and special circumstances result in solutions, not brick walls. This attitude of working together applies in class and administration." One MBA adds, "The Dean encourages all of the faculty to be available to students for questions. They are always available when I need them either by their office hours, e-mail, or special appointment." Students also appreciate that "this is a growing program. As a student, I can see many opportunities for future MBA students." As for now, students are already enjoying a great "hometown feeling" that helps students manage "the stress of returning to school while raising a family and performing at work."

Career and Placement

The Career Center at Lamar has "great resources," but because the MBA program is relatively small, "MBA students must work hard to get career placement advice. More recruiters for MBA students would be a great help. The school brings in many speakers and alumni specifically for MBA students, and that is a great help." Students are satisfied that "the school is working on and needs to continue working on developing the Placement Office and networking for MBA students." Students who can get to the school during the day have a more positive outlook on the office, as many of its services and events—such as lunchtime Executive in Residence seminars—are available primarily during standard business hours. The Career Center offers one-on-one career advising, personal assessments, and online job search resources.

Employers who most frequently hire graduates include: Ernst & Young, Melton & Melton LLP, Merrill Lynch, and Chase.

ADMISSIONS CONTACT: DEBBY PIPER, GRADUATE ADMISSIONS OFFICE
ADDRESS: P. O. BOX L0078 BEAUMONT, TX 77710 UNITED STATES
PHONE: 409-880-8356 • FAX: 409-880-8414
E-MAIL: GRADMISSIONS@LAMAR.EDU • WEBSITE: MBA.LAMAR.EDU

Student Life and Environment

"There are a lot of events to participate in around the Lamar campus," and "With the campus being smaller it is actually easier to be involved in several different groups. There are tons of leadership opportunities." Administrators and student groups "are working to involve students in networking opportunities such as socials, a mentoring program with alumni, and through guest speakers." How many MBAs get involved is another question entirely; most attend classes in the evenings and have little time to spare. One student writes, "I work 50 to 60 hours a week and attend class at night, study when I can during the week, and commit most of the weekend to school other than coaching a soccer team. As a father of four, this commitment takes time away from my family, but with an understanding wife, we are managing. The long and short of it is I don't have time for a social life on campus."

Regardless of how many hours students spend there, the Lamar campus "offers a great atmosphere for learning. This campus has traditionally been a commuter school, but it is now transitioning to a campus-centered institution. There is campus day care and increasing opportunity for extracurricular and social participation." Lamar "is adding new state-of-the-art facilities such as the dining facility, residence halls, and recreational sports facilities" in its effort to make the campus more homey and accommodating. A student adds, "The school is also working to clean up the surrounding area by buying vacant property surrounding the campus." Hometown Beaumont is "a wonderful place to raise a family. The economy is booming, and the university contributes by providing a skilled workforce to meet the expanding labor force in the area."

Admissions

Lamar University requires all applicants to provide GMAT scores, undergraduate transcripts, essays, and TOEFL scores (for students whose native language is not English). An interview, letters of recommendation, personal statement, resume, and evidence of computer experience are all recommended but not required; all are taken into account in rendering an admissions decision. Applicants must earn a score of at least 950 under the formula (200 multiplied by GPA plus GMAT) or a score of 1000 under the formula (200 multiplied by GPA for final 60 semester hours of undergraduate work plus GMAT). In both cases, a minimum GMAT score of 450 is required for unconditional admission; students with scores between 400 and 450 qualify for conditional admission. International applicants must provide proof of financial support.

FINANCIAL FACTS

Annual tuition (in-state/out-of-state)	$4,296/$10,968
Fees	$1,367
Cost of books	$1,382
Room & board (on/off-campus)	$5,888/$6,932
% of students receiving aid	52
% of first-year students receiving aid	50
% of students receiving loans	20
% of students receiving grants	45
Average award package	$4,944
Average grant	$1,505
Average student loan debt	$850

ADMISSIONS

Admissions Selectivity Rating	72
# of applications received	52
% applicants accepted	62
% acceptees attending	53
Average GMAT	482
Range of GMAT	450–540
Average GPA	3.13
TOEFL required of international students	Yes
Minimum TOEFL (paper/computer)	525/200
Application fee	$25
International application fee	$75
Regular application deadline	7/1
Regular notification	rolling
Deferment available	Yes
Maximum length of deferment	1 year
Transfer students accepted	Yes
Transfer application policy	Accept 6 hours from another AACSB MBA program
Non-fall admissions	Yes
Need-blind admissions	Yes

EMPLOYMENT PROFILE

Career Rating	76	Grads Employed by Function	%	Avg. Salary
Primary Source of Full-time Job Acceptances		Finance	76	$57,500
School-facilitated activities	2 (20%)	Marketing	7	$85,000
Unknown	8 (80%)	Consulting	7	NR
		General Management	7	NR

LONG ISLAND UNIVERSITY—C.W. POST CAMPUS
COLLEGE OF MANAGEMENT

GENERAL INFORMATION
Type of school	Private
Academic calendar	Trimester

SURVEY SAYS...
Students love Brookville, NY
Solid preparation in:
Finance
General management
Teamwork
Doing business in a global economy

STUDENTS
Enrollment of parent institution	8,500
Enrollment of business school	310
% male/female	58/42
% out-of-state	2
% part-time	62
% minorities	15
% international	59
Average age at entry	27
Average years work experience at entry	6

ACADEMICS
Academic Experience Rating	**69**
Student/faculty ratio	15:1
Profs interesting rating	73
Profs accessible rating	74
% female faculty	23
% minority faculty	23

Joint Degrees
Dual JD/MBA 3 years, BS/MBA 4 years.

Academics

Long Island University's C.W. Post Campus boasts "one of the top business programs on Long Island." It offers two paths to an MBA to its mostly part-time student population. In the Campus MBA program, students take "flexible night classes" Monday through Thursday. As a general rule, 48 credit hours are required to graduate. Depending on your undergraduate coursework, though, you can complete the program in as few as 36 hours. The other option is the Saturday MBA program, which features intensive, all-day classes and takes between 15 and 23 months to complete, again depending on your undergraduate work. Students in the Campus MBA program may supplement their curricula with Saturday classes. C.W. Post's advanced certificate program is also worth noting. It requires four additional electives and allows students to acquire further expertise in six areas including accounting and taxation, finance, and international business.

One of the best things about C.W. Post is its class sizes. "Classes are not too large, which makes for a better learning environment," explains one student. For the most part, "support from the advisors and faculty is great" as well. Professors are "responsible, nice, and professional." They are "knowledgeable in their respective fields" and "willing to help students" outside of class.

One student describes the administration as "very helpful." Another calls it "terrible." Additional complaints include the cumbersome registration process. Also, gripes about the narrow range of elective courses are a hardy perennial here. "We have to take many core courses to graduate," says one student.

Career and Placement

C.W. Post affords its students a variety of placement services. The Office of Professional Experience and Career Planning offers self-assessment diagnostics, career counseling, resume and job-search advisement, mock interviews, job fairs, recruiting events, and online databases. Also, a broad graduate assistantship program provides advanced research opportunities. However, some students here report that career resources are "nonexistent." "Get better companies to job fairs," demands one student. "I don't see that many events to help facilitate job placement for C.W. Post graduates," observes another.

CAROL HAFFORD, DIRECTOR OF GRADUATE AND INTERNATIONAL ADMISSIONS
ADDRESS: 720 NORTHERN BOULEVARD BROOKVILLE, NY 11548 UNITED STATES
PHONE: (516) 299-3952 • FAX: (516) 299-2418
E-MAIL: CAROL.HAFFORD@LIU.EDU • WEBSITE: WWW.LIU.EDU/BUSINESS

Student Life and Environment

The MBA students at C.W. Post describe themselves as "friendly, smart, active," and "interesting." Virtually everyone here is a part-timer, attending classes in the evenings and on Saturdays. That's the nature of the program. Many students choose C.W. Post because it's close to home. There's also a tremendous population of international students. "In recent years, C.W. Post has focused on recruiting students from overseas and it has made the learning experience more global." Students vary quite a bit in their levels of experience. There are older types with fat resumes and others who "have no business experience and cannot bring real-life examples to the class discussions."

C.W. Post is "a beautiful school" spread out across a few hundred acres. Green, rolling lawns and heavily wooded areas proliferate the area. The location of the campus on the north shore of Long Island is definitely a plus. It's not far from some fabulous beaches and, at the same time, relatively "close to New York City." Parking is about the only problem. Students gripe, "The parking situation needs to improve drastically."

Socially, this is a commuter school. Beyond the MBA association and the occasional function during business hours, there are few clubs or activities. With work and families, and with the lights of Manhattan beckoning, most students "have busy lives."

Admissions

Your grades and your GMAT scores don't have to be terrifically high to get admitted to C.W. Post. Prerequisites for admission include competence in business communications, mathematics, and computers, as demonstrated through undergraduate work, successful completion of a related workshop, or successful completion of a waiver exam. In addition to transcripts and a GMAT score, you need to submit two letters of recommendation and a resume. There's also an essay. If your first language isn't English, you need to submit official results for the TOEFL. The minimum score requirement is 550 on the paper-based test, or 215 on the computer-based test, or 71 on the Internet-based test. Students who completed undergraduate degrees from institutions that teach primarily in English don't have to submit TOEFL scores.

FINANCIAL FACTS

Annual tuition	$15,030
Fees	$1,250
Cost of books	$2,100
Room & board	$10,000
% of students receiving aid	80
% of first-year students receiving aid	70
% of students receiving loans	75
% of students receiving grants	15
Average grant	$3,000

ADMISSIONS

Admissions Selectivity Rating	**68**
# of applications received	143
% applicants accepted	84
% acceptees attending	47
Average GMAT	465
Range of GMAT	400–610
Average GPA	3.05
TOEFL required of international students	Yes
Minimum TOEFL (paper/computer)	550/215
Application fee	$30
International application fee	$30
Regular application deadline	8/7
Regular notification	8/7
Deferment available	Yes
Maximum length of deferment	1 year
Transfer students accepted	Yes
Transfer application policy 6 credits within the last five years from an AACSB accredited School.	
Non-fall admissions	Yes
Need-blind admissions	Yes

Applicants Also Look At
Hofstra University, St. John's University.

LOUISIANA STATE UNIVERSITY
E. J. OURSO COLLEGE OF BUSINESS

GENERAL INFORMATION

Type of school	Public
Environment	Metropolis

SURVEY SAYS...
Friendly students
Good social scene
Smart classrooms

STUDENTS

Enrollment of parent institution	26,071
Enrollment of business school	341
% male/female	70/30
% out-of-state	12
% minorities	10
% international	10
Average age at entry	23
Average years work experience at entry	1.6

ACADEMICS

Academic Experience Rating	**96**
Student/faculty ratio	1:1
Profs interesting rating	88
Profs accessible rating	73
% female faculty	27
% minority faculty	3

Joint Degrees
JD/MBA 4 years.

Prominent Alumni
Harry Hawks, Executive VP and CEO, Hearst-Argyle Television; D. Martin Phillips, Sr. Managing Director, EnCap Investments, LLC; Ross Centanni, Chairman, President & CEO, Gardner Denver, Inc.; Richard F. Gill, Executive Vice President of the Shaw Group, Inc.; John H. Boydstun, President, Capitol One Banking Segment.

Academics

Looking for an MBA that offers "the perfect combination of academics, athletics, and the South?" Well, look no further than the Flores MBA, part of the E. J. Ourso College of Business at Louisiana State University, which offers a "respected academic program along with very favorable financial aid," not to mention "the camaraderie of the students," "the beautiful campus," and "excellent" football. Many here note the "reasonable tuition" and flexible programs as the driving force behind their decision to enroll. "My undergraduate degree was in engineering, and LSU had the only MBA program in the state that did not require me to take undergraduate business courses before starting the program," a student says. In fact, according to the school, "49 percent" of their students "hold non-business undergraduate degrees, including education, engineering, journalism, geography, political science, criminal justice, kinesiology, and history," to name a few. This results in a student body with an impressive—and varied—set of undergraduate backgrounds. Another boon of being in the Flores MBA Program is "real work experience" the program offers both in the classroom and around campus. "On Fridays, we have speakers come in from all over the country, which really lends a practical, applicable side to the LSU MBA," one student explains. Another adds, "The internal auditing program, without a doubt, is one of the high-lights of the MBA program." When it comes to professors, however, feelings are a little mixed. "Many teachers may be well-qualified academically," one student notes, "but they are completely unable to teach, or relay information to the students effectively." Another student agrees, adding, "The level of the courses is roughly that of an undergraduate degree. The professors are hit and miss. Some teach for the love of it, and it shows. Some are there only for the paycheck." That said, others have been "very impressed with the profes-sors" who "go out of their way to get to know each student and are always available for help when you need it." Another student admits: "The courses were challenging, but not impos-sible. As with most things, to succeed one must put forth effort." Students also tell us that the Flores MBA Program is keen on expanding. "In the past year and a half, the MBA office has made numerous hires and expanded its services, especially in corporate relations and recruiting. These advances are making contacting corporate recruiters and finding more specialized professions easier than ever." Additionally, the "electives offerings are improv-ing." Good news for whichever side of the spectrum of opinion you might fall on. Less divi-sive are the views on the school's "wonderful" and "very accessible" administration. "They are constantly assessing the curriculum to ensure that our students have the greatest prepa-ration upon graduation," one student says.

Change is indeed on its way to the Flores MBA Program. Many students point out that "the school is in the midst of a multimillion dollar building campaign that will greatly improve its facilities," which they hope will also improve "the quality of the programs overall" and "the standards of new students." ("Request work experience, higher GMAT, and more extracurricular work in general," a die-hard student suggests.) Regardless, enthusiasm for the construction runs high. "I have seen the approved plans for the new building, and it will be an incredible boost to the reputation of the Flores MBA and the icing on the cake for our recent Wall Street Journal ranking!" a student enthuses.

Career and PLacement

Options abound for jobseekers in the Flores MBA Program thanks to a multi-faceted career services department and strong alumni connections. An abundance of events, from alumni receptions to career expos to speaking engagements, are available to MBA students not only through the Flores Program, but the E. J. Ourso College of Business itself. Many find that the "Distinguished Speaker Series" is particularly helpful because "we have business leaders, often LSU MBA Alumni, speak to our students about current industry trends and offer career advice as well as networking!" Others opine that the

STEPHANIE CANCIENNE HEDGE, ASSOCIATE DIRECTOR OF ENROLLMENT & ADMINISTRATION
ADDRESS: E. J. OURSO COLLEGE OF BUSINESS, 3176 PATRICK F. TAYLOR HALL BATON ROUGE,
LA 70803 U.S. • PHONE: 225-578-8867 • FAX: 225-578-2421
E-MAIL: BUSMBA@LSU.EDU • WEBSITE: MBA.LSU.EDU

career center offers "good" recruitment and job placement for those "who want to stay in Louisiana," and some note that "though vastly improving already, it could be better." Lucky for them, help is on the way. "The MBA office here at LSU just added two new members that are responsible solely for placing us in great jobs, and they are already helping many of us find the jobs that are just right," one student explains. Another adds, "My graduate assistantship is awesome and there couldn't be better or more helpful alumni as far as networking is concerned."

Student Life and Environment

The "culturally rich state" of Louisiana has plenty to offer to students, but it's "being on the campus of a major university" that "affords students the great opportunities that come with a university such as performing arts and sports." And have we mentioned LSU's "national championship football team?" ("[Despite being] in graduate school, students still care more about football than education," a student notes.) Students here find themselves among a "diverse group" set in a "productive atmosphere of graduate students who are willing and able to learn and at the same time bring unique and realistic views to the classroom." Many note that those with a cutthroat attitude might do well to look elsewhere. "The school day does not end at the end of class," one student explains. "Students regularly get together to work on school projects, study, or even to socialize. The atmosphere is a close community with students who are willing to help each other out." Additionally, many here appreciate what the school does to get the social ball rolling. "Our MBA Association holds monthly socials where we can all meet outside of class and just hang out. For instance, our social this month is bowling. We will all get together at the bowling alley and talk about things other than school. This friendship spills over into our academic life and our careers." All in all, students find that it's "very easy to make friends here" and "life is never dull" in Baton Rouge. That said, LSU's reputation as a party school can carry over into graduate classes. Some find Flores students to be "young" and "immature." "They just party and don't work hard," one student says. Ultimately, it seems you can find what you're looking for here, whether raucous or relaxed, there's something for everyone. "As a married student, I would say that the MBA program is very conducive to married life, and although I spend many hours studying, I still feel like I have a good school/life balance."

Admissions

In considering applicants, the Flores MBA Program requires prospective students to submit two sets of undergraduate transcripts (with a minimum GPA of 3.0), GMAT scores (the Class of 2009 had an average GMAT score of 640), record of previous work experience (not required, but considered "desirable"), a one-page resume, one letter of recommendation (this is optional, but recommended), and, in the case of international students, a financial statement and TOEFL scores (minimum score: 550 written, 213 computer-based, or 79 internet-based).

FINANCIAL FACTS

Annual tuition (in-state/ out-of-state)	$2,982/$11,281
Fees	$5,682
Cost of books	$1,500
Room & board (on/off-campus)	$6,498/$10,768

ADMISSIONS

Admissions Selectivity Rating	96
# of applications received	144
% applicants accepted	57
% acceptees attending	80
Average GMAT	637
Range of GMAT	590–690
Average GPA	3.43
TOEFL required of international students	Yes
Minimum TOEFL (paper/computer)	550/213
Application fee	$25
International application fee	$25
Transfer students accepted	Yes
Transfer application policy Applicants must have attended an AACSB accredited school and meet the entrance requirements for the Flores MBA Program.	
Need-blind admissions	Yes

Applicants Also Look At

Emory University, Rice University, Tulane University, University of Houston, University of Mississippi.

EMPLOYMENT PROFILE

Career Rating	78	Grads Employed by Function	%	Avg. Salary
Primary Source of Full-time Job Acceptances		Finance	47	$61,117
School-facilitated activities	24 (56%)	Human Resources	5	$62,500
Graduate-facilitated activities	4 (9%)	Marketing	16	$73,367
Unknown	15 (35%)	MIS	21	$61,744
Percent employed	91	Consulting	2	$67,000
		Other	9	$35,000

Top 5 Employers Hiring Grads
PricewaterhouseCoopers; Chevron; Ernst & Young; Ochner Health System; The Shaw Group

LOYOLA COLLEGE IN MARYLAND
SELLINGER SCHOOL OF BUSINESS AND MANAGEMENT

GENERAL INFORMATION
Type of school	Private
Affiliation	Roman Catholic/Jesuit
Environment	Village
Academic calendar	Semester

SURVEY SAYS...
Solid preparation in:
Doing business in a global economy

STUDENTS
Enrollment of parent institution	6,035
Enrollment of business school	791
% male/female	100/0
% part-time	100
Average age at entry	28

ACADEMICS
Academic Experience Rating	**79**
Student/faculty ratio	12:1
Profs interesting rating	87
Profs accessible rating	73
% female faculty	28
% minority faculty	10

Academics

Loyola's Sellinger School of Business and Management offers the aspiring MBA a distinct, challenging, and flexible program. With evening classes held on both the Timonium and Columbia campuses, full-time working professionals can really take advantage of the self-paced curriculum. The average time to degree completion is less than three years, with some qualified and dedicated students finishing within twelve to fifteen months. Candidates whose undergraduate coursework involved business may be eligible for course waivers. Available concentrations include accounting, finance, general business, international business, marketing, management, and management information systems.

Loyola manages to attract "extremely accessible" professors who know how to provide "practical knowledge to complement the academic theories of business." They cultivate a "very supportive environment" and "continuously seek student and outside feedback to [ensure] courses are relevant to today's business environment." Importantly, the "majority of professors are at the top of their fields" and have "an extensive background in real-world business." Many employ teaching methods that encourage students to "think in a different way rather than regurgitate information." Though students are quick to heap praise on their instructors, their enthusiasm is tempered by one qualifier. While the tenured faculty is continually described as "top-notch," some do warn that the adjunct faculty is "barely prepared."

Student opinion is decidedly mixed when it comes to Loyola's administration. As one disgruntled respondent shared, "The financial offices make more mistakes than a fourth grader with a calculator." Conversely, others assert that they are "very concerned about the well-being of their student" noting that "[administrators] make themselves readily available to students by having extended office hours and [by] being located at all satellite campuses." And an impressed second-year candidate shared, "The dean even called to inform that I will need to take two specific courses in order to graduate."

Career and Placement

Loyola's Career Center provides comprehensive services, equipping graduates with the necessary tools to succeed in the job market. Experienced officers help students identify and explore possible career paths. They also offer resume critiques and practice interviews, allowing students to sharpen their skills and apply for a job with supreme confidence. The Career Center grants access to a number of online resources and connects students with a handful of job fairs throughout the Baltimore area. Impressively, MBA candidates are privy to a network of approximately 1000 Loyola alumni. These alums become invaluable mentors, providing industry knowledge and acumen along with indispensable career advice. Lastly, there is an on-campus recruitment program, attracting roughly 150 from local, regional, national, and international corporations.

In the 2007–2008 academic year, the top five recruiters at Loyola College were T. Rowe Price; Northrop-Grumman; Legg Mason-Wood Walker; the U.S. government; and Verizon.

Student Life and Environment

Loyola's MBA program is offered on a part-time basis only, a factor that does impact student life. Indeed, the population is comprised primarily of "professionals" who maintain "busy personal and work schedules." Due to time constraints "there is limited interaction with other students outside of the classroom and study groups." However, one eager respondent did note that students do sometimes "go out for drinks after class."

Despite a scarcity of social opportunities, Loyola's MBA candidates speak highly of one another. They are quick to define their peers as "highly motivated," "friendly" and "career-driven." And while "fellow students are competitive," they also prove themselves to be "amazing team players" who are "very supportive of each other and…create an atmosphere where everyone is committed to coming to class each week with a desire to learn as much as we can from each other." As one respondent sums up, "Doing well and receiving good grades are important to Loyola students."

Importantly, the school attracts a healthy "mix of new graduates and working adults with broad backgrounds and an extremely diverse experience base—from government [and] non-profit to commercial and private sector." Certainly this diversity within the student body enhances the learning experience by allowing "for different perspectives to be heard." And ultimately, all of this works to create an "environment very conducive not only to learning but making friends and connections too."

Admissions

A complete application to the Loyola College MBA program includes: a completed application form; a personal statement; a resume; an official GMAT score report; official transcripts for all degree work and for any postsecondary academic work completed within five years of application; as well as international documents, where appropriate. Applicants with a 3.25 undergraduate GPA and five years of work experience may waive the GMAT requirement, as may students with an advanced degree in any other discipline (e.g., an MA, a PhD, a JD, etc.). Interviews and letters of recommendation are optional.

FINANCIAL FACTS

Annual tuition	$9,450
Fees	$50
Cost of books	$630
Room & board (off-campus)	$13,365
% of students receiving aid	38
% of first-year students receiving aid	62
% of students receiving loans	33
% of students receiving grants	12
Average award package	$16,120
Average grant	$10,920
Average student loan debt	$26,550

ADMISSIONS

Admissions Selectivity Rating	**75**
# of applications received	558
% applicants accepted	81
% acceptees attending	85
Average GMAT	536
Range of GMAT	440–680
Average GPA	3.34
TOEFL required of international students	Yes
Minimum TOEFL (paper/computer)	550/215
Application fee	$50
International application fee	$50
Regular application deadline	rolling
Regular notification	rolling
Deferment available	Yes
Maximum length of deferment	1 year
Transfer students accepted	Yes
Transfer application policy Only classes from another AACSB accredited school will be counted, total 6 credits.	
Non-fall admissions	Yes
Need-blind admissions	Yes

LOYOLA MARYMOUNT UNIVERSITY
COLLEGE OF BUSINESS ADMINISTRATION

GENERAL INFORMATION
Type of school	Private
Affiliation	Roman Catholic/Jesuit
Environment	Metropolis
Academic calendar	Semester

SURVEY SAYS...
Solid preparation in:
Entrepreneurial studies

STUDENTS
Enrollment of parent institution	8,979
Enrollment of business school	303
% male/female	60/40
% part-time	76
% minorities	35
% international	21
Average age at entry	27
Average years work experience at entry	4

ACADEMICS
Academic Experience Rating	**89**
Student/faculty ratio	5:1
Profs interesting rating	93
Profs accessible rating	77
% female faculty	24
% minority faculty	19

Joint Degrees
MBA/JD 4 years, MBA/SELP
(Systems Engineering) 4 years.

Academics

The part-time MBA program at Loyola Marymount University "is by far the most accommodating program for working professionals in the Los Angeles area," students assert. One argues that "The evening classes, small class size, strong academics, and flexible schedules make LMU an obvious choice" for mid-career business types looking for a boost, as does "the very convenient location for residents on the Westside of Los Angeles." A "widely recognized entrepreneurship program" also draws its fair share of students.

Loyola Marymount is a Jesuit school, meaning the curriculum focuses on "educating the whole person." As one student observes, "All the other MBA schools talked about how much money their graduates made. This school talked about teaching me to live up to Jesuit ideals of philanthropy, loyalty, and justice. It suited my value system." "High ethical and moral standards" infuse all course offerings here. Students tell us that the program also excels in management, finance, and operations.

Entrepreneurship is the most prominent program here, however, as indicated by its number 11 national ranking by *Entrepreneur* magazine. Students praise "everything from the classes to the extracurricular activities to the guest speakers" within the program and tell us, "If someone comes into the program knowing they want to develop their own business, they definitely have all the tools they will need here. They will be able to graduate with a viable business plan in hand."

LMU offers a full-time MBA program as well as a part-time program. The former is especially appealing to LMU business undergraduates, who place out of certain MBA prerequisites and thereby complete their graduate degrees more quickly. All students conclude their study here with a series of integrative experiences, the last of which is the year-long Corporate Management Systems, through which "students are given the opportunity to spend a few weeks abroad making presentations and learning about how business is done in other countries."

Career and Placement

LMU serves two distinct student bodies: a majority of part-timers who already have full-time jobs, and a minority who attend full-time and will be looking for job placement post-MBA. The MBA Career Services Office (CSO) doesn't see much of the former, whose employers frequently foot the bill for their MBAs. The latter benefit from resume and cover-letter seminars, interview and salary-negotiation workshops, and career counseling. An MBA Mentor program pairs students with area execs, while the annual Meet the Firms event brings employers to campus to meet with prospective employees and interns. The CSO also offers the CareerLeader assessment tool and access to Vault.com and Monstertrak.com. The office maintains an online bulletin board for job postings.

Students tell us that "the career services department is limited," with some going so far as to say the office "needs a huge overhaul...The career services department offers little beyond what someone in a graduate program should already know when it comes to looking for a new job. Connections with recruiters and alumni should be made more readily available." A few counter: "LMU is working on delivering more to its students. As the program is growing, so are the resources available to the students. The career center is beginning to deliver more for its students, which is where the greatest improvement opportunity existed."

ADMISSIONS CONTACT: ELYNAR MORENO, MBA COORDINATOR
ADDRESS: ONE LMU DRIVE, MS 8387 LOS ANGELES, CA 90045-2659 UNITED STATES
PHONE: 310-338-2848 • FAX: 310-338-2899
E-MAIL: MBAPC@LMU.EDU • WEBSITE: MBA.LMU.EDU

Student Life and Environment

The LMU campus is "very accommodating," students report, telling us, "The facilities are top notch, there are computer facilities and multimedia stations available in every classroom." Students appreciate that "The school is nice and quiet, and still students have a social life outside of school. The school has social events that are free of cost to students." They also note, however, that "It's [largely] a part-time program, so there isn't a whole lot of structure to it besides classes, but the students are very self-organizing, and sociable, so there is no lack of academic support or networking opportunities." The program offers "frequent speakers or events planned for students and/or alumni to attend," including "networking parties to help students get to know each other."

LMU is in "a good location, close to downtown Los Angeles and close to the beach." One student reports: "The school's beauty and location are two of the greatest strengths. It is hard to feel stressed out when you can walk around and see views of the Los Angeles Basin, Pacific Ocean, Marina Del Rey, and Century City skyline. The laid-back atmosphere…is welcoming."

LMU students "are very friendly, very willing to help, and seem to be there to learn and improve their own lives as opposed to wanting to compete and run the world. They are realistic about expectations and prefer an environment where people work together to achieve success as opposed to working against each other." Most are "working professionals with busy schedules" who have "very diverse backgrounds with regards to their careers, origins, and viewpoints."

Admissions

Applicants to the LMU MBA program must provide the admissions office with the following materials: two official copies of transcripts for all post-secondary schoolwork; an official score report for the GMAT; two letters of recommendation; and a completed application form. International students must additionally provide an official TOEFL score report (if English is not their first language) and documentation demonstrating the financial means to support themselves while attending the program. Work experience "is not required but will enhance the application," according to the school. Applicants may be admitted for fall or spring semester. Applications are processed on a rolling basis, with admissions decisions typically made within two weeks of delivery of all application materials.

FINANCIAL FACTS

Annual tuition	$26,514
Fees	$540
Cost of books	$1,300

ADMISSIONS

Admissions Selectivity Rating	**81**
# of applications received	283
% applicants accepted	58
% acceptees attending	61
Average GMAT	573
Range of GMAT	530–610
Average GPA	3.23
TOEFL required of international students	Yes
Minimum TOEFL (paper/computer)	600/250
Application fee	$50
International application fee	$50
Regular application deadline	rolling
Regular notification	rolling
Deferment available	Yes
Maximum length of deferment	1 year
Transfer students accepted	Yes
Transfer application policy Students from other Jesuit MBA Programs may transfer core and electives through the Jesuit Transfer Network or 6 units from AACSB schools	
Non-fall admissions	Yes
Need-blind admissions	Yes

Applicants Also Look At

Pepperdine University, University of California—Irvine, University of California—Los Angeles, University of Southern California.

LOYOLA UNIVERSITY—CHICAGO
GRADUATE SCHOOL OF BUSINESS

GENERAL INFORMATION

Type of school	Private
Affiliation	Roman Catholic/Jesuit
Environment	Metropolis
Academic calendar	Quarter

SURVEY SAYS...
Students love Chicago, IL
Cutting edge classes

STUDENTS

Enrollment of parent institution	15,545
Enrollment of business school	749
% male/female	48/52
% part-time	75
% minorities	22
% international	19
Average age at entry	27
Average years work experience at entry	5

ACADEMICS

Academic Experience Rating	**77**
Profs interesting rating	85
Profs accessible rating	88

Joint Degrees
MBA/JD 4–6 years, MBA/MSISM 2–4 years, MBA/MSIMC 2–4 years, MBA/MS (Nursing) 2–4 years, MBA/MSHR 2–4 years, MBA/MSA 2–4 years, MBA/MSF 2–4 years.

Prominent Alumni
Robert L. Parkinson, Jr., President and CEO, Baxter International Inc.; Brenda Barnes, President and CEO, Sara Lee Corporation; Michael R. Quinlan, Retired Chairman of the Board and CEO, McDonald's; John B. Menzer, President and CEO, Wal-Mart International; John Rooney, President and CEO, US Cellular.

Academics

Like many big-city business schools, Loyola University of Chicago capitalizes on its location. Chicago, students here agree, has "a first-rate business environment . . . there is no better city." The city not only provides students with opportunities unthinkable at schools in more isolated locations but also serves to attract "top-notch faculty" who are "among the top in the country. Professors come from diverse backgrounds. Many have worked internationally and have valuable insight to provide in class. Others have been at top executive positions with top global companies." It's possible to find a faculty this strong in Podunk, but it's not likely.

A Jesuit university, Loyola is institutionally committed to "teaching how to think, rather than teaching mechanics" as well as to a curricular "emphasis on ethics and ethical leadership." The idea is to train students who are flexible enough to adapt; as one student puts it, "We live in a world where change is the norm, so to be able to navigate change and apply what we learn to new situations is critical." Flexibility is also a hallmark of the design of Loyola's part-time program, which is frequently ranked among the nation's top 20. Students tell us that Loyola's classes "fit my busy work schedule" while the quarterly calendar with relatively few required courses "allows flexibility to take courses that are of interest across disciplines rather than requiring specific courses."

Loyola offers a broad range of graduate business degrees. Students tell us that "the accounting department is very strong," that the MS in human resources is "all encompassing," and that the MS in integrated marketing communications "offers a holistic approach to advertising, marketing, PR and the customer experience." A good student/faculty ratio "provides for closer contacts of students with their professors" while a curricular emphasis on teamwork develops skills "important in modern business environments." Students also appreciate the "integration of high technology courses in the graduate programs, which introduces prospective graduates to situations likely to be encountered in the real world of business or administration."

Career and Placement

The Business Career Center at Loyola is dedicated exclusively to undergraduate and graduate students in business. Some here recount good experiences with the office; one student writes, "They have hooked me up with two great internships, and I have been talking to multiple companies about full-time work which was done through the BCC." Others aren't as impressed. As one puts it, "With the wealth of great companies in the area and Loyola alumni out in the workforce, I was often underwhelmed by the opportunities presented to the GSB students at Loyola. Many companies had events with DePaul and other campuses but were not recruiting at Loyola. My best career help came directly from professors." Some wonder how much the BCC can accomplish on its own, noting that "While LUC is a fine school, holding its own against many of the other schools located in Chicago . . . with close proximity to U of Chicago and Northwestern, most companies choose to recruit there. In line with the outdated thinking 'You'll never get fired for buying IBM,' most firms feel the same way about those two schools. This is unfortunate, but the truth."

Employers who most frequently hire Loyola MBAs include: Northern Trust, Federal Reserve Bank, Deloitte Touche Tohmatsu, Eli Lilly and Company, Sara Lee, Grant Thornton, Crain's Chicago Business, Archdiocese of Chicago, and Solo Cup.

Student Life and Environment

Loyola's Graduate School of Business "is located in the heart of Chicago" and "has two buildings where classes are held" where "the facilities are great. Classrooms are equipped with the latest technology, costing the university thousands per classroom. The libraries are very large and have resources that you need." A "new dorm building right next to the GSB" is very convenient for those who choose to live in school housing; students report that "the campus is safe" and that security is good. Those who live off campus report that the location "is easily accessible. There is good public transportation and regular shuttle services between the two campuses at downtown Chicago."

Business classes at Loyola "take place in the evening" (with a few weekend classes), so "Sometimes it feels like a commuter school in the sense that the students come to class and then leave to focus on their own personal/work lives. However, if you seek out clubs and organizations, a social life is available." Indeed, "there has, in the last year, been a significant increase in the school's coordinating activities for the students to network. Lots of mixers, several outings to local sport events and an increase in a sense of 'community' as opposed to 'just school.'" Full-time students even report "more opportunities than I can take advantage of. There are lectures, guest speakers, networking events, career fairs, study abroad programs, and social outings."

Admissions

Applicants to Loyola's Graduate School of Business must submit the following materials: a completed application form; one set of official transcripts for all completed undergraduate and graduate course work; an official GMAT test score report (applicants with a minimum of 10 years' managerial experience may submit an essay requesting a GMAT waiver); two letters of recommendation; a personal statement of goals; and a current resume. International applicants must submit all of the above materials as well as a Declaration and Certification of Finances form. International students whose first language is not English must submit official score reports for either the TOEFL or IELTS exams. Applicants whose transcripts are in a language other than English must have the transcripts translated and analyzed by an outside credentialing service.

FINANCIAL FACTS

Annual tuition	$29,835
Fees	$320
Cost of books	$800
Room & board (on/off-campus)	$13,000/$13,965
% of students receiving aid	87
% of first-year students receiving aid	63
% of students receiving loans	87
% of students receiving grants	11
Average award package	$14,370
Average grant	$7,369
Average student loan debt	$34,775

ADMISSIONS

Admissions Selectivity Rating	76
# of applications received	737
% applicants accepted	81
% acceptees attending	55
Average GMAT	560
Range of GMAT	510–610
Average GPA	3.34
TOEFL required of international students	Yes
Minimum TOEFL (paper/computer)	550/213
Application fee	$50
International application fee	$50
Regular application deadline	7/15
Regular notification	Rolling
Deferment available	Yes
Maximum length of deferment	1 year
Transfer students accepted	Yes
Transfer application policy Up to 9 hours can transfer from AACSB-accredited institutions.	
Non-fall admissions	Yes
Need-blind admissions	Yes

Applicants Also Look At

DePaul University, Illinois Institute of Technology, Northern Illinois University, Northwestern University, University of Chicago, University of Illinois at Chicago, University of Illinois at Urbana-Champaign.

EMPLOYMENT PROFILE

Career Rating	68	Grads Employed by Function	%	Avg. Salary
Primary Source of Full-time Job Acceptances		Finance	8	$60,595
School-facilitated activities	17 (12%)	Human Resources	2	$51,200
Graduate-facilitated activities	104 (76%)	Marketing	5	$70,518
Unknown	16 (12%)	MIS	1	$56,660
Percent employed	22	Operations	1	$57,333
		Consulting	4	$43,200
		General Management	1	$93,400
		Other	5	$65,176

Top 5 Employers Hiring Grads
Accenture; Euromonitor International; Grant Thornton; Ernst & Young; Loyola University Chicago

LOYOLA UNIVERSITY—NEW ORLEANS
JOSEPH A. BUTT, S.J. COLLEGE OF BUSINESS ADMINISTRATION

GENERAL INFORMATION

Type of school	Private
Affiliation	Roman Catholic/Jesuit
Environment	City
Academic calendar	Semester

SURVEY SAYS...
Cutting edge classes
Solid preparation in:
General management

STUDENTS

Enrollment of parent institution	4,874
Enrollment of business school	70
% male/female	92/8
% out-of-state	5
% part-time	85
% minorities	4
% international	1
Average age at entry	25
Average years work experience at entry	2

ACADEMICS

Academic Experience Rating	**76**
Student/faculty ratio	13:1
Profs interesting rating	91
Profs accessible rating	96
% female faculty	25
% minority faculty	15

Joint Degrees
MBA/JD 4–5 years.

Academics

With a program small enough to provide a "family-like environment," Loyola University—New Orleans serves a largely local student body seeking a "personalized education experience" at an institution with "a solid academic reputation." Just how comfortable is it? Many of the students we surveyed happily identified themselves as former Loyola undergrads who couldn't wait to get back here to pursue graduate work.

Loyola offers a general MBA. The school also offers a combined MBA/JD, which typically takes 4 to 5 years to complete. The MBA is divided into four components: a basic core, designed for the needs of students with little undergraduate background in business (business majors can place out of some or all of these courses); an advanced core; electives; and a capstone course called Global Strategy, which emphasizes case study and integrative analysis. Flexibility "to accommodate working students" is the key in this program. Students may attend on either a part-time or full-time basis and, since classes meet only once weekly in the evening, have some latitude in fashioning their class schedules. The curriculum is designed to "challenge you to think and think of things from different perspectives."

Students report that their "outstanding" professors "are very enthusiastic about the subject matter, which makes class time so much more valuable. It is clear that the priority of professors is teaching and working with the students." Better still, small class sizes mean "You get one-on-one time to discuss issues at length with your professors." The scale of the program also allows administrators to provide more personalized service. Students tell us that they are "really active and helpful in assisting students to achieve their academic goals. They try to accommodate students as best as possible to ensure that the proper classes are offered and that there are interesting business electives to take."

Career and Placement

Loyola maintains a Counseling and Career Services Center to serve all undergraduate and graduate students of the university. Services include self-assessment instruments, career counseling, internship and job placement services, and guidance in resume writing, interviewing, job search, and salary negotiation skills. The office organizes on-campus recruiting events. Students remind us that "we don't only use the Career Center on the main campus; we all network with each other and recent alumni to pass on applicable contacts to each other." The MBA Association also contributes by organizing networking events.

In recent years, Loyola MBAs have been placed with: AmSouth Bank, BearingPoint, Clear Channel Radio, Entergy, Freeport-McMoRan, Harrah's, Hibernia Bank, Northrop Grumman, Prudential Financial Services, Qualified Health Services, Ritz Carlton, Trumpet Advertising and Marketing, U.S. Department of Commerce, and Whitney Bank.

ADMISSIONS CONTACT: STEPHANIE MANSFIELD, MBA MARKETING AND COMMUNICATIONS
ADDRESS: 6363 ST. CHARLES AVENUE, CAMPUS BOX 15 NEW ORLEANS, LA 70118 UNITED STATES
PHONE: (504) 864-7965 • FAX: (504) 864-7970
E-MAIL: SMANS@LOYNO.EDU • WEBSITE: BUSINESS.LOYNO.EDU/MBA

Student Life and Environment

Loyola's MBA program is a small evening program in which students are "supportive and friendly." "Everyone wants to see everyone else succeed." It's not as close as your typical cohort-based daytime program, however—in part because students simply don't spend as much time together. "More barbeques and [other] functions would help." Even if the school did step up the level of activities, though, there's no guarantee it would foster greater student involvement.

Loyola is located in the fashionable uptown section of New Orleans. The campus sustained no flooding during Hurricane Katrina. In fact, damage to the campus was relatively minor, with the school Recreational Complex taking the biggest hit. The school was closed during the Fall 2005 semester but reopened in January 2006. More than 90 percent of its undergraduate population returned. Students today report that the campus is small but pretty and that "the library is the best! The school understands that a library isn't just about books any more and offers lots of technical resources that can help you find any kind of information you need."

Loyola draws a student body representing "diverse backgrounds." One MBA writes, "I have really enjoyed getting to know the other students. Everyone's background is so different that we are able to learn from many different perspectives. There is some noticeable difference between the older, experienced students and the younger, straight-out-of-school students in both their personal and academic styles, but nothing that is impossible to work with." Students here tend to be "intellectually curious team players as opposed to cutthroat competitors." Many have full-time jobs.

Admissions

Loyola requires the following of applicants to its MBA program: official transcripts for all past postsecondary academic work; an official score report for the GMAT; two letters of recommendation; a 400-word personal statement of purpose; and a resume. International students whose first language is not English must also submit TOEFL scores (the minimum acceptable score is 237; scores can be no more than 2 years old); all international students must provide an affidavit demonstrating sufficient financial resources to support themselves during their tenure at the university. Work experience, though not required, is strongly recommended. Interviews are optional.

FINANCIAL FACTS

Annual tuition	$18,264
Fees	$856
Cost of books	$1,500
Room & board (off-campus)	$8,000
Average grant	$5,000

ADMISSIONS

Admissions Selectivity Rating	**74**
# of applications received	41
% applicants accepted	91
% acceptees attending	63
Average GMAT	527
Range of GMAT	500–550
Average GPA	3.34
TOEFL required of international students	Yes
Minimum TOEFL (paper/computer)	580/237
Application fee	$50
International application fee	$50
Regular application deadline	6/15
Regular notification	Rolling
Deferment available	Yes
Maximum length of deferment	1 academic year
Transfer students accepted	Yes
Transfer application policy 6 credit hours from an AACSB-accredited program.	
Non-fall admissions	Yes
Need-blind admissions	Yes

Applicants Also Look At
Louisiana State University.

EMPLOYMENT PROFILE	
Career Rating	79

MARIST COLLEGE
SCHOOL OF MANAGEMENT

Academics

For more than 30 years, Marist College has offered working professionals the opportunity to pursue an MBA degree on a part-time basis. Today, the school continues to operate a part-time, campus-based program, while also distinguishing itself as "one of the few AACSB-accredited graduate schools that offered an MBA program fully online, while being affordable." While part-time students in other MBA programs complain about the difficulties of balancing home life, work, and school, the Marist "program [is] tailored to those working long hours and still offer[s] a strong reputation with a decent curriculum." The flexibility of the program is perhaps its most attractive feature, allowing students to take traditional or online courses, or a blend of the two. Indeed, students tell us that "being able to mix online courses as well as traditional in-class courses is very beneficial for students who also work full time."

The curriculum at Marist is divided into foundation courses, core courses, and electives; however, foundation courses may be waived for students who have an undergraduate degree in business. Taking two courses per semester and one course in the summer, many students are able to earn their MBA in just 2 years. To accommodate the schedule of working professionals, traditional classroom courses are scheduled one evening per week, Monday through Thursday, on the Marist College campus, as well as in off-site classrooms. Online classes are available 24 hours a day, 7 days a week, and have no on-campus requirement whatsoever. "The high quality of the program and professors" draws many students to the school, and online students are welcome to meet with faculty in person while taking the course. Students say Marist professors are, on the whole, "accessible and very helpful."

The school is technologically and organizationally equipped to help online students plan and execute a quality educational program. A student shares, "Enrollment is a breeze, and the Assistant Dean who works with online students is very helpful." Another adds, "The administration was very helpful in getting [me] access to courses to meet my academic plan." Online classes are very similar to classroom courses in that students must be prepared to turn in assignments, take exams, participate in class, and meet deadlines. Course work is fully multimedia and includes group projects, case studies, computer simulations, and presentations. Students insist that they build a sense of community via the Internet, and "Group projects illuminate personalities pretty well even over the web." A current student enthuses, "I completed my program completely online. I have found many students to be actively engaged and willing to collaborate via online chat, e-mail, and over the phone."

Whether online or in the classroom, students say the program is high quality and challenging. One shares, "I started here after moving away from Chicago, where I attended a top-10 MBA program (Kellogg). I find the classes to be rigorous and academically competitive. I was worried that the courses would seem much easier than Kellogg['s], but my fears were misplaced." Even so, the program is fairly structured, and some students say they'd like to have the option of "more concentrations within the program" that are "structured to specific disciplines" while "removing some courses that aren't as beneficial to one's future goals."

Career and Placement

Ninety-five percent of Marist students work full-time while completing their MBA. Ranging from relatively young professionals to senior managers, most students plan to stay with their current company upon termination of the program. For those who are

ADMISSIONS CONTACT: KELLY HOLMES, DIRECTOR OF ADMISSION
ADDRESS: 3399 NORTH ROAD POUGHKEEPSIE, NY 12601 UNITED STATES
PHONE: 845-575-3800 • FAX: 845-575-3166
E-MAIL: GRADUATE@MARIST.EDU • WEBSITE: WWW.MARIST.EDU/MANAGEMENT/MBA

looking for a new position, MBA students have access to the Marist College Career Services Office, which hosts career-building workshops, career conferences, career fairs, and a host of online resources. The 2007 Spring Career Conference at Marist included a number of regional employers, including: Affinity Group/Mass Mutual, Aldi, CVS Pharmacy, First Investors Corporation, Gap, Gunn Allen Financial Corporation, Household Finance, IBM, MetLife, Morgan Stanley, Northwestern Mutual Financial Network, Ryder Transportation, Target, United Parcel Service, Wells Fargo, and Worldwide Express.

Student Life and Environment

Because a large percentage of Marist courses are taught via the Internet, the student community is largely virtual. Even so, Marist students have the opportunity to get to know their classmates through the phone and Internet, describing them as "hardworking, intelligent [people], with work and family obligations." Those who attend classes on campus tell us the school promotes a "good sense of community" and "attracts people who are just plain nice and helpful both to work and teach and as students." While the business school is located on Marist's lively undergraduate campus, there aren't many social or recreational activities targeted at business students. Indeed, some would like to see "more opportunities for socializing, networking, out-of-classroom learning (speakers, etc.)."

Marist is located in Poughkeepsie, New York, a small city about 90 minutes from both New York City and Albany. A picturesque campus environment, the school is located near the Catskill Mountains, and the surrounding area is a paradise for hiking, cross-country skiing, mountain biking, and other outdoor activities. There are also a number of attractions in the town of Poughkeepsie, including the historic Barbadon Theater and Mid-Hudson Civic Center, which show opera, ballet, Broadway shows, and popular performers.

Admission

To apply to the graduate program at the Marist School of Management, students must possess an undergraduate degree in any discipline. Whether applying to the online or on-campus program, all applicants must submit a completed graduate school application, an application fee, two letters of recommendation, responses to the essay questions, official GMAT scores, and official transcripts from undergraduate study.

FINANCIAL FACTS

Annual tuition	$11,970
Cost of books	$1,398
% of students receiving aid	21
% of first-year students receiving aid	20
% of students receiving loans	12
% of students receiving grants	7
Average award package	$14,869
Average grant	$1,656

ADMISSIONS

Admissions Selectivity Rating	**71**
# of applications received	67
% applicants accepted	85
% acceptees attending	70
Average GMAT	532
Range of GMAT	470–575
Average GPA	3.42
TOEFL required of international students	Yes
Minimum TOEFL (paper/computer)	550/213
Application fee	$50
International application fee	$50
Regular application deadline	7/1
Regular notification	7/15
Deferment available	Yes
Maximum length of deferment	1 year
Transfer students accepted	Yes
Transfer application policy No more than six credit hours of core courses accepted from AACSB accredited programs.	
Non-fall admissions	Yes
Need-blind admissions	Yes

Applicants Also Look At

Fairfield University, Pace University, University of Connecticut.

EMPLOYMENT PROFILE

Career Rating	81	Grads Employed by Function	% Avg. Salary
Percent employed	92	General Management	92 $65,000

MARQUETTE UNIVERSITY
COLLEGE OF BUSINESS ADMINISTRATION

Academics

The MBA program at Marquette University pursues "transformative education," and students tell us that it succeeds on this front. One tells us, "The Global Environment of Business Class that I took exemplified the school's mission. I definitely look at international business in a new light after taking that class. It's not too often that a business class can shape perspectives like that." This ability, along with Marquette's "strong academic reputation," its "proximity to Fortune 500 companies," and the "Christian ethics" infused through the school's Jesuit traditions all attract a largely part-time student body to the school.

Marquette's busy MBAs appreciate "the flexibility afforded by the part-time MBA program. It is invaluable," allowing students "to take classes at night and on the weekends, allowing us to work full time while attending school." An efficient faculty and administration also help; according to one student, "The accessibility and assistance from professors and the staff in the Graduate School of Management are among the program's great strengths. They help and guide us to make the best choices for our individual situations." Professors "recognize that the students are working and will always make time to meet them." In the debit column, "Electives for grad students are very limited and therefore getting a specialization on your MBA is very difficult without going past your graduation date." Students also wish that the school would "offer more online or blended courses," noting optimistically that "the program has started to experiment with this approach."

MU teaches a broad curriculum that "exposes students to a number of different types of problems, whether they are strategic or pragmatic." In addition, students tell us, "Each course blends different facets of real problems faced in industry with theoretical knowledge to fully dissect the issues and understand them." Marquette offers a number of unique joint degrees, including an MBA/JD in sports business, an MBA/MS in political science, and a Healthcare Technology Management Program offered in collaboration with the Medical College of Wisconsin.

Career and Placement

The Career Services Center at Marquette provides counseling and placement services to all undergraduates and graduate students at the university. The office organizes workshops, one-on-one counseling sessions, on-site recruiting events, and job databases. In addition, the College of Business offers career management services through its Hire Learning Program. A few students here describe the office as "second to none," but that's definitely the minority opinion; most tell us that Marquette's MBA program "could improve on providing job opportunities. Because most people in the program are employed, it does not have any on-campus interviewing. However, there are some full-time students and students looking to change careers and opportunities to interview with companies." A recent career fair promoted by exclusively for MBAs drew "primarily local firms, of various sizes. Almost all participating companies were looking for recent undergraduates for entry-level positions, rather than experienced business graduate students."

Student Life and Environment

Marquette offers MBA classes in three locations: downtown Milwaukee, Waukesha, and Kohler. In all locations, "many students work full time and do not have the time to enjoy the [available] opportunities" to get involved in campus life. As one student explains, "The workload is substantial; it's like taking on a part-time job for 20 to 30 hours a week."

ADMISSIONS CONTACT: DR. JEANNE SIMMONS, ASSOCIATE DEAN
ADDRESS: PO BOX 1881, STRAZ HALL SUITE 275 MILWAUKEE, WI 53201-1881 UNITED STATES
PHONE: 414-288-7145 • FAX: 414-288-8078
E-MAIL: MBA@MARQUETTE.EDU • WEBSITE: WWW.MARQUETTE.EDU/GSM

On a positive note, the fact that nearly 90 percent of all students work full time presents excellent networking opportunities.

For those who can make the time, opportunities to get involved "are abundant for students who want to be involved," particularly at the Milwaukee campus. MBAs report that "Basketball is the major sport on campus, and I like the fact that tickets for the Marquette Fanatic Student Section are offered to graduate students. In my opinion, this helps MBAs to feel more included in the campus community." Some MBAs even find time to attend the many on-campus theater and musical productions.

Marquette MBAs "are hard-working and personable" and are also "very helpful to other students. It's a great group to learn with." The typical student is "in his mid to late twenties and is in a serious relationship. Some have just started having families. All are career-oriented and take the MBA program very seriously. Most are already in management positions." There "is some ethnic and racial diversity," and "everyone seems to get along."

Admissions

Applicants to the Marquette MBA program must provide the admissions office official transcripts for all previous post-secondary academic work, an official GMAT score report, a personal essay, and a resume. International students are additionally required to submit three letters of recommendation and an official score report for the TOEFL or another acceptable English proficiency exam. Two letters of recommendation are required for the Executive MBA program and for the MS programs in applied economics and engineering management; letters of recommendation are optional for the MBA and MS in accounting and human resource programs. Marquette encourages applicants to apply for full admission but also offers a temporary-admission option, good for one semester only. Students applying to campuses other than the downtown campus must remember to specify their campus of choice on their application.

FINANCIAL FACTS

Annual tuition	$17,000
Fees	$0
Cost of books	$750

ADMISSIONS

Admissions Selectivity Rating	**75**
# of applications received	323
% applicants accepted	86
% acceptees attending	74
Average GMAT	572
Average GPA	3.26
TOEFL required of international students	Yes
Minimum TOEFL (paper/computer)	550/NR
Application fee	$50
International application fee	$50
Regular application deadline	Rolling
Regular notification	Rolling
Deferment available	Yes
Maximum length of deferment	1 year
Transfer students accepted	Yes
Transfer application policy We accept transfers from most Jesuit Schools will also accept up to 6 approved credits from AACSB schools.	
Non-fall admissions	Yes

Applicants Also Look At

DePaul University, Loyola University—Chicago, University of Wisconsin—Madison, University of Wisconsin—Milwaukee.

MASSACHUSETTS INSTITUTE OF TECHNOLOGY
SLOAN SCHOOL OF MANAGEMENT

GENERAL INFORMATION
Type of school	Private
Environment	City
Academic calendar	Semester

SURVEY SAYS...
Good peer network
Happy students
Solid preparation in:
Teamwork
Quantitative skills
Entrepreneurial studies

STUDENTS
Enrollment of parent institution	10,233
Enrollment of business school	781
% male/female	69/31
% out-of-state	80
% minorities	7
% international	32
Average age at entry	28
Average years work experience at entry	5

ACADEMICS
Academic Experience Rating	**99**
Student/faculty ratio	7:1
Profs interesting rating	88
Profs accessible rating	80
% female faculty	19
% minority faculty	13

Joint Degrees
SM or MBA in Management, SM in Engineering 2 years.

Academics

The MIT Sloan MBA Program has "both the best entrepreneurial program of any business school in the world and the most fantastic technology available," students insist. And that's hardly all the school offers; on the contrary, students tell us that MIT Sloan is "the best all-around program in allowing students to learn to their innovative endeavors while still teaching and offering the most academically challenging traditional MBA curriculum of all schools."

MIT expertly exploits the synergies of its location in a great city and its affiliation with a great university. Students brag about "Sloan's ties to the real business world. In the last week alone, I listened to three Fortune 500 CEOs speak on campus, and had dinner with a partner from a local VC firm and a partner from a local law firm. Many of the professors have incredibly deep experience and connections to industry and bring great insight along those dimensions." They are especially impressed with "how connected MIT Sloan is with companies in a non-recruiting session," which they justly see as "a real point of differentiation" for the program. MIT's Herculean status in the worlds of math, engineering, and science contribute substantially to the MBA program. "There are very low barriers between schools; interdisciplinary work and entrepreneurship are actively encouraged between business and engineering," one student writes. MIT's many strengths make possible such programs as the Leaders for Manufacturing Program—"an operations and logistics-focused program" that students call "the best dual-degree program in business and engineering in the country"—and the Biomedical Enterprise Program, to which "Anyone who is interested in business within the life sciences should apply. This is a top-notch program that allows students to study business and science while providing the opportunity to interact in a close setting with industry leaders."

Throughout the program, MIT Sloan emphasizes "a strong hands-on approach to learning" and cooperative work. "At MIT Sloan, practically everything is done in teams," students tell us. The workload "is what you expect of MIT: rigorous and quantitative." Most don't mind the challenge; as one explains, "Although the workload is heavy, people actually want to prepare just for the opportunity to participate in discussions in where faculty are posing questions to the most pressing business issues. A place like MIT Sloan is a reason why people want to continue their education." The cherry on the sundae is global travel; "Everyone travels on trips or treks, both foreign and domestic. I am headed to Japan for 10 days with 200 of my classmates. These are student-planned trips that are excellent ways to get to see other cultures and get business exposure around the world."

Career and Placement

MIT Sloan's Career Development Office provides MBAs with a range of career management resources, including seminars, self-assessment tools, library materials, and online databases and services. Students tell us that "the CDO is great for traditional MBA jobs such as banking, consulting and the major corporations and tech companies, but not as good with smaller and tougher markets such as private equity and venture capital." They also observe: "The new focus on entrepreneurship means that a lot of MIT Sloan students are starting companies or working at early-stage startups right after school. The CDO is still figuring out how to deal with these students." Supplementing the CDO, "Clubs have a huge impact on career choices, setting up relationships, bringing in speakers, etc. Alumni are also a great resource, and a fantastic channel for connecting. Many Sloanies are looking to work for startups, tech, or smaller firms without traditional recruiting seasons, and alumni are very helpful in this regard."

ADMISSIONS CONTACT: ROD GARCIA, ADMISSIONS DIRECTOR
ADDRESS: 50 MEMORIAL DRIVE, E52-126 CAMBRIDGE, MA 02139 UNITED STATES
PHONE: 617-258-5434 • FAX: 617-253-6405
E-MAIL: MBAADMISSIONS@SLOAN.MIT.EDU • WEBSITE: MITSLOAN.MIT.EDU/MBA

Employers most likely to hire MIT Sloan MBAs include Bain & Company, Booz Allen Hamilton, The Boston Consulting Group, Citi, Dell, Fidelity, Goldman Sachs, Google, IBM, Lehman Brothers, and McKinsey & Company.

Student Life and Environment

MIT Sloan keeps students plenty busy with work, but they still somehow find time to "participate in clubs and set up the many conferences we host. For example, the Sports Conference this spring had general managers from each of the top four professional sports (basketball, hockey, baseball, and football) sit on a panel about leadership and winning moderated by Peter Gammons. How cool is that?" Students tell us that MIT Sloan "provides more opportunities than anyone could expect. I find that I spend about 50 percent of my time on academics and the other 50 percent working with clubs and local companies, a perfect balance that allows me to take what I've learned in the classroom and apply it in a real-world setting." It's easy to get overwhelmed; according to one student, "School is a blur with so many classes, activities, guest speakers, etc. In terms of social activities, I think you have to pick your spots. Otherwise you will fall behind in your coursework and job search, but the options are pretty limitless here."

About the only area of dissatisfaction here concerns the school's facilities, and that problem will soon be addressed; the school is currently constructing a new business school building that is scheduled to open in fall 2010.

Admissions

Completed applications to the MIT Sloan MBA program include a cover letter, two letters of recommendation, post-secondary transcripts (self-reported prior to interview; if called for an interview, applicants must provide official transcripts), a current, resume, four personal essays, supplemental information, and GMAT or GRE scores. The school requires additional materials from applicants to the Entrepreneurship Program, the Leaders for Manufacturing Program, and the Biomedical Enterprise Program. The nature of the program favors candidates with strong quantitative and analytical skills, as well as those with strong personal attributes including leadership, teamwork, and ability to make decisions and pursue goals.

FINANCIAL FACTS

Annual tuition	$46,784
Fees	$250
Cost of books	$1,800
Room & board	$27,690
% of students receiving aid	75
% of first-year students receiving aid	63
% of students receiving loans	69
% of students receiving grants	27
Average award package	$46,213
Average grant	$21,084
Average student loan debt	$55,400

ADMISSIONS

Admissions Selectivity Rating	**98**
# of applications received	3,896
% applicants accepted	14
% acceptees attending	61
Average GMAT	710
Range of GMAT	665–760
Average GPA	3.5
Application fee	$230
International application fee	$230
Regular application deadline	1/10
Regular notification	10/28, 1/13
Application Deadline/Notification	
Round 1:	10/28 / 01/13
Round 2:	01/07 / 04/09
Need-blind admissions	Yes

EMPLOYMENT PROFILE

Career Rating	96	Grads Employed by Function	% Avg. Salary
Primary Source of Full-time Job Acceptances		Finance	26 $103,016
School-facilitated activities	219 (76%)	Marketing	8.1 $93,854
Graduate-facilitated activities	58 (20%)	Operations	5 $102,529
Unknown	10 (4%)	Consulting	40 $114,891
Average base starting salary	$107,990	General Management	6 $105,056
Percent employed	94	Other	2 $107,000

Top 5 Employers Hiring Grads
McKinsey & Company; Bain & Company; Boston Consulting Group; Booz Allen Hamilton; Lehman Brothers

McMaster University
DeGroote School of Business

GENERAL INFORMATION
Type of school   Public

SURVEY SAYS...
Friendly students
Good social scene
Good peer network
Solid preparation in:
Accounting
Teamwork
Communication/interpersonal skills
Presentation skills

STUDENTS
Enrollment of parent institution	33,202
Enrollment of business school	315
% male/female	66/34
% part-time	36
% international	10
Average age at entry	27
Average years work experience at entry	3.6

ACADEMICS
Academic Experience Rating	**75**
Student/faculty ratio	7:1
Profs interesting rating	66
Profs accessible rating	89
% female faculty	15

Prominent Alumni
Karen Maidment, Chief Financial & Administrative Officer, BMO; David Feather, President, Mackenzie Financial Servives Inc.; Paul Cummings, President and CEO, Auto World Imports; Rebecca Repa, VP, Redevelopment & Diagnostic, St.Joseph's Hosp.; Stephen Smith, Past President/CEO, Westjet Airlines.

Academics

The DeGroote School of Business at McMaster University offers conventional full-time and part-time MBAs, but its co-op program (with paid work terms) truly distinguishes it from the competition. It is a program that, in the words of one student, is "vital to the school's differentiation factor." Through co-op, students with no business experience can enter DeGroote and 2 years later emerge with an MBA and significant professional experience.

DeGroote's co-op program is especially "friendly to young grads," as it carries no prerequisite of professional experience though 46 percent have some work experience. Students appreciate that the program "offers a great way for fresh graduates to gain specialized work experience while concurrently completing their degree. The ability to simultaneously learn theory and apply it in the business world is priceless." The program also suits some already in the midst of their careers. One student revels in the fact that co-op offers "the best way to get a job in a different field" than his experience was in.

DeGroote also offers an accelerated MBA program for individuals with an undergraduate business degree. Students enter at what is traditionally the program's second year and have eight months of intensive study. Students tell us that DeGroote offers "good networking" with the biotech and pharmaceutical industries, and they praise the "innovative" curriculum for its emphasis on "leadership and ethical culture." The program also stresses "team building and cross-functional teamwork," thereby building necessary business communication skills. Some here lament that "quantitative material is afforded seemingly little attention . . . the material covered is cursory," while others observe that "first-year courses are too much like undergraduate [business] courses." Qualified students can enter the MBA program from any undergraduate discipline.

Even those who see problems, however, agree that the school is headed in the right direction. One student commends, "I have been tremendously impressed with the direction [the Dean] has taken the school in recent years." Another agrees, "No question about it, the leaders of our program are putting it on the map." Students like that the current Dean "is not from the academic world and has brought a practical perspective to the school and courses. . . . He knows what he is talking about." They also love that "the price of the program (compared to other programs in the Ontario area) is low." Sums up one MBA, "Given . . . the cost of the program, I felt that McMaster offered a far superior return on investment than most business schools."

Career and Placement

DeGroote's Centre for Business Career Development "is an excellent resource for students." The center shows an "aggressive ambition" that "is necessary in this job market, and is beginning to pay dividends" for students. The office provides coaching and recruitment services throughout the MBA program and partners with many high end and notable Canadian employers to "deliver seamless, on-campus company information sessions and career recruiting," according to the school's website. Some here feel that "more diverse career opportunities would be nice. Currently, our on-campus recruitment is very focused on accounting and finance jobs, and they do this very well. However, opportunities in other areas such as consulting and marketing leave something to be desired."

Employers most likely to hire DeGroote MBAs include: Accenture, Bank of Nova Scotia, Bell Canada, BMO, Canadian Tire, CIBC World Markets, Gennum Corporation, Hydro One, PricewaterhouseCoopers, Scotiabank, Canadian Tire Financial Services, Eli Lilly, Scotia Capital, ArcelorMittal Dofasco, The Ministry of Health, TD Securities, and Telus.

Student Life and Environment

Students enjoy a "very social atmosphere" at DeGroote. One reports, "We all spend a lot of time with each other, whether it's outside of school or just grabbing coffee. You can always find someone to get coffee within Innis (our business library) at any time of day or night." They also tell us that "life on campus is excellent. It is a home away from home for anyone who wants to make it so. Facilities are open at all hours, the environment is comfortable, and the school has gone out of its way to make MBAs a priority (e.g., the entire top floor of the building is now an MBA study space)."

Academics here "are challenging but still provide us with free time to pursue other interests as well." A new recreation center that opened recently "is state of the art" while classrooms are "modern and well equipped." The DeGroote MBA Association "plans frequent events and activities"; "There are several MBA intramural sports teams" and "opportunities to participate in case competitions." No wonder students tell us that life here is "quite busy" and things move at a "fast pace. Fortunately, there is always help when you need it."

Hometown Hamilton "is not the most attractive place to live in general, but the location of the school in the west end of the city is quite safe and attractive. The mid-range size of the school in comparison to other Canadian universities gives it the best of both worlds: small-school networking with larger-school sports and community involvement." McMaster University is located within close proximity to the vibrant and diverse city of Toronto.

Admissions

The Admissions Staff at DeGroote focuses primarily on applicants' final 2 years of undergraduate work (minimum 3.0 GPA strongly preferred) and their GMAT scores in assessing candidates. The process is highly holistic in nature. Work experience and demonstrated community leadership skills are also considered, as are evidence of ethical maturity and business aptitude. Applicants to the co-op program are assessed by interview for communication skills, initiative, leadership potential, and general experience. Applicants must submit official transcripts for all previous undergraduate and graduate work, an official score report for the GMAT, two letters of recommendation, and a current resume. One year of post-collegiate work experience is required of applicants to the full-time and part-time programs; applicants to the co-op program need not have prior professional experience. International students whose first language is not English must submit an official score report for the TOEFL (minimum score:100, internet-based test; 250, computer-based test; or 600, paper-based test strongly preferred).

FINANCIAL FACTS

Annual tuition	$11,200
Cost of books	$1,500
Room & board	
(on/off-campus)	$5,500/$4,300
% of students receiving aid	30
% of first-year students	
receiving aid	38
% of students receiving grants	27
Average award package	$3,400
Average grant	$2,500

ADMISSIONS

Admissions Selectivity Rating	**85**
# of applications received	359
% applicants accepted	65
% acceptees attending	66
Average GMAT	619
Average GPA	3.0
TOEFL required of	
international students	Yes
Minimum TOEFL	
(paper/computer)	600/250
Application fee	$150
International application fee	$150
Regular application deadline	6/15
Regular notification	Rolling
Non-fall admissions	Yes

Applicants Also Look At
University of Toronto, York University.

EMPLOYMENT PROFILE

Career Rating	81	Grads Employed by Function	%	Avg. Salary
		Finance	23	$55,417
		Marketing	19	$63,987
		General Management	23	$73,473
		Other	35	$74,807

Top 5 Employers Hiring Grads
Courtyard Group; KPMG; Eli Lilly; TD Financial Group/TD Canadian Trust; Local Health Integration Networks; Courtyard Group

MERCER UNIVERSITY—ATLANTA
EUGENE W. STETSON SCHOOL OF BUSINESS AND ECONOMICS

Academics

Designed for the convenience of its predominantly professional student body, Mercer University in Atlanta offers a number of accommodations to suit busy MBAs. Classes here meet only once a week, on weekday evenings or on Saturday. Eight-week sessions help students proceed through the program at a steady pace, while five separate admissions entry points mean students can begin the program at virtually any time of the year. As the school's website asserts, "The program is tailored to meet the needs of individuals already employed as managers," as well as those "preparing for advancement into middle-management and administrative levels."

Mercer is a Baptist university with its main campus an hour south of Atlanta, in Macon, Georgia, and a graduate and professional campus in Atlanta. The school draws on its roots to provide a program that "focuses on ethical leadership and problem-solving skills" in order to give students a "competitive edge" in today's business world. This goal is further achieved through "the establishment of a real-world experience base by maintaining continuous interaction with community organizations, profit and non-profit, through seminars and special programs for practicing managers and administrators." The school's location in a major metropolis is a great asset in achieving this goal.

The heart of the Mercer MBA in Atlanta is a core curriculum covering managerial economics, managerial accounting, marketing, management information systems, corporation finance, operations management science, and ethics. A concluding simulation student seminar and electives are also part of the program. Prior to beginning core course work, incoming Mercer students may be required to complete a sequence of four non-graduate-level foundation courses covering micro- and macro-economics, accounting and finance, management and marketing, and business law. Equivalent courses previously completed at the undergraduate level may allow students to place out of these requirements.

Mercer MBAs appreciate their "professional" and "personable" professors who are "helpful outside the class, open to feedback, [and] truly care that the students are learning." One respondent exclaims, "They push you!" Students also love "the timeliness of the program" and the "state-of-the-art equipment in the lecture rooms," but wish that "more class options were available throughout the school year."

Career and Placement

The Office of Career Services at Mercer "provides support to students and alumni in the areas of decision-making and networking," according to the school catalog, which also notes that "students and alumni can view and be informed of ongoing full-time, part-time, and internship opportunities by registering online with SUCCESSTRAK. Annual career days, an academic majors fair, a senior kick-off event, and presentations on resume design and other job-search topics" are all offered here. Students here tell us that "recruiting and corporate partnerships" all could use improvement.

ADMISSIONS CONTACT: KAREN GOSS HERLITZ, ASSISTANT VICE PRESIDENT FOR ADMISSIONS
ADDRESS: MERCER UNIVERSITY, 3001 MERCER UNIVERSITY DRIVE ATLANTA, GA 30341-4155 U.S.
PHONE: 678-547-6417 • FAX: 678-547-6367
E-MAIL: ATLBUSADM@MERCER.EDU • WEBSITE: WWW.MERCER.EDU/BUSINESS

Student Life and Environment

Mercer's Atlanta campus is "primarily a commuter campus" where classes "are held in the evenings to accommodate working individuals." Although most students spend very little time on campus, a few would like to see a stronger MBA community and call for "more graduate associations, especially for minorities and women."

Mercer MBAs are "mostly full-time workers in the professional world" who "generally have substantial real-world experiences to contribute." This mélange of professionals makes for "good networking because there's lots of different people in different fields." Students also appreciate the "diverse mix of cultural ethnicities" drawn to Mercer's Atlanta campus.

Hometown Atlanta is one of the great cities of the Southeast, a corporate and cultural mecca that is home to Coca-Cola, The Home Depot, Delta, and a slew of other business giants. The city is awash in restaurants, clubs, live music venues, theaters, culture of every shape and form, and great professional athletics. Top that off with the fact that the weather's fantastic.

Admissions

Applicants to the Stetson MBA program at Mercer must provide the school with a completed application form, two sets of official transcripts from each postsecondary academic institution attended, a resume, and an official GMAT score report showing test results no more than five years old. In addition, international applicants whose first language is not English must demonstrate English proficiency through TOEFL scores. All students who received undergraduate degrees abroad must, at their own expense, provide an independent evaluation (and, where appropriate, a translation) of their undergraduate records. International students must additionally demonstrate the ability to finance their education at Mercer.

FINANCIAL FACTS

Annual tuition	$13,776
Fees	$160
Cost of books	$1,000
Room & board (off-campus)	$9,450
% of students receiving aid	60
% of first-year students receiving aid	60
% of students receiving loans	60
% of students receiving grants	1
Average award package	$12,666
Average grant	$1,140
Average student loan debt	$20,000

ADMISSIONS

Admissions Selectivity Rating	74
# of applications received	165
% applicants accepted	62
% acceptees attending	73
Average GMAT	503
Range of GMAT	450–610
Average GPA	3.0
TOEFL required of international students	Yes
Minimum TOEFL (paper/computer)	550/213
Application fee	$50
International application fee	$100
Regular application deadline	7/1
Regular notification	Rolling
Deferment available	Yes
Maximum length of deferment	5 years
Transfer students accepted	Yes
Transfer application policy Will consider up to two courses.	
Non-fall admissions	Yes
Need-blind admissions	Yes

Applicants Also Look At

Georgia State University, Kennesaw State University, University of Georgia.

EMPLOYMENT PROFILE

Career Rating	83	Grads Employed by Function	%	Avg. Salary
Percent employed	86	Finance	11	$69,000
		Human Resources	2	$83,000
		Marketing	21	$79,781
		MIS	5	$76,833
		Operations	12	$80,281
		Consulting	2	$112,000
		General Management	10	$69,528
		Other	27	$69,953

MERCER UNIVERSITY—MACON
EUGENE W. STETSON SCHOOL OF BUSINESS AND ECONOMICS

Academics

Baptist-affiliated Mercer University provides its MBAs a program that "focuses on ethical leadership and problem-solving skills" in order to give students a "competitive edge" in today's business world. Nearly all the students in this program attend part-time while working full-time. According to the school, "The program is tailored to meet the needs of individuals already employed as managers," as well as those "preparing for advancement into middle-management and administrative levels."

Incoming Mercer students should have at least 18 hours of undergraduate work in business with a grade of C or better; those lacking these credentials will need to complete an additional nine hours of graduate electives. All students must demonstrate mastery in statistics, microeconomics, and principles of finance, either through examination or successfully completed undergraduate work. Students lacking these credentials are required to take the appropriate foundation classes before beginning work on their MBA.

The heart of the Mercer MBA is a 12-course core curriculum covering financial reporting, operations management, applied microeconomic analysis, global macroeconomic environment, management and business law, corporate finance, accounting, leadership, and ethics. A seminar in strategic management, an integrative capstone class, and electives (available in accounting, economics, general business, management, MIS, and marketing) are also part of the program.

Students praise the MBA program for providing "lots of individual attention," an outcome of the school's choice to "keep class sizes small." The "solid faculty make themselves available," which is helpful since "some of the course work is hard for people who work full-time to get done." A surprising number of students here warn that class times are too often inconvenient for full-time workers, and some suggest class time could be used more wisely ("Lectures are too long!" says one). They also point out that "it would be nice to have a wider selection of classes," although they recognize that "at so small a school, it would be hard to offer more without increasing costs."

Career and Placement

The Office of Career Services at Mercer "provides support to students and alumni in the areas of decision-making and networking," according to the school catalog, which also notes that "students and alumni can view and be informed of ongoing full-time, part-time, and internship opportunities by registering online with SUCCESSTRAK. Annual career days, an academic majors fair, a senior kick-off event, and presentations on resume design and other job-search topics" are all offered here. Students in the MBA program would like to see the services improved.

ADMISSIONS CONTACT: ROBERT (BOB) HOLLAND, JR., DIRECTOR OF ACADEMIC ADMINISTRATION
ADDRESS: 1400 COLEMAN AVENUE, SSBE MACON, GA 31207 UNITED STATES
PHONE: 478-301-2835 • FAX: 478-301-2635
E-MAIL: HOLLAND_R@MERCER.EDU • WEBSITE: WWW2.MERCER.EDU

Student Life and Environment

"Most people in the MBA program work," so "there is limited outside contact" among Mercer MBAs, "but everyone is very close in class." The pace of life here is always a little frantic because most students are juggling full-time jobs and school obligations, but "it is especially frantic around finals and midterms, in part due to the number of classes each professor teaches."

Mercer students include "a mix of people from off campus who have full-time jobs and graduate assistants, as well as other Mercer employees." They "contribute a vast array of experience that enriches the program," students tell us. The school's Baptist affiliation tends to help the school attract minorities.

Hometown Macon, a city of about 125,000, is home to three other colleges and universities, making it a serious college town. The city offers all the typical school-town prerequisites, including clubs, bowling alleys, bars, cheap eats, and plenty of shopping. Medicine is big business here, as is education; insurance is another major player, as both GEICO and the Georgia Farm Bureau Federation maintain major operations in Macon.

Admissions

Applicants to the Stetson MBA program at Mercer must provide the school with a completed application form, two sets of official transcripts from each postsecondary academic institution attended, a resume, and an official GMAT score report showing test results no more than five years old. In addition, international applicants whose first language is not English must demonstrate English proficiency both through TOEFL scores and, upon arrival at the school, a test administered by the English Language Institute of Mercer University. All students who received undergraduate degrees abroad must, at their own expense, provide an independent evaluation (and, where appropriate, a translation) of their undergraduate records. International students must additionally demonstrate the ability to finance their education at Mercer.

FINANCIAL FACTS

Annual tuition	$20,000
Fees	$483
Cost of books	$2,000
Room & board (off-campus)	$7,000

ADMISSIONS

Admissions Selectivity Rating	**69**
# of applications received	15
% applicants accepted	100
% acceptees attending	100
Average GMAT	520
Range of GMAT	450–600
Average GPA	3.5
TOEFL required of international students	Yes
Minimum TOEFL (paper/computer)	550/213
Application fee	$50
International application fee	$50
Regular application deadline	rolling
Regular notification	rolling
Non-fall admissions	Yes
Need-blind admissions	Yes

MIAMI UNIVERSITY (OH)
RICHARD T. FARMER SCHOOL OF BUSINESS

Academics

The Richard T. Farmer School of Business at Miami University has completely revamped its MBA program over the last few years, and it finally rolled out its new-and-improved program for the 2005–2006 academic year. The new Farmer MBA is an accelerated 14-month full-time-only program (the school will introduce its new part-time program in 2006–2007) that emphasizes practical experience: All participants complete a nine-month extended internship and a capstone international field study. Early reviews are extremely positive. In one student's opinion, "This has to be one of the most progressive and relevant program designs available."

Miami's MBA program kicks off with a four-month "Summer Boot Camp," an intensive survey of graduate-level material in accounting, economics, information systems, marketing, organizational behavior, and statistics. Boot Camp lays the groundwork for the "highly integrated" classes of the Fall and Spring semesters. Fall semester focuses on internal enterprise by "investigating processes and functions within the business itself," according to the school's website. External enterprise, "those relationships or factors which affect the business but which are not found within the company itself, such as supply-chain management, vendor partnerships, and capital acquisition," is the focus of Spring classes. Throughout both semesters, students participate in an extended internship that sends them off-campus one day per week.

Students here brag that "our administration is of the highest quality—comprised of seasoned businesspeople who understand what the market's needs are for skills and qualities of tomorrow's MBA." They also appreciate the fact that "the program utilizes a group of consulting business partners (some of the most seasoned and recognized business leaders in their fields) who advise on the program design and career opportunities for its students. The program offers a unique opportunity for all of its students to mentor under these respectable business leaders, where a rapport can be built and subsequent networks can be expanded." Instructors also earn high praise for "always being willing to help. They are enthusiastic and passionate about their subjects, whether customer acquisition or strategy or new product development and integration."

Career and Placement

Miami's Office of Career Services "does an exceptional job bringing a diverse group of *Fortune* 500 companies in for recruiting," students report, observing that "the setup of the interviewing schedule allows each student a fair opportunity to interview for any position with any company on campus, but also requires responsibility, research, and awareness on the student's part." The office provides a number of other standard career-placement services, but students tell us that their careers receive their greatest push from the internships and mentoring relationships incorporated into the MBA program itself. One writes, "The exposure to top executives (Jeff Immelt, Brad Alford, John Faraci), the Mentorship program, and the integrated internship—it's all great. No other school places you with a *Fortune* 25 company for a whole year, but that's what this school did for me."

ADMISSIONS CONTACT: RITA MORROW, ASST. DIR. MBA PROGRAM
ADDRESS: 107 LAWS HALL OXFORD, OH 45056 UNITED STATES
PHONE: 513-529-6643 • FAX: 513-529-6992
E-MAIL: MIAMIMBA@MUOHIO.EDU • WEBSITE: MBA.MUOHIO.EDU

Student Life and Environment

Miami has upgraded its MBA program in recent years. It hasn't upgraded its facility yet, but it is in the process of doing just that. The school breaks ground on the $30 million Farmer Hall in the summer of 2006 and expects to have the new business center open for the Fall semester of 2008.

Students love the Miami campus, which one describes as "among the nicest I've seen." Hometown Oxford "is pretty nice. It is a college town so something is always going on, but the town is still very laid-back and residents are quite friendly. The atmosphere is light, young, vibrant, and active." The city is "also only 45 minutes away from Cincinnati, and with so many people commuting, the city is very accessible."

The Miami MBA student body "seems to be split. Half are very involved in the program, half are here to get their degree." Regardless of their level of commitment, everyone here "grows really close because of the small size of the class. We get along very well and know what to expect from one another."

Admissions

Admission to the MBA program at Miami University requires a minimum undergraduate GPA of 2.75, with a minimum GPA of 3.00 for the final two full years (i.e., four semesters) of undergraduate study; applicants must provide two official transcripts of all postsecondary academic work. GMAT scores are also required. Miami admissions officers also consider work experience (a minimum of three years post-undergraduate professional experience is typically required) and personal qualities as reflected in the essays, two letters of recommendation, and an interview. International students must meet all of the above requirements and must, in addition, demonstrate English competency through the TOEFL and the Test of Written English (TWE). Transcripts in languages other than English must be translated and must bear the official seal of the issuing institution.

FINANCIAL FACTS

Annual tuition (in-state/ out-of-state)	$9,643/$22,402
Fees	$2,223
Cost of books	$1,000
Room & board	$6,300
% of students receiving aid	100
% of first-year students receiving aid	100
% of students receiving loans	37
% of students receiving grants	100
Average award package	$17,543
Average grant	$2,800
Average student loan debt	$19,480

ADMISSIONS

Admissions Selectivity Rating	**84**
# of applications received	50
% applicants accepted	58
% acceptees attending	93
Average GMAT	558
Range of GMAT	510–610
Average GPA	3.2
TOEFL required of international students	Yes
Minimum TOEFL (paper/computer)	550/213
Application fee	$35
International application fee	$35
Regular application deadline	3/15
Regular notification	4/1
Deferment available	Yes
Maximum length of deferment	2 years
Non-fall admissions	Yes
Need-blind admissions	Yes

Applicants Also Look At

Indiana University—Bloomington, The Ohio State University, University of Cincinnati, University of Dayton, Xavier University.

EMPLOYMENT PROFILE			
Career Rating	**82**	**Grads Employed by Function**	**% Avg. Salary**
Primary Source of Full-time Job Acceptances		Marketing	23 $68,167
School-facilitated activities	10 (62%)	MIS	12 $100,000
Graduate-facilitated activities	4 (25%)	Consulting	23 $80,000
Unknown	2 (13%)	Other	42 $57,500
Average base starting salary	$67,625	**Top 5 Employers Hiring Grads**	
Percent employed	4	Huron Consulting; AC Nielsen; Procter & Gamble; Kroger	

MILLSAPS COLLEGE
ELSE SCHOOL OF MANAGEMENT

Academics

Reflecting the spirit and friendliness of the Millsaps undergraduate institution, the Else School of Management at Millsaps College offers a rigorous MBA program in a refreshingly intimate atmosphere. The student/faculty ratio at Millsaps is very low, with many classes taught in teams by two or more professors. In fact, "in class sizes of less than 20, we often have 2 PhDs or 1 PhD and a JD." These numbers allow for an engaging and productive classroom experience: "Classes focus on participation and discussion," and "students are eager to learn as well as participate in class."

While professors at Millsaps actively engage in research and professional activities, they "really love teaching and their students," and "are available outside of class through e-mail or meetings. They give students the one-on-one attention that you'd expect at a small school." For students who are struggling with course work or wish to solicit professional advice, professors "always have an open-door policy and are very open to questions, comments, or suggestions." No matter what subjects they teach, "all the professors know a lot about their fields, but they also know about other fields so they help us relate all aspects of business together." According to one student, "they prepare us for the real world, not just the academics."

While the academic atmosphere at Millsaps is friendly and supportive, students make it clear that "the course work is challenging." Overall, students value the preparation this workload gives them; in particular, students appreciate the fact that "the program really focuses on effective oral and written communications skills." In fact, "several weekend communications seminars are part of the core curriculum." A current student tells us that applicants should "expect to write, write, and then write some more!"

Working students say that Millsaps is particularly suited to their unique needs: "The classes are conveniently scheduled and the school's proximity to the downtown central business district makes it very easy to get to classes easily and on time." In fact, 90 percent of the MBA classes at the Else School are offered in the evening to accommodate work or internships. The library is also "open at all hours to facilitate all schedules." "Professors understand that working students have obligations other than school and exert every effort to help students who have missed class."

Career and Placement

"Millsaps has an excellent academic reputation within the state and certainly within the local community," making it a great choice for students who wish to launch or promote their careers in the Jackson region. One second-year student explains, "I chose this school based on three factors: its reputation, the kind of students that it produces, and the respect that a degree from Millsaps garners." Many students who attend Millsaps are already working in Jackson and have chosen to pursue an MBA at Millsaps to increase their opportunities at their current companies. For recent college grads who want to build their professional experience, Millsaps offers academic credit for internship experiences in a professional environment. Students may receive additional assistance through the Millsaps College Career Center, which offers resume and interview counseling, career-development services, and internship placement. The school also organizes a variety of career-development opportunities, community-service activities, and professional development seminars.

ADMISSIONS CONTACT: BILL BRISTER, DIRECTOR OF GRADUATE BUSINESS ADMISSIONS
ADDRESS: 1701 NORTH STATE STREET JACKSON, MS 39210 UNITED STATES
PHONE: 601-974-1253 • FAX: 601-974-1260
E-MAIL: MBAMACC@MILLSAPS.EDU • WEBSITE: WWW.MILLSAPS.EDU/ESOM

Student Life and Environment

A "friendly, very Southern atmosphere" permeates the Else School campus, whose location in Jackson makes for plenty of social and cultural opportunities. While most students hail from the state of Mississippi, the student body is nevertheless "a diverse bunch that has the utmost respect for individuals from various backgrounds." Given the school's flexible evening schedule and supportive academic environment, it's not surprising that many Millsaps students are older professionals; however, there is also a decent population of younger students, of whom "quite a few are actually right out of undergraduate [programs]."

There are several business honoraries chartered at Millsaps College, including Beta Gamma Sigma, Beta Alpha Psi, and the Financial Management Association. For those looking for a little fun, the Else School hosts several annual events for MBAs: "The dean attempts to pull the MBA students into the school activities; for example, we had a tailgating party for homecoming." However, since the program is largely part-time, students admit that "working full-time and being in school part-time doesn't leave much time for social activities." In general, "most of the students go to class and then go home to their families." A second-year student admits, "Besides group work and the occasional holiday party or community-service activity, there is not as much social interaction as I would like."

Admissions

Admission to Millsaps is rolling. To apply, prospective students must submit an application form, GMAT scores, two letters of recommendation, and official transcripts from all previously attended graduate and undergraduate institutions. Along with their application materials, students must submit an essay detailing their reasons for pursuing an MBA. The Else School also requires a personal interview for all applicants. Prospective students do not need to have studied business as an undergraduate, but students with no background in accounting may be required to take undergraduate courses to catch up. There is no minimum GMAT score requirement for admission to the MBA program, although a score of 500 or better is preferred.

FINANCIAL FACTS

Annual tuition	$26,400
Cost of books	$550
% of students receiving aid	85
% of first-year students receiving aid	100
% of students receiving grants	90

ADMISSIONS

Admissions Selectivity Rating	75
# of applications received	110
% applicants accepted	91
% acceptees attending	96
Average GMAT	560
Range of GMAT	500–730
Average GPA	3.39
TOEFL required of international students	Yes
Minimum TOEFL (paper/computer)	550/230
Application fee	$25
International application fee	$25
Deferment available	Yes
Maximum length of deferment	1 year
Transfer students accepted	Yes
Transfer application policy	Student in Good Standing. 6 hours from a non-AACSB program; 12 hours from a AACSB accredited program
Non-fall admissions	Yes
Need-blind admissions	Yes

EMPLOYMENT PROFILE			
Career Rating	69	Grads Employed by Function	% Avg. Salary
Percent employed	8	Finance	2 NR
		Marketing	2 NR
		MIS	2 NR
		Global Management	1 NR
		Non-profit	1: NR

MINNESOTA STATE UNIVERSITY—MANKATO
COLLEGE OF BUSINESS

Academics

The MBA program at Minnesota State University—Mankato's College of Business employs an unusual calendar. Each semester here is divided into two eight-week modules, during which students complete two-credit courses that meet once a week. The school's goal in creating this system is to afford maximum flexibility to the school's busy students. MBAs here can take one or two classes per module, and they can skip a module entirely when necessary without losing too much ground. A student who takes the maximum number of classes per module can complete the program in about two years. One student writes, "The most attractive part of this program was the class schedule. I am a working individual, so classes from 6:00 to 9:00 P.M. are a great option for me, because I don't have to take off from work to attend classes!"

MSU Mankato's MBA program allows students to concentrate in international business (international study opportunities are available) or leadership and organizational change. Students may also fashion their own concentrations in consultation with a faculty advisor. An executive lecture series and executive seminars give students the chance "to learn from, as well as interact with, top executives." Students appreciate that the curriculum "places more emphasis on real life. Theories are great, but theories won't get you through life. Tying current business trends to course work makes the material applicable to life today and allows business students to use course information in their current jobs." They also approve of the school's "attempts to teach course-work fundamentals as well as up-to-date problems, situations, and changes that are currently affecting businesses today."

Mankato MBAs report that "most classes have moderate reading, and many use case studies. The class formats are split between lecture and interactive learning. The class sizes are just great, and the level of feedback from the professors and from the other students' insights really makes a difference." The financial burden of attending is lessened by the "many great opportunities for graduate assistantships, which pay for tuition while giving you work experience."

Career and Placement

MSU Mankato's Career Development Center serves all undergraduate students, graduate students, and alumni of the school. The MBA program is relatively new, with its first graduating class being Spring 2006 so there is still plenty of room for growth. The College of Business has recently partnered with CareerBeam which allows MBA students to access more than 20,000 business sources across 50 job categories. Students here should consider mining another valuable resource: the faculty. One student explains, "I am sure not every student takes advantage of this, but I have talked with many professors regarding career path, industry insight, corporate contacts, etc., and they all have been extremely useful developing postgraduate career prospects. I have about five months left in the program and have secured numerous interviews and a few job offers."

ADMISSIONS CONTACT: LIZ OLMANSON, ADMINISTRATIVE ASSISTANT
ADDRESS: MSU MBA PROGRAM, 150 MORRIS HALL MANKATO, MN 56001 UNITED STATES
PHONE: 507-389-2967 • FAX: 507-389-5497
E-MAIL: MBA@MNSU.EDU • WEBSITE: WWW.COB.MNSU.EDU

Student Life and Environment

Mankato, students tell us, is "a great college town with a warm and friendly community, and a growing university with a vast support system from local businesses and leaders." The town of 45,000 is located about 65 miles southwest of Minneapolis. The surrounding region is "the health care, commercial, and cultural center of south-central Minnesota," according to the school's website. Residents have easy access to parks and ski facilities; outdoor activities are very popular here. MSU's athletic teams, which compete in the North Central Conference, enjoy strong support from area residents. The Twin Cities can be reached in less than one and a half hours by automobile.

MSU Mankato's MBAs generally work full-time in addition to attending school, so they "don't have any time to enjoy campus life. Most of us try to spend as little time on campus as possible." Some students complain that "there are few programs outside of class to provide learning and application experiences. Groups, clubs, or other opportunities focused toward the graduate student body would enrich the graduate experience." Most, however, acknowledge that they wouldn't take advantage of such opportunities because they lack the time to do so.

Admissions

Applicants to the MBA program at MSU Mankato's College of Business must submit all of the following materials to the College of Graduate Studies: a completed application form; two official transcripts from one's degree-granting institution(s); and official score reports for the GMAT and, if applicable, the TOEFL. International applicants must also complete a Financial Statement Form demonstrating that they have sufficient funds to pay for the program. Most international applicants are required to have their undergraduate transcripts evaluated by a well-regarded credential evaluation service. All applicants must also submit a separate MBA program application form, a resume, and two letters of reference to the College of Business. Admission to the MBA program is competitive. Applicants are assessed holistically. Relevant factors include test scores (a score of at least 500 on the GMAT and 550 on the paper version of the TOEFL are recommended), undergraduate GPA, work experience, and quality of letters of reference.

FINANCIAL FACTS

Annual tuition	$8,092
Fees	$523
Cost of books	$900
Room & board (on-campus)	$5,600
% of students receiving aid	10
% of first-year students receiving aid	10
% of students receiving loans	10
Average award package	$16,000

ADMISSIONS

Admissions Selectivity Rating	79
# of applications received	40
% applicants accepted	72
% acceptees attending	94
Average GMAT	527
Range of GMAT	440–660
Average GPA	3.25
TOEFL required of international students	Yes
Minimum TOEFL (paper/computer)	550/210
Application fee	$40
International application fee	$40
Regular application deadline	6/1
Regular notification	7/1
Deferment available	Yes
Maximum length of deferment	1 year
Transfer students accepted	Yes
Transfer application policy	Students may transfer up to six credits from a regionally accredited institution.
Non-fall admissions	Yes
Need-blind admissions	Yes

MISSOURI STATE UNIVERSITY
COLLEGE OF BUSINESS ADMINISTRATION

GENERAL INFORMATION
Type of school	Public
Environment	City

SURVEY SAYS...
Students love Springfield, MO
Solid preparation in:
Marketing
General management
Computer skills

STUDENTS
Enrollment of parent institution	21,000
Enrollment of business school	401
% male/female	43/57
% out-of-state	5
% part-time	45
% minorities	4
% international	33
Average age at entry	27
Average years work experience at entry	3

ACADEMICS
Academic Experience Rating	**68**
Student/faculty ratio	20:1
Profs interesting rating	84
Profs accessible rating	69
% female faculty	32
% minority faculty	4

Prominent Alumni
David Glass, former CEO of Wal-Mart and CEO of KC Royals; Todd Tiahrt, Congressman; Richard McClure, President, Uni Group, Inc.; Jim Smith, former President, American Banking Association; Terry Thompson, former President, Jack Henry.

Academics

Why choose Missouri State University's College of Business Administration (COBA) for your MBA? Well, how about the "accessibility, flexibility, reputation, and affordability" of the program for starters? Many students here also point out that this "well-managed" program has the "highest accreditation of all the business schools in the area," which goes a long way come job-hunting time. Along with having "the best price in the region," COBA also offers a "very flexible program." "It allowed me the freedom to tailor my MBA exactly to my needs," one student says. Part of this flexibility is evidenced by its "excellent" Accelerated Master's degree option that, according to the school, "enables outstanding Missouri State University undergraduate students to begin taking graduate course work in their junior or senior year and thus combine components of the undergraduate and graduate curriculum." Not too bad a deal, if you ask us, and it certainly accounts for the substantial number of MSU undergrads becoming COBA grads. "It provided an easy transition from my undergraduate to graduate work," one such student explains.

Another enticing component of COBA is its partnership with the International School of Management Studies in Chennai, India, that allows Indian students to "complete their foundation courses in India" and then "complete the remaining credits at MSU." "That way, I get an international MBA," one student explains. Others appreciate the "challenging courses" and the "outstanding" professors who "have an interest in teaching." "MSU employs intelligent professors that make an effort to be readily available outside the class for questions and/or comments," a student adds. Most describe the administration as "excellent" and find that the school "runs rather smoothly."

Thanks to MSU's "convenient rural location" and its rising academic reputation, it's a "large school with a small-school feel." However, despite this some students find themselves left out of the mix. "I do feel disconnected from it," one student says, "because I have never had the same teacher twice or established any consistent 'class' or group to associate with." Others are more concerned with course offerings. "I would have preferred a more developed entrepreneurial department with more small business-oriented courses to choose from." That said, for the courses that are available students appreciate the "ease of registering" and the "very positive and helpful staff." Some wouldn't mind seeing the school take a more proactive role in enhancing its visibility through "more advertising and marketing." But many here find that things are well on their way. One student sums it up, saying, "I think the school is in a transition period in right now. However, I believe they are making progress."

Career and Placement

MSU is quick to point out that "The Career Center doesn't work like an employment agency." "Instead," they say, "our mission focuses upon education: We attempt to teach people job-searching skills that they can use throughout their lives." In line with this, career advisors are available to students by appointment and work to both "link" them with employers and educate them in "researching companies, occupations, or geographic locations...[so that they] won't be dependent upon someone else doing it for them." Students here can also opt to register their resumes with the Career Center so that when employers do come calling for MBAs, the office can send them info on a number of qualified individuals. Additionally, the Career Center holds career fairs where "about 90 recruiters come on campus each year to interview students." According to the school, approximately three-fourths of graduates work in Missouri after graduation, which accounts for the strong local ties MSU possesses.

ADMISSIONS CONTACT: TOBIN BUSHMAN, GRADUATE COLLEGE COORDINATOR
ADDRESS: 901 S. NATIONAL AVENUE SPRINGFIELD, MO 65897 UNITED STATES
PHONE: 417-836-5335 • FAX: 417-836-6888
E-MAIL: GRADUATECOLLEGE@MISSOURISTATE.EDU • WEBSITE: WWW.COBA.MISSOURISTATE.EDU

Student Life and Environment

COBA students are an "intelligent" and "mostly friendly" bunch who appreciate the "culturally diverse learning experience" the MBA program offers. Despite the prevalence of "business guys" roaming the halls, most find that students here, while being competitive, are only so "against themselves" and "not really against other students." "They try very hard for the 'A,' but are very open to helping classmates succeed as well," one student states. Others opine that "Overall they lack the drive to do well. When it is possible to do just the minimum that road is taken." The student body is "primarily recent graduates or people in their early 30s," who "come from a variety of cultural backgrounds" thanks to "a large international population," all of who appreciate the "low cost of living" in Springfield.

Outside of class, the "compact campus" facilitates getting to know your fellow student. "Our campus community is safe and inviting, and allows for exploration into various activities and academic endeavors," one student says. Another adds that "Activities are planned for the University almost every night of the week, including lectures, panel discussions, public affairs conferences, free movie nights, Broadway shows, and athletic events (all sports Division I)." However, some believe that student involvement would take an upswing if "faculty members sponsored and recommended activities." "Life at school is very segmented from the rest of my life," one student explains. "Coming from a non-business background put me on the outside of events and other clubs." Others would like to see the improved "gym facilities" and "public transportation," but all in all, students seem more than content in "The Queen City of the Ozarks."

Admissions

Admissions officers for COBA look for applicants with a Bachelor's or Master's degree from an accredited school with a GPA of at least 2.75 for the last two years (or 60 semester hours) of academic work, a GMAT score of at least 400 (or GRE equivalent) with a minimum score in the 20th percentile for both the verbal and written portions of the test, and a minimum value of 1,000 based on this formula (200 times your GPA for the last 60 semester hours of your degree plus your GMAT score). That said, the school will consider applicants "who do not meet the normal admission requirements, but who possess high promise (usually based upon a successful record of managerial performance at increasing levels of responsibility)" for probationary admission. Additionally, international students who are not native speakers of English must submit TOEFL scores of 550 or higher.

FINANCIAL FACTS

Annual tuition (in-state/ out-of-state)	$4,536/$9,072
Fees (in-state/out-of-state)	$206/402
Cost of books	$875
Room & board (on/off-campus)	$4,806/$5,200
% of students receiving aid	55
% of students receiving loans	53
% of students receiving grants	34
Average award package	$8,909
Average grant	$3,112
Average student loan debt	$16,500

ADMISSIONS

Admissions Selectivity Rating	67
# of applications received	286
% applicants accepted	63
% acceptees attending	68
Average GMAT	510
Range of GMAT	400–760
Average GPA	3.45
TOEFL required of international students	Yes
Minimum TOEFL (paper/computer)	550/213
Application fee	$35
International application fee	$30
Regular application deadline	rolling
Regular notification	rolling
Deferment available	Yes
Maximum length of deferment	1 Semester
Transfer students accepted	Yes
Transfer application policy With advisor permission	
Non-fall admissions	Yes

Applicants Also Look At

Arkansas State University, Central Missouri State University, Southeast Missouri State University, University of Arkansas at Little Rock, University of Missouri—Kansas City, University of Missouri—Columbia, University of Missouri—St. Louis.

EMPLOYMENT PROFILE

Career Rating	74	Grads Employed by Function	% Avg. Salary
Primary Source of Full-time Job Acceptances		Accounting	10 $47,265
School-facilitated activities	30%	Finance	9 $41,875
Graduate-facilitated activities	20%	Human Resources	3 $33,456
Unknown	50%	Marketing	12 $43,667
		MIS	12 $48,920
		Operations	10 $41,000
		Consulting	12 $39,810
		General Management	20 $40,988
		Other	12 $43,210

Top 5 Employers Hiring Grads
BKD; State of Missouri; Cerner; Boeing; Wal-Mart

MONMOUTH UNIVERSITY
SCHOOL OF BUSINESS ADMINISTRATION

Academics

The School of Business Administration at Monmouth University has long been a boon to area professionals looking to fast-track their careers. Now, thanks to "a lot of initiatives occurring to improve Monmouth's standing as a leading educational institution," the school is beginning to expand its appeal.

Among these innovations is the addition of a full-time accelerated MBA program that can be completed in one year. The school has also broadened its concentration offerings to include not only real estate and health care management (as it has in the past) but also accounting and finance. Finally, the school is expanding its selection of course formats, adding hybrid courses with an online component to its roster of traditional classroom courses.

Students here appreciate "the small-school atmosphere in getting to know and interact with your classmates," noting in contrast that "Larger universities...are very impersonal, where students are treated as numbers and figures, not as living people." Cost, convenience, and reputation with local employers all figure into students' choice of MU, as does location; as one student explains, "Being close to New York and Philadelphia helps the school develop the students to what the major employers need." MU professors "bring substantial prior work experience" to the classroom and "are very supportive. They have an interest in seeing their students learn." Students warn that the faculty can be hit-or-miss, though; one MBA informs us, "There are some very good professors and a few professors that are so awful they give poor professors a bad name."

Mostly, though, students appreciate how this program "recognizes that students have busy lives outside of school, as many work. Every effort is made to use the e-campus electronic classroom meeting-place for supplemental class work like group discussions. This allows students to log in as their time permits to contribute to discussions with classmates; the discussions are moderated by knowledgeable professors. This use of electronic tools allows for group work that allows for care of your own harried life schedules." Some here warn that "Hybrid courses have a mixed performance" but report that the school is working hard to iron out the kinks in the system.

Career and Placement

Career services are provided to Monmouth MBAs by the Life and Career Advising Center, which serves the entire university. The office administers aptitude tests and career inventories and provides a contact point between students and alumni and businesses. One-on-one counseling services are also available. According to one student, "The placement director at the University is energetic and caring, but I do not get the impression that there is a full-scale service for placement at the graduate level. This is important to me as a 'career changer,' but my understanding is that I am in the minority."

Companies recruiting business grads at MU in the fall of 2007 included AXA Advisors, Empire Technologies, Meridian Health, Northwest Mutual Financial, PriceWaterhouseCoopers, and UPS.

Student Life and Environment

For the many part-time MBA students here with major commitments outside of school, participation in extracurriculars is a rarity. As one student aptly puts it, "I am attending night school, so all I ever see is the parking lot and the classroom." Even those who spend more time on campus say that "The school lacks any central graduate business student grouping. Perhaps an orientation each semester and a graduate business school lounge might lend some cohesiveness. Also, I'd like to see some emphasis on job placement for the graduate business school students." Most here, though tell us that they are "not looking for a full college experience again, so what I am getting now is making me happy."

Monmouth's student body is "very diverse"; most here "seem to be in their late 20s to early 30s and up." Quite a few told us that they attended MU as undergraduates and that this experience figured heavily in their decisions to return for an MBA. Some of these are "younger recent graduates" who "seem less focused, as if they are entering undergrad all over."

Admissions

Minimum requirements for conditional admission to the Monmouth MBA program include either a GMAT score of at least 500, or a formula score of at least 1000 under the formula [(undergraduate GPA ? 200) + GMAT score] with a minimum GMAT score of 450. Students who hold graduate degrees in other areas (PhD, Ed D, MD, JD, CPA) may be exempted from the above admissions requirements. Conditional admission may be granted to a few who do not meet any of the above requirements at the program director's discretion. International students whose native language is not English must submit official TOEFL score reports in addition to all required documents listed above (minimum score 550 paper, 213 computer, 79 Internet). The school will also consider results in the IELTS (minimum score 5), Cambridge (all grades of A, B, and C are considered passing grades), or MELAB (minimum score 77).

FINANCIAL FACTS

Annual tuition	$13,392
Fees	$628
Cost of books	$1,000
Room & board (off-campus)	$13,817
% of students receiving aid	88
% of first-year students receiving aid	88
% of students receiving loans	51
% of students receiving grants	70
Average award package	$12,834
Average grant	$3,822
Average student loan debt	$33,028

ADMISSIONS

Admissions Selectivity Rating	71
# of applications received	162
% applicants accepted	78
% acceptees attending	69
Average GMAT	518
Range of GMAT	460–580
Average GPA	3.18
TOEFL required of international students	Yes
Minimum TOEFL (paper/computer)	550/225
Application fee	$50
International application fee	$50
Regular application deadline	7/15
Regular notification	rolling
Deferment available	Yes
Maximum length of deferment	1 year
Transfer students accepted	Yes
Transfer application policy Transfer credits must be within 7 years.	
Non-fall admissions	Yes
Need-blind admissions	Yes

MONTCLAIR STATE UNIVERSITY
SCHOOL OF BUSINESS

Academics

Affordability, "proximity to New York City," and "a program that caters to part-time students" are the main attractions at the MBA program at Montclair State University. The school offers a full-time program, with classes in the evenings and Saturdays; a part-time evening program; and an accelerated Saturday program. Approximately one-quarter of the student body attends full-time.

The Montclair MBA is a 48-credit sequence including nine credits of introductory management classes, a 15-credit functional core (covering accounting, finance, marketing, and information management), 9 credits of advanced business courses, 12–18 credits of electives (some of which may be used to create an area of concentration), and a three-credit capstone course in advanced strategic management. Up to 15 hours of these classes can be waived based on prior academic work or through challenge examinations. Concentrations are available in accounting, economics, finance, international business, management, marketing, and MIS.

Montclair professors "have a good amount of practical knowledge and integrate current topics well, without going into overkill mode. The program design offers a good balance of individual and group assignments, papers, exams, and presentations." Instructors earn praise for being "understanding of students' other obligations, but without being pushovers," and for "bringing great real-world experience to [the] classroom." Administrators earn praise for soliciting student evaluations of their professors, and for actually listening to these comments: students claim that "some professors have actually been removed from the program upon student request." Administrators are also very approachable; one student states, they "hold lunches that are a great environment for conversation. They're really good at listening to students."

Career and Placement

The MSU Career Development Center serves all undergraduates and graduates at the school. MBAs are not impressed; one writes, "We need to establish an alumni club or organization and a career/campus recruiting office." Another agrees, "It would be nice to have a career services center active for MBAs. In all my years attending I have yet to have anyone from the MBA office or career office offer a meeting, discussion, or follow-up on my studies." Living near New York City, "the greatest free market in the world," makes it a little easier for students to find internships and jobs on their own. Most MSU MBAs attend while pursuing full-time careers; their employers include Abbott Laboratories, ADP, AT&T Wireless Services, Bank of New York, Con Edison, Deloitte Consulting, Goldman Sachs, Gucci, Kodak, the *New York Times*, the Office of the New Jersey Attorney General, PricewaterhouseCoopers, Prudential Financial, Sodexho USA, Thomson Financial, United Parcel Service, and Wyeth-Ayerst Research.

Student Life and Environment

Montclair is "mostly a commuter campus," with "about 75 percent of the students attending part-time and working full-time." As a result, "Most people don't get involved in activities because there are higher priorities (work, family, the rest of life)." The part-time student body arrives with "an interesting array of backgrounds and work experiences," we're told. The large number of part-time commuters means "group work can be difficult because we all have different schedules, but we figure out how to work together."

The town of Montclair has several major parks and lots of quiet streets. It boasts four movie theaters, an art museum and several art galleries, lots of artisan shops, two off-Broadway theater companies, a host of funky restaurants, and an abundance of coffee shops. Students remark that they often see no need to venture into New York City proper, as they are able to partake in a range of cultural activities without ever leaving the Montclair vicinity. Cross-town public transportation is also pretty good, and access to and from NYC is frequent, easy, and cheap.

Those MBAs who live on campus and attend full-time "tend to be the international students." They tell us that "overall, campus life is good. We have many graduate- and undergraduate-level clubs and organizations to choose from. There is something for everyone at MSU." Full-timers and commuters alike appreciate the fact that "there is a diner on campus, proof that this is a Jersey school."

Admissions

Applicants to the MSU/MBA program "must have at least earned a bachelor's degree from a regionally accredited college or university (or the foreign equivalent)" and must submit two official copies of transcripts for all academic work completed after high school; an official score report for the GMAT (applicants holding a terminal degree—a PhD, MD, or JD, for example—are exempt from the GMAT requirement); a personal statement of professional goals; two letters of recommendation from "persons qualified to evaluate the applicant's promise of academic achievement and potential for professional growth;" and a completed application form. International students whose first language is not English must submit an official score report for the TOEFL. Of these elements, the undergraduate GPA and the GMAT score are among the most important factors that the Admissions Department considers. The average GMAT score of the 2005 entering class was 500, and the average GPA was 3.24. Prior work experience is "strongly recommended" but is not required.

FINANCIAL FACTS

Annual tuition (in-state/ out-of-state)	$9,466/$12,778
Fees	$1,143
Cost of books	$1,200
Room & board (on/off-campus)	$8,250/$12,500
% of students receiving aid	26
% of first-year students receiving aid	32
% of students receiving loans	22
% of students receiving grants	6
Average award package	$12,862
Average grant	$2,596
Average student loan debt	$26,629

ADMISSIONS

Admissions Selectivity Rating	**70**
# of applications received	117
% applicants accepted	83
% acceptees attending	100
Average GMAT	493
Range of GMAT	470–600
Average GPA	3.3
TOEFL required of international students	Yes
Minimum TOEFL (paper/computer)	380/207
Application fee	$60
International application fee	$60
Regular application deadline	rolling
Regular notification	rolling
Deferment available	Yes
Maximum length of deferment	1 year
Transfer students accepted	Yes
Transfer application policy Up to 15 credits.	
Non-fall admissions	Yes
Need-blind admissions	Yes

Applicants Also Look At
Farleigh Dickinson University, Metropolitan College of New York, Rutgers, The State University of New Jersey, Seton Hall University.

EMPLOYMENT PROFILE

Career Rating	65	Grads Employed by Function	% Avg. Salary
Primary Source of Full-time Job Acceptances		Finance	28 $60,000
School-facilitated activities	10	Marketing	16 $75,000
Graduate-facilitated activities	90	MIS	8 $60,000
Percent employed	15	Operations	4 $65,000
		Consulting	4 $50,000
		General Management	40 $80,000

Top 5 Employers Hiring Grads
Roche Laboratories; Schering Plough; Morgan Stanley; Johnson & Johnson; Prudentia

Monterey Institute of International Studies
Fisher Graduate School of International Business

Academics

As its name indicates, the graduate business program at the Monterey Institute "focuses on international business" from its curriculum (which includes "a three-semester advanced language component") to the composition of its student body (one American student calls it "the most international environment I have ever been in, and I have been living abroad since the end of high school. Half the students in every class are international students."). The Fisher School excels in entrepreneurship studies, receiving a top-10 ranking from Entrepreneur magazine and the Princeton Review in 2006. Students praise its offerings in language, country and political risk assessment, cross-cultural negotiation, and corporate responsibility.

MIIS offers a "small and personal" program that is nonetheless large enough to accommodate "the ability to customize degrees, classes, specializations, and extracurricular activities." A number of our respondents noted the dual-degree programs available here, which include an MBA/MA in international environmental policy, several MBA/MA options in international policymaking, and an MBA/MA in translation. The program's size is not without its drawbacks, however. One student explains: "Being a small school with limited resources strains the ability of the faculty to offer core courses every semester. Also, being in a small town also isolates the school from strong local internship opportunities. The faculty does a great job in their respective fields, but often has to teach classes outside of their specialties. Overall, the academic experience is great, but somewhat different than most other business schools. The focus is more on language studies, negotiation and cross-cultural issues, leaving less emphasis on the core business studies."

In addition to the above-mentioned areas, the MIIS curriculum also focuses "on ethics, corporate social responsibility, and environmental issues," an aspect of the program students find appealing. They also love how "This place is pretty laid-back, and everyone from the security folks to the Dean wants to see you succeed. Ain't no sabotaging here in Monterey!" Finally, MBAs appreciate "the strong alumni network and mentor program."

Career and Placement

The Career Management Center (CMC) for the Fisher MBA program offers "a customized approach to each individual's goals, skill set, [and] educational and personal background," according to the school. The office "acts as an 'executive search firm'" to help students "target potential employers and enhance their added-value" through online career assessments; one-on-one consultations; and workshops in interviewing skills, salary negotiation, internship, and networking. Students report that the office "is slowly pulling things together, but our size and location, and the fact that no one has heard of us, definitely limits the number of recruiters coming to campus."

Employers who most frequently hire MIIS graduates include: Accenture, Bank of America, Cargill, Central Intelligence Agency, Cisco Systems, CTB McGraw Hill, Daimler Chrysler, Deutsche Bank, Deloitte & Touche Consulting, EMDAP (Emerging Markets Development Advisors Program), Ernst & Young, Frost & Sullivan, Hewlett Packard, HSBC (Hong Kong Shanghai Bank Company), Intel, JP Morgan, LanguageLine Services, Paul Kagan & Associates, PriceWaterhouse Coopers, Seagate Technology, Silicon Graphics, Inc., Sun Microsystems, Target, Ubisoft, US Dept of Commerce, US Dept of Labor, US Dept of State, US Peace Corps, Wells Fargo, and West Marine.

ADMISSIONS CONTACT: CAROLINE MANSI, ENROLLMENT MANAGER
ADDRESS: 460 PIERCE STREET MONTEREY, CA 93940 UNITED STATES
PHONE: 831-647-4123 • FAX: 831-647-6405
E-MAIL: ADMIT@MIIS.EDU • WEBSITE: FISHER.MIIS.EDU

Student Life and Environment

The MIIS MBA program is a small one; "The entering business class is about 50 students. We all know each other well and freely mingle inside and outside of class well. For the size of the school, it does very well to give each student as many opportunities to gain both intellectually and professionally as possible." MBAs report: "There is a lot of interaction between business school students and the students of other schools. The student council organizes happy hours every month to encourage the interaction between students of all schools as well as professors." They also tell us, "There are many clubs on campus, including a golf club, scuba club, international trade and development club, women in business club, language clubs, and many others." Languages are very important, and thanks to the translation and interpretation school, one gets many opportunities to practice his second language throughout the day.

The campus here "is well equipped. All classrooms have brand-new furniture, and most have multimedia equipment. The library is top-notch; I rely on its internal collection, on the collection of the consortium to which it belongs, and on its interlibrary loan services. However, the campus has no gym and no discount arrangements, which is a shortcoming." Quality of life in the Monterey region "is excellent," although "because of Monterey's large student population, rents are high and housing quality is low." Monterey "is a beautiful and quiet place" that "has rich nature," but "it is isolated from centers of business activity." San Jose is about an hour's drive to the north; San Francisco is two hours off.

Admissions

Proficiency in a second language is required by the MIIS graduate business program; students are required to demonstrate reading and listening proficiency in their second language during New Student Orientation. The MBA Plus program, which is designed for students with limited proficiency in a second language, provides an intensive language immersion program in the summer prior to enrollment in the MBA program, allowing students to gain the needed language skills. Applicants whose native language is not English must demonstrate proficiency through TOEFL or IELTS testing. Applicants must have achieved a minimum 3.0 undergraduate GPA and must submit an official score report for the GMAT. Letters of recommendation, a resume, and a personal statement are also required. An interview, while not required, are strongly recommended.

FINANCIAL FACTS

Annual tuition	$27,750
Fees	$200
Cost of books	$900
Room & board (off-campus)	$8,550
% of students receiving aid	88
% of first-year students receiving aid	90
% of students receiving loans	48
% of students receiving grants	83
Average award package	$19,041
Average grant	$6,893
Average student loan debt	$32,920

ADMISSIONS

Admissions Selectivity Rating	**74**
# of applications received	130
% applicants accepted	75
% acceptees attending	51
Average GMAT	551
Range of GMAT	510–590
Average GPA	3.3
TOEFL required of international students	Yes
Minimum TOEFL (paper/computer)	550/213
Application fee	$50
International application fee	$50
Regular application deadline	3/15
Regular notification	5/1
Transfer students accepted	Yes
Transfer application policy Credits must be from an AACSB accredited college or university.	
Non-fall admissions	Yes
Need-blind admissions	Yes

Applicants Also Look At
Pepperdine University, Stanford University, Thunderbird, University of California—San Diego, University of California—Berkeley, University of Pennsylvania, University of South Carolina.

EMPLOYMENT PROFILE

Career Rating	70	Grads Employed by Function	%	Avg. Salary
Primary Source of Full-time Job Acceptances		Finance	39	$64,333
School-facilitated activities	6 (21%)	Marketing	21	$76,667
Graduate-facilitated activities	12 (43%)	Operations	11	$61,000
Unknown	10 (36%)	Consulting	11	$82,500
Percent employed	78	General Management	7	$42,500
Average base starting salary	$64,000	Other	11	NR

Top 5 Employers Hiring Grads
HSBC; Intel; Eastman Kodak Company; Coldwell Banker; Wells Fargo

NATIONAL UNIVERSITY OF SINGAPORE
BUSINESS SCHOOL

Academics

"Asia is fast becoming the center of global business activity," students at the National University of Singapore Business School remind us, and "NUS is one of the best schools, both to learn about how business is conducted in Asia and to network with corporations established in the region." The school is "considered one of the best universities in the world and the topmost business school in Asia." The school's location "offers a strategic advantage," because Singapore "is the financial hub of Asia and the hub of all Asian business. "NUS Business School gives the best possible value" and prepares students for a solid business career overall, "where the regional job market, especially for a career in finance, is quite good."

NUS' graduate business programs offer "a global perspective with an Asian outlook" augmented by "the ability to be part of a multicultural society in Singapore. You can enhance your understandings of, and contacts within, the Chinese, Indian, and Southeast Asian business cultures here." Students also extol "the excellent facilities, especially the libraries and auditoriums," the "very strong faculty," and the excellent "value."

NUS has long offered a part-time program. It recently added a full-time program that "has increased class sizes; the school administration has been able to handle it very well and there have been no logistical or administrative issues." Students have the option to pursue a general MBA or one with a specialization in either real estate management or health care management. Either way, they must complete a 10-course core module that "provides a holistic view of the entire business world" while giving us "exposure to all different fields of management." All of the modules "are very important, the type of courses you'd take even if they were electives."

Students also tell us that the program and the entire environment are very flexible. "We are free to do what we want (obviously within the parameter of rules), which helps us in being as creative as we want. Professors are eager to help us in various international events and competitions. This is a great impetus for students that brings out the best in them." Students tell us that "administrators are open to discussion on improving the course and integrates new business concepts in the curriculum," which they appreciate.

Career and Placement

The Career Services Office (CSO) "is a strong point of the NUS Business School," students report. One writes, "I was surprised to see so many companies coming over for on-campus recruitment." Another adds, "The CSO is changing so fast and for the better. Many job postings" are available to choose from. Some here feel that the office could do a better job bringing recruiters to campus; others counter that those who complain mostly "come from places where the placement cells actually ensure that companies come and recruit on the same day. That is not the way it works in Singapore and most of rest of the world."

Companies most likely to hire NUS MBAs include: ExxonMobil Asia Pacific, Hewlett-Packard Singapore, International Enterprise Singapore, KPMG International, Ministry of Trade and Industry, National Computer Board, NEC Singapore PTE LTD, Proctor & Gamble, Philips Electronics, Shell Eastern Petroleum, Singapore Police Force, Sony Systems Design International, and Swiss Bank Corporation.

ADMISSIONS CONTACT: MR. LIM YUE WEN, DIRECTOR (GRADUATE STUDIES)
ADDRESS: BIZ 2 BUILDING, 1 BUSINESS LINK, LEVEL 5 SINGAPORE, 117592 SINGAPORE
PHONE: 011-65-65161499 • FAX: 011-65-68724423
E-MAIL: MBA@NUS.EDU.SG • WEBSITE: MBA.NUS.EDU

Student Life and Environment

The NUS program carries a moderate workload, allowing for a "fantastic balance between studies and fun." The workload also means that "students have time to think about career moves, take part in business plan competitions and do some job searching." Extracurricular events include "lots of competitions, amazing speakers from the industry, lots of different activities with student clubs," and "wonderful parties like International Day and the Deepawali celebration." An annual Graduate Business Conference "brings us all together." In the past, the conference has featured such noteworthy keynote speakers as Jimmy Carter and former GM Chairperson John Smale.

On campus, "The MBA lounge is the place to be if you [want to] be a part of the 'in' group. Discussions . . . range from politics, business ethics, case studies, and the venue for the next 'jam' session (basically music, booze, and fun)." Some students complain that "the layout of the school is not ideal, because it is spread out over too many buildings."

NUS draws a "mature and serious" student body of professionals "who are obviously occupied with how their careers are going and who are earnest in wanting to learn." These "well-traveled" MBA candidates are highly international; India and China are heavily represented, while students from the United States, Switzerland, Norway, Korea, and other far-flung locations fill out the student body. In terms of background, students "come from engineering, commerce, medicine, architecture, and many more fields. As the median work experience is about 4 years, there is a good quality of contribution that people make in the class."

Admissions

NUS seeks applicants who "have leadership capabilities and the strong desire and drive for academic and management excellence" and who are "motivated, mature, focused and have a desire to make a positive impact on business and society," according to the school's website. Applicants to the NUS School of Business must provide the Admissions Office with transcripts for all undergraduate and graduate work, GMAT scores, TOEFL or IELTS scores (for non-native English speakers), two letters of recommendation, and a resume demonstrating at least 2 years of professional experience after obtaining their first degree or equivalent. Shortlisted applicants will be interviewed and may be required to take further evaluation tests. Interviews are conducted face-to-face or via phone for candidates located overseas.

FINANCIAL FACTS

Annual tuition	$24,286
Fees	$24,660
Cost of books	$600
Room & board	
(on/off-campus)	$9,171/$9,000
% of students receiving aid	34
% of first-year students	
receiving aid	40
% of students receiving grants	34
Average award package	$10,714
Average grant	$31,160

ADMISSIONS

Admissions Selectivity Rating	**95**
# of applications received	1,473
% applicants accepted	23
% acceptees attending	59
Average GMAT	653
Range of GMAT	620–680
TOEFL required of	
international students	Yes
Minimum TOEFL	
(paper/computer)	620/260
Regular application deadline	3/31
Regular notification	5/31
Application Deadline/Notification	
Round 1:	12/31 / 03/01
Round 2:	03/31 / 05/31
Deferment available	Yes
Maximum length of	
deferment	1 year
Transfer students accepted	Yes
Transfer application policy	
Admission and credit transfer applications are evaluated on a case-by-case basis.	
Non-fall admissions	Yes
Need-blind admissions	Yes

Applicants Also Look At

China Europe International Business School (CEIBS), INSEAD, Melbourne Business School, Nanyang Technological University (Singapore).

EMPLOYMENT PROFILE

Career Rating	**82**	**Grads Employed by Function**	**% Avg. Salary**
Primary Source of Full-time Job Acceptances		Finance	43 $72,531
School-facilitated activities	25 (40%)	Marketing	18 $52,316
Graduate-facilitated activities	38 (60%)	MIS	7 $52,262
Percent employed	100	Operations	18 $47,174
		Consulting	7 $37,619
		Other	7 $43,571

Top 5 Employers Hiring Grads

Adventity; Hong Leong Group; Citigroup; HSBC; Motorola

NEW JERSEY INSTITUTE OF TECHNOLOGY
SCHOOL OF MANAGEMENT

GENERAL INFORMATION

Type of school	Public
Environment	Metropolis
Academic calendar	Semester

SURVEY SAYS...

Friendly students
Helpful alumni
Happy students
Solid preparation in:
General management
Teamwork
Presentation skills
Quantitative skills
Doing business in a global economy

STUDENTS

Enrollment of parent institution	8,828
Enrollment of business school	205
% male/female	80/20
% out-of-state	25
% part-time	35
% minorities	19
% international	25
Average age at entry	33
Average years work experience at entry	5

ACADEMICS

Academic Experience Rating	**84**
Student/faculty ratio	13:1
Profs interesting rating	71
Profs accessible rating	64
% female faculty	5

Academics

The New Jersey Institute of Technology MBA program "offers a technology-focused curriculum" that "is best suited for future managers/leaders in the technical/IT field." Students enrolled in this "affordable, convenient" program tell us that an "interesting curriculum focused on practical knowledge" "provides a very good blend of business and technology management" supplemented by "first-rate facilities." The school offers a 48-credit MBA that can be completed in two years by full-timers or four years by part-timers. An 18-month accelerated Executive MBA is open to managers and professionals; the program meets on alternate Saturdays. The availability of "both in-class and online course options makes the school very flexible."

NJIT's curriculum focuses on the development and interrelation of four themes: the transition toward a knowledge-based economy, the emergence of the digital firm, the increasing globalization of business, and the primacy of innovation in gaining a competitive advantage in the modern business world. All students here complete a 27-credit core curriculum, followed by a six-credit module in knowledge and information management, a six-credit module in technology and innovation, and nine credits to be applied toward a concentration. Concentrations are available in e-commerce, finance, infrastructure management, marketing, MIS, operations management, and transportation and logistics. The school also offers "appealing independent study opportunities."

Students report that the faculty is mixed in quality. As one of them notes, "Most professors I've encountered are decent to good. Some professors are outstanding. The overall academic experience has been very solid so far." Another explains, "There are professors who have demanding workloads that keep you up all night trying to meet deadlines and grade incredibly hard and there are those that give moderate workloads and demand far less." Many agree that "the only area that the graduate degree program can improve in is the diversification of classes. Many classes in the later modules are not available for various reasons. Most of these reasons are very valid, but when you want to take one class and it won't be offered until two semesters from now, it can leave you scrambling for another class that can take its place." EMBA students tell us that their program "is well administered and continues to get better. The program is extremely aggressive in its schedule and scope and the professors and administrators are cognizant of the fragile balance between work, family, and school."

Career and Placement

NJIT maintains a Career Resources Center to serve all undergraduates and graduates at the university. The center includes a library, self-assessment exams, and online job postings. Counseling services are also available. Some of the companies recruiting MBAs on the NJIT campus in 2005 included ASCO Power Technologies, BAE Systems CNIR, IBM, Keyence Corporation of America, Lucent Technologies, Peri Software Solutions Inc., Schindler Elevator Corporation, Sensor Products, Sozoh Technologies, Inc, Stryker Orthopaedics, Telcordia Technologies, and Vonage.

Student Life and Environment

Students who take their classes on the NJIT campus tell us that "academic life here consists of a strong learning culture. The supporting facilities are excellent. There is less emphasis on extracurricular activities." One MBA adds, "Commuters will find themselves driving to school and home with the lack of fun things to do after hours. Living on campus is another story. You can find things to do almost all the time. However, most grad students don't live on campus."

ADMISSIONS CONTACT: OFFICE OF UNIVERSITY ADMISSIONS, OFFICE OF UNIVERSITY ADMISSIONS
ADDRESS: FENSTER HALL - ROOM 100, UNIVERSITY HEIGHTS NEWARK, NJ 07102 UNITED STATES
PHONE: 973-596-3300 • FAX: 973-596-3461
E-MAIL: ADMISSIONS@NJIT.EDU • WEBSITE: WWW.NJIT.EDU

NJIT is located in Newark, NJ, meaning that it is not much more than a stone's throw from downtown New York City. Thus, students have access not only to endless entertainment opportunities but also to an equally robust supply of business resources.

NJIT's student body consists of "an ethnically diverse group of working professionals ranging in age from 30 to 45. Most are married with children and have extremely active lives. The range of professional business experience varies greatly. The majority of the students have low to middle-management positions. However . . . the class is committed to learning and to the overall objective of career development through the program. In general, students are friendly and helpful. The classroom dynamic is robust and healthy and as a result lends itself to thoughtful discussion."

Admissions

All applications to the NJIT MBA program must, at minimum, include complete transcripts for all work done at the undergraduate level and an official score report for the GMAT (although applicants who already hold a master's or doctoral degree from an accredited university are exempt from the GMAT requirement). Students entering the program must also demonstrate competency in economics, finance, information systems, and quantitative methods; these requirements may be met with undergraduate work or through completion of pre-degree foundation courses. International students whose first language is not English are required to submit scores for the TOEFL exam. All students may provide supplemental application materials, including up to three letters of recommendation, a personal statement, and a description of work experience or a resume, if they wish.

FINANCIAL FACTS

Annual tuition	$12,730
Fees	$1,624
Cost of books	$1,400
Room & board	$9,264
% of students receiving aid	64
% of first-year students receiving aid	71
% of students receiving loans	26
% of students receiving grants	34
Average grant	$10,000
Average student loan debt	$10,000

ADMISSIONS

Admissions Selectivity Rating	**86**
# of applications received	249
% applicants accepted	51
% acceptees attending	54
Average GMAT	522
Range of GMAT	480–550
Average GPA	3.5
TOEFL required of international students	Yes
Minimum TOEFL (paper/computer)	525/213
Application fee	$60
International application fee	$60
Regular application deadline	rolling
Regular notification	rolling
Non-fall admissions	Yes

NEW MEXICO STATE UNIVERSITY
COLLEGE OF BUSINESS

GENERAL INFORMATION

Type of school	Public
Environment	City
Academic calendar	Semester

SURVEY SAYS...
Friendly students
Cutting edge classes
Happy students
Solid preparation in:
Accounting
General management

STUDENTS

Enrollment of parent institution	17,000
Enrollment of business school	1,900
% male/female	51/49
% out-of-state	10
% part-time	80
% minorities	60
% international	20
Average age at entry	28
Average years work experience at entry	4

ACADEMICS

Academic Experience Rating	**77**
Student/faculty ratio	30:1
Profs interesting rating	76
Profs accessible rating	89
% female faculty	17
% minority faculty	10

Prominent Alumni
John J. Chavez, Former Cabinet Secty, Dept of Tax & Revenue; Robert D. Chelberg, Retired, U.S. Army Lt. General; John M. Cordova, Former Dir. of Mktg, Milwaukee Brewers; Andres Gutierrez, Founder/Mgr Dir of New Co Production; James Hawkins, Exec. Vice President, Ranchers Bank.

Academics

The College of Business at New Mexico State University is "extremely technologically savvy," a quality that serves it well in a state that is home to several air force bases, major NASA operations, two national laboratories, Spaceport America, and several big tech players (Intel, for one, has a large manufacturing plant in Albuquerque). The tech sector is, in fact, the fastest-growing employer in the Las Cruces area.

NMSU incorporates technology in all disciplines, and has developed several specialized degrees. The school also "concentrates on entrepreneurs because of its abundant resources. It's planning new ways to convert these resources into products." NMSU is a participant in the Space Alliance Technology Outreach Program (SATOP), "which creates interactions between students and the corporate people and gives a very good exposure to the aerospace industry."

Many students simply appreciate the convenience of the program, praising its "wonderfully located campus with a very unique and culturally diverse academic program." The school serves both full-time and part-time MBAs, and fully understands and meets the needs of traditional and nontraditional students when it comes to education. NMSU has even "created an MBA cohort program for the Los Alamos National Laboratory. Every other weekend a NMSU professor comes to Los Alamos. We are enrolled in two classes per semester and each class meets once a month for two 5-hour sessions. This schedule is wonderfully convenient, and communication is ongoing throughout the months." A school that comes to you—you can't beat that for convenience.

Instructors at NMSU "are well respected in their fields and apply real-world applications to their lectures and assignments," while "The administration is always very responsive whenever a conflict arises." A "socially and ethnically diverse student population" informs class discussion. One student sums up, "I have had a very positive overall academic experience. Every single administrator and faculty member has treated me with the utmost respect and professional courtesy."

Career and Placement

NMSU's Placement and Career Services Office provides university students with on-campus employment, internship listings, career listings, workshops, advising, job fairs, and online research tools. The school holds a number of job fairs and other recruiting events throughout the year, but all are primarily targeted toward undergraduates. As a result, relatively few of the many companies that visit campus seek MBAs.

Recent employers of NMSU MBAs include: Accenture, ElPaso Electric, Ernst & Young, Agilent Technologies, ConocoPhilips Company, General Motors, Hewlett-Packard, IBM, Intel, KPMG International, NASA, Los Alamos National Laboratories, Qwest, Sandia National Laboratory, TXU Energy, and Wells Fargo.

ADMISSIONS CONTACT: DR. BOBBIE GREEN, DIRECTOR, MBA PROGRAM
ADDRESS: 114 GUTHRIE HALL, MSC 3GSP LAS CRUCES, NM 88003-8001 UNITED STATES
PHONE: 505-646-8003 • FAX: 505-646-7977
E-MAIL: GRADINFO@NMSU.EDU • WEBSITE: BUSINESS.NMSU.EDU/MBA

Student Life and Environment

NMSU "is a great place to continue your education and the Las Cruces area is second to none," students report, adding that "Las Cruces is a very slow-paced, small-town type environment. It is, however, slowly changing due to this area being designated as one of the top-10 places to retire in the nation." The school is located "in its own private corner of the city, and it is very safe, clean, and spirit oriented."

Many who attend the MBA program work part-time as well; one such student writes, "This is a focused and relevant MBA that meets my needs as a nontraditional student who holds down a full-time civil engineering job." When they can manage to take a break from their responsibilities, they "enjoy attending college sporting events and special events at the Pan American Center on campus. The campus is also a nice place to take a long walk for exercise or leisure, strolling from pond to pond." The campus includes excellent facilities for workouts and for study. Some here point out that "NMSU could definitely improve in how it caters to students with families. Child care is only available to students with very low incomes, or at the standard child care rates in this city. There also don't seem to be any family-oriented extracurricular activities."

The NMSU MBA population includes "a large portion of international students, who come because of the affordability and friendly environment. Classes with widely diversified cultures and nations contribute to the discussions related to international trade and global business management." Students "have diverse work experience, which makes interaction between students interesting and useful" and results in "a very professional approach to problem-solving case studies or application of curriculum covered in course material."

Admissions

Applicants to the NMSU MBA program must apply for admission to the university's graduate school before they can be admitted to the GMAT program. Admission to the graduate school requires that the applicant hold a 4-year undergraduate degree from an accredited institution with a GPA of at least 3.0 (some exceptions to the GPA requirement are possible; contact school for details). International applicants must earn at least a 530 on the paper-based TOEFL or a 197 on the computer-based TOEFL. Applicants to the MBA program must meet one of the following criteria: a minimum GMAT score of 400 and a minimum score of 1400 under the formula (GPA multiplied by GMAT); possession of a graduate degree from an accredited institution; or completion of at least 4 years of full-time professional work and an undergraduate GPA of at least 3.25.

FINANCIAL FACTS

Annual tuition (in-state/ out-of-state)	$4,543/$14,172
Cost of books	$1,000
Room & board (on/off-campus)	$5,200/$7,000
% of students receiving aid	22
% of first-year students receiving aid	10
% of students receiving loans	30
% of students receiving grants	8
Average award package	$350,000
Average grant	$30,000

ADMISSIONS

Admissions Selectivity Rating	**75**
# of applications received	102
% applicants accepted	69
% acceptees attending	100
Average GMAT	500
Range of GMAT	480–760
Average GPA	3.25
TOEFL required of international students	Yes
Minimum TOEFL (paper/computer)	530/197
Application fee	$30
International application fee	$50
Regular application deadline	7/1
Regular notification	8/4
Application Deadline/Notification	
Round 1:	11/30 / 2/15
Round 2:	2/1 / 3/30
Round 3:	3/15 / 4/15
Round 4:	4/15 / 5/15
Deferment available	Yes
Maximum length of deferment	1 year
Transfer students accepted	Yes
Transfer application policy	
A maximum of 12 Semester credits from AACSB schools.	
Non-fall admissions	Yes
Need-blind admissions	Yes

EMPLOYMENT PROFILE

Career Rating	73	Grads Employed by Function	% Avg. Salary
		Finance	2 NR
		Marketing	5 NR
		Operations	2 NR
		Consulting	2 NR
		General Management	7 NR
		Quantitative	2 NR

NEW YORK UNIVERSITY
LEONARD N. STERN SCHOOL OF BUSINESS

GENERAL INFORMATION
Type of school   Private
Environment   Metropolis
Academic calendar   Semester

SURVEY SAYS...
Students love New York, NY
Good social scene
Good peer network
Happy students
Solid preparation in:
Finance
Quantitative skills

STUDENTS
Enrollment of
business school   2,861
% male/female   58/42
% part-time   71
% minorities   16
% international   39
Average age at entry   27
Average years work
experience at entry   5

ACADEMICS
Academic Experience Rating   **95**
Student/faculty ratio   4:1
Profs interesting rating   87
Profs accessible rating   98
% female faculty   21

Joint Degrees
JD/MBA 4 years, MA/MBA (French
Studies) 3 years, MA/MBA (Politics)
3 years, MPA/MBA (Public
Administration) 3 years, MA/MFA
MBA/MS (Mathematics in Finance).

Prominent Alumni
Richard Fuld, Chairman/CEO,
Lehman Brothers Holdings, Inc.;
Kathryn B. Swintek, Head of
Leveraged Finance, N. America, BNP
Bank; Robert Greifeld,
President/CEO, NASDAQ.

Academics

In name, culture, and spirit, the Stern School of Business at New York University is defined by the city that surrounds it. "Smack in the middle of all the great New York industries," students at NYU tell us that "the city and its offerings are as much a part of the program as is its course curriculum." Traditionally recognized as a powerhouse in the field of finance, students say you can't beat NYU's financial and accounting programs: "I started with no knowledge of how capital markets work and I now consider myself well above average, even in NYC!" In fact, academics are "of the highest caliber" in almost every field and are spearheaded by a talented teaching staff that includes "a Nobel laureate, the preeminent bankruptcy expert, and a financial statements professor who literally wrote the CFA book on the subject." Promoting an equal emphasis on theory and practice, the teaching staff is a "good balance between tenured academic (i.e., research oriented) professors and clinical (i.e., practical, real-world experience) professors." "The faculty and administration have tailored the course load so that MBA students are not overwhelmed by the combination of academics and the job search."

The evening program at NYU is "the highest ranked part-time MBA program in the nation," benefiting students with its stellar reputation as well as its diverse and accomplished student body. As one student explains, "Everyone is working so there are always new viewpoints on the business world being interjected into our conversations. Also, rather than meeting only future bankers and consultants, there's been a wide range of careers represented." The school also offers a Westchester and weekend MBA program, though some feel "The quality of offerings, professors, and administrative help is higher for the weekday night classes than for the Saturday classes."

Despite the intensity of the urban environment, the atmosphere at Stern is surprisingly friendly and noncompetitive. On the whole, NYU students are "hardworking, driven, diverse, and above all, incredibly friendly and helpful." Faculty are "very accessible" and willing to help students grow personally and professionally. A current student shares, "The professors are generally very approachable. Professor Damodaran teaches a class on valuation with over 250 students but he always finds time to answer my most mundane questions." Even the higher-ups are described as responsive and easily accessible; for example, "The Dean knows all of us by name and has had lunch with each of us throughout our time here."

Career and Placement

Bright, well trained, and ready for action, NYU grads are in high demand. A current student marvels, "First-years only have a few weeks to adjust to academic demands before companies start flooding campus. In the meantime, the Office of Career Development prepares them for the job search by refining their networking and interviewing skills and by polishing their resumes." Thanks to "Stern's strong ties with finance recruiters in the area," many students have employment offers by the end of their first year; however, "For those who are still looking for a full-time position, the second-year job search begins earlier than the first-year internship search, but it is over for many before the Christmas break." Be warned, however, that "Part-time students [do not have] access to recruiting events. The administration has been working to better meet part-time students' needs" through its Career Center for Working Professionals.

Hundreds of companies recruit at Stern. Some of the top companies are: American Express, Banc of America Securities, Booz Allen Hamilton, Citigroup, Colgate, Deloitte Touche Tohmatsu, Deutsche Bank, Ernst & Young, General Electric Company, Goldman

ADMISSIONS CONTACT: ANIKA DAVIS PRATT, ASSISTANT DEAN, MBA ADMISSIONS
ADDRESS: 44 WEST 4TH STREET, SUITE 6-70 NEW YORK, NY 10012 UNITED STATES
PHONE: 212-998-0600 • FAX: 212-995-4231
E-MAIL: STERNMBA@STERN.NYU.EDU • WEBSITE: WWW.STERN.NYU.EDU

Sachs, IBM, JPMorgan Chase, Johnson & Johnson, Lehman Brothers, L'Oréal, McKinsey & Company, MTV Networks, Pfizer, Standard & Poor's, and Unilever.

Student Life and Environment

Located downtown and just a few paces from Wall Street, the city's high-energy atmosphere seeps into the student body at Stern. As one student explains, "Going to Stern is all about a cultural fit. Students have very well-balanced lives; we work hard and play harder." On campus, students are involved in the school community, taking advantage of the "limitless opportunities to be involved and take leadership roles in clubs." More than your typical college town, "Being in the heart of the city makes student life at Stern completely unique." Not surprisingly, the school boasts a "great social atmosphere," and students get together for myriad extracurricular events, from the Thursday evening "beer blast" to more refined events such as "dinners at Japanese restaurants organized by the Japan Business Association, the Global Business Conference organized by the Emerging Markets Association, and happy hours organized by a number of clubs."

Even part-time students (many of whom have families or preexisting social lives) say Stern makes an effort to keep them in the loop. Attests a current part-timer, "Since I am only on campus for 2 nights a week, a lot of the social interaction with my peers occurs at events on weekends. However, there have been many events and conferences which have allowed me to interact with other part-time students as well as the full-time student community."

Admissions

NYU's Admission's Committee strives to create a business school community that is as vibrant and diverse as New York City itself. In addition to having a strong academic background, Stern students are leaders in a wide range of fields, bringing diverse expertise and experiences to the program. The entering class of 2008 numbers just over 400 and boasts an average undergraduate GPA of 3.4. The class's average GMAT score was 700, with a range of 640–750.

FINANCIAL FACTS

Annual tuition	$39,800
Fees	$2,022
Cost of books	$1,460
Room & board	$19,444
Average award package	$43,840
Average student loan debt	$61,066

ADMISSIONS

Admissions Selectivity Rating	**98**
# of applications received	4,021
% applicants accepted	17
% acceptees attending	54
Average GMAT	700
Range of GMAT	650–750
Average GPA	3.39
TOEFL required of international students	Yes
Application fee	$200
International application fee	$200
Regular application deadline	3/15
Regular notification	3/15
Application Deadline/Notification	
Round 1:	11/15 / 2/15
Round 2:	1/15 / 4/1
Round 3:	3/15 / 6/1
Non-fall admissions	Yes
Need-blind admissions	Yes

EMPLOYMENT PROFILE			
Career Rating	**94**	**Grads Employed by Function% Avg. Salary**	
Primary Source of Full-time Job Acceptances		**Top 5 Employers Hiring Grads**	
School-facilitated activities	263 (77%)	Lehman Brothers	NR
Graduate-facilitated activities	66 (19%)	Citigroup/Citibank	NR
Unknown	14 (4%)	American Express	NR
Percent employed	94	Deutsche Bank	NR
		JP Morgan Chase	NR

NORTH CAROLINA STATE UNIVERSITY
COLLEGE OF MANAGEMENT

Academics

"The greatest strength of the MBA program at North Carolina State is its focus on technology," many students at this small, new graduate business program in Raleigh tell us. NCSU's program is tailor-made to fit the needs of businesses in nearby Research Triangle Park, where communications, technology, and pharmaceutical firms are always looking to hire "the engineers and scientists to whom this program caters."

NCSU's focus on technology and engineering allows it to offer some unique areas of concentration. The school is "very strong in the integration of marketing and technical knowledge" thanks to its "unique Product Innovation Management program," for example. A biotechnology and pharmaceutical program is another standout; both the faculty and student body benefit from the school's proximity to GlaxoSmithKline, Novartis, and other big regional pharmaceutical players. Students here also boast about the "outstanding supply-chain management program, which carries a great reputation in the region."

Students describe NCSU professors as "hit and miss," but with more hits than misses. They're generally "very energetic about the subjects they teach," "have a wealth of experience from the real world that they use to help teach," and "are easy to contact outside of class and quick to return phone calls." Students appreciate a pedagogical approach across the curriculum that is "focused more on practical team projects and less on business case study." "Strong emphases on communications and presentations skills" and "cross-functional insight into business" are also highly valued. On the downside, "being at a state-funded school [means] budget crunches have hit hard and cut back a lot of nice extras" here.

About two-thirds of all students attend part-time. Full-timers find internships between their first and second year. As one second-year full-time student observes, "Having done an internship this past summer and continued it part-time into the school year, I can definitely say that school is much tougher than real life. I don't know what other scale I can use, other than to say that school appears to be preparing me for difficult situations I may face in the future."

Career and Placement

The program at NCSU "has some very strong industry connections, so students have very well-known companies to choose from for employment," MBAs tell us. In 2005, internship placements included positions with CAT, Chevron Texaco, Cree, Delphi, Duke Energy, Heard & Associates, IBM, Halliburton, the Hoop Group, Last Mile, MCNBC, MTS Sensors, Murphy Family SAS, Ventures, Northrop Grumman, Progress Energy, Red Hat, Starquest Dance, Talecris, and VF Corporation. Graduating MBAs found work with BB&T, Bechtel, Boston Scientific, Capital One, Chevron Texaco, Cisco, Credit Suisse, Duke Energy, First Boston, IBM, John Deere, Last Mile, Nortel, RBC Centura, Red Hat, SAS, Sigmon, Team Pharma, Tech Engage, Teleflex, and Withers.

ADMISSIONS CONTACT: PAM BOSTIC, MBA PROGRAM DIRECTOR
ADDRESS: MBA PROGRAM OFFICE/CAMPUS BOX 8114 RALEIGH, NC 27695-8114 UNITED STATES
PHONE: 919-515-5584 • FAX: 919-515-5073
E-MAIL: MBA@NCSU.EDU • WEBSITE: WWW.MBA.NCSU.EDU

Student Life and Environment

The majority of NCSU's MBAs are part-time students, most of whom work in addition to attending school. One such student explains, "We don't have a lot of free time. We enjoy the experience of being in school, but work, classes, and the constant group meetings for classes limit the amount of free time." Full-time students "generally do not work at the same time" and so "usually have more free time to concentrate on things outside of school." As one of these students explains, "Our academic work and social life is well balanced. Almost every fortnight the entire class has a party. All the students in the class are constantly working on group projects and we have formed good study groups, which help us a lot by dividing the work among ourselves and thus making us able to accomplish everything."

Full-timers and part-timers alike agree that "Raleigh, NC, is a great city. The weather here is outstanding. And there are plenty of available activities, such as attending NC State football and basketball games." Located in central North Carolina, Raleigh allows for easy escapes to the beach (about two hours away by car) or the mountains (about three hours away, in the other direction). Raleigh is part of a greater metropolitan area known as the Triangle that is also home to University of North Carolina, Duke University, and numerous other smaller colleges and universities.

The MBA program at NCSU draws a "friendly, professional, mature, experienced, and extremely helpful" student body. A "strong sense of sharing our experience and supporting each other as we face many challenges" helps students survive the sometimes intense demands of the program. China, Belarus, India, Turkey, Romania, Bulgaria, and Jamaica are among the nations represented in the student body here.

Admissions

Admission to NCSU's MBA program is "highly competitive." Successful candidates typically have strong undergraduate academic records and solid GMAT scores, work experience "demonstrating management potential, leadership skills, creativity," the ability to work in teams, and a genuine interest in technology as it relates to management issues. Interviews are required prior to admission; the school contacts applicants who are deemed potential candidates for the program.

FINANCIAL FACTS

Annual tuition (in-state/ out-of-state)	$10,893/$22,816
Fees	$1,368
Cost of books	$1,000
Room & board (on/off-campus)	$6,000/$11,000
Average award package	$22,121
Average grant	$8,348
Average student loan debt	$28,723

ADMISSIONS

Admissions Selectivity Rating	88
# of applications received	152
% applicants accepted	47
% acceptees attending	59
Average GMAT	608
Range of GMAT	590–650
Average GPA	3.33
TOEFL required of international students	Yes
Minimum TOEFL (paper/computer)	600/250
Application fee	$65
International application fee	$75
Regular application deadline	3/2
Regular notification	4/2
Application Deadline/Notification	
Round 1:	10/10
Round 2:	01/05
Round 3:	03/02
Early decision program?	Yes
ED Deadline/ Notification	10/10 / 11/10
Deferment available	Yes
Maximum length of deferment	1 year
Transfer students accepted	Yes
Transfer application policy May accept up to 12 hours of transfer credit.	
Need-blind admissions	Yes

Applicants Also Look At

Clemson University, Duke University, The University of North Carolina at Chapel Hill, University of North Carolina at Charlotte, University of Pittsburgh, University of South Carolina, Wake Forest University.

EMPLOYMENT PROFILE

Career Rating		73
Primary Source of Full-time Job Acceptances		
School-facilitated activities	20 (63%)	
Graduate-facilitated activities	12 (37%)	
Average base starting salary	$72,568	
Percent employed	17	

Grads Employed by Function	%	Avg. Salary
Finance	17	$66,808
Marketing	21	$63,333
Operations	28	$83,613
Consulting	21	$71,257
General Management	10	$71,333
Other	3	$80,000

Top 5 Employers Hiring Grads
Chevron; LuLu Press; Nortel; GlaxoSmithKline; Manhattan Associates

NORTHEASTERN UNIVERSITY
COLLEGE OF BUSINESS ADMINISTRATION

Academics

Northeastern University offers a broad range of full-time and part-time MBA options. The full-time program follows a 24-month curriculum that includes a cooperative work experience; specializations are available in finance, marketing, and operations and supply chain management. Part-time programs include a conventional Evening MBA, an Executive MBA, and a High Tech MBA.

For full-timers, the highlight of the program is the six-month Corporate Residency (often referred to simply as 'co-op'), during which students undertake a residency with a Boston-area business. One student puts it simply: "The six month co-op program is the best asset of the university. Through co-op I was able to affect changes at an international company and use that experience to earn a great job placement for after graduation. I wouldn't have landed my new job without the co-op experience." While "issues can arise due to the six month co-op, because you are still working in the fall when every other MBA in the nation is interviewing at large companies, banks, and consulting firms for top jobs"—making it "difficult to work out a schedule to interview for the job of your future while committing to the internship of the present"—most students cite co-op as their primary reason for choosing Northeastern.

Part-time programs do not include a co-op component at Northeastern but have much to recommend them all the same. The High Tech MBA "provides a relevant and credible education" with a schedule that "allows the flexibility to keep a full-time job that requires significant travel." One participant explains that the program "has a full-time class load (three to four classes per semester: fall, spring, and summer) with part-time flexibility (classes meet every other week Tuesday night and all day Saturday), and students complete the program in 21 months. The curriculum is preset, covering the broad spectrum of business functions and no specific specialty." Likewise, students in the EMBA program say it "has the right combination of content and environment" with "a significant level of engagement and interaction among the cohort each year."

Students in all programs tell us, "The faculty, the network, and the location are the school's greatest strengths. Our professors have been world class and well connected. NU is located in the heart of Boston. That is tough to beat." Dual campuses mean "easy access for many students. Classes in the satellite campus in downtown Boston are always filled with people who work in the financial district. Also, because NU has two campuses, it is more convenient for most people than going to Suffolk (only in downtown Boston) and Boston College (about an hour's commute on the subway from downtown Boston and most other points in Boston)." The school offers a variety of online MBA options.

Career and Placement

Northeastern's six-month co-op program means that the school has "good relationships ...with a wide variety of employers" in the Boston area, and these relationships pay dividends for the efforts of the school's Career Center. Co-op employers in 2006 included Carrier, Cyprus Tree Investment, GE Supply, Gilette, Harvard Pilgrim Health Care, Hasbro, Kidde Fenwal, MasterFoods USA, Sovereign Bank, TD Securities, Thermo Fisher Scientific, UV Partners, and Wolfe Laboratories. Co-op definitely provides students with a leg up when it comes time for their co-op companies to hire new full-timers, students here agree.

Employers most likely to hire Northeastern MBAs after graduation include AC Nielsen, Amazon, Bayer Consumer Care, Citigroup, Dunkin' Brands, Fidelity, Kaiser Permanente, Liberty Mutual, Lindt & Sprungli, Mellon Financial Corporation, Proctor & Gamble/Gillette, Raytheon Corporation, and Washington Mutual.

ADMISSIONS CONTACT: EVELYN TATE, DIRECTOR, RECRUITMENT AND ADMISSIONS
ADDRESS: 350 DODGE HALL, 360 HUNTINGTON AVENUE BOSTON, MA 02115 UNITED STATES
PHONE: 617-373-5992 • FAX: 617-373-8564
E-MAIL: GSBA@NEU.EDU • WEBSITE: WWW.MBA.NEU.EDU

Student Life and Environment

The Northeastern campus "is a great place to be even when you're not in class." The Marino Center "is a superb gym and is one of the centers of campus life," and "Students participate in any number of activities and are encouraged to form their own groups" elsewhere on campus, creating "an environment that fosters learning, but it also fosters socializing and fun." Also, "Because of the sheer number of employers and outside experts visiting NU, there is always a worthwhile event going on." Students in part-time programs rarely have time for such diversions, however; they "come right from work and all are tired but power through the class." EMBA participants "attend classes all day on one day per week, on alternating Fridays and Saturdays. The support staff takes care of all of your needs: food, books, and travel are all arranged for you, so you just show-up and never have to focus on anything trivial."

The wide variety of programs available at NU draws a diverse student body that includes plenty of techies, mid-career professionals, business neophytes looking to fast track their careers, and internationals.

Admissions

All applicants to the Northeastern MBA program must provide the Admissions Office with the following: a completed online application; sealed copies of official transcripts for all post-secondary schools attended; a current resume; three essays; two professional letters of recommendation; and an official GMAT score report. In addition, international students whose first language is not English must submit TOEFL results. All international students must submit transcripts that have been translated with U.S. grade equivalents assigned for work completed, as well as a certified Declaration and Certification of Finances Statement. Neither an undergraduate degree in business nor previous work experience are required for admission to the program, although those lacking both are unlikely candidates for admission; the school advises such students to take college-level introductory business courses prior to or while applying to the school. The school prefers candidates with a minimum of two years' professional experience.

FINANCIAL FACTS

Annual tuition	$33,300
Fees	$402
Cost of books	$1,700
Room & board	
(off-campus)	$15,000
% of students receiving aid	68
% of first-year students	
receiving aid	94
% of students receiving loans	28
% of students receiving grants	63
Average award package	$26,328
Average grant	$16,250
Average student loan debt	$52,962

ADMISSIONS

Admissions Selectivity Rating	84
# of applications received	319
% applicants accepted	52
% acceptees attending	50
Average GMAT	589
Range of GMAT	540–640
Average GPA	3.2
TOEFL required of	
international students	Yes
Minimum TOEFL	
(paper/computer)	600/250
Application fee	$100
International application fee	$100
Regular application deadline	4/15
Regular notification	5/15
Application Deadline/Notification	
Round 1:	11/30 / 02/15
Round 2:	02/01 / 03/30
Round 3:	03/15 / 04/15
Round 4:	04/15 / 05/15
Transfer students accepted	Yes
Transfer application policy	
We may award a limited number of transfer credits for MBA courses taken at AACSB-accredited institutions.	
Need-blind admissions	Yes

Applicants Also Look At

Babson College, Boston College, Boston University, Fordham University.

EMPLOYMENT PROFILE

Career Rating	80	Grads Employed by Function	% Avg. Salary
Primary Source of Full-time Job Acceptances		Finance	51 $67,889
School-facilitated activities	12 (31%)	Marketing	26 $67,000
Graduate-facilitated activities	25 (64%)	MIS	3 $65,000
Unknown	2 (5%)	Operations	3 $58,000
Average base starting salary	$66,300	Consulting	8 $55,000
Percent employed	72	General Management	6 $66,250
		Other	3 $75,000

Top 5 Employers Hiring Grads
W.R. Grace & Co.; Ocean Spray Cranberries, Inc.; Gillette/Procter & Gamble; EMC

NORTHERN ARIZONA UNIVERSITY
THE W.A. FRANKE COLLEGE OF BUSINESS

Academics

Whether you're in a hurry or in a big hurry to collect your MBA, Administration at Northern Arizona University can accommodate you. The school's MBA program for students with undergraduate degrees in business takes a mere 10 months to complete. Even those who lack a business background can hustle through the NAU MBA, however, thanks to an accelerated foundation course program (called the Common Body of Knowledge) that allows students to earn an MBA in 18 months or less.

NAU offers two graduate options: the MBA and the MBA-ACC. In the MBA program, students can emphasis in accounting, finance, general management, marketing analysis and distribution management, geographic information systems, or a custom emphasis. Geographic information systems is the specialty of the house, students tell us; MBAs also tell us that "the accounting department is fantastic." Throughout the program, teamwork and an integrative cross-disciplinary approach to the material are stressed.

Students here report that the program is "intense and fun at the same time," leaving them "better prepared and more knowledgeable in regards to the major business functions, such as marketing, management, finance, and accounting." Professors "offer challenging work, but they are always available for further instruction beyond classroom hours." One MBA writes, "Our professors strive to enrich students' professional and business skills to prepare them for success in the work force. Professors are welcoming and know students on a first-name basis, which makes communication easier and more fluid." Administrators are "helpful and resourceful when meeting student needs." On the downside, some feel the school's small size can narrow students' options too much; "The school could . . . provide more variety of elective courses to differentiate student skills," writes one student.

Career and Placement

The Gateway Student Success Center at NAU provides career services to all students at the university through counseling and placement services. Students also work directly with the MBA Director in their efforts to find career opportunities. The school reports that average starting salaries for graduates are up 28 percent since 2004. Still, some here complain that "the school could improve on providing a stronger network of alumni to connect graduates with potential job opportunities."

In the past, NAU MBAs have gone on to work at such major corporations as American Express, American Management Systems, AT&T, the Federal Reserve Bank, General Dynamics, Hewlett-Packard, Honeywell, IBM, Intel, Intuit, Motorola, Nestlé, Rockwell International, Safeway Stores, Sandia National Laboratory, State Farm Insurance, Walgreen Co., and W.L. Gore & Associates. Others have signed on with smaller firms and still others have pursued academic careers. The school currently reports that employers who most frequently hire graduates include: Vanguard Investments, Intel, Pulte Homes, Countrywide Bank, and Shea Homes.

Student Life and Environment

Students in the NAU MBA program are the beneficiaries of a "wonderful" new building that "offers all the students a great place to study." The "modern-yet-retro" facility includes plenty of open space, designed to encourage students to linger after class in order to break off into study groups or simply to hang out and socialize.

Student life here "is balanced between schoolwork and activities outside of school." One MBA observes, "During the week, school comes first along with opportunities to go to

ADMISSIONS CONTACT: JERI DENNIS, PROGRAM COORDINATOR
ADDRESS: MBA PROGRAM OFFICE, P.O. BOX 15066 FLAGSTAFF, AZ 86011-5066 UNITED STATES
PHONE: 928-523-7342 • FAX: 928-523-7996
E-MAIL: MBA@NAU.EDU • WEBSITE: WWW.FRANKE.NAU.EDU/MBA

the gym or engage in other recreational activities. Some weekends are full of schoolwork, but most weekends include time to go outside and engage in recreational activities," which typically include "lots of outdoor recreation (skiing, hiking, fishing, running, and visiting the Grand Canyon)" thanks to the school's "superb" location amid the San Francisco peaks. MBAs point out that "the emphasis is really placed on undergraduates at NAU," explaining why many grad students "engage in activities that we set up outside the student-run clubs."

NAU MBAs "come from a variety of backgrounds," which gives students a chance "to meet so many different people" and, as a result, "learn quite a bit about other cultures and how they function." Most here "like to share their opinions, and there is a lot of respect among classmates," who are "supportive and help to create a culture of helpfulness, professionalism, and team orientation."

Admissions

All applicants to the MBA program at NAU must complete an application for graduate admission as well as a supplemental application to the MBA program. They must also submit official transcripts for all postsecondary academic work, an official GMAT score report, a personal essay describing the applicant's background and career ambitions, and three letters of recommendation. In addition to the above, international students must submit an official TOEFL score report and an official Test of Spoken English score report. Successful applicants should score a minimum of 450 on the GMAT, with both verbal and quantitative scores above the twenty-fifth percentile. Under the formula [GMAT score multiplied by (GPA for final 64 undergraduate semester hours multiplied by 200)] applicants should score at least 1050. Incoming students must be proficient in mathematics through introductory calculus, must have mastery of basic business-related computer applications, and must have either completed an undergraduate degree in business or complete the school's Common Base of Knowledge course sequence before commencing work on the MBA.

FINANCIAL FACTS

Annual tuition (in-state/ out-of-state)	$6,516/$16,198
Fees	$3,500
Cost of books	$1,200
Room & board	$6,825

ADMISSIONS

Admissions Selectivity Rating	**76**
# of applications received	43
% applicants accepted	67
% acceptees attending	72
Average GMAT	534
Range of GMAT	470–570
Average GPA	3.36
TOEFL required of international students	Yes
Minimum TOEFL (paper/computer)	550/213
Application fee	$50
International application fee	$50
Regular application deadline	6/1
Regular notification	6/15
Deferment available	Yes
Maximum length of deferment	1 year
Transfer students accepted	Yes
Transfer application policy 6 hours toward electives only	
Non-fall admissions	Yes
Need-blind admissions	Yes

Applicants Also Look At

Arizona State University, University of Arizona.

EMPLOYMENT PROFILE	
Career Rating	69

NORTHERN KENTUCKY UNIVERSITY
COLLEGE OF BUSINESS

GENERAL INFORMATION
Type of school	Public
Environment	Metropolis

SURVEY SAYS...
Solid preparation in:
Presentation skills
Doing business in a global economy

STUDENTS
Enrollment of parent institution	14,000
Enrollment of business school	236
% part-time	85
Average age at entry	28
Average years work experience at entry	5

ACADEMICS
Academic Experience Rating	**70**
Student/faculty ratio	20:1
Profs interesting rating	80
Profs accessible rating	88

Joint Degrees
MBA/JD 5 years.

Academics

Its location "10 minutes from downtown Cincinnati, Ohio" and "affordable [overall cost] relative to other AACSB-accredited schools in the area" draws enthusiastic students to Northern Kentucky University's College of Business. About 85 percent of the students here attend part-time, and those who do appreciate that "classes are offered in the evenings"—most courses meet from 6:00 to 9:00 P.M. once a week—"so that [students] can attend all required classes without cutting into [their] work schedules." NKU also offers two 7-week summer sessions that run on accelerated evening schedules. While class times are convenient, students say that NKU's "greatest strength" is "the course work itself. NKU is very challenging and very strict with academics. Although it is not so easy to prepare for class at times, this has helped prepare me well for my professional career by pushing me to the limit." Class sizes are "small," and professors are "passionate about their subject areas" and "always willing to stay [after class] with you and meet whenever you need to." They're also, for the most part, "flexible and understand that most graduate students also work full-time and have a family." Many have "very relevant real-life experience to impart," and their ranks "include the former director of human resources of a major public utility, a consultant who specializes in turning businesses around, and a finance professor who works as a Certified Financial Planner on the side. No, Jack Welch does not teach here, but those [who] do are knowledgeable and do a good job." Students love that NKU "allows specialization of the MBA" and cite its Entrepreneurship Institute, International Business Center, and finance programs as major strengths.

Overall, students find NKU to be a place where "The student is the top priority." "The staff has always been quick [when] answering my questions and available when I need them," a student writes.

Career and Placement

"There is a wonderful Career Center on campus, but it is primarily focused on meeting the needs of undergraduates," NKU business students tell us. That being said, students admit that, for the most part, they "already have jobs, so career placement is not a large need." Most are looking to move up the ranks with their current employer; those looking to jump ship turn to their fellow students for job leads. Which isn't to say there aren't those who'd like a little more help in the area of job placement: "I think we need more career counselors within the MBA program for those of us who do not come from a traditional business background," one student tells us. Another would like NKU to "improve job [placement] opportunities through alumni relations."

Student Life and Environment

Many at NKU are "on the 'slow' track to finish because of the demands of family and jobs." As such, the school differs from institutions that "have the same students begin and end the program together"; most here "meet different students each semester." Despite this, students report that their "classmates are great people who, through this MBA program, have become real friends." Such friendships are forged largely without the assistance of clubs or activities geared toward graduate students: "I'm a commuter, so most of my time at school is in class, in the library, or meeting to do group work," a typical student writes. While NKU's campus "has food/coffee stands in almost every building" and "computers everywhere with free printing," drawbacks include a "mostly concrete" aesthetic and difficult parking "at certain times of the day."

Students describe their "hardworking" peers as "friendly" but "competitive." NKU strongly recommends that potential applicants obtain 2 years of work experience before

ADMISSIONS CONTACT: MBA OFFICE
ADDRESS: COLLEGE OF BUSINESS, NUNN DRIVE HIGHLAND HEIGHTS, KY 41099 UNITED STATES
PHONE: 859-572-6657 • FAX: 859-572-6177
E-MAIL: MBUSINESS@NKU.EDU • WEBSITE: COB.NKU.EDU/MBA

applying, and, by all accounts, its student body is "very diverse" in employment backgrounds. "Most [students here] are mid-20s to mid-30s," but "age ranges from 20 to 50." "Quite a few are married with children" and "Most have significant work experience." When students seek common ground, they need look no further than their objective: "We are all here for the same reason: to get an MBA," one student writes. That being said, most students are "eager to learn and get the most from their MBA experience, not just a credential."

Admissions

To gain admission to NKU, applicants must obtain a bachelor's degree from a regionally accredited institution and possess a cumulative undergraduate GPA of at least 2.50 on a 4.00 scale; he or she must also obtain a score of at least 450 on a GMAT taken within the last 5 years and, if applicable, obtain a score of at least 550 on the paper version of the TOEFL (or at least 213 on the computer version of the test). Applicants will be admitted if he or she obtains at least 1,000 points via the formula 200 multiplied by GPA plus GMAT score. In lieu of admission via the formula above, a student will be admitted if he or she obtains at least 1,050 points via the formula 200 multiplied by GPA for student's last 60 semester hours plus GMAT score. Exceptions to the GMAT include: GRE score within the last 5 years, possession of a Master degree, M.D., or Ph.D., or similar advanced degree.

FINANCIAL FACTS

Cost of books	$0
% of students receiving aid	33
% of students receiving loans	23
% of students receiving grants	10
Average award package	$8,356
Average grant	$3,359
Average student loan debt	$27,880

ADMISSIONS

Admissions Selectivity Rating	**74**
# of applications received	105
% applicants accepted	70
% acceptees attending	62
Average GMAT	530
Range of GMAT	440–630
Average GPA	3.23
TOEFL required of international students	Yes
Minimum TOEFL (paper/computer)	550/213
Regular application deadline	8/1
Regular notification	rolling
Deferment available	Yes
Maximum length of deferment	0
Transfer students accepted	Yes
Transfer application policy Up to 9 hours from regionally accredited institutions.	
Non-fall admissions	Yes
Need-blind admissions	Yes

Applicants Also Look At
University of Cincinnati, Xavier University.

NORTHWESTERN UNIVERSITY
KELLOGG SCHOOL OF MANAGEMENT

Academics

At the Kellogg School of Management at Northwestern University, you can almost feel the cooperation in the air. "It's the kind of atmosphere that even if you don't know people, you will say 'hi' in the halls," reports one student. This "collaborative," "collegial," and "student-led environment" at Kellogg means that students' input is always sought, and their voices and desires have a huge impact on the course the school takes both academically and socially. Students agree that this crash-course in democracy is "the best way to train tomorrow's business leaders" and note that it also lends the school "a certain energy around the campus that brings excitement to each and every day."

One facet of the cooperative spirit is that both professors and students receive regular performance evaluations. However, it seems the results are rarely negative as the majority of students here praise them as "bright, accomplished, fair, and engaging." Students aren't exempt from the scrutiny of their peers, either. Through a web-based program called LeadNet, Kellogg students are able to receive "confidential, detailed, and honest feedback on how they work in teams" from fellow students, faculty, and staff. According to the school, this produces an unparalleled ability to "respond to and give confidential peer feedback, something excellent managers do well."

Another major draw to the program is the school's 1-year MBA program that allows students to earn their MBAs in just 12 months. "Kellogg's 1-year program is one-of-a-kind," one student says. "It's the best return on investment and offers great flexibility combined with small classes and highest quality students." There is, of course, the traditional 2-year program available as well. In addition to the 1-year MBA program, another unique facet at Kellogg is the Master of Management and Manufacturing (MMM), offered in conjunction with the McCormick School of Engineering and designed to aid students who wish to pursue "management roles in product-driven companies."

Kellogg offers a lengthy list of majors in which students can specialize, from biotechnology management to technology industry management, though some students feel that "application of technology is a little slow compared to other schools." Conversely, students single out the "breadth of the marketing, strategy, and finance departments."

Overridingly, students feel confident in regards to their prospective futures thanks to Kellogg's "overall atmosphere, solid reputation and ranking, [and] strength across academic disciplines."

Career and Placement

Recent recruiters with a presence at Kellogg include Merrill Lynch, Microsoft, UBS, JPMorgan Chase, and Booz Allen Hamilton; most students are confident that their school has a "sterling reputation among corporate recruiters." It helps, too, that professors are "student focused" and fellow students are "willing to go out on a limb to help . . . with recruiting, career advice, and schoolwork." While students agree that the team-focused environment ensures that "networking at Kellogg is tremendous."

ADMISSIONS CONTACT: BETH FLYE, ASSISTANT DEAN, ADMISSIONS AND FINANCIAL AID
ADDRESS: DONALD P. JACOBS CENTER, 2001 SHERIDAN ROAD EVANSTON, IL 60208 UNITED STATES
PHONE: 847-491-3308 • FAX: 847-491-4960
E-MAIL: MBAADMISSIONS@KELLOGG.NORTHWESTERN.EDU
WEBSITE: WWW.KELLOGG.NORTHWESTERN.EDU

Student Life and Environment

Kellogg is situated in Evanston, Illinois, along the shores of Lake Michigan, with only a short commute on the El (elevated train) to downtown Chicago. Most here appreciate this proximity since there aren't "a lot of activities in the city of Evanston." However, don't confuse the city for the campus as "There is a lot going on [at] school." One student explains, "There are dozens, maybe hundreds of clubs at school—special interest, sports, academic, career, spouse/children, politics and government, nonprofit, gay and lesbian, etc." Though the student body is "alive and energetic," some find that diversity, "both ethnically and in terms of people from industries other than consulting," could be improved.

The school has been steadily undergoing multiple renovations to its facilities over the years, including "new classrooms wired for network access," "group study rooms," "quiet study rooms," a "computer training facility" and "expanded computer lab," "free-standing computer terminals," a "student lounge," "lockers," and a "sky-lit atrium." Others note that "off-campus living facilities are outdated, but they're working on it!"

Admissions

Admissions Officers at Kellogg have the unenviable job of whittling a pile of approximately 4,500 applications down to an admitted class of just less than 600. During this process, they look for work experience, academic excellence, and personality. The school's Admissions Board conducts thousands of interviews each fall. For the entering class of 2006, the average GMAT score was 703. The average amount of employment time was just over 5 years for admitted students. In addition, 34 percent of Kellogg students hail from outside of the United States, and for those applicants, TOEFL scores are required. The average TOEFL score for enrolled students is 279 on the computer-based exam.

FINANCIAL FACTS

Annual tuition	$43,935
Room & board	$14,190
% of students receiving aid	67
Average award package	$50,312
Average grant	$11,888
Average student loan debt	$77,940

ADMISSIONS

Admissions Selectivity Rating	97
# of applications received	4,148
Average GMAT	704
Average GPA	3.45
TOEFL required of international students	Yes
Application fee	$225
International application fee	$225
Regular application deadline	1/5
Regular notification	3/26
Application Deadline/Notification	
Round 1:	10/20 / 1/8
Round 2:	1/5 / 3/26
Round 3:	3/9 / 5/7
Deferment available	Yes
Non-fall admissions	Yes
Need-blind admissions	Yes

EMPLOYMENT PROFILE

Career Rating	97	Grads Employed by Function	% Avg. Salary
Primary Source of Full-time Job Acceptances		Finance	24 NR
School-facilitated activities	310 (70%)	Marketing	23 NR
Graduate-facilitated activities	102 (23%)	Operations	1 NR
Unknown	31 (7%)	Consulting	35 NR
Percent employed	97	General Management	7 NR
		Other	7 NR

Top 5 Employers Hiring Grads

McKinsey & Co; Bain & Company; The Boston Consulting Group; Booz Allen Hamilton; Morgan Stanley

THE OHIO STATE UNIVERSITY
MAX M. FISHER COLLEGE OF BUSINESS

GENERAL INFORMATION

Type of school	Public
Environment	Metropolis
Academic calendar	Quarter

SURVEY SAYS...
Friendly students
Good peer network
Smart classrooms
Solid preparation in:
Teamwork

STUDENTS

Enrollment of parent institution	59,900
Enrollment of business school	570
% male/female	71/29
% out-of-state	44
% part-time	53
% minorities	17
% international	33
Average age at entry	27
Average years work experience at entry	4.2

ACADEMICS

Academic Experience Rating	**91**
Student/faculty ratio	5:1
Profs interesting rating	83
Profs accessible rating	92
% female faculty	20
% minority faculty	14

Joint Degrees
MBA/JD 4 years, MBA/MHA 3 years, MBA/MD 5 years, MBA/PharmD 5 years, MLHR/MA (Education) 3 years.

Prominent Alumni
Mr. Leslie Wexner, Chair/CEO/Founder, Limited, Inc.; Mr. Jesse J. Tyson, President, ExxonMobil Inter-America Inc.; Mr. Lionel Nowell, Executive Vice President/CFO, Pepsi Bottling Gr; Ms. Tami Longaberger, CEO, The Longaberger Company; Mr. Russell Klein, Chief Marketing Officer, Burger King Corp.

Academics

Ranked among the nation's top-25 MBA programs and among the top 10 such programs at public universities, the Fisher MBA program at Ohio State University offers both "great value" and "high-quality classroom training." With a student/faculty ratio of 5 to 1, Fisher is able to offer "a lot of personal attention" as well. One student writes of a factor that convinced him to attend: "The students and faculty seemed on very familiar terms."

OSU excels in a broad range of disciplines. Students agree that Fisher is "one of the best schools in the operations and supply department" and also that the school has "great finance and logistics programs" and is strong in marketing. MBAs here appreciate "the flexibility within the curriculum to design [one's] own major" as well as the "emphasis on group learning" that serves as the program's pedagogic foundation. While the "smaller program size . . . allows the students to get to know each other, as well as the professors, far more intimately than at most business schools," students also benefit from being on "a large university campus," which "lets students tap many resources available at large schools such as OSU."

Fisher operates on a quarterly academic calendar, which makes for a fast-paced learning environment. Some find it overwhelming, revealing that "if you don't have knowledge of a subject before coming into the class, you're screwed because you don't have time to learn it." "If you want to hide behind a laptop or sit in the back row, you have every opportunity to do it." Others handle the system better. The fact that many find time for extracurriculars (see "Student Life and Environment" below) indicates that, for most students, the workload is manageable. Professors' teaching skills "vary greatly . . . but the administration seems very anxious and willing to adjust the line-up from year to year based off our recommendations. For each quarter there is a formal Fisher-driven evaluation on each professor. . . . The great majority of professors seems to be very receptive to this system and will alter their teaching styles if necessary and/or possible." It's also "not uncommon for Fisher to replace one or two 'core' faculty teachers each year if students overwhelmingly feel that he or she is not working out." Students add that professors, regardless of their teaching ability, make themselves available and that "most, if not all, are tightly integrated into the Columbus/outside business community. All of them are known and respected by managers of the companies" that students interview with.

Career and Placement

Fisher's "second-to-none" Career Services Office attracts "a large number of companies in and around Columbus." Students tell us that "operations is the one field that the best companies come to Fisher for." Some here regret that while regional recruiting is quite good, "There are almost no companies from other parts of the country." Others, however, counter that "there is ample support for students interested in positions outside of the Midwest. Many of the finance students are pursuing investment banking opportunities in the Northeast with great success." Students here also benefit from "a fantastic alumni base that is always willing to help out current students."

Companies most likely to extend offers to OSU MBAs in 2006 included: American Greetings, Capital One, Defense Finance and Accounting Services, Emerson, Johnson & Johnson, Kimberly-Clark, Limited Brands, Motorola, Nationwide, Nestlé, Oracle Consulting, PricewaterhouseCoopers, Procter & Gamble, and United Stationers.

Student Life and Environment

"Many students are active in various organizations" and extracurricular projects at Fisher, including "the Fisher Board Fellows, which allow you to interact with members from the Board of Directors of various companies large and small within Columbus . . . the Initiative for Managing Services, whereby students from the first year full-time program get an

ADMISSIONS CONTACT: DAVID SMITH, EXECUTIVE DIRECTOR, GRADUATE PROGRAMS OFFICE
ADDRESS: 100 GERLACH HALL, 2108 NEIL AVENUE COLUMBUS, OH 43210-1144 UNITED STATES
PHONE: 614-292-8511 • FAX: 614-292-9006
E-MAIL: MBA@FISHER.OSU.EDU • WEBSITE: FISHERMBA.OSU.EDU

insight into diverse fields of business management from marketing to human resources, way before their summer internship actually starts . . . and Fisher Professional Services, which provides consulting services to various companies in and around Columbus (predominantly) and is growing rapidly. Students, both first and second year do these consulting projects and assignments along with their regular course work and internships." One MBA adds, "Student organizations are very active. The Finance Club took students interested in a Wall Street career to New York to network with a variety of investment banks. The Marketing Association organized a networking trip to Chicago and Milwaukee. Most career-type organizations provide students a large number of opportunities to interact with companies."

Fisher's facilities are "brand new and all resources are state of the art." "The school is well equipped technologically, and the professors definitely utilize the tech resources. Notes and all other materials are available in hard copy and digital format. Communications are frequent and through e-mail from them as well." Prospective students should know that the OSU campus is a bit sports crazed. One student explains, "Being a Buckeye is like a religion, and you're quickly indoctrinated upon arrival. People have a lot of fun going to all kinds of Buckeye sports events. We also have an event of the week that brings together everyone for a moment of relaxation—much needed after a tough week!" "Students and faculty all seem to love, not just like, being Buckeyes and working alongside one another," one MBA says. Another agrees: "The administration keeps a close ear to student feedback and takes quick action to mend issues. And the students themselves are a joy to learn from."

Admissions

The Admissions Office at Fisher requires applicants to provide two official copies of transcripts for all undergraduate and graduate institutions attended, GMAT scores, three letters of recommendation, essays, and a resume of work experience. Interviews are conducted at the request of the Admissions Department. In addition to the above, international applicants whose first language is not English must provide proof of English proficiency (the school accepts several standardized tests, including the TOEFL, MELAB, and IELTS; minimum acceptable scores are 600 on the paper-based TOEFL, 250 on the computer-based TOEFL, 86 on the MELAB, and 8 on the IELTS) and an affidavit of financial support.

FINANCIAL FACTS

Annual tuition (in-state/ out-of-state)	$18,696/$32,049
Fees	$783
Cost of books	$2,586
Room & board (on/off-campus)	$6,378/$7,200
% of students receiving aid	74
% of first-year students receiving aid	84
% of students receiving loans	57
% of students receiving grants	60
Average award package	$26,409
Average grant	$17,609

ADMISSIONS

Admissions Selectivity Rating	**96**
# of applications received	749
% applicants accepted	30
% acceptees attending	62
Average GMAT	661
Range of GMAT	630–700
Average GPA	3.41
TOEFL required of international students	Yes
Minimum TOEFL (paper/ computer/internet)	600/250/100
Application fee	$60
International application fee	$70
Regular application deadline	rolling
Regular notification	rolling
Deferment available	Yes
Maximum length of deferment	1 year
Need-blind admissions	Yes

Applicants Also Look At

Duke University, Indiana University—Bloomington, Michigan State University, Northwestern University, Purdue University, The University of North Carolina at Chapel Hill, University of Michigan.

EMPLOYMENT PROFILE

Career Rating	89	Grads Employed by Function	%	Avg. Salary
Primary Source of Full-time Job Acceptances		Finance	23	$84,579
School-facilitated activities	77 (74%)	Marketing	21	$84,329
Graduate-facilitated activities	27 (26%)	Operations	15	$87,400
Average base starting salary	$84,674	Consulting	16	$92,000
Percent employed	96	General Management	10	$87,643
		Other	3	$90,000

Top 5 Employers Hiring Grads
Nationwide; Abbott; Limited Brands; Wipro Technologies; Deloitte Consulting; Emerson; Procter & Gamble

OLD DOMINION UNIVERSITY
COLLEGE OF BUSINESS AND PUBLIC ADMINISTRATION

Academics

The MBA program at Old Dominion University serves a predominantly local student population for whom cost and convenience are major priorities. Students here also appreciate that "program options are deeper here than at others in the area."

Choices are indeed myriad in the ODU College of Business and Public Administration. Students may pursue a traditional MBA or an MS in Accounting, an MA in Economics, an MPA, a Master of Urban Studies, an MS in Computer Science, along with two PhD options. Furthermore, they may take classes part-time or full-time; in the daytime, evenings, or weekends; and at the main campus in Norfolk, at any of several satellite campuses; or in virtual classrooms at the Northern Virginia Higher Education Center, where students participate in a lockstep, cohort program. MBA students may choose a concentration in financial analysis and valuation, international business, public administration, information technology and enterprise integration, business and economic forecasting, or maritime and port management, or they may opt for a general MBA without a concentration. A variety of study abroad options and independent research projects round out the choices here.

Whatever option they pursue, students praise the program's many conveniences. They appreciate the way in which "Electronic communication allows submittal of questions and assigned work, as well as distribution of reference material. The system is set up well to allow easy contact with the instructors and classmates." Because so many are employed, students are especially grateful that "the school works very well with people who work full-time, with great class schedules on nights and weekends." Professors here "are a truly outstanding group, with many who have been successful professionally and are now teaching. Their combination of real-world experience and academic theory allows for a richness of education." Professors are also easily accessible "7 days a week," while administrators "always return telephone calls." As one student aptly asks, "What more can you expect from a school?"

Career and Placement

Old Dominion offers career services to its MBA through the university Career Development Center. The university dedicates one counselor in the CDC Office to serve MBAs; she assists students in finding both internship and full-time positions, helps with resume and cover letter preparation, and provides individual career consultation. MBA students also benefit from an MBA Association comprised of both current students and alumni. The association organizes numerous career-promoting events over the course of the school year, including seminars, forums, social events, community service, and an annual dinner.

Student Life and Environment

ODU's MBA program is located in Constant Hall, a thoroughly renovated facility that features 21 mediated wireless classrooms, executive education facilities, and a computer lab dedicated to business students. The new facilities are just part of a plan "to help transform this school from a commuter-oriented school to a traditional urban university." The university is "expanding by adding other facilities" as well, but students report that ODU is still a long way from becoming a conventional residential school with a full and active campus life.

For now, the ODU MBA "is very commuter oriented," meaning that most students "don't spend a lot of time at school." One student says, "Unfortunately, I don't have enough time to experience much of what the school has to offer due to full-time work

ADMISSIONS CONTACT: MS. SHANNA A. WOOD, MBA PROGRAM MANAGER
ADDRESS: CONSTANT HALL 1026 NORFOLK, VA 23529 UNITED STATES
PHONE: 757-683-3585 • FAX: 757-683-5750
E-MAIL: MBAINFO@ODU.EDU • WEBSITE: WWW.ODU-MBA.ORG

along with school requirements," and another adds, "I don't spend a lot of time at school because I am married with kids." Most students live in and around Norfolk, a naval town with a population of approximately a quarter-million. Surrounding cities and suburbs including Virginia Beach, Newport News, Hampton, and Chesapeake make this a substantial metropolitan area. Top regional employers include the military, Sentara Health Care, American Systems Engineering, Amerigroup, Manpower, Geico Direct, Gold Key Resorts, Stihl, Norfolk Southern, and the Christian Broadcasting Network.

ODU's MBA program attracts "many current and former military personnel" (military personnel who receive any form of tuition assistance are charged the in-state rate for all tuition charges regardless of their home state), as well as students who "run a broad range of race, age, experience, and sociopolitical background." Students are "generally likeable, easygoing, and friendly, and willing to help out in a team effort."

Admissions

All applicants to the MBA program at ODU must submit the following materials: a completed application (paper or online) including statement of personal objectives and resume; an official GMAT score report; official transcripts for all undergraduate and graduate work; a letter of recommendation (from a professor if you are currently a student; from a supervisor if you are currently employed); and a tuition-rate-determination form (to determine eligibility for in-state tuition). International students whose first language is not English must also submit an official score report for the TOEFL. Applications generally take 4 to 6 weeks to process once all materials have arrived at the Admissions Office. Incoming students who have not completed college-level calculus are required to complete an equivalent undergraduate course during their first semester of MBA work. ODU considers the trend of undergraduate grades as well as overall cumulative GPA; those who showed marked improvement in junior and senior years can overcome poor performance as underclassmen. Returning adults with considerable work experience may earn up to six credits toward the MBA for skills and knowledge accrued through work; credits are awarded on the basis of evaluation, examination, certifications, or portfolio.

FINANCIAL FACTS

Annual tuition (in-state/ out-of-state)	$6,840/$17,160
Fees	$185
Cost of books	$800
Room & board (on/off-campus)	$6,500/$7,500
Average grant	$14,500

ADMISSIONS

Admissions Selectivity Rating	**76**
# of applications received	235
% applicants accepted	71
% acceptees attending	69
Average GMAT	545
Average GPA	3.25
TOEFL required of international students	Yes
Minimum TOEFL (paper/computer)	550/213
Application fee	$40
International application fee	$40
Regular application deadline	6/1
Regular notification	Rolling
Application Deadline/Notification	
Round 1:	11/01 / 12/01
Round 2:	03/01 / 04/01
Round 3:	06/01 / 07/01
Deferment available	Yes
Maximum length of deferment	1 year
Transfer students accepted	Yes
Transfer application policy We accept up to 12 credit hours from AACSB accredited MBA programs only.	
Non-fall admissions	Yes
Need-blind admissions	Yes

PACIFIC LUTHERAN UNIVERSITY
SCHOOL OF BUSINESS

GENERAL INFORMATION
Type of school	Private
Affiliation	Lutheran
Environment	City

SURVEY SAYS...
Cutting edge classes
Smart classrooms
Solid preparation in:
General management
Doing business in a global economy

STUDENTS
Enrollment of parent institution	3,661
Enrollment of business school	84
% part-time	100
Average age at entry	31
Average years work experience at entry	6

ACADEMICS
Academic Experience Rating	**75**
Student/faculty ratio	6:1
Profs interesting rating	80
Profs accessible rating	87
% female faculty	46
% minority faculty	12

Joint Degrees
MBA/MS (Nursing) 2.5 years.

Academics

With an average of 15 students per class, the School of Business at Pacific Lutheran University offers "classes size small enough to actually get personal attention and learn from other students as well as the faculty members." This, a strong local reputation, and a "school schedule [that] really caters to working professionals" are among the top reasons students choose the MBA program at PLU.

PLU accommodates a broad swath of the professional world through a wide range of offerings. Students may pursue an accelerated 16-month MBA for the Knowledge Economy, which focuses on technology and innovation management, or they may pursue the same degree through the conventional part-time evening program. They may opt for an MBA in Health Care Management, or they may pursue an MBA in Entrepreneurship and closely held business. An MBA in general management is also offered. The curriculum includes 36 credit hours of required core courses and 9 credit hours of electives. It can be completed in 20 months, although most students take longer. Students appreciate "the emphasis on leadership" in this "robust curriculum." Busy professionals also love that "the curriculum is set up so you can graduate very quickly with only 9 units a semester and 2 nights a week. This is probably the quickest legitimate MBA program in Washington."

A unique feature of the PLU MBA is the 10-day international experience, the cost of which is covered largely by tuition. (Students may be responsible for one or two meals per day; travel and hotel are included.) The program may include a trade mission trip organized by the Tacoma World Trade Center, or may involve travel to an international destination to meet with foreign business leaders to study global business best practices.

As one student sums up, "The administration, faculty, and academic experience are why I chose PLU. The past 2 years have strengthened my overall skills and provided me an educational experience I will never forget. The school impressed me on my first visit and impresses me even more today with their skill and knowledge base."

Career and Placement

The Career Development Office at PLU provides placement and counseling services for all undergraduates, graduate students, and alumni. The office acts as a liaison between current students and alumni in order to establish mentoring relationships. It also assists students with internship and career placement, and it works with the PLU Business Network, an alumni association, to schedule social events throughout the school year. Another significant networking opportunity is the MBA Executive Leadership Series, a series of addresses delivered by area execs. Among recent speakers are Belo Corp. President Ray Heacox and Pyramid Breweries CEO Scott Barnum.

Employers who most frequently hire Pacific Lutheran MBAs include Boeing, Microsoft, Weyerhaeuser, State Farm Insurance, and Intel.

ABBY WIGSTROM-CARLSON, DIRECTOR OF GRADUATE PROGRAMS & EXTERNAL RELATIONS
ADDRESS: OFFICE OF ADMISSIONS, PACIFIC LUTHERAN UNIVERSITY TACOMA, WA 98447 U.S.
PHONE: 253-535-7151 • FAX: 253-536-5136
E-MAIL: PLUMBA@PLU.EDU • WEBSITE: WWW.PLU.EDU/MBA

Student Life and Environment

The MBA program at PLU is unusually small; only 65 students were enrolled for the 2005–2006 academic year. Although most attend full-time, classes are scheduled at the convenience of part-time students during weekday evenings, resulting in "flexible evening schedules for working professionals." Students tell us that "classes go by fairly quickly and they are set up on a rotational schedule so you only have each class once every 10 days or so. This allows a good amount of prep time. The reading is fairly light, but most of the projects are group assignments, which can be tough for [those with] busy lives."

Students appreciate that PLU "is committed to making the school better. Many great changes have happened since my arrival, including a new, modern, updated facility; free Wi-Fi access; outstanding, well-equipped rooms; and real-life practical experience from the faculty. I am getting a better education than I had expected, and my expectations coming in were high," declares one student. They also enjoy a homey environment; one student notes, "It is a small school, [and] there are always people looking out for your safety."

As part of the PLU student body you'll find "accountants, doctors, bankers, and lawyers" who together form "a big family and enjoy spending time together." Students tell us that "the age range is broad, and the experience they bring adds to the learning experience." Most "are working professionals with families" along with "a few international students who do not work outside of school." Students also remark on noticing "a higher percentage of school employees enrolled in the program than one might expect."

Admissions

According to the school, Admission Officers of the PLU MBA program look for candidates who "have demonstrated proven success in a challenging undergraduate or master's-level program," "desire academic, personal, and career challenges," "communicate clearly and demonstrate leadership capability in a variety of settings," "serve in their community, workplace, church, or school," and "bring a unique perspective to the classroom environment." Applicants must provide the school with the following materials: official transcripts covering all undergraduate and graduate work; an official GMAT or GRE score report; a current resume; a completed application form; two letters of recommendation; and a 300-word statement of personal goals. Candidates whose native language is other than English must also submit an official TOEFL or IELTS score report. International transcripts must be submitted to Educational Perspectives for evaluation. All international applicants are required to submit an I-20 as well as a Declaration of Finances.

FINANCIAL FACTS

Annual tuition	$19,755
Fees	$0
Cost of books	$1,800
Room & board	$6,765
% of students receiving aid	50
% of students receiving loans	22
% of students receiving grants	30
Average award package	$10,281
Average grant	$4,717
Average student loan debt	$15,563

ADMISSIONS

Admissions Selectivity Rating	**73**
# of applications received	52
% applicants accepted	73
% acceptees attending	68
Average GMAT	520
Average GPA	3.23
TOEFL required of international students	Yes
Minimum TOEFL (paper/computer)	573/230
Application fee	$40
International application fee	$40
Regular application deadline	rolling
Regular notification	rolling
Deferment available	Yes
Maximum length of deferment	1 year
Transfer students accepted	Yes
Transfer application policy Minimum of 24 Semester hours in residence.	
Non-fall admissions	Yes
Need-blind admissions	Yes

Applicants Also Look At
Seattle Pacific University, Seattle University, University of Washington.

```
┌─────────────────────────────────────────────────┐
│              EMPLOYMENT PROFILE                   │
│  Career Rating              84                    │
│                                                   │
└─────────────────────────────────────────────────┘
```

PENNSYLVANIA STATE UNIVERSITY
SMEAL COLLEGE OF BUSINESS

GENERAL INFORMATION
Type of school	Public
Environment	Town

SURVEY SAYS...
Good social scene
Good peer network
Smart classrooms
Solid preparation in:
Communication/interpersonal skills
Presentation skills

STUDENTS
Enrollment of parent institution	42,294
Enrollment of business school	86
% male/female	67/33
% out-of-state	65
% minorities	18
% international	35
Average age at entry	28
Average years work experience at entry	4.5

ACADEMICS
Academic Experience Rating	**98**
Student/faculty ratio	4:1
Profs interesting rating	93
Profs accessible rating	97
% female faculty	14

Joint Degrees
Science BS/MBA 5 years, MHA/MBA 3 years, JD/MBA 5 years.

Prominent Alumni
John Arnold, Chairman and CEO, Petroleum Products Corporation; J. David Rogers, Chairman and CEO, JD Capital Management; James R. Stengel, CMO, Proctor and Gamble Corporation.

Academics

Many factors combine to convince MBAs at Penn State's Smeal College of Business that their program offers "one of the best returns on investment in the world." The "reasonable tuition and amazing financial assistance from the program" certainly play a large part, not to mention the school's small-town location, which provides "a cheap place to live and study, so costs are minimal." There's also "the world-class education provided by professors who are extremely respected in their industry," and, last but not least, "the benefit of the Penn State network with the largest active alumni base in the country." One student describes the alumni as "rabidly loyal to the school and very willing to help current students. . . . They also come back for football tailgates, so students have a great opportunity to connect with many alumni in person."

The Smeal MBA is "a very small program" (between 75 and 110 students in each incoming class) that "facilitates a more personalized education" through "great access to professors and professional development opportunities." Students love the "many opportunities to build close relationships with a world-class faculty." One student explains, "MBAs are on a first-name basis with all faculty and staff. Everyone really goes out of their way to make sure you are on the right path in virtually everything." Administrators "join the students daily for coffee and are tremendously responsive to our needs. They also join us for social events and attend outside events." Students are especially pleased that "the new Dean is committed to transforming this program into a national powerhouse."

Smeal excels in supply chain management; students tell us that finance is another strength of the program, as is business-to-business marketing (a product of Smeal's Institute for the Study of Business Markets, which "brings the thought leaders from around the world together to face the challenges in today's B2B markets"). They warn that "the first year at Smeal is packed. Students coming into the program should expect to be in class 16 hours a week and working outside the classroom around 20 hours." Things don't let up that much during the second year, but students don't mind; they tell us that the program "prepares students for the challenges they will face once they re-enter the workforce in a management capacity. Students develop both technical and leadership skills and are well positioned to lead business in the future. In addition, the collaborative culture of the program translates well into successful behaviors in the business world."

Career and Placement

Career Services is a mixed bag at Penn State. Students grumble that "due to the small size of our MBA program, the school struggles to bring in a large number of recruiters in various disciplines." However, they also point out that "career services have been upgraded recently." They also point out that "the school sponsors treks to Philadelphia and New York City to enable/facilitate students to connect with recruiters and alumni," and that "through a school database, you can quickly identify key alumni contacts at every major company in the world." Overall, most agree the placement picture here is pretty good.

Companies most likely to employ Smeal MBAs include: Air Products & Chemicals, Amazon.com, Avaya, Bank of America Corporation, Bear Stearns, CIGNA, Citigroup, Dell, DuPont, ExxonMobil, Ford Motor Company, Hewlett-Packard, Honeywell International, IBM, Intel, Johnson & Johnson, Kennametal, KPMG International, Pfizer, Praxair, PricewaterhouseCoopers, Solectron, and Time Inc.

Student Life and Environment

State College, Pennsylvania, may not have Manhattan's glitz and glamour, but it is "a beautiful town and a fantastic place to spend 2 challenging years of your life." The town provides "great nightlife and a downtown bar scene," while the school provides the football beloved by so many here. Major events such as Thon and Arts Fest pepper the academic calendar, and students report that "outside of the classroom, opportunities abound for cross-cultural learning (student organizations host numerous events), philanthropic involvement (Habitat for Humanity, etc.), and social events (we went skydiving at the beginning of the semester!)." In 2005, the business school "moved into a new, state-of-the art $68 million building that takes advantage of cutting-edge technology available today. The building helps strengthen a sense of community that is already very evident at Penn State." On the downside, students tell us that "activities can be limited due to the small size of the school. There are always demands for more clubs, but not always enough students available. Several students and spouses started a partners club this year, which should help new students with domestic partners."

Admissions

The Smeal admission's website notes that Admissions Officers work hard to optimize class composition for each entering class. Diverse backgrounds in terms of both professional and life experience are sought so that a wide range of perspectives inform group work and class discussion. Applicants to the program must submit the following materials: a completed online application form; official copies of all transcripts for all postsecondary academic work; an official GMAT score report; two letters of recommendation from individuals who can assess your past professional performance; personal essays; a resume; and an interview. In addition to all of the above, international applicants must also submit an official score report for the TOEFL; and evidence of sufficient funds to cover at least 1 year's expenses while in the program (approximately $40,000 to $45,000). The school admits some students directly from undergraduate programs, but most students enter with at least 4 years of professional experience.

FINANCIAL FACTS

Annual tuition (in-state/ out-of-state)	$17,110/$28,712
Fees	$1,410
Cost of books	$2,500
Room & board	$10,000
% of students receiving aid	78
% of first-year students receiving aid	79
% of students receiving grants	78
Average award package	$24,627
Average grant	$24,627

ADMISSIONS

Admissions Selectivity Rating	95
# of applications received	527
% applicants accepted	29
% acceptees attending	57
Average GMAT	651
Range of GMAT	610–700
Average GPA	3.32
TOEFL required of international students	Yes
Minimum TOEFL (paper/computer)	600/250
Application fee	$75
International application fee	$75
Regular application deadline	4/15
Regular notification	5/31
Application Deadline/Notification	
Round 1:	12/1 / 1/31
Round 2:	2/1 / 3/31
Round 3:	4/15 / 5/31
Early decision program?	Yes
ED Deadline/ Notification	12/01 / 01/31
Deferment available	Yes
Maximum length of deferment	1 year
Transfer students accepted	Yes
Transfer application policy A maximum of six elective credits may be transferred	
Need-blind admissions	Yes

Applicants Also Look At

Indiana University—Bloomington, Michigan State University, Purdue University, University of Maryland—College Park.

EMPLOYMENT PROFILE

Career Rating	90	Grads Employed by Function	%	Avg. Salary
Primary Source of Full-time Job Acceptances		Finance	47	$80,926
School-facilitated activities	44 (85%)	Human Resources	2	NR
Graduate-facilitated activities	8 (15%)	Marketing	23	$91,388
Average base starting salary	$83,098	Operations	17	$86,378
Percent employed	90	Consulting	7	$73,750
		General Management	4	NR

Top 5 Employers Hiring Grads
Dell Inc.; DuPont; Air Products; IBM Corporation; Pfizer

Pennsylvania State University—Erie, The Behrend College
Sam and Irene Black School of Business

GENERAL INFORMATION
Type of school	Public
Environment	Village
Academic calendar	Semester

SURVEY SAYS...
Good peer network
Cutting edge classes
Solid preparation in:
General management
Teamwork
Communication/interpersonal skills

STUDENTS
Enrollment of parent institution	4,446
Enrollment of business school	137
% male/female	53/47
% out-of-state	5
% part-time	69
% minorities	1
% international	2
Average age at entry	26
Average years work experience at entry	4

ACADEMICS
Academic Experience Rating	**79**
Student/faculty ratio	6:1
Profs interesting rating	78
Profs accessible rating	86
% female faculty	22
% minority faculty	22

Academics

Thanks to its "good institutional name and reputation," Penn State Erie, The Behrend College draws an "intelligent, diverse, competitive" group of students to its comprehensive and broad-based MBA program. A general degree that aims to develop the critical-thinking skills necessary for a career in mid- and upper-level management, the MBA curriculum consists of 48 units, or 14 courses. Of these, 18 units form the foundation core courses, comprising four introductory classes: Business, Government, and Society; Costs, Competition, and Market Performance; Demand, Operations, and Firm Performance; and Integrated Business Analysis. After completing these courses, students must complete 18 credits of advanced required courses and 12 credits of elective course work. For those who have already taken business courses, the program can be streamlined through the omission of certain foundation courses.

Depending on their previous academic preparation, full-time students can usually complete the MBA curriculum in three semesters, whereas part-time students usually require 3 to 4 years to complete the program. You'll find a pretty decisive split on the Penn State campus between "those who are relatively fresh out of undergrad with little/no work experience," and returning students "who are married with children and have 10-plus years of work experience (often in technical backgrounds)." In fact, many of the younger students have come to the program directly out of the undergraduate college, as the school offers talented business majors the opportunity to complete MBAs with one additional year of study. A lively mix, students enjoy the diversity within the student body, telling us, "My fellow students are intelligent people. We learn a lot off of each other due to our diverse professional and undergraduate backgrounds."

Professors join the Penn State Behrend faculty from a variety of distinguished professional and academic backgrounds, and "The majority are outstanding" in the classroom. There is no predominant teaching methodology at the school, and "Professors are different, but each is able to teach a particular course in a dynamic way." The result is a diversified and useful academic experience. A second-year student adds, "Each class has given me valuable information, especially those that I thought were not relevant in my profession. Those particular classes have pushed me beyond my comfortable boundaries and allowed me to succeed." Enrolling roughly 90 new students annually, the program is fairly small, and the school prides itself on establishing supportive relationships between professors and students. A current student attests, "The professors are a pleasure to be around, and they understand that the student body is not only diverse in its gender and race but its work experience and age as well."

While the program has historically maintained a limited enrollment, many students mention that the program has grown considerably in recent years, increasing average class sizes and causing some administrative distress. However, many feel "The program is moving in the right direction," reassuring us that school officials are "always looking for ways to improve" and will probably have "all the bugs worked out in a few years."

Career and Placement

A high percentage of Penn State Behrend students are currently employed in a professional positions and are pursuing an MBA with the intention of improving their career opportunities at their current companies. In fact, a considerable number of Penn State Behrend students receive tuition assistance from their employers. Even so, "A significant portion of those students desires a career change upon graduating." For those, the Penn State—Behrend Academic Advising and Career Development Center serves both the

ADMISSIONS CONTACT: ANN M. BURBULES, GRADUATE ADMISSIONS COUNSELOR
ADDRESS: 4701 COLLEGE DRIVE ERIE, PA 16563 UNITED STATES
PHONE: 814-898-7255 • FAX: 814-898-6044
E-MAIL: PSBEHRENDMBA@PSU.EDU • WEBSITE: WWW.BEHREND.PSU.EDU

undergraduate and graduate population at the college, including students in the MBA program. The CDC hosts career fairs, on-campus recruiting and interview events, seminars, and workshops. A growing number of organizations participate in Penn State Behrend career fairs each year. In 2005, the MBA graduates who responded to the CDC's placement survey reported an average salary of $59,214, with a salary range between $42,000 and $65,000.

Student Life and Environment

In the Sam and Irene Black School MBA program, students are "interesting, easy to work with, helpful, and enjoyable to be around," making class time and study groups a pleasure rather than a chore. A current student shares, "I have a lot of fun with classmates working on projects and activities although I am only there two days a week." While there are plenty of student organizations and activities associated with the larger university, a majority of MBA students "are commuters who have difficulty scheduling classes and meeting time commitments around work and family obligations." These students "only spend time at school for class time and group work/study time" and generally do not participate in extracurricular clubs or activities. As a result, "Getting to know everyone is difficult" and students admit, "There is little social interaction other than going out for 2 hours at the very end of the semester." Life at Penn State Behrend is nonetheless agreeable, boasting a "very friendly atmosphere, very amicable personnel and students, very attractive campus setting." Currently, the school is located in a new $30-million Research and Economic Development Center, and students agree that "the new business building is a great asset to the MBA program."

Admissions

Students may apply to begin study at Penn State in the fall, spring, or summer semester. Admissions decisions are made on a rolling basis. To apply, students must submit two official transcripts, official GMAT scores, a statement of purpose, an application fee, and three recommendation forms. Candidates with the highest GMAT scores and GPA are given priority in admissions. Candidates are evaluated based on the strength of their combined GMAT score and GPA; therefore, a lower GMAT score can be compensated for by a higher GPA, or vice versa.

FINANCIAL FACTS

Annual tuition (in-state/ out-of-state)	$11,664/$18,108
Fees	$552
Cost of books	$1,536
Room & board (on/off-campus)	$0/$9,378
% of students receiving aid	87
% of first-year students receiving aid	83
% of students receiving loans	76
% of students receiving grants	29
Average award package	$17,391
Average grant	$8,333
Average student loan debt	$17,725

ADMISSIONS

Admissions Selectivity Rating	79
# of applications received	60
% applicants accepted	62
% acceptees attending	95
Average GMAT	527
Range of GMAT	460–600
Average GPA	3.41
TOEFL required of international students	Yes
Minimum TOEFL (paper/computer)	550/213
Application fee	$45
International application fee	$45
Regular application deadline	7/10
Regular notification	rolling
Deferment available	Yes
Maximum length of deferment	2 years
Transfer students accepted	Yes
Transfer application policy 10 credits of relevant graduate work completed at an accredited institution.	
Non-fall admissions	Yes
Need-blind admissions	Yes

EMPLOYMENT PROFILE

Career Rating	76	Grads Employed by Function	%	Avg. Salary
Primary Source of Full-time Job Acceptances		Consulting	50	$45,000
School-facilitated activities	3 (75%)	Other	50	$65,250
Graduate-facilitated activities	1 (25%)	**Top 5 Employers Hiring Grads**		
		Deloitte Consulting; Paradigm Wave;		

PEPPERDINE UNIVERSITY
GRAZIADIO SCHOOL OF BUSINESS AND MANAGEMENT

Academics

Pepperdine's Graziadio School of Business and Management offers a range of program options for full-time students, working individuals, and accomplished execs. Full-time programs include a traditional MBA, an international program, and two joint-degree programs: an MBA/Master of Public Policy and an MBA/JD. About three in four students here attend part-time, and those looking to schedule their education around a full-time job can do so with either morning or evening classes. The school encourages mid-level managers to take advantage of its executive MBA program and senior-level executives to take advantage of its presidential and key executive MBA program; both programs meet on weekends. The school's Master of Science in Organization Development is also geared toward those with significant professional experience and is composed of eight 1-week sessions at various locations in California and abroad.

Across programs, the Graziadio curriculum focuses on "keeping up with the changing global economy while doing business in an ethical manner." Course work on organizational behavior is "very strong," though students tell us that "employers aren't so worried about that if you want to do something like high finance." "Small class sizes" are the norm here, and "Most grades are based on group presentations and papers rather than testing." While most students enjoy this setup, a few gripe that "people can get by without doing much work at all if others in the group do the work" and describe the atmosphere as "too nonchalant." By all accounts, Graziadio "professors genuinely care" about students and "have tons of real-world experience." Staff members are reportedly "helpful," though some here describe the overall administration of the school as "slightly disjointed." A few students would also like Graziadio to recruit students with "higher GMAT" scores in order to boost its standing in the b-school community.

Career and Placement

Graziadio boasts the largest b-school alumni network in Southern California; the school has over 30,000 alumni, and over 3,600 of them occupy prominent positions at major organizations. It is not surprising, then, that students cite the opportunities the school provides to "network" as one of its major strengths. However, many students also characterize the school's Career Services as a significant weakness. As one student explains, "The current staff is helpful in identifying alumni whom [students] can connect with, but is little help in . . . helping students target employers that fulfill their desired profession." A few Graziadio students tell us that "Recruiting/Career Services is improving." A multipurpose online tool provided by the school allows students to manage most of their job search in a single place.

Employers who frequently hire Graziadio graduates include: NASA, Mattel, Countrywide Financial, KPMG International, AT&T, Boston Consulting Group, Nestlé, Princess Cruises, The Walt Disney Company, Wellpoint, Wells Fargo, Farmer's Insurance, Cintas, and Wilmington Trust. Students here, however, maintain that few "great companies actively recruit—I have to go to those companies myself and bang on [their] door."

ADMISSIONS CONTACT: DARRELL ERIKSEN, DIRECTOR OF ADMISSIONS
ADDRESS: 6100 CENTER DRIVE LOS ANGELES, CA 90045 UNITED STATES
PHONE: 310-568-5535 • FAX: 310-568-5594
E-MAIL: GSBM@PEPPERDINE.EDU • WEBSITE: WWW.BSCHOOL.PEPPERDINE.EDU

Student Life and Environment

Students at Graziadio report that "all classes have a group project element so we spend a lot of time outside of class with other students," adding that these interactions "usually go beyond academic levels; classmates usually hang out together outside of school." Of the "well-educated" and "energetic" students here, a sanguine student writes: "I know these are people I will keep in contact with for the rest of my life." A student in the financial industry adds: "We have so many international students; I'll have friends all over the world now." "It is challenging, rewarding, and fun," a student coming from the field of pharmaceutical marketing writes. "Days are long, and I work hard, but I enjoy being at school. I look forward to seeing my classmates. I usually have one or two meetings in a day—for team projects and/or extracurricular activities. I generally spend all day on campus."

Just which Pepperdine campus a Graziadio student calls home, however, varies. The university's primary campus is in Malibu, but it also maintains graduate campuses in West Los Angeles, Encino, Irvine, Long Beach, Pasadena, Santa Clara, and Westlake Village; each of Graziadio's different programs is offered on one or more of these campuses. Students on the primary campus in Malibu describe it as "beautiful and peaceful." "It's a great place to come study, but it's so secluded that you end up wanting to actually leave Malibu and head into areas where there's more life." To that end, some here claim that "hitting the bars and clubs in Santa Monica and Hollywood happens at least once a week, if not twice a weekend." "Talks by industry professionals" (including "some fairly big-time CEOs"), "information sessions by local companies for recruitment purposes, and, sometimes, club events" also mix things up. Students believe, however, that the school could provide "more social activities" for students in the different programs "to network better [and] to build a better sense of school unity for the business school."

Admissions

The Admissions staff at Graziadio provides prospective applicants with one-on-one consultations regarding their suitability for its programs. This acts as a prescreening process; therefore, the school is more selective than its admit rate would suggest.

FINANCIAL FACTS

Annual tuition	$34,544
Fees	$30
Cost of books	$1,400
Room & board (off-campus)	$15,000
% of students receiving aid	58
% of students receiving loans	31
% of students receiving grants	35
Average award package	$27,800
Average grant	$21,311
Average student loan debt	$62,374

ADMISSIONS

Admissions Selectivity Rating	**79**
# of applications received	401
% applicants accepted	80
% acceptees attending	49
Average GMAT	635
Range of GMAT	590–680
Average GPA	3.22
TOEFL required of international students	Yes
Minimum TOEFL (paper/computer)	600/250
Application fee	$50
International application fee	$50
Regular application deadline	5/1
Regular notification	Rolling
Early decision program?	Yes
ED Deadline/ Notification	12/15 / 01/15
Deferment available	Yes
Maximum length of deferment	1 year
Transfer students accepted	Yes
Transfer application policy No more than 2 courses may be transferred, contingent upon approval of policy committee.	
Need-blind admissions	Yes

EMPLOYMENT PROFILE

Career Rating	79	Grads Employed by Function	%	Avg. Salary
Primary Source of Full-time Job Acceptances		Finance	39	$74,111
School-facilitated activities	15 (35%)	Marketing	37	$70,813
Graduate-facilitated activities	24 (56%)	Operations	5	$78,000
Unknown	4 (9%)	Consulting	7	$79,667
Average base starting salary	$74,834	General Management	12	$85,000
Percent employed	26	**Top 5 Employers Hiring Grads**		
		Roth Capital Partners; AT&T; Citibank (Banamex); Walt Disney Internet Group; IBM		

PITTSBURG STATE UNIVERSITY
GLADYS A. KELCE COLLEGE OF BUSINESS

Academics

For many an MBA student in Kansas, there's no place like home at the Kelce College of Business, which "provides a great atmosphere to receive an education." You'll find many a native Kansan here thanks to the school's "close to home" location; however its real draw is its "excellent reputation" as one of the best business schools in the area. Students here appreciate the "small class sizes" and "enlightening" curriculum, along with the "flexible study options" that allow students to earn their degrees on either a full-time (12 months of study) or part-time (two and a half years of study) basis.

The "high quality of the courses" offered are bolstered by "great" professors who "take time to get to know you as a student, and come off as real people that are there to facilitate your learning." "I have been really impressed by my professors," one student explains. "They usually have extensive real-world experience, and they are able to bring their insights into the classroom. I have found most of my professors have a good sense of humor which is often the best way to keep students' attention." Another adds, "The professors [each] have different strengths, but [many] have a business leaning rather than a purely academic one." Some here would like to see professors with "more real-world experience," and note that despite the faculty being "very well seasoned," they might almost be too much so when it comes to "age."

PSU's administration also gets glowing reviews. "The school administrators...take an active role in your learning experience," one student says. The school is "well organized" and many note that "difficult situations" are handled with ease by an "understanding and helpful" staff. The main issue that students report is the need for "a new building" and "more access to study or work areas." But in line with the hands-on nature of a school that students describe as "already looking ahead toward the future," "a brand-new business school...is already in the plans."

Career and Placement

The Career Services office at PSU states that their mission is "to proactively educate students and alumni to make informed career decisions and provide them with counseling, teaching, training, resources, plus consultation and employment-related services necessary to optimize their life span career development; and to support institutional outcomes through employment data collection." This attitude, combined with a "career-oriented" MBA program, accounts for a high degree of success when it comes to graduates looking for work. "Pitt State concentrates on making its education both useful to the students and to local businesses," one student explains. "Finding a job does not usually seem to be a problem for Pitt State graduates." This is further bolstered by PSU's "many high-profile alumni" and the "good working relationship" the school has with the local community. That said, when looking beyond the local community, some students find their career options limited. "The majority of companies at the university's career fair are ones I have never even heard of," a student laments.

Student Life and Environment

Students say that Pittsburg State "offers a traditional MBA with great on-campus clubs, sports, and other educational and extracurricular activities." School spirit runs high, particularly during football season, and the MBA Program Director "does a good job encouraging students to be involved." "Pitt State is truly a community," one student explains, "almost a town within a town. Everyone knows each other here!" This is helped in a large way by the school's popular standing in Pittsburg, Kansas. "The town is such a strong supporter of the college," one student notes. "The people are friendly and helpful."

ADMISSIONS CONTACT: JAIME VANDERBECK, ADMINISTRATIVE OFFICER-GRADUATE STUDIES
ADDRESS: 1701 SOUTH BROADWAY PITTSBURG, KS 66762-7540 UNITED STATES
PHONE: 620-235-4223 • FAX: 620-235-4219
E-MAIL: CGS@PITTSTATE.EDU • WEBSITE: WWW.PITTSTATE.EDU/KELCE

By and large, students here are "amazed" at the number of school-run clubs, activities, and volunteering opportunities. As one student attests, "There is always something going on." That said, finding time for activities can sometimes prove challenging for MBA candidates. Many find that the assortment of "assignments, submissions, exams, and quizzes" keeps them "pretty busy."

The student body is comprised of a "culturally diverse" "variety of foreign and domestic students," all of whom are "extremely well-qualified" due to their "educational backgrounds and work experience." There is also a "blend of younger students and those who have come back to school [from the working world]." All in all, "most students are intent on making the most out of their education." "I feel that students in the business school are extremely focused," one student states. Students describe themselves as "friendly" and "willing to lend a helping hand." "We all seem to have the attitude that we are in this together," one student says. "Fellow students are always a pleasure to work with in groups and tend to be supportive during heavy workload periods," another adds. No surprise that many here tell us that they have "built some great relationships" during their time at Pittsburg State University. However, some international students complain that when they step off campus, they find themselves surrounded by "rednecks, racists, and rustic rascals." Additionally, they also find that they are "handicapped" if they don't have a car. Students with families would like to see the school "offer more childcare facilities to enable the attraction of more students from the working environment."

Admissions

Students looking to apply to Kelce must present official copies of undergraduate transcripts (those who didn't major in business will be required to take foundation courses to bring them up to speed), a completed application for admission to the Graduate School of Pittsburg State University, GMAT scores (a minimum of 400 is required), and, if the applicant's native language isn't English, a TOEFL score of at least 550 (or 213 on the computer-based exam). The school states that for unconditional admission, students "must submit a minimum of 1,050 points based on the following formula: 200 times the overall undergraduate grade point average plus the GMAT score."

FINANCIAL FACTS

Annual tuition (in-state/ out-of-state)	$4,288/$10,546
Cost of books	$1,200
Room & board (on/off-campus)	$4,844/$7,266
% of students receiving aid	50
% of first-year students receiving aid	25
% of students receiving loans	25
% of students receiving grants	15
Average award package	$8,500
Average grant	$3,500

ADMISSIONS

Admissions Selectivity Rating	**72**
# of applications received	270
% applicants accepted	76
% acceptees attending	67
Average GMAT	510
Range of GMAT	400–710
Average GPA	3.5
TOEFL required of international students	Yes
Minimum TOEFL (paper/computer)	550/213
Application fee	$35
International application fee	$60
Regular application deadline	7/15
Regular notification	8/1
Deferment available	Yes
Maximum length of deferment	1 year
Transfer students accepted	Yes
Transfer application policy Up to 9 Semester hours may be transferred from another accredited program.	
Non-fall admissions	Yes
Need-blind admissions	Yes

EMPLOYMENT PROFILE

Career Rating	61	Grads Employed by Function% Avg. Salary	
Primary Source of Full-time Job Acceptances		Marketing	24 $44,000
School-facilitated activities	43 (72%)	MIS	22 $45,000
Unknown	17 (28%)	General Management	54 $45,000
Percent employed	25	**Top 5 Employers Hiring Grads**	
		Deloitte & Touche; Sprint; Kock\h; Walmart; AllState	

PORTLAND STATE UNIVERSITY
SCHOOL OF BUSINESS ADMINISTRATION

Academics

MBA students choose Portland State, "the acknowledged leader in MBA education in this area," for its "interdisciplinary approach to sustainable development," "location and low costs," and flexible options for "working professionals," including "evening classes" and part-time and online MBA programs. These students are not disappointed. They remark that the "well-designed" and "well-run" new MBA-plus program, which has replaced the traditional MBA, represents "a very innovative approach to developing the students' soft skills as well as technical skills." The 72-credit program consists of seven foundation courses in business perspectives and leadership development, seven courses in business disciplines including financial management and organizational management, three integrated application courses that include opportunities for business simulation and real-world consultancy, and 16 elective credits that may constitute a specialization such as finance or lead to a certificate in sustainability, real estate development, or food marketing and logistics. Some students would prefer an even "broader range of specialization areas," including a "marketing specialization program." One degree candidate says, MBA-plus "courses link together across topics very well. . . . Themes repeat across marketing, finance, accounting, operations, etc." Credits may also be accrued at study abroad programs in Marseille, Copenhagen, Palian and Beijing, China, and Asolo, Italy. The Graduate School of Business also offers the 49-credit MSFA (Master of Science in Financial Analysis) and 75-credit, East Asia–focused MIM (Master of International Management) degrees.

Unlike at many other schools, students say they are "happy" with administrators and faculty. "On-campus operations are well run" (although "The school is still sorting out how best to run the online courses") and "Professors are intelligent, caring role models." The "few who share administrative and teaching roles" are especially "inspiring." In particular, Director of Leadership Development and Professor Carolyn McKnight "is phenomenal. . . . She has very innovative ideas for the department based on [her] professional and academic experience," and is a proponent of the "managerial intelligence" training that characterizes the new MBA-plus program. Students differ, however, in their satisfaction with the school's material resources. Several gripe that the "aging" "facilities need updating" and the program should "streamline the technology a bit more." Others praise the technology available to students, noting, "All classrooms support multimedia presentations, and many support broadcast to and interaction with remote students."

Student Life and Environment

Student life at the School of Business Administration is defined by the cohort system in which students take all classes with a set group of peers. MBA candidates call the SBA environment "the antithesis of the Ivy: experience trumps intellect; cooperation trumps competition." The typical student, if such a person exists, is a "good-natured," youngish West Coaster with a science or techie background and "a desire to better" himself or herself rather than crush others on the way to the top. The "bright, fun, challenging, and fabulous" students do, however, reflect substantial diversity in interests and experience: "To my left is a nonprofit executive director with a donut shack on the side," demonstrates one student, and "To my right [is] a drag-show-producing math savant." Going against the grain, there are even "at least five kids in my cohort who could make—and rock—*The Apprentice.*"

This high level of individuality and creativity reflects the mood and character of PSU's "great location." A small Pacific Rim city whose residents are "focused on the environment and sustainability" and attuned to their neighbors across the ocean, Portland is also

JOHN STOECKMANN, GRADUATE BUSINESS PROGRAMS ADMISSIONS COORDINATOR
ADDRESS: 631 SW HARRISON ST PORTLAND, OR 97201 UNITED STATES
PHONE: 503-725-8001 • FAX: 503-725-2290
E-MAIL: MBAINFO@PDX.EDU • WEBSITE: WWW.GRADBUSINESS.PDX.EDU

the hub of Silicon Forest, a prominent high-tech region that boasts Intel and IBM corporate garrisons. The housing costs, anything-goes lifestyle, and lush scenery compare favorably to what you'd find in Palo Alto, and SBA's Food Industry Leadership Center thrives on the agricultural wealth of the region.

Career and Placement

In order to facilitate the connections that power student job searches, the school's business-only Career Center presides over internships, mentorships with local corporate leaders, and other pre-graduation opportunities that smooth the way to job offers. One of the school's most interesting networking programs is embedded in the curriculum itself: BA 506 Business Project places MBA candidates as consultants in Portland-area businesses for an average of 4 months and average profit of about $50,000 to the organizations. Students may request projects that fulfill a particular area of specialization, such as finance or sustainability. Not surprisingly, SBA-minted MBAs often head to surrounding high-tech companies such as IBM, Intel, and Xerox.

Admissions

A typically successful application includes a GMAT score in the mid-600s and GPA between 3.0 and 3.5, as well as 5 or more years of work experience. In many ways, the application requirements are more hassle-free than you might expect: For instance, PSU requires only a one-page statement of intent rather than the multiple short essay questions that fill other schools' forms.

Because PSU is a public university, residents of Oregon and bordering Washington counties receive more than 25 percent off their tuition bills. Residency criteria are strict, excluding those who have moved to Oregon to attend school; be sure you meet them before banking on in-state prices.

FINANCIAL FACTS

Annual tuition (in-state/ out-of-state)	$17,000/$21,000
Fees	$2,400
Cost of books	$2,000
Room & board	$12,700

ADMISSIONS

Admissions Selectivity Rating	86
# of applications received	219
% applicants accepted	64
% acceptees attending	96
Average GMAT	610
Range of GMAT	570–650
Average GPA	3.14
TOEFL required of international students	Yes
Minimum TOEFL (paper/computer)	550/213
Application fee	$50
International application fee	$50
Regular application deadline	4/1
Regular notification	5/30
Early decision program?	Yes
ED Deadline/ Notification	01/01 / 04/01
Transfer students accepted	Yes
Transfer application policy Maximum of 1/3 of the total number of PSU credits may transfer from a US accredited university.	
Need-blind admissions	Yes

Applicants Also Look At
Oregon State University, University of Oregon, University of Washington.

EMPLOYMENT PROFILE

Career Rating	76	Grads Employed by Function	% Avg. Salary
Primary Source of Full-time Job Acceptances		Finance	9 $61,500
Unknown	22 (100%)	Human Resources	1 $48,000
Percent employed	32	Marketing	2 $55,000
		Operations	1 $66,000
		Consulting	1 $57,000
		General Management	3 $51,667
		Other	1 $55,000

PURDUE UNIVERSITY
KRANNERT SCHOOL OF MANAGEMENT

GENERAL INFORMATION

Type of school	Public
Environment	Town
Academic calendar	Semester

SURVEY SAYS...

Smart classrooms
Solid preparation in:
Operations
Teamwork
Quantitative skills

STUDENTS

Enrollment of parent institution	39,228
Enrollment of business school	143
% male/female	85/15
% minorities	8
% international	45
Average years work experience at entry	4.4

ACADEMICS

Academic Experience Rating	**88**
Student/faculty ratio	2:1
Profs interesting rating	80
Profs accessible rating	89
% female faculty	17
% minority faculty	10

Joint Degrees

BS/MBA (Management) 5 years,
PharmD/MSIA 6 years, BS/MBA
(Industrial Engineering) 5 years,
BS/MBA (Mechanical Engineering) 5
years.

Prominent Alumni

Joseph Forehand, Chairman/CEO,
Accenture; Marshall Larsen,
President/COO, Goodrich; Marjorie
Magner, Chairman/CEO, Global
Consumer Group, Citigroup; Albert
Nahmad, Chairman, CEO, Watsco,
Inc.; Jerry Rawls, CEO, Finisar.

Academics

If you are looking for a technical and progressive MBA program with strong ties to the Midwestern business community, you'll find a good match at the Krannert School of Management at Purdue University. While the program provides a thorough education in all aspects of business and management, Krannert attracts many students for its "strength and rankings of finance, operations, and quantitative methods programs." A 60-unit course of study, roughly half the MBA program is comprised of core course work. Maintaining a "strong quantitative focus" throughout the first year, students appreciate the fact that "core classes are taught by professors [who] are nationally and internationally respected in their fields." However, be prepared for the fact that the program is extremely rigid at first, as "All but two core classes occur in first year with little opportunity for electives." On top of that, students warn us that "the workload is tremendous, especially in the core classes, and there is an air of competitiveness."

Despite the challenges, don't be scared away. Students reassure us that "Krannert's program through the first year is challenging," mostly due to a heavy course load. "But as a rule, the teachers are effective in teaching the material and preparing students for the real world." Another adds, "Professors are top-notch in their fields and very approachable outside of the classroom. In fact, students routinely take advantage of a program that allows students to take their favorite professors out to lunch." On top of that, a friendly and laid-back vibe permeates the campus, despite the curricular demands. Students promise us that the program is "competitive to a point," but that most are "more concerned about getting the most out of the program than beating everyone else for the grades."

Once they have survived the core curriculum, the norm reverses in the second year, during which the "schedule is almost completely electives and is designed around the individual." Within their elective choices, students are encouraged to pursue a specialization in an area such as accounting, finance, marketing, strategic management, operations management, information systems, e-business, or human resource management. With dynamic and progressive course offerings, "Krannert also does a great job of adapting the curriculum to meet the needs of the dynamic corporate world." A student elaborates, "The leadership of the Krannert program is very much in tune with the needs of corporate America and is quick to implement necessary changes to accommodate those needs." However, some lament the fact that "no course work is aimed at not-for-profit or green learning; most material taught is aimed at manufacturing." In addition to the standard curriculum, Krannert runs a variety of special programs to keep abreast of current trends in business, including the Friday Management Development Series.

Career and Placement

Students can prepare for interviews, contact employers, research companies, and career counseling through Krannert Graduate Career Services. Students say "The companies recruiting at Purdue now are primarily the 'heavy hitters' you'd like to see;" although some international students say they could use more support in looking for positions. The mean base salary for last year's Purdue graduates was $83,661. Seventy-three percent of students also received a signing bonus with their offer of employment, averaging an additional $14,114.

ADMISSIONS CONTACT: CARMEN CASTRO-RIVERA, DIRECTOR OF ADMISSIONS
ADDRESS: RAWLS HALL, ROOM 2020, 100 S. GRANT STREET WEST LAFAYETTE, IN 47907 U.S.
PHONE: 765-494-0773 • FAX: 765-494-9841 • E-MAIL: MASTERS@KRANNERT.PURDUE.EDU
WEBSITE: WWW.KRANNERT.PURDUE.EDU/PROGRAMS/MASTERS

The top employers for the class of 2006 were: Air Products, American Axle & Manufacturing, Analog Devices, Bank of America, Citigroup, Cummins, Dell, Discover Financial, Eaton, EchoStar, Eli Lilly and Company, Ford Motor Company, General Electric Company, Guidant, Hewlett-Packard, Honeywell, IBM, Intel, Johnson & Johnson, Kimberly-Clark, Liberty Mutual, Motorola, Northrop Grumman, Praxair, Procter & Gamble, Raytheon, Roche Diagnostics, United Technologies.

Student Life and Environment

At Krannert School of Management, students are "kind, smart, open and very team oriented." Students love the fact that "everyone in the program seems to follow the 'Work Hard, Work Together, Work Right' mantra that Krannert advertises." The environment is further enhanced by the professional diversity within the program, as students hail from "many different work backgrounds, including those from engineering and the sciences." A current student explains, "My peers also bring a wealth of experiences to the classroom. I have several friends in the program that served in Iraq, one who worked at a nuclear power plant, and one who ran his own business in California."

During the week, most students are busy keeping up with the heavy workload. However, they say it's not too unpleasant because "The common areas provide a great place to study and share ideas with other students. . . . There's always someone around to help you out with whatever course you're working on." When is time to relax, they don't have to look far: "Since it is a smaller program, students are all very close. There are bowling leagues, athletic clubs, and numerous social outings." In fact, "Starting Thursday night the schedule becomes a little more relaxed. There are usually group meetings over the weekends but there is still plenty of time to get recharged for the next week." On top of that, West Lafayette, Indiana, is a "small but safe college town" with "many outdoor activities" in the surrounding area.

Admissions

To apply to Krannert School of Management, all candidates must submit an official undergraduate transcript, GMAT scores, a resume, letters of recommendation, and several admissions essays. In 2006, the entering class had a mean GPA of 3.27 on a 4.0 scale, and a mean GMAT score of 661. Women comprised 29 percent of the entering class. While some students have significantly more or less professional experience before the class of 2006, the average post-college work experience was 4.4 years.

FINANCIAL FACTS

Annual tuition (in-state/ out-of-state)	$15,276/$30,010
Fees	$500
Cost of books	$1,900
Room & board (off-campus)	$7,500
% of first-year students receiving aid	54
Average award package	$18,268
Average grant	$5,500

ADMISSIONS

Admissions Selectivity Rating	87
# of applications received	765
% applicants accepted	56
% acceptees attending	34
Average GMAT	661
Range of GMAT	620–700
Average GPA	3.3
TOEFL required of international students	Yes
Minimum TOEFL (paper/computer)	575/230
Application fee	$55
International application fee	$55
Regular application deadline	3/1
Regular notification	4/15
Application Deadline/Notification	
Round 1:	11/01 / 12/15
Round 2:	01/01 / 03/01
Round 3:	03/01 / 04/15
Round 4:	05/01 / 06/15
Early decision program?	Yes
ED Deadline/ Notification	11/01 / 12/15
Deferment available	Yes
Maximum length of deferment	1 year
Need-blind admissions	Yes

Applicants Also Look At

Indiana University—Bloomington, The Ohio State University, The University of North Carolina at Chapel Hill, The University of Texas at Austin, University of Chicago, University of Michigan, University of Southern California.

EMPLOYMENT PROFILE

Career Rating	88	Grads Employed by Function	% Avg. Salary
Percent employed	96	Finance	32 $80,035
		Marketing	17 $82,792
		MIS	4 $82,703
		Operations	17 $89,358
		Consulting	19 $87,154
		General Management	5 $85,625
		Other	2 NR

Top 5 Employers Hiring Grads

Intel; Discover Financial; Procter & Gamble

QUEEN'S UNIVERSITY
QUEEN'S SCHOOL OF BUSINESS

Academics

Queen's University quickly burst onto many prospective MBAs' radars in 2004, when *BusinessWeek* magazine named it the number one international MBA program. The school was no secret to Canadian and international employers, though; in fact, their high regard for Queen's MBAs contributed substantially to the lofty BW ranking.

Queen's has taken a unique route to the top: specialization. The Queen's MBA is officially called the "Queen's MBA for Science and Technology," a designation that accurately indicates the program's focus. Although the curriculum looks like that of a standard MBA program, all students and professors here have considerable backgrounds in science, mathematics, technology, and/or engineering. Their backgrounds inform every aspect of instruction and class discussion here. "The analytical strength in the class is unbelievable," students agree.

Queen's offers a great return on investment, thanks to a 12-month calendar that allows students "to return to the work force faster." Like most one-year MBAs, the Queen's MBA "is very intense and the course load is pretty heavy." A "very strong team-based learning" approach permeates all classes. All students here are assigned to a single team for the duration of the program, and "a significant portion of a student's overall marks is derived from group work." The idea is to model the team atmosphere in which students will work throughout their careers.

With between 60 and 80 students each year, Queen's runs "a very small program" that "allows the administration and students to get to know each other very well." The result is a happy student body: MBAs tell us that the "amazing administration couldn't be more helpful. It is amazingly receptive to any requests." Likewise, professors are regarded as "warm-hearted, committed, responsible, open-minded, and talented." Most of all, students appreciate the school's "excellent reputation, which is on the upswing across the world."

Career and Placement

Career and placement services to MBA students at Queen's University are provided by personal career managers, who offer "one-on-one coaching to help you explore your career options and chart your career path." Career managers assist students with practice interviews, resume counseling, and self-assessment instruments. Numerous online job postings are available through the Student Career Services Office, which also coordinates student-alumni contacts. Students appreciate the office's hard work but feel that "on-campus recruitment companies lack variety and this needs to improve." Some note that "Kingston is a small town, and that may be why we have fewer connections with companies compared with schools in big cities."

Typically, about one-fourth of Queen's MBAs find their first post-degree jobs in finance. The same number take positions with high tech and telecommunications firms. Around 16 percent go into management consulting, and just under 10 percent find work in manufacturing and bio-pharmaceuticals. About half the graduating class typically has a position by graduation day.

Student Life and Environment

Queen's one-year curriculum means "a hectic academic schedule" that leaves little free time. As one student notes, "Despite efforts to balance our lifestyles as students, our lives are school. Since the program is only one year long, our friends and families are very accepting of this fact." Life here generally consists of "classes followed by preparation assignments, exams, projects, and presentations."

There are opportunities to blow off steam, however: "the school organizes numerous social events such as a cruise and hockey games," for example. Most popular of all is the "Point Four" club, a "tradition that has the whole class going out for drinks every Thursday night. This tradition is continued in numerous cities in Canada after graduation." The origin of the club's name, incidentally, is the notion that "going out one day a week will only reduce your grade by 0.4 percent."

MBAs in this high-caliber program are "very bright and intelligent" and the community "friendly and close-knit," qualities that are assets to the team-oriented approach to learning. While some feel that "the science and technology background sometimes hinders the very technical ones who cannot think out of the box," few would argue with the assertion that everyone here is "very strong analytically and mathematically." The international nature of the student body means that "people can talk about issues in North America as easily as issues in Africa or Asia."

Admissions

Minimum requirements for admission to the Queen's MBA for Science and Technology program include: a four-year undergraduate degree in an engineering, technology, or science discipline, plus two years of relevant work experience; or, a four-year undergraduate degree in some other discipline, plus two years work experience in a science- or technology-related area. Most admitted students have an undergraduate grade point average (GPA) of at least 3.3 and a GMAT score of at least 600. Students whose first language is not English must submit a score for the TOEFL, IELTS, or MELAB. A cover letter and resume, three letters of reference, and three short-answer essays—all of which can be completed online—are also required. Applicants from the USA must obtain a student visa from the Canadian government in order to attend the school; the school warns that this process can take up to three months.

FINANCIAL FACTS

Annual tuition (in-state/ out-of-state)	$58,139/$63,151
Cost of books	$0
Room & board	$27,065

ADMISSIONS

Admissions Selectivity Rating 60*

Average GMAT	650
Range of GMAT	560–770
TOEFL required of international students	Yes
Minimum TOEFL (paper/computer)	600/250
Application fee	$0
International application fee	$0
Application Deadline/Notification	
Round 1:	11/30
Round 2:	01/15
Round 3:	03/23
Deferment available	Yes
Maximum length of deferment	1 year
Non-fall admissions	Yes
Need-blind admissions	Yes

EMPLOYMENT PROFILE

Career Rating	84	Grads Employed by Function	%	Avg. Salary
		Finance	29	$82,200
		MIS	12	$77,750
		Consulting	24	$93,900
		Other	19	$65,000

QUINNIPIAC UNIVERSITY
SCHOOL OF BUSINESS

GENERAL INFORMATION
Type of school	Private
Environment	Town

SURVEY SAYS...
Solid preparation in:
Teamwork
Presentation skills

STUDENTS
Enrollment of parent institution	7,216
Enrollment of business school	151
% male/female	58/42
% out-of-state	22
% part-time	68
% minorities	7
% international	13
Average age at entry	27
Average years work experience at entry	6

ACADEMICS
Academic Experience Rating	**83**
Student/faculty ratio	16:1
Profs interesting rating	87
Profs accessible rating	72
% female faculty	32
% minority faculty	16

Joint Degrees
JD/MBA 4 years, JD/MBA (Health Care Mgt.) 4.5 years.

Prominent Alumni
William Weldon, Chairman/CEO, Johnson & Johnson; Murray Lender, Co-Founder, Lender's Bagels; Bruce Dumelin, CFO (retired), Bank of America; Joseph Onorato, CFO (retired), Echlin, Inc.; Terry Goodwin, VP/Mgr. (retired), Equity Trading Goldman Sachs.

Academics

Quinnipiac University is devoting considerable effort to developing its MBA program—students brag about its "exceptional resources," professors who "go above and beyond their duties," and "a new director of the business school who has worked very hard to make QU more competitive and to bring new employers to recruit"—and students respond with enthusiastic praise. A mix of area full-time professionals studying on a part-time basis and full-time undergraduates taking advantage of the five-and-a-half year BA/MBA program populates the program, which offers not only a conventional MBA but also an MBA in health care management, an MS is accounting, and an MS in computer information systems.

The QU MBA program benefits from "high-tech equipment for presentations, a Financial Technology Center for real-time trading, TV screens that constantly keep us up-to-date on current news," and "classroom facilities are one of the best I've seen; they played a large part in my selection of the school." Students tell us that professors "are also a strong resource; they like to question students and speak with them about their particular field." Proximity to New York City drives the school's focus toward finance, and indeed QU has "great resources for the financial industry" and "has been great at providing work opportunities for all of the students in many diverse fields in the business world."

The program's design encourages frequent collaborative work; as one MBA explains, "You constantly have a group project that ends with a presentation. This prepares you for presentation in the real world, as well as building your skills to work with others." Professors "encourage part-time students (those working full-time) to work with a full-time student. By combining the two, you get the additional knowledge that comes with experience, but you also have the book-smart approach to the situation. It is believed that by combining the two, all parties learn more from each other, without one being fully reliant on the other. Each one has to be able to contribute to the group meetings and the overall project."

Career and Placement

Quinnipiac MBAs tell us that the university "has decentralized its career services" so that "each college has its own career service team. For the School of Business, the career service team actively works on developing employer relationships while assisting students on campus in their job/internship search. Students have access to powerful job databases and search engines." Observes one student, the School of Business "has an extremely devoted team that works diligently to host network receptions, maintain a career website, assist with resumes, and regularly communicate with students." Many of Quinnipiac's part-time students are concurrently employed by such prominent area concerns as SBC-SNET, Anthem Blue Cross/Blue Shield, Yale New Haven Hospital, the Hopsital of St. Raphael, Bayer, and United Technologies.

ADMISSIONS CONTACT: JENNIFER BOUTIN, ASSISTANT DIRECTOR OF GRADUATE ADMISSIONS
ADDRESS: 275 MOUNT CARMEL AVE, AB-GRD HAMDEN, CT 06518-1940 UNITED STATES
PHONE: 203-582-8672 • FAX: 203-582-3443
E-MAIL: GRADUATE@QUINNIPIAC.EDU • WEBSITE: WWW.QUINNIPIAC.EDU/x197

Student Life and Environment

Quinnipiac "has a beautiful campus located right outside of Sleeping Giant State Park" that "is safe and offers a great environment for learning and social life." As one student explains, "When you step foot on QU grounds, you just want to grab a book and start studying. The beauty of the school is like being in a movie where all you do is study and hang out with friends in a really nice college." On the downside, "Parking is always a problem," and "The common library is beautiful, but there is not enough space for students, especially during midterms and finals."

Graduate life here "is heavily focused around academics and education," although opportunities for extracurricular engagement are available. The director of the program "aims to get everyone connected and does so through a variety of ways. He hosts meet and greets and other programs throughout the semester for everyone to get involved in. All the students are connected and stay so through a variety of ways, like going out for dinners, meeting for classes etc." There are "a limited number of graduate clubs," but most here feel that "the graduate population is not very interested in participating in additional activities or socials."

QU MBAs are "bright, creative, and energetic," with lots of "late 20-somethings" in this "good mix of people with families, working professionals, joint undergraduate students, full-time students, and middle-aged people." Most are "extremely friendly and helpful, and many would be good contacts to have for the future."

Admissions

Quinnipiac processes MBA applications on a rolling basis. A complete application includes official transcripts for all post-secondary academic work, a current résumé, an official GMAT score report, two letters of recommendation, and a completed application form. The school's website states that desired candidates have achieved at least a 3.0 undergraduate GPA and earned at least a 500 on the GMAT; it also notes that full-time professional work experience is preferred. International applicants must provide an official statement of sufficient financial support and, if their native language is not English, TOEFL scores. Many Quinnipiac MBAs enter through the five-year program, which is open to Quinnipiac undergraduates only; the school expects such students to have a minimum undergraduate GPA of 3.0 with at least a 3.25 GPA in their major. Five-year MBA applicants are required to submit GMAT scores unless their cumulative undergraduate GPA is at least 3.5.

FINANCIAL FACTS

Annual tuition	$16,200
Fees	$540
Cost of books	$1,200
Room & board (off-campus)	$13,082
% of students receiving aid	34
% of first-year students receiving aid	43
% of students receiving loans	27
% of students receiving grants	13
Average award package	$22,224
Average grant	$10,469
Average student loan debt	$25,831

ADMISSIONS

Admissions Selectivity Rating	**79**
# of applications received	107
% applicants accepted	60
% acceptees attending	69
Average GMAT	550
Range of GMAT	510–580
Average GPA	3.2
TOEFL required of international students	Yes
Minimum TOEFL (paper/computer)	575/233
Application fee	$45
International application fee	$45
Regular application deadline	Rolling
Regular notification	Rolling
Deferment available	Yes
Maximum length of deferment	1 year
Transfer students accepted	Yes
Transfer application policy	
9 graduate transfer credits allowed from AACSB accredited schools.	
Non-fall admissions	Yes
Need-blind admissions	Yes

Applicants Also Look At
Fairfield University, Rensselaer Polytechnic Institute, University of Connecticut, University of Hartford.

RADFORD UNIVERSITY
COLLEGE OF BUSINESS AND ECONOMICS

GENERAL INFORMATION

Type of school	Public
Environment	Village

SURVEY SAYS...

Cutting edge classes
Solid preparation in:
Marketing
General management
Teamwork

STUDENTS

Enrollment of parent institution	9,000
Enrollment of business school	80
% male/female	70/30
% part-time	30
% minorities	32
% international	29
Average age at entry	24
Average years work experience at entry	3

ACADEMICS

Academic Experience Rating	**78**
Student/faculty ratio	3:1
Profs interesting rating	84
Profs accessible rating	82
% female faculty	25
% minority faculty	10

Academics

The College of Business and Economics at Radford University is home to a large undergraduate population; nearly one in four RU undergrads majors in a business-related area. The much smaller MBA program capitalizes on the resources and strengths of the school's undergraduate program to provide a solid generalist graduate degree. As one student assessed the program says, "The school is affordable, and it is good for someone who does not plan on conquering the world, but rather [someone who] wants to stay in their community and better themselves," though some grads do go on to work for major firms around the world.

Because of the size of the program, MBAs at Radford enjoy "small classes with plenty of personal attention." One student notes, "after only one semester, I am already convinced going to this school was the right decision for future endeavors. Professors are easily accessible and responsive to students' needs, and the administration is very attentive." Radford's curriculum focuses on "the presentation experience" and a large dose of writing; "there are lots of challenging papers assigned," students warn. Because of the nature of the program (classes are held almost exclusively in the evening), the program tends to be a little more lecture-based and academic than others. Some feel that "they need more opportunities to work with outside companies and more real-life examples of local companies and speakers" in order to gain more practical experience within the program.

What Radford isn't is a place to forge a high degree of expertise in one area. That's because "it is a basic MBA program that does not allow for specialization." Some students see this as a drawback; one writes, "I would like more marketing courses because I would like to go into the marketing field upon graduation. This program only offers one marketing course." Others feel they are best served by the program's broad approach; one student explains, "My analytical business-diagnosing skills and presentation skills have been greatly enhanced by this MBA program." Radford's curriculum consists of eight required courses and two electives; the greatest number of electives are available in economics, finance, and management. Aggressive students can complete the degree in as little as 12 months, although some students work full-time and accordingly attend the program on a part-time basis. MBA courses are offered in two locations: the main campus in Radford, Virginia, and the Roanoke Higher Education Center in Roanoke, Virginia.

Radford's "tough but fair" professors "are excellent and even inspiring. Students find that they want to do their best work for all of them." They also "have a good sense of humor," which comes in handy during those long three-hour classes following a full work day.

Career and Placement

The Center for Experiential Learning and Career Development at Radford University offers a variety of resources to undergraduates, graduates, and alumni. These include a virtual resume, internship, and job database "where students and employers come together to post and view resumes and position openings," as well as workshops in resume and portfolio development, career fairs, and career-assessment tools. On-campus recruiters include Ameriprise Financial, DMG Securities, Ferguson Enterprises, Northwestern Mutual, State Farm, Wachovia, and the federal government.

ADMISSIONS CONTACT: DR. CLARENCE ROSE, DIRECTOR, MBA PROGRAM
ADDRESS: MBA OFFICE, BOX 6956 RADFORD, VA 24142 UNITED STATES
PHONE: 540-831-6905 • FAX: 540-831-6655
E-MAIL: RUMBA@RADFORD.EDU. • WEBSITE: COBE-WEB.ASP.RADFORD.EDU

Student Life and Environment

Radford's MBA program serves two identifiable populations. One consists of full-time workers who live in the area or in nearby Roanoke. The second, which is also substantial, is made up of "students fresh from Radford undergraduate programs." Wrote one of the professional students of his younger peers, "Some of their writing skills have not been up to graduate-level quality, which can be a real problem in team situations. All of these issues should be taken care of through the admissions process."

The Radford campus "has many formally organized activities," but most students are too busy to participate. The campus is small and pretty, attributes appreciated by the school's MBAs. Those who attend classes at the Roanoke Higher Education Center tell us that "the RHEC is a newly remodeled, high tech, and comfortable facility more suited to providing an appropriate atmosphere for educating older MBA students." Students at both campuses praise the school's "excellent website, telecommunications equipment, [and] library."

Hometown Radford is a small town in the Blue Ridge Mountains; Roanoke is about 45 miles away. The area is most amenable to outdoor enthusiasts, as it provides easy access to the Appalachian Trail, the New River, and Clayton Lake. Shopping, restaurants, nightlife, and such are not in great supply, students warn, although the proximity of Roanoke helps to make up for this deficiency. Charleston, West Virginia, and Greensboro, North Carolina, are also within a reasonable driving distance.

Admissions

Admission to Radford's MBA program requires successful completion of an undergraduate degree with a minimum GPA of 2.75. Applicants must also submit an official report of GMAT scores, TOEFL scores (international students), two letters of recommendation, a resume of work experience, a personal statement of purpose, and "evidence of creativity and leadership." Also, "applicants must also have taken accredited collegiate preparation in the following foundation areas (or equivalents): fundamentals of financial accounting, fundamentals of managerial accounting, principles of economics I and II, organizational behavior, essentials of marketing, introduction to business finance, business statistics, and business calculus." Students can earn credit for some of these prerequisites through CLEP testing. Competency with computers is also a prerequisite.

FINANCIAL FACTS

Annual tuition (in-state/ out-of-state)	$6,686/$12,466
Cost of books	$1,000
Room & board	6,218

ADMISSIONS

Admissions Selectivity Rating	**83**
# of applications received	90
% applicants accepted	89
% acceptees attending	100
Average GMAT	505
Range of GMAT	400–680
Average GPA	3.0
TOEFL required of international students	Yes
Minimum TOEFL (paper/computer)	550/213
Application fee	$40
International application fee	$40
Regular application deadline	rolling
Regular notification	rolling
Deferment available	Yes
Maximum length of deferment	1 year
Transfer students accepted	Yes
Transfer application policy Maximum of six credit hours.	
Non-fall admissions	Yes
Need-blind admissions	Yes

Applicants Also Look At

Virginia Tech.

RENSSELAER POLYTECHNIC INSTITUTE

LALLY SCHOOL OF MANAGEMENT AND TECHNOLOGY

GENERAL INFORMATION

Type of school	Private
Environment	City
Academic calendar	Semester

SURVEY SAYS...

Friendly students
Good social scene
Cutting edge classes
Solid preparation in:
General management
Doing business in a global economy
Entrepreneurial studies

STUDENTS

Enrollment of parent institution	7,299
Enrollment of business school	49
% male/female	69/31
% part-time	35
% minorities	16
% international	28
Average age at entry	28
Average years work experience at entry	4

ACADEMICS

Academic Experience Rating	**78**
Student/faculty ratio	15:1
Profs interesting rating	65
Profs accessible rating	83
% female faculty	18
% minority faculty	2

Prominent Alumni

George M. Low, NASA, Apollo administrator; James Q. Crowe, Founder and Builder of telecom industry compaines; Denis Tito, Founder, Wilshire Associates; Ray Tomlinson, Inventor of e-mail in 1971; Marcian E. "Ted" Hoff, Inventor of Silicon Chip.

Academics

The Rensselaer Polytechnic Institute Lally School of Management and Technology is located in Troy, New York, a historic town along the Hudson River. Once a major center of the Industrial Revolution (during the 1800s), Troy now finds itself at the center of a technological revolution. Rensselaer's sterling reputation as a school that turns out technical superstars has influenced Lally's direction. The Lally MBA program combines technological innovation and a focus on entrepreneurship in a team-oriented curriculum that cuts across all business functions.

The students enrolled in the Lally MBA program appreciate being in an "entrepreneurship program friendly to those with technical backgrounds." Rensselaer's state-of-the-art facilities include the Center for Entrepreneurship, the Business Incubator Program, and the RPI tech-park, so it's no surprise that the Lally School's strength is in technological entrepreneurship. The school's mantra is that "technology creation and commercialization do not occur in an ivory tower; they happen in a competitive, increasingly global marketplace. Our students and faculty have a passion for taking ideas and turning them into real-world products." Students here concur: "Everybody at Rensselaer thinks about initiating a company." One student adds, "This makes it one of the best schools in providing a technology-driven MBA."

A few years ago, Lally introduced a dynamic new MBA curriculum that identifies critical areas for advancing business through innovation and mimics real-world decision making. The curriculum is based on "streams of knowledge" and modeled after their signature course, "Developing Innovative Products and Services," in which student teams develop a new product or service, write a business and marketing plan, and learn how to market and sell it. Students love this program, arguing that it "prepares future business leaders and strategic thinkers. Most courses incorporate projects that are applied to real businesses in the community." Some of the groups have even taken their products to compete in the "Tech Valley Collegiate Business Plan Competition" sponsored by the school's own Severino Center for Technological Entrepreneurship. There, teams compete for the money to make their theoretical venture a reality. Some groups from these classes have "actually now established themselves as startups!" Some students point out that "even if you don't have a desire to start your own company, the experiences you gain can be used in established tech companies."

However, none of this means that traditional business school curriculum is lacking. The school has a strict core curriculum, which takes up the entire first year of the MBA program, and a summer internship is encouraged. In the second year, there are only three required classes; that year is primarily dedicated to specialization. While professors are "hit or miss" pedagogically, they're always focused on the student: "Even in the larger classes, you can tell that the professors really know who everyone is." At the moment, students would like to be allowed "more freedom to take electives" and would like to see "more seminars and more of a focus on financial market topics." And despite the assurances of most students that all the Rensselaer facilities boast top-of-the-line technology, some students would like to see Lally "upgrade some of its classrooms." Fortunately, the administration here is "bend-over-backward supportive of students and their needs. This program at Lally is growing and developing, so our input is extremely valuable. I don't know of any other school where [student] input is acted on within a semester."

ADMISSIONS CONTACT: JILL M TERRY, ASSISTANT DEAN OF MASTER'S PROGRAMS
ADDRESS: 110 EIGHTH STREET- PITTSBURGH BUILDING 3216 TROY, NY 12180-3590 UNITED STATES
PHONE: 518-276-6565 • FAX: 518-276-2665
E-MAIL: LALLYMBA@RPI.EDU • WEBSITE: LALLYSCHOOL.RPI.EDU

Career and Placement

Though the emphasis at Lally is so much about creating jobs rather than looking for them, Career Services reports that they've managed to place plenty of their students. The average salary for Lally's MBA graduates in 2006 was around $66,400; 43 percent of those who completed the MBA were employed in the Northeast region of the United States; iconic companies such as IBM, GE, and 3M frequently hire Lally graduates. According to some students, the weakest link in the employment chain is Lally's "circle of alumni," which is not as involved as most current students would like.

Student Life and Environment

Including Lally's "interesting mix of nationalities, talents, and backgrounds," Troy is home to just about 55,000 people. The city benefits from its proximity to Albany, which, despite what New York City likes to believe, is still the capital of the state. And students who manage to make time in their hectic academic schedule point out that there are "tons of cultural opportunities like readings, speakers, and music on campus and in town. We have a brewpub in town making great beer. There is a good live music scene." The school, along with student-run groups, tries to facilitate student interaction as well. "We have regular social functions that get both classes together and try to involve faculty as well. Since it's a smaller program, it's pretty close knit, and a lot of students organize social activities and invite the entire class."

Admissions

Though the majority of Lally's admitted students come from some sort of technical background, 35 percent do not. The average age for an admitted student is 28, the average work experience is about 4 years, the average GMAT is 629, and the average undergraduate GPA is 3.41.

FINANCIAL FACTS

Annual tuition	$36,950
Fees	$1,830
Cost of books	$1,815
Room & board	$10,000

ADMISSIONS

Admissions Selectivity Rating	**87**
# of applications received	91
% applicants accepted	74
% acceptees attending	48
Average GMAT	619
Average GPA	3.2
TOEFL required of international students	Yes
Minimum TOEFL (paper/computer)	600/250
Application fee	$75
International application fee	$75
Regular application deadline	7/1
Regular notification	Rolling
Early decision program?	Yes
ED Deadline/ Notification	1/15 / 02/15
Deferment available	Yes
Maximum length of deferment	1 year
Need-blind admissions	Yes

Applicants Also Look At
Babson College, Carnegie Mellon, Cornell University, Georgia Institute of Technology, Massachusetts Institute of Technology.

EMPLOYMENT PROFILE

Career Rating	78	Grads Employed by Function	%	Avg. Salary
Primary Source of Full-time Job Acceptances		Finance	20	$77,500
School-facilitated activities	5 (29%)	Marketing	20	$54,677
Graduate-facilitated activities	12 (70%)	MIS	10	$91,000
Unknown	1 (1%)	Operations	5	$80,000
Percent employed	67	Consulting	25	$73,960
		General Management	10	$52,500
		Other	10	$44,000

Top 5 Employers Hiring Grads
Blue Slate Solutions; Agora Games; Smith Barney; Morgan Stanley; IBM

RICE UNIVERSITY
JESSE H. JONES GRADUATE SCHOOL OF MANAGEMENT

GENERAL INFORMATION

Type of school	Private
Environment	Metropolis
Academic calendar	Semester

SURVEY SAYS...

Solid preparation in:
Finance
Accounting
Communication/interpersonal skills
Presentation skills

STUDENTS

Enrollment of parent institution	5,145
Enrollment of business school	408
% male/female	70/30
% out-of-state	26
% part-time	44
% minorities	10
% international	29
Average age at entry	27
Average years work experience at entry	4

ACADEMICS

Academic Experience Rating	**89**
Student/faculty ratio	9:1
Profs interesting rating	86
Profs accessible rating	96
% female faculty	18
% minority faculty	20

Joint Degrees

MBA/MD 5 years, MBA/MS (Bioengineering) 22 months, MBA/MS (Chemical Engineering) 22 months, MBA/MS (Civil Engineering) 22 months, MBA/MS (Computational and Applied Mathematics) 22 months, MBA/MS (Computer Science) 22 months, MBA/MS (Electrical Engineering) 22 months, MBA/MS (Environmental Engineering) 22 months, MBA/MS (Materials Science) 22 months, MBA/MS (Mechanical Engineering) 22 months, MBA/MS (Statistics) 22 months.

Academics

The Jones Graduate School of Management at Rice University is "one of the top schools in the world for finance" as well as "a core school for [recruiting by] most of the world's top energy companies," students in this prestigious program brag. That latter distinction has much to do with Rice's location in Houston, America's oil capital. One student explains, "If I could pick up Rice and put it anywhere in the country, I would put it right back in Houston. There are more MBA-level jobs in Houston than in many other states combined. The demand for Rice graduates in this area is incredible."

In addition to its stellar offerings in finance, Rice also has "a strong entrepreneurship program" and a "great" strategy curriculum, and it "excels in accounting as well as communication." Overall this is "a very technical, quantitatively rigorous MBA" with "unbelievable facilities." One unique feature here is "the Rice Alliance program, which integrates business/science/engineering disciplines in the areas of new technology and entrepreneurship such as nanotechnology, which is a strong discipline at Rice." In 2008, the Rice Alliance Business Plan Competition awarded over $675,000 in prize money.

Rice "is a small program, so you get the personal attention that you need," and students get to enjoy "the feel of a well-knit community. When I walk down the hall, I have to say hello to 95 percent of the people I see because I know them from somewhere or another," says one MBA. The faculty here includes "CEOs, CFOs, and board members of *Fortune* 500 companies in Houston" who "are very accessible and helpful outside of class." What's more, "The professors continue to get better" here, as "The program office and the Dean have a strong role in attracting new profs to Jones." "The new program office is very interested in the students' needs and [is] committed to working with students to make their experience better." It helps that "the administration is readily available to partner with students" on whatever they need. The administration also works hard to attract "highly touted keynote speakers" who "routinely visit the Jones school to give us the latest in business planning, experience, and analytics."

Career and Placement

"Top investment banks like Goldman Sachs, Lehman Brothers, and other bulge brackets are recruiting more Rice MBAs each year. The majority of students have two to three offers for full-time positions" upon graduation. If there is a weakness here, it is that "there is heavy emphasis on the energy industry. I would like to see more technology companies from California and financial institutions from cities like New York and Boston to come and recruit at Rice," says one MBA. In the asset column, "Recruitment from real estate firms has picked up due to word of the technical nature of the program." Students tell us "The alumni network is wonderful, and both undergrads of Rice and Rice MBA alums are more than happy to help with a job search."

Employers who most frequently hire Rice MBAs include: Chevron; ExxonMobil; Deutsche Bank; Citi; ConocoPhillips.

ADMISSIONS CONTACT: MELISSA BLAKESLEE, DIRECTOR OF ADMISSIONS
ADDRESS: MBA ADMISSIONS, PO BOX 2932 - MS 531, JONES SCHOOL HOUSTON, TX 77252-2932 U.S.
PHONE: 888-844-4773 • FAX: 713-348-6147
E-MAIL: RICEMBA@RICE.EDU • WEBSITE: WWW.JONESGSM.RICE.EDU

Student Life and Environment

"Rice doesn't feel like school, it feels like a family," students tell us, reporting that "every week, we have social network events where the faculty and professors all unwind. It's a great balance between social life and school." Those events include Partios, which are "parties on the patio every Thursday, often sponsored by recruiting companies" that draw a crowd with "free beer (yes, beer) and pizza." Another fave is the Coffee Colloquium, a free breakfast every Monday and Wednesday morning that provides "a chance to meet professors and other students. and get the latest news." Students get involved here in the "variety of student activities and professional clubs that truly contribute to the overall student experience."

Aside from the fun stuff, first-year students must deal with a "mountain of assignments, case studies, and teamwork projects" that can be "overwhelming" because "They all have to be done now!" First-year course work, in particular, can be "rough, with little available time to socialize or network off campus." "If you think your communication and presentation skills are excellent, be prepared for a lesson in humility," warns one student. The workload eases up during the second year of the program, allowing students more time to devote to such opportunities as the Wright Fund, "a student-run fund with market value of over $850,000" that gives them "hands-on and real-world knowledge in investment management."

The Jones School "is also located in the most beautiful building on the Rice University campus. With its technology, the school is a wonderful place to be stuck in working on a team project for hours on end." Students want you to know that "the general perception that Houston is an ugly city" is accurate, but also that Rice is located "in the nicest, most beautiful part of Houston, with 100-year-old oak trees that line the roads, and within walking distance to the Museum District and Rice Village. This is the ritzy, old-money area of Houston."

Admissions

Applicants to the Jones school must provide the Admissions Committee with official copies of all undergraduate and graduate transcripts, GMAT scores, two letters of recommendation, two personal essays, and a resume. An interview is also required. The school considers "leadership experience and team-based experiences" in evaluating candidates and seeks "unique qualities that the candidate will contribute to the program." International applicants must also demonstrate English proficiency and provide proof of sufficient financial support to pay for their education and expenses while studying at the Jones School. While post-undergraduate professional experience is not required, the school prefers candidates with at least 2 years of such experience.

Prominent Alumni

James S. Turley, Chairman/CEO, Ernst & Young LLP; Subha Barry, First Vice President, Merrill Lynch & Co., Inc.; Keith Anderson, CIO, Soros Fund Management; Doug Foshee, President/CEO, El Paso Corporation; Hamd Alkayat, Assistant Minister, Ministry of Education in Iraq.

FINANCIAL FACTS

Annual tuition	$36,000
Fees	$2,234
Cost of books	$1,500
Room & board (on/off-campus)	$12,000/$15,500
% of students receiving aid	84
% of first-year students receiving aid	71
% of students receiving loans	56
% of students receiving grants	70
Average award package	$38,071
Average grant	$16,370
Average student loan debt	$48,675

ADMISSIONS

Admissions Selectivity Rating	91
# of applications received	566
% applicants accepted	39
% acceptees attending	56
Average GMAT	642
Range of GMAT	600–680
Average GPA	3.25
TOEFL required of international students	Yes
Minimum TOEFL (paper/computer)	600/250
Application fee	$100
International application fee	$100
Application Deadline/Notification	
Round 1:	11/12 / 12/14
Round 2:	01/14 / 02/15
Round 3:	02/25 / 03/28
Round 4:	04/07 / 05/02
Deferment available	Yes
Need-blind admissions	Yes

EMPLOYMENT PROFILE

Career Rating	90		
Primary Source of Full-time Job Acceptances		Grads Employed by Function	% Avg. Salary
School-facilitated activities	75 (70%)	Finance	50 $89,719
Graduate-facilitated activities	32 (30%)	Marketing	16 $86,300
Average base starting salary	$89,006	Operations	4 $81,500
Percent employed	95	Consulting	9 $97,070
		General Management	9 $88,778
		Other	12 $85,250

Top 5 Employers Hiring Grads
Chevron; ExxonMobil; Deutsche Bank; Citi; ConocoPhillips

ROCHESTER INSTITUTE OF TECHNOLOGY
E. PHILIP SAUNDERS COLLEGE OF BUSINESS

Academics

Rochester Institute of Technology is among the nation's top engineering/science schools, so it should come as no surprise that the RIT MBA "concentrates on both business and technology," with a "practical, rather than theoretical, structure and philosophy" that students find appealing. RIT's "blend of engineering and business for the MBA program" results in "course material that is highly applicable to existing industry issues," students tell us.

RIT's approach to getting students in and out of the program is every bit as practical as its approach to curriculum. One MBA reports, "The school has practices in place that allow you to get your degree more quickly. It recognizes undergraduate course work for waiving courses, for example, and it has programs in place where you can get your degree in 1 year (full-time). Also, the program is structured in a way that makes it easier for people who are working full-time to get their degree" by allowing them to place out of foundation courses through examination. Part-timers tell us the program "is very well structured to our needs. Almost all classes are in the evening (or at least offered in the evening), and because other students are in a similar situation, professors and teammates are used to being flexible with meeting times." The only impediment to total convenience, students tell us, is that required courses for concentrations aren't offered as frequently as they might be. "Many are only offered once a year, making it difficult to schedule them," warns one MBA.

RIT's MBA curriculum "heavily utilizes case studies, which is nice." A quarterly academic schedule "is fast, competitive, and very challenging," but students generally like the way it keeps the curriculum moving quickly forward. Students also appreciate "the heavy focus on technology" (RIT has "great facilities with first-rate technology" to support this focus) and "the almost endless possibilities to combine concentrations and classes." Entrepreneurship and market research earn students' approval; unique offerings here include environmentally sustainability management, software project management, and telecommunications.

Career and Placement

RIT provides placement and counseling services through the university-wide Office of Cooperative Education and Career Services. Students tell us that their job searches are abetted by the school's great reputation; one MBA reports, "I am getting calls for jobs because I have RIT on my resume. I was hired for my current job by an RIT alum (didn't know it before the interview, though)." The alumni network is universally praised for its assistance during and after the program. Students are less uniform in their praise of the placement office, telling us that job fairs "are too heavily weighted toward tech and government employers looking for only one or two hires. Not enough companies [are] looking for business employees."

Employers who recently hired RIT MBAs include: Bausch & Lomb, Bose, Capital One Financial Services, Cypress Semiconductor Corporation, Danka Office Imaging Company, Deloitte Touche Tohmatsu, Eastman Kodak, Fluor, Frontier Corporation, General Electric Company, Global Crossing, Heidelberg Digital, Hewlett-Packard, IBM, Lockheed Martin, Motorola, Paychex, PricewaterhouseCoopers, Proctor & Gamble, Prudential Securities, RCN Telecom Services, and Xerox.

ADMISSIONS CONTACT: DIANE ELLISON, DIRECTOR, PART-TIME & GRADUATE ENROLLMENT
ADDRESS: 105 LOMB MEMORIAL DRIVE ROCHESTER, NY 14623 UNITED STATES
PHONE: 585-475-7284 • FAX: 585-475-5476
E-MAIL: GRADINFO@RIT.EDU • WEBSITE: WWW.RITMBA.COM

Student Life and Environment

Under RIT's quarterly calendar, "The general course load is three classes. Some people take four, but that makes it hard to really learn the stuff without getting overworked." Classes here "are generally taught at night (6:00 P.M. to 9:20 P.M.) once a week. Some courses are also taught during the daytime, and some are even offered online." The school's facility "has recently been extensively remodeled and is beautiful. It has a lot of glass on the front of the first floor, new computer labs, new wall coverings and flooring, and more solid oak trim." Students "meet before class and socialize in the lounge on the first floor or in the graduate student lounge on the second floor. Students also gather before class around the lounge chairs that are interspersed in the upstairs hallways and discuss course work." They also bond through "the many clubs that are available to all," although many are too busy with work and personal obligations to participate. Hometown Rochester "is a lot of fun" with "a great downtown life," although "The local weather is awful." Diversions include "skiing, bars, parks, casinos, and day trips" to Buffalo and Canada.

RIT students include a large number who come "straight from undergraduate programs, meaning they are not always able to contribute that much practical knowledge to class discussion." They are "smart, friendly, and motivated without being overly competitive." The program is "evenly split between full-time and part-time, evenly split between men and women, and evenly split between American and international."

Admissions

RIT accepts applications to its MBA program for all four quarters; most full-time students enter the program in the fall. Online application is available. All applicants must have an undergraduate degree from an accredited university or college and must be able to demonstrate proficiency in algebra, statistics, and computer literacy. A completed application includes an official copy of the applicant's undergraduate transcript, an official GMAT score report, a current resume, and a personal statement. International students whose transcripts are not in English must have their transcripts translated and interpreted by an accredited service. They must also submit an official score report for the TOEFL.

FINANCIAL FACTS

Annual tuition	$30174
Fees	$207
Cost of books	$1,500
Room & board (on-campus)	$10,000
% of students receiving aid	24
% of first-year students receiving aid	32
% of students receiving grants	24
Average grant	$10,644

ADMISSIONS

Admissions Selectivity Rating	**75**
# of applications received	254
% applicants accepted	84
% acceptees attending	62
Average GMAT	598
Range of GMAT	540–650
Average GPA	3
TOEFL required of international students	Yes
Minimum TOEFL (paper/computer)	580/237
Application fee	$50
International application fee	$50
Regular application deadline	8/1
Regular notification	rolling
Deferment available	Yes
Maximum length of deferment	1 year
Transfer students accepted	Yes
Transfer application policy	Transfer up to 3 courses if relevant to program. Grade of B or better
Non-fall admissions	Yes
Need-blind admissions	Yes

ROLLINS COLLEGE
CRUMMER GRADUATE SCHOOL OF BUSINESS

Academics

With an "excellent reputation" in the region, a "great alumni network" and "strong connections to central Florida businesses including Walt Disney World, Darden Restaurants, Morgan Stanley, SunTrust and Universal Orlando," and "numerous global projects," the Rollins MBA has a lot to offer America's future business tycoons. And with four separate programs—each geared to the needs of a distinct demographic—just about anyone and everyone, from the business neophyte to the experienced manager, can benefit.

Rollins' sole full-time MBA program is its early advantage MBA (EAMBA), which is aimed primarily at recent college grads with little or no work experience—although working stiffs on sabbatical are also welcome. The school also offers three part-time programs: the professional MBA, open to anyone currently employed full-time; the Saturday MBA, designed for mid- to senior-level professionals (minimum 5 years of work experience required); and the executive MBA, which meets on alternate Fridays and Saturdays and is open only to those with at least 10 years of professional experience.

Students in all programs praise the "wonderful faculty," who bring a lot to the table with "a high level of professionalism, competence, and real-world experience," as well as their "down-to-earth personalities. They're willing to go the extra mile to assist students." MBAs also appreciate that the curriculum "allows business students to be creative. How often do you get to hear of students having fun and being creative at business school? At Rollins it happens." International business is one of the program's main focal points; each year about 130 students participate in 12-week international consulting projects.

Crummer promotes "numerous presentations and meetings with business leaders" to the great benefit of students; those in the part-time programs, however, note that these events typically occur at times inconvenient to students with full-time jobs. In the EAMBA, students tell us they benefit from "a team environment that helps prepare students for the real world." Team spirit is built from the beginning of the program, as students endure the grueling core curriculum in cohorts. MBAs also praise "the wide range of available courses and a good number of concentrations for a school of this size. Academics are rigorous."

Career and Placement

The Career Management Center handles placement services for Rollins MBAs, offering a variety of in-person and online counseling and recruiting services. In 2006, the mean salary for a graduating EAMBA was $60,000; the median salary was $50,000. That's not bad for a group that typically enters the program with no real work experience.

Top employers of Crummer MBAs include: The Walt Disney Company, Radiant, CNL Group, FedEx, Harris Corporation, Johnson & Johnson, Marriott International, Darden Restaurant Group, AT&T, Siemens Westinghouse, CIA, Dynetech, Citigroup, Universal Studios, General Mills, Tupperware, and SunTrust Bank. Students are generally satisfied with the school's ties to the business community, its alumni connections, and its recruiting efforts, although some complain that "we don't get enough recruiting companies outside of banking, financial services, and Disney."

ADMISSIONS CONTACT: STEPHEN GAUTHIER, ASSOCIATE DEAN
ADDRESS: 1000 HOLT AVE. - 2722 WINTER PARK, FL 32789-4499 UNITED STATES
PHONE: 407-646-2405 • FAX: 407-646-2522
E-MAIL: MBAADMISSIONS@ROLLINS.EDU • WEBSITE: WWW.CRUMMER.ROLLINS.EDU

Student Life and Environment

Full-time students at Crummer report that "there is a real sense of belonging and inclusion at the business school. Through the wide range of student-run organizations, our students network with business professionals, volunteer in the community, develop themselves professionally, and socialize with each other." The school provides "plenty of activities and speakers on campus," most often "scheduled around lunchtime so students do not have to leave the business school." Students tell us that "these are great networking events, as well as being informative." Once classes are over, students enjoy "a very social atmosphere on and around campus. Rollins is located on a beautiful campus in a great town where there is lots of shops, restaurants, and fun things to do. It's a great environment to be in."

Part-time students, naturally, are not as involved in campus life, since "Everyone in our program has a full-time job and does not have a lot of time for outside the classroom activities. Still, most students have found ways to get involved in one way or another." Part-timers tell us that many of them "try to get to class early, sometimes even 30 minutes early to set up our computers and chat with the professors, who are always around. This helps with networking and camaraderie." Regardless of their program, students tell us that "classes are intense but interesting. You really need to be prepared, or you can easily get called out by your professor or fellow students for not putting the needed prep work in. Even subjects like accounting are taught from the perspective of the skills a business executive would need to use."

Admissions

Applicants to Crummer's EAMBA program must provide the school with the following: official transcripts for all undergraduate, graduate, and professional school work; an official GMAT score report; personal essays; two 'confidential evaluations' (letters of recommendation); and a resume. Interviews are conducted at the school's invitation only. Applicants to the executive MBA program must meet all of the above requirements in addition to a required interview, and they must also submit proof of their employer's support for their participation. PMBA and SMBA applicants must interview as part of the application process as well.

FINANCIAL FACTS

Annual tuition	$26,800
Fees	$60
Cost of books	$2,200
Room & board (off-campus)	$15,000
% of students receiving aid	50
% of first-year students receiving aid	48
% of students receiving grants	50
Average award package	$15,154
Average grant	$15,154
Average student loan debt	$28,900

ADMISSIONS

Admissions Selectivity Rating	**80**
# of applications received	190
% applicants accepted	62
% acceptees attending	67
Average GMAT	571
Range of GMAT	510–650
Average GPA	3.2
TOEFL required of international students	Yes
Application fee	$50
International application fee	$50
Regular application deadline	Rolling
Regular notification	Rolling
Deferment available	Yes
Maximum length of deferment	1 year
Transfer students accepted	Yes
Transfer application policy	
The school accepts up to 6 credits transferred from an MBA program that is accredited by the AACSB.	
Non-fall admissions	Yes
Need-blind admissions	Yes

Applicants Also Look At

Florida State University, Stetson University, University of Central Florida, University of Florida, University of Miami, Vanderbilt University, Wake Forest University.

EMPLOYMENT PROFILE

Career Rating	80	Grads Employed by Function	%	Avg. Salary
Primary Source of Full-time Job Acceptances		Finance	52	$53,800
School-facilitated activities	68%	Marketing	25	$50,000
Graduate-facilitated activities	32%	MIS	5	$0
		Operations	2	$60,000
		Consulting	7	NR
		General Management	5	$300,000
		Other	4	$51,000

ROWAN UNIVERSITY
THE ROHRER COLLEGE OF BUSINESS

Academics

Rowan University's MBA program, the school tells us, "offers a variety of course scheduling options for both part-time and full-time students." "As working adults, we have been treated like valued customers," one student notes, pointing out that the once-a-week, three-hour classes (mostly week nights, with some classes held on Saturday mornings) best fit her busy work schedule. Because most students attend part-time, a Rowan degree usually takes between three and six years to complete; those enrolled full-time have the option of completing the program in a single year.

The Rowan MBA curriculum commences with 27 hours of required core courses covering fundamental general-management skills. The curriculum also leaves room for nine hours of electives; students may choose to take a variety of courses that match their career needs or may use these courses to specialize in finance, accounting, management marketing, or entrepreneurship. MBAs tell us that "every class involves group work, which teaches students to work well with each other and share work. This skill set has helped in the workforce as well."

The program has been growing in recent years, a fact that students acknowledge and appreciate. The school recently earned AACSB accreditation, placing it among the nation's top programs. Students tell us that "there has been an increase in the quality of the program, and [they] were delighted when the Rowan program was accredited in 2003. Enrollment has increased, and [they] see a great future for Rowan's MBA program." One graduating BA/MBA student told us that "although the program started at a low level, it is now getting tougher and tougher to get into." The increased standards, we're told, have paid dividends in more challenging classes and more illuminating in-class discussions.

Rowan MBAs love that "we are able to access the library's databases from our home computers. It's great to be able to look up material 24/7. Also, online and tele-registrations have reduced the hassle of registering to zero." Technology remains in the spotlight in the classroom; "Rowan teaches computer skills that have proven invaluable in the workforce," students tell us, although they also complain that "the audiovisual capabilities are terrible in all but one classroom. It is a very limiting feature when trying to receive information or do presentations." Overall, students feel that Rowan "is a great regional school whose current programs and commitment to expansion of the program will continue to take great strides in drawing students from outside this region."

Career and Placement

Rowan maintains a Career and Academic Planning Center "to provide developmental advising" to all students in their pursuit of academic and professional goals. The CAPC serves the entire school; there is no office dedicated specifically to MBAs or to business students on the undergraduate and graduate levels. CAPC Services include one-on-one counseling, workshops, online self-assessment and job databases (CampusRecruiter, Career Key), career publications, and employer directories. Services are available to alumni as well as to current students. It should be noted that most current students are full-time workers looking to advance within their current places of work; relatively few students seeking MBAs are actively searching for new jobs.

ADMISSIONS CONTACT: THE GRADUATE SCHOOL, DIRECTOR OF GRADUATE ADMISSIONS
ADDRESS: MEMORIAL HALL, 201 MULLICA HILL ROAD GLASSBORO, NJ 08028 UNITED STATES
PHONE: 856-256-4050 • FAX: 856-256-4436
E-MAIL: MBA@ROWAN.EDU • WEBSITE: WWW.ROWAN.EDU/MBA

Student Life and Environment

Rowan serves mostly part-time students. That's not to say the opportunities to socialize and network aren't there; as one BA/MBA student explains, "As an undergraduate, I found many activities that were available to students who lived on and off campus. I enjoyed my four years living on campus. Rowan had activities for everyone, including day and evening events, student government, community-service efforts, fraternities, and campus-wide events. As a graduate student, however, I am a working professional, so I do not have any time to participate in the activities available."

Rowan's suburban New Jersey home town of Glassboro is a mere half-hour's drive from Philadelphia; the Jersey shore is less than an hour to the east, and Atlantic City is only 50 miles away. New York; Washington, DC; and the Chesapeake are all within easy travel distances. The Rowan campus is in the middle of an ambitious expansion program, with makeovers planned for most facilities and several new buildings going up. Students praise the new athletic center and enjoy watching Rowan's Division III excellent men's and women's basketball teams.

Admissions

Rowan's graduate b-students are required to complete seven foundation courses, or their undergraduate. Those courses are foundations of accounting, statistics I, principles of finance, principles of marketing, calculus, operations management, and on economics. Applicants to the MBA program must submit official transcripts for all undergraduate work (with a minimum GPA of 2.5. overall or 2.8 for final 60 semester hours), GMAT or GRE scores, two letters of recommendation, a personal statement of career objectives, evidence of computer proficiency, and a resume. International students whose first language is not English must also provide TOEFL (or equivalent) scores.

FINANCIAL FACTS

Annual tuition	$10,624
Fees	$2,058
Cost of books	$700
Room & board (on-campus)	$6,044

ADMISSIONS

Admissions Selectivity Rating	**75**
Average GMAT	501
Average GPA	3.36
TOEFL required of international students	Yes
Minimum TOEFL (paper/computer)	550/213
Application fee	$50
International application fee	$50
Regular application deadline	Rolling
Regular notification	Rolling
Deferment available	Yes
Maximum length of deferment	1 year
Transfer students accepted	Yes
Transfer application policy Student may transfer up to 9 credit hours.	
Non-fall admissions	Yes
Need-blind admissions	Yes

Applicants Also Look At

Rutgers, The State University of New Jersey.

RSM ERASMUS UNIVERSITY

Academics

Future international business moguls choose RSM Erasmus for two simple reasons: The school provides "the most international MBA" experience in the world, and Rotterdam is in the heart of the EEC, with "easy access" to Germany and the "EU labor market." RSM provides a "very challenging, positive learning environment," but its intensive 15-month MBA program is not for the faint of heart. The "workload is heavy," and the curriculum is front loaded (students take 11 general management courses in the first two semesters). During this period, the day "starts at 9:30 A.M. with classes and ends at 7:00 P.M. with some group work or . . . [an] assignment." Overworked students take comfort in the fact that their professors are "excellent! They clearly enjoy teaching their subject matters, and because they are from all over the world, we get different perspectives in class." Students also point out that "the small class size means we have more opportunities to form close relationships with the program staff." During the third semester, students choose an advanced course from one of four areas of specialization (finance, marketing, strategy, or IT), then plunge into a summer associateship. The final semester is an elective curriculum; about a third of students fulfill these credits in one of 30 international exchange programs. All academic work in residency at RSM is conducted in English.

With one eye trained on the executive job market and the other on skill development and business knowledge, Rotterdam is what "b-school should be"; that is, "practical and academic at the same time." The Personal Leadership Development program, a mandatory 15-month experiential course, adds additional value. One student sums it up: "In hindsight I would not have gone to any other business school. RSM offers the right balance of soft and hard skills." "The school [also] has a strong sense of social responsibility." "I am now equipped to be a stronger and more sensitive businessperson," writes one satisfied student.

Career and Placement

Students say RSM's "Career Services Department is currently understaffed. They are encouraging, but they lack manpower." For less-motivated students, this might "be an issue." Regardless, RSM Erasmus MBAs can look forward to bright and lucrative careers. While the school is responsible for connecting students with about three-quarters of internships and half of post-MBA jobs, students also find significant career opportunities within the alumni network and elsewhere. Top employers of RSM grads are ABN Amro, Barclays Capital, Campina, Coca-Cola, Eli Lilly and Company, General Electric Company, Hewlett-Packard, ING, Interbrand, Johnson & Johnson, KPN, L'Oréal, McKinsey & Company, Novartis, Orange, Philips, Reckitt Benckiser, Roland Berger, Strategy Consultants, Shell Oil Company, and Siemens Business Services. Newly minted grads report a mean base salary of $104,426, with women earning slightly more than men.

Student Life and Environment

RSM "Students form a strong and very connected group," students say. "Everyone is automatically a member of every club. It's your responsibility to contribute as much or as little to the events. For example, though you may not be in any entrepreneurial courses, you are automatically invited to [hear] every entrepreneurial speaker on campus. And once you arrive, you are welcome in the room." The collegial atmosphere is "perfect and wonderful," says one MBA candidate. "I'd like to go back to the first semester and to start again." Even so, students are "extremely driven." "Almost half want to be entre-

ADMISSIONS CONTACT: RICK RUDOLPH, SENIOR MARKETING & ADMISSIONS MANAGER
ADDRESS: BURGEMEESTER OUDLAAN 50 - J BUILDING 3062 PA ROTTERDAM, NETHERLANDS
PHONE: 011-31-10-4082222 • FAX: 011-31-10-4529509
E-MAIL: INFO@RSM.NL • WEBSITE: WWW.RSM.NL/MBA

preneurs or have owned businesses." RSM's "inspiring and challenging" students don't shrink from competition or from giving "positive and constructive criticism."

Diversity is no afterthought here—it's the reason MBA candidates choose RSM. Students say that the "international perspective was a big draw. Several other [schools] claimed to be international, but mostly had over 50 percent from one or two backgrounds." RSM, on the other hand, "has 42 nationalities and only small clusters from the same backgrounds." This means that students learn "a lot from classmates," and "There is no ruling racial group in our class." "It is just great!" enthuses one student. "A mix of cultures brings so many good things out of each student that it is almost like magic. The amount of kindness that I've experienced is just overwhelming." Demographically speaking, students are overwhelmingly European and Asian, with large Indian and Taiwanese communities; the average student is in his or her late 20s, with an undergraduate background in business or economics and more than 5 years of pre-MBA work experience. A quarter of MBA candidates are women. Partners and spouses "have banded together" to form "a supportive network," "and routinely have nights out on the town."

Admissions

RSM Erasmus admits more than half of all its applicants—good news to the self-selected pool of MBA candidates whose passion for international business and culture brings them to RSM. Admission is no cakewalk—successful applicants report an average GMAT score of 620 and a minimum of 2 years' work experience—but the numbers give good reason for optimism. The most recent application requires essays on career goals, hobbies and interests, and difficult decisions—slightly more personal topics than appear on American applications. Submit translations of your academic transcripts if they are written in languages other than Dutch and English, and prepare for an interview if you make the first cut. Admission is rolling.

FINANCIAL FACTS

Annual tuition	$52,626
Cost of books	$800
Room & board (off-campus)	$7,000
% of students receiving aid	55
% of first-year students receiving aid	55
% of students receiving loans	30
% of students receiving grants	25
Average award package	$38,914
Average grant	$14,920

ADMISSIONS

Admissions Selectivity Rating	**84**
# of applications received	447
% applicants accepted	53
% acceptees attending	47
Average GMAT	640
Range of GMAT	580–760
Minimum TOEFL (paper/computer)	600/250
Application fee	$50
International application fee	$50
Regular application deadline	7/15
Regular notification	rolling
Deferment available	Yes
Maximum length of deferment	1 year
Need-blind admissions	Yes

Applicants Also Look At

ESADE, HEC School of Management-Paris, IESE Business School, IMD (International Institute for Management Development), INSEAD, London Business School, Nyenrode Business Universiteit.

EMPLOYMENT PROFILE

Career Rating	87	Grads Employed by Function	% Avg. Salary
Primary Source of Full-time Job Acceptances		Finance	30 NR
School-facilitated activities	37 (51%)	Human Resources	1 NR
Graduate-facilitated activities	35 (45%)	Marketing	25 NR
Unknown	3 (4%)	MIS	1 NR
Average base starting salary	$104,426	Operations	5 NR
		Consulting	27 NR
		General Management	10 NR
		Other	1 NR

Top 5 Employers Hiring Grads
Fortis Bank; AT Kearney; ABN Amro; Bain & Company; ExxonMobil

RUTGERS, THE STATE UNIVERSITY OF NEW JERSEY
RUTGERS BUSINESS SCHOOL—NEWARK AND NEW BRUNSWICK

GENERAL INFORMATION
Type of school   Public
Academic calendar   Trimester

SURVEY SAYS...
Friendly students
Good peer network
Cutting edge classes
Helpful alumni
Happy students
Smart classrooms
Solid preparation in:
Communication/interpersonal skills
Presentation skills

STUDENTS
Enrollment of parent institution	50,000
Enrollment of business school	1,098
% male/female	56/44
% out-of-state	28
% part-time	89
% minorities	11
% international	25
Average age at entry	27
Average years work experience at entry	4.3

ACADEMICS
Academic Experience Rating	**86**
Student/faculty ratio	15:1
Profs interesting rating	88
Profs accessible rating	93
% female faculty	22
% minority faculty	35

Joint Degrees
BA/MBA, BS/MBA, MPH/MBA, MD/MBA, JD/MBA, MS/MBA (Biomedical Sciences), MPP/MBA, MCRP/MBA.

Prominent Alumni
Thomas A. Renyi, Chairman & CEO, The Bank of New York Mellon; Gary M. Cohen, President, BD Medical; Irwin M. Lerner, Retired Chairman of the Board, Hoffmann-La Roche; Nicholas J. Valeriani, Worldwide Chairman, Johnson & Johnson; Ralph Izzo, President/CEO, PSEG.

Academics

A "renowned international business program," "marketing professors who are well-known in their respective fields," and perhaps most of all "a top-rated pharmaceutical MBA program" draw a strong applicant pool to the MBA program at Rutgers Business School. Programs are also offered in Accounting, Finance, and Supply Chain Management. The school's location "in a metropolitan area with easy access to New York City and Philadelphia" is another one of Rutgers' prized assets. But for many New Jersey natives, the low in-state tuition is the greatest attraction; coupled with the quality of the program, the cost of attending RBS allows Garden Staters to realize a substantial return on investment here.

A full-time Rutgers MBA requires a minimum of 60 class-hour credits. The newly revised full-time curriculum introduced in fall 2007 includes 19 credits of core courses, 6 credits of foundation courses, 3 credits in team consulting, and 32 credits of electives. The part-time curriculum varies slightly from the full-time curriculum but follows the same general approach. Concentrations are available in six primary disciplines, including finance, management and global business, information technology, marketing, pharmaceutical management and supply chain management.

Students love the fact that Rutgers offers "terrific professors who know real-life situations and bring that experience to the classroom," and "an administration that is constantly active and involved." "Proximity to New York City" and "connections within the pharmaceutical industry" translate into plenty of job opportunities for graduates. The school's website boasts that the region "has the highest concentration of corporate headquarters for U.S. metro areas of comparable size." Part-time students appreciate that "the workload is perfect—not too overwhelming, but still substantial. We learn a lot and I feel that we will be well prepared when we graduate."

Career and Placement

The Office of Career Management provides counseling and placement services to Rutgers' full-time and part-time MBAs and MQF students as well as to alumni of those programs. Students report that the office provides "great career forums that network students with alumni." In 2008, students completing their first year in the program found summer internships in the following industries: pharmaceutical, 42 percent; finance, 20 percent; manufacturing, 13 percent each; consumer goods, 19 percent; non-profit and energy utilities, 3 percent each. Recent employers of Rutgers MBAs include The Bank of New York, Mellon (Becton, Dickinson, and Company), Bristol-Myers Squibb, Celgene Corp., Citigroup, Church & Dwight, Daiichi Sankyo, Deloitte, Dendrite International, Ethicon, Inc., Johnson & Johnson, Kraft Foods, KPMG, Lockheed Martin, Merrill Lynch, Novartis Pharmaceuticals, Pfizer, Praxair, Reckitt Benckiser, Sanofi-Aventis, Siemens Corp., Strategyx, Stryker, Toys "R" Us, Tyco International USA.

Student Life and Environment

Rutgers Business School boasts an extremely diverse student body. Women constitute more than one-third the population here—an unusually high proportion for an American MBA program. The international population is substantial: 40 countries are represented among the graduate business student population. Students tell us that their peers "come from greatly diverse backgrounds, both culturally and professionally" and that "although they are competitive, they are always willing to help one another." Approximately 25 percent of the student body attends full-time. The majority part-timers tell us that "social contact is limited, as people are tired after work and want to go home. We are very busy juggling work, school, and family (those of us who have one). Involvement outside of class is usually limited to one study group per class per week."

Full-time classes are offered at the Rutgers' Newark campus; part-time classes are available at the two main campuses in Newark and New Brunswick and also at satellite sites in Jersey City, Morristown, and Princeton. New Brunswick is among the nation's premier health care centers, providing an optimal setting for the school's pharmaceutical management-related programs. Newark is a large city located about a half hour away from central Manhattan by train. New Jersey Transit makes travel to and from New York City relatively easy, convenient, and affordable. It certainly beats driving in the area.

Admissions

The admissions committee serving the Rutgers MBA program gives primary consideration to evidence of academic promise. Undergraduate transcripts and transcripts for any graduate work are scrutinized both for the student's performance in class and for the quality and rigor of the program pursued. GMAT scores also figure into the committee's assessment of a candidate's readiness. Admissions officers also consider applicants' professional history, recommendations from supervisors, evidence of leadership and civic involvement, and the personal essay. The school "seeks a diverse student body to bring to the classroom varying experiences and backgrounds;" appraisal of students' personal histories allows it to achieve this goal. Applicants must submit a completed application form, official transcripts for all postsecondary academic work, an official GMAT score report, a current resume, two letters of professional reference, and an essay. International applicants must meet all of the above requirements and must submit an official score report for the TOEFL, professional translations of all transcripts not in English, and appropriate financial documentation.

FINANCIAL FACTS

Annual tuition (in-state/ out-of-state)	$18,825/$30,027
Fees	$1,995
Cost of books	$3,000
Room & board	$12,000

ADMISSIONS

Admissions Selectivity Rating	**88**
# of applications received	205
% applicants accepted	54
% acceptees attending	57
Average GMAT	637
Range of GMAT	600–660
Average GPA	3.3
TOEFL required of international students	Yes
Minimum TOEFL (paper/computer)	600/250
Application fee	$60
International application fee	$60
Regular application deadline	5/1
Regular notification	rolling
Deferment available	Yes
Maximum length of deferment	1 year
Transfer students accepted	Yes
Transfer application policy Students may transfer a maximum of 18 applicable credits earned in an MBA program at an AACSB-accredited school.	
Non-fall admissions	Yes
Need-blind admissions	Yes

Applicants Also Look At

City University of New York—Baruch College, Fordham University, New York University, Penn State University, Seton Hall University.

EMPLOYMENT PROFILE

Career Rating	87	Grads Employed by Function	% Avg. Salary
Primary Source of Full-time Job Acceptances		Finance	13 $79,692
School-facilitated activities	28 (74%)	Marketing	15 $73,867
Graduate-facilitated activities	1 (3%)	MIS	4 $70,000
Unknown	9 (23%)	Operations	1 $85,000
Average base starting salary	$78,921	Consulting	4 $78,750
Percent employed	86	General Management	1 $80,000
		Top 5 Employers Hiring Grads	
		Johnson & Johnson Companies; Hoffman-La Roche; Bristol Meyers Squibb; StrategyX; Church & Dwight	

RUTGERS, THE STATE UNIVERSITY OF NEW JERSEY—CAMDEN
SCHOOL OF BUSINESS

Academics

Why attend Rutgers' MBA program? According to students, because of its "reputation," "reputation," "reputation." "The tuition is reasonable and the education is of the highest caliber for a New Jersey public university," one student explains. Add to this an MBA program that requires "only 57 total credits" for the degree, and "only three courses needed for a concentration," and the deal gets sweeter. "Convenience" is another popular factor, meaning that many students are from Camden or nearby cities and towns. "The location is perfect for where I live," one student says. "It's close to everything (Philadelphia, the New Jersey Shore, and even New York City)."

"The expectations for students are high" at Rutgers—Camden School of Business thanks to "the opportunity to learn cutting-edge, real-world applications from experienced professionals." It's these professionals who enable students here to fulfill such expectations. "The Faculty is very impressive and they bring a well of knowledge to the classroom," one student notes. Another adds, "The professors are very approachable—they understand that we are working professionals and that we all have families, jobs, and a life away from Rutgers. They are very understanding and supportive, yet still challenging." Many students with families or jobs take advantage of Rutgers' "part-time" course offerings, particularly in the "evening" and also appreciate the "great ability to accelerate [their] degrees via summer and winter sessions." Such flexibility results in "a wide variety of students from a number of different backgrounds."

The administration also gets high marks from students for "going the extra mile to make sure each student is satisfied with his or her experiences at the university." "If a problem develops, the professionals at Rutgers are eager to solve it in a timely fashion," one student notes. "You never experience the 'isolated' feeling at this school." Others praise the "great facilities," but would like to see the school "offer more classes" "online" and at its other, off-campus locations. Some would also like the "course classifications" process to run more smoothly. "Two of my arguably finance-based Special Topics courses (Raising Capital and Corporate Restructuring) were classified as Management courses, depriving me of a desired concentration in Finance," one student says. However, as one student adds, "It may not be the most attractive school, but I believe the quality of education ranks close to if not among elite MBA programs."

Career and Placement

The Career Services office at Rutgers—Camden offers a multitude of offerings to job-seeking students, including career coaching, assessment inventories, on-campus recruiting, job fairs, web-based job postings, and resume and credentials help at their career resource center. MBA graduates can join "The Graduates Club," which the school describes as a "state-of-the-art online community that [combines the features of] a traditional off-line alumni club" that "aims to become the foremost meeting place for graduates of the world's leading programs." MBA students can also join Rutgers' Alumni Career Network, "a database of over 1,200 alumni from Camden, New Brunswick, and Newark offering career information and support to current students and alumni." Another option for MBA grads is the Rutgers—Camden alliance with Drake Beam Morin ("a provider of career management and transition services) that offers "online resources such as career consultations, resume/cover letter writing, career assessments, networking, discussion boards, and more." "Many students are well known in their industries and each student wants to get as much out of class as possible," one student says.

Student Life and Environment

Many students here agree that "the business school is like a family," since despite the "many different backgrounds and experiences, [they] all have something in common: ambition!" Students note that most of their "competitive," "motivated," and "mature" peers "are established in their discipline and are looking for the opportunity to take their career to the next level." In line with this focused approach to education, these "overworked MBA students are generally only on campus for classes," meaning that a school-based social life can be "hard to find." Despite this, while they're in class together students find each other "friendly" and "helpful." "They're just swell," one student adds. After class, those who don't head home say, "The school offers a number of different clubs and activities." For those leading a double-life as student and family person, "Rutgers—Camden does a great job of allowing students to balance work life and home life with a quality MBA education."

According to some students, Camden "isn't the nicest place to be." However, "great public transportation" and "good facilities" go a long way to offset this. However, some would like to see "transport from the subway and train station to campus" improve. Others mention that the campus itself could use some "landscaping." "[The school needs to] plant some trees and acquire more of the surrounding property to better define the campus," one student says. But despite this, the school's location is its biggest asset thanks to a short distance from Philadelphia, New York, Boston, and Washington, DC. "There is an abundance of things to do outside of class because of the proximity to Philadelphia," a student explains.

Admissions

Applicants to the Rutgers—Camden MBA program must submit the following: an online application (available via the school's website), original undergrad and—if applicable—graduate transcripts, a personal statement, two letters of recommendation, GMAT scores (the GMAT is "waived for applicants with an MD degree), and a current resume (optional, but recommended). Students with an LSAT score in the 80th percentile may submit that instead of the GMAT. International applicants are required to submit a minimum TOEFL score of 213 on the computer version, 550 on the paper version, or 22 (writing), 23 (speaking), 21 (reading), and 17 (listening) on the internet version. International applicants must also submit a Financial Statement Documentation (also available via the school's website).

FINANCIAL FACTS

Annual tuition (in-state/ out-of-state)	$15,921/$24,067
Fees	$1,438
Room & board (on-campus)	$6,716

ADMISSIONS

Admissions Selectivity Rating	**78**
# of applications received	228
% applicants accepted	61
% acceptees attending	55
Average GMAT	560
Average GPA	3.2
TOEFL required of international students	Yes
Minimum TOEFL (paper/computer)	550/230
Application fee	$60
Deferment available	Yes
Maximum length of deferment	1 Semester
Transfer students accepted	Yes
Transfer application policy We will transfer courses from AACSB-accredited schools.	
Non-fall admissions	Yes
Need-blind admissions	Yes

Applicants Also Look At

Drexel University, Rowan University, Temple University, University of Delaware.

EMPLOYMENT PROFILE

Career Rating	71	Top 5 Employers Hiring Grads
		Lockheed Martin; Aramark; Deloitte & Touche; JP Morgan Chase; Computer Sciences Coporation

SACRED HEART UNIVERSITY
JOHN F. WELCH COLLEGE OF BUSINESS

GENERAL INFORMATION

Type of school	Private
Affiliation	Roman Catholic
Academic calendar	Trimester

SURVEY SAYS...
Cutting edge classes
Solid preparation in:
General management
Doing business in a global economy

STUDENTS

Enrollment of parent institution	5,775
Enrollment of business school	183
% male/female	62/38
% out-of-state	23
% part-time	86
% minorities	27
% international	15
Average age at entry	28
Average years work experience at entry	6

ACADEMICS

Academic Experience Rating	**72**
Profs interesting rating	87
Profs accessible rating	89
% female faculty	21
% minority faculty	29

Joint Degrees
MSN/MBA.

Academics

The John F. Welch College of Business at Sacred Heart University "has a great reputation" and is making "strides . . . to make it one of the best business schools" in the area. SHU has built its MBA program on the back of its "amazing" undergraduate business program, reproducing the "small class size and personal attention" that mark the undergrad experience here. Students believe this combination leads to "a successful graduate experience as well." "As an undergraduate at Sacred Heart University, I was impressed with the quality of education," relates one of the BA/MBA students. "The professors are highly educated individuals who apply real-world material to the subject matter. In addition, the faculty is highly focused on teaching each individual student and does not consider the students only numbers."

The Welch school offers a number of MBA options. BA/MBA students can complete both their undergraduate and graduate degrees in business in 5 years. An MBA for liberal arts majors allows nonbusiness majors to complete their BA and MBA in 6 years' time. A part-time evening program serves area professionals. The school also offers MBA studies overseas at its campus in Luxembourg. Students on the Fairfield campus may pursue concentrations in accounting, finance, and general management; on the Luxembourg campus, concentrations in finance and general management are available. Students report that "course offerings in the areas of international business, accounting, finance, and marketing show that the curriculum taught at our business school reflects the changing nature of business in the world. I think the school is well equipped to develop MBAs for the twenty-first century, where doing business across borders and cultures is going to be the deciding factor for success of future enterprises."

Students are also bullish on the school's future, praising the "dedication to growth, which can be seen in the recent AACSB accreditation and naming ceremony with Jack Welch."

Career and Placement

SHU's Office of Career Development offers a range of services to MBA students. Staff provides assistance in resume creation and critique, conducts seminars in interview skills, maintains online job postings, and organizes on-campus job fairs and interview sessions. Career Development recently hired a full-time Assistant Director whose primary focus is on MBA student internships and job placement. During the 2007-2008 school year, 29 employers interviewed on campus, including PriceWaterhouseCoopers, General Electric, Target, Ernst & Young, Sikorsky, Heineken, and Legg Mason.

ADMISSIONS CONTACT: MEREDITH WOERZ, DIRECTOR OF GRADUATE ADMISSIONS
ADDRESS: 5151 PARK AVENUE FAIRFIELD, CT 06825 UNITED STATES
PHONE: 203-365-7619 • FAX: 203-365-4732
E-MAIL: GRADSTUDIES@SACREDHEART.EDU • WEBSITE: WWW.SACREDHEART.EDU

Student Life and Environment

Students find plenty to do, telling us that "there are many activities for students to participate in" along with "clubs such as Graduate Counsel, Commuter Counsel, cultural clubs, business-related clubs (such as Students in Free Enterprise), and much more." One full-time student adds, "There are plenty of events such as committee meetings, alumni events, and public speaking events that students can attend." Best of all, according to some, is that "professors participate in extracurricular activities along with students and provide mentoring in an informal setting."

Students on the Luxembourg campus "all work 40-plus hours a week," darting on campus only "for evening and Saturday courses." On the Fairfield campus, students "are mostly from Fairfield and New Haven counties, but some of them drive all the way from New York State." Students tell us that their classmates challenge them "to work harder, especially when you work in groups, because you want to do your part."

Admissions

Applicants to the MBA program at SHU's Welch College of Business must submit the following materials: a completed application form; official transcripts from all undergraduate institutions attended; a personal statement of career and academic goals; two letters of recommendation; a current professional resume; and an official GMAT score report. International applicants, including applicants to the MBA program in Luxembourg, must submit transcripts in English; foreign language transcripts must be translated and analyzed by an approved professional service. Applicants whose first language is not English (except those with a degree from an English-language institution) must submit an official score report for the TOEFL. Students should anticipate at least a 3-month wait in the issuance of student visas for the Luxembourg program. The Luxembourg program runs approximately nine 6-week sessions per year; students may apply for admission and begin the program during any session. The Fairfield campus operates on a trimester calendar.

FINANCIAL FACTS

Annual tuition	$24,000
Fees	$360
Cost of books	$3,000
Room & board (off-campus)	$10,000

ADMISSIONS

Admissions Selectivity Rating	**67**
# of applications received	52
% applicants accepted	71
% acceptees attending	70
Average GMAT	438
Range of GMAT	400–500
Average GPA	3.35
TOEFL required of international students	Yes
Minimum TOEFL (paper/computer)	550/213
Application fee	$50
International application fee	$100
Deferment available	Yes
Maximum length of deferment	1 year
Transfer students accepted	Yes
Transfer application policy Transferred credits are reviewed by the Program Director.	
Non-fall admissions	Yes
Need-blind admissions	Yes

Applicants Also Look At

Fairfield University, University of Connecticut.

SAGINAW VALLEY STATE UNIVERSITY
COLLEGE OF BUSINESS AND MANAGEMENT

GENERAL INFORMATION

Type of school	Public
Academic calendar	Year round

SURVEY SAYS...

Cutting edge classes
Solid preparation in:
General management
Doing business in a global economy
Entrepreneurial studies

STUDENTS

Enrollment of parent	
institution	9,662
Enrollment of	
business school	95
% male/female	62/38
% part-time	58
% minorities	3
% international	92
Average age at entry	30
Average years work	
experience at entry	6.3

ACADEMICS

Academic Experience Rating	**67**
Student/faculty ratio	7:1
Profs interesting rating	71
Profs accessible rating	72
% female faculty	14
% minority faculty	7

Academics

Saginaw Valley State University combines the personal attention and small class sizes you'd expect to get at a private college with the attractive tuition price you can only find at a public school. The result is a "great value" education that prepares students for upper-level business positions in a friendly, teamwork-oriented environment. Saginaw offers both a full-time and part-time MBA. You'll benefit from small classes and "more focus on students in terms of teacher-student relationships." In addition, cooperation is highly encouraged among the student body, as the school "integrates team work and leadership as a requirement in each class." In fact, there is a "group element in 95 percent of all the courses offered. This group element makes interacting with your classmates a necessity and allows you to get an extremely well-rounded view of the world encompassing all issues, not just business." Fortunately, "everybody is extremely friendly and works well with each other," and "the students come from diverse backgrounds and cultures," which makes group projects particularly rewarding.

In the mission statement, the Saginaw Valley College of Business and Management pledges to provide a "relevant, interactive, and quality business education" to its students. To that end, students say Saginaw Valley truly delivers. Bringing real-world relevance to the academic setting, "the professors at Saginaw Valley come from various backgrounds throughout the world and incorporate their research into the classroom." Teaching quality varies between "some very good professors and a few that could be replaced." However, the overall academic experience is excellent. A current student confirms, "I've been very happy with each professor that I have had. They all have practical experience in the field in which they are instructing." In addition, Saginaw students really appreciate the unique "ability to work on research with professors," which adds depth and personal relationships to the MBA coursework.

No matter what your personal needs or professional goals, "The administration and professors are great at custom-building the program around the student's needs." In fact, all core coursework is taught through a hybrid/online and in-person work, in order to accommodate students' varying schedules. A student says, "The education I have received to this point has been tremendously helpful in my work life and my personal life." When it comes to the inevitable round of paperwork, the "administration is very helpful and accessible. Applying and communication with the school [was] easy and smooth." A student adds, "After graduating from a large university for my undergraduate education, I was pleasantly surprised when I arrived at Saginaw Valley State University. The administrative staff has been approachable and unspeakably accommodating." The good news doesn't stop there. Students also dole out praises for "Saginaw Valley's world-class facilities. The school is widely integrated with high-tech multimedia applications to aid classroom learning." In addition, "the library is very impressive for the school's size."

JILL WETMORE, ASSISTANT DEAN, COLLEGE OF BUSINESS AND MANAGEMENT
ADDRESS: 7400 BAY ROAD UNIVERSITY CENTER, MI 48710 UNITED STATES
PHONE: 989-964-4064 • FAX: 989-964-7497
E-MAIL: CBMDEAN@SVSU.EDU • WEBSITE: WWW.SVSU.EDU/CBM

Career and Placement

SVSU's Career Planning and Placement Office hosts on-campus interviews, offers resume and cover letter critiques, and organizes a range of career fairs for Saginaw students and graduates. The larger university also hosts a number of career fairs and recruiting events, which have recently drawn employers such as Abraham and Gaffney, PC; Chase; Hantz Group Financial Services; Prudential; and Wells Fargo.

In addition to these services, business students would like to see more job placement assistance for MBA graduates, including "more job fairs and developing closer ties to big corporations. These would help students better plan their careers pre-graduation." However, Saginaw students believe strongly in the value of their education, reminding us that "the program is quickly evolving and growing. Employers are starting to recognize the high value that a Saginaw Valley State University education has."

Student Life and Environment

The newest campus in Michigan's fifteen state colleges, Saginaw Valley State is located on more than 750 acres in the tri-city area. The school's large undergraduate and graduate community hosts a large range of clubs and activities, though the majority of MBA candidates say they don't have much time for extracurricular activities. In the part-time program, students are "usually working outside the home and working on their MBA at the same time." The double life doesn't leave much room for socializing, and most students come to campus for class and not much more. However, if you'd like to go out on the town, students point out that, "SVSU is central located in the middle of three vastly different cities each with its own night-life scene."

In this vibrant and academic community, "countless cultural, social, economic, and occupational segments are represented" within the business school. The school also attracts a large international population, which adds a distinctive range of opinions and cultures to the campus. A current student attests, "My fellow students could best be described as widely diverse. My undergraduate education at Michigan State University's College of Engineering had a very diverse atmosphere, but this environment is even more culturally varied."

Admissions

Saginaw Valley admits students based on an admissions index number, calculated using each applicant's GPA and GMAT scores. Therefore, a lower GMAT score can potentially be counter-balanced by a higher GPA, and vice versa. GMAT scores, however, must be above 450 to be considered for admission. In addition to official transcripts and test scores, applicants must also submit a statement of purpose, two professional letters of reference, and a current resume.

FINANCIAL FACTS

Annual tuition (in-state/ out-of-state)	$6,198/$11,890
Fees	$256
Cost of books	$1,500
Room & board	$6,630
% of students receiving aid	45

ADMISSIONS

Admissions Selectivity Rating	**64**
# of applications received	76
% applicants accepted	95
% acceptees attending	58
Average GMAT	505
Range of GMAT	490–520
Average GPA	3.14
TOEFL required of international students	Yes
Minimum TOEFL (paper/computer)	525/197
Application fee	$25
International application fee	$60
Regular application deadline	rolling
Regular notification	rolling
Deferment available	Yes
Maximum length of deferment	7 Semesters
Transfer students accepted	Yes
Transfer application policy may transfer 6 credits	
Non-fall admissions	Yes
Need-blind admissions	Yes

Applicants Also Look At

Central Michigan University, Michigan State University, Northwood University, University of Michigan—Flint.

EMPLOYMENT PROFILE	
Career Rating	73

SAINT JOSEPH'S UNIVERSITY
ERIVAN K. HAUB SCHOOL OF BUSINESS

GENERAL INFORMATION
Type of school	Private
Affiliation	Jesuit
Environment	Metropolis
Academic calendar	Semesters

SURVEY SAYS...
Cutting edge classes
Solid preparation in:
Teamwork
Communication/interpersonal skills
Presentation skills

STUDENTS
Enrollment of parent institution	7,535
Enrollment of business school	941
% male/female	56/44
% out-of-state	1
% part-time	85
% minorities	16
% international	1
Average age at entry	28
Average years work experience at entry	5.4

ACADEMICS
Academic Experience Rating	**72**
Student/faculty ratio	20:1
Profs interesting rating	76
Profs accessible rating	89
% female faculty	29
% minority faculty	15

Joint Degrees
DO/MBA (Osteopathic Medicine).

Academics

The Erivan K. Haub School of Business at Saint Joseph's University "has a great and long tradition of being a place for the top students in the Philadelphia area. At Saint Joe's you know you are getting one of the best educations available," due in part to "the Jesuit mission of cura personalis, or care for the whole person" which imbues the program with "the Jesuit philosophy of duty and service to others. This is extremely positive. There is high attention to ethics." A "great faculty and good facilities" are also part of the mix here.

The vast majority of Saint Joe's MBAs attend on a part-time basis, and these Philly-area professionals love the flexibility of the program, which allows students to complete the program at their own pace. Strength in a variety of areas broadens students' choices; we're told that Haub is home to "a great accounting department" and that the Master of Science in Financial Services offered here is quite useful because it "covers all required course work to permit sitting for the Certified Financial Planning exam. " Students also tell us that the school has "the best MS in Human Resource Management program available to working adults in the region." Some here, however, complain that "the curriculum isn't as flexible as it needs to be, especially for part-time students who work for a living. Some also feel that the school "should update the curriculum for some courses (the MBA Information Technology and Empowering Human Potential core required courses come immediately to mind)" to bring content in line with twenty-first-century business realities.

Saint Joe's keeps MBA classes small to "allow interaction on many levels. You can't hide from the teacher or your classmates." Professors "are knowledgeable and surprisingly accessible." One MBA elaborates, "I have trouble with math, and both professors helped to ensure that any questions I had about concepts or theory were answered. The course work is intriguing, challenging, and applicable to the problems facing society today. . . . I have been able to apply 90 percent of what I learn in class to my job and personal life." Saint Joe's offers concentrations in 10 areas: accounting, decision and system sciences, finance, health and medical services, human resource management, international business, international marketing, management, marketing, and nonprofit management.

Career and Placement

The Career Development Center at Saint Joe's serves all undergraduates, graduate students, and alumni. Students tell us the office is "typical of parochial Philadelphia colleges like La Salle and Temple," with a recruiting base largely from the Philadelphia area. While some wish for a broader range of recruiters, others "think SJU caters to its students' wants, and most want to stay in the Philly area. That's why they came to school here in the first place. If you are unsure about what you want to do after MBA, Career Services has a great assessment system, where they meet and counsel you on where you would be a good fit." Saint Joe's MBAs also benefit from "tremendous alumni networking."

ADMISSIONS CONTACT: SUSAN KASSAB, DIRECTOR
ADDRESS: 5600 CITY AVENUE, MANDEVILLE HALL 392 PHILADELPHIA, PA 19131 UNITED STATES
PHONE: 610-660-1318 • FAX: 610-660-1224
E-MAIL: GRADSTAFF@SJU.EDU • WEBSITE: WWW.SJU.EDU/HSB

Student Life and Environment

Saint Joe's offers its MBA program in two locations. The school's main campus is located "on the outskirts of the city, so you have that city feel without the dangers of a city." Students love the "small campus in a big city" and report that "the decor of the architecture and the outlay of the campus are inviting and serene. Students all smile and are genuinely happy and safe." A satellite site is located at Ursinus College in Collegeville; students here describe a conventional evening-program experience, with little extracurricular life on and around campus.

Saint Joe's graduate business programs "sponsor events throughout the semester to encourage networking." An esprit de corps is further enhanced by the fact that "the school has a very fanatical sports fan base." While extracurricular agendas are relatively light, most students here are good with that. One student writes, "Life at school is fine. It does not interfere with professional or family commitments. The program is very understanding that there are other commitments at this juncture of life."

Admissions

Applicants to the Haub MBA program must submit the following materials to the school: an official transcript from each undergraduate and graduate institution at which credits were earned; an official GMAT score report (not more than 7 years old); two letters of recommendation; a current resume; and a personal statement of 250 to 500 words outlining career objectives and the value of an MBA in reaching those objectives. International applicants must submit all of the following as well as a statement of financial support. International applicants who attended undergraduate institutions at which English was not the language of instruction must have their transcripts translated and interpreted by World Education Service. Students whose first language is not English must submit an official TOEFL score report. Saint Joe's admits MBA students for fall, spring, and summer terms.

FINANCIAL FACTS

Annual tuition	$15,603
Fees	$0
Cost of books	$800
Average award package	$15,603

ADMISSIONS

Admissions Selectivity Rating	**76**
# of applications received	237
% applicants accepted	65
% acceptees attending	79
Average GMAT	526
Average GPA	3.23
TOEFL required of international students	Yes
Minimum TOEFL (paper/computer)	550/213
Application fee	$35
International application fee	$35
Regular application deadline	Rolling
Regular notification	Rolling
Deferment available	Yes
Maximum length of deferment	1 year
Transfer students accepted	Yes
Transfer application policy Must provide a completed application including original test scores.	
Non-fall admissions	Yes
Need-blind admissions	Yes

Applicants Also Look At

Drexel University, La Salle University, Penn State University—Great Valley, Temple University, Villanova University.

SAINT LOUIS UNIVERSITY
JOHN COOK SCHOOL OF BUSINESS

GENERAL INFORMATION
Type of school	Private
Affiliation	Roman Catholic
Environment	Metropolis
Academic calendar	Semester

SURVEY SAYS...
Good peer network
Solid preparation in:
Doing business in a global economy

STUDENTS
Enrollment of parent institution	12,309
Enrollment of business school	427
% male/female	69/31
% out-of-state	39
% part-time	80
% minorities	8
% international	3
Average age at entry	27
Average years work experience at entry	3.8

ACADEMICS
Academic Experience Rating	**83**
Student/faculty ratio	15:1
Profs interesting rating	84
Profs accessible rating	76
% female faculty	7
% minority faculty	2

Joint Degrees
JD/MBA 3.5 years, MBA/MS (Health Administration) 2 years, MD/MBA 5 Years.

Prominent Alumni
August A. Busch, IV, President, Anheuser-Busch, Inc; Mark Lamping, CEO, New Meadowlands Stadium Company; Robert Ciapciak, General Partner, Edward Jones; Alison Talbot, VP of Operations, Miss Elaine; Patrick J. Sly, Executive Vice President, Emerson Electric Co.

Academics

"The John Cook School of Business at St. Louis University gets you the most bang for the buck," students in this Jesuit-affiliated MBA program insist. Indeed, compared to some of the higher profile MBA programs in the area, SLU is "reasonably priced," and the savings are further enhanced for those who pursue the school's recently implemented full-time one-year MBA. SLU also offers a part-time MBA to serve the needs of area professionals. Students in both programs cite the "strong ethical values" of the curriculum as another major incentive to choose SLU.

Students in the new one-year MBA praise the "innovative program that really tries to integrate the whole MBA learning process," warning that it is "intense" but ultimately worth the hard work. The administration earns praise for its responsiveness to student feedback during this early stage of the program's development. As one MBA tells it, "This administration is far and away the most flexible and willing to listen of any I've ever encountered. With the one-year program in its second year, the administration is constantly encouraging students to help make the program better by providing feedback. The administration is very clearly committed to continuous improvement." Part-time students also praise the administration, reporting that it has "created a very easy environment for part-time students to get into and get going on the MBA. They make sure to resolve any problems quickly and effectively."

In past surveys, students have complained that the SLU faculty is too academically oriented. This is changing, though, as SLU has made "a push lately to get professors with real-world experience. As a graduate student with 5+ years of work experience, I appreciate learning from the professors with real-world experience much more than from the 'typical' college professor. The main difference lies in the specific insights the teachers with real-world experience can provide. They typically have plenty of war stories to share and a lot can be learned from listening to their past experiences." While many "need to sharpen their lecturing skills," instructors are generally "easy to work with, and much is learned in most classes."

Career and Placement

The Career Resources Center at the John Cook School of Business provides career services and counseling for all MBAs here. The center offers self-assessments, personal advising, resume and cover letter assistance, mock interviews, networking workshops and counseling, and access to multiple online and hard-copy databases and reference sources. Students tell us that the school's regional reputation and alumni network are its most effective career-enhancing assets. "SLU has a good reputation in the area, which helps in getting a job," one student tells us. About one-quarter of all SLU MBAs pursue careers in finance and accounting; about as many build careers in marketing and sales. The manufacturing sector claims about one-third of each graduating class; nonprofits attract about one-fifth of each class. Recent employers of SLU MBAs include Accenture, Anheuser Busch Companies, Inc., Covidien, Ernst & Young, Edward Jones, Emerson, JC Penney Company Inc., Kaiser Permanente, Mayo Clinic, Nestle Purina PetCare Company, Northrop Grumman Corporation, and RubinBrown.

ADMISSIONS CONTACT: NANCY BISCAN, PROGRAM COORDINATOR
ADDRESS: 3674 LINDELL BLVD. SUITE 132 ST. LOUIS, MO 63108 UNITED STATES
PHONE: 314-977-6221 • FAX: 314-977-1416
E-MAIL: GRADBIZ@SLU.EDU • WEBSITE: GRADBIZ.SLU.EDU

Student Life and Environment

Saint Louis University is, of course, located in St. Louis, "a great city" with plenty of opportunities for career professionals and entrepreneurs. Full-time students exploit the city's many assets during "business school networking events such as hockey games, baseball games, etc." Because the Jesuit tradition seeks to educate the whole person, SLU brings numerous cultural events to campus. Through the campus ministry, opportunities for service and spiritual growth are readily available. SLU competes in 16 NCAA Division I sports; the men's basketball and soccer teams both draw hefty crowds. Part-timers enjoy the same extracurricular opportunities but rarely have the time to engage in clubs, daytime guest speakers and symposia, and other such events.

The SLU campus offers "excellent facilities: library, gym, buildings, etc." Classrooms "are equipped with computer/multimedia resources" and the school is conveniently "located right in downtown St. Louis, yet it is still safe, like it's in own little world" because the "beautiful campus" is self-contained. The school's midtown location provides students easy access to the Fox Theatre, the Sheldon Concert Hall, the Grandel Square Theatre, and the Powell Symphony Hall.

SLU MBAs represent "a wide range of work experiences. Some people are in their forties and have worked for Boeing or Anheuser Busch for years. Others are just out of college. Everyone is friendly and cooperative." Some feel that most full-time students "are a little younger and less experienced in the working world" than they ought to be, and that their "lack of professional experience" limits the quality of in-class discussion.

Admissions

St. Louis University accepts both online and paper-and-pencil applications; an Adobe Acrobat file of the application can be downloaded at the school's website. All applications must include a completed application form, a personal statement (500 word maximum), two letters of recommendation (at least one professional), official transcripts for all post-secondary academic work, a current resume, and an official GMAT score report. International applicants must provide all of the above plus certification of financial support and, for non-native English speakers, an official TOEFL score report representing a score no more than two years old. The part-time program admits students prior to the fall session, the spring intersession, and the two summer sessions. Full-time applicants must enter at the start of the summer session.

FINANCIAL FACTS

Annual tuition	$48,785
Fees	$360
Cost of books	$1,250
Room & board (on/off-campus)	$0/$11,000
% of students receiving aid	100
% of first-year students receiving aid	100
% of students receiving grants	100
Average grant	$11,723

ADMISSIONS

Admissions Selectivity Rating	85
# of applications received	77
% applicants accepted	78
% acceptees attending	60
Average GMAT	585
Range of GMAT	540–620
Average GPA	3.5
TOEFL required of international students	Yes
Minimum TOEFL (paper/computer)	570/230
Application fee	$90
International application fee	$90
Deferment available	Yes
Maximum length of deferment	1 year
Transfer students accepted	Yes
Transfer application policy For part-time MBA only; up to 6 credit hours from another AACSB accredited school.	
Non-fall admissions	Yes
Need-blind admissions	Yes

Applicants Also Look At
Washington University in St. Louis.

EMPLOYMENT PROFILE

Career Rating	75	Grads Employed by Function	%	Avg. Salary
Primary Source of Full-time Job Acceptances		Finance	24	$47,150
School-facilitated activities	9 (41%)	Marketing	24	$73,013
Graduate-facilitated activities	11 (50%)	MIS	10	$53,000
Unknown	2 (9%)	Operations	14	$63,000
Percent employed	78	Consulting	7	$60,000
		General Management	10	$50,500
		Other	11	$72,000

Top 5 Employers Hiring Grads
Anheuser Busch Companies, Inc.; Nestle Purina PetCare Company; Covidien; Ernst & Young; Accenture

SAN DIEGO STATE UNIVERSITY
GRADUATE SCHOOL OF BUSINESS

GENERAL INFORMATION

Type of school	Public
Environment	City
Academic calendar	Semester

SURVEY SAYS...

Students love San Diego, CA
Cutting edge classes
Happy students
Solid preparation in:
Entrepreneurial studies

STUDENTS

Enrollment of parent institution	32,693
Enrollment of business school	700
% male/female	60/40
% out-of-state	12
% part-time	55
% minorities	15
% international	19
Average age at entry	28
Average years work experience at entry	5

ACADEMICS

Academic Experience Rating	**84**
Student/faculty ratio	35:1
Profs interesting rating	86
Profs accessible rating	70
% female faculty	14
% minority faculty	3

Joint Degrees

MBA/MA (Latin American Studies)
3–4 years, MBA/JD 4 years.

Academics

A solid return on investment—especially for California natives—and a "great reputation in international business and entrepreneurship" are among the major attractions at San Diego State University's Graduate School of Business. Entrepreneurship is a particular strength, with the prestigious Entrepreneurial Management Center helping SDSU earn a "high ranking among all entrepreneurship programs." A sports business MBA program "that partners with Major League Baseball, National Football League, and National Basketball Association teams" is another big draw.

Potential SDSU business grads have a number of choices to consider. The conventional MBA program here presupposes that students did not study business as undergraduates. Thus, it includes 19 foundation credits that cannot be waived (because the program is cohort-based). Students who studied business as undergraduates, however, are more suitable candidates for the MSBA program. Students "really like the way it is set up. It allows you to finish in one year and specialize in an area." The Sports Business Management MBA has its own separate program. SDSU also offers an MS in accounting ("one of the few accredited accounting programs in the state," one student writes) and an Executive MBA program.

Students praise SDSU as an "efficient school" where "the faculty is very attuned with latest trends in the business world, and professors can offer very practical experience in the classroom based on their consulting work." Faculty instruction is supplemented by "guest lecturers who are well-respected and powerful." Throughout the curriculum, students here "do a lot of group work, which facilitates good student relationships and teamwork." Students appreciate that "classes are taught in an open and participatory environment" that fortunately is "not overly competitive. Quality of life is important to the people attending and working in the community, and they aim to balance academic achievement with living well." The school's city of San Diego location also means that a steady supply of local business leaders are always on hand, whether as mentors or potential employers.

Career and Placement

Career and placement services for SDSU MBAs are handled through the Career Services Office of the university; there is no dedicated Career Services Office for the MBA program. Supplemental services are provided through the MBA Association and the Entrepreneurial Management Center. Students see Career Services here as a weak area, with comments that "on-campus recruiting needs to be improved." As far as the effectiveness of the alumni network goes, students are split. Some see it as a strength, while others feel the school should work harder to "foster better communication between the students and alumni for employment purposes."

SCOTT OR S.TEMORES-VALDEZ, ASSOCIATE DIRECTOR OF THE MBA AND MS PROGRAMS
ADDRESS: 5500 CAMPANILE DRIVE SAN DIEGO, CA 92182-8228 UNITED STATES
PHONE: (619) 594-8073 • FAX: (619) 594-1863
E-MAIL: SDSUMBA@MAIL.SDSU.EDU • WEBSITE: WWW.SDSU.EDU/BUSINESS

Student Life and Environment

SDSU "provides an interesting, active environment, allowing students to be as involved or as isolated as they choose." Business students at this school are presented with "an incredible array of options to create the ultimate experience." Most important to business students, "There are many clubs to join that are great networking, social and career opportunities." In addition to these "great clubs" are "large events and a variety of cultural activities to participate in" while enjoying a "nice campus. . .that seems always to be striving for continual improvement."

The city of San Diego brings a lot to the table as well. It's "an outstanding place to live" with plenty of opportunity for those who wish to stick around after they graduate. Biotechnology, software development, and wireless communications industries all thrive here. The city is widely regarded as a leading laboratory for entrepreneurial development, and the U.S. military has a huge presence.

SDSU attracts "a great mix of enthusiastic people who are excited about furthering their education." This "intelligent, multi-cultural, driven, diverse" population includes "some who have many years of work experience and others who have only recently finished their undergraduate degrees." True to the Californian character, "Many here don't appear to be very competitive, which makes the atmosphere pretty relaxed and easy going. Still, the students are often the quietly successful type, so you never know what they are capable of until you ask them."

Admissions

Nearly 1,500 potential MBAs apply to SDSU's "highly competitive" program every year. The Admissions Committee considers a number of factors, including GMAT score (minimum score of 540 is required; the average score of an admitted student is 609); GPA for the final sixty course hours of undergraduate academic work (minimum 2.85 for American students, 3.0 for international students (for their entire four year degree); average GPA for admitted students was 3.3); letters of recommendation, resume (work experience is preferred but not required); and personal statement. None of the final three is required, but each "can enhance an application," according to the school's website. International students whose first language is not English must also submit official TOEFL scores; a minimum paper-and-pencil test score of 550 or an Internet-based test score of 79 is required. Applications are accepted for both the Fall and Spring terms. They are processed on a rolling basis, so it's best to apply as early as possible.

FINANCIAL FACTS

Annual tuition (in-state/ out-of-state)	$3,758/$11,894
Cost of books	$1,260
Room & board	$9,391

ADMISSIONS

Admissions Selectivity Rating	**88**
# of applications received	807
% applicants accepted	48
% acceptees attending	61
Average GMAT	609
Range of GMAT	560–620
Average GPA	3.3
TOEFL required of international students	Yes
Minimum TOEFL (paper/computer)	550/213
Application fee	$55
International application fee	$55
Regular application deadline	4/15
Regular notification	5/15
Transfer students accepted	Yes
Non-fall admissions	Yes
Need-blind admissions	Yes

Applicants Also Look At

University of California—San Diego, University of San Diego.

SAN FRANCISCO STATE UNIVERSITY
COLLEGE OF BUSINESS

Academics

Affordable, convenient, and exceptionally well located, San Francisco State University is a great place to get a broad-based MBA, while adding depth and distinctiveness to the program through specialized coursework in specific business disciplines. Offering the MBA on a full-time and part-time basis, working students appreciate SF State's "flexible program," which creates "no distinction between full-time and part-time students." In addition, the curriculum's flexibility gives students the opportunity to tailor the program and "focus on topics you are interested in." To that end, San Francisco State provides lots of great academic options. For example, the school boasts a strong accounting program, as well as an "excellent and growing program in sustainable business." The school's international business department also draws its share of praises, and syudents find the "IBUS department faculty to be extremely engaged and willing to spend time discussing a multitude of topics outside of class."

San Francisco State recently opened a new graduate business facility in downtown San Francisco (the school's main campus is located in a residential neighborhood in the city's outskirts). Thanks to this strategic move, SF State now boasts one of the best business school locations in the Bay Area, offering students unparalleled "proximity to the financial district and the access that provides to global and entrepreneurial leaders in technology, biotech, finance, sustainable business, and more." Fortunately, "the administration in the new facility has been very helpful and efficient, and have worked hard to make the transition to the new campus as smooth as possible." In this and every way, students say the program is "run very smoothly—good communication, quick responses to questions."

Academically, the SF State experience is rewarding. Uniting academic theory and practical insights, the "professors generally have a high level of working knowledge for their areas and they do indeed bring that to their lectures. Here and there you have instructors who rely too much on PowerPoint, but this honestly doesn't happen that often." Despite the program's sizable student body, students nonetheless benefit from the "availability and accessibility" of SF State professors, who "don't disappear between classes and are for the most part engaged with the success of the students... Most really want you to succeed, are patient, and very, very approachable."

Career and Placement

An up-and-coming business program, SF State has improved placement possibilities for its students in recent years, thanks to its prime location, growing reputation, and heightened focus on career development. In fact, the school recently expanded the career services programs for MBA graduates, and now provides "a high level of service to students." The career services staff offers "optional seminars and provides one-on-one assistance with resumes," and also coordinates career fairs and campus networking events.

A recent Graduate Business Career Fair at SF State drew a large number of prominent companies, including Bechtel, Charles Schwab, CNET Networks, Hyatt SF Hotels, Kelly Financial Resources, Media Zone, Target Corporation, Ritz-Carlton Club, and UPS. In addition, "the accounting department has two "Meet the Firms" nights where graduating students are recruited and interviewed. Most accounting students are hired through this program." Despite these noteworthy offerings, a current student laments, "My only wish is that more Fortune 500 firms visit the campus to recruit, because they would be pleasantly surprised how much talent is here."

ADMISSIONS CONTACT: MS. ARMAAN MOATTARI, ASSISTANT DIRECTOR OF ADMISSIONS
ADDRESS: 835 MARKET STREET, SUITE 550 SAN FRANCISCO, CA 94103 UNITED STATES
PHONE: 415-817-4300 • FAX: 415-817-4340
E-MAIL: MBA@SFSU.EDU • WEBSITE: MBA.SFSU.EDU

Student Life and Environment

Drawing a mix of students from the Bay Area, as well as "a lot of international students," SF State's student community is friendly, diverse, and cooperative. Unfortunately, the student community is somewhat fragmented, as "none of the graduate students live at the downtown campus." After hours, full-time and international students are eager to hang out with their classmates, whereas "the students who work full time don't tend to socialize much, though they are friendly in class." On top of that, "due to the flexibility of the class schedule, there isn't as much opportunity to form strong networks as students have in cohort-based schools. A lack of social events and spaces further compounds this problem." On the other hand, the school's enviable urban location means there is "lots to see, lots of international students, easy to get to and from (school is on top of a subway station)." In fact, some students feel "the student life has improved since we moved downtown since all the MBA students have classes in the same building. A group of students meet up to network and socialize every Thursday night after classes."

While they can't complain about the school's stellar new campus (there is even a Starbucks in the building), students mention that "it is very difficult for students at the downtown campus to take advantage of many of the resources offered at the Main University Campus (libraries, bookstore, student organizations, and events), leaving MBA students feeling a bit cut-off from the full student experience." Of course, most quickly note that "the proximity to the financial district and the cultural offerings of downtown SF more than make up for this."

Admissions

To apply to the graduate business programs at San Francisco State, students must have an undergraduate degree with a minimum GPA of 3.0 in the last 60 semester units (or 90 quarter units). The current incoming class had an average undergraduate GPA of 3.3, and an average GMAT score of 560. In addition to transcripts and test scores, it is required that candidates submit letters of recommendation and a current resume for consideration.

FINANCIAL FACTS

Annual tuition (in-state/ out-of-state)	$6,498/$14,634
Cost of books	$2,000
Room & board (on/off-campus)	$12,000/$14,000

ADMISSIONS

Admissions Selectivity Rating	**84**
# of applications received	900
% applicants accepted	40
% acceptees attending	70
Average GMAT	560
Range of GMAT	500–740
Average GPA	3.3
TOEFL required of international students	Yes
Minimum TOEFL (paper/computer)	570/230
Application fee	$55
International application fee	$55
Regular application deadline	4/1
Regular notification	5/15
Transfer students accepted	Yes
Transfer application policy Applicants need to apply to the program and waive out the foundation requirements.	
Non-fall admissions	Yes

Applicants Also Look At

California State University—East Bay, Golden Gate University, Saint Mary's College of California, San José State University, University of San Francisco.

EMPLOYMENT PROFILE	
Career Rating	**86**
Percent employed	90

SAN JOSE STATE UNIVERSITY
LUCAS GRADUATE SCHOOL OF BUSINESS

GENERAL INFORMATION

Type of school	Public
Environment	Metropolis
Academic calendar	Semester

SURVEY SAYS...
Students love San Jose, CA
Good social scene
Happy students
Solid preparation in:
General management
Operations
Entrepreneurial studies

STUDENTS

Enrollment of parent institution	28,400
Enrollment of business school	347
% male/female	45/55
% out-of-state	1
% part-time	65
% minorities	3
% international	25
Average age at entry	31
Average years work experience at entry	8

ACADEMICS

Academic Experience Rating	**74**
Student/faculty ratio	28:1
Profs interesting rating	72
Profs accessible rating	73
% female faculty	29
% minority faculty	26

Joint Degrees
MBA/MSE.

Academics

Students at the AACSB-accredited Lucas Graduate School of Business at San Jose State University tell us that their school offers "part-time convenience" in the "center of the Silicon Valley" and a "workload that is manageable for full-time professionals." In addition, students enjoy a "high-quality academic program" whose hallmarks are "affordability" and "flexibility."

San Jose State's full-time, 1-year MBA program is just one of four Master of Business Administration degrees that the school offers, and is "designed for non-working individuals who prefer an intensive, cohort style of learning" and who want to complete the MBA degree in less time than it would normally take. San Jose State also offers a traditional on-campus MBA program that is designed for "students who prefer the educational atmosphere provided by a university setting." The on-campus program provides semester-length courses that meet once a week and a limited number of 6-week courses are available during the summer. An accelerated, off-campus program is usually preferred by students who want an "executive" style of learning. Classes are delivered year-round in six 8-week sessions, which allows students to complete six (or more) courses in a year's time. Finally, a Master's of Business Administration/Master's of Science in Engineering dual-degree program is tailored to working students and may be completed in 32 months.

The MBA program at San Jose State combines "case studies, lecture, research, team projects, computer analysis, student presentations, and presentations by members in the business community" to "provide 'simply the best' business education to a diverse, talented group of individuals from all over the world." Students in all programs benefit from "awesome" professors who are "knowledgeable and humorous." A "smooth administration" is available to answer students' questions. Students love that "guest speakers from over 100 Silicon Valley firms address College of Business classes" and say the school "takes advantage of its Silicon Valley location by hiring local professionals to teach part-time." "No courses are taught by teaching assistants." Overall, students say San Jose State is a "good value for the money."

Career and Placement

One of the obvious strengths of attending a school close to so many "high-tech companies" is that "most of the students work for companies like Oracle, Google, and Juniper Networks," which creates "great social networks and contacts" as well as a short commute to class for the "bulk" of students. The school claims that "80 percent of [its] graduate students are full-time business professionals in Silicon Valley companies." There is also an entrepreneurial culture evident amongst San Jose's graduate students. Many have start-up experience, work for start-ups, or have begun their own companies after graduation.

Additionally, San Jose provides students in the 1-year accelerated program with "direct exposure to Silicon Valley companies" and a challenging curriculum. Students say the program is "very geared toward the Pacific Rim business climate." Other areas in which students said the school could improve include the school's "standing with local companies," and frequency of "alumni events."

Employers who have hired San Jose MBAs include Abercrombie & Fitch, Adobe Systems, AltaVista, AMD, American Red Cross, Apple, AT&T, Charles Schwab, Chevron, Citibank, Cisco, Disneyland, Dow Jones & Company, eBay, Eastman Kodak, General Electric Company, Goodyear, HP, H&R Block Financial Advisers, Compaq, Intel, Lucent Technologies Merrill Lynch, Microsoft, Morgan Stanley, Netscape, Nordstrom, PepsiCo, Sprint, Staples, Starbucks, Symantec Corporation, T-Mobile, Texas Instruments, Toyota, Toys "R" Us, Visa, Wells Fargo, Xerox, Yahoo!.

Student Life and Environment

Students are "diverse," "highly intelligent," and "professionally experienced" at San Jose State. Student life is "busy, busy!," and because so many students work full-time and attend classes on one of the off-campus sites, there is the opinion among the student body of feeling scattered. "I do not spend much time on campus," one commuter says. Students recommend "integrating the 1-year MBA with the main campus," and they would also like to see more electives and more "interactive activities." Students appreciate the MBA Association's efforts to "promote social interaction among all MBA students, their families, faculty, and administrators" by organizing a variety of activities, including workshops, lectures, social mixers, and an annual BBQ lunch. When students want to head off campus, San Jose State's "downtown setting [makes] for an exciting" and "social atmosphere" full of interesting diversions.

Admissions

Applicants to Lucas must submit the following materials: official transcripts covering undergraduate work; an official GMAT score report; personal statement; resume; and a completed application form. Candidates who have earned a degree from a university in which the language of instruction was not English must submit an official TOEFL score report. Priority for admission will be given to applicants with better than a 3.0 GPA (on a 4.0 scale) in their last 60 semester units or 90 quarter units of course work and a score of at least 500 on the GMAT, with scores in the verbal and quantitative sections in the 50th percentile or above. Recently admitted had an average undergraduate GPA of 3.29 and an average GMAT score of 562.

FINANCIAL FACTS

Annual tuition (in-state/ out-of-state)	$4,274/$10,376
Cost of books	$1,386
Room & board (on/off-campus)	$9,505/$9,734
% of students receiving aid	1
% of first-year students receiving aid	10
% of students receiving loans	1
% of students receiving grants	2
Average award package	$12,226
Average grant	$2,427

ADMISSIONS

Admissions Selectivity Rating	**81**
# of applications received	448
% applicants accepted	55
% acceptees attending	58
Average GMAT	562
Range of GMAT	510–600
Average GPA	3.29
TOEFL required of international students	Yes
Minimum TOEFL (paper/computer)	550/213
Application fee	$55
International application fee	$55
Regular application deadline	5/1
Regular notification	7/1
Transfer students accepted	Yes
Transfer application policy Applicant must meet admission requirements. Up to 20% of units can be transferred from AACSB accredited institution.	
Non-fall admissions	Yes
Need-blind admissions	Yes

Applicants Also Look At

California State University—East Bay, San Francisco State University, Santa Clara University, University of California—Berkeley.

EMPLOYMENT PROFILE

Career Rating	73	Grads Employed by Function	%	Avg. Salary
Primary Source of Full-time Job Acceptances		Finance	29	$67,500
School-facilitated activities	6 (86%)	Marketing	14	$65,000
Unknown	1 (14%)	Operations	14	$65,000
Percent employed	67	Communications	14	NR
		General Management	14	$85,000

SANTA CLARA UNIVERSITY
LEAVEY SCHOOL OF BUSINESS

GENERAL INFORMATION
Type of school	Private
Affiliation	Roman Catholic/Jesuit
Environment	City
Academic calendar	Quarters

SURVEY SAYS...
Students love Santa Clara, CA
Friendly students
Good peer network
Cutting edge classes
Helfpul alumni
Happy students
Solid preparation in:
General management
Teamwork

STUDENTS
Enrollment of parent institution	8,397
Enrollment of business school	1,126
% male/female	66/34
% part-time	82
% minorities	15
% international	22
Average age at entry	30
Average years work experience at entry	7

ACADEMICS
Academic Experience Rating	**83**
Student/faculty ratio	16:1
Profs interesting rating	86
Profs accessible rating	67
% female faculty	18
% minority faculty	10

Joint Degrees
JD/MBA 4 years.

Academics

The Leavey School of Business at Santa Clara University combines "Jesuit values, primarily in the quality of education and the emphasis on high integrity," with a Silicon Valley location that draws "the cream of the crop to the faculty, such as the former 3Com CEO." The result is a unique MBA program that "caters to part-time students" but also has plenty to offer full-timers.

Customer service is the name of the game at Leavey, where "the dean runs the school as if it was a company in itself. He provides quarterly reports of the progress of school and reviews student evaluations as a measure of the progress." Administrators "do everything they can to keep up with the changing trends in business and business schools. For example, this year, they introduced international exposure for the student. Every summer, one or two student groups visit another country to meet with business leaders and financial institutions to understand how business is done in that country. This year, the group went to China. Next year, one group will go to China and another, to Germany." Professors take a similar student-first approach; they are "eager to help students in the classroom and to introduce them to colleagues for future employment opportunities. They are always available for personal/professional consultation."

Leavey's curriculum employs "a great case-study approach" that "is structured to maximize teamwork abilities." Students find this pedagogical approach immediately applicable to their professional lives. MBAs also "love the 'experimental' classes that students can choose as electives, such as Spirituality and Leadership, which really gets you to focus on your inner self and become a better, less stressed person." Students tell us the school excels in accounting, general management, and marketing. Asked where the school should improve, one student comments, "For some reason, the school is not so well recognized as other schools in the area, namely Stanford and Berkeley. But I have been quite impressed with SCU so far. The campus is good and the academic standards are excellent. I think the school will stand to gain if marketed better."

Career and Placement

Students appreciate the "great Bay Area network" connected to SCU; MBAs here benefit from "a terrific level of interaction with leaders and innovators in Silicon Valley." The Graduate Business Career Services Office capitalizes on these connections to help students procure internships ("The quarter system allows for some interesting internship opportunities in the area because local employers know some students can be available part-time or full-time for a quarter or two," explains one student) and post-graduation jobs. Even so, students feel the service isn't all it could be. As one observes, "Since most students are working, there are limited resources devoted to the internship/career placement program. Also, SCU also does not do enough promotion of the program out in the business community. Its reputation is only good regionally, despite its high ranking as a part-time business program."

The top ten employers of graduates of the class of 2004 were Applied Materials, Inc.; Cisco Systems, Inc.; eBay; Hewlett-Packard; KLA-Tencor Corporation; Silicon Valley Bank; Sun Microsystems; VERITAS Software; Wells Fargo; and Xilinx.

ADMISSIONS CONTACT: JENNIFER TAYLOR, DIRECTOR, GRADUATE BUSINESS ADMISSIONS
ADDRESS: 223 KENNA HALL, 500 EL CAMINO REAL SANTA CLARA, CA 95053-0001 UNITED STATES
PHONE: 408-554-4539 • FAX: 408-544-4571
E-MAIL: MBAADMISSIONS@SCU.EDU • WEBSITE: WWW.SCU.EDU/BUSINESS

FINANCIAL FACTS

Annual tuition	$19,278
Fees	$165
Cost of books	$1,000
Room & board (off-campus)	$13,000
Average grant	$1

ADMISSIONS

Admissions Selectivity Rating	**79**
# of applications received	395
% applicants accepted	80
% acceptees attending	64
Average GMAT	624
Range of GMAT	540–720
Average GPA	3.28
TOEFL required of international students	Yes
Minimum TOEFL (paper/computer)	600/250
Application fee	$75
International application fee	$100
Regular application deadline	6/1
Regular notification	rolling
Early decision program?	Yes
ED Deadline/ Notification	03/01 / 04/15
Deferment available	Yes
Maximum length of deferment	2 quarters
Transfer students accepted	Yes
Non-fall admissions	Yes
Need-blind admissions	Yes

Student Life and Environment

MBAs report that SCU "provides a safe, clean, study environment coupled with a very caring and personal staff. The school really treats students as 'customers' and caters to their needs, offering extended library hours during exams. The staff wants the students to succeed." Part-timers also appreciate that "the schedule is really terrific [and] works for working folks as well as commuters." A new facility is in the works, we're told, which is a good thing; students agree that "the current facility is old and cramped."

SCU's "gorgeous and safe campus" offers a number of top amenities, including "a state-of-the-art gym and pool, great recreation areas, and a late-night venue called The Bronco with a pool table and a large television and several couches," as well as "campus-wide wireless access, [and] a peaceful rose garden and a church for when you need serenity." Although most students are part-timers with numerous other commitments outside school, MBAs here do occasionally socialize. One writes, "There are quarter-end bar nights which are great for relaxing after your last final with current classmates, catching up with past classmates, and meeting new people." Another student points out that "life at school can be great for those who do the work to get involved. It can be a commuter school if that is all a student wants to get out of it. [But] there is always something social to do on the weekends, either sponsored by the school or just going out with other MBA students."

"Many students here have jobs," which "provides the best opportunity for networking and recruiting after graduation, as you have gained so many resources at numerous organizations," students here tell us. MBAs range from the mid 20s to the mid 40s. Their "backgrounds are extremely diverse; they come from such areas as financial services, banking, semiconductors, software, technology management, finance, and human resources, to name a few." Engineers from the Silicon Valley are the single most visible contingent.

Admissions

Applicants to Leavey MBA programs at SCU must provide the Admissions Office with all of the following: official transcripts for all postsecondary academic work; official GMAT score reports reflecting scores no more than five years old; a completed application and a copy of same; two letters of recommendation; and personal essays. A third essay is optional. Candidates whose first language is not English must also submit official score reports for the TOEFL (minimum required score: 600 paper-based test, 250 computer-based test). Work experience is not a prerequisite to admission, although a minimum of two years of experience is recommended; on average, admitted students have between five and seven years of post-undergraduate professional experience. All applicants must demonstrate competency in four areas: college algebra, calculus, and oral communications. SCU uses targeted advertising and recruiting events to enhance its minority and disadvantaged populations.

Applicants Also Look At

San José State University, University of California—Davis, University of California—Berkeley, University of San Francisco.

EMPLOYMENT PROFILE	
Career Rating	**86**
Primary Source of Full-time Job Acceptances	
School-facilitated activities	4 (12%)
Graduate-facilitated activities	30 (88%)
Average base starting salary	$88,680
Percent employed	64

SEATTLE PACIFIC UNIVERSITY
SCHOOL OF BUSINESS AND ECONOMICS

GENERAL INFORMATION

Type of school	Private
Affiliation	Free Methodist
Environment	Metropolis
Academic calendar	Quarters

SURVEY SAYS...

Friendly students
Cutting edge classes
Solid preparation in:
Doing business in a global economy

STUDENTS

Enrollment of parent institution	3,830
Enrollment of business school	132
% male/female	57/43
% part-time	90
% international	7
Average age at entry	31
Average years work experience at entry	7

ACADEMICS

Academic Experience Rating	**74**
Student/faculty ratio	17:1
Profs interesting rating	86
Profs accessible rating	95
% female faculty	25
% minority faculty	5

Academics

Students in the Puget Sound region looking for a "great local school" with a "positive atmosphere" would be wise to investigate the School of Business and Economics at Seattle Pacific University, which runs two programs for graduate students: an MBA and a Master of Science in Information Systems Management (MSISM). The school offers a variety of concentrations for students in its MBA program, including: management of business processes, finance, e-business, human resource management, and information systems management. Most classes here meet one evening each week, and students can fill up or scale back on classes as their outside responsibilities fluctuate. A first-year student writes, "The flexibility that the school offered in setting my class schedule was a major selling point. The school also offered two classes in Christian ethics that I thought would be interesting considering some of the recent corporate scandals." SPU introduces "ethical considerations" into "all" b-school classes, which, students tell us, is something the school has done "since long before it was a trendy issue."

Students say their professors are, for the most part, "very impressive." "Most of them have had or still have a successful business" and can provide "concrete examples" of the "theories taught in class." Their ranks include several "former CEOs," and "Many are still very connected." While one student cautions that "not all professors are top-notch—I had a Managerial Communications course in which we studied junior-high grammar," most here focus on the positive: "I've only had one or two course experiences where I felt the instructor wasn't helping me learn at the highest level," a third-year student avows. Professors "bend over backwards to provide a positive learning experience" and are "very accessible" outside of the classroom. They're also "understanding of the fact that most students in the program are also working full-time as well as juggling family commitments."

SPU is unusual in that its administration draws even greater praise than its professors, with one student describing it as "the best-administered school I have ever seen or heard about." By all accounts, it's "really easy to get things taken care of" here. Not only is it "easy to sign up for classes," but also the administration "will add class sections if interest is high for a particular class," which allows students to "take the classes and go back to work." That being said, students still harbor a few complaints; specifically, the school "could do better getting big-name CEOs to speak" at its speaker series, and "The business school computer lab [should be] open more hours."

Career and Placement

SPU has great connections with area businesses, and students cite "mentorship and internship opportunities" as a major strength. The school, however, does not leverage its connections for jobs at graduation. Students tell us that "placement services are intentionally restricted" as "many companies [are] paying tuition for their employees [to] attend SPU," and "SPU would not want to discourage [such] companies from [doing so] by giving the impression that it supported career transition[s] for employed students at graduation." Students say that "those of us who attend full-time without working are at a disadvantage versus those who attend schools without this limitation." Most here believe that, "given the large percentage of students who plan career transitions after graduation anyway," SPU's stance on placement "is not valid and should be abandoned in favor of a strong placement assistance program to include the invitation of interested companies to recruit on campus."

ADMISSIONS CONTACT: DEBBIE WYSOMIERSKI, ASSOCIATE GRADUATE DIRECTOR
ADDRESS: 3307 THIRD AVE. W., SUITE 201 SEATTLE, WA 98119-1950 UNITED STATES
PHONE: 206-281-2753 • FAX: 206-281-2733
E-MAIL: MBA@SPU.EDU • WEBSITE: WWW.SPU.EDU/SBE

Student Life and Environment

"Exceedingly helpful and accommodating" students who are "interested in getting to know you" "create a great learning environment" at SPU. Students describe their peers as "high-integrity people" who are both "supportive and competitive. They expect and bring the best out of one another." SPU students represent "a good variety of ages," though most are "married with children" and "trying to balance full-time work and a graduate program." Across the board, students here are "very driven and dedicated to getting the most out of the program at SPU." "A large portion of the students are employed at Boeing," the result of cross-pollination with the on-site MBA SPU offers at Boeing's nearby Everett, Washington, facility.

Many students "just go to classes and go back home," so "At school it is all work. There is limited time to socialize outside of class. This is the nature of [having a] full-time job and school [commitments]." Fortunately, the campus is "attractive" and "There are plenty of good options for eating" in the vicinity.

Admissions

When reviewing applicants, SPU's School of Business and Economics looks for an undergraduate GPA of 3.0 on a 4.0 scale and at least 1 year of continuous, full-time work experience. In addition, applicants to the MBA program should obtain a score of 490 or greater on the GMAT, and applicants to the MSISM program should obtain a score of 450 or greater on the verbal section of the GRE as well as a score of 525 or greater on the quantitative section of the test. A GPA or standardized test score that does not meet the guidelines listed above will be considered and may be accepted if other areas of the application are strong. Domestic students may apply for the fall, winter, spring, or summer term; international students may apply for any term with the exception of Summer.

FINANCIAL FACTS

Annual tuition	$15,000
Fees	$0
Cost of books	$1,200
Room & board (off-campus)	$10,829
Average grant	$1,200

ADMISSIONS

Admissions Selectivity Rating	**68**
# of applications received	32
% applicants accepted	88
% acceptees attending	43
Average GMAT	530
Range of GMAT	460–550
Average GPA	3.54
TOEFL required of international students	Yes
Minimum TOEFL (paper/computer)	565/225
Application fee	$50
International application fee	$50
Regular application deadline	8/1
Regular notification	8/31
Deferment available	Yes
Maximum length of deferment	2 quarters
Transfer students accepted	Yes
Non-fall admissions	Yes
Need-blind admissions	Yes

Applicants Also Look At
Seattle University, University of Washington.

SEATTLE UNIVERSITY
ALBERS SCHOOL OF BUSINESS AND ECONOMICS

Academics

The MBA program at Seattle University offers full-time and part-time degrees, but students here agree that the school "caters to the working student, maintaining a stronger focus on its evening MBA program than other schools that have day and evening programs." It's an approach that makes good sense, given that four-fifths of the students here are part-time students who typically have full-time jobs.

Students here appreciate that SU's curriculum "allows a tailored approach (as opposed to a track program), meaning that you can take the courses that are most meaningful to you and your future." Many evening programs offer a rather Spartan spread of options, but Seattle University bucks that trend; it provides "a good selection of electives" to evening students. Also, because the program is not lockstep, "Students can take a quarter off or take fewer credits when professional obligations make that necessary." The quarterly schedule is also a convenience in this regard, although it does mean that course material must be mastered over a relatively short period. Fortunately, "Professors here balance the workload, knowing that most of us have full-time jobs." One student sums up, "The school's culture is to treat students as customers and to deliver excellent customer service."

A Jesuit school, Seattle University incorporates "a focus on social justice" and "a push toward ethics and ethical business practices" into the curriculum and also has "community service opportunities built into the program," an aspect students here find very appealing. One student notes, "I want an all-encompassing education—not just a textbook knowledge about how to be a good manager. I want to be a good, well-rounded corporate citizen. Seattle University has all the right ingredients." MBAs here also love "the study abroad program, with its trips to China, Korea, Japan, Italy, and France." But perhaps most of all, they love the engaged faculty who "are very down-to-earth and willing to go the extra mile to make sure the students understand the materials. No matter whether it's meeting outside of class, staying after class late, or an endless e-mail correspondence, the professors have a caring mindset."

Career and Placement

When it comes to career advancement, "The greatest strength of this program is probably the reputation SU has in the business community in the Seattle area." There are lots of high-powered employers in the city, so that's a major plus. Students' enthusiasm is tempered; they tell us that "career and placement services are not as visible as they could be, and often the jobs that are publicized are with a limited group of employers or require much more experience than the standard younger MBA student has. Additionally, all the jobs are very near the campus while students come from all over, some as far as 60 miles away. An expanded geographical offering of available jobs would be helpful."

Top employers of Seattle University MBAs include: Washington Mutual, Paccar, Expeditors, PricewaterhouseCoopers, Deloitte Touche Tohmatsu, Amazon.com, Weyerhaeuser, Wells Fargo, Boeing, Moss Adams, InfoSpace, Holland American Line, Russel Investment, Microsoft, GMI, T-Mobile, Banner Bank.

ADMISSIONS CONTACT: JANET SHANDLEY, DIRECTOR, GRADUATE ADMISSIONS
ADDRESS: 901 12TH AVENUE, PO BOX 222000 SEATTLE, WA 98122-1090 UNITED STATES
PHONE: (206) 296-2000 • FAX: (206) 296-5656
E-MAIL: GRAD-ADMISSIONS@SEATTLEU.EDU • WEBSITE: WWW.SEATTLEU.EDU/ASBE

Student Life and Environment

Most students at Albers "work full-time and attend school part-time, which means the environment is very different from that of a mostly full-time student base. For those who work and go to school it's great; you get to go to school with people who understand what you're going through, and everyone is very supportive of each others' busy schedules." Many here "try to gather before classes in the Atrium. I know of some students who come early from work to 'hang out' with their fellow MBA students before class. Professors are there too. It is a friendly environment that makes you feel like you are . . . more than a number in the school." While the administration allocates "the majority of its funding to undergraduates," Albers' Graduate Student Council "has been working to increase funding in order to increase graduate student activities and functions. We have talks about the different business environments by leaders in that environment. They help students understand the problems and potential of those industries."

SU maintains a satellite campus in Bellevue, which students say is "a bit drab and not as full of life as the Seattle campus but is darn convenient for those who work on the East Side." One student who attends classes there notes, "With the volume of people that we meet through our leadership courses and study abroad trips. I think that the East Side campus can be a great place to take classes and to network with students that you meet through other parts of the program. And the East Side campus really isn't that bad. It has a computer lab and wireless Internet as well as a place to grab something to eat" before class, with "coffee or vending-machine snacks."

Admissions

Applicants to the MBA program at the Albers School must submit the following materials: an official undergraduate transcript reflecting at least the final 2 years (60 semester credits/90 quarter credits) of academic work; transcripts reflecting any post-baccalaureate academic work, regardless of whether it led to a degree; an official GMAT score report; a current resume; and a completed application form. International students whose first language is not English must also submit an official TOEFL score report (237 minimum computer-based score for unconditional admission; students with scores of 227 to 233 may be admitted but must complete a Culture Language Bridge Program). Minimum standards for admission are typically a GMAT score of 500 and an undergraduate GPA of 3.0; students who do not meet these minimums are encouraged to submit personal statements and/or letters of reference in support of their applications.

FINANCIAL FACTS

Annual tuition	$17,415
Fees	$0
Cost of books	$1,107
Room & board (on-campus)	$7,158
% of students receiving aid	30
% of first-year students receiving aid	34
% of students receiving loans	27
% of students receiving grants	4
Average award package	$18,628
Average grant	$6,169
Average student loan debt	$28,339

ADMISSIONS

Admissions Selectivity Rating	**78**
# of applications received	276
% applicants accepted	71
% acceptees attending	75
Average GMAT	573
Range of GMAT	520–620
Average GPA	3.29
TOEFL required of international students	Yes
Minimum TOEFL (paper/computer)	580/237
Application fee	$55
International application fee	$55
Regular application deadline	8/20
Regular notification	
Deferment available	Yes
Maximum length of deferment	1 year
Transfer students accepted	Yes
Transfer application policy	

Applicants must meet standard admission requirements. University will accept 9 quarter credits from AACSB accredited schools. Students transferring from an accredited Jesuit MBA program (JEBNET) may transfer up to 50% of credits.

Non-fall admissions	Yes
Need-blind admissions	Yes

Applicants Also Look At

Harvard University, Pacific Lutheran University, Seattle Pacific University, University of San Francisco, University of Washington, Washington State University, Western Washington University.

SETON HALL UNIVERSITY
STILLMAN SCHOOL OF BUSINESS

GENERAL INFORMATION
Type of school	Private
Affiliation	Roman Catholic
Environment	Village
Academic calendar	Semester

SURVEY SAYS...
Cutting edge classes
Solid preparation in:
Communication/interpersonal skills
Presentation skills
Computer skills
Doing business in a global economy

STUDENTS
Enrollment of parent institution	9,700
Average age at entry	26
Average years work experience at entry	4

ACADEMICS
Academic Experience Rating	**71**
Student/faculty ratio	25:1
Profs interesting rating	77
Profs accessible rating	86
% female faculty	21

Joint Degrees
MBA/JD 3.5–4 years, MBA/MSN 2.5–5 years, MBA/MA (Diplomacy & International Relations) 2.5–5 years.

Prominent Alumni
James O'Brien, Owner, Carlton Hill Hedge Fund; Gerald P. Buccino, Chairman/CEO, Buccino & Associates; Michael Wilk, Partner, Ernst & Young; Stephen Lalor, Partner, Ernst & Young; Steve Waldis, Owner, Synchonos.

Academics

Stillman School of Business at Seton Hall University offers students a location close to New York City along with "high academic standards," a "wonderful reputation," "comfortable class size," a streamlined course plan, and a Catholic tradition of service to community. It also offers one of the few MBA level concentrations in sports management in the country.

The MBA program at Seton Hall requires "42 credits rather than traditional 60." One student claims, "There are great opportunities for learning at a challenging pace and level." Four "hub" courses covering business basics such as marketing, economics, management, and finance are required, along with one course each in international perspectives and social responsibility. One student says, "Social responsibilities and morals are a vital part of the curriculum." This focus, students believe, "sets Seton Hall apart from the rest of institutions out there." Another student adds, "Group projects . . . tend to be a focus at the school and are often illuminating of the human condition—interesting!" There's also a capstone course, integrating ideas and topics studied across the business disciplines. In addition to sports management, students may concentrate in accounting, finance, financial markets, institutions and instruments, health care administration, information systems, international business, management, marketing, and pharmaceutical management. Students may also pursue double concentrations combining two of these areas. In addition, students must complete 20 hours of volunteer work with a community organization of their choice as a graduation requirement for the MBA.

In keeping with the streamlined nature of Seton Hall's programs, study abroad opportunities are offered as 10-day immersion experiences, rather than whole semesters. In recent years students have studied in countries including Italy, China, Poland, Czechoslovakia, France, and Spain. In addition, at the New Jersey campus, the school maintains several practically oriented Centers for Excellence, in areas such as entrepreneurship, securities trading, international business, sports polling, and sports management, which students are encouraged to explore. Programs combining the MBA with a JD or a Master of Science in Nursing are also offered.

Students, most of whom work full-time and attend part-time, appreciate the quality of teaching at Seton Hall, the scheduling choices, and the atmosphere. The administration "has made accommodations for me and my wife to enroll in classes that would have exceeded our allowable credits in a single semester. Additionally, [the] request of a professor has opened an independent study class in business leadership," says one individual. The professors "exemplify a good balance between academic scholarship and practical experience. They are approachable, down-to-earth, serious, and passionate about their disciplines," many students agree, and "They are very embracing and always willing to help in any way possible." One definite strong point of the program is the "very personalized attention by the faculty."

Career and Placement

The Career Center at Stillman School of Business offers help with career assessment and planning, tips on interviewing and networking, and a mentoring program. Given that most students already work full-time and that the school is located just 14 miles from the business hub of New York City, students find that personal networking and being near an active business city often is more useful. "The location of the school is excellent because it is close to the city and other areas where major corporations are based," one student points out. "Since most students are working, it seems like the Career Center for-

ADMISSIONS CONTACT: CATHERINE BIANCHI, DIRECTOR OF GRADUATE ADMISSIONS
ADDRESS: GRADUATE ADMISSIONS - STILLMAN SCHOOL OF BUSINESS, 400 SOUTH ORANGE AVENUE
SOUTH ORANGE, NJ 07079-2692 UNITED STATES • PHONE: 973-761-9262 • FAX: 973-761-9208
E-MAIL: MBA@SHU.EDU • WEBSITE: WWW.BUSINESS.SHU.EDU

gets about MBA students," many feel. "The Stillman School could improve on its alumni network," one students says. "There are a lot of very [wealthy,] successful alumni who have lost touch with the school due to the fact that no one has reached out to them," and "The school should do more to get the word out about how good it is."

Merrill Lynch, the New Jersey Nets, PricewaterhouseCoopers, Prudential Financial, Madison Square Garden, the New York Yankees, and Tiffany & Co. are among those who have employed Seton Hall graduates.

Student Life and Environment

Most students in the MBA program are busy with family and commitments off campus. "Business school students go to class and then go home," says one student, and others agree with the students who say, "I feel like I am part of a community when I go to Seton Hall." That community is, most agree, centered around classwork and academic projects. Students are "motivated professionals at all stages of their career who ask questions, make great comments, and stay engaged in class," who are "diverse" as well as "determined, disciplined, dedicated, freethink[ing], gregarious-natured [individuals with] dynamic personalities. They are "friendly, helpful, competitive, motivating, and adaptive," as well as "not afraid of a heavy workload, looking to share and learn experiences, and [looking for] an education [that will] challenge ideas and processes."

The Catholic tradition of service to and engagement with the community plays out as an inclusive aspect of the college atmosphere, as well. "Being Jewish in a Catholic school worried me at first, but I never had an issue, and people accepted me from the beginning," one student admits.

Admissions

Scores on the GMAT, letters of recommendation, a personal essay about background and goals, and copies of transcripts are required for admission to Stillman School of Business at Seton Hall. The TOEFL is also required for all international applicants. In 2006, the average GMAT score among accepted applicants was 565, with the range of scores for those accepted running between 500 and 700. The average GPA was 3.30. Seton Hall accepted slightly more than half of those who applied in that year, and those students averaged 4 years of work experience in addition to their academic credentials.

FINANCIAL FACTS

Annual tuition	$20,328
Fees	$610
Cost of books	$1,458
Room & board (off-campus)	$10,200
% of students receiving aid	10
% of first-year students receiving aid	5
% of students receiving grants	3
Average grant	$20,328

ADMISSIONS

Admissions Selectivity Rating	**72**
# of applications received	271
% applicants accepted	86
% acceptees attending	66
Average GMAT	555
Range of GMAT	510–600
Average GPA	3.22
TOEFL required of international students	Yes
Minimum TOEFL (paper/computer)	607/254
Application fee	$75
International application fee	$75
Regular application deadline	6/1
Regular notification	Rolling
Deferment available	Yes
Maximum length of deferment	1 academic year
Transfer students accepted	Yes
Transfer application policy Students are eligible to transfer up to a maximum of 12 credits.	
Non-fall admissions	Yes
Need-blind admissions	Yes

Applicants Also Look At

Columbia University; Farleigh Dickinson University; Metropolitan College of New York; Fordham University; Montclair State University; New York University; Pace University; Rutgers, The State University of New Jersey.

SHIPPENSBURG UNIVERSITY
JOHN L. GROVE COLLEGE OF BUSINESS

GENERAL INFORMATION

Type of school	Public

SURVEY SAYS...

Friendly students
Cutting edge classes
Happy students
Smart classrooms
Solid preparation in:
Finance
Accounting

STUDENTS

Average age at entry	32
Average years work experience at entry	5

ACADEMICS

Academic Experience Rating	**62**
Profs interesting rating	63
Profs accessible rating	62

Academics

The MBA program at the Shippensburg University's John L. Grove College of Business exploits twenty-first century technology to the great convenience of its busy student body. Two-thirds of each course in the program is taught in an electronic classroom; videoconferencing technology allows the classes to be broadcast to remote sites so that students and professors in different locations can interact. Area employers may even have their electronic conference rooms added to the school's roster of videoconferencing sites, thus allowing employees to complete the program from their workplaces. The other third of the course content is presented via the Internet, which permits students to complete the work at their own pace. For added convenience, all classes are recorded on digital video and uploaded to the program's website so that students may later stream the classes online.

The Shippensburg MBA consists of 30 credits, meaning "You can do the whole program in one year," which is exactly what some students here are after. Most students attend part-time though, taking two or more years to earn the degree. Students whose undergraduate degree was in an area other than business typically must take up to eight prerequisite undergraduate-level courses (in accounting, business statistics, economics, finance, information management, operations, organizational behavior, and marketing) prior to beginning course work on the MBA proper. The MBA curriculum consists of eight required classes (managerial accounting, global management finance, entrepreneurship, international business, organizational leadership, information management, supply chain, and strategic management) and two electives.

Students tell us that Shippensburg professors "tend to be very friendly and like to see success. They bond well with successful students who show that they are interested in doing well and learning the material." Some concede that "It takes money to keep really, really good professors here and we do not have it!" but quickly add that "The professors that we do have are very good and dedicated." The online component of the program stresses independent learning, which many students appreciate; as one student explains, "Because we have to teach ourselves, we end up learning a lot." Students also love the convenience of taking classes in remote locations; many attend a learning center in Harrisburg near their places of employment. Students also note approvingly that "because this is a new program, the administration takes suggestions seriously. And the technology is great, when it works."

Career and Placement

The Career Development Center (CDC) of Shippensburg University serves current students and alumni of the university. The office offers counseling services, organizes job search programs, provides seminars in job-search skills, and publishes a bi-weekly newsletter announcing upcoming on-campus interviews. Employers who have recruited on the Shippensburg campus in the past include Advantica, Allegis Group, CACI International, Capital Blue Cross, Citibank, Edward Jones Investments, Ernst & Young, Federated Mutual Insurance, Fulton Bank, G E Fanuc Automation, Highmark, Inc., IBM, Integrated Management Solutions, KPMG International, LLP, Lockheed Martin, Nationwide Insurance, Northwestern Mutual Financial Network, the Pennsylvania Department of Revenue, PricewaterhouseCoopers, Raytheon, The Vanguard Group, Vectron International, and Wells Fargo.

ADMISSIONS CONTACT: GRADUATE ADMISSIONS OFFICE,
ADDRESS: 1871 OLD MAIN DRIVE SHIPPENSBURG, PA 17257 UNITED STATES
PHONE: 717-477-1213 • FAX: 717-477-4016
E-MAIL: GRADUATE@SHIP.EDU • WEBSITE: WEBSPACE.SHIP.EDU/MBA

Student Life and Environment

Shippensburg is a public university that is home to over 6,500 undergraduate students and about 1,000 graduate students. The campus, spread over 200 acres, is located 40 miles southwest of Harrisburg, not far from the Pennsylvania Turnpike. The school is accredited by the AACSB. Many MBA students attend the Dixon University Center in Harrisburg, where they participate in Shippensburg-based classes via teleconferencing technology.

Most students in the MBA program attend part-time and have little time for extracurricular involvement. While some feel "the department needs to have more clubs and social events for the students to join," most are happy to restrict their involvement to class-related activities. The majority of students here are "older, married adults who are employed full-time." They share the common bond of "all working toward the same goal" and "don't feel in competition with each other in the least." In fact, there's a "definite sense of community within the school." Some here tell us that "the students who take classes on campus at Ship tend to be more immature than those at Harrisburg. The Harrisburg people tend to be working professionals, whereas Shippensburg has more students who came straight from undergrad to the MBA program."

Admissions

The Admissions Office at Shippensburg University requires applicants to submit official copies of transcripts for all undergraduate work and a current resume. GMAT scores are required for applicants that have less than 5 years of work experience from the date of their undergraduate degree; students required to take the GMAT must submit an official GMAT score report. In addition, applicants must either have work experience or undergraduate credits in computer usage, oral and written communication, and quantitative analysis. A personal statement and letters of recommendation are both optional. International applicants must not only meet all of the above requirements, but must also submit an international student application, an evaluation of their transcripts by a professional evaluating service (either Educational Credential Evaluators (ECE) or World Education Services (WES)); an official score report for the TOEFL; and an affidavit of support accompanied by a current bank statement. Applicants who do not meet Shippensburg's admissions requirements may seek special consideration. Some such students do receive provisional admissions status, which allows them to enter the program and continue contingent upon success in their initial MBA course work.

FINANCIAL FACTS

Annual tuition (in-state/ out-of-state)	$3,107/$4,972
Fees (in-state/out-of-state)	$544/$580

ADMISSIONS

Admissions Selectivity Rating 60*

Minimum TOEFL (paper/computer)	550/213
Application fee	$30
International application fee	$30
Regular application deadline	rolling
Regular notification	rolling
Deferment available	Yes
Maximum length of deferment	1 year
Transfer students accepted	Yes
Transfer application policy Up to 9 credits may transfer.	
Non-fall admissions	Yes

SOUTHEAST MISSOURI STATE UNIVERSITY
DONALD L. HARRISON COLLEGE OF BUSINESS

GENERAL INFORMATION

Type of school	Public
Environment	Town
Academic calendar	Semester

SURVEY SAYS...

Good peer network
Solid preparation in:
Communication/interpersonal skills
Presentation skills

STUDENTS

Enrollment of parent institution	10,250
Enrollment of business school	117
% male/female	50/50
% out-of-state	10
% part-time	38
% minorities	3
% international	15
Average age at entry	25
Average years work experience at entry	5

ACADEMICS

Academic Experience Rating	**75**
Student/faculty ratio	19:1
Profs interesting rating	71
Profs accessible rating	88
% female faculty	40
% minority faculty	10

Joint Degrees

MBA/MS (International Business and Economics).

Academics

The Donald L. Harrison College of Business at Southeast Missouri State University (SEMO) offers students plenty of "bang for their buck." In 2003, *U.S. News & World Report* reported that the school produces some of the "least indebted students" in the nation. As one MBA student says, "It's not Kellogg, but it's as good as you'll find for the money. I was an MBA at another university for a semester and transferred because the education there was not up to par with the tuition charged. SEMO, which charges much less, has provided a much better value." Harrison MBAs can choose from seven different degree options: accounting, environmental management, finance, general management, industrial management, international business, and a recently added concentration in health administration. MBAs praise "the variety of available disciplines of study, given the size of the institution," although they also warn that "there should be a wider variety of courses offered each semester." One student adds, "Sometimes you may be very limited to what [courses] you will be able to take. For instance, I can't take any summer courses because the courses that will be offered are ones that I have already taken." Internships play an integral role in the Harrison MBA—at least for its younger full-timers. The school notes, "Students have the opportunity to participate in internship assignments (and receive full credit as an elective course) that bring our graduate students into contact with the managerial practice of business. Our students have benefited from internships with American Express Financial, Coca-Cola, KPMG International, Merrill Lynch, [and] Northwestern Mutual Life, to name just a few." Many Harrison MBAs have jobs (they attend evening classes), and so, do not participate in the internship program. Students love Harrison's small classes and the focus on in-class discussion. One older MBA student writes, "As a nontraditional student with over 30 years [of] business experience, my reflections and experiences were sometimes sought [after] and discussed as another means to broaden the overall picture of the real work place. I felt valued as a contributor by most professors and younger students. Diversity and variety seemed to be positive influences in most of my classes. Students were supportive of each others' efforts." However, some other students feel that "some professors do not demand enough from students, especially in the area of presentation and revision of work. Overall, this school's MBA program should be more challenging."

Career and Placement

Harrison placement services are provided by SEMO's Career Linkages Office, which serves all undergraduates and graduate students at the university. In conjunction with the Alumni Affairs office, Career Linkages has established the Southeast Career Alumni Network to facilitate job searches. The office also offers the standard array of services including counseling, workshops, and online support. Students are unimpressed; they feel that "the biggest area the MBA administration must improve on is the career center. The business school doesn't have a career center. We must use the undergraduate career center that focuses on attracting jobs for undergraduates. Obtaining a job through the career center at Southeast is nearly impossible. All work must be self-initiated and completed." Recently, the business school has initiated "Saint Louis Interview Days," which facilitate interviews for students on site in greater Saint Louis. Harrison MBAs who seek new jobs after graduation most often find themselves working for Accenture, Boeing, Bausch & Lomb, Dow Jones & Company, PricewaterhouseCoopers, TG Missouri, and Texas Instruments. About one in ten students finds a job outside the United States.

Student Life and Environment

"Life at school is good!" one Harrison MBA reports. The student body is tight and the surrounding town of Cape Girardeau is pleasant and quiet. Another student explains, "Cape

FINANCIAL FACTS

Annual tuition (in-state/ out-of-state)	$5,400/$9,504
Cost of books	$500
Room & board	$5,200
Average award package	$11,200
Average grant	$11,200

ADMISSIONS

Admissions Selectivity Rating	**71**
# of applications received	65
% applicants accepted	89
% acceptees attending	78
Average GMAT	500
Range of GMAT	430–618
Average GPA	3.27
TOEFL required of international students	Yes
Minimum TOEFL (paper/computer)	550/213
Application fee	$20
International application fee	$100
Regular application deadline	rolling
Regular notification	rolling
Deferment available	Yes
Maximum length of deferment	1 year
Transfer students accepted	Yes
Transfer application policy May transfer 9 hours authorized by Director of MBA Program.	
Non-fall admissions	Yes
Need-blind admissions	Yes

Applicants Also Look At

Missouri State University (Formerly SW MSU), Saint Louis University, Southern Illinois University— Carbondale, University of Missouri— Columbia, University of Missouri— St. Louis.

Girardeau is a fairly small town, so there are some limitations on recreational activity. In warm months, there are many lakes, parks, and trails nearby to enjoy. The people in the community are friendly overall." One MBA student says, "Even though Cape Girardeau is a relatively small town, there is actually quite a lot to do, and it is close to Memphis and St. Louis for people who want to get to a city every once in a while." Campus life centers on the MBA Association, which "has holiday parties, happy-hour gatherings, intramural sports teams, [and] sponsors speakers." One student says, "I must give credit to the MBA Association because they work hard to create a positive social atmosphere for students." However, other MBAs believe that is pretty much the only school-related extracurricular. One student writes, "It seems the only student organization that MBA students are a part of is the MBA Association. This may be because MBA students have busy schedules." Other students feel that "the administration needs to work at creating more community. Although the student-run MBA Association does well, the administration does little to make new students feel welcomed." Students agree that "[SEMO's campus] is nice and fairly attractive [with] good facilities on-campus for student recreation, exercise, leisure, activities, and so on. The library resources are adequate and [continue to] improve—considering the budget crisis of the past couple years. The surrounding community is fairly supportive of the university and recognizes the impact it plays on its economy." Although one student comments, "For those who work during the day and study at night, some of the facilities are not open (for example, the bookstore). Sometimes the working student just simply cannot get to campus before it closes and has to take time off work to get necessary books for class." Students agree, "[The Harrison student body] comes from a wide array of backgrounds: rural, urban, suburban, international, and so on. The mix of such a diversity of students offers a relatively interesting student population." The school notes, "Approximately 16 percent of our MBA students and half of our alumni are international students. Since Southeast Missouri State University launched its MBA program in fall 1996, students from more than 25 countries have studied in the program. Currently, students from more than eight countries represent their nations and bring the world to the classroom."

Admissions

Harrison admissions officers use a formula to establish a floor for all MBA applicants: (200 × GPA [on a four-point scale] + GMAT score). Applicants must score at least 1,000 to be considered for admission. In addition, applicants must score at least 400 on the GMAT and must have earned at least a C in all required foundation courses for the GMAT program. These foundation courses are applied calculus, financial management, introductory statistics, management and organizational behavior, management information systems, principles of financial accounting, principles of macroeconomics, principles of managerial accounting, principles of marketing, and principles of microeconomics. Students without the requisite undergraduate work may place out of foundation courses through local and/or CLEP exams.

EMPLOYMENT PROFILE		
Career Rating	**91**	**Top Employers Hiring Grads**
Percent employed	95	Boeing

SOUTHERN ILLINOIS UNIVERSITY—CARBONDALE
COLLEGE OF BUSINESS AND ADMINISTRATION

GENERAL INFORMATION
Type of school	Public
Environment	Town
Academic calendar	Semester

SURVEY SAYS...
Friendly students
Helpful alumni
Happy students
Smart classrooms
Solid preparation in:
Doing business in a global economy

STUDENTS
Enrollment of parent institution	21,589
Enrollment of business school	134
% male/female	61/39
% part-time	48
% minorities	10
% international	10

ACADEMICS
Academic Experience Rating	**74**
Student/faculty ratio	12:1
Profs interesting rating	74
Profs accessible rating	66

Joint Degrees
MBA/JD 3–4 years, MBA/MS (Agribusiness Econmics) 1–2.5 years, MBA/MA (Communications) 1–2.5 years.

Academics

The College of Business and Administration at Southern Illinois University—Carbondale offers both a traditional MBA and off-campus EMBA options in Hong Kong, Singapore, and Taiwan. All programs are AACSB-accredited. About half the graduate students at SIUC attend full-time. While part-time students can manage the program as well, the mixed schedule of daytime and nighttime classes limits their options somewhat.

SIUC MBAs report that "the school is famous for its finance department" and that it offers "good courses in the Management of Information Systems." Classes here "are very interactive, with only 20 to 30 students in a class," and "professors work to extend the understanding of the discipline in all classes. Also, most professors seek to design classes in an unorthodox manner to develop skills needed for business." Many students cite the low cost of attending as their primary reason for choosing SIUC; relatively low tuition rates are made effectively lower by the availability of "a lot of assistantships for students." SIUC maintains a relationship with ESC-Grenoble, which allows SIUC MBAs to study for a Masters of International Business (MIB) in France.

Entering students who lack the required knowledge base for an MBA program are required to complete up to 37 hours of foundation courses prior to beginning work on their MBA. It helps that students with degrees outside business may receive credit for any equivalent undergraduate business classes in which they earned a grade of C or better. Such students must present both a transcript and a course syllabus for each course in order to be considered for the exemption. Students with undergraduate degrees in business generally are exempt from all foundation course work.

Full-time students who arrive with undergraduate business degrees under their belt can finish the 33-semester hour MBA program in 12 months. The MBA curriculum includes seven core courses and four electives. Students may also pursue electives in finance, marketing, international business, management information systems, and organizational behavior. Those who wish to concentrate in a particular area can opt to take all of their electives in one discipline.

Career and Placement

Southern Illinois University maintains a separate Business Placement Center to serve the College of Business and Administration. The office serves undergraduates, graduates, and alumni of the school. The office coordinates an annual job fair, maintains e-recruiting resources, and provides career counseling to students. Some here feel that "The career center could use a more hands-on effort with graduates. The only contact I had was through e-mail notices of career center activities." On-campus recruiters include 7-Eleven, Aldi, Archer Daniels Midland (ADM), CBIZ Business Solutions, Deloitte Touche Tohmatsu, Disney, Ernst & Young, Federated Insurance, KPMG International, MB Financial, MMP&W, PricewaterhouseCoopers, Regions Financial Corporation, State Farm Insurance, Swink, Fiehler & Company, Watkins Uiberall, and Woodbury Financial.

Student Life and Environment

An overall student population of more than 20,000 keeps the SIUC campus hopping. As one MBA student explains, "There are lots of things to do here, such as [hearing] guest speakers and seminars to attend. The school often has forums for students to express their opinions on politics. They also offer fun events like concerts, and many students are avid sports fans, so sporting events are social gatherings." The campus recreation center "is very good, with basketball courts, swimming pools, racquetball courts, etc. There are also weight rooms and many cardiovascular fitness machines, and the staff that works at the Rec Center is very helpful." As if all that weren't enough, "The Student Center is an excellent facility for throwing pots, woodworking, and metal smithing." Even the surrounding campus "is beautiful, with forests all around where you can go hiking if the weather allows."

The city of Carbondale has a population of about 26,000, and the surrounding county is home to nearly 60,000 Illinoisans. St. Louis is the closest big city; it's less than 100 miles to the west. Both Chicago and Kansas City are just over 300 miles away. Major employers in the area include Nascote Industries, West Teleservices, Southern Illinois Healthcare, and the Maytag Corporation.

SIUC MBAs include "many international students. There are more young students than in many MBA programs, but not at the expense of competence." To some "it seems that almost every other student in the MBA program is a recent graduate of SIUC. Although they come from varied backgrounds…they are very similar," especially in that "few seem to have undergraduate degrees in business."

Admissions

All applicants to the MBA program at SIUC must provide the admissions department with a completed application to the university's graduate school; a separate application to the College of Business; official transcripts for all postsecondary academic work; an official score report for the GMAT; and three letters of recommendation. International applicants must also provide an official score report for the TOEFL (minimum score: 550 paper, 213 computer), a financial statement for graduate international students, and a photocopy of their passport. Work experience is not required; however, students with work experience do receive special consideration. All applications are assessed individually and holistically. Admission to the program requires a minimum undergraduate GPA of 2.7 (on a four-point scale) over the applicant's most recent 60 semester hours.

FINANCIAL FACTS

Annual tuition (in-state/ out-of-state)	$5,760/$11,520
Fees	$1,414
Cost of books	$840

ADMISSIONS

Admissions Selectivity Rating	**74**
# of applications received	78
% applicants accepted	69
% acceptees attending	63
Average GMAT	507
Range of GMAT	440–570
Average GPA	3.39
TOEFL required of international students	Yes
Minimum TOEFL (paper/computer)	550/213
Application fee	$35
International application fee	$35
Regular application deadline	3/15
Regular notification	6/1
Deferment available	Yes
Maximum length of deferment	1 year
Transfer students accepted	Yes
Transfer application policy Maximum number of transfer credits accepted for core curriculum is 6.	
Non-fall admissions	Yes

Applicants Also Look At

Eastern Illinois University, University of Illinois at Urbana-Champaign, University of Missouri—Columbia, Western Illinois University.

SOUTHERN ILLINOIS UNIVERSITY—EDWARDSVILLE
SCHOOL OF BUSINESS

GENERAL INFORMATION

Type of school	Public
Environment	Metropolis

SURVEY SAYS...
Helpful alumni
Happy students
Solid preparation in:
General management
Computer skills

STUDENTS

Enrollment of parent institution	13,398
Enrollment of business school	188
% part-time	100
Average age at entry	27
Average years work experience at entry	5.7

ACADEMICS

Academic Experience Rating	**77**
Student/faculty ratio	5:1
Profs interesting rating	83
Profs accessible rating	61
% female faculty	43
% minority faculty	16

Prominent Alumni
Fernando G. Aguirre, President/CEO, Chiquita Brands International; John Shimkus, U.S. Representative (IL) 19th District; Ralph Korte, President, Korte Construction Company; Deanna L. Daughhetee, President, American Equity Mortgage, Inc.; Steven F. McCann, Executive Vice President/CFO, Long's Drugs.

Academics

Students are drawn to the business programs at Southern Illinois University Edwardsville by "the cheapest tuition in the St. Louis metro area," the convenience of "a lot of night and weekend classes," and "the good reputation" of the program, bolstered by its AACSB accreditation. SIUE offers a general MBA as well as specialized master's programs in accountancy, marketing research, economics, finance, and computer management and information systems.

SIUE's MBA program is designed for part-time working professionals. Students are required to take 42 credit hours in quantitative analysis, decision making for managers, negotiation and interpersonal skills, and courses in accounting, finance, economics, marketing, computer management and information systems, production, and strategic management.

Students may take 12 credit hours of electives in functional areas, pursue a concentration in project management, or a specialization in management of information systems. Some of the elective requirements may be fulfilled by writing an independent thesis. All students must complete a comprehensive exam to graduate.

MBA students at SIUE tell us that "professors are very knowledgeable and well-prepared for classes." Overall, they "are very interested in providing an excellent learning environment." While "the administration of the School of Business is first-rate," the "administration of the university as a whole is not as impressive." Students warn that "There is far too much red tape and far too many walls built into the system." Some here also feel that "the physical classroom environment needs an overhaul for the MBA student. We need something much different than the kindergarten desks-in-a-row. Some professors have made efforts to improve this, but for the most part it is very poor, not conducive for most adults who work all day at a desk." Students also would like to see the program incorporate online classes.

Career and Placement

Business students at SIUE are served by the university's Career Development Center, which provides career counseling and placement services for all students and alumni. Services include individual counseling, resume referral, on-campus interview sessions, workshops on various career-related skills, and a Career Resources Center with both online and hard-copy materials. SIUE holds two annual career fairs, one in the fall and one in the spring.

Student Life and Environment

SIUE is located in Edwardsville, a city of 22,000 strong that's just twenty miles northeast of St. Louis, Missouri. St. Louis provides copious opportunities for work, shopping, and entertainment. The school's location in a major metropolitan area also means that it serves a potential market of nearly three million people. Major employers in the area include Anheuser-Busch, BJC Healthcare, Boeing, Edward Jones, and Mansanto.

The university is home to more than 13,000 students and sits on a meandering campus that features woodlands, lakes, and rolling hills. Students note that "the campus is very nice and has all the amenities you could need." Most business students "don't spend a lot of time on campus," though, as "We commute and attend evening and weekend classes. This is very helpful to those of us in the working world" but it dampens student participation in the school community at large.

SIUE business students "come from impressively diverse backgrounds," are "pleasant to work with," and "have a great deal of real-world knowledge to share." Most "have children and full-time jobs, yet they have decided to come back to school and finish their degrees. Their commitments outside the classroom force them to be creative with their time-management skills and this, in turn, becomes a valuable tool that they can use in the business world." The student body includes "people from various cultures, which makes class interesting. They are also very easy to talk to!"

Admissions

Applicants to the MBA program at SIUE must apply for admission to the Graduate School, and send appropriate supporting materials, including official transcripts and GMAT score. Applicants who hold a PhD, MD, or the equivalent in a recognized field are not required to submit a GMAT score. International students must also earn a minimum of 550 on the paper-based TOEFL or 213 on the computer-based TOEFL.

Admission is based on a variety of factors including undergraduate GPA, GMAT score, and previous work in other graduate programs. At least two years of work experience is recommended. Students are expected to enter the program with competencies in computer software and statistics.

FINANCIAL FACTS

Annual tuition (in-state/ out-of-state)	$5,670/$14,175
Fees	$687
Cost of books	$1,000
Room & board (on-campus)	$7,000
% of students receiving aid	43
% of first-year students receiving aid	5
% of students receiving loans	22
% of students receiving grants	12
Average award package	$8,386
Average grant	$2,773
Average student loan debt	$15,050

ADMISSIONS

Admissions Selectivity Rating	**76**
# of applications received	192
% applicants accepted	65
% acceptees attending	82
Average GMAT	509
Range of GMAT	450–560
Average GPA	3.26
TOEFL required of international students	Yes
Minimum TOEFL (paper/computer)	550/213
Application fee	$30
Regular application deadline	Rolling
Regular notification	Rolling
Deferment available	Yes
Maximum length of deferment	1 year
Transfer students accepted	Yes
Transfer application policy From an AACSB accredited school and up to 9 hours.	
Non-fall admissions	Yes
Need-blind admissions	Yes

Applicants Also Look At

Saint Louis University, University of Missouri—St. Louis, Washington University in St. Louis.

SOUTHERN METHODIST UNIVERSITY
COX SCHOOL OF BUSINESS

Academics

A contemporary and challenging business program situated in a lively, commerce-oriented city, Southern Methodist University's Cox School of Business is touted by students as the "best program offered in Dallas/Fort Worth area" in its balance of "course offerings, rankings, network ability and recognition, and faculty quality." All MBA students are initially enrolled in the general management concentration, taking a series of courses that provide a thorough introduction to business theory, including "very deep and modernized topics in the area of finance and accounting." Once they have finished the core curriculum, students may tailor their education through one or two academic concentrations, including strategic leadership, marketing, finance, information technology, and accounting. Students appreciate the fact that SMU is highly focused on the latest trends and on a practical approach to business education, saying "Teachers bring relevant material to the class and challenge students every day."

Responding to the increasingly global economy, Cox offers a "forward-thinking, cutting-edge program with a strong focus on the international marketplace." In 2000, Cox inaugurated the Global Leadership Program, a partnership with more than 90 leading businesses and government organizations throughout Asia, Latin America, and Europe. All full-time MBA students participate in the Global Leadership Program, and take a seminar in their first semester, which provides a comprehensive study of the culture, politics, and business in Asia, Latin America, or Europe. At the end of the second semester, students travel to the region for a 2-week, hands-on immersion into global commerce and culture. For those who wish to further enhance their international acumen, the school operates a number of international exchange programs with universities in China, Japan, Singapore, Australia, Belgium, Denmark, Spain, Argentina, Brazil, and Mexico, among others.

In addition to the traditional, 2-year, full-time MBA, the school offers two part-time programs: the professional MBA for students who wish to work full-time while pursuing the MBA and the executive MBA for students who already have advanced business experience. Students in the part-time programs appreciate the camaraderie they feel among their classmates as well as the support of the faculty. One student assures, "They realize that we are all working professionals, and [they] are always there to lend a hand." Whether full-time or part-time, many say the greatest benefit of the program is "the way the b-school administration cares about the individual students." A current student shares, "Before I was even accepted, the Admissions staff and administration made me feel as if I was a part of the school."

Career and Placement

For those hoping to work in Texas or the Southwest region, Southern Methodist University is an excellent choice; the school maintains a "great reputation and alumni network in the Dallas/Fort Worth area, Texas, and the Southwestern U.S. cities." In fact, 80 percent of graduates took jobs in the Southwest last year, many in hometown Dallas. Since Dallas itself is a "very corporate city," many stay put after graduation. However, some feel the school is too Dallas-centric and "would improve the value to its graduates by increasing the number of companies recruiting for positions in Houston, Austin, and San Antonio."

Cox graduates have a high job-placement rate, and the majority of students take finance/accounting or marketing/sales positions, comprising 56 percent and 19 percent of last year's graduates, respectively. In 2006, the average salary of a Cox graduate was $83,978.

ADMISSIONS CONTACT: PATTI CUDNEY, DIRECTOR, MBA ADMISSIONS
ADDRESS: P.O. BOX 750333 DALLAS, TX 75275 UNITED STATES
PHONE: 214-768-1214 • FAX: 214-768-3956
E-MAIL: MBAINFO@COX.SMU.EDU • WEBSITE: WWW.COXMBA.COM

Student Life and Environment

On the Cox campus, you'll find "a great group of people, most in their 20s, some in their 30s, with different backgrounds and interests, but all outgoing." Conversation and camaraderie are not limited to the classroom, and "The school makes a strong effort to have students interact outside the classroom. They host events all the time to mingle with fellow students, professors, alumni, and even guests that people bring." For those who wish to augment the academic experience through a club or recreational activity, "there are plenty of chances for anyone who wishes to get involved with extracurricular activities to do so." However, many part-time students say the demands of work and study are overwhelming. A second-year student laments, "Being in the professional MBA program I wish I had more time to take advantage of all the school offers."

Located in Dallas, Texas, the campus is within striking distance of every form of entertainment imaginable, including restaurants, museums, shopping, and seven major sports teams. On the flip side, the school's pleasant campus offers relief from the bustling city. A current student enthusiastically sums it up: "The campus is beautiful—shady tree-lined streets with really attractive people in one of the most pro-business cities with an awesome nightlife. Seriously, who could ask for anything more!?"

Admissions

Successful applicants to SMU have leadership experience, a strong academic record, and competitive scores on the GMAT. Last year, the average GMAT score for accepted applicants was 640. Personal qualities are also heavily weighed, and Cox admits students with a history of professional and personal growth, demonstrated achievements, proven academic abilities, and leadership potential. Although an academic background in business is not a requirement for admission, SMU recommends students enter the program with a working knowledge of calculus, accounting, statistics, and microeconomics. Qualified applicants are offered the opportunity to interview with the Admissions staff.

Admissions criteria differ slightly for students seeking admission to Cox's part-time programs. In addition to the aforementioned, applicants to the PMBA program must have at least 2 years of professional work experience and a strong basic knowledge of accounting, statistics, and microeconomics. Applicants to the executive MBA program are expected to have a minimum of 8 years of experience in mid- to upper-level management and to currently hold a senior-level title.

FINANCIAL FACTS

Annual tuition	$35,530
Fees	$3,480
Cost of books	$1,650
Room & board (off-campus)	$13,900
% of students receiving grants	52
Average grant	$20,282

ADMISSIONS

Admissions Selectivity Rating	89
# of applications received	393
% applicants accepted	47
% acceptees attending	44
Average GMAT	640
Range of GMAT	600–680
Average GPA	3.3
TOEFL required of international students	Yes
Minimum TOEFL (paper/computer)	600/250
Application fee	$75
International application fee	$75
Regular application deadline	4/15
Regular notification	6/1
Application Deadline/Notification	
Round 1:	11/15 / 01/15
Round 2:	01/15 / 03/15
Round 3:	03/01 / 05/01
Round 4:	04/15 / 06/01
Deferment available	Yes
Maximum length of deferment	1 year
Need-blind admissions	Yes

Applicants Also Look At

Rice University, Texas A&M University—College Station, Texas Christian University, The University of Texas at Austin, Vanderbilt University, Washington University in St. Louis.

EMPLOYMENT PROFILE

Career Rating	89	Grads Employed by Function	%	Avg. Salary
Primary Source of Full-time Job Acceptances		Finance	56	$83,450
School-facilitated activities	29 (50%)	Human Resources	1	$0
Graduate-facilitated activities	27 (47%)	Marketing	19	$87,400
Unknown	2 (3%)	Operations	3	$0
Average base starting salary	$83,978	Consulting	10	$90,000
Percent employed	91	General Management	6	$82,750
		Other	1	$0

Top 5 Employers Hiring Grads
Frito-Lay; JP Morgan Chase; AT&T; American Airlines; Texas Instruments

ST. JOHN'S UNIVERSITY
THE PETER J. TOBIN COLLEGE OF BUSINESS

Academics

A large business school in New York City, St. John's University provides a strong, general management MBA, which can be tailored to fit individual student interests through a range of concentrations and co-curricular activities. St. John's recently updated their curriculum, which now consists of eight required courses, followed by four field courses and two non-field courses in the student's chosen area of concentration. Through the school's extensive elective offerings, students may pursue a specialization in taxation, decision sciences, finance, insurance financial management, international business, marketing management, and risk management, among a number of other fields. In addition, Tobin operates several unique co-curricular activities, including a multi-million dollar student-managed investment fund, as well as an extensive service learning and economic development program. A Catholic-affiliated school, St. John's commitment to service has been fundamental to the program since its early days, and the school distinguishes itself from other business programs through its ethical approach to academics. A student explains, "St. John's is grounded in morals and values, and the well-being of their students is always a top priority."

With a total enrollment of over 650 graduate students, you might be surprised to learn that St. John's faculty are "accessible outside of class" and are "willing to give home and cellular phone numbers so that they can be reached at any time with an questions students may have." Drawing intellectuals and business professionals from the New York community, "professors are excellent with both high academic credentials but also real-world experience." However, while students appreciate the skill demonstrated by the senior faculty, many say they'd like to see more case studies, practical instruction, and contemporary theory integrated into the curriculum. For example, a student suggests the school provide more instruction in "accounting and computer application methods, especially for finance students."

St. John's offers the MBA program on their campus in Jamaica, Queens, and on a satellite campus on Staten Island. In addition, the School of Risk Management is located in the Financial District in Manhattan. No matter where you study, the "proximity to Manhattan" is definitely among the school's major selling points, putting students in position for jobs and internships at a wide range of companies. For those who aren't entirely focused on the Big Apple, the school operates an MBA program in Rome, Italy, with an evening class schedule geared towards part-time students. Students may complete their entire MA or MBA in Rome, or simply spend a semester abroad. With the increasing need for internationally trained business professionals, "having the opportunity to study abroad while pursuing an MBA" is another attractive aspect of a St. John's education.

Career and Placement

The Career Center at St. John's University helps students and alumni define and achieve their career goals through workshops, seminars, and campus recruiting events. Serving the entire St. John's community, the Career Center hosts industry-specific and broad-based career fairs and interview days on all three New York campuses. They also host a series of Saturday speakers, who discuss careers in various professional fields.

Among the greatest advantages to St. John's is the "proximity to NYC and the career opportunities that comes with it;" however, business students must also take a proactive approach to the career search if they want to land a plum position. A current student elaborates, "On one hand, you can do the bare minimum and still come out with your

MBA with a mediocre job waiting for you. While on the other, you can give it all you've got and come out of SJU with that amazing six-figure-to-start career."

At the Rome campus, the "career center staff [are] able to assist students that intend to remain and work in Italy upon graduation;" however, the university points out that Italian language skills are necessary for most jobs in Italy.

Student Life and Environment

St. John's University's main campus is located on 100 acres in Jamaica, Queens. The Queens campus is home to most of the university's facilities, including the library (which includes the business school's research collection) and athletic buildings. On all three New York campuses, St. John's attracts a largely local crowd, which reflects the diversity of the greater New York metropolitan area. While many students join the program with years of professional experience, "approximately 50–65 percent seem young (early to mid-20s) with little work experience but recent academic experience. This makes class discussion an interesting mix of theory and experience." Catering to the school's majority of part-time students, most classes are taught at night.

St. John's Italian campus boasts its share of attractions, most notably, its lovely European location. Plus, the smaller student body creates a laid-back and friendly atmosphere. A student at the Rome campus says, "Since there are only about 70–100 students total we are a very tight-knit group and extremely helpful whenever one is in need."

Admissions

To apply to the Tobin School of Business, students must submit official undergraduate transcripts, a current resume, and official GMAT scores, no more than five years old. Currently, the average GMAT score for accepted applicants is 540, and the average GPA is 3.2 on a 4.0 scale. An undergraduate business degree is not a pre-requisite of the program; in fact, 37 percent of current students joined the program from other major disciplines.

FINANCIAL FACTS

Annual tuition	$23,850
Fees	$250
Cost of books	$3,000
Room & board	
(on/off-campus)	$12,000/$15,000
% of students receiving aid	30
% of first-year students	
receiving aid	14
Average award package	$14,914
Average grant	$1,812

ADMISSIONS

Admissions Selectivity Rating	77
# of applications received	644
% applicants accepted	59
% acceptees attending	62
Average GMAT	530
Range of GMAT	440–630
Average GPA	3.2
TOEFL required of	
international students	Yes
Minimum TOEFL	
(paper/computer)	580/NR
Application fee	$40
International application fee	$40
Regular application deadline	6/1
Regular notification	Rolling
Deferment available	Yes
Maximum length of	
deferment	1 year
Transfer students accepted	Yes
Transfer application policy	
Must use regular application.	
Individual review of transfer credits.	
Non-fall admissions	Yes
Need-blind admissions	Yes

Applicants Also Look At

City University of New York—Baruch College, Fordham University, Hofstra University, New York University, Pace University.

EMPLOYMENT PROFILE

Career Rating	85	Top 5 Employers Hiring Grads
		Merrill Lynch; Pricewaterhouse Coopers; Citigroup; Deloitte and Touche; Goldman Sachs

ST. MARY'S UNIVERSITY
BILL GREEHEY SCHOOL OF BUSINESS

GENERAL INFORMATION

Type of school	Private
Affiliation	Roman Catholic
Environment	Metropolis
Academic calendar	Semester

SURVEY SAYS...

Students love San Antonio, TX
Friendly students
Cutting edge classes
Happy students
Solid preparation in:
Teamwork

STUDENTS

Enrollment of parent institution	3,904
Enrollment of business school	91
% male/female	60/40
% part-time	81
% minorities	10
Average age at entry	33
Average years work experience at entry	3

ACADEMICS

Academic Experience Rating	**83**
Student/faculty ratio	10:1
Profs interesting rating	81
Profs accessible rating	65
% female faculty	36
% minority faculty	4

Joint Degrees

JD/MBA.

Prominent Alumni

Bill Greehey, Chairman, Nustar Energy.

Academics

There are big days ahead for the MBA program at St. Mary's University. Thanks to a $25 million donation from Valero Energy chairman Bill Greehey, the university has planned major upgrades to the faculty, curriculum, and student scholarship support in the business school. The school of business—renamed in Greehey's honor in March of 2006—is one of the major beneficiary of the local philanthropist's largesse. Whatever improvements are made will only add to some already commendable assets here, including "a unique international entrepreneurship program" a "solid financial planning curriculum," and a professional accounting curriculum.

Prerequisites to MBA study at Greehey begin with the completion of six undergraduate-level fundamentals courses. Students arriving with undergraduate degrees in business can place out of these courses, as can students who demonstrate proficiency through CLEP and DANTES examinations. After completing or placing out of these fundamentals courses, students must complete a 30 semester-hour program that includes five core courses (in human resources, accounting/finance, international business, informational technology, and marketing). Tracks are offered in financial planning, professional accountancy and general management as well as a joint JD/MBA. (Note that the financial planning concentration requires two additional classes, meaning that students who choose this option must complete 36 semester hours to graduate.)

MBAs here praise the faculty for "focusing on teaching and understanding" and "providing real-life experience. They bring a lot of outside experience to the classroom." St. Mary's has always been known for its personal touches, and students confirm that "classes are small and the program as a whole is small. This allows for a lot of individual attention from professors and administrators." Students here appreciate this "laid- back program with not too much pressure" but wish that the administration was sometimes a little less laid back. They tell us that administrators "are very disorganized. They lose papers way too often."

Career and Placement

The Career Services Center at St. Mary's University serves all undergraduate students, graduate students, and alumni of the school. The office provides one-on-one advisement with career counselors, a library of career-related materials including hard-copy and online job search databases, special events (Resume Drive, Business Etiquette Dinner, Mock Interview Day), a career fair, and connections to an alumni mentoring program. Students tell us that "the strong alumni network" is one of the biggest attractions of a St. Mary's degree. Employers interviewing on the St. Mary's campus in the spring of 2006 included BNSF Railway; Fisher, Herbst, & Kemble; USAA; Valero Energy; and Walgreens.

ADMISSIONS CONTACT: DR. RICHARD MENGER, MBA PROGRAM DIRECTOR
ADDRESS: ONE CAMINO SANTA MARIA SAN ANTONIO, TX 78228-8507 UNITED STATES
PHONE: 210-436-3101 • FAX: 210-431-2220
E-MAIL: LBAGLEY@STMARYTX.EDU • WEBSITE: WWW.STMARYTX.EDU/MBA

Student Life and Environment

St. Mary's student body includes "many Hispanic women working toward improving their careers." The school has traditionally served the Hispanic community well; over half of all undergraduates here are Hispanic. On the whole, students "are diverse in age and cultures, all striving toward a common goal." Many "have careers and a family." Their classmates describe them as "team-oriented, hard-working, and friendly."

With over one million residents within city limits and almost as many living in the metropolitan area, San Antonio is the third-largest city in Texas and one of the larger cities in the country. The military and the petroleum industry both have major presences here. With nearly 20 million visitors every year, San Antonio is also a major player in the nation's tourism trade. Students speak highly of the city, although they warn that "the school is located in a very rough part of town."

Admissions

Applicants to the MBA program at St. Mary's must apply to the graduate school for admission. Applications are reviewed by the MBA program director, who makes recommendations to the Graduate Council. The council is then responsible for the final admissions decisions. Candidates must submit all of the following materials to the graduate admissions office: a completed application form; an official score report for the GMAT; two sets of official transcripts for all postsecondary academic work; two letters of recommendation "from individuals well acquainted with your academic/professional ability" (graduates of St. Mary's University are exempt from this requirement); and a completed health form (required by Texas State Law). An interview may also be required; candidates for whom an interview is required will be notified by the school. International applicants must provide all of the above materials as well as a signed financial statement; and, an official score report for the TOEFL (minimum acceptable score: 570 paper-based, 230 computer-based, 67 Internet; students with lower TOEFL scores may be allowed to attend the English Language School in order to meet minimum language proficiency requirements). Admitted students may receive regular admission, which is unconditional. Students may also receive conditional admission, which allows them to enroll in no more than nine hours of classes, after which their admission status is reappraised; or they may receive special admission as a nondegree seeking student. They may also receive auditor status, which is a noncredit option for students who are not working toward a graduate business degree.

FINANCIAL FACTS

Annual tuition	$19,500
Fees	$500
Cost of books	$750
Room & board	
(on/off-campus)	$6,000/$7,500
% of students receiving grants	26
Average grant	$24,000

ADMISSIONS

Admissions Selectivity Rating	**86**
# of applications received	65
% applicants accepted	62
% acceptees attending	100
Average GMAT	595
Range of GMAT	525–720
Average GPA	3.42
TOEFL required of	
international students	Yes
Minimum TOEFL	
(paper/computer)	570/230
Application fee	$0
International application fee	$0
Regular application deadline	Rolling
Regular notification	Rolling
Deferment available	Yes
Maximum length of	
deferment	1 year
Transfer students accepted	Yes
Transfer application policy	
May accept a maximum of 6	
Semester hours from AACSB-	
accredited programs.	
Non-fall admissions	Yes
Need-blind admissions	Yes

Applicants Also Look At

University of Texas Health Science Center at San Antonio.

STANFORD UNIVERSITY
STANFORD GRADUATE SCHOOL OF BUSINESS

GENERAL INFORMATION

Type of school	Private
Environment	City
Academic calendar	Quarter

SURVEY SAYS...

Good social scene
Good peer network
Cutting edge classes
Solid preparation in:
General management
Communication/interpersonal skills
Entrepreneurial studies

STUDENTS

Enrollment of parent institution	14,890
Enrollment of business school	740
% male/female	65/35
% minorities	20
% international	36
Average years work experience at entry	3.9

ACADEMICS

Academic Experience Rating	**98**
Student/faculty ratio	6:1
Profs interesting rating	82
Profs accessible rating	98
% female faculty	17
% minority faculty	9

Joint Degrees

JD/MBA, MBA/MA (Education), MBA/MS (Environment and Resources), MBA/MPP (Public Policy).

Prominent Alumni

Phil Knight, Founder and Chairman, Nike Inc.; Miles White, CEO/Chairman, Abbott Laboratories; Charles Schwab, Founder and Chairman, Charles Schwab & Co.; Jean-Pierre Garnier, CEO, GlaxoSmithKline; Richard Fairbank, CEO/Chairman, Capital One Financial Corporation.

Academics

Students are attracted to Stanford's "culture of entrepreneurship and social welfare," as well as its "strength in general management" and finance. "It's simply the best," explains one student, and the numerous students who turned down Harvard Business School for Stanford presumably agree. Anticipation runs high for the "exciting new curriculum," which debuts this year and will feature "a high degree of customization," mandatory "overseas experience," and a "leadership development program." The new second-year program offers a choice to take 16 out of more than 100 electives, ranging from "Strategy and Global Supply Networks" to "Entrepreneurial Design for Extreme Affordability," "Biodesign Innovation," "Managing Talent," and "Urban School System Reform." Overseas work encompasses international internships known as the Global Management Immersion Experience (GMIX), study trips ("Trips for 2007/2008 include Australia, Brazil, China, Ghana, Italy, Korea, Middle East, Russia, Scandinavia, Singapore/Malaysia, South Africa, and U.K./Ireland"), International Service Learning trips through the Public Management Program, and an exchange program with China's Tsinghua University School of Economics and Management. "This new curriculum is a huge differentiation point versus other b-schools, as Stanford is truly integrating new business trends and practices into not just course offerings but the entire methodology of education." "I wish I could reapply and start all over," comments one second-year.

"The weakest part of the school" may be the "overly bureaucratic" administration. Although one student sees administrators as "out of touch" and "cold-hearted," another says that the new curriculum proves they are "open to new ideas." As for faculty, "There's a highly academic culture among professors that places less value on teaching," says one student, "but it frankly hasn't affected the quality of my academic experience at all. My professors have mostly been very good and very accessible." "The professors are outstanding," affirms another student. "If you want to learn from accomplished, extremely successful businesspeople, . . . this is where they teach!" Another says, "I regularly eat lunch with one of the most successful venture capitalists in the Valley, who happens to be teaching my entrepreneurship elective."

Career and Placement

As far as job placement, there really is a Stanford difference. "If you want to learn how to effectively start and/or run a business, I would be hard pressed to find a school with more resources and a better network," says one student. Sure enough, about 10 percent of the class goes into entrepreneurship immediately after graduation. Stanford's outstanding relationship with high tech, private equity, and venture capital means that 21 percent of grads go into these fields. Location is everything—a slight majority of students stay on the West Coast, and more than a tenth go abroad, while only about a fifth work in the MBA-saturated Northeast. The median first-year salary for grads is $110,000. Students tell us that Stanford creates "a sense of perspective in its students that extends past their future professional lives. Stanford graduates well-rounded MBAs who will likely do well in many aspects of life, not just their job."

Student Life and Environment

Students describe the Stanford environment as a "cooperative culture" of "excellence without the arrogance," and are awed by the talent and diversity of their classmates. "My peers come from backgrounds in everything from international development to finance to consulting to education to entrepreneurship. Hearing their experiences and working with them is what has made the program." Students are more likely to have undergraduate

ADMISSIONS CONTACT: DERRICK BOLTON, DIRECTOR OF MBA ADMISSIONS
ADDRESS: 518 MEMORIAL WAY STANFORD, CA 94305-5015 UNITED STATES
PHONE: 650-723-2766 • FAX: 650-725-7831
E-MAIL: • WEBSITE: WWW.GSB.STANFORD.EDU

degrees in the humanities and social sciences and to possess advanced degrees than students at many other schools. They "are not just competent in one area but they are also intellectuals and athletes and musicians and entrepreneurs and board members and highly socially adept. Stanford GSB is a beautifully humbling experience because you are truly amongst the best of the best." Grades are not disclosed, and students are "collaborative"; they "reach out to help each other without being asked." Social life here is very active. These students "know how to juggle academic work with other club activities and partying," and many "want to spend the 2 years getting to know their classmates as well as possible."

The spacious campus has the feel and many of the luxuries of an exclusive resort. Gardens and palm trees surround university buildings, the weather is fine, sports facilities are excellent, and few strangers venture onto campus. "This morning I had a breakfast meeting with a designer from the design firm IDEO about a business I am working on with classmates, then went to the pool for a workout with some friends who are doing the Wildflower Triathlon with me," reports one student. Stanford is the hub of Silicon Valley, "a perfect location for someone looking to get into high tech," and for many entrepreneurs-in-training, that's excitement enough. One student tells us that "everyone talks about starting their own ventures." If neighboring Palo Alto feels "a bit boring and yuppity, . . . fortunately, San Francisco is only 30 minutes away" by car.

Admissions

The GSB Admissions Office says that candidates should not include academic recommendations unless they reflect work experience (as a TA or research assistant, for example). The top criteria for admission are "intellectual vitality," "demonstrated leadership potential," and "personal qualities and contributions"—Stanford looks for community leaders—so the "impact [you made] on [your] workplace" matters much more than your job responsibilities. Students report a broad range of GMAT scores, with a median of 720 (the GRE is also acceptable in some cases), and a median TOEFL score of 283.

FINANCIAL FACTS

Annual tuition	$48,921
Cost of books	$3,714
Room & board	
(on/off-campus)	$19,932/$22,602
% of students receiving aid	74
% of first-year students	
receiving aid	80
% of students receiving loans	59
% of students receiving grants	62
Average award package	$48,915
Average grant	$18,341
Average student loan debt	$72,500

ADMISSIONS

Admissions Selectivity Rating	99
# of applications received	5,741
% applicants accepted	8
% acceptees attending	79
Average GMAT	721
Range of GMAT	700–750
Average GPA	3.6
TOEFL required of	
international students	Yes
Minimum TOEFL	
(paper/computer)	600/250
Application fee	$250
International application fee	$250
Application Deadline/Notification	
Round 1:	10/22 / 01/24
Round 2:	01/07 / 04/03
Round 3:	03/21 / 05/15
Deferment available	Yes
Need-blind admissions	Yes

Applicants Also Look At
Harvard University.

EMPLOYMENT PROFILE

Career Rating	99	Grads Employed by Function	% Avg. Salary
Primary Source of Full-time Job Acceptances		Finance	39 $130,053
School-facilitated activities	160 (58%)	Marketing	14 $104,000
Graduate-facilitated activities	115 (42%)	Operations	5 $96,076
Percent employed	94	Strategic Planning	8 $111,153
		Consulting	5 $115,168
		General Management	3 $124,375
		Venture Capital	2 $142,500
		Other	5 $90,208

Top 5 Employers Hiring Grads
Amazon.com; Bain and Co.; Booz Allen Hamilton Inc.; Goldman Sachs; Google

STATE UNIVERSITY OF NEW YORK AT BINGHAMTON
SCHOOL OF MANAGEMENT

GENERAL INFORMATION
Type of school	Public
Environment	Town
Academic calendar	Semester

SURVEY SAYS...
Smart classrooms
Solid preparation in:
General management
Teamwork
Presentation skills
Computer skills

STUDENTS
Enrollment of parent institution	14,716
Enrollment of business school	114
% male/female	68/32
% out-of-state	7
% part-time	4
% minorities	6
% international	41
Average age at entry	23
Average years work experience at entry	1.8

ACADEMICS
Academic Experience Rating	**85**
Student/faculty ratio	6:1
Profs interesting rating	86
Profs accessible rating	70
% female faculty	18
% minority faculty	1

Joint Degrees
MS/MBA (Engineering) 5 years,
BA/MBA (Arts & Sciences) 5 years.

Academics

"Close proximity to New York City," an "excellent reputation in New York and elsewhere" (not just for the MBA program but for the entire school, as "SUNY has a worldwide reputation"), and a "small incoming class with a diverse population" that ensures students won't get lost in the crowd are among the top reasons given for choosing the MBA program at Binghamton University. It also doesn't hurt that it "all comes with an extremely reasonable price tag."

The four-semester MBA program at Binghamton University employs "an extremely team-based approach" to education "that replicates real-world business in a way many other business programs do not," students here inform us. This is especially true in the first year, during which the program covers core essentials. One student explains, "The first year of the program requires students to stick with a set group of students to work on projects, presentations, papers, and cases. It can be difficult at times, but the lessons learned are crucial for the real world." Students also feel that "the cohort teams are really good for discussing with prospective employers, as it shows the ability to work together with many diverse people to come to one end result." The school also offers a Fast Track MBA to Binghamton undergraduates; the program allows them to earn both a BA and an MBA in five years, no small feat considering that a Binghamton MBA requires 70 credits, "more than any other university."

For a state school, BU provides excellent service. Students tell us that "The school really tries to adapt to the latest management concepts and ideals" and that administrators "continually make improvements to meet all of our needs." Professors here "want to see their students succeed and are happy to give the time to help them with any hardship they may face in the MBA program." The only knock on them is that "Many are foreign," so that "sometimes it is difficult to understand what is being said due to accents." Most often, however, instructors "can communicate easily with the students, and they do not use their native language even when conversing with students from the same country, which is very professional." Another asset to the program is that "the alumni that are in highly respected companies are great, and everyone really tries to pull for other Binghamton students."

Career and Placement

For a small program, Binghamton does a good job of bringing some major recruiters to its relatively remote location. One student informs us that "we have powerhouse recruiters from Credit Suisse, Goldman Sachs, the big four accounting, all the engineering firms, as well as many others. Without question the recruiting at this school is on an incredible climb upwards. More and more powerhouse companies are coming to Binghamton, who in the past have not." The Career Development Center here offers counseling services, career workshops, resume-development services, resume-referral services, a career-resource library, and access to the alumni network.

Top employers of Binghamton MBAs include Ernst & Young, Deloitte, KPMG, Lockheed Martin, and Target. Ninety percent of all graduates remain in the Middle Atlantic States or New England. The average starting salary for a Binghamton MBA graduating in 2007 was $54,409, with those in finance and accounting doing best (average starting salary $64,666).

Student Life and Environment

"First-year classes for the fall are all held in the evenings" at Binghamton, which "leads to very long days, especially for those who also have part-time jobs" and thus hampers extracurricular involvement. As students progress through the program, however, the school offers "many opportunities for interested students to get involved, from the GSO (Graduate Student Organization) to the GMA (Graduate Management Association)." The latter "implements various activities throughout the year: coffee hours, open bars, networking events," "horseback riding, bowling, etc." The university also "has a great Division I athletic department that provides exciting competitions for the students to attend," and many do.

The city of Binghamton "has lots of things going for it besides the downtown bar scene. For one thing there is a hometown hockey team and baseball team, an opera house, numerous playhouses, and theaters, too. We are also the carousel capital of the United States. Binghamton is ethnically diverse as well, there are often ethnic festivals going on throughout the Southern Tier. Plus if you are a golf fan, we were home to a PGA tour event for 35 years, and now we are home to a Champions Tour Event." Also, "living expenses here are not much," especially when compared to the cost of living in much of the rest of the state.

Admissions

Applicants to the Binghamton MBA program must submit two copies of official undergraduate transcripts for all college work, two letters of recommendation, a personal statement, a resume, and GMAT scores. Work experience, while preferred, is not required. Additionally, international students must submit a certified statement of financial responsibility and TOEFL scores (minimum acceptable score is 580). A basic understanding of calculus is "strongly recommended" for all incoming students; strong calculus skills are necessary for those interested in studying finance or operations management.

To attract minority applicants, the School of Management offers the Clifford D. Clark Graduate Fellowship Program for Underrepresented Minority Students. According to the school, "These fellowships are granted to students entering both master's and doctoral degree programs and carry stipends of between $6,800 and $12,750 (depending on discipline) for the academic year plus a full-tuition scholarship. Renewals or graduate assistantships may be awarded in subsequent years, depending upon availability of funds."

FINANCIAL FACTS

Annual tuition (in-state/ out-of-state)	$7,100/$11,340
Fees	$1,019
Cost of books	$1,500
Room & board (on/off-campus)	$0/$6,800
% of students receiving aid	62
% of first-year students receiving aid	44
% of students receiving loans	30
% of students receiving grants	28
Average award package	$8,275
Average grant	$8,275
Average student loan debt	$23,047

ADMISSIONS

Admissions Selectivity Rating	83
# of applications received	223
% applicants accepted	70
% acceptees attending	54
Average GMAT	617
Range of GMAT	580–640
Average GPA	3.39
TOEFL required of international students	Yes
Minimum TOEFL (paper/computer)	580/237
Application fee	$60
International application fee	$60
Regular application deadline	3/15
Regular notification	rolling
Deferment available	Yes
Maximum length of deferment	1 year
Need-blind admissions	Yes

Applicants Also Look At

Albany Law School, City University of New York—Baruch College, State University of New York—University at Buffalo, SUNY—College at Geneseo, Syracuse University, TEST.

EMPLOYMENT PROFILE

Career Rating	80	Grads Employed by Function	% Avg. Salary
Primary Source of Full-time Job Acceptances		Finance	24 $63,833
School-facilitated activities	20 (80%)	Marketing	24 $52,167
Unknown	6 (20%)	MIS	16 $62,375
Average base starting salary	$58,350	Operations	4 $59,000
Percent employed	67	Consulting	28 $57,800
		Other	4 $65,000

Top 5 Employers Hiring Grads
Protiviti; KPMG; Lockheed Martin; Deloitte; Ernst & Young

State University of New York—Oswego

School of Business

GENERAL INFORMATION

Type of school	Public
Academic calendar	Semester

SURVEY SAYS...
Friendly students
Smart classrooms
Solid preparation in:
Accounting
Teamwork
Presentation skills
Quantitative skills

STUDENTS

Enrollment of parent institution	8,660
Enrollment of business school	66
% male/female	44/56
% part-time	35
% minorities	6
% international	29
Average age at entry	26
Average years work experience at entry	5

ACADEMICS

Academic Experience Rating	**67**
Student/faculty ratio	19:1
Profs interesting rating	73
Profs accessible rating	85
% female faculty	12
% minority faculty	35

Prominent Alumni
Al Roker, NBC Meteorologist; Alice McDermott, Award Winning Author; Ken Auleta, New Yorker Columnist & critically acclaimed author; Kendis Gibson, CNN Anchor; Heraldo Munoz, Ambassador of Chile to the United Nations.

Academics

Students who enroll in the School of Business at SUNY Oswego can expect several things: excellent value for their money, intimate classes, knowledgeable professors, state-of-the-art facilities, and an excellent hockey team. As one student puts it, "In most areas, the school of business is at the top of its class. The classes are challenging and worthwhile. Most professors are really good at their areas. They are also widely available to help students both inside and out of class." According to most of the students, the "very small classes promote learning and student-professor interaction."

Designed as a degree in general management, an MBA from SUNY Oswego provides a solid grounding in the basics of modern business organization. The school says that "this program is intended to be equally applicable to private, public, and governmental sectors of management." The core subjects required of students include management, accounting, marketing, organization, law, and finance. In addition, students can choose to specialize in a specific field such as international management, manufacturing management, organizational leadership, or financial services. Core requirements include management information systems, managerial finance, marketing management, management science I, international business, global perspectives on organizational management, and management policy. A wide range of electives is also available to students at SUNY Oswego, including management economics, database development, collective bargaining, industrial and organizational psychology, industrial sociology, principles of forecasting, business research, futures and options markets, database development, project management, public-sector accounting, and advanced auditing.

Students find their course work both rigorous and exciting. As one puts it, "the professors are excellent and the classes are fun and challenging." Another says, "the course load is challenging, requiring solid communication and organization skills. Many professors are conducting research on global trade, accounting, and management science. My academic experience has been very positive. I would suggest Oswego to all prospective business students (undergraduate or graduate)."

Career and Placement

Although Oswego has a lot to offer—lovely campus, low cost, quality education, intimate program—most students wish it would go further in strengthening its Career Services department. There is little aid specifically for prospective MBAs, and the job search is often directed almost entirely by the student. As one puts it, "Connecting with employers is a difficult task. Linking up with quality employers looking for graduates with postgraduate degrees needs to be addressed."

ADMISSIONS CONTACT: GRADUATE OFFICE, DAVID W. KING, DEAN GRADUATE STUDIES
ADDRESS: 602 CULKIN HALL, SUNY OSWEGO OSWEGO, NY 13126 UNITED STATES
PHONE: 315-312-3692 • FAX: 315-312-3577
E-MAIL: MBA@OSWEGO.EDU • WEBSITE: WWW.OSWEGO.EDU/BUSINESS/MBA

Student Life and Environment

Students at SUNY Oswego rave about their "beautiful campus," which, they proudly point out, is also extremely "technologically advanced and mostly wireless." The typical MBA's social life is strong, and there are "plenty of bars around for an active nightlife." As one student says, "At Oswego, I had the opportunity to make new friends from all over the world. The social life is active and I consider myself lucky." For the most part, students claim to be "very active on campus. There is a multitude of clubs and organizations to choose from." Students enjoy their "great gyms to work out in or play a game of racquetball." Plus—as is typical in upstate New York—the school's athletic life centers on their "excellent hockey team, instead of football." As one student puts it, "what's excellent about living on campus here is that there is every resource that you could possibly need available on campus. There are new buildings and renovations, from a new student center to the newly renovated freshman residence hall and new business center with technology classrooms."

Admissions

To be considered for admission to the small MBA program at the School of Business at SUNY Oswego, a candidate must have a minimum GPA of 2.6 out of 4.0. The minimum required score for the GMAT is 450, unless the applicant's native language is not English, in which case the minimum score is 400. Taking the TOEFL test is also required for students whose native language is not English.

FINANCIAL FACTS

Annual tuition (in-state/ out-of-state)	$7,100/$11,340
Fees	$764
Cost of books	$800
Room & board	$9,470
% of students receiving aid	73
% of first-year students receiving aid	32
% of students receiving loans	42
% of students receiving grants	19
Average award package	$20,644
Average grant	$339
Average student loan debt	$23,824

ADMISSIONS

Admissions Selectivity Rating	67
# of applications received	84
% applicants accepted	76
% acceptees attending	48
Average GMAT	501
Range of GMAT	290–650
Average GPA	3.11
TOEFL required of international students	Yes
Minimum TOEFL (paper/computer)	560/220
Application fee	$50
Regular application deadline	4/15
Regular notification	6/1
Deferment available	Yes
Maximum length of deferment	1 year
Transfer students accepted	Yes
Transfer application policy Two classes may be transferred into the program	
Non-fall admissions	Yes
Need-blind admissions	Yes

Applicants Also Look At

Albany Law School, State University of New York—University at Buffalo, TEST.

EMPLOYMENT PROFILE

Career Rating	70	Grads Employed by Function	%	Avg. Salary
		Finance	10	$38,000
		Human Resources	5	NR
		MIS	5	NR
		Operations	10	NR
		General Management	5	NR
		Quantitative	5	NR
		Non-profit	10:	NR

STATE UNIVERSITY OF NEW YORK—UNIVERSITY AT ALBANY
SCHOOL OF BUSINESS

GENERAL INFORMATION
Type of school   Public
Environment   City

SURVEY SAYS...
Solid preparation in:
Finance
General management
Teamwork
Communication/interpersonal skills
Presentation skills

STUDENTS
Enrollment of parent institution	17,000
Enrollment of business school	285
% male/female	40/60
% out-of-state	40
% part-time	75
% minorities	16
% international	36
Average age at entry	28
Average years work experience at entry	5

ACADEMICS
Academic Experience Rating	**73**
Student/faculty ratio	30:1
Profs interesting rating	72
Profs accessible rating	63
% female faculty	12
% minority faculty	1

Joint Degrees
MS/MBA (Science Nanoscale Engineering) 2 years.

Prominent Alumni
Kimberly Welsh, Managing Director, Morgan Stanley; Dale Carleton, Vice Chairman (Retired), State Street Corporation; Steve Rotella, President/CEO, Chase Manhattan Mortgage Corp.; Harold Cramer, VP, Exxon Mobil Fuels; Anthony McCarthy, Global CIO, Investment Banking, Deutsche Bank.

Academics

Students in the MBA programs at State University of New York—University at Albany School of Business love that the school "constantly updates the curriculum to mirror current business trends." In its full-time and various part-time programs, Albany uses "a combination of classroom instruction and applied experience" to prepare students for the business world of tomorrow.

About one in four MBA students at Albany attend the program full-time. This number includes the majority of international students, who account for approximately 20 percent of the student body. The full-time program takes two years to complete. The first year is dedicated to core competencies; students undertake in-depth study in accounting, economics, finance, human resources, information systems, and marketing. Case studies play a central role in classroom study, as do reading assignments and classes that divide time between lectures and discussions. Group projects supplement the curriculum and offer students opportunities to develop important teamwork skills. The first year culminates in a one-week integrative course that addresses social, legal, and political issues in international business. According to students, the first-year curriculum "is heavily weighted toward global business and the changing economy."

The second year of the full-time program—which also allows students to develop an area of specialization—focuses on technology, an area in which Albany excels. Students praise the school's "cutting-edge use of technology and IT knowledge" and note that "everyone learns IT here." Students' work in this area reaches its high point in an information systems-based field project during which students provide consulting services to such organizations as the Albany Medical Center, DuPont, GE, KeyCorp, PepsiCo, Tiffany & Co., Towers Perrin, and a variety of regional nonprofits. The field project consumes one-third of the second-year curriculum, with a hands-on approach that prepares students for full-time employment.

Albany also offers several part-time options. In the Evening MBA Program, classes convene once a week in three-hour sessions. The program is "extremely flexible" and allows students to enter during the Fall, Spring, or Summer semester. Evening MBA program students may use elective classes to develop a specialization in management information systems, management, marketing, finance, new venture development, or tax. A Weekend MBA Program is also available; its classes meet every other weekend, with classes held on Friday afternoons and all day Saturday. It now also includes a one-week international business experience. This program meets off campus at a satellite facility in Saratoga. Students may enter the program in the fall only, and enrollment is limited to 24 students per year.

Career and Placement

Albany's School of Business maintains its own Career Services Office, whose work is supplemented by the school's Career Development Center, which serves the entire university. The Career Services Office provides workshops on cover letter writing, resume writing, interviewing, developing job-search skills, and honing business-related social skills. MBAs who graduate from Albany receive job offers from many small and medium-sized businesses as well as from such business giants as Accenture, Bear Stearns, Deloitte Consulting, Deutsche Bank, Ernst & Young, Goldman Sachs, IBM, KPMG & International, Merrill Lynch, and PricewaterhouseCoopers. Results from a recent survey indicate that MBAs typically receive initial offers in the $60,000 range.

Student Life and Environment

Most students in the Albany MBA program attend part-time; they have little time to devote to extracurricular life because of their commitments to course work, careers, and family. The program attracts "many area IT professionals and their coworkers," but the student body is fairly diverse, with participants "from many different fields, industries, career levels, and cultural backgrounds." Students tell us that "it is a wonderful experience to be in a classroom with people that have very diversified backgrounds."

Nearly 17,000 students are enrolled in the nine degree-granting schools and colleges at the State University of New York at Albany. Like all large state universities, it pursues the mission of offering an affordable education to state residents while also providing the state and country with cutting-edge research. The university was founded in 1844; undergraduate business study was not added to the curriculum until 1970. Graduate business programs began a few years later. Facilities include classrooms and computer labs equipped with the latest high-tech accoutrements; these serve the program's focus on technology well. Students appreciate the facilities but note that "the campus buildings should be spruced up a bit. The buildings are old and unattractive."

Admissions

Applicants to the MBA program at the State University of New York at Albany School of Business must provide the graduate admissions department with all of the following: official copies of transcripts for all postsecondary academic work, an official score report for the GMAT, a resume, three letters of recommendation, and a personal statement of purpose. International applicants must provide all of the above plus an official score report for the TOEFL (minimum acceptable score: 600 paper-based; 250 computer-based); and a financial affidavit accompanied by appropriate supporting documentation to demonstrate the applicant's "ability to meet all educational and living expenses for the entire period of intended study." Furthermore, international academic transcripts in languages other than English must be accompanied by a certified English translation.

FINANCIAL FACTS

Annual tuition (in-state/ out-of-state)	$7,100/$11,340
Fees	$1,220
Cost of books	$1,000
Room & board (on/off-campus)	$9,000/$7,500
% of students receiving aid	34
% of first-year students receiving aid	32
% of students receiving grants	34
Average award package	$7,600
Average grant	$3,400

ADMISSIONS

Admissions Selectivity Rating	**85**
# of applications received	261
% applicants accepted	61
% acceptees attending	96
Average GMAT	578
Range of GMAT	550–660
Average GPA	3.39
TOEFL required of international students	Yes
Minimum TOEFL (paper/computer)	600/250
Application fee	$75
International application fee	$75
Regular application deadline	5/1
Regular notification	6/1
Deferment available	Yes
Maximum length of deferment	1 year
Transfer students accepted	Yes
Transfer application policy We accept up to 50% transfer credit in each program of study	
Non-fall admissions	Yes
Need-blind admissions	Yes

Applicants Also Look At
Fordham University, State University of New York at Binghamton, State University of New York—University at Buffalo.

EMPLOYMENT PROFILE

Career Rating	72	Grads Employed by Function	%	Avg. Salary
Primary Source of Full-time Job Acceptances		Finance	31	$50,000
School-facilitated activities	28 (78%)	Human Resources	24	$55,000
Graduate-facilitated activities	8 (22%)	Consulting	31	$60,000
Average base starting salary	$55,500	General Management	14	$55,000
Percent employed	62	**Top 5 Employers Hiring Grads**		
		Deloitte Consulting; KPMG; New York State; Price Waterhouse Coopers		

STATE UNIVERSITY OF NEW YORK—UNIVERSITY AT BUFFALO
SCHOOL OF MANAGEMENT

Academics

Students come to the "very affordable" and "reputable" State University of New York—University at Buffalo School of Management to get a great education at a great price. Teamwork defines the Buffalo experience. First-year students spend 8–12 hours a week in their assigned study groups, a commitment that represents "the second most important aspect of the program next to class attendance," according to the university. One student warns that the "UB business school is highly dedicated to working in teams. If you are an individualistic individual you will most likely not like this environment." Ten study groups make up a cohort. The members of a cohort take core management courses together during the first year. Of these courses, students say statistics arguably "has the heaviest workload." Students take "one or two [additional] electives each semester."

For most students, the second year is about customization. University at Buffalo offers a variety of specialized tracks, including entrepreneurship, accounting-corporate reporting and control, finance, global services and supply management, information assurance, information systems and e-business, international management, management consulting, marketing management, supply chains and operations management, and workforce management. UB's highly regarded finance major is bolstered by semesters and workshops at SUNY's Levin Institute in Manhattan. Much of the faculty is simply "outstanding," and "Most courses are of moderate workload." Students also rate the administration as "one of the best," willing to "bend over backward to help current students." MBA candidates wish for a dedicated library, and increased "course offerings," made possible by "more teachers."

Career and Placement

Student opinion is divided on the helpfulness of UB's Career Resource Center (CRC). Enthusiastic students say the office "goes beyond the requirements to make sure that students are totally prepared for all aspects of the recruiting process. From the minute that you walk in the door, they have a checkpoint system to make sure that you are on track for obtaining a job after graduation." Alumni networking events such as a "cruise on Lake Erie" "allow MS/MBA students to discuss real-world industry experiences and how best to prepare for the job market."

Detractors contend that while the CRC "is great for students with [fewer] than 5 years of work experience" and its "technological resources are excellent," it doesn't draw "big recruiters outside the accounting discipline" and is too focused on the local area. Additionally, students say the CRC "does a poor job of prepping companies for on-campus job fairs; many company reps come unprepared to discuss opportunities with MS/MBA students." "I know many people who submitted resumes through the CRC for internships and did not get phone calls. However, when they later submitted them themselves, they did get phone calls," says a second-year. Average starting salary for the class of 2007 was $54,282. Top employers include Deloitte Touche Tohmatsu, Ernst & Young, M&T Bank, PepsiCo, and PricewaterhouseCoopers

ADMISSIONS CONTACT: JAIMIE FALZARANO, ASSISTANT DIRECTOR OF GRADUATE PROGRAMS
ADDRESS: 203 ALFIERO CENTER BUFFALO, NY 14260 UNITED STATES
PHONE: 716-645-3204 • FAX: 716-645-2341
E-MAIL: SOM-APPS@BUFFALO.EDU • WEBSITE: MGT.BUFFALO.EDU

Student Life and Environment

The collegiality of the classroom environment at SUNY Buffalo spills over into the social life on campus, and the "competitive, cheerful" students spend their weekends "unwinding and getting to know each other" better. A bevy of organized activities exist for just this purpose. "The Graduate Management Association has a free happy hour each Friday to make sure students interact outside of the classroom. Additionally, they host at least one major social every month." "There are lots of student clubs and athletic activities, so [students] can get to know people with similar interests." The city of Buffalo, which boasts a conveniently "low cost of living," offers diversions like "Buffalo Sabres and Bills" games. Students say "There is always something to do at UB."

Buffalo's "hardworking and diverse" MBA students often come in "fresh," i.e., "with no [full-time] work experience." Some students gripe that this makes for "a challenging team environment when someone with years of experience enters" a study group. The cultural expertise of international students, who make up approximately 40 percent of the class, is highly valued: "We have country forums every month where students from a particular country can talk about their culture, traditions, and most importantly, the business practices in their country." American students tend to be "from the local area," and students say the school should "make a stronger effort to recruit minorities not represented in the business profession." One student notes that the school "needs more effort in European and Latin American recruitment," and recommends that the School of Management "offer financial aid for international students whose global experiences are not represented."

Admissions

Average GMAT and TOEFL scores for the class of 2009 were 619 and 256 respectively; the average student holds 2 years of work experience. International students (except in the case of a limited list of 16 Indian universities) must supplement 3-year degrees with an additional year of scholarship. The Admissions Office warns that criteria will be more selective for its future classes, which will be 43 percent smaller at just 100 students.

FINANCIAL FACTS

Annual tuition (in-state/ out-of-state)	$7,100/$11,340
Fees	$1,315
Cost of books	$1,025
Room & board	$9,300
% of students receiving aid	25
% of first-year students receiving aid	20
% of students receiving grants	25
Average award package	$14,000
Average grant	$5,000

ADMISSIONS

Admissions Selectivity Rating	89
# of applications received	369
% applicants accepted	45
% acceptees attending	49
Average GMAT	619
Range of GMAT	540–710
Average GPA	3.3
TOEFL required of international students	Yes
Minimum TOEFL (paper/computer)	573/230
Application fee	$50
International application fee	$50
Application Deadline/Notification	
Round 1:	11/15 / 12/21
Round 2:	2/1 / 2/29
Round 3:	3/10 / 4/4
Round 4:	5/1 / 5/23
Deferment available	Yes
Maximum length of deferment	1 year
Need-blind admissions	Yes

Applicants Also Look At

Boston University, Canisius College, City University of New York—Baruch College, State University of New York at Binghamton, The University of Texas at Dallas, University of Pittsburgh, University of Rochester.

EMPLOYMENT PROFILE

Career Rating	79	Grads Employed by Function	% Avg. Salary
Primary Source of Full-time Job Acceptances		Finance	43 $50,500
School-facilitated activities	48 (67%)	Human Resources	8 $61,300
Graduate-facilitated activities	23 (32%)	Marketing	20 $56,250
Unknown	1 (1%)	MIS	8 $54,000
Average base starting salary	$54,282	Operations	11 $55,286
Percent employed	75	Consulting	5 $64,000
		General Management	5 $52,333

Top 5 Employers Hiring Grads
M & T Bank; Citi; PriceWaterhouseCoopers; Ernst & Young; Fisher-Price

STETSON UNIVERSITY
SCHOOL OF BUSINESS ADMINISTRATION

Academics

One of the advantages of small programs like the Stetson University School of Business Administration—which sometimes hosts fewer than 20 students—is that you really "get to know each other." As one student says, "The faculty and administration at Stetson are easily accessible and extremely supportive. Everyone is on a first-name basis, and the individual attention makes me feel as if my money was well spent." Many claim that the "nicest thing is that the school is small, and class sizes are small." One student says, "I have had a great experience at Stetson and am glad that I chose this school for my graduate-level classes. The professors always have time to talk to you and help you [and]. . . the administration is great and will help you whenever you need it."

The school, which is located on campuses throughout central Florida, "offers classes in three locations to serve the needs of not just the full-time student but also the working student." The locations are situated "throughout central Florida, including Orlando and Tampa, two of the largest metropolitan areas in Florida and two major job markets." Other students point out that "the proximity of the school to major job markets like Orlando, Tampa, and Jacksonville is a major strength of the program" that helps to draw "Many international students and working professionals with a passion for business!"

Stetson's MBA offers a general business management degree, though students can choose to specialize in a number of different areas. According to the school, "[The] programs are designed not to make you a technical specialist, but rather to provide you with a range of knowledge needed by the professional manager." The MBA program is divided into two parts: the business foundation and the advanced-level courses. Students appreciate the focus of the program along with its "current curriculum" taught by "very knowledgeable" and "concerned" professors. Others have been extremely impressed by "the professional experience that the faculty brings from their diverse backgrounds" and how "Everyone is encouraged to work in teams and [to] get to know each other."

Stetson also offers several special programs for its business students including the Family Business Center, the Joseph C. Prince Entrepreneurial Program, and the Roland George Investments Program. Stetson also has a summer school abroad program in Innsbruck, Austria, that is open to students in all majors and concentrations. Still, many students would like to see "an entrepreneurship program for students interested in that field" as well as more offerings in "economics" and "stock market overview." Another complaint is the uneven distribution of classes among the campuses. Though DeLand houses the main campus, many students complain that "the course offerings at the Celebration campus in Orlando and the Law School campus in Gulfport are not as plentiful as in DeLand."

Career and Placement

Stetson's Career Management Office offers a variety of services to its MBA students including "individual career counseling, career planning and development in the classroom, resume referrals, internship development, full-time placement, on-campus recruiting, mock interviews, and the Business and Industry Speaker Series presentations." However, some students still express dissatisfaction with the office, feeling it "needs improvement."

ADMISSIONS CONTACT: DR. FRANK A. DEZOORT, DIRECTOR, GRADUATE BUSINESS PROGRAMS
ADDRESS: 421 NORTH WOODLAND BOULEVARD, UNIT 8398 DELAND, FL 32723 UNITED STATES
PHONE: 386-822-7410 • FAX: 386-822-7413
E-MAIL: MBA@STETSON.EDU • WEBSITE: WWW.STETSON.EDU/BUSINESS

Student Life and Environment

With campuses in DeLand (20 minutes north of Orlando), Celebration (located in Orlando), and Gulfport (near St. Petersburg), Stetson University has the advantages of pleasant weather, active campus life, vital student athletics, and an extremely friendly student body. As a "values-centered, comprehensive, private liberal arts university," Stetson promises on its website that all of its students will be "challenged by [the] academic programs in more than 40 disciplines. Just as importantly, [students] will learn about life and all the opportunities it holds." As one student says, "We have a well-rounded class with a global perspective. The facilities are modern, and the campus is beautiful. The class sizes are small, and the competition is stiff." Many note the wide variety of activities on campus. "The school has so many clubs, sororities, fraternities, and intramurals," enthuses one student, while another explains his reasons for staying out of the fray: "The market keeps me plenty busy (and fishing on my boat)."

Besides the fact that "the student body feels like a small community where most people know each other," students are impressed that they've "met so many wonderful people while going to Stetson." To take a break from MBA stress, students decompress with their peers at beaches, bars, restaurants, and clubs. And then there's the omnipresent Disney World, "conveniently located less than 30 minutes from Daytona, which offers students wonderful, inexpensive nightlife and vacation spots."

Admissions

All applicants to Stetson's MBA program must have received a BA from an accredited college or university. Stetson is quick to point out that "the undergraduate degree need not be in business administration" since "the course of study is specifically designed to accommodate the non-business as well as the business degree holder." (According to the school, this combination of an "MBA with a non-business undergraduate degree is considered outstanding career preparation in many fields.") MBA applicants must submit GMAT scores, undergraduate transcripts, three letters of recommendation, a medical report, and a recent photograph of themselves in order to be considered.

FINANCIAL FACTS

Annual tuition	$18,000
Fees	$0
Cost of books	$1,400

ADMISSIONS

Admissions Selectivity Rating	**71**
# of applications received	209
% applicants accepted	90
% acceptees attending	83
Average GMAT	529
Range of GMAT	425–690
Average GPA	3.5
TOEFL required of international students	Yes
Minimum TOEFL (paper/computer)	550/213
Application fee	$25
International application fee	$25
Regular application deadline	5/31
Regular notification	6/30
Application Deadline/Notification	
Round 1:	01/01 / 1/11
Round 2:	3/1 / 3/15
Round 3:	5/1 / 5/15
Round 4:	8/1 / 8/12
Deferment available	Yes
Maximum length of deferment	1 year
Transfer students accepted	Yes
Transfer application policy Maximum 6 credit hours from AACSB	
Non-fall admissions	Yes
Need-blind admissions	Yes

EMPLOYMENT PROFILE	
Career Rating	75

SUFFOLK UNIVERSITY
SAWYER BUSINESS SCHOOL

GENERAL INFORMATION

Type of school	Private
Environment	Metropolis
Academic calendar	Semester

SURVEY SAYS...

Students love Boston, MA
Solid preparation in:
Doing business in a global economy

STUDENTS

Enrollment of parent institution	9,231
Enrollment of business school	703
% male/female	59/41
% out-of-state	5
% part-time	84
% minorities	6
% international	56
Average age at entry	27
Average years work experience at entry	4.1

ACADEMICS

Academic Experience Rating	**68**
Student/faculty ratio	15:1
Profs interesting rating	73
Profs accessible rating	85
% female faculty	30
% minority faculty	16

Joint Degrees

MBA/MS (Accounting) 1.5–2 years,
MBA/MS (Finance) 1.5–2 years,
MBA/MS (Taxation) 1.5–2 years,
JD/MBA 4–5 years.

Prominent Alumni

Robert Mudge, New England Region President, Verizon; Tara Taylor, VP, State Street Global Advisors; Edward J. Boudreau, Chmn, John Hancock Advisers, Inc; Peter Gicheru, Finance Controller, Coca-Cola South Africa.

Academics

When singing the praises of their Boston-based business school, Suffolk University students immediately mention the kindness and quality of their professors. Among the school's talented teaching staff "Most—over 95 percent—hold PhDs, and all are extremely passionate about the subject they are teaching." However, they aren't just knowledgeable; they are also dedicated educators. One current student adds, "One word describes Suffolk faculty: that is 'commitment.' Rain, snow, or sunlight, professors are available at any time through e-mail, phone, or by appointment." In fact, the entire institution is very student oriented. In addition to seeking help from their professors, Suffolk offers "many mentoring programs, networking programs, and advisors who are willing to help."

Boasting a sizable part-time population, many students choose Suffolk University because of its flexible scheduling options, which allows students to take courses at the main campus, at one of the many "satellite locations outside of Boston," or via the Internet. In that and many ways, Suffolk, "really caters to creating the optimal experience for someone who is working full-time and going to school part-time." Whether studying full-time or part-time, all Suffolk MBAs are required to take three introductory courses, plus 24 units of core course work in areas such as management, economics, and marketing. After completing these requirements, Suffolk students have a great deal of liberty in planning their educations, because the school offers more than 100 electives in areas such as accounting and finance, entrepreneurship, health administration, information systems, international business, and marketing.

A large percentage of the school's full-time students hail from outside the United States, which adds a "fresh, firsthand, and global intelligence to the classroom." Students appreciate the international angle, describing themselves as "a business-focused 'United Nations'—working together to learn about business and our place it." The school further demonstrates its commitment to an international business education through core and elective course work, including a series of global-travel seminars. These week-long courses are conducted in a foreign country and "At least two professors attend and really take part in the learning experience with the students."

Students further praise Suffolk's "commitment to group work and real business cases/studies," saying the teaching methodology reflects the fact that "important business decisions are not made [by] taking a written exam but by how you react in a situation and under pressure." Students have the chance to stretch their wings in the classroom thanks to "smaller class sizes, typically 25 to 35, where I . . . have the opportunity to share my working and leadership experiences as well as hearing about my peers'." Because of the practical focus, Suffolk students feel they are well prepared to start or to advance in their career after graduation. A student sums it up: "What will set a Suffolk University MBA grad apart from the others is the in-depth training we receive on crucial skills such as networking and follow-up protocols, self-assessment and self-evaluation skills, goal setting, speech and presentation skills, resume writing, interviewing skills, and business etiquette. The expertise and confidence gained from this knowledge is well worth the tuition."

Career and Placement

Suffolk prides itself on preparing students for the real world, and effective, long-term career planning is a major piece of the puzzle. In fact, every student at Suffolk must take an introductory course aptly named Effective Career Planning, designed to help students evaluate their professional skills and career paths and to make a solid plan for what they

ADMISSIONS CONTACT: JUDITH L. REYNOLDS, DIRECTOR OF GRADUATE ADMISSIONS
ADDRESS: 8 ASHBURTON PLACE BOSTON, MA 02108 UNITED STATES
PHONE: 617-573-8302 • FAX: 617-305-1733
E-MAIL: GRAD.ADMISSION@SUFFOLK.EDU • WEBSITE: WWW.SUFFOLK.EDU/BUSINESS

wish to accomplish with an MBA. In addition, the Suffolk MBA EDGE offers professional development events throughout the academic year. These events run the gamut from seminars on power lunches and the professional image to MBA networking week and Technology Day. MBA EDGE also hosts a number of career services events such as workshops on resume writing and salary negotiations.

Ideally located in downtown Boston, "There are numerous top Boston-based businesses that recruit at Suffolk University." However, some suggest that the school could broaden its scope of opportunities. "I would like to see the school bring in top recruiters in the investment banking and private equity sectors, and I know I am not alone in that desire. A Suffolk MBA can get a job in these sectors but it requires a great deal of leg work," explains a student.

Student Life and Environment

Whether you call it networking or socializing, "Suffolk stresses getting to know your peers and receiving the best education at the same time." With an admissions process that emphasizes personal qualities as well as academic excellence, "Suffolk University does an excellent job of handpicking the candidates for this program," admitting students who are "inquisitive travelers, inventive thinkers, creative problem-solvers and just plain down-to-earth." Thanks to the international focus and part-time programs, the school boasts a "very diverse culture with respect to age, ethnicity, gender, and employment background."

In addition to the friendships they make within the school of business, Suffolk MBAs also participate in "a graduate school association that often holds events at neighboring pubs and restaurants." Located in the heart of downtown Boston, "The campus has a constant buzz about it." A few blocks from Boston Commons and all the downtown restaurants, nightlife, and public transportation, the "terrific location" is what attracts many students to Suffolk in the first place.

Admissions

To apply to Suffolk University Sawyer School of Business, students must submit undergraduate transcripts, a resume, and a completed application, including essays. Those applying to the full-time program must have at least 1 year of work experience; however, the average admit has logged 3 years in a professional position. Part-time applicants are expected to have spent more time in the professional world and average 5 to 7 years of work experience. Applicants must also submit GMAT scores, though exceptions may be made for practicing CPAs, and attorneys.

FINANCIAL FACTS

Annual tuition	$29,490
Fees	$20
Cost of books	$1,010
Room & board (off-campus)	$12,000
% of students receiving aid	59
% of first-year students receiving aid	60
% of students receiving loans	32
% of students receiving grants	38
Average award package	$21,698
Average grant	$6,437

ADMISSIONS

Admissions Selectivity Rating	70
# of applications received	463
% applicants accepted	71
% acceptees attending	48
Average GMAT	499
Range of GMAT	450–550
Average GPA	3.2
TOEFL required of international students	Yes
Minimum TOEFL (paper/computer)	550/213
Application fee	$50
International application fee	$50
Regular application deadline	6/15
Regular notification	rolling
Deferment available	Yes
Maximum length of deferment	1 year
Transfer students accepted	Yes
Transfer application policy same as for regular applicants	
Non-fall admissions	Yes
Need-blind admissions	Yes

Applicants Also Look At
Babson College, Bentley College, Boston College, Boston University, Northeastern University.

EMPLOYMENT PROFILE

Career Rating	84	Grads Employed by Function	% Avg. Salary
Primary Source of Full-time Job Acceptances		Finance	33 $67,700
School-facilitated activities	4 (13%)	Human Resources	5 $89,000
Graduate-facilitated activities	27 (87%)	Marketing	10 $72,500
		Operations	10 $57,500
		Consulting	5 $70,000
		Communications	5 $34,000
		General Management	5 $80,000
		Other	5 $60,000
		Non-profit	22: $41,000

Top 5 Employers Hiring Grads
State Street Corporation; PricewaterhouseCoopers; Raytheon; Exxonmobil; Massachusetts Institute of Technology

SYRACUSE UNIVERSITY
MARTIN J. WHITMAN SCHOOL OF MANAGEMENT

GENERAL INFORMATION

Type of school	Private
Environment	City
Academic calendar	Semester

SURVEY SAYS...
Smart classrooms
Solid preparation in:
Operations
Teamwork
Entrepreneurial studies

STUDENTS

Enrollment of parent institution	19,084
Enrollment of business school	344
% male/female	71/29
% part-time	70
% minorities	9
% international	40
Average age at entry	25
Average years work experience at entry	2

ACADEMICS

Academic Experience Rating	**86**
Student/faculty ratio	4:1
Profs interesting rating	70
Profs accessible rating	85
% female faculty	19
% minority faculty	7

Joint Degrees
MBA/Juris Doctorate 4 years,
MBA/MS (Public Administration) 3
years.

Prominent Alumni
Martin J. Whitman, Founder, Third
Avenue Value Fund; Dick Clark,
Chairman/CEO, Dick Clark
Productions; Dan D'Aniello,
Founding Partner, Carlyle Group;
The Honorable Alfonse D'Amato,
former U.S. Senator; Arthur Rock,
venture capitalist, Arthur Rock &
Company.

Academics

A tiny MBA program at a "great, nationally recognized" university, the Whitman School of Business at Syracuse University provides a thorough business education in an intimate academic setting. With fewer than 30 students per entering class, students benefit from uniformly small class sizes, and "the opportunity to develop relationships with every classmate as well as professors." These relationships are incredibly valuable, as "Professors get to know students on a personal level and help out in every way they can." One student elaborates, "By talking with faculty and administration, I have been put in close personal contact with a number of prominent alumni and have even been offered internship positions at some of the top firms in their respective fields due to these alumni relationships."

Whitman's challenging 54-unit curriculum includes a year of core course work in essentials like economics and finance. Core courses extend into the second year; however, by the final semester, course work is comprised entirely of electives, and students may complete a concentration in accounting, entrepreneurship, finance, general management, supply chain management, or marketing management. In addition to the traditional program, the school offers an accelerated MBA for students with a business background. Students may also pursue a joint-degree with any other graduate department at the university, including "a great JD/MBA program with a lot of connections in and around New York City."

Mixing traditional lectures with hands-on projects, Whitman's curriculum introduces Syracuse students to both the practical and theoretical sides of business. A student shares, "Our leadership class was mostly lectures and reading and more of an in-class discussion that did not require intensive study. Our GEM class [involved] creating a whole new business from scratch, presenting to a venture capitalist and having a certain number of deliverables ready in 3 months." As a result of this variety, "The workload can be anywhere from easy to killer depending on deadlines and classes." Fortunately, students find lots of support: "Professors are regularly available, but especially on days they know students will need them—they are in their offices later than most students remain at school."

A great option for those early in their careers, Syracuse does not require previous professional experience for entry into the MBA program and "The majority of the MBA students in my class have had less than 5 years work experience, so [they] are fairly young." As one student explains, "I had internship experiences but no professional work experience. Syracuse University was one of the only universities that allowed me to get a quality MBA earlier in life when I have the time to go to school versus later in life when family and work become a higher priority than education."

Career and Placement

Career placement is taken seriously at Syracuse. During their studies, students hone their skills through internships at local companies, and "Every week there is some event for students to take part in, whether it is a guest speaker or networking reception." When it comes to permanent placements, "The school's strong accounting and supply chain [management] programs are well recognized nationally, and students in those fields get good job offers." However, with a young and largely international student body, placements can occasionally be more difficult. A current student explains, "Part of the problem is that because they accept students with little to no work experience, it is also tougher to place those MBA students in jobs, specifically international students in finance and marketing fields."

ADMISSIONS CONTACT: CAROL J. SWANBERG, DIRECTOR OF ADMISSIONS AND FINANCIAL AID
ADDRESS: 721 UNIVERSITY AVENUE - SUITE 315 SYRACUSE, NY 13244-2450 UNITED STATES
PHONE: 315-443-9214 • FAX: 315-443-9517
E-MAIL: MBAINFO@SYR.EDU • WEBSITE: WHITMAN.SYR.EDU

In 2006, 71 percent of students were employed within 3 months of graduation. Companies that offered positions to graduates include: Bear Stearns, ChinaTrust Commercial Bank, Citigroup, Deloitte Touche Tohmatsu, Ellis Deming Development, Ernst & Young, Health Net, JPMorgan Chase, PricewaterhouseCoopers, Rockefeller & Co., Samsung SDI, and Verizon Wireless. Another nice perk is that the school "pays for CFA testing and travel expenses for job interviews."

Student Life and Environment

You might be surprised how much you'll learn from your classmates on this tiny but diverse campus. A student praises, "Many of the students have international backgrounds and offer an international/alternative perspective to traditional North American ways of thinking." Despite students' cultural differences, the environment is noncontentious and friendly, and "People here really care for others, especially new students." There are many ways to fill your free time at Syracuse, and students say the "Many academic, social, and cultural activities to choose from [make] the experience rewarding." When they aren't hitting the books, students "plan trips together (to national and international destinations), events together (i.e., bowling night, international day), and involve the faculty as well (i.e., student versus faculty softball)."

While the city of Syracuse isn't the most happening location, students reassure us that communities outside Syracuse are "clean, crime-free, and cater to professionals. We have golf courses and ski resorts around the area that cater to people with those interests. There is also plenty to do in term of hiking, camping canoeing." In addition, many Syracuse students "take part in charity work around the city, offering their business skills and acumen to small business owners who may not always have a solid business background."

Admissions

Admission to Syracuse is competitive. Last year's entering class (for the full-time program) had an average GMAT score of 619, with a range of 560–700 and an average undergraduate GPA of 3.3. To apply to the accelerated program, students must have an undergraduate degree in business, a GMAT score of 650 or better, and 4 or more years of professional work experience. Reviews are made on a rolling basis and students are notified of their acceptance or nonacceptance within 4 to 6 weeks.

FINANCIAL FACTS

Annual tuition	$30,360
Fees	$874
Cost of books	$1,325
Room & board	$12,490
% of students receiving aid	75
% of first-year students receiving aid	81
% of students receiving loans	19
% of students receiving grants	75
Average award package	$30,453
Average grant	$23,199
Average student loan debt	$48,546

ADMISSIONS

Admissions Selectivity Rating	88
# of applications received	197
% applicants accepted	50
% acceptees attending	48
Average GMAT	615
Range of GMAT	580–640
Average GPA	3.36
TOEFL required of international students	Yes
Minimum TOEFL (paper/computer)	600/250
Application fee	$65
International application fee	$65
Regular application deadline	
Regular notification	
Application Deadline/Notification	
Round 1:	01/15 / 02/15
Round 2:	03/01 / 04/01
Round 3:	05/01 / 06/01
Deferment available	Yes
Maximum length of deferment	1 year
Need-blind admissions	Yes

Applicants Also Look At

Boston University, Cornell University, New York University, Penn State University, University of Illinois at Urbana-Champaign, University of Rochester, University of Wisconsin—Madison.

EMPLOYMENT PROFILE

Career Rating	83	Grads Employed by Function	%	Avg. Salary
Primary Source of Full-time Job Acceptances		Finance	46	$48,727
School-facilitated activities	13 (76%)	Marketing	1	NR
Graduate-facilitated activities	4 (24%)	Operations	1	NR
Average base starting salary	$58,059	Consulting	17	$73,500
Percent employed	89	Other	1	NR

Top 5 Employers Hiring Grads
Ernst & Young; PricewaterhouseCoopers; Bear Stearns & Co.; Deloitte Consulting; BDO Seidman

TEMPLE UNIVERSITY
THE FOX SCHOOL OF BUSINESS AND MANAGEMENT

Academics

Temple University's Richard J. Fox School of Business and Management boasts more than 5,500 students and 154 full-time faculty, making it one of the largest business schools in the world. Despite its large size, the MBA program is an intimate one with "only 30 full-timers." The small size of the full-time program has many benefits, particularly when it comes to access to the faculty. As one student explains, "The administration is readily available, and you get lots of individualized attention." The "outstanding, very dedicated, [and] extremely knowledgeable" professors are central to students' satisfaction with program, and students appreciate that "the course work and curriculum are organized well." Very few students have gripes about the administration, but even those who do felt that they were heard. As one student says, "They do a great job [of] soliciting and acting on feedback from students to improve the program. They are very committed to the MBA program and its continued success."

Working students can take advantage of Fox's part-time MBA, and the executive MBA and international MBA programs cater to more seasoned professionals interested in a specific focus. The IMBA and health care programs are known for being particularly strong at Fox, but students also have many positive things to say about some of the school's other curricular offerings. The Finance Department earns great reviews, with students citing "professors who have years of industry experience behind them," who modify the course structure to address "needs and changes in the industry."

Students routinely say that a combination of price and reputation is what drew them to Fox. Most feel that the quality of instruction is "comparable to any top business school in the country." The school's integrated approach to the core curriculum is thought to be "highly beneficial," with each course building on content learned in earlier classes. One student notes that professors "communicate with each other [and] work hard to integrate the courses with each other." After completing core and elective courses, degree candidates get some real-world experience by participating in the Enterprise Management Consulting Practice (EMC). Students say this "consulting practicum in the second year of the program will help [students] apply all of the skills learned through the program." Students are assigned to teams to assist on a real-life consulting project for some influential start-ups, corporations, and nonprofit organizations.

Career and Placement

Students may be thrilled with the academics at Fox, but they are less enthusiastic about the career services resources. Many students complain that the Career Services Office "has little external experience in order to guide students who are looking to change careers." Others feel that the absence of a large recruiting presence is a matter of brand recognition, with "very few companies aware of the strength of the full-time Temple program." Despite the school's large alumni network, students feel that alums were hampered by their companies' recruiting policies. One student explained that "if the company doesn't recruit at Temple, then the Temple alum is not likely to help current Temple students in their internship and career search." The school is aware of the shortcomings within Career Services, and many students concede that the "administration is trying very hard to improve in this area."

Although students may feel that Career Services leaves something to be desired, this certainly doesn't hinder them in their pursuit of employment. Last year, 66 percent of students looking for a job had received and accepted offers by graduation; 3 months after graduation, 88 percent had received and accepted offers. Most graduates entered the financial or consulting industries, and the mean base salary (not including bonuses) was $77,936.

ADMISSIONS CONTACT: WILLIAM MCDONALD, DIRECTOR, ENROLLMENT MANAGEMENT
ADDRESS: 1515 MARKET STREET, SUITE 400 PHILADELPHIA, PA 19102 UNITED STATES
PHONE: 215-204-5890 • FAX: 215-204-1632
E-MAIL: FOXINFO@TEMPLE.EDU • WEBSITE: WWW.FOX.TEMPLE.EDU/MBAMS

Student Life and Environment

Fox touts its Philadelphia location as one of its major benefits; certainly the school's location in the center of the Northeast Corridor puts it within easy reach of a host of multinational companies, and public transportation provides easy access to the business hubs of New York and Washington, DC. Fox has facilities on two campuses, the Main Campus and the Center City Campus; however, most students say that they spend the majority of their time at Center City.

Most students at Fox are enrolled in the part-time program and "just come for class and then leave." However, the full-time program is made up of a "tight group of students who work well together in class and outside of class." Fox's full-time students especially appreciate the school's supportive, teamwork-focused environment, particularly when "compared to the competitive nature found [at schools] across town." "We share job leads and help each other network," says one full-time student. "This cohort has really bonded." The full time students are the most socially active outside of class, and there are "many opportunities to party hard." However, there aren't as many student organizations on campus as some would like, mostly because it's hard to maintain student involvement: "The part-time students . . . do not participate in activities, and full-time students are only in school for 2 years."

Admissions

In a recently admitted class the average undergraduate GPA hovered around 3.5, and the average GMAT was approximately 651. Students had an average of 3.5 years of work experience. TOEFL scores for international applicants are required.

FINANCIAL FACTS

Annual tuition (in-state/ out-of-state)	$17,010/$25,145
Fees	$750
Cost of books	$1,200
Room & board	$15,000
% of students receiving aid	75
% of first-year students receiving aid	75
% of students receiving loans	73
% of students receiving grants	25
Average award package	$60,000
Average grant	$10,000
Average student loan debt	$45,000

ADMISSIONS

Admissions Selectivity Rating	88
# of applications received	366
% applicants accepted	67
% acceptees attending	64
Average GMAT	623
Range of GMAT	580–660
Average GPA	3.33
TOEFL required of international students	Yes
Minimum TOEFL (paper/computer)	575/230
Application fee	$50
International application fee	$50
Regular application deadline	6/1
Regular notification	rolling
Deferment available	Yes
Maximum length of deferment	1 year
Transfer students accepted	Yes
Transfer application policy Reviewed on a case by case basis for the Professional MBA.	
Non-fall admissions	Yes
Need-blind admissions	Yes

Applicants Also Look At

Penn State University; Rutgers, The State University of New Jersey; Thunderbird; University of Maryland—College Park; University of Pennsylvania; University of South Carolina; Wake Forest University.

EMPLOYMENT PROFILE

Career Rating	84	Grads Employed by Function	% Avg. Salary
Primary Source of Full-time Job Acceptances		Finance	34 $74,000
School-facilitated activities	15 (29%)	Marketing	18 $85,338
Graduate-facilitated activities	30 (59%)	Consulting	11 $97,755
Unknown	6 (12%)	Other	36 $82,712
Average base starting salary	$80,964	**Top 5 Employers Hiring Grads**	
Percent employed	90	Advanta; Boenning and Scattergood; Ernst & Young; KPMG; Accentur	

TENNESSEE TECHNOLOGICAL UNIVERSITY
COLLEGE OF BUSINESS

Academics

Tennessee Technological University offers a flexible, affordable, and student-oriented MBA, designed to meet the needs of working professionals. Tech's MBA is a general management program, with an emphasis on practical and interactive learning through research, case studies, computer simulation, business mentoring, workshops, consulting assignments, field trips, and more. "Professors encourage professional growth by designing classes to build teamwork among students in a global atmosphere," while simultaneously weaving appropriate co-curricular experiences into the MBA. For example, students pursuing a concentration in finance have the opportunity to manage a real investment portfolio during their studies. Students also have the opportunity to augment their education by working at the school's external-focused centers, designed to transfer technology and knowledge from the school community to the business world. These centers include the Business Media Center, the J.E. Owen Center for Information Technology Research, and the Small Business Development Center. With a name like "Tech," it's not surprising that the school is also "leading the way in combining education and technology."

At Tech, the classroom experience is top-notch and professors "go out of their way to make the material interesting." If you have questions, doubts, or just want to talk over a concept, you'll find professors are " surprisingly accessible." In fact, at this small school, "it is easy to get to know your professors and administration" as both the faculty and staff take a genuine interest in the student experience. A case in point, a current MBA candidate shares, "Tennessee Tech extended a warm welcome when I applied to the MBA program. The director, Dr. Bob Wood, met personally with me and helped me develop a strategy both for classes chosen and handling homework load." On that note, busy professionals should keep in mind that, despite the prevalence of "very cool and easy-going professors," Tech is "very demanding in terms of course deadlines."

If your work schedule suddenly changes or you don't have time to visit campus for class, "TTU also runs an excellent distance program that has the feel and personal touch of a campus degree." A current online student shares, "I feel as though Tech is also spending lots of time to improve their DMBA website. They just recently released a new version for the DMBA and it is getting better and better." Another adds, "The MBA program support staff have been very help to me as a distance student. They have hand-carried paperwork that needed signatures from person to person for me so that I didn't have to take a couple of days off work in order to travel to the university." Whether online or in the classroom, one thing unites all of Tech's MBA offerings: "This school provides a very high quality education at a very reasonable price."

Career and Placement

Tennessee Tech's Career Services Center serves the entire campus community, including the business school. Throughout the year, the center hosts on-campus interviews and career fairs. A recent career fair drew large employers such as AFLAC, Axciom Digital, Honda, 21st Mortgage Corporation, Denso, Alstom, Lennox, Greystone Healthcare Management, Regions Financial Corporation, Sonoco Products Company, Schneider Electric, Enterprise, Unifirst Corporation, and State Farm Insurance. A number of these employers were specifically seeking MBA graduates. According to the business school literature, Tennessee Tech is usually successful in placing all candidates who are seriously seeking employment after graduation.

ADMISSIONS CONTACT: DR. BOB WOOD, ASSISTANT DEAN
ADDRESS: BOX 5023 TTU, 1105 N. PEACHTREE COOKEVILLE, TN 38505 UNITED STATES
PHONE: 931-372-3600 • FAX: 931-372-6544
E-MAIL: MBASTUDIES@TNTECH.EDU • WEBSITE: WWW.TNTECH.EDU/MBA

Student Life and Environment

Thanks to the flexible scheduling and affordable tuition price, Tech draws a fairly diverse group of students, who "range in age from 20s to 50s. The majority is working professionals intent on getting a good education." Within the business school, there is a "very social life with frequent Pizza session in class and end of the semester outing." In fact, "students at Tech tend to bond together. They study together, hang out together, and go out together." A current student writes, "One of the things I like best about Tech is that the school is just small enough to encourage a tight group of people. When you go out, everybody knows your name." To add to the appeal, "the campus is beautiful with buildings easily accessible on foot," and is located in the "darling, small town" of Cookeville, Tennessee, seventy miles from Nashville.

At this medium-sized, public college, "it is easy to get involved on campus as an undergrad but there aren't any activities/organizations to join as a graduate student." However, there are a number of extracurricular activities aimed specifically at graduate business students, including the MBA Association, study abroad programs, investment challenge courses, and the Rural Economic Development Conference, for which MBA students assist in planning. Needless to say, online MBA students say that the campus itself does not play a large role in their graduate school experience. However, "the MBA program (led by Prof. Bob Wood) does try to do one or two events a semester that involve distance students (e.g., hockey game and group tours)."

Admissions

To be admitted to Tennessee Tech's MBA programs, you need an undergraduate degree with a minimum GPA of 2.5 on a 4.0 scale. A minimum GMAT score of 450 is also required. In addition, students must meet a computer efficiency requirement, and competency requirements in accounting, business law, economics, finance, marketing, managements, and statistics. Students who did not major in business can fulfill these competency requirements through college coursework or through pre-MBA, self-study CD courses.

FINANCIAL FACTS

Annual tuition	$23,790
Fees (in-state/ out-of-state)	$10,410/$13,380
Cost of books	$1,500
Room & board (on/off-campus)	$6,530/$8,400
% of students receiving aid	50
% of first-year students receiving aid	45
% of students receiving grants	25
Average award package	$14,228
Average grant	$1,500
Average student loan debt	$9,000

ADMISSIONS

Admissions Selectivity Rating	**71**
# of applications received	141
% applicants accepted	84
% acceptees attending	75
Average GMAT	528
Range of GMAT	450–780
Average GPA	3.27
TOEFL required of international students	Yes
Minimum TOEFL (paper/computer)	550/213
Application fee	$25
International application fee	$30
Regular application deadline	rolling
Regular notification	rolling
Deferment available	Yes
Maximum length of deferment	1 year
Transfer students accepted	Yes
Transfer application policy TTU will transfer 9 hours or less from an AACSB accredited school.	
Non-fall admissions	Yes
Need-blind admissions	Yes

Applicants Also Look At

Middle Tennessee State University, University of Tennessee.

EMPLOYMENT PROFILE				
Career Rating	73	**Grads Employed by Function**	**%**	**Avg. Salary**
Primary Source of Full-time Job Acceptances		Finance/Accounting	50	NR
Average base starting salary	$46,178	Marketing	10	NR
Percent employed	95	MIS	5	NR
		General Management	20	NR
		Other	15	NR

Texas A&M International University

College of Business Administration

GENERAL INFORMATION

Type of school	Public
Academic calendar	Semester

SURVEY SAYS...

Friendly students
Cutting edge classes
Happy students
Smart classrooms
Solid preparation in:
Finance
General management
Teamwork

STUDENTS

Enrollment of parent institution	5,188
Enrollment of business school	161
% male/female	64/36
% part-time	78
% minorities	33
% international	58
Average age at entry	29
Average years work experience at entry	6

ACADEMICS

Academic Experience Rating	**63**
Student/faculty ratio	20:1
Profs interesting rating	78
Profs accessible rating	63
% female faculty	10
% minority faculty	76

Academics

The College of Business Administration at Texas A&M International University "is dedicated to the delivery of a high quality professional and internationalized education to a graduate student population that is drawn from a wide variety of countries and cultures," according to the college's website, which also points out that "these programs [are intended to] contribute to the students' success in leadership positions in both domestic and international settings." This AACSB-accredited school offers a general MBA, an MBA in international banking (MBA-IBK), an MBA in international trade (MBA-IT), and a PhD in International Business Administration.

All MBA programs at TAMIU require mastery of eight foundation areas: accounting, information systems, quantitative methods, economics, finance, management, marketing, and operations. Students may fulfill these requirements by completing corresponding undergraduate courses at TAMIU, by showing evidence of equivalent course work at another undergraduate institution, or by having earned an undergraduate business degree from an AACSB-accredited program. Waivers are only granted for course work completed within the previous seven years.

TAMIU's general MBA is taught in both English and Spanish. The 30-hour program allows students to concentrate in one of the following areas: accounting, information systems, international business, international finance, international trade economics, logistics, and management marketing. The strong international focus of the program "gives students the opportunity to immerse themselves in an international environment in which we can analyze situations of different countries. The diversity of the student body helps." Students also praise the "extremely optimistic" professors who "honestly care about their students and are always willing to offer a helping hand." One student writes, "Teachers are very good and highly cooperative, with great academic ability. They have the knowledge to impart, help the students and, offer their valuable suggestions to guide their further course of action."

Students also point out that "the small size of the program is a great strength. The student population is not big, so there is enough opportunity to interact with your professors and get to know everyone in your college." MBAs here appreciate how "professors acknowledge that the majority of the class works full-time and also goes to school, so they make the assignments challenging, but not impossible." In addition to the abovementioned degrees, TAMIU also offers a master of professional accountancy (MPAcc), a master of science in international logistics (MS/IL), a master of science in information systems (MS/IS), and a doctorate in international business administration (PhD/BA).

Career and Placement

The Texas A&M International Career Services Office provides counseling and placement services to the entire undergraduate and graduate student body. The office organizes on-campus recruiting events, career expos, and job fairs. It also offers one-on-one counseling, workshops, library services, and resume review.

ADMISSIONS CONTACT: IMELDA LOPEZ, GRADUATE ADMISSIONS ADVISOR
ADDRESS: 5201 UNIVERSITY BLVD. LAREDO, TX 78041 UNITED STATES
PHONE: 956-326-2485 • FAX: 956-326-2479
E-MAIL: LOPEZ@TAMIU.EDU • WEBSITE: WWW.TAMIU.EDU/COBA

Student Life and Environment

Around 40 percent of TAMIU's MBA students attend full-time, providing a sizeable base for clubs, organizations, and extracurricular activity. Students tell us that "campus life offers a diverse field of organizations. New clubs and sports are always developing." They also report that "seminars provided by the school are good. Many important speakers visit the campus to deliver inspirational speeches on important current topics, including politics, finance, economics, and health." Part-timers generally "don't get to spend much time on campus, but rather just get here for class at night and leave once classes are done." They "visit the computer labs and library to do research and work," but otherwise spend little extra time socializing.

Hometown Laredo "is poised at the gateway to Mexico," placing it "at an enviable crossroads of international business and life." 156 miles south of San Antonio and 153 miles north of Monterrey, Mexico, this city of over 150,000 is the fastest growing in the state of Texas. The area's growth has been spurred by Laredo's increasing role as a center for international manufacturing and trade. Top employers in the area, outside of education and government, include the Laredo Medical Center, the H-E-B Grocery Company, Doctor's Hospital, Laredo Candle, and area banks.

TAMIU's "friendly, frank, cheerful and helpful" students "enjoy the challenge of studying in a foreign country and expect the experience to give them a better professional future." More than half the MBAs here are international students; most of whom are Mexican and Latin American. Almost twenty percent of the international student body comes from Asia.

Admissions

Applying to the TAMIU MBA program is a two-step process, as applicants must be admitted to both the university at large and the College of Business in order to enroll in the MBA program. Applicants must submit the following materials to the Office of Graduate Admission: a completed application; an official copy of transcripts for all postsecondary academic work undertaken; and an official score report for the GMAT. Applicants must also provide a statement of purpose, a resume, and two letters of recommendation. The TOEFL is required of all students who completed undergraduate study in a country where English is not the language of instruction; a minimum score of 550 paper-based or 213 computer-based is required. International students must also submit documentation demonstrating the ability to support themselves financially while studying at TAMIU.

FINANCIAL FACTS

Annual tuition (in-state/ out-of-state)	$1,170/$6,174
Fees	$2,324
Cost of books	$2,825
Room & board (on/off-campus)	$6,630/$5,814
% of students receiving aid	24
% of first-year students receiving aid	23
% of students receiving loans	22
% of students receiving grants	23
Average award package	$4,400
Average grant	$1,117

ADMISSIONS

Admissions Selectivity Rating	61
# of applications received	61
% applicants accepted	98
% acceptees attending	70
Average GMAT	385
Average GPA	3.2
TOEFL required of international students	Yes
Minimum TOEFL (paper/computer)	550/213
Application fee	$25
International application fee	$25
Regular application deadline	4/30
Regular notification	
Deferment available	Yes
Maximum length of deferment	1 yr
Transfer students accepted	Yes
Transfer application policy In terms of the application process, this remains the same as first-time applicants. However, for F1 applicants, it is critical these applicants be in-status at their current institutuion.	
Non-fall admissions	Yes
Need-blind admissions	Yes

Applicants Also Look At

Texas A & M University—Corpus Christi, Texas A&M University—Commerce, The University of Texas—Pan American.

EMPLOYMENT PROFILE	
Career Rating	69

TEXAS A&M UNIVERSITY—COLLEGE STATION
MAYS BUSINESS SCHOOL

Academics

The top-ranked Mays Business School at Texas A&M University—College Station combines a one-size-fits-all approach with specialization options to provide its small student body a cost-effective and streamlined, yet flexible, MBA degree. This inexpensive public school offers one of the 10 quickest returns on investment, according to *BusinessWeek*. *Financial Times* ranked it the fourth best value in U.S. graduate business education. One MBA agrees, "The education you receive is top notch for the cost."

All Mays students complete a 49-credit core sequence over a 16-month period. This core covers accounting, business communication, finance, global management, information and operations management, marketing, negotiations, and management, all with "an emphasis on character and ethics, a very appealing aspect of the program." This mandatory curriculum that combines "business competencies, communications, international issues, teamwork, and ethics" means all Mays MBAs "are prepared to be strategic thinkers, effective communicators, and accountable team members and leaders in today's global marketplace," according to the school.

Those seeking specialization are welcome to remain at Mays for an additional semester, participate in study abroad, or undertake other enrichment opportunities. The school offers specialization in 11 predefined areas (students speak most highly of accounting, marketing, management, and real estate). MBAs may also design specializations of their own. Other unique aspects of the program include the Technology Transfer Challenge, in which MBAs compete to develop commercial applications for promising new technologies. The school writes, "The Challenge's design is based on state-of-the-art knowledge management theory, demonstrating how knowledge management principles can be used to help evaluate the potential of patents and other raw technologies. It demands a level of creativity not possible with traditional case competitions."

Students here love the "low cost and excellent financial aid," as well as the school's vision. One MBA exclaims, "The school continues to replace weak faculty in an effort to improve. And the program is definitely improving, with great faculty leading the way." They also appreciate that it's a "conservative, strong program with high starting salaries and great recruiting companies." Naturally, though, a few see its small size as a drawback. One such student opines, "The Mays MBA Class of 2006 is only 70 students strong. If the school is ever to be mentioned amongst Harvard, Texas, and Michigan, then it will have to expand to upwards of 500 students."

Career and Placement

A&M's legendary alumni network works its magic for MBAs. Students exploit this valuable asset through publications, a website, newsletters, and on- and off-campus events. The Mays Graduate Business Career Services (GBCS) Office also provides one-on-one counseling, online assessment tools, and frequent workshops on crafting resumes and cover letters, networking, interviewing, and negotiating your salary.

Hundreds of companies recruit on the College Station campus each year—just how many come for the purpose of interviewing MBAs is less clear. What counts is that the results are pretty impressive. Employers of Mays MBAs include BP, CattleSoft, Chevron Phillips, China National Petroleum Corp, CIA, Citibank, Citigroup, DuPont, Eagle Pass Winery, the Federal Reserve Bank, First Houston Mortgage, Ford, Hewlett-Packard, Johnson-Lancaster & Associates, Procter & Gamble, Smith Barney, Solutions Inc., Sovico Trading Ltd., USAA, Wal-Mart, and World Savings. In 2007, the mean starting salary of a Mays MBA was $87,475. One student sums up, "One of the greatest facets of a Texas A&M education is the high salary upon graduation with relatively low tuition costs."

ADMISSIONS CONTACT: WENDY FLYNN, DIRECTOR OF MBA ADMISSIONS
ADDRESS: 4117 TAMU COLLEGE STATION, TX 77843-4117 UNITED STATES
PHONE: 979-845-4714 • FAX: 979-862-2393
E-MAIL: MAYSMBA@TAMU.EDU • WEBSITE: MBA.TAMU.EDU

Student Life and Environment

Although "school requires much of a student's time" at A&M, "the lifestyle in College Station is still very enjoyable." Furthermore, "those who wish to participate in social activities will not be disappointed," MBAs write, since "there are weekly events organized, as well as plenty of hot spots to frequent." It will come as no surprise to anyone who knows anything at all about the school that "football is the major activity" and that A&M is "big into traditions, and it really enhances the life here." Overall, MBAs here agree that "Texas A&M is very conservative and an excellent environment to learn quality business practices."

With a substantial international population, Mays' student body is "very diverse in ethnicity, education, and experience," although not so much in gender. MBAs tend to be "boisterous in class, friendly and intelligent, [and] proactive in regards to career advancement and networking." All "have some special skills which make them unique. If one is good in math, another is very good in communications." One MBA observes, "Fellow students are like good coworkers at the office: During class and study time they work hard, but after class, they know how to have fun."

Admissions

With a limited number of slots available, the Mays MBA program can keep admissions very competitive. Successful applicants typically have at least two years of post-college, full-time work experience, good GMAT scores ("quant and verbal sections must have scores at least at the 50th percentile for consideration," notes the Admissions Office), and evidence of leadership, management experience, and professional potential. All applicants must submit a current resume, three letters of recommendation from professional sources, and application essays. International students must provide TOEFL scores (minimum 600 on the paper-and-pencil test, 250 on the computerized test for admission). A&M "aggressively seeks to enhance diversity on all levels in the program, and has programs in place to recruit all students who will bring diversity to our program."

FINANCIAL FACTS

Annual tuition (in-state/ out-of-state)	$7,333/$17,341
Fees	$7,982
Cost of books	$2,114
Room & board (on/off-campus)	$0/$9,651
% of students receiving aid	75
% of first-year students receiving aid	75
% of students receiving loans	65
% of students receiving grants	75
Average award package	$17,281
Average grant	$4,968
Average student loan debt	$26,300

ADMISSIONS

Admissions Selectivity Rating	96
# of applications received	463
% applicants accepted	30
% acceptees attending	57
Average GMAT	665
Range of GMAT	590–740
Average GPA	3.44
TOEFL required of international students	Yes
Minimum TOEFL (paper/computer)	600/250
Application fee	$50
International application fee	$75
Application Deadline/Notification	
Round 1:	11/1 / NR
Round 2:	1/4 / NR
Round 3:	2/28 / NR
Round 4:	4/15 / NR
Deferment available	Yes
Maximum length of deferment	1 year
Need-blind admissions	Yes

Applicants Also Look At

Arizona State University, Brigham Young University, Rice University, The University of Texas at Austin, University of Maryland—College Park, University of Notre Dame, Vanderbilt University.

EMPLOYMENT PROFILE

Career Rating	89	Grads Employed by Function	% Avg. Salary
Primary Source of Full-time Job Acceptances		Finance	32 $90,619
School-facilitated activities	34%	Human Resources	4 $68,667
Graduate-facilitated activities	66%	Marketing	18 $88,700
Average base starting salary	$87,475	Operations	13 $81,178
Percent employed	100	Consulting	18 $91,617
		General Management	12 $85,313

Top 5 Employers Hiring Grads

Citigroup; Dell; Bearing Point; Exxon Mobil; Microsoft.

Texas A&M University—Corpus Christi

College of Business

GENERAL INFORMATION

Type of school	Public
Environment	Village
Academic calendar	Semester

SURVEY SAYS...

Friendly students
Cutting edge classes
Happy students
Smart classrooms
Solid preparation in:
Finance
General management
Teamwork

STUDENTS

Enrollment of parent institution	8,579
Enrollment of business school	152
% male/female	45/55
% part-time	44
% minorities	15
% international	62
Average age at entry	27

ACADEMICS

Academic Experience Rating	**63**
Profs interesting rating	84
Profs accessible rating	86
% female faculty	27
% minority faculty	21

Academics

"Cost and location," along with strong word of mouth—students hear "very good reviews from previous MBA students in comparison to other schools"—drive MBA traffic toward the College of Business at Texas A&M University—Corpus Christi (TAMUCC), an AACSB-accredited MBA program. Convenience is another important factor. One student offers that the school is "flexible with my work schedule"; another agrees that with all MBA classes held at night, it is "easy to integrate school and work."

The school offers two areas of concentration: international business, and health care management. While students tout TAMUCC's "strong accounting program" (the school offers a Master of Accounting in addition to the MBA), some feel that "it would be great to have more management or operations electives" here. As a general rule, "A lot of courses are in the catalog but are not offered and have not been for several years (according to my advisor)." Those with undergraduate degrees in business can complete the TAMUCC MBA in 30 semester hours. Those with degrees in other areas must also complete some or all of six foundation courses covering material typically taught at the undergraduate level.

TAMUCC professors "are available to the students. If you can't meet at their office time, they are always available for an appointment." "I have had profs give me their home number for questions on projects," one student says. Students appreciate the "strong real-life academic instruction" that professors impart. Most "are able to incorporate real-life skills in all aspects of their courses. The things we learn we can actually apply in our jobs," one student relates. To keep students competitive in the job market, professors here "generally try to incorporate many teaching methods that are in use at top business schools like Harvard," by requiring students "to perform many case studies in addition to textual readings. There is a strong emphasis on preparing us to be great oral and written communicators by requiring presentations and papers weekly in multiple classes."

Career and Placement

The TAMUCC Career Services office provides counseling and placement services for all undergraduates, graduate students, and alumni of the university. Frequent seminars and presentations are offered on such topics as "How to Job Search in the 'Hidden Market,'" "The Second Interview and Salary Negotiation," and "How to Get a Federal Job." The office also provides career counseling, computer-based self-assessments, job search advisement, online and hard-copy job postings, a career resource library and computer lab, videotaped mock interviews, and job fairs and on-campus recruiting events. Students tell us that the program would benefit from even more "job fairs and more actively getting companies to recruit here." Top employers in the area include the Naval Air Station Corpus Christi, Christus Spohn Health System, the Corpus Christi Army Depot, H-E-B Grocery Co., Bay Limited, SSP Partners/Circle K, Driscoll Children's Hospital, APAC, First Data, and Gulf Marine Fabricators.

Student Life and Environment

"Most graduate students work full-time, have families, and attend school part-time" at TAMUCC, "so their involvement with the school and school activities is minimal." Even so, students report that "group projects are usually done on campus." Those who do have time to participate in campus activities will find that "there is much to do here other than schoolwork." One student explains, "Our calendar is full of events and opportunities. I cannot stress how friendly and happy the ambiance is at TAMUCC."

TAMUCC "has a great campus" located on a 240-acre island surrounded by Corpus

ADMISSIONS CONTACT: SHARON POLANSKY, DIRECTOR OF MASTER'S PROGRAMS
ADDRESS: 6300 OCEAN DRIVE UNIT 5808 CORPUS CHRISTI, TX 78412-5808 UNITED STATES
PHONE: 361-825-2655 • FAX: 361-825-2725
E-MAIL: SHARON.POLANSKY@TAMUCC.EDU • WEBSITE: WWW.COB.TAMUCC.EDU

FINANCIAL FACTS

Annual tuition (in-state/ out-of-state)	$2,583/$7,587
Fees	$1,169
Cost of books	$675
Room & board (on/off-campus)	$8,648/$9,971

ADMISSIONS

Admissions Selectivity Rating	**63**
# of applications received	69
% applicants accepted	93
% acceptees attending	91
Average GMAT	459
Range of GMAT	410–500
Average GPA	3.1
TOEFL required of international students	Yes
Minimum TOEFL (paper/computer)	550/213
Application fee	$40
International application fee	$70
Regular application deadline	7/15
Regular notification	rolling
Deferment available	Yes
Maximum length of deferment	1 year
Transfer students accepted	Yes
Transfer application policy Possibility of transferring in 6 credits from an accredited school.	
Non-fall admissions	Yes
Need-blind admissions	Yes

Christi Bay and Oso Bay; downtown Corpus Christi is about 10 miles away. Students "are all over the place before classes. You can hear them talking and sharing ideas and enjoying the atmosphere" of this "island university." The library "has plenty of computer labs that are adequate for the campus size and . . . subscribes to many online research databases," which can be used extensively in b-school. Students tell us that "many new buildings are being built and lots of money is pouring into the school." As a bonus, "the university is closely linked with" the surrounding community.

Corpus Christi has a population of about a quarter-million. Its seaside location makes it a popular destination for vacationers and tourists; the city receives 5 million visitors annually. TAMUCC itself attracts a "very diverse group," made up of "young, old, Hispanic[s], foreigners, and your typical Texan[s]." One student reports, "My accounting class has almost 50 percent international students from South Korea, China, Japan, Thailand, Phillipines, Russia (Moscow), Turkey, and France." Students here are, "in general, smart people who choose to pursue their master's at night, while working during the day. Everyone is extremely friendly, and you get to know each other because of the small class sizes, which range from 6 to 44. The median class size is probably around 18." There are "a lot" of military personnel in the program, not surprising, given the large military presence in Corpus Christi.

Admissions

All applicants to the TAMUCC MBA program must submit the following materials: official transcripts for all undergraduate and graduate work; an official score report for the GMAT (test score can be no more than 5 years old); two letters or recommendation; a current resume or curriculum vitae; a personal essay stating your reasons for pursuing the MBA; and a completed application form. In addition, international students whose first language is not English must submit an official score for the TOEFL (minimum score: 550, paper-based test; 213, computer-based test) and an evaluation of non-English language transcripts executed by Education Credential Evaluators, Inc., International Education Research Foundation, Inc., or World Education Services. All international applicants must submit an I-34 form or other notarized confirmation of adequate financial support, a copy of their current visa, and proof of medical insurance.

Texas Christian University
The M. J. Neeley School of Business

Academics

Students at Texas Christian University's M.J. Neeley School of Business have at least four MBA degree programs to choose from. There's the full-time program, in which students generally attend day classes and which requires 54 credit hours to complete, and the evening or professional MBA, which requires students to attend class 2 nights a week for 48 credit hours. For those who hold a bachelor's degree in business, there is an accelerated MBA option requiring just 36 credits, and for students who have substantial work experience TCU offers an executive MBA option with classes meeting on Fridays and Saturdays. Joint-degrees in education and physics are also offered, along with a 2-year master's program in international management. Citing "the value of their education versus the cost," students laud the breadth of academic options offered and note that TCU has "great resources to customize programs to individual needs."

The core MBA curriculum focuses on both strategic and analytical management skills, with managing financial resources, managing people, and market-driven strategy among the topics covered. Integrative team projects that combine the skills learned in these classes are required, and about 20 credit hours are available for concentrations and electives which may include work at the school's centers for excellence in leadership, supply chain management, professional communication, and capital management. Study abroad opportunities are also offered in Germany, Mexico, Italy, and Chile. Overall, students say "The first-year experience is great," but some students feel "The second year has left a lot to be desired." "If the first year can be described as having a lot of overlap and being tightly integrated, the second year is sort of anarchic." "A lot of the courses like global strategy, ethics, [and] information technology strategy are almost complete jokes. The school just does not put forward the best or right professors to teach these courses at a graduate level."

Throughout the curriculum, "a great deal of emphasis is placed on real-world experience. Consulting projects are offered and students are encouraged or required to participate. And the faculty is generally flexible to accommodate your work schedule if you decide to work an internship during the academic year." In fact, most students find that "the M.J. Neeley School staff and faculty are helpful, willing, energetic, smart people who enjoy students' questions." Neeley's "excellent" professors "are easily accessible and are eager to help you achieve your goals." As one student says, "The faculty places many challenges before us." Students also laud the "great administration" for being "very helpful and interested in your individual success and experience." Both faculty and staff "[show] so much care toward each student to make sure his/her experience is fulfilling."

Career and Placement

Neeley's location in the heart of Fort Worth, close to the center of the vibrant Dallas/Fort Worth metroplex, is an asset students value when it comes time to launch their post-MBA job search. The school does its part too, with "an excellent Career Services" staff available for individual consultations and access to a database of job openings for MBAs online. The Career Center also conducts targeted career management seminars on topics such as networking, writing a cover letter, developing leadership skills, and the like. The Career Services staff is "very helpful and interested in your individual success and experience," students say. These "supportive and helpful Career Counselors," along with a good reputation among area businesses, are a formidable combination when it comes to job placement. In 2006, nearly 90 percent of graduating MBAs had received at least one job offer before graduation. Sabre Holdings, Frito Lay, PepsiCo., Alcan Labs, and Goldman Sachs are among those who hire TCU graduates.

Student Life and Environment

Students say that Neeley has the "best facilities in the area," a "beautiful" campus, and "easy" parking, all of which complement campus life. Student opinion about their classmates is split, with some students describing the vibe on campus as a "very friendly, good, team-based atmosphere" with "classmates [who are] more like family. We all look out for each other." Other students observe "young, immature, bright, resilient party people with a strong 'beer factor'" who are "inexperienced in team environments." One student remarks that most of his classmates "are looking for a piece of paper with three letters on it: MBA. There is definitely a lack of effort overall." While most students agree that "the top students are extremely motivated and intelligent," they also observe that "there is a steep decline after the top 25 percent in terms of work ethic and intellectual capability." Unsurprisingly, then, "getting better MBA candidates" was an area cited as being in need of improvement by many. Academic differences notwithstanding, campus life and life in Fort Worth in general, garnered praise from students across the board. Dallas/Fort Worth is "very fun, [with] lots of activities for all students. Good athletic events, churches, and nightlife. [There's] something for everyone," students agreed.

Admissions

GMAT scores, undergraduate GPA, personal statements, letters of recommendation, a resume, and TOEFL scores for students whose native language is not English are all required to apply for admission at TCU. According to the school's website, TCU looks for "a history of setting and achieving challenging goals in every aspect of your life" when making admissions decisions. In 2006, accepted students had an average GMAT score of 624 with an average GPA of 3.22, plus 4 years of work experience. Those pursuing the executive MBA option had an average of 16 years of work experience.

FINANCIAL FACTS

Annual tuition	$25,950
Fees	$3,350
Cost of books	$1,600
Room & board (off-campus)	$12,000
% of students receiving aid	98
% of first-year students receiving aid	96
% of students receiving loans	48
% of students receiving grants	98
Average award package	$28,150
Average grant	$18,593

ADMISSIONS

Admissions Selectivity Rating	84
# of applications received	125
% applicants accepted	71
% acceptees attending	55
Average GMAT	608
Range of GMAT	570–640
Average GPA	3.29
TOEFL required of international students	Yes
Minimum TOEFL (paper/computer)	550/213
Application fee	$75
International application fee	$75
Application Deadline/Notification	
Round 1:	11/15 / 12/15
Round 2:	1/15 / 2/15
Round 3:	3/1 / 4/1
Round 4:	4/15 / 5/15
Early decision program?	Yes
ED Deadline/ Notification	11/30 / 12/15
Deferment available	Yes
Maximum length of deferment	1 year
Transfer students accepted	Yes
Transfer application policy Maximum transferable credits are six Semester hours from an AACSB accredited institution.	
Need-blind admissions	Yes

Applicants Also Look At

Baylor University, Rice University, Southern Methodist University, Texas A&M University—College Station, The University of Texas at Austin, Tulane University.

EMPLOYMENT PROFILE

Career Rating	85	Grads Employed by Function	%	Avg. Salary
Primary Source of Full-time Job Acceptances		Finance	52	$67,000
School-facilitated activities	61%	Marketing	14	$78,666
Graduate-facilitated activities	39%	Operations	17	$68,400
Average base starting salary	$70,477	Consulting	3	$68,583
Percent employed	97	General Management	10	$76,000
		Other	4	$0

Top 5 Employers Hiring Grads

American Airlines; AT&T; Accenture; Citigroup; Sabre Holdings

TEXAS SOUTHERN UNIVERSITY
JESSE H. JONES SCHOOL OF BUSINESS

Academics

Students at the Texas Southern University's Jesse H. Jones School of Business have a lot of great things to say about their program, not the least of which is the school's focus on "diversity and entrepreneurship." Students enrolled in the MBA program at this historically black college have four degree tracks to choose from. JHJ offers an MBA degree with a general business concentration, an MBA with a health care administration concentration, a dual MBA/JD degree, and a Master's of Science degree in Management Information Systems. Whatever degree program they ultimately choose, students across the board speak of a "very intense program with very friendly and accessible staff members" and a "challenging" curriculum. "Professors are awesome," students say, and they "love the relationship between students and professors." In fact, one of the most common reasons that students choose Texas Southern is because of the school's visionary and "awesome" professors. Of these luminaries, students say, "They are highly competitive and knowledgeable about their professions," and students appreciate the "quality of their experience and expertise." Also, as one student points out, the professors show a distinct "ability to steer students' creativity and innovation." Despite these accolades, a few students commented that there could be "more professors" and that the "administration needs major work."

Beyond the "convenience" and "academic excellence" along with "a unique perspective" that Texas Southern offers, other strengths cited by students were the school's "location, cost, [and] small classes." "My MBA class is like a small family," one student said. While the small class sizes are a boon when it comes to gaining access to faculty, students say it can also be a limitation, especially when it comes to course selection. "We need more marketing courses," one student says. One student believes the problem is that "the business school does not fully challenge the academic potential of the students." Another adds that the school needs to "broaden the curriculum and course offerings," and that the administration should "design classes around the application of curriculum." But on the whole, however, student comments lean more toward the positive. "My overall academic experience has been great," one student says. "It's a good school," another sums up.

Career and Placement

According to the school, Texas Southern is a "major historically black college and university located in a leading international business environment." Located in Houston, Texas, the school prides itself—and students enjoy the benefits of—its "location, location, location," which any business student knows is a key component to landing the right job post-graduation. Hometown Houston offers "good career and placement" according to students. The largest city in Texas and the fourth largest city in the United States, Houston and its "booming economy" attract "31,000 new jobs among the 18 *Fortune* 500 companies and thousands of energy-related firms headquartered here," according to the school's website.

The Cooperative Education and Placement Services Center at Texas Southern University works every year to capitalize on the school's great location, and bring more companies on campus to recruiting events. The center hosts information sessions throughout the year where students can meet with company representatives to learn more about opportunities with their firm. Some of the companies that have conducted sessions recently are: Black & Decker, CITGO, Continental Airlines, Shell Oil Company, Target, Pfizer, and Kraft Foods. Other companies have visited the campus as part of a career development series, and they include: Wells Fargo, JPMorgan Chase, American Express Company, Merrill Lynch, and ING.

Student Life and Environment

When it comes to student life at Texas Southern, it's literally all about the students. Given Texas Southern's small class size and "intimate" learning environment, it's no wonder that student life at the school is characterized by a sense of "community" and a "welcoming" atmosphere. In fact, the "intimacy of the students in the program" is a common theme running throughout student comments about Texas Southern. Students say the class is like a "tight-knit family," characterized by "supportive instructors" and "diverse," "open communications." Students here appreciate the "unique perspective" their peers bring to the campus, and note that they "cut across every strata—social, economic, business experience, [and] age." Despite their differences, these "talented," and "career-oriented" students "have similar goals and objectives," commonalities that are bolstered by the school's "encouragement of teamwork" and "smart, competitive, and fun" learning environment. It helps that students in the program are "nice and professional" and "encouraging and compassionate about education." It's clear that Texas Southern's "professional, career-focused, results-driven, friendly, and down-to-earth" MBAs feel they are in good company.

Admissions

Students seeking admission to any of Texas Southern's four degree programs will need to submit, along with the application fee and completed application, official transcripts from all colleges and universities previously attended; GRE, GMAT and TOEFL scores; a personal statement; a current resume; and two letters of recommendation. There is an English Proficiency Requirement. Each graduate student who is admitted must have an analytical writing score of 3.5 or higher on the GRE or GMAT exam or enroll in a graduate-level English class. Admission is for the fall semester only. Conditional admission may be offered to students who do not meet all of the application requirements but demonstrate promise and ability.

FINANCIAL FACTS

Annual tuition (in-state/ out-of-state)	$5,856/$13,266
Fees	$4,930
Cost of books	$1,045
Room & board (on/off-campus)	$6,056/$6,336
% of students receiving aid	10
% of first-year students receiving aid	5
% of students receiving loans	10
Average grant	$8,000

ADMISSIONS

Admissions Selectivity Rating	73
# of applications received	56
% applicants accepted	52
% acceptees attending	86
Average GMAT	417
Range of GMAT	389–566
Average GPA	3.11
TOEFL required of international students	Yes
Minimum TOEFL (paper/computer)	550/213
Application fee	$50
International application fee	$78
Regular application deadline	7/15
Regular notification	
Early decision program?	Yes
ED Deadline/ Notification	4/30 / 05/30
Deferment available	Yes
Maximum length of deferment	1 year
Transfer students accepted	Yes
Transfer application policy	
Apply similar to regular applicants	
Need-blind admissions	Yes

Applicants Also Look At

Sam Houston State University, University of Houston, University of Houston—Clear Lake, University of Houston—Victoria, University of Phoenix.

EMPLOYMENT PROFILE

Career Rating	62
Primary Source of Full-time Job Acceptances	
School-facilitated activities	88%
Graduate-facilitated activities	12%
Percent employed	18

Grads Employed by Function	% Avg. Salary
Finance	7 NR
Human Resources	16 NR
Marketing	24 NR
MIS	4 NR
Operations	9 NR
Consulting	6 NR
Entrepreneurship	5 NR
General Management	19 NR
Global Management	2 NR
Other	2 NR
Non-profit	6: NR

Top 5 Employers Hiring Grads

Wal Mart; Enterprise-Rent-a-Car; Haliburton; Wells Fargo; JP Morgan

TEXAS TECH UNIVERSITY
JERRY S. RAWLS COLLEGE OF BUSINESS ADMINISTRATION

Academics

"Academics are on the rise" at Texas Tech University's Rawls College of Business, where the main attraction is a slew of special concentrations and unique joint-degree programs. One future attorney says, "Texas Tech is one of the few schools that offers a 3-year joint JD/MBA program, [in] which I am currently enrolled. Most schools offer these degrees in a minimum of 4 years." The health organization management specialization and MD/MBA are also huge draws for many students (not to mention the school's "great facilities" and "reasonable price"). Rawls's proximity to the School of Law and School of Medicine facilitate these partnerships. Joint-degrees are also available in architecture, foreign languages, personal financial planning, and environmental toxicology. The "energy commerce department is excellent" and provides a rare training opportunity for future oil execs. Other notable concentrations include agribusiness, entrepreneurship, and statistics. Students gave less than rave reviews to the accounting department, which one student says "has completely ruined my chances of becoming CPA-eligible, as I am an MBA student, and they no longer allow MBA students to take graduate accounting courses."

The Rawls faculty consists of many "well-published, tenured, and highly regarded members of the academic community"—"passionate" teachers who "are interested in the students, not just [in] the research." The faculty "comes from all parts of the world," and "Their experiences and industry knowledge bring a complete understanding to the subject matter." One student cautions that "some male professors are still outdated in their ideas about women. They are not against women in power positions, but they sometimes make assumptions about women." Professors are "accommodating" to students who "lack a business background" and "are always willing to put in the extra hour for anyone who needs extra help." Students had mostly positive things to say about the administration, noting that it has done "everything possible to ensure that students can be enrolled in their appropriate classes. It has made registration a breeze." Some students wish the administration would make "more inclusion of other cultures, ethnicities, and women" in the faculty and classroom a priority.

Career and Placement

"TTU has a strong alumni base that tries to hire new graduates," students say. "It is not uncommon for several alumni to be employed at the same company." The new Career Management Center serves both undergraduates and graduates, and "Many students, even graduate students, find jobs" thanks to the center's services. Some students complain that the CMC "does not put much effort into obtaining job opportunities for [international students]" and that when grad students ask about working in companies with little or no relationship to Rawls, "We are often told that . . . it is out of the question." Eighty percent of Rawls MBAs take jobs in Texas and the Southwest. The vast majority of grads enter the finance industry, but the highest-paid grads are the 5 percent who go into manufacturing jobs. Top employers include Cintas, Deloitte Touche Tohmatsu, Enterprise Rent-A-Car, ExxonMobil, Halliburton, JPMorgan Chase, Lockheed Martin, National Instruments, Plains Capital, PricewaterhouseCoopers, Rolled Alloys, Sherwin Williams, Southwest Bank of Texas, Texas Bank, Texas Tech, USAA, Wal-Mart, and Wells Fargo.

Student Life and Environment

"Texas Tech has the best people in the world, hands down," students say. "People are very laid-back, friendly, and always willing to help. That is what I love about Texas Tech and Lubbock." Another student agrees, "You can't walk across campus without someone saying 'hello.' Everyone is always smiling, which makes life on campus much more enjoyable." One student asks, "Where else can you meet a total stranger on campus who is willing to walk you to the building that you just cannot seem to locate?!"

"Due to the accelerated MBA for TTU undergrads, the graduate students do not really differ from undergraduate students," says one MBA candidate. Grad students tend to be "conservative," "friendly, charismatic" Texas Tech grads who "are still in their early 20s and [enjoy] partying and going out" and often have little work experience. Some students say "The social scene is much more important than working." While this is great news for students who fit the party mold, one student complains, "I went Greek in undergrad and I loved my sisters in the Tri-Deltas, but I don't want to relive those days again."

Rawls students love the "secluded west Texas" city of Lubbock, "a very social town" where everyone is "supportive of Texas Tech and the students." Students say that "nightlife around the campus is great for after-school networking." Lubbock may be "in the middle of nowhere," which makes landing internships difficult, but most students feel the advantages far outweigh any inconveniences. In particular, "The cost of living is extremely cheap"; "three-bedroom/two-bath homes rent for under $1000 a month." In addition, "The weather is fair, which makes for a lot of outdoor activities."

Admissions

The outlook is good for applicants to Rawls, which has an 82-percent MBA acceptance rate. Successful candidates boast a mean GMAT score of around 528, a mean GPA of 3.4, and 2 years' average work experience. Those who'd like to get a taste of Rawls before committing can take up to 12 credit hours as nonmatriculated students.

FINANCIAL FACTS

Annual tuition (in-state/ out-of-state)	$4,600/$11,320
Fees	$3,000
Cost of books	$1,500
Room & board (on/off-campus)	$6,000/$6,000
% of students receiving aid	100
% of first-year students receiving aid	100
% of students receiving grants	100
Average grant	$2,000
Average student loan debt	$15,192

ADMISSIONS

Admissions Selectivity Rating	**73**
# of applications received	363
% applicants accepted	81
% acceptees attending	77
Average GMAT	528
Range of GMAT	470–580
Average GPA	3.43
TOEFL required of international students	Yes
Minimum TOEFL (paper/computer)	550/213
Application fee	$50
International application fee	$60
Regular application deadline	rolling
Regular notification	rolling
Deferment available	Yes
Maximum length of deferment	1 year
Transfer students accepted	Yes
Transfer application policy Six hours may transfer	
Non-fall admissions	Yes
Need-blind admissions	Yes

Applicants Also Look At

Texas A&M University—College Station, The University of Texas at Austin.

EMPLOYMENT PROFILE

Career Rating	77	Grads Employed by Function	%	Avg. Salary
Primary Source of Full-time Job Acceptances		Finance	44	$44,788
Unknown	28 (100%)	Marketing	16	$52,333
Average base starting salary	$53,072	MIS	6	$58,000
Percent employed	68	Operations	6	$45,000
		Consulting	6	$58,000
		General Management	16	$61,667
		Other	6	$70,000

Top 5 Employers Hiring Grads

Ryan & Co.; Texas Instruments; Chevron Phillips; Comerica Bank; Price Waterhouse Coopers

THUNDERBIRD
SCHOOL OF GLOBAL MANAGEMENT

GENERAL INFORMATION

Type of school	Private
Academic calendar	Trimesters

SURVEY SAYS...
Friendly students
Good social scene
Good peer network
Solid preparation in:
General management
Teamwork
Communication/interpersonal skills
Doing business in a global economy

STUDENTS

Enrollment of parent institution	1,245
Enrollment of business school	548
% male/female	69/31
% out-of-state	84
% minorities	9
% international	46
Average age at entry	28
Average years work experience at entry	5

ACADEMICS

Academic Experience Rating	**77**
Student/faculty ratio	26:1
Profs interesting rating	78
Profs accessible rating	84
% female faculty	24
% minority faculty	24

Joint Degrees
MBA/MIM (International Management) 1.5–2 years.

Prominent Alumni
Frances Sevilla-Sacasa, President, US Trust Corporation; Luis Moreno, President, Inter-American Development Bank; Mark Emkes, Chairman/CEO, Bridgestone Americas Holding; Lewis Lucke, Ambassador, Kingdom of Swaziland; Bill Burrus, President/CEO, Accion USA.

Academics

There is one overriding reason to pursue an MBA at Thunderbird: it is "the single most globally oriented program in the United States, bar none." In today's business environment, "having specialized knowledge of the global business is a must," and Thunderbird's consistently high rankings in international business draws a community of talented students from across the world. At a school where "over 60 percent of students were born outside the United States or have worked outside the United States," students compare the environment to "a mini U.N. or maybe mini LA," where cultural exchange is highly encouraged. A current student enthuses, "The students and faculty are passionate about international business, and it creates this overwhelming and awe-inspiring feeling of community and an 'Oh my God! I can't believe there is a school like this' feeling."

When it comes to the teaching staff, "Professors are as global as the students," and the "learning opportunities from both faculty and students are outstanding." More than just your average professionals, professors at Thunderbird are veritable experts in their fields, and "Textbooks for many subjects are written by professors at this school." What's more, they consistently are described as student oriented, "really solid, accessible, and for the most part, 'on your side.'" A student elaborates, "They manage to hold their expectations high, while also taking personal responsibility for how well students understand the material."

Students warn that the "workload is heavy," especially in the first year; however, the atmosphere isn't cutthroat. A student assures, "Student collaboration is common and encouraged—there is not the sense that ego-driven, competitive students prevail here." Throughout the core MBA curriculum, course material maintains its focus on global business, and "All of my classes have in some way or form integrated this purpose and help reinforce the materials from other courses." In addition, Thunderbird offers a range of special, internationally focused course offerings on topics such as international market and country analysis. Before graduating, all MBA candidates must be proficient in one foreign language in order to confer their degree.

Many students note that the school has been going through some administrative changes in recent years, which has "resulted in academic class changes, professor departures, and other jarring events that the students were, overall, not informed of and not prepared for." However, most feel that the rocky road will smooth over shortly; and they are quick to point out that the academic programs remain top-notch.

Career and Placement

The Career Management Center at Thunderbird is actively involved in a student's career choices from day one—in fact, students meet with a Career Counselor before they even begin the program. Students note that "the administration seems very focused on finding employment for students," which they demonstrate through more than 150 corporate visits annually, including government, NGO, and intelligence organizations. The CMC also hosts a series of career-related events throughout the academic year. It further helps that "the alumni network is also very strong," with many Thunderbird graduates retaining great memories of and respect for their alma mater. However, the region isn't necessarily the best fit in terms of career opportunities, as "Phoenix does not offer much in terms of a multitude of activities or jobs for international business students." Fortunately, should your dream job materialize on campus, "The student body is so diverse concerning employment interests that it is very rare for two students to be competing for the same employment position."

For the 2006–2007 academic year, Thunderbird MBAs were offered jobs with an average salary of $107,937 (an aggregate of the average base salary of $80,979, an average signing bonus of $12,283, plus an average for other guaranteed compensation of $14,486.) Thirty-four percent chose to work outside the United States. The top employers of 2006–2007 graduates were Hilti, Cisco, Deutsche Post World Net, Bristol-Myers Squibb Company, Johnson & Johnson, American Express, Deloitte, General Electric, Sungard, and IBM.

Student Life and Environment

While Thunderbird is a graduate-only program, campus life might feel something like undergrad. Most Thunderbird students live on campus (many without a car), and "All students are involved in campus clubs or other activities." In addition, students gather for "multiple parties every week," rugby games with the school team, and a plethora of ongoing social and cultural events. A student says, "Culture nights here are the bomb: Korean drums, Capoeira, Thai and Indian dances, cultural[ly] based fashion shows, and abundant food. Learning to love the fabulous cultures around us is one of the great pleasures of Thunderbird." Believe it or not, students say the cafeteria food isn't half bad, and many note that "we also have a pub on campus, which is a great place to meet students that you probably wouldn't meet in class."

While they hail from across the world and every imaginable background, Thunderbird students can nonetheless be characterized as "friendly, collaborative, lively, and highly motivated," or alternately as "worldly, traveled, sophisticated." They take their studies seriously, but Thunderbird students also know when its time to relax, and "friendly discussion over a beer is more likely to be about climbing a mountain in Japan or teaching English in Italy than it is to be about high finance." When they aren't dedicating themselves to school-related activities, "Weekend trips to nearby attractions are common, and even in the busiest of times, students find time to help in the community and to treat themselves to dinners out."

Admissions

To apply to Thunderbird, students must submit a completed application including three personal essays, GMAT scores and (for international students) TOEFL test scores, two letters of recommendation, official transcripts, and a resume. Because a large portion of Thunderbird course work is driven by case studies and practical, hands-on examples, students must have at least 2 years of professional work experience to be considered for the program.

FINANCIAL FACTS

Annual tuition	$37,740
Fees	$1,260
Cost of books	$1,590
Room & board	
(on/off-campus)	$9,205/$9,305
% of students receiving aid	80
% of first-year students	
receiving aid	72
% of students receiving loans	49
% of students receiving grants	44
Average award package	$27,564
Average grant	$13,888
Average student loan debt	$26,609

ADMISSIONS

Admissions Selectivity Rating	79
# of applications received	595
% applicants accepted	72
% acceptees attending	59
Average GMAT	598
Range of GMAT	550–640
Average GPA	3.31
TOEFL required of	
international students	Yes
Minimum TOEFL	
(paper/computer)	600/250
Application fee	$125
International application fee	$125
Regular application deadline	3/3
Regular notification	Rolling
Application Deadline/Notification	
Round 1:	1/7 / Roll
Round 2:	3/3 / Roll
Round 3:	4/28 / Roll
Round 4:	06/30 / Roll
Deferment available	Yes
Maximum length of	
deferment	1 year
Non-fall admissions	Yes
Need-blind admissions	Yes

Applicants Also Look At

Harvard University, The University of Texas at Austin, University of California—Los Angeles, University of South Carolina, Vanderbilt University.

EMPLOYMENT PROFILE

Career Rating		81	
Primary Source of Full-time Job Acceptances			
School-facilitated activities	84 (65%)		
Graduate-facilitated activities	45 (35%)		
Average base starting salary	$80,979		
Percent employed	62		

Grads Employed by Function	%	Avg. Salary
Finance	22	$76,080
Human Resources	3	$94,000
Marketing	29	$82,049
Operations	7	$85,680
Consulting	22	$79,518
General Management	10	$96,265
Other	7	$73,500

Top 5 Employers Hiring Grads
Cisco; Johnson & Johnson; Sungard; Hilti; Deloitte

TULANE UNIVERSITY
FREEMAN SCHOOL OF BUSINESS

GENERAL INFORMATION
Type of school	Private
Environment	City
Academic calendar	Semester

SURVEY SAYS...
Friendly students
Good social scene
Good peer network
Happy students
Smart classrooms
Solid preparation in:
Finance

STUDENTS
Enrollment of parent institution	11,256
Enrollment of business school	210
% male/female	74/26
% out-of-state	79
% part-time	34
% minorities	18
% international	26
Average age at entry	26
Average years work experience at entry	4

ACADEMICS
Academic Experience Rating	**77**
Student/faculty ratio	22:1
Profs interesting rating	79
Profs accessible rating	87
% female faculty	38
% minority faculty	5

Joint Degrees
MBA/MD 5 years, MBA/JD 4 years, MBA/MA (Latin American Studies) 2.5 years, MBA/MA (Health Administration) 2.5 years, MBA/MA (Political Science) 2.5 years, MACCT/JD 4 years, MACCT/MBA 2 years, MACCT/JD 3.5 years, MBA/MA (English) 2.5 years.

Academics

A lot has changed but also stayed the same for MBA students at Tulane. Students note that being "part of the first class in a new curriculum following Hurricane Katrina," they can "see the value in the changes that were made even though there have been a few bumps in the road while the changes have been implemented." "Class size" is still "one of the strong points about Tulane," with sizes "around 50 students." And many happily report that "Tulane has . . . recovered from Hurricane Katrina as [has] New Orleans." "Courses in finance, international business, and entrepreneurship" are strong—particularly finance (many here take "at least a supporting concentration in finance") and entrepreneurship (which is "nationally ranked")—though some find "a limitation of course variety because of the small enrollment."

MBAs appreciate the "at-home atmosphere" at Tulane's Freeman School between students and their "knowledgeable, outgoing, and sometimes brilliantly innovative" professors. They "want students to ask questions and visit them in their office," explains one student. Despite a general feeling of administrative uncertainty after the hurricane, students are confident that "once the faculty turnover has settled down, things will be excellent." But until then, they note, "The professors we have had, are top-notch." And this helps to keep the stress low during the school's intensive 7-week academic terms. Be warned: the heavy course work starts on day one and doesn't let up until exam day.

Before the hurricane, Tulane had experienced impressive growth, and while there are no plans to change that outlook, "enrollment has been lower." Despite this, Tulane is rising with the city. As one student explains, "Some of my classmates decided to transfer to other schools after they evacuated, [but] most of them came back to New Orleans," proving that "the attractiveness of the city and the school" are tough to resist. In light of all this, the school has been "very responsive and receptive to students" who acknowledge that "change is a part of life here." One thing that probably will not change is Freeman's overriding mission of "providing the skills that will be directly applicable to your career."

Career and Placement

Career prep begins as soon as students arrive at the Freeman School; orientation includes training in the use of eRecruiting, Tulane's online student information-management system. Subsequent training in interviewing, resume building, internship hunting, and salary negotiation follows and is offered throughout the program. Tulane also maintains a database (called the Career Consultants Network) of Freeman alumni willing to counsel current students. Job fairs and other recruiting events pepper Freeman's academic calendar.

The school's best efforts notwithstanding, students are less than 100-percent satisfied with their Career Office. One MBA explains that although "the CMC has a horrible reputation . . . it is what the students make of it." Most students concede that "the New Orleans economy is a drawback, but with aggressive . . . networking students have the opportunity to land very good jobs." "Many students in my class have landed great jobs in New York, Houston, Dallas, and a few in New Orleans, among other places," says one student.

Companies most likely to hire Freeman MBAs include Bank of America, Citibank, Credit Suisse, D&T Management Solutions, Entergy, FedEx, First Union Securities, Jackson & Rhodes, JPMorgan Chase, PA Consulting, Reliant Energy, Towers Perrin, and TXU.

BILL D. SANDEFER, DIRECTOR OF GRADUATE ADMISSIONS AND FINANCIAL AID
ADDRESS: 7 MCALISTER DRIVE, SUITE 401 NEW ORLEANS, LA 70118 UNITED STATES
PHONE: 504-865-5410 • FAX: 504-865-6770
E-MAIL: FREEMAN.ADMISSIONS@TULANE.EDU • WEBSITE: FREEMAN.TULANE.EDU

Student Life and Environment

In 2003 the school completed building Goldring/Woldenberg Hall II and the facility earned top marks from all students, who found it "attractive and technologically advanced—amazing." With all the "latest and greatest technology, including a trading floor, digital media theater, 60-inch plasma TVs . . . [and] a number of breakout rooms for students to use for group work," students found plenty of room to host speakers, club meetings, and social functions. And even after all that's gone on, students still report that "the facility is state of the art and has recovered from damage of the hurricane." Students also enthusiastically agree that "New Orleans is a great place to live, and our alumni are great." We have several school-sponsored events that are usually well organized, though in New Orleans style," MBAs report. They add, "Social functions are extremely fun and occur quite often. We usually have a great turnout for each and every one, which makes for great friendships and networking opportunities within the MBA program."

Students here are "very outgoing socially and creative in applying their skills towards real life." One student explains, "For example, we meet every Thursday for 'Think and Drink' and have a 'Social Chair' as a VP position in student government. We also consult with businesses, volunteer, and network more than any other school I see at conferences." One student approvingly notes, "Student organizations also invite speakers [and] do community consulting and other helpful jobs for the communities in New Orleans." "Being in New Orleans, Tulane offers outstanding life outside of the classroom," says one student. "Great food, great music, great festivals, great easygoing people . . . who could ask for anything better?"

Admissions

Freeman reviews applications to its graduate programs in three separate rounds, and the school encourages students to apply as early as possible to maximize their chances of gaining admission. The following is required to apply: an undergraduate transcript, an affidavit of support, GMAT scores, TOEFL scores (for international students), two letters of recommendation, a current resume, personal statement, and interview. Minority recruitment efforts include Destination MBA, the National Black MBA Association Career Fair, targeted GMASS searches, and minority fellowships.

Prominent Alumni

Burdon Lawrence, Chairman, Kirby Corp.; Wayne Downing, General, Natl Director of Security for Combating Terrorism; Ray Nagin, Mayor, City of New Orleans; Larry Gordon, Film Producer, former pres. of 20th Century Fox.

FINANCIAL FACTS

Annual tuition	$33,750
Fees	$1,600
Cost of books	$1,600
Room & board	$11,000
% of students receiving aid	80
% of first-year students receiving aid	74
% of students receiving loans	42
% of students receiving grants	47
Average award package	$41,055
Average grant	$9,350
Average student loan debt	$67,010

ADMISSIONS

Admissions Selectivity Rating	**89**
# of applications received	159
% applicants accepted	61
% acceptees attending	72
Average GMAT	656
Range of GMAT	540–730
Average GPA	3.26
TOEFL required of international students	Yes
Minimum TOEFL (paper/computer)	600/250
Application fee	$125
International application fee	$125
Regular application deadline	5/1
Regular notification	6/1
Application Deadline/Notification	
Round 1:	11/15 / 12/15
Round 2:	01/15 / 02/15
Round 3:	03/15 / 04/15
Round 4:	05/01 / 06/01
Need-blind admissions	Yes

Applicants Also Look At

Emory University, Rice University, Southern Methodist University, The University of North Carolina at Chapel Hill, The University of Texas at Austin, Vanderbilt University, Washington University in St. Louis.

EMPLOYMENT PROFILE

Career Rating	**84**	**Grads Employed by Function**	**%**	**Avg. Salary**
Primary Source of Full-time Job Acceptances		Finance	55	$71,417
School-facilitated activities	54%	Marketing	14	$80,000
Graduate-facilitated activities	46%	Consulting	10	$70,000
Average base starting salary	$73,375	General Management	20	$63,333
Percent employed	93	Other	1	$115,000
		Top 5 Employers Hiring Grads		
		TXU corporation		

THE UNIVERSITY OF AKRON
COLLEGE OF BUSINESS ADMINISTRATION

Academics

Offering a flexible and comprehensive MBA program and boasting an "excellent reputation for business," The University of Akron attracts students from Ohio and beyond who wish to augment their undergraduate degrees or professional experiences with an MBA. The school's low tuition combined with a generous scholarship program makes the program affordable; in fact, "The school supports a lot of students financially," making it a highly appealing choice for many qualified students.

Before they begin their studies, the university conducts a one-on-one consultation with future business students to help them tailor the program to their needs. For those with a more limited business background, the program begins with a series of eight foundational courses. These courses form the cornerstone of the MBA program, establishing a common background and introducing students to the vocabulary they will share throughout their studies. Foundational courses are followed by core courses, which are designed to create breadth within the program, in areas such as leadership and international business. After that, students add depth to their studies by choosing an area of concentration. For the particularly ambitious types, "The University of Akron offers great opportunities through a joint-degree program with its law school. Students can pursue a JD/MBA, JD/MTax, or a JD/MSM-HR simultaneously!"

Thanks to the school's sizable international population, "Group work at The University of Akron presents a valuable opportunity to not only meet diverse people, but also to explore the unique perspective and immense knowledge that others can contribute." A satisfied second-year student shares, "The class discussions require everyone's input, and the respect [shown] for other's opinions is extremely professional. I will actually miss the classes after graduation . . . but not the long weekends writing case studies." Promoting a friendly atmosphere inside and outside the classroom, "Professors are outstanding to talk to outside of class." However, students mention that the program tends to take an academic (rather than practical) approach to business education."

Working students find the program at The University of Akron particularly amenable, as "There is a lot of flexibility in terms of the timings of courses offered and also variety." On the whole, students report that the school is run smoothly, saying the university's "new Dean seems very dynamic and a person who would bring about far-reaching changes in a place that is already full of life and enthusiasm." They also give kudos to the Academic Advising Office, "which is always available to help students with scheduling classes and other problems that we as students encounter on a daily basis."

Career and Placement

The University of Akron Center for Career Management serves the school's undergraduate and graduate community; however, there is no job placement office associated with the business school in particular. As a result, some complain that "there is no serious networking or career counseling or job placement structure here." However, through the CCM, business students can get help with cover letters and resumes, research corporations and positions, and receive one-on-one counseling with career advisors. The CCM also hosts a number of career fairs and on-campus recruiting events annually. Among the companies who recruited at The University of Akron this year are: Allstate Insurance Company, Ameriprise Financial, Bank of America, CareerBuilder.com, Charles Schwab, CVS/Pharmacy, Diebold, Enterprise Rent-A-Car, Northwestern Mutual Finance Network, PERI Software Solutions, Rite Aid, the U.S. Social Security Administration, Target, UPS, Ernst & Young, FedEx, Frito-Lay, INROADS, Linens 'n Things, Lone Star Steel, and

National Interstate Insurance Company. The school's large international population also suggest that the "university should strive to bring those companies on campus which could sponsor international students to work for them."

Student Life and Environment

The student body at The University of Akron is "culturally diverse, friendly, and competitive," creating a laid-back but stimulating atmosphere on campus. Business students enjoy the university's "beautiful and green campus" and appreciate the modern amenities in the business building. A student elaborates, "The wireless computer network is extremely fast and reliable, and all of the classrooms have brand-new multimedia systems." Due to the school's active evening program, a large number of students are "part-time, have day jobs, and are married. A lot of them have children too." Balancing a demanding career and family life with the demands of an MBA program is obviously a challenge. As a result, a large percentage of students say, "There is not a whole lot of time for socialization with other students because of everything else going on."

Full-time students, on the other hand, enjoy the "lively" campus atmosphere and say you'll be "surprised to see how many full-time students there are in the grad program." In the past few years, the larger university "offers students many improved resources for both academic and leisure activities." For example, there are "lots of frats and sports activities," and "The gym/wellness center is a great place to burn off steam." Many students say they chose The University of Akron because they are already based in the area; however, this does not prevent them from recognizing the benefits of this laid-back town. A current student tells us, "The downtown area provides several different types of bars and restaurants. Highland Square and Fairlawn areas also provide shops and different activities to do during time away from classes and studying."

Admissions

To apply to The University of Akron's MBA program, prospective students must submit a completed application, undergraduate transcripts, GMAT scores, and, if English is a second language, TOEFL scores. Be sure to double check your application: Admissions Officials remind us that these materials make a lasting impression and "Spelling errors are noted." Currently, The University of Akron requires a GPA of at least 2.75 for entry, though some successful applicants with significant professional experience have been admitted with lower grades. The previous incoming class presented average GMAT scores of 570 and an average of 5 years of professional experience.

FINANCIAL FACTS

Annual tuition (in-state/ out-of-state)	$14,481/$23,302
Fees	$798
Cost of books	$1,200
Room & board	$10,000
% of students receiving aid	23
% of first-year students receiving aid	23
Average award package	$26,839

ADMISSIONS

Admissions Selectivity Rating	**69**
# of applications received	125
% applicants accepted	90
% acceptees attending	54
Average GMAT	547
Range of GMAT	449–590
Average GPA	3.2
TOEFL required of international students	Yes
Minimum TOEFL (paper/computer)	550/213
Application fee	$30
International application fee	$40
Regular application deadline	8/1
Regular notification	8/15
Deferment available	Yes
Maximum length of deferment	2 years
Transfer students accepted	Yes
Transfer application policy Up to 24 credits of foundation courses and nine credits of the core may transfer from AACSB accredited schools.	
Non-fall admissions	Yes
Need-blind admissions	Yes

Applicants Also Look At

Case Western Reserve University, Cleveland State University, John Carroll University, Kent State University, The Ohio State University, University of Cincinnati, Youngstown State University.

EMPLOYMENT PROFILE

Career Rating	**74**	**Grads Employed by Function% Avg. Salary**	
Primary Source of Full-time Job Acceptances		Finance	22 $53,750
School-facilitated activities	3 (17%)	Human Resources	12 $43,500
Graduate-facilitated activities	15 (83%)	Marketing	22 $46,000
Percent employed	86	General Management	44 $50,900

Top 5 Employers Hiring Grads

The Goodyear Tire & Rubber Company; First Energy Corp.; National City Bank; Enterprise; Dominion

THE UNIVERSITY OF ALABAMA AT BIRMINGHAM
SCHOOL OF BUSINESS

GENERAL INFORMATION

Type of school	Public
Environment	Metropolis
Academic calendar	Semester

SURVEY SAYS...
Cutting edge classes
Smart classrooms
Solid preparation in:
Accounting
Quantitative skills

STUDENTS

Enrollment of parent institution	16,000
Enrollment of business school	398
% male/female	56/44
% out-of-state	5
% part-time	66
% minorities	5
% international	17
Average age at entry	27
Average years work experience at entry	4

ACADEMICS

Academic Experience Rating	**72**
Student/faculty ratio	30:1
Profs interesting rating	86
Profs accessible rating	85
% female faculty	16
% minority faculty	12

Joint Degrees
MBA/MPH (Public Health) 2–3 years, MBA/MS (Health Administration) 2–3 years, MBA/MS (Nursing) 2-3 years.

Prominent Alumni
John Bakane, CEO, Mills; Daryl Byrd, CEO/President, Iberia Bank; Susan Story, CEO/President, Gulf Power Company; James Woodward, Chancellor, UNC; Stephen Zelnak, CEO/President, Martin Marietta Materials.

Academics

The School of Business at the The University of Alabama at Birmingham offers its students concentrations in finance, information technology management, and health care management. "It's a great program" with a "metropolitan" location. Generally known for its medical and health sciences—with highly respected and well-funded research programs, and for strong schools of medicine and nursing—UAB offers in the School of Business several combined degree programs, including MBA/Master of Public Health, MBA/Master of Science in Health Administration and MBA/Master of Science in Nursing.

Students without a business background are required to take foundational courses in subjects including organizational behavior, corporate finance, marketing concepts, and microeconomic analysis. These comprise 21 of the 51 credits required for graduation. Five advanced courses in specific areas including a seminar in marketing policy and at least one course relating to international business are also required, and the remaining classes focus on the student's area of specialization. There are opportunities for study abroad after completing 36 credit hours through agreements with schools in Spain, Italy, and England.

Students praise the "strong academics," the flexible scheduling, and especially the quality of their professors "who have a great deal of academic and real-world experience." The program also has an "excellent reputation as a quality MBA program," and students agree that "the school's prestige," which is based on solid teaching and good administration, "is growing." "The professors really know their field. They bring real-world experience to the classroom." The administration also is a "very solid team, focused on improving the business school."

The university points with pride to the high ranking of its graduates when taking CPA and CFA exams—finance graduates of UAB pass the CFA exam at a rate 20 percent higher than the national average, for example—but some students feel that there may be too much emphasis on the numbers side of business practice. "The experience has been great in reference to understanding the mathematical side of business," but "I would like to have some classes that focus on terminology with not so much math work," one student says.

Career and Placement

There is a Career Services Office located in the School of Business building at UAB, which offers career counseling, coaching, practical workshops on areas such as resume writing and job searching, and an online database of jobs as well as a database to which students may upload their resumes. About three quarters of UAB's MBA student are working professionals, and most candidates for the degree have several years of work experience, so perhaps it's not surprising that they ask for "better recruitment programs for business. The career fairs are heavy in sciences and social sciences," one student believes. However, "location in a metro setting in the Southeast," is a plus: Birmingham is the largest city in Alabama and one of the largest cities in the Southeast. "It is a good state university, and it is located in a great city," which are factors that students agree are helpful in their job searches.

Regions Bank, Alabama Power, Wal-Mart, Baptist Health Systems, AT&T; and Blue Cross and Blue Shield Association are among those who have hired UAB graduates.

ADMISSIONS CONTACT: CHRISTY MANNING, MBA PROGRAM COORDINATOR
ADDRESS: 1530 3RD AVENUE SOUTH BEC 210 BIRMINGHAM, AL 35294-4460 UNITED STATES
PHONE: 205-934-8815 • FAX: 205-934-9200
E-MAIL: CMANNING@UAB.EDU • WEBSITE: WWW.BUSINESS.UAB.EDU/MBA

Student Life and Environment

Most students pursuing an MBA take classes in the late afternoons and evenings at UAB. Opinions are mixed on whether this allows them the opportunity to connect with campus life and their fellow students or if it's more of a hindrance. "I'm part-time so I don't really have a chance to attend activities for full-time students. I'm at campus for school, group meetings, and study time," explains one student. Happy with the level of activity and interaction or not, most find their fellow students "friendly and enjoyable to be around," and "good, hardworking people" who are also "very diverse. "Extremely intelligent, but not very socially oriented," says another student. "Most of all our students have lots of work experience." In common with many MBA programs, UAB appeals to those who already live nearby: "Most work full-time. Most live full-time in [the] community," one student reports.

Birmingham itself has changed over the years from a center for manufacturing, once known as the Pittsburgh of the South for its steel industry, to a center for the information technology business, and for medical research, with a quality of life that ranks it high on most national surveys.

Admissions

Academic GPA rank and scores on the GMAT are considered very important by those making admissions decisions for the graduate business programs at UAB, followed by work experience and personal essays. A minimum score of 480 on the GMAT is required. In 2006 the average score for those admitted is 553, and the average GPA is 3.2. Non-native English speakers must score at least 550 on the TOEFL, and all students are required to have passed a course in business calculus with a grade of C or better in the 5 years preceding admission, or to pass a proficiency exam or, once admitted, to schedule a course in it. At least 2 years of work experience is prefferred for admission; the average student admitted has 4 years.

ADMISSIONS

Admissions Selectivity Rating	74
# of applications received	276
% applicants accepted	81
% acceptees attending	77
Average GMAT	553
Range of GMAT	510–600
Average GPA	3.2
TOEFL required of international students	Yes
Minimum TOEFL (paper/computer)	550/213
Application fee	$50
International application fee	$75
Regular application deadline	7/1
Regular notification	8/1
Deferment available	Yes
Maximum length of deferment	1 year
Transfer students accepted	Yes
Transfer application policy	

Must meet UAB MBA admission requirements, transfer courses must be from AACSB accredited program and equivalent to our required courses.We will accept up to 25% of the degree program in transfer work with a minimum "B" grade.

Non-fall admissions	Yes
Need-blind admissions	Yes

Applicants Also Look At
Samford University.

EMPLOYMENT PROFILE	
Career Rating	76

THE UNIVERSITY OF ALABAMA AT TUSCALOOSA
MANDERSON GRADUATE SCHOOL OF BUSINESS

Academics

Offering a unique combination of "national reputation and Southern hospitality," the Manderson Graduate School of Business at the The University of Alabama at Tuscaloosa treats its MBAs to a small and rigorous program that "stresses the technical aspect of many of the fields covered in the curriculum." The school is well positioned to do so, given that "facilities are fantastic" here, with "a high level of technology in the classroom. Every student has a laptop, and there is a wireless cloud for the business school. You can log on anywhere inside or outside the facilities." Manderson's tech emphasis means that "those with highly quantitative abilities will almost certainly enjoy many of the classes and do quite well, and will quickly acclimate to the workplace upon graduation."

The MBA program at Tuscaloosa is full-time only, with concentrations offered in five areas. Students speak highly of the finance and enterprise consulting programs; several (who apparently don't require sleep) praised the joint JD/MBA program. Professors here are "fantastic. Most write leading textbooks in their subject areas. Better still, they are highly accessible and willing to work as hard as students, and they passionately desire to help students grow as leaders." The program itself is "very rigorous, with high levels of interaction with students and a strong team atmosphere." Some students told us that the workload "sometimes seems impossible."

Administrators here "respond to changes in the marketplace, totally dropping something or taking on something new full force because they know that it will be needed for success in the marketplace." The school also does a great job of keeping "the greatest alumni in the country" in the loop, an endeavor students especially appreciate when it comes time to find a job.

Career and Placement

Students tell us that "currently, the Manderson program is very regional as far as career placement. However, the administration recognizes this weakness and is working to fix that issue in a variety of creative ways. Given their dedication and gung-ho attitudes, expect the program to see quick results." The school has the proper building blocks; MBAs report that "career administrators are awesome, sending constant correspondence regarding our progress and upcoming events." Top employers of Manderson MBAs include Accenture, the AEA Group, Southern Company, Capgemini, Lithonia Lighting, Mercedes-Benz, Proctor & Gamble, International Paper, FedEx, Johnson & Johnson, AmSouth, Regions Bank, and KPMG.

Student Life and Environment

"Life as an MBA student is busy" at Tuscaloosa, as students "have 15 credit hours per semester, and the work is challenging." Students tell us that "although classes usually only last for half the day, the rest of the afternoon and much of the evening in spent going over material. Most of the material is so detailed and comprehensive that it takes tremendous effort at times to meet professors' expectations." In addition, "Team projects are a key part of our grade," and they, too, demand time. The heavy workload helps build a tight campus community; students "go out together, study together, and end up being involved in most aspects of each others' lives." Even when the school day is done, they continue to hang out; "On the evenings and weekends, the MBAA Association, Net Impact, and NAWMBA offer events and socials. Well-known speakers are brought in on almost a weekly basis."

ADMISSIONS CONTACT: MR. BLAKE BEDSOLE, MANAGER, ADMISSIONS AND STUDENT SERVICES
ADDRESS: BOX 870223 TUSCALOOSA, AL 35487-0223 UNITED STATES
PHONE: 205-348-9122 • FAX: 205-348-4504
E-MAIL: MBA@CBA.UA.EDU • WEBSITE: WWW.CBA.UA.EDU/MBA

UA Tuscaloosa students fully embrace the school's football program, "which is very much an essential part of the experience at the university and is a huge part of the traditions. This is a school that is heavily involved in its athletics." Students also tell us that "the school has a beautiful campus that offers countless opportunities to get involved" and that "Tuscaloosa is a great college town, incredibly fun," with "restaurants and bar/grill locations as well as retail and a grocery store on 'the Strip,' which is within walking distance of the b-school complex." The larger city of Birmingham is close enough to provide occasional nights out as well as internship opportunities and professional contacts.

Manderson MBAs tend to be "young, unmarried, and straight out of college," meaning that "many have never worked full-time out of school. This results in a relatively immature class with little appreciation for the opportunity cost of being here." Fortunately, students are "highly intelligent and motivated," so they're capable of managing the challenging work required of them. They're also "competitive yet willing to lend a helping hand at a moment's notice. It's a friendly atmosphere."

Admissions

Applicants to the Manderson MBA program must submit three copies of the completed application form; two copies of a personal statement detailing their past accomplishments and future ambitions; a copy of their current resume; an official GMAT or GRE score report (score must be less than 5 years old); three letters of recommendation; and two official transcripts from each postsecondary institution attended. International applicants must also supply an immigration and visa information form; certification of finances; and, for those applicants whose first language is not English, an official TOEFL score report (score must be less than 2 years old). The Admissions Committee requires an admissions interview, except in rare cases. The school reports that it formulates each incoming class "to represent a diversity of academic, work, cultural, and international experiences that reflects today's workplace. An applicant's background that has the potential to make a unique or missing contribution to an incoming MBA class's make-up can be the deciding admissions factors that supercedes other factors." Incoming students are expected to know how to use Microsoft Office software.

FINANCIAL FACTS

Annual tuition (in-state/ out-of-state)	$5,700/$16,518
Fees	$2,000
Cost of books	$950
Room & board	$9,000
% of students receiving aid	93
% of first-year students receiving aid	90
% of students receiving loans	33
% of students receiving grants	66
Average grant	$9,063

ADMISSIONS

Admissions Selectivity Rating	88
# of applications received	175
% applicants accepted	55
% acceptees attending	64
Average GMAT	615
Range of GMAT	575–650
Average GPA	3.39
TOEFL required of international students	Yes
Minimum TOEFL (paper/computer)	550/213
Application fee	$35
International application fee	$35
Regular application deadline	4/15
Regular notification	Rolling
Application Deadline/Notification	
Round 1:	01/05 / 01/20
Round 2:	02/15 / 03/01
Round 3:	04/15 / 05/01
Round 4:	07/01 / 07/15
Early decision program?	Yes
ED Deadline/Notification	
Fall (Rolling up to Jan. 5) / 01/20	
Deferment available	Yes
Maximum length of deferment	1 year
Transfer students accepted	Yes
Transfer application policy	
Rare, but up to 12 credit hours accepted for transfer from AACSB accredited programs.	
Need-blind admissions	Yes

Applicants Also Look At

Auburn University, Louisiana State University, University of Florida, University of Georgia, University of Mississippi, University of Tennessee, Vanderbilt University.

EMPLOYMENT PROFILE

Career Rating	**84**	**Grads Employed by Function**	**% Avg. Salary**
Primary Source of Full-time Job Acceptances		Finance	29 $60,376
School-facilitated activities	32 (56%)	Human Resources	2 $0
Graduate-facilitated activities	25 (44%)	Marketing	22 $58,150
Average base starting salary	$60,170	MIS	8 $65,000
Percent employed	90	Operations	13 $60,882
		Consulting	4 $0
		General Management	9 $50,000
		Other	13 $69,166

Top 5 Employers Hiring Grads
Accenture; Regions Bank; KPMG; Procter and Gamble; Southern Company

UNIVERSITY OF ALBERTA
SCHOOL OF BUSINESS

Academics

With only 60 students admitted per year, the University of Alberta's 2-year MBA program is highly selective. Students spend the majority of their first year completing core requirements in accounting, business strategy, economics, finance, management science, marketing, and organizational behavior. Teamwork is a central part of the program, and students are assigned to teams at orientation so that they can get to know each other "without the demands of the program that will soon be upon them." In their second year, students are allowed to take elective courses and pursue a specialization in natural resources and energy, international business, technology commercialization, leisure and sports management, or public management. Alberta's diverse offerings are what draw many students to the campus. In fact, Alberta is the "only program in Canada to offer a specialization in leisure and sport management" and "The natural resources and energy specialization is one of only a couple in the world." However, in order to complete a specialization, students must submit a letter of application during the first semester. Alberta offers several MBA joint-degree programs, including MBA/Master of Agriculture, MBA/Master of Engineering, MBA/Master of Forestry, and an MBA/LLB.

Students have rave reviews for their professors, a group of "brilliant academics" who "really care about your performance" and "obviously enjoy teaching MBA students." Students characterize the support provided by the MBA Office as "unbelievable." "We are always aware of what upcoming deadlines are upon us," one student says. "And when we need help with finding courses that work best for us, the staff is extremely helpful."

Although some students feel the school had a tendency to be bureaucratic, one student cites "the welcoming experience I had by the administrative staff" as a "significant motivating factor for me to attend this program." MBA candidates appreciate the small class sizes, particularly in the second-year specialization courses, but some say there's a disconnect between theory and real-world practice.

Part-time students say "The school is really geared to full-time students who have access to the administration during the day and who can attend daytime tutorials." Other part-time students feel there could be "better adaptations and accommodations," as the program's demands on their time are often "extreme." Many students mentioned facilities as an area that could be improved, mostly as a result of the "rapid growth at the university." Students say the facilities are "old" and often "cramped," and that study facilities need upgrading. However, the university is working to address these problems, and "new buildings are on the way!" Overall, students are happy with life at Alberta; as one student put it, "I could not have made a better personal choice."

Career and Placement

The University of Alberta has the highest job-placement rating in Canada, with 93 percent of graduates finding employment within 3 months of graduation. Students praise the "the strength of the networks" built by the school. A wide variety of companies have a presence on campus, including HSBC, KPMG International, Caterpillar, ATCO Electric, the Alberta Government, and the Canadian Soccer Association.

Students accepted jobs in many different industries, with equal percentages going to marketing/sales, consulting, general management, and finance/accounting. The average salary for students who accepted employment 3 months after graduation was $58,373. Some students mentioned that the school could provide "more not-for-profit/arts management information," but, by and large, the students were pleased with the services provided by the Career Office.

ADMISSIONS CONTACT: JOAN WHITE, EXECUTIVE DIRECTOR, MBA PROGRAMS
ADDRESS: 2-30 BUSINESS BUILDING EDMONTON, AB T6G 2R6 CANADA
PHONE: 780-492-3946 • FAX: 780-492-7825
E-MAIL: MBA@UALBERTA.CA • WEBSITE: WWW.MBA.NET

Student Life and Environment

Students at Alberta are nothing if not busy. Life on campus is described as "hectic but fun," with "no shortages of extracurricular activities to get involved in." Among other things, the university organizes holiday get-togethers, and hosts a very popular intramural sports league, and for students who like to party, "There's no shortage of that, either!" The campus, "large in both area and in students," is situated in Edmonton, "one of the most dynamic and red-hot economies in North America." Although Edmonton provides many opportunities for eager MBA students, the "booming economy" can be problematic when it comes to housing, as there is more demand than supply.

The student body is "all ages, and from all over the world." Described as "helpful, intelligent, friendly," the students at Alberta are "high-achieving people willing to work with and help each other." The student body is also very diverse, with almost 50 percent international enrollment. Classes are "very tightly knit," a closeness that starts "right from the orientation." Although the students are "very competitive," most describe their classmates as "very willing to take time to help other students." As with most MBA programs, there is a dividing line between the full-time and part-time students. The full-time students "tend to be younger and have less work experience" than the part-timers, who generally work full-time and take classes at night. However, whether full-time or part-time, most students agreed that their fellow degree candidates were "genuinely nice people."

Admissions

In a recently admitted class, students at the 25th percentile had GPAs of 3.0 and GMAT scores of 550. Students at the 75th percentile had GPAs of 3.5 and a GMAT score of 610. Students had an average of 7 years of work experience.

FINANCIAL FACTS

Annual tuition (in-state/ out-of-state)	$11,000/$22,000
Fees	$750
Cost of books	$1,300
Room & board (on/off-campus)	$7,000/$9,500
% of students receiving aid	50
% of first-year students receiving aid	80
% of students receiving grants	50
Average grant	$4,450

ADMISSIONS

Admissions Selectivity Rating	**85**
# of applications received	180
% applicants accepted	54
% acceptees attending	54
Average GMAT	600
Range of GMAT	550–640
Average GPA	3.3
TOEFL required of international students	Yes
Minimum TOEFL (paper/computer)	600/250
Application fee	$100
International application fee	$100
Regular application deadline	4/30
Regular notification	rolling
Deferment available	Yes
Maximum length of deferment	1 year
Need-blind admissions	Yes

Applicants Also Look At

McGill University, The University of British Columbia, University of Calgary, University of Toronto, University of Western Ontario Richard Ivey School of Business, York University.

EMPLOYMENT PROFILE

Career Rating	**80**	Grads Employed by Function	% Avg. Salary
Primary Source of Full-time Job Acceptances		Finance	38 $67,333
School-facilitated activities	7 (21%)	Marketing	10 $68,333
Graduate-facilitated activities	19 (56%)	MIS	3 NR
Unknown	8 (24%)	Operations	7 NR
Average base starting salary	$70,000	Consulting	17 $77,740
Percent employed	95	General Management	14 $53,558
		Other	10 $88,000

Top 5 Employers Hiring Grads
Ernst & Young; North American Construction Group; TELUS; TD Waterhouse; Accenture

UNIVERSITY OF ARIZONA
ELLER COLLEGE OF MANAGEMENT

GENERAL INFORMATION
Type of school	Public
Environment	Metropolis
Academic calendar	Semester

SURVEY SAYS...
Smart classrooms
Solid preparation in:
Finance
Teamwork
Communication/interpersonal skills
Presentation skills
Entrepreneurial studies

STUDENTS
Enrollment of parent institution	37,000
Enrollment of business school	329
% male/female	80/20
% out-of-state	55
% part-time	64
% minorities	17
% international	27
Average age at entry	26
Average years work experience at entry	4

ACADEMICS
Academic Experience Rating	**83**
Student/faculty ratio	5:1
Profs interesting rating	82
Profs accessible rating	96
% female faculty	32
% minority faculty	22

Joint Degrees
JD/MBA 5 years, MD/MBA 5 years, MBA/MS (International Management) 2–4 years, MS MIS/MBA 3 years, MBA/PharmD 5 years, MBA/MMF 2–3 years, MBA/MS (Engineering and Optical Science) 2-3 years.

Academics

Getting your MBA at The University of Arizona is a warm and sunny experience. With 120 graduate students in the full-time program, "Eller is well known for its close-knit community with a small class size" as well as for a high ranking for its entrepreneurship, MIS, and finance programs. The intimate academic setting really pays off at Eller, where the student body brings its own unique cultural and professional experiences to the classroom. A student says, "People ranging from 22 to 45 (age) are enrolled in the MBA program. They include army personnel, farmers, and lawyers, and [many] are international. The experiences they bring to the table are phenomenal."

The Eller curriculum provides a rigorous business education, with an "emphasis on group work and case studies." Since a majority of the teaching staff joins Eller with a blend of academic credentials and real-world know-how, they lend practical insight to theoretical topics. Students explain, "We have knowledgeable professors who have prepared us well for the business world, including former executives with a great deal of experience." Academics are manageable but the "time commitment is challenging" especially for students who work while attending school; however, students reassure that when the going gets rough, professors are "extremely helpful and go out of their way to assist students." A current student exclaims, "Most of the professors work from home on weekends and reply to e-mails almost instantaneously—this surprises me!"

A startup spirit pervades the campus, and many students come to The University of Arizona for the high-ranked entrepreneurial program. Through the McGuire Entrepreneurship Center, students can pursue a nine-unit concentration in entrepreneurship, with course work in new venture finance, competitive advantage and industry analysis, and venture development. Those looking for a special, diversified education have also found a good match at Eller, as it "is surrounded by strong schools in the university, and it has made a good effort of providing dual degrees between MBA and other science/law-based programs." These dual-degree programs allow students to "further customize their educations and [the programs] provide [students] with additional assets in today's working world." Eller doubles its appeal with a low, public school price tag, as well as a "generous scholarship program," which makes an Eller MBA highly affordable.

Career and Placement

The Office of Career Development aims to provide highly personalized service to each individual student, helping them to plan and achieve their career goals. The office further supports students in their job search through professional development workshops, interview preparation, resume preparation, and professional mentoring. In 2007, 80 percent of students were placed upon graduation, making an average salary of $59,250. Last year, the biggest employers were E & J Gallo Winery, Emerson Electric Company, Ernst & Young LLP, FedEx Services, Intel Corporation, The Dial Corporation, and US Airways Inc.

Located in the heart of Tucson, Arizona, Eller is "really close to the companies and lots of job opportunities." Despite the excellence of the MBA program, some students are disheartened because it's "hard to get recruiters from top companies interested because we do not have the brand name of some schools." However, the Eller administrators are aware of this limitation, and the "Challenges associated with being small and not well recognized nationally are being handled on an ongoing basis," including the recent addition of new companies such as PriceWaterhouse Coopers, Deloitte Consulting, and Texas Instruments. In fact, "New Career Officers have recently been hired," and students believe that career placement opportunities will continue to improve.

Student Life and Environment

Between work, school, networking, and socializing, "life's hectic" at Eller. Blending work with pleasure, Eller "is academically challenging yet provides a lot of social activities allowing students to interact and form firm friendships." A student adds, "Every day there is something new that I look forward to. I spend more time in school than at home, and I just love doing that!" For friendship and future business purposes, the Eller student body is appealing, as "students are friendly, organized, and very culturally diverse, creating a strong sense of global awareness in the environment. Also, I have noticed that they have a high level of business integrity, and many of them have an entrepreneurial nature."

In the pleasant, low-cost, Southwestern city of Tucson, Arizona, the warm and sunny Eller campus is an ideal location for graduate students on a tight budget. Close to the Saguaro National Park and surrounded by beautiful desert scenery, Eller students further benefit from low-cost "great outdoor activities, such as hiking and cycling." The charming and laid-back college campus also boasts a "great recreation center."

Admissions

The admissions process at The University of Arizona is highly quantitative, analyzing each applicant's ability to handle the analytic portions of the program as evidenced by their GMAT scores, undergraduate record, and work experience. The Admissions Committee carefully evaluates each applicant's intellectual capacity, professional experience and career progression, and personal qualities that demonstrate leadership, integrity, initiative, and potential.

In most cases, students must have a GPA of at least 3.0 to be considered for admission; however, the Class of 2008 presented much higher averages, with an average undergraduate GPA of 3.49 and an average GMAT score of 624. There are three rounds of admissions deadlines at Eller, with rolling admissions in the intervening periods, though students are highly encouraged to apply in first round, especially if they are international students or scholarship applicants. All qualified applicants are interviewed by an Admissions Official, either in person or via telephone.

Prominent Alumni

Mark Hoffman, CEO, Commerce One; Thomas Kalinske,, President, Knowledge Universe; Chairman, LeapFrog; Jim Whims, Managing Partner, Tech Fund; Stephen Forte, Sr. VP, Flight Operations, United Airlines; Cephas Bowles, General Manager, WBGO-FM Jazz Radio.

FINANCIAL FACTS

Annual tuition (in-state/ out-of-state)	$15,044/$25,851
Fees	$224
Cost of books	$800
Room & board	$8,400
% of students receiving grants	70
Average grant	$17,939

ADMISSIONS

Admissions Selectivity Rating	85
# of applications received	193
% applicants accepted	108
% acceptees attending	64
Average GMAT	603
Range of GMAT	460–750
Average GPA	3.33
TOEFL required of international students	Yes
Minimum TOEFL (paper/computer)	600/250
Application fee	$50
International application fee	$50
Regular application deadline	4/15
Regular notification	5/15
Application Deadline/Notification	
Round 1:	11/15 / 12/15
Round 2:	02/15 / 03/15
Round 3:	04/15 / 05/15
Early decision program?	Yes
ED Deadline/ Notification	11/15 / 12/15
Deferment available	Yes
Maximum length of deferment	1 year
Need-blind admissions	Yes

Applicants Also Look At

Arizona State University, Babson College, The University of Texas at Austin, Thunderbird, University of California, Irvine, University of Colorado at Boulder, Wake Forest University.

EMPLOYMENT PROFILE

Career Rating	82	Grads Employed by Function	% Avg. Salary
Primary Source of Full-time Job Acceptances		Finance	28 $63,294
School-facilitated activities	16 (52%)	Human Resources	2 NR
Graduate-facilitated activities	15 (48%)	Marketing	22 $67,965
Average base starting salary	$75,003	MIS	9 $66,000
Percent employed	80	Operations	9 $69,000
		Consulting	9 $88,333
		Other	16 $108,937

Top 5 Employers Hiring Grads

Intel Corporation; China Trust Bank; Dial Corporation; Raytheon; US Airways; Emerson; Ernst & Young; FedEx Services; Intel Corporation; PriceWaterhouse Coopers.

UNIVERSITY OF ARKANSAS—FAYETTEVILLE
SAM M. WALTON COLLEGE OF BUSINESS

GENERAL INFORMATION
Type of school	Public
Environment	Town
Academic calendar	Jan. Start

SURVEY SAYS...
Students love Fayetteville, AR
Cutting edge classes
Happy students
Smart classrooms
Solid preparation in:
Finance
Quantitative skills

STUDENTS
Enrollment of parent institution	18,648
Enrollment of business school	86
% male/female	88/12
% out-of-state	5
% part-time	67
% minorities	2
% international	6
Average age at entry	29
Average years work experience at entry	6.7

ACADEMICS
Academic Experience Rating	**89**
Student/faculty ratio	24:1
Profs interesting rating	81
Profs accessible rating	84
% female faculty	19
% minority faculty	17

Joint Degrees
MBA/JD 4 years.

Prominent Alumni
S. Robson Walton, Chairman, Wal-Mart Stores Inc.; William Dillard Sr., Chairman, Dillards Inc.; Frank Fletcher, Entrepreneur; Jack Stephens, Stephens Inc.; Thomas F. McLarty, Former U.S. Presidental Advisor.

Academics

From the moment you arrive, it's clear that students at the University of Arkansas' have a prime location "next to the largest retail corporation in the world." And that's a good thing, since "with Wal-Mart headquarters just a few miles away and multiple vendor offices in the vicinity," the school can easily fulfill its mission of "providing students with real world experiences—especially in supply chain and marketing at Wal-Mart." Students can't resist drawing comparisons to their neighbor and benefactor; one student writes, "The school offers good quality at low cost. It's the Wal-Mart of schools." And Wal-Mart money, students agree, has made Walton College "the most technologically advanced of any school in the U of A system. The classrooms and facilities are second to none."

In order to maximize return on students' investment, Walton offers a 16-month MBA program. Though 4 months longer than the previous version, students find this "better than the old 1-year program" since it "now includes a summer internship, study abroad, or corporate consulting project." Also, one student adds, "The extra time in the program helps give you more time to find a job that is a good fit." The core is covered in two 8-week integrated modules in the fall and the spring starts with a 5-week strategic management course followed by an 11-week consulting project, during which students apply classroom lessons to the real-world problems of local companies ("There are many employment opportunities with Fortune 500 companies in the local area who are eager to hire from the U of A").

MBAs report that "the classes are challenging, and you are expected to work hard." They love the school's "local reputation and contacts, especially if you want to get involved in the retail/Wal-Mart vendor industry." Students also appreciate how "The administration is dedicated to bringing the best teachers together with the best students. They want us to succeed in the class and in life." Accordingly, most students agree that the faculty is "way more knowledgeable, professional, helpful, and approachable than I ever expected." Another explains, "Most of the classes are very interactive, and a top-notch faculty applies and teaches the most current tools to solve today's business problems. They really do challenge us to think outside the box." They also have high hopes for the program's future; as one student comments, "Unlike Wal-Mart right now the stock of a Walton School of Business Diploma is growing at an exponential rate. I think you will find that the people leading business into the future will be from the U of A's Walton College of Business. And let me tell you they are sharp, very sharp. They don't call us Razorbacks for nothing!"

Career and Placement

Since the U of A is so "well known" within the business world, Career Development wouldn't have to do much to help students. However, the Career Center at Walton offers students a number of job fairs each year, some aimed specifically at a particular function (supply chain management, engineering, IT), and others that are open to the entire campus. Students single out the "exceptional" paid graduate assistantship program which allows them to work "on or off campus in offices of international companies, research labs, or with professors." "The work experience you gain through the graduate assistantship program is priceless," says one student.

Top employers of Walton MBAs include J.B. Hunt, Masterfoods, Tyson Foods, Unilever, and, of course, Wal-Mart. About three in five graduates remain in the area; approximately 10 percent find jobs outside of the United States.

Student Life and Environment

The old real estate cliché holds true; it's all about "location, location, location." In Fayetteville, students enjoy a "close proximity to Wal-Mart headquarters and 'Vendorville' (all Wal-Mart suppliers, including Newell-Rubbermaid, Procter & Gamble, and Unilever, have offices here) in one of the fastest-growing region in the country (according to the Milken Institute)," both of which create "great opportunities for newly minted MBAs." In addition, students agree, "Fayetteville is a great town to be in. There is plenty to do socially after hours," says one student. Check out Dixon Street, a near-doppelganger for Bourbon Street, that lines the way to the U of A with bars, shops, and restaurants. And then there are always the football games.

According to students, MBAs form a tight-knit and "unique" community at the university. The rigors of the accelerated academic program also help forge an esprit de corps, but there's more to it than that. One student explains, "The students in the Walton College of Business have formed a collegial and cohesive group. The small size of the program and efforts of the MBA program administration have fostered a supportive and team-oriented approach to our business education." Add into the mix a healthy dose of diversity with "many" students hailing from "China, India, South Korea, Bulgaria, and various states in the U.S." and coming from backgrounds in "engineering, business, law, and arts and sciences." In addition, "Some students have owned their own businesses or worked for large corporations" and "almost everyone . . . has worked or studied abroad."

Admissions

The Walton Admissions Committee reports that successful applicants on average have undergraduate GPAs of 3.4, GMAT scores of 620, and, for international students, TOFEL scores of 550 (paper-based test) or 213 (computer-based test). Preference is given to those with at least 2 years of work experience (or substantial extracurricular involvement in their undergraduate programs). In addition, aim for three letters of recommendation and a compelling personal statement. The school mentions that "underrepresented minorities are encouraged to apply, and special financial assistance is available to minority students."

FINANCIAL FACTS

Annual tuition (in-state/ out-of-state)	$9,261/$21,910
Fees (in-state/ out-of-state)	$3,795/$7,589
Cost of books	$13,348
% of students receiving aid	100
% of first-year students receiving aid	100
% of students receiving grants	100

ADMISSIONS

Admissions Selectivity Rating	91
# of applications received	152
% applicants accepted	70
% acceptees attending	81
Average GMAT	559
Range of GMAT	550–630
Average GPA	3.27
TOEFL required of international students	Yes
Minimum TOEFL (paper/computer)	550/213
Application fee	$40
International application fee	$50
Regular application deadline	9/15
Regular notification	10/15
Early decision program?	Yes
ED Deadline/ Notification	04/01 / 05/01
Deferment available	Yes
Maximum length of deferment	1 year
Transfer students accepted	Yes
Transfer application policy Max 6 hours, electives from an AACSB accredited school.	
Non-fall admissions	Yes
Need-blind admissions	Yes

Applicants Also Look At

Arkansas State University, The University of Texas at Austin, University of Arkansas at Little Rock, University of Central Arkansas, University of Missouri—Columbia, University of Oklahoma, Vanderbilt University.

EMPLOYMENT PROFILE	
Career Rating	78

THE UNIVERSITY OF BRITISH COLUMBIA
SAUDER SCHOOL OF BUSINESS

GENERAL INFORMATION

Type of school	Public
Academic calendar	Unique

SURVEY SAYS...

Students love Vancouver, BC
Friendly students
Good social scene
Good peer network
Solid preparation in:
Accounting
Teamwork

STUDENTS

Enrollment of parent institution	47,000
% international	58
Average age at entry	29
Average years work experience at entry	6

ACADEMICS

Academic Experience Rating	89
Student/faculty ratio	20:1
Profs interesting rating	98
Profs accessible rating	77
% female faculty	17

Joint Degrees

MBA/LLB 4 years, MBA/MAPPS
(Master of Arts, Asia Pacific Policy
Studies) 2 years, MBA/CMA 2 years.

Academics

The Sauder School of Business at the University of British Columbia offers both a 15-month full-time and 28-month part-time MBA in the Robert H. Lee Graduate School. The full-time program convenes at the school's 100-acre campus west of Vancouver's downtown core; the part-time program meets at the school's downtown campus in Robson Square.

Sauder's full-time program commences with a fully integrated core curriculum that "integrates 11 subjects to create one hectic but excellent learning environment." Students describe this intensive 13-week sequence, which imposes a heavy workload and requires a high level of complex analysis, as a boot camp-like experience. The remainder of the program is devoted primarily to specialization electives and professional development. Students tell us that finance is the school's strongest area, although supply chain management, entrepreneurship, and international business also earn praise. An "option to partake in international exchange and an internship" during the final six months of the program means students can leave UBC with two unique and valuable experiences; the former reinforces the international focus of the curriculum as a whole.

Part-time students at Sauder experience the same faculty and curriculum as do full-timers, including the rigorous Integrated Core. The chief difference is scheduling; the part-time program is offered on Friday evenings and on weekends to accommodate students' work schedules. Students in both the full-time and part-time programs describe professors as "a mixed bag. Some are excellent scholars, some are accomplished business leaders, but others don't seem fit to teach master's level courses. Thankfully this last group is a minority." They also tell us that "The support the MBAs receive from the dean, the library staff, the career center, and the MBA office is unbelievable" and that "UBC also has excellent research facilities."

Career and Placement

UBC's Hari B. Varshney Business Career Centre offers "both personal consultation and a structured program" to help students identify goals and develop strategies to meet those goals. Self-assessment, coaching sessions, skills-training programs in resume-writing, interviewing, and networking, recruiting events that bring "corporate recruiters from prominent companies" to campus to interview job candidates, and job postings all figure into the mix here. Some here tell us that "The career center is also very helpful when it comes to finding internships, preparing for interviews or just researching industries," while others complain that the office still needs to improve its performance "if the school wants to be taken seriously at a global level."

Employers likely to hire UBC MBAs include Accenture, BC Hydro, Bell Mobility, Best Buy/Future Shop, BP, Business Objects, Cadbury, Elecronic Arts, Elli Lilly, Fraser Health Authority, GE, Health Canda, Hilti, Honeywell, HSBC, Intrawest, Kodak, Kraft, L'Oreal, Lululemon Athletica, Nike Inc, Nokia, Pepsi Bottling Group, Pivotal Corporation, PMC-Sierra, PricewaterhouseCoopers, Royal Bank Canada, Teekay Shipping Corporation, Telus, Terasen, Vancity, Vancouver Coastal Health, Vancouver International Airport Authority, Vancouver Port Authority, VANOC, and Weyerhauser.

MASTERS PROGRAMS OFFICE, ROBERT H. LEE GRADUATE SCHOOL, SAUDER SCHOOL OF BUSINESS
ADDRESS: #160 - 2053 MAIN MALL VANCOUVER, BC V6T 1Z2 CANADA
PHONE: 604-822-8422 • FAX: 604-822-9030
E-MAIL: MBA@SAUDER.UBC.CA • WEBSITE: WWW.SAUDER.UBC.CA/MBA

Student Life and Environment

The Sauder School "treats the MBA students extremely well. We're spoiled, in fact," with loads of opportunities for career-building extracurricular clubs, recreation, and study-related travel. One student reports: "I have traveled to Nashville and Hamilton, and before this degree is completed I will have been to London (Ontario), Harvard, Philadelphia, and Porto Fino, Italy. Each of these trips is heavily subsidized by our dean. It is his mission to get as many students involved in activities that help promote the Sauder name." The full-time program also has "an excellent social rep who is constantly creating new excuses for us to take a night off from studying." Hometown Vancouver "is amazing," students tell us. "There is always a group of students going for a run, a bike, a hike or a sail," and skiing is accessible during much of the year, thanks to the proximity of Whistler Mountain.

The full-time program at Sauder draws "a very diverse group" that is "nearly 60 percent international, bringing to the classroom "diverse backgrounds of experience and culture." While "quite competitive," students here are quite willing to "help each other with course issues." The school has "a great MBA office to assist students with any problems. It also has a language center to help international students edit their papers and improve their proficiency in English."

Admissions

Admission to the Sauder MBA program is extremely competitive. All applicants must submit official transcripts for undergraduate work (students who attended schools where English was not the primary language must arrange for a certified translation of their transcripts to be delivered to UBC), official GMAT score reports, evidence of English proficiency (TOEFL scores for students whose first language is not English) essays, a resume, and three letters of reference. Interviews are by invitation only; the school interviews roughly half its applicant pool. The school's brochure notes, "Competitive applicants generally have more than two years of full-time post-baccalaureate work experience for admission to the program." On average, students enter the program with six years' full-time professional experience. Applications are processed on a rolling basis; the process favors those who apply early. Admitted students may not defer admission.

FINANCIAL FACTS

Annual tuition	$30,000
Cost of books	$2,200

ADMISSIONS

Admissions Selectivity Rating	84
# of applications received	366
% applicants accepted	64
% acceptees attending	54
Average GMAT	620
Range of GMAT	550–760
Average GPA	3.3
TOEFL required of international students	Yes
Minimum TOEFL (paper/computer)	600/250
Application fee	$125
International application fee	$125
Regular application deadline	4/30
Regular notification	Rolling
Need-blind admissions	Yes

Applicants Also Look At
McGill University, University of Toronto, University of Western Ontario, York University.

EMPLOYMENT PROFILE

Career Rating	87	Grads Employed by Function	% Avg. Salary
Percent employed	94	Finance	24 $92,500
		Human Resources	1 NR
		Marketing	11 $71,000
		MIS	4 $67,000
		Operations	6 $60,000
		Consulting	15 $76,000
		General Management	19 $70,000
		Other	20 NR

UNIVERSITY OF CALGARY
HASKAYNE SCHOOL OF BUSINESS

GENERAL INFORMATION

Type of school	Public
Academic calendar	Semester

SURVEY SAYS...

Students love Calgary, AB
Smart classrooms

STUDENTS

Enrollment of parent institution	28,200
Enrollment of business school	280
% male/female	67/33
% part-time	75
% international	27
Average age at entry	30
Average years work experience at entry	6

ACADEMICS

Academic Experience Rating	**80**
Student/faculty ratio	3:1
Profs interesting rating	68
Profs accessible rating	84
% female faculty	25

Joint Degrees

MBA/LLB 4 years, MBA/MSW 2 years, MBA/MD 5 years, MBA/MBT 2 years.

Prominent Alumni

Al Duerr, President/CEO, Al Duerr & Associates; Charlie Fisher, President/CEO, Nexen; Hal Kvisle, President/CEO, Trans Canada; Brett Wilson, Managing Director/First Energy Capital; Byron Osing, Chairman, Launchworks Inc.

Academics

The University of Calgary's Haskayne School of Business boasts more than 3,000 full- and part-time students enrolled in bachelor's, master's, PhD, and executive education programs. Despite its large size, intimacy is the name of the game with the MBA program. "It is a relatively small-sized MBA program—around 30 full-time," says one candidate, "so it is good for students." Haskayne is one of the top business schools in the world, and has received top rankings from several sources. Students echo these accolades, describing their classmates as "knowledgeable," the administration as "friendly and helpful," and the professors as having "strong academic backgrounds." One student says, "I am very happy with the close support" provided by the faculty.

Aside from the traditional MBA, Haskayne offers many degrees, including the Alberta/Haskayne Executive MBA (offered jointly with the University of Alberta), a PhD, and an interdisciplinary Master of Science in Sustainable Energy Development in Quito, Ecuador. Students praised the school's "focus on the oil and gas industry," as well as their "expertise in finance." Haskayne also offers several joint-degrees with other faculties within the University of Calgary, including the MBA/MBT, JD/MBA, MD/MBA, and MSW/MBA. Some students wish that "the Haskayne school would be more strict with academic enrollment." "The class age is getting younger and those coming in have very little tangible work experience."

The Haskayne MBA is a 20-course program, which consists of 10 core courses, 2 integrative courses, and 8 electives. Up to two electives can be taken outside the School of Business with approval from the MBA office. Students appreciate the program's flexibility, and the "ability to tailor your course work, activities, [and] job searches to your future career field." Another says: "Coming from an engineering background and wanting to transition into investment banking, I have found this school very accommodating." Students also have an opportunity to engage in a mentorship program in their second year, and 43 senior executives from 32 companies were participating as mentors in 2006–2007. One student who benefited from the program said, "This was the most helpful career development opportunity I have taken advantage of while at Haskayne. My mentor was an ideal match for me and highly networked into the business community."

Career and Placement

Students are very enthusiastic about the career opportunities afforded by Haskayne's "close ties to the business community," and the Career Center earns praise for its "help concerning resume writing and interview skills." In surveys, the school's location is consistently listed as one of its major benefits. It's "in the heart of the current hottest (economically speaking) city in Canada," and the city is in "close proximity to major companies' headquarters." Another student said, "There are plenty of quality jobs available for MBA students . . . high-profile oil and gas companies and investment banks are a staple at recruitment drives."

There is a strong multinational recruiting presence on campus, and students enjoy a great deal of "opportunity upon graduation," particularly in the energy and financial sectors, where "salary and benefits are far superior to many other industries." Companies that frequently hire graduates include Nexen, Enbridge, Suncor Energy, CIBC World Markets, Scotia Bank, Shell Canada, Imperial Oil, and Deloitte Touche Tohmatsu. The mean base salary (without bonus) is $95,351, and 93 percent of students reported accepting offers by three months after graduation. As one student said, "It is an MBA employee's market right now."

ADMISSIONS CONTACT: MICHAEL MCKINLAY, ADMISSIONS COORDINATOR
ADDRESS: 2500 UNIVERSITY DRIVE, NW CALGARY, AB T2N 1N4 CANADA
PHONE: 403-220-3808 • FAX: 403-282-0095
E-MAIL: MBAREQUEST@MGMT.UCALGARY.CA • WEBSITE: WWW.HASKAYNE.UCALGARY.CA/MBA

Student Life and Environment

Students tout the "diversity of the class" and the lack of "the hostile competitive environment" at Haskayne, which has "made for a better learning experience." Because of the small class size, students know each other well and "spend many hours outside of class together." Others echoed that sentiment, describing their classmates as "like family." Life in Calgary is described as "on the go," and although the MBA Society plans social events for students like skiing and bowling, some students note that the heavy workload makes it difficult to get involved with extracurricular activities.

The biggest complaint among students is the scarce housing, which is described as "difficult (and expensive!)" and "a nightmare." Students praise the facilities, particularly the "great gym at the school with modern equipment" and the MBA Lounge, where "most of the students spend the whole day." There are always people there "to help you or just to chat." As is the case with many other schools, the part-time students feel segregated from the full-time students. "As a part-time student, I am little involved in campus life," one student says. Other part-timers agree, explaining that "you attend your courses and go home."

Admissions

Fall 2006, the average GMAT score for Haskayne first-years was 614, and the average GPA was 3.30. Students had an average of 6 years of work experience. The average age of the Fall 2006 entering class was 30.

FINANCIAL FACTS

Annual tuition (in-state/ out-of-state)	$11,450/$20,350
Fees	$843
Cost of books	$2,000
Room & board	$12,000
% of first-year students receiving aid	75
Average grant	$5,000

ADMISSIONS

Admissions Selectivity Rating	85
# of applications received	200
% applicants accepted	60
% acceptees attending	54
Average GMAT	614
Range of GMAT	550–680
Average GPA	3.3
TOEFL required of international students	Yes
Minimum TOEFL (paper/computer)	600/250
Application fee	$100
International application fee	$130
Regular application deadline	5/1
Regular notification	Rolling
Application Deadline/Notification	
Round 1:	11/15 / 01/15
Round 2:	01/15 / 03/01
Round 3:	03/01 / 05/01
Round 4:	05/01 / 06/15
Deferment available	Yes
Maximum length of deferment	1 year
Transfer students accepted	Yes
Transfer application policy	
We can accept up to nine courses.	
Need-blind admissions	Yes

Applicants Also Look At

Queen's University, The University of British Columbia, University of Alberta, University of Western Ontario, York University.

EMPLOYMENT PROFILE

Career Rating	93	Grads Employed by Function	% Avg. Salary
Primary Source of Full-time Job Acceptances		Finance	31 NR
School-facilitated activities	44%	Human Resources	3 NR
Graduate-facilitated activities	56%	Marketing	11 NR
Percent employed	93	MIS	3 NR
		Operations	36 NR
		Consulting	14 NR
		Other	2 NR

UNIVERSITY OF CALIFORNIA—BERKELEY
HAAS SCHOOL OF BUSINESS

GENERAL INFORMATION
Type of school	Public
Environment	City
Academic calendar	Semester

SURVEY SAYS...
Good social scene
Good peer network
Happy students

STUDENTS
Enrollment of parent institution	32,714
Enrollment of business school	1,404
% male/female	66/34
% out-of-state	70
% part-time	64
% minorities	4
% international	32
Average age at entry	29
Average years work experience at entry	5.4

ACADEMICS
Academic Experience Rating	**96**
Student/faculty ratio	12:1
Profs interesting rating	80
Profs accessible rating	98
% female faculty	25

Joint Degrees
MBA/MPH (Public Health), MBA/JD
3–4 years, MBA/MIAS 3 years.

Prominent Alumni
Arun Sarin, CEO, Vodafone; Barbara Desoer, Exec VP, Bank of America; Paul Otellini, CEO of Intel; Bengt Baron, CEO, V & S Group (Absolut Vodka), Sweden; Ishmael Benavides, Minister of Agriculture, Peru.

Academics

The Haas School of Business at the University of California—Berkeley offers students "a truly interactive environment," one in which "professors learn from the students as well as the other way around" thanks to students' substantial input into the program. The full-time program in particular is designed to provide students with an unusual degree of autonomy; explains one student, "Student initiative comes into play in every aspect of the program, from scheduling speakers to career search." Students here also design and run, with faculty oversight, a number of electives every semester. The result of all this freedom is that "students are forced to become entrepreneurs as part of their education." The small size of the program (only 250 full-time students and about as many part-timers) contributes to the experience by "forcing a collaborative environment where competition is put aside in order to help one another."

Haas backs up its unique approach to graduate business education with a strong curriculum and a solid faculty. The school excels in social entrepreneurship, corporate social responsibility, general management, and technology; this last area capitalizes on Berkeley's location "across the bay from San Francisco and just one hour from Silicon Valley." The faculty includes a number of stars; boasts one MBA, "Our finance professor is serving as the president of the San Francisco Federal Reserve. Our Dean was on leave as [Governor] Arnold Schwarzenegger's Finance Director. They don't get better than this." Better still, "not only are the professors outstanding in their fields, but they are also highly approachable and willing to make changes to the class to meet the students' needs." Semesters move along quickly here; "The academic pace is very fast," students observe, "but the workload is not overwhelming." While the core "is solid," most here prefer the "awesome electives that give you some great opportunities outside the classroom."

Career and Placement

When it comes time to find a career, Berkeley MBAs benefit from their program's high profile and sound reputation. As is often the case at such schools, the Haas Career Center provides a broad range of excellent services. Students here benefit from one-on-one advisement, access to numerous online job databases, industry clubs, workshops, seminars, a mentoring program in which second-year students counsel first years in their search for internships, and a strong, global alumni network.

Employers most likely to hire Berkeley MBAs include Bank of America; the Clorox Company; Deloitte Google; Apple; Bain & Co.; Boston Consulting Group; Abbott; Genentech; Amazon; Lehman, Yahoo!; Johnson & Johnson; McKinsey & Company; Microsoft; and Wells Fargo.

Student Life and Environment

For full-time students, "student clubs are at the heart of the school" because they help organize student input to the program. Explains one MBA, "Nothing happens at Haas without student involvement. Just about every full-time student is heavily involved in all aspects of the school. From student government to admissions to industry clubs to sports and wine clubs, everyone is able to express their interests and tap their fellow students for more information or just someone to share a good meal." The administration "fully supports club activities and has our needs on their minds continuously. It is only with their aid that we have been able to accomplish so much in our short time here."

ADMISSIONS CONTACT: PETER JOHNSON, DIRECTOR OF INT'L ADMISSIONS, FULL-TIME MBA PROG
ADDRESS: 430 STUDENT SERVICES BUILDING #1902 BERKELEY, CA 94720-1902 UNITED STATES
PHONE: 510-642-1405 • FAX: 510-643-6659
E-MAIL: MBAADM@HAAS.BERKELEY.EDU • WEBSITE: WWW.HAAS.BERKELEY.EDU

Between classes, clubs, and other extracurricular options, "live is very busy" for full-time students at Haas. There are "groups constantly getting together to go to arts festivals, AIDS walks, golfing, cycling, surfing, skiing, attending seminars, hearing guest lecturers, and hiking, to name just a few activities. The opportunities are endless and everyone loves being here." Thursday nights "are a tradition at Haas. We have BoW (Bar of the Week) in Berkeley and San Francisco, so there are always fun places to check out as you get to know the area." Students also appreciate their "access to the Bay Area's business, culture, natural beauty, and geographic diversity. Networking opportunities abound because so many business and thought leaders either live in the area or pass through here."

The "great, resourceful, creative, and mellow" students of Haas are "warm, but with a competitive edge—in the best sense of the word." Students speculate that "Haas' long-standing 'no grade-disclosure' policy" results in "students who are extremely helpful to each other, making certain that learning is truly a collaborative process." Indeed, our survey respondents all agree that "students at Haas are extremely team-oriented. They very much work together to get things done. The Berkeley MBA attracts top-notch students from all over the world and we mutually benefit from one another's experiences." Adds one student, "Given how diverse the work experiences are here, I find myself learning from those around me every day. These are truly the type of people I want to work with and for after graduation."

Admissions

Applicants to Haas graduate programs must submit all the following materials to the admissions department: official copies of transcripts for all postsecondary academic work, an official GMAT score report, letters of recommendation, a personal statement, and a resume. Interviews are conducted on an invitation-only basis. In addition to the above materials, international applicants whose first language is not English must also submit official score reports for the TOEFL (minimum score of 570 for the paper-based test, 230 for the computer-based test). The school considers all of the following in determining admissions status: "demonstration of quantitative ability; quality of work experience, including depth and breadth of responsibilities; opportunities to demonstrate leadership, etc.; strength of letters of recommendation; depth and breadth of extracurricular and community involvement; and strength of short answer and essays, including articulation of clear focus and goals."

FINANCIAL FACTS

Annual tuition (in-state/ out-of-state)	$26,881/$37,950
Cost of books	$2,500
Room & board	$20,012
% of students receiving aid	75
% of first-year students receiving aid	70
% of students receiving loans	59
% of students receiving grants	27
Average award package	$33,856
Average grant	$17,420
Average student loan debt	$54,098

ADMISSIONS

Admissions Selectivity Rating	99
# of applications received	3,276
% applicants accepted	14
% acceptees attending	53
Average GMAT	710
Range of GMAT	680–740
Average GPA	3.57
TOEFL required of international students	Yes
Minimum TOEFL (paper/computer)	570/230
Application fee	$175
International application fee	$175
Regular application deadline	3/12
Regular notification	5/14
Application Deadline/Notification	
Round 1:	11/5 / 1/29
Round 2:	12/11 / 3/19
Round 3:	1/31 / 4/30
Round 4:	3/12 / 5/14
Need-blind admissions	Yes

Applicants Also Look At
Columbia University, Harvard University, New York University, Northwestern University, Stanford University, University of California—Los Angeles, University of Pennsylvania.

EMPLOYMENT PROFILE

Career Rating	98	Grads Employed by Function% Avg. Salary	
Primary Source of Full-time Job Acceptances		Finance	35 $99,529
School-facilitated activities	154 (72%)	Marketing	23 $98,315
Graduate-facilitated activities	53 (25%)	MIS	1 NR
Unknown	7 (3%)	Operations	1 $96,667
Average base starting salary	$101,859	Consulting	19 $112,348
Percent employed	94	General Management	16 $104,497
		Other	2 $85,400

Top 5 Employers Hiring Grads
Google; Deloitte; Bain & Co.; Bank of America; McKinsey & Co./Abbott/Citi/Yahoo!

UNIVERSITY OF CALIFORNIA—DAVIS
GRADUATE SCHOOL OF MANAGEMENT

Academics

With a class size of fewer than 60 students, the full-time daytime MBA program at UC, Davis "is the closest thing to a private education, combined with all the resources of the University of California." It's a combination students here appreciate. One student says, "UC, Davis Graduate School of Management is based on a team-oriented and collaborative environment. I didn't feel that a school focused on . . . intense competition was truly reflective of the qualities that would serve me well in my post-MBA career. The GSM's emphasis on ideas to action through teamwork has been everything I hoped for."

UC, Davis excels in a surprising range of disciplines, given the size of the program. Students describe a "renowned organizational behavior program" and say the school is especially strong in finance. Also, "If you want to be an entrepreneur, there is no other school you should even consider applying to. There are more opportunities for viable startups moving through the UC, Davis campus than the GSM can even handle!" The school's Consulting Center "allows students to take on real-life projects for credit," while recent changes to the curriculum have created "a strong and quickly evolving focus area (via classes, concentrations, centers of excellence, student organizations, and dual degrees) in corporate social responsibility and business sustainability."

The Davis business faculty "is top-notch. Their expertise is almost always available for students to draw on. We have a formal student-faculty mentoring program, most professors have an open-door policy, and their offices are in our building. They have been willing to sponsor clubs, teach new courses that students request, aid in job searches, employ students as research and teaching assistants, attend social events, etc." Students love how "The administration eagerly pursues feedback from students and then implements effectual change. We work together to better the school based on changing business and social trends and the goals of the current student body. It is very encouraging to see a suggestion implemented quickly that improves the quality of our educational experience."

Career and Placement

Students report that "as a small school, our Career Services resources are more limited than other programs," so "Finding a post-MBA career takes more student initiative than may be required at bigger schools." While the office "is excellent for finding finance jobs," it "leaves a little to be desired in other areas." Also, "Being in the Sacramento area really hurts our ability to recruit companies. Services are improving, though." On another positive note, "While being a small program limits the breadth of alumni contacts, the value of the contacts derived from our small feel far outweighs the downside."

Employers that most frequently recruit Davis MBAs include: AT&T, Blue Cross and Blue Shield Association, CalPERS, CalSTRS, Clorox, Deloitte Touche Tohmatsu, eBay, E&J Gallo Winery, Gartner Consulting, Hewlett-Packard, IBM, Intel, Kaiser Permanente, MRSI Consulting, National Forest Service, PricewaterhouseCoopers, and Wells Fargo.

Student Life and Environment

At the top of Davis MBAs' wish list is a new facility, as the program currently is housed "in a small older building." Ground was broken in December, 2007, and the new building will be ready in fall 2009. When it arrives, the new facility "will include a conference center, restaurant, etc., and will be located across from the famous Mondavi Center [for the performing arts]."

Davis MBAs "are given the opportunity to become involved in a large number of clubs," thanks to the small size of the program. One student writes, "As the leader of the UC—Davis chapter of Challenge for Charity, I know that I can literally call 30 to 50 percent of my classmates on the weekend for help with an event or project and they'd be willing to help. I think that would be extremely difficult to find at bigger schools." Extracurricular events "range from career/academic panels to wine appreciation classes to flag football games. We work hard and play hard here, and everyone is included." While "there are no specific activities for partners/spouses, they are always encouraged to join in and come to events."

Davis "is a growing midsize city. It is called 'bike town U.S.A.' because there is no need to own a car (this is rare in California). . . . There is a diverse mix of restaurants, including Thai, Chinese, Japanese, Mexican, Czech, Bavarian, French, European, Indian, American fare, and others." The city is located "20 minutes from downtown Sacramento, 90 minutes from San Francisco, and 2 hours from Lake Tahoe." Another student says, "The environment in Davis is awesome. It has high quality of life, elementary schools are great, everybody bikes around, there's no violence," and there's "huge diversity."

Admissions

Admissions Officers for the full-time MBA program at UC—Davis consider the following factors in assessing candidates: academic potential, professional potential, and personal qualities. Full-time work experience is not required for admission, but most students have at least a few years of work experience. Applicants must submit the following materials: a completed application form (online or hard copy); a current resume; a list of outside activities and honors; three personal essays; official transcripts from each undergraduate and graduate institution attended; two letters of recommendation; and an official GMAT score report. Applicants whose native language is not English must submit an official TOEFL score report or IELTS reflecting a score no more than 2 years old. Applications to the full-time program are accepted for the fall semester only.

FINANCIAL FACTS

Annual tuition	$12,245
Fees	$22,629
Cost of books	$1,707
Room & board	$13,349
% of students receiving aid	100
% of first-year students receiving aid	100
% of students receiving loans	62
% of students receiving grants	67
Average award package	$24,955
Average grant	$11,387
Average student loan debt	$37,000

ADMISSIONS

Admissions Selectivity Rating	97
# of applications received	337
% applicants accepted	26
% acceptees attending	65
Average GMAT	674
Range of GMAT	650–700
Average GPA	3.39
TOEFL required of international students	Yes
Minimum TOEFL (paper/computer)	600/250
Application fee	$125
International application fee	$125
Regular application deadline	3/12
Regular notification	5/31
Application Deadline/Notification	
Round 1:	11/14 / 01/31
Round 2:	01/16 / 3/31
Round 3:	03/12 / 5/31
Round 4:	05/14 / 6/30
Early decision program?	Yes
ED Deadline/Notification	11/14 / 01/31
Deferment available	Yes
Maximum length of deferment	1 year
Transfer students accepted	No
Transfer application policy A maximum of 12 quarter units from a University of California campus or 6 quarter units from another university.	
Need-blind admissions	Yes

Applicants Also Look At

Stanford University, The University of Texas at Austin, University of California—Irvine, University of California—Los Angeles, University of California—Berkeley, University of Southern California.

EMPLOYMENT PROFILE

Career Rating	88	Grads Employed by Function	% Avg. Salary
Primary Source of Full-time Job Acceptances		Finance	30 $81,336
School-facilitated activities	23 (59%)	Marketing	23 $81,438
Graduate-facilitated activities	16 (41%)	MIS	8 $127,333
Average base starting salary	$85,555	Operations	8 $67,500
Percent employed	89	Consulting	23 $83,125
		General Management	8 $93,280

Top 5 Employers Hiring Grads
Agilent Technologies; Blue Shield; Pacific Gas & Electric; Pricewaterhouse Coopers; Trianz

UNIVERSITY OF CALIFORNIA—IRVINE
THE PAUL MERAGE SCHOOL OF BUSINESS

GENERAL INFORMATION

Type of school	Public
Environment	City
Academic calendar	Sept–June

SURVEY SAYS...

Good social scene
Cutting edge classes
Happy students
Smart classrooms
Solid preparation in:
Accounting

STUDENTS

Enrollment of parent institution	24,000
Enrollment of business school	800
% male/female	68/32
% part-time	74
% international	34
Average age at entry	28
Average years work experience at entry	4.5

ACADEMICS

Academic Experience Rating	**89**
Student/faculty ratio	7:1
Profs interesting rating	82
Profs accessible rating	95
% female faculty	25

Joint Degrees

MD/MBA 5–6 years.

Prominent Alumni

Lisa Locklear, Vice President,
Ingram Micro; Darcy Kopcho,
Executive Vice President, Capital
Group Companies; George
Kessinger, Pres. and CEO, Goodwill
Industries International; Norman
Witt, Vice President Community
Development, The Irvine C.

Academics

At the University of California—Irvine's Paul Merage School of Business, "The buzz is growing so quickly you can just feel that UC—Irvine is about to explode." Students across the board had rave reviews for the school, calling it "a great experience." Students praise an "intimate environment" that includes monthly lunches with the Dean, and "faculty and staff who actually remember you." The "experienced professors" all are "very knowledgeable in their fields. Some are not as good teachers but [are] great research[ers]. We also have professors [who] are full-time professionals" that "provide valuable insights" and are "very committed to teaching first-year students the basic skills needed to succeed." Students also reserved high praise for the administration, which is "very involved in our day-to-day needs." As one student put it, "They really make us feel wanted."

Aside from the full-time MBA, Merage offers a fully employed MBA, an executive MBA, and a health care executive MBA. Merage also offers a doctoral program, with degrees available in accounting, finance, information systems, marketing, operations and decision technologies, organization and management, and strategy. The full-time MBA program has 13 core courses, after which students are allowed to take a range of elective courses to tailor their program to their specific career goals. Students say the school excels at disciplines like finance and marketing, but that it's "missing out on the opportunity to really expand the course offerings to include topics like CSR [corporate social responsibility] and globalization."

Unique elements of the Merage experience include the opportunity to study abroad at one of 10 different business schools throughout Europe, South America, and Asia, as well as the Merage MBA Field Project. Available to second-year students, the Field Project is a 10-week corporate program in which student teams work directly with company managers while receiving guidance from a faculty expert. Students appreciate the school's heavy focus on teamwork, commenting that "it's common to see groups of students working together on campus," and that "it's not a competitive environment like other MBA programs." As one student gushed, "The school is in an upswing . . . everything is great. I really love it here!"

Career and Placement

UC—Irvine students have a "special advantage" when it comes to employment opportunities because of their proximity to University Research Park, which is located next to the campus. Host to a slew of big-name corporations like America Online, Cisco Systems, and McKinsey & Company, the park "attracts companies interested in hiring UCI students and collaborating with faculty on research projects." Although students appreciate the wide variety of companies that recruit for summer internships (149 in 2006), some students mentioned that the career center could do a better job of "helping students with their job search outside of Southern California." However, many students saw "dramatic improvement" in the university's support of the Career Center, as well as the recent overhaul of its strategy.

Many large companies have a recruiting presence on campus, including Microsoft, KPMG International, Intel, Buena Vista Home Entertainment, Accenture, Bristol-Myers Squibb Company, and Honda Motor Company. Almost half of the 2006 graduates went into the finance/accounting industry, and the remaining students went into either marketing or consulting. Fifty-eight percent of students had a job offer by graduation, and 83 percent had accepted an offer within 3 months after graduation.

ADMISSIONS CONTACT: CHRISTINE HOYT, ASSISTANT DIRECTOR RECRUITMENT AND ADMISSIONS
ADDRESS: SB 220 IRVINE, CA 92697-3125 UNITED STATES
PHONE: 949-824-4622 • FAX: 949-824-2235
E-MAIL: MBA@MERAGE.UCI.EDU • WEBSITE: WWW.MERAGE.UCI.EDU

Student Life and Environment

It's all about the location at UC—Irvine. Nestled in famous Orange County, Merage students truly feel that "you can't beat the O.C." Although Irvine itself is described as a "safe and quiet town," the nearby beach cities of Newport and Laguna are "awesome destinations" for "sunny days and wild nights." With "nearby beach, golf courses, and relatively close places to ski/snowboard," students have plenty of ways to blow off steam and hang out with their classmates.

Student life at Merage is very social, and the students describe each other as "proactive [about] socializing together outside of school" and, a little more bluntly, "party animals, smart and friendly." Students can take advantage of the abundance of extracurricular activities on campus. With a range of activities that include "functional/career clubs to corporate social responsibility clubs," students have "many opportunities to get involved." Outside of clubs, students mentioned the weekly happy hours, which are well attended and give "everyone a chance to get to know each other better."

For most of the students, housing is "a very special aspect" of the Merage experience. With plenty of space on campus, "most MBAs will get housing if they want it," at a cost that is "lower than private market." First-years are usually assigned to live in the same apartment complex, which students describe as "gorgeous" and beneficial to students' social lives. Students say the housing situation contributes to "a family atmosphere that really strengthens the community bonds."

Admissions

The average undergraduate GPA of recently admitted students was 3.37, and their average GMAT score was 687. The average age of the students was 28, and most had around 5 years of work experience. International students make up 34 percent of the student body.

FINANCIAL FACTS

Annual tuition (in-state/ out-of-state)	$26,187/$37,394
Cost of books	$2,947
Room & board (on/off-campus)	$11,039/$14,425
% of students receiving aid	80
% of first-year students receiving aid	84
% of students receiving loans	54
% of students receiving grants	67
Average award package	$22,500
Average grant	$10,784
Average student loan debt	$45,500

ADMISSIONS

Admissions Selectivity Rating	**92**
# of applications received	600
% applicants accepted	40
% acceptees attending	43
Average GMAT	670
Range of GMAT	600–740
Average GPA	3.3
TOEFL required of international students	Yes
Minimum TOEFL (paper/computer)	600/250
Application fee	$150
International application fee	$150
Application Deadline/Notification	
Round 1:	11/1 / 01/15
Round 2:	12/15 / 03/01
Round 3:	02/01 / 04/01
Round 4:	04/15 / 06/15
Non-fall admissions	Yes
Need-blind admissions	Yes

Applicants Also Look At

University of California—Davis, University of California—Los Angeles, University of California—Berkeley, University of Southern California, University of Washington.

EMPLOYMENT PROFILE

Career Rating	76	Grads Employed by Function	%	Avg. Salary
Primary Source of Full-time Job Acceptances		Finance	28	$70,266
School-facilitated activities	39 (68%)	Human Resources	3	NR
Graduate-facilitated activities	18 (32%)	Marketing	25	$74,928
Average base starting salary	$76,407	MIS	3	NR
Percent employed	31	Consulting	33	$79,222
		General Management	3	NR
		Other	3	$75,666

Top 5 Employers Hiring Grads

PricewaterhouseCoopers; Deloitte & Touche; KPMG; Johnson & Johnson; Yahoo!

University of California—Los Angeles
Anderson School of Management

GENERAL INFORMATION
Type of school	Public
Environment	Metropolis
Academic calendar	Quarters

SURVEY SAYS...
Students love Los Angeles, CA
Friendly students
Good social scene
Good peer network
Happy students

STUDENTS
Enrollment of parent institution	38,896
Enrollment of business school	1,557
% male/female	69/31
% out-of-state	31
% part-time	54
% minorities	26
% international	31
Average age at entry	28
Average years work experience at entry	4.6

ACADEMICS
Academic Experience Rating	**97**
Profs interesting rating	83
Profs accessible rating	91
% female faculty	20
% minority faculty	23

Joint Degrees
MBA/JD, MBA/MD, MBA/DDS, MBA/MPH, MBA/MA (Latin American Studies), MBA/MA (Urban Planning), MBA/MS (Computer Science), MBA/MS (Public Policy), MBA/MS (Library and Information Science), MBA/MS (Nursing), MBA/MS (Public Health).

Prominent Alumni
Jeff Henley, Chairman, Oracle Corporation; William Gross, Founder & Chief Investment Officer, PIMCO; Chris Zyda, International CFO, Amazon; Lisa Brummel, Vice President of Home Products, Microsoft; Mitch Kupchak, General Manager, Los Angeles Lakers.

Academics

Future business mavens show their innate decision-making powers when choosing to pursue an MBA at UCLA Anderson School of Business, an institution touted as the "best school in Southern California as far as reputation" that has the added benefit of being a "great value since it's a public school." Among its many advantages, UCLA boasts a prime location in Los Angeles, offering access to Hollywood and the entertainment industry, as well as "greater exposure to Asia and greater name recognition in Asia" than is typically found in East Coast schools. Students also choose Anderson for the "emphasis on entrepreneurial topics in the curriculum" and the fact that a "culture of leadership and cooperation is reinforced throughout the courses and student activities."

Students report that the school's "intellectually top-notch faculty," make learning engaging as well as useful, as professors are "well respected in their fields and effective in class." In addition to their skill in the classroom, UCLA professors are lauded as friendly, accessible, and "committed to our learning experience." But don't mistake the affable atmosphere for an easy ride. The pace is "fast and furious" especially at the beginning, as there is an "extremely heavy workload the first quarter of the first year."

Throughout the program's rigorous core courses and elective offerings, Anderson strives to make "theoretical material relevant to real-world situations." Professors are "on top of current industry trends and have interesting/dynamic lectures reflecting their specialized industry knowledge." Applying classroom concepts to practical scenarios, the culmination of an Anderson MBA is a 20-week course entitled Applied Management Research, through which students work in groups to build a business plan, conduct a management field study, or collaborate on a special project.

Through the school's numerous research centers, students have access to specialized academic and extracurricular activities, classes, and association with expert faculty. The various student-run clubs and academic organizations further enhance the curricular experience through events and seminars. For example, "150 events, from hosted dinners to strategy workshops, are hosted by the Entrepreneur Association each year." Anderson also operates several international exchange programs, through which students earn course credit at universities in Asia, Europe, Australia, and Latin America.

Career and Placement

With the reputation as the "best in the West," UCLA students have full "access to top recruiters in entertainment and technology" and can look for a job during the plethora of "on-site recruiting events with all the top firms." Offering "amazing placement services," the Parker Career Management Center brings more than 300 companies to recruit on campus each year.

In 2006, a whopping 97 percent of UCLA students who were looking for a job had received an offer within 3 months of graduation, and 93.4 percent had accepted an offer. A second-year student attests, "I already have several very competitive job offers from the top-tier firms in the industry in which I wish to work." Consulting was the most popular career choice (as it has been for several years at UCLA), drawing 14 percent of graduates. The next most popular fields were entertainment, with 11.8 percent of graduates, and real estate, with 10.5 percent of graduates. The average salary for a new graduate was $92,011.

MAE JENNIFER SHORES, ASST. DEAN AND DIR. OF MBA ADMISSIONS & FINANCIAL AID
ADDRESS: 110 WESTWOOD PLAZA, GOLD HALL, SUITE B201 LOS ANGELES, CA 90095-1481 U.S.
PHONE: 310-825-6944 • FAX: 310-825-8582
E-MAIL: MBA.ADMISSIONS@ANDERSON.UCLA.EDU • WEBSITE: WWW.ANDERSON.UCLA.EDU

Student Life and Environment

Although it is a competitive, top-tier school, UCLA "has a reputation as having a laid-back student body where there's not a lot of competitiveness/mean-spiritedness among the students." Does it live up to its image? Absolutely. UCLA business students are "friendly, social, outgoing, intellectually curious and have amazing pedigrees—minus the egos that are often associated with top backgrounds." Others describe them as "brilliant party animals" who are "fun loving yet have very high standards for the quality of their work." A lively collegiate environment, "social events, networking events, study groups, classes, lunch, clubs meetings" are well attended; and "Most activities are student run with minimal support from administration," a situation well suited to entrepreneurial graduate students.

If you want to blow off steam with your classmates, "There are social activities every week, multiple times a week," including a "social party for the whole business school every Thursday evening." However, given the school's demanding workload, "Some people attend every one of them, and some people attend very few." A second-year student admits, "It can be a 'fun in the sun' school to some extent, but I spend a whole lot more time with formulas and models than I do with a surfboard." Even so, students are sure to take advantage of their fabulous location. A current students shares, "Weekends are filled with more than waves and beer. Sunshine affords great hiking all year long, such as Runyon Canyon, and many of us escape at least once per quarter to nearby sunny San Diego or up north for a weekend of cultural exuberance in San Francisco."

Admissions

UCLA receives thousands of applications for an entering class of just 360 students. Admissions Officials insist that there is no specific skill set or "cookie cutter" profile for a successful applicant to Anderson. Rather, the Admissions Committee evaluates each applicant's unique ability to be a leader in management and to contribute to the community at UCLA. As such, there are no minimum requirements for GMAT scores or undergraduate GPA, and there is no minimum requirement for previous work experience—though these factors are heavily considered in an admissions decision. Other factors that influence an admissions decision are TOEFL scores (when applicable), achievements, awards, letters of recommendation, college and community involvement, and previous leadership experience. Prospective students also have the option of scheduling an interview at UCLA.

FINANCIAL FACTS

Fees (in-state/ out-of-state)	$36,860/$39,050
Cost of books	$11,230
Room & board (off-campus)	$13,407
% of students receiving aid	70
% of first-year students receiving aid	75
% of students receiving loans	70
% of students receiving grants	60
Average award package	$55,139
Average grant	$15,000
Average student loan debt	$93,000

ADMISSIONS

Admissions Selectivity Rating	97
# of applications received	3,151
% applicants accepted	23
% acceptees attending	49
Average GMAT	704
Range of GMAT	680–730
Average GPA	3.55
TOEFL required of international students	Yes
Minimum TOEFL (paper/computer)	600/260
Application fee	$175
International application fee	$175
Regular application deadline	4/28
Regular notification	6/23
Application Deadline/Notification	
Round 1:	11/03 / 01/26
Round 2:	01/05 / 03/24
Round 3:	02/21 / 05/19
Round 4:	04/28 / 06/23
Early decision program?	Yes
ED Deadline/ Notification	11/03 / 01/26
Deferment available	Yes
Maximum length of deferment	case by case basis
Need-blind admissions	Yes

Applicants Also Look At

Duke University, Harvard University, Northwestern University, Stanford University, University of California—Berkeley, University of Pennsylvania.

EMPLOYMENT PROFILE

Career Rating	95	Grads Employed by Function	% Avg. Salary
Primary Source of Full-time Job Acceptances		Finance	41 $100,811
School-facilitated activities	188 (72%)	Human Resources	1 $90,000
Graduate-facilitated activities	73 (28%)	Marketing	25 $91,577
Average base starting salary	$99,237	MIS	1 $87,500
Percent employed	93	Operations	2 $86,750
		Consulting	15 $112,703
		General Management	5 $98,431
		Other	10 $96,102

Top 5 Employers Hiring Grads
Yahoo! Inc.; Deloitte Consulting; Google; Citigroup; Merrill Lynch & Co.

UNIVERSITY OF CALIFORNIA—RIVERSIDE
A. GARY ANDERSON GRADUATE SCHOOL OF MANAGEMENT

Academics

Combine the Southern California climate with a "fantastic school" and it's easy to understand why the A. Gary Anderson Graduate School of Management at UC—Riverside gets such high marks from students. One raves, "I am having the time of my life [and] . . . feel very privileged to be here." Many MBA candidates here are taking their first steps in the business world, as applicants are not required to have work experience—which can be a good or bad thing depending on who you talk to. One thing students do agree on is the "challenging" classes, bolstered by the "very accessible" professors who "care very much about their students' learning and understanding of the course material." However, some students would like to see them "chase the new trends of business aggressively."

The six components of an MBA from AGSM are the core courses, an internship, the communication workshop, the electives, a "capstone course," and a case project or thesis. Though the core courses take up more time than any other single component, students are most enthusiastic about the "wide diversity of electives," which are all seminar size and designed to "encourage participative learning." One student explains, "I love coming to a small school like UCR's AGSM. You get real interaction with professors, and all of the students know each other, which allows for tighter bonds and networks." There are 10 areas of electives, and students are allowed to take up to nine courses from any area, such as accounting, entrepreneurial management, finance, general management, human resources management/organizational behavior, international management, management information systems, management science, marketing, and production and operations management.

Most students agree that "discussion is greatly encouraged" in class. A fair number of courses "require presentation with business formal attire" and some "even require group debate." One student notes, "It gives you some pressure, but it's fun." Some lament the feeling that the university "does not attach [enough] importance to our business school," and hope for this to change in the near future. Others, though conscious that the school is a "research-oriented university," wouldn't mind getting more "attention from some professors" who they find to be "mostly researchers and not lecturers."

Career and Placement

Aside from recent budget cuts, the thing that has most students at AGSM are up in arms about is the Career Resources Center. As one student says, "The school desperately needs a stronger Career Counseling Center designed just for the MBA students." Another adds, "I really think the school should begin to target the school's alumni more. There are many UCR MBAs in the industry and they could be a real resource and asset to the school." The MBA now has its own Career Services, which should help alleviate many of the students' concerns regarding "job placement," "internships," and "professional networking."

ADMISSIONS CONTACT: CINDY ROULETTE, MBA STUDENT AFFAIRS OFFICER
ADDRESS: ANDERSON HALL RIVERSIDE, CA 92521-0203 UNITED STATES
PHONE: (951) 827-4551 • FAX: (951) 827-3970
E-MAIL: MBA@UCR.EDU • WEBSITE: WWW.AGSM.UCR.EDU

Student Life and Environment

In recent years Riverside, California has undergone both something of a renaissance and an influx of people. Gone are the days of quiet orange groves, and in their place resides the veritable capital of the Inland Empire. Whether your tastes run to the great outdoors or to great shopping, students find "plenty of unique hangouts, interesting shopping, and a wide variety of eats to fit anyone's desires (and budget)." Some MBA students feel that they "lack social activities" within the program, though in many instances this could be blamed on the large amount of "homework" these students undertake. That said, as the university (and those that surround it) continue to grow, students can expect more avenues to their social outlets to open.

The school itself is housed in a 30,000-square-foot building that features "state-of-the-art research and teaching facilities." MBA students agree that their "computer lab is very nice" and relish that they, as MBAs, "have priority over all computers in the lab." Other students gripe that they're stuck in "a small building that consists of one lecture room and one classroom. Our school has suffered greatly from the previous budget cuts." Still, the building must have something going for it because "MBA students rarely venture onto the main campus at [UC Riverside], unless it's to go to the library or bookstore."

Students report that "most people are very nice, and it is easy to meet new people if you try." These "very laid-back and friendly" students have formed "a tight-knit community here because our graduate program is so small." "I pretty much know and am friends with every other MBA student," says one. Due to the proximity of students, there is "a level of competition between students during academic competitions and presentations," but most happily note that "it is healthy and in good fun."

Admissions

At AGSM, students from all undergraduate majors and levels of business experience are eligible for admission. In fact, more than 30 percent of all incoming students come from a background other than business and have little—if any—experience in the business world. According to the school, "There is no minimum GPA or GMAT requirement for MBA admission consideration." However, they also say "Satisfying minimal standards does not guarantee admission, since the number of qualified applicants far exceeds the number of places available," meaning that you'd best do your best. It is worth noting that because the school doesn't require prior work experience, all prospective MBAs must complete an internship "to ensure your success upon graduation."

FINANCIAL FACTS

Annual tuition (in-state/ out-of-state)	$0/$12,245
Fees	$23,455
Cost of books	$1,650
Room & board	$8,954
% of students receiving aid	45
% of first-year students receiving aid	46
% of students receiving grants	45
Average award package	$21,573
Average grant	$14,276

ADMISSIONS

Admissions Selectivity Rating	78
# of applications received	263
% applicants accepted	59
% acceptees attending	28
Average GMAT	569
Range of GMAT	540–610
Average GPA	3.35
TOEFL required of international students	Yes
Minimum TOEFL (paper/computer)	550/213
Application fee	$60
International application fee	$75
Regular application deadline	5/1
Regular notification	6/1
Transfer students accepted	Yes
Transfer application policy A maximum of 8 graduate units taken in residence may be transferred.	
Non-fall admissions	Yes
Need-blind admissions	Yes

Applicants Also Look At

California State Polytechnic University—Pomona, California State University—Fullerton, Pepperdine University, University of California—Irvine, University of California—San Diego.

EMPLOYMENT PROFILE

Career Rating	66	Grads Employed by Function% Avg. Salary		
Primary Source of Full-time Job Acceptances		Finance	30	$44,900
School-facilitated activities	12 (30%)	Human Resources	10	$31,200
Graduate-facilitated activities	29 (70%)	Marketing	20	$30,900
Percent employed	47	**Top 5 Employers Hiring Grads**		
		Deloitte & Touche; Ernst & Young; Cathay Bank - Taiwan; IEHP		

UNIVERSITY OF CENTRAL ARKANSAS
COLLEGE OF BUSINESS ADMINISTRATION

GENERAL INFORMATION
Type of school	Public
Environment	Town
Academic calendar	Semester

SURVEY SAYS...
Students love Conway, AR
Helpful alumni
Happy students
Solid preparation in:
Operations
Teamwork
Computer skills
Entrepreneurial studies

STUDENTS
Enrollment of parent institution	12,800
Enrollment of business school	84
% male/female	62/38
% out-of-state	35
% part-time	56
% minorities	16
% international	32
Average age at entry	26
Average years work experience at entry	4

ACADEMICS
Academic Experience Rating	**61**
Student/faculty ratio	28:1
Profs interesting rating	62
Profs accessible rating	61
% female faculty	19
% minority faculty	19

Academics

University of Central Arkansas operates a number of graduate business programs, including full-time and part-time MBA programs, a master of accountancy, and a master's program in community and economic development. One testament to the quality of education at University of Central Arkansas is that many undergraduate students choose to return to the university for a graduate degree, directly out of college or many years later. A current student writes, "I attended UCA for my undergrad degree and it is such a good fit for me that it was an easy decision to stay."

Before students can begin the MBA program at UCA, they must complete prerequisite coursework in accounting, economics, and finance. After they have completed the prerequisites, the MBA program consists of ten business courses. Students also have the option of pursuing an international specialization through an additional six credit hours in an approved elective or internship experiences related to international business. Focused on advanced, general management principles, the MBA coursework is quite traditional. In fact, a number of students say they'd like a more interactive business school experience, as UCA's program includes "no group work, few papers, and hardly any projects."

When it comes to the teaching staff, student opinions run the gamut; however, a current student assures us, "With the exception of a small portion of my professors, I have had great relationships with all my teachers. I feel I have been given a solid education at UCA, facilitated by small class sizes, a large college atmosphere, and attentive professors." With an entering class of just 50 students each year, class sizes are small and instructors generally encourage students to add their personal experiences to academic material. As a result, "classroom discussion is rarely dry. We all get along well and enjoy each other's thoughts and input, whether in or out of the classroom."

University of Central Arkansas is rapidly expanding its offerings and campus facilities. When it comes to the school's leadership, students appreciate the fact that "our president is seen everywhere and only a handful of students don't know him by name." The College of Business is likewise on the up-and-up. A student writes, "The administration is in a transition to make the College of Business one of the best in the state. The transition is not complete, but it is well on its way." A case in point, plans are currently in the works for a new business school building, including state-of-the-art case study classrooms, a student commons, and a professional conference room.

Career and Placement

Attracting a large part-time population of students who already have professional jobs, the College of Business doesn't dedicate many resources to career planning and placement. However, business students can use the University of Central Arkansas Career Services office, which offers resume writing assistance, campus interviews, current job listings, career fairs, and workshops for job seekers. Even so, those who'd like to start a new career after graduation say the business school could do more to "help with job placement and recruitment." After graduation, UCA students can keep networking with other alums through the MBA Alumni Association or at events like the MBA Scholarship Golf Classic.

ADMISSIONS CONTACT: DAVID KIM, MBA DIRECTOR
ADDRESS: COLLEGE OF BUSINESS, UNIVERSITY OF CENTRAL ARKANSAS CONWAY, AR 72035 U.S.
PHONE: 501-450-5316 • FAX: 501-450-5302
E-MAIL: DAVIDK@UCA.EDU • WEBSITE: WWW.UCA.EDU/DIVISIONS/ACADEMIC/MBA

Student Life and Environment

Located "right in the middle of Arkansas," UCA boasts a "beautiful" campus with ever-improving facilities, including a "brand new medical and self-wellness center." Plans are under way to keep the positive changes going, and currently "the student center is being expanded to house more eating establishments and office/meeting space" and the student recreation center is constructing a new, Olympic-size swimming pool. On the larger campus, "there are hundreds of student organizations that any student can get involved in." However, most MBA students feel they are "left to fend for themselves," with few networking events or campus activities expressly for them.

Within the MBA program, "the students are divided between professionals and those who did their undergraduate work here"—the former group usually comprised of younger, recent graduates. Those who did their undergraduate degree at UCA tend to feel more connected to the university than those who entered the university to pursue an MBA or masters degree. Both full-time and part-time students at UCA are "all are very busy between their personal, business, and academic activities." As a result, "there is not much time for socializing." The surrounding town of Conway is a growing city of 50,000, which offers modest recreational activities for students. However, be advised that "you have to travel over 30 miles to get a drink" after class.

Admissions

To be considered for admission at University of Central Arkansas, students must submit a minimum GMAT score of 500 and a minimum undergraduate GPA of 2.7. Along with their application, students must submit a two-page statement of purpose. Last year's entering class had an average GMAT score of 524 and an average undergraduate GPA of 3.27.

FINANCIAL FACTS

Annual tuition (in-state/ out-of-state)	$5,748/$10,572
Fees	$298
Cost of books	$1,000
Room & board (on/off-campus)	$6,578/$6,300

ADMISSIONS

Admissions Selectivity Rating	72
# of applications received	64
% applicants accepted	83
% acceptees attending	83
Average GMAT	524
Range of GMAT	460–620
Average GPA	3.28
TOEFL required of international students	Yes
Minimum TOEFL (paper/computer)	550/213
Application fee	$25
International application fee	$40
Deferment available	Yes
Maximum length of deferment	3 years
Transfer students accepted	Yes
Transfer application policy A maximum of 6 graduate hours is transferrable from a AACSB institution.	
Non-fall admissions	Yes

Applicants Also Look At

Arkansas State University, University of Arkansas at Little Rock, University of Arkansas—Fayetteville.

UNIVERSITY OF CENTRAL FLORIDA
COLLEGE OF BUSINESS ADMINISTRATION

GENERAL INFORMATION
Type of school	Public
Environment	City
Academic calendar	Semester

SURVEY SAYS...
Students love Orlando, FL
Friendly students
Smart classrooms
Solid preparation in:
General management
Teamwork

STUDENTS
Enrollment of parent institution	48,699
Enrollment of business school	516
% male/female	61/39
% out-of-state	8
% part-time	51
% minorities	18
% international	12
Average age at entry	31
Average years work experience at entry	8

ACADEMICS
Academic Experience Rating	**71**
Student/faculty ratio	37:1
Profs interesting rating	64
Profs accessible rating	82
% female faculty	15
% minority faculty	12

Joint Degrees
MBA/MS (Sport Business Management) 21 months.

Prominent Alumni
Kenneth G. Dixon, CPA, Real Estate Developer; J. D. Atchison, Exec. VP, Sea World; Andrew J. Fore III, Exec. Director, Citigroup Business Services; Nan McCormick, Partner, Sr. VP, CB Richard Ellis; Laurette Koellner, President, The Boeing Co.

Academics

Students pursuing an MBA at the University of Central Florida have four options: the traditional MBA, a lockstep evening program designed for working professionals; the full-time one-year MBA, a daytime program for freshly minted BAs as well as mid-career professionals looking to jumpstart their careers; an Executive MBA, designed for current executives and managers with at least five years experience; and a Professional MBA, which reduces the EMBA experience requirement from five years to three. In addition, the school offers a variety of master's degrees in business, including a well-regarded program in sport business management.

UCF draws a predominantly local student body that turns to the school because it is "affordable and convenient." Some cite the program's "emphasis on diversity and community service" as further incentives to attend. Others tout the "outstanding professors" whose "actual work experience for almost all of their classes is their greatest strength" but who are also "always willing to help students whether it be with class material or outside counsel." The one-year program appeals to "individuals who want to move right into their MBA before or while beginning their career search."

UCF is a relatively "younger school, so many of the facilities are well equipped with up-to-date computer systems and fully functional (as opposed to antiquated buildings on older campuses)." Resources "are excellent; there are computer and study labs with peer help available 24/7, the online resources are great, teachers are always available, advisors help with planning, and courses are easy to find and register for." Like many newer schools, UCF is constantly developing, and students tell us that "The MBA program has made goods step in helping with the selection of electives by introducing various certificate programs (i.e., entrepreneurship). However, it could still offer more, especially in terms of international business considering the number of foreign students." Students see UCF's Orlando location as a big plus, "providing a variety of outside opportunities to get experience while in school."

Career and Placement

UCF's Office for Corporate Partnerships & Career Management (OCPCM) provides counseling and placement services to MBA and other graduate business students. The office includes a Career Information Library stocked with job binders, salary surveys, employer databases, and other reading materials. Workshops are offered in resume writing, job search strategies, interviewing techniques, and federal employment opportunities. Counselors are also available to assist with internship and full-time job searches.

Employers who most frequently hire UCF MBAs include Embarq, Fairwinds Credit Union, GlaxoSmithKline, Harris Corporation, Lockheed Martin, Northrup Grumman, Northwestern Mutual Financial Network, Protiviti, and Siemens. Just over one quarter of UCF MBAs find work in finance and accounting (mean starting salary: $52,188). Marketing/sales and operation/production each claim just over one-fifth of each graduating class.

Student Life and Environment

For full-time MBAs at UCF, "There is always something to do, something to see, something to learn. The UCF campus is always alive." Classes meet "early in the morning, and then most students have graduate assistantships where they work in the afternoon. There are group projects due nearly every week, so the ability to get to campus quickly and easily is imperative. Fortunately, although the university has nearly 50,000 students, the graduate business school does not have a crowded feel. In fact, it sometimes seems

ADMISSIONS CONTACT: JUDY RYDER, DIRECTOR OF GRADUATE ADMISSIONS
ADDRESS: P.O. BOX 161400, BA I, ROOM 240 ORLANDO, FL 32816 UNITED STATES
PHONE: 407-823-4723 • FAX: 407-823-0219
E-MAIL: CBAGRAD@BUS.UCF.EDU • WEBSITE: WWW.BUS.UCF.EDU

like a separate bubble, but in a way that promotes intense focus and cooperation on common goals." The school hosts " many different types of clubs, societies, and groups to join" to keep students busy when they're not in class or studying.

Students love UCF's "blue skies with nearly constant sunshine and green grass. It is a genuine pleasure simply to walk to class" across this "beautiful campus." As one student puts it, "There are four Starbucks locations and three different places to get pizza. What else do you need to know?" For those who need to know more: UCF has "excellent resources ranging from a great library to an enormous gym to restaurants and more," "the new stadium and arena are awesome," and the campus is host to "lots of activities, concerts, comedy, etc." As an added bonus, the school's "sports teams are becoming more recognized nationally."

Not all students have time to enjoy campus amenities. UCF's part-timers typically "don't do much outside of academics at my school" because they're simply too busy. They are working professionals whose experience "helps make the part-time program what it is. The interaction of the students and the professors is at a high level that keeps you wanting to attend class." In both the part-time and full-time programs "there is a broad range of students of all races and backgrounds," infusing each cohort with "different personalities and backgrounds that provide different points of view. Our class helps each other out a lot."

Admissions

Applicants to the UCF College of Business MBA program must complete an online application to the UCF School of Graduate Studies. Additionally, applicants must submit official transcripts for each university or college attended, an official GMAT score report, a personal essay, a current resume, and three letters of recommendation. International students whose first language is not English must also submit TOEFL scores (minimum score: 577 paper-based; 233 computer-based; 90-91 Internet-based); all international students need to provide translations of non-English documents and an accredited course-by-course evaluation of transcripts from institutions that do not employ the American grading system. UCF requires a minimum GMAT score of 540 (550 for the one-year full-time program) for its MBA programs; requirements for other Master's programs are less restrictive. An undergraduate GPA of at least 3.0 over the final 60 semester hours of coursework (3.3 for the One-Year MBA) is also required.

FINANCIAL FACTS

Annual tuition (in-state/ out-of-state)	$6,480/$23,952
Fees	$180
Cost of books	$1,500
Room & board (on/off-campus)	$8,500/$14,000

ADMISSIONS

Admissions Selectivity Rating	**84**
# of applications received	308
% applicants accepted	53
% acceptees attending	88
Average GMAT	550
Range of GMAT	540–620
Average GPA	3.3
TOEFL required of international students	Yes
Minimum TOEFL (paper/computer)	575/233
Application fee	$30
International application fee	$30
Regular application deadline	6/15
Regular notification	Rolling
Early decision program?	Yes
ED Deadline/Notification	Fall Only: 1/15 / 03/15
Transfer students accepted	Yes
Transfer application policy	

Transfer applicants must be from a regionally or nationally accredited university. May transfer in up to 9 hours.

Need-blind admissions	Yes

Applicants Also Look At

Florida State University, Rollins College, University of Florida, University of South Florida.

EMPLOYMENT PROFILE

Career Rating	73	Grads Employed by Function	% Avg. Salary
Primary Source of Full-time Job Acceptances		Finance	28 $52,188
School-facilitated activities	7 (39%)	Human Resources	6 $40,000
Graduate-facilitated activities	11 (61%)	Marketing	22 $47,500
Average base starting salary	$51,379	Operations	22 $61,250
Percent employed	12	Consulting	11 $47,500
		General Management	11 $47,500

Top 5 Employers Hiring Grads

Harris Corporation; Lockheed Martin; Marcus & Millichap; Protiviti; Target Corporation

THE UNIVERSITY OF CHICAGO
GRADUATE SCHOOL OF BUSINESS

Academics

"The emphasis on [students] learning the basics rather than some predigested goo" along with "an unbeatable faculty" are "what make the University of Chicago's Graduate School of Business (GSB) one of the best, especially in hard-core areas such as finance and accounting," students tell us. A "rigorous quantitative program that compels students to think critically and analytically" is the hallmark of a Chicago MBA, although students hasten to add that GSB also "emphasizes persuasion, communication, and negotiation skills."

Chicago offers a full-time, part-time evening, part-time weekend, and executive MBA program. All three tracks share "top-notch" faculty, wide-ranging academic options, and an approach that "doesn't chase new trends in business but instead relies on teaching sound fundamentals that can then be applied to any situation." The programs differ in some details; full-time students, for example, enjoy a grade nondisclosure policy that creates a conducive environment for "teamwork and sharing of ideas." Full-time students must also complete the Leadership Exploration and Development (LEAD) program, which "provides analytic frameworks for leadership that are very helpful in determining the best way to use [one's] strengths and where to improve." While neither grade nondisclosure nor LEAD is included in the part-time curriculum, part-timers enjoy "great flexibility," noting that "most classes have several sessions taught by the same professor during the same quarter, enabling students to make up class sessions if for some reason they cannot attend their normal session." GSB's weekend executive and regular MBAs have "students flying to Chicago from across the U.S. and world to attend classes on Saturdays. This connects a much broader and more diverse group of people than other MBA programs can."

Chicago's faculty includes Nobel laureates and cutting-edge researchers "who also excel in the classroom." One accounting student reports, "Both my corporate tax strategy professor and my M&A accounting professor consult for corporate and government clients, so they have intimate knowledge of how to apply what they teach in the real world." GSB is best known for its faculty in finance, economics, and accounting, but students note that the school should work to "increase awareness of its excellence in marketing, entrepreneurship, and general management disciplines." Many students also "do a one-term or full-year exchange program at a foreign business school," and "These international career development opportunities are a big part of the experience for many GSB students."

Career and Placement

The GSB Career Services Office doesn't have to work hard; as one student explains, "The network and doors that open up to a graduate from Chicago GSB are outstanding. Gaining an MBA from this school carries a lot of weight and in the job market no one will question your education." That doesn't mean that Career Services slacks off, however; on the contrary, it "is an excellent resource and deserves praise," and does a good job attracting recruiters in consulting, accounting, and finance including McKinsey & Company, Lehman Brothers, Citigroup, The Boston Consulting Group, UBS, A.T. Kearney, Credit Suisse, Goldman Sachs, Merrill Lynch, Bear Stearns, and Booz Allen Hamilton.

Chicago GSB also excels at "preparing career changers. You learn from the best faculty in the world to attain the skills you need to succeed in your given career. The alumni, and especially second-year students at the school, are available to answer any questions.

ROSEMARIA MARTINELLI, ASSOCIATE DEAN, STUDENT RECRUITMENT & ADMISSIONS
ADDRESS: 5807 SOUTH WOODLAWN AVENUE CHICAGO, IL 60637 UNITED STATES
PHONE: 773-702-7369 • FAX: 773-702-9085
E-MAIL: ADMISSIONS@CHICAGOGSB.EDU • WEBSITE: CHICAGOGSB.EDU

Career Services does an excellent job of helping you identify your transferable skills to your new targeted career . . . I would highly recommend the school for people looking to change careers."

Student Life and Environment

"The social aspect of University of Chicago is often overlooked," students in the full-time program tell us, reporting that "There are all kinds of opportunities to get together with other students in social or more formal settings, including school-sponsored happy hours, etc." Although "MBAs here work as hard as students at any other b-school, we know how to have fun too." One student writes, "If anything, there are too many programs and opportunities to be involved. You need to carefully consider them all to properly juggle [your] schedule." And with "the great city of Chicago is at our doorstep," students don't have to look far to find a wide range of fun diversions.

The school is located on Chicago's South Side in the Hyde Park neighborhood, which "is too often made out to be a scary place when, in fact, it's not. There is a pretty unique mixture of socioeconomic groups here, so you can drive by a building with three poor families living in it and four blocks later be at a stop sign next to a million-dollar (or more) home. The fact is that it's on the South Side of Chicago so people automatically say, 'bad, scary neighborhood.'" Part-time students attend classes at the Gleacher Center, "a beautiful building" in downtown Chicago, just off the Magnificent Mile. For students whose activities keep them in the Hyde Park area, GSB's Charles M. Harper Center boasts a "winter garden," a "dramatic foyer in the center of the building" where "People can catch up, do work, or just relax for a moment."

Admissions

Admission to Chicago's Graduate School of Business is extremely competitive. Admissions Officers scrutinize a wide array of qualifications, including academic record (quality of curriculum, scholarships, special honors, etc.), work experience (quality as well as quantity), and overall "fit"(interpersonal skills, unique experiences, philanthropic activity). Applicants must provide the Admissions Office with transcripts for all postsecondary academic work, an official GMAT score report, letters of recommendation, personal essays, and TOEFL/IELTS scores (for international students only). Interviews are required for all candidates. Applicants to the full-time program interview on a "by invitation only" basis.

FINANCIAL FACTS

Annual tuition	$44,500
Fees	$639
Cost of books	$2,100
Room & board	$18,900
% of students receiving aid	77
% of first-year students receiving aid	75
% of students receiving loans	79
% of students receiving grants	25
Average award package	$54,218
Average grant	$22,336
Average student loan debt	$84,034

ADMISSIONS

Admissions Selectivity Rating	60*
Average GMAT	708
Average GPA	3.5
TOEFL required of international students	Yes
Minimum TOEFL (paper/computer)	600/250
Application fee	$200
International application fee	$200
Application Deadline/Notification	
Round 1:	10/17 / 01/03
Round 2:	01/9 / 03/26
Round 3:	03/12 / 05/14
Deferment available	Yes
Maximum length of deferment	1 year
Need-blind admissions	Yes

EMPLOYMENT PROFILE

Career Rating	96	Grads Employed by Function	% Avg. Salary
Primary Source of Full-time Job Acceptances		Finance	55 NR
School-facilitated activities	443 (88%)	Marketing	8 NR
Graduate-facilitated activities	61 (12%)	Operations	1 NR
Percent employed	95	Consulting	25 NR
		General Management	5 NR

Top 5 Employers Hiring Grads
McKinsey & Company; Lehman Brothers; Merrill Lynch Co.; Deutsche Bank; The Boston Consulting Group

UNIVERSITY OF CINCINNATI
COLLEGE OF BUSINESS

Academics

Offering an efficient, one-year MBA program, the University of Cincinnati is a great place to jumpstart your career with a general business degree, or pursue a specialized graduate program that will prepare you to work in a specific industry. Described as "rigorous but manageable," the school's "one-year MBA program is very attractive to those who are taking time off of their career to pursue extra education." If you don't want to drop out of the workforce, even for just a year, the school offers part-time evening and weekend programs as well. These programs are flexible and suited to a working student; if you can't make it to campus on certain evenings, "core classes are recorded and available for viewing online." Keep in mind, however, that while these programs are designed to accommodate busy schedules, they're no walk in the park. Part-timers should "plan on 24 hours of coursework and homework per week" in addition to their professional and personal commitments.

Depending on your career interests, there are lots of educational avenues at UC. Within the MBA program, students may choose to tailor their education by taking classes within nine areas of concentration, including Operations Management and International Business. In addition, "the study abroad opportunities are plentiful" and every year, the school offers seminars in important international business locations, such as France, India, China, Thailand, and Germany. UC also offers four joint degree and various master's programs. Of particular note, University of Cincinnati's joint degree in arts administration is "unique among business schools in North America" and confers a special prestige, considering the school's fine reputation in the arts and their world-famous music conservatory. At this "top research organization," students may also pursue their specific interests through the school's research centers, like the Goering Center for Family and Private Business, and the Center for Entrepreneurship Education and Research.

In the classroom, you'll be treated to "several standout professors supported by a solid core that ensures rewarding class experiences." The majority of UC faculty is "recognized as leaders in their fields" who bring real-world expertise to the learning environment—though some students feel they would benefit from a more hands-on, case-based approach across the curriculum, rather than lecture. If you are struggling, most professors are "willing to provide extra assistance when needed." Evening classes can sometimes be a bit over-stuffed, but during the daytime, "classes are often very small and the teachers really care about their students and support you whenever you have problems and need them." On the whole, "the academic experience is very intense, but the faculty and staff try to keep everyone at ease."

Career and Placement

MBA Career Services offers workshops, counseling, career panels, mock interviews, and other services for career seekers. Their efforts clearly pay off, as 80 percent of UC graduates have accepted a job within three months of graduation. Recently, students held internships or took jobs at companies including Procter & Gamble, Citi, Deloitte & Touche, Ernst & Young, Johnson & Johnson, Kendle International, Dunnhumby, Duke Energy, Rivercities Capital Fund.

Most students who come to University of Cincinnati plan to stay in the region, and the majority of jobs and internships placements are made within the larger metropolitan area. In fact, 100 percent of last year's internship placements were with Cincinnati companies. Unfortunately, students who'd like to consider a wider geographical region feel the school needs to "tap into other regions, especially the close ones like Chicago, Cleveland, and the Northeast."

Student Life and Environment

As at many schools that have traditional and part-time programs, you'll see a bit of a split within the UC student body. Generally speaking, "the full-time MBA program is characterized by younger students, most just out of undergrad, with limited work experience. Part-time students are mostly older, more diverse, and knowledgeable about various fields." Especially among younger students, "the social setting is pretty good, and most of the students are open to out-of-class experiences."

UC is an urban campus; however, the school grounds have recently received a facelift, and now have "a lot more green space and new workout facility." In addition, the "computer lab and library are excellent." Outside of attending class, the business school and the larger university provide a range of extracurricular and recreational options to those who are interested. A current student explains, "For me it was important to have things to do in my spare time beside school. There are a lot of opportunities on and around campus to go out, relax. The new recreation center was just perfect for me." Adds another, "There are a lot of socializing options around the school and all over the city. The school has also developed a strong football culture over the last few years and that has gone on to strengthen the community."

Admissions

This year's MBA class submitted an average GPA of 3.22 and an average GMAT score of 565, plus more than four years of full-time work experience. UC considers any student with an undergraduate degree for their master's and MBA programs, regardless of discipline. UC admits students whose success in their undergraduate studies, in addition to professional experience, will make them successful in the MBA program. GMAT scores, GPA, work history, communication skills (written and oral), and teamwork experience are among the most important factors in an admissions decision.

FINANCIAL FACTS

Annual tuition (in-state/ out-of-state)	$21,400/$26,804
Fees	$2,004
Cost of books	$3,500
Room & board (on/off-campus)	$14,000/$15,500
% of students receiving aid	76
% of first-year students receiving aid	76
% of students receiving loans	37
% of students receiving grants	67
Average award package	$19,169
Average grant	$12,370

ADMISSIONS

Admissions Selectivity Rating	77
# of applications received	216
% applicants accepted	71
% acceptees attending	64
Average GMAT	565
Range of GMAT	520–630
Average GPA	3.22
TOEFL required of international students	Yes
Minimum TOEFL (paper/computer)	600/250
Application fee	$40
International application fee	$40
Application Deadline/Notification	
Round 1:	1/08 / 3/08
Round 2:	4/08 / 6/08
Round 3:	7/08 / 8/08
Early decision program?	Yes
ED Deadline/Notification	Fall, 01/15 / 03/15
Deferment available	Yes
Maximum length of deferment	1 year
Transfer students accepted	Yes
Transfer application policy	Transferring from an AACSB accredited institution, no more than 12 credit hours.
Need-blind admissions	Yes

Applicants Also Look At
Indiana University—Bloomington, Miami University (OH), Northern Kentucky University, The Ohio State University, University of Dayton, Wright State University, Xavier University.

EMPLOYMENT PROFILE

Career Rating	70	Grads Employed by Function	% Avg. Salary
Primary Source of Full-time Job Acceptances		Finance	50 $56,800
Graduate-facilitated activities	16 (100%)	Marketing	20 $62,500
Percent employed	62	MIS	20 $63,750
		Operations	10 $55,000

Top 5 Employers Hiring Grads
Kendle International; Ernst & Young; Procter & Gamble, Convergys, Dunhhumby.

UNIVERSITY OF CONNECTICUT
SCHOOL OF BUSINESS

Academics

An "innovative curriculum" that emphasizes experiential learning is the hallmark of the MBA program at the University of Connecticut, providing students with "tremendous opportunities to integrate classroom learning with real-life business problem-solving." No wonder students tell us that UConn "offers a high-level education at state school cost, along with many highly appealing academic programs." To top it all off, a "premium location close to financial centers such as Boston, New York City, and Hartford" makes the job-search process at the end of the program that much easier.

Experiential learning opportunities at UConn include various "learning accelerators," which include "consulting assignments for a variety of Connecticut firms"; the Student Managed Fund, which "provides students an opportunity to put their financial skills into practice by investing $1 million of real cash"; and the GE edgelab, which partners the university with GE to "leverage the expertise and research backgrounds of distinguished UConn School of Business faculty and MBAs to provide unbiased perspective and strategic insights to GE businesses."

UConn's strengths include "an exceptional real estate department," a "highly rated operations and information management department," a "terrific marketing department," and a solid finance program. Students also report that "new initiatives in entrepreneurship are being implemented," and that "an international concentration is under discussion." Students in all areas benefit from small classes that promote "individualized attention from faculty and the opportunity to build a closer network with peers."

The school supplements this with "excellent facilities." The program is growing, and students say "The school's administration is handling the business school's expansion very well. I am constantly surprised by their accessibility and by the fact that they know everyone's name."

Career and Placement

Connecticut MBAs agree that their Career Services Office does a good job of bringing insurance industry and finance recruiters to campus, but in other areas they see shortcomings. One student writes,: "The school needs to improve placement in larger investment banking firms. Not enough is done to help students contact alumni [who] would be willing to help them. They only just now got an alumni database together that students can access." For others, placement in internships is "the issue many people are facing right now. More needs to be done to ensure that first-years have a summer internship and second-years have a job." Some here feel that "the Career Services Office is "overworked," and that the office "needs a larger staff that can recruit companies to recruit students on campus."

Employers who most frequently hire Connecticut MBAs include United Technologies, CIGNA, IBM, Travelers, GE, The Hartford, Citigroup, ESPN, Aetna, General Dynamics and PricewaterhouseCoopers.

Student Life and Environment

"Facilities are excellent within the business school" at UConn, which recently relocated its MBAs to "a brand-new building with state-of-the-art equipment." Students tell us that "food selection on campus is great, group meeting space is great, and there is plenty of easily accessible space to meet for team projects." A "new student union is great and provides lots of activities for commuter students."

ADMISSIONS CONTACT: SURESH NAIR, ASSOCIATE DEAN
ADDRESS: 2100 HILLSIDE ROAD UNIT 1041 STORRS, CT 06269-1041 UNITED STATES
PHONE: 860-486-2872 • FAX: 860-486-5222
E-MAIL: UCONNMBA@BUSINESS.UCONN.EDU • WEBSITE: WWW.BUSINESS.UCONN.EDU

Life on campus in Storrs "is very fun. People help each other out, there aren't really any cliques, and everyone talks to everyone. We are one big happy 'family.' Every Thursday night our whole class goes to happy hour together, and it's a great way to unwind after a week of classes." Also, the program's Graduate Business Association "works hard and provides many events." The active campus life helps make up for the fact that Storrs "is in the middle of nowhere" and is "pretty small, so if anyone wants big-city style, this may not be the place for them." Students say they feel "very safe around campus."

UConn provides on-campus housing for some MBAs. Students love the convenience, telling us that "the shuttle comes right to the door, the apartments are clean, and the building is quiet." Not all students live on or near campus, of course. Many "have a long commute or are married and/or have children, and they tend to be less involved in activities on campus, but those that live on campus or are younger/single socialize a lot." UConn draws MBAs "from all over the world, and they make the program ethnically diverse. UConn has a great engineering program, a law school, and a medical school. Many of those students cross over into the MBA program. It makes for a wonderful experience in the classroom."

Admissions

UConn classifies its MBA admissions as "highly competitive." Applicants typically have GMAT scores of at least 560 and an undergraduate GPA of at least 3.0. They have at least 2 full years of post-undergraduate professional experience and have completed a college-level calculus course. Students who don't meet these standards are nonetheless encouraged to apply, particularly if their professional or life experiences will enrich the classroom experience. Applicants must submit the following materials: an application form, completed online; official transcripts from the student's degree-granting undergraduate institution and from any graduate programs attended; an official GMAT score report; two letters of recommendation from professional supervisors or mentors; and a current resume.

International applicants must meet the above requirements and must also submit professional translations and interpretations of transcripts in languages other than English. Students whose native language is not English must submit an official TOEFL score report (minimum score: 575, paper-based test; 233, computer-based test; 90–91, Internet-based test).

FINANCIAL FACTS

Annual tuition (in-state/ out-of-state)	$7,992/$20,772
Fees	$1,518
Cost of books	$3,000
Room & board (on/off-campus)	$8,684/$9,500
% of students receiving aid	57
% of first-year students receiving aid	66
% of students receiving loans	21
% of students receiving grants	37
Average award package	$23,000
Average grant	$14,000

ADMISSIONS

Admissions Selectivity Rating	83
# of applications received	305
% applicants accepted	61
% acceptees attending	48
Average GMAT	603
Range of GMAT	560–660
Average GPA	3.39
TOEFL required of international students	Yes
Minimum TOEFL (paper/computer)	575/233
Application fee	$65
International application fee	$65
Regular application deadline	4/15
Regular notification	
Deferment available	Yes
Maximum length of deferment	1 year
Transfer students accepted	Yes
Transfer application policy	
All students requesting to transfer are required to meet with the Director of the MBA Program. A maximum of 15 credits are accepted.	
Need-blind admissions	Yes

Applicants Also Look At

Boston University, New York University, State University of New York—University at Buffalo, University of Massachusetts—Amherst, University of Pittsburgh, Yale University.

EMPLOYMENT PROFILE

Career Rating	82	Grads Employed by Function	% Avg. Salary
Primary Source of Full-time Job Acceptances		Finance	37 $70,364
School-facilitated activities	1 (2%)	Marketing	12 $66,875
Graduate-facilitated activities	24 (48%)	MIS	15 $67,000
Percent employed	86	Operations	2 NR
		Consulting	7 $62,333
		General Management	17 $80,000
		Other	10 NR

Top 5 Employers Hiring Grads
The Hartford; GE; PricewaterhouseCoopers; ING; Blum Shapiro Consulting

UNIVERSITY OF DAYTON
SCHOOL OF BUSINESS ADMINISTRATION

Academics

An "exceptional integrated core curriculum," "excellent faculty," a "strong alumni base," and "a marvelous Marianist-centered campus life" attract students to the MBA program at the University of Dayton, a mid-size Catholic university in southwestern Ohio. Students here assure us that their School of Business Administration offers "one of the best kept secrets in the world of MBA programs."

They are especially enthusiastic about the program's "exceptional process-oriented 'integrated' approach to the core curriculum," which they deem "extremely unique." This integrated approach "allows students to break out of the strict mold of marketing and management," and enroll in "courses involving the integration of two major disciplines (i.e. operations management paired with managerial accounting)." In doing so, students get "the opportunity to have two (or more) senior faculty teaching a class rather than just one (not to mention possibly one executive-in-residence or more)." "Class participation is expected" in all of these classes, forcing "students to think about the interaction between different disciplines, and how decisions or actions in one will affect another."

Dayton MBAs also love the "guaranteed real-world consulting project experience" that, coupled with the school's "integration of its entire curriculum with area industry and its leveraging of professors with industry experience," ensures that students confront "real-life examples in class and elsewhere." Facilities "are terrific," and professors are "a diverse group made up of career teachers, professionals who teach part-time, and retired business leaders. All are accessible and offer a lot to the program." Students busy with careers appreciate that "the program is organized well" and UD "allows for a great amount of flexibility, so you can complete it at your own pace." The Dayton MBA curriculum consists of the integrated core, electives, and a two-semester capstone segment. Students may use their electives to develop a concentration in accounting, business intelligence, entrepreneurship, finance, international business, management information systems, operations management, marketing, and technology-enhanced business/e-commerce. The school is especially noted for its work in finance (driven by the Davis Center for Portfolio Management) and entrepreneurship (Dayton houses the Crotty Center for Entrepreneurial Leadership).

Career and Placement

MBAs at University of Dayton are served by the Career Services Office, which assists undergraduates, graduates, and alumni in their development and placement needs. The office provides graduate students with the following services: career advisement; job search and résumé critiquing workshops, career fairs, online résumé referral, on-campus recruiting events, and contact with the alumni career network. Employers who typically recruit on the Dayton campus include ACNielsen, Deloitte Touche Tohmatsu, Xerox, Ernst & Young, Ethicon Endo-Surgery, Federal-Mogul, Fifth Third Bank, FM Global, GE, Georgia-Pacific, NCR, NVR/Ryan Homes, PricewaterhouseCoopers, Procter & Gamble, Lexis Nexis, and USG Corporation.

Student Life and Environment

The degree to which a student is involved in extracurricular life at Dayton "depends on whether you are a full-time or part-time student. Full time students are still connected to undergraduates and the university, while part-time students don't feel as connected." As one part-timer explains, "If someone were interested in getting involved, there are plenty of opportunities, but MBA students typically do not take advantage of these due to a lack of time. Many of us have full-time jobs." Those who can indulge in campus fun report

ADMISSIONS CONTACT: JANICE GLYNN, DIRECTOR MBA PROGRAM
ADDRESS: 300 COLLEGE PARK AVENUE DAYTON, OH 45469-2234 UNITED STATES
PHONE: 937-229-3733 • FAX: 937-229-3882
E-MAIL: MBA@UDAYTON.EDU • WEBSITE: WWW.SBA.UDAYTON.EDU/MBA

that they enjoy "a very modern gym that contains a pool, track, climbing wall, free weight room, aerobic room, and numerous other things" as well as "a tremendous amount of school spirit at the University of Dayton. Here, I feel like part of a family. I believe UD has struck the perfect balance of being an extremely social campus while upholding academic excellence." Full-timers and part-timers alike note that "the campus is very inviting. There are several places to study before and after class and also places to meet with groups, with plenty of resources for graduate students." Students also report that the school "recently implemented a graduate student social networking event that was very well received. Several more are planned for the upcoming year."

The Dayton MBA program consists of "a diverse mix of individuals from many different walks of life: Some are right out of college, some have been out for 25 years, some have 10-plus years work experience, some have none. In general people are able to share real life examples [that] make the learning environment better."

Admissions

All applications to the University of Dayton MBA program must include official transcripts for all postsecondary academic work, an official GMAT score report, a completed application form, and a current resume or curriculum vita. Personal statements are encouraged but not required. Letters of recommendation from employers or professors are not required either; however, the admissions committee will consider them if they are submitted. International applicants must meet all of the above requirements and must also provide a translation of any non-English language transcripts and official scores for the TOEFL (minimum score of 550 paper exam, 213 computer exam required for unconditional admission; students with lower scores may be admitted under the condition that they successfully complete English as a Second Language training).

FINANCIAL FACTS

Annual tuition	$694 per credit hour
Cost of books	$650
Average grant	$1,000

ADMISSIONS

Admissions Selectivity Rating	**76**
# of applications received	329
% applicants accepted	80
% acceptees attending	80
Average GMAT	555
Average GPA	3.26
TOEFL required of international students	Yes
Minimum TOEFL (paper/computer)	550/213
Application fee	$0
International application fee	$50
Regular application deadline	Rolling
Regular notification	Rolling
Deferment available	Yes
Maximum length of deferment	1 year
Transfer students accepted	Yes
Transfer application policy Students may request up to 6 Semester hours of approved graduate transfer credit.	
Non-fall admissions	Yes
Need-blind admissions	Yes

Applicants Also Look At
Wright State University, Xavier University.

EMPLOYMENT PROFILE	
Career Rating	**87**
Percent employed	85

UNIVERSITY OF DENVER
DANIELS COLLEGE OF BUSINESS

GENERAL INFORMATION

Type of school	Private
Environment	Metropolis
Academic calendar	Quarter

SURVEY SAYS...

Students love Denver, CO
Cutting edge classes
Solid preparation in:
Teamwork
Communication/interpersonal skills

STUDENTS

Enrollment of parent institution	11,117
Enrollment of business school	411
% male/female	64/36
% out-of-state	20
% part-time	53
% minorities	7
% international	16
Average age at entry	26
Average years work experience at entry	4.27

ACADEMICS

Academic Experience Rating	**77**
Student/faculty ratio	30:1
Profs interesting rating	81
Profs accessible rating	85
% female faculty	15
% minority faculty	9

Joint Degrees

JD/MBA 3–4 years, JD/IMBA 3–4 years, JD/MSRECM 3–4 years, IMBA/MA (Global Finance, Trade, and Economic Integration) 2–3 years.

Prominent Alumni

Joseph Saunders, Chairman and CEO of Visa; Andrew Daly, Former President, Vail Resorts; Tom Marsico, CEO and CIO of Marisco Capital Management; W. Patrick McGinnis, President and CEO, Nestle Pur; Andrew C. Taylor, Chairman and CEO, Enterprice Ren.

Academics

At the University of Denver's Daniels College of Business, future business leaders benefit from an excellent combination of "academic rigor, high-quality faculty, and values-based and ethically focused curriculum." The Daniels MBA provides a balanced educational experience and is nationally renowned for its focus on business ethics. Students say the school lives up to its good reputation: "Ethics and values are emphasized in every class," giving "every student at Daniels a strong sense of purpose and challenging us to examine our motivation and action in our daily lives and careers."

Students appreciate the school's practical approach to learning, telling us that "the professor's at DU work hard to keep things focused on business applications." A current student confirms, "I am learning things that I take back to work immediately and feel well prepared to contribute at a higher level at my company." The program also maintains "high expectations and focus on writing and communication in all subject areas," which can make the course work particularly time consuming. Even so, students assure us that "class work, depending on the class, ranges from easy to moderately hard, but the environment is certainly not cutthroat."

As the reputation of the Daniels MBA grows, the school continually strives to strengthen the quality of its education along with its program rankings. As a result, "The professors and administration are always asking for feedback, and new programs are continuously presenting themselves." Students appreciate the school's commitment to the student experience, saying professors "genuinely care about their students and want us to succeed." In fact, ambitious MBA candidates are pleased to report that "professors eagerly take students on as a graduate assistants to help them with research and to further augment what they are learning."

In addition to attracting a large number of international students, the University of Denver operates a program that "gives high-achieving undergraduate business students the opportunity to continue on to get their MBA in only 1 extra year." As a result, the student body includes a number of younger students, some of whom have yet to enter the workforce. However, with a student population of over 950, there is plenty of diversity on the Daniels campus. A current student attests, "DU is a well-rounded school with diversity in race, ethnicity, and age. This diversity, especially in age, offers me perspectives on business in more ways than I could have ever found anywhere else."

Career and Placement

Boasting the "best reputation in the Denver area," students at Daniels say they enjoy a competitive edge in the local business community. To maximize that edge, The Suitts Center for Career Services provides a variety of resources for job seekers, including professional development workshops, career advising, company tours and career shadowing, alumni and executive mentoring, as well as extensive print and online job search tools. As one student explains, "They have programs to help anyone willing to put the time and energy into perfecting a resume, mock interview, etc. They will go as far as you need them to."

Fifty-four percent of last year's graduating class (both U.S. citizens and international students) had accepted a job offer within 3 months of graduation at a mean base salary of about $56,000. Twenty-five percent took jobs in sales/marketing, and another 25 percent of the class accepted jobs in finance/banking. The following companies are among those who hired Daniels MBA students in 2006: AIMCO, Allstate Insurance Company, Axcent Sports, Booz Allen Hamilton, Edward Jones, Ernst & Young, Fast Enterprises, G2

Analytics, Hitachi Consulting, Northwest Airlines, Oppenheimer Funds, Pitney Bowes, Starbucks, and United Parcel Service.

Student Life and Environment

With a large student body comprised of "dedicated, hardworking, interesting, fun, intelligent, friendly people," the University of Denver boasts an incredibly dynamic and vibrant campus atmosphere. In addition to their studies, Daniels students enjoy a lively social scene: "Because so many of the students are young and unmarried, Daniels has a collegiate feel which gives you a chance to meet and become friends with a lot of new people."

Networking is practically built into the program as, "the school provides various social events for students to gather outside of class which helps to enrich the relationships." For example, "Bar nights for grad students are frequent and the Graduate Board (GBSA) does a wonderful job of getting involvement in activities from students." Many students also mention that a "bimonthly happy hour is held for all business students,"which is not only a reliable stress-buster but a great career opportunity, as "Many of these happy hours are also hosted by regional companies that use them as a marketing and recruiting opportunity."

Hometown Denver is a great place to work and study, with "fantastic weather," ample recreation and outdoor activities, and plenty of business and industry. University of Denver's campus is similarly first rate, boasting a "wonderful recreation center and tremendous facilities." With the school's enviable location right at the foot of the Rocky Mountains, it's no surprise that in addition to work and studies, "everybody skis."

Admissions

Daniels admits students who demonstrate a commitment to advanced learning, leadership potential, and strong ethical standards. Admissions are selective, and decisions are based on a qualitative review of a candidate's personal, professional, and intellectual preparedness. Last year's entering class submitted a mean GMAT score of 597 and had an average undergraduate GPA of 3.18. Full-time students entered with an average of 5 years professional work experience, whereas part-time students had 11 years of relevant professional experience, on average. Once a completed application is submitted, candidates receive a response in 3 to 6 weeks.

FINANCIAL FACTS

Annual tuition	$34,920
Fees	$755
Cost of books	$1,698
Room & board	$9,900
% of students receiving aid	81
% of first-year students receiving aid	95
% of students receiving loans	50
% of students receiving grants	50
Average award package	$9,250
Average grant	$7,000

ADMISSIONS

Admissions Selectivity Rating	82
# of applications received	349
% applicants accepted	67
% acceptees attending	37
Average GMAT	588
Range of GMAT	540–618
Average GPA	3.15
TOEFL required of international students	Yes
Minimum TOEFL (paper/computer)	570/230
Application fee	$100
International application fee	$100
Regular application deadline	3/15
Regular notification	5/1
Application Deadline/Notification	
Round 1:	01/15 / 03/01
Round 2:	03/15 / 05/01
Round 3:	05/15 / 07/01
Deferment available	Yes
Maximum length of deferment	1 year
Transfer students accepted	Yes
Transfer application policy 8 quarter hours (6 Semester hours) toward electives.	
Non-fall admissions	Yes
Need-blind admissions	Yes

Applicants Also Look At

Arizona State University, Boston University, Brigham Young University, Thunderbird, University of Arizona, University of Colorado at Boulder, University of Colorado Denver.

EMPLOYMENT PROFILE

Career Rating	72	Grads Employed by Function	% Avg. Salary
Primary Source of Full-time Job Acceptances		Finance	33 $62,184
School-facilitated activities	18 (30%)	Marketing	23 $67,231
Graduate-facilitated activities	40 (67%)	Operations	5 $63,333
Unknown	2 (3%)	Consulting	18 $62,000
Average base starting salary	$64,026	General Management	12 $77,000
Percent employed	33	Other	9 $49,000

Top 5 Employers Hiring Grads
Aimco; Oppenheimer Funds, Inc; The Interger Group; Sun Microsystems; Hitachi Consulting Corp

UNIVERSITY OF FLORIDA
HOUGH GRADUATE SCHOOL OF BUSINESS

GENERAL INFORMATION
Type of school	Public
Environment	City
Academic calendar	Semester

SURVEY SAYS...
Good social scene
Good peer network
Solid preparation in:
Finance
Communication/interpersonal skills
Quantitative skills

STUDENTS
Enrollment of parent institution	53,000
Enrollment of business school	962
% male/female	73/27
% out-of-state	22
% part-time	86
% minorities	11
% international	21
Average age at entry	27
Average years work experience at entry	3.7

ACADEMICS
Academic Experience Rating	**96**
Student/faculty ratio	10:1
Profs interesting rating	87
Profs accessible rating	96
% female faculty	17
% minority faculty	19

Joint Degrees
MBA/JD 4 years, MBA/MS Medical Sciences, MBA/PhD Medical Sciences, Biotechnology, MBA/Doctor of Pharmacy, MBA/PhD Medical Sciences, MBA/MD.

Prominent Alumni
William R. Hough, President, William R. Hough & Co.; Cesar Alvarez, CEO/Managing Partner; John Dasburg, Chairman/CEO, ASTAR; Laurie Burns, President, Bahama Breeze; Hal Steinbrenner, General Partner, New York Yankees.

Academics

Offering "a wide range of ways to earn an MBA, including a 1-year program, a 2-year program, an executive MBA, an online degree, and the South Florida program," the Warrington College of Business at the University of Florida "not only serves different types of students but also allows students to expand their professional alumni network" through interaction with a wide variety of peers. Students here also appreciate the relatively small size of the program, which ensures "small class sizes" and "great interaction with professors, resulting in more individualized attention from faculty." And, as a state school, Florida delivers it all "at a low cost," resulting in "a great return on investment."

Students report that Warrington boasts "excellent finance and real estate programs." One student explains, "The real estate department offers not only an excellent curriculum but also has additional mentorship opportunities and networking trips outside of the standard MBA program," while "The finance professors are some of the most intelligent individuals I have ever had the pleasure of meeting." Students here also tout a "very strong management program" and an "underrated program in marketing." Across disciplines, "The wide variety of courses and concentrations can tailor to anyone's needs or interests," a benefit of students' access to "the resources of a monstrous learning institution."

Florida boasts "a strong faculty who facilitate learning and are very approachable" and are also "often leaders in their respective fields and are willing to speak with you about industry experiences and contacts." A "great alumni network" shepherded by a "helpful Director of Alumni Affairs" is "very helpful in providing mentoring opportunities and contacts for potential job opportunities." While "some of the facilities here are somewhat outdated," a "recent gift to the graduate business school" means that "a multimillion-dollar facility will be built in the next year or two and will provide a substantial boost to an already world-class program."

Career and Placement

The Graduate Business Career Services office at Florida "works hard to help students with their career search" and "tries to be as innovative as possible to assist students with their search" through such programs as 'Day in the Life,' which "allows MBAs to go to UF business partners' offices and experience a day at that business. This allows the students the ability to get an inside track to making contacts at potential employers, to make good impressions, and to get a feel for corporate culture." Some here wish the office did a better job of attracting on-campus recruiters; some see this as the result of the program's size. One MBA explains, "One of GBCSO's challenges is the size of the graduate program. Even though UF is one of the largest universities in the nation, the MBA program is one of the smallest. Therefore, it is a little more difficult to get recruiters to come to see a smaller group of potential recruits."

Employers who most frequently hire Florida MBAs include: FPL, Accenture, IBM, Wachovia, Bank of America, Jabil Circuits, Lennar Homes, Pratt & Whitney, Lockheed Martin, Cintas, CSX, Johnson & Johnson, ExxonMobil, Ryder, Deloitte Touche Tohmatsu, Raymond James, BB&T, Citicorp, Ernest & Young, Capital One, and Target.

ADMISSIONS CONTACT: MICHELLE LOVELL, ASSOCIATE DIRECTOR OF ADMISSIONS
ADDRESS: 134 BRYAN HALL, P.O. BOX 117152 GAINESVILLE, FL 32611-7152 UNITED STATES
PHONE: 877-435-2622 • FAX: 352-392-8791
E-MAIL: FLORIDAMBA@CBA.UFL.EDU • WEBSITE: WWW.FLORIDAMBA.UFL.EDU

FINANCIAL FACTS

Annual tuition (in-state/ out-of-state)	$7,478/$22,603
Fees	$500
Cost of books	$2,660
Room & board (on/off-campus)	$7,910/$8,330
% of students receiving aid	58
% of first-year students receiving aid	61
% of students receiving loans	23
% of students receiving grants	56
Average award package	$19,596
Average grant	$9,643
Average student loan debt	$11,372

ADMISSIONS

Admissions Selectivity Rating	**94**
# of applications received	337
% applicants accepted	43
% acceptees attending	66
Average GMAT	680
Range of GMAT	650–710
Average GPA	3.39
TOEFL required of international students	Yes
Minimum TOEFL (paper/computer)	600/250
Application fee	$30
International application fee	$30
Regular application deadline	4/15
Regular notification	Rolling
Deferment available	Yes
Maximum length of deferment	1 year
Non-fall admissions	Yes
Need-blind admissions	Yes

Applicants Also Look At

Emory University, Georgetown University, The University of North Carolina at Chapel Hill, The University of Texas at Austin, University of Georgia, University of Notre Dame, University of Southern California.

Student Life and Environment

"Campus life is great" at Florida, where in 2006 "We won the football national championship, and may repeat as basketball champs too." It isn't just about sports here, though; "There are constantly social events and alumni events around the state for us to attend," and the Gainesville area is "a terrific place to go to school," with "a diverse range of things to do. If you're a runner, you can run almost anywhere in town or on campus with great weather year round. If you enjoy nature, there are many great resources and activities to enjoy in the area from springs and lakes to beaches not too far away. There's always something exciting happening on campus from plays, concerts, and lectures to Gator athletics—which are reason enough to go to UF." All in all, students enjoy "an incredible split of academics and fun" with "great opportunities to network and socialize both in and out of school."

Academic life at UF "is hectic, as our courses are organized into 7-week modules. Most of the assignments are team-based, requiring additional time to schedule meetings and develop a single document." As a result, "the MBA lounge is always full of working teams." Fortunately, the close-knit nature of the student body makes "creating study groups and seeking help extremely easy. The relationship between the students and the faculty and staff make it a unique place to study"; students are catered to "as customers of their product." Students here also benefit from "the great diversity among the prior work experiences of classmates. We have engineers, linguistics majors and lawyers in addition to many business majors."

Admissions

Applicants to Florida MBA programs must submit the following materials to the Admissions Office: official copies of transcripts for all undergraduate and graduate programs attended; an official score report for the GMAT (scores may be no more than 5 years old); a resume showing meaningful post-undergraduate professional experience (at least 2 years for the full-time MBA, at least 8 years for the executive MBA; two letters of recommendation from those in a position to evaluate professional performance; and essays. Interviews are conducted by invitation only. International applicants whose first language is not English must submit an official score report for the TOEFL (minimum score: 600 on the written version; 250 on the computer version). The school conducts a Graduate Minority Campus Visitation program, a 'Women in Business' Recruiting Day, and a Diversity Recruitment Day in its efforts to attract underrepresented demographics.

EMPLOYMENT PROFILE

Career Rating	**84**	**Grads Employed by Function**	**%**	**Avg. Salary**
Primary Source of Full-time Job Acceptances		Finance	47	$66,522
School-facilitated activities	25 (51%)	Human Resources	10	$73,250
Graduate-facilitated activities	17 (35%)	Marketing	10	$71,750
Unknown	7 (14%)	Operations	10	$59,500
Average base starting salary	$66,669	Consulting	10	$69,085
Percent employed	96	Other	13	$67,002

Top 5 Employers Hiring Grads

Exxon Mobil; KPMG; Starwood; Wachovia; Bank of America

UNIVERSITY OF GEORGIA
TERRY COLLEGE OF BUSINESS

GENERAL INFORMATION
Type of school	Public
Environment	City
Academic calendar	Semester

SURVEY SAYS...
Good social scene
Good peer network
Solid preparation in:
Accounting
Communication/interpersonal skills

STUDENTS
Enrollment of parent institution	33,660
% male/female	70/30
% out-of-state	50
% minorities	10
% international	30
Average age at entry	27
Average years work experience at entry	4

ACADEMICS
Academic Experience Rating	**92**
Student/faculty ratio	25:1
Profs interesting rating	84
Profs accessible rating	89

Joint Degrees
JD/MBA 4 years.

Prominent Alumni
Mason Hawkins, Chairman/CEO, Southeastern Asset Management; George Slusser, President, Coldwell Banker Commercial.

Academics

You'll get a lot of bang for your buck at the University of Georgia's Terry MBA program. Despite small class sizes, world-class faculty, and top-ranked programs in insurance/risk management, real estate, MIS, and accounting, UGA tuition is inexpensive, and the school is "very generous with financial aid." All totaled, University of Georgia is an incredible value. A student jokes, "Compared to Wake or Vandy, UGA might as well be free."

Spearheaded by professors who are "accessible, understanding, progressive, and committed," UGA students describe the academic program as "challenging and relevant." Joining the faculty from a range of impressive backgrounds, UGA students are taught "statistics by the ex-CFO of Kodak, economics by the nation's best economist, entrepreneurship by an MS, MBA, PhD, and doctorate holder all from Harvard, and law by America's best property-rights favoring lawyer." Attesting to the thoroughness and strength of the program, a current student shares, "I have 8 years of experience in my career and, so far, many of my experiences have been taught, or at least simulated, in most of my classes." While their credentials are undisputable, Terry professors are "very helpful, and most make time readily for students with questions or needs."

University of Georgia operates two full-time MBA programs: a 2-year, program for students who do not have an undergraduate degree in business, and an accelerated, 11-month program for students holding a business degree from an AACSB-accredited institution. For 2-year students, the first year consists of foundational course work, followed by a summer internship. In the second year, students tailor their studies through elective course work. Students on the 11-month track take a crash course/review of business topics during the summer months before joining 2-year students in the second year of electives.

While UGA provides thorough training on business essentials, it is not a hard-nosed, quantitative program; rather, professors at Terry "place a tremendous value on the soft skills and the development of a well-rounded individual" through "a strong leadership and personal development component." The academic curriculum is further enhanced by "requirements that allow us to build our skills both inside and outside of the classroom including community-service hour requirements, club activity requirements, career coaching, and leadership training seminars." Through the Terry International Business program, the school runs week-long international trips during spring break, with lectures, company visits, and cultural exposure.

Career and Placement

The Terry MBA Career Resource Center recently partnered with Stanton Chase International, an executive search firm that is ranked in the top 1 percent of firms nationwide. Through Stanton Chase, students have access to two on-site career consultants four days a week, as well as access to Stanton Chase's 56 offices in 34 countries.

In addition to recruiting, the Career Resource Center works individually with MBA students to develop an effective strategy to target the companies and positions that are in line with each student's career goals. Last year the placement rate within 3 months of graduation was 92 percent, and the mean base salary was $68,791 with an average signing bonus of $8,302. While UGA students certainly feel that their school cares about placing them in top positions, they say that UGA could improve by offering "more diverse jobs, not just finance and accounting."

Student Life and Environment

This school sustains a tight-knit intellectual and social community. "The caliber of the individuals and the cohesion within the program are what truly brings value to the MBA experience" at UGA. "My classmates range in age from 22 to 39, and the relationships I have built with them are ones that will last for years to come," says a current student. Hailing from "diverse backgrounds," the student body includes "deep-sea divers, army officers who served in Afghanistan, a geography professor, a chemist, lawyers, engineers, hoteliers, entrepreneurs, CPAs, finance professionals, consultants, real estate professionals, CNN/CNBC media professionals, logisticians, fresh undergrads, and many more." Generally speaking, students are social and friendly, and "regularly hang out" outside of the classroom.

Through the MBA program, there is always something happening on campus, and "The business program has linked arms with the music, education, and law schools during different events to provide more networking opportunities." Through the university, there are "football games, night life, community service, arts and exhibitions, cultural interactions" and more. Surrounding Athens offers "great nightlife, culture, weather, sports, and restaurants." In fact, some say, "There are so many really good activities to get involved in that . . . 2 years is just too short." Even "Beyond those activities, we have an active group of students who enjoy being around one another and are a close-knit group," sums up one student.

Admissions

Applicants to UGA are evaluated for academic and intellectual ability, personal qualities, professional experience, and management potential. The school evaluates these factors based on a student's academic transcripts, admissions essays, GMAT scores, professional resume, honors and activities, letters of recommendation, and, for international students, TOEFL scores. In addition, because personal factors are highly important to the program, personal interviews with Admissions Staff are highly encouraged, though not mandatory. Current students take note of the stellar community at UGA, saying, "Our Admissions Office is very good at bringing the right group of people together to benefit both the school and the students."

UGA usually receives about 400 applications for the MBA program. Last year's entering class had an average GMAT score of 651 and a GPA of 3.3, with professional work experience of 4.4 years. Work experience is very important and heavily weighed in an application. If a student has less than 2 years of experience, chances of admission are limited. University of Georgia admits students on a rolling basis, so students (especially those seeking scholarships and assistantships) are encouraged to apply early.

FINANCIAL FACTS

Annual tuition (in-state/ out-of-state)	$8,182/$27,036
Fees (in-state/ out-of-state)	$1,126/$1,072
Cost of books	$1,000
Room & board (on/off-campus)	$12,400/$16,500
% of students receiving aid	77
% of first-year students receiving aid	82
% of students receiving grants	77
Average grant	$13,916

ADMISSIONS

Admissions Selectivity Rating	93
# of applications received	285
% applicants accepted	41
% acceptees attending	68
Average GMAT	653
Range of GMAT	560–700
Average GPA	3.39
TOEFL required of international students	Yes
Minimum TOEFL (paper/computer)	577/233
Application fee	$62
International application fee	$62
Regular application deadline	5/12
Regular notification	Rolling
Deferment available	Yes
Maximum length of deferment	1 year
Non-fall admissions	Yes
Need-blind admissions	Yes

Applicants Also Look At

Emory University, Georgia Institute of Technology, The University of North Carolina at Chapel Hill, The University of Texas at Austin.

EMPLOYMENT PROFILE

Career Rating	85	Grads Employed by Function	% Avg. Salary
Primary Source of Full-time Job Acceptances		Finance	37 $69,971
School-facilitated activities	28 (57%)	Marketing	24 $72,773
Graduate-facilitated activities	21 (43%)	MIS	2 NR
Average base starting salary	$71,908	Operations	4 NR
Percent employed	82	Consulting	25 $73,206
		General Management	4 NR
		Other	4 NR

Top 5 Employers Hiring Grads
The Home Depot; Bank of America; FedEx; CapGemini; IBM

UNIVERSITY OF HARTFORD
THE BARNEY SCHOOL OF BUSINESS

Academics

"Class flexibility and reputation" draw area business students to the MBA program at the University of Hartford's Barney School. As one explains, "The program was created for working students. The program structure allows me to continue with my career and still attend school." The school's many full-time workers especially enjoy the convenience of the school's "No Hassle MBA program," under which "the MBA advisor takes full care to register No Hassle MBA students for all of their classes. In addition, books are waiting for graduate students in the No Hassle program on the first night of classes during each term. There is no need to wait on lines at the bookstore or other cumbersome activities typical of registration each term." Students tell us that "The No Hassle option really does work. I don't have to worry about anything but showing up for class. My ID, parking permits, registration, and books are all taken care of for me."

The Barney School benefits from a location that is both convenient to area working people and advantageous to full-time students seeking summer work and internships. Hartford is one of the nation's insurance centers and is also home to numerous financial, manufacturing, and technological concerns (it should be noted that several students feel that finance is among the weaker disciplines here). Most who teach here "have real-life experience, not just book experience, and bring this to the classroom." That expertise, combined with the professional experience of students, makes for "a high quality of class dialogue and discussion among peers from various sectors." One student reports: "In my Capstone course, I am in the company of other full-time professionals who include engineers, insurance industry professionals, an actuary, government executives, retail executives, self-employed entrepreneurs, and business analysts, to name a few."

Several students report that classroom facilities here need an upgrade. One tells us, "Classrooms have a very dated look to them," with "desks and chairs rather than tables and chairs," which would "make the classrooms more team-friendly." They would also like to see an expansion of the curriculum, with additions made in project management, "a hot topic and a necessity in industry today. Also, more courses in operations management and international studies would be pertinent." Students praise the current curriculum for its "global viewpoint" and "engaging and practical" approach to the material. They also love the recently initiated study abroad options, describing them as "great opportunities for the students who can afford to go."

Career and Placement

Placement and career-counseling services are provided to Barney MBAs by the Career Services Office (CSO), which serves the entire undergraduate and graduate student body of the university. Services include resume and cover-letter writing workshops, seminars on networking and interviewing strategies, job banks, on-campus interviewing, and job fairs. Students warn that the office "is primarily for undergraduate students. It's rare that there is an event that would be of any interest to an MBA." Independently of the CSO, the Barney School offers a series of Saturday morning "enrichment workshops" covering such subjects as business presentations, negotiations, career planning, and job search strategies. The school also sponsors a mentoring program for MBAs.

ADMISSIONS CONTACT: CLAIRE SILVERSTEIN, DIRECTOR OF MBA PROGRAM
ADDRESS: 200 BLOOMFIELD AVENUE, CENTER FOR GRADUATE & ADULT SERVICES, CC231 WEST
HARTFORD, CT 06117 UNITED STATES
PHONE: 860-768-4444 • FAX: 860-768-4821
E-MAIL: ADMISSIONS@HARTFORD.EDU • WEBSITE: BARNEY.HARTFORD.EDU

FINANCIAL FACTS

Annual tuition	$10,710
Cost of books	$0
% of students receiving aid	29
% of first-year students receiving aid	48
% of students receiving loans	20
% of students receiving grants	6
Average award package	$15,312
Average grant	$4,563

ADMISSIONS

Admissions Selectivity Rating	**72**
# of applications received	178
% applicants accepted	79
% acceptees attending	53
Average GMAT	510
Range of GMAT	450–720
Average GPA	3
TOEFL required of international students	Yes
Minimum TOEFL (paper/computer)	550/213
Application fee	$45
International application fee	$45
Regular application deadline	Rolling
Regular notification	Rolling
Deferment available	Yes
Maximum length of deferment	1 year
Transfer students accepted	Yes
Transfer application policy	Based on Individual Cases.
Non-fall admissions	Yes

Student Life and Environment

The Barney School attracts "friendly, smart, motivated" people, "about half of whom are in their twenties and the other half are in their forties. Generally, they are working people looking to take that next step." They arrive from "various industries such as insurance, banking, and financial services." About one in five attends full time; about half of full-time students are international students who "appear to enjoy the university environment and are engaged in various programs as this institution." Students also point out that the "good mix of international and domestic students allows you to develop better understanding of international issues." Full-time students "work in a cohort environment" that allows them to "bond deeply and quickly." Part-timers tell us that there is generally "no out-of-class mingling, which is fine for most classmates because no one has time between working and family life."

The University of Hartford campus offers "many arts and music activities to attend" through the Hartt School Program, which mounts theatre productions, concerts, and similar events. Students also have access to lecture series and other campus-wide activites. Most here, however, simply "take classes after work and then go home," with "participation in the activities at this institution limited to group meetings, project analysis, and data gathering (i.e., using the school's library and computer resources)."

Admissions

The Barney admissions office requires all MBA applicants to submit: official transcripts from all previously attended post-secondary schools; two letters of recommendation; official GMAT results; a current resume; a letter of intent describing the applicant's academic and career goals; and, a completed application. Applicants with at least three years of continuous work experience may apply for a GMAT waiver, as may applicants who have already successfully completed another master's program. International students must submit TOEFL scores and a Guarantor's Statement of Financial Support in addition to the above. Applications are processed on a rolling basis; because space in each incoming class is limited, it greatly benefits applicants to apply as early as possible.

UNIVERSITY OF HOUSTON
C.T. BAUER COLLEGE OF BUSINESS

GENERAL INFORMATION
Type of school	Public
Environment	Metropolis
Academic calendar	Semester

SURVEY SAYS...
Students love Houston, TX
Friendly students
Good peer network
Cutting edge classes

STUDENTS
Enrollment of parent institution	34,663
Enrollment of business school	579
% male/female	56/44
% out-of-state	26
% part-time	89
% minorities	10
% international	33
Average age at entry	28
Average years work experience at entry	3

ACADEMICS
Academic Experience Rating	**82**
Student/faculty ratio	3:1
Profs interesting rating	85
Profs accessible rating	79
% female faculty	26
% minority faculty	20

Joint Degrees
MBA/JD 4–6 years, MBA/MIE (Industrial Engineering) 2–5 years, MBA/MA (Spanish) 2–5 years, MBA/MS (Hospitality Management) 2–5 years; MBA/MSW, 3–5 years, MBA/MS (International Management) 3–5 years.

Prominent Alumni
G. Edmond Clark, President/CEO, FedEx Trade Netoworks, Inc.; Karen Katz, President/CEO, Neiman Marcus Stores; Duy-Loan T. Le Senior Fellow, Texas Instruments; David M. McClanahan, President/CEO, CenterPoint Energy; Mark G. Papa, Chairman/CEO, EOG Resources, Inc.

Academics

Marshaled by a team of experienced business leaders and located in a patently commerce-friendly city, Bauer College of Business enjoys "prominence in the Houston business community" and distinguishes itself from other Texas schools through its "very strong academic focus on the energy industry." If you want to learn about business straight from the mouth of high-power executives, you'll have ample opportunity at Bauer, where "professors are knowledgeable and generally have experience from industry, not just academia." A current student enthuses, "My professors in the past year, for example, included the senior M&A executive for a global Fortune 500 company, and a former Treasurer of Exxon-Mobil."

Each entering student is assigned to a "cohort," which is a group of students that works through the MBA curriculum together. Providing continuity throughout the program, as well as an excellent opportunity to begin networking, "the cohorts allow you to get to know the other students and each semester's classes are tied together very well." In fact, many Bauer students say the "most valuable part of class is often the insight that your colleagues bring to the table." Drawing students from "almost every industry" you'll meet plenty of energy industry folks, with "other experiences are sprinkled throughout: high tech, real estate, non-profit, health care, government, aerospace, banking, commodities trading, all contributing to a very diverse experience."

Another benefit to the University of Houston is the ample extracurricular opportunities to enhance your education. Special programs like the Leadership and Ethics Week, "the Distinguished Lecture series, the Rockwell Career Center, and the active students organizations also enrich the academic experience." For future investors, the school also offers "excellent Financial Services Management program that involves participation in the Cougar Fund. This fund is a mutual fund that affords students enrolled in the concentration the opportunity to serve as portfolio managers and analysts for over a year." To put the icing on the cake, University of Houston's "administration is so well run that you hardly ever have an issue or question that is not answered even before you can come up with them."

Career and Placement

After graduation, Bauer students have plenty to look forward to: "the city of Houston has lots of career opportunities and Bauer has an exceptional reputation. Our graduates are synonymous with hard work and dedication." In fact, the Houston job market is so hopping that a current student tells us, "Several of my classmates have offered me very well paying jobs at their companies. Most of my close friends work in management positions at major Fortune 500 companies."

In addition to the networking that naturally takes place between students, the Rockwell Career Center is always busy helping students make connections. Their full events calendar includes "two huge and industry-diverse career fairs specifically for Business and MBAs." Among the numerous companies that bought booths at recent career fairs are A-AIG, Allied Waste, Cameron, CenterPoint Energy, Central Intelligence Agency, Chevron, Chevron Phillips, CITGO Petroleum, Commerce Bank, Compass Bank, Continental Airlines, Deloitte Consulting, EC Power, El Paso Corporation, Intel Corporation, Koch, Merrill Lynch Commodities, Million Air, Nabors Industries, Prudential Financial, Sears Holdings, Sequent Energy Management, Serenity Systems, Shell Oil, Smith Barney, Spectra Energy, Suez Energy, SunGuard Consulting, Tesoro Corporation.

ADMISSIONS CONTACT: ALBA VILLEGAS, PROGRAM COORDINATOR
ADDRESS: 334 MELCHER HALL, ROOM 330 HOUSTON, TX 77204-6021 UNITED STATES
PHONE: 713-743-0700 • FAX: 713-743-4807
E-MAIL: HOUSTONMBA@UH.EDU • WEBSITE: WWW.BAUER.UH.EDU/MBA

Student Life and Environment

Bauer students describe their classmates as "bright, ambitious, stimulating people with diverse personal, cultural, and professional backgrounds. They range from recent undergrads to successful executives." It's fortunate that students express such respect for their cohorts, because networking, group work, and collaboration are fundamental to the Bauer experience. Happily, "students are respectful of one another, and group projects generally go well." In fact, the spirit of work and collaboration seems to permeate the entire Bauer community, and "the academic advisors, career center, Dean's office, and even Starbucks, work long late hours, just like the students."

Hailing from across the greater Houston metropolitan area, "the MBA students are virtually all commuters. There are strong student chapters [and] professional organizations, but in general, MBA students do not participate much in campus life." Even study groups tend to form away from campus, that is, if they physically form at all. A student in the evening program explains, "I do a lot of collaboration with classmates via conference call and e-mail. Since Houston is so large, commuting to campus for every group meeting would be challenging. Working in virtual teams is a huge plus for those of us with a lot going on." But don't fret if you'd like to make a friend or two in business school; social life isn't totally non-existent. As proof, a student shares this perspective: "While a lot of student gatherings on the weekend are for group work, I would venture to say that students form very strong relationships with others from our classes and some of us do meet up socially [when] we have the time." In addition, the commuter vibe may soon be a thing of the past, as "recent and ongoing campaigns have been focused on creating a family atmosphere, where more MBA students live in new on-campus housing and commuting students spend more time on campus to socialize. These efforts have largely been successful, and even professors will occasionally attend after-hours functions."

Admissions

The University of Houston prides itself on diversity, and therefore, they understand that the strengths of each student vary. However, on the whole, the school seeks to admit students with a strong academic background, quantitative aptitude, management potential, and diversity of experiences. There are no minimum test scores or GPA required for admission; however, average Bauer admits had GMAT scores of 600 and an undergraduate GPA of 3.30. Entering students have an average of five years' work experience; however, two are generally considered the minimum acceptable years of professional experience.

FINANCIAL FACTS

Annual tuition (in-state/ out-of-state)	$6,343/$11,347
Fees	$3,480
Cost of books	$1,400
Room & board (on-campus)	$7,550
% of students receiving aid	52
% of first-year students receiving aid	47
% of students receiving loans	45
% of students receiving grants	33
Average award package	$18,168
Average grant	$3,763
Average student loan debt	$29,658

ADMISSIONS

Admissions Selectivity Rating	**81**
# of applications received	384
% applicants accepted	84
% acceptees attending	74
Average GMAT	543
Range of GMAT	490–590
Average GPA	3.23
TOEFL required of international students	Yes
Minimum TOEFL (paper/computer)	603/250
Application fee	$75
International application fee	$150
Regular application deadline	5/1
Regular notification	6/1
Deferment available	Yes
Maximum length of deferment	1 year
Non-fall admissions	Yes
Need-blind admissions	Yes

Applicants Also Look At

Rice University, Texas A&M University—College Station, The University of Texas at Austin, University of Houston—Clear Lake, University of St. Thomas.

UNIVERSITY OF HOUSTON—VICTORIA
SCHOOL OF BUSINESS ADMINISTRATION

GENERAL INFORMATION
Type of school   Public

SURVEY SAYS...
Students love Victoria, TX
Happy students
Solid preparation in:
General management
Quantitative skills

STUDENTS
Enrollment of parent institution	2,827
Enrollment of business school	681
% male/female	46/54
% out-of-state	4
% part-time	80
% minorities	59
% international	10
Average age at entry	33
Average years work experience at entry	2

ACADEMICS
Academic Experience Rating	**71**
Student/faculty ratio	25:1
Profs interesting rating	87
Profs accessible rating	65
% female faculty	25
% minority faculty	61

Academics

The options are abundant for MBAs at the University of Houston—Victoria. Students here can pursue a traditional MBA, or they can also choose from among several other degree options: a Global MBA, with a focus on international business and management; a Master's of Economic Development and Entrepreneurship, with a focus on start-ups and entrepreneurial enterprises; and a fourth-year bridge MBA, designed for students who earned three bachelor's degrees abroad. UHV also allows students several choices of venue: Many programs are available not only at the main campus in Victoria but also at satellite campuses in Sugar Land and Katy (the Cinco Ranch campus). All classes are available to distance learners online.

The highlight of the UHV MBA curriculum, students agree, is the MBA Conference; it's "the culmination of everything that has been learned in the MBA program and applied to an original team case. Each team is competing for top honors and must present its findings at the MBA conference to faculty and students. It is truly a team effort." The competition "really helps us to recapture all the concepts that we have learned through out the program," students say.

Many students—especially those with full-time jobs—opt to take advantage of the well-supported distance-learning options here. Explains one, "Because the course material was online, and because my work in the oil business carried me to very remote locations (e.g., jungles of the Amazon, the Andes mountains, the Caribbean, offshore on a drilling platform), I was always 'present and accounted for.' I could not have finished the MBA if it had not been for the use of technology at UHV." Distance learning allows such students to participate in their courses "while literally working in the global economy, making it easy to learn how the MBA material integrates with the real world." Even those who don't have to trot around the globe appreciate how "we don't waste the time commuting to and from campus, and that results in much more time to devote to researching and studying the material."

Career and Placement

UHV's MBA program maintains an online Career Opportunities Center that houses a collection of job-search resources. Students here also have access to the Career Planning and Placement Office, which serves the entire university community. Students note, however, that the school "is clearly lacking many elements in MBA career placement services. As a relatively new program, they are still working to develop contacts and organize this aspect." As this is a nontraditional program, on-campus recruiting is minimal. However, several employers have expressed interest in applicants from UHV including 3M, AXA Financial Advisors, Banco Popular, Colgate-Palmolive, DuPont, GE, Goldman Sachs, Johnson & Johnson, JPMorgan Chase, PricewaterhouseCoopers, the United States Securities and Exchange Commission, and Wachovia.

ADMISSIONS CONTACT: LINDA PARR, ADMISSIONS COORDINATOR
ADDRESS: 3007 N BEN WILSON ST. VICTORIA, TX 77901 UNITED STATES
PHONE: 361-570-4119 • FAX: 361-570-4114
E-MAIL: PARRL@UHV.EDU • WEBSITE: WWW.UHV.EDU/BUS

Student Life and Environment

UHV holds MBA classes on three campuses. As one student explains, "The UHV main campus is located in Victoria, Texas. There are also large satellite campuses located in South Houston and West Houston. All facilities have state-of-the-art equipment and all campuses offer online courses that run concurrently with the face-to-face classes." Classes "are scheduled at convenient times, and most of the lecturers are understanding in extending our assignment deadlines during personal emergencies. Most of the heavy workload is in a few courses in the second year, but otherwise it is easy to keep up with the classwork." One student sums it up like this: "Life at UHV is unique. You can be as involved or uninvolved as you choose. The technology resources are wonderful, especially the online research tools. The facilities are always clean and attractive inside and out."

Students describe their peers as "mature, experienced, leaders in their communities, smart, current, and well-respected." Many are hard-working professionals with families who still find time and energy to make school a priority. Team projects aren't a problem here, as "it is easy to form teams with enthusiastic students that are willing to share the work together. The diversity of the students allows different views of attacking business problems." One student tells us that the school "is a good fit for students that really want to learn, but not for students who just want to check the box that an MBA was completed."

Admissions

Applicants to the UHV MBA program are eligible for unconditional admission to the program if they have a four-year undergraduate degree from an accredited institution, earned a GPA of at least 2.5, and a GMAT score of at least 450. Students with an admissions index of at least 1,400—calculated under the formula (GPA x 200) + (GMAT x 2)—also qualify for unconditional admission. Students who fail to meet these requirements may qualify for conditional admission. Those students who have previously earned a graduate or professional degree (e.g. MD, PhD, JD) are generally exempted from the GMAT requirement. Under certain circumstances, the school will accept a recent (i.e., less than 5 years old) GRE score in lieu of a GMAT score; a combined verbal-quantitative score of at least 900 is required. A GMAT waiver may also be granted to applicants who meet all the following requirements: an undergraduate GPA of at least 3.0; a grade of B or better in two qualifying courses offered by UHV; and at least two years of relevant professional experience. Such students must submit a personal statement describing their career objectives.

FINANCIAL FACTS

Annual tuition (in-state/ out-of-state)	$4,548/$10,020
Fees	$2,436
Cost of books	$1,200

ADMISSIONS

Admissions Selectivity Rating	**61**
# of applications received	230
% applicants accepted	99
% acceptees attending	78
Average GMAT	438
Range of GMAT	370–450
Average GPA	2.94
TOEFL required of international students	Yes
Minimum TOEFL (paper/computer)	550/213
Application fee	$0
International application fee	$0
Deferment available	Yes
Maximum length of deferment	1 year
Transfer students accepted	Yes
Transfer application policy Up to 6 hours of graduate business coursework may be accepted with approval.	
Non-fall admissions	Yes
Need-blind admissions	Yes

Applicants Also Look At

University of Houston, University of Houston—Clear Lake.

EMPLOYMENT PROFILE	
Career Rating	**88**
Percent employed	79

UNIVERSITY OF ILLINOIS—CHICAGO
LIAUTAUD GRADUATE SCHOOL OF BUSINESS

GENERAL INFORMATION

Type of school	Public
Environment	City
Academic calendar	Semester

SURVEY SAYS...

Students love Chicago, IL
Friendly students
Good social scene
Cutting edge classes
Solid preparation in:
Accounting

STUDENTS

Enrollment of parent	
institution	25,000
Enrollment of	
business school	344
% male/female	54/46
% out-of-state	41
% part-time	71
% minorities	18
% international	32
Average age at entry	28
Average years work	
experience at entry	5

ACADEMICS

Academic Experience Rating	**75**
Student/faculty ratio	13:1
Profs interesting rating	71
Profs accessible rating	83
% female faculty	26
% minority faculty	8

Joint Degrees

MBA/MS (Accounting) 3–6 years,
MBA/MPH 3–6 years, MBA/MSN
(Nursing) 3–6 years, MBA/MA
(Economics) 3–6 years, MBA/MIS
(Management Information Systems)
3–6 years, MBA/MD 5 years.

Academics

Offering an "affordable," "socially progressive" MBA program in the stellar city of Chicago, the University of Illinois at Chicago's Liautaud Graduate School of Business is an "outstanding value" in graduate business education. The program consists of 54 credit hours—roughly 13 or 14 courses—half of which are dedicated to the school's core curriculum. These six courses lay the foundation for the Liautaud MBA and are generally taken during the first two semesters of course work. After completing the core course work," Liautaud students take up to 30 credit hours of advanced electives. Due to the school's "flexibility and the option of various concentrations," students have the opportunity to focus their studies on one or two areas of interest—including a "highly ranked" entrepreneurship program—allowing them to graduate with targeted business savvy. Students may also take two courses in the Professional Topics Series, which address emerging trends in business. Some recent offerings include Cross-Functional Teams, The Chicago Exchanges, and Corporate Strategy.

There are a wide variety of professors and teaching styles at Liautaud and "Like any school, some professors are much better than others." Students across the board, however, are "very impressed with the level of personal attention available with professors and administrators," especially "for a large school." The curriculum is enhanced by considerable group work and case studies; students praise the fact that "course projects have been very challenging and have given [us] hands-on experience in real-life [business] situations." Moreover, students say their classmates contribute to the overall learning experience since "Most of them are experienced and knowledgeable in their field and bring professionalism to the class."

Liautaud students rave about the school's prime location in the commerce-friendly city of Chicago. In addition to the opportunities they gain in the classroom, students benefit from the fact that the school is "tied closely into the Chicago business community and successful Chicago business people." Noteworthy businesspeople often come to the campus, though "Visiting speakers are often scheduled prohibitively for part-time students." All students appreciate the myriad advantages that come with being in a "huge urban city with lots of learning opportunities," although some note that the "facilities could be upgraded/updated" and are "not conducive to learning." As one student jokes, "[The] library is louder than a heavy metal concert."

Career and Placement

Through Liautaud's Career Services Office, students have access to a number of professional development seminars on topics such as salary negotiation, personal branding, resume building, networking, and on-campus interviews. The center also offers advising, career development assistance (like mock interviews), and alumni and employer contacts, including an alumni mentor program, roundtable recruiting, and career fairs. Students' experiences with the Career Services Office is a mixed bag. Some observe that the school fails to tap into local resources and "needs to do better job of facilitating alumni interaction," while others claim that "the new Career Center is excellent in partnering students with potential employers and taking students through resume preparation, mock interview."

While the school continues to "work on providing better career opportunities" for students, the following companies have recently hired LGSB graduates: Abbott Laboratories, Allstate Insurance Company, Information Resources, Baxter, Caterpillar, Deloitte Touche Tohmatsu, Hewitt Associates, Morningstar, State Farm, Lockheed Martin, Nuveen Investments, UBS Financial, HSBC, Caremark, and Navigant Consulting.

Students Life and Environment

Because a large percentage of Liautaud students commute to school, there is something of a split amongst the student body and their perception of campus life. Part-time students are more likely to jet home rather than hang out after class, making it "difficult to foster a sense of community." Full-time students take a more active role in the campus community, participating in case competitions, conferences, and activities put on by the MBA Student Association. When it comes to their peers, students appreciate their classmates for being "friendly and intellectual without being overly competitive." "Minority groups are strongly represented" on campus, as are part-time students, "which aids in making contacts." As one student reports, "Overall, it is a campus filled with fun and academic activities. There is always something to do at Liautaud. The campus life is never boring here."

When students need to head off campus, "all of the amenities of Chicago [are] just beyond the campus perimeter." One student attests, "Apart from academics, I have always enjoyed hanging out with my fellow classmates for a bar night, movie night, or even a casual dinner." With a plethora of restaurants, bars, shopping, and cultural activities just a stone's throw away, there is always something to do after class—and usually someone ready and willing to join you.

Admissions

To apply to the University of Illinois at Chicago's Liautaud Graduate School of Business, you must submit a completed application (including several essay questions), an application fee, official transcripts from your undergraduate institution, GMAT scores, a current resume, two letters of recommendation, and, for international students, TOEFL test scores. Liautaud looks for candidates who demonstrate academic ability and strong management potential. The ideal candidate possesses the ability to lead, work in a team, conceptualize and analyze complex problems, and formulate solutions. To be considered for admission, Liautaud requires a B average on the last 60 hours of undergraduate course work (3.0 on a 4.0 scale). When analyzing an applicant's academic record, the school looks for evidence of analytic and quantitative skills.

Prominent Alumni

Charles B. Edlestein, Managing Director, Credit Suisse First Boston, LLC; William L. Gaultier, Principal, E-Storm international; Dennis P. Neumann, Chairman, Bank of New York Capital Funding; Raymond Roman, Sr. VP, Consumer Service Solutions, Dell; Jeffrey R. Rosenthal, CFO, Fortress Investment Group, LLC.

FINANCIAL FACTS

Annual tuition (in-state/ out-of-state)	$15,098/$30,218
Fees	$3,122
Cost of books	$1,389
Room & board (on-campus)	$11,250

ADMISSIONS

Admissions Selectivity Rating	87
# of applications received	404
% applicants accepted	48
% acceptees attending	50
Average GMAT	610
Range of GMAT	570–650
Average GPA	3.18
TOEFL required of international students	Yes
Minimum TOEFL (paper/computer)	570/230
Application fee	$50
International application fee	$60
Regular application deadline	5/15
Regular notification	rolling
Deferment available	Yes
Maximum length of deferment	one Semester
Transfer students accepted	Yes
Transfer application policy Maximum of 12 Semester hours may transfer.	
Non-fall admissions	Yes
Need-blind admissions	Yes

Applicants Also Look At

DePaul University, Loyola University—Chicago, Northwestern University, University of Chicago.

EMPLOYMENT PROFILE

Career Rating	63	Grads Employed by Function	% Avg. Salary
Primary Source of Full-time Job Acceptances		Finance	55 $55,627
School-facilitated activities	17 (90%)	Marketing	10 $60,000
Graduate-facilitated activities	2 (11%)	MIS	20 $79,500
Average base starting salary	$63,176	Consulting	15 $75,000
Percent employed	21	**Top 5 Employers Hiring Grads**	
		Bosch; Jones Lang LaSalle; Navigant Consulting; CNA Financial Serivces; UBS Finacial Services	

UNIVERSITY OF ILLINOIS AT URBANA-CHAMPAIGN
COLLEGE OF BUSINESS

Academics

You get a lot of bang for your buck at University of Illinois at Urbana-Champaign. Despite the school's low price tag, UIUC's College of Business offers an unbeatable mix of "strong academics, intimate class sizes, and a tight-knit, community environment." The unique, first-year curriculum takes a decidedly integrated approach to business education. Instead of taking individual courses in accounting, finance, and marketing, students march through a series of intensive, interdisciplinary courses that progressively cover all business essentials. The result is "a well-rounded experience that ensures the basics within each discipline are mastered." Be forewarned: The program is intense. Students caution, "This school is by no means a walk in the park—we have four 7-week semesters in the first year, which makes the curriculum that much more rigorous under the time constraints." However, they also reassure us that the heavy workload is eased by the fact that "the professors are very accommodating and accessible, while the MBA administration is also very accessible."

In their second year at UIUC, students identify a professional concentration in finance, marketing, information technology, operations management, general management, or a customized concentration. After the broad-based approach in the first year, the second year allows students to add depth and specificity to their studies. A unique component of the curriculum is the "Illinois Business Consulting, which gives students the opportunity to work with actual clients while in school." Through this student-run and faculty-supported consulting business, students have the chance to work on projects for a range of clients, from major players like the Ford Motor Company to new ventures to nonprofit organizations.

Peers are an important part of the educational experience at UIUC, as group assignments are a major component of the curriculum. Fortunately, students describe their classmates as interesting, diverse, and "very hardworking due to the rigorous workload, but also not as competitive or 'type A' as in other programs." Thanks to the prevalence of international students, "Every day is a class in international culture and customs!" While the cultural differences have been known to cause some stress during group assignments, most savvy business students see these challenges as an excellent opportunity to hone key social and negotiation skills. In the words of a current student: "This program offers an amazing opportunity—for someone that takes it—to learn about other cultures in a very informal setting."

Career and Placement

Through the MBA Career Services Office, students at University of Illinois have access to extensive online job-search resources, on-campus interviews, and a variety of professional development activities, including mock interviews, resume critiques, and workshops. The Career Services Office hosts two annual campus career fairs as well as special trips to Chicago, where students have the opportunity to meet with recruiters and UIUC alumni.

Ideally located and well respected in the region, students at UIUC say they benefit from "great networking, especially in Chicago and the Midwest." In fact, 97 percent of last year's graduates received a job offer within 3 months of graduation. The mean base salary for UIUC grads after graduation was $82,693 per year, with a range between $50,000 and $145,000. The most popular career fields were finance/accounting and marketing, which drew 30 percent and 18 percent of graduates, respectively. In 2006, the top hiring companies were: AT&T, BearingPoint, Capital One, Capgemini, Flowserve, Ford Motor Company, IBM, IllinoisVENTURES, Ingersoll Rand, Intel, International Truck and Engine Corporation, LG Electronics, Mercer Human Resource Consulting, Samsung, and Walgreen Co.

ADMISSIONS CONTACT: JAQUILIN WILSON, DIRECTOR OF ADMISSIONS
ADDRESS: 405 DAVID KINLEY HALL, 1407 W. GREGORY DRIVE URBANA, IL 61801 UNITED STATES
PHONE: 217-244-7602 • FAX: 217-333-1156
E-MAIL: MBA@UIUC.EDU • WEBSITE: WWW.MBA.UIUC.EDU

Student Life and Environment

Part of a large university and located in lively college town, UIUC's College of Business feels a little like returning to college. Taking advantage of the rich campus environment, business students enjoy tailgating and football games, replete with a beautiful main quad that "gives you that all-American feeling of 'college life.'" The fun doesn't stop there. Within the business school, "There are a lot of activities to choose from." "Scheduled weekly events include intramural sports, bowling, and social events at local establishments." Students warn, however, "with schoolwork and all the activities" available on campus, the UIUC experience "teaches you the true meaning of 'time management.'"

While many UIUC students take advantage of the school's proximity to Chicago (just a 2-hour drive away), they also exclaim, "It is surprising how much there is to do at a campus in the middle of the corn fields of central Illinois!" In fact, "Downtown Champaign (near the bus/train station) has been completely revitalized and has a number of trendy bars that would do Chicago proud. The selection of ethnic restaurants is similarly impressive with an amazing array of Japanese, Korean, Thai, and Chinese restaurants." Drawing friendly, young professionals, the student body at UIUC "is a social bunch who gather weekly to strengthen their ties and networks." Students also enjoy a small bonus within their busy schedule: "Since there's no class on Fridays [though there are often professional development activities], everyone convenes at a local establishment on Thursday nights to celebrate the end of a long, 4-day week."

Admissions

The Admissions Committee at the University of Illinois at Urbana-Champaign begins reviewing completed applications in December and will notify applicants of a decision within 4 to 6 weeks. Last year's entering class had an average undergraduate GPA of 3.4 and an median GMAT score of 652. Forty percent of entering students were business majors in college, and had more than 4 years of professional work experience before entering the program. UIUC does not have a minimum required GMAT score or GPA for admission. If you have taken the GMAT more than once, the Admissions Committee will only consider your highest score. There are no academic prerequisites for the program.

Prominent Alumni

Mike Tokarz, Chairman, The Tokarz Group; Tom Siebel, Founder, Chairman/CEO, Siebel Systems, Inc.; Jan Klug Valentic, Executive VP, Young and Rubican; Alan Feldman, President/CEO, Midas, Inc.; Bruce Holecek, CEO, Hobbico.

FINANCIAL FACTS

Annual tuition (in-state/ out-of-state)	$17,500/$26,500
Fees	$2,410

ADMISSIONS

Admissions Selectivity Rating	87
# of applications received	537
% applicants accepted	42
% acceptees attending	46
Range of GMAT	580–680
Average GPA	3.4
TOEFL required of international students	Yes
Application fee	$60
International application fee	$75
Regular application deadline	3/1
Regular notification	Rolling
Early decision program?	Yes
ED Deadline/ Notification	12/01 / 02/15
Need-blind admissions	Yes

EMPLOYMENT PROFILE

Career Rating	88	Grads Employed by Function	%	Avg. Salary
Percent employed	97	Finance	29	$87,556
		Human Resources	3	$75,000
		Marketing	15	$74,800
		MIS	2	$60,000
		Operations	5	$79,600
		Consulting	23	$84,726
		General Management	12	$76,000
		Other	11	$145,000

Top 5 Employers Hiring Grads

AT & T; General Electric; Deutsche Post World Net; Sears Holding Corp; Ford Motor Company

THE UNIVERSITY OF IOWA
HENRY B. TIPPIE SCHOOL OF MANAGEMENT

Academics

"Quality, location, and price" combine to make the MBA program at the University of Iowa's Henry B. Tippie School of Management an exceptional value. So exceptional, in fact, that "the school is ranked number one by Forbes in terms of speed of payback [on investment]." Students know how good they have it; one writes, "The Tippie School of Management at the University of Iowa appeared to be the complete package: passionate professors, rigorous academics, individual attention, ambitious yet inclusive student body, and a successful Career Services Department. When recruiting, Tippie treats you first class, and this does not change once you enter the program!"

Finance is the area in which Tippie's reputation is the strongest; marketing is another of the school's strengths. Both full-time and part-time students complete a comprehensive core curriculum before undertaking a concentration. Students report that instruction is best in concentration courses but that, throughout the curriculum, "Academics are strenuous and relevant. There is meaning in what we learn." The program is "very focused on the core skills and knowledge set rather than on chasing fads or flights of fancy." The relatively small size of the program means that it's a very personalized experience. "Professors, administrators, and classmates know one another personally and service is given on a one-on-one basis." Students also recognize drawbacks to the size of their program, telling us that "it prevents us from being ranked highly by publications that rely heavily on feedback from a random pool of potential employers because we don't send a great deal of people to California or New York."

Tippie professors "are both good teachers and cutting-edge researchers." Professors typically "have business experience through consulting, owning consulting companies, or [working] in business before teaching. They are not afraid to challenge you to work to your potential. Most really care about preparing you and try to give you the edge to be successful." They also "concentrate on our learning; an A is great, but learning the material is more important than a grade." Administrators "are passionate about the success of this program, and are in touch with students' needs."

Career and Placement

Tippie's MBA Career Services Office is "committed" to students and is "very strong in helping [students] find a job or internship," given the constraints created by the relatively small size of the MBA program. Many students feel that Tippie "needs to be a larger program so that we can attract more company representatives to campus for interviewing." As one student puts it, "Many companies don't want to come to campus for 65 students per class."

Employers who most frequently hire Tippie MBAs include: Aegon, Ameriprise, Best Buy Co., Inc., Boeing Corporation, Caterpillar, Discover Financial,Eaton, First National Bank, Goldman Sachs, JP Morgan Chase, Meredith Corporation, Motorola, Northwest Airlines, Orbitz, Pearson Educational Measurement, Principal Financial, Sears Holding, Waddell & Reed Investment Management Co., Whirlpool Corporation, Kohler Co., HNI Corporation, ESP International, Aviva, HSBC, Advanta Corporation.

Student Life and Environment

Because the Tippie MBA is "a small program at a large university, everyone is encouraged to get involved in many different things. There is a great sense of community among those in the program." Full-time students, in particular, are "really involved with campus activities like case competitions, social nights out, international celebrations, volunteer opportunities, sporting events, cultural and performing arts events, and more."

ADMISSIONS CONTACT: MARY SPREEN, DIRECTOR OF MBA ADMISSIONS AND FINANCIAL AID
ADDRESS: W160 PBB, HENRY B. TIPPIE SCHOOL OF MANAGEMENT, THE UNIVERSITY OF IOWA IOWA
CITY, IA 52242-1000 UNITED STATES
PHONE: 319-335-1039 • FAX: 319-335-3422
E-MAIL: TIPPIEMBA@UIOWA.EDU • WEBSITE: WWW.BIZ.UIOWA.EDU/MBA

Because "Iowans love their football . . . for most home games the MBA Association has a company-sponsored tailgate. The tailgates are fun and also allow for some networking with the sponsoring company."

Thank God It's Thursday (there are no MBA classes held on Fridays) is a tradition here that "typically involves going to bars, but we also use TGIT events to build ourselves professionally. For example: We hold a wine tasting and invite the medical, law, and pharmacy students; we take private tours at the Museum of Art; students participate in golf lessons; or we have an occasional Texas Hold 'Em tournament (you never know when you'll have to entertain an important client in Vegas)."

The MBA program "holds most of its classes in a brand-new building across from the fairly new general business building." Students say, "It's very nice, and there is almost always something going on besides classes, whether it is an executive speaker, alumni event, awards ceremony, or a student organization function." Because Tippie "has a tremendous international community," students enjoy "social activities that include dinners for events like Diwali, Lunar New Year, and Thanksgiving where we share our cultures."

Admissions

Applicants to the Tippie MBA program must submit official transcripts for all completed postsecondary academic work; an official GMAT score report; a current resume; two personal essays (topics provided in application packet); and three letters of recommendation. International students whose first language is not English must submit an official score report for either the TOEFL or the IELTS. Full-time students may apply for admission in the fall only; part-time students may begin study in either the fall or spring semesters. An admission interview is required of all full-time candidates. The school recommends, but does not require, a minimum of 2 years of postundergraduate professional experience for applicants to the full-time program.

FINANCIAL FACTS

Annual tuition (in-state/ out-of-state)	$13,162/$24,142
Fees	$778
Cost of books	$2,200
Room & board	$11,900
% of students receiving aid	54
% of first-year students receiving aid	54
% of students receiving grants	54
Average award package	$20,510
Average grant	$4,044
Average student loan debt	$27,700

ADMISSIONS

Admissions Selectivity Rating	**94**
# of applications received	205
% applicants accepted	50
% acceptees attending	64
Average GMAT	652
Range of GMAT	600–710
Average GPA	3.34
TOEFL required of international students	Yes
Minimum TOEFL (paper/computer)	600/250
Application fee	$60
International application fee	$85
Regular application deadline	7/15
Regular notification	Rolling
Deferment available	Yes
Maximum length of deferment	1 year
Transfer students accepted	Yes
Transfer application policy Maximum number of nine transferable credits from AACSB-accredited programs only.	
Non-fall admissions	Yes
Need-blind admissions	Yes

Applicants Also Look At

Indiana University Southeast, Purdue University, Texas A&M University—College Station, The University of Texas at Austin, University of Illinois at Urbana-Champaign, University of Minnesota, University of Wisconsin—Madison.

EMPLOYMENT PROFILE

Career Rating	89	Grads Employed by Function	% Avg. Salary
Primary Source of Full-time Job Acceptances		Finance	50 $71,300
School-facilitated activities	17 (65%)	Human Resources	4 NR
Graduate-facilitated activities	9 (35%)	Marketing	25 $82,083
Average base starting salary	$73,702	Operations	13 $71,533
Percent employed	90	Consulting	4 NR
		General Management	4 NR

Top 5 Employers Hiring Grads
HNI Corporation; Northwest Airline; Best Buy Co., Inc.; Discover Financial; Eaton Corporation

UNIVERSITY OF KANSAS
SCHOOL OF BUSINESS

GENERAL INFORMATION
Type of school	Public
Environment	City
Academic calendar	Semester

SURVEY SAYS...
Students love Lawrence, KS
Happy students
Solid preparation in:
Doing business in a global economy

STUDENTS
Enrollment of parent institution	29,260
Enrollment of business school	321
% male/female	76/24
% out-of-state	26
% part-time	69
% minorities	24
% international	10
Average age at entry	30
Average years work experience at entry	5

ACADEMICS
Academic Experience Rating	**74**
Student/faculty ratio	7:1
Profs interesting rating	73
Profs accessible rating	86
% female faculty	25
% minority faculty	9

Joint Degrees
MBA/MA (East Asian Languages and Cultures) 2 years, MBA/MA (Latin American Studies) 2 years, MBA/MA (Russian, Eastern European and Eurasian Studies) 2 years, MBA/MA (Management) 2 years, MBA/JD 4 years, MBA/PharmD 7 years, MBA/PM 2 years.

Prominent Alumni
Kent C. McCarthy, Private Client Services Division, Goldman Sachs; Ketchum Kreig, Google, VP International Marketing; Ronald G. Harper, Chairman/CEO of MPSI; Robert S. Kaplan, Lecturer at Harvard, Director of Goldman Sachs Grp; Edward A. Kangas, Former Chairman and CEO, Deloitte and Touche.

Academics

Students at the University of Kansas' School of Business describe their institution as "the best business school in the Midwest," and they have good reason to be so complimentary. "Positive, up-tempo, friendly, and lots of work," the Kansas program is "vastly underrated" and a "truly wonderful" grad school experience. The students characterize the professors as "second to none" and are impressed with their academic and professional backgrounds." KU profs, who are "active in the business world within their fields," exhibit "a great blend of teaching skills and real-world experience."

Students are held to a high standard and are "expected to be well prepared, well read, and well spoken in course discussions." The "fantastic" administration receives high praise as well. One MBA candidate reported that "if you want to try something different or want to attend a conference, they support you 100 percent of the time." Students also mention the administration's constant efforts "to improve facilities, encourage student involvement and input, and expand the faculty and curriculum."

On top of the full-time MBA offered at KU, the school also offers an evening-professional MBA, a Master's in Accounting, Master's in Finance, and several dual-degree MBAs, including a JD/MBA, MBA/MIM, MBA-PharmD, MBA/PM (petroleum management), as well as three international-themed dual degrees involving Latin American, European, and Asian studies. KU also has an extensive PhD program in which students can concentrate in accounting, information systems, finance, marketing, decision sciences, and management. KU's "focus on the global business environment" is a huge draw for many applicants, who feel that the school provides "an exceptional international business program for being in the middle of the United States and far from the coasts." Reasonable fees also are a major plus, and many students feel they're receiving a great deal of value for their money.

As one might expect from a school that focuses a great deal on international business, KU has an international program that allows students to obtain real-world experience in the global marketplace. The KU School of Business partners with the Center for International Business Education and Research to facilitate study abroad with an array of businesses across the globe. In the past few years students have traveled to India, China, Germany, France, Brazil, and Mexico as part of the program. With these types of experiences available to students, it's no wonder they describe the KU program as a "good value for the money that offered many options in terms of international experience."

Career and Placement

On its website the school boasts that "KU Business alumni are chief officers and senior executives of dozens of Fortune 500 companies." Fortunately for KU students who aspire to such heights, Kansas City is home to many large corporations, including Sprint and Hallmark, and the metropolitan area was named one of the "Top 20 Areas to Start and Grow a Company" by Inc.com. KU also has a second campus (Edwards Campus) located in nearby Overland Park, which was named one of the top 10 cities for doing business by Business Development Outlook.

Students give glowing reviews to the school's Career Services Department, which does a "fantastic job of preparing students for the job-search process and facilitating that process through two massive career fairs, many interview and resume workshops, one-on-one counseling, and more." One student says, "I already have a job waiting for me when I complete the master's program, thanks to the business school's Career Services and KU's strong reputation in the region."

ADMISSIONS CONTACT: DEE STEINLE, ADMINISTRATIVE DIRECTOR OF MASTER'S PROGRAMS
ADDRESS: 206 SUMMERFIELD HALL, 1300 SUNNYSIDE AVENUE LAWRENCE, KS 66045 U.S.
PHONE: 913-897-8587 • FAX: 785-864-5376
E-MAIL: BSCHOOLGRAD@KU.EDU • WEBSITE: WWW.BUSINESS.KU.EDU

Approximately 86 percent of Kansas students accepted job offers before graduating in 2006, and by 3 months after graduation, that number had grown to 86 percent. The average salary for graduates was $58,955 (not including bonus). The majority of students accepted jobs in marketing and finance, although there were quite a few who went into operations and consulting. A range of companies recruit on campus, and the ones who hire graduates most frequently include Deloitte Touche Tohmatsu, Payless Shoe Source, Sprint, Capgemini, Ernst & Young, and KPMG International.

Student Life and Environment

KU students enjoy life on campus, which many describe as "great." The only complaint is that "there are really more things that I'd like to be able to participate in than I have time to do!" One student described life at KU as "filled with a variety of activities, including extracurriculars (Net Impact, MBA Ambassadors), social events put on by MBA student organizations, working for the MBA Admissions Office, and of course, course work."

Although the majority of the class is "ambitious and concentrated on their future," students are also "very fun people." There is diversity among the MBA candidates, and the students "vary from people straight out of undergrad to people 35 years old, and they all have different goals and lifestyles, but they communicate well and make the classes enjoyable by opening up discussion without judging others." Some say their classmates "are the very best part about my experience in the KU MBA program." Overall, students are more than satisfied with their experiences at KU. As one student said, "I cannot thank KU enough for preparing me to excel in my future endeavors."

Admissions

Applications are accepted at anytime, up until posted application deadlines. KU is now accepting applications for all programs for the Fall 2007 semester. In a recently admitted class, students' average undergraduate GPA was around 3.3, and the average GMAT was approximately 600. Students had an average of 5 years of work experience.

FINANCIAL FACTS

Annual tuition (in-state/ out-of-state)	$8,493/$17,187
Fees	$2,596
Cost of books	$1,500
Room & board	$5,750
% of students receiving aid	70
% of first-year students receiving aid	70
% of students receiving loans	90
% of students receiving grants	50
Average award package	$5,000
Average grant	$5,000

ADMISSIONS

Admissions Selectivity Rating	**77**
# of applications received	129
% applicants accepted	80
% acceptees attending	81
Average GMAT	580
Range of GMAT	500–770
Average GPA	3.28
TOEFL required of international students	Yes
Minimum TOEFL (paper/computer)	53/20
Application fee	$60
International application fee	$60
Regular application deadline	6/1
Regular notification	Rolling
Deferment available	Yes
Maximum length of deferment	1 year
Transfer students accepted	Yes
Transfer application policy Maximum number of transferable credit hours is six.	
Non-fall admissions	Yes
Need-blind admissions	Yes

Applicants Also Look At

Iowa State University, University of Iowa, University of Missouri—Columbia, University of Nebraska—Lincoln, University of Oklahoma.

EMPLOYMENT PROFILE

Career Rating	67	Grads Employed by Function	% Avg. Salary
Primary Source of Full-time Job Acceptances		Finance	17 $75,000
School-facilitated activities	55%	Marketing	16 $55,000
Graduate-facilitated activities	39%	Operations	38 $60,000
Unknown	6%	Consulting	25 $62,000
Percent employed	17	Other	4 $62,000

Top 5 Employers Hiring Grads

Marketsphere; Sprint; 3M; Amdocs; Payless Shoesource

UNIVERSITY OF KENTUCKY
GATTON COLLEGE OF BUSINESS AND ECONOMICS

GENERAL INFORMATION
Type of school	Public
Environment	City
Academic calendar	Semester

SURVEY SAYS...
Students love Lexington, KY
Good social scene
Cutting edge classes
Solid preparation in:
Teamwork
Communication/interpersonal skills

STUDENTS
Enrollment of parent institution	26,545
Enrollment of business school	181
% male/female	75/25
% out-of-state	29
% part-time	57
% minorities	12
% international	10
Average age at entry	27
Average years work experience at entry	2.7

ACADEMICS
Academic Experience Rating	**82**
Student/faculty ratio	3:1
Profs interesting rating	72
Profs accessible rating	86
% female faculty	15
% minority faculty	5

Joint Degrees
MBA/JD 4 years, MBA/BS (Engineering) 5 years, MBA/MD 5 years, MBA/PharmD 4 years, MBA/MA (International Relations) 3 years.

Prominent Alumni
Chris Sullivan, Chairman of the Board, Outback Steakhouse; Paul Rooke, Executive VP, Lexmark International, Inc.; Gretchen Price, VP, Finance & Accounting, Global Operations, P&G; Greg Burns, Chairman/CEO, O'Charley's, Inc.; James E. Rogers, Jr., Chairman, President, Cinergy Corp.

Academics

Educating business students for more than 80 years, the Gatton College features bachelor's, master's and doctoral degrees within three academic units: the School of Management, the Von Allmen School of Accountancy, and the Department of Economics. There are three majors offered in the MBA program: marketing, finance, and IT.

Students praise Gatton's "approachable" faculty and staff, describing support from them as "top-notch." "They go above and beyond to make sure every student is given the resources to succeed," says one MBA candidate. "Having an MBA center dedicated to us has been one the best academic experiences I've had." The professors are leaders in their field and are "published in respected journals." They are "very dedicated to helping us learn the course work," and are remarkably open with the candidates. "They give us access to their published, unpublished, and even working papers. They have done this without making their own material the main basis of assignments and exams, which I like, because it lets them be more unbiased," one student says. Several students say the program would benefit greatly from the professors and administrators doing "a better job of working together and becoming a cohesive unit," because the "lack of communication between the two groups causes some problems for the students."

Gatton has undergone a major change recently, making the transition to an 11-month immersion MBA. The new program is designed "for both business and non-business students but is much more challenging for those without a business background." The arduous program boasts "a unique structure and opportunities for PDMA and Six Sigma certification." Because the program is only a year long, students do not have a summer off to participate in an internship. To address this, the school has implemented a program called Project Connect, which pairs teams of students with a company to work on real-world projects during the course of the year. In 2006, participating companies included Lexmark, Humana, Fifth Third, Tempur-Pedic, and United Technologies.

The part-time students aren't that thrilled with the program's transition, expressing concern that "working professionals seeking an MBA from Gatton aren't provided the same opportunities and resources as those students in the 11-month program." However, there's agreement that all of the students are "driven, intelligent, hardworking, studious."

Career and Placement

There are 103 students in Gatton's MBA program, and 229 companies participated in recruiting last year, so it's no wonder students say "Career placement is getting better." However, some feel the Career Center needs to "focus more on separating undergrad recruiting from MBA recruiting."

Career services at the University of Kentucky are based in the James W. Stuckert Career Center. Among other services, the Career Center hosts a mentoring program and specialized MBA workshops. The mentoring program provides students with networking contacts, including alumni, friends of UK, and employers. Through mentoring contacts, students can participate in informational interviews and shadowing, as well as ask for career advice. The Career Center also hosts several career fairs throughout the year, with the Business Career Fair held in the fall semester, followed by the Spring Career and Internship Expo. To help students prepare for these events, Gatton offers MBA workshops whose topics include resume writing, interviewing, networking, salary negotiations, etiquette, and more.

ADMISSIONS CONTACT: BEVERLY KEMPER, MBA ACADEMIC COORDINATOR
ADDRESS: 145 GATTON COLLEGE OF BUSINESS AND ECONOMICS LEXINGTON, KY 40506-0034 U.S.
PHONE: 859-257-7722 • FAX: 859-323-9971
E-MAIL: KEMPER@UKY.EDU • WEBSITE: GATTON.UKY.EDU

Last year the average salary for a Gatton graduate was $50,098. Recruiting employers included Humana, the Department of Labor, Proctor & Gamble, Ryder, and Toyota. Finance is the most popular of the three Gatton majors, with almost half of graduates taking jobs in finance. Fifty-eight percent of candidates accepted offers before they graduated, and by 3 months after graduation, 75 percent had accepted offers.

Student Life and Environment

Located on a 687-acre campus near downtown Lexington, the University of Kentucky has an enrollment of 26,000 students and is a nationally recognized research institution. Students enjoy life in Lexington, and among Gatton's strengths they list "the local area, local quality of life, temperate climate, [and] good facilities." Lexington is the second largest city in Kentucky and has an international reputation for its bluegrass horse farms, and is home to the renowned Keeneland Race Track. Another big draw for Lexington residents is the UK men's basketball team, a perennial powerhouse. The student body isn't particularly diverse, with students describing their peers as "mostly middle-class White Americans, with a majority being conservative." However, despite "not [being] an extremely diverse group," students are tolerant and "very accepting of differences."

Gatton students tend to form close bonds because of the short duration of the program. As one student says, "The program is only 11 months, so we spend a lot of time around each other." The result is a "family atmosphere" that's conducive to collaboration. "Everyone I have interacted with has been very friendly and willing to offer advice or any help they could," one MBA candidate says. "I was happily surprised to discover this, as I assumed classmates would be more cutthroat."

Admissions

In the fall of 2006, the average undergraduate GPA was 3.4, and the average GMAT was 598. Sixty-seven percent of the student population was male, out of a class of 94, and 17 states and 4 countries were represented. Students had an average of 2.6 years of work experience, and their average age was 26.

FINANCIAL FACTS

Annual tuition (in-state/out-of-state)	$8,212/$16,700
Fees (in-state/out-of-state)	$6,000/$7,000
Cost of books	$2,500
Room & board (on/off-campus)	$8,250/$9,100
% of students receiving aid	29
% of first-year students receiving aid	29
% of students receiving grants	29
Average award package	$13,482
Average grant	$13,482

ADMISSIONS

Admissions Selectivity Rating	89
# of applications received	212
% applicants accepted	64
% acceptees attending	80
Average GMAT	609
Range of GMAT	530–690
Average GPA	3.38
TOEFL required of international students	Yes
Minimum TOEFL (paper/computer)	550/213
Application fee	$40
International application fee	$55
Regular application deadline	6/1
Regular notification	Rolling
Transfer students accepted	Yes
Transfer application policy	File must be completed and applicant is considered as a regular applicant only for Evening program.
Need-blind admissions	Yes

Applicants Also Look At

Eastern Kentucky University, Indiana University—Bloomington, The Ohio State University, University of Cincinnati, University of Louisville, University of Tennessee, Xavier University.

EMPLOYMENT PROFILE

Career Rating	70	Grads Employed by Function	% Avg. Salary
Primary Source of Full-time Job Acceptances		Finance	41 $46,690
School-facilitated activities	11 (39%)	Marketing	22 $44,583
Graduate-facilitated activities	17 (61%)	MIS	4 NR
Average base starting salary	$46,991	Operations	7 NR
Percent employed	65	Consulting	4 NR
		General Management	7 NR
		Other	15 $49,068

Top 5 Employers Hiring Grads
Alltech Biotechnology; Department of Labor; Tempur-Pedic; Bellerive Development Company

UNIVERSITY OF LOUISIANA—LAFAYETTE
B. I. MOODY III COLLEGE OF BUSINESS

GENERAL INFORMATION
Type of school	Public
Environment	City
Academic calendar	Semester

SURVEY SAYS...
Cutting edge classes
Solid preparation in:
General management
Computer skills

STUDENTS
Enrollment of parent institution	16,800
Enrollment of business school	184
% male/female	52/48
% out-of-state	5
% part-time	75
% minorities	10
% international	40
Average age at entry	26
Average years work experience at entry	5

ACADEMICS
Academic Experience Rating	**76**
Student/faculty ratio	20:1
Profs interesting rating	73
Profs accessible rating	83
% female faculty	40
% minority faculty	12

Prominent Alumni
Mike DeHart, Stuller Management Services, Inc.; Stefni Lotief, UL Women's SoftBall Coach; Greg Roberts, Dir. of Aviation, Lafayette Airport; Dr. Ross Judice, Acadian Ambulance and Air Med, EVP and CMO.

Academics

Convenience and local reputation are the reasons most aspiring businesspeople choose the Moody MBA program at the University of Louisiana—Lafayette. The majority of Moody students work full time in the area and attend classes in the evenings, thus limiting their choices of programs in which to enroll. Few mind though, as Moody is "a really good school," especially "for students who work full-time," and offers a "cozy college atmosphere" where "just about everyone knows everyone else," and the faculty "really cares about the students."

Students at Moody report that the school has a "great reputation in the computer sciences" and is "the best and closest" when it comes to the health care industry. In fact, ULL offers an MBA with a concentration in health care administration, an appealing option to the area's many health care professionals. Professors have a lot of experience in their fields and "can relate to what we need better than those who just teach us with no experience to back it up." Among students' few complaints was that the relatively small size of the program limits course selection. "Schedule conflicts are common, and this is causing me to graduate at a later date than I anticipated," writes one student.

The Moody MBA requires students to complete 33 semester hours consisting of 27 hours of required core courses and 6 semester hours of electives (the health care MBA also consists of 33 semester hours but divides those hours between business and health care administration classes). Students who did not major in business as undergraduates are typically required to complete an additional 15 semester hours in foundation courses; these courses are prerequisite to, but do not count toward, the graduate degree.

Career and Placement

The Moody MBA program coordinates with the university's Career Services Center and the Internship Office to offer MBA N-Work, a service dedicated to finding jobs for past and current students. The Career Services Center offers Moody students on-campus job fairs and other placement services, but its primary mission is to serve undergraduates. The MBA Association is probably students' most effective conduit to employment. It should be noted that many Moody MBAs are currently employed, often by companies funding their graduate education, and thus are not actively seeking jobs. Top employers of Moody MBAs include Stuller, Lafayette General Medical Center, The Schumacher Group, Schlumberger, Acadian Ambulance Service and Air Med Services, Our Lady of Lourdes Regional Medical Center, Chevron, Texaco, and Louisiana Health Care Group Lafayette.

Student Life and Environment

Most students in the Moody MBA program attend part time, with lives so full of family and work obligations that they rarely linger unnecessarily on campus. Don't expect the hustle and bustle of a Northeastern b-school here, however; even the busiest MBAs tell us that "the school has a very laid-back attitude." That's simply the way life is in this section of Louisiana, known as Acadiana; students tell us that "in this part of the state, things are very relaxed and fun, and school is no different. We work hard, of course, but the overall feeling is more relaxed than, I assume, other business schools to be." Hometown Lafayette is "a great place to live" with an "excellent culture" that is "very attractive" to students. Students who can find time for campus events tell us that the schools "provide great opportunities to network and learn more about specific fields of work and study" and that the MBA Association does an especially good job "hosting socials and banquets and helping students and faculty get to know each other."

ADMISSIONS CONTACT: DR. C. EDDIE PALMER, DEAN OF THE GRADUATE SCHOOL
ADDRESS: MARTIN HALL, ROOM #332, P. O. BOX 40200 LAFAYETTE, LA 70504-0200 U.S.
PHONE: 337-482-6965 • FAX: 337-482-1333
E-MAIL: GRADSCHOOL@LOUISIANA.EDU • WEBSITE: MOODY.LOUISIANA.EDU

Moody MBAs are "are competitive and, for the most part, have a positive attitude toward learning," although "Some are happy to settle for B's and socialize too." Students note that the school draws "an ethnically diverse" population and that "the 'joie de vivre' of the Cajun students at UL promotes a friendly but competitive atmosphere that you won't find elsewhere." While most students here are "older people coming back to school," Moody also has a number of students "just out of undergraduate school." Most feel their classmates "are mature and very helpful," a good thing since "In this program there are a lot of group projects. In every group I have been in, everyone pulls their own weight."

Admissions

Applicants to the Moody MBA program must meet the following minimum requirements for admission: a bachelor's degree from an accredited U.S. college or university or an equivalent degree from a foreign school; a minimum overall undergraduate GPA of 2.75; an "acceptable" score on the GMAT (average score for the 2006 entering class was approximately 500; analytical writing scores are also considered); three letters of recommendation from people capable of assessing your academic ability and potential to succeed in a graduate program; a written personal statement (up to 750 words describing why you wish to pursue an MBA); a current resume (include degrees earned, employment history, honors and awards received, summary of computer skills, and list of overseas travel and foreign language abilities); and, for international students, TOEFL scores. The school prefers but does not require previous work experience. The school accepts electronically submitted applications.

FINANCIAL FACTS

Annual tuition (in-state/ out-of-state)	$3,300/$9,446
Fees	$538
Cost of books	$1,200
Room & board (on/off-campus)	$3,750/$6,750
% of students receiving aid	20
% of first-year students receiving aid	10
% of students receiving loans	40
% of students receiving grants	10
Average award package	$8,800
Average grant	$3,000
Average student loan debt	$5,000

ADMISSIONS

Admissions Selectivity Rating	82
# of applications received	150
% applicants accepted	47
% acceptees attending	80
Average GMAT	530
Range of GMAT	470–540
Average GPA	3.25
TOEFL required of international students	Yes
Minimum TOEFL (paper/computer)	550/213
Application fee	$25
International application fee	$30
Regular application deadline	6/30
Regular notification	8/1
Early decision program?	Yes
ED Deadline/Notification	Applications processed as soon as received.
Deferment available	Yes
Maximum length of deferment	1 year
Transfer students accepted	Yes
Transfer application policy	Can transfer in a maximum of 9 credit hours. Must apply through regular process.
Non-fall admissions	Yes
Need-blind admissions	Yes

Applicants Also Look At

Louisiana State University, Louisiana Tech University, Loyola University— New Orleans, McNeese State University, Nicholls State University, Tulane University, University of New Orleans.

EMPLOYMENT PROFILE

Career Rating	75

UNIVERSITY OF LOUISVILLE
COLLEGE OF BUSINESS

GENERAL INFORMATION

Type of school	Public
Environment	Metropolis
Academic calendar	Year-round

SURVEY SAYS...
Students love Louisville, KY
Cutting edge classes
Solid preparation in:
General management
Entrepreneurial studies

STUDENTS

Enrollment of parent institution	21,841
Enrollment of business school	389
% male/female	63/37
% part-time	100
Average age at entry	31
Average years work experience at entry	7

ACADEMICS

Academic Experience Rating	**87**
Student/faculty ratio	11:1
Profs interesting rating	82
Profs accessible rating	71
% female faculty	18
% minority faculty	8

Joint Degrees
BA/MBA, BS/MBA (Economics), BSBA/MBA.

Prominent Alumni
Robert Nardelli, Chairman/CEO, Chrysler, LLC; David Jones, Founder/Chairman, Humana; James Patterson, Founder/Chairman, Long John Silver's, Rally's; Dan Ulmer, Chairman/President, Terry Forcht, Owner.

Academics

The College of Business at the University of Louisville offers two primary MBA options. The first is the new Professional MBA, a two-year accelerated program offered in two formats (two nights per week and occasional Saturdays, or all-day Saturday), and taught in six-week modules across 14 terms, including a consecutive two-term capstone project, five professional development Saturdays per year, and six elective choices. The second is the IMBA, an integrated, two-year lockstep program that focuses primarily on entrepreneurship. The IMBA is also scheduled for the convenience of working students, meeting twice weekly in the evenings. The university also offers a number of joint-degree MBA programs. Both MBA programs offer a cohort-based team learning environment in a two year, year-round format, and guarantee no tuition increase for students who complete the program with their cohort.

Students tell us that "Most of the professors have an innovative approach to teaching, and they look for ways to make their classes better. If I were to restart the program three years after graduating, I am sure it would be a unique experience." Students appreciate that this approach "is essential given the ever-changing business environment," adding that "We may not be a Harvard or Wharton, but we still produce some of the world's leaders in business. In addition, the program offers a great work/life balance." Students praise their professors for "demonstrating meaningful real-world knowledge through prior experiences. The course work they present is very applicable to situations I face as a manager at a bank each day."

Louisville's IMBA is a lockstep program with an entrepreneurial focus. All courses and meeting times are mandatory. This approach allows for greater integration within the curriculum; classes can be team-taught to highlight the interconnectedness of two or more business disciplines, for example. It also allows the school to vary course lengths. Because all students are taking all courses together, scheduling need not be restrained by traditional semester intervals, and students love the results. One participant writes, "I feel that it's designed to give me everything I wanted in a graduate business program. Everything that I have learned thus far has been applied in my professional life."

Career and Placement

Louisville MBAs receive career counseling and placement services from the Ulmer Career Management Center, an all-new, state-of-the-art, 3,800 square foot facility that includes a career management resource library, conference rooms, and interview rooms. The office provides resume assistance, training seminars on interviewing skills, and on-campus recruiting events supported by CareerLeader tools and Symplicty software. Students confess that "the school still needs to improve in its career management for graduate students. Although some jobs have been posted, the majority are geared towards undergraduates or students who have graduated from the MBA program and already have several years of experience." On the bright side, students find that attending Louisville creates "many networking opportunities. Most classmates have full-time jobs and experience in the 'real world.' You can make connections with students throughout Louisville that will stay with you a long time." Opportunities to network are also enhanced in the Professional MBA through the capstone project, which is a team-based, external consulting project.

ADMISSIONS CONTACT: KEVIN KANE, DIRECTOR, MASTERS PROGRAMS
ADDRESS: COLLEGE OF BUSINESS LOUISVILLE, KY 40292 UNITED STATES
PHONE: 502-852-3969 • FAX: 502-852-4901
E-MAIL: K0KANE01@GWISE.LOUISVILLE.EDU • WEBSITE: BUSINESS.LOUISVILLE.EDU/MBA

Student Life and Environment

Most MBAs at Louisville "have little involvement with the rest of campus (library, gym, etc.) because most work full-time and attend classes in the evenings." Students spend so little time on campus that "they are secluded from other graduate students and, to a certain extent, from the other MBA students," though the recent creation of the Professional MBA program should offer more opportunities to network and utilize campus facilities with other members of their cohort. Even the busiest MBAs, however, know that "our basketball team is nationally recognized and dominates both the school and the town during the season." Those who find time to spend on campus boast that it is "very accommodating, with a recently renovated state-of-the-art library and a great athletic program (activities MBAs can attend when not studying!)." One student notes, "Although it's an urban campus, you would never know it given the quaint, friendly atmosphere." MBA 'campus life' will be enhanced in 18-24 months with the planned relocation of the College's graduate business programs to the heart of downtown Louisville.

The metropolitan Louisville area is home to over one million people. Students describe it as "a city full of opportunities for recent or upcoming MBA grads. Openings for MBAs are frequently e-mailed to students by school officials, which is a great service." A recent Wall Street Journal supplement ranked Louisville "the nation's fourth best city for job opportunities for recent graduates." Papa John's, YUM!, Humana Health Insurance, UPS Worldport, and GE all have a large presence in the city; some are headquartered here. Students report that the area surrounding the school "is not the best residential area, it's not good housing. There is good, safe housing about 15 minutes from campus, though, over in the Highlands."

Admissions

Admission to the University of Louisville MBA program is, without a doubt, competitive. Students in the program rank in the top third of MBA candidates nationwide. Applicants must submit all of the following to the Admissions Office: a completed application; an official copy of all undergraduate transcripts; an official GMAT score report; a one-page personal statement; two letters of recommendation from professors (or employers for applicants who have been out of school for a substantial period); and a current resume. International students must provide, in addition to the above, an official TOEFL score report (minimum score: 170 computer-based test, 550 paper-and-pencil test). All candidates must be proficient in computer and quantitative skills prior to the commencement of their MBA work.

FINANCIAL FACTS

Annual tuition (MBA/IMBA)	$30,000/$27,000
Fees	$0
Cost of books	$1,000
Room & board (on/off-campus)	$10,000/$12,000
Average award package	$13,661
Average grant	$7,257
Average student loan debt	$32,911

ADMISSIONS

Admissions Selectivity Rating	**92**
# of applications received	195
% applicants accepted	46
% acceptees attending	94
Average GMAT	570
Range of GMAT	420–710
Average GPA	3.32
TOEFL required of international students	Yes
Minimum TOEFL (paper/computer)	550/213
Application fee	$50
International application fee	$50
Regular application deadline	5/31
Regular notification	rolling
Deferment available	Yes
Transfer students accepted	Yes
Transfer application policy	

Up to 9 credits are accepted from an AACSB accredited MBA program, reviewed on a case by case basis.

Non-fall admissions	Yes
Need-blind admissions	Yes

Applicants Also Look At

Bellarmine University, Indiana University Southeast.

EMPLOYMENT PROFILE

Career Rating	64	Grads Employed by Function	%	Avg. Salary
Primary Source of Full-time Job Acceptances		Finance	40	$55,500
School-facilitated activities	1 (20%)	MIS	20	$80,000
Percent employed	73	Operations	20	$50,000
		Consulting	20	$42,000

Top 5 Employers Hiring Grads
Humana; BBT; Invesco; Arnold and Porter, LLP; Link-Belt Construction Equipment Company

UNIVERSITY OF MARYLAND—COLLEGE PARK
ROBERT H. SMITH SCHOOL OF BUSINESS

GENERAL INFORMATION
Type of school	Public
Environment	Metropolis
Academic calendar	Semester

SURVEY SAYS...
Friendly students
Solid preparation in:
General management
Teamwork
Communication/interpersonal skills
Quantitative skills
Doing business in a global economy

STUDENTS
Enrollment of parent institution	36,014
Enrollment of business school	1,201
% male/female	67/33
% out-of-state	77
% part-time	80
% minorities	24
% international	36
Average age at entry	28
Average years work experience at entry	5.1

ACADEMICS
Academic Experience Rating	**93**
Student/faculty ratio	7:1
Profs interesting rating	93
Profs accessible rating	77
% female faculty	28
% minority faculty	20

Joint Degrees
MBA/MS 21 months–5 years,
MBA/JD 3–5 years, MBA/MA
(Public Management) 2.3–5 years,
MBA/MA (Social Work) 2.3–5 years,
MBA/MS (Nursing) 3–5 years.

Prominent Alumni
Carly Fiorina, Former Chairman/CEO,
Hewlett Packard; Robert Basham,
Founder, Outback Steakhouse; Ro
Parra, Senior Vice President,
Americas, Dell Inc.; Richard
Schaeffer, Chairman NYMEX
Holding; Kevin Plank, Founder &
President, Under Armour.

Academics

A large school with a commanding reputation in the DC and Baltimore metropolitan areas, the Robert H. Smith School of Business offers a wide range of MBA options to a diverse student body of more than 1,000 graduate students. Depending on their professional experience, work schedule, and academic objectives, students can apply to Smith's full-time MBA program, Executive MBA, Accelerated MBA, or the part-time Evening MBA or Weekend MBA. While each of these programs differs in terms of class schedules, enrollment, admissions requirements, overall length, and location, they share an emphasis on the "digital economy," the integration of technology and business, and entrepreneurship. At the same time, real-world experience is paramount to a Smith education, and the school "allows many opportunities for students to learn outside the classroom, such as case competitions, consulting projects, and international teams." In addition to the aforementioned, "the school has a special program called the Mayer Fund where 12 selected MBA students from the entire school get to manage a $1.2 million endowment fund." Adding to the school's dynamic atmosphere is its urban location (Smith maintains campuses in College Park, Washington DC, Baltimore, and Rockville), which helps "attract some top-notch students to join the school, and also allows the school to offer many opportunities for growth outside the classroom."

Smith attracts a team of "incredible" faculty, who "are at the top of their fields in the industry and in research." Fortunately, the classroom experience does not play second fiddle to the faculty's research interests; at Smith, professors are "not only experts in their fields, but are also superb teachers (a rare combination)." In fact, evening students tell us that Smith professors "are very good at holding the attention of the class, even late at night when everyone is tired and the material is dry." Drawing talent from the local business community, most Smith "professors have been very involved in both the Baltimore and Washington business communities" throughout their career, adding an important practical dynamic to the classroom. In addition to their expertise, Smith professors "are also just great people to be around; very personable and approachable. They work as hard for us as we work for them." Administrators, for their part, get mixed reviews. While some students feel the school runs smoothly, others complain that Smith's directorship is "unresponsive" to student concerns.

Career and Placement

A large percentage of Smith's part-time students plan to stay at their current company after graduation (in fact, many are receiving tuition reimbursement for their studies.) However, for students seeking a new position or career change after graduation, the Smith School of Business boasts "excellent job placement rates" and lots of deep ties in the local community. On campus, Smith's Office of Career Management offers a full range of professional development resources, including career and communication coaching, an online job database, an active alumni network, research materials, and more. Students can get highly individualized assistance from one of the office's professional staff.

In 2006, the school placed 95 percent of graduating MBAs, and in 2007, they achieved a 92 percent placement rate. Recent companies that have recruited Smith grads include American Express Financial Advisors, Bank of America, Barclays Capital, Capital One, Chase Card Services, Citigroup, Deloitte Services, DuPont, Fannie Mae, FedEx, IBM, Intel Corporation, Lockheed Martin, McKinsey & Company, Morgan Stanley, Motorola, The Washington Post, and The World Bank.

ADMISSIONS CONTACT: LEANNE DAGNALL, ASSOCIATE DIRECTOR, MBA & MS ADMISSIONS
ADDRESS: 2417 VAN MUNCHING HALL, UNIVERSITY OF MARYLAND COLLEGE PARK,
MD 20742-1871 UNITED STATES • PHONE: 301-405-2559 • FAX: 301-314-9862
E-MAIL: MBA_INFO@RHSMITH.UMD.EDU • WEBSITE: WWW.RHSMITH.UMD.EDU

Student Life and Environment

Smith has MBA programs on four campuses in College Park, Rockville, Washington DC, and Baltimore. At each campus, you'll find a different range of resources and opportunities; however, in general, Smith facilities are excellent. For example, students who attend class at the Ronald Reagan Building in Washington DC describe it as a "top-notch business atmosphere" with "recently renovated rooms with electronic everything." The school's reputation and selective admissions draws a group of students who are "intelligent, well informed, confident, hardworking, kind, and dependable." You'll also find a range of professional experience amongst the student body, with some students who are "young and fresh without much work experience, while others are seasoned and settled in their careers."

In College Park, there is a wide range of student organizations for full-time MBA students, including the Entrepreneurship Club and the China Business Association. In addition, students and administrators are "working to ensure more community service is woven into student life." When it comes to having fun, students report a lively and social atmosphere among MBAs, including "great happy hours and frequent memorable cultural and variety nights." Luckily, part-time students don't miss out on the fun; while their schedules leave little downtime, part-timers still find time for "happy hours after class, if we are still awake… We also have parties on weekends."

Admissions

To apply to Smith, students must submit an official copy of their undergraduate transcripts, official GMAT scores, two letters of recommendation, and a set of personal essays. In the full-time program, the entering class had GMAT scores ranging from 580–730, and an average undergraduate GPA of 3.3. The part-time class submitted GMAT scores between 550–670, and an average undergraduate GPA of 3.26. Students have an average of six years' professional work experience before beginning the part-time program.

FINANCIAL FACTS

Annual tuition (in-state/ out-of-state)	$14,454/$23,814
Fees	$14,761

ADMISSIONS

Admissions Selectivity Rating	89
# of applications received	1,349
% applicants accepted	55
% acceptees attending	59
Average GMAT	650
Range of GMAT	600–700
Average GPA	3.34
TOEFL required of international students	Yes
Minimum TOEFL (paper/computer)	600/250
Application fee	$60
International application fee	$60
Regular application deadline	Rolling
Regular notification	Rolling
Application Deadline/Notification	
Round 1:	11/1 / 01/15
Round 2:	12/15 / 2/01
Round 3:	1/15 / 3/15
Round 4:	03/15 / 05/01
Early decision program?	Yes
ED Deadline/ Notification	11/1, 12/15 / 02/01
Need-blind admissions	Yes

Applicants Also Look At

Carnegie Mellon, Georgetown University, The University of North Carolina at Chapel Hill, The University of Texas at Austin, University of Virginia.

EMPLOYMENT PROFILE

Career Rating	90	Grads Employed by Function	%	Avg. Salary
Primary Source of Full-time Job Acceptances		Finance	48	$88,363
School-facilitated activities	56 (75%)	Human Resources	1	$90,000
Graduate-facilitated activities	19 (25%)	Marketing	20	$84,352
Average base starting salary	$88,629	MIS	2	$78,666
Percent employed	92	Operations	1	$90,000
		Consulting	24	$93,138
		General Management	2	$81,909
		Other	2	$95,000

Top 5 Employers Hiring Grads

Campbell Soup Company; Deloitte Consulting; PricewaterhouseCoopers; Wachovia; JP Morgan

UNIVERSITY OF MASSACHUSETTS—AMHERST
ISENBERG SCHOOL OF MANAGEMENT

GENERAL INFORMATION

Type of school	Public
Environment	Town
Academic calendar	Semester

SURVEY SAYS...
Good social scene
Good peer network
Happy students
Smart classrooms
Solid preparation in:
Teamwork
Communication/interpersonal skills

STUDENTS

Enrollment of parent institution	25,593
Enrollment of business school	890
% male/female	49/51
% out-of-state	77
% part-time	92
% minorities	4
% international	28
Average age at entry	29
Average years work experience at entry	4

ACADEMICS

Academic Experience Rating	**96**
Student/faculty ratio	12:1
Profs interesting rating	86
Profs accessible rating	89
% female faculty	33
% minority faculty	21

Joint Degrees

MBA/MS (Sport Management) 2 years, MBA/MS (Hospitality & Tourism Management) 2 years, MBA/MA (Public Policy) 2.5 years, MBA/MS (Industrial Engineering) 3 years, MBA/MS (Civil Engineering) 3 years, MBA/MS (Environmental Engineering) 3 years, MBA/MS (Mechanical Engineering) 3 years.

Academics

Bargain hunters can't say enough about the full-time MBA program at UMass—Amherst's Isenberg School of Management. As a state school, UMass already charges relatively low tuition, but the deal gets even better here as "Tuition is waived for most students" as part of a graduate assistantship program. This program pays double dividends by allowing students "to work with professors on a regular basis and learn information that is not easily taught in a classroom setting. Many of the faculty [members] are engaged in great research projects that the assistants are able to take part and aid in."

UMass keeps its MBA program trim, and "The small class size certainly promotes camaraderie and special relationships among classmates. Everyone, especially the faculty, knows who we are and is generally very happy to help us out with anything," comments one student. The program accommodates a high degree of individualization through "a great system of double MBA majors, in which full-time MBAs are allowed to interact with other people with a variety of interests and take advantage of other academic resources." The school offers dual-degree programs in sports management, hospitality and tourism management, public policy and administration, and four different engineering fields (industrial, mechanical, civil, and environmental).

Isenberg's full-time program "is structured in such a way so that the cohort works together as a unit instead of pitting us against each other." The first year of the program is "very intense" while the second year is "flexible." Instruction is targeted at "practical application of concepts, not for memorization."

Career and Placement

Students report that the MBA Career Management Office at UMass "needs some improvements, but it was reorganized at the beginning of this school year. We now have a career person dedicated to the MBA students. The benefit of this is already being felt, and I expect it to continue to improve in the coming year or two," one student informs us. Currently, "Many venture capitalists visit campus and will hold seminars or lunch meetings for the students," but "Larger corporations are underrepresented in the area of recruiting." Some acknowledge that the program's size presents a potential stumbling block to improvement. One student explains, "While the small class sizes allow for the high personal attention, it's hard to get recruiters to come to campus. The small size also seems to work against the school in some of the ranking systems, which is unfortunate as the program has been outstanding so far."

Employers who most frequently hire UMass—Amherst MBAs include MassMutual Financial Group, United Technologies Corporation, PricewaterhouseCoopers, Carrier Corporation, Babson Capital, Baystate Medical Center, and Deloitte Touche Tohmatsu.

Student Life and Environment

The full-time program at Isenberg "is very busy," as it operates on a quarter system instead of semesters. "It seems that there are always papers, projects, or homework to do, but due to our numerous study groups the work is less formidable," says one student. MBAs "work very hard but find time to unwind as well. Some get to speaker presentations, some catch hockey games, some enjoy the bar scene." Students appreciate that "the first-year track program creates an instant community, providing a working and social environment that make the transition from work to school that much easier through the added resource of peers experiencing the same thing." The b-school facility "is well-equipped with breakout rooms for group work and study sessions." Students often "find themselves weaving in and out of several breakout rooms, finding answers and helping each other out. We may be divided into groups, but we still value others' help," one tells

ADMISSIONS CONTACT: ERIC N. BERKOWITZ, ASSOCIATE DEAN, PROFESSIONAL PROGRAMS
ADDRESS: 305 ISENBERG SCHOOL OF MANAGEMENT, UNIVERSITY OF MASSACHUSETTS AMHERST,
MA 01003 UNITED STATES • PHONE: 413-545-5608 • FAX: 413-577-2234
E-MAIL: GRADPROG@SOM.UMASS.EDU • WEBSITE: WWW.ISENBERG.UMASS.EDU/MBA

us. The program hosts "a fair number of clubs, such as the Graduate Business Association, the Graduate Student Senate, Women in Business, Net Impact, etc. that are active and putting on events monthly. There are many ways for people to be involved if they want to be."

UMass is "a large university within a small town" with "good sporting events, interesting restaurants, and big cities not too far" away. Hartford is about an hour's drive to the south; Boston and New York City are both close enough for day trips. The town of Amherst "is very liberal," and much of the surrounding area "is very gay-friendly." The town has "a few good places for night activities." Northampton, for example, which is "the next town over, has even more locations for nightlife and is only a free short bus ride for anyone without a car."

Admissions

Applicants to the full-time MBA program at the Isenberg School must submit all of the following materials to the Admissions Department: a completed application form; a personal statement; an official GMAT score report; two official copies of transcripts of all undergraduate and graduate institutions attended at which at least six credits were completed; two letters of recommendation; and a current resume. International applicants whose first language is not English must submit an official TOEFL score report (minimum score: 600, paper-based test; 250, computer-based test). The Admissions Department reports that it seeks students with "demonstrated academic ability, personal drive, self-confidence and enthusiasm, potential to thrive in a small personal program, and 2 to 4 years of professional work experience." To attract underrepresented demographics, the school offers "a mentoring program for diverse graduate students, participation in the National Black MBA and National Society of Hispanic MBA conferences," and "coordination with university ALANA and GLBT representatives to continually promote and improve our program."

Prominent Alumni

Eugene M. Isenberg, Chairman/CEO, Nabors Industries, Ltd.; Michael G. Philipp, Chairman, Credit Suisse Inc.; Nancy S. Loewe, CFO, GE Industrial Consumer & Industrial Division; Jeffrey C. Taylor, Founder, monster.com, Founder/CEO, aeons.com; Vivek Paul, Partner, Texas Pacific Group Ventures.

FINANCIAL FACTS

Annual tuition (in-state/ out-of-state)	$2,035/$11,385
Fees (in-state/ out-of-state)	$7,737/$9,523
Cost of books	$2,500
Room & board (on/off-campus)	$8,500/$9,500
% of students receiving aid	95
% of first-year students receiving aid	88
% of students receiving grants	4
Average award package	$23,488

ADMISSIONS

Admissions Selectivity Rating	94
# of applications received	224
% applicants accepted	28
% acceptees attending	56
Average GMAT	642
Range of GMAT	610–680
Average GPA	3.3
TOEFL required of international students	Yes
Minimum TOEFL (paper/computer)	600/250
Application fee	$40
International application fee	$65
Regular application deadline	2/1
Regular notification	
Deferment available	Yes
Maximum length of deferment	1 year
Need-blind admissions	Yes

Applicants Also Look At

Babson College, Bentley College, Boston College, Boston University, Northeastern University, Syracuse University, University of Connecticut.

EMPLOYMENT PROFILE

Career Rating		84
Percent employed		93

Grads Employed by Function	%	Avg. Salary
Finance	32	$70,000
Marketing	32	$78,000
MIS	11	$68,000
Operations	16	$86,300
Consulting	5	$86,000

Top 5 Employers Hiring Grads
EMC; Eaton Corp; The Hartford; MassMutual; Carrier UTC

UNIVERSITY OF MASSACHUSETTS—BOSTON
GRADUATE COLLEGE OF MANAGEMENT

GENERAL INFORMATION
Type of school — Public
Environment — Metropolis
Academic calendar — Semesters

SURVEY SAYS...
Cutting edge classes
Solid preparation in:
Teamwork
Communication/interpersonal skills
Presentation skills

STUDENTS
Enrollment of parent institution	13,000
Enrollment of business school	497
% male/female	52/48
% out-of-state	46
% part-time	63
% minorities	22
% international	36
Average age at entry	30
Average years work experience at entry	6

ACADEMICS
Academic Experience Rating	**87**
Student/faculty ratio	13:1
Profs interesting rating	86
Profs accessible rating	91
% female faculty	35
% minority faculty	38

Joint Degrees
MBA/MS (Accounting) 3 years,
MBA/MS (Finance) 3 years,
MBA/MS (International
Management) 3 years, MBA/MS
(Information Technology) 3 years.

Prominent Alumni
Thomas M. Menino, Mayor, City of
Boston; Joseph Abboud, Fashion
Designer; James Kantelis, CEO,
Sprague Energy Corp.; Mark Atkins,
CEO, Invention Machine; Joseph
Kennedy, U.S. Congressman.

Academics

"Bang for the buck" is hardly the only reason for choosing the MBA program at UMass—Boston, but it's such a huge perk that few students can resist citing it as one of their primary motivations for attending. Many chose this program over more prestigious but also more expensive private school alternatives. One MBA tells us he is getting an "education similar to programs [that cost] two to three times more money." Students don't have to sacrifice quality to get value here, since "we can tap into the best educational resources in the world with professors from BC, BU, Northeastern, Harvard, and all the other schools in the Boston area."

Students report that UMass—Boston boasts "strong" human resources and information technology concentrations as well as "a strong accounting program with lots of accounting firms who recruit here." The school also offers "a tremendous international program focusing on leadership, integrity, and diplomacy." Throughout the program the quality of instruction is "very high"; professors are "accessible, helpful, and challenge their students." "All are knowledgeable," and although "A few do not have the gift of teaching, most are generous with their time outside of class and are available by e-mail just about any time."

UMass—Boston offers both a full-time and part-time MBA. Students rave that they have found "the most convenient part-time program and the best value in Boston." "Flexible class schedules" are enhanced by "sympathy for, empathy with, and accommodations made for [students'] full-time employment status by faculty and administration." They also point out that "being in downtown Boston and convenient to public transportation makes this an excellent environment." Students of all types appreciate how the low cost "yields a diverse group" of "highly qualified" students, "many of whom have undergraduate degrees from universities with competing business schools." On the downside, "The campus and facilities are outdated," meaning that "the physical plant is in desperate need of an overhaul."

Career and Placement

Students tell us that "the administration is extremely helpful and offers a lot of extra networking events throughout the year with area employers" at UMass—Boston. Students in finance are especially well served, as the school is "networked in with leadership of the largest institutions in Boston's financial district." Students in other disciplines, on the other hand, sometimes feel that the school could "improve by building a strong network of alumni" and by "providing more placement opportunities after graduation." The College of Management Career Center serves both undergraduates and graduate students in business. The school offers graduate students placement services as well as advice on salary negotiation.

Employers most likely to hire UMass—Boston MBAs include: Bank of America, Fidelity Investments, Investor Bank and Trust, Raytheon, and State Street.

Student Life and Environment

UMass—Boston "is a commuter school" with "most of the campus life geared toward undergraduates," but there are opportunities for students (especially full-time students) to get involved outside of classes. There are the recently implemented "international celebrations," which are "great for cultural awareness and fun" along with numerous clubs (although many meetings are at 5:00 P.M., hardly ideal for working students). Still, "Life at UMass is fun. It is relaxed and so diverse that everyone fits in. The campus is located

ADMISSIONS CONTACT: WILLIAM KOEHLER, GRADUATE PROGRAM DIRECTOR
ADDRESS: 100 MORRISSEY BOULEVARD, MBA OFFICE BOSTON, MA 02125-3393 UNITED STATES
PHONE: 617-287-7720 • FAX: 617-287-7725
E-MAIL: MBA@UMB.EDU • WEBSITE: WWW.MANAGEMENT.UMB.EDU

on Boston Harbor, so it is not unusual to see students studying outside by the harbor. There are lots of activities at the university covering almost all fields and interests."

Unfortunately, students refer to UMass—Boston's facilities as "problematic." "The classrooms are very outdated and uncomfortable" and "are not that clean" with furniture that "is very old and not well maintained." As one MBA here observes, "The facilities do not match the level of the professors. Hopefully over time this discrepancy will get smaller." Students tell us that the Graduate Center at Healey Library is an excellent resource.

Students here "all come from different ethnic and social backgrounds, and our work experience varies. But our goals are all the same: educational achievement and the desire to learn." One student explains, "Our Director of Admissions is very keen on bringing in a diverse background of students, from various professional and academic backgrounds. My class is not overloaded with one type of student." Most here "are full-time employees. But there are full-time students also. I like the diversity of my classes because my fellow students are from different countries, religions, cultures, backgrounds and have different work experience, so you learn a lot."

Admissions

Applicants to the University of Massachusetts—Boston MBA program must submit all of the following materials: a completed online application; official transcripts from all higher education institutions attended, undergraduate and graduate, whether you received a degree or not; official GMAT scores; three letters of recommendation from employers, professors or character references; and two essays as described in the university graduate admission packet, one describing why you chose UMass—Boston and a second describing your professional objectives and the role of an MBA in achieving them. The first (approximately one page in length) should describe why you have chosen to apply to UMass—Boston. International applicants must submit all of the above plus: bank statements (in English) showing $31,034 in available cash; a letter of support if another party is providing your funds, a Declaration and Certification of Finances (DCF) form, and official TOEFL scores.

FINANCIAL FACTS

Annual tuition (in-state/ out-of-state)	$2,590/$9,758
Fees (in-state/ out-of-state)	$6,896/$10,235
Cost of books	$1,000
Room & board (off-campus)	$10,000
% of students receiving aid	65
% of first-year students receiving aid	55
% of students receiving loans	62
% of students receiving grants	21
Average grant	$17,000
Average student loan debt	$16,500

ADMISSIONS

Admissions Selectivity Rating	88
# of applications received	386
% applicants accepted	39
% acceptees attending	64
Average GMAT	581
Range of GMAT	530–640
Average GPA	3.34
TOEFL required of international students	Yes
Minimum TOEFL (paper/computer)	600/250
Application fee	$40
International application fee	$60
Regular application deadline	6/1
Regular notification	7/1
Application Deadline/Notification	
Round 1:	03/01 / 03/15
Round 2:	06/01 / 07/01
Deferment available	Yes
Maximum length of deferment	1 Semester
Transfer students accepted	Yes
Transfer application policy	Same applicant procedure. Transfer credits and waivers will be considered.
Non-fall admissions	Yes
Need-blind admissions	Yes

Applicants Also Look At

Babson College, Bentley College, Boston College, Boston University, Northeastern University, Suffolk University, University of Massachusetts—Amherst.

EMPLOYMENT PROFILE				
Career Rating		86	Top 5 Employers Hiring Grads	
Average base starting salary		$77,000	State Street Corporation	5
Percent employed		85	Bank of America	3
			Ernst & Young	5
			Fidelity Investments	3
			PriceWaterhouseCoopers	3

UNIVERSITY OF MASSACHUSETTS—DARTMOUTH
CHARLTON COLLEGE OF BUSINESS

GENERAL INFORMATION
Type of school	Public
Environment	Town

SURVEY SAYS...
Helfpul alumni
Happy students
Smart classrooms
Solid preparation in:
Accounting
Presentation skills

STUDENTS
Enrollment of business school	250
% male/female	50/50
Average age at entry	26
Average years work experience at entry	6

ACADEMICS
Academic Experience Rating	**61**
Profs interesting rating	73
Profs accessible rating	61
% female faculty	10
% minority faculty	16

Joint Degrees
JD/MBA.

Academics

The AACSB-accredited MBA program at the University of Massachusetts—Dartmouth is "building its reputation, giving students a great deal of pride in feeling that they are part of something that will be much bigger in the future." For the present, UMass Dartmouth excels at providing its mix of local part-timers and international full-timers a convenient MBA program that can be completed in as little as one year or as many as five years.

All students here must complete a eight-course sequence of core requirements that cover fundamental concepts in accounting, information technology, finance, organization, operations, strategy, and marketing. Four electives are also required; students completing all three electives in a single "concentration stream" may earn an MBA with a concentration. Concentrations are available in accounting, business information, e-commerce, finance, international business, management, marketing, and operations. Students without concentrations graduate with a general MBA.

Entering students who have not satisfactorily completed undergraduate classes in business may be required to complete up to three foundation courses prior to enrolling in any of the 12 courses credited toward the MBA. Completion of an equivalent undergraduate course with a grade of at least a B typically qualifies students to skip a foundation course. Students with undergraduate degrees in business are generally exempt from foundation requirements.

UMass Dartmouth MBA students praise their program's "fine academic facilities and equipment" as well as the school's "favorable student-professor ratio." Administrators and professors are "very helpful and nice" and have a way of "making everything easier to understand." The net result of these positive factors is a "satisfying academic experience."

Career and Placement

The Career Resource Center at UMass Dartmouth serves all students and alumni of the university. The center provides counseling services, job postings, access to job search engines, and workshops in interviewing, resume writing, and career search. The CRC also maintains the Alumni Career Network and organizes on-campus recruiting events. MBA students receive additional career counseling from the MBA program coordinator. The majority of UMass Dartmouth MBAs attend while working full-time; the primary goal of many is to advance at their current place of employment rather than to find a new career. Thus, many MBAs here do not utilize the university's Career Services.

Student Life and Environment

Part-time students constitute the majority in UMass Dartmouth's MBA program, and they are drawn almost exclusively from the surrounding area. These "motivated, interesting and intelligent individuals" include a number of students who are "relatively older, with years of experience in the professional world. Many of them bring their experiences to bear in our classroom discussions." The school also hosts a number of full-timers, many of them "international students with different backgrounds, most of whom are younger than 30." Their ranks include "lots of scholarship students from Germany." MBAs from both populations bond well. As one explains, "I have found my fellow students to be team-oriented and I have made lasting friendships. We have formed informal study groups and we have helped each other through difficult class times."

All classes at UMass Dartmouth are offered in the evenings in order to accommodate students with jobs. Many part-timers juggle family and career responsibilities with work and accordingly spend as little time on campus as possible. "Generally, because the school is

ADMISSIONS CONTACT: NANCY LUDWIN, MBA COORDINATOR
ADDRESS: 285 OLD WESTPORT ROAD NORTH DARTMOUTH, MA 02747-2300 UNITED STATES
PHONE: 508-999-8543 • FAX: 508-999-8776
E-MAIL: GRADUATE@UMASSD.EDU • WEBSITE: WWW.UMASSD.EDU/CHARLTON

FINANCIAL FACTS

Annual tuition (in-state/ out-of-state)	$12,150/$22,680

ADMISSIONS

Admissions Selectivity Rating 60*	
Average GMAT	500
Average GPA	3.39
TOEFL required of international students	Yes
Application fee	$40
Regular application deadline	rolling
Regular notification	rolling
Deferment available	Yes
Maximum length of deferment	1 Semester
Need-blind admissions	Yes

oriented toward commuter students and people who take night classes, there really is no campus life for MBA students per se," explains one part-time student. Full-timers socialize more often; they "come together before and after class and perform some teamwork and long discussions. Outside the classroom, there are many social activities, from karate courses to chess, from sport activities to art. It is easy to find many things (to do)."

The main UMass Dartmouth campus is located in the southeast corner of the state, about one hour's drive from Boston and about a half hour away from Providence, Rhode Island. Wholesale trade helps fuel the local economy, as do fishing, cranberry farming, retail, and the remnants of the region's once-robust manufacturing industry.

Admissions

UMass Dartmouth considers all of the following in evaluating candidates for its MBA program: previous undergraduate and graduate academic record; GMAT scores or scores on an equivalent test; two letters of recommendation (one from a faculty member and one from an employer preferred); a personal statement of 200 to 300 words describing one's academic and career goals; and employment experience. TOEFL scores are required of all international applicants whose first language is not English. UMass Dartmouth offers certificate programs that, for some, provide a backdoor entry to the MBA program. One such student writes, "I came here because they offer certificate programs. I entered a certificate program first, then applied again to be a formal MBA student."

Students already in possession of a master's degree may apply for a post-master's certificate. Students complete five classes in one of the following: e-commerce, finance, general management, leadership, marketing, or supply chain management.

UNIVERSITY OF MASSACHUSETTS—LOWELL

COLLEGE OF MANAGEMENT

GENERAL INFORMATION
Type of school	Public
Environment	City

SURVEY SAYS...
Cutting edge classes
Solid preparation in:
Accounting
Quantitative skills

STUDENTS
Enrollment of parent institution	12,000
Enrollment of business school	316
% male/female	58/42
% out-of-state	54
% part-time	96
% minorities	8
% international	23
Average age at entry	32
Average years work experience at entry	6

ACADEMICS
Academic Experience Rating	**81**
Student/faculty ratio	12:1
Profs interesting rating	77
Profs accessible rating	83
% female faculty	27
% minority faculty	27

Academics

Cost and convenience are the reasons students most often cite for choosing the MBA program at the University of Massachusetts—Lowell (UML) College of Management. They also have faith in its quality. As one student declares, "I know I will feel confident and proud to receive my MBA/IT from UML." Lowell MBAs may attend the program full-time; most, however, attend part-time. Distance-learning options are available for nearly all classes offered here. Classes meet after 6:00 P.M. on weekdays.

The UML MBA commences with 12 hours of foundation courses in subjects traditionally covered in undergraduate business programs. Students who have completed equivalent undergraduate classes within the last 5 years and have earned at least a B may receive a waiver for some or all of these courses; alternately, students may attempt to place out of these classes through written exams. The curriculum also includes seven core courses in accounting, finance, analysis of customers and markets, MIS, operations, managing organization design and change, and strategy. The program concludes with three electives, which students may use to develop a concentration in accounting, finance, or information technology. They may also take an MBA in general business. Students speak highly of the IT offerings here, telling us that "if you're interested in business in a technology- or engineering-based company, UMass—Lowell is perfect."

UML professors "are firm but fair, available, and they have real-world experience." Just understand that "the curriculum is not easy." One MBA observes, "Some professors are much more in tune with current events and practices than others. The ones who can make their topics relevant to current topics tend to have the most stimulating classes. I have been able to use much of what I've learned already and apply it to my company, and it's paid off in a big way in some cases. If I left today without the degree, I can tell you that what I've learned has already had a positive impact in my professional life." Students appreciate that "most of the professors and the curriculum are practical for people who work full-time and also have families."

Career and Placement

The UML Career Services Office provides counseling and placement services to all undergraduates, graduates, and alumni of the university. The office organizes a variety of job fairs throughout the school year. It also provides practice interviews, counsels students on resume writing and job-search skills, schedules corporate information sessions on campus, and offers access to online job search engines such as MonsterTRAK. The office coordinates the efforts of the University Career Advisory Network, which is essentially an online community of alumni and current students.

Employers who most frequently hire UMass—Lowell MBAs include: Bank of America, Banknorth, Fidelity, Putnam Investments, Raytheon, Wyeth, Gillette (P&G), U.S. Air Force, U.S. Government, Dana Farber Cancer Institute, and CR Bard.

Student Life and Environment

UML MBAs largely fall into the category of "working professionals [who] take classes at night" who "have no idea (and don't care, frankly) what activities [are available] on campus." They're "just interested in taking classes, not joining clubs or spending time with other students." Those who do spend time on campus tell us that "the campus and student facilities are comfortable. A lot of effort has been made to make UML a nice place to be. Ten years ago it wasn't anything special, but now it is." One MBA adds, "The gym and coffee shop are excellent."

ADMISSIONS CONTACT: GARY M. MUCICA, DIRECTOR, GRADUATE MANAGEMENT PROGRAMS
ADDRESS: ONE UNIVERSITY AVENUE, PA 303 LOWELL, MA 01854-2881 UNITED STATES
PHONE: 978-934-2848 • FAX: 978-934-4017
E-MAIL: KATHLEEN_ROURKE@UML.EDU • WEBSITE: WWW.UML.EDU/MBA

Despite the upgrades to the university at large, some here feel that the MBA facilities are in need of a makeover. One student explains, "The school needs to improve facilities. A lot of the equipment is old and outdated, and classrooms are not set up for students to have a laptop at their desk (no electrical plugs)." They also warn that "the new online computer program for scheduling, fees, bills, etc. leaves a lot to be" desired. It's set up to be "self-service" but is simply "not easy to work with." Students who take online classes say UML "could improve by offering interactive audio and video," which would "remove the feeling of isolation you sometimes feel when taking online classes." One student tempers his comment by adding, "This is true with most universities today; but as an IT professional, I am sure it will change in the near future."

Plenty of MBAs here chose the business school because they "really enjoyed" their undergraduate experience here. Among the "working professionals" at UML are some who "are back in school after a long layoff." Overall, the "motivated, friendly, and engaging" folks are generally "a pleasure to interact with on an intellectual and personal basis." Most "are understanding of personal needs/issues when it comes to professional or family conflicts and are able to work around them when it comes to group projects."

Admissions

The MBA program at the University of Massachusetts—Lowell requires applicants to submit the following materials: an official transcript of undergraduate grades; an official GMAT score report; three letters of recommendation from "employment-related sources" demonstrating a minimum of 2 years of relevant work experience; a current resume; and a one-page essay describing academic and career objectives. Applicants must complete prerequisite courses in microeconomics and statistics prior to entering the program. According to the school's website, "An aptitude for management decision-making and demonstrated academic ability are the most important qualifications for admission." International students whose first language is not English must submit an official score report for the TOEFL; a minimum score of 550 on the paper-based exam is required. UMass—Lowell admits new students for both the fall and spring terms.

FINANCIAL FACTS

Annual tuition (in-state/ out-of-state)	$1,637/$6,425
Fees (in-state/ out-of-state)	$6,603/$10,037
Cost of books	$1,000
Room & board	$6,978
% of students receiving aid	10
% of first-year students receiving aid	10
% of students receiving loans	10

ADMISSIONS

Admissions Selectivity Rating	83
# of applications received	175
% applicants accepted	73
% acceptees attending	80
Average GMAT	550
Range of GMAT	505–615
Average GPA	3.26
TOEFL required of international students	Yes
Minimum TOEFL (paper/computer)	600/250
Application fee	$20
International application fee	$35
Regular application deadline	rolling
Regular notification	rolling
Deferment available	Yes
Maximum length of deferment	1 year
Transfer students accepted	Yes
Transfer application policy	
Must be fron an AACSB accredited program. Maximum of 12 tranfer credits.	
Non-fall admissions	Yes
Need-blind admissions	Yes

Applicants Also Look At

Bentley College, Boston University, Northeastern University, Suffolk University, University of Massachusetts—Amherst, University of Massachusetts—Boston, Worcester Polytechnic Institute.

EMPLOYMENT PROFILE

Career Rating	64	Grads Employed by Function	% Avg. Salary
Percent employed	6	Finance	21 NR
		Marketing	8 NR
		MIS	13 NR
		Operations	28 NR
		General Management	10 NR
		Other	12 NR
		Non-profit	8: NR

UNIVERSITY OF MEMPHIS
FOGELMAN COLLEGE OF BUSINESS AND ECONOMICS

GENERAL INFORMATION

Type of school	Public
Environment	City
Academic calendar	Semester

SURVEY SAYS...
Solid preparation in:
General management
Computer skills
Doing business in a global economy

STUDENTS

Enrollment of parent institution	20,379
Enrollment of business school	273
% out-of-state	35
% part-time	64
% minorities	8
% international	25
Average age at entry	30
Average years work experience at entry	5

ACADEMICS

Academic Experience Rating	**76**
Student/faculty ratio	29:1
Profs interesting rating	79
Profs accessible rating	86
% female faculty	22
% minority faculty	4

Joint Degrees
MBA/JD 4 years.

Academics

Fogelman College of Business and Economics at the University of Memphis is a no-nonsense professional MBA program designed for working people "from all walks of business life" who are looking to further their careers but who don't have a lot of time or energy to waste. The school has a solid reputation among locally based businesses like FedEx. One student holds Memphis in such high regard that she has two degrees from there: "The University of Memphis is where I received my BBA in accounting. I liked my experience there, and I knew that an MBA from there would open many doors in the company that I work for."

Students say their "very knowledgeable" professors "present concepts completely" and help them relate the course material to practice. "Each of them has done extensive research in their field and [is] noted to be among the best in the country for their area of expertise." Another student says: "Every professor is interested in the development of each student into future managers and business leaders." The administration does not receive the same ringing endorsement, however. Some take issue with the allocation of funds in certain areas. One student was succinct and blunt: "Solid professors, good academic experience, but really bad administration that spends money" excessively.

Some students also have difficulty with course selection and enrollment; many required or desired classes are offered only once per semester under limited enrollment, and these courses "often conflict with each other." Since pretty much all of the courses take place in the evenings to accommodate the vast majority of students who have day jobs, there's very little leeway in terms of scheduling. But these night classes also give part-time and full-time students the opportunity to interact with each other through "small classes and heavy teamwork," something not found in a lot of MBA programs. "A lot of projects are team based, so you get to know classmates very well." One student takes away warm feelings about the camaraderie he felt at the school: "I have a new set of best friends. I never thought it was possible after reaching age 40."

In keeping with the no-frills approach to the program, however, the facilities tend toward the sparse side. Several students expressed disdain for the academic buildings and equipment and spoke of the need for "more technology in the classroom." One student said the classrooms "need better seating. The desks were made for 4th graders."

Career and Placement

Some students say the program needs better ties to "big industries" to provide those students seeking out new or nonlocal careers with better job prospects. Fortunately for the students looking to stay in the area (and there are many), "There are several excellent companies in the area, also, that recruit heavily," and since the student body is, as one student puts it, "not nearly as competitive as I expected," everyone is "very supportive" and happy to help each other land available positions. Another boon to the school's local reputation is the recently formed partnership with the Leadership Academy. The partnership, known as the Community Internship, gives MBA students the chance to team with Leadership Academy fellows on projects designed to benefit the community.

Student Life and Environment

The school is located in the midtown area of Memphis, which "is great for students because there are a lot of social establishments nearby" offering "a lot of things for students to do recreationally." Of course, there are the well-traveled destinations like Graceland (check out Elvis' gaudy yellow and black rec room), Sun Studios, and the famous Beale Street, with its string of live-music joints and soul food. And the National

ADMISSIONS CONTACT: GREGORY W. BOLLER, DIRECTOR OF MASTER'S PROGRAMS
ADDRESS: GRADUATE SCHOOL ADMINISTRATION BUILDING RM. 216 MEMPHIS, TN 38152-3370 U.S.
PHONE: 901-678-2911 • FAX: 901-678-5023
E-MAIL: GRADSCH@MEMPHIS.EDU • WEBSITE: FCBE.MEMPHIS.EDU

Civil Rights Museum, located at the old Lorraine Motel where Martin Luther King, Jr., was shot to death in 1968, is a haunting must-see for tourists and locals alike. Overall, "The University of Memphis, like the city of Memphis, is greatly underrated," one student says.

Since "Most graduate students work and commute," little time is left for a social life outside of the classroom, but there's a foundation for friendship and networking among the "outgoing" and "friendly" individuals that attend Fogelman. Though some think "The school could put more effort into organized activities for students outside of class," the "busy" nature of the student body doesn't lend itself to much free time anyway, so complaints are few. Everyone is in agreement over the variety of backgrounds provided by their classmates: "The graduate population is very diverse, which makes things more interesting." "You have a great opportunity to meet people from various backgrounds (educational and ethnic)," another student says.

Admissions

Admittance to the professional MBA program at the Fogelman College of Business and Economics is not terribly selective, and the admissions requirements are fairly standard. Applicants to the school's professional MBA program must submit the following materials: a completed application (either online or via mail); an official copy of undergraduate transcripts from all colleges and universities attended (even if you did not graduate); a copy of your current resume; a statement of personal interest; a 1,000-word essay answering one of the acceptable questions provided on the school's admissions website; two letters of recommendation; and an official GMAT or GRE score report. Interviews and previous work experience are optional. In addition to the above documents, international students whose primary language is not English must also provide an official score report for the TOEFL (minimum score: 550, paper-based test; 213, computer-based test).

FINANCIAL FACTS

Annual tuition (in-state/ out-of-state)	$6,990/$17,818
Fees	$360
Cost of books	$2,000
Room & board (on/off-campus)	$8,000/$12,000

ADMISSIONS

Admissions Selectivity Rating	**78**
# of applications received	107
% applicants accepted	76
Average GMAT	530
Range of GMAT	530–700
Average GPA	3.2
TOEFL required of international students	Yes
Minimum TOEFL (paper/computer)	550/213
Application fee	$35
International application fee	$60
Regular application deadline	7/1
Regular notification	rolling
Deferment available	Yes
Maximum length of deferment	1 year
Non-fall admissions	Yes

EMPLOYMENT PROFILE

Career Rating	75

UNIVERSITY OF MIAMI
SCHOOL OF BUSINESS ADMINISTRATION

GENERAL INFORMATION
Type of school	Private
Environment	Town

SURVEY SAYS...
Friendly students
Good social scene
Smart classrooms
Solid preparation in:
Quantitative skills

STUDENTS
Enrollment of parent institution	15,449
Enrollment of business school	240
% male/female	67/33
% out-of-state	19
% part-time	2
% minorities	38
% international	32
Average age at entry	25
Average years work experience at entry	2

ACADEMICS
Academic Experience Rating	**84**
Student/faculty ratio	6:1
Profs interesting rating	94
Profs accessible rating	74
% female faculty	28
% minority faculty	19

Joint Degrees
JD/MBA 3.5–4.5 years, MD/MBA.

Prominent Alumni
Ralph Alvarez, President/COO, McDonald's Corporation; Gerald Cahill, Chairman/CEO, Carnival Corporation; Matthew Rubel, CEO, Payless Shoe Source; Jack Creighton, Former Chairman/CEO, United Airlines; Ray Rodriguez, President/COO, Univision Network.

Academics

A rigorous MBA program with a strong international focus, the University of Miami School of Business Administration prides itself on attracting a diverse and multinational faculty and student body, and on offering challenging and relevant course work for today's global professional. The school offers a full-time 48-credit program, which must be completed over the course of two years. The program is targeted to individuals who want to advance their career. Since there are no summer courses in either program, students are encouraged to do an internship.

The program boasts a lockstep curriculum, in which the entire entering class moves through required course work in unison. As a result, students form strong professional, scholarly, and social relationships with their classmates. On this campus, a third of students hail from outside the United States and comprise "a wide range of ages," so these relationships form an integral part of the learning experience at the University of Miami. A current student enthuses, "fellow classmates interest me, challenge me, and contribute to a productive class/team environment." With a "small student to teacher ratio," the environment is truly collaborative and "people work together on every aspect of education and life."

Elective classes are available to students. While students say the program is excellent, some feel it could be improved by becoming "much more challenging" and incorporating a heavier workload. Students in the two-year program may choose to focus their electives to receive a concentration in accounting, computer information systems, finance, international business, management, management science, or marketing. In general, students have high praises for University of Miami professors, especially for those in their area of concentration. One student reports, "The professors in my chosen concentration of management science are outstanding and have prepared me very well for my career post-graduation. The school has afforded me opportunities within management science that are not available elsewhere and has helped me to pursue different career paths."

Career and Placement

The Ziff Graduate Career Service Center at the University of Miami is available to graduate business students only and offers career advising, online and on-campus recruiting, a career library, and periodic workshops on resume writing and job search strategy. Boasting the sixth largest alumni network in the world, University of Miami students have access to a large, international employment base. Students report that, "on-campus recruiting is sufficient for students with no real work experience," while more advanced professional positions are harder to come by.

ADMISSIONS CONTACT: SYLVANA ZAVALA, ASSOCIATE DIRECTOR
ADDRESS: PO BOX 248505 CORAL GABLES, FL 33124-6524 UNITED STATES
PHONE: 305-284-4607 • FAX: 305-284-1878
E-MAIL: MBA@MIAMI.EDU • WEBSITE: WWW.BUS.MIAMI.EDU/GRAD

Student Life and Environment

For a business student, you couldn't ask for a more comfortable lifestyle and environment than at the University of Miami. With a "perfect location" on the university's Coral Gables campus, the business school is housed in an "absolutely beautiful" $24-million facility, in which, "Each classroom has big, comfy leather executive chairs for the students and great computers for the professor." There is even "a lounge for graduate business students that has free coffee and bagels every morning."

The campus vibe is highly social, as "most everyone moved to Miami from different states/cities, and it was very easy to make new friends who will last a lifetime." On top of that, "There is a great student run organization, Graduate Business Student Association, that arranges and sponsors many events. It is easy to meet new people and make many friends." For those who like to get involved, "There are clubs for every concentration plus a few others. A lot of the students form intramural teams for flag football, soccer, and softball." Students are quick to mention that "The football team is a big deal here and everyone goes to the games together, and the business school always has a tailgate before the games." Situated in Miami, the party capital of the Southeast, "there is a very active social life both on and off campus," as students further enjoy world-class cultural and recreational opportunities—not to mention, perfect weather—in their immediate vicinity.

Admissions

To apply to the MBA program, students must submit a completed application, official transcripts from any undergraduate and postgraduate course work, a current resume, one letter of recommendation, official GMAT score reports, and TOEFL test scores for non-native speakers of English. Students are evaluated on the strength of all application materials. Students wishing to enter the program do not need to have undergraduate business degrees. Admissions decisions are made on a rolling basis until the class is full, though students are encouraged to apply at least three months before the beginning of the term. Students who wish to be considered for merit-based scholarships, fellowships, or graduate assistantship are advised to apply early, as they are limited and available for fall applicants only.

FINANCIAL FACTS

Annual tuition	$34,176
Fees	$274
Cost of books	$1,200
Room & board	
(on/off-campus)	$7,610/$9,556
% of students receiving aid	60
% of first-year students	
receiving aid	71
% of students receiving loans	38
% of students receiving grants	42
Average award package	$32,241
Average grant	$19,735
Average student loan debt	$40,000

ADMISSIONS

Admissions Selectivity Rating	82
# of applications received	444
% applicants accepted	59
% acceptees attending	36
Average GMAT	631
Range of GMAT	530–750
Average GPA	3.2
TOEFL required of	
international students	Yes
Minimum TOEFL	
(paper/computer)	550/213
Application fee	$50
International application fee	$50
Application Deadline/Notification	
Round 1:	12/1 / 12/23
Round 2:	02/2 / 02/27
Round 3:	06/1 / 06/26
Early decision program?	Yes
ED Deadline/	
Notification	10/17 / 12/3
Deferment available	Yes
Maximum length of	
deferment	1 year
Need-blind admissions	Yes

EMPLOYMENT PROFILE

Career Rating	76	Grads Employed by Function	% Avg. Salary
Primary Source of Full-time Job Acceptances		Finance	33 $59,576
School-facilitated activities	36 (43%)	Marketing	10 $60,100
Graduate-facilitated activities	46 (55%)	Operations	3 $72,733
Average base starting salary	$61,655	Consulting	3 $67,667
Percent employed	72	General Management	7 $62,786
		Other	8 $60,878

Top 5 Employers Hiring Grads

Bacardi; Bayview Financial Group; PWC; Stanford Financial Group; JP Morgan Chase Securities Inc.

UNIVERSITY OF MICHIGAN—ANN ARBOR
STEPHEN M. ROSS SCHOOL OF BUSINESS

Academics

After the 2004 $100 million donation from Stephen M. Ross—the largest gift ever bestowed upon any U.S. business school—the school has been witness to an exponential increase in both construction and curriculum, including a new $145 million facility and a revised MBA curriculum whose benefits include carefully sequenced core courses, more electives, and the opportunity to focus on specific areas of interest prior to internship interviews. Most students agree that the program "ranks high in everything," but note that it is "extremely strong in corporate strategy, entrepreneurial studies, management accounting, marketing, organizational behavior, nonprofit organizations, social venturing, and venture capital/private equity/entrepreneurial finance."

Much of the program's strength comes from the "great professors who respond to the individual classes' needs and interests." Students appreciate that the "helpful and challenging" faculty "push you to think," adding that "classes are a great mix of lecture and performance." Because the business school does not require students to specialize, MBAs "have a lot of flexibility in the second-year schedule to focus on the classes [they] want." Just keep in mind the rigorous core curriculum must be completed before students can take on the multitude of electives the school has on offer. (Some of these courses are so "popular" that the administration works "with the professor to expand the number of sections they teach in order to give the most opportunity to people to take the class.)

MBAs add that the workload is fairly heavy, but "That's what we're paying for." One student explains, "We take five classes per semester, and each class usually meets twice a week for 1 and a half hours at a time. For every 1-and-a-half-hour class, there's probably about that much preparation time that is put in outside of class." As a major research institution, Michigan gives its MBAs access to world-class research facilities. And don't forget about the "breadth and depth" of the "second-to-none" opportunities offered, such as "dual degrees, academic programs, International Multidisciplinary Action Projects, and [access to] institutes such as The William Davidson Institute for International Studies and the Zell Lurie Institute for Entrepreneurial Studies."

On the aesthetic front, many note that "classrooms need to be upgraded" and that "facilities could be improved." The good news in this is that the school's administration "is driven to improve the school" and has "a strategic plan for the school." And that $100 million mentioned earlier has come a long way to make these students' hopes for the campus become a foreseeable reality.

Career and Placement

The university is home to a "powerful and active alumni movement," meaning that MBA graduates have exceptional access to career opportunities; "Alums seem to go out of their way to help you." U of M's Student Career Services Office at the Ross School of Business, serves both undergraduates and graduate students, and reports that an impressive 90.6 percent of recent MBA graduates received their first job offer within 3 months of graduating.

Top employers of Michigan MBAs include Citigroup, Booz Allen Hamilton, Dell, McKinsey & Company, American Express Company, JPMorgan Chase, A.T. Kearney, Eli Lilly and Company, Bain & Company, Ford Motor Company, Medtronic, 3M, Cummins, General Mills, Guidant Corporation, Intel, Kraft Foods, Lehman Brothers, Microsoft, National City Corporation, and SC Johnson.

ADMISSIONS CONTACT: SOOJIN KWON KOH, DIRECTOR OF ADMISSIONS
ADDRESS: 701 TAPPAN STREET ANN ARBOR, MI 48109-1234 UNITED STATES
PHONE: 734-763-5796 • FAX: 734-763-7804
E-MAIL: ROSSMBA@UMICH.EDU • WEBSITE: WWW.BUS.UMICH.EDU

FINANCIAL FACTS

Annual tuition (in-state/ out-of-state)	$38,100/$43,100
Fees	$189
Cost of books	$8,170
Room & board	$10,884
% of students receiving aid	75
% of first-year students receiving aid	75
% of students receiving loans	64
% of students receiving grants	56
Average award package	$62,343
Average grant	$17,224
Average student loan debt	$67,576

ADMISSIONS

Admissions Selectivity Rating	98
# of applications received	2,983
% applicants accepted	20
% acceptees attending	70
Average GMAT	700
Range of GMAT	640–760
Average GPA	3.3
TOEFL required of international students	Yes
Minimum TOEFL (paper/computer)	600/250
Application fee	$180
International application fee	$180
Regular application deadline	3/1
Regular notification	3/2
Application Deadline/Notification	
Round 1:	11/01 / 1/15
Round 2:	1/3 / 3/15
Round 3:	3/1 / 5/15
Deferment available	Yes
Maximum length of deferment	1 year
Transfer students accepted	Yes
Transfer application policy	
Transfer applicants are welcome to apply, but no credits will transfer into our program.	
Need-blind admissions	Yes

Student Life and Environment

"If you like college towns, you will love Ann Arbor," students at U of M agree. In addition, on campus you'll find the "friendliest group of people I've ever met," says one student. "This is my new extended family." And this family has no shortage of social opportunities. "There's happy hour every Thursday, tailgates every Football Saturday, and numerous club parties in between," explains one student. "You can't beat Michigan football, hockey, and basketball." With "jazz [clubs], dance clubs, and restaurants" in the city, students find a "heck of a lot of fun" everywhere they go. Some even venture to Detroit. But beware the winter months, warn students: "The weather is cold . . . and students do spend too much time studying because there's not much else to do when it's 15 degrees out."

The MBA program offers "abundant opportunities to get involved, from professional to social clubs, newspaper, admissions, and career counseling. There's even a wine-tasting club." One student mentions that "without the energy the other students provide, many of the clubs/activities would not happen and our experience here would not be as rich." And students work together here to find a "good work-life balance." "We work quite hard, but on Thursday evenings, practically all MBAs flock to the b-school happy-hour bar, Mitch's," says one. "No weekend goes by without lots of prep for class, several group meetings, and at least one party or social/fun activity." The program also "provides lots of opportunities for spouses to get together. It also has joint programs with other schools in the university, which provide meaningful activities."

Admissions

Applications to the University of Michigan MBA program must include undergraduate transcripts, GMAT test scores (on average, successful applicants score 700), TOEFL test scores (for international students), letters of recommendation, a personal statement, and a resume. The school also looks at an applicant's record of success, clarity of goals, and management and leadership potential. The program does require previous work experience and, though not required, interviews are "highly recommended." There are many minority recruitment efforts, such as the Consortium for Graduate Study in Management, Robert F. Toigo Fellowships in Finance, National Society of Hispanic MBA Conference, National Black MBA Conference, and many more.

Applicants Also Look At

Duke University, Northwestern University, University of Chicago, University of Pennsylvania.

EMPLOYMENT PROFILE

Career Rating	98	Grads Employed by Function	%	Avg. Salary
Primary Source of Full-time Job Acceptances		Finance	25	$93,317
School-facilitated activities	265 (73%)	Marketing	28	$93,779
Graduate-facilitated activities	96 (27%)	Operations	2	$99,143
		Strategic Planning	4	$3,287
		Consulting	31	$111,044
		General Management	6	$99,947
		Other	4	$84,333

Top 5 Employers Hiring Grads

Citigroup; Lehman Brothers Inc; Deloitte Consulting; A.T. Kearney; Kraft Foods

UNIVERSITY OF MICHIGAN—FLINT
SCHOOL OF MANAGEMENT

Academics

Offering two programs designed with the needs of working students in mind, the University of Michigan—Flint satisfies MBAs with a winning combination of convenience, "excellent professors," and the "name recognition" that comes with a University of Michigan degree. Prospective MBAs choose between a traditional evening MBA program, in which cohorts convene for weekly classes, and the *NetPlus!* a mixed mode MBA program, complemented by "weekend residencies every 6 weeks in order to receive some classroom interaction and perspective." One student writes, "The mixed media *NetPlus!* program available at the University of Michigan—Flint is unsurpassed by any other program. It offers the best of both worlds for my busy life." UM—Flint's traditional MBA is typically completed in 20–32 months; the *NetPlus!* program takes 15–24 months to complete.

No matter which program they choose, students will find a curriculum that "focuses on the importance of international business" while requiring "lots of projects and case studies." Each program commences with four foundation courses (waivers are available for those who have completed equivalent undergraduate or graduate courses, followed by eight core courses (three functional, four external environment/managerial support, and one capstone class), two general electives, or three concentration-specific electives. Flint offers six areas of concentration: accounting, health care management, lean manufacturing, international business, organizational leadership, and finance.

Professors here, we're told, "are exceptional. One cannot say enough about their knowledge in terms of course work and their real world application." In terms of workload, professors "are demanding but very understanding of working professionals. They pile the work on, but know when it's pushing to the limit. Grading is fair, an A is not automatic, but if solid work is put in you aren't beat up on minor things." The administration is "outstanding." One student reports, "Although I live over an hour from campus, I have never had a problem getting help from someone in the MBA office, with everything from financial aid to contacting a professor in an emergency."

Career and Placement

UM—Flint's Career Development Center focuses primarily on serving the school's undergraduate population. Limited services, including resume posting, online job boards, and counseling are available to Flint's MBAs, but few use them. Some here complain that the school "needs to develop contacts with recruiting companies and hold job fairs," but many simply don't care; they have jobs and see the MBA as a means to improve their current situation, not as a stepping stone to a new career.

ADMISSIONS CONTACT: D. NICOL TAYLOR, MBA, MBA PROGRAM DIRECTOR
ADDRESS: SCHOOL OF MANAGEMENT, UM-FLINT, 3139 WILLIAM S. WHITE BLDG, 303 EAST
KEARSLEY STREET FLINT, MI 48502-1950 UNITED STATES
PHONE: 810-762-3163 • FAX: 810-237-6685
E-MAIL: UMFLINTMBA1@UMICH.EDU • WEBSITE: MBA.UMFLINT.EDU

FINANCIAL FACTS

Annual tuition	$12,998
Fees	$348
Cost of books	$1,000
Average award package	$15,472
Average grant	$2,273

ADMISSIONS

Admissions Selectivity Rating	**83**
# of applications received	132
% applicants accepted	51
% acceptees attending	79
Average GMAT	535
Range of GMAT	470–580
Average GPA	3.22
TOEFL required of international students	Yes
Minimum TOEFL (paper/computer)	550/213
Application fee	$55
International application fee	$55
Regular application deadline	Rolling
Regular notification	Rolling
Deferment available	Yes
Maximum length of deferment	1 year
Transfer students accepted	Yes
Transfer application policy AACSB accredited, "B" or better, grad level, 9 credit hours only.	
Non-fall admissions	Yes
Need-blind admissions	Yes

Student Life and Environment

For students attending all MBA classes on campus, "The life of the school is fast paced, requiring lots of classmates to work in teams to finish projects. The program focuses a lot of time on projects and case studies." Because "Most professors want a lot out of you," the pace here "can be kind of hectic." For the many students who work full-time and manage family obligations in addition to their graduate work, "Life at school is limited to what is required in the classroom."

Students in the *NetPlus!* program participate in "weekend residencies every 6 weeks to receive some classroom interaction and perspective." They tell us that "the residencies are great because they provide more interaction. The group studies and chances to work with a diverse group of people is a benefit." MBAs note that "the campus is beautiful," "safe, and brightly lit," but it is "located in the middle of downtown Flint," a "bad city." Some complain that "the campus is sort of spread out." Campus facilities earn high marks from all students.

Flint MBAs are "professional, ambitious, and intelligent," not to mention "friendly, helpful, and funny." Most "are working adults returning to school in order to learn management techniques because either they are new managers, or want to move up the corporate ladder." According to at least one international student, the student body can be a little "provincial." "Many students are from the counties surrounding Flint, and not many have international experience." Not only does this sometimes impede class discussion, but it also "can make it hard for a foreign student to make contacts with fellow students. They've lived in Michigan all their lives and have all their friends at arm's reach. They have little need and incentive to make more contacts other than in the study groups."

Admissions

All applicants to the School of Management at the University of Michigan—Flint must provide the school with official copies of all undergraduate and graduate transcripts, GMAT scores, TOEFL scores (international students), three letters of recommendation (preferably from employers and/or professors), a statement of purpose (in response to the question: "What are your career objectives and how will an MBA contribute to achieving those goals), and a resume. Work experience is preferred; the average student arrives with 3 years of professional experience. The school catalog notes that "admission decisions are guided by a desire to draw participants from diverse organizations and backgrounds, balancing class composition to ensure diverse, wide-ranging experiences and perspectives." An online application is available.

UNIVERSITY OF MISSISSIPPI
SCHOOL OF BUSINESS ADMINISTRATION

GENERAL INFORMATION

Type of school	Public
Environment	Village
Academic calendar	Semester

SURVEY SAYS...

Students love University, MS
Friendly students
Good peer network
Solid preparation in:
Quantitative skills

STUDENTS

Enrollment of parent institution	14,000
Enrollment of business school	59
% male/female	72/28
% out-of-state	37
% part-time	22
% international	6
Average age at entry	26
Average years work experience at entry	2

ACADEMICS

Academic Experience Rating	**68**
Student/faculty ratio	30:1
Profs interesting rating	84
Profs accessible rating	65
% female faculty	18

Academics

The University of Mississippi—known affectionately as "Ole Miss" to its many students and supporters—offers students two MBA options. The first is an intensive, one-year full-time MBA, which does not require post-undergraduate professional experience for admission; the other is the two-year professional MBA for working adults, which gives strong preference to students with at least two years of post-undergraduate business-related employment.

Ole Miss' one-year program runs 11 months, commencing in July and ending in May. The curriculum consists of 13 prescribed courses, taught cohort-style with an emphasis on "the integration of subjects into real business applications." Students warn that the program is intense. As one explains, "Overall, you have to be very serious if you want to be in a one-year program. Don't let the kind recruiters fool you: You are in for hell if you are not 100 percent committed...There is hardly any time to breathe. This is only for the extremely serious." Instructors "expect a lot out of us," and even "The administration is concerned with our performance and takes measures to continually monitor our progression through the classes. Overall, the academic experience is rigorous." One student concurs, "The program could use more breaks. Or, they could lengthen it to ease the stress."

The part-time MBA at Ole Miss is more flexible, using "alternate methods of delivering course content" that include interactive CD-ROMs, DVDs, videoconferencing, conference calls, and Internet learning. Some on-campus sessions are required, but most of the program can be completed remotely. In both the part-time and full-time program, "Professors all have business backgrounds and have been tenured for a long time, or they have short academic careers and long, successful business careers in the fields they teach." Instructors typically employ "real-world examples and tie your education from them into your own work experiences. Dictation seldom happens. Discussion of the assigned readings is the primary classroom focus."

Career and Placement

Ole Miss MBAs receive career support from the university's Career Center. Students report that many of the best career opportunities come via the alumni network, which is "very supportive. The Ole Miss 'brand' is well-respected in the Southeast." Employers that recruit on the Ole Miss campus include Acxiom, Allstate, Bancorp South, FedEx, Harrah's, IBM, International Paper, Regions Bank, and the Tennessee Valley Authority.

Student Life and Environment

The swift pace of the full-time MBA program means that many students "study so much that it is hard to have a life. But when there are small breaks, the potential to have a great time is definitely there." First and foremost, is Ole Miss football and the requisite tailgate parties beforehand, but there's much more to the social scene than sports. The school "offers a wide variety of activities socially and academically that you can become involved in. This place has a lot of great traditions." Students appreciate the Ole Miss grounds, which one describes as "a walking campus that promotes and produces beautiful people!"

ADMISSIONS CONTACT: DR. JOHN HOLLEMAN, DIRECTOR OF MBA ADMINSTRATRION
ADDRESS: 319 CONNER HALL UNIVERSITY, MS 38677 UNITED STATES
PHONE: 662-915-5483 • FAX: 662-915-7968
E-MAIL: JHOLLEMAN@BUS.OLEMISS.EDU • WEBSITE: WWW.OLEMISSBUSINESS.COM

FINANCIAL FACTS

Annual tuition (in-state/ out-of-state)	$7,000/$13,000
Cost of books	$5,000
Room & board (on/off-campus)	$8,800/$10,000
Average grant	$1,469

ADMISSIONS

Admissions Selectivity Rating	**82**
# of applications received	189
% applicants accepted	54
% acceptees attending	45
Average GMAT	562
Range of GMAT	500–610
Average GPA	3.65
TOEFL required of international students	Yes
Minimum TOEFL (paper/computer)	600/NR
Application fee	$25
Regular application deadline	3/1
Regular notification	4/1
Non-fall admissions	Yes
Need-blind admissions	Yes

Hometown Oxford is a small, Southern college town distinguished by the university and the residences of several famous writers, including John Grisham. The town has become a travel destination for many, not only for Ole Miss sporting events but also for festivals such as the Double Decker Arts Festival and conferences as the Faulkner & Yoknapatawpha Conference (named after the author William Faulkner, who made his home in Oxford, and the fictional county in which much of his work is set). The city of Memphis is just 70 miles to the north.

Full-timers at Ole Miss tend to be "very young. The majority are 22 years old. Some have had internships, but none have actually worked. It's very difficult to have a discussion about business if you've never been involved in one. The few students with work experience talk 95 percent of the time." The student community is close. As one student explains, "One thing about going through an MBA 'boot camp' like this is that you come together very quickly. Because you're all suffering together, people are very friendly and quick to help you out."

Admissions

All applicants to the full-time MBA program at Ole Miss must provide an official transcript of undergraduate work showing a minimum 3.0 GPA for the final 60 semesters hours of academic work; an official GMAT score report (the school lists 550 as the cut-off for "acceptable" scores); two letters of recommendation; and a 400-word personal statement of purpose. Students who have not completed prerequisite course work in undergraduate business disciplines will be required to complete such courses successfully before commencing work on their graduate degrees. International students must meet all of the above requirements and submit TOEFL scores (minimum acceptable score is 600). Applicants to the professional MBA program "with two or more years of post-baccalaureate degree professional work experience" receive "particular consideration" from the Admissions Committee. The professional MBA program is "very competitive."

EMPLOYMENT PROFILE			
Career Rating	74	**Grads Employed by Function**	**% Avg. Salary**
		Finance	15 NR
		Marketing	15 NR
		MIS	20 NR
		Consulting	10 NR
		Entrepreneurship	5 NR
		General Management	5 NR
		Internet/New Media	25 NR

UNIVERSITY OF MISSOURI—COLUMBIA
COLLEGE OF BUSINESS

GENERAL INFORMATION
Type of school	Public
Environment	City
Academic calendar	Semester

SURVEY SAYS...
Happy students
Smart classrooms
Solid preparation in:
Marketing
Finance
Presentation skills

STUDENTS
Enrollment of parent institution	28,253
Enrollment of business school	207
% male/female	61/39
% out-of-state	38
% part-time	3
% minorities	4
% international	29
Average age at entry	25
Average years work experience at entry	2

ACADEMICS
Academic Experience Rating	**83**
Student/faculty ratio	20:1
Profs interesting rating	85
Profs accessible rating	69
% female faculty	12
% minority faculty	3

Joint Degrees
MBA/MS (Industrial Engineering) 3 years, MBA/JD 4 years, MBA/MA (Health Administration) 3 years.

Academics

Boasting modern facilities, a cool campus culture, talented students, and superbly friendly faculty and staff, the University of Missouri is a great place to earn a degree while enjoying the best aspects of academic life. With just 200 graduate students in the business program each year, "class sizes are kept low so there is a lot of student-teacher interaction." As a result, the academic environment is highly supportive, and "the professors are wonderful at providing help outside of the classroom for both class-related items and professional development." In addition, students dole out praise for the school's super-friendly administrators, whom they describe as "very congenial and efficient" as well as highly responsive to student needs. A current student attests, "The administration has a great flow of communication. I can go to them when I need assistance with class work or if I simply want advice."

While the majority of students focus on management, marketing, finance, or management information systems, "Mizzou" likes to stay on top of the trends—"Whenever a new market trend emerges, it is incorporated into the classroom environment, either in a class or in a seminar." Course work is just one component of this highly integrated program, which also draws heavily on teamwork, networking, and hands-on projects. For example, the school boasts something called the Integrated Business Perspectives project, where "students work together without a classroom setting and do a case analysis that involves several functions, instead of simply the one that you are studying." In general, Mizzou's "programs are designed to encourage networking between students, alumni, and faculty"; work outside the classroom is as important as work within it. Students dole out endless praise for the caliber of their talented classmates, whom they characterize as "very active in the program, extremely bright, hardworking, and [possess] diverse talents and career aspirations that make for a great learning environment."

Given the focus on extracurricular learning, Mizzou "strikes a great balance between exceptional in-class learning while not making the workload too rigorous." Students feel they are definitely learning techniques that will be essential outside the classroom. "However, the reasonably manageable workload provides the opportunity to do outside research and independent study that pertain to my niche interests." Even so, don't expect to coast through the program. Mizzou MBAs definitely keep busy with "a great amount of networking, socializing, teamwork, and career development activities outside of the classroom. So, when you factor in all the MBA-related events, classes, studying, and outside events, you will spend 40 hours a week involved with the program."

Career and Placement

The MBA program at Mizzou "does a great job of polishing young businesspeople into professionals," and students at the University of Missouri feel confident entering the workforce after graduation. In addition to course work, "professional development opportunities add the finesse that is needed to succeed in a competitive business environment."

Through the Career Services Office, students have access to career and internship fairs, career-building workshops, and online job databases. The office also maintains contact with a number of recruiting firms across the United States. The school has an especially excellent reputation in the state of Missouri, and "several recruiters are discovering the value of students who come out of this university, so the on-campus recruiting opportunities are phenomenal!" Some students, however, feel that the school is still too regionally focused, and that "Career Services could offer more [recruiting opportunities with] companies outside of Missouri."

ADMISSIONS CONTACT: BARBARA SCHNEIDER, DIRECTOR OF RECRUITING AND ADMISSIONS
ADDRESS: 213 CORNELL HALL COLUMBIA, MO 65211 UNITED STATES
PHONE: 573-882-2750 • FAX: 573-882-6838
E-MAIL: MBA@MISSOURI.EDU • WEBSITE: MBA.MISSOURI.EDU

Student Life and Environment

A MBA at Mizzou is "not only about academics; it's also about socializing, networking, and finding out who you really are." The students form a "very tight-knit" group. Most hail from Missouri yet come from "very diverse backgrounds ethnically and education-ally." After class, students are enthusiastic to "kick back and relax together"; they also "love to celebrate the diversity of the program with special international days, language partner programs, and impromptu dinners and cultural activities."

Extracurricular opportunities are ample, and "about half of the students are involved in the MBA Association. Through this organization, students participate in philanthropy activities (such as Big Brothers, Big Sisters, and Relay for Life), professional development activities (networking receptions, workshops, and alumni events), and social events (weekly happy hours, parties, and wine tastings)." Students with families should take note, however: The programs primarily cater to a younger set, and while "some spouses come to MBA events, most are left out."

On campus, MBA students enjoy "an outstanding library, tons of cultural events, beautiful architecture, and lots of brand new student housing," as well as a state-of-the-art rec center. On top of that, "The business school is housed in a brand-new, technologically-advanced building that is full of resources for the students." According to students here, there's no better location than Columbia, Missouri, which many characterize as "a very forward-thinking city, perfect for both families and younger singletons." The consummate college town, Columbia is home to a host of "schools, parks, libraries, hike-and-bike trails, and arts programs, as well as standard college-town nightlife and activities."

Admissions

The University of Missouri evaluates prospective students based on the strength of their undergraduate work, leadership skills, and GMAT scores. Work experience is not a requirement of the program, but is a factor that is considered in the admissions decision. In the previous year, successful applicants to University of Missouri's graduate business program submitted an average GPA of 3.45 and an average GMAT score of 630. Applicants must submit an MU Graduate School Application and MBA Department Application. Admissions decisions are made on a rolling basis, and students are usually notified of a decision within six weeks of submitting all of the necessary application materials. Students can enter in the Fall, Spring, or Summer terms and graduate in three or four semesters depending upon their academic background.

FINANCIAL FACTS

Annual tuition (in-state/ out-of-state)	$8,963/$21,672
Fees	$965
Cost of books	$940
Room & board (off-campus)	$8,100
% of students receiving aid	55
% of first-year students receiving aid	45
% of students receiving grants	16
Average award package	$13,000
Average grant	$4,800

ADMISSIONS

Admissions Selectivity Rating	86
# of applications received	332
% applicants accepted	62
% acceptees attending	53
Average GMAT	630
Range of GMAT	590–660
Average GPA	3.45
TOEFL required of international students	Yes
Minimum TOEFL (paper/computer)	550/213
Application fee	$45
International application fee	$60
Regular application deadline	rolling
Regular notification	rolling
Deferment available	Yes
Maximum length of deferment	1 year
Transfer students accepted	Yes
Transfer application policy Students my waive up to 24 credit hours and may transfer 6 credit hours from an AACSB MBA program.	
Non-fall admissions	Yes
Need-blind admissions	Yes

EMPLOYMENT PROFILE

Career Rating	83	Grads Employed by Function	% Avg. Salary
Primary Source of Full-time Job Acceptances		Finance	43 $58,585
School-facilitated activities	29 (73%)	Marketing	3 $50,000
Graduate-facilitated activities	11 (27%)	Operations	3 $49,500
Percent employed	91	Consulting	33 $53,363
		General Management	6 $63,000
		Other	12 $57,125

University of Missouri—Kansas City

Henry W. Bloch School of Business and Public Administration

Academics

"A convenient location" and "a strong reputation" in the region attract students to the Henry W. Bloch School of Business and Public Administration at the University of Missouri—Kansas City, a large public institution serving nearly 15,000 undergraduates and graduate students. As you would expect of a school named after a founder of tax-preparation giant H & R Block, accounting is among the strongest programs here. Many also praise the finance emphasis, pointing out that "many of the professors [in this discipline] are distinguished and have impressive backgrounds in publications."

The Bloch MBA requires a minimum of 30 semester hours of course work, and students who enter the program with deficiencies in core skills (e.g. students who did not satisfactorily complete a business major at the undergraduate level) may be required to complete up to 18 additional semester hours as well as introductory classes in mathematics and computer applications. All students must complete a minimum of 18 semester hours outside their area of emphasis. Twelve semester hours are required to complete an emphasis; emphases are available in entrepreneurship, finance, general management, international business, leadership and change in human systems, management information systems, marketing, and operations management.

Students appreciate the "availability of experiential learning" throughout the program and observe that "the quality of the faculty is very high and the overall program is quite thorough." Small class sizes encourage strong relationships between students and teachers—a boon for those MBAs hoping to develop a mentor while here. UMKC's administration "is not very noticeable, which is a good thing. They don't get in the way. They are accessible, though."

Career and Placement

UMKC's Career Services Center, which serves the entire university population, recently opened a satellite office at the Bloch School to serve business graduates and undergraduates. Unfortunately, the office only stays open until 5:00 P.M., making it difficult for Bloch's many part-time students who hold full-time jobs to benefit from its services. It's only an issue for some—many students here have little interest in leaving their current employers—but it is a nuisance for those it affects. Recently, the Bloch School has begun offering some services online. Employers who recruit on the UMKC campus include Ameriprise Financial Services, Inc., Cerner, Commerce Bank, Eli Lilly & Company, Etelligent Consulting Inc., the Farmers Insurance Group, the Federal Bureau of Investigation, the Federal Reserve, First Investors Corp., the Internal Revenue Service, John Hancock Financial Services, State Street, US Bank, Wells Fargo, and Zen Infotech.

Student Life and Environment

"Most MBA students are working professionals during the day and students at night" at UMKC. "Many are married and have kids, most are hard working and competitive," and nearly all are "looking for more out of their careers." This population is supplemented by "a significant international presence" and "some executive students. UMKC is an urban school that fits the mold." For the most part, students' careers and familial obligations leave them "minimal time for extracurricular interaction." They attend classes, participate in team projects, and try to make time for study groups. Aside from that, they do not spend much time on campus.

ADMISSIONS CONTACT: JENNIFER DEHAEMERS, DIRECTOR OF ADMISSIONS
ADDRESS: 5100 ROCKHILL ROAD KANSAS CITY, MO 64110 UNITED STATES
PHONE: 816-235-1111 • FAX: 816-235-5544
E-MAIL: BLOCH@UMKC.EDU • WEBSITE: WWW.BLOCH.UMKC.EDU

The Bloch School is located in a renovated and expanded facility that is also one of the city's historic mansions. The building has been updated to meet the requirements of twenty-first century business education. Students have access to modern classrooms and to computer and research laboratories.

The Kansas City metropolitan area sprawls over six counties in two states, Missouri and Kansas. The region is home to nearly two million residents, placing it among the 30 largest metropolitan regions in the country. Naturally, numerous companies and national organizations are headquartered in the city. They include American Century, Applebee's, Aquila, Black and Veatch, Ferrallgas, Hallmark, H & R Block, Interstate Bakeries, Russell Stover, and Sprint.

Admissions

Applicants to the MBA program at the University of Missouri—Kansas City must submit official copies of transcripts for all academic work completed after high school and an official score report for the GMAT. The school will consider graduate-level admissions tests other than the GMAT (e.g. LSAT, GRE) so long as scores exceed the fiftieth percentile in all parts of the exam. Candidates must also provide the admissions committee with all of the following: a completed application form (available online); a current resume showing both work history and professional certifications; a personal statement of purpose in pursuing the MBA; and a summary of the candidate's current commitments to work (i.e., hours of work per week, amount of business travel). International students must provide all of the above and must also provide an official score report for the TOEFL; a minimum score of 550 on the paper-based exam or 213 on the computer-based exam is required.

FINANCIAL FACTS

Annual tuition (in-state/ out-of-state)	$5,164/$13,334
Fees	$615
Cost of books	$742
Room & board (on/off-campus)	$9,376/$8,660
% of students receiving aid	36
% of first-year students receiving aid	35
% of students receiving loans	26
% of students receiving grants	16
Average award package	$13,673
Average grant	$3,656
Average student loan debt	$27,846

ADMISSIONS

Admissions Selectivity Rating	**82**
# of applications received	151
% applicants accepted	67
% acceptees attending	80
Average GMAT	544
Range of GMAT	490–580
Average GPA	3.28
TOEFL required of international students	Yes
Minimum TOEFL (paper/computer)	550/213
Application fee	$35
International application fee	$50
Regular application deadline	5/1
Regular notification	Rolling
Deferment available	Yes
Maximum length of deferment	1 year
Transfer students accepted	Yes
Transfer application policy	We will accept up to 6 hours of grad credit from an AACSB accredited institution.
Non-fall admissions	Yes
Need-blind admissions	Yes

Applicants Also Look At
Rockhurst University, University of Kansas.

UNIVERSITY OF MISSOURI—ST. LOUIS
COLLEGE OF BUSINESS ADMINISTRATION

GENERAL INFORMATION
Type of school	Public
Environment	Metropolis
Academic calendar	Semester

SURVEY SAYS...
Cutting edge classes
Smart classrooms
Solid preparation in:
Operations

STUDENTS
Enrollment of parent institution	12,100
Enrollment of business school	462
% male/female	62/38
% out-of-state	18
% part-time	72
% minorities	1
% international	15
Average age at entry	29
Average years work experience at entry	5

ACADEMICS
Academic Experience Rating	**72**
Student/faculty ratio	12:1
Profs interesting rating	75
Profs accessible rating	85
% female faculty	22
% minority faculty	4

Academics

Students looking to earn one of the three "affordable" MBAs (evening, professional, and international) offered at the University of Missouri—St. Louis's College of Business Administration will find themselves doing so at the largest AACSB-accredited business school in the St. Louis region, and the only AACSB-accredited business school to offer an online MBA. The predominantly part-time program is completed through mostly night courses, and with a large population of older students returning to school after several years in the workplace, "most have become very efficient in time management."

The course of study in the evening MBA provides a solid foundation in the functional areas of business with emphasis areas available in accounting, finance, information systems, logistics and supply chain management, management, marketing, and operations management. The professional MBA program is a much smaller cohort of working individuals who take all of their classes together. One student says this arrangement allows her "to feel more comfortable and enables me to take more risks (presenting, sharing ideas) than in a traditional class setting." Another value-add is the school's reputable program in logistics/supply chain management. The International MBA is a unique two-year program in which students spend the first year studying overseas at a partner institution and the second year on campus at UM-St. Louis.

The "accessible" professors at UMSL get fairly positive reviews, though the instruction methods are not without their detractors. Many remain unchallenged by the courses, which tend to "overlap," "They are pretty much doing Finance 101, Marketing 101, etc.," one student grumbles. Another doesn't like what he sees as an overemphasis on group projects, which must be coordinated outside the classroom: "This is night school for people with jobs and families; we don't have time to do group projects in every class . . . once or twice is enough to teach teamwork concepts!"

Another gripe is the lack of "real-world interaction" opportunities offered by the school, such as required internships and more business leaders in the classroom. "I think my academic experience will be pure[ly] academic, without any real business insight," one student says. But another thinks the "strong international presence" at UMSL "contributes to my understanding of the global marketplace. If I have a question about how to effectively penetrate the European market and capture the broadest consumer base possible, I ask my classmate from France." The school's strong reputation in the St. Louis area allows for numerous internships, and students say the faculty mambers are willing to use their connections with top local employers and alumni channels to help students put their knowledge to use in more practical settings. Criticisms aside, students here recognize that they're getting a "quality education for a reasonable price."

Career and Placement

The counseling at the Career and Placement Center at UMSL is "very limited." One student finds that "there is virtually no placement assistance that is geared toward grad students that already have some experience," with most career events featuring recruiters looking for undergraduate (and sometimes MBA) students only. "It doesn't seem like our Career Services Department has contacts in the real world other than to collect and post job descriptions and availability," says a graduating student.

ADMISSIONS CONTACT: THOMAS EYSSELL, ASSOCIATE DEAN AND DIRECTOR OF GRADUATE STUDIES
ADDRESS: ONE UNIVERSITY BOULEVARD, 250 UNIVERSITY CENTER ST. LOUIS, MO 63121-4499 U.S.
PHONE: 314-516-5885 • FAX: 314-516-7202
E-MAIL: MBA@UMSL.EDU • WEBSITE: MBA.UMSL.EDU

Student Life and Environment

Life in St. Louis, "a baseball town," is pretty much what you make of it, and since the majority of (American) students here have lived in the area for a while, they're typically pretty settled in. "The most popular question asked at a party: 'What high school did you go to?'" says a student. The breakdown of students tends to divvy up into "married working professionals," international and exchange students who "are likely to have their own community (friendship) within their origin or with other international students," and the smallest subset, full-time American students.

Though everyone is easy to talk to, "even though ages of the students may vary widely," "Social unity is not a characteristic" of the college, and there's no doubt that the primary focus for most students at UMSL is to go to class and then leave. This is just as well for the school, which isn't exactly chomping at the bit to provide activities that most students wouldn't attend anyway. "I don't think students even know what organizations UMSL has," says a student, and for those that do, most events are not grad student–specific, so people show only "marginal student involvement." The facilities, while functional, are "not aesthetically pleasing," and the gym and parking situations leave much to be desired.

Admissions

Though professional experience is not required for admittance into the traditional MBA program, it does play a factor in admissions decisions. In order to gain nonrestricted admittance to any of the school's MBA programs, an applicant must submit a GMAT score of at least 500 (50th percentile) overall and must have an undergraduate GPA of at least 3.0. Applicants who score below the 30th percentile on either the verbal or quantitative component of the GMAT generally are not accepted. Applicants also must submit an official copy of undergraduate transcripts from all institutions where course work was completed (this should come directly from the schools themselves); a current resume; an official GMAT score report; a personal statement; and two letters of recommendation.

In addition to the above documents, international students whose primary language is not English must also provide an official score report for the TOEFL (minimum score: 550, paper-based test; 213, computer-based test).

FINANCIAL FACTS

Annual tuition (in-state/ out-of-state)	$6,316/$16,313
Fees	$1,287
Cost of books	$3,000
Room & board (on/off-campus)	$5,600/$6,180
% of students receiving aid	53
% of first-year students receiving aid	48
% of students receiving loans	32
% of students receiving grants	24
Average award package	$10,139
Average grant	$6,159
Average student loan debt	$5,933

ADMISSIONS

Admissions Selectivity Rating	74
# of applications received	106
% applicants accepted	80
% acceptees attending	71
Average GMAT	550
Range of GMAT	470–590
Average GPA	3.2
TOEFL required of international students	Yes
Minimum TOEFL (paper/computer)	550/213
Application fee	$35
International application fee	$40
Regular application deadline	7/1
Regular notification	rolling
Deferment available	Yes
Maximum length of deferment	1 year
Transfer students accepted	Yes
Transfer application policy Maximum of nine hours of acceptable graduate credit allowed to transfer in.	
Non-fall admissions	Yes
Need-blind admissions	Yes

EMPLOYMENT PROFILE

Career Rating	70	Grads Employed by Function	%	Avg. Salary
		Finance	50	$51,600
		Consulting	17	$42,500
		Communications	16	$43,000
		Other	17	$48,000

UNIVERSITY OF NEVADA—LAS VEGAS
COLLEGE OF BUSINESS

Academics

The College of Business at the University of Nevada—Las Vegas offers both a full-time day and full-time and part-time evening MBA as well as a cohort-based weekend Executive MBA program for more experienced professionals. Roughly half the students in these programs attend the college full time.

UNLV's evening MBA consists of 48 credit hours, 33 of which are devoted to core courses. Students must devote five electives to a single area in order to achieve a concentration; the college offers concentrations in finance, management information systems, service marketing, and venture management. An accelerated program is open only to evening students who score at least a 600 on the GMAT (with a score exceeding the 50th percentile in both verbal and quantitative skills) and an undergraduate business degree from an AACSB-accredited university. Students who meet these conditions may be allowed to waive up to six of the ten required core courses.

The 18-month Executive MBA program offers a general management degree; in order to preserve the program's cohort-based approach to learning, all students follow the same curriculum. The program begins with a week of intensive work; afterwards, students meet every Friday and Saturday from 8:30 A.M. to 5:30 P.M. Applicants to the program must have at least seven years of professional experience, at least three of which have been spent in "a key decision-making role."

UNLV also offers combined-degree programs in hotel administration, dental medicine, management information system and a JD/MBA. Students point out that the "hotel concentration feeds off the Las Vegas resort market."

Career and Placement

The UNLV College of Business Career Services Center serves only graduate students in business. According to the College's website, the office seeks to help students define career goals, develop a career plan, market themselves, develop job-search skills, sharpen interviewing skills, and contact alumni. The office serves as a liaison to the local business community, maintains a number of hard-copy and online job databases, and organizes lectures and on-campus recruiting events.

Employers most likely to hire UNLV MBAs include Bechtel Nevada, Bechtel SAIC, Citibank, Harrah's Entertainment Inc., Pulte Homes, US Bank, and Wells Fargo. A plurality of the class of 2004 wound up in the finance sector, and almost everyone had found employment by graduation.

Student Life and Environment

Las Vegas is one of America's top tourist destinations, primarily because "it's fun every single night." Those who live here know that Vegas has a lot more to offer than just gambling, over-the-top floor shows, and cheap buffets. The Las Vegas metropolitan region is home to 1.8 million residents, many of whom never set foot inside a casino. The city boasts all the amenities of a midsize metropolis and adds to the mix a perennially sunny climate and proximity to plenty of outdoor fun; Lake Mead, the Colorado River, and the Hoover Dam are all within a half-hour's drive of the city. Some fabulous skiing and hiking awaits residents on Mount Charleston, less than an hour northwest of Sin City.

UNLV does its part to keep things interesting, providing "new cultural and entertainment attractions to the community every day," according to the college's website. Prominent lecturers and touring performing artists regularly stop by this desert campus.

Admissions

Applicants to the MBA program at UNLV must submit the following to the Admissions Committee: official transcripts for all postsecondary academic work undertaken; an official score report for the GMAT; two letters of recommendation; a personal essay; and a resume. An interview is required for admission to the Executive MBA and full-time day programs, but not for other graduate programs. The TOEFL is not required of students who completed degree programs conducted in English or the U.S., U.K., Australia, Canada, or New Zealand. All international applicants must provide financial certification documents.

FINANCIAL FACTS

Annual tuition (in-state/ out-of-state)	$0/$8,674
Fees	$456
Cost of books	$800
Room & board (on/off-campus)	$5,000/$7,000
% of students receiving aid	55
% of students receiving loans	25
% of students receiving grants	3
Average award package	$16,633
Average grant	$2,954
Average student loan debt	$34,309

ADMISSIONS

Admissions Selectivity Rating	**92**
# of applications received	177
% applicants accepted	38
% acceptees attending	96
Average GMAT	597
Range of GMAT	550–630
Average GPA	3.24
TOEFL required of international students	Yes
Minimum TOEFL (paper/computer)	550/213
Application fee	$60
International application fee	$75
Regular application deadline	6/1
Regular notification	7/1
Deferment available	Yes
Maximum length of deferment	One semester
Transfer students accepted	Yes
Transfer application policy Total of 6 credits from an AACSB accredited school.	
Non-fall admissions	Yes
Need-blind admissions	Yes

EMPLOYMENT PROFILE

Career Rating	67	Grads Employed by Function	%	Avg. Salary
		Finance	40	$52,000
		Human Resources	2	$50,000
		Marketing	20	$45,000
		MIS	3	$50,000
		Operations	2	$65,000
		Consulting	3	$60,000
		General Management	10	$50,000
		Other	10	$35,000

UNIVERSITY OF NEVADA—RENO
COLLEGE OF BUSINESS ADMINSTRATION

Academics

The University of Nevada—Reno's College of Business offers graduate business programs designed to serve the needs of its largely local and mostly part-time student body. As high tech, distribution, hospitality, tourism, and gambling dominate western Nevada's business landscape, UNR's business school curriculum takes note of this, offering specializations in accounting, finance, gaming management, international business, and supply chain management. All MBA students are required to follow a core curriculum intended to provide them with a foundation in statistics, marketing, economics, and finance; the core curriculum takes up roughly half the credits required for the degree.

Students must also take classes in managing computer-based systems and understanding changing business environments, and must choose courses from several other areas of business before moving into their area of specialization. Specialized classes make up about one quarter of the credits required for the degree.

UNR's ranking as one of the top 150 research institutions in the U.S. attracts business professors who are "very accessible and helpful" as well as "skilled in blending real-world experience with academic theory," with an ability "to promote critical thinking and teamwork." Nearly three-quarters of the students are in part-time programs, but that "doesn't mean that the course material is less rigorous," students agree. In fact, "This program challenges you since the classes are condensed" and "Some classes have overloaded us with homework and projects," one student grumbles. If they were to make improvements, some students would start with what they describe as a limited class selection, offering "too many accounting/finance classes and not enough other subjects." Fortunately, faculty and administration are "always willing to listen to your goals and dreams, and help to custom design the MBA program you need to follow." In fact, "The greatest strength of the school is its practical, hands-on curriculum." One student echoes the sentiments of his classmates when he says, "I am getting a great education at such a bargain!"

Career and Placement

In 2005, 3 months after graduation, an impressive 99 percent of the College of Business MBA holders at UNR were employed, with an average starting salary of $50,000. While some students do not find the Career Connections Center very active ("I didn't even know we had one," said one), others take advantage of career fairs, recruiting appointments, and networking among fellow students to find jobs. A reported snag in the process is that "students do not have much of an opportunity to mingle with one another due to the late-night classes and the fact that most students work at least part-time," one points out. The Career Connections Center does offer a variety of workshops targeted to the general university population on topics such as resume writing, effective networking, and developing interviewing skills in which MBA student may participate. The school's 2006 graduates were recruited by the following companies: Gentech, The Peppermill Casinos, Wells Fargo, the Bureau of Land Management, Coventry Health Care, and International Game Technology.

ADMISSIONS CONTACT: VICKI KRENTZ, COORDINATOR OF GRADUATE PROGRAMS
ADDRESS: MAILSTOP 0024 RENO, NV 89557 UNITED STATES
PHONE: 775-784-4912 • FAX: 775-784-1773
E-MAIL: VKRENTZ@UNR.EDU • WEBSITE: WWW.COBA.UNR.EDU/MBA

Student Life and Environment

UNR College of Business students are a "very diverse group of people, racially, cultural-ly, and in the range of experiences they have had prior to school." "About 50 percent have a science or engineering background; about 50 percent have a business or liberal arts background," students say. This range of experience is a real benefit both inside and outside the classroom: "I have had the opportunity to meet many people from various backgrounds. The diverse student body makes attending classes well worth the time."

UNR's campus sits on a hill north of downtown, and the original campus design (it's the oldest university in Nevada) was modeled on Thomas Jefferson's ideal of an academic village. But students here—"mostly married with children, employed full-time, non-career changers who are looking for advancement within their current organization"—rarely have time to take in the scenery. Despite their busy schedules, UNR's "friendly" students help create a welcoming atmosphere on campus. "My fellow students are mature and respectful. They are always willing to help anyone who is unsure about any-thing," says one student.

Since "students commute to the campus, live off campus and tend to be local profes-sionals," students say it's sometimes difficult to build connections. However, "I like the fact that the restaurants and coffeehouse are open late for night students. They really try!" pointed out one such student, echoing the thoughts of many of his classmates.

Admissions

Two or more years of work experience, a minimum GPA of 2.75 on a 4.0 scale, and a GMAT score of at least 500 are required for admission to the College of Business at UNR. A resume, two letters of reference, and a two- to three-page personal statement concern-ing background and goals are also needed. A minimum TOEFL score of 550 is required from non-native English speakers. In 2007, the average GMAT score for those admitted was 577, and the average length of work experience was five years. A full 77 percent of those who applied were accepted, and about three-quarters of them pursued their degrees on a part-time basis. Of the 219 students enrolled in graduate programs in 2007, approximately 49 percent were women.

ADMISSIONS	
Admissions Selectivity Rating	**71**
# of applications received	116
% applicants accepted	84
% acceptees attending	61
Average GMAT	577
Average GPA	3.1
TOEFL required of international students	Yes
Minimum TOEFL (paper)	550
Application fee	$60
Regular application deadline	3/15
Regular notification	rolling
Deferment available	Yes
Maximum length of deferment	1 year
Non-fall admissions	Yes

EMPLOYMENT PROFILE	
Career Rating	67

UNIVERSITY OF NEW HAMPSHIRE
WHITTEMORE SCHOOL OF BUSINESS AND ECONOMICS

Academics

Things are changing at the University of New Hampshire's Whittemore School of Business and Economics: In 2005–2006, the school introduced a brand-new MBA program designed to streamline the degree-earning process. The new program hustles full-time students through in less than one year (through an "intense program" that leaves "little time for anything else," according to the school's website), while part-timers graduate in fewer than two years. Students here frequently cite the speed with which the program can be completed as one of its biggest draws.

Whittemore's full-time program begins in late August with a five-week term, during which students study management, accounting, and organizational behavior. The second term, which runs for three months, consists entirely of required courses in economics, marketing, information systems and enterprise integration, and financial management. Term three is split between two required courses (one in organizations and leadership, the other in managerial decision making) and two electives. Term four consists of two required courses covering operations management and business strategy, and electives. This provides student teams the opportunity to work on a real-world project with a major company, such as Fidelity Investments or Liberty Mutual Life. The program concludes with term five, during which students complete a consulting project. Students can take electives in marketing and supply chain management, entrepreneurial venture creation, or financial management. Many students single out the entrepreneurship classes as a highlight of the program.

Whittemore's part-time program follows a similar curriculum to the full-time program, although it replaces the consulting project with two electives. The part-time program offers the same selection of concentrations as the full-time program.

MBAs at Whittemore detect an "an emphasis on academic greatness that fosters a great study environment." They report approvingly that "the faculty is always willing to help out" and that "the school offers lots of resources for going into the workplace," and "professors are, for the most part, very good and have extensive experience and research in their fields. The experience from the Whittemore School of Business and Economics is one of academic intensity as well as a lot of fun."

Career and Placement

Business students at UNH have their own placement service which works in partnership with the university-at-large placement office, the University Advising and Career Center. Placement staff work with business undergraduates, graduates, and alumni to forge career strategies, identify potential employers, and navigate the recruitment process. Recent employers of Whittemore School graduates include Anthem Blue Cross Blue Shield, AT&T, Boise Cascade, Chubb Life-America, Cigna, Credit Suisse, Fidelity Investments, GE, IBM, LL Bean, Inc., The McGraw-Hill Companies, Osram Sylvania, Pfizer, Raytheon, Sprague Energy, Timken Aerospace, Verizon, and Westinghouse.

ADMISSIONS CONTACT: GEORGE ABRAHAM, DIRECTOR, GRADUATE AND EVECUTIVE PROGRAMS
ADDRESS: 116 MCCONNELL HALL, 15 COLLEGE ROAD DURHAM, NH 03824 UNITED STATES
PHONE: 603-862-1367 • FAX: 603-862-4468
E-MAIL: WSBE.GRAD@UNH.EDU • WEBSITE: WWW.MBA.UNH.EDU

Student Life and Environment

"Most of us are in the same boat here: all fresh out of undergrad with no business knowledge whatsoever," explains one full-time student. "This alone gives us a strong bond. But add myriad team-building exercises and an intense workload, and we've become very close in our time together thus far." MBAs here describe themselves as "overachievers—we were hand-picked by the program's creator—but we manage to maintain a balance between our academic lives and our social lives." Outside the classroom, students participate in international competitions, such as I2P Idea to Product and the NASA Means Business Competition. Discipline-related clubs are also available. Like full-timers, part-timers tend to be young; however, they typically have full-time jobs, and their extracurricular experiences are more limited.

The UNH campus and surrounding area provide "a fun, beautiful environment to be in. The seasons are amazing, and the skiing is great." Durham is "a small college town" with "a few bars, three or four pizza places, and a cell phone service provider," but fortunately "Portsmouth and the beaches are close by." Students tell us that "it is desirable to take trips down to Boston for some excitement."

Admissions

Applicants to the MBA program at UNH's Whittemore School must provide the Admissions Department with all of the following: official copies of transcripts for all postsecondary academic work; an official score report for the GMAT; three letters of reference focusing on the candidate's "strengths, weaknesses, and potential for academic and managerial success"; responses to essay questions, which the school deems a "crucial" aspect of the application; a current resume; and any evidence of leadership skills that the applicant wishes to provide. Applicants to the Executive MBA program must undergo an admissions interview. Applicants to other MBA programs may request an interview but are not required to do so. (It is, however, "strongly recommended" that such applicants who have "one or more weak components in their profile" schedule an appointment.) Two years of work experience is "recommended but not required" for the full-time and part-time MBA programs; a minimum of seven years of professional experience is required for the Executive MBA program. International applicants must meet all of the above requirements and must submit an official score report for the TOEFL (minimum required score: 550 paper-based test, 213 computer-based test).

FINANCIAL FACTS

Annual tuition (in-state/ out-of-state)	$17,000/$28,000
Fees	$1,506
Cost of books	$2,250
Room & board (on/off-campus)	$9,240/$9,500
% of students receiving aid	81
% of first-year students receiving aid	81
% of students receiving loans	44
% of students receiving grants	72
Average award package	$8,544
Average grant	$7,173

ADMISSIONS

Admissions Selectivity Rating	79
# of applications received	155
% applicants accepted	88
% acceptees attending	78
Average GMAT	559
Range of GMAT	490–600
Average GPA	3.24
TOEFL required of international students	Yes
Minimum TOEFL (paper/computer)	550/213
Application fee	$60
International application fee	$60
Regular application deadline	7/1
Regular notification	rolling
Early decision program?	Yes
ED Deadline/ Notification	04/1 / 05/15
Deferment available	Yes
Maximum length of deferment	1 year
Transfer students accepted	Yes
Transfer application policy A maximum of nine credits may be considered for transfer credit.	
Non-fall admissions	Yes
Need-blind admissions	Yes

Applicants Also Look At
Babson College, Bentley College, Boston University, Suffolk University.

EMPLOYMENT PROFILE

Career Rating	78	Grads Employed by Function	%	Avg. Salary
Primary Source of Full-time Job Acceptances		Finance	57	$57,968
School-facilitated activities	3 (21%)	Other	43	$56,727
Graduate-facilitated activities	11 (79%)			

Top 5 Employers Hiring Grads
Sprague Energy; Raytheon; Bank of America; MITRE; Citigroup

THE UNIVERSITY OF NORTH CAROLINA AT CHAPEL HILL

KENAN-FLAGLER BUSINESS SCHOOL

GENERAL INFORMATION

Type of school	Public
Environment	Town
Academic calendar	Semester

SURVEY SAYS...

Friendly students
Good social scene
Good peer network
Solid preparation in:
Teamwork

STUDENTS

Enrollment of parent institution	23,000
Enrollment of business school	568
% male/female	72/28
% out-of-state	74
% minorities	17
% international	28
Average age at entry	29
Average years work experience at entry	5.6

ACADEMICS

Academic Experience Rating	**96**
Student/faculty ratio	5:1
Profs interesting rating	89
Profs accessible rating	99
% female faculty	22
% minority faculty	1

Joint Degrees

MBA/JD 4 years, MBA/MS (Regional Planning) 3 years, MBA/MS (Health Care Administration) 3 years, MBA/MS (Information Sciences) 3 years.

Prominent Alumni

Claire Babrowski, Exec VP/COO, Toys; Hugh McColl, Former chairman/CEO, Bank of America; Brent Callinicos, VP/Treasurer, Google, Inc.; Gary Parr, Deputy Chairman, Lazard Freres and Co.; Paul Clayton, President/CEO, Jamba Juice.

Academics

The University of North Carolina at Chapel Hill's Kenan-Flagler Business School offers a practical and progressive MBA program, with a faculty and staff "committed to making sure the curriculum reflects what students need to be successful after graduation." The program begins with a rigorous core curriculum that covers the full cycle of running a business. With an emphasis on case study and group work, students appreciate a core curriculum that is "extremely well-integrated, so that what you learn in one class will show up in a different context in another class." They also appreciate their school's staunch commitment to education, explaining, "When the core faculty is teaching, that's all they are doing—no research or travel—so they are available and willing to talk with students as much as needed." Consistently small class sizes further ensure that the "personal attention you receive from administrative staff and faculty is outstanding." A current student reassures, "On several occasions, I've been working late and had a question—there was always someone to help me out."

In the second semester, students begin to take elective course work, gaining "more in-depth knowledge of emerging business issues." The school is noted for "extremely strong marketing, entrepreneurship, and real estate programs," and for its unique sustainable energy concentration. Committed to innovation, 20 percent of the school's elective offerings change annually in response to new business trends. An excellent choice for those considering a career change or looking to expand upon their current professional experience, "The Kenan-Flagler MBA is not targeted [at] individuals who just want a generic management degree, but [at] those who want a degree tailored to their area of specialization." Students can further specialize their studies through courses "taken from other graduate programs within the broader university."

A former CEO, Kenan-Flagler's Dean Steve Jones runs the school like a well-oiled business venture, and consequently the administration is surprisingly responsive to student suggestions and concerns. UNC's administrators "take action when requests are made to change curriculum and administrative situations." When it comes to academics, "Student feedback is taken in the middle and at the end of the course. The feedback is incorporated into the new version of the course quickly."

Career and Placement

Boasting a stellar reputation "coupled with one of the best startup/tech communities on the East Coast," Kenan-Flagler students enjoy great job-placement opportunities through the school's Career Management Center. The CMC also lends a hand with one-on-one career counseling, peer counseling, and group training sessions on topics such as writing a resume, salary negotiations, and how to work a career fair. Students also have access to the school's alumni base, which is "strong and actively participates in recruiting and networking."

Last year, the mean base salary for Kenan-Flagler grads (U.S. citizens) was $93,004, with a high of $125,000. Eighty-seven percent of graduates also received signing bonuses. Real estate, marketing, investment banking, and consulting are the most popular career choices, and a plethora of companies recruit on the UNC campus. Here is an abbreviated list of companies who hired three or more Kenan-Flagler students last year: American Express, Bain & Company, Bank of America, The Boston Consulting Group, Citi, Credit Suisse, CSE Consulting, Deloitte Consulting, DuPont, Eli Lilly and Company, Goldman Sachs, IBM Corporation, Johnson & Johnson, JPMorgan, Kraft Foods, Lehman Brothers, Lowe's Companies, McKinsey & Company, McNeil Consumer & Specialty Pharmaceuticals, Morgan Stanley, Procter & Gamble, Wachovia Securities.

ADMISSIONS CONTACT: SHERRY WALLACE, DIRECTOR, MBA ADMISSIONS
ADDRESS: CB #3490, MCCOLL BUILDING CHAPEL HILL, NC 27599-3490 UNITED STATES
PHONE: 919-962-3236 • FAX: 919-962-0898
E-MAIL: MBA_INFO@UNC.EDU • WEBSITE: WWW.KENAN-FLAGLER.UNC.EDU

Student Life and Environment

Located in a beautiful college town and blessed with an extraordinarily affable student body, life is good at UNC Chapel Hill. "Everyone goes the extra mile to help and contribute to the overall atmosphere," says one student. Another student observes, "The one word I'd have to use to describe the students at KFBS is 'dynamic.' I've been really impressed with the depth and diversity of their backgrounds, work experiences, and what they contribute to class."

While the workload is considerable, the life of a UNC MBA student is "very busy but very balanced." In addition to schoolwork, "Students at UNC are very involved in extracurricular and community activities." For example, "The Business School has its own Habitat House at which students volunteer every weekend." Students assure us that the social life outside of class is "vibrant, including tailgating on the lawn, black-tie casino night, and MBA Olympics against Duke." Off campus, "The Chapel Hill area is a great place for outdoors activities and the town has lots of bars and nightlife." Going out with fellow students is a popular pastime, and "Chapel Hill is especially great for single students because there's so much to do and so many people to meet." However, those who have already tied the knot are happy too: "I'm married, and I've found that KFBS is very accepting and helpful for the married students."

Admissions

The Kenan-Flagler School of Business admits students who demonstrate leadership and organizational skills, communication ability, interpersonal skills, teamwork ability, analytic and problem-solving skills, drive and motivation, prior academic performance, career progression, and career goals. The school recommends at least 2 years of full-time work experience before entering the program. No specific course work is necessary, but students must have knowledge of financial accounting, statistics, macroeconomics, and calculus. Last year's entering class had a median GMAT score of 690, a median GPA of 3.3, and professional work experience averaging 5.3 years. Qualified candidates are invited to interview from September through April.

FINANCIAL FACTS

Annual tuition (in-state/ out-of-state)	$18,375/$36,749
Fees	$2,773
Cost of books	$4,540
Room & board	$16,300
% of students receiving aid	79
% of first-year students receiving aid	80
% of students receiving loans	69
% of students receiving grants	64
Average award package	$42,295
Average grant	$11,370
Average student loan debt	$70,366

ADMISSIONS

Admissions Selectivity Rating	93
# of applications received	1,714
% applicants accepted	39
% acceptees attending	42
Average GMAT	681
Range of GMAT	650–720
Average GPA	3.27
TOEFL required of international students	Yes
Minimum TOEFL (paper/computer)	600/250
Application fee	$135
International application fee	$135
Regular application deadline	3/7
Regular notification	4/21
Application Deadline/Notification	
Round 1:	10/26 / 12/10
Round 2:	12/07 / 02/4
Round 3:	01/4 / 03/17
Round 4:	03/07 / 04/21
Early decision program?	Yes
ED Deadline/Notification	Oct. 26th / 12/10
Deferment available	Yes
Maximum length of deferment	1 yr emergency only
Need-blind admissions	Yes

Applicants Also Look At

Duke University, Northwestern University, University of Michigan, University of Virginia.

EMPLOYMENT PROFILE

Career Rating	93
Primary Source of Full-time Job Acceptances	
School-facilitated activities	171 (80%)
Graduate-facilitated activities	42 (20%)
Average base starting salary	$92,505
Percent employed	90

Grads Employed by Function	%	Avg. Salary
Finance	46	$92,155
Human Resources	3	$86,666
Marketing	23	$87,273
Consulting	12	$108,146
General Management	8	$92,812
Other	6	$86,416

Top 5 Employers Hiring Grads
Bank of America; Citi; Deloitte Consulting; Lehman Brothers; Dell

THE UNIVERSITY OF NORTH CAROLINA AT CHARLOTTE
BELK COLLEGE OF BUSINESS

Academics

A "wise investment" for future business leaders, UNCC Charlotte offers a selection of high-quality, affordable, flexible, and student-oriented graduate programs through the Belk College of Business. For MBA candidates, the school offers two distinct options: the Full-Time MBA, a seventeen-month cohort program on UNC Charlotte's main campus, and the Flexible MBA, which offers evening classes in Charlotte uptown, as well as the main campus. Flexible is, indeed, the key word, as the school allows students to complete the coursework in 18 to 36 months—or even longer, if necessary—so you are free to take "classes at your preferred pace." If your professional schedule really heats up, the school also offers virtual classes. A student shares, "I'm even taking one course in the evenings live over the Internet this term and I love it. The flexibility and choices for constructing your own educational experience are wonderful." Even paying for your education is super student-friendly and flexible at Belk College; since 2008, students are able to "split tuition payments up throughout the semester."

While all MBA students get a thorough introduction to essential business principles, the UNCC education is greatly enriched by "the diversity of concentrations within the MBA program and its relationships within the local business community." Students praise the school's programs in supply chain management and real estate (for which the school offers a specific certificate program), as well as the strength of the finance and communications faculty. Belk also offers an MBA in Sports Marking and Management, a unique graduate program that incorporates a full-time internship in the sports industry, as well as special electives in various sports fields.

Academic and administrative departments work hard to "accommodate business students at an individual level," and "the faculty and administrators are very accessible and show obvious concern" for each student's success. A current student writes, "I love that if I have a question about anything, from a homework problem to internship opportunities, the Belk College faculty and support staff are always available and willing to help." Academics focus on practical as well as theoretical business principles, and "most professors are or have held high level positions in their respective fields." In the words of a student: "I haven't had a bad professor yet; although some are more eccentric than others. My overall experience has been excellent."

The curriculum is challenging and "it's generally pretty hard to get A's" at Belk College. A current student shares, "I appreciate the fact that my classes and professors push me to think on my own instead of spoon-feeding me information that they expect to be regurgitated on quizzes or exams." Still, the MBA is manageable and "life is, for the most part, laid back. You have to get your work done, but professors understand when work occasionally takes time away from studying."

Career and Development

Many part-time MBA candidates hope their new degree will help them move up the ladder with their current employer. To that end, Belk College is highly successful, arming graduates with a slew of new skills and professional contacts in Charlotte. Since joining the program last year, a student says, "My supervisor at my current job has commented numerous times on my development."

In addition, Belk College offers a variety of career development services, including career counseling and career fairs, and workshops on topics like interviewing and business etiquette. The school also works its "ties to the local business community" to schedule an interesting campus speaker's series. For those looking for contacts within the local community, UNCC offers superb "networking opportunities with classmates and Charlotte professionals."

Student Life and Environment

Three-quarters of Belk students are working professionals, who "range in age from fresh out of undergrad, to early-to-mid 40s." In particular, many Belk College students come from the banking industry; though there are "many who are from other interesting companies in the area (NASCAR, Real Estate companies, health care)." On the whole, students "bring a lot of different views and experiences into discussions" and "the diversity and quality of the student body gets better every year" at Belk College.

As you'll find at many graduate and professional programs, UNCC is "very decentralized; school is incidental, and most people's lives take place separately." Older students admit that, "in the evenings and weekends program, most of us with families have little time for socializing." While the hands-off attitude works for some students, many say they "would like to see more social events/functions for the younger crowd." A student writes, "Charlotte is a fun city; I'd like to share some of that fun with my classmates." In the meantime, those who'd like a little extracurricular stimulation can participate in the MBA Association, which hosts speaker series and social events.

Admissions

For admission to Belk College, students are evaluated based on their undergraduate record, GMAT scores, resume, personal essays, and three letters of recommendation. The average GMAT score for entering students currently hovers around 575. Work experience is strongly recommended, but not required.

FINANCIAL FACTS

Annual tuition (in-state/ out-of-state)	$10,000/$20,000
% of students receiving aid	53
% of students receiving loans	16
% of students receiving grants	15

ADMISSIONS

Admissions Selectivity Rating	**91**
# of applications received	174
% applicants accepted	66
% acceptees attending	61
Average GMAT	591
Range of GMAT	550–640
Average GPA	3.3
TOEFL required of international students	Yes
Minimum TOEFL (paper/computer)	557/220
Application fee	$55
International application fee	$55
Regular application deadline	rolling
Regular notification	rolling
Deferment available	Yes
Maximum length of deferment	1 year
Transfer students accepted	Yes
Transfer application policy With permission, it may be possible to transfer graduate level work from an AACSB-accredited university	
Non-fall admissions	Yes
Need-blind admissions	Yes

EMPLOYMENT PROFILE			
Career Rating	**81**	**Grads Employed by Function**	**% Avg. Salary**
		Finance	35 NR
		Human Resources	2 NR
		Marketing	7 NR
		MIS	5 NR
		Operations	14 NR
		Consulting	12 NR
		General Management	5 NR
		Other	18 NR

THE UNIVERSITY OF NORTH CAROLINA AT GREENSBORO
JOSEPH M. BRYAN SCHOOL OF BUSINESS AND ECONOMICS

Academics

The Bryan MBA program at The University of North Carolina—Greensboro offers a very affordable price, a great location, and a tremendous faculty. The MBA program requires 36 credit hours plus an additional 12 hours of prerequisite coursework (which can be waived). "UNCG has a very flexible evening program which allows students to work during the day and attend classes at night." There's also a day program for students with a limited amount of professional experience that emphasizes practical learning experiences and includes a capstone consulting course.

Courses are taught in seven-week modules, and in addition to lectures, group projects, and case studies, students at UNCG frequently work on projects with local firms and interact with bigwigs from area industries. "The flexibility of the program structure" is outstanding and electives are very abundant. Students can specialize by taking up to 25 percent of their courses in a host of areas including finance, advanced accounting, entrepreneurship management, and international business. Bryan's weeklong study-abroad programs in Brazil and Germany are another great perk. They allow students to tour cultural and business centers and attend roundtable discussions with business leaders and professors. If you want more substantial experience overseas, semester-long exchange programs with over 40 institutions around the world are also available.

UNCG's "efficient and accommodating" administration reportedly runs the school "very well." The MBAs here also think quite highly of their professors and the "non-tenured professionals" who teach many elective courses. "The fact that I have access to this quality of faculty at a reasonably priced school is fantastic," beams one impressed student. Outside of class, professors are "willing to help either through phone calls or through scheduled meetings."

Facilities are hit or miss. The wireless network is very good and the school's cafe "provides an excellent area to study and meet with other students." The library is certainly adequate. "The main business building is a little dated," though." "Most classrooms are antiquated and need to be upgraded with outlets for laptops." The school is in the process of renovations.

Career and Placement

UNCG has a "good reputation" in the region and career prospects are reportedly pretty bright. "The setting in Greensboro has been changing over the past few years," explains one student. "More people are moving in and more jobs are available." Career Services is "excellent" and "very proactive in providing opportunities to network with local employers." "Evaluation, coaching, and mentoring programs" are readily available. A summer internship program allows day students to gain practical experience and, perhaps more importantly, get paid. There are several on-campus recruiting events and a lot of the MBA social events include alumni, who help tremendously with networking. Also, Bryan's unique targeted recruiting service works to actively partner with local employers and promote current students for their specific needs. Companies that employ Bryan MBAs include Volvo, Lincoln Financial Group, Wachovia, BB&T, Hanes, Tyco Electronics, American Express, Deloitte, AT&T, IBM, and Moses Cone Health System.

ADMISSIONS CONTACT: THOMAS KELLER, DIRECTOR OF MARKETING
ADDRESS: PO BOX 26165 GREENSBORO, NC 27402-6165 UNITED STATES
PHONE: 336-334-5390 • FAX: 336-334-4209
E-MAIL: MYBRYANMBA@UNCG.EDU • WEBSITE: WWW.MYBRYANMBA.COM

Student Life and Environment

In the smaller day program at UNCG, students are usually "only a few years out of undergrad" and they average one or two years of work experience. Evening students are an older crowd. Their average age is 31 and they have around eight years of career experience. Students here describe themselves as "smart, driven," and "extremely motivated" "business folks who want to climb the corporate ladder." There is a large group of international students and the population as a whole comes "from various lifestyles" and "a wide array of backgrounds and disciplines." The variety of educational and working backgrounds "leads to very interesting and stimulating classroom discussions."

The first week for day students is a thorough four-day orientation. UNCG even calls it "Boot Camp." Day students are "energetic" and often more "idealistic" than their peers in the evening program. They also tend to have stronger bonds with each other. "There is essentially no campus life among the students" in the evening program. For them, "life outside of school is totally separate." "Everyone just wants to go to class, get done, and go home. After already working eight hours then taking a three-hour class everyone is tired."

The surrounding midsize city of Greensboro is very affordable and it's calm enough to be "a good place for studying." If you prefer to socialize, though, Greensboro is also full of entertainment options. The downtown area boasts a good number of lively bars and restaurants and the city is part of North Carolina's Triad metropolitan region (which also includes High Point and Winston-Salem), home to 11 colleges and universities. The location provides easy access to mountain getaways, golf, and North Carolina's two largest cities, Charlotte (a major banking center) and Raleigh (the state capital).

Admissions

You have to submit transcripts, a GMAT score, three letters of recommendation, and an essay. You also must have completed college algebra and you need to demonstrate some basic computer literacy. Previous work experience is preferred but not required. International students must also submit TOEFL scores and an affidavit of financial support. UNCG states on its website that the lowest GMAT score it will accept is a 550 and the lowest grade-point average it will accept is a 3.0. Don't take that as gospel, though. At least some successful applicants fail to meet those benchmarks. It's also worth noting that fellowships, scholarships, and graduate assistantships are available to defray the already low tuition.

FINANCIAL FACTS

Annual tuition (in-state/ out-of-state)	$4,522/$15,572
Fees	$1,571
Cost of books	$1,200
Room & board (on/off-campus)	$5,297/$8,066
% of students receiving aid	40
% of first-year students receiving aid	48
% of students receiving grants	28
Average grant	$6,000

ADMISSIONS

Admissions Selectivity Rating	91
# of applications received	170
% applicants accepted	32
% acceptees attending	95
Average GMAT	572
Range of GMAT	530–600
Average GPA	3.34
TOEFL required of international students	Yes
Minimum TOEFL (paper/computer)	550/213
Application fee	$45
International application fee	$45
Regular application deadline	7/1
Regular notification	rolling
Deferment available	Yes
Maximum length of deferment	1 year
Transfer students accepted	Yes
Transfer application policy They must be in good standing at a fellow AACSB Accredited MBA Program and may transfer no more than 12 Semester credit hours of approved coursework	
Non-fall admissions	Yes
Need-blind admissions	Yes

Applicants Also Look At

Appalachian State University, North Carolina State University, The University of North Carolina at Chapel Hill, Wake Forest University.

EMPLOYMENT PROFILE	
Career Rating	83

THE UNIVERSITY OF NORTH CAROLINA AT WILMINGTON
CAMERON SCHOOL OF BUSINESS

Academics

The Cameron School of Business at UNC Wilmington offers a part-time evening and weekend program leading toward the MBA. In the fall of 2007, the school began a full-time international degree program, which offers dual degrees with several universities in Spain, Russia, and other countries. It requires residency abroad, and is open to those with undergraduate degrees in business.

Students from any undergraduate background may enroll in the evening MBA program, and in recent years approximately 70 percent of those students have come from academic fields other than business. "The administration understands the pressures involved with full-time employment and classwork," one student says. "The administration and professors are willing to help ease this stress, but still require a high level of participation and learning."

Though the program is part-time in the sense that classes meet in the evenings and on weekends, Cameron requires courses to be taken in sequence, and it employs an integrated-project model. Students are assigned to groups to work on exercises and practical presentations, and "Students will generally hang around after class meetings with assigned work teams to discuss upcoming projects or deadlines."

The evening MBA program consists of 49 credit hours, which, with the exception of three courses in special topics toward the end of the program, are mainly in prescribed courses. These include subjects such as macroeconomics, business law, and behavioral management. Communications, decision making, teamwork, organizational change, and ethics are stressed in cross-disciplinary activities, which require students to integrate the skills they're learning, both in strategic exercises and real-world problems posed by local business partners.

Special topics may include study in new product development, technology management, investment analysis, and strategic information systems. An executive challenge situation designed to test students' leadership skills is required near the end of the course work.

"Practical application with actual business" is a strength of the curriculum at Cameron, students say, and "Projects with local small businesses are . . . very beneficial in helping the students tie all the classroom materials in to real-life situations." But one student complains that "the quality of instruction has ranged from excellent to awful." Several students echo the concern that "at times, especially for experienced students, some professors still act like they are teaching undergrads," although, "Overall, the professors are very helpful and accessible."

One student says that "the program is small enough for faculty to really care about you and your success, as opposed to some of the larger schools that appear to be about status alone." Many feel the administration could benefit from some reorganization, but "The MBA program administrators can best be typified as supportive and student focused," and that "the program is evolving and changing as the needs of students change."

Career and Placement

There is a dedicated Career Services representative at the school of business at UNCW, and MBA students may also use the general university's career services, such as online databases, career workshops, and career fairs. Almost all Cameron students work full-time while earning their degrees, and many are sponsored by local employers. Those who do seek career assistance would like "more interaction with the business community to

ADMISSIONS CONTACT: KATHY ERICKSON, GRADUATE PROGRAMS ADMINISTRATOR
ADDRESS: 601 SOUTH COLLEGE ROAD WILMINGTON, NC 28403-5920 UNITED STATES
PHONE: 910-962-3903 • FAX: 910-962-3815
E-MAIL: GRADSTUDIES@UNCW.EDU • WEBSITE: WWW.CSB.UNCW.EDU/MBA/INDEX.STM

assist in job placement," and a Career Services Office that is "more ambitious about marketing itself" to business.

General Electric Company, Corning, International Paper, New Hanover Regional Medical Center, the U.S. Coast Guard, United Parcel Service, and First Citizens Bank are among the employers who have recruited Cameron School graduates.

Student Life and Environment

Students at the Cameron School of Business seem to appreciate both town and gown, not surprising as most work full-time in the region.

"Wilmington is a great city for families," one man points out, and "There is plenty of life outside of schoolwork here." Another student praises the "friendly people, beautiful beaches, and [the] tons of restaurants and things to do." As one student explains, "Learning at UNCW takes place in a very laid-back atmosphere." Another notes that although "lacking in racial diversity, there is strong diversity in experience levels, age, and industry segment, coupled with an extremely collaborative and supportive environment." Life in the program isn't "cutthroat . . . everyone wants to see each other do well and graduate."

What would students like to see improved? "Job placement, parking, class-time child care!" is the resounding cry, in addition to "more [academic] specialization. The program is currently a general MBA program." But students agree with their classmate who says "UNCW offers a good 2-year evening program in a great area, with a beautiful campus, and a fine reputation."

Admissions

GMAT scores, transcripts, letters of recommendation, a resume, TOEFL scores for those who need prove fluency in English, and a year of work experience are required for admission to the MBA program at UNCW. The program also requires a three-semester hour course in introductory calculus, or its equivalent, and while the school would prefer that students have this before admission, arrangements can be made to take the classes during the student's first term at the university. In 2006 the average GMAT score for those accepted was 555, and the average GPA was 3.50; students had more than 6 years of work experience on average.

FINANCIAL FACTS

Annual tuition (in-state/ out-of-state)	$4,696/$9,267

ADMISSIONS

Admissions Selectivity Rating	88
# of applications received	147
% applicants accepted	44
% acceptees attending	92
Average GMAT	555
Average GPA	3.5
TOEFL required of international students	Yes
Minimum TOEFL (paper/computer)	500/213
Application fee	$45
International application fee	$45
Regular application deadline	2/1
Regular notification	Rolling
Deferment available	Yes
Maximum length of deferment	1 year
Non-fall admissions	Yes

THE UNIVERSITY OF NORTH DAKOTA
COLLEGE OF BUSINESS AND PUBLIC ADMINISTRATION

Academics

With just 100 students in the graduate program, University of North Dakota is a convenient and affordable place to get an MBA, while also benefiting from an intimate, student-friendly atmosphere. Incorporating a practical perspective into classroom material, "UND is very focused on offering students the resources they need for a flourishing future." Most professors "have great experiences prior to their professorships and do an excellent job of sharing these experiences" within their students. Thanks to the low enrollment, it's easy to make contact with the school's faculty and staff, and "class sizes are small enough, allowing students to interact more openly." What's more, "the professors are always accessible and all have an open-door policy with a positive attitude when someone interrupts their research." A satisfied student shares, "I feel that a number of my professors are great mentors and will be lifelong connections." In the same vein, students say administrators are friendly, accessible, and efficient, and "academic advisers are more than happy to assist you" with questions about coursework and schedules.

Located in the middle of a large agricultural zone, the professors at UND have an understanding of both rural business and big-city business, which makes UND somewhat unique among business schools. The curriculum also focuses on business technology—a focus that is supported by the school's state-of-the-art classroom facilities, a marketing research center, and modern computer labs. The North Dakota MBA program consists of 32 credit hours, with the opportunity to focus your studies through a concentration in accounting or international business. For students enrolled in the undergraduate business program, UND allows them to begin coursework toward an MBA during their last two years of undergraduate studies. Therefore, these students have the opportunity to earn a bachelor's degree and an MBA in just five years. However, the school also goes out of its way to cater to working professionals, who have quite different scheduling, personal, and academic needs than recent graduates. In fact, convenience is central to the University of North Dakota experience, and because classes are offered during the day, in the evening, or via the distance education, they "can easily be fit into your busy schedule," no matter what you do.

Career and Placement

Career Services at University of North Dakota helps coordinate job and internship placements for the UND undergraduate and graduate community. Among other functions, the office offers career counseling and professional development workshops, an annual career fair each fall, and on-campus interview sessions throughout the spring. Some MBA students feel that the College of Business and Public Administration might improve its services by hosting "its own career fair, separate from the campus career fair," which would help MBA candidates link up with corporations specifically seeking their skill set.

After graduation, about 20 percent of MBA students take jobs in manufacturing and another 20 percent take military jobs. The third most popular career field is financial services, which attracts roughly 12 percent of graduates. The placement percentage for the entire business school (undergraduate and graduate combined) is 97.2 percent. Current UND alumni hold top positions at Coca-Cola, Bank of America, General Motors Defense, Modern Information Systems, Nodak Electric Cooperative, Legacy Consulting, and Alerus Financial ND.

ADMISSIONS CONTACT: MICHELLE GARSKE, GRADUATE ADVISOR/ACCREDITATION COORDINATOR
ADDRESS: 293 CENTENNIAL DRIVE, STOP 8098 GRAND FORKS, ND 58202 UNITED STATES
PHONE: 701-777-4853 • FAX: 701-777-2019
E-MAIL: MBA@UND.NODAK.EDU • WEBSITE: WWW.BUSINESS.UND.EDU/MBA

Student Life and Environment

The largest university in the region, University of North Dakota offers a pleasant, collegiate atmosphere to a student population of 13,000 undergraduate and graduate students. While many commute, graduate business students have the option of living in the school's nice apartments or dormitories, and all graduate students enjoy access to the university's myriad facilities; in particular, the "wellness center gym facility is outstanding." Students are friendly with one another, and the "social atmosphere contributes to the great learning environment at UND." For those who'd like to participate, the MBA Student Association hosts weekly roundtable discussions and social activities. In addition, if you want to blow off steam, UND students "take pride in our hockey team" and games are well attended.

The population of Grand Forks numbers just under 100,000, which is large enough to create a substantial business and cultural community, while at the same time maintaining a more laid-back, small-town feeling. A student explains: "The life in Grand Forks is not as diversified as that in the big cities. However, we have good social events and networks with the companies around Midwest." An international student adds that North Dakota is "a safe and easygoing place where foreign students can easily concentrate on their studies and be familiar with American culture."

Admissions

For admission to the graduate business program, University of North Dakota requires a minimum undergraduate GPA of 3.0 and a minimum GMAT score of 500. Students who fail to meet the minimum admissions standards but show potential for success may be admitted on a provisional basis if their GMAT score is high enough to balance out a lower GPA, or vice versa. However, under no circumstance will a student with a GMAT score below 450 be admitted to the program. In recent years, the average GMAT score for full-time students was 511 and the average GMAT score for part-time students was 545.

FINANCIAL FACTS

Annual tuition (in-state/out-of-state)	$6,510/$15,537
Fees	$553
Cost of books	$3,600
Room & board (on-campus)	$3,980
% of students receiving aid	14
% of first-year students receiving aid	48
% of students receiving loans	6
% of students receiving grants	2
Average award package	$10,552
Average grant	$3,924

ADMISSIONS

Admissions Selectivity Rating	77
# of applications received	37
% applicants accepted	84
% acceptees attending	71
Average GMAT	525
Range of GMAT	420–700
Average GPA	3.17
TOEFL required of international students	Yes
Minimum TOEFL (paper/computer)	550/213
Application fee	$35
International application fee	$35
Regular application deadline	Rolling
Regular notification	Rolling
Deferment available	Yes
Maximum length of deferment	1 year
Transfer students accepted	Yes
Transfer application policy	
Up to nine credits of approved coursework can be transferred.	
Non-fall admissions	Yes
Need-blind admissions	Yes

Applicants Also Look At
North Dakota State University,
University of Minnesota.

EMPLOYMENT PROFILE	
Career Rating	64

UNIVERSITY OF NORTH FLORIDA
COGGIN COLLEGE OF BUSINESS

Academics

Serving a diverse group of working professionals from the Jacksonville and North Florida region, students come to Coggin College of Business for its "excellent in-state tuition, convenience, and location." However, a Coggin education is more than just an efficient way to get a diploma in your hand. At this large college, class sizes are small and the teaching staff is knowledgeable and student-oriented. A current student says, "Professors are very committed to meeting students' needs. Overall [this] has been a very positive academic experience and [I] would enroll here again." In addition to the faculty, the "administration office is very committed to helping with school or personal issues." In particular, students point out the efforts of the school's "great president, who is looking to make the university grow."

For MBA students, UNF offers a general business degree, which can be tailored to a student's educational interests in a number of contemporary and traditional areas of concentration, including accounting, e-commerce, human resource management, finance, international business, construction management, and logistics. The school also operates a number of centers and institutes, as well as some unique curricular and extracurricular options. For example, the Osprey Financial Group is a student-managed investment fund, through which students can earn elective credits for their work researching and reporting on financial markets in support of the fund.

Coggin enrolls about 450 students in its MBA program, and 80 percent of the student body works full time while attending school. In fact, the program is specifically designed for working professionals and, to accommodate their needs, all MBA classes are taught one day a week, in the afternoon or evening. While the school caters to the working student, keep in mind that "the projects are quite time-consuming" and often require group work, so the decision to enroll should not be taken lightly. For those who can take time off from work (or are studying full time), the school also offers an excellent range of abroad programs through their partnerships with numerous universities in France, Germany, Belgium, China, Poland, and Sweden. Students may choose to participate in semester-long programs, or participate in a short-term study program at select universities.

In addition to the traditional MBA program, University of North Florida offers a unique Global MBA, in conjunction with four other international universities. This program allows students to mix traditional academics with residential experiences in the United States, China, Germany, and Poland. Global MBA participants join a cohort of about forty students, which spends a semester at a university in each of these four countries. Global MBA students add a unique dimension to the North Florida campus during their semester in Jacksonville. New cohort starts every fall.

Career and Placement

The Career Management Center serves Coggin students and alumni, offering services like career counseling, recruiting and networking events, resume assistance, and internship programs. The center also prints individual business cards for Coggin students.

While it serves the whole university, the Career Management Center hosts a number of networking events just for Coggin students. Companies who have attended previous events include: Adams & Harper P.A., Alluvion Staffing, ATS Executive Search, Bank of North Florida, CitiGroup, Client Focused Media, COACH, CSX, Crowley, Educational Tools, Inc., EverBank, Fidelity Investments, Fidelity National Information Services, GEICO, Henry Schein, IDEAL, LBA, Liberty Mutual, Merrill Lynch, Morgan Stanley,

ADMISSIONS CONTACT: KIERSTEN JARVIS, THE GRADUATE SCHOOL COORDINATOR
ADDRESS: 1 UNF DRIVE JACKSONVILLE, FL 32224-7699 UNITED STATES
PHONE: 904-620-1360 • FAX: 904-620-1362
E-MAIL: KIERSTEN.JARVIS@UNF.EDU • WEBSITE: WWW.UNF.EDU/COGGIN

MPS/Parker&Lynch, Northwestern Mutual Financial Network, PSS World Medical, Staples, State Farm, Tensolite Company, The Suddath Companies, Total Military Management, Trailer Bridge, VyStar Credit Union, Website Pros. Inc.

Student Life and Environment

University of North Florida's flexible scheduling and contemporary programs draw "people from a variety of backgrounds and with diverse experiences." There are "not many 'traditional' full-time MBA students and those who have limited work experience." Instead, most students are "focused professionals seeking an advanced degree sprinkled with some students coming directly from the undergraduate programs." In this serious environment, group work is a pleasure, since most students "are friendly and helpful and all will do their best to pull their own weight."

Coggin is "really a commuter school," where students arrive for classes in the evening then head home in the greater North Florida region. While they don't spend much time on campus, students nonetheless note that the "university has nice facilities" and a "comely" environment. Plus, the business school maintains an appealing "small-town atmosphere," where "you tend see students and professors you know a lot around campus." In addition to curricular activities, the business school brings students together for speakers, as well as academic and social clubs such as the Student Business Advisory Council, Toastmasters, Finance and Investment Society, Economics Society, and International Business Society.

Admissions

Admission to all programs, with the exception of the GlobalMBA, is based upon a candidate's undergraduate grade point average (GPA) and GMAT score. Currently, the average GMAT score for entering students is 520. The average age of an entering MBA candidate is 29 years old, with an average of three years of work experience. Admission for the Global MBA varies slightly, and includes a full set of prerequisites in each of the following seven areas: business law, financial accounting, corporate finance, macroeconomics, microeconomics, management, and marketing.

FINANCIAL FACTS

Annual tuition (in-state/ out-of-state)	$6,390/$20,583
Cost of books	$800
Room & board (on/off-campus)	$7,071/$10,398
% of students receiving aid	27
% of first-year students receiving aid	34
% of students receiving loans	88
% of students receiving grants	28
Average award package	$3,407
Average grant	$1,064

ADMISSIONS

Admissions Selectivity Rating	81
# of applications received	276
% applicants accepted	60
% acceptees attending	75
Average GMAT	527
Range of GMAT	480–560
Average GPA	3.15
TOEFL required of international students	Yes
Minimum TOEFL (paper/computer)	550/213
Application fee	$30
International application fee	$30
Regular application deadline	7/1
Regular notification	rolling
Deferment available	Yes
Maximum length of deferment	1 Semester
Transfer students accepted	Yes
Transfer application policy On a case by case basis	
Non-fall admissions	Yes
Need-blind admissions	Yes

EMPLOYMENT PROFILE

Career Rating	60*	Grads Employed by Function	% Avg. Salary
Primary Source of Full-time Job Acceptances		Finance	33 $48,125
School-facilitated activities	2 (11%)	Human Resources	13 $52,300
Graduate-facilitated activities	16 (89%)	Marketing	12 $37,300
		Operations	21 $49,800
		General Management	8 $43,500
		Other	13 $35,600

Top 5 Employers Hiring Grads
KPMG; CSX Transportation; PricewaterhouseCoopers; Deloitte; RSM McGladrey

University of Northern Iowa
College of Business Administration

GENERAL INFORMATION
Type of school	Public
Environment	Town
Academic calendar	Trimester

SURVEY SAYS...
Friendly students
Good peer network
Happy students
Solid preparation in:
General management
Teamwork

STUDENTS
Enrollment of parent institution	10,835
Enrollment of business school	57
% male/female	50/50
% out-of-state	50
% part-time	72
% international	50
Average age at entry	28
Average years work experience at entry	5

ACADEMICS
Academic Experience Rating	**89**
Student/faculty ratio	25:1
Profs interesting rating	88
Profs accessible rating	73
% female faculty	17
% minority faculty	19

Prominent Alumni
Nancy Aossey, CEO, International Medical Corporation; Mark Baldwin, CEO, Iowa Laser Technology; Kevin Lentz, Sr. VP, Cuna Mutual Insurance; Gary Rolling, President/CEO, J-Tec Associates, Inc.; Kyle Selberg, VP Marketing, Principal Financial Group.

Academics

Combining state-of-the-art facilities, "impossibly friendly" faculty, and a low, public school price tag, it's no wonder that University of Northern Iowa students feel theirs is "the best business program in the Midwest." A friendly environment is balanced with a high caliber of academics creating "a small-college feel and university opportunities" at UNI. Professors are "knowledgeable, efficient, friendly, concerned, creative, and provide a learning- and result-oriented atmosphere with as little psychological pressure as possible." One current student tells us, "Most of the professors are above standard academically speaking and are willing to help the students as much as possible." Another adds, "It's a great value and the faculty are very accessible. They are passionate about their work and strive to continually improve programs." On that note, the university is dedicated to offering course work that addresses current issues in business, and one of the school's greatest strengths is "the diversity of the classes and the desire to incorporate current issues and trends into the various classes."

Committed to providing a thorough but expeditious education, the University of Northern Iowa's curriculum can be tailored to fit the objectives and needs of each individual student. In fact, before beginning the program, every student's educational and professional background is evaluated to determine which foundational courses he/she will be required to take in order to complete the degree. As a result, students entering the program with business experience may be able to complete the program more quickly, and thereby save on tuition costs. In this and other ways, the school's "great and efficient administration," displays its' commitment to students' needs. By all accounts, "the school is running smoothly" and "the administration is very active in making sure all students have the resources they need to succeed in the program and beyond."

All courses in the graduate program at the University of Northern Iowa are offered in the evening to accommodate students who work full-time or who wish to pursue an internship during business hours. Of UNI master's students, "The majority are working or have work experience" and are able to directly integrate their course work into their current positions. In terms of practical, hands-on components, the MBA at UNI culminates in the business capstone experience, a one-credit course in which the student serves as a consultant to a local company under the advisement of a UNI faculty member. In addition, students may gain real-world experience through one of the school's two-week international programs in Hong Kong and Paris, France.

Career and Placement

In the Cedar Falls area, UNI is "well known for its finance and business degrees," giving graduates a step-up in the local market. For extra support, the Academic Advising and Career Services Center at UNI offers workshops, resume reviews, cover letter advice, mock interviews, and Internet resources for job seekers. Recruiters visit the campus throughout the year, and the school also hosts the Fall Career Fair Day and the Spring Job and Internship Fair for job seekers.

Student Life and Environment

UNI's MBA Program offers "excellent facilities and technology," to undergraduate and graduate business students. A surprisingly diverse community, "MBA students at the University of Northern Iowa represent a wide variety of ethnic, cultural and educational backgrounds, as well as a breadth of future endeavors. The diversity helps to create a dynamic and intellectually challenging learning environment." As one current student enthuses: "I was amazed at the diversity of students in the MBA program (in regards to) marital status, age, ethnicity, and work experience. This was great for classroom discussion." Despite the diversity within the student body, everyone finds a place, as "Life at the University of Northern Iowa is well suited to a variety of needs."

Outside the classroom, "There are a wide variety of activities offered through the university at large. In addition, there are a large number of extracurricular and social activities offered." Students note that "the athletic teams are spectacular at UNI" and a source of pride for the whole school community. A number of academic organizations are represented on campus, including the Economics Club, Accounting Club, American Marketing Association, as well as honor organizations such as Beta Gamma Sigma and Mu Kappa Tau, among others. However, the level of extracurricular involvement is laid back and entirely up to each student. "If a student is interested in community or campus involvement, there are numerous groups to join. If the student would rather not be involved, there is no pressure to join extracurricular activities."

Admissions

Applicants to the University of Northern Iowa must submit official GMAT scores, transcripts from all colleges and universities attended, and three essays that address the applicant's professional and personal background. The Admissions Committee selects applicants based on their communication skills, demonstrated leadership potential, intellectual capability, and academic success during undergraduate and graduate work. The Admissions Committee considers each applicant's particular accomplishments individually, and admissions essays are strongly weighted in a decision. Applicants must have a bachelor's degree from an accredited university or college. In the past three years, successful applicants have submitted GMAT scores averaging 560–580.

FINANCIAL FACTS

Annual tuition (in-state/ out-of-state)	$6,246/$14,554
Fees	$838
Cost of books	$2,000
Room & board	$6,800

ADMISSIONS

Admissions Selectivity Rating	**85**
# of applications received	51
% applicants accepted	59
% acceptees attending	93
Average GMAT	580
Range of GMAT	530–610
Average GPA	3.3
TOEFL required of international students	Yes
Minimum TOEFL (paper/computer)	600/250
Application fee	$30
International application fee	$50
Regular application deadline	7/20
Regular notification	rolling
Deferment available	Yes
Maximum length of deferment	1 year
Transfer students accepted	Yes
Transfer application policy Students may transfer up to 11 hours of AACSB accredited graduate credit.	
Non-fall admissions	Yes
Need-blind admissions	Yes

Applicants Also Look At

Iowa State University, University of Iowa, University of Minnesota, University of Nebraska—Lincoln.

EMPLOYMENT PROFILE	
Career Rating	**94**
Percent employed	100

UNIVERSITY OF NOTRE DAME
MENDOZA COLLEGE OF BUSINESS

Academics

Students come the University of Notre Dame to become part of the "Notre Dame family," and few leave disappointed; the MBA program at the Mendoza College of Business fosters a strong sense of community that, coupled with the campus-wide school spirit, quickly makes Notre Dame feel like home. Add "outstanding professor-student interaction" and "great potential for alumni networking" and you understand why student satisfaction levels are so high here.

The Mendoza MBA program "excels at providing an overall business understanding," students tell us. The school offers a 2-year full-time program that "is perfect for non-business undergraduate majors to gain a well-rounded understanding of business fundamentals," as well as a 1-year program for those with exceptionally strong business backgrounds. Students say, "Ethics is a hallmark of the school and it can be seen in every course," and "The school's reputation for producing ethical graduates is more important in recent years than ever before."

Mendoza implemented a modular curriculum a few years back, and "The 2007 class is the first to complete our entire course work under the current 'module' system. The module system will allow Notre Dame MBAs to be better prepared than were previous classes. Although "There was some negative press after the transition," "now that the transition is completed, Notre Dame will move quickly [back] up the rankings." The faculty here "is top-notch." Their research, publications, work experience, and generally great personalities inspire confidence in their ability to prepare [students] for the business world."

Career and Placement

"The majority of recruiting is Midwest based" at Notre Dame, and while some complain about the dearth of New York finance-sector recruiters, most students feel that "the Career Office does a good job of locating companies from various regions." Mendoza MBAs recognize that "our small class size hinders our ability to get a large selection of companies from each region, but they are represented." However, "The situation is greatly improving, with some bulge-bracket and many middle-market banks already recruiting on campus. This will improve over time as the school moves toward its long-term mission of improving rank."

Of course, Notre Dame's storied alumni network helps with placement. Students tell us that "the Career Development Office recently made it easier for current MBA students to get in contact with alumni. Prior to this, it was a very prolonged process that involved Career Development responding to individual student's requests for alumni contact information in their respective field." These contacts can be invaluable. As one student reports, "I went to a conference with several classmates for the weekend where we met a ND alum recruiter for a major corporation. . . .We were invited over his house to talk and have a couple of drinks. This is what you get at Notre Dame: family. And our family is everywhere in every kind of position." No wonder students brag that "becoming a member of the alumni network is worth more than the cost of tuition."

Companies recruiting Mendoza MBAs include: Avaya Systems, DaimlerChrysler, Deloitte Touche Tohmatsu, Ernst & Young, Ford Motor Company, GE, Hewlett-Packard, Honeywell, IBM, Intel, Johnson & Johnson, Kraft Foods, PricewaterhouseCoopers, SAP, Sandler O'Neill, Sprint, Textron Financial, The Gallup Organization, Western & Southern Life, and Whirlpool.

Student Life and Environment

There's no doubt that Notre Dame is a very social campus, but the extent to which MBAs can partake in that social life depends on whether they're in their first or second year of the program. First year is "very difficult" with a massive workload. Many students "spend twice as much time on schoolwork" during their first year, and find it difficult to "juggle [classes] with career pursuits." Those who can carve out some leisure time agree that "Notre Dame has a culture that is contagious! It's not hard to keep yourself busy with a broad range of activities, whether it's class, a group meeting, intramural game, community-service event, or a football tailgate. There's never a dull moment." Football unites the campus and provides more than mere entertainment; it also "lures large corporations for networking events." Also, alumni return to campus for football games "for years after graduation and usually for life." Hometown South Bend is a small town, with only a "few good places to go out." The "students make up for it, though. We host a lot of social gatherings."

Mendoza MBAs benefit from "a strong esprit de corps" built on team projects and "an ethical foundation that is reinforced constantly so that it actually has an effect." Most are "married, with families and children, and have been working in industry for 7 to 10 years." They represent "more diverse backgrounds than some of the 'big' schools back East, meaning we have folks from engineering, the public sector, and other nontraditional or non-business backgrounds. These are very sharp people who may have had the 'wrong' undergrad pedigree but are every bit as bright as those at any b-school anywhere."

Admissions

Applicants to Mendoza's 2-year MBA program must provide the Admissions Department with all of the following: proof of an undergraduate degree from an accredited college or university; official transcript(s); GMAT scores; a current resume; three essays (topics provided by school); and two letters of recommendation. Transcripts and/or resume must demonstrate familiarity with basic quantitative processes and accounting methods. A background in statistics is strongly recommended. International students must also provide TOEFL scores and visa documentation. Applicants to the 1-year program must present academic transcripts showing successful completion of 6 credit hours each of mathematics, accounting, and economics and 3 credit hours each of marketing and MIS. All applicants must have at least 2 years of meaningful work experience.

FINANCIAL FACTS

Annual tuition	$35,490
Fees	$2,025
Cost of books	$1,300
Room & board (on-campus)	$7,650
% of students receiving aid	84
% of first-year students receiving aid	85
% of students receiving loans	64
% of students receiving grants	64
Average award package	$41,569
Average grant	$17,753
Average student loan debt	$57,874

ADMISSIONS

Admissions Selectivity Rating	91
# of applications received	664
% applicants accepted	44
% acceptees attending	44
Average GMAT	673
Range of GMAT	590–740
Average GPA	3.2
TOEFL required of international students	Yes
Minimum TOEFL (paper/computer)	600/250
Application fee	$100
International application fee	$100
Application Deadline/Notification	
Round 1:	11/15 / 12/15
Round 2:	1/15 / 2/15
Round 3:	3/15 / 4/15
Round 4:	5/1 / 6/1
Early decision program?	Yes
ED Deadline/ Notification	11/15 / 12/15
Deferment available	Yes
Maximum length of deferment	1 year
Non-fall admissions	Yes
Need-blind admissions	Yes

Applicants Also Look At

Georgetown University, Northwestern University, The University of Texas at Austin, University of Michigan, Vanderbilt University.

EMPLOYMENT PROFILE

Career Rating	88	Grads Employed by Function	% Avg. Salary
Primary Source of Full-time Job Acceptances		Finance	39 $82,312
School-facilitated activities	89 (62%)	Marketing	17 $87,542
Graduate-facilitated activities	30 (21%)	MIS	1 NR
Unknown	25 (17%)	Operations	5 $80,786
Average base starting salary	$86,000	Consulting	17 $86,050
Percent employed	98	General Management	9 $80,046
		Other	12 $94,025

Top 5 Employers Hiring Grads
IBM; United Airlines; Huron Consulting; OfficeMax; Whirlpool

UNIVERSITY OF OKLAHOMA
MICHAEL F. PRICE COLLEGE OF BUSINESS

Academics

With "great facilities," a low student/faculty ratio, and "a connection to the Oklahoma City market," the Price College of Business at the University of Oklahoma "offers great value" to Midwestern students, particularly if they're interested in working in the energy or banking sectors. Students tell us that Price's size is a good fit for all, offering "the feel of a very small school with small classes fostering interaction with professors, [while] at the same time you are attending a large university with great traditions, outstanding athletic programs, and a very strong and loyal network of alumni across the United States."

Price offers both a full-time MBA and a part-time professional MBA with evening classes held from 6:00 P.M. to 9:40 P.M. Monday through Thursday. Both programs offer concentrations in entrepreneurship, corporate finance, investment management, business process integration, risk management, management information systems, and supply chain management. Students speak especially highly of the school's offerings in entrepreneurship, finance, and MIS.

MBAs here report that "the faculty is very intelligent, but many are focused on research." As one student puts it, "A lot of the teachers for required courses are too 'academic.' The entrepreneurship teachers are the exception. They give real-life lessons and bring great personal experience to the students." Another student adds, "Some departments are better than others at integrating industry into teaching. The best provide students opportunities to work on projects with local companies as well as major corporate sponsors for practical concept application." On a positive note, "The staff and resources provided at the University of Oklahoma are unmatched! They are dedicated in equipping students with information and knowledge that will help provide opportunities that aren't found elsewhere." Students also tell us that "the business communication center is wonderful."

Career and Placement

Primary responsibility for career counseling and placement services falls to the MBA Student Support Center at Price. The center provides one-on-one mentoring, assistance with resume preparation and interviewing skills, and contacts with corporate recruiters. Students tell us that "our school has a very strong alumni network that cares about current and past students" and that the school does a good job of attracting recruiters in the field of finance; other areas are not as well served, they complain. One MBA warns, "Any students not interested in working in finance for an oil company or local bank should not count on the student support center in their job search." Summer internship programs like the Price Scholars program (which sends students to New York City) and International Internship programs "are good, but relatively few students are selected, and the others are really left to fend for themselves."

Employers who most frequently hire Price MBAs include: ExxonMobil, Bank of Oklahoma, OGE, RiskMetrics, ConocoPhillips Company, SBC, American Airlines, Devon Energy, Schlumberger, KPMG International, Ernst & Young, and Liquidnet.

Student Life and Environment

The Price MBA program "is housed in the new wing of the business school, a facility nicer than those of most Fortune 500 companies. The classrooms have computers, dual projectors, [and] DVD and audio systems." As if all that wasn't enough, "The business school is right next to the football stadium, which provides covered parking for faculty and students. Graduate student housing is brand new, and the Student Fitness Center is huge and has all of the latest equipment." Extracurricular life here is subdued; part-

ADMISSIONS CONTACT: GINA AMUNDSON, DIRECTOR OF GRADUATE PROGRAMS
ADDRESS: 1003 ASP AVENUE, PRICE HALL, SUITE 1040 NORMAN, OK 73019-4302 UNITED STATES
PHONE: 405-325-4107 • FAX: 405-325-7753
E-MAIL: GAMUNDSON@OU.EDU • WEBSITE: PRICE.OU.EDU/MBA

timers and full-timers with jobs tell us that the MBA program is "round the clock," with "not much time for extracurricular activities." Many here make time for football, because "Everybody here loves it. It brings people and the town together."

Students tell us that OU's campus "is beautiful and well manicured" and in the process of a major revitalization. "I have lost count of the number of construction projects due to donations," writes one student. OU is located in Norman, "a great town: small but not too small. People are friendly, and the living expenses are very low. It is true that the town dies out during the summer, but as an MBA student you will hold an internship, and you probably will not be in town." Furthermore, Norman is "just 20 minutes from downtown Oklahoma City."

Admissions

Applicants to the Price MBA program must submit the following materials to the Office of Admissions and Records: an application for admission to the university; an official transcript from every undergraduate and graduate institution attended; and, for international applicants, a financial statement as well as an official TOEFL score report (minimum score: 213, computer-based test; 550, paper-based test) if English is not their first language. In addition, all applicants must also submit the following materials to the MBA Admissions Office: a completed supplemental application for graduate study in business; an official score report for the GMAT; a current resume; a personal statement of career and educational goals; and three letters of recommendation. Applicants to the full-time program must have an undergraduate GPA of at least 3.2 and a GMAT score of at least 600. Two years of work experience is preferred but not required.

FINANCIAL FACTS

Annual tuition (in-state/ out-of-state)	$4,752/$17,094
Fees (in-state/ out-of-state)	$4,830/$6,088
Cost of books	$1,209
Room & board	$7,654

ADMISSIONS

Admissions Selectivity Rating	**81**
# of applications received	89
% applicants accepted	72
% acceptees attending	67
Average GMAT	596
Range of GMAT	550–635
Average GPA	3.42
TOEFL required of international students	Yes
Minimum TOEFL (paper/computer)	600/250
Application fee	$40
International application fee	$90
Regular application deadline	7/1
Regular notification	Rolling
Deferment available	Yes
Maximum length of deferment	1 year
Transfer students accepted	Yes
Transfer application policy Students may transfer into our PT MBA program from other AACSB accredited institutions.	
Need-blind admissions	Yes

Applicants Also Look At

Oklahoma State University, Texas A&M University—College Station, The University of Texas at Austin.

EMPLOYMENT PROFILE

Career Rating	86	Grads Employed by Function	% Avg. Salary
Primary Source of Full-time Job Acceptances		Finance	30 $82,850
School-facilitated activities	12 (55%)	Human Resources	4 $65,000
Graduate-facilitated activities	10 (45%)	Marketing	4 $65,000
Average base starting salary	$71,833	MIS	13 $65,000
Percent employed	97	Operations	26 $60,000
		Consulting	13 $70,500
		General Management	4 $55,000
		Other	6 $77,000

Top 5 Employers Hiring Grads
KPMG; UBS; RiskMetrics; Raytheon; Shell

UNIVERSITY OF OREGON
CHARLES H. LUNDQUIST COLLEGE OF BUSINESS

Academics

A green-oriented, left-coast business program in the pretty city of Eugene, University of Oregon offers a small but diverse MBA program at a low, public school price. The location and regional reputation are among the school's most attractive features, although many students say they chose Oregon because they wanted to study sustainable business or participate in "one of the best sports business programs nationally."

No matter what your field of interest, Oregon's extensive core curriculum ensures that every student receives a strong foundation in the quantitative principles of business. During the first year, full-time MBA students also participate in the Strategic Planning Project over the course of two terms. Through this experiential learning program, small groups of Oregon students work as consultants to major Northwest businesses, including such big names as Adidas, Amazon.com, Hewlett Packard, and Intel.

After finishing the core curriculum, students take elective coursework, with the option of focusing their studies in accounting/financial analysis, innovation/entrepreneurship, finance/securities analysis, marketing, sports business, or sustainable supply chain management. Your academic experience will depend on your field of study; however, the "bright and accessible" teaching staff gets high marks in almost every area. However, with small, intensive classes, professors "don't let you just sit back and take in the class to float through. They expect you to participate, make presentations, and contribute." Despite the challenges of the curriculum, "a collaborative environment is fostered to breed the entrepreneurial spirit." A second-year student explains, "We encourage competition in the classroom and on the field but collaborative learning continues right up until exam time."

An extraordinarily pleasant campus atmosphere, "each classroom is high tech" and "the facilities are fantastic and enhance the learning in countless ways." With numerous research centers and resources, students assure us, "if you want to learn about something, you can find a resource to learn it." To give one example, "the entrepreneurship center gives students access to a breadth of resources and contacts as well as numerous opportunities for additional external education experiences."

Career and Placement

When it's time to begin the job hunt, University of Oregon students benefit from the efforts of the school's active career service center and "strong reputation in Seattle, Portland and San Francisco." Due to the school's small-town "location and the program's small size, on-campus recruiting is virtually nonexistent." However, "the career services office is fantastic about organizing company visits in Portland, Seattle, and San Francisco, as well as providing shuttle service to MBA career fairs held in Portland for programs throughout the Pacific Northwest." In addition, the Ducks have a great many loyal graduates, and "the alumni are always willing to help current students." Beyond the local offerings, the school hosts "a networking trip to New York City for students in the sports marketing program."

The average salary for the 2006 graduating class was $59,073, with a range from $30,000 to $120,000. However, U of O students point out that many students prefer to take their "dream job" in sports for a lower income, or plan to work in nonprofit areas, which can make entering salaries look lower for Oregon graduates than for graduates of other schools. In fact, they assure us that Oregon graduates are highly competitive and that "there are more jobs available than there are MBA candidates." A second-year student confides, "Specifically for accounting, recruiting is amazing! All Big 4 visit almost monthly, many regional and local firms are just as competitive in recruiting."

ADMISSIONS CONTACT: PERRI McGEE, ADMISSIONS ASSISTANT
ADDRESS: 1208 UNIVERSITY OF OREGON EUGENE, OR 97403-1208 UNITED STATES
PHONE: 541-346-1462 • FAX: 541-346-0073
E-MAIL: INFO@OREGONMBA.COM • WEBSITE: WWW.OREGONMBA.COM

Student Life and Environment

At University of Oregon, you'll find a slew of young recent graduates, as well as a "slightly older, 30-plus crowd, who have more experience" in the workplace. Old or young, married or single, everyone remarks on the business school's incredibly collegial atmosphere. With fewer than 200 students in the graduate business programs (and just over 100 pursuing an MBA), "the small class sizes allow the student to develop long-lasting friendships and future networking opportunities."

When it comes to social life, you can choose your own adventure at the University of Oregon. Depending on your lifestyle, "you can strictly stay to school work and use your free time to yourself, or you can enter many clubs and groups and consume your time within those." To connect with classmates, "the program offers weekly social activities for its students and the B-school and law school often have social activities together." In addition, the Ducks have "a strong athletics program so football and basketball seasons are fun." Older students note that the "school is very supportive of married students and family life," and spouses are welcome to join in campus activities, such as intramural sports.

Around Eugene, "housing is convenient and affordable," and "public transportation is everywhere (lots of free buses for students)." Of particular note, outdoor activities are plentiful, as "skiing is only a short drive away, the coast is within two hours, running trails can be found all over town and there are great places to go hiking."

Admissions

To be accepted to the MBA program at the University of Oregon, students must have a minimum GMAT score of 600 and a minimum 3.0 GPA on a 4.0 scale. However, when making an admissions decision, this small school considers factors beyond the numbers, examining the quality of an applicant's leadership and professional experiences, the rigorousness of their undergraduate curriculum, letters of recommendation, and interview feedback.

FINANCIAL FACTS

Annual tuition (in-state/ out-of-state)	$11,592/$16,344
Fees	$1,950
Cost of books	$1,050
Room & board (on/off-campus)	$10,880/$12,445
% of students receiving aid	69
% of first-year students receiving aid	71
% of students receiving loans	53
% of students receiving grants	41
Average award package	$23,195
Average grant	$12,368
Average student loan debt	$22,637

ADMISSIONS

Admissions Selectivity Rating	86
# of applications received	143
% applicants accepted	64
% acceptees attending	64
Average GMAT	626
Range of GMAT	600–660
Average GPA	3.3
TOEFL required of international students	Yes
Minimum TOEFL (paper/computer)	600/250
Application fee	$50
International application fee	$50
Regular application deadline	3/15
Regular notification	4/15
Application Deadline/Notification	
Round 1:	11/15 / 12/15
Round 2:	2/15 / 3/15
Round 3:	3/15 / 4/15
Early decision program?	Yes
ED Deadline/ Notification	11/15 / 12/15
Deferment available	Yes
Maximum length of deferment	1 year
Need-blind admissions	Yes

Applicants Also Look At

Arizona State University, Indiana University—Bloomington, Penn State University, University of Colorado at Boulder, University of Massachusetts—Amherst, University of Washington, University of Wisconsin—Madison.

EMPLOYMENT PROFILE

Career Rating	79	Grads Employed by Function	% Avg. Salary
Primary Source of Full-time Job Acceptances		Finance	17 $65,000
School-facilitated activities	11 (58%)	Marketing	52 $49,444
Graduate-facilitated activities	7 (37%)	MIS	5 $74,000
Unknown	1 (5%)	Consulting	11 $61,600
Average base starting salary	$55,718	General Management	5 $40,000
Percent employed	76	Other	5 $70,000

Top 5 Employers Hiring Grads
NIKE; Symantec; Relay Worldwide; Adidas; Washington Mutual

UNIVERSITY OF OTTAWA
TELFER SCHOOL OF MANAGEMENT

Academics

The MBA program at the University of Ottawa's Telfer School of Management is well integrated with top area employers. Students tell us, "The school has a very strong reputation with the federal government," as well as "close links with the Canadian high-tech industry. Ottawa is considered 'Silicon Valley North.'" MBAs here "interact with business leaders on a regular schedule, are encouraged to consult with governmental organizations, and never feel 'isolated in a classroom' from the real world." A "wide alumni network" also "provides excellent and current knowledge in all areas," keeping the program grounded in real-world issues and strategies.

Ottawa offers both a "12-month intensive" full-time program and a part-time program. Both teach "a broad, cross-functional curriculum" that places "a focus on leadership and performance management" and "reflects private and public sector influences." All students participate in a consulting project in which they "deal with a real project provided and coordinated by a real company, along with [a] senior professor and a mentor who is a certified consultant." Students tell us that throughout the curriculum, "There's a lot to learn, and, definitely, you have to learn it more on your own. The Greek way [of] teaching, i.e., having a mentor that spoon feeds, is nonexistent in this school, so [you] can get very respectable professors, but they will not give you everything; you have to go out on your own and dig for at least 50 percent of what you should learn."

Ottawa is a bilingual school, with instruction available in English and French. The Telfer School of Management offers a general management MBA, with a consulting project chosen by the student group.

Career and Placement

Ottawa's Telfer School of Management Career Centre offers one-on-one counseling, supplemented with an intensive self-assessment program. The office has access to online job search tools and exclusive job postings.

Employers who most frequently hire Ottawa MBAs include Accenture, Bank of Nova Scotia, Bell Canada, BMO Nesbitt, Business Development Bank of Canada, Canada Mortgage and Housing Corporation (CMHC), Canadian Commercial Corporation (CCC), CIBC, Clarica, Costco, Deloitte Touche Tohmatsu, Ernst & Young, IBM Canada, KPMG International, Kraft Foods, Labatt, Laurentian Bank of Canada, L'Oréal, National Bank of Canada, Natural Research Council of Canada (NRC), Nortel, PepsiCo, PricewaterhouseCoopers, Primerica Financial Services, Public Service Alliance of Canada, RBC Royal Bank, SwiftTrade Securities, TD Waterhouse Investment, Toyota Canada, Veritaaq Technology House, and Xerox Canada.

Student Life and Environment

The Telfer MBA is cohort based with English, French, full-time and part-time cohorts. It also has an exchange program with some of the top schools in France. We get really good students who bring a totally different perspective of the world. The American way of doing things surprises them, and the European way surprises us." Starting in September 2007, the Telfer School of Management will move into their state-of-the-art Desmarais Building. Named in honor of Paul G. Desmarais, a University of Ottawa alumnus and one of Canada's most distinguished corporate leaders, the 12-story structure offers management students an unparalleled learning environment.

"Life is easy to manage" in Ottawa. The campus "is located downtown and within easy reach [of] parking for the students. It is absolutely safe and friendly. There are two gyms and several pubs and cafes located nearby." The school "truly feels like home." Not that the students, even the part-timers, have much time to go out. A full-timer tells us that "academics always take precedence" and that "social life is not very strong, since the program is a 1-year intensive program." Part-timers, meanwhile, are typically too busy with work, family, and schoolwork on top of all that to play an intramural sport or hit the happy hours. One part-timer writes, "The course workload is quite heavy, given that I'm part of the part-time cohort. School was not flexible for those who needed to lighten their course load because of work or family obligations during the first two-thirds of the program. [There is] more flexibility for the elective courses."

Admissions

All applicants to the Telfer MBA program must submit the following materials to admissions: a completed online application form, printed out; official academic transcripts from all postsecondary institutions attended; a current resume reflecting at least 2 years' professional or managerial experience; two letters of recommendation (at least one from a recent employer); a 500-word personal statement describing goals in pursuing the MBA; an official GMAT score report demonstrating at least 50th percentile performance, with a strong showing in each subsection and a minimum score of 4.5 on the analytical writing section; proof of language proficiency for the applicant's desired program (English or French). English proficiency may be demonstrated through the TOEFL (minimum score of 250 on the computer-based test; minimum score of 5 on the Test of Written English; minimum score of 50 on the Test of Spoken English), IELTS (minimum score of 7 in at least three of four categories and minimum score of 6 in the fourth category), or CANTEST (minimum score of 14, with no individual test score below 4.0 and a minimum score of 4.5 on the oral section). The school reserves the right to request an interview of applicants.

FINANCIAL FACTS

Annual tuition (in-state/ out-of-state)	$15,739/$28,856
Fees	$945
Cost of books	$1,500
Room & board (on/off-campus)	$4,625/$5,760
Average grant	$4,750

ADMISSIONS

Admissions Selectivity Rating	**83**
# of applications received	241
% applicants accepted	67
% acceptees attending	73
Average GMAT	611
Range of GMAT	550–760
Average GPA	3.1
TOEFL required of international students	Yes
Minimum TOEFL (paper/computer)	600/250
Application fee	$75
International application fee	$75
Regular application deadline	4/1
Regular notification	Rolling
Transfer students accepted	Yes
Transfer application policy	
A maximum of 24 credits could be retained for graduate courses in management completed in a Canadian MBA program or AACSB accredited program.	
Need-blind admissions	Yes

EMPLOYMENT PROFILE

Career Rating	90	Grads Employed by Function	% Avg. Salary
Average base starting salary	$72,222	Finance	9 NR
Percent employed	92	Human Resources	2 NR
		Marketing	4 NR
		MIS	13 NR
		Operations	4 NR
		Consulting	13 NR
		General Management	13 NR
		Other	42 NR

UNIVERSITY OF THE PACIFIC
EBERHARDT SCHOOL OF BUSINESS

GENERAL INFORMATION
Type of school	Private
Environment	City
Academic calendar	Semester

SURVEY SAYS...
Friendly students
Good social scene
Helfpul alumni
Solid preparation in:
Teamwork
Communication/interpersonal skills
Presentation skills

STUDENTS
Enrollment of parent institution	6,250
Enrollment of business school	50
% male/female	70/30
% out-of-state	17
% part-time	28
% minorities	36
% international	10
Average age at entry	24
Average years work experience at entry	1.5

ACADEMICS
Academic Experience Rating	**87**
Student/faculty ratio	19:1
Profs interesting rating	83
Profs accessible rating	63
% female faculty	29
% minority faculty	12

Joint Degrees
MBA/JD 4 years, MBA/Peace Corps 3.5 years, MBA/PharmD 4 years.

Prominent Alumni
A.G. Spanos, Real Estate Development; David Gerber, MGM/UA, Film & TV Production; Dave Brubeck, Jazz Composer/Musician; Jaime Lee Curtis, Actress; Chris Isaak, Rock Musician/Actor.

Academics

At the Eberhardt School of Business at the University of the Pacific, a small cohort of MBAs enjoys a surprising range of degree options, including an 18-month accelerated full-time program, and joint-degree programs in law and pharmacology. The school also offers a unique master's international Peace Corps/MBA, which includes two years of on-campus study and a two-year Peace Corps assignment.

In all programs, "small class sizes that allow professors to engage students in their education" and a "strong emphasis on field experience" distinguish an Eberhardt degree. Field experience opportunities include participation in an annual global business couse that has taken students to South Korea, Singapore, Chile, Malaysia, Spain, Ireland, France, England, Finland, and Estonia.

Eberhardt offers specialization in four areas: finance, marketing, management, and entrepreneurship. Classes are taught by professors who "have great experience in different industries and apply their experiences to the applications of the course." Students appreciate how "the team aspect of business is stressed within the classroom. The students here apply it to all aspects of Pacific. They have made this a great learning experience." They also give the administration a thumbs up, telling us that administrators "have always been helpful in achieving goals, as well as providing solutions to any problems faced in the past. They've always been reliable."

Career and Placement

Eberhardt MBAs receive career assistance through the Career Management Center. In addition to teaching a required semester-long Career Development course, CMC professionals lead monthly career development team meetings, one-on-one career counseling, online recruiting tools, and access to alumni and employers. Many here commend the office's "major push on networking and finding a job before you graduate. The ESB Career Management Center is very helpful."

More than twenty employers visit the Pacific campus to recruit MBAs each year for career and internship positions. Employers who most frequently hire Eberhardt MBAs include Accenture, Clorox, Chevron, Google, E&J Gallo, Kaiser Permanente, Ernst & Young LLP, and state and federal government agencies.

Student Life and Environment

Both the size and the nature of the Eberhardt MBA contribute to a low-key extracurricular scene. With many classes held at night and many students commuting to campus, there can be a lack of social activity, but as the school is moving to a single cohort of full-time students, this will likely change. The MBA Association does its best, "trying to gather students every Thursday for socializing, wine tasting, movie nights, bar nights, trips, and other community services as a means of helping others and getting together." An MBA reports, "About half the MBA population goes to these events. They're usually fun."

The Pacific community at large offers a great deal more, and MBAs are welcome to partake. One student writes, "Within the university, there are many different schools which include pharmacy, education, engineering, and music (to name a few). By being in a diverse environment, business students can meet other students who come from a wide variety of backgrounds." The campus "has a strong Greek influence, as well as lots of clubs and organizations. If anyone wants to get involved, one does not need to look hard." Another agrees, "Overall, I'm having a great experience at Pacific. Clubs provide a great opportunity to get involved in the community and meet other students. The school also

CHRISTOPHER LOZANO, ESB DIRECTOR, STUDENT RECRUITMENT & ADMISSIONS
ADDRESS: MBA PROGRAM OFFICE, 3601 PACIFIC AVENUE STOCKTON, CA 95211 UNITED STATES
PHONE: (800) 952-3179 • FAX: (209) 946-2586
E-MAIL: MBA@PACIFIC.EDU • WEBSITE: WWW.BUSINESS.PACIFIC.EDU/MBA

has a lacrosse team that I joined and really enjoy." MBAs approve of the beautiful campus, which "is built much like many of the campuses on the East Coast: brick buildings and ivy-covered walls." The campus so closely follows the Ivy League model, in fact, that moviemakers often use it as a stand-in for Harvard or Yale. On campus, "Students have access to many facilities including the Conservatory, Pacific Theatre, an Olympic swimming pool, track, and many others." The only downside: "While the campus is generally a safe place to be, the surrounding area can be dangerous at night. Campus police do a good job of keeping the university safe, but an escort service would be nice."

Eberhardt MBA's tend to be "young and excited, eager sharks waiting to venture into the depths of the unknown [but] with little to no experience in the work field." Their shark-like qualities notwithstanding, students tend to be "very supportive and enthusiastic about the program." A considerable number "come from other countries such as France, Brazil, and the Philippines, and they bring a wide array of experiences to the education."

Admissions

Applicants to Eberhardt must submit official transcripts for all undergraduate, graduate, and professional schools attended; two letters of recommendation (one from an instructor, one from a work supervisor); GMAT scores; a completed application; and an interview. The Admissions Committee studies grade trends and ranks students by formula score, applying the formula [(undergraduate GPA $\times$ 200) + GMAT score] and looking for scores of at least 1,200. International students must also submit TOEFL scores (minimum 550 paper-and-pencil, 213 computer-based) and a Certification of Finances. Prior to beginning the MBA program, students must have completed the following prerequisite courses: intro microeconomics, intro macroeconomics, probability and statistics, and calculus.

FINANCIAL FACTS

Annual tuition	$32,040
Fees	$500
Cost of books	$1,600
Room & board	$12,000
% of students receiving aid	85
% of first-year students receiving aid	85
% of students receiving loans	60
% of students receiving grants	50
Average award package	$20,500
Average grant	$8,129

ADMISSIONS

Admissions Selectivity Rating	85
# of applications received	54
% applicants accepted	56
% acceptees attending	53
Average GMAT	552
Range of GMAT	510–610
Average GPA	3.39
TOEFL required of international students	Yes
Minimum TOEFL (paper/computer)	550/213
Application fee	$75
International application fee	$75
Regular application deadline	3/1
Regular notification	Rolling
Deferment available	Yes
Maximum length of deferment	1 year
Transfer students accepted	Yes
Transfer application policy Students may transfer up to 2 advanced courses from another AACSB accredited MBA Program.	
Need-blind admissions	Yes

Applicants Also Look At

California State University—Sacramento, San Diego State University, San Francisco State University, University of California—Davis, University of California—Los Angeles, University of San Francisco, University of Southern California.

EMPLOYMENT PROFILE

Career Rating	81	Grads Employed by Function	% Avg. Salary
Percent employed	100	Finance	50 NR
		Marketing	19 NR
		Consulting	25 NR
		Other	6 NR

Top 5 Employers Hiring Grads
Accenture; Clorox; University of the Pacific; California Department of Finance; Google

UNIVERSITY OF PENNSYLVANIA
WHARTON SCHOOL GRADUATE DIVISION

Academics

The University of Pennsylvania's Wharton School, one of the premier MBA programs in the world, is best known for its "strong finance reputation," but the curriculum's "strong emphasis on quantitative analysis" extends "across many disciplines, not just finance but marketing, entrepreneurship, operations, international business, real estate, etc." as well. All areas present a "holistic program with a mix of case studies, traditional lecture formats, experiential learning opportunities, and strong co-curricular programs."

Students brag that Wharton "provides all the resources necessary for us to succeed, and then some," reporting that "the difficult part here is deciding between which resources—lectures, seminars, simulations, clubs, special events—one can fit into one's schedule." Writes one student, "The breadth and depth of the academic curriculum and the extracurricular activities is so huge that I would need at least six MBA years to experience 20 percent of it all." A heavy workload, described as "difficult for everyone but the most brilliant to manage," makes those choices even tougher. But what impresses students most here is the degree to which students themselves contribute to the learning experience. Wharton uses a "co-production model of learning" that "requires engagement from all participants in the Wharton community." One MBA observes, "Students sometimes add more value than assigned readings. Students make Wharton. 'Student-run' is an understatement." Another agrees, "The 'co-production model' is not just a buzz word; it really exists here."

Under the Wharton pedagogic system, "Classes build on each other. Professors are known to coordinate timing of discussing certain topics to ensure that the student has mastered the concept in another class." Much work here is done in teams. To promote cooperation and reduce competitiveness, Wharton policy currently forbids grade disclosure to recruiters. Students report that the policy "fosters an environment of helping at the school." Nondisclosure apparently has little impact on students' motivation to work. One notes, "The school has high expectations for each admit, and the overall performance of the students rises to that expectation."

Career and Placement

Wharton is a brand that pretty much sells itself, so it's no surprise that the school's career services are highly regarded and widely appreciated by students. Each year brings the following career placement services to the campus: over 200 employer information sessions; almost 300 recruiting companies; and, more than 5,000 job-board postings. Wharton's Career Management Services Office also offers resume review and distribution, mock interviews, internship placement, one-on-one counseling, and over 25 career treks both in and outside the U.S. No wonder students praise the "fantastic career opportunities and resources." About 47 percent of Wharton MBAs take jobs in the finance sector; 28 percent wind up in consulting; and 7 percent find jobs in the information technology arena.

ADDRESS: 420 JON M. HUNTSMAN HALL, 3730 WALNUT STREET PHILADELPHIA, PA 19104-6340 U.S.
PHONE: 215-898-6183 • FAX: 215-898-0120
E-MAIL: MBA.ADMISSIONS@WHARTON.UPENN.EDU • WEBSITE: WWW.WHARTON.UPENN.EDU/MBA

Student Life and Environment

Life at Wharton offers "an amazing number of choices in terms of classes, activities, clubs, etc." It's an atmosphere students tell us is filled with a constant stream of unique opportunities they wouldn't otherwise have. One student cites these personal examples: "At Wharton I have done a four-week study trip to greater China; a consulting project to an Israeli company that wanted to enter the U.S. market; a marketing consulting project for AOL for the mobile location-based services product; a leadership venture to Ecuador next spring to learn about teamwork through a mountain climbing expedition; dozens of fantastic speakers; and finally, some great parties." MBAs appreciate that their "partners are involved in almost all campus-related activities here." One reports, "My wife and one-year-old daughter enjoy going to activities every Wednesday and Friday with the Wharton Kids Club. This has proved to be very helpful in providing an environment where my wife can make lots of friends in a new city, and my daughter can play with other kids her own age."

Hometown Philadelphia "is underrated but still needs work." One Bay Area native notes, "I was worried about Philadelphia after living in San Francisco, but I have been pleasantly surprised by the depth of culture, fun, and good food." Wharton's new facility, Huntsman Hall, is "top-of-the-line" but MBAs gripe that "sharing the building with undergraduates leads to scarce group study rooms. Most students do not use the library because it is overrun with undergrads." Still, Wharton does most things right. You realize this when you ask students what most needs improving here and all they can think to mention is "full-size lockers for each student."

Admissions

Wharton is among the most selective MBA programs in the country. On average, the school receives between 7 and 10 applications for each available slot. The school's website notes that "approximately 75 to 80 percent of all applicants are qualified for admission." Applicants are evaluated holistically by at least three members of the Admissions Committee. All prior academic experience, including graduate work and certifications, is considered. GMAT scores also figure into the decision. Quality of professional experiences, career choices, and stated goals for entering the program are all carefully reviewed. Committee members also look for evidence of leadership, interpersonal skills, entrepreneurial spirit, and good citizenship. International students must demonstrate competency in English through essays and interviews. Wharton offers three rounds of an admission each year; the first two rounds are equal with regard to a candidate's admissibility. The third round offers admission on a space-available basis and is generally more competitive.

FINANCIAL FACTS

Annual tuition	$41,950
Fees	$7,772
Cost of books	$4,172
Room & board (on-campus)	$18,054
% of students receiving aid	80
% of students receiving loans	67
% of students receiving grants	45
Average financial award	$49,000
Average grant	$13,480
Average student loan debt	$48,350

ADMISSIONS

Admissions Selectivity Rating	**99**
# of applications received	7,328
% applicants accepted	17
% acceptees attending	70
Average GMAT	712
Range of GMAT	660–760
Average GPA	3.54
TOEFL required of international students	Yes
Application fee	$235
International application fee	$235
Application Deadline/Notification	
Round 1:	10/09 / 12/18
Round 2:	01/08 / 03/26
Round 3:	03/05 / 05/14
Deferment available	case-by-case
Maximum length of deferment	case-by-case
Need-blind admissions	Yes

EMPLOYMENT PROFILE

Career Rating	99	Grads Employed by Function	%	Avg. Salary
Primary Source of Full-time Job Acceptances		Finance	48	NR
School-facilitated activities	477 (70%)	Marketing	7	NR
Graduate-facilitated activities	197 (29%)	Operations	1	NR
Unknown	7 (1%)	Consulting	30	NR
Average base starting salary	$105,000	General Management	4	NR
Percent employed	93	Other	9	NR

Top 5 Employers Hiring Grads

McKinsey & Company; Boston Consulting Group; Bain & Company; Goldman, Sachs & Company; Morgan Stanley

UNIVERSITY OF PITTSBURGH
JOSEPH M. KATZ GRADUATE SCHOOL OF BUSINESS

Academics

Boasting a "good hometown reputation," ample elective offerings, and a "team-building approach to learning," the University of Pittsburgh's Joseph M. Katz Graduate School of Business is an excellent MBA program for both full-time students and working professionals. Stressing real-world applications of academic theory, Katz professors "are in tune with issues being faced out there, which they incorporate into their classes or target their research towards." In addition to classroom instruction, "The school is very big on scheduling guest speakers to share real world examples with the students." "Recently a woman from Deloitte's consulting section came to speak about being a woman in the business world."

In 1963, Katz became the first university to offer a 1-year MBA program. Designed for students with a strong background in economics or business, the 1-year MBA continues to draw students. Katz also operates a part-time program, through which business professionals can complete an MBA during the evening. According to students in the part-time program, professors are "accommodating to the needs of part-time students and try to manage the course in a manner that will not overwhelm." This includes "spreading apart their due dates and exams to make sure students aren't incredibly overloaded." Students say, "The high caliber of people who are in the part time program really make the class time so much more contextual and rewarding because we're directly applying the information we're learning to work circumstances." The 2-year, full-time program, on the other hand, is designed for students who need a longer and more thorough introduction to business, and the program incorporates highly individualized coaching and mentoring. Whether studying part-time, full-time, or on the accelerated track, Katz students quickly discover that "the academics are quite challenging"; however, the school maintains a "friendly learning atmosphere," and struggling students are pleased to find that "professors are always willing to work with students."

When it comes to the school's higher-ups, many students report that "the administrative team is very good and are able to help tackle any student issues or problems," while others feel that "the administration does not value part time students very much." However, "The arrival of the new dean last year has been the turning point," marking a new and more positive era in the school's management, and "creating a new sense of unity" between part-time and full-time students. Other non-academic staff also received kudos from students: "The advisor staff and Admissions Office personnel are almost bend-over-backwards friendly."

Career and Placement

All students at Katz receive one-on-one personalized mentoring to help them develop their "soft skills" within a managerial context. Through Career Services, students can seek further career preparation, including assistance researching positions, interviewing, negotiating offers, and seeking promotions. Career opportunities are enhanced by the fact that "the school has very strong ties with many companies in Pittsburgh and the western Pennsylvania region in general," and by all reports the "Career Counselors are very helpful if you engage them."

Last year, 71 percent of students seeking employment had received an offer by graduation, and 95 percent had received an offer within 3 months of graduating. Jobs in the manufacturing industry have been the most popular for several years, drawing 28 percent of last year's class. Another 19 percent of graduates took jobs in the financial services industry. The following companies are among the many that hired 2006 Katz grads:

ADMISSIONS CONTACT: KELLY R. WILSON, ASSISTANT DEAN AND DIRECTOR
ADDRESS: 276 MERVIS HALL, ROBERTO CLEMENTE DRIVE PITTSBURGH, PA 15260 UNITED STATES
PHONE: 412-648-1700 • FAX: 412-648-1659
E-MAIL: MBA@KATZ.PITT.EDU • WEBSITE: WWW.KATZ.PITT.EDU

Bayer Healthcare, Capital One, Cisco Systems, Del Monte Foods, Deloitte Touche Tohmatsu, Deutsche Bank, Ford Motor Company, General Electric, GlaxoSmithKline, H.J. Heinz Company, Hewlett-Packard, JPMorgan Chase, NBC, Northrop Grumman, Samsung, SBI Holdings, St. Clair Hospital, U.S. Patent and Trademark Office, Washington Mutual, Wilshire Associates, and Wyeth Pharmaceuticals.

Student Life and Environment

There is "a good work/life balance" at Katz, where the friendly atmosphere and reasonable workload allow students to succeed academically while maintaining a healthy extracurricular and social life. There is always something happening on campus, as "The school has a golf club, ski/snow sports club, various academic clubs and a Student Executive Board to arrange activities to benefit the student body as a whole." Students in the part-time program find their time is more limited, as most "are busy juggling careers, family, and the MBA." However, Katz students appear to be comfortable with their hectic lifestyle, as one student explains: "Most are working full-time and understand how busy life can get, but still find time socialize with classmates after class during the week or on weekends."

On campus, Katz students enjoy a beautiful, three-story building, often a hub of activity thanks to "a small cafe located in the main building. Students come here straight from work to eat and socialize before class." The surrounding city of Pittsburg offers plenty of restaurants and nightlife, especially for sports fans: "Pittsburgh is a sports-loving community with the Steelers, the Penguins, and the Pirates, as well as all the Pitt teams."

Admissions

Applicants to the Joseph M. Katz Graduate School of Business are evaluated for admission based on their undergraduate GPA, GMAT scores, and previous work experience. In addition, the Admissions Committee evaluates qualitative parts of the application, including career goals, recommendations, admissions essays, management potential, leadership skills, and community-service experience. While an interview is not required, 97 percent of last year's entering class was interviewed. Students are encouraged to enter the program with at least 2 years of professional work experience.

FINANCIAL FACTS

Annual tuition (in-state/ out-of-state)	$14,838/$22,208
Fees	$2,650
Cost of books	$1,050
Room & board (off-campus)	$13,200
% of students receiving aid	46
% of first-year students receiving aid	39
% of students receiving grants	0
Average award package	$13,000

ADMISSIONS

Admissions Selectivity Rating	87
# of applications received	800
% applicants accepted	60
% acceptees attending	60
Average GMAT	615
Range of GMAT	540–680
Average GPA	3.31
TOEFL required of international students	Yes
Minimum TOEFL (paper/computer)	600/250
Application fee	$50
International application fee	$50
Regular application deadline	12/1
Regular notification	2/1
Application Deadline/Notification	
Round 1:	11/01 / 12/15
Round 2:	12/01 / 02/01
Round 3:	0/15 / 03/15
Round 4:	03/01 / 04/15
Transfer students accepted	Yes
Transfer application policy	
Accepting up to 17 credits from an AACSB MBA program, provided that credits were not used to complete a previous MBA degree.	
Need-blind admissions	Yes

Applicants Also Look At
Carnegie Mellon, Duquesne University, Penn State University, The Ohio State University, University of Illinois at Urbana-Champaign, University of Maryland—College Park, University of Pennsylvania.

EMPLOYMENT PROFILE			
Career Rating	87	**Grads Employed by Function**	**% Avg. Salary**
Primary Source of Full-time Job Acceptances		Finance	27 $69,300
School-facilitated activities	33 (60%)	Marketing	10 $61,000
Graduate-facilitated activities	22 (40%)	MIS	6 $75,000
Average base starting salary	$74,000	Operations	13 $76,300
Percent employed	93	Consulting	17 $71,000
		Top 5 Employers Hiring Grads	
		Ford Motor Company; KPMG; Deloitte; Del Monte Foods; Giant Eagle.	

UNIVERSITY OF PORTLAND
PAMPLIN SCHOOL OF BUSINESS ADMINISTRATION

GENERAL INFORMATION

Type of school	Private
Affiliation	Roman Catholic
Environment	Metropolis
Academic calendar	Semester

SURVEY SAYS...
Students love Portland, OR
Happy students
Smart classrooms
Solid preparation in:
Teamwork
Entrepreneurial studies

STUDENTS

Enrollment of parent institution	3,600
Enrollment of business school	138
% male/female	60/40
% out-of-state	32
% part-time	65
% minorities	15
% international	30
Average age at entry	29
Average years work experience at entry	5

ACADEMICS

Academic Experience Rating	**78**
Student/faculty ratio	13:1
Profs interesting rating	76
Profs accessible rating	62
% female faculty	33
% minority faculty	19

Prominent Alumni
Dr. Robert B. Pamplin. Jr., Philanthropist/Entreprenuer; Fidele Baccio, Co-Founder Bon Apetite.

Academics

The Pamplin MBA at the University of Portland is structured to suit the needs of its largely part-time student body. A flexible schedule built around evening classes accommodates a student body that typically is also part of the full-time work force of Portland. About 30 percent of the students here have full-time status; their numbers primarily include international students and students in the five-year BBA/MBA program.

For students with undergraduate degrees in non-business areas, the Pamplin MBA begins with a Foundation Core, a series of college-level courses covering basic principles of economics, marketing, finance, and accounting. Students who majored in business during college skip the Foundation Core and proceed directly to the Integration Core, a cross-disciplinary sequence focusing on "solving common business problems." The Advanced Core, covering advanced analysis of statistics, information systems, finance, marketing, and international business follows. Students may use electives to establish a concentration in entrepreneurship, finance, global business, health care, management, or marketing. Alternatively, students can design their own concentrations in consultation with a faculty advisor. Students may also choose electives from a variety of disciplines and graduate with a degree in general management.

Students praise the Pamplin School for its willingness to experiment and innovate. The school "has the flexibility to allow students to take classes in any area of business," writes one student, adding that she is "working on earning a CPA and CMA licenses in addition to my MBA. There were no other programs in this area that offered all of this!" Another student approvingly notes that "UP seems to always hire guest professors to offer new classes, such as special 'Summer only' classes in areas like real estate or nonprofit accounting and management." Participation in JEBNET, "a network of 30 universities nationwide," allows students who must relocate to complete their MBAs at another school without losing credits.

Portland business professors "are very good. They all have their doctorates, have decades of professional experience in their fields, know other professionals in their respective fields, and invite these professionals into class to give real-world examples of what we are learning." Students also value the school's "great local reputation." The program is "administered extremely well, with regular communications from the school, including schedules, a newsletter, etc. The same cannot be said for the university at large, unfortunately."

Career and Placement

The University of Portland's Office of Career Services provides career and placement services for the school's undergraduate students, graduate students, and alumni. Office staff maintain job and internship listings, company research, and lists of alumni contacts. The office also organizes resume-writing and interviewing workshops, job fairs, and networking events. Students feel that the office, like much of the university, "sees UP primarily as an undergraduate institution and provides services accordingly" and believe that the school "should network better with local companies to get them to recruit on campus." Employers that recruit on campus include Black and Veatch, Deloitte Touche Tohmatsu, Ernst & Young, KPMG, and PricewaterhouseCoopers.

ADMISSIONS CONTACT: MELISSA MCCARTHY, MBA PROGRAM COORDINATOR
ADDRESS: 5000 N. WILLAMETTE BLVD. PORTLAND, OR 97203 UNITED STATES
PHONE: 503-943-7225 • FAX: 503-943-8041
E-MAIL: MBA-UP@UP.EDU • WEBSITE: BUSINESS.UP.EDU

Student Life and Environment

"There are no real clubs on campus" for Pamplin MBAs, "and no one seems to care. Because of the scheduling—classes are from 4:00 P.M. to 7:00 P.M. or 7:00 P.M. to 10:00 P.M. Monday through Thursday—it is almost impossible to get out into the community and attend business-related events, or even most school events, since they are scheduled right during the middle of most of our classes." One student observes, "The University of Portland's MBA program is mostly attended by working professionals who are only on campus long enough to go to class and then go home to their families. While there is not really a sense of community with this group, there is a strong sense of pride that we are attending the best MBA program in the city, and one of the best in the Northwest."

The average Pamplin student "is about 29 years old. There are a few of us with a couple of years of work experience but the majority of the students have been out for four or five years and there are also others who have been out for eight to fifteen years." The program is "diverse both ethnically and financially, populated by people who are always willing to help while at the same time are very competitive."

The city of Portland is among the most appealing in the Pacific Northwest. An arts Mecca, the city also hosts numerous fine restaurants, great shopping, and major-league professional basketball. The city's location provides easy access to numerous locations ideal for outdoor activity.

Admissions

Applicants to the MBA program at the University of Portland must meet the following minimum requirements: an undergraduate GPA of at least 3.0; a GMAT score of at least 500; and an "admission index" of at least 1,100 under the formula [(undergraduate GPA x 200) + GMAT score]. Work experience, though strongly recommended, is not required; applicants with at least three years of post-baccalaureate professional experience are considered optimal candidates for the program. International students must score at least 570 on the TOEFL paper test or 230 on the computer-adaptive version of the TOEFL. All applications to the University of Portland must include a completed application form, a personal statement of goals, official transcripts for all postsecondary academic work, an official GMAT score report, and two letters of recommendation. International students must submit all of the above as well as an official TOEFL score report and a financial statement that indicates they will have adequate support throughout the duration of study. This is required before the I-20 form will be issued to them.

FINANCIAL FACTS

Annual tuition	$27,900
Fees	$1,260
Cost of books	$600
% of students receiving aid	55
% of first-year students receiving aid	25
% of students receiving loans	40
% of students receiving grants	43
Average award package	$11,531
Average grant	$6,741
Average student loan debt	$30,000

ADMISSIONS

Admissions Selectivity Rating	**77**
# of applications received	77
% applicants accepted	50
% acceptees attending	31
Average GMAT	540
Average GPA	3.3
TOEFL required of international students	Yes
Minimum TOEFL (paper/computer)	570/230
Application fee	$50
International application fee	$50
Regular application deadline	rolling
Regular notification	rolling
Deferment available	Yes
Maximum length of deferment	1 year
Transfer students accepted	Yes
Transfer application policy 9 Semester hours of transfer credit from AACSB accredited program, or all credits in the Jesuit Transfer Agreement.	
Non-fall admissions	Yes
Need-blind admissions	Yes

Applicants Also Look At
Portland State University, Willamette University.

UNIVERSITY OF RHODE ISLAND
COLLEGE OF BUSINESS ADMINISTRATION

GENERAL INFORMATION
Type of school	Public
Environment	Village
Academic calendar	Semesters

SURVEY SAYS...
Students love Kingston, RI
Friendly students
Happy students
Smart classrooms
Solid preparation in:
Accounting

STUDENTS
Enrollment of parent institution	15,095
Enrollment of business school	174
% male/female	76/24
% out-of-state	52
% part-time	88
% international	38
Average age at entry	29

ACADEMICS
Academic Experience Rating	**77**
Student/faculty ratio	4:1
Profs interesting rating	86
Profs accessible rating	62
% female faculty	24

Joint Degrees
MBA/PharmD 7 years,
MBA/Engineering 5 years, MBA/MS
(Oceanography) 16 months.

Academics

The College of Business Administration at the University of Rhode Island offers a one-year, full-time MBA program with "a very compact curriculum that focuses on the most important fields." Students "like the one-year aspect," noting that "it costs less and is more efficient" than traditional two-year programs. The school also offers a part-time program, which is favored by area students who wish to continue their careers while attending school. The full-time program convenes on URI's main campus in Kingston, while the evening classes for part-time students meet at the Allen Shawn Feinstein College of Continuing Education in Providence. URI's relatively small graduate business program—fewer than 200 students pursue MBAs here—allows students to forge close relationships with their professors.

URI's one-year full-time MBA is a non-thesis program consisting of 45 class-hour credits. The entire curriculum is integrated, with only six credits of electives allowed. Students love how the program is "designed to have us working with real-life small businesses" by "setting up consulting relationships with local companies." They also tell us that "the program incorporates teamwork into every aspect of the program, which is a great strength," and that "all the professors are very competent and demand student participation in class." Some wish that "the core curriculum would offer a little more flexibility" so that "we could develop concentrations for our MBAs," or that faculty would "do a better job of creating a competitive atmosphere and challenging the students to improve the overall quality of the program." Some also feel that "the focus of the program is too regional, preparing you for working in Rhode Island (vs. NYC or Boston)" and that "a greater focus on global business would improve the program."

Part-time MBA students must complete at least 36 class-hour credits. Students lacking in foundation skills may be required to take up to 17 additional credits of prerequisite classes covering undergraduate business material. The part-time curriculum is similar to the full-time curriculum, although it allows students a few more elective options.

Career and Placement

Career and placement services are provided to URI MBAs by the university's Career Services Office, which serves the entire university population. All MBA students receive a BEACON ("Become Employed at Career Online Network") account in order to access the university's online recruitment system, which is powered by MonsterTRAK. BEACON notifies students by e-mail when opportunities that fit their skill set are posted; it also enables students to monitor the on-campus interviewing schedule and to search a database of job postings. Other services available to grad students include one-on-one counseling; personal assessments; workshops on resume writing, interviewing, and job search skills; mock interviews; resume review; job and internship fairs; and networking events.

ADMISSIONS CONTACT: LISA LANCELLOTTA, COORDINATOR, MBA PROGRAMS
ADDRESS: 7 LIPPITT RD., BALLENTINE HALL KINGSTON, RI 02881 UNITED STATES
PHONE: 401-874-5000 • FAX: 401-874-4312
E-MAIL: MBA@URI.EDU • WEBSITE: WWW.CBA.URI.EDU/MBA

FINANCIAL FACTS

Annual tuition (in-state/ out-of-state)	$12,711/$34,914
Fees	$2,905
Cost of books	$3,500

ADMISSIONS

Admissions Selectivity Rating	**74**
# of applications received	68
% applicants accepted	76
% acceptees attending	75
Average GPA	3.21
TOEFL required of international students	Yes
Minimum TOEFL (paper/computer)	575/233
Application fee	$50
International application fee	$50
Regular application deadline	4/15
Regular notification	rolling
Deferment available	Yes
Maximum length of deferment	1 year
Transfer students accepted	Yes
Transfer application policy Can take up to 20% of total credits from another AACSB accredited college/university.	
Non-fall admissions	Yes
Need-blind admissions	Yes

Applicants Also Look At

Babson College, Bentley College, Boston University, Bryant University, Northeastern University, Suffolk University, University of Connecticut.

Student Life and Environment

URI's College of Business has "great technology in the classrooms." Larger classes are held in a tiered-seating facility equipped with touch-screen controls, a computer, a projector, audiovisual equipment, and both wired and wireless Internet access. Smaller classrooms boast many of the same amenities. The business facility also has two computer labs with 40 computers each, a seminar room, and two conference rooms. Wireless service is supported throughout Ballentine Hall, home to the College of Business.

URI is located in Kingston, where "the beach is close" and "apartments are clean and spacious as well as low cost." It's not hard to find housing close to campus. Many students "live in houses on the beach, the type of places that are rented to vacationers in the summer." The school itself makes up a large portion of the town of Kingston, but larger cities and big-city fun are within easy reach. Providence sits a short drive from campus, and Boston, MA and New Haven, CT are both easily reachable by car or train.

URI's campus "is mostly populated by undergrads," and students in the MBA program also "are mostly young—either recent grads or only a few years out of school. Everyone is very nice and social, easy to talk to, and willing to work as a team." "Some are married" and "many have an international background or are exchange students," although "there are also plenty of local kids here, too."

Admissions

URI offers many components of its application online and encourages applicants to submit materials online whenever possible. Students may provide all of the following materials via the Internet: a current resume, a personal statement of purpose, and letters of recommendation (applicants e-mail referees, who then send their recommendations directly to the school). Students must also provide the admissions office with official transcripts for all postsecondary academic work and an official score report for the GMAT (scores must be no more than five years old). International applicants must provide all of the above plus an official TOEFL score report (scores must be no more than five years old); the minimum required score for admission is 575 on the paper-based test, 233 on the computer-based test. The school notes that applicants with a GPA below 3.0 and GMAT scores below the 50th percentile "have a low probability of admission," but allows that grades and test scores are not the sole criteria for admission. The school seeks candidates with demonstrated strength in quantitative skills, work experience ("valued," but not required, according to university materials), leadership potential, motivation, and communication skills.

UNIVERSITY OF RICHMOND
ROBINS SCHOOL OF BUSINESS

GENERAL INFORMATION

Type of school	Private
Environment	Metropolis
Academic calendar	Semester

SURVEY SAYS...
Good peer network
Happy students
Smart classrooms
Solid preparation in:
Accounting

STUDENTS

Enrollment of parent institution	4,322
Enrollment of business school	148
% male/female	100/0
% part-time	100
Average age at entry	28
Average years work experience at entry	5

ACADEMICS

Academic Experience Rating	**87**
Student/faculty ratio	2:1
Profs interesting rating	89
Profs accessible rating	68
% female faculty	20
% minority faculty	1

Joint Degrees
JD/MBA 3–4 years.

Prominent Alumni
David Beran, Senior Vice President, Philip Morris USA; Lyn McDermid, Chief Information Officer, Dominion Resources; Larry Marsh, Managing Director, Lehman Bros.; Bruce Kay, VP, Markel Corp.

Academics

Offering "an excellent MBA program for part-time working students," the University of Richmond is ideal for business professionals looking to expand their skill set and advance their career opportunities. The curriculum is "geared toward business in the real world and not just conceptual skills" and, from the first day of classes, practical applications of business issues are stressed. In fact, the program begins with the opening residency, a case-based course that introduces students to business topics through a "live" case.

In the classroom, professors "are not strict academics, but bring an extensive amount of background from the professional world;" "classes focus on cases and discussions more so than on lectures and books." Group work and student participation is encouraged, and the classroom environment is characterized by "rich discussions and a laid back atmosphere that fosters contributions from all points of view." Students tell us that "the atmosphere is collaborative and genuinely friendly" and "the professors are terrific and interested in learning from us as we learn from them."

"The past two associate deans of the school have been very progressive," one student asserts, "and as a result they have been able to create a strong, relevant, and current MBA program." This program includes course work in current topics such as leadership, ethics, and international business. A unique requirement of the Richmond MBA is that all students must participate in the international residency, a weeklong consulting project in a foreign country in Asia, Latin America, or Central or Eastern Europe.

Given the program's focus on working students, professors are sensitive to the needs of part-time students. All classes are taught at night and students "can even meet with some faculty on Sunday afternoons." Even so, students warn us that the "workload is slightly overboard given that 95 percent of us are trying to juggle school with very demanding day jobs." However, one student contests: "The school is academically challenging but not busy work; it is work that actually helps me to be more successful at work. I feel more knowledgeable regarding the global economy and trends than ever before."

Career and Placement

Many students choose University of Richmond based on the advice of their colleagues and employers, as it has a "fine reputation for being a challenging program that allows its graduates to advance in their careers." While the school is very efficient at accomplishing this goal, students complain that "because the program is part-time and most students go through the program while continuing to work full-time during the day, there is no career office to help in a job search besides the general one that's focused on undergraduate students." In fact, "the careers services branch is strong for undergrads and the law school," but "the school has made little effort to attract area employers to campus to target MBA students or program graduates." Many suggest that while "a formal office may not be needed, it would be nice to have a few faculty members who function as career counselors and are able to attract employers to campus specifically for MBAs when appropriate." Even so, students say they benefit immensely from the school's strong standing in the local community, as well as its "great reputation throughout the Southeast with a growing national reputation."

DR. RICHARD S. COUGHLAN, ASSOCIATE DEAN FOR GRADUATE AND EXECUTIVE PROGRAMS
ADDRESS: MBA OFFICE, ROBINS SCHOOL OF BUSINESS UNIVERSITY OF RICHMOND, VA 23173 U.S.
PHONE: 804-289-8553 • FAX: 804-287-1228
E-MAIL: MBA@RICHMOND.EDU • WEBSITE: BUSINESS.RICHMOND.EDU/MBA

Student Life and Environment

With a lovely academic environment—even for graduate students screeching in after a long day of work—the University of Richmond's "campus is beautiful and the classrooms have the latest in technology tools." Generally speaking, the Richmond MBA caters to "very hard working professionals from the Richmond area." However, professionally speaking, students hail from a wide variety of backgrounds, "from the military to corporate America to government and nonprofit."

As the program is primarily part-time, there "is not much campus activity associated with the program. Its classes and that's it." Even so, you might be surprised to learn that U of R students "are relatively social, so they gather on their own a great deal." A student explains: "We don't have all the bells and whistles of a normal, full-time MBA program, such as student clubs and organizations. That's not to say we're not social and never get together after classes, though." Another adds, "We have a good time with each other, get to know each other really well, and enjoy our experience." Even those who have little time outside the program find that "the international residency program, where you spend a week abroad with your classmates working on a business case [in] a foreign company, is a great bonding experience." However, some would like to see "more activities catered to families with children. I have not seen any such activities advertised by the business school; if they are, they aren't very noticeable."

Admissions

Applicants to the Robins School of Business must submit a completed application form, official GMAT scores, official transcripts from each college and university attended, and a current resume. As the program is designed for working professionals, students are required to have at least two years of relevant work experience after completion of their bachelor's degree, though the average student applies with more than 4 years of experience. There are no minimum GPA or GMAT requirements. As a point of reference, in the past year accepted students had an average GMAT score of 587 and an average undergraduate GPA of 3.15. While the majority of students attend part-time, students may apply to complete the program full-time, or apply to the JD/MBA joint-degree program. Applicants to either the full-time or joint-degree program may be considered without prior work experience.

FINANCIAL FACTS

Annual tuition	$28,970
Fees	$0
Cost of books	$4,780
Room & board (off-campus)	$9,360
% of students receiving aid	40
% of first-year students receiving aid	45
% of students receiving loans	24
% of students receiving grants	23
Average award package	$15,160
Average grant	$9,250
Average student loan debt	$43,170

ADMISSIONS

Admissions Selectivity Rating	**78**
# of applications received	83
% applicants accepted	77
% acceptees attending	73
Average GMAT	592
Range of GMAT	540–650
Average GPA	3.24
TOEFL required of international students	Yes
Minimum TOEFL (paper/computer)	600/250
Application fee	$50
International application fee	$50
Regular application deadline	5/1
Regular notification	6/1
Deferment available	Yes
Maximum length of deferment	1 year
Transfer students accepted	Yes
Transfer application policy Maximum of 12 hours of transfer credit accepted from other AACSB-accredited schools.	
Need-blind admissions	Yes

Applicants Also Look At

College of William & Mary, University of Virginia, Wake Forest University.

UNIVERSITY OF ROCHESTER
WILLIAM E. SIMON GRADUATE SCHOOL OF BUSINESS ADMINISTRATION

GENERAL INFORMATION

Type of school	Private
Environment	Village
Academic calendar	Quarter

SURVEY SAYS...

Helpful alumni
Solid preparation in:
Finance
Accounting
Quantitative skills
Computer skills

STUDENTS

Enrollment of parent institution	8,730
Enrollment of business school	661
% male/female	70/30
% out-of-state	57
% part-time	32
% minorities	8
% international	55
Average age at entry	26
Average years work experience at entry	4.3

ACADEMICS

Academic Experience Rating	**91**
Student/faculty ratio	10:1
Profs interesting rating	85
Profs accessible rating	92
% female faculty	15

Joint Degrees

MBA/MS (Public Health) 3 years,
MD/MBA 5 years.

Prominent Alumni

Rene Jones, CFO, M&T Bank;
Ronald Fielding, Senior Vice
President, OppenheimerFunds;
Robert Keegan, CEO, Goodyear Tire
Company; Mark Grier, Chairman,
Prudential Insurance Co.; Mark Ain,
Founder and CEO, Kronos
Incorporated.

Academics

One student sums it up perfectly: Simon is "definitely a school on the rise." Though founded in the 1960s under an already well-established parent institution, it's only been in recent years that the school has started to make the strides necessary to become a world-class institution. Students here say the "rigorous" academic workload is as heavy as you make it out to be, though "If you don't stay on top of your work, you will get lost very quickly." It's this flexibility and trust on the part of the school of which students speak most highly: "You have the unique ability to [tailor] your education to whatever way you see fit by utilizing all of the resources and opportunities available," one student said.

The "top-notch" faculty at Simon is a high point for students, and "To be able to speak directly with some of the leaders in their various fields is really impressive." Another student adds: "The small class size, combined with professor quality/availability, is an unbelievably strong combination." However, a few others caution that accessibility doesn't always translate into helpfulness when it comes to making students understand material they might have trouble understanding. And some professors aren't as successful as others when it comes to venturing or teaching outside of their field.

Students enjoy their classes and find them "challenging," but one notes that "there is not a wide variety offered after the core is complete." A robust program in finance and accounting is highly regarded, and the school's "economics-based approach to analyzing all business problems" is an invaluable tool for students as they prepare to enter the workforce.

At this up-and-coming school, the administration has the difficult task of increasing the breadth of the program and generating buzz, while simultaneously acting to keep things running smoothly, a job they have more than proven themselves up to. Those who attend Simon rave about its administration, which is "quick to fix any problem." Also praised is the "awesome" Dean ("an invaluable resource for networking and personal guidance"), who holds several town hall-style meetings per quarter "to find out what the students want."

Career and Placement

On the whole, Career Services at Simon generally is well received for what the office provides students, but there's no question that more diversity in recruiting (in terms of both the number of companies interviewing on campus and the number of cities in which programs are available) would be welcome. International and more experienced students also feel that more could be done to aid them in their search for employment. Boston and New York are heavily favored areas for recruitment, but the school's biggest asset tends to be the alumni: "In recent years, alumni have been responsible for opening up big hiring pipelines with major firms such as Citibank and J&J. This trend is continuing with openings to major players such as McKinsey."

Other companies that typically hire Simon grads include M&T Bank, Deloitte Touche Tohmatsu, and Xerox.

GREGORY V. MACDONALD, EXECUTIVE DIRECTOR FOR MBA ADMISSIONS AND ADMIN
ADDRESS: 305 SCHLEGEL HALL ROCHESTER, NY 14627-0107 UNITED STATES
PHONE: 585-275-3533 • FAX: 585-271-3907
E-MAIL: ADMISSIONS@SIMON.ROCHESTER.EDU • WEBSITE: WWW.SIMON.ROCHESTER.EDU

Student Life and Environment

It's an "academically competitive" crowd here; "intelligent," "friendly," and "helpful to a point, but it is business school, so when crunch time hits, if you're all in the same class and they're not your immediate friends, you might have to search harder for help." Simon is home to a very large number of international students, many of whose language and writing skills leave something to be desired in team projects, where they can be a "burden," according to one student. She adds, "I would not have come to this school had I fully understood the impact of this."

However, since it's a small school, the overall crowd tends to be very "close-knit" and familiar with each other, students say. Although some are wholly focused on school and their career search, many are very social outside of classroom, either in the "active bar/club atmosphere" or at school-sponsored events. As a younger crowd, "There are very few people at the school who are married or have a significant other," and many people socialize with students from neighboring grad schools and universities. Rochester "could never be called a charming town," and the cold weather and heavy snow can be an unpleasant surprise for many non-Northeasterners, but the city does have an ample night life and great cultural activities, including fairs, festivals, theater, films, music, and art galleries.

Admissions

As a general rule, students with the best combination of GPA, applicable test scores, and relevant team/leadership experience (either through internships, post-baccalaureate work, or extracurricular activities) will have the first opportunity to enter the programs, according to the school's website. Applicants to the school's MBA program must submit the following materials: an online application, including three required essays; an official copy of undergraduate transcripts from all institutions where course work was completed; two letters of recommendation; a current resume; an official GMAT score report; and an interview (if requested by the Admissions Committee). In addition to the above documents, international students whose primary language is not English must also provide an official score report for the TOEFL, unless they have studied for at least one full academic year in a college or university where English is the language of instruction.

FINANCIAL FACTS

Annual tuition	$36,840
Fees	$950
Cost of books	$1,800
Room & board	$14,760

ADMISSIONS

Admissions Selectivity Rating	**93**
# of applications received	643
% applicants accepted	41
% acceptees attending	43
Average GMAT	673
Range of GMAT	640–710
Average GPA	3.52
TOEFL required of international students	Yes
Application fee	$125
International application fee	$125
Application Deadline/Notification	
Round 1:	12/1 / 2/15
Round 2:	1/8 / 3/30
Round 3:	4/1 / 5/15
Round 4:	6/1 / 7/15
Early decision program?	Yes
ED Deadline/ Notification	11/01 / 01/15
Transfer students accepted	Yes
Transfer application policy No more than 9 credit hours, may not be core courses.	
Non-fall admissions	Yes
Need-blind admissions	Yes

Applicants Also Look At
Carnegie Mellon, Columbia University, Cornell University, Indiana University—Bloomington, New York University.

EMPLOYMENT PROFILE			
Career Rating	**89**	**Grads Employed by Function**	**% Avg. Salary**
Primary Source of Full-time Job Acceptances		Finance	42 $85,828
School-facilitated activities	53 (77%)	Marketing	21 $80,987
Graduate-facilitated activities	15 (21%)	Operations	7 $80,000
Unknown	1 (2%)	Consulting	8 $87,503
Percent employed	92	General Management	20 $84,043
		Top 5 Employers Hiring Grads	
		Citigroup; Barclays Capital; Johnson & Johnson; Deloitte; Info Sys Technologie	

UNIVERSITY OF SCRANTON
KANIA SCHOOL OF MANAGEMENT

GENERAL INFORMATION
Type of school	Private
Affiliation	Roman Catholic/Jesuit
Environment	City

SURVEY SAYS...
Solid preparation in:
General management
Communication/interpersonal skills
Presentation skills

STUDENTS
Enrollment of parent institution	5,615
Enrollment of business school	83
% male/female	60/40
% part-time	57
% minorities	2
% international	35
Average age at entry	30
Average years work experience at entry	2

ACADEMICS
Academic Experience Rating	**79**
Student/faculty ratio	12:1
Profs interesting rating	95
Profs accessible rating	73
% female faculty	36
% minority faculty	2

Academics

Jesuit values add a unique flavor to the graduate business programs at the University of Scranton, which emphasizes a contemporary approach to business while simultaneously exploring topics in ethics and social responsibility. University of Scranton's MBA is designed to ensure that every candidate gains valuable knowledge in a breadth of essential business areas. In addition to traditional academics, "the school's leadership is very in tune with the needs of the students, as well as focused on what will be required of a MBA graduate in today's market place." Therefore, the program puts particular weight on the integration of technology and business, and maintains "a strong focus on globalization" throughout the curriculum. Of particular note, the business school's building, Brennan Hall, is the university's most high-tech facility, including an auditorium (fully wired for audio-visual presentations), an executive center, simulated trading floor, well-equipped computer labs for student use, and a pleasant student lounge.

Jesuit philosophy influences the character of the business school community, inspiring a cooperative and supportive academic environment, which focuses attention on educating the whole individual. At the University of Scranton, it's not difficult to solicit extra help or a bit of advice, as "the professors are always available for questions, problems, or just to talk." A current student writes, "The administration and professors have all been very helpful. They are readily available for whatever you may need. They have made me feel very comfortable and reassured knowing that they are there for you." Likewise, teamwork and cooperation is encouraged between students, fostering "a very positive environment," which students liken to "a company where everyone works as a team." In summary, a student tells us, "The community at the University of Scranton is its greatest strength. The school would not be the same if I didn't feel at home every time I walked on campus."

Kania's MBA program can be completed on a part-time basis, and therefore, a majority of students work full time while enrolled in the program. Drawing hardworking professionals from the local community, Kania students are "diverse, friendly, and bring many real-world experiences that contribute in a positive way to discussions." Generally speaking, part-time students are well integrated into the MBA program. Some, however, say they would like more weekend classes, as well as a "wider range of courses and resources to graduate students who work full time during the day." For students who would like to attend the program full time, the school operates an "excellent graduate assistantship program," which can help offset the cost of education.

Career and Placement

From a career standpoint, University of Scranton's location has both pluses and minuses. On the one hand, Scranton is within striking distance of several major metropolitan centers on the East coast, putting students in the running for positions in Philadelphia, New York, or Pittsburg. However, because Scranton is a smaller city, there are fewer job and internship opportunities in the region. Fortunately, Scranton MBAs are first in line for local positions, as the school boasts "the best reputation among business schools in Northeastern PA."

The office of Career Services at the University of Scranton assists the school's undergraduate and graduate students in locating internships and full-time employment. Throughout the year, they hold workshops on various professional development topics and also maintain an online job database, which lists current vacancies. Students say they could use a bit more assistance from the Career Services center when it comes to looking

ADMISSIONS CONTACT: JAMES L. GOONAN, DIRECTOR, GRADUATE ADMISSIONS
ADDRESS: 800 LINDEN STREET SCRANTON, PA 18510-4631 UNITED STATES
PHONE: 570-941-7600 • FAX: 570-941-5995 • E-MAIL: GRADUATESCHOOL@SCRANTON.EDU
WEBSITE: ACADEMIC.SCRANTON.EDU/DEPARTMENT/GRADSCH/GMBA.HTM

for a job; however, they also point out that the "Jesuit tradition and help from other Jesuit schools is a big plus."

Student Life and Environment

The Kania School of Management is located on the university's "scenic," 58-acre campus in downtown Scranton. In addition to the beautiful and modern business facilities, students can take advantage of all the resources available through the larger campus, including numerous libraries and wide-ranging wireless Internet. The sense of community is among the most appealing aspects of the Scranton MBA program, and "life at the University of Scranton is very vibrant among the students." In fact, many students mention the school's unique, family-like atmosphere, which tends to attract "very diverse and extremely friendly" people.

Many graduate students commute to the University of Scranton in the evenings, and therefore "spend very little time on campus." However, there are also many students who play an active role in the student community. A case in point, a current student tells us, "I am heavily involved in activities in the business school. I am a graduate assistant, so I know most of the faculty pretty well. I am an officer of the MBA Club, and I coordinate socials and presentations for the MBA students and faculty to go to." For those who'd like to mingle with their classmates, the MBA Student Association "works to get all the MBA students involved outside of the classroom. They have socials and presentations a few times a semester in order to get the MBA student socializing."

Admissions

When evaluating applicants for admission, the University of Scranton evaluates candidates on four major factors: previous academic performance, standardized test scores, letters of recommendation, and previous work experience. While all these factors play a role in an admissions decision, academic performance and GMAT scores are the most heavily weighted.

FINANCIAL FACTS

Annual tuition	$17,472
Fees	$2,500
Cost of books	$1,733
Room & board (on/off-campus)	$10,950/$14,495
% of students receiving aid	10
Average award package	$26,278

ADMISSIONS

Admissions Selectivity Rating	**69**
# of applications received	492
% applicants accepted	76
% acceptees attending	35
Average GMAT	510
Average GPA	3.3
TOEFL required of international students	Yes
Minimum TOEFL (paper/computer)	500/173
Application fee	$50
International application fee	$50
Regular application deadline	rolling
Regular notification	rolling
Deferment available	Yes
Maximum length of deferment	2 years
Transfer students accepted	Yes
Transfer application policy A transfer from an AACSB-accredited school Jesuit school, otherwise 6 credits max.	
Non-fall admissions	Yes

EMPLOYMENT PROFILE	
Career Rating	79

UNIVERSITY OF SOUTH CAROLINA
MOORE SCHOOL OF BUSINESS

GENERAL INFORMATION
Type of school   Public
Environment   City
Academic calendar   Semester

SURVEY SAYS...
Good social scene
Good peer network
Solid preparation in:
Operations
Teamwork
Doing business in a global economy

STUDENTS
Enrollment of parent
institution   28,000
Enrollment of
business school   700
% male/female   66/34
% out-of-state   80
% part-time   59
% minorities   10
% international   21
Average age at entry   27
Average years work
experience at entry   3.4

ACADEMICS
Academic Experience Rating   **83**
Student/faculty ratio   30:1
Profs interesting rating   82
Profs accessible rating   93
% female faculty   22
% minority faculty   3

Joint Degrees
JD/IMBA 4 years, JD/MHR 3 years,
JD/MACC 3 years.

Prominent Alumni
Larry Wilson, CEO, IT Company;
Shigeru Sekine, President, Nikko
Chemicals; Keilie Cooper Johnson,
Sr. Product Manager, Glazo Smith
Kline; Whitney MacEachern, VP Latin
American Affairs, Citigroup; Larry
Kellner, President, Continental
Airlines; William M. Ginn, CEO, exec-
utive officer, Sumitomo Mitsui
Banking Corporation, Chairman, CEO,
SMBC Leasing and Financing, Inc.;
David B. Holl, president and CEO,
Mary Kay Inc.; Gary M. Parsons,
Chairman, XM Satellite Radio..

Academics

"If international exposure is what you are looking for, the Moore School of Business is top-notch," MBAs at University of South Carolina agree, citing "the international focus of all course matter from the very beginning of the curriculum." Moore's flagship program is its international MBA (IMBA), in which "The MBA is integrated with foreign language studies and international focus. It's more than just an MBA plus international electives or an MBA plus language study." IMBA students choose from among two program tracks. The language track emphasizes multilingualism, international internships, and geopolitical issues. The global track focuses more intensely on political, business, and economic issues that impact international investment; it, too, includes an international internship.

All students complete a core curriculum that "is well integrated with respect to individual disciplines (accounting, management, etc.) and international realities." Moore also offers several specialized master's degrees and a professional MBA. Students cite finance, accounting, and operations as Moore's strongest areas ("We learn more in operations here than most managers would within 2 years on the job," one student opines), while marketing and information systems are sometimes deemed "less than satisfactory."

Students place their international internships in the asset column, telling us that "the school gives 5 months for an international internship to every student." The experience is "second to none." Professors also score high marks with students: "[They] have fabulous forward-thinking planning about curriculum possibilities for the electives that are offered after the internship, during the second year. The professors want to maintain cutting-edge competitive advantages in what they impart to students as 'deep skills sets.'" Moore's administration "is excellent," placing it in stark contrast to the administration of the university at large, which students deem "two stone-throws away from Neanderthal. Even for a state university it is average at best." Students also complain that "the school really needs to improve its facilities and separate the IMBA program from the rest of the university." "A new building is supposedly on its way in the next several years. Let's just hope this occurs."

Career and Placement

Students tell us that Moore's Career Management "has actually turned things around in the last 2 or 3 years" and is now "Outstanding. Resources for finding jobs and job search help are both readily available." Students report that "the Graduate Career Management Office does a fantastic job of focusing their company contact efforts on employers requested by current students, and they present many on-campus opportunities for students in addition to offering $300 per student in the second year to attend an approved job fair or recruiting event." Students are especially pleased that "there have been more multinational companies coming to school this year," although they note that these companies "generally hire for local jobs and are not open to putting students in international locations."

Students observe that "the international students who come to the Moore School find it very difficult to find employment in the U.S. because most of the companies will not

REENA LICHTENFELD, DIRECTOR, GRADUATE ADMISSIONS & ENROLLMENT MGMT.
ADDRESS: 1705 COLLEGE STREET COLUMBIA, SC 29208 UNITED STATES
PHONE: 803-777-4346 • FAX: 803-777-0414
E-MAIL: GRADADMIT@MOORE.SC.EDU • WEBSITE: MOORESCHOOL.SC.EDU

sponsor a work visa." One such international student notes, "Approximately 99 percent of the companies coming to recruit on campus are looking either for U.S. citizens or permanent residents. I am a Romanian citizen and would like very much to work somewhere in Europe, but none of the companies present on campus seem to have any opportunities for me in this direction." Top employers of Moore MBAs include: Ingersoll Rand, CHEP, Citibank, Bank of America, Hilti, BBandT, PPG, Michelin, ExxonMobil and Liberty Mutual.

Student Life and Environment

Moore places its core classes into cohorts, and "This, along with class size, makes students an extremely close group." Students endure a first semester with "an extremely heavy and accelerated course load," but afterwards "Things ease up," and by second year "Things can be very relaxed, and students may find that they can easily balance part-time work and school." Students also find time for extracurriculars "or finance clubs that organize different social events, tours, wine tastings, and other activities. Moreover, students are enjoy getting to know each other at events like tailgates, birthday parties, or other get-togethers. The balance between studies and relaxation is very good, especially during the second year."

Admissions

Applications to the IMBA program at Moore must include: an official application to the USC Graduate School, including letters of recommendation and personal essays; official transcripts documenting all postsecondary academic work; and satisfactory GMAT scores. At least 2 years of meaningful professional experience is strongly preferred. International applicants whose first language is not English must submit official score reports for the TOEFL, unless they have a degree from an American college or university. In addition to the IMBA, the Moore School also offers a Master of Accountancy, a Master of Human Resources, a Master of Arts in Economics, and a Professional MBA. Admissions requirements are most stringent for the IMBA program and personal interview may be required.

FINANCIAL FACTS

Annual tuition (in-state/ out-of-state)	$35,000/$52,000
Fees	$525
Cost of books	$2,000
Room & board (on/off-campus)	$13,000/$15,000
% of students receiving aid	82
% of first-year students receiving aid	89
% of students receiving loans	72
% of students receiving grants	47
Average award package	$12,000
Average grant	$14,000
Average student loan debt	$36,000

ADMISSIONS

Admissions Selectivity Rating	**87**
# of applications received	325
% applicants accepted	58
% acceptees attending	56
Average GMAT	638
Range of GMAT	570–710
Average GPA	3.3
TOEFL required of international students	Yes
Minimum TOEFL (paper/computer)	600/250
Application fee	$50
International application fee	$50
Application Deadline/Notification	
Round 1:	11/15 / 12/07
Round 2:	02/15 / 03/08
Round 3:	05/15 / 06/08
Early decision program?	Yes
ED Deadline/Notification	Summer II
for IMBA, Nov. 15 / 12/07	
Transfer students accepted	Yes
Transfer application policy	
Can transfer up to a maximum of 12 credit hours.	
Non-fall admissions	Yes
Need-blind admissions	Yes

Applicants Also Look At

Duke University, Georgetown University, The University of North Carolina at Chapel Hill, The University of Texas at Austin, Thunderbird, University of Georgia, Wake Forest University.

EMPLOYMENT PROFILE

Career Rating	88	Grads Employed by Function	% Avg. Salary
Primary Source of Full-time Job Acceptances		Finance	39 $81,095
School-facilitated activities	54%	Human Resources	1 $67,200
Graduate-facilitated activities	46%	Marketing	25 $77,437
Average base starting salary	$76,000	MIS	1 NR
Percent employed	88	Operations	4 $70,333
		Consulting	11 $64,742
		General Management	6 $75,493
		Other	9 $69,833

Top 5 Employers Hiring Grads
Bank of America; Clariant; Ingersoll Rand; Exxon Mobil; Liberty Mutual

UNIVERSITY OF SOUTH DAKOTA
BEACON SCHOOL OF BUSINESS

GENERAL INFORMATION
Type of school	Public
Environment	Village
Academic calendar	Semester

SURVEY SAYS...
Good peer network
Solid preparation in:
Finance
Accounting
Communication/interpersonal skills
Quantitative skills

STUDENTS
Enrollment of parent institution	8,400
Enrollment of business school	199
% male/female	50/50
% out-of-state	15
% part-time	55
% minorities	3
% international	10
Average age at entry	26

ACADEMICS
Academic Experience Rating	**73**
Student/faculty ratio	15:1
Profs interesting rating	85
Profs accessible rating	71
% female faculty	15
% minority faculty	5

Joint Degrees
JD/MBA 3 years.

Prominent Alumni
John Thune, US Senator from South Dakota.

Academics

Boasting both convenience and quality, University of South Dakota serves the local community with the only AACSB-accredited business program in the state. For South Dakotans, there is no better package than a USD MBA, as the "school is cheap, has small class sizes along with faculty that is always available to help out, is close to home, and has just as many opportunities as a bigger graduate school would have." Operating a full-time MBA program at the school's main campus in Vermillion, as well as a part-time cohort program at a satellite campus in Sioux Falls and a part-time online program, many students say the school's convenient location was one of the main factors in their decision to attend USD. However, the school's accreditation, reputation, and special East Asian Institute also draws a smattering of international students to the Vermillion campus.

While this state school is low cost, it maintains high-quality academic programs. Drawing a team of experienced professors from across the nation, USD "faculty are overall very easy to talk to, are accessible outside of class, and are focused on learning." A student writes, "The professors seem very eager to help us learn. Often times I have asked many questions and they were willing to spend the time answering questions, even if it was not directly related to the coursework." When it comes to the administration, "it is easier to be in contact with the directors of the program, as well as the dean, because the school is small." A current student adds, "The way I look at it is, if a faculty member with a PhD is willing to stay at this school and teach here in this small town, there is more passion for educating students here than at some other schools."

Before students can begin the MBA program at USD, they must complete a series of prerequisite courses in business essentials. Undergraduate business majors will easily meet these requirements; however, students coming to the program from other disciplines should expect to take introductory economics, accounting, statistics, and finance courses before they begin the MBA, or else be prepared to pass a challenge exam in these subjects. Once they have begun the official MBA curriculum, students will be versed in managerial and high-level business topics, with the option of specializing in health services administration, or simply pursuing a general MBA.

Throughout the MBA curriculum, students appreciate the fact that "classroom environments are small, making it easier to interact and get to know everyone at least on an acquaintance level." In both the daytime and evening programs, discussion is encouraged, and students learn a lot from their cohorts. While some have more limited career experiences, many others join the MBA program midway through careers as "software engineers, CFO, directors, and analysts." A student details, "My fellow students have great ideas and have great experiences to share with the class."

Career and Placement

The University of South Dakota Career Development Center offers a range of services to undergraduate and graduate students, including career and life coaching, resume review and cover letter assistance, and mock interviews. Their full events calendar includes various career fairs and campus recruiting events. This year, recruiters from various companies visited the business school, including Wells Fargo Financial and Federated Insurance. In addition, you'll be able to accomplish some useful networking right on campus, because USD professors "have done their own research and teaching at other major universities as well as abroad. They have many contacts."

ADMISSIONS CONTACT: DR. ANGELINE LAVIN, MBA PROGRAM DIRECTOR
ADDRESS: 414 E. CLARK, SCHOOL OF BUSINESS VERMILLION, SD 57069 UNITED STATES
PHONE: 866-890-1622 • FAX: 605-677-5058
E-MAIL: MBA@USD.EDU • WEBSITE: WWW.USD.EDU/BUSINESS/MBA

Student Life and Environment

University of South Dakota is a smaller state university with a friendly vibe and nice facilities. The full-time MBA program takes place on the school's main campus in Vermillion, where graduate students can take advantage of all the resources and facilities available at the school's peaceful, 200-acre campus. While the surrounding town of Vermillion isn't a hub of urban activity, there are plenty of outdoor activities in the surrounding area (and throughout the state) to satisfy your recreational needs.

The part-time program, on the other hand, is located in Sioux Falls. In this larger city environment, most students work full time and attend class in the evenings. As a result, the campus atmosphere is a bit more pared down, though students nonetheless report a friendly and collaborative environment. In and outside of classes, "everyone gets along for the most part, and their behavior is professional." MBA students "are all very outgoing; they understand when to have fun and when to get down to business."

Admissions

To apply to the University of South Dakota, students must submit official GMAT scores and undergraduate transcripts, as well as two letters of recommendation, a statement of purpose, and a current resume. International applicants must have a TOEFL score of at least 550 (paper version) or 213 (computer version) as well as a score of at least 79 on the IBT or 6.0 on the IELTS. Qualified full-time students may also choose to apply for one of the competitive Graduate Assistantships, which helps offset the costs of the USD education.

FINANCIAL FACTS

Annual tuition (in-state/ out-of-state)	$4,133/$12,187
Fees	$4,688
Cost of books	$1,300

ADMISSIONS

Admissions Selectivity Rating	70
# of applications received	202
% applicants accepted	75
% acceptees attending	60
Average GMAT	555
Average GPA	3.34
TOEFL required of international students	Yes
Minimum TOEFL (paper/computer)	550/213
Application fee	$35
International application fee	$35
Regular application deadline	6/1
Regular notification	rolling
Deferment available	Yes
Maximum length of deferment	3 years
Transfer students accepted	Yes
Transfer application policy	Maximum of 9 credit hours from an accredited institution may be transferred.
Non-fall admissions	Yes
Need-blind admissions	Yes

EMPLOYMENT PROFILE

Career Rating	71
Percent employed	95

UNIVERSITY OF SOUTHERN CALIFORNIA
MARSHALL SCHOOL OF BUSINESS

GENERAL INFORMATION

Type of school	Private
Environment	Metropolis
Academic calendar	Semester

SURVEY SAYS...
Good social scene
Good peer network
Helpful alumni
Solid preparation in:
Doing business in a global economy

STUDENTS

Enrollment of parent institution	33,408
Enrollment of business school	1,267
% male/female	66/34
% out-of-state	45
% part-time	64
% minorities	8
% international	26
Average age at entry	28
Average years work experience at entry	5

ACADEMICS

Academic Experience Rating	**94**
Student/faculty ratio	3:1
Profs interesting rating	75
Profs accessible rating	88
% female faculty	18
% minority faculty	3

Joint Degrees
Dual degree programs: MBA/DDS (Dental Surgery), (MBA/MA) East Asian Area Studies; MSG/MBA (Gerontology), MBA/MSISE (Industrial and Systems Engineering), MBA/MA (Jewish Communal Service), JD/MBA; MD/MBA; MBA/MPL (Planning), PharmD/MBA (Pharmacy), MBA/MRED (Real Estate Development), MBA/MSW (Social Work); MBA/EdD; JD/MBT (Law and Business Taxation).

Academics

Offering "international business learning opportunities not available elsewhere" as well as solid programs in entrepreneurship, real estate, marketing, and entertainment, the University of Southern California's Marshall School of Business excels in a broad range of areas. Best of all, perhaps, USC boasts "the most amazing alumni network in the nation," a huge asset when the time for job searches arrives. As one student explains, "I have never met another Trojan anywhere in the world who wasn't excited to meet another fellow Trojan!" "The Trojan Network is enormous and expansive, providing a lifetime equity of resources."

Marshall offers a 2-year full-time program as well as a part-time evening MBA, an executive MBA, and a 1-year international MBA (called the IBEAR MBA). The school "combines a rigorous curriculum" with "the personal attention of a private college." The MBA program here "has a strong emphasis on providing students an international perspective on business issues. It is more than just saying 'We think it is important that you consider other cultures.' At Marshall, it's mandatory that all students work on a consulting project for a company overseas and travel to that region through the PRIME program. As a result of PRIME and other programs, I've had meaningful work, educational, and fun experiences in Singapore, Thailand, Vietnam, and in Western Europe."

Marshall professors "are outstanding. They bring new research into the classroom and encourage students to actively participate in class." The faculty represents "a mixture of academics and recent career switchers from their fields in business . . . they do a very good job giving us a base to learn from." Course work is demanding; one student warns, "Marshall is much more difficult than I expected. I have 9 years of work experience and consider myself a fairly bright individual. If I put in a decent amount of work and keep up with the reading, I can get a B-plus in our classes with relative ease, but it really is difficult to break the A barrier." Administrators "are committed to growth and innovation as an institution." As a result, "Chaos is inherent when new programs and classes are initiated. . . . This is a leading school's greatest challenge, and USC Marshall does everything in its power to attend to students' individual needs as well as meet their own goals and expectations."

Career and Placement

Marshall's Career Resources Center "has already made incredible changes" since bringing on a new director in 2004. "The resources and energy the Career Coaches bring to the students are head and shoulders above what students at [another prominent area business school] have. While I'm sure the CRC will continue to improve and bring in more high-profile companies, it is already a premier organization." Students praise the center's 1-week winter inter-term program for first-years, through which "students learn how to fine tune their resume and interview skills. Additionally, they learn about networking, discover their inner interests, and come up with a value proposition. I believe this gives Marshall students a leg up in recruiting."

Companies most likely to employ Marshall MBAs include: Deloitte Touche Tohmastu, Wells Fargo, Mattel, The Walt Disney Company, Warner Brothers, Bank of America, Countrywide, Neutrogena, JPMorgan Chase, Intel, Booz Allen Hamilton, McKinsey & Company, Ernst & Young, Nissan North America, and Goldman Sachs.

Student Life and Environment

Full-time students tell us that "there are numerous professional and social club opportunities in which to be involved at Marshall." Several point out that "being involved with the community is easy and fun due to the Challenge 4 Charity Club, which schedules regular volunteer days for junior achievement and hosts parties at popular LA night clubs where the entry fees are donated to the Special Olympics." One student adds, "With the numerous clubs and organizations, USC students are really only limited by the amount of time and energy they possess. Personally, I wanted to take a leadership role in the community, and have had the opportunity to do just that. That makes my schedule a little bit more hectic than normal, but that was a personal decision. Really, life at Marshall is as challenging as one has the ambition to make it." Throughout the program and the campus, students enjoy "a very communal atmosphere. Football season is amazing."

Los Angeles is a great hometown, "a fun and vibrant city" with "fabulous weather all year round." Students note that "living in LA requires a car" and tell us that there are "nice apartments by the ocean for a decent price" within a 20-minute commute of the campus. The city provides many opportunities "to spend time together outside of class." "There are parties or small get-togethers almost every weekend."

Admissions

The Marshall Admissions Office warns that its MBA programs are "highly selective," and that the Admissions Committee "carefully assesses each candidate on a number of dimensions, including prior academic, professional, and personal accomplishments." All applicants must provide the school with official transcripts for all postsecondary academic work, an official GMAT score report, an official TOEFL score report (for international students who have not previously attended an English-language undergraduate or graduate program), an online application, a current resume, three required essays (a fourth optional essay is available), and two letters of recommendation (at least one from a direct supervisor is preferred).

Prominent Alumni
Cho Yang Ho, Chairman/CEO, Korean Air Lines Co., Ltd.; Stephen C. Goodall, CEO, J.D. Power and Associates; J. Terrence Lanni, Chairman/CEO, MGM MIRAGE; Paul Orfalea, Founder/Chairman Emeritus, Kinko's; Robert B. McKnight, Chairman/CEO, Quicksilver Inc.

FINANCIAL FACTS
Annual tuition	$35,212
Fees	$598
Cost of books	$1,344
Room & board	$13,146

ADMISSIONS
Admissions Selectivity Rating	96
# of applications received	1,651
% applicants accepted	29
% acceptees attending	47
Average GMAT	689
Range of GMAT	640–740
Average GPA	3.3
TOEFL required of international students	Yes
Minimum TOEFL (paper/computer)	600/100
Application fee	$150
International application fee	$150
Regular application deadline	4/1
Regular notification	5/25
Application Deadline/Notification	
Round 1:	12/01 / 02/01
Round 2:	1/15 / 03/30
Round 3:	2/15 / 04/27
Round 4:	04/01 / 05/25
Need-blind admissions	Yes

Applicants Also Look At
Columbia University, New York University, Stanford University, University of California—Los Angeles, University of California—Berkeley, University of Michigan.

EMPLOYMENT PROFILE
Career Rating	91	Grads Employed by Function	%	Avg. Salary
Percent employed	94	Finance	44	$88,167
		Marketing	20	$87,348
		Operations	1	NR
		Consulting	15	$97,497
		General Management	1	NR
		Other	19	$84,723

Top 5 Employers Hiring Grads
Amgen; General Electric; Mattel; Bank of America Securities; Proctor & Gamble

UNIVERSITY OF SOUTHERN MAINE
SCHOOL OF BUSINESS

GENERAL INFORMATION

Type of school	Public
Environment	Town
Academic calendar	Semester

SURVEY SAYS...

Students love Portland, ME
Friendly students
Solid preparation in:
Accounting
Teamwork
Quantitative skills
Computer skills

STUDENTS

Enrollment of parent institution	10,478
Enrollment of business school	136
% male/female	44/56
% out-of-state	25
% part-time	74
% minorities	5
% international	22
Average age at entry	30
Average years work experience at entry	5

ACADEMICS

Academic Experience Rating	**70**
Student/faculty ratio	20:1
Profs interesting rating	78
Profs accessible rating	64
% female faculty	21
% minority faculty	5

Joint Degrees

MBA/BS 5 years, BS/MSA (Accounting) 5 years, MBA/MS (Nursing) 3–4 years, JD/MBA 4–5 years.

Academics

The MBA program at the University of Southern Maine focuses its attention primarily on students "who wish to advance their careers and contribute to their companies." It serves a largely part-time student body whose members hold full-time jobs in the area and seek a degree that will help them "develop cross-functional business solutions to real-world problems [and] cultivate a broad critical perspective, interpersonal skills, and the analytical tools of management." USM's full-time student body is primarily enrolled in the 3-2 MBA program, which allows undergraduates to earn a bachelor's degree and an MBA in five years.

Part-time students can complete USM's 33-credit sequence in two years, although some take longer. The curriculum consists of nine three-hour core courses and two three-hour electives. "All classes are held in the evening" so that working students can attend the MBA program, which students appreciate. One such student writes, "This school is well-located for part-time students and it caters well to them. The administration strongly supports the students." Because of the limited number of electives available, students cannot fashion an area of concentration here, a situation some would like to see addressed. One says, "I work in the financial services industry and would love to be able to come out of USM with a finance concentration MBA."

USM professors "are well integrated into the local business community, opening up several great opportunities for enriching projects." Their quality as classroom instructors varies; "Some seem to teach to the lowest common denominator, but generally they are good to very strong," students tell us. They single out instructors in operations, accounting, and finance for their expertise and "ability to inspire learning in their students." Many agree the b-school facility "needs to be vastly improved," adding that "the school desperately needs a new building of their own with more modern, comfortable facilities."

Career and Placement

USM's website states: "Because many of our students are already employed in management positions, we do not have a formal placement service for MBA or MSA students." The site adds that "opportunities for employment often come to our attention," and these opportunities "are passed on to students for consideration." Students may use the services of the USM Career Services Office, which serves the entire university population. Students may also work with the Office of Graduate Studies, which employs a career advisor to administer career assessments, counsel students in resume building and interviewing skills, and arrange networking opportunities.

Student Life and Environment

Because "the University of Southern Maine is mainly a commuter college," "there is really very little in the way of organized outside activities. We all have a local life outside of school which demands our time." One student observes, "There isn't a whole lot of school spirit and clubs like at other universities. The only club I've heard of for the MBA program is the MBA Association. Unfortunately, any clubs that students are asked to participate in have meetings when many students are in class. That also goes for most networking opportunities that are available." Extracurricular life isn't totally dead, though; according to one MBA, "The school does try to bring students together for occasional special events, and many professors hold off-campus gatherings on the last night of class that provide a good networking opportunity with other students."

USM's MBA program is a small one, the majority of whose students attend part time. They are "good-natured, intelligent individuals" who are "motivated but not extremely driven in a business sense. They are hard-working and striving for knowledge," creating "a positive learning environment." The mix of "older students with families and substantial professional backgrounds and younger students with less work experience but more recent educational experience" is a "positive mix," students say. They also love that "the academic community is quiet and the scenery is wonderful, very relaxing."

Portland is home to the School of Business' main campus. With a population just under a quarter of a million, Portland is the largest city in Maine. It serves as the state's financial, business, and retail center; its major industries include tourism, telecommunications, technology, light manufacturing, and insurance.

Admissions

All applicants to the MBA program at USM must submit a completed application, two copies of official transcripts for all postsecondary work (including work at USM), GMAT scores, three letters of recommendation, a resume, and a personal essay. In addition, international students must also submit a certificate of finances and, if English is not their first language, TOEFL scores. Fully admitted students must have a formula score of 1,100 under the formula [(undergraduate GPA × 200) + GMAT score] and a minimum GMAT score of 500. The GMAT requirement is waived for students who have completed a terminal degree (e.g. PhD, JD, MD). The admissions office considers rigor of undergraduate field of study, reputation of undergraduate institution, potential, likelihood of enhancing the educational environment at USM, demonstrated leadership, evidence of creativity, and record of accomplishment in business in making its admissions decisions. Prior to commencing the MBA program, all students must complete, or demonstrate competency in, the following 'foundation' areas: managing organizational behavior, IT/MIS, economics, accounting, probability and statistics, finance, marketing, and management science. Students with deficiencies in these areas will be notified at the time of their admission.

FINANCIAL FACTS

Annual tuition (in-state/ out-of-state)	$4,860/$13,572
Fees	$561
Cost of books	$1,000
Room & board (on-campus)	$7,800
% of students receiving aid	68
% of first-year students receiving aid	47
% of students receiving loans	35
% of students receiving grants	47
Average award package	$8,779
Average grant	$5,479

ADMISSIONS

Admissions Selectivity Rating	73
# of applications received	60
% applicants accepted	100
% acceptees attending	68
Average GMAT	544
Range of GMAT	490–580
Average GPA	3.3
TOEFL required of international students	Yes
Minimum TOEFL (paper/computer)	550/213
Application fee	$50
International application fee	$50
Regular application deadline	8/1
Regular notification	Rolling
Deferment available	Yes
Maximum length of deferment	1 year
Transfer students accepted	Yes
Transfer application policy A maximum of nine Semester hours of transfer credit may be accepted.	
Non-fall admissions	Yes
Need-blind admissions	Yes

Applicants Also Look At

University of Maine, University of New Hampshire, EMBA.

THE UNIVERSITY OF TAMPA
JOHN H. SYKES COLLEGE OF BUSINESS

Academics

MBAs considering the John H. Sykes College of Business at the University of Tampa have three options: a full-time program that can be completed in 16 months, a part-time program that is typically completed in about three years, and a six-term Saturday professional MBA program. Roughly one-third of the student body attends full time.

MBA programs as Sykes include foundation courses, which are designed to prepare students with the fundamentals of business, both theories and practices. All full- and part-time MBA students must meet the foundation requirements prior to taking the integrated core courses. The integrated core curriculum here "stresses case studies and group work, allowing students to obtain knowledge and corporate values." All students also complete course work leading to a concentration, a leadership development program centered on mentoring and one-on-one coaching, and a capstone team project in which students create a strategic business assessment and present it to the top leadership of an area company. Concentrations are available in accounting, economics, entrepreneurship, finance, information systems management, international business, management, marketing, and non-profit management and innovation.

"Teamwork and leadership skills" are "the focus of this MBA program," students tell us. Professors here "have a genuine interest in students' success and academic endeavors" and "find ways to stimulate our thinking. They're not just giving us required material. If one doesn't understand the class material, he or she can always talk to professor during consultation hours. If even that is not enough, there is free tutoring available." Students praise Sykes' "strong relationship with the business community" and its "ability to include local area businesses in projects." Many, however, complain that "the school doesn't offer enough electives each semester," making it difficult to complete some concentrations.

Career and Placement

UT's Office of Career Services provides Sykes MBAs with a battery of services, including assessment tests, workshops in business etiquette and business dress, one-on-one counseling, and job fairs. Attendees of a recent on-campus career fair included Tampa Electric, Franklin Templeton, Ernst & Young, Deloitte Services, Inc., HSBC, Citigroup, Geico, Smith Barney, Depository Trust and Clearing Corp., Am South Bank, and Sun Trust Bank.

Student Life and Environment

A "beautiful campus" with "state-of-the-art facilities" makes the University of Tampa a pleasant and supportive place for students pursuing their MBAs. Many here do not get to enjoy the extra amenities very often, however. Part-time students have too many other responsibilities (e.g. work, family) to linger on campus a second longer than necessary, although they do appreciate that "there are plenty of places to relax or grab a bite to eat for a student coming from a full-time job to school."

Full-time students "are typically on campus all day. Many live on campus." And since there are "a lot of activities to do," why shouldn't they? For example, "There is the Student Organization of MBAs (SOMBA), which meets about once every two weeks. Any MBA student can come, and pizza and sodas are served. The Dean of Graduate Studies always comes. Meetings have a very relaxed yet very productive atmosphere: We talk about how to promote our school, what events we would like to happen and how to organize them, and what we would like to see different in our school." An MBA lounge is another "great feature because it is a place where MBA students can study and meet for group projects. You can usually always find a seat there because it isn't flooded with undergrads."

Sykes MBAs are predominantly from the Southeast U.S., although "a lot of international students" are in the mix as well. This "enthusiastic, diverse group of professionals from all around the globe, brought together to share in growth and learning" is "competitive, but in a cooperative atmosphere: lots of e-mails, phone calls, and meetings." Full-time students tend to have "little to no work experience," while "evening classes have many working professionals in them." Nearly everyone feels that Tampa Bay is the place to be, a metropolis that "is showing very strong signs of healthy growth to use MBAs in the coming years."

Admissions

Admission to the full-time and part-time MBA programs at Sykes is based on under-graduate work (a minimum GPA of 3.0 is required of degree-seeking students; non-degree seeking students need a minimum GPA of 3.0 for their final 60 hours of undergraduate credit); GMAT score (a minimum score of 500 is required) or GRE score (a minimum combined verbal-quantitative score of 1,000 is required); demonstration of proficiency in mathematics, computers, and written and oral communications skills; and professional experience. International students must demonstrate proficiency in English by scoring at least 577 on the written TOEFL or 230 on the computer-based TOEFL. Admission to the Saturday MBA program requires relevant work experience. Applicants to the Saturday MBA program are required to have five years of relevant work experience, including two years in a management position. Applicants to all programs must submit two letters of recommendation, a resume, and a personal statement.

FINANCIAL FACTS

Annual tuition	$7,200
Fees	$70
Cost of books	$622
Room & board (on/off-campus)	$7,616/$4,800
% of students receiving aid	55
% of first-year students receiving aid	18
% of students receiving loans	41
% of students receiving grants	32
Average award package	$11,501
Average grant	$9,908
Average student loan debt	$21,903

ADMISSIONS

Admissions Selectivity Rating	**74**
# of applications received	362
% applicants accepted	55
% acceptees attending	72
Average GMAT	523
Range of GMAT	470–560
Average GPA	3.35
TOEFL required of international students	Yes
Minimum TOEFL (paper/computer)	577/230
Application fee	$40
International application fee	$40
Regular application deadline	7/15
Regular notification	
Early decision program?	Yes
ED Deadline/ Notification	Spring 11/01 / 11/15
Deferment available	Yes
Maximum length of deferment	1 year
Transfer students accepted	Yes
Transfer application policy Up to 9 hours from an AACSB accredited school.	
Non-fall admissions	Yes
Need-blind admissions	Yes

Applicants Also Look At
University of Florida, University of South Florida.

EMPLOYMENT PROFILE			
Career Rating	**75**	**Grads Employed by Function**	**% Avg. Salary**
Average base starting salary	$55,833	Finance	35 $55,192
Percent employed	20	Human Resources	4 $82,500
		Marketing	17 $63,750
		MIS	15 $83,929
		General Management	15 $78,929
		Other	13 $58,333

THE UNIVERSITY OF TENNESSEE AT CHATTANOOGA
COLLEGE OF BUSINESS

Academics

Change is coming to the MBA program at The University of Tennessee at Chattanooga. The school recently revamped its MBA curriculum, with changes to be implemented in the fall of 2006. The new curriculum increases the length of the program from a minimum of 30 class hours to a minimum of 36 class hours. The school has reduced the number of foundation/background courses (classes that cover pre-MBA material and which can be waived by students with undergraduate business degrees), increased the number of core and elective options, and added a second capstone class (in entrepreneurship). Students admitted after August 2006 must complete the new curriculum to graduate.

UTC's predominantly part-time student body will most likely be satisfied with the changes so long as the school maintains "a reputation for academic rigor" and, perhaps more importantly, the "great convenience of evening class scheduling, which makes it possible to work full-time while attending." As one student observes, "The program is tailored to individuals who work full-time. The faculty and staff go above and beyond to help make the program feasible without compromising the quality of the academics." Even without the coming upgrades, students here are "very impressed" by the perception that "for a small school, this program has some professors who are high profile and important in their field, yet also accessible to the students. The professors really seem to love teaching."

Other assets here include "modern classroom facilities and computer labs" and "an administration that is professional and meticulous." While some here feel that the school should get a little pickier about "whom they select for the program, because some students are not quite ready" and others wish that "there were more options for students who aren't engineers, computer scientists, or in the manufacturing and production industries," most here recognize UTC as "an excellent value for the money. The professors have real-world experience and want to help you be as prepared as possible. The work for each course is designed to give real-world experience and help you understand better the macro business perspective. Overall this is an excellent school that will only get better as more money is funded toward it."

Career and Placement

UTC maintains a Career Resource Center for all students. The center houses a library of job-search related materials, including literature, annual reports, and job postings. The school's Placement and Student Employment Center also hosts on-campus recruitment interview sessions, one major annual career fair, and a number of special career fairs each year. Students and alumni may post their resumes online with the Placement Center.

Student Life and Environment

Students at UTC tell us that they experience an "excellent atmosphere for learning." Facilities "have integrated multimedia capability and are thoroughly up-to-date" and "small class sizes are conducive to student participation and enhance learning." Students here "for the most part take classes at night and are not a part of the life of the university." And while "the Grad School is attempting to create more of a community for all of the graduate students on campus by distributing interest surveys and planning activities," "not that many people participate."

ADMISSIONS CONTACT: MARK FAIRCHILD, GRADUATE PROGRAM LIAISON
ADDRESS: GRADUATE SCHOOL, DEPARTMENT 5305, 615 MCCALLIE AVENUE CHATTANOOGA, TN
37403 UNITED STATES • PHONE: 423-425-4667 • FAX: 423-425-5223
E-MAIL: MARK-FAIRCHILD@UTC.EDU • WEBSITE: WWW.UTC.EDU/BUSINESS

Many simply don't have the time for extracurricular commitments. Most students here "are working professionals who are committed to achieving the highest grade possible." These "hard workers are here to learn everything they can," and they "take the MBA program very seriously." Work and family obligations leave them with just enough time to study, but not to do much else. Students report that "there seem to be a lot of engineers in the program, but there are also many people from local insurance companies and other businesses in the area. It is not unusual to have classes with engineers, nurses, teachers, computer science professionals, etc."

Chattanooga is located on Tennessee's southern border, about halfway between Nashville and Atlanta. The city is home to a number of colleges and universities. UTC, the second-largest school in The University of Tennessee system, is the biggest. Others include Tennessee Temple University and Covenant College (located just outside the city, on Lookout Mountain).

Admissions

Applicants to the MBA program at UTC must provide the Admissions Committee with two official copies of transcripts for all academic work completed after high school and an official GMAT score report. The academic record must show either a minimum GPA of 2.5 for the applicant's entire undergraduate career or a GPA of at least 3.0 during the senior year in order for the applicant to gain unconditional admission. Successful applicants must have a minimum "admissions index" score of 950, calculated under the formula [(undergraduate GPA x 200) + GMAT Score] and a minimum score of 450 on the GMAT. Students who do not meet the above-mentioned qualifications may still earn conditional admission. International students whose first language is not English must submit an official score report for the TOEFL (minimum grade required: 550, paper-based; 213, computer-based).

FINANCIAL FACTS

% of students receiving aid	72
% of first-year students receiving aid	70
% of students receiving loans	61
% of students receiving grants	4
Average grant	$9,500

ADMISSIONS

Admissions Selectivity Rating	**70**
# of applications received	122
% applicants accepted	78
% acceptees attending	59
Average GMAT	512
Range of GMAT	470–570
Average GPA	3.21
TOEFL required of international students	Yes
Minimum TOEFL (paper/computer)	550/213
Application fee	$30
International application fee	$35
Regular application deadline	Rolling
Regular notification	Rolling
Deferment available	Yes
Maximum length of deferment	1 year
Transfer students accepted	Yes
Transfer application policy Students can transfer up to six hours from an AACSB accredited school.	
Non-fall admissions	Yes
Need-blind admissions	Yes

Applicants Also Look At

East Tennessee State University, Georgia State University, Middle Tennessee State University, Tennessee Tech University, University of Georgia, University of Tennessee, Vanderbilt University.

THE UNIVERSITY OF TENNESSEE AT KNOXVILLE
COLLEGE OF BUSINESS ADMINISTRATION

GENERAL INFORMATION

Type of school	Public
Environment	City
Academic calendar	Semester

SURVEY SAYS...

Students love Knoxville, TN
Friendly students
Good social scene
Good peer network
Happy students
Solid preparation in:
Teamwork

STUDENTS

Enrollment of parent institution	25,474
Enrollment of business school	140
% male/female	66/34
% out-of-state	32
% minorities	8
% international	18
Average age at entry	26
Average years work experience at entry	3.5

ACADEMICS

Academic Experience Rating	**87**
Student/faculty ratio	4:1
Profs interesting rating	71
Profs accessible rating	86
% female faculty	18
% minority faculty	9

Joint Degrees

JD/MBA 4years, MBA/MS (Engineering) 2 years + 6 week summer session, MBA/MS (Sport Management) 2 years.

Prominent Alumni

Ralph Heath, VP/COO, Lockheed Martin Aeronautics; Kiran Patel, CFO, Solectron; Joseph O'Donnell, CEO, Artesyn Technology; Bob Hall, CEO, Jewelry Television by ACN; Scott Parish, CFO, Alcon Entertainment.

Academics

The University of Tennessee's College of Business Administration has an easy time attracting the MBA-seeking masses with its 17 month program. Though "compressed in time," the school assures that "this program maintains all of the quality instruction that has made our graduates attractive to corporate recruiters." And students agree wholeheartedly that this is one of the school's "greatest strengths." "It is so stressful and fun at the same time that I think these 17 months would be one of the best times in my life," says one student.

UTK was the first MBA program in the nation to implement an integrated core curriculum, taught by a "cross-functional faculty team," that some students praise for always "moving and changing," making it "much more like business." They also appreciate that since "Classes for first-year students are lockstep," they have the opportunity to "become very familiar with peers." Meanwhile, others find it "frustrating" as "It hinders learning because it is all over the place." The list of possible concentrations for students includes finance, logistics, marketing, operations management, entrepreneurship, JD/MBA, an MS/MBA in engineering and in sports management. "So far," one student says, "I have learned volumes and have been exposed to a plethora of different real-world case scenarios. I feel that this has been a fabulous investment."

The extras are what makes the program stand out. The school offers a cultural exchange program for "academic purposes" and "credit hours" that has been hosted in locations as far-flung as Prague and Chile. After-class activities "provide the opportunity to hear speakers or participate in activities that enhance the learning experience," and "Professors always make themselves available to the students, sometimes even missing a lunch if time is pressing." In addition, "There are plenty of finance courses now included in the core curriculum" and "a large focus on entrepreneurship." All in all, students appreciate the emphasis placed on "great teamwork" and how the school is "very up-to-date with the current happenings in the business world." "I love how much attention is put in communication and presentation skills," one student explains. "The true-to-life work atmosphere allows us to prepare very well for real jobs."

Career and Placement

Although it had something of a rocky past, students praise Career Services now, noting that "under new direction" it really began "picking up." However, they do feel that more could be done to promote "the value of our program to more Fortune 100 companies." For the 2005–2006 year, the average salary for MBA graduates was $69,392.

Companies who have recruited on campus recently include Accenture, Amazon.com, AmSouth Bank, Burke, Deloitte Touche Tohmatsu, Eli Lilly and Company, FedEx, Hewlett-Packard, Milliken & Company, New York Life, and Wells Fargo, among many others.

ADMISSIONS CONTACT: DONNA POTTS, DIRECTOR OF ADMISSIONS, MBA PROGRAM
ADDRESS: 527 STOKELY MANAGEMENT CENTER KNOXVILLE, TN 37996-0552 UNITED STATES
PHONE: 865-974-5033 • FAX: 865-974-3826
E-MAIL: MBA@UTK.EDU • WEBSITE: MBA.UTK.EDU

Student Life and Environment

Knoxville, Tennessee is consistently recognized as one of the "best places to live in the United States" and UT is noted for being "a very large university in a growing, mid-major city." This may have something to do with the fact that it's nestled between the Great Smokey Mountains and the Cumberland Mountains, or that it's about a 2-hour drive from five national parks, seven state parks, and seven lakes. It is the largest city in east Tennessee and the third largest in the state. The shelter of the mountain ranges ensures that the climate is relatively temperate, with an annual average temperature of about 60 degrees (F). Students call the "downtown scene" "excellent with lots of bars, clubs, and entertainment venues." Even students coming from big cities have come to enjoy life in a smaller city. "I am enjoying the pace of life and getting to relive college to a certain degree, but this time I have a plan and more responsibility," one former New Yorker says.

Football consumes much of a UTK MBA's free time, but rest assured that "besides football games, there's plenty to do." Students say that "there are events taking place every-day, whether cultural or athletic," and that the social scene is "what you make of it." That is, if you plan on taking a break from the books. Despite staying busy with the 17-month program, many are able to find "a good balance between school and social life." "I have made great contacts," says one student. Another agrees, "They are the greatest bunch of people I have ever met! They are very smart but fun at the same time. I know for sure that I will miss my MBA life a lot after graduation."

Admissions

For the 80-odd students of the class of 2007, 66 percent were male, 34 percent were female, with 18 percent of the student body consisting of international students. The average age of an incoming student was 26, and the average undergraduate GPA was a 3.35. In addition, the average GMAT score was 600 and the average amount of work experience was 3 years. The international students came from places as diverse as Brazil, China, India, Japan, South Korea, Taiwan, and Thailand.

FINANCIAL FACTS

Annual tuition (in-state/ out-of-state)	$5,376/$15,156
Fees	$1,000
Cost of books	$3,000
Room & board (on/off-campus)	$7,400/$12,500
% of students receiving aid	43
% of first-year students receiving aid	27
% of students receiving grants	14
Average award package	$17,784
Average grant	$8,514

ADMISSIONS

Admissions Selectivity Rating	**88**
# of applications received	230
% applicants accepted	45
% acceptees attending	62
Average GMAT	600
Range of GMAT	560–640
Average GPA	3.3
TOEFL required of international students	Yes
Minimum TOEFL (paper/computer)	600/250
Application fee	$35
International application fee	$35
Regular application deadline	2/1
Regular notification	Rolling
Need-blind admissions	Yes

Applicants Also Look At

Arizona State University, Penn State University, University of Georgia, Vanderbilt University, Wake Forest University.

EMPLOYMENT PROFILE

Career Rating	77	Grads Employed by Function	%	Avg. Salary
		Finance	17	$54,300
		Marketing	22	$52,000
		Operations	31	$59,800
		Consulting	6	$60,300
		General Management	20	$53,600
		Other	4	$45,200

THE UNIVERSITY OF TEXAS AT ARLINGTON
COLLEGE OF BUSINESS

GENERAL INFORMATION
Type of school	Public
Environment	Metropolis
Academic calendar	Semester

SURVEY SAYS...
Good peer network
Cutting edge classes
Smart classrooms

STUDENTS
Enrollment of parent institution	25,297
Enrollment of business school	776
% male/female	54/46
% part-time	66
% minorities	28
% international	35
Average age at entry	31
Average years work experience at entry	5

ACADEMICS
Academic Experience Rating	**85**
Student/faculty ratio	20:1
Profs interesting rating	85
Profs accessible rating	78
% female faculty	16
% minority faculty	5

Joint Degrees
May combine any two degrees (usually MBA and specialized program).

Prominent Alumni
Gen. Tommy Franks, U.S. Army (ret.); John Goolsby, President CEO (ret.), Howard Hughes Corporation; Roy Williams, Chief Scaut Exec. (ret.), Boy Scouts America; Jerry Thomas, President/CEO, Decision Analyst, Inc.; Jackie Fouse, Sr. VP, CFO & Corp Strategy, Bunge, Ltd.

Academics

Savvy business students looking for maximum return on investment say you'll get "a high quality education for a reasonable price" at the University of Texas at Arlington. The school maintains an outstanding reputation in the Dallas-Fort Worth metropolitan area, and also attracts students for its unique fields of study, including an MBA concentration in real estate business and a rigorous master's program in quantitative finance. The accounting program also enjoys high repute, and "UT Arlington ranks in the top three schools in which the students pass all the sections of the CPA exam the first time around."

UT Arlington offers a number of MBA options for working professionals and for full-time students, both in Forth Worth and at the school's Arlington campus. In addition to the traditional MBA, which can be completed on a full-time or part-time basis, the school operates an accelerated 15-month Executive MBA for working professionals, and a part-time Cohort MBA, which offers a unique team-based approach to business study with a lockstep curriculum. You can even participate in a "wonderful" online MBA program through UT Arlington.

No matter if you are a full- or part-time student, you'll find yourself in classes with "a bright and disciplined group of folks," who are "focused on doing their best and con- tributing their part to the overall academic experience." Cohort students appreciate a particular sense of camaraderie, because "the lockstep program is crucial in getting to know [your] peers, and building and maintaining networks which can be used in future business endeavors." Of particular note, professional students feel that UT Arlington caters to their unique needs, helping them to balance the diverse challenges of work, school, and family life. At UT Arlington, both faculty and administrators "realize we have careers and lives, respect that, and work with us to make our learning experience the best it can be."

Academically, every professor has "an outstanding academic background, an impressive work history, and certifications in their field. Many are also authors, contributing to the advancement of their professions, while also putting their opinion out there to be criti- cized by their peers." In addition to full-time staff, "there is a good relationship between professors and companies around the DFW area; in many cases, executives have been invited as guest speakers." Although UT Arlington is a large public school, it isn't belea- guered by excessive administrative headaches. On the contrary, a current student attests, "Overall, I'm very pleased with the way the Business School is run. I haven't had any problems getting into the classes that I was interested in, and the professors have been very helpful."

Career and Placement

Thanks to the school's great regional reputation and the dedicated efforts of the career center, it's relatively easy to start a new career after finishing your MBA at UT Arlington. A current student praises, "The career services center in the College of Business provid- ed me with resume preparation, mock interviews, and made it simple for me, through the electronic networking system, to set up on-campus interviews with industry lead- ers." In addition, "the school offers an employment fair that connects the school with other companies."

There are myriad opportunities in Dallas and Fort Worth, and "the school has established a very good rapport with businesses around the metroplex, who easily absorb fresh graduates!" Getting to know your business school instructors can also be a beneficial first step, as "professors also maintain a vast network of former students that proves helpful for current students when they begin their job hunt." An accounting graduate adds these positive comments: "I was heavily recruited by the Big 4 accounting firms, as well as small local firms, middle-market firms, and "industry" firms with accounting departments (which is every firm). The opportunity that I had with being placed with a company was extraordinary."

Student Life and Environment

On this diverse, metropolitan campus, "each student is different from the next." Representing a "wide cross-section of society," UT Arlington attracts students of "every race, a range of ages," and students who are "married, single, and with children." You'll also find "a large number of foreign students in this MBA program," which most see as an advantageous way to "globalize your Business School experience." The one uniting factor is that "most everyone works, and brings with him or her a breadth of knowledge and experience."

Despite the diversity, UT Arlington students can nonetheless be grouped into two major categories: "married working professionals working to improve themselves," and "students that entered the program shortly after obtaining an undergraduate degree." In both groups, most students commute to UT Arlington (keep in mind that "there is no public transportation [to Arlington], so we need cars"); however, students say there is still plenty of campus life, if you're looking for a more traditional college experience. In fact, a current MBA candidate insists, "The school overall is moving from a "commuter" school to a more traditional school. More students are living on campus [and] more activities and organizations are starting." In addition, the larger university is home to "many interdisciplinary groups that offer multiple activities on campus: theater, recitals, sports, and so forth." However, weekends quiet down around Arlington, so "be ready to commute to Fort Worth or Dallas to accommodate your night-life plans."

Admissions

UT Arlington carefully considers both quantitative and qualitative factors in every admissions decision. Admissions requirements vary by program; however, for the traditional, two-year program, the average GMAT score and GPA for students entering the MBA program are 550 and 3.25, respectively. Work experience is not a requirement, but 2–5 years is preferred. To be considered for admission, students must also submit test scores and transcripts, as well as a statement of purpose, recommendations, and a resume.

FINANCIAL FACTS

Annual tuition (in-state/ out-of-state)	$11,802/$20,430
Fees (in-state/ out-of-state)	$2,058/$2,253
Cost of books	$1,000
Room & board (on/off-campus)	$4,800/$6,000
% of students receiving aid	20
Average award package	$8,500
Average grant	$1,000
Average student loan debt	$23,475

ADMISSIONS

Admissions Selectivity Rating	**80**
# of applications received	1,212
% applicants accepted	56
% acceptees attending	44
Average GMAT	550
Range of GMAT	470–620
Average GPA	3.25
TOEFL required of international students	Yes
Minimum TOEFL (paper/computer)	550/213
Application fee	$30
International application fee	$60
Regular application deadline	6/10
Regular notification	Rolling
Early decision program?	Yes
ED Deadline/ Notification	Rolling / 6/15
Deferment available	Yes
Maximum length of deferment	1 year
Transfer students accepted	Yes
Transfer application policy	
Maximum number of transferable credits is nine from an AACSB accredited university.	
Non-fall admissions	Yes
Need-blind admissions	Yes

THE UNIVERSITY OF TEXAS AT AUSTIN
McCOMBS SCHOOL OF BUSINESS

GENERAL INFORMATION
Type of school	Public
Environment	Metropolis
Academic calendar	Semester

SURVEY SAYS...
Students love Austin, TX
Good social scene
Good peer network
Solid preparation in:
Communication/interpersonal skills
Doing business in a global economy
Entrepreneurial studies

STUDENTS
Enrollment of parent institution	50,170
Enrollment of business school	1,091
% male/female	72/28
% out-of-state	37
% part-time	53
% minorities	8
% international	25
Average age at entry	28
Average years work experience at entry	5

ACADEMICS
Academic Experience Rating	**95**
Student/faculty ratio	6:1
Profs interesting rating	97
Profs accessible rating	77
% female faculty	26
% minority faculty	8

Joint Degrees
MBA/JD, MBA/MS (Manufacturing and Decision Systems Engineering), MBA/MS (Nursing), MBA/MA (Public Affairs), MBA/MA (Advertising), MBA/MA (Asian Studies), MBA/MA (Communication Studies), MBA/MA (Journalism), MBA/MA (Latin American Studies), MBA/MA (Middle Eastern Studies), MBA/MA (Radio-Television-Film), MBA/MA (Russian, East European, and Eurasian Studies).

Academics

The MBA program at the McCombs School of Business earns its stellar national reputation with "top 15 rankings in all the major concentrations" and excellent placement results, but it's the program's add-ons that have students here excited. McCombs students aren't simply satisfied to master their program's demanding curriculum; this school "attracts really driven and talented young professionals" anxious to "take advantage of all the MBA program has to offer, such as the MBA Investment Fund, Venture Fellows, Plus Program, MootCorp, the Austin Technology Incubator, etc."

McCombs' Plus Program "gets a lot of press" for "connecting students with their dream companies to work on consulting projects solving real business issues." One student reports that the program "enabled me to receive one-on-one professional coaching for teamwork, presentation skills, and interviewing. It has enabled me to do real projects with companies that I have always been curious about like REI. It has helped me get mergers and acquisition training that helped me learn the language prior to the interview season. It is a great way for me to branch out and build my exposure to new things." All these characteristics make Plus "very beneficial for career switchers," MBAs here agree.

Yet there are some here who insist that Plus "is not the crown jewel of the program." They point instead to several other programs, such as Venture Fellows, "a leadership and academic program that allows students the opportunity to learn more about the venture capital and private equity communities" through guest speakers and internships with local private equity and venture capital firms. They also trumpet the MBA Investment Fund, which "manages $15 million of all private dollars. No public or university money is managed here and the students have to report to private investors while managing the fund." Finally, there's the students' "widespread interest in global trips. With such a diverse student body and the importance of globalization, interest in international affairs is growing every day. Students can choose to study abroad for a semester and tons of students choose to participate in global trips--two-week excursions, part business/part culture—to large business development centers around the globe."

Students report strong offerings across the board, with pronounced strength in entrepreneurship, finance, and marketing. The faculty offers "both practitioners and academics that add to the overall learning experience," although they warn that "There are some incredible professors here, but those are the classes that are really hard to get into. If Texas can attract better teachers as opposed to just researchers (or develop them), it should be a top-ten school."

Career and Placement

McCombs' status as a high-ranking program ensures a robust recruitment season for MBAs. Students note that "the Texas MBA program offers one of the few specializations in energy finance and has considerable contacts in the energy industry, including major energy companies (ExxonMobil, Shell, El Paso, TXU, etc.). The MBA program also offers significant access to the major investment banks and their energy groups." Also, "The MBA alumni base is strong and supportive."

Top employers of McCombs MBAs include 3M, Accenture, Alliance Residential Co., Alvarez & Marsal,Bank of America Securities, Booz Allen Hamilton, Boston Consulting Group, Cambridge Associates, Capgemini U.S. LLC, Chase, Chevron, Citigroup, ConocoPhillips, Dell, Deloitte Consulting, Dimensional Fund Advisors, Discover Financial, Eli Lilly & Co., Everest Group, Exxon Mobil Corp., Frito-Lay, Hewlett-Packard, Hoover's, IBM, J.P. Morgan, Johnson & Johnson International, KPMG, Lehman Brothers, McKinsey &

Co., Mercer Management Consulting, Merrill Lynch, Microsoft Corp., Progressive Insurance, USAA Real Estate Co., Wachovia Securities, and Walmart.

Student Life and Environment

The McCombs MBA program works hard to build community fast. As one student explains, "The Texas MBA program offers new students the opportunity to meet classmates before classes start through the McCombs Adventure Program. This summer students traveled to Morocco, Costa Rica, Chile, and Napa Valley." The trend continues through students' first semester. "At the beginning, classes are back to back with your own cohort," writes one student. "After the first semester, people do one core class and the rest electives. People are more united at the beginning of the MBA given the constant interaction. As semesters progress, people get to gather in groups and have classes with other graduate or undergraduate peers."

Life on the Austin campus provides "a good combination of work and play. The first semester is brutal and filled with busy work, but the rest of the semesters offer more options for classes and a better learning environment. Plenty of social and cultural events throughout the year offer the opportunity for networking and building up the strong community here at McCombs." In addition, "Austin is a vibrant city that is perfect for business school students. The attractive nightlife and social network of students make the transition from the professional world to business school very smooth."

Admissions

The McCombs School accepts online applications only. A completed application must include: a resume detailing work history (two years of post baccalaureate work experience is strongly recommended); personal essays; official copies of transcripts for all post-secondary academic work; letters of recommendation; an official score report for the GMAT; and, for international students whose first language is not English, an official score report for the TOEFL. Programs designed to increase minority and disadvantaged populations at McCombs include: Jump Start, which "targets undergraduate seniors who are academically qualified for a top-ranked MBA but lack the required work experience"; Explore McCombs, a three-day preview of the school for qualified African-American, Hispanic-American, and Native-American applicants; participation in the Consortium for Graduate Study in Management, a thirteen-university alliance working to facilitate excellence in graduate business education for minority students; attending the annual conferences of the National Society for Hispanic MBAs (NSHMBA) and the National Black MBA; and Women's MBA Weekend, a three-day preview of the program for women considering an MBA.

Prominent Alumni

Jim Mulva, President/CEO, Conoco Phillips; William Johnson, Chairman, President & CEO, Heinz; Don Evans, former U.S. Secretary of Commerce; Sara Martinez Tucker, President/CEO, Hispanic Scholarship Fund; Gerard Arpey, Chairman, President & CEO, American Airlines.

FINANCIAL FACTS

Annual tuition (in-state/ out-of-state)	$14,882/$31,686
Fees	$7,536
Cost of books	$1,477
Room & board (off-campus)	$13,500
% of students receiving aid	54
% of first-year students receiving aid	54
% of students receiving loans	53
% of students receiving grants	22
Average award package	$42,456
Average grant	$14,564
Average student loan debt	$62,808

ADMISSIONS

Admissions Selectivity Rating	94
# of applications received	1,548
% applicants accepted	34
% acceptees attending	50
Average GMAT	673
Range of GMAT	640–710
Average GPA	3.38
TOEFL required of international students	Yes
Minimum TOEFL (paper/computer)	620/260
Application fee	$125
International application fee	$125
Regular application deadline	4/1
Regular notification	5/1
Deferment available	Yes
Maximum length of deferment	1 year
Need-blind admissions	Yes

Applicants Also Look At

Duke University, Harvard University, Northwestern University, The University of North Carolina at Chapel Hill, University of California—Berkeley, University of Michigan, University of Pennsylvania.

EMPLOYMENT PROFILE

Career Rating	91	Grads Employed by Function	%	Avg. Salary
Primary Source of Full-time Job Acceptances		Finance	39	$93,149
School-facilitated activities	155 (71%)	Marketing	26	$87,024
Graduate-facilitated activities	51 (24%)	MIS	2	$96,250
Unknown	11 (5%)	Operations	3	$86,714
Average base starting salary	$93,649	Consulting	20	$106,205
Percent employed	94	General Management	8	$92,135
		Other	2	$80,500

Top 5 Employers Hiring Grads
Dell; Citigroup; Deloitte Consulting; Chevron; Merrill Lynch

THE UNIVERSITY OF TEXAS AT DALLAS
SCHOOL OF MANAGEMENT

Academics

No matter what your age, background, or educational goals, UT Dallas is likely to offer an MBA program that will be a good match for your objectives and lifestyle. The school has been conferring MBA degrees since the early 1980s, and currently offers a part-time Professional MBA, an Executive MBA, and a Global Online MBA, as well as various PhD and MS programs. In addition, the school established a 16-month, full-time Cohort MBA in 1996. Through this program, "the school has an unbeatable value proposition for B-School students: 16 months, rigorous curriculum, excellent faculty and situated in the heart of a vibrant commercial ecosystem." Sound good? That's not all: "the icing on the top of the cake happens to be the extremely low cost of tuition."

While UTD's relatively new MBA programs have already garnered national attention for quality, you'll still enjoy the benefit of an atmosphere that is "young, dynamic, and open to change." A current student adds, "I am a professional student but when I go to school I feel that I am a high school kid again. The energy, enthusiasm and quest for knowledge makes me feel young and energetic." However, as the school ages, its reputation and rigorousness also seem to be on an upward trajectory. A student elaborates, "The school has really upped the ante, and the course work has double or tripled in recent years. The classes really demand that you learn the material and are able to demonstrate knowledge and fluency." At the helm of the academic experience is a fleet of talented, diverse, and "incredibly knowledgeable" faculty. A student details, "Many of the professors have a variety of life experiences to draw on when lecturing. I have had an Accounting instructor who used to design weapons for the military and a Marketing professor who has been an actor/talk show host. This variety brings a point of view that would never be found in a textbook."

Administration is smooth and efficient, and "even though UTD is a larger public university, it has a small-school feel in that you are not just a number. It would be quite difficult for a person to fall through the cracks." Nonetheless, UTD is a big school, so classes (especially in the evenings) can be uncomfortably over-stuffed with students. UT Dallas makes up for this unfortunate shortcoming through unmatched flexibility, offering students the ability "to complete your degree during the week, weekend, day, night, or online each semester as your life changes." The curriculum is likewise flexible and easy to tailor. After completing foundational courses, "the School of Management offers a broad array of electives, which allows the student to either specialize in a particular field or diversify and learn about several subjects."

Career and Placement

UTD business students have access to the university Career Center, as well as the SOM Career Management Center (CMC), which focuses exclusively on the business school. In addition to career workshops and counseling, the CMC hosts frequent panels and speaker sessions. At UTD, "almost every day it seems like some CEO is coming and speaking with the students in a panel. Placement is great of the Cohort MBA."

Many prominent companies recruit on campus, including American Express, Boeing, Cisco Systems, Deloitte, McKesson, State Farm Insurance, and Texas Instruments Incorporated, among many others. However, students worry that the school's largely regional reputation doesn't do justice to its world-class graduates. A current student laments, "The business school is excellent at UTD and I don't think the majority of the country recognize how good the school is." Even so, most graduates are sitting pretty, with an average starting salary in excess of $70,000 in recent years.

ADMISSIONS CONTACT: MONICA POWELL, PHD, ASSISTANT DEAN
ADDRESS: 800 WEST CAMPBELL ROAD RICHARDSON, TX 75080-3021 UNITED STATES
PHONE: 972-883-6595 • FAX: 972-883-4095 • E-MAIL: MPOWELL@UTDALLAS.EDU
WEBSITE: SOM.UTDALLAS.EDU/GRADUATE/MBA/FULLTIMEMBA

Student Life and Environment

UTD students share the drive and determination you'd expect to find at a top business program; however, they hail from a diverse cross-section of society. A student elaborates, "There is a huge mixture at UTD as far as work experience, cultural background, and gender. Some students are single, some are married with children, and others are just beginning their families." International students comprise 50 percent of the graduate population, a reflection of "the changes that are taking place in business due to globalization." Most students view their international classmates as yet another major advantage to the program, since students often have "the opportunity to share our diverse experiences and learn from each other" both in and out of the classroom.

For the many students who commute to UTD, campus life doesn't amount to much more than classes and library time. Still, the business school has a lively, hard-working atmosphere, and "the lounge areas are always bustling with students." On the larger university campus, there are "many clubs and organizations," and "from 24-hour gym facilities to a fantastic student union, where there is always something fun going on."

Admissions

UTD admissions standards are high. Currently, admission to the full-time Cohort MBA is particularly competitive, admitting just 25 percent of applicants. Admissions rates and requirements depend on the program to which you are applying. However, for the full-time program, the 2006 entering class had an average GMAT score of 650 and an average undergraduate GPA of 3.64 on a 4.0 scale. In addition to transcripts and test scores, students are required to submit personal essays and recommendation letters.

FINANCIAL FACTS

Annual tuition (in-state/ out-of-state)	$13,462/$26,172
Fees	$300
Cost of books	$2,000
Room & board	$7,500
% of students receiving aid	94
% of first-year students receiving aid	75
% of students receiving grants	94
Average award package	$15,000
Average grant	$15,000

ADMISSIONS

Admissions Selectivity Rating	93
# of applications received	191
% applicants accepted	40
% acceptees attending	70
Average GMAT	650
Range of GMAT	600–680
Average GPA	3.39
TOEFL required of international students	Yes
Minimum TOEFL (paper/computer)	550/213
Application fee	$50
International application fee	$100
Regular application deadline	5/1
Regular notification	6/15
Application Deadline/Notification	
Round 1:	01/15 / 03/01
Round 2:	03/01 / 04/15
Round 3:	06/01 / 06/15
Deferment available	Yes
Maximum length of deferment	1 year
Need-blind admissions	Yes

Applicants Also Look At

Southern Methodist University, The University of Texas at Arlington, The University of Texas at Austin, University of Dallas, University of North Texas.

EMPLOYMENT PROFILE

Career Rating	82	Grads Employed by Function	%	Avg. Salary
Primary Source of Full-time Job Acceptances		Finance	27	$55,250
School-facilitated activities	11 (73%)	Marketing	27	$58,875
Graduate-facilitated activities	4 (27%)	MIS	6	NR
Average base starting salary	$61,429	Operations	33	$70,020
Percent employed	94	General Management	7	NR

Top 5 Employers Hiring Grads

Deloitte; Countrywide; Blockbuster; PriceWaterhouse; Bank of America

THE UNIVERSITY OF TEXAS—PAN AMERICAN
COLLEGE OF BUSINESS ADMINISTRATION

Academics

The College of Business Administration at The University of Texas—Pan American offers both an evening Professional MBA program and an online MBA program. The college and the MBA program are accredited by the American Assembly of Collegiate Schools of Business (AACSB).

Students with an undergraduate background in business can complete UTPA's evening MBA program in two years. The program typically requires 36 credit hours, although students lacking academic background in some business-related areas are required to complete additional foundation courses that cover principles of accounting, economics, management, marketing, statistics, and finance. Students praise the program's "good study environment" with "very modern classrooms" as well as its diverse student population. One tells us that "UTPA is the University that educates most Mexican-Americans in the country, and it has a strong Hispanic MBA." They also appreciate that the program is "very affordable" and "has a great reputation" in the area. Students may develop an area of specialization by completing nine credit hours in one of the following disciplines: accounting, economics, finance, management, management information systems, or marketing. They may also choose to write a thesis instead of taking six of the nine hours of required electives; thesis topics must be approved by the academic committee.

The online MBA is administered jointly with seven other UT campuses (Arlington, Brownsville, Dallas, El Paso, Permian Basin, San Antonio, and Tyler). The online curriculum consists of 48 course hours. Students with sufficient backgrounds in business may have up to four core courses waived, reducing the number of required hours to 36.

UTPA professors "are genuinely interested in helping students in whatever is requested" and "will allow you the freedom to both learn as much as you want and explore your particular interests. The professors are all happy to be teaching you." Administrators are "making a concerted effort to improve the experience of the students" but "can be a bit slow to work with."

Career and Placement

Because UTPA's MBA program is relatively small, graduate students here share a career services office with business undergraduates. That office, called the Center for Advisement, Recruitment, Internships, and Retention (CARIR), provides career counseling services, job-related reference materials, and assistance in internship placements. The office participates in numerous regional and national online job databases, which students may access through their UTPA accounts. CARIR also organizes on-campus recruitment events each semester, although most of the recruitment is geared toward undergraduate students. Employers seeking MBAs at a recent Career Fair included Burton McCumber and Cortez, Luby's, and Valley Baptist Health System.

ADMISSIONS CONTACT: DR. KIA KOONG, DIRECTOR OF MBA PROGRAM
ADDRESS: 1201 WEST UNIVERSITY DRIVE EDINBURG, TX 78541-2999 UNITED STATES
PHONE: 956-381-3313 • FAX: 956-381-2970
E-MAIL: MBAPROG@UTPA.EDU • WEBSITE: WWW.COBA.PANAM.EDU/MBA/INDEX.HTM

Student Life and Environment

The typical UTPA MBA "works all day, goes to class half the night, and gets home just in time to put the kids to bed and have a late supper." He or she "is dedicated to the program and has the kind of work and world experience that high test scores can never make up for." There is "great diversity, especially culturally" here, as "most students speak Spanish as a second language and a high percent come from a variety of universities around the world. It is a great experience!" As one student explains, "Students' classroom comments often sound like a United Nations meeting! One of my classes has students from India, Mexico, Texas, China, Japan, Taiwan, Turkey, France, Romania, and I'm sure I've missed a couple others."

UTPA is a commuter school attended by part-time students with full time jobs, so "student life usually consists of a spouse and a child" when work and school aren't eating up their time. Those who can engage in extracurricular life praise "the new state-of-the-art gym," the "many mixers for students to attend," and "events from poker tournaments to trips to Europe."

UTPA is located in Edinburg, Texas, a city of nearly 58,000 in the southernmost section of the state. Students report that the location provides "great opportunities for those interested in a growing economy, proximity to the border, and industry." Education and health care are the area's major employment sectors; retail trade capitalizes on the city's location near the Mexico border.

Admissions

Applicants to University of Texas Pan American must submit all the following materials to the Admissions Committee: an application to the UTPA Graduate School; sealed copies of official transcripts for all previously attended post-secondary institutions; a sealed copy of an official GMAT score report. In addition, international students whose first language is not English must submit a sealed copy of an official TOEFL score report. The school requires applicants to receive a score of at least 1000 under the formula [(undergraduate GPA for final 60 semester hours of academic work ? 200) + GMAT score] and have an undergraduate GPA of at least 3.0 and score at least 400 on the GMAT in order to receive unconditional admission to the program. Those required to take the TOEFL must score at least 500. Those who fail to meet these benchmarks are generally denied admission. They may appeal this decision and may be subsequently admitted on the basis of "strong supporting documentation" such as letters of recommendation, resume, and "other relevant information indicating that the applicant should be successful in the Program (e.g., publications, presentations, etc.)."

FINANCIAL FACTS

Annual tuition (in-state/ out-of-state)	$2,797/$8,900
Fees (in-state/out-of-state)	$314/$402
Cost of books	$1,500
Average grant	$9,999

ADMISSIONS

Admissions Selectivity Rating	**75**
# of applications received	78
% applicants accepted	47
% acceptees attending	73
Average GMAT	450
Average GPA	3
TOEFL required of international students	Yes
Minimum TOEFL (paper/computer)	500/173
Application fee	$35
International application fee	$35
Regular application deadline	7/1
Regular notification	Rolling
Transfer students accepted	Yes
Transfer application policy Accept max. 3 courses	
Non-fall admissions	Yes
Need-blind admissions	Yes

THE UNIVERSITY OF TEXAS AT SAN ANTONIO
COLLEGE OF BUSINESS

GENERAL INFORMATION

Type of school	Public
Environment	Metropolis
Academic calendar	Semester

SURVEY SAYS...
Students love San Antonio, TX
Solid preparation in:
Finance
Quantitative skills

STUDENTS

Enrollment of parent institution	28,533
Enrollment of business school	360
% male/female	60/40
% part-time	72
% minorities	36
% international	10
Average age at entry	29
Average years work experience at entry	4

ACADEMICS

Academic Experience Rating	**83**
Student/faculty ratio	26:1
Profs interesting rating	79
Profs accessible rating	71
% female faculty	31
% minority faculty	50

Prominent Alumni
Gilbert Gonzalez, US Depart Arg. Undersecretary for Rural Dev; Ernest Bromley, President/CEO, Bromley & Associates; Jeanie Wyatt, CEO, South Texas Money Management; James Clingman, Chairman, San Antonio region of JPMorgan Chase & Co.; John McMurray, Chief Enterprise Risk Officer, Washington Mutual; A.J. Rodriguez, Deputy City Manager, City of San Antonio.

Academics

The "affordable" University of Texas at San Antonio College of Business has a "solid" regional reputation" and it's "very accessible to working professionals." The "well-designed MBA program" here requires 33 hours of course work (beyond preparatory core courses). There's also a thesis option, which tacks on an additional six hours. In addition to the general MBA, you can choose among 10 areas of concentration including accounting, health care management, marketing management, and real estate finance. UTSA also offers an Executive MBA, an MBA in International Business, a PhD in business administration, and a bevy of master's programs. Students brag that their "professors, curriculum, process, and flexibility far outweigh those of other programs in town." They also laud the "very hands-on" nature of the program. "The vast majority of students are completing their courses while working full time," explains one student, "so there is a very strong student-driven emphasis on practical skills, not only as they might apply in case studies, but as they apply in the actual work that is done by students."

There are "some very exceptional professors and some really lousy lecturers who do not seem to be qualified to teach" but, on the whole, professors are "engaging." "The quality of the faculty is probably the best kept secret in Texas," claims one happy student. Professors frequently bring substantial "real-world experience" to the classroom and they are "very attentive" once class is over. "They always emphasize office hours and promote asking for help," says one student. "It is encouraging to know that professors are always available and interested in helping students sort out individual problems or discuss research interests." Part-time students add that "professors will work with you if your job interferes with your school." A few students consider the administration "a bureaucratic nightmare" but most report that UTSA is "a well-oiled machine." The "efficient and helpful" staff is "ready and willing to help any time it is needed," they say. "There is a friendly atmosphere and supportive attitude permeating all levels."

Complaints among students at UTSA include the registration process. One student says the school "seems to be growing too fast and [is] not able to successfully catch up." "The library is awful." "Not enough places to study, not enough light, not enough books," gripes one student. Parking is also "a big issue" and the aesthetics around campus certainly are not the greatest. The architecture "can be best described as 'neo-brutalism' with its emphasis on concrete."

Career and Placement

MBA students at UTSA are really divided when it comes to the quality of Career Services. Satisfied students tell us that the staff "has been outstanding in directing students to potential employers, hosting information sessions, and providing on-campus interviews." They boast that "tons of recruiters" from Houston and other cities in Texas hire graduates. They say that career fairs bring "close to 100 companies each semester." They also note that "Valero, Ernst & Young, Deloitte, KPMG, and many other local and regional accounting firms" harvest many recruits here. Career Services does receive criticism from some students." "From my experience, there are few strong relationships between employers and our business school," laments one student. Unhappy students also charge that UTSA concentrates "only on San Antonio–based businesses."

ADMISSIONS CONTACT: MONICA RODRIGUEZ, MANAGER OF GRADUATE ADMISSIONS
ADDRESS: ONE UTSA CIRCLE SAN ANTONIO, TX 78249-0603 UNITED STATES
PHONE: 210-458-4330 • FAX: 210-458-4332
E-MAIL: GRADUATESTUDIES@UTSA.EDU • WEBSITE: BUSINESS.UTSA.EDU/GRADUATE

Student Life and Environment

Students say that the MBA program here is pretty heavily geared toward working professionals. It's possible to attend full time but the population is "largely part time" and "most students take longer than two years to get a degree." On one hand, "UTSA is a great place for part-time students" and it accommodates working students "very well." For example, courses are typically offered on weekday evenings at both the main UTSA campus on the northern edge of the city and at the school's downtown campus. However, many full-timers feel overlooked and complain that "the school caters to part-time MBA students" too much.

Students at UTSA describe themselves as "very competitive, determined individuals" who are "looking to add extra education to their repertoire." They're also a very diverse group. "People from all around the world with different jobs, backgrounds, and home lives" attend UTSA. "Classes tend to be very diverse in terms of age, race, occupation, and virtually any other metric," explains one student. "The mixing of individuals in different fields adds a unique flavor to each classroom setting." You'll find some recent college grads here but many students are "older" and established in their careers. They "have families and jobs" and they attend UTSA because of its proximity to their homes and their existing places of employment. Consequently, "it's a commuter school." There's "not much social interaction between the students" and there are few activities outside of class hours beyond assigned group work. It's definitely possible to move here and make a rich social life for yourself, though. "Enchanting" San Antonio is reportedly "very welcoming for newcomers" and a "fiesta year round."

Admissions

Admitted students at the 25th percentile have GMAT scores in the low 500s. Admitted students at the 75th percentile have GMAT scores around 600. Work experience is not a requirement but it's certainly helpful. If your background and training isn't in business, you'll have to take some core courses (e.g., accounting, finance). If it's been seven years since you completed core courses, you may still have to take some core courses or you may be able to test out. It's a case-by-case decision. Also, be prepared to demonstrate competence with spreadsheets and commonly used business applications.

FINANCIAL FACTS

Annual tuition (in-state/
out-of-state) $6,386/$17,099

ADMISSIONS

Admissions Selectivity Rating	83
# of applications received	174
% applicants accepted	57
% acceptees attending	75
Average GMAT	585
Range of GMAT	520–600
Average GPA	3.21
TOEFL required of international students	Yes
Minimum TOEFL (paper/computer)	500/173
Application fee	$45
International application fee	$80
Regular application deadline	7/1
Regular notification	Rolling
Deferment available	Yes
Maximum length of deferment	2 terms
Transfer students accepted	Yes
Non-fall admissions	Yes
Need-blind admissions	Yes

Applicants Also Look At

St. Mary's University, Texas A&M University—Corpus Christi, The University of Texas at Austin.

EMPLOYMENT PROFILE

Career Rating	61	Grads Employed by Function	%	Avg. Salary
Primary Source of Full-time Job Acceptances		Finance	46	$51,605
School-facilitated activities	4 (31%)	Marketing	8	$57,000
Graduate-facilitated activities	4 (31%)	MIS	8	$52,000
Unknown	5 (38%)	General Management	23	$64,667
Percent employed	47	Other	15	$45,521

THE UNIVERSITY OF TOLEDO
COLLEGE OF BUSINESS ADMINISTRATION

Academics

Offering a "good education at a very competitive price with convenient scheduling," the College of Business Administration at The University of Toledo fits the needs of area businesspeople in search of a quality MBA. One student explains, "The program is very accommodating toward people who work full-time. The majority of classes are taught at night, so I have been able to continue to work full-time while taking one or two classes at night." And, with a "low cost of living and low tuition fees when compared to other business schools," a UT MBA isn't a wallet buster.

UT distinguishes its MBA program with a number of cutting-edge concentrations. Students here may specialize in CRM and marketing intelligence, human resource management, information systems, operations and supply chain management, and professional sales as well as in the more traditional areas of administration, finance, international business, and marketing. Still, students warn that despite this apparent variety of choices, "The grad-level courses are fairly limited, [with] not enough variety/electives available to really customize our education. Classes are usually only offered once per semester at one specific time, so time conflicts between class and work schedules are quite common."

Students agree that "the greatest strengths of the UT MBA program come from its people. Overall, students are helpful, and it is easy to make connections through classmates. Professors follow a 40-40-20 rule with their time: 40 percent on research, 40 percent on preparing for classes, and 20 percent on advising students. This allows teachers to be student-centric." One student adds, "Receiving individual attention is a norm, be it in the Advising Office or from a professor."

Career and Placement

MBA students at Toledo may choose from an assortment of career support options. The school coordinates both academic graduate assistantships and corporate assistantships with employers like ProMedica Health System, Therma-Tru Doors, SSOE, Mercy Medical, Paramount Medical, and Goodwill. The school also sponsors regular networking events at which current students can meet and greet alumni. Finally, the Business Career Programs Office organizes on-campus recruiting, conducts mock interviews, performs resume reviews, provides counseling services, and manages a biannual Business Career Fair that brings more than 90 recruiters to campus.

Recent employers of UT MBAs include Calphalon, Chrysler, Dana Corp., DTE Energy, Ernst & Young, GM Powertrain, KeyBank, Heartland Information Systems, Hickory Farms, National City Corporation, Owens Corning, Owens Illinois, and Pilkington.

Student Life and Environment

"Life at UT is comfortable," students assure us. One praises, "Classrooms are clustered centrally so travel time between classes is quick. Most buildings have a computer lab, and the library has many quiet places to study. The fitness center is one of the largest I've seen for a college, and workouts are great. There aren't too many students crowding resources, so long lines are never a problem." If there's one area that needs help, students tell us it's the traffic and parking. One student warns, "There's an extreme lack of parking available. . . On days/nights when a major event such as a basketball or football game is going on, the school allows outsiders (nonstudents) to park on campus for a fee. This usually keeps students from being able to go to class as there's so much spillover of vehicles sometimes that parking in grass or restricted areas is common. I've had to turn

ADMISSIONS CONTACT: DAVID CHATFIELD, DIRECTOR MBA & EMBA PROGRAMS
ADDRESS: COLLEGE OF BUSINESS ADMINISTRATION, THE UNIVERSITY OF TOLEDO TOLEDO, OH
43606-3390 UNITED STATES • PHONE: 419-530-2775 • FAX: 419-530-7260
E-MAIL: MBA@UTOLEDO.EDU • WEBSITE: WWW.UTOLEDO.EDU/BUSINESS

around and go home, missing class, due to not being able to park or to get through traffic in a timely manner to park." To top it off, "The traffic situation on campus is horrendous."

Most students attend UT's MBA program on a part-time basis, arriving after a full day of work. Consequently, they have little time or inclination to participate in activities other than classes and group projects. Full-time students tell us that "there are many organizations to be involved in if you choose to. There are also department social functions quite frequently that are highly advertised." As for evenings and weekends, they are "what you make of them. Most people settle for simply just going to house parties or campus bars, which grows old fast. The downtown area offers good times, but most of that area is dead."

Toledo MBAs "come from diverse backgrounds, including majors, universities, religions, and ethnicity." While they "are competitive in their pursuit of high-quality jobs," they also enjoy "an atmosphere of mutual respect and teamwork between students in the program. Students are very comfortable approaching other students for help in their studies. In exchange, it is expected that every student pulls his or her own weight on the many team-based assignments." About one in three students originates from outside the United States, "providing a unique and interesting perspective on major business topics of the day."

Admissions

Applicants to the MBA program at UT must submit the following materials: a completed application; official copies of transcripts from each undergraduate and graduate institution attended; three letters of recommendation (letters should speak to academic potential); and an official score report for the GMAT. In addition to the above, all international applicants must submit a financial statement and supporting documents. International applicants from countries in which English is not the primary language must submit an official score report for the TOEFL. Students are encouraged to complete their applications online.

FINANCIAL FACTS

Annual tuition (in-state/ out-of-state)	$10,147/$18,958
Fees	$1,180
Cost of books	$1,200
Room & board (on/off-campus)	$0/$5,830
Average grant	$17,646

ADMISSIONS

Admissions Selectivity Rating	**72**
# of applications received	190
% applicants accepted	71
% acceptees attending	65
Average GMAT	510
Range of GMAT	450–780
Average GPA	3.2
TOEFL required of international students	Yes
Minimum TOEFL (paper/computer)	550/213
Application fee	$45
International application fee	$45
Regular application deadline	rolling
Regular notification	rolling
Deferment available	Yes
Maximum length of deferment	1 Semester
Transfer students accepted	Yes
Transfer application policy Maximum 9 credit hours with at least a B from an AACSB-accredited school.	
Non-fall admissions	Yes
Need-blind admissions	Yes

Applicants Also Look At
Bowling Green State University, The University of Findlay.

THE UNIVERSITY OF TULSA
COLLEGE OF BUSINESS ADMINISTRATION

Academics

A small private school with a great local reputation, the College of Business Administration at The University of Tulsa offers a well-rounded MBA curriculum, an enviably low student/faculty ratio, and an intimate and supportive academic atmosphere. A true teaching college, TU professors are dedicated to their students and "very willing to help, often giving a home or cell phone number for after-hours questions." A current student insists, "Every professor that I have ever taken a course with knows me by name and makes themselves available for help, even if I do not currently have a course with them." Another agrees, "Young professors and senior professors alike all truly are dedicated to our learning experience. They strive for us to succeed."

The TU curriculum is fairly structured, consisting of 18 credit hours of foundation courses in subjects such as accounting concepts, economic concepts, statistics, and marketing (though students with an educational background in business may be able to waive some of the core requirements). After the foundation is complete, students take 25 credit hours of advanced curriculum courses in more specific subject areas, including classes like behavioral sciences in administration and management information systems. Finally, students complete the degree requirements with elective course work—some in more unusual subject areas such as nursing, athletic training, accounting, taxation, statistics, management, and quantitative methods. Throughout the curriculum, practical applications to business are emphasized, and TU professors "all have valuable work experience to share with their students and are extremely intelligent."

In order to meet the needs of a diverse student population, the school offers flexible scheduling and the opportunity to pursue a degree part-time, full-time, and online. In addition to the traditional MBA, the school also offers a couple of opportunities to pursue a joint degree, including the JD/MBA which, through overlapping course content, can reduce the degree requirements for both programs by up to 16 credit hours. Professors "assign quite a bit of reading each week" and students warn that "6 hours of course work plus a demanding full-time job is difficult." Even so, they reassure us that the "Faculty [are] aware that many of the students work and are very helpful."

Although it is a private school, many students can comfortably afford their University of Tulsa MBA because "TU offers great graduate assistantships to pay for tuition and provides a great stipend." In addition to coordinating assistantships, students appreciate the fact that the "administration is concerned with improving the university and attracting high-caliber students." In fact, students are sure that their top-notch program will soon be recognized, and "as the school grows, it will be able to offer even more opportunities."

Career and Placement

The University of Tulsa enjoys a "very good reputation in the community," and current students say its "easy to get jobs through your professors and get involved with high-powered executives in the business community." On campus, the Office of Career Services offers workshops on resume writing, interviewing, and negotiating, as well as career assessment and counseling. The Office of Career Services also sponsors on-campus interviews and annual career fairs, through which more than 200 companies visit the TU campus. In addition, TU students may access the Office of Career Services online database of more than 2,500 employers and companies.

In recent years, companies that have interviewed students at the College of Business Administration include: American Airlines, Chevron, PricewaterhouseCoopers, Ernst & Young, IBM, Koch Industries, MCI, Phillips Petroleum, and State Farm. When it comes to recruiting, students feel that TU could expand their reputation nationally, explaining "TU has great relationships with companies in the Midwest/central region of the United States, but there are few recruiters that come to TU from the coasts."

Student Life and Environment

As with the academic experience, social life at TU is defined by the school's intimate atmosphere. A current student explains, "TU has a great student life because of the small size. It is easy to make friends even in different colleges across the campus because there are so many activities and ways to get involved." Through the business school and beyond, extracurricular activities are "plentiful and well advertised," and students appreciate the school's "beautiful campus with many new facilities." "All of the sports facilities are brand new on campus and foster a fun game atmosphere for attending sporting events." However, married students and students with families (who comprise a large percentage of the student population) feel the school could improve by providing "more activities for students and their families or partners."

TU students enjoy life in hometown Tulsa, describing it as "a fantastic city with a huge amount of growth potential." Thanks to the school's small size and cosmopolitan atmosphere, students benefit from "the perfect mixture of big-city social life and small-city relationships" at TU. When it comes to their classmates, "Tulsa and TU both have a vibrant population" and students hail from diverse backgrounds personally and professionally. On the business school campus, you'll find students who "are married with children and have worked in corporations for 5 years," and others who are "single socialites straight from undergrad."

Admissions

To apply to the MBA program at the University of Tulsa, students must submit official GMAT scores, undergraduate transcripts, a current resume, three letters of recommendation from professional or academic sources, and a completed graduate school application form. Younger applicants may be pleased to learn that professional work experience isn't required for entry into the program, nor is an undergraduate degree in business. Students may apply to enter during the fall, spring or summer term.

FINANCIAL FACTS

Annual tuition	$15,408
Fees	$54
Cost of books	$1,300
Room & board (on/off-campus)	$7,850/$8,813
% of students receiving aid	59
% of first-year students receiving aid	67
% of students receiving loans	22
% of students receiving grants	43
Average award package	$10,402
Average grant	$7,151
Average student loan debt	$25,681

ADMISSIONS

Admissions Selectivity Rating	76
# of applications received	84
% applicants accepted	86
% acceptees attending	85
Average GMAT	573
Range of GMAT	530–610
Average GPA	3.39
TOEFL required of international students	Yes
Minimum TOEFL (paper/computer)	575/232
Application fee	$40
International application fee	$40
Regular application deadline	Rolling
Regular notification	Rolling
Deferment available	Yes
Maximum length of deferment	1 year
Transfer students accepted	Yes
Transfer application policy	Up to 6 credit hours may be transferred.
Non-fall admissions	Yes
Need-blind admissions	Yes

Applicants Also Look At

Oklahoma State University, University of Oklahoma.

EMPLOYMENT PROFILE

Career Rating	70	Grads Employed by Function	%	Avg. Salary
Percent employed	30	Finance	52	$53,572
		Human Resources	3	NR
		Marketing	13	$59,000
		Consulting	16	$81,666
		General Management	10	$63,333
		Other	6	$30,000

Top 5 Employers Hiring Grads
Bank of Oklahoma; KPMG; Williams

UNIVERSITY OF UTAH
DAVID ECCLES SCHOOL OF BUSINESS

Academics

The David Eccles School of Business (DESB) at the University of Utah is a "smaller, and still very personable" program that "is striving hard to compete with larger, more well-known business schools." By many students' accounts, it is succeeding in its efforts. The school is particularly strong in the field of entrepreneurship, in which it offers "a lot of resources and opportunities for entrepreneurs." It sponsors the Utah Entrepreneur Challenge and run a Venture Development Fund. DEBS is also home to the Lassonde New Venture Center, a "great experience that allows business students to partner with researchers on campus to commercialize technology."

Entrepreneurship isn't the only game in town here, however. DESB has become strong in operations management over the past few years, as "Professors of top schools have been hired" in the field. Students also note that the university at large accommodates MBAs who are interested in health care and international business. (Students tell us that Utah has a "good Middle East Center.") A "focus on technology management and corporate strategy" throughout the curriculum leaves students feeling prepared for the challenges of the twenty-first-century business environment.

DEBS offers "a small daytime program (120 students)" that lets students "get to know the faculty and other students really well and get personalized instruction and attention." In addition to professors who know their students "by name," "The courses and structure allow for a flexible program that can be customized to individual needs." A part-time professional MBA program, with classes held in the evening, offers additional convenience and flexibility. In either program, "The faculty are extremely accessible, and I have been impressed by how they want to help the students succeed," says one student. The majority take an interest in students' schooling "outside of the classroom. For example, one of my professors has gone above and beyond in using his professional network to place students with top firms in the field. This same attitude is pervasive throughout the administration and faculty."

Career and Placement

The Office of Career Services for Graduate Business Students works in conjunction with the university's Career Services Office to provide counseling and career placement services including career fairs and on-campus recruiting events. Many students, however, report dissatisfaction with the services, telling us that "students typically do not find jobs until the last minute, and most jobs are within Utah. Those who want to get out of the state have a very difficult time doing so." As one MBA studying health services management observes, the majority of placement opportunities "are in the fields of accounting and finance. For those of us who don't do the number-crunching thing, opportunities are further apart." Students also feel that "the alumni network needs to improve so that students who are graduating have people to turn to when they are looking for jobs."

Employers who most frequently hire Utah MBAs include Ford Motor Company, KPMG International, PacifiCorp, Select Portfolio Services, Zions Bank, UBS, Utah Jazz, Albertsons, St. Mark's Hospital, McLean Quality, Mercer Health, MyFamily.com, Daifuku, and George S. Mays Consulting.

Student Life and Environment

Utah's different MBA programs have different cultures; full-time day students "have the time to engage in activities outside of the classroom" while "Professional MBAs work full-time so they rarely, if ever, engage in extracurriculars." Full-timers report that "there are so many activities and clubs and so few students that you quickly find yourself involved to a degree that would be difficult to imagine at other schools." These "activities include basketball and football games, golf clinics, visits to local businesses, and conferences. . . . Networking opportunities are endless, and, of course, we have the 'Attitude Adjustment Networking' event," a four-time-a-year at which "students and spouses meet and mingle." Otherwise, though, "Family activities are lacking" here.

The DESB MBA program holds classes in several buildings. One "is fully modern and fabulous; the other two are not. The school is in the midst of a capital campaign to help construct new buildings." The Utah campus is "beautiful" and "close to the mountains." Students agree that the "Wasatch Mountains can't be beat for convenient, year-round outdoor recreation." Some here even credit the ski-friendly mountains with attracting some of the program's prominent faculty.

Utah's full-time students "are friendly and always willing to help each other—there is very little overt competitiveness. Many students are married with families, but still find time to socialize, at least on campus." According to one student there are "two specific types of people who attend here." One is "Mormon, married, and has kids." The other is "outdoorsy, outgoing, adventurous, and is living here to get a great education and ski the best mountains in the U.S." Because of the nature of the program, there is a pronounced entrepreneurial trend among students. The evening program draws area professionals.

Admissions

The Eccles Admissions Department requires applicants to provide the following: an undergraduate transcript demonstrating a GPA of at least 3.0 (students failing to meet this requirement may gain entry based on evaluation of their performance during the final two years of undergraduate work); proof of successful completion of a college-level statistics course; GMAT scores (minimum 50th percentile score in math required); two recommendations, submitted online; responses to essay questions; and a resume. International students whose first language is not English must take the TOEFL (minimum score: 600, paper-based test; 250, computer-based test). Two years of post-undergraduate professional experience are strongly encouraged but not required. The school reports that it administers "several privately donated scholarships reserved for underrepresented groups and to help us build the gender, ethnic, and geographic diversity of our student body."

FINANCIAL FACTS

Annual tuition (in-state/ out-of-state)	$10,688/$23,680
Fees (in-state/out-of-state)	$720/$763
Cost of books	$1,500
Room & board (on/off-campus)	$8,500/$11,000
% of students receiving aid	44
% of first-year students receiving aid	44
% of students receiving grants	44
Average award package	$14,350
Average grant	$14,350

ADMISSIONS

Admissions Selectivity Rating	86
# of applications received	154
% applicants accepted	56
% acceptees attending	67
Average GMAT	595
Range of GMAT	560–640
Average GPA	3.43
TOEFL required of international students	Yes
Minimum TOEFL (paper/computer)	600/250
Application fee	$45
International application fee	$65
Regular application deadline	2/15
Regular notification	3/15
Transfer students accepted	Yes
Transfer application policy In special circumstances, up to 6 credit hours may be transferred into the program from another program.	
Need-blind admissions	Yes

Applicants Also Look At
Arizona State University, Brigham Young University.

EMPLOYMENT PROFILE

Career Rating	78	Grads Employed by Function	%	Avg. Salary
Primary Source of Full-time Job Acceptances		Finance	39	$53,409
School-facilitated activities	19 (63%)	Marketing	14	$69,000
Graduate-facilitated activities	10 (33%)	MIS	3	$57,000
Unknown	1 (3%)	Operations	7	$49,500
Average base starting salary	$58,089	Consulting	7	$60,000
Percent employed	85	General Management	7	$68,500
		Other	21	$59,000

Top 5 Employers Hiring Grads
ATK; GE Capital Financial; Boart-Longyear; Comcast; Zions Bank

THE UNIVERSITY OF VERMONT
SCHOOL OF BUSINESS ADMINISTRATION

GENERAL INFORMATION

Type of school	Public
Environment	City
Academic calendar	FA/SP

SURVEY SAYS...

Students love Burlington, VT
Solid preparation in:
Operations

STUDENTS

Enrollment of parent institution	12,239
Enrollment of business school	67
% male/female	55/45
% part-time	70
% international	15
Average age at entry	30
Average years work experience at entry	4

ACADEMICS

Academic Experience Rating	**84**
Student/faculty ratio	2:1
Profs interesting rating	87
Profs accessible rating	67
% female faculty	37

Prominent Alumni

Doug Goldsmith, CFO/VP, Finance & Admin, Rock of Ages; Elisabeth Robert, Pres, CFO & Treasurer, VT Teddy Bear, Inc.; Katherine B. Crosett, Kalex Enterprises, Inc.; tech wrtng; Alexander D. Crosett, III, Kalex Enterprises, Inc.

Academics

Small, friendly, and as "green" as the rolling hills of Vermont, UVM's business school offers a practical, stimulating, and balanced approach to business education. Bringing "a wealth of information and experience" to the classroom, UVM "professors are current and professionals in their area of study." With only 67 students in the MBA program, the teaching staff is "extremely accessible, and classes are a great small size." In fact, it's easy to receive one-on-one mentorship and guidance, as UVM's teaching staff is "accessible, supportive, willing to give constructive criticism and advice, both for school, work, and career questions." The pleasant vibe is echoed throughout the school community, where "advisors and staff are also very helpful and friendly."

The MBA curriculum at UVM begins with six core courses in organization and management, marketing, accounting, production and operations management, corporate finance, and the legal environment of business. After that, students take 10 advanced-level courses, tailoring their coursework to their individual interests. A feature of Vermont's MBA is "the ability to attain a general management concentration while being able to take classes in other colleges (Environment, Public Administration, Community Development) to meet electives." However, while the program's small size is certainly a benefit in the classroom, it limits the range of courses the business school is able to offer. "There is a definite finance/accounting slant" within the course selection, and students suggest that the university add more operations, entrepreneurship, and international business courses. Students would also like to see "more focus on technology, especially business applications, enterprise software, and use of collaboration tools (e.g., SharePoint) within the student body."

UVM offers a traditional MBA, which can be completed on a full-time or part-time basis, as well as an accelerated program. Working students really appreciate the fact that "most classes are at night to accommodate part-time commuters." Full-time students also benefit from the school's evening schedule, which allows them time to pursue internships. Fortunately, the surrounding town of "Burlington provides a lot of interesting and unique opportunities both inside and outside of business." With this progressive small city as a backdrop, UVM is highly "involved in green business," and "students are aware of sustainable business practices due to the university's emphasis on environmental studies." On the whole, students at UVM are "ambitious, analytical, [and] intellectual," and they "bring a lot to the table in terms of experience, insight, and determination." Encouraging participation and drawing on the experience of the student body, "classes are dynamic and discussion is facilitated well by the professors."

Career and Placement

The School of Business Career Services offers resume-building assistance, cover letter preparation, interview coaching, and a recruiting database, as well as an extensive library of books about job hunting, which all come in handy during the career fairs and a Spring Career Week. The UVM MBA is set up for working students, with all classes starting after 5 p.m. Therefore, most students in the MBA program are already employed and, consequently, students complain that "there are virtually no career services in place for graduate students." Some students also feel that the administration should encourage "much more interaction between the MBA program and area businesses." However, as the only AACSB-accredited program in the region, UVM has a corner on the local market.

MICHAEL GORDON, ASSOCIATE DEAN FOR GRADUATE PROGRAMS
ADDRESS: 55 COLCHESTER AVE, BURLINGTON, VT 05405 UNITED STATES
PHONE: 802-656-4119 • FAX: 802-656-4078
E-MAIL: STUDENTSERVICES@BSAD.UVM.EDU • WEBSITE: WWW.BSAD.UVM.EDU/_COMM/MBA

Student Life and Environment

The laid-back Vermont lifestyle and "dynamic" university environment make UVM a highly appealing place to study. Maybe it's the calming effect of the Vermont's natural beauty, but the school attracts students who are "motivated to excel but lead a balanced lifestyle." A current student adds, "UVM feels like a second home. Class schedules are very comfortable, and there are a lot of options for spending time both on and off campus." However, "most students balance full-time jobs and part-time school responsibilities, and are very busy." As a result, "the social network is not very strong."

Despite the lack of a more formal graduate school culture, social relationships often form in the classroom because "the group/team activities build the strong bonds that exist between students. That organically grows into events outside of school and off campus." On top of that, "an MBA association has been restarted, and students go out once a month for drinks and to chat." A student offers, "MBA students at UVM are some of the friendliest people I've ever met. Everyone is more than willing to offer their opinions on classes and professors as well as potential career opportunities and contacts." When looking for a little recreation or down time, the beautiful town of "Burlington is a dream," offering plenty of outdoor activities as well as a lively, collegiate atmosphere.

Admissions

At the University of Vermont, there is no minimum GMAT score or undergraduate GPA required for admission; however, test scores and undergraduate record are considered in an admissions decision. Students are also evaluated on the quality of their undergraduate institution, perceived rigor of undergraduate coursework, quality and quantity of business experience, letters of recommendation, statement of purpose, and post-graduate work. The average GMAT for accepted students is 600 and the average GPA is 3.2.

FINANCIAL FACTS

Annual tuition (in-state/ out-of-state)	$10,422/$26,306
Fees	$1,632
Cost of books	$700
Room & board	$8,024
% of students receiving aid	20
% of first-year students receiving aid	26
% of students receiving loans	5
% of students receiving grants	11
Average award package	$10,000
Average grant	$5,200

ADMISSIONS

Admissions Selectivity Rating	80
# of applications received	46
% applicants accepted	76
% acceptees attending	77
Average GMAT	603
Range of GMAT	520–700
Average GPA	3.24
TOEFL required of international students	Yes
Minimum TOEFL (paper/computer)	550/213
Application fee	$40
International application fee	$40
Regular application deadline	rolling
Regular notification	rolling
Deferment available	Yes
Maximum length of deferment	1 year
Transfer students accepted	Yes
Transfer application policy Transfer credit is reviewed based upon each individual set of circumstances.	
Non-fall admissions	Yes
Need-blind admissions	Yes

Applicants Also Look At

Bentley College, Boston College, Boston University, Georgetown University, University of Connecticut, University of Massachusetts—Amherst, University of New Hampshire.

University of Virginia
Darden Graduate School of Business Administration

Academics

Offering a unique, challenging, and spirited MBA program, the Darden School of Business at the University of Virginia distinguishes itself through "the outstanding reputation of the faculty and students, the rigorous and exciting case method, and the broad focus on general management that the school offers." Hailed as "one of the toughest programs in the world," the hallmark of a Darden education is the case-based curriculum—an intensive, discussion-based teaching method with an emphasis "on experiential learning in a collaborative environment and through teamwork." Sounds fun, but students warn that "the first-year curriculum is rigorous, and the case method demands students be prepared and take leadership positions." Not to mention that curricular requirements are incredibly time consuming. First-year students typically spend the day at school: Classes run from 8:00 A.M. to 2:00 P.M. and related activities can run until 10:00 P.M.

It's a challenge, but a Darden education is well worth the effort as "you really gain mastery of the material." Encouraging a lively and interactive classroom environment, the school's savvy professors "are outstanding at leading a case conversation and covering all of the key learning points." A second-year student raves, "The faculty at Darden has revolutionized my life. They have challenged me to think differently, to go deeper to find solutions to complex problems and stimulate my mind each day." Darden really distinguishes itself in its commitment to the student experience: "Professors at Darden are there because they want to teach. Students are the priority, not research." A current student enthuses, "Professors have enormous levels of experience and are ridiculously available outside class. I've gone in unscheduled and been able to spend over an hour working on an issue—the professor just made the time."

Teamwork is integral to the Darden experience, and each new student is assigned to a learning team of 5 or 6 students with whom they prepare for class each day. Working together, students say that Darden's "intense and competitive" academic atmosphere is counterbalanced by the fact that "Darden has an extremely helpful and collegial environment." In this stimulating campus setting, "The common thread running through the student body is a general sense of appreciation for the atmosphere, enthusiasm toward the learning experience, and a desire to collaborate with the learning experience through student-led review sessions, informal help sessions, etc."

Career and Placement

Students say "the Career Development Center has improved to a great extent," bringing a "record number of recruiters and companies on grounds this [past] fall." The center offers a variety of services to MBA students, including Career Discovery Forums, individual career consultations, a professional development series, and workshops and special events. Through the Career Development Center, students also have access to the Darden Networking Partnership, a database of nearly 2,000 alumni who have volunteered to help fellow grads in career searches.

In 2006, 87 percent of graduates seeking employment had received a job offer by graduation, and 95 percent had received a job offer within 3 months of graduation. Finance was the most popular career choice, drawing 41 percent of students; consulting drew 20 percent. Among the top recruiters were: A.T. Kearney, Booz Allen Hamilton, Deloitte Touche Tohmatsu, The Boston Consulting Group, Everest, General Mills, Johnson & Johnson, Kraft Foods, Bank of America, Citigroup, Merrill Lynch, McKinsey & Company, Bain and Company, Standard and Poor's, UTC, Progressive, Danaher Corp., Mass Mutual Financial Group, Goldman Sachs, Lehman Brothers, DuPont, General Electric, JPMorgan Chase, The McGraw-Hill Companies, Centex, Target, Dell, EDS, Intel, and Sprint Nextel.

ADMISSIONS CONTACT: SARA E. NEHER, DIRECTOR OF ADMISSIONS
ADDRESS: P.O. BOX 6550 CHARLOTTESVILLE, VA 22906 UNITED STATES
PHONE: 434-924-7281 • FAX: 434-243-5033
E-MAIL: DARDEN@VIRGINIA.EDU • WEBSITE: WWW.DARDEN.VIRGINIA.EDU

Student Life and Environment

For those who thrive under pressure, Darden is an ideal environment as "The rhythm is extremely hectic, but the atmosphere is jovial, and there is a real palpable energy and excitement about learning in the place." In fact, Darden students seem to take a masochistic pleasure in the hectic pace of life where "Sleep is a rare commodity." In the hearty words of one first-year student: "Although the workload seems unbearable at times, and I have to schedule phone calls with my spouse, I really wouldn't trade this experience for any other." While acknowledging the rigors of the workload, students continually emphasize the kindness of the Darden community, where "Everything from the computer services to the dining hall is done for the students and with their best interests at heart."

When it comes to extracurricular activities, students reassure us that "even with the demanding workload students are very active in clubs, social events, MBA case competitions, and the community." They also manage to sneak in a moment of socializing during the daily First Coffee, "a break between classes in which you can catch up with classmates in other sections, friends, or professors. Everyone in the Darden community comes by for a cup of joe (partners and children included at times)." When it's time to relax, "Saturdays during the fall are a time for attending football games, the Chili Cook-Off, or the International Food Festival." Another favorite is "the Thursday Night Drinking Club where the majority of students meet up at a different bar every Thursday." An ideal college town, "Charlottesville is a great place to live; it has a really low cost of living without sacrificing culture."

Admissions

Darden evaluates a student's readiness for business school in three broad areas: academics, professional experience, and personal qualities and characteristics. These competencies are measured through the applicant's undergraduate record, GMAT scores, resume and work experience, letters of recommendation, and admissions essays. In addition, interviews are required and are considered an important part of the application. While there are no minimum requirements for admission, last year's entering class had a mean GMAT of 688. The mean GPA was 3.33, and every person had full-time work experience before entering the program.

FINANCIAL FACTS

Annual tuition (in-state/ out-of-state)	$37,500/$42,500
Fees	$102
Cost of books	$2,800
Room & board	$17,200
% of students receiving aid	88
% of first-year students receiving aid	91
% of students receiving loans	85
% of students receiving grants	47
Average award package	$38,100
Average grant	$15,995
Average student loan debt	$62,585

ADMISSIONS

Admissions Selectivity Rating	96
# of applications received	2,468
% applicants accepted	29
% acceptees attending	45
Average GMAT	688
Average GPA	3.3
TOEFL required of international students	Yes
Minimum TOEFL (paper/computer)	650/270
Application fee	$190
International application fee	$190
Application Deadline/Notification	
Round 1:	11/07 / 02/08
Round 2:	01/08 / 03/08
Round 3:	02/08 / 05/08
Transfer students accepted	Yes
Transfer application policy	
Transfer students are accepted but credits cannot be transferred.	
Need-blind admissions	Yes

EMPLOYMENT PROFILE

Career Rating	97	Grads Employed by Function	% Avg. Salary
Primary Source of Full-time Job Acceptances		Finance	38 $97,616
School-facilitated activities	207 (78%)	Marketing	11 $90,458
Graduate-facilitated activities	59 (22%)	Consulting	23 $111,970
Average base starting salary	$100,575	General Management	26 $100,373
Percent employed	95	Other	2 $89,143

Top 5 Employers Hiring Grads
Danaher; Bank of America; Booz Allen; Goldman; McKinsey

UNIVERSITY OF WASHINGTON
MICHAEL G. FOSTER SCHOOL OF BUSINESS

GENERAL INFORMATION
Type of school	Public
Environment	Metropolis
Academic calendar	Quarter

SURVEY SAYS...
Students love Seattle, WA
Friendly students
Good peer network
Solid preparation in:
Finance
Accounting
Teamwork

STUDENTS
Enrollment of parent institution	39,251
Enrollment of business school	436
% male/female	55/45
% out-of-state	60
% part-time	50
% minorities	9
% international	34
Average age at entry	29
Average years work experience at entry	5

ACADEMICS
Academic Experience Rating	**94**
Student/faculty ratio	8:1
Profs interesting rating	87
Profs accessible rating	93
% female faculty	32
% minority faculty	8

Joint Degrees
MBA/MP (Accounting) 3 years, JD/MBA 4 years, MBA/MAIS 3 years, MBA/MHA (Health Administration) 3 years.

Prominent Alumni
William Ayer, CEO, Alaska Airlines; Dan Nordstrom, Former CEO, Nordstrom.com; Charles Lillis, Former CEO, Media One Group; Gary Neale, Chairman, Nisource; Yoshihiko Miyauchi, CEO, Orix.

Academics

The Foster School of Business at the University of Washington draws on its Seattle locale to inform the focus of its program. The curriculum emphasizes a global perspective (especially as it pertains to countries in the Pacific Rim), and there is an overall focus on technology reflecting UW's proximity to such tech heavyweights as Microsoft and Amazon ("Think tons of Microsoft alums"). There are also numerous opportunities to learn about entrepreneurship, in keeping with the city's relaxed and independent vibe. In fact, many students choose UW for its "entrepreneurship and technology focus." This plays out in case studies, projects, and real-world examples drawn from these areas during core courses, as well as in areas of concentration.

Those core courses comprise about half of the Foster MBA program. Foundation subjects such as accounting, finance, human resources, ethics, and marketing are included in the required core. Toward the end of the first year, each student selects three Bridge Electives, which allow closer exploration of areas available for concentration in the second year of the program. Students say, "All classes require a good bit of teamwork." "The level of involvement is left up to individuals, but most take part in a lot of the activities." Most students take an internship between their first and second years and return for the second year to specialize in fields such as entrepreneurship and innovation, international business, e-commerce, or marketing.

Washington's MBA students are happy with the quality of teaching, as well as the support from the university's administration. "UW has excellent professors who value teaching and helping students learn. That means everything!" The "mix of case and lecture method and small class size" also are helpful, as are professors who "go beyond to make sure that students get all the education they want." That same student adds, "I haven't met more dedicated professors than the professors at UW." Another MBA candidate says, "The core professors are superstars—far and away the best instructors I've ever had in my life." The evening MBA program is also well staffed: The "Evening program generally is taught by full-time established professors who are very good at their fields, and have made themselves available via e-mail if 'in person' is not convenient for working students."

Career and Placement

The Business Connections Center in the University of Washington program offers network events, career-evaluation tools, a mentorship program with local business leaders, an online jobs data base, and personal career counseling. They "excel at connecting students with alums and other business leaders in the community and elsewhere. They stress the importance of networking and help students to establish a network." The center boasts "great connections to the Seattle business community," and "relationships with world-class companies like Microsoft, Starbucks, [and] Amazon.com." "In most cases, students are extremely successful in landing desirable internships and jobs."

Students also say there's room for improvement: "UW could improve getting access to companies and jobs outside the Pacific Northwest," one student says, and others' comments echo his opinion. He adds, "UW concentrates on networking with local companies, and doesn't seem to put much effort [into] encouraging students to recruit with national companies outside the Northwest."

AT&T Wireless, Alaska Airlines, Hewlett-Packard, Washington Mutual, Intel, Microsoft, Hitachi Consulting, Samsung, Starbucks, Tektronix, and Wells Fargo are among the companies that recruit on campus.

Student Life and Environment

Students find much to like about their classmates, the lifestyle, and the opportunities offered at the University of Washington. "UW has a collaborative, rigorous, and challenging academic environment, plus a sense of work/life balance that many schools do not have," says one student. "When I visited [before enrolling], I met several students, faculty, and staff, who all impressed me with their intelligence, enthusiasm, kindness, and humor. I knew that this was the type of community I wanted to be a part of."

"Smart people without the attitude," is how another MBA candidate described his classmates. Another says, "One of the greatest things about the MBA program is that there were activities and clubs for my wife. Some of these activities were social, while others were community-related." But improving the "quality of child care or providing child care for all students" is area that needs to be addressed, student agree.

Another issue is facilities. "The buildings are the ugliest ones on campus," one student complains. Another says, "UW is behind the curve for business school facilities. A new building is in the works but will not be completed for several more years." Another student adds, "The business school buildings are getting up there in terms of age and facilities. There is a plan to upgrade these, but it probably won't happen while I am a student there. Future students will certainly benefit from the improvements, though."

Admissions

Those making admissions decisions for the Foster MBA program look for leadership potential, academic strength, communicative ability, and intellectual ability. They evaluate quantitative and language skills through transcripts, GMAT scores, GPAs, and, if needed, TOEFL scores. UW does not have minimum GMAT score or GPA requirement. "If a student is lacking in one area but strong in others, he or she may still be admitted," the school says on its website. For the class admitted in 2006, the average GMAT score was 679, and the average GPA was 3.5. These students averaged 5 and a half years of work experience.

FINANCIAL FACTS

Annual tuition (in-state/ out-of-state)	$20,300/$30,500
Fees	$550
Cost of books	$3,350
Room & board (on/off-campus)	$15,340/$15,780
% of students receiving aid	70
% of first-year students receiving aid	84
% of students receiving loans	68
% of students receiving grants	44
Average award package	$13,420
Average grant	$8,567
Average student loan debt	$22,344

ADMISSIONS

Admissions Selectivity Rating	94
# of applications received	861
% applicants accepted	42
% acceptees attending	61
Average GMAT	679
Range of GMAT	630–720
Average GPA	3.38
TOEFL required of international students	Yes
Minimum TOEFL (paper/computer)	600/250
Application fee	$75
International application fee	$75
Regular application deadline	10/15
Regular notification	12/10

Application Deadline/Notification

Round 1:	10/15 / 12/10
Round 2:	11/15 / 01/25
Round 3:	01/15 / 03/30
Round 4:	03/15 / 05/10
Transfer students accepted	Yes

Transfer application policy
  The status of a transfer student is determined on a case by case basis.

Need-blind admissions	Yes

Applicants Also Look At

Arizona State University, Stanford University, The University of Texas at Austin, University of California—Irvine, University of California—Los Angeles, University of California—Berkeley, University of Southern California.

EMPLOYMENT PROFILE

Career Rating	90	Grads Employed by Function	% Avg. Salary
Primary Source of Full-time Job Acceptances		Finance	18 $85,972
School-facilitated activities	42 (57%)	Marketing	23 $83,478
Graduate-facilitated activities	27 (36%)	MIS	1 NR
Unknown	5 (7%)	Operations	1 NR
Average base starting salary	$87,138	Consulting	12 $91,000
Percent employed	91	General Management	11 $78,455

Top 5 Employers Hiring Grads
Microsoft; Hitachi Consulting; Accenture; Amazon.com; Autodesk

UNIVERSITY OF WEST GEORGIA
RICHARDS COLLEGE OF BUSINESS

GENERAL INFORMATION

Type of school	Public
Environment	City
Academic calendar	Semester

SURVEY SAYS...

Friendly students
Smart classrooms
Solid preparation in:
General management
Operations

STUDENTS

Enrollment of parent institution	10,677
Enrollment of business school	73
% male/female	53/47
% out-of-state	41
% part-time	77
% minorities	41
% international	24
Average age at entry	30

ACADEMICS

Academic Experience Rating	**62**
Student/faculty ratio	18:1
Profs interesting rating	89
Profs accessible rating	62
% female faculty	34
% minority faculty	20

Academics

The MBA program at University of West Georgia is designed primarily to address the needs of part-time students who work full-time in the area (the school's Carrollton and Newman campuses are both located about 40 miles from Atlanta). A number of full-time students also attend. Their ranks include American students making the jump directly from undergraduate programs and international students who "usually return to their own country after graduation," according to the school catalogue.

West Georgia offers both an MBA and a masters of professional accounting. Either program can be completed in 12 months by a full-time student who is entering with an undergraduate degree in business. Students whose undergraduate work is in a non-business related discipline typically must complete 24 semester hours of preparation-level course work (covering the basics of marketing, statistics, information systems, corporate finance, business law, accounting theory, microeconomics, and macroeconomics) or complete a set of modules and assessments in lieu of taking courses. Excluding prep-level courses, the MBA requires 30 semester hours of course work, 24 of which are dedicated to required classes. Students may choose elective courses from the fields of economics, information technology, finance, international business, cost accounting, theory and philosophy of management, and business and society.

Students attending classes at the Carrollton campus tell us that "the school has a lot of good professors who are from all over the country and the world. The teachers are very knowledgeable in what they do." Professors are also "surprisingly easy to reach, and most are willing to provide time and energy to help students succeed." Small classes create a "great learning environment," as do "the many guest speakers who lecture about their field or a topic in [their] field."

University of West Georgia also offers a web MBA, in which "all classes are taught online via the Web." Admission to the web MBA program requires a minimum of two years of post-baccalaureate professional work experience (though admission to the traditional MBA program carries no such requirement). The web MBA curriculum roughly mirrors the conventional MBA curriculum; however, no electives are available to web MBA students. One student in the program tells us that "I chose the web MBA program because it was affordable and allowed me flexibility in my study schedule. I travel during the week and would not be able to attend classes in a traditional setting."

Career and Placement

MBA students at West Georgia use the Department of Career Services, which provides "a comprehensive career development and employment plan for all students and alumni" of the school. The office provides assistance with job searches and career strategy, resume referrals, and help with finding internships. It also coordinates on-campus recruitment events, maintains job listings and a career resource library, offers seminars and workshops in resume writing and interviewing, and organizes career and job fairs.

Student Life and Environment

The University of West Georgia campus in Carrollton "is attractive and well located. It's outside of Atlanta but within an easy commute [from] work." Students enjoy "a relaxed, easygoing mood on the campus and in the MBA program," although they complain that "parking on campus is horrible." Because the program here is small and predominantly part-time, there is little extracurricular life for MBAs.

The conventional MBA program includes "a great diversity of international students." One MBA writes, "I have classes with students from Bulgaria, Turkey, India, and Colombia. I didn't have this much diversity as an undergraduate in a school of 25,000 students." Most of the American students in the program "have little work experience, and many have lived in Georgia all their lives." Students in the web MBA bring more experience to their studies, partly due to the nature of the requirements. Writes one student in the program, "We have a diverse group in our virtual team. The fact that our ages, life experiences, and backgrounds are so different seems to add to our focus and enables us to leverage individual strengths when tackling group projects. I'd say we are a friendly bunch, [and] willing to lean on each other when necessary, but also [to] hold each individual accountable for [his or her] share of work."

Admissions

All applicants to the MBA program at the University of West Georgia must submit official copies of transcripts for all postsecondary academic work, an official GMAT score report, and letters of recommendation. Applicants must meet the following minimum requirements to be considered for admission with "regular status": an analytical writing score of at least 3.0 on the GMAT, a total GMAT score of at least 450, and an admissions score of at least 950 under the formula [(undergraduate GPA × 200) + GMAT score] or a score of at least 1,000 under the formula [(undergraduate GPA for final 60 semester hours of undergraduate work × 200) + GMAT score]. International students whose first language is not English must earn at least a 550 on the paper-based TOEFL or at least a 213 on the computer-based TOEFL. Students not meeting these minimum requirements may be granted admission with "provisional status." Such students are "reviewed for retention on regular status after completing nine hours toward the MBA," according to the school.

FINANCIAL FACTS

Annual tuition (in-state/ out-of-state)	$2,448/$9,774
Fees	$960
Cost of books	$1,545
Room & board (on-campus)	$5,776
% of students receiving aid	38
% of first-year students receiving aid	34
% of students receiving loans	28
% of students receiving grants	7
Average award package	$6,907
Average grant	$3,121
Average student loan debt	$19,444

ADMISSIONS

Admissions Selectivity Rating	**60***
Average GMAT	520
Range of GMAT	410–530
Average GPA	3.2
TOEFL required of international students	Yes
Minimum TOEFL (paper/computer)	550/213
Application fee	$30
International application fee	$30
Regular application deadline	7/1
Early decision program?	Yes
ED Deadline/ Notification	Rolling / 08/30
Deferment available	Yes
Maximum length of deferment	1 year
Transfer students accepted	Yes
Transfer application policy	
A maxium of 6 Semester hours of graduate credit may be transferred from another accredited institution.	
Non-fall admissions	Yes
Need-blind admissions	Yes

UNIVERSITY OF WISCONSIN—MADISON
SCHOOL OF BUSINESS

GENERAL INFORMATION

Type of school	Public
Environment	City
Academic calendar	Semester

SURVEY SAYS...
Friendly students
Good social scene
Good peer network
Smart classrooms
Solid preparation in:
Finance
Teamwork

STUDENTS

Enrollment of parent institution	42,041
Enrollment of business school	450
% male/female	71/29
% out-of-state	63
% part-time	50
% minorities	9
% international	25
Average age at entry	28
Average years work experience at entry	4

ACADEMICS

Academic Experience Rating	**94**
Student/faculty ratio	3:1
Profs interesting rating	80
Profs accessible rating	93
% female faculty	22
% minority faculty	9

Joint Degrees
JD/MBA 4 years.

Prominent Alumni
Steve Bennett, President/CEO, Intuit; Curt Culver, Chairman/CEO, MGIC; Tadashi Okamura, Chairman, Toshiba Corporation; Thomas J. Falk, Chairman of the Board/CEO, Kimberly Clark Corp.; John P. Morgridge, Chairman, Cisco Systems.

Academics

The University of Wisconsin—Madison offers a unique and challenging MBA program, well suited to highly focused students with clear career goals. Whereas most MBA programs require a wide array of course work in general management topics, the Wisconsin curriculum is designed around career specializations, through which students focus their studies on a single business area such as real estate, entrepreneurship, brand management, or marketing research. Through their career specialization, students work within the business school's Centers for Expertise, which "ensure that students have lots of exposure to alumni, specific industry news, and professionals at various levels." A current student explains, "I chose the University of Wisconsin because they have a specialized program in marketing research that would give me the specialized skill set to continue in this field."

While career specializations are the hallmark of the Wisconsin curriculum, "The program emphasizes strong learning within a specific discipline while allowing flexibility to learn cross-functional skills." Before beginning their studies within a specific center, students must complete the general management core curriculum, which provides a solid foundation in management essentials. Even so, those looking for a more varied education will probably find a better match elsewhere. Students warn that "The specified 'center' does make it difficult at times to expand into other departments." Throughout the curriculum, applied learning is an important component of the Wisconsin MBA, and students participate in live business projects for a wide range of companies. For example, students may conduct market research for leading companies, manage stock portfolios, or manage a portfolio of real estate securities.

The business school draws a team of top-notch faculty "committed to up-to-date teaching styles and topics." Student input here is valued. "Feedback is taken from the students at the end of every semester and the recommended changes are implemented for the next incoming class," says one MBA. "It's a constantly evolving and improving program that is viewed as a collaborative effort between the administration and students." On the whole, "Wisconsin represents a culture of collaboration and teamwork," and students reassure us that "when students compete, there is a general collegiate respect for one another." Another major perk of a UW education is its public school price tag, made better by the fact that through assistantships "The tuition is covered, benefits are covered, and you get a stipend." A student exclaims, "You might find it hard to catch your breath, but it's a great way to avoid loans."

Career and Placement

During the first semester at Wisconsin, students take a 6-week course to help them plan and initiate their internship search, including instruction on resume writing, interviewing, researching companies and more. After that, students have access to the Career Center's Internet database as well as one-on-one career advising with professional counselors. However, the program's unique in-depth focus is what really makes the difference in career placement. A current student explains, "Access to corporate recruiters is unprecedented since we have a program which consists of specializations, rather than a generic MBA. You get put on a niche career track right away, so recruiters know exactly what they're getting during interviews."

With strong ties in the region, 60 percent of students take jobs in the Midwest. However, for those looking to expand their horizons, students reassure us that "last year and the current year, we have been utilizing our alumni and board member connections to send a significant number of finance students out to New York for positions with bulge bracket

ADMISSIONS CONTACT: SEANN SWEENEY, ASSISTANT DIRECTOR OF MBA MARKETING & RECRUITING
ADDRESS: 3150 GRAINGER HALL, 975 UNIVERSITY AVENUE MADISON, WI 53706 UNITED STATES
PHONE: 800-390-8043 • FAX: 608-265-4192
E-MAIL: MBA@BUS.WISC.EDU • WEBSITE: WWW.BUS.WISC.EDU/MBA

firms." Currently, the top 15 recruiters at UW are: Proctor & Gamble, General Electric Company, Kraft Foods, Johnson & Johnson, Guidant, Abbott Laboratories, Nestlé, Best Buy, General Mills, SC Johnson, R.W. Baird, IBM, Cisco, UBS, and Starbucks.

Student Life and Environment

When they aren't hitting the books, Wisconsin students say there are "plenty of activities to become involved in, such as fundraising events, guest lecturers and social get-togethers." Even if you aren't into extracurricular activities, it's easy to get to know your classmates, because "In addition to clubs, classes, and social events, most students are well connected with the other students in their centers." Most Wisconsin students maintain a balanced perspective on life, work, and studies. A current student elaborates, "The students in the business school are very serious about their studies and put in long, dedicated hours to get things done. Then they go party. It takes a mature kind of mindset to be able to effectively balance the two." Another chimes in, "It's not uncommon to work on group projects until two or three in the morning."

At this famous university, the business school is located "in the middle of campus with the 35,000 other students, so there is a constant buzz of activity." The consummate college town, students love Madison, "a city with a thriving arts and cultural scene, and plenty of opportunities for recreation and entertainment." And the school's downtown location means "you get the undergraduate as well as the professional demographic all within seven blocks." With so many entertainment options, it's no surprise that "most of the MBA students go out every Thursday night for a beverage—a great way to get to know everyone."

Admissions

The University of Wisconsin—Madison seeks students from diverse personal, professional, and cultural backgrounds, who have demonstrated success in business and management. Last year's class had an average GMAT score of 656 and average work experience of 4 years. In addition to their academic and professional achievements, Wisconsin looks for students who demonstrate intellectual curiosity, motivation, leadership, communication skills, and analytical ability. An applicants fit with their chosen career specialization, academic record, standardized test scores, and work experience are among the most important factors in an admissions decision.

FINANCIAL FACTS

Annual tuition (in-state/ out-of-state)	$10,240/$25,678
Fees	$858
Cost of books	$930
Room & board (on-campus)	$10,520
% of students receiving aid	73
% of first-year students receiving aid	75
% of students receiving grants	24
Average award package	$18,149
Average grant	$19,283

ADMISSIONS

Admissions Selectivity Rating	**95**
# of applications received	447
% applicants accepted	33
% acceptees attending	73
Average GMAT	656
Range of GMAT	620–690
Average GPA	3.37
TOEFL required of international students	Yes
Minimum TOEFL (paper/computer)	600/250
Application fee	$45
International application fee	$45
Application Deadline/Notification	
Round 1:	11/1 / 12/21
Round 2:	1/23 / 3/7
Round 3:	3/26 / 5/9
Round 4:	5/15 / 6/13
Need-blind admissions	Yes

Applicants Also Look At

Indiana University—Bloomington, Northwestern University, Purdue University, University of Chicago, University of Michigan, University of Minnesota.

EMPLOYMENT PROFILE

Career Rating	92	Grads Employed by Function	% Avg. Salary
Primary Source of Full-time Job Acceptances		Finance	35 $87,177
School-facilitated activities	66 (73%)	Human Resources	6 $76,500
Graduate-facilitated activities	24 (27%)	Marketing	27 $84,083
Average base starting salary	$82,000	MIS	1 NR
Percent employed	96	Operations	6 $83,400
		Consulting	10 $79,333
		General Management	2 NR
		Other	13 $66,917

Top 5 Employers Hiring Grads
GE; General Mills; Abbott Vascular; CUNA Mutual Group; Kraft

UNIVERSITY OF WISCONSIN—MILWAUKEE
SHELDON B. LUBAR SCHOOL OF BUSINESS

GENERAL INFORMATION

Type of school	Public
Environment	City
Academic calendar	Semester

SURVEY SAYS...
Students love Milwaukee, WI
Helpful alumni
Smart classrooms

STUDENTS

Enrollment of parent institution	29,358
Enrollment of business school	311
% male/female	62/38
% part-time	70
Average age at entry	27
Average years work experience at entry	4.6

ACADEMICS

Academic Experience Rating	**80**
Student/faculty ratio	4:1
Profs interesting rating	78
Profs accessible rating	64
% female faculty	30
% minority faculty	1

Joint Degrees
MHRLR (Human Resources and Labor Relations) 2–7 years, MBA/MS (Nursing) 3–7 years, MS-MIS/MBA 3–7 years.

Prominent Alumni
Keith Nosbusch, CEO, Rockwell Automation; James Ziemer, President/CEO, Harley-Davidson Co.; Robert Probst, Exec VP, Tamarack Petroleum; Mary Ellen Stanek, Managing Director, Robert Baird & Co; Dennis Glaso, President/CEO, Jefferson Pilot Corporation.

Academics

Students choose the MBA program at the University of Wisconsin—Milwaukee's Sheldon B. Lubar School of Business because it is convenient and affordable, and because it can be completed on a flexible schedule. Students here agree that "the greatest strength of the program is the school's ability to accommodate the full-time working student via flexible class times, and the next greatest strength is the low cost." MBAs here also appreciate that the university "has a strong connection to the surrounding community, and the school and community often work together on initiatives to make both better places."

Offering classes in the evening, UW—Milwaukee's MBA program is designed for the part-time student who can complete the program in two years by taking three courses per semester (provided the student has an undergraduate degree in business—students with non-business degrees must complete introductory courses before beginning work on the MBA). The program offers the option of graduating with a career-focused concentration in health care management, international business, supply chain management, or managing change. Students may also opt for a general MBA. Either way, students are required to complete 39 to 42 semester credits.

UW—Milwaukee offers "a great atmosphere" with "classes that are filled with discussion and group work." Instruction is "very case study-focused so you get a lot of real world applications for the concepts you are learning." Students also appreciate "the many different academic resources available here, including the computer labs, library, and faculty." Some complain, however, that "many of the courses seem limited in scope" and that "some core courses could be combined to form one comprehensive course. "Students tell us that the program could benefit from "improv[ing] the quality of the courses," "more mandatory academic counseling," and "better instructors" for "a handful of classes."

UW—Milwaukee students may also opt to pursue the MBA at Waukesha. This program, taught by the same faculty who teach at the Milwaukee campus, is a cohort-based program that takes 16 months to complete. The program consists of 24 to 27 semester credits worth of core courses and 12 credits of electives, which are chosen as a group by each cohort.

Career and Placement

The Sheldon B. Lubar School of Business Career Services Center serves undergraduates, graduate students, and alumni of the UW Milwaukee business school. The staff includes two career advisors and a director of career services. The office schedules on-campus interviews online via the eRecruiting system; coordinates internships; organizes career fairs; maintains a list of job postings; conducts workshops on resume writing, interviewing, and job-search skills; and hosts company information sessions.

Student Life and Environment

UW—Milwaukee is "mainly a commuter school," with "the majority of all students (graduate and undergraduate) living off campus. Some drive one hour each way to class." As one MBA candidate puts it, "Students tend to identify as members of society first, and students at this school second. Even though people come to class and leave, there are no slackers here. They are dedicated, sincere academics." Students "range in age from 22 to 40. Many are married or engaged, and all are friendly. Most are employed by major firms around Milwaukee (Briggs, GE Medical, Harley, Kohler, SC Johnson, US Bank, etc.) and want to differentiate themselves."

The UW—Milwaukee campus is not without its amenities. Students report that "the library is great for research, the student union is great for relaxing and eating, and parking isn't all that difficult. The school offers a comfortable atmosphere." There are "lots of student activities going on in the union for the campus at large," though "business school activities seem more career-focused, more concerned with additional learning and career opportunities than with socialization. There are not as many social opportunities for graduate students as there are for undergrads." Students also point out that some "campus services do not revolve around the evening class time period, nor are there standard accommodations for those who attend classes from 5:30 P.M. to 8:10 P.M. or 6:00 P.M. to 8:40 P.M."

UW—Milwaukee is located "on the east side of the city" and "it would be difficult to find a better location. There is always plenty to do, with bars and clubs everywhere. There is plenty of live music as well."

Admissions

Applicants to UW—Milwaukee's MBA program must apply to the university's Graduate School, which refers b-school applications to the School of Business Administration for review and recommendation. The Graduate School Admissions Office makes all final admissions decisions. All applicants must submit a completed application form, an official GMAT score, two official copies of transcripts for all undergraduate work, and two copies of a personal statement. Students must achieve a minimum undergraduate GPA of 2.75 and have a "satisfactory" score on the GMAT to be considered for "admission in good standing." Applicants who fail to meet these minimum requirements may be granted "admission on probation" status. International students must meet all of the above requirements and must also submit an official TOEFL score report (the minimum required score is 550 on the paper test, 213 on the computer test, and 79 on the internet-based test).

FINANCIAL FACTS

Annual tuition (in-state/ out-of-state)	$10,523/$28,188
Cost of books	$900
Room & board (on/off-campus)	$9,000/$10,000
% of students receiving aid	60
% of first-year students receiving aid	41
% of students receiving loans	52
% of students receiving grants	8
Average award package	$14,276
Average grant	$8,400
Average student loan debt	$20,369

ADMISSIONS

Admissions Selectivity Rating	**82**
# of applications received	223
% applicants accepted	54
% acceptees attending	69
Average GMAT	546
Range of GMAT	490–600
Average GPA	3.24
TOEFL required of international students	Yes
Minimum TOEFL (paper/computer)	550/213
Application fee	$45
International application fee	$85
Regular application deadline	Rolling
Regular notification	Rolling
Deferment available	Yes
Maximum length of deferment	1 year
Transfer students accepted	Yes
Transfer application policy The application process is the same for all applicants.	
Non-fall admissions	Yes
Need-blind admissions	Yes

Applicants Also Look At
Marquette University, University of Wisconsin—Madison, University of Wisconsin—Whitewater.

EMPLOYMENT PROFILE

Career Rating	61	Grads Employed by Function	%	Avg. Salary
		Finance	35	$57,091
		Marketing	2	$46,500
		MIS	13	$69,750
		General Management	40	$63,845
		Other	10	$51,000

Top 5 Employers Hiring Grads
US Bank; KPMG; Deloitte & Touche LLP; Northwestern Mutual; Quad/Graphics

UNIVERSITY OF WISCONSIN—WHITEWATER
COLLEGE OF BUSINESS AND ECONOMICS

GENERAL INFORMATION

Type of school	Public
Environment	Village
Academic calendar	Semester

SURVEY SAYS...

Solid preparation in:
Marketing
General management
Communication/interpersonal skills
Computer skills
Doing business in a global economy

STUDENTS

Enrollment of parent institution	10,720
Enrollment of business school	560
% male/female	45/55
% out-of-state	10
% part-time	85
% minorities	1
% international	28
Average age at entry	34
Average years work experience at entry	7

ACADEMICS

Academic Experience Rating	**72**
Student/faculty ratio	28:1
Profs interesting rating	87
Profs accessible rating	71
% female faculty	29
% minority faculty	22

Academics

University of Wisconsin—Whitewater's "well-regarded" and "inexpensive" MBA program is a two-sided affair, but you won't find any students complaining. The first side is its traditional classroom-based MBA program. The other side is its online MBA degree option, which students praise for its "quality of education and flexibility of hours." Classes are also offered "at a few remote locations," which students laud for its "convenience." "I've taken classes online, at Whitewater, and at their Madison, Wisconsin location," one student says. Another agrees: "They're ahead of the curve for implementing technologies to support the educational system. The system is designed for great convenience....I really like the fact that I can take courses in person or, if I choose, online." The option of fulfilling the requirements of your MBA according to your schedule is a huge draw, so much so that "There are even soldiers in Iraq who are taking UW—Whitewater courses online."

While the school "isn't as famous as UW—Madison," most students insist that its "reputation" in the "business field" more than makes up for it. Many appreciate that the Economics program is part of the Business school, allowing "multifunctional disciplines." UW—Whitewater offers "strong" programs in finance and accounting in a "safe environment." Students are equally positive about their "excellent" professors, who they believe to be "some of the most highly sought after in the nation." The "bright" faculty "strives to help students learn" and "most are available for students 100 percent of the time." Students also appreciate that the "teaching methods are very effective," meaning "you learn a lot quickly without sacrificing all of your time."

For those attending class via the World Wide Web, there are a few more shades of grey. "Some of the professors have been great and very interactive," one student explains. "Others have been phantom professors. After taking four classes, I'd say it is about 50–50. There really is no middle ground though. The professors have either been really good or really absent." A fellow online student has a sunnier view: 'I have been exceptionally satisfied with the amount of time and effort that the administration, professors, and dean have given to me personally. They are quick to respond to emails and call back in a timely manner. Since my program is online, I don't have any face-to-face conversations. However, they treat me as though I were in their office."

While most agree that "everything runs like butter," there are a few complaints. "Brand presence is lacking," one student notes. Others would like to see the school hire faculty with "real world" experience. I'd prefer experienced adjunct professors who are at the top of their field who work in an office environment so that we can get the true insight into what we need to learn," a student explains. On the technological front, "hiring a larger IT service force" would be welcomed due to some "server outages." However, the MBA program will take further prominence within the UW system once its "new business school" is completed. "It will be an excellent monument and addition to the Whitewater campus," one student says.

Career and Placement

UW—Whitewater's Career Services office offers a number of services to current students and alumni, including career counseling, career groups, a resource center and classes, workshops and presentations, career fairs, employer presentations, online job postings, on-campus interviews, and resume, cover letter, and interviewing advice. Few students had much to say about this area, most likely because of the large number of students who participate in the online MBA program, meaning they aren't on campus to take advan-

ADMISSIONS CONTACT: DONALD K. ZAHN, ASSOCIATE DEAN
ADDRESS: 800 WEST MAIN STREET WHITEWATER, WI 53190 UNITED STATES
PHONE: 262-472-1945 • FAX: 262-472-4863
E-MAIL: ZAHND@UWW.EDU • WEBSITE: WWW.UWW.EDU

tage of the career office. However, some who attend the school in person would like to see some improvement.

Student Life and Environment

Though some students find that "Whitewater is definitely not a popular vacation spot," the "hardworking," "dependable," and "diverse" students that populate it provide "a wide variety of experiences" to their MBA program peers. The student body is comprised of "many minorities and older returning students," along with a "handful" of younger students that came "directly after their undergraduate programs." "I am probably the youngest student at 23 years old," one student explains. "I would say most students in this program have been working for 5+ years after undergraduate." Many are "very active in sports, arts, and, most importantly, participating in their education with a positive attitude." Students also always seem ready to lend a hand. "I have not in two years met anyone who does not pull their share of the workload during group projects, nor anyone who does not offer to take on more," one student says.

But what of those attending online? Well, it's about the same, really. "Since this is an online program, people often have other work or social commitments they must meet," one student explains. "The other students have been great to work with and very understanding of others' situations." As an online student, the campus is what you make of it, however many note that even though they can't experience Whitewater firsthand, it's clear there's no lack of things to do. As one student explains, "My campus email account is always getting filled up with all kinds of junk mail from the different campus groups."

Admissions

According to UW—Whitewater, applicants to the MBA program must have one of the following: a minimum GPA of 2.75 for all undergraduate work; a minimum GPA of 2.9 for at least half of all undergraduate work; or a Master's degree or higher from a regionally accredited school. In addition, applicants must submit GMAT scores with a minimum composite score of 1000 based on the formula [(GPA x 200) + GMAT], or a minimum composite score of 1050 based on the formula [(GPA from last half of undergrad program x 200) + GMAT]. Student who do not speak English as their native language are required to submit TOEFL scores of at least 550. However, the school does state that exceptions to these requirements may be made on a "case-by-case basis," so if you feel you have a convincing argument but lack the grades and test scores to back it up, it's worth stating your case to the admissions committee.

FINANCIAL FACTS

Annual tuition (in-state/ out-of-state)	$7,456/$18,092
Cost of books	$2,800
Room & board (on-campus)	$3,700
Average grant	$500

ADMISSIONS

Admissions Selectivity Rating	**69**
# of applications received	173
% applicants accepted	81
% acceptees attending	86
Average GMAT	479
Range of GMAT	300–700
Average GPA	3.2
TOEFL required of international students	Yes
Minimum TOEFL (paper/computer)	550/213
Application fee	$56
Regular application deadline	Rolling
Regular notification	Rolling
Deferment available	Yes
Maximum length of deferment	1 year
Transfer students accepted	Yes
Transfer application policy Nine credits may be transferred into the program.	
Non-fall admissions	Yes
Need-blind admissions	Yes

Applicants Also Look At

Marquette University, University of Wisconsin—Madison, University of Wisconsin—Oshkosh, University of Wisconsin—Parkside, University of Wisconsin—Milwaukee.

EMPLOYMENT PROFILE	
Career Rating	71

VALPARAISO UNIVERSITY
COLLEGE OF BUSINESS ADMINISTRATION

GENERAL INFORMATION

Type of school	Private
Affiliation	Lutheran

SURVEY SAYS...

Cutting edge classes
Solid preparation in:
Accounting
General management
Presentation skills
Doing business in a global economy

STUDENTS

Enrollment of	
business school	69
% male/female	60/40
% part-time	60
% minorities	15
% international	1
Average age at entry	29
Average years work	
experience at entry	5.4

ACADEMICS

Academic Experience Rating	**84**
Student/faculty ratio	2:1
Profs interesting rating	81
Profs accessible rating	90
% female faculty	33
% minority faculty	19

Joint Degrees

MBA/JD 4 years.

Academics

A fresh and fairly new MBA program (the first class entered in 2002), the College of Business Administration at Valparaiso University provides a strong "values-centered education" to a small class of about 85 graduate students. The Valparaiso MBA provides a thorough introduction to business topics; however, the focus on ethics and environmental stewardship is what makes a Valpo education unique. Throughout the core curriculum and elective offerings, "Professors take every opportunity to stress these concerns and develop thoughtful and caring future business leaders."

Classes at Valparaiso are small and dynamic, taught by "innovative faculty who understand the business world and incorporate those aspects into their classrooms." Students laud their teachers' ability to "engage students, involve their own personal experiences, and develop thoughts through class discussion." Indeed, group work and discussion are integral to the learning experience at Valparaiso, so students appreciate that their classmates "come from a variety of backgrounds and are able to share numerous experiences in course discussions that provide value and growth not only in the academic areas, but in the 'real world' areas." A current student attests, "I have found all of my courses to be well-run and relevant to today's business environment."

The Valparaiso MBA is specially designed to accommodate both full- and part-time students, offering 2-unit courses in short 7-week blocks. Students can complete the program in as few as 1 or as many as 5 years, and throughout their studies, students can enroll in core courses alongside elective or "enhancement" courses. Enhancement courses run the gamut from Brand Management to Global Supply Chain Management; however, some students would like to see the program include more specialized business topics. A current student explains, "Our program is small and fairly young, and thus it is not yet able to offer a large range of diverse courses. All the necessities are there of course, but as we expand hopefully there will be more focused and deeper courses in particular areas."

When it comes to the higher-ups, students agree that the "administrative system is set up well," even allowing "students the freedom to take care of their own registration and accounts." A current MBA candidate enthuses, "The overall program runs very smoothly, almost by itself. From application, to advising, to registration—it all flows."

Career and Placement

With just a few years in operation, students admit that "the word has not spread about Valpo," and the business community is just beginning to catch on to this new source of talented recruits. However, with the power of the Valparaiso name behind it and the strength of the MBA curriculum, students know it's just a matter of time before their program begins to draw its rightful share of attention from recruiters.

Many Valpo students are already employed when they begin their MBA and plan to continue at their current company after graduation. However, those who are looking for a new position have access to the Valparaiso University Career Center. The Career Center serves the school's graduate and undergraduate community and offers a variety of professional development workshops and career counseling, an annual campus career fair, and a job search database. The Career Center also helps students contact employers and schedule on-campus interviews. According to statistics published by the Career Center, the MBA program had an overall placement rate of 97.4 percent (including students who were previously employed, those who entered new positions, and those who continued with more graduate work).

Erin L. C. Nickelsburg, Assistant Director Graduate Programs in Management
Address: 104 Urschel Hall, 1909 Chapel Drive Valparaiso, IN 46383 United States
Phone: 800-599-0840 • Fax: 219-464-5789
E-mail: mba@valpo.edu • Website: www.valpo.edu/mba

Student Life and Environment

While they come from different academic, professional, and personal backgrounds, "Students interact well with each other" at Valparaiso and find the academic atmosphere to be both stimulating and pleasant. "Since the program is fairly new, there are not many clubs and activities targeted to graduate MBA students." On top of that, many students are busy balancing the demands of work, school, and family; as a result, "Valpo MBA students tend to keep to themselves" and don't make time to hang out with their classmates. Not surprisingly, many students feel that Valpo should do more to promote extracurricular interaction "through more networking events and otherwise encouraging students to get together outside of class." Since the MBA program is so small, students also suggest that the business school could "promote more interaction between the different graduate schools."

For those seeking fun and friendship there is "a small group of people will gather after class at the end of the week to socialize." In addition, the school has made a modest effort to encourage non-academic interaction and "There have been some fun activities for MBA students outside of class," such as trips to see the Chicago Bulls. However, with such an engaged and effective administration at its helm, the program will surely grow its extracurricular offerings as the program expands.

Admissions

Admissions decisions are made on a rolling basis and—thanks to the program's 7-week course schedule—there are six different entry dates during the year. When making an admissions decision, Valparaiso assesses the whole person, weighing the strength of an applicant's undergraduate and postgraduate academic performance, applicable professional experience, letters of recommendation, and GMAT scores. In addition, Valparaiso requests a one-page personal statement explaining why the applicant wants to pursue an MBA at Valpo. The entering class of 2006 had an average GMAT score of 580 and an average GPA of 3.32. The average age was 27, and the average amount of professional work experience among admits was 3.6 years.

FINANCIAL FACTS

Annual tuition	$20,900
Fees	$60
Cost of books	$1,000
% of students receiving aid	69
% of first-year students receiving aid	33
% of students receiving grants	69
Average student loan debt	$11,887

ADMISSIONS

Admissions Selectivity Rating	**92**
# of applications received	187
% applicants accepted	28
% acceptees attending	63
Average GMAT	600
Average GPA	3.22
TOEFL required of international students	Yes
Minimum TOEFL (paper/computer)	575/236
Application fee	$30
International application fee	$50
Deferment available	Yes
Maximum length of deferment	1 year
Transfer students accepted	Yes
Transfer application policy	
Up to 6 credit hours may be transferred.	
Non-fall admissions	Yes
Need-blind admissions	Yes

VANDERBILT UNIVERSITY
OWEN GRADUATE SCHOOL OF MANAGEMENT

Academics

MBA students at Vanderbilt praise the "small class size, warm culture, and strong finance faculty" at the first-rate Owen Graduate School of Management. "There is competition here, and fellow students and faculty do not let you off easily, but they also help you through the challenges," one student explains. "Whether it is helping you prepare for an interview that they are preparing for themselves or tutoring you in finance because you tutored them in marketing, students are there for each other." It's not just the student body immersed in community spirit; the administration and faculty also join in. One MBA writes, "The beauty of going to a smaller school like Owen is that our professors know the students well, and we know our professors well. I believe this gives us a competitive advantage because we can graduate not only with fellow student contacts, but also faculty contacts." Students also appreciate that "the school is run very much like a business." "The professors are evaluated based on student feedback . . . [and] part of a professor's compensation and tenure decision is based on these reviews," notes one student. "Most of the professors at Vanderbilt have years of experience and are very easy to meet with or talk to outside of class."

Such personal touches are rarely accompanied by top-rate research, but Owen is also a leader in a variety of fields thanks to its professors' cutting-edge work. The faculty excels in finance and marketing, along with e-commerce, operations management, and organizational management. One MBA writes, "The greatest strengths of Owen are the various strong concentrations, along with a well-organized academic calendar. Moreover, if we want, we can take more electives depending on personal special interest." The strength of other Vanderbilt divisions adds further value to the program, since "Owen offers jointly taught courses with other highly ranked programs in the Vanderbilt system like the law, medical, and engineering schools." Some do wish, though, that Owen would improve "the speed at which [it] adds new classes."

Vanderbilt's MBAs rate the professors as "stellar" and the academic curriculum as "very rewarding and challenging." Many here note the "real-world practices and situations" that are incorporated "into the courses," which not only make them "fun" but encourage "active participation among students." Across the board, students love that the school is "designed for the students and all activities have that in mind. From administration through Career Management Office, everything is set up to help students succeed." One student sums it up concisely, "I couldn't have chosen a better MBA program."

Career and Placement

Owen's Career Management Center "has been completely transformed and is more confident with their opportunities and placements of students." Many find that "the CMC office does a great job" and trusts its "creativity" in how it deals with "the changing needs of the students." That said, there's always more work to be done, and "Although the school does a spectacular job in career management, it should work"—and is working—"on attracting more companies to actively recruit at the school."

Employers most likely to hire Owen MBAs include American Express, Banc America Securities, Citigroup, Dell, Deloitte Touche Tohmatsu, Deutsche Bank, Eli Lilly and Company, Emerson Electric, Ford Motor Company, Gaylord Entertainment, GE Capital, Harrah's Entertainment, Hewlett-Packard, The Home Depot, Honeywell, IBM, Johnson & Johnson, Mattel, Merrill Lynch, Procter & Gamble, Smith Barney, Sara Lee, Southern Company, SunTrust Bank, Unilever, and Wachovia.

ADMISSIONS CONTACT: JOHN ROEDER, DIRECTOR OF ADMISSIONS
ADDRESS: 401 21ST AVENUE SOUTH NASHVILLE, TN 37203 UNITED STATES
PHONE: 615-322-6469 • FAX: 615-343-1175
E-MAIL: ADMISSIONS@OWEN.VANDERBILT.EDU • WEBSITE: OWEN.VANDERBILT.EDU

Student Life and Environment

The place changes but the cliché remains the same: students at Vanderbilt "work hard and play hard." But with an MBA curriculum this time-consuming, that's very welcome news to students here. "At Vanderbilt, you don't only live with books," explains one student. "The community helps you to keep a balanced life, so you also have time to play sports or meet outside the school." As one student put it, "One minute you're doing bond arbitrage, another minute you're playing flag football with the same great people." "My classmates are very intelligent and work really hard yet save enough energy to have fun," One student states, "Aside from business clubs, we have a variety social and interest clubs. This year students have started Owen Culinary Society that once a month prepares a dinner for about 40 students—cooked by the students. Also we have weekly kegs in the lobby sponsored by faculty or recruiting companies."

Students also make time to enjoy hometown Nashville, "a terrific place to go to school." The city "has the best music scene in the country," one MBA who's "not even a huge country music fan" writes, noting that "there's all types of music here because Nashville attracts incredible musicians." Another appreciates that "it is not too expensive to live in and it is very easy to navigate." Nashville also offers "good food, great parks, and a surprising number of very good employment opportunities." The city is home to big-league hockey and football teams, as well as an AAA minor league baseball team.

Admissions

Vanderbilt bases admissions decisions on several factors, namely the applicant's "caliber of undergraduate institution, difficulty of major, quality and duration of prior work experience, professional responsibilities and accomplishments, career advancement, career goals, extracurricular/professional/community involvement, leadership potential, interpersonal skills, communication skills, team orientation, diversity, and cross-cultural awareness/understanding/experience/appreciation." The school encourages minorities and disadvantaged students to apply and attend its "Diversity Weekend," which the school states is "open to all prospective students, but specially targeted to prospective U.S. minority students."

FINANCIAL FACTS

Annual tuition	$39,992
Fees	$602
Cost of books	$1,668
Room & board (off-campus)	$3,894
% of students receiving aid	83
% of first-year students receiving aid	80
% of students receiving loans	57
% of students receiving grants	58
Average award package	$41,569
Average grant	$18,442
Average student loan debt	$75,899

ADMISSIONS

Admissions Selectivity Rating	89
# of applications received	759
% applicants accepted	47
% acceptees attending	60
Average GMAT	644
Range of GMAT	602–690
Average GPA	3.27
TOEFL required of international students	Yes
Minimum TOEFL (paper/computer)	600/250
Application fee	$100
International application fee	$100
Regular application deadline	3/3
Regular notification	4/1
Application Deadline/Notification	
Round 1:	11/15 / 01/15
Round 2:	01/07 / 03/07
Round 3:	03/03 / 04/21
Round 4:	05/15 / NR
Deferment available	Yes
Maximum length of deferment	1 year
Need-blind admissions	Yes

Applicants Also Look At

Duke University, Emory University, Georgetown University, Indiana University—Bloomington, The University of North Carolina at Chapel Hill, The University of Texas at Austin, University of Virginia.

EMPLOYMENT PROFILE

Career Rating	90	Grads Employed by Function	%	Avg. Salary
Primary Source of Full-time Job Acceptances		Finance	43	$90,553
School-facilitated activities	87 (66%)	Human Resources	6	$87,250
Graduate-facilitated activities	34 (26%)	Marketing	18	$78,900
Unknown	11 (8%)	Operations	5	$91,517
Average base starting salary	$89,268	Consulting	20	$100,760
Percent employed	84	General Management	7	$76,556

Top 5 Employers Hiring Grads

Bank of America; Citigroup; Deloitte Consulting; General Electric; Capgemini

VILLANOVA UNIVERSITY
SCHOOL OF BUSINESS

GENERAL INFORMATION

Type of school	Private
Affiliation	Roman Catholic
Environment	Village
Academic calendar	Semester

SURVEY SAYS...

Good peer network
Solid preparation in:
Communication/interpersonal skills

STUDENTS

Enrollment of parent institution	10,274
Enrollment of business school	679
% part-time	94
Average age at entry	28
Average years work experience at entry	5

ACADEMICS

Academic Experience Rating	**81**
Student/faculty ratio	12:1
Profs interesting rating	80
Profs accessible rating	81
% female faculty	22

Joint Degrees

JD/MBA 3–4 years.

Academics

MBA students at Villanova University consider their School of Business to be "the most reputable business school in Philadelphia not named 'Wharton,'" with "a good overall philosophy and a good approach to education" that emanates from the university's Augustinian tradition. Students are also impressed by VU's strong "alumni connections in major cities on the Eastern Seaboard, especially in New York City." Students here feel confident that "the Villanova name will serve [them] well after graduation."

Most MBAs at Villanova attend part-time, primarily in the school's professional MBA (PMBA) program, which they describe as "a very robust program conducted at a pace that is conducive to people who cannot devote the time needed for a 2-year intensive program." PMBA students also like that their program offers a specialization option; "The international business specialization options" are especially appealing. Villanova's PMBA maintains a sense of class unity by kicking off with a Leadership Weekend; one participant notes, "In the part-time program, it is easy to not meet fellow students, but this course offers students the opportunity to meet multiple students, making group work and class discussion easier throughout the program."

VU's FTE MBA is a cohort-based program with a prescribed curriculum of 12 classes. Students "truly love the cohort aspect," telling us that "our class is extremely close and the caliber of student is high." Program requirements "are largely the same as a professional MBA, although we do not take electives during the program. However, we may return for electives/specialty courses that would be listed as a postgraduate certificate." Full-timers "are segregated from the PMBA students" because of the cohort nature of their program.

Participants in both programs agree that "the greatest strength of Villanova is the professors," whose ranks include "many who have their own businesses on the side or are active consultants with regional or national business clients. Their ability to show real-world examples of theories and principles is key to the value of a Villanova MBA." The school's "ambitious administration is actively seeking to enhance the school's reputation," a fact that pleases students here.

Career and Placement

Villanova's MBA candidates say the Career Services Office "leaves something to be desired." Students report that "recruiting efforts are 98 percent targeted toward undergraduate students." Reinforcing that perception is that fact that the office's website lists placement data for undergraduates only, though the school says it is actively working to provide recruiting opportunities for graduate business students. The school participates in joint recruiting ventures such as the Graduate Business Talent Finder Fair, which allows employers to recruit for jobs and internships from 11 Philadelphia-area MBA programs.

Student Life and Environment

Villanova's business school facility "is very conveniently located for working professionals to access via car or public transportation from downtown Philadelphia or the suburbs." Students also like how "the building [where classes are held] has a place to purchase cooked meals or sandwiches and snacks as well as a Pete's Coffee Shop open late, all very convenient for working professionals who go to class directly from the office." The actual classroom facilities, however, "are subpar. Electrical outlets do not work, and many Ethernet ports are broken. The wireless routers are offline more than they are online."

ADMISSIONS CONTACT: TOM KEGELMAN, ASSOCIATE DIRECTOR
ADDRESS: 800 LANCASTER AVENUE - BARTLEY HALL VILLANOVA, PA 19085 UNITED STATES
PHONE: 610-519-4336 • FAX: 610-519-6273
E-MAIL: GRADBUSINESS@VILLANOVA.EDU • WEBSITE: WWW.GRADBUSINESS.VILLANOVA.EDU

The majority part-time population here "all work full-time, meaning our interactions with school are primarily during class and group study hours." PMBA students tell us that "professors are very understanding of the things we are all trying to balance, and are very flexible and work with each student to make the most of the class." Classmates are "friendly and make themselves available to work on group learning projects and presentations."

FTE MBA students enjoy a more robust extracurricular life. They tell us that "students are encouraged to get active in the community, as the school provides opportunities for MBA students to provide pro-bono services to nonprofits." As one student explains, "There is a huge amount of community-based activities [available] in addition to a myriad of school-related clubs and groups. I like being surrounded by these constant giving-back activities and reinforcement of good human behavior."

Villanova draws "a broad range of students, from age to background to personal life." There are "some just out of college, and many with 2 to 6 years [of] work experience. Many students have work experience in finance and pharmaceuticals (both big in the Philadelphia area)." Across the board, "Students tend to be very helpful, willing to answer questions and share thoughts. They also make sure to have someone copy notes if a student misses class, even if they aren't asked to do so. It is a very equal environment, and everyone wants each other to get ahead." In terms of students who are married versus students who are single, "It varies. Some have kids and are married, some aren't married and don't have kids." Spouses "are encouraged to come to social functions," which students appreciate. Students say the student body has "a good mix of women and men."

Admissions

Applicants to Villanova's MBA programs must submit official transcripts for all postsecondary academic work, an official GMAT score report, an official TOEFL score report (international students whose first language is not English only), two personal essays (at a maximum of 600 words each), two letters of recommendation, a resume, and a completed application.

FINANCIAL FACTS

Annual tuition	$12,000
Fees	$60
Cost of books	$800

ADMISSIONS

Admissions Selectivity Rating	**81**
# of applications received	256
% applicants accepted	69
% acceptees attending	78
Average GMAT	595
Average GPA	3.4
TOEFL required of international students	Yes
Minimum TOEFL (paper/computer)	600/250
Application fee	$50
International application fee	$50
Regular application deadline	11/30, 3/31, 6/30
Regular notification	Rolling
Deferment available	Yes
Maximum length of deferment	One year
Transfer students accepted	Yes
Transfer application policy Up to nine credits from AACSB accredited MBA Programs.	
Non-fall admissions	Yes
Need-blind admissions	Yes

Applicants Also Look At
Drexel University, Temple University.

VIRGINIA COMMONWEALTH UNIVERSITY
SCHOOL OF BUSINESS

GENERAL INFORMATION

Type of school	Public
Environment	Metropolis
Academic calendar	Semester

SURVEY SAYS...

Good peer network
Cutting edge classes

STUDENTS

Enrollment of parent institution	30,452
Enrollment of business school	220
% male/female	70/30
% part-time	74
% international	25
Average age at entry	27
Average years work experience at entry	4.7

ACADEMICS

Academic Experience Rating	**79**
Student/faculty ratio	20:1
Profs interesting rating	75
Profs accessible rating	87
% female faculty	15
% minority faculty	5

Joint Degrees

BS/MS (Accountancy) 5 years,
BS/MBA (Engineering),
PharmD/MBA, MBA/MSIS.

Academics

"The greatest strength [of the MBA program] is the school's connection with the local business community" at Virginia Commonwealth University, a school that capitalizes on "the many major corporations headquartered in Richmond." Students here report that "networking with prospective employers is widely available" and that "networking with other students working in various industries" is also one of the program's great benefits. A "strong regional reputation" increases the likelihood that networking opportunities here will yield positive results.

Although "VCU might be the biggest university in the state of Virginia," its MBA program is designed to create "an individualized experience. You're not just a cog or a number. You get the great facilities and resources of a big school with the close, personal touches of a small school." Those touches include "professors who are here to teach. They truly want the students to excel. Every teacher makes a strong effort to make sure each student masters the material. There is no such thing as remote teaching here; it's really hands-on, make-a-connection"-style learning. VCU professors "incorporate real-world insight into their course material and the information is there for the taking."

VCU's MBA program design also earns high marks from students for its "integrated approach rather than a silo subject-based approach" with "multiple topics per module." This type of approach allows students "to better understand how to tie multiple disciplines together to become an effective business executive." VCU's cross-functional approach includes a heavy emphasis on information technology across the curriculum.

VCU offers both a full-time and part-time MBA. With four out of five students attending part-time, students say that "the blend of part-time and full-time students provides opportunities to share different perspectives on various topics among students"). The school also offers an executive MBA that participants describe as "an exceptionally well-run program. From administration down to support staff, they do a tremendous job to help ensure each student gets the best possible education." Students here also agree that the price is right.

Career and Placement

The VCU Career Center serves all undergraduate and graduate students at the university. The office provides a wide range of counseling and placement services. Area businesses also contact the School of Business directly to post internship and career opportunities available to MBA students here. Students can keep up to date on such notifications by subscribing to the School of Business Listserv. About 80 percent of VCU's MBA students attend part-time; nearly all work part-time or full-time, many with companies with whom they intend to remain after graduation.

Student Life and Environment

A typical day in the life of a full-time MBA student at VCU, according to one such student, includes a morning internship (typically running from 9:00 A.M. to 1:00 P.M.), an extended study and preparation period through mid- to late-afternoon, "attending an employer speaker series sponsored by the graduate school networking group or employer information meet-and-greet sponsored by the Career Center," or grabbing "a snack at the Student Commons" or a local restaurant during the dinner hour, classes from 7:00 to 9:40 P.M., and then more studying until bedtime. Part-timers follow a slightly different schedule: Most work full-time jobs, arrive at campus just in time for class, and then either study or try to squeeze in some quality family time before hitting the sack. No matter what type of student you're talking about, it's a very full schedule.

ADMISSIONS CONTACT: JANA P. McQUAID, DIRECTOR, GRADUATE STUDIES IN BUSINESS
ADDRESS: 301 WEST MAIN STREET, PO BOX 844000 RICHMOND, VA 23284-4000 UNITED STATES
PHONE: 804-828-4622 • FAX: 804-828-7174
E-MAIL: GSIB@VCU.EDU • WEBSITE: WWW.GSIB.VCU.EDU

VCU students tell us that campus life involves "many things happening all the time. You can watch free movies at night, go to the gym, pool, tennis, etc." or hit the "eateries and cafés on every corner," which include the "fine dining at Shafer Court for the price of a canteen." The school is enjoying a period of major renovation. Says one b-student, "The building in which I have attended all of my classes is being torn down next year after a new, state-of-the-art business school opens." Students brag that "the area around the business school is one of the most attractive places in the area for young students to live," offering access to anything you could need. They also appreciate that "the campus is safe." One student observes, "If you like small cities that offer everything that big cities do without the traffic and headaches, you will like the location."

Admissions

Applicants to all MBA programs at VCU must submit a completed application, official transcripts for all postsecondary academic work, an official GMAT score report, a resume, a personal statement, and three letters of recommendation. International applicants must also provide proof of English proficiency (the school accepts both the TOEFL and the IELTS and evidence of sufficient financial support to cover the cost of attending and expenses while at VCU. The school reports that "students who were admitted to and completed course work at other AACSB-accredited institutions may apply to VCU and seek transfer of up to 6 semester hours of work toward the VCU graduate degree. Students must have earned no less than a B in each class to be transferred. The decision to transfer courses is left to the discretion of the Director of Graduate Studies in Business."

FINANCIAL FACTS

Annual tuition (in-state/ out-of-state)	$7,224/$15,904
Fees	$1,680
Cost of books	$1,000
Room & board (on/off-campus)	$5,000/$8,000

ADMISSIONS

Admissions Selectivity Rating	**83**
# of applications received	216
% applicants accepted	53
% acceptees attending	61
Average GMAT	567
Range of GMAT	490–640
Average GPA	3.2
TOEFL required of international students	Yes
Minimum TOEFL (paper/computer)	600/250
Application fee	$50
International application fee	$50
Regular application deadline	7/15
Regular notification	8/1
Early decision program?	Yes
ED Deadline/Notification	Fall Term 04/01 / 05/01
Deferment available	Yes
Maximum length of deferment	1 year
Transfer students accepted	Yes
Transfer application policy Students may apply to VCU and seek transfer of up to six Semester hours of work from other AACSB accredited institutions..	
Non-fall admissions	Yes
Need-blind admissions	Yes

Applicants Also Look At

College of William & Mary, James Madison University, University of Richmond, Virginia Tech.

Virginia Polytechnic Institute and State University
Pamplin College of Business

Academics

A small business program within a large university, the Pamplin College of Business offers an appealing blend of academic excellence, affordable tuition, and an intimate student atmosphere. Depending on your needs and career experience, the school offers a number of MBA options, including a full-time MBA, a part-time MBA, and an executive MBA, each offered in a different Virginia location. All programs provide an advanced education in marketing, management, finance, and leadership, with the option of pursuing an area of concentration in a particular business field. The school also operates a dual-degree program with an international focus, offered jointly with Thunderbird School of Global Management in Arizona or Institute National Des Telecommunications (INT) in France. In addition, a number of special programs help add depth and distinctiveness to a Pamplin MBA. For example, the SEED program (Student-managed Endowment for Educational Development) allows business students to manage about $4 million of Virginia Tech's endowment through stock investment.

Thanks to its low graduate enrollment, Pamplin offers uniformly small class sizes and plenty of personal attention. In both full-time and part-time programs, "professors are more than willing to meet with students outside of class" and "are very knowledgeable, easily accessible and always ready to help." Despite their uniform accessibility, some of the teaching staff may have passed their prime. A student explains, "I have had some really inspiring professors, but I have also had the opposite, ones who have taught for so long that they just go through the motions." In addition to academics, the "school has great support functions, be it administration, HR, IT or any other department...Everyone is on their toes to help and guide the students in all administrative affairs." The downside to the smaller student body is that the school cannot offer as diverse a course selection as larger schools. Many would also like to see the school "widen the scope of concentrations offered"—recently, in fact, the school cut the marketing concentration, because there weren't enough participating students. However, students point out that "the program is also willing to help create a concentration tailored toward the students' wants and goals through work-studies and outside courses." On that note, "the program [is] also very helpful in providing fellowships and assistantships," which can be an excellent way to offset the costs of the education while also providing valuable professional experience.

Career and Placement

Pamplin takes the job search seriously, offering personalized career counseling and placement assistance for students at every professional level. Through the MBA Program Office, students can participate in career talks and workshops, company field visits, mentoring programs, and alumni symposia, among many other useful offerings. During the first semester of their second year, full-time students are also required to take a one-unit course called Job Search Strategy.

Future students should be aware that this small program does not attract as many recruiters as other large graduate programs might, and for "people doing MBA in Finance there are no companies that come to campus." Many international students also complain that the school does not offer enough assistance for those seeking positions that will sponsor them for professional work visas. On the flip side, Pamplin students benefit from the fact that "the size of the school attracts many recruiters, despite a relatively small MBA program." MBA students can also augment Pamplin's career services by using the extensive services offered through the university's Career Services center.

ADMISSIONS CONTACT: MELANIE JOHNSTON, ASSOCIATE DIRECTOR
ADDRESS: 1044 PAMPLIN HALL, VIRGINIA TECH BLACKSBURG, VA 24061 UNITED STATES
PHONE: 540-231-6152 • FAX: 540-231-4487
E-MAIL: MBA_INFO@VT.EDU • WEBSITE: WWW.MBA.PAMPLIN.VT.EDU

FINANCIAL FACTS

Annual tuition (in-state/ out-of-state)	$7,361/$13,556
Fees (in-state/ out-of-state)	$1,625/$1,795
Room & board (off-campus)	$7,200
% of students receiving aid	80
% of students receiving loans	30
% of students receiving grants	56
Average award package	$21,490
Average grant	$8,470
Average student loan debt	$10,757

ADMISSIONS

Admissions Selectivity Rating	**87**
# of applications received	132
% applicants accepted	58
% acceptees attending	47
Average GMAT	629
Range of GMAT	590–660
Average GPA	3.42
TOEFL required of international students	Yes
Minimum TOEFL (paper/computer)	550/213
Application fee	$45
International application fee	$45
Regular application deadline	2/1
Regular notification	rolling
Deferment available	Yes
Maximum length of deferment	2 year
Need-blind admissions	Yes

Applicants Also Look At

College of William & Mary, George Mason University, The George Washington University, University of Maryland—College Park, University of Virginia, Virginia Commonwealth University.

Student Life and Environment

Pamplin offers a number of MBA programs in various Virginia locations, with the main campus located in Blacksburg. To each of these campuses, the school draws students from "a wide variety of different ethnicities, backgrounds, ages, and genders, which makes class much more interesting." A current student elaborates, "We have a diverse cohort made up of about 50 percent international students, mostly from India, China, and France." Despite diversity, everyone works together with ease, and "fellow students are very friendly and helpful…No one faces any issues being in groups with anyone for the class assignments, and everyone is extremely polite." In fact, friendships quickly extend beyond the classroom as "most students venture outside their nationality and peer groups without hesitancy. Many have active social lives and make an effort to get to know the other students."

On that note, many Pamplin students are able to find some downtime amidst their busy schedule, enjoying "very social lives while working extremely hard at our school work." When they aren't hitting the books or preparing a presentation, "students get together out of class to hike on the Appalachian trail, bike, play golf, or just socialize at a pub/cafe." In the immediate area, the "Blue Ridge Mountains offer excellent hiking, trail running, rock climbing, kayaking, and mountain biking within close proximity to Blacksburg." While Blacksburg is a smaller city, you'll nonetheless find "a lot of good places to hang out and spend your Saturday nights." What's more, commuters and campus residents will like the fact that "Blacksburg has an excellent public transportation system and is pedestrian- and bicycle-friendly."

Admissions

Admissions criteria at Pamplin vary by program. For the full-time MBA, last year's entering class had an average GMAT score of 640. For part-time and professional MBA students, the average GMAT score was 600. Students in all programs submitted an average GPA of 3.0. During the admissions process, applicants may be contacted for a personal interview.

EMPLOYMENT PROFILE

Career Rating	82	Grads Employed by Function	%	Avg. Salary
Primary Source of Full-time Job Acceptances		Finance	28	$53,999
School-facilitated activities	17 (81%)	MIS	10	$72,500
Graduate-facilitated activities	4 (19%)	Operations	14	$71,500
Average base starting salary	$64,921	Consulting	33	$67,977
Percent employed	92	General Management	5	$59,000
		Other	10	$72,500

Top 5 Employers Hiring Grads

Cap Gemini; Deloitte & Touche; Ernst & Young; Booz Allen Hamilton; Capital One

WAKE FOREST UNIVERSITY
BABCOCK GRADUATE SCHOOL OF MANAGEMENT

Academics

A small program in a private university setting, the Babcock Graduate School of Management at Wake Forest University provides a business education that is focused on teamwork, entrepreneurship, experiential learning, and hands-on management. No matter what their academic preparation or business interest, all students are required to take the first-year core courses, which include such essentials as International Business Management, Financial Management, Macroeconomics, Operations Management, and Quantitative Methods. In the second year, students choose a career concentration within the broader areas of consulting/general management, finance, entrepreneurship, marketing, operations management, information technology management (available only as a secondary concentration), or an individually designed concentration in an area such as health care management.

With only 80 students per class, Wake Forest maintains "an intimate feel and incredible exposure to top-notch faculty and alums in incredible positions." Students love the "entrepreneurial, collegial atmosphere that provides everyone with the opportunity to excel and invoke innovation and change." In fact, students say the school's small size works to their advantage in many ways, including "the development of stronger relationships with peers, better rapport with the faculty, and higher levels of access to the resources on campus." While a Wake Forest education comes with a private school price tag, students appreciate the little perks, like the fact that "everyone gets a [laptop] computer and [is] linked into the same network. This makes school assignments very easy to complete, and our IT support staff is fantastic."

Focusing on quantitative skills and boasting strong programs in IT and strategy, students say the workload at Wake Forest can be "very intense." However, the academic stress is counterbalanced by the fact that "professors are extremely dedicated to providing a positive learning environment and experience." A current student explains: "The school fosters a competitive environment which is key in the business world today; however, it also encourages a helpful and empowering attitude in individuals. If anyone is ever falling behind in a particular course or not understanding material, study groups are immediately formed."

Despite their years of experience in the classroom, Wake Forest professors are "surprisingly up to date on their integration of current business trends into classroom study." The curriculum is further augmented by a series of school-sponsored events and lectures, providing "excellent opportunities to hear reputable outside speakers talk on relevant business topics."

Career and Placement

The Career Management Center at Wake Forest works closely with students to define their goals and help make corporate contacts. The university also maintains a list of more than 5,000 MBA alumni, among the school's approximately 6,300 total MBA graduates, who are considered active and accessible in helping current students find positions. Babcock students acknowledge that there is a trade-off in attending a smaller school, as "Increased class size would help attract more companies, but would decrease intimacy." Even so, students assure us that "the school is small; however it pulls in many large companies to recruit on campus."

Having built strong ties in the finance industry, Wake Forest is currently "placing a strong emphasis on marketing and consulting." But on the whole, students report, "The Career Services team has done a fantastic job of assembling a wide variety of professional opportunities." In 2006, the mean salary for graduating students was $80,311. Fifty-two

ADMISSIONS CONTACT: STACY POINDEXTER OWEN, DIRECTOR OF ADMISSIONS
ADDRESS: WORRELL PROFESSIONAL CENTER, ROOM 2119, 1834 WAKE FOREST RD. WINSTON-
SALEM, NC 27106 UNITED STATES • PHONE: 336-758-5422 • FAX: 336-758-5830
E-MAIL: ADMISSIONS@MBA.WFU.EDU • WEBSITE: WWW.MBA.WFU.EDU

percent of grads took jobs in finance and accounting, and 20 percent took jobs in marketing and sales.

Student Life and Environment

Life at Wake Forest is a mix of work, play, and professional development, and students enjoy plenty of "well-balanced days with strong academics and a warm, friendly class." Drawing "a diverse mix of individuals across all kinds of work experience, backgrounds, race, nationality, and even age," Wake Forest students describe their classmates as "smart, fun, socially vibrant, extremely supportive, and helpful in both academic and personal issues." Encouraging an intimate and tight-knit culture, the sense of community at Wake Forest "permeates every level of [students'] academic and social lives."

Outside the classroom, "There are many student-run activities for personal and career development. These include minority interest clubs, business function clubs, and social clubs." As a result, students enjoy "multiple outlets to be a leader in a club, work with admissions, and help the surrounding community." Notable student-run activities include social enterprise projects and trips, the Wake Forest MBA Marketing Summit and an accompanying MBA Marketing Case Competition, and the Elevator Competition, a business plan/venture capital event. When looking for a little down time, "Winston is a good town with plenty to do—good restaurants, good bars, good climate, and it's close to the beach and mountains." A current student enthuses, "One of the best things is that I am always busy, whether it's from being immersed in challenging studies or hanging out with new friends."

Admissions

Wake Forest admits students who have proven academic ability, professional experience, and community involvement. Sought-after qualities include focus, motivation, leadership ability, strong values, and teamwork skills. Postgraduate work experience is highly important to an admissions decision. Last year, the entering class had an average GMAT score of 647, with a range of 610 to 680 (25th to 75th percentile), and average work experience of 3.3 years.

For students who want to take part in a unique accelerated admissions process, Wake Forest offers "Done in a Day" admissions, wherein prospective candidates come to campus for one of several panel interview sessions. These applicants forego completing the admissions essays, and they receive an admissions decision within 24 hours of their interview.

FINANCIAL FACTS

Annual tuition	$33,400
Fees	$150
Cost of books	$1,500
Room & board (off-campus)	$7,000
% of students receiving aid	84
% of first-year students receiving aid	84
% of students receiving loans	56
% of students receiving grants	73
Average award package	$33,999
Average grant	$15,282
Average student loan debt	$56,743

ADMISSIONS

Admissions Selectivity Rating	88
Average GMAT	632
Range of GMAT	590–660
Average GPA	3.1
TOEFL required of international students	Yes
Minimum TOEFL (paper/computer/internet)	600/250
Application fee	$75
International application fee	$75
Regular application deadline	5/1
Regular notification	Rolling
Early decision program?	Yes
ED Deadline/Notification	11/01 / 11/22
Need-blind admissions	Yes

Applicants Also Look At

Duke University, Indiana University—Bloomington, The University of North Carolina at Chapel Hill, University of Notre Dame, University of Virginia, Vanderbilt University.

EMPLOYMENT PROFILE

Career Rating	88	Grads Employed by Function	%	Avg. Salary
Primary Source of Full-time Job Acceptances		Finance	45	$84,541
School-facilitated activities	67%	Marketing	27	$75,480
Graduate-facilitated activities	33%	MIS	3	$0
Average base starting salary	$81,012	Operations	7	$81,000
Percent employed	78	Consulting	18	$81,050

Top 5 Employers Hiring Grads

Bank of America and Banc of America Securities; Scotia Capital; Alltel; Booz Allen; Fedex

WASHBURN UNIVERSITY
SCHOOL OF BUSINESS

GENERAL INFORMATION
Type of school	Public
Academic calendar	Semester

SURVEY SAYS...
Cutting edge classes
Solid preparation in:
Finance
Accounting

STUDENTS
Enrollment of parent institution	7,000
Enrollment of business school	74
% male/female	40/60
% out-of-state	2
% part-time	86
% minorities	8
% international	1
Average age at entry	31
Average years work experience at entry	5

ACADEMICS
Academic Experience Rating	**83**
Student/faculty ratio	20:1
Profs interesting rating	85
Profs accessible rating	91
% female faculty	29
% minority faculty	18

Joint Degrees
MBA/JD 4 years.

Prominent Alumni
Greg Brenneman, CEO/President, Burger King; Mayo Schmidt, CEO/President, Saskatchewan Wheat Pool; Dale Pond, VP Marketing, Lowe's; Ken Calwell, VP Marketing, Domino's Pizza.

Academics

Located in Topeka, Kansas, Washburn University's broad-based MBA program seeks to improve a student's skills in quantitative analysis, teamwork, and technology while providing a strong academic foundation in accounting, economics, finance, information systems, management, marketing, legal and ethic issues, and global business. Attracting many working professionals as well as a considerable population of full-time, international students, Washburn teaches students how to think like business leaders and gives them the skills and confidence they need to succeed in the business world. "Upon completion of the program, I will feel confident in my abilities to provide outstanding analysis, negotiation, coordination, troubleshooting and communications skills," attests a student. "I have learned to demonstrate ethical and professional conduct coupled with excellent leadership skills."

The MBA program begins with the core-level curriculum, which covers quantitative methods and accounting. After completing the core, students begin the upper-level curriculum, comprising 30 semester hours in more specialized business topics. While eight courses in the upper-level curriculum are required, students may also take two or more electives in an area of special interest. However, be forewarned that elective offerings comprise a very small portion of the MBA program. In fact, students looking for more specialized business knowledge say the school should offer "more classes targeted to specific areas of study instead of a general overview." A current student admits, "The diversity of electives is nonexistent. Our electives would be more appropriately named requirements."

Quality teaching is fundamental to the Washburn experience, and the school's top-notch faculty is "a diverse group that have many years of experience in teaching." A dynamic classroom environment, professors "provide insight, facilitate discussion and group work resembling the workplace, and use situation analysis to make points." On top of that, students appreciate the fact that the small program facilitates personal relationships with the faculty. A current student elaborates, "Your professors will know your name. They will answer your call or e-mail. They have a genuine desire to see you succeed and do well."

Drawing students from a variety of academic and professional backgrounds, Washburn MBAs are "high-energy, results-oriented, self-motivated team players." The majority of students also work full-time while completing their MBA, which means that class discussions are loaded with real-world insights. Despite the rigors of balancing life, school, and a personal life, Washburn professors go out of their way to accommodate working students. A student explains, "It is geared toward the nontraditional working student and has a lot of flexibility for students who have to travel for their jobs." Another agrees, "Professors demand a lot, but most have been very aware and accommodating to school/life balances."

Career and Placement

Many MBA students at Washburn are currently employed and plan to stay with their current company after graduation from the program. However, those looking for a new position can receive assistance through the Washburn University Career Services Office, which serves the undergraduate and graduate community at the school, as well as alumni. Though Career Services, students have access to numerous career fairs and interview days, interview and resume preparation assistance, and job search information. A number of prominent companies have offices in Topeka, including Blue Cross and Blue

DR. BOB BONCELLA, MBA DIRECTOR / PROFESSOR OF INFORMATION SYSTEMS
ADDRESS: 1700 SW COLLEGE, HENDERSON ROOM 114 TOPEKA, KS 66621 UNITED STATES
PHONE: 785-670-1308 • FAX: 785-670-1063
E-MAIL: MBA@WASHBURN.EDU • WEBSITE: WWW.WASHBURN.EDU/BUSINESS/MBA

Shield Association, Burlington Northern & Santa Fe Railway, Hills Pet Foods, Southwestern Bell, Western Resources, Frito-Lay, Goodyear, and as well as a variety of smaller companies and medical resources.

Student Life and Environment

Students appreciate the amiable and non-competitive culture on the Washburn campus, describing their classmates as "friendly, personable, and enthusiastic." Group work is an important part of the Washburn MBA, giving students ample opportunity to meet and work with their classmates throughout the course of the program. Students enjoy interacting with their talented cohorts, telling us, "Almost everyone pulled their weight with regard to team projects, and the interaction of differing opinions and backgrounds was very interesting."

Of the 120 graduate students in Washburn's MBA program, about 80 percent are full-time professionals who take classes at night. As a result, there isn't much of a social buzz on campus, and most students don't participate in extracurricular activities. In fact, one student who came directly to the program out of undergrad laments, "I wish there were more of a social atmosphere outside of the classroom, but other students are too busy."

However, as a part of a larger college and university, there are plenty of ways to enjoy campus life at Washburn and, for those who are interested, "There is strong encouragement for involvement in activities and in the community." In addition to campus clubs and activities, MBA students can take advantage of the school's excellent facilities, including a new Student Recreation and Wellness Center, an art museum, and an observatory. The surrounding capital city of Topeka is a low-cost, medium-sized city of about 150,000 inhabitants, and an excellent place to balance the rigors of work and school.

Admissions

To be considered for admission to the Washburn MBA, students must submit official undergraduate transcripts, a completed application form, official GMAT scores, and two letters of recommendation from academicians, employers, or other sources who can attest to your ability to succeed in graduate school. Students with outstanding promise but incomplete applications may be considered for provisional admission to the program. International students make up 15 percent of the student population and, in addition to the preceding materials, must submit the International Student Application and TOEFL scores. Students from all major fields are welcome at Washburn.

FINANCIAL FACTS

% of students receiving aid	25
% of first-year students receiving aid	10
% of students receiving grants	20

ADMISSIONS

Admissions Selectivity Rating	**83**
# of applications received	34
% applicants accepted	88
% acceptees attending	93
Average GMAT	530
Range of GMAT	470–590
Average GPA	3.3
TOEFL required of international students	Yes
Minimum TOEFL (paper/computer)	550/213
Application fee	$40
International application fee	$60
Regular application deadline	7/1
Regular notification	7/1
Transfer students accepted	Yes
Transfer application policy Up to nine hours of MBA hours from an AACSB accredited school may be accepted upon approval.	
Non-fall admissions	Yes
Need-blind admissions	Yes

Applicants Also Look At

Kansas State University, University of Kansas.

EMPLOYMENT PROFILE

Career Rating	85	Grads Employed by Function% Avg. Salary
Percent employed	100	**Top 5 Employers Hiring Grads**
		Payless Shoesource 15
		Security Benefit Comanies 10
		Westar Energy 8

WASHINGTON STATE UNIVERSITY
COLLEGE OF BUSINESS

GENERAL INFORMATION
Type of school	Public
Environment	Town
Academic calendar	Semester

SURVEY SAYS...
Friendly students
Good peer network
Smart classrooms
Solid preparation in:
General management
Teamwork

STUDENTS
Enrollment of parent institution	18,000
Enrollment of business school	55
% male/female	60/40
% out-of-state	13
% minorities	12
% international	50
Average age at entry	25

ACADEMICS
Academic Experience Rating	**69**
Student/faculty ratio	40:1
Profs interesting rating	66
Profs accessible rating	82

Joint Degrees
JD/MBA 4 years.

Academics

Washington State's College of Business has gained a strong national reputation for its "fantastic" study environment and "relatively low tuition," but its many attributes are no secret to WSU undergrads. Many students like the school so much that they decide to remain Cougars. "I completed my undergrad at WSU and enjoyed the experience so much that I wanted to complete my graduate degree here as well," one student says.

The school offers classes at WSU's main campus in Pullman, and at its satellite campuses in Spokane, Vancouver, Washington, and the Tri-Cities area in the southeastern part of the state. Course work is offered in accounting, finance; insurance and real estate; information systems; management and operations; marketing; and hospitality business management. Master of Accounting, Master of Business Administration (MBA), Master of Technology Management, and Doctor of Philosophy (in business administration) degrees are available.

The recently revamped MBA program is "directed toward non-business undergraduate majors" and "accepts students with less than 1 year [of work] experience." Opinions of the intro-level courses are mixed: One student said his first semester was "a bit weak." Though difficult, it was "really just busywork." By all accounts, things pick up from there, with course work "designed around the issues and direction of the changing business world." There's an "emphasis on teamwork," and assignments are connected to "real-life experience." Professors are "highly experienced." One student says, "The quality of [the] faculty is by far the biggest asset." Professors maintain close contact with students through a "cohort system that allows for smaller classes and greater [student] teacher interaction." This can be a mixed blessing, however. While the faculty includes "some of the best research minds" in the field, some professors "don't know the first thing about teaching," one student says. Fortunately, "The program coordinators listen to and respect student feedback." The school's administrative staff is "on a first-name basis with all the students." They "will go out of their way to help you solve/remedy a problem," though their "speed of handling affairs" could improve.

Career and Placement

The Carson Center for Professional Development encourages student involvement in meaningful extracurricular activities. The center also polishes students' resume and interviewing skills and utilizes "alumni and faculty connections" to help students gain real-world experience through jobs and internships. These efforts are, for the most part, successful. The "proud alumni base" is particularly helpful; many here believe that WSU's greatest strength is the "dedication to each other" shown by fellow Cougars. Some students, however, would like to see more direct "interaction with outside companies." Another student says the program is "so new [that] they do not have the reputation with employers that some other MBA programs have."

Student Life and Environment

Students at WSU hail from "extremely diverse backgrounds." However, as most students "lack real working experience," this diversity is generally of the cultural variety: "About half" the students in some years are foreign-born, and "All of the students are friendly and intelligent." Students describe their classmates as "mature individuals"—the average age at entry into the program is 25—"who are attending business school to better themselves for their future careers." They're "open-minded," perhaps to a fault: "They do not have very strong opinions about much in the world," one student reports. Many have part-time jobs on campus, and almost all are "willing to help others" with course

ADMISSIONS CONTACT: CHERYL OLIVER, MBA@WSU.EDU
ADDRESS: PO BOX 644744 PULLMAN, WA 99164-4744 UNITED STATES
PHONE: 509-335-7617 • FAX: 509-335-4735
E-MAIL: MBA@WSU.EDU • WEBSITE: WWW.WSU.EDU/MBA

work. While a few students believe that "the course load is usually too heavy to take part in extracurricular activities," "Most manage their time very well." Students say that because of the smaller groups in the cohort system, peers in the program "turn into life-long friends."

There are two camps here. The first could be described as the nothing-to-do camp, which claims that life here "is just going to school for classes and returning home [to] study—there's not much entertainment in this city." The other camp says Pullman is a "wonderful college town," and that the campus is "very lively." The campus reportedly has a "perfect gym" that houses "great sports programs." Some students are "involved in organized sports and activities with [the] professors and administration." One student writes, "I am involved in two organizations on campus (MBA Association and Delta Sigma Pi business fraternity). I currently hold two jobs totaling 25 hours a week. I live with other MBA students so that we can do much [of] our homework together."

Admissions

WSU's MBA program accepts applications from those with a bachelor's degree from a regionally accredited undergraduate institution. All undergraduate fields of study are considered. To be qualified for regular admission, an applicant must have a GPA of 3.0 on a 4.0 scale for the final 60 hours of undergraduate course work, or for 12 or more credits of recognized graduate-level course work. International applicants also must have a score of 580 or better on the TOEFL. GMAT scores and three letters of recommendation are required of all applicants. In addition to the above requirements, to be qualified for regular admission to the Master of Accounting program, an applicant must have a bachelor's degree in business administration with a concentration in accounting.

FINANCIAL FACTS

Annual tuition (in-state/ out-of-state)	$10,000/$19,000
Fees	$683
Cost of books	$1,080
Room & board	$8,720
Average grant	$4,000

ADMISSIONS

Admissions Selectivity Rating	82
# of applications received	128
% applicants accepted	58
% acceptees attending	38
Average GMAT	570
Range of GMAT	480–650
Average GPA	3.72
TOEFL required of international students	Yes
Minimum TOEFL (paper/computer)	580/237
Application fee	$50
Regular application deadline	1/10
Regular notification	1/10
Transfer students accepted	Yes
Transfer application policy Transfer students will only be able to apply 6 credits of elective coursework to the WSU MBA on a case by case basis.	
Non-fall admissions	Yes
Need-blind admissions	Yes

EMPLOYMENT PROFILE

Career Rating	66	**Grads Employed by Function% Avg. Salary**	
Primary Source of Full-time Job Acceptances		Finance	16 $29,750
Graduate-facilitated activities	2 (17%)	Marketing	8 $45,000
Unknown	10 (83%)	MIS	8 $60,750
		Operations	8 $65,000
		Consulting	16 $60,000
		General Management	33 $38,250
		Other	8 $13,000

WASHINGTON UNIVERSITY IN ST. LOUIS
JOHN M. OLIN SCHOOL OF BUSINESS

Academics

Offering the unbeatable combination of a strong reputation, small class sizes, and a dedicated and talented teaching staff, students at Washington University's Olin School of Business say theirs is the "best and most recognized business school in St. Louis." Get ready to hit the ground running: "Since the MBA program is front loaded with many classes," the first semester can be "very challenging." In fact, during the first semester, students complete all but two required core courses, which comprise a third of the required units for the MBA. After that, students can take advantage of the flexible curriculum to tailor their studies through ample elective course work, including a "strong program in international business and brand management."

Despite the "grueling schedule which doesn't seem to let up," Olin's decidedly "collaborative atmosphere" and consistently small class sizes make the experience both manageable and intimate. At Olin, students have "the ability to truly learn and get involved in the learning process, both from fellow classmates and the professors." As one current student explains, "After completing each class I can truly say that I have learned something new and useful, which makes the grueling schedule bearable." A diverse and talented faculty, Olin professors "each bring a unique perspective and personality to the classroom," teaching material that is "contemporary and relevant to the business world."

Boasting a student body that is "hardworking, competitive, driven, and opinionated," fellow students play a very large role in the Washington University experience, especially in the beginning of the program. Employing a cohort study system, "The first semester is based largely on loads of group work with a pre-selected group of four to five students." These groups are selected by the administration to ensure a diversity of background and experience amongst team members, which most students find extremely edifying.

At this small, private school "The entire program is very student-centered," and the "administration is extremely open to student suggestions." Program administrators even handle all the red tape, "taking pressure off students for items like financial aid, course selection, or other issues that may take away from time that can be used for course work." Even in the classroom student concerns are taken seriously, and "Teachers issue evaluation forms every 6 weeks so that they can adapt teaching styles midway through their courses if students feel it is needed."

Career and Placement

At Olin, the focus on career planning and placement begins in the first semester, during which all first-year students must take a course entitled Career Developer, which helps refine their career goals through expert panels, self-assessments, and instruction in "soft skills" like emotional intelligence. Thereafter, the Weston Career Center offers a host of resources, including an alumni and corporate database, advising by professional career counselors, skill-building activities, and workshops on topics such as interviews, evaluating offers, and cover letter and resume editing. Some feel "The school could bring more recruiters to campus" but appreciate the fact that "alumni are always happy to help and the Career Center does an excellent job making sure that [students] are positioned to talk to recruiters even if [they] have to go to their city."

In 2006, graduates from Washington University received a median base salary of $82,000, with an average signing bonus of $14,065. Over half of students (53 percent) took positions in the Midwest. Jobs in financial services, consumer products, and manufacturing drew the most students, at 21 percent, 15 percent, and 14 percent respectively. Top employers included IBM, Johnson & Johnson, AT&T, General Mills, Merrill Lynch, and Samsung.

Student Life and Environment

With a student body that is "friendly, eager to learn and approachable," it's easy to fit in at the Olin School of Business. A current student raves: "They're a great bunch, whether in class, in our cohort groups, or relaxing at the bar!" Despite the challenging course material, the average Olin student "works hard but realizes that every sane and normal person should put the books aside for a while to have some fun." A first-year student explains, "You could study here 24/7 if you wanted to but most students are able to find a nice balance." On weekends, business students enjoy a weekly get-together with free food and a keg, thanks to the school-sponsored "Friday Afternoon Clubs."

On campus, the environment is both pleasant and stimulating, as "The facilities are top-notch, and the school is always buzzing with activity, from conferences to club meetings." As one current student explains, "Our day actually starts when we get out of class as we meet with our groups, go to speaker events, company info sessions, club events, work on practicum projects, and much more." Located next to Forest Park in the center of St. Louis, Missouri, "There are tons of restaurants and bars very close by, and housing is VERY affordable in the area."

Admissions

Olin looks for self-directed, disciplined professionals who will be highly involved in the MBA community as demonstrated by their academic proficiency, leadership potential, communication skills, and history of participation in extracurricular activities. To apply to Olin, students must submit a completed application form (which includes several essays and a resume), official transcripts from college, two letters of recommendation, GMAT scores, and, for international students, TOEFL scores. Though there are no official minimums for entry into the program, last year's incoming class had an average GMAT score of 654 and an average GPA of 3.37. There is also no minimum work requirement, though the average work experience for students in last year's entering class was 4.3 years.

FINANCIAL FACTS

Annual tuition	$37,900
Fees	$820
Cost of books	$2,500
Room & board (on/off-campus)	$0/$16,500

ADMISSIONS

Admissions Selectivity Rating	94
# of applications received	973
% applicants accepted	33
% acceptees attending	47
Average GMAT	674
Range of GMAT	640–710
Average GPA	3.38
TOEFL required of international students	Yes
Application fee	$100
International application fee	$100
Application Deadline/Notification	
Round 1:	11/05 / 01/25
Round 2:	01/14 / 03/28
Round 3:	03/03 / 05/23
Round 4:	05/01 / 06/30
Deferment available	Yes
Maximum length of deferment	1 year
Transfer students accepted	Yes
Transfer application policy	With approval, up to 9 credits from an AACSB-accredited graduate program.
Need-blind admissions	Yes

Applicants Also Look At

Emory University, Georgetown University, Indiana University—Bloomington, The University of North Carolina at Chapel Hill, The University of Texas at Austin, University of Michigan, Vanderbilt University.

EMPLOYMENT PROFILE

Career Rating	89	Grads Employed by Function	% Avg. Salary
Primary Source of Full-time Job Acceptances		Finance	37 $80,728
School-facilitated activities	64 (74%)	Marketing	31 $89,453
Graduate-facilitated activities	22 (26%)	Operations	5 $86,875
Average base starting salary	$85,583	Consulting	12 $85,403
Percent employed	94	General Management	13 $91,475
		Other	2 NR

Top 5 Employers Hiring Grads
Citi; Emerson; Johnson & Johnson; Nestle Purina Pet Care; First National Bank of Omaha

WAYNE STATE UNIVERSITY
SCHOOL OF BUSINESS ADMINISTRATION

GENERAL INFORMATION
Type of school	Public
Environment	Metropolis
Academic calendar	Semester

SURVEY SAYS...
Cutting edge classes
Solid preparation in:
Accounting
General management

STUDENTS
Enrollment of parent institution	33,240
Enrollment of business school	1,255
% male/female	60/40
% part-time	89
Average age at entry	28
Average years work experience at entry	5

ACADEMICS
Academic Experience Rating	**65**
Student/faculty ratio	38:1
Profs interesting rating	70
Profs accessible rating	82
% female faculty	21
% minority faculty	33

Joint Degrees
JD/MBA 3 years.

Prominent Alumni
Paul Glantz, President/CEO, Proctor Financial, Corp.; Honorable Jack Martin, CFO, US Dept. of Education; Sandra E. Pierce, President/CEO, Charter One Bank MI & IN; James H. Vandenberghe, Vice Chairman, Lear Corp.

Academics

Located in the heart of Detroit and associated with a "large, research-based university," the School of Business Administration at Wayne State University provides a progressive MBA program to a serious population of working professionals. The MBA curriculum consists of a minimum of 12 courses (or 36 credits) split between core courses and elective course work. However, students who do not have an educational background in business may be required to take up to eight foundation courses before beginning the core. After completing the foundation and core courses, students complete their credit requirements with electives in accounting, finance, marketing, human resources management, international business, leadership and organizational behavior, management information systems, quality management, and taxation. While the school doesn't offer specific concentrations, students say the elective offerings are impressive: "The excellent quality of the international business electives are the greatest strengths that WSU's MBA program has to offer its students."

Ninety percent of students in the graduate program at Wayne State University are working professionals, pursuing a graduate degree in the evenings while working part-time or full-time during the day. In order to "effectively accommodate working students," graduate courses are offered in the afternoon and evening, on Saturdays, and online. The extremely flexible schedule includes classes at the 203-acre, landscaped main campus, as well as at the satellite campus in Farmington Hills. Students can even pursue the MBA online, or through a combination of on-site and online courses.

Drawing students with strong career goals and diverse career experience, the varied composition of the student body brings an additional dynamic to the classroom, and many report, "The interaction with a diverse student body has been a very positive experience." Located in America's auto city, "A large percentage of Wayne State University MBA students come from the automotive industry and many are engineers by trade." Nevertheless, "other fields such as finance, telecommunications, pharmaceuticals, IT, advertising, and others are well represented." Students immediately apply class lessons to their jobs, saying the MBA course work "is pertinent to my profession, and I take what I learn and use it every day in the workplace."

Thinking like the business mavens they are training to be, Wayne State's students say, "The cost/benefit of attending this school versus another public university is excellent; it's half the cost, and the professors are just as qualified." There are nearly 60 full-time professors teaching courses in the MBA program, whom students describe as "open-minded teachers who are knowledgeable and enthusiastic about the subject matter." What's more, the professors are "very approachable and encouraging," fostering a non-competitive atmosphere in the classroom. In addition to course work, the school keeps the business program relevant to the modern business world, hosting field trips and inviting distinguished business executives to speak to the student community. Lastly, Wayne State University is the 29th largest public, doctoral-granting institution in the United States.

Career and Placement

Dedicated solely to students in the School of Business Administration, the SBA Planning and Placement Office offers career counseling and professional development assistance to undergraduate and graduate students, as well as alumni of Wayne State. The center hosts a variety of on-campus interviews, career days, and meet-and-greet events, and

ADMISSIONS CONTACT: LINDA S. ZADDACH, ASSISTANT DEAN OF STUDENT AFFAIRS
ADDRESS: OFFICE OF STUDENT SERVICES, 5201 CASS, ROOM 200 DETROIT, MI 48202 UNITED STATES
PHONE: 313-577-4505 • FAX: 313-577-5299
E-MAIL: L.S.ZADDACH@WAYNE.EDU • WEBSITE: WWW.BUSADM.WAYNE.EDU

benefits from the fact that the school's "ties to the business community are strong." The center also offers career counseling services and comprehensive online resources.

A vast majority of Wayne State students are already working in a full-time, professional capacity when they begin their MBA. In fact, 70 percent of Wayne State graduate students are receiving tuition reimbursement from their current company. Therefore, many students are more focused on progressing in their current job, rather than making a career change or finding new positions. Whether seeking a new career or continuing in their current job, 90 percent of Wayne State graduates stay in Michigan, most in the Detroit area.

Student Life and Environment

Balancing schoolwork, a full-time career, and family life can be incredibly challenging; even so, most Wayne State students maintain a positive, go-getter attitude throughout their studies. A current student explains, "Since most people have jobs, and are thus part-time students, everyone is busy—but at the same time very determined to get through the degree." Thanks to their demanding schedules, few Wayne State students have time for extracurricular or social activities at school. However, for those who can make the time, there are a number of student clubs and honor societies at the School of Business Administration, including the MBA Association. Plus, the larger university lends a sense of excitement and action to the business school atmosphere, as there are a plethora of "young adults all over campus studying and moving from one class to another."

Students take advantage of the recreation center and the undergraduate and graduate libraries campus, and at mealtimes there are "pretty good places to eat nearby and a lounge with machines and a microwave in the library." Wayne State's business-minded grad students are pleased with the school's strategic "location, location, location, in the heart of Detroit, near downtown." However, students also warn that the current classrooms are a bit run-down and that the school "needs more security in the buildings." The School of Business Administration has responded to student and faculty needs by beginning renovations of its current building and adding undercover security, since the facility is open daytimes through late evening for classes. A new state-of-the-art, technologically advanced building is scheduled for groundbreaking in 2009.

Admissions

One of the largest part-time MBA programs in the world, there are over 1,250 students enrolled in Wayne State's graduate program. For entry, students must score at least 450 on the GMAT and have an undergraduate GPA of at least 2.5. The Admissions Committee also evaluates a student's leadership potential and professional experience when making an admissions decision. Students may apply for admission in the fall, spring, or summer semesters.

FINANCIAL FACTS

Annual tuition (in-state/ out-of-state)	$8,417/$17,181
Fees	$813
Cost of books	$1,200
Average grant	$5,373

ADMISSIONS

Admissions Selectivity Rating	**72**
# of applications received	351
% applicants accepted	72
% acceptees attending	69
Average GMAT	510
Average GPA	3.15
TOEFL required of international students	Yes
Minimum TOEFL (paper/computer)	550/213
Application fee	$50
International application fee	$50
Regular application deadline	8/1
Regular notification	Rolling
Deferment available	Yes
Maximum length of deferment	One semester
Transfer students accepted	Yes
Transfer application policy Meet admission standards	
Non-fall admissions	Yes

EMPLOYMENT PROFILE

Career Rating	83	Grads Employed by Function	% Avg. Salary
Primary Source of Full-time Job Acceptances		Finance	25 $75,900
School-facilitated activities	75%	Human Resources	2 NR
Percent employed	98	Marketing	3 $53,500
		MIS	3 NR
		Operations	3 NR
		General Management	7 $58,600
		Other	57 NR

WEBER STATE UNIVERSITY
JOHN B. GODDARD SCHOOL OF BUSINESS AND ECONOMICS

GENERAL INFORMATION

Type of school	Public
Environment	Village

SURVEY SAYS...

Good peer network
Cutting edge classes
Happy students
Smart classrooms

STUDENTS

Enrollment of parent institution	18,303
Enrollment of business school	241
% part-time	100
Average age at entry	30
Average years work experience at entry	4.3

ACADEMICS

Academic Experience Rating	**81**
Student/faculty ratio	10:1
Profs interesting rating	79
Profs accessible rating	78
% female faculty	20

Joint Degrees

MBA/MA (Health Administration).

Academics

The MBA program at Weber State University's John B. Goddard School of Business and Economics is specially designed to meet the needs of working professionals looking to advance their careers in business. The curriculum consists of hybrid courses which combine classroom instruction with online tools, helping to enhance delivery of class material and reduce class time. All MBA classes are taught in the evenings, and the extremely flexible curriculum allows students to switch between full-time and part-time study and even arrange leaves of absence, as necessary. Therefore, Weber State is an excellent choice for returning students, as "Nontraditional students are able to complete the courses while continuing on with their busy personal lives."

Students who completed an undergraduate degree in business in the past 10 years are eligible for the fast-track MBA, a streamlined 36-credit-hour curriculum. Full-time students can complete this program in as little as 1 year. Those who do not have an undergraduate degree in business—comprising roughly half of the current business students at Goddard—are eligible for The Goddard School MBA, a 54 credit-hour program. However, if you are hoping to power through your MBA while working full-time, "The classes are structured so that I as a part time student can take two classes per semester consecutively so that I work really hard and fast and study one class at a time."

Given their professional background, students at Goddard are looking for solid, practical business expertise, and appreciate the fact that "all of the professors have great, real-life, industry knowledge to apply to their teaching skills." Fulfilling the role of academic instructor as well as professional mentor, "The professors at Weber State are much more involved in the lives and education of their students. These professors take time to get to know their students and provide guidance when students are in need." While students say there can be some headaches associated with the larger university administration, the business school is well run and student friendly. Like Weber State's affable teaching staff, "The administration seems attentive to our needs and open to our thoughts and concerns."

Not surprisingly, the academic atmosphere at Goddard is influenced by the fact that the vast majority of students are professionals. Students insist that their classmates add depth to the learning experience, describing their peers as "smart, sophisticated, and enlightening. They spur thoughts and dialogues that are unique and beneficial." "Almost every student in the program works full-time, so there is an immediate application of the subjects taught." In fact, "All students are already networking because they are almost all currently employed." Plus, there is a wide range of diversity, which further enhances the classroom discussions. A current student attests, "The undergraduate degrees in my program range from nursing to family studies. Our discussions are interesting and help me see things from different perspectives."

Career and Placement

Within the Wattis Business Building, Goddard operates a Career Services Office exclusively for business students. Staff at the Career Services Office work with Human Resources Directors to place graduates in new positions, coordinate on-campus recruiting events and interviews, and host seminars, workshops, and provide personal counseling services to business students. Their annual career fair is the largest in the region. Though most students enroll at Weber State University while continuing to work in a professional capacity, those looking for a new position reported an average starting salary of $55,025 following graduation.

ADMISSIONS CONTACT: DR. MARK A. STEVENSON, MBA ENROLLMENT DIRECTOR
ADDRESS: 2750 N. UNIVERSITY PARK BLVD. MC102 LAYTON, UT 84041-9099 UNITED STATES
PHONE: 801-395-3519 • FAX: 801-395-3525
E-MAIL: MBA@WEBER.EDU • WEBSITE: WEBER.EDU/MBA

Student Life and Environment

Attracting a student body that is "educated, diverse, older, mature, married, busy," life at Weber State is anything but the typical college experience. In fact, students estimate that, "Most (98 percent) of my classmates are working adults with jobs. I guess that 75 percent of them have mortgages and families." As a result, most don't have time to get involved in extracurricular activities on campus, and there is "not much social interaction between students, just classwork." However, if you enjoy a lively academic atmosphere and meeting diverse and talented people, you'll have your share of fun.

For those who can find the time, "There are many opportunities to get involved in different activities" through the larger university and the business school. As the school is sensitive to the curricular needs of older students, it also understands their unique social and personal needs; in fact, "The university does a good job of providing activities, such as family-friendly movies and comedy, that the family can attend. There is also collegiate football, basketball, etc. that the family can attend for a reasonable cost."

Admissions

To apply to the Goddard School of Business and Economics, students must possess a bachelor's degree from an accredited university. The primary criteria for selection are the student's undergraduate record and GMAT performance. Current students have an average GMAT score between 560–570 and an average GPA of 3.4 on a 4.0 scale. Other factors, such as work experience and professional progression will also be considered by the Admissions Committee. Each application is evaluated individually for the applicant's ability to succeed, potential for success, and possible strengths to contribute to the program. Currently, Goddard has a 60–70 percent admissions rate.

FINANCIAL FACTS

Annual tuition (in-state/ out-of-state)	$5,931/$14,149
Cost of books	$2,000
Room & board (on/off-campus)	$2,900/$4,000
Average grant	$3,900

ADMISSIONS

Admissions Selectivity Rating	**77**
# of applications received	116
% applicants accepted	83
% acceptees attending	91
Average GMAT	573
Range of GMAT	540–610
Average GPA	3.45
TOEFL required of international students	Yes
Minimum TOEFL (paper/computer)	550/213
Application fee	$30
International application fee	$30
Regular application deadline	6/15
Regular notification	6/22
Deferment available	Yes
Maximum length of deferment	1 year
Transfer students accepted	Yes
Transfer application policy Transfer credits from AACSB-accredited programs accepted; from non-AACSB-accredited programs on a case-by-case basis.	
Non-fall admissions	Yes
Need-blind admissions	Yes

Applicants Also Look At
University of Utah, Utah State University.

WEST VIRGINIA UNIVERSITY
COLLEGE OF BUSINESS AND ECONOMICS

Academics

West Virginia University offers two distinct MBA options, each designed for a specific demographic. For young students with little professional experience and a desire to move forward quickly, WVU has designed a full-time MBA program that can be completed in just over a year. For more experienced students with a stronger business background and ongoing professional obligations, WVU offers a part-time executive MBA in eight West Virginia cities.

Both MBA options stress the integral nature of technology in modern business. One student observes, "The greatest strength of this program is the broad use of technology in the classes. I would have rated myself as an advanced user of information technology in my role of managing a number of databases before this class, and yet I have learned so much more and become even more comfortable with technology and common software packages." Although the curricula for the two programs vary, both stress the importance of teamwork and cover all major functions of business study.

The full-time program, located in Morgantown, begins with a pre-professional session designed to polish necessary business skills. It then moves through the curriculum thematically, covering such subjects as business planning, organizational skills, implementation, control, and change. Students "take one class for a period of weeks, and then a different class begins. It's a really great structure that allows you to fully concentrate on the material." The program's emphasis on "practical thinking and experience," MBAs tell us, is helpful. One explains, "I am young and do not have much business and working experience, and the MBA program has done an excellent job of easing me into the business atmosphere while challenging me to go further." Professors "make themselves available to help each student, even into the late hours of the evening, and go above and beyond the call of duty for the WVU MBA students"—another plus.

The part-time EMBA brings students to a satellite classroom, where interactive technology allows them to participate in classes with each other and the professor. Classes are videotaped to accommodate working professionals who miss class due to travel. An MBA tells us that "given the complexity of coordinating things, it is amazing how well everything has worked. Any time you are heavily dependent on technology, you expect a certain amount of inconvenience, but I have been pleasantly surprised at how well-maintained the systems are and how committed the school has been to making sure that we are all comfortable with the learning experience." Students also appreciate that "professors visit the various sites during the classes so that we actually meet them and each site gets to experience being remote and being on-site." They also tell us, "The online support given is outstanding. Anything and everything you need to know can be found by a simple Internet connection." A student complains that "too many group projects are required, meaning that additional travel to a central meeting place (one hour for me) was a common occurrence. Usually 20 to 40 percent of your grade is based upon group efforts. This undercuts a lot of the convenience of the program."

Career and Placement

The College of Business and Economics at WVU has its own dedicated Career Development Center to serve business undergraduates and graduate students. The office provides counseling services, workshops, seminars, and on-campus recruiting events.

ADMISSIONS CONTACT: GERALD BLAKELY, DIRECTOR OF GRADUATE PROGRAMS
ADDRESS: P.O. BOX 6027 MORGANTOWN, WV 26506-6027 UNITED STATES
PHONE: 304-293-7932 • FAX: 304-293-8905
E-MAIL: MBA@WVU.EDU • WEBSITE: WWW.BE.WVU.EDU

FINANCIAL FACTS

Annual tuition (in-state/ out-of-state)	$11,776/$32,080
Cost of books	$1,800
Room & board	$9,080

ADMISSIONS

Admissions Selectivity Rating	**86**
# of applications received	171
% applicants accepted	31
% acceptees attending	100
Average GMAT	488
Range of GMAT	240–680
Average GPA	3.37
TOEFL required of international students	Yes
Minimum TOEFL (paper/computer)	580/237
Application fee	$50
International application fee	$50
Regular application deadline	3/1
Regular notification	3/15
Early decision program?	Yes
ED Deadline/ Notification	10/15 / 10/30
Deferment available	Yes
Maximum length of deferment	1 year
Transfer students accepted	Yes
Transfer application policy Applicants request transfer credits and the admission committee reviews the request.	
Non-fall admissions	Yes
Need-blind admissions	Yes

Applicants Also Look At

Marshall University; Rutgers, The State University of New Jersey; Syracuse University; Temple University; University of Kentucky; University of Pittsburgh; Virginia Tech.

Students tell us that the office seems geared mostly toward the needs of undergraduates. One writes, "The largest improvement to the program could be made with career services tailored specifically to the MBA students. The MBA program would benefit greatly by bringing reputable companies to directly meet with business students. The accounting program at WVU has an excellent relationship with the big four accounting firms. The MBA program should seek to achieve a similar relationship with a selected group of organizations."

Student Life and Environment

WVU is a pretty typical large state university, with plenty of extracurricular options for those who seek them. One student notes, "There are many things that WVU offers as special activities. They offer movies, up-all-night activities, that sort of thing. They also have a lot of shows and performers that come to campus." Football games "are always great," and "keg parties, bar crawls, and burning couches are fairly regular affairs. This is a renowned party school." Most MBAs, though, "do not have as much time to enjoy these activities as [they] did as undergrads." Hometown Morgantown "is the kind of wonderful town that you never tire of. It offers absolutely anything and everything you could want, while still holding true to a small-town atmosphere. You would have to search long and hard to match all that it offers."

It's a different story for EMBAs, whose students are "not very focused on campus life. Most people have non-university centered lives."

WVU MBAs are "a diverse group," with "work experience from a number of industries, government, and health care. Some are managers, directors, or vice presidents, while others are in staff positions. They are all willing to share their experiences and opinions." One student writes, "Even though we are so different in the class, we all pull together and work as a team and learn from each other just as much as we learn in the classes. It has been amazing."

Admissions

Applicants to the MBA program must submit official transcripts for all postsecondary academic work, an official GMAT score report, and a resume. Letters of recommendation and a statement of purpose are optional. All students must have full use of a laptop PC that meets prescribed minimum software, memory, and processor-speed requirements; contact the school or visit the website for details. Applicants to the EMBA program must have at least two years of "significant work experience." For applicants with less than five years experience, GPA and GMAT figure most heavily in the admissions decision. Professional experience, especially managerial experience, is the greater factor for applicants with at least five years of experience.

EMPLOYMENT PROFILE	
Career Rating	72

WESTERN CAROLINA UNIVERSITY
COLLEGE OF BUSINESS

GENERAL INFORMATION

Type of school	Public
Environment	Rural
Academic calendar	Semester

SURVEY SAYS...

Smart classrooms
Solid preparation in:
Accounting
General management
Presentation skills

STUDENTS

Enrollment of parent institution	9,056
Enrollment of business school	93
% male/female	47/53
% out-of-state	27
% part-time	63
% minorities	12
% international	24
Average age at entry	26
Average years work experience at entry	4

ACADEMICS

Academic Experience Rating	**77**
Student/faculty ratio	12:1
Profs interesting rating	75
Profs accessible rating	63
% female faculty	31
% minority faculty	12

Academics

Students may pursue the Western Carolina University MBA at the school's main campus in Cullowhee or at its resident credit center in Asheville. WCU also offers a master of accountancy at the Asheville campus and a master of entrepreneurship and a master of project management as web-based programs.

WCU keeps MBA class sizes below 35 students, with many classes having as few as 15 students. Small classes free professors to employ a range of teaching techniques including team projects, case studies, in-class discussion, and lecture. Students tell us that the small size of their program means that "administration and professors are always available and easy to talk to. Most students have very good relationships with their professors. Since the MBA program here at Western is not too large, students can get to know their professors other than just in the classroom."

The WCU MBA curriculum consists of 24 credits in core courses covering managerial accounting, decision support systems, managerial economics, financial management, organizational behavior and analysis, quantitative analysis for business, strategic management, and marketing management. Students must also successfully complete 12 hours of course work in electives. Elective classes are available in the following areas: accounting; business law; information systems; economics; entrepreneurship; finance; international business; management; and marketing. Instruction is provided by "professors who are at the PhD level and are experienced teachers," though some here "wish the instructors had more experience with big business." The administration earns student praise for being "helpful in every way it can be, from signing students up for classes to sending out job vacancies from businesses."

Career and Placement

The Office of Career Services and Cooperative Education handles counseling and placement services for all undergraduate and graduate students at WCU. Services include a career library, co-op placement, one-on-one counseling, interviewing workshops, resume critiquing, online job listings, career-related personality assessment, career days, and on-campus recruitment events. Companies recruiting on campus in 2004 included Allegis Group, BB&T, Builders First Source, Cintas Corporation, Consolidated Electrical Distributors, Edward Jones, Ferguson Enterprises, Home Trust Bank, and Liberty Mutual.

Student Life and Environment

Western Carolina's main campus is located in Cullowhee, which has a "small-town atmosphere that makes it easy to focus on your studies." Cullowhee is surrounded by a rural valley between the Great Smoky Mountains and the Blue Ridge Mountains. Nearby amenities include the Blue Ridge Parkway, the Cherokee Indian Reservation, Great Smoky Mountain National Park, and a number of resorts offering golf, fishing, skiing, and other outdoor activities. Not everyone sees the town's merits, however. Complains one MBA, "To me, the town WCU is a little small. Some people enjoy that there aren't a lot of buildings and cars and people, but I enjoy larger cities with a little more going on. However, Asheville, NC is only 45 minutes away, and [it has] a lot to offer." For a real taste of city life, Atlanta, Georgia, lies two and a half hours to the southwest.

ADMISSIONS CONTACT: KENNETH PLACE, DIRECTOR OF MBA PROGRAM
ADDRESS: 379 BELK BUILDING CULLOWHEE, NC 28723 UNITED STATES
PHONE: (828) 227-3588 • FAX: (828) 227-7414
E-MAIL: KPLACE@EMAIL.WCU.EDU • WEBSITE: WWW.WCU.EDU/COB/MBA

WCU's MBA program includes "many students from all over the world, including Germany, Ireland, Egypt, and India" who "are very friendly and are as curious about our culture as we are of theirs." Writes one American MBA, "Here at WCU, I have learned a lot about different cultures by just simply getting to know my fellow students. It has been a fun and educational experience for me." The program also attracts many "younger part-time students with families." Most have been "pleasantly surprised by the qualities of [their] fellow students" who are, as one student puts it, "bright, friendly, motivated, and interesting people. They come from a variety of backgrounds and work experiences and are well-rounded."

WCU hosts "many clubs and organizations" and has "a movie theater on campus," all of which help to foster a "close-knit community" among full-time students. The many part-timers here, however, have little time for such diversions; explains one, "My life at school is insignificant compared to my life at work and [as] a mother of three children. However, if I had the time, there would be many opportunities to do really cool stuff at school. I read the announcements of events longingly."

Admissions

Applicants to the MBA program at Western Carolina University must submit official copies of transcripts for all academic work completed after high school and an official score report for the GMAT, and two letters of recommendation. International applicants must also submit official score reports for the TOEFL and achieve a minimum score of 79–80 on the Internet-based test, 550 on the paper test, or 213 on the computer test. International applications are due by April 1 for the fall semester and by September 1 for the spring semester.

FINANCIAL FACTS

Annual tuition (in-state/ out-of-state)	$2,314/$11,899
Fees	$2,122
Cost of books	$1,067
Room & board (on/off-campus)	$5,546/$7,468
% of students receiving aid	49
% of first-year students receiving aid	76
% of students receiving loans	12
% of students receiving grants	40
Average award package	$7,804
Average grant	$2,747
Average student loan debt	$19,261

ADMISSIONS

Admissions Selectivity Rating	75
# of applications received	51
% applicants accepted	71
% acceptees attending	72
Average GMAT	531
Range of GMAT	490–580
Average GPA	3.19
TOEFL required of international students	Yes
Minimum TOEFL (paper/computer)	550/213
Application fee	$40
International application fee	$40
Regular application deadline	rolling
Regular notification	rolling
Deferment available	Yes
Maximum length of deferment	1 year
Transfer students accepted	Yes
Transfer application policy	
Up to 6 hours of graduate credit may be transferred from an AACSB institution.	
Non-fall admissions	Yes
Need-blind admissions	Yes

Applicants Also Look At

Appalachian State University, University of North Carolina at Charlotte.

WICHITA STATE UNIVERSITY
BARTON SCHOOL OF BUSINESS

Academics

At the W. Frank Barton School of Business at Wichita State University, students benefit from a traditional, management-based MBA program that offers a broad range of course work in accounting, economics, finance, management, and marketing. Depending on a student's academic background (those who studied business as an undergraduate may be able to waive some requirements), the MBA is comprised of 36 to 48 credit hours, beginning with a core curriculum that covers business fundamentals. Throughout the core curriculum, particular attention is given to understanding the organization as an integrated system. Later, students may choose an area of concentration, taking up to 9 credit hours of electives in finance, marketing, entrepreneurship, technology and operations management, or health care administration.

The school offers a fast-paced executive MBA program for high-level professionals, as well as a traditional MBA program. Whether enrolled in the accelerated or traditional program, a majority of students work full-time while attending school in the evenings. In fact, "Most of them are professionals with aircraft industries in the Wichita area," which means a double dose of work and responsibility. However, the school is aware of its students' special needs and "is very adept at offering programs that fit the schedules of its students." On top of that, students reassure us that the workload is manageable—"substantial at times, but for the most part, the average workload is within the expected output of a graduate program."

Reporting on the great classroom experience, WSU students generally describe their professors as "candid, well spoken, knowledgeable, prepared, and fun." Unfortunately, students admit that a few staff members don't deserve such rave reviews. "There are some professors' classes I wish I could get a refund on, simply because the professors seem to be there only to earn a paycheck or a boosted ego," grumbles one student. In addition to their professors, classmates form an essential part of the learning experience at WSU. Drawing "a mix of mid-career business people and young business students," Wichita State students enjoy the fact that "everyone is very opinionated, which makes for great class discussions."

The "only AACSB-accredited school in the Wichita area," WSU is an excellent match for those who work or wish to start a career in the region, and WSU promotes a great deal of "community involvement with local businesses and entrepreneurs." Students appreciate the fact that "the school brings in wonderful special speakers and has a good reputation in the community." For example, "Recently, the CEOs of Wal-Mart and PepsiCo visited the business school." Beyond Kansas, the school also runs an "international project with Berlin School of Economics, where students taking the advanced strategic management course go to Berlin, Germany for one week and do the project there in conjunction with Berlin students."

Career and Placement

The Career Services office at Wichita State University serves the school's undergraduate and graduate community, including the business school. Through Career Services, students have access to career counseling, an online job database, and an alumni database. The office also hosts several campus career fairs and on-campus interviews.

ADMISSIONS CONTACT: DOROTHY HARPOOL, DIRECTOR OF GRADUATE STUDIES IN BUSINESS
ADDRESS: 1845 N. FAIRMOUNT WICHITA, KS 67260-0048 UNITED STATES
PHONE: 316-978-3230 • FAX: 316-978-3767
E-MAIL: MBA@WICHITA.EDU • WEBSITE: WICHITA.EDU/MBA

At Wichita State, "Many students seem to be earning their MBAs in order to receive a raise or progress upward with their current employers," with a number of them also receiving tuition assistance. For those looking for a position with a new company after graduation, major employers in Wichita include Bank of America, Boeing, Bombardier Aerospace Learjet, Cargill Meat Solutions, Cessna Aircraft Company, The Coleman Company, Hawker Beechcraft, INTRUST Bank, Koch Industries, Spirit AeroSystems, Via Christi Health Systems, and York International.

Student Life and Environment

Those looking for a close-knit and community-oriented business school may be disappointed by "commuter-school" Wichita State. While they get a great business education, students admit that "the opportunities for networking are not particularly strong, as most students are too busy with work and families to attend mixers or be involved on campus." On the other hand, the atmosphere is pleasantly casual and friendly, and the community is "very diverse with local, national, and international students." A current student shares: "Even though we come from very different backgrounds and experiences, everyone seems to be incredibly open-minded and accepting to all students in the program."

The university provides plenty of extracurricular and recreational opportunities. In fact, students assure us that "if you want to do an activity and you look for one, you can find one." A case in point: One student who went from part-time to full-time status in his second year tells us, "I was surprised when I concentrated life to studies. . . . I learned a lot that I missed when I was working in my first year." Off campus, Wichita is a pleasant, low-cost, medium-sized city with plenty of cultural, financial, shopping, performing arts, festivals, and entertainment options for graduate students.

Admissions

To be considered for admissions at Wichita State University, students must possess a 4-year degree from an accredited college or university and be proficient in word processing, spreadsheet, and presentation software. Admissions decisions are made by evaluating the following: official GMAT scores, undergraduate transcript, an applicant's personal goals statement, two letters of recommendation, and a current resume. For the traditional MBA, career experience is a plus in an application package but is not required. Applicants to the executive MBA must have at least 5 years of relevant work experience. Students may apply for entry in the spring and fall semesters.

FINANCIAL FACTS

Cost of books	$1,200
Average grant	$6,000

ADMISSIONS

Admissions Selectivity Rating	**81**
# of applications received	98
% applicants accepted	61
% acceptees attending	78
Average GMAT	559
Average GPA	3.35
TOEFL required of international students	Yes
Minimum TOEFL (paper/computer)	570/230
Application fee	$35
International application fee	$50
Regular application deadline	7/1
Deferment available	Yes
Maximum length of deferment	1 year
Transfer students accepted	Yes
Transfer application policy Only AACSB accredited classes may be transferred in.	
Non-fall admissions	Yes
Need-blind admissions	Yes

EMPLOYMENT PROFILE	
Career Rating	70

WILFRID LAURIER UNIVERSITY
SCHOOL OF BUSINESS AND ECONOMICS

GENERAL INFORMATION
Type of school   Public

SURVEY SAYS...
Good peer network

STUDENTS
Enrollment of parent institution	
Enrollment of business school	488
% male/female	70/30
% part-time	84
% international	5
Average age at entry	30
Average years work experience at entry	7

ACADEMICS
Academic Experience Rating	**74**
Profs interesting rating	71
Profs accessible rating	83

Joint Degrees
MBA/CMA (Certified Management Accountant), MBA/CFA (Certified Financial Anaylist), MBA/FCIP (Fellow Chartered Insurance Professional), 3.3 years part-time study.

Academics

As Canada's largest full classroom-contact MBA program, there is something for everyone at the School of Business and Economics at Wilfrid Laurier University. Whether you want to take courses during the week, during the weekend, during the day, at night, on a part-time basis, on a full-time basis, at the Waterloo campus, or at the satellite campus in Toronto, chances are there is going to be an MBA format option at Laurier that suits your needs. In addition, the school's many MBA options cater to students from all professional and academic backgrounds. At Laurier, business executives have the opportunity to get a high-speed degree though the school's accelerated MBA program, while students with no previous work experience may apply to the "co-op" program, designed to help business newcomers develop their managerial and organizational skills. In addition, many students come to Laurier because it offers "the ability to get a professional designation (i.e., CMA, CFA) along with the MBA" through several joint-degree programs.

No matter how, when, or where they pursue an MBA, Laurier students appreciate the school's commitment to the case-based learning method, which "requires that you understand both the theory and then apply them in real-world situations." Emphasizing practical competence over strict academic theory, "The Laurier experience builds your thinking skills and allows you to attack complex problems from many angles." Discussion and debate are fundamental to the program, and "Almost all courses include a group work component which promotes the teamwork abilities within each student." This interaction is an undeniable asset to the MBA education, since many "Students are already at the manager/director level in their careers." A current student praises the professors, saying, "Not only do they contribute to the learning experience due to their vast work experiences, but they are very willing to help out both within the classroom and outside of it (networking)."

The core curriculum takes an "integrated" approach to business topics, which "allows you to cement concepts since you are dealing with them in multiple courses at the same time." After completing the core, students can tailor their education through a concentration in a number of fields (such as finance, accounting, brand communication management, supply chain management, or international business to name a few) by completing at least four courses in that subject area. They may also add breadth to their education through one of the school's international programs in Europe and Asia, or through the school's ample list of special seminars.

At the top of their field, Laurier professors are an excellent "mix of tenured professors and recognized, practicing professionals." Most "are PhDs and have recent/relevant consulting or real business experience." Friendly, down to earth, and well run, administrators at Laurier "communicate frequently with students and have always responded to questions very quickly."

Career and Placement

Career Services for the School of Business and Economics Graduate Programs provides assistance to MBA and MABE students and alumni. Their services include one-on-one career counseling and specialized workshops on topics such as resume writing, networking, interviewing, and cocktail and dining etiquette. Career Services also hosts special events, such as executive recruiter panels.

Students agree that their school enjoys a great reputation in Canada, telling us that "employers love Laurier MBA students because they are much better educated and

Maureen Ferraro or Susan Manning-Faber, MBA Marketing Coordinator's
Address: 75 University Avenue West, Waterloo, On N2L3C5 Canada
Phone: 519-884-0710 • Fax: 519-886-6978
E-mail: mbawlu@wlu.ca • Website: www.wlu.ca/mba

friendlier to work with." The following companies are among the extensive list of organizations recruiting Laurier MBAs from 2004 to 2005: Accenture, American Express Canada, Bank of Canada, Canada Revenue Agency, CIBC World Markets, CPP Investment Board, Dell Canada, Deloitte Touche Tohmatsu, FedEx Canada, GE Canada, General Mills Canada, General Motors Canada, IBM Canada, The Loyalty Group, Managerial Design, Manulife Financial, National Bank Financial, Proctor & Gamble, Raytheon Canada, RLG International, Scotiabank Group, and TD Securities.

Student Life and Environment

With such a large and diverse student population, it's hard to summarize life at Laurier. Not surprisingly, there is something of a split between students who attend the program part-time and those who chose to pursue their studies full-time. There are two campuses in the Wilfrid Laurier University MBA program. One is on the Waterloo-based university campus and the other is a satellite campus right in downtown Toronto. Part-timers attending school at the Toronto MBA campus sometimes feel a little cut off from the main campus. However, Toronto students are required to participate in MBA events and competitions at the Waterloo campus.

In both locations, the majority of students are "mature with an established career and family life." For most, "Life happens off campus," and students admit that there isn't much enthusiasm for campus activities or after-hours socializing. "Social activities with the satellite or main campus are limited due to work/family commitments in addition to academic demands," explains a current MBA candidate.

With many personal and professional commitments, most students at Laurier are talented multitaskers, who "are very good at balancing personal, work, and school life." However, they warn that the many group assignments, homework, and classes can make it difficult to juggle your educational, professional, and personal life. A student laments, "You have to be tough skinned to do an MBA on a part-time basis at WLU."

Admissions

To be considered for admission to Wilfrid Laurier University's MBA program, students must possess a 4-year, undergraduate degree (in any field of study) with at least a B average in the last 10 half-credit courses taken. Except for the MBA with co-op option (for which no work experience is required), applicants must have at least 2 years of full-time work experience to apply for an MBA at Laurier. Students must also submit a GMAT score of at least 550. In addition to test scores and transcripts, students must send three letters of recommendation from professional and academic references.

FINANCIAL FACTS

Annual tuition (in-state/ out-of-state)	$17,100/$20,470
Cost of books	$5,120

ADMISSIONS

Admissions Selectivity Rating	**82**
# of applications received	474
% applicants accepted	69
% acceptees attending	65
Average GMAT	600
Range of GMAT	550–710
Average GPA	3.3
TOEFL required of international students	Yes
Minimum TOEFL (paper/computer)	573/230
Application fee	$100
International application fee	$100
Regular application deadline	5/1
Regular notification	rolling
Deferment available	Yes
Maximum length of deferment	1 year, case by case
Non-fall admissions	Yes
Need-blind admissions	Yes

Applicants Also Look At
Brock University, McMaster University, Queen's University, University of Toronto, York University.

EMPLOYMENT PROFILE

Career Rating	79

WILLAM PATERSON UNIVERSITY
CHRISTOS M. COTSAKOS COLLEGE OF BUSINESS

GENERAL INFORMATION
Type of school   Public
Academic calendar   Semester

SURVEY SAYS...
Friendly students
Solid preparation in:
General management
Communications/interpersonal skills

STUDENTS
Enrollment of parent institution
Enrollment of MBA program

ACADEMICS
Academic Experience Rating   73
Student/faculty ratio   4:1
Profs interesting rating   79
Profs accessible rating   76
% female faculty   20
% minority faculty   30

Academics

Located in Wayne, New Jersey, the Christos M. Cotsakos College of Business augments the traditional MBA curriculum with a number of experiential learning programs, which add depth and relevance to the academic experience. The MBA core curriculum is divided into two sections: lower core and upper core—though the former may be waived for those who majored in business as undergraduates. In addition to the core, students must take 15 credits of electives, including an international component, and may choose to pursue a concentration in accounting, finance, marketing or music management. Future record company executives take note: "William Paterson has one of the best reputations for music," and the school's "proximity to NY" makes it a particularly attractive choice for those interested in the music business. Other unique features of the business school are the mentoring program, the sales center facility, and the ETRADE Financial Learning Center, which hosts one of the few active trading rooms found in an academic institution.

In the classroom, the William Paterson experience is rewarding, spearheaded by "excellent professors who truly care about your success." Faculty is "accessible, helpful, challenging, and enlightening, and they all seem devoted to and knowledgeable in their subject area." In particular, practical instruction is incorporated into classroom lessons with ease because the "faculty has a lot of on-the-job experience and are able to incorporate case work very smoothly." A student enthuses, "I love the new challenges I must face with each class because what I am learning in the classroom, I use everyday in my profession." Like the teaching staff, the administration is "wonderful" and very responsive to student needs. In particular, "the MBA director is great to work with—he will solve any problem very quickly." If you have a question or concern, "it rarely takes more than a day to get a reply on an email, and most of the time it is within an hour of sending."

Most students at William Paterson graduated from college somewhat recently; however, you'll find a nice "mix of recent undergrads, 30-somethings who are professionally successful, and 40-plus-year-olds who want to improve their skill-sets." For full-time students who would like some professional experience while offsetting tuition costs, WPU offers "financial assistance in a form of Graduate Assistantship." However, even without financial assistance, this public school has an attractive price tag, which ensures a high "educational quality at a reasonable price."

Career and Placement

Located less than 20 miles from Manhattan, William Paterson's Wayne campus places students within striking distance of New York City jobs and internship opportunities. To help with the process, the Career Development and Gloria S. Williams Advisement Center serves undergraduate and graduate students, providing career decision-making and job-search assistance. The center also coordinates on-campus recruiting events. In addition, the MBA program maintains an online job resources center, which lists current vacancies and internship opportunities in some of the region's top business employers. Students can post their resume on the site, browse jobs, or search the large alumni database. This service is also open to William Paterson alumni and faculty.

ADMISSIONS CONTACT: TINU ADENIRAN, ASSISTANT DIRECTOR
ADDRESS: 300 POMPTON RD. WAYNE, NJ 07470 UNITED STATES
PHONE: 973-720-2237 • FAX: • E-MAIL: GRADUATE@WPUNJ.EDU
WEBSITE: WWW.WPUNJ.EDU/COB

FINANCIAL FACTS	
Cost of books	$600

ADMISSIONS	
Admissions Selectivity Rating	**60***
Average GMAT	480
Average GPA	3.12
TOEFL required of international students	Yes
Minimum TOEFL (paper/computer)	515/213
Application fee	$50
International application fee	$50
Deferment available	Yes
Maximum length of deferment	One semester
Non-fall admissions	Yes

Student Life and Environment

Christos M. Cotsakos College of Business is located on its own modern and "beautiful campus," separate from the school's main undergraduate school in Wayne. The Cotsakos building includes a "great library" and fabulous computer facilities as well as classrooms that incorporate the "latest technologies." In addition, William Paterson gets a thousand gold stars for this unusual advantage: "The parking there is exceptional; we do not have to deal with construction, traffic, or no parking. There is always a spot for you, due to the fact that we are located on our own campus."

"A warm, friendly environment for learning," WPU attracts students who are "very diverse from different age groups, but always willing to help." "The majority of B-school students commute" at WPU, so campus life is largely limited to classes. Most students are comfortable with this arrangement. However, some students would like the school to "offer more activities for graduate students to participate in…. Perhaps they could offer some classes during the day for individuals who may be able to attend class during the day and not just during evening hours."

Admissions

To be admitted to William Paterson University, students must submit a GMAT score of at least 500, or meet an admissions index criteria in which a lower GMAT score is balanced by a higher GPA. In some cases, students with a high undergraduate grade point average in a business field may be eligible to waive the GMAT requirement. All applicants must also submit two letters of recommendation and some applicants are also asked to interview. Fortunately, the school's administration is committed to making the application process straightforward and user-friendly. A new student explains, "The administration has worked with me from the time I applied, to before and after the GMAT, to the present day hiccups I may occasionally run into."

WILLAMETTE UNIVERSITY
ATKINSON GRADUATE SCHOOL OF MANAGEMENT

Academics

Willamette University is an excellent place for early-career professionals to get their feet wet in the world of business. This small MBA program is "tailored more to those students with less work experience"; therefore, business theory and academic course work is heavily augmented by hands-on projects. Of the numerous experiential learning programs at Willamette, many mention the excellence of the school's Practical Applications for Careers and Enterprise program (or PACE program), through which students develop business plans for venture capitalist approval and provide management consulting for a client organization. Through such projects, students develop their skills in "teamwork, time-management, managing expectations, presentation, HR, organizational development, market research, delegation, consulting, and a view of the world of an entrepreneur." A current student attests, "My overall experience has allowed me to grow a lot, and given me the skills that I will need to leverage into the workplace."

In the classroom, professors "make it a point to stay on top of the latest trends and make learning about business fun." Group work is fundamental to the core curriculum, during which students "are paired with 12 other students for the first year to work on various team assignments." Boasting a student body that is "motivated, driven, ethical, friendly, and non-competitive," team-building opportunities are among the most attractive aspects of the Willamette MBA. One student describes it this way: "One of the biggest benefits of Atkinson is the ability to gain cross-cultural understanding. Herding cats? Try reaching consensus in a group made up of people from India, Japan, Romania, and Texas." Another adds, "For being a small school in Oregon's pristine nature, the program is intellectually diverse with a global outlook."

While the program is excellent for newbies, those with a more extensive professional background are less satisfied with Willamette, complaining that "students with previous work experience shouldn't have to be forced to take a career class." Though the class does provide tools needed for successful transitions to internships and future professional positions. For more experienced students, Atkinson recently opened a professional MBA program in Portland, Oregon. However, full-timers also warn us that the school is still ironing out the kinks: "The same professors are used at both locations, and it is obvious to full-time students that the professors feel very overwhelmed and compromised for out-of-class availability." To address these growing pains, the school has hired additional faculty.

Career and Placement

When it's time to look for a job, Willamette students benefit from their school's "great regional reputation" and loyal alumni network. "If you want to work in the Pacific Northwest after graduation, our alumni network is going to be so valuable to you," insists a current student.

From day one, career development is taken seriously, and a course entitled Achieving Your Career Goals is a required part of the core curriculum. In addition, Career Services at Willamette helps MBAs define and achieve their career goals through career counseling, career fairs, professional organizations, peer advisors, workplace site visits, networking events, Internet resources, and more. Career Services also operates a mentorship program, which "allows for additional contacts and networking opportunities." While they are loaded down with tools and resources, students suggest you be somewhat of a self-starter when it comes to the career search, as "on-campus recruiting seems almost nonexistent." Many Northwest companies prefer to interview at their own site and through the Northwest MBA Career Day consortium while working with the school's career services office.

ADMISSIONS CONTACT: JUDY O'NEILL, ASSISTANT DEAN AND DIRECTOR OF ADMISSION
ADDRESS: 900 STATE STREET SALEM, OR 97301 UNITED STATES
PHONE: 503-370-6167 • FAX: 503-370-3011
E-MAIL: MBA-ADMISSION@WILLAMETTE.EDU • WEBSITE: WWW.WILLAMETTE.EDU/MBA

In 2006, 66 percent of full-time MBA students had accepted a job offer by graduation, and 88 percent had accepted a job offer within three months of graduation. Companies that recently hired Willamette grads include Digimarc, Ernst & Young, The Gallup Organization, Harrah's Lake Tahoe, Intel, Kaiser Permanente, Microsoft, Nordstrom, Russell Investments, Saber, The Boeing Company, US Bank, and Vision Plastics.

Student Life and Environment

Life as a Willamette MBA is "intense, rewarding, and worthwhile." Be prepared for some late nights and coffee drinking. "The first year is a pressure cooker," and students say you can expect 80 or more hours of academic activities per week. Fortunately, studying and socializing go hand-in-hand at Willamette, where students "spend a lot of time working together, and, hence, we also relax together."

In this tiny program, "Students build strong relationships in the first-year core classes," and during the course of their 22 months of study, students "become a big family." In addition, "There is a good camaraderie among business students and law students, whose college is directly across the street from the Atkinson building. We participate in joint courses, which diversify the perspectives and group learning in class. The two graduate schools even participate in extracurricular functions together, such as a bowling league."

Outside the classroom, "There are more than enough ways to get involved and be social with our classmates," whether it's tipping back a beer at the bar or playing on an intramural sports team. An oft-mentioned pleasure is the weekly Thursday Night Out, "where staff, faculty, students, and spouses/others network and socialize," at a local venue. While Salem is a small town, students say it enjoys an idyllic location close to the charming city of Portland and lies "only an hour from the beach and an hour and a half from the mountains."

Admissions

Applicants to the Early Career MBA must submit the application, GMAT or GRE score, references, and undergraduate transcripts. Qualified applicants are invited to interview. Last year's entering class had a mean GMAT score of 598 and a mean undergraduate GPA of 3.3. Thirty-eight percent of Willamette MBAs studied liberal arts or social sciences in college. The Early Career MBA program is designed for students with little or no professional experience. Applicants to the MBA for Professionals Program must submit the application, GMAT score, references and undergraduate transcripts. A minimum of three years of professional experience is required for the MBA for Professionals Program.

FINANCIAL FACTS

Annual tuition	$25,200
Fees	$50
Cost of books	$1,200
Room & board (on/off-campus)	$12,000/$11,000
% of students receiving aid	89
% of first-year students receiving aid	89
% of students receiving loans	60
% of students receiving grants	67
Average award package	$24,650
Average grant	$13,000
Average student loan debt	$35,523

ADMISSIONS

Admissions Selectivity Rating	80
# of applications received	191
% applicants accepted	70
% acceptees attending	55
Average GMAT	598
Range of GMAT	550–650
Average GPA	3.32
TOEFL required of international students	Yes
Minimum TOEFL (paper/computer)	570/230
Application fee	$50
International application fee	$50
Regular application deadline	5/1
Regular notification	Rolling
Application Deadline/Notification	
Round 1:	01/11 / Roll
Round 2:	03/01 / Roll
Round 3:	05/01 / Roll
Deferment available	Yes
Maximum length of deferment	1 year
Transfer students accepted	Yes
Transfer application policy	
Up to six credits of MBA course work to the Early Career program with the approval of Dean.	
Need-blind admissions	Yes

Applicants Also Look At
Arizona State University, Bentley College, College of William and Mary, Oregon State University, Purdue University, University of Oregon, University of Portland.

EMPLOYMENT PROFILE

Career Rating	82	Grads Employed by Function	% Avg. Salary
Primary Source of Full-time Job Acceptances		Finance	39 $54,136
School-facilitated activities	22 (56%)	Human Resources	11 $53,941
Graduate-facilitated activities	17 (44%)	Marketing	25 $66,857
Percent employed	89	Operations	14 $64,550
		Consulting	11 $53,333

Top 5 Employers Hiring Grads
Saber Consulting; Nautilus; Ashland Partners; Accenture; Intel Corporation

WORCESTER POLYTECHNIC INSTITUTE
DEPARTMENT OF MANAGEMENT

GENERAL INFORMATION
Type of school	Private
Academic calendar	Semester

SURVEY SAYS...
Cutting-edge classes
Solid preparation in:
Finance
Accounting
General management
Presentation skills
Quantitative skills

STUDENTS
Enrollment of parent institution	4,157
Enrollment of business school	238
% male/female	57/43
% out-of-state	71
% part-time	97
% minorities	29
% international	57
Average age at entry	31
Average years work experience at entry	7

ACADEMICS
Academic Experience Rating	**81**
Student/faculty ratio	11:1
Profs interesting rating	83
Profs accessible rating	84
% female faculty	46
% minority faculty	4

Joint Degrees
BS/MBA 5 years.

Prominent Alumni
Paul Allaire, Chairman/CEO, Xerox Corporation; Judith Nitsch, President, Judith Nitsch Engineering, Inc.; Windle Priem, President/CEO, Korn/Ferry International; Stephen Rubin, President/CEO, Intellution, Inc.; Ronald Zarella, President, GM North America.

Academics

The MBA program at Worcester Polytechnic Institute unites a broad-based degree in business essentials with highly specialized instruction on technology and technology management. One of the oldest technical universities in the United States, "WPI is an engineering school first and foremost" that built its reputation on its strong programs in science and technology. Given the school's legacy, students agree that "the addition of a technology-oriented business program is a natural progression that WPI is uniquely suited to provide." The 49-credit hour MBA program begins with foundation courses, such as economics and accounting, followed by a set of core courses, designed to integrate foundational concepts. Naturally, all course work is taught from a technological perspective and practical applications to business theory are emphasized. After completing the core requirements, students tailor their education through a concentration in challenging fields such as information security management, operations management, or technological innovation. In addition to electives offered through the business school, WPI students can enroll in graduate-level electives in other departments, including computer science, biomedical engineering, and electrical engineering. While students choose WPI for its highly pointed focus on technical subject areas, they also suggest that the school make an effort to "team with other universities nationwide to provide an even more diverse curriculum."

Offering the opportunity to pursue an MBA entirely online or through a mix of classroom and online courses, many students gravitate to Worcester Polytechnic Institute for its flexible scheduling options. At Worcester, busy professionals appreciate "the ability to take classes remotely even if my career required me to travel around the world from time to time." Offering a web-based program since 1998, students reassure us that the school maintains high academic standards, even for virtual students. In the words of one, "I am currently an online student and find the online classes very thorough, organized, and convenient." As if we would expect any less, students also report that "the technical support is phenomenal. They make the whole thing work so seamlessly that you feel spoiled. If all IT/IS departments were this effective, the world would be a much more efficient place."

In the classroom, students appreciate the quality of the teaching staff, saying their professors are "extremely up to date and have a genuine affection toward their students. They work very hard to make the experience positive and exciting." The program's extensive project-based work "gives a good amount of experience in applying the theories taught and prepares students well for applying lessons in the real world." Teamwork is also a crucial part of the learning experience, and even online courses include "virtual teams," who meet via the Internet. Across the board, students agree that "WPI is a well-run institution that exhibits a high degree of consistency." A current student adds, "The administration is also top-notch. They have an unusually quick response time to problem resolution and provide excellent advice."

Career and Placement

A high percentage of WPI students work full-time, many receiving tuition reimbursement from their current company while pursuing the MBA. Therefore, most will continue at the same company after completing the WPI program. However, those considering a career change can receive support and guidance through the university's Career Development Center, which serves the undergraduate, graduate, and alumni population. The CDC offers career counseling, workshops, and assessments, and maintains contact with regional employers and WPI alumni. The CDC also hosts several annual campus career fairs.

ADMISSIONS CONTACT: NORM WILKINSON, DIRECTOR, GRADUATE MANAGEMENT PROGRAMS
ADDRESS: 100 INSTITUTE ROAD WORCESTER, MA 01609 UNITED STATES
PHONE: 508-831-5218 • FAX: 508-831-5720
E-MAIL: GMP@WPI.EDU • WEBSITE: WWW.MGT.WPI.EDU

According to statistics published by the Career Development Center, MBA graduates in 2005 were offered an average salary of $91,500.

Student Life and Environment

At WPI, students are "mostly male in their 30s," pursuing a degree part-time or online while continuing to work in a professional capacity. Those who attend classes on campus enjoy the company of their classmates, saying they "come from various backgrounds and work experiences, but all seem bright and eager to be part of the MBA program." There are plenty of clubs and activities offered through the larger university—though be forewarned that the technology focus extends well beyond the classroom. A student elaborates, "Like most schools there are the sports and social clubs, but there are also many opportunities for students with a passion for science to feed their 'inner geek.'"

Set on 80 acres in the small New England town of Worcester, Massachusetts, the WPI campus boasts a pleasant collegiate atmosphere, excellent student facilities, and, of course, first-rate technological resources. A part-time student shares, "Being part-time, I spend time on campus once or twice a week and find the classrooms and student center to be quite usable and very inviting." Since there isn't a virtual campus (yet), most distance students aren't involved in the community and "do not go to campus except to meet with professors." While they certainly keep busy with school and work, some say they'd like the school to "find ways to connect the off-campus part-time students with on-campus activities."

Admissions

The MBA program at Worcester Polytechnic Institute accepts students whose academic and professional record demonstrates the ability to excel in a challenging, technology-focused graduate program. Students are analyzed on the basis of their academic and professional performance, as well as their career goals and personal statement. In addition, all applicants must have demonstrated capacity to succeed in a technology-driven management program; therefore, a minimum of three semesters of college-level math or two semesters of college-level calculus are a prerequisite of the program. To apply, students must submit undergraduate transcripts, official GMAT scores, three letters of recommendation, and a completed application form.

FINANCIAL FACTS

Annual tuition	$25,529
Fees	$85
Cost of books	$1,100
Room & board (off-campus)	$8,100
% of students receiving aid	65
% of first-year students receiving aid	75
% of students receiving loans	33
% of students receiving grants	65
Average award package	$4,800
Average grant	$35,000

ADMISSIONS

Admissions Selectivity Rating	**79**
# of applications received	158
% applicants accepted	72
% acceptees attending	46
Average GMAT	611
Range of GMAT	580–690
Average GPA	3.32
TOEFL required of international students	Yes
Minimum TOEFL (paper/computer)	550/213
Application fee	$70
International application fee	$70
Regular application deadline	8/1
Regular notification	rolling
Deferment available	Yes
Maximum length of deferment	1 year
Transfer students accepted	Yes
Transfer application policy Accepted transfer applicants may transfer in up to 9 prior graduate-level credits toward MBA.	
Non-fall admissions	Yes
Need-blind admissions	Yes

Applicants Also Look At

Babson College, Bentley College, Boston College, Boston University, Massachusetts Institute of Technology, Northeastern University, University of Massachusetts—Amherst.

EMPLOYMENT PROFILE

Career Rating	**97**		
Primary Source of Full-time Job Acceptances		**Grads Employed by Function% Avg. Salary**	
School-facilitated activities	1 (50%)	Operations	50 $105,000
Graduate-facilitated activities	1 (50%)	Communications	50 $78,000
Average base starting salary	$91,500		

XAVIER UNIVERSITY
WILLIAMS COLLEGE OF BUSINESS

GENERAL INFORMATION

Type of school	Private
Affiliation	Roman Catholic/Jesuit
Environment	Metropolis
Academic calendar	Semester

SURVEY SAYS...

Cutting-edge classes
Happy students
Solid preparation in:
General management

STUDENTS

Enrollment of parent institution	6,644
Enrollment of business school	994
% male/female	68/32
% out-of-state	10
% part-time	75
% minorities	49
% international	10
Average age at entry	30
Average years work experience at entry	7

ACADEMICS

Academic Experience Rating	**86**
Student/faculty ratio	26:1
Profs interesting rating	83
Profs accessible rating	94
% female faculty	37
% minority faculty	8

Joint Degrees

MBA/MA (Health Services Administration) 3 years, MBA/MS (Nursing) 3 years.

Prominent Alumni

George Schaefer, President/CEO, Fifth Third Bancorp; Robert J. Kohlhepp, Vice Chairman, Cintas Corporation; John Lechleiter, President/CEO, Eli Lilly & Company; Carlos Alcantara, President/CEO Chalaco; Mary Jean Ryan, F.S.M. MEA., President/CEO, SSM Health Care.

Academics

The Williams College of Business at Xavier University combines three things that students respect: "academic excellence," a "strong reputation," and "scheduling convenience" to fit in the lives of working professionals. All students at Xavier are required to have a foundation in basic business skills courses, which comprise 20 of the 36 to 60 credit hours required for graduation. Students may then concentrate in e-business, finance, business administration, international business, management information systems, or marketing. They may take courses offered in the evening, generally meeting one day a week, or they may choose a weekend MBA option. With substantial work experience (and usually financial support from an employer), students may also choose an executive MBA option, which meets one full day a week for 19 months.

Whatever option they choose, students like the fact that Xavier has "the best reputation in the Midwest for an MBA," and they find the quality of teaching upholds that reputation. "Professors are very passionate about their respective subjects, and most seem to have tremendous past work experience to help shed light on them," a student says. "Talented faculty who are experts in their areas," and "instructors who understand what is happening in the real world and have experience to share" make students feel their investment in working toward an MBA is worthwhile. Xavier is a private school based on centuries of Jesuit educational tradition, and students find "no hard-bitten civil servants here. Professors get who their students are," and "they have high expectations" as well being as "accessible outside the classroom and going the extra mile when you need help." Some, however, "wish classes were more in-depth and more technical," and they would like to see Xavier "offering more graduate-level electives and concentrations that apply to the business community."

Across the board, students praise a concerned administrative staff. "They are very good about facilitating learning rather than just throwing you out there and hoping you can swim," one student points out, and another offers that "Xavier's administration of the MBA program is exceptional. From communication with students to outside seminars and career development and skills workshops, Xavier goes above and beyond to provide students with the tools they need to succeed." When problems do arise, "Any road bumps encountered along the way" are "quickly resolved," and "This school makes all administrative matters a snap," students agree.

Career and Placement

Three out of four MBA students at Williams College of Business attend part-time because they are already working; still, many feel the Professional Development Center, as well as Xavier's alumni network, is helpful to them as they consider new opportunities. In addition to the career fairs, workshops, and networking events offered by the center, students may also tap into the networking resources of other members of a consortium of Jesuit business schools. "Strong alumni ties to corporate community," is an aspect many students point to as an asset, although "helping students with job placements and internships outside of Cincinnati" is an area that some students feel needs improving. In general, though, students are satisfied with the assistance they receive in career planning and placement. "The administration is constantly keeping students in the loop regarding career opportunities," one student says, summing up the feelings of colleagues.

GE, Proctor & Gamble, Hewlett-Packard, Fifth Third Bank, Convergys, and International Paper are among the companies which have employed Xavier's MBA graduates.

Student Life and Environment

In common with most graduate programs where the majority of students attend part-time, there's a mixed bag of feelings about student life among those in Xavier's MBA program. Besides course work "The only other interaction is maybe going out for a beer after class"; one student says, "We spend time in classes together but have other lives, and so we do not interact or network as much I would like in order to make connections that would help my career advancement," though the school does provide options. "Everyone is going through the same experience, and everyone is understanding of this. Everyone is helpful in classes and out. Easy to network with and helpful in that respect as well." Most Xavier MBA students agree that "students are hardworking but friendly. Most are open to, and expect to, learn from other students and their experiences. Everyone strives to do well and is [more] interested in helping others succeed [than hoping they fail]." It's no surprise that the program is made up of "very driven, type-A personalities." Students find that "Xavier has the feeling of a small town where everyone knows everyone. It has a relaxed atmosphere where academics are a priority."

Admissions

Williams College of Business at Xavier offers paper and online application methods. Either way, students must submit a resume, transcripts, and scores on the GMAT, with an optional personal statement. While prior work experience is not required for the weekend and weeknight MBA programs, the executive MBA requires that students have substantial management experience, or hold a PhD, JD, or other higher-level degree. Those admitted to that program recently have 8 years of work experience. Across all programs, the average undergraduate GPA of those admitted in 2006 is 3.2, and the average GMAT score is 550.

FINANCIAL FACTS

Annual tuition	$11,790
Fees	$0
Cost of books	$900
% of students receiving aid	23
% of students receiving loans	23
% of students receiving grants	38
Average award package	$13,358
Average grant	$755
Average student loan debt	$30,130

ADMISSIONS

Admissions Selectivity Rating	**89**
# of applications received	666
% applicants accepted	32
% acceptees attending	92
Average GMAT	550
Range of GMAT	500–590
Average GPA	3.33
TOEFL required of international students	Yes
Minimum TOEFL (paper/computer)	550/213
Application fee	$35
International application fee	$35
Deferment available	Yes
Maximum length of deferment	1 year
Transfer students accepted	Yes
Transfer application policy 6 hours of core curriculum from AACSB accredited programs only. Up to 18 hours of core curriculum from AACSB accredited Jesuit MBA Network Schools.	
Non-fall admissions	Yes
Need-blind admissions	Yes

Applicants Also Look At

Miami University (OH), Northern Kentucky University, University of Cincinnati.

EMPLOYMENT PROFILE

Career Rating	86	Grads Employed by Function% Avg. Salary	
Percent employed	75	Finance	21 $65,505
		Marketing	14 $98,875
		MIS	9 $67,700
		Operations	4 $67,000
		General Management	5 $58,000
		Global Management	3 NR
		Other	7 $51,175
		Internet/New Media	1 NR

Top 5 Employers Hiring Grads
Procter & Gamble; Fidelity Investments; Federal Home Loan

YALE UNIVERSITY
SCHOOL OF MANAGEMENT

Academics

An MBA program "outside the box," Yale University's School of Management distinguishes itself though an unparalleled "emphasis on social issues and integrity" coupled with the prestige and quality of the Yale name. "Top ranked for social enterprise and nonprofit management" as well as for its finance programs, the school aims to educate global leaders for business and society, promoting purpose, creativity, passion, and accountability among its students and faculty. Attracting a diverse and accomplished student body, Yale's talented business students are "not number-crunching machines or ultra-competitive politicians"; rather they are intelligent leaders and innovators, who "strive for excellence, but still care about the ethical implications of how things are done."

The core MBA curriculum at Yale recently underwent a serious overhaul, the result of which is a first-year program that presents a "highly interdisciplinary, integrated approach to learning the fundamentals of business management." Built around eight multidisciplinary courses called Organizational Perspectives, the new core curriculum is cutting edge—the product of the "commitment to curriculum innovation among faculty and administration." In fact, the new program is so enticing that a second-year student laments, "I totally have 'core envy' and wish I could go back and take the core as it currently is!"

Beyond core courses, "a wide range of electives provide ample opportunity to expand my horizons." Plus, lucky Yale students "don't have to worry about getting into classes; this semester 99.9 percent of second-year students got into all of their first-choice classes." Part of a renowned university, there are "many different ideas and paths here outside the traditional-stereotype MBA track," including the "opportunity to integrate classes from other schools at Yale." In particular, many students mention the school's "strong joint-degree program with the Yale School of Forestry and Environmental Studies."

When it comes to faculty, Yale draws big names in every subject area, and some "classes are taught by 'executives in residence'—the former CEO of JPMorgan Capital or the co-founder of Marakon Associates." The rigorous course work is counterbalanced by the fact that "the professors are excellent instructors and are very accessible outside of class." On top of that, the "warm, interpersonal dynamic" on campus creates the perfect salve for business school slavery. In addition, students dole out praises for the school's "open and innovative" administration—especially the dynamic Dean Podolny, who "makes it a priority to be available for the students, be it through monthly breakfasts or over e-mail in which he responds within 24 hours."

Career and Placement

The Career Development Office at the Yale School of Management helps place students in a variety of positions and industries. Through the CDO, students have access to one-on-one career counseling, mock interviews, and special workshops on resume writing, career searches, networking, and negotiation. The CDO also hosts career fairs, company presentations, and on-campus interviews. Needless to say, Yale students enjoy a "huge brand name," which adds some serious sparkle to your postgraduate career search.

In 2006, 46 percent of Yale grads took jobs in financial services, and another 15 percent in consulting. The top hiring companies were: Lehman Brothers, Citigroup, Washington Mutual, General Electric Company, Hartford Financial Services, Merrill Lynch, American Express Company, Standard & Poor's, Technoserve, Banc of America Securities, Barclay's Capital, JPMorgan Chase, Johnson & Johnson, MBIA, PepsiCo, and Proctor & Gamble. Grads in 2006 earned a median base salary of $95,000 with a median signing bonus of $20,000.

ADMISSIONS CONTACT: BRUCE DELMONICO, DIRECTOR OF ADMISSIONS
ADDRESS: 135 PROSPECT STREET , P.O. BOX 208200 NEW HAVEN, CT 06520-8200 UNITED STATES
PHONE: 203-432-5635 • FAX: 203-432-7004
E-MAIL: MBA.ADMISSIONS@YALE.EDU • WEBSITE: WWW.MBA.YALE.EDU

Student Life and Environment

The friendliness, talent, and diversity of the student body is one of the most unique and enviable aspects of a Yale education. Hardly cookie-cutter future executives, "Students come from a wide range of backgrounds, have a variety of job and life experiences, and have a broad range of professional and personal interests, passions, and hobbies." On the whole, Yale students are "more liberal in their thinking and progressive in their politics" than you would traditionally find at a business school program. This year's class tried to level the playing field with the addition of a Conservative Club—though, to date, they have only two members.

An active academic and social environment, "students are usually involved in half a dozen different clubs, consulting and research projects. Often, students spend as much on organizing and participating nonclass activities as in actual class time." From dinners to ski trips, there are tons of regular social events for business students, including an "excellent happy hour every Thursday, with faculty and administrators joining in the fun."

Yale is "a great place to make lifelong friendships," boasting a highly friendly and inclusive atmosphere. A current student exclaims, "It is hard to have a party without inviting the whole class—both because you want to include everyone, and because it is such a tight-knit group!" Off campus, there is plenty of nightlife in this bustling college town, and students admit that "the small city of New Haven facilitates stronger networking and relationship-building with classmates." However, when they are ready for the bright lights, Yale is situated "close enough to New York and Boston to take advantage of the big city during the weekends."

Admissions

The Admissions Committee at Yale University School of Management seeks accomplished students with highly diverse professional and academic experience. Recent admits come from a range of backgrounds (69% private, 22% public, and 9% government), including such unlikely fields as jewelry design, athletics, medicine, nonprofit organizations, and the performing arts. The school does not publish any specific admissions standards; however, the class of 2008 had an average GMAT score of 701 and an average college GPA of 3.4. Women comprise 38 percent of the entering class at Yale School of Management.

Prominent Alumni

John Thornton, Former Co-COO/President, Goldman Sachs; Nancy Peretsman, EVP and Managing Director, Allen & Company; Indra Nooyi, Chairman and CEO, PepsiCo Inc.; Fred Terrell, Managing Partner/CEO, Provender Capital Group; Timothy Collins, CEO/Senior Managing Director, Ripplewood Holding.

FINANCIAL FACTS

Annual tuition	$42,000
Fees	$1,932
Cost of books	$7,200
Room & board	$13,320
% of students receiving aid	73
% of first-year students receiving aid	84
% of students receiving loans	67
% of students receiving grants	20
Average award package	$39,927
Average grant	$19,427
Average student loan debt	$82,949

ADMISSIONS

Admissions Selectivity Rating	98
# of applications received	2,776
% applicants accepted	15
% acceptees attending	44
Average GMAT	700
Average GPA	3.47
TOEFL required of international students	Yes
Minimum TOEFL (paper/computer)	600/250
Application fee	$200
Application Deadline/Notification	
Round 1:	10/24 / 01/18
Round 2:	01/9 / 04/04
Round 3:	03/14 / 05/09
Need-blind admissions	Yes

Applicants Also Look At

Harvard University, University of Pennsylvania.

EMPLOYMENT PROFILE

Career Rating	95	Grads Employed by Function	%	Avg. Salary
Primary Source of Full-time Job Acceptances		Finance	52	$98,169
School-facilitated activities	65%	Marketing	13	$98,238
Graduate-facilitated activities	34%	MIS	1	NR
Unknown	1%	Consulting	19	$104,288
Average base starting salary	$99,307	General Management	13	$98,658
Percent employed	88	Other	1	NR

Top 5 Employers Hiring Grads
Citigroup; Standard & Poors; IBM; JP Morgan; Lehman Brothers

Part III-B
Business School Data
Listings

ARIZONA STATE UNIVERSITY— WEST
SCHOOL OF GLOBAL MANAGEMENT & LEADERSHIP

ADMISSIONS CONTACT: GRADUATE PROGRAMS ADMISSIONS
ADDRESS: P.O. BOX 37100, PHOENIX, AZ 85069-7100
PHONE: 602-543-6201 • FAX: 602-543-6249
E-MAIL: GRADPROGRAMS@ASU.EDU
WEBSITE: WWW.WEST.ASU.EDU/SGML/GRAD

STUDENTS
Enrollment of Parent Institution: 55,000 **Enrollment of Business School:** 180 **% Male/female:** 100/0 **% Part-time:** 100 **Average Age at Entry:** 35 **Average Years Work Experience at Entry:** 9

ACADEMICS
Student/faculty Ratio: 20:1 **% Female Faculty:** 29 **% Minority Faculty:** 12

ADMISSIONS
Admissions Selectivity Rating: 77

# of Applications Received: 45 **% Applicants Accepted:** 93 **% Acceptees Attending:** 100 **GMAT Range (25th to 75th percentile):** 450–700 **Average GMAT:** 590 **Average GPA:** 3.5 **TOEFL Required of Int'l Applicants:** Yes **Minimum TOEFL (paper/computer):** 600/250 **Application Fee:** $50 **Non-fall Admissions:** Yes **Applicants Also Look At:** Arizona State University, Northern Arizona University, University of Arizona.

EMPLOYMENT PROFILE
Grads Employed by Industry:.......%
Finance 15
Human Resources...........................1
Marketing 20
MIS 6
Operations.......................................24
Strategic Planning...........................1
Consulting...6
Communications 1
General Management 7
Other...10

ARKANSAS STATE UNIVERSITY
COLLEGE OF BUSINESS

ADMISSIONS CONTACT: DR. THOMAS WHEELER, DEAN, GRADUATE SCHOOL
ADDRESS: PO BOX 60, STATE UNIVERSITY, AR 72467
PHONE: 870-972-3029 • FAX: 870-972-3857
E-MAIL: GRADSCH@CHOCTAW.ASTATE.EDU
WEBSITE: BUSINESS.ASTATE.EDU

GENERAL INFORMATION
Type of School: Public **Environment:** Town **Academic Calendar:** Semester

STUDENTS
Enrollment of Business School: 104

ACADEMICS
Student/faculty Ratio: 25:1 **% Female Faculty:** 24 **% Minority Faculty:** 1

FINANCIAL FACTS
Tuition (in-state/out-of-state): $1,488/$3,744 **Books and Supplies:** $2,100 **Room & Board:** $3,500 **Average Grant:** $6,427

ADMISSIONS
Admissions Selectivity Rating: 60*

# of Applications Received: 53 **% Applicants Accepted:** 85 **% Acceptees Attending:** 80 **TOEFL Required of Int'l Applicants:** Yes Minimum TOEFL: 550 **Regular Application Deadline:** rolling **Regular Notification:** rolling

ARKANSAS TECH UNIVERSITY
SCHOOL OF BUSINESS

ADDRESS: ATU, DOC BRYAN #141, RUSSELLVILLE, AR 72801
PHONE: 479-968-0343 • FAX: 479-964-0522
E-MAIL: TECH.ENROLL@ATU.EDU
WEBSITE: WWW.ATU.EDU

GENERAL INFORMATION
Type of School: Public

ADMISSIONS
Admissions Selectivity Rating: 60*

TOEFL Required of Int'l Applicants: Yes **Minimum TOEFL (paper/computer):** 173/500 **Application Fee:** $0 **International Application Fee:** $25 **Non-fall Admissions:** Yes

Ashridge (United Kingdom)
Ashridge Business School

Admissions Contact: MBA Admissions, MBA Admissions
Address: Berkhamsted, Hertfordshire, HP4 1NS England
Phone: 001 44 1442 841483 • *Fax:* 001 44 1442 841144
E-mail: MBA@ASHRIDGE.ORG.UK
Website: WWW.ASHRIDGE.ORG.UK

GENERAL INFORMATION
Academic Calendar: Jan.–Dec.

STUDENTS
Enrollment of Business School: 55 **% Male/female:** 61/39 **% Part-time:** 53 **% International:** 73 **Average Age at Entry:** 35 **Average Years Work Experience at Entry:** 13

ACADEMICS
Student/faculty Ratio: 1:1 **% Female Faculty:** 30
Prominent Alumni: Mark Harris, Chief Exec, National Lottery Commission; Rob Williams, Finance Director, The Economist; Nigel Pears, Operations & Safety Director, First Group PLC; Sue Latham, Director of Nursing, Clemintine Hospital.

FINANCIAL FACTS
Tuition: $58,603 **Books and Supplies:** $880 **Room & Board:** $19,860 **Average Award Package:** $50,000

ADMISSIONS
Admissions Selectivity Rating: 77
# of Applications Received: % Applicants Accepted: % Acceptees Attending: 100 **GMAT Range (25th to 75th percentile):** 520–640 **Average GMAT:** 565 **Average GPA: TOEFL Required of Int'l Applicants:** Yes **Minimum TOEFL (paper/computer):** 600/250 **Application Fee:** $0 **International Application Fee:** $0
Deferment Available: Yes **Maximum Length of Deferment:** One year **Non-fall Admissions:** Yes

EMPLOYMENT PROFILE
Primary Source of Full-time Job Acceptances

School-facilitated Activities 5 (20%)
Graduate-facilitated Activities 1 (4%)
Unknown.......................................19 (76%)
Percent Employed 88
Grads Employed by Industry:.......%
Finance 8
Marketing 4
Operations.......................................4
Consulting......................................24
Entrepreneurship............................8
General Management 36
Global Management 4
Non-profit 4
Top 5 Employers Hiring Grads: DHL, Standard Chartered Bank, Prem Group, RTL, Talisma Corporation.

Ball State University
Miller College of Business

Admissions Contact: Dr. Gayle Hartleroad, Director of Student Services
Address: WB 147, Muncie, IN 47306
Phone: 765-285-5329 • *Fax:* 765-285-8818
E-mail: MBA@BSU.EDU
Website: WWW.BSU.EDU/MBA

GENERAL INFORMATION
Type of School: Public **Environment:** City **Academic Calendar:** Semester

STUDENTS
Enrollment of Parent Institution: 18,161 **Enrollment of Business School:** 173 **% Male/female:** 73/27 **% Out-of-state:** 11 **% Part-time:** 68 **% Minorities:** 4 **% International:** 15 **Average Age at Entry:** 27 **Average Years Work Experience at Entry:** 4

ACADEMICS
Student/faculty Ratio: 30:1

FINANCIAL FACTS
Tuition (in-state/out-of-state): $8,272/$21,040 **Fees:** $675 **Books and Supplies:** $1,700 **Room & Board (on/off campus):** $9,000/$9,500

ADMISSIONS
Admissions Selectivity Rating: 70
# of Applications Received: 41 **% Applicants Accepted:** 78 **% Acceptees Attending:** 191 **GMAT Range (25th to 75th percentile):** 420–720 **Average GMAT:** 532 **Average GPA:** 3.32 **TOEFL Required of Int'l Applicants:** Yes **Minimum TOEFL (paper/computer):** 550/213 **Application Fee:** $35 **International Application Fee:** $40
Regular Application Deadline: rolling **Regular Notification:** rolling **Deferment Available:** Yes **Maximum Length of Deferment:** 2 years **Transfer Students Accepted:** Yes **Non-fall Admissions:** Yes **Need-Blind Admissions:** Yes **Applicants Also Look At:** Butler University, Indiana University—Kokomo, Indiana University—Purdue University at Fort Wayne, Indiana University—Purdue University Indianapolis.

Bilkent University
Facutly of Business Administration

Admissions Contact: Ilham Bayhan-Cipil, MBA Coordinator
Address: _sletme Fakultesi MAZ18, Ankara, 06800 Turkey
Phone: 0090-312-2902817 • *Fax:* 0090-312-2664958
E-mail: CIPIL@BILKENT.EDU.TR
Website: WWW.MAN.BILKENT.EDU.TR

FINANCIAL FACTS
Tuition: $12,090 **Fees:** $0 **Books and Supplies:** $300 **% of Students Receiving Grants:** 33

Admissions Selectivity Rating: 60*
Regular Application Deadline: 6/6

BOISE STATE UNIVERSITY
COLLEGE OF BUSINESS AND ECONOMICS

ADMISSIONS CONTACT: J. RENEE ANCHUSTEGUI, PROGRAMS ADMINISTRATOR &
ACADEMIC ADVISOR
ADDRESS: BUSINESS GRADUATE STUDIES, 1910 UNIVERSITY DRIVE B318,
BOISE, ID 83725-1600
PHONE: 208-426-3116 • FAX: 208-426-1135
E-MAIL: GRADUATEBUSINESS@BOISESTATE.EDU
WEBSITE: COBE.BOISESTATE.EDU/GRADUATE

GENERAL INFORMATION
Type of School: Public Environment: City Academic Calendar:
Semester

STUDENTS
Enrollment of Parent Institution: 18,876 Enrollment of Business
School: 175 % Male/female: 68/32 % Out-of-state: 20 % Part-
time: 50 % Minorities: 1 % International: 7 Average Age at Entry:
31 Average Years Work Experience at Entry: 6.3

ACADEMICS
Student/faculty Ratio: 28:1 % Female Faculty: 20 % Minority
Faculty: 7
Prominent Alumni: Jan Packwood, President & COO, Idaho Power Co.;
William Glynn, President, Intermountain Gas; Steve Heyl, VP Strategic
Planning, Arby's; Norm Schlachter, VP Finance, Micron Technology;
Mary Schofield, Controller, Boise Division, Hewlett-Packard.

FINANCIAL FACTS
Tuition (in-state/out-of-state): $0/$8,168 Fees: $6,240 Books and
Supplies: $2,000 Room & Board (on/off campus): $6,800/$7,200 %
of Students Receiving Aid: 30 % of First-year Students Receiving
Aid: 12 % of Students Receiving Loans: 18 % of Students
Receiving Grants: 12 Average Award Package: $20,020 Average
Grant: $22,130 Average Student Loan Debt: $12,000

ADMISSIONS
Admissions Selectivity Rating: 90
# of Applications Received: 163 % Applicants Accepted: 44 %
Acceptees Attending: 48 GMAT Range (25th to 75th percentile):
532–640 Average GMAT: 583 Average GPA: 3.4 TOEFL Required of
Int'l Applicants: Yes Minimum TOEFL (paper/computer): 587/240
Application Fee: $55 International Application Fee: $55
Regular Application Deadline: 6/1 Regular Notification: 7/15
Early Decision Program: Yes ED Deadline/notification: FA 02/15;
SP 08/01 / 3/31 Deferment Available: Yes Maximum Length of
Deferment: 1 year Transfer Students Accepted: Yes Non-fall
Admissions: Yes Need-Blind Admissions: Yes Applicants Also Look
At: Brigham Young University, Idaho State University.

EMPLOYMENT PROFILE
Primary Source of Full-time Job Acceptances
School-facilitated Activities 3 (15%)
Graduate-facilitated Activities 8 (40%)
Unknown...9 (45%)
Percent Employed 100
Grads Employed by Industry: ......% avg. salary:
Finance 55 $40,545
Marketing 5 $45,000
MIS 5 $104,000
Operations.......................................5 $115,000
Other...30 $60,833
Top 5 Employers Hiring Grads: Blue Cross of Idaho, Wells Fargo.

BRADLEY UNIVERSITY
FOSTER COLLEGE OF BUSINESS ADMINISTRATION

ADMISSIONS CONTACT: DR. EDWARD SATTLER, DIRECTOR OF GRADUATE
PROGRAMS
ADDRESS: BAKER HALL, PEORIA, IL 61625
PHONE: 309-677-2253 • FAX: 309-677-3374
E-MAIL: ADE@BRADLEY.EDU
WEBSITE: WWW.BRADLEY.EDU/FCBA/INDEX.HTML

GENERAL INFORMATION
Type of School: Private Environment: City Academic Calendar:
Semester

FINANCIAL FACTS
Tuition: $8,832 Fees: $15 Books and Supplies: $700

ADMISSIONS
Admissions Selectivity Rating: 60*
# of Applications Received: 47 % Applicants Accepted: 100 %
Acceptees Attending: 57 TOEFL Required of Int'l Applicants: Yes
Minimum TOEFL (paper/computer): 500 Application Fee: $50
Regular Application Deadline: Rolling Regular Notification: Rolling
Deferment Available: Yes Maximum Length of Deferment: 1 year
Non-fall Admissions: Yes Need-Blind Admissions: Yes Applicants
Also Look At: Illinois State University, University of Phoenix On-Line.

CALIFORNIA STATE UNIVERSITY—
BAKERSFIELD
SCHOOL OF BUSINESS AND PUBLIC
ADMINISTRATION

ADMISSIONS CONTACT: DEBBIE BLOWERS, EVALUATIONS
ADDRESS: 9001 STOCKDALE HIGHWAY, BAKERSFIELD, CA 93311-1099
PHONE: 661-664-3036 • FAX: 661-664-3389
E-MAIL: ADMISSIONS@CSUB.EDU
WEBSITE: WWW.CSUBAK.EDU/BPA/

GENERAL INFORMATION

Type of School: Public **Environment:** Village **Academic Calendar:** Quarter Schedule

STUDENTS

Enrollment of Parent Institution: 6,700 **Enrollment of Business School:** 84 **% Male/female:** 33/67 **% Part-time:** 86 **% Minorities:** 25 **% International:** 25 **Average Age at Entry:** 32

ACADEMICS

Student/faculty Ratio: 17:1 **% Female Faculty:** 10 **% Minority Faculty:** 10

FINANCIAL FACTS

Tuition (in-state/out-of-state): $2,126/$6,646 **Books and Supplies:** $2,200 **Room & Board (on/off campus):** $4,950/$7,679

ADMISSIONS

Admissions Selectivity Rating: 87

# of Applications Received: 80 **% Applicants Accepted:** 28 **% Acceptees Attending:** 73 **GMAT Range (25th to 75th percentile):** 490–570 **Average GMAT:** 530 **Average GPA:** 3.3 **TOEFL Required of Int'l Applicants:** Yes **Minimum TOEFL (paper):** 550 **Application Fee:** $55

Regular Application Deadline: rolling **Regular Notification:** rolling **Non-fall Admissions:** Yes

CALIFORNIA STATE UNIVERSITY— LOS ANGELES
COLLEGE OF BUSINESS AND ECONOMICS

ADMISSIONS CONTACT: JOAN WOOSLEY, ADMISSIONS OFFICER
ADDRESS: 5151 STATE UNIVERSITY DRIVE, LOS ANGELES, CA 90032
PHONE: 323-343-3904 • FAX: 323-343-6306
E-MAIL: ADMISSIONS@CALSTATELA.EDU
WEBSITE: CBE.CALSTATELA.EDU

GENERAL INFORMATION

Type of School: Public **Environment:** Metropolis **Academic Calendar:** Quarter

STUDENTS

Enrollment of Parent Institution: 18,849 **Enrollment of Business School:** 330 **% Male/female:** 47/53 **% Part-time:** 100 **% Minorities:** 50 **Average Age at Entry:** 31

ACADEMICS

Student/faculty Ratio: 20:1

FINANCIAL FACTS

Tuition (in-state/out-of-state): $3,949/$12,096 **Books and Supplies:** $500 **Average Grant:** $12,000

ADMISSIONS

Admissions Selectivity Rating: 84

# of Applications Received: 388 **% Applicants Accepted:** 43 **% Acceptees Attending:** 52 **Average GMAT:** 560 **Average GPA:** 3

TOEFL Required of Int'l Applicants: Yes **Minimum TOEFL (paper/computer):** 550/213 **Application Fee:** $55

Regular Application Deadline: 6/15 **Regular Notification:** 1/1 **Non-fall Admissions:** Yes

CALIFORNIA STATE UNIVERSITY— SACRAMENTO
COLLEGE OF BUSINESS ADMINISTRATION

ADMISSIONS CONTACT: JEANIE ALLAM, GRADUATE PROGRAM ACADEMIC COUNSELOR
ADDRESS: 6000 J STREET, SACRAMENTO, CA 95819-6088
PHONE: 916-278-6772 • FAX: 916-278-4233
E-MAIL: CBAGRAD@CSUS.EDU
WEBSITE: WWW.CSUS.EDU/CBAGRAD/INDEX.HTML

GENERAL INFORMATION

Type of School: Public **Environment:** Metropolis **Academic Calendar:** Semester

STUDENTS

Enrollment of Parent Institution: 28,375 **Enrollment of Business School:** 311 **% Male/female:** 56/44 **% Part-time:** 63 **% Minorities:** 49 **% International:** 10 **Average Age at Entry:** 30 **Average Years Work Experience at Entry:** 3

ACADEMICS

Student/faculty Ratio: 13:1 **% Female Faculty:** 28

Joint Degrees: Master of Business Administration and Juris Docotrate (MBA/JD)McGeorge School of Law, University of Pacific: Full-time; approx 4.5 years needed to complete combined program. **Prominent Alumni:** Dennis Gardemeyer, Executive Vice President/Zuckerman-Hertog; Tom Weborg, Chief Executive Officer/Cucina Holdings; William Keever, President/Vodafone Airtouch; Margo Murray, President, CEO/MMHA The Mangers' Mentors Inc.; Scott Syphax, President, CEO/Nehemiah Corporation.

FINANCIAL FACTS

Tuition (in-state/out-of-state): $3,310/$9,160 **Books and Supplies:** $1,700 **Room & Board (on/off campus):** $9,400/$8,400

ADMISSIONS

Admissions Selectivity Rating: 81

# of Applications Received: 247 **% Applicants Accepted:** 61 **% Acceptees Attending:** 66 **GMAT Range (25th to 75th percentile):** 420–750 **Average GMAT:** 575 **Average GPA:** 3.1 **TOEFL Required of Int'l Applicants:** Yes **Minimum TOEFL (paper/computer):** 550/213 **Application Fee:** $55 **International Application Fee:** $55

Regular Application Deadline: 4/1 **Regular Notification:** 5/30 **Transfer Students Accepted:** Yes **Non-fall Admissions:** Yes **Need-Blind Admissions:** Yes

CALIFORNIA STATE UNIVERSITY— STANISLAUS
GRADUATE SCHOOL OF BUSINESS

ADDRESS: MBA ADMISSIONS OFFICE, 801 MONTE VISTA AVE., TURLOCK, CA 95382
PHONE: (209) 667-3568 • FAX: (209) 667-3080
E-MAIL: MBAPROGRAM@CSUSTAN.EDU
WEBSITE: WWW.CSUSTAN.EDU/MBA/DEPT/INDEX.HTML

GENERAL INFORMATION
Type of School: Public

ADMISSIONS
Admissions Selectivity Rating: 60*
Regular Application Deadline: 6/30 **Regular Notification:** 6/30

CANISIUS COLLEGE
RICHARD J. WEHLE SCHOOL OF BUSINESS

ADMISSIONS CONTACT: LAURA MCEWEN, DIRECTOR, GRADUATE BUSINESS PROGRAMS
ADDRESS: CANISIUS COLLEGE, 2001 MAIN ST, BAGEN HALL 201, BUFFALO, NY 14208-1098
PHONE: 716-888-2140 • FAX: 716-888-2145
E-MAIL: GRADUBUS@CANISIUS.EDU
WEBSITE: WWW.CANISIUS.EDU/MBA

GENERAL INFORMATION
Type of School: Private **Affiliation:** Roman Catholic-Jesuit **Environment:** Metropolis **Academic Calendar:** Semester

STUDENTS
Enrollment of Parent Institution: 4,979 **Enrollment of Business School:** 261 **% Male/female:** 51/49 **% Part-time:** 74 **% Minorities:** 9 **% International:** 9 **Average Age at Entry:** 28

ACADEMICS
% Female Faculty: 13 **% Minority Faculty:** 8
Joint Degrees: Bachelor and MBA 5 years.

FINANCIAL FACTS
Tuition (in-state/out-of-state): $32,251/$32,251 **Books and Supplies:** $500 **Room & Board:** $8,300

ADMISSIONS
Admissions Selectivity Rating: 60*
GMAT Range (25th to 75th percentile): 410–550 **Average GMAT:** 474 **Average GPA: TOEFL Required of Int'l Applicants:** Yes **Minimum TOEFL (paper/computer):** 500/200 **Application Fee:** $25 **Regular Application Deadline:** rolling **Regular Notification:** rolling **Deferment Available:** Yes **Maximum Length of Deferment:** 1 year **Transfer Students Accepted:** Yes **Non-fall Admissions:** Yes **Applicants Also Look At:** State University of New York—University at Buffalo.

CENTRAL MICHIGAN UNIVERSITY
COLLEGE OF BUSINESS ADMINISTRATION

ADMISSIONS CONTACT: PAMELA STAMBERSKY, MBA ADVISOR
ADDRESS: 252 ABSC-GRAWN HALL, MOUNT PLEASANT, MI 48859
PHONE: 989-774-3150 • FAX: 989-774-1320
E-MAIL: MBA@CMICH.EDU
WEBSITE: WWW.CBA.CMICH.EDU

GENERAL INFORMATION
Type of School: Public **Environment:** Town **Academic Calendar:** Semester

STUDENTS
Enrollment of Parent Institution: 26,788 **Enrollment of Business School:** 118 **% Male/female:** 60/40 **% Out-of-state:** 20 **% Part-time:** 48 **% International:** 20 **Average Age at Entry:** 28 **Average Years Work Experience at Entry:** 3

ACADEMICS
Student/faculty Ratio: 23:1 **% Female Faculty:** 20 **% Minority Faculty:** 10

FINANCIAL FACTS
Tuition (in-state/out-of-state): $11,640/$25,000 **Books and Supplies:** $1,600 **Room & Board:** $7,236

ADMISSIONS
Admissions Selectivity Rating: 76
# of Applications Received: 116 **% Applicants Accepted:** 67 **% Acceptees Attending:** 76 **Average GMAT:** 530 **Average GPA:** 3.3 **TOEFL Required of Int'l Applicants:** Yes **Minimum TOEFL (paper/computer):** 550/213 **Application Fee:** $35 **International Application Fee:** $45
Regular Application Deadline: Rolling **Regular Notification:** Rolling **Deferment Available:** Yes **Maximum Length of Deferment:** one semester **Transfer Students Accepted:** Yes **Non-fall Admissions:** Yes

CLARION UNIVERSITY
COLLEGE OF BUSINESS ADMINISTRATION

ADMISSIONS CONTACT: DR. ROBERT S. BALOUGH, DIRECTOR OF MBA PROGRAM
ADDRESS: 302 STILL HALL, CLARION UNIVERSITY, CLARION, PA 16214
PHONE: 814-393-2605 • FAX: 814-393-1910
E-MAIL: MBA@CLARION.EDU
WEBSITE: WWW.CLARION.EDU/MBA

GENERAL INFORMATION
Type of School: Public **Environment:** Village **Academic Calendar:** Semester

STUDENTS
Enrollment of Parent Institution: 6,338 **Enrollment of Business School:** 36 **% Male/female:** 64/36 **% Out-of-state:** 8 **% Part-time:** 14 **% Minorities:** 6 **% International:** 31 **Average Age at Entry:** 23 **Average Years Work Experience at Entry:** 6.25

ACADEMICS

% Female Faculty: 18 **% Minority Faculty:** 23

FINANCIAL FACTS

Tuition (in-state/out-of-state): $5,888/$9,422 **Fees (in-state/out-of-state):** $1,778/$1,843 **Books and Supplies:** $3,650 **Room & Board (on/off campus):** $5,246/$4,000

ADMISSIONS

Admissions Selectivity Rating: 66

# of Applications Received: 36 **% Applicants Accepted:** 86 **% Acceptees Attending:** 65 **Average GMAT:** 489 **Average GPA:** 3.4 **TOEFL Required of Int'l Applicants:** Yes **Minimum TOEFL (paper/computer):** 550/213 **Application Fee:** $30 **International Application Fee:** $30

Regular Application Deadline: rolling **Regular Notification:** rolling **Deferment Available:** Yes **Maximum Length of Deferment:** 1 year **Transfer Students Accepted:** Yes **Non-fall Admissions:** Yes **Need-Blind Admissions:** Yes

CLARK ATLANTA UNIVERSITY
SCHOOL OF BUSINESS ADMINISTRATION

ADMISSIONS CONTACT: SARBETH J. FLEMING, DIRECTOR OF ADMISSIONS AND STUDENT AFFAIRS
ADDRESS: 223 JAMES P. BRAWLEY DRIVE, ATLANTA, GA 30314
PHONE: 404-880-8447 • FAX: 404-880-6159
E-MAIL: SFLEMING@CAU.EDU • WEBSITE: WWW.SBUS.CAU.EDU

GENERAL INFORMATION

Type of School: Private **Affiliation:** Methodist **Environment:** City **Academic Calendar:** Semester

STUDENTS

Enrollment of Parent Institution: 5,000 **Enrollment of Business School:** 120 **% Male/female:** 38/62 **% Part-time:** 10 **% Minorities:** 90 **% International:** 10 **Average Age at Entry:** 28 **Average Years Work Experience at Entry:** 5

ACADEMICS

Student/faculty Ratio: 11:1 **% Female Faculty:** 39 **% Minority Faculty:** 92

FINANCIAL FACTS

Tuition: $19,127 **Fees:** $550 **Books and Supplies:** $800 **Room & Board:** $4,875 **% of Students Receiving Aid:** 95 **% of First-year Students Receiving Aid:** 95 **% of Students Receiving Loans:** 95 **% of Students Receiving Grants:** 95 **Average Award Package:** $32,000 **Average Grant:** $32,000 **Average Student Loan Debt:** $65,000

ADMISSIONS

Admissions Selectivity Rating: 66

# of Applications Received: 134 **% Applicants Accepted:** 67 **% Acceptees Attending:** 69 **GMAT Range (25th to 75th percentile):** 340–520 **Average GMAT:** 430 **Average GPA:** 3.0 **TOEFL Required of Int'l Applicants:** Yes **Minimum TOEFL:** 175 **Application Fee:** $40 **International Application Fee:** $55

Regular Application Deadline: 4/1 **Regular Notification:** Rolling **Deferment Available:** Yes **Transfer Students Accepted:** Yes **Need-Blind Admissions: Applicants Also Look At:** Emory University, Georgia State University, Kennesaw State University.

EMPLOYMENT PROFILE

Primary Source of Full-time Job Acceptances

School-facilitated Activities 7 (25%)
Graduate-facilitated Activities 15 (50%)
Unknown..7 (25%)

Grads Employed by Industry: ......% avg. salary:

Finance 30 $82,000
Human Resources.........................7 $75,000
Marketing 52 $80,000
Operations......................................7 $75,000
Other...4 $50,000

Top 5 Employers Hiring Grads: Chevron/Texaco, Coca Cola, American Express, Union Pacific, Delta Airlines.

CLEVELAND STATE UNIVERSITY
JAMES J. NANCE COLLEGE OF BUSINESS ADMINISTRATION

ADMISSIONS CONTACT: BRUCE M. GOTTSCHALK, MBA PROGRAMS ADMINISTRATOR
ADDRESS: 2121 EUCLID AVENUE, BU 219, CLEVELAND, OH 44115
PHONE: 216-687-3730 • FAX: 216-687-5311
E-MAIL: CBACSU@CSUOHIO.EDU
WEBSITE: WWW.CSUOHIO.EDU/CBA/MBA

GENERAL INFORMATION

Type of School: Public **Environment:** City **Academic Calendar:** Semester

STUDENTS

Enrollment of Parent Institution: 15,450 **Enrollment of Business School:** 641 **% Male/female:** 60/40 **% Out-of-state:** 40 **% Part-time:** 78 **% Minorities:** 18 **% International:** 31 **Average Age at Entry:** 26 **Average Years Work Experience at Entry:** 5

ACADEMICS

Student/faculty Ratio: 27:1 **% Female Faculty:** 22 **% Minority Faculty:** 15

Joint Degrees: JD/MBA 4 years, MBA/MSN 3 years. **Prominent Alumni:** Monte Ahuja, Chairman,President& CEO, Transtar Industries; Michael Berthelot, Chairman& CEO Transtechnolgy Corporation; Ted Hlavaty, Chairman & CEO, Neway Stamping&Manufacturing; Thomas Moore, President, Wolf Group; Stephen F. Kirk, President, Lubrizol Additives.

FINANCIAL FACTS

Tuition (in-state/out-of-state): $10,536/$20,016 **Fees:** $50 **Books and Supplies:** $1,300 **Room & Board (on/off campus):** $10,000/$12,000 **% of Students Receiving Aid:** 4 **% of First-year**

Students Receiving Aid: 8 **% of Students Receiving Loans:** 55 **% of Students Receiving Grants:** 1 **Average Award Package:** $20,000

ADMISSIONS

Admissions Selectivity Rating: 71

# of Applications Received: 464 **% Applicants Accepted:** 72 **% Acceptees Attending:** 60 **GMAT Range (25th to 75th percentile):** 460–590 **Average GMAT:** 500 **Average GPA:** 3.1 **TOEFL Required of Int'l Applicants:** Yes **Minimum TOEFL (paper/computer):** 550/213 **Application Fee:** $30 **International Application Fee:** $30 **Regular Application Deadline:** 7/1 **Regular Notification:** rolling **Deferment Available:** Yes **Maximum Length of Deferment:** 12 months **Transfer Students Accepted:** Yes **Non-fall Admissions:** Yes **Need-Blind Admissions:** Yes **Applicants Also Look At:** Case Western Reserve University, John Carroll University, Kent State University, The University of Akron, University of Phoenix.

EMPLOYMENT PROFILE

Primary Source of Full-time Job Acceptances

School-facilitated Activities 30 (46%)
Graduate-facilitated Activities 15 (23%)
Unknown...20 (31%)
Percent Employed 15

Grads Employed by Industry:.......% avg. salary:

Finance 21 $61,300
Human Resources..........................4 $54,000
Marketing 9 $63,400
MIS 6 $65,200
Operations.....................................18 $61,700
Consulting......................................1 $57,000
General Management 3 $64,000
Other..3 $53,000

Top 5 Employers Hiring Grads: Progressive Insurance, National City Bank, Key Bank, AmTrust Bank, Sherwin Williams.

COASTAL CAROLINA UNIVERSITY
WALL COLLEGE OF BUSINESS

ADMISSIONS CONTACT: DR. RICHARD L. JOHNSON, ASSOCIATE PROVOST FOR GRADUATE STUDIES
ADDRESS: P. O. BOX 261954, CONWAY, SC 29528-6054
PHONE: 843-349-2192
E-MAIL: ADMISSIONS@COASTAL.EDU
WEBSITE: WWW.COASTAL.EDU/BUSINESS

GENERAL INFORMATION

Type of School: Public

STUDENTS

Enrollment of Parent Institution: 7,872 **Enrollment of Business School:** 52 **% Male/female:** 61/39 **% Out-of-state:** 30 **% Part-time:** 56 **% Minorities:** 17 **% International:** 13 **Average Age at Entry:** 27 **Average Years Work Experience at Entry:** 5

ACADEMICS

% Female Faculty: 44 **% Minority Faculty:** 11

FINANCIAL FACTS

Tuition (in-state/out-of-state): $9,624/$10,488 **Fees:** $80 **Books and Supplies:** $2,790 **Room & Board:** $7,412 **% of Students Receiving Aid:** 61 **% of First-year Students Receiving Aid:** 56 **% of Students Receiving Loans:** 52 **Average Award Package:** $18,166

ADMISSIONS

Admissions Selectivity Rating: 60*

GMAT Range (25th to 75th percentile): 490–580 **Average GMAT:** 539 **Average GPA:** 3.6 **TOEFL Required of Int'l Applicants:** Yes **Minimum TOEFL:** 575 **Application Fee:** $45 **International Application Fee:** $45 **Regular Application Deadline:** rolling **Regular Notification:** rolling **Transfer Students Accepted:** Yes **Non-fall Admissions:** Yes **Need-Blind Admissions:** Yes **Applicants Also Look At:** Clemson University, University of South Carolina, Winthrop University.

COLORADO STATE UNIVERSITY— PUEBLO
MALIK & SEEME HASAN SCHOOL OF BUSINESS

ADMISSIONS CONTACT: JON VALDEZ, OFFICE MANAGER
ADDRESS: 2200 BONFORTE BOULEVARD, PUEBLO, CO 81001
PHONE: 719-549-2461 • FAX: 719-549-2419
WEBSITE: HSB.COLOSTATE-PUEBLO.EDU

GENERAL INFORMATION

Type of School: Public

STUDENTS

Enrollment of Business School: 95 **% Male/female:** 58/42 **% Out-of-state:** 61 **% Part-time:** 20 **% Minorities:** 39 **% International:** 61 **Average Age at Entry:** 26 **Average Years Work Experience at Entry:** 5

ACADEMICS

Student/faculty Ratio: 7:1 **% Female Faculty:** 20 **% Minority Faculty:** 53

ADMISSIONS

Admissions Selectivity Rating: 63

# of Applications Received: 47 **% Applicants Accepted:** 100 **% Acceptees Attending:** 96 **Average GMAT:** 460 **Average GPA:** 3.2 **TOEFL Required of Int'l Applicants:** Yes **Application Fee:** $35 **Deferment Available:** Yes **Maximum Length of Deferment:** 1 year **Transfer Students Accepted:** Yes **Non-fall Admissions:** Yes **Applicants Also Look At:** University of Colorado—Colorado Springs.

COLUMBUS STATE UNIVERSITY
D. ABBOTT TURNER COLLEGE OF BUSINESS

ADMISSIONS CONTACT: MS. KATIE THORNTON, GRADUATE ADMISSIONS
ADDRESS: 4225 UNIVERSITY AVE, COLUMBUS, GA 31907
PHONE: 706-568-2035 • FAX: 706-568-5091
E-MAIL: ADMISSIONS@COLSTATE.EDU
WEBSITE: DATCOB.COLSTATE.EDU

GENERAL INFORMATION
Type of School: Public **Academic Calendar:** Semester

STUDENTS
Enrollment of Parent Institution: Enrollment of Business School:
48 **% Male/female:** 33/67 **% Minorities:** 56

ACADEMICS
Student/faculty Ratio: 12:1

FINANCIAL FACTS
Tuition (in-state/out-of-state): $3,500/$14,000 **Fees:** $876 **Books and Supplies:** $1,000 **Average Grant:** $3,000

ADMISSIONS
Admissions Selectivity Rating: 86
# of Applications Received: 33 **% Applicants Accepted:** 36 **%
Acceptees Attending:** 100 **Average GMAT:** 500 **Average GPA:** 3.4
TOEFL Required of Int'l Applicants: Yes **Minimum TOEFL
(paper/computer):** 550/213 **Application Fee:** $25 **International
Application Fee:** $25
Regular Application Deadline: 7/20 **Regular Notification:** Rolling
Transfer Students Accepted: Yes **Non-fall Admissions:** Yes **Need-Blind Admissions:** Yes

CRANFIELD UNIVERSITY
CRANFIELD SCHOOL OF MANAGEMENT

ADMISSIONS CONTACT: EILEEN FISHER, ADMISSIONS EXECUTIVE
ADDRESS: CRANFIELD SCHOOL OF MANAGEMENT, CRANFIELD, BEDFORD, MK43
   0AL ENGLAND
PHONE: 0044-1234-754431 • FAX: 0044-1234-752439
E-MAIL: MBAADMISSIONS@CRANFIELD.AC.UK
WEBSITE: WWW.CRANFIELDMBA.INFO

GENERAL INFORMATION
Type of School: Public **Academic Calendar:** Year Long

STUDENTS
Enrollment of Business School: 233 **% Male/female:** 77/23 **% Part-time:** 45 **% International:** 84 **Average Age at Entry:** 31 **Average Years Work Experience at Entry:** 8

ACADEMICS
Student/faculty Ratio: 2:1 **% Female Faculty:** 25
Prominent Alumni: Ted Tuppen, CEO Enterprise Inns; Nigel Doughty, CEO Doughty Hanson; John McFarlane, CEO ANZ Banking Grp; Andy

Bond, Chief Executive, Asda; Michael Wemms, Chairman House of Fraser.

FINANCIAL FACTS
Tuition: $52,555 **Books and Supplies:** $1,100 **Room & Board:**
$10,500 **% of Students Receiving Aid:** 78 **% of First-year Students
Receiving Aid:** 78 **% of Students Receiving Grants:** 78 **Average
Grant:** $19,000

ADMISSIONS
Admissions Selectivity Rating: 89
# of Applications Received: 462 **% Applicants Accepted:** 48 **%
Acceptees Attending:** 59 **GMAT Range (25th to 75th percentile):**
620–680 **Average GMAT:** 660 **Average GPA: TOEFL Required of Int'l
Applicants:** Yes **Minimum TOEFL (paper/computer):** 600/250
Application Fee: $0 **International Application Fee:** $0
Regular Application Deadline: Rolling **Regular Notification:** Rolling
Deferment Available: Yes **Maximum Length of Deferment:** 2 years
Need-Blind Admissions: Yes **Applicants Also Look At:** IESE
Business School, Instituto de Empresa, University of Cambridge,
University of Oxford, University of Warwick.

EMPLOYMENT PROFILE
Primary Source of Full-time Job Acceptances

School-facilitated Activities	31 (49%)
Graduate-facilitated Activities	31 (49%)
Unknown	2 (2%)
Average base starting salary	$111,400
Percent Employed	97
Grads Employed by Industry:	**% avg. salary:**
Finance	5 $119,600
Human Resources	5 $199,400
Marketing	18 $121,800
MIS	3 $119,600
Operations	13 $137,600
Strategic Planning	3 $215,300
Consulting	15 $137,600
General Management	8 $149,500
Other	30 $98,500

Top 5 Employers Hiring Grads: Arcelor Mittal Steels, American
Express, Johnson & Johnson, HBOS, UBS.

CREIGHTON UNIVERSITY
COLLEGE OF BUSINESS ADMINISTRATION

ADMISSIONS CONTACT: GAIL HAFER, COORDINATOR OF GRADUATE BUSINESS
   PROGRAMS
ADDRESS: COLLEGE OF BUSINESS ADMINISTRATION, ROOM 212C, 2500
   CALIFORNIA PLAZA, OMAHA, NE 68178
PHONE: 402-280-2853 • FAX: 402-280-2172
E-MAIL: COBAGRAD@CREIGHTON.EDU
WEBSITE: COBWEB.CREIGHTON.EDU

GENERAL INFORMATION

Type of School: Private **Affiliation:** Roman Catholic **Environment:** Metropolis

STUDENTS

Enrollment of Parent Institution: 6,723 **Enrollment of Business School:** 118 **% Male/female:** 58/42 **% Part-time:** 84 **% Minorities:** 1 **% International:** 31 **Average Age at Entry:** 25 **Average Years Work Experience at Entry:** 3

ACADEMICS

Student/faculty Ratio: 2:1 **% Female Faculty:** 10

Joint Degrees: Master of Business Administration/Juris Doctor (3 years); Master of Business Administration/Doctor of Pharmacy (4 years; Master of Business Administration/Master of International Relations (3 years); Master of Business Administration/Master of Science-Information Technology Management with emphasis in Digital Business/Juris Doctor(3 years).

FINANCIAL FACTS

Tuition: $10,206 **Fees:** $764 **Books and Supplies:** $1,600 **Room & Board (on/off campus):** $7,000/$6,000 **% of Students Receiving Aid:** 15 **% of First-year Students Receiving Aid:** 8 **Average Award Package:** $19,653

ADMISSIONS

Admissions Selectivity Rating: 72

# of Applications Received: 24 **% Applicants Accepted:** 96 **% Acceptees Attending:** 78 **Average GMAT:** 570 **Average GPA:** 3.4 **TOEFL Required of Int'l Applicants:** Yes **Minimum TOEFL (paper/computer):** 550/213 **Application Fee:** $40 **International Application Fee:** $40

Regular Application Deadline: Rolling **Regular Notification:** Rolling **Deferment Available:** Yes **Maximum Length of Deferment:** 1 year **Transfer Students Accepted:** Yes **Non-fall Admissions:** Yes **Applicants Also Look At:** University of Nebraska—Omaha.

DePaul University
Kellstadt Graduate School of Business

Admissions Contact: Robert Ryan, Assistant Dean
Address: 1 East Jackson Blvd, Suite 7900, Chicago, IL 60604
Phone: 312-362-8810 • Fax: 312-362-6677
E-mail: kgsb@depaul.edu
Website: www.kellstadt.depaul.edu

GENERAL INFORMATION

Type of School: Private **Affiliation:** Roman Catholic **Environment:** Metropolis **Academic Calendar:** Quarters

STUDENTS

Enrollment of Parent Institution: 23,148 **Enrollment of Business School:** 1,682 **% Male/female:** 74/26 **% Part-time:** 97 **% Minorities:** 8 **% International:** 18 **Average Age at Entry:** 28 **Average Years Work Experience at Entry:** 5.1

ACADEMICS

Student/faculty Ratio: 11:1 **% Female Faculty:** 24 **% Minority Faculty:** 23

Joint Degrees: MBA/JD 2.8 years. **Prominent Alumni:** Jim Jenness, CEO, Kellogg's; Richard Driehaus, President, Driehaus Capital Management; Edward Bosowski, President, USG Corporation; Daniel Ustian, Chairman, President and CEO, Navistar Internationa.

FINANCIAL FACTS

Tuition (in-state/out-of-state): $36,920 **Fees:** $200 **Books and Supplies:** $1,300 **Room & Board (on/off campus):** $12,316/$10,800 **Average Award Package:** $21,120 **Average Grant:** $16,080 **Average Student Loan Debt:** $46,005

ADMISSIONS

Admissions Selectivity Rating: 71

# of Applications Received: 750 **% Applicants Accepted:** 84 **% Acceptees Attending:** 58 **GMAT Range (25th to 75th percentile):** 452–640 **Average GMAT:** 547 **Average GPA:** 3.1 **TOEFL Required of Int'l Applicants:** Yes **Minimum TOEFL (paper/computer):** 550/213 **Application Fee:** $60 **International Application Fee:** $60

Regular Application Deadline: 7/1 **Regular Notification:** Rolling **Deferment Available:** Yes **Maximum Length of Deferment:** One year **Transfer Students Accepted:** Yes **Non-fall Admissions:** Yes **Need-Blind Admissions:** Yes **Applicants Also Look At:** Loyola University—Chicago, Northwestern University, The University of Chicago.

EMPLOYMENT PROFILE

Primary Source of Full-time Job Acceptances

School-facilitated Activities 9 (50%)
Graduate-facilitated Activities 9 (50%)
Average base starting salary $63,000

Grads Employed by Industry: ......% avg. salary:

Finance 12 $74,833
Marketing 2 $72,500
Consulting......................................1 $93,000
General Management 1 $83,000

Top 5 Employers Hiring Grads: Lehman Brothers, Grant Thornton, Motorola, Northern Trust, Morningstar.

Drake University
College of Business and Public Administration

Admissions Contact: Danette Kenne, Director of Graduate Programs
Address: 2507 University Avenue, Aliber Hall, Suite 211, Des Moines, IA 50311
Phone: 515-271-2188 • Fax: 515-271-2187
E-mail: cbpa.gradprograms@drake.edu
Website: www.cbpa.drake.edu/aspx/Programs/ProgramDetail.aspx?id=6

GENERAL INFORMATION

Type of School: Private **Environment:** Metropolis **Academic Calendar:** Semester

STUDENTS

Enrollment of Parent Institution: 5,617 **Enrollment of Business School:** 167 **% Male/female:** 20/80 **% Part-time:** 97 **Average Age at Entry:** 28

ACADEMICS

Student/faculty Ratio: 19:1 **% Female Faculty:** 19 **% Minority Faculty:** 5

Joint Degrees: MBA/Pharm D 6 years, MBA/JD 3 years, MPA/JD 3 years, MPA/Pharm D 6 years. **Prominent Alumni:** Robert D, Ray, Former Governor State of Iowa; Sherrill Milnes, Opera; Daniel Jorndt, Former Chairman/CEO Walgreen's; Dwight Opperman, Former CEO of West Publishing; Marie Wilson, President of MS Foundation for Women.

FINANCIAL FACTS

Tuition: $9,400 **Fees:** $412 **Books and Supplies:** $800 **Room & Board:** $7,350

ADMISSIONS

Admissions Selectivity Rating: 60*

# of Applications Received: 98 **% Applicants Accepted:** 61 % **Acceptees Attending:** 65 **TOEFL Required of Int'l Applicants:** Yes **Minimum TOEFL (paper/computer):** 550/213 **Application Fee:** $25 **International Application Fee:** $25

Regular Application Deadline: 7/6 **Regular Notification:** Rolling **Deferment Available:** Yes **Maximum Length of Deferment:** one term **Transfer Students Accepted:** Yes **Non-fall Admissions:** Yes **Need-Blind Admissions:** Yes **Applicants Also Look At:** Iowa State University, University of Iowa.

EASTERN ILLINOIS UNIVERSITY
LUMPKIN COLLEGE OF BUSINESS AND APPLIED SCIENCES

ADMISSIONS CONTACT: DR. CHERYL NOLL, COORDINATOR, GRADUATE BUSINESS STUDIES
ADDRESS: 600 LINCOLN AVENUE, 4025 LUMPKIN HALL, CHARLESTON, IL 61920-3099
PHONE: 217-581-3028 • FAX: 217-581-6642
E-MAIL: MBA@EIU.EDU
WEBSITE: WWW.EIU.EDU/~MBA

GENERAL INFORMATION

Type of School: Public **Environment:** Village **Academic Calendar:** Fall, Spring, Summer

STUDENTS

Enrollment of Parent Institution: 12,000 **Enrollment of Business School:** 113 **% Male/female:** 50/50 **% Out-of-state:** 4 **% Part-time:** 56 **% Minorities:** 8 **% International:** 6 **Average Age at Entry:** 26 **Average Years Work Experience at Entry:** 4

ACADEMICS

Student/faculty Ratio: 22:1 **% Female Faculty:** 24 **% Minority Faculty:** 20

FINANCIAL FACTS

Tuition (in-state/out-of-state): $6,262/$18,785 **Fees:** $2,363 **Books and Supplies:** $325 **Room & Board (on/off campus):** $7,000/$8,000 **% of Students Receiving Aid:** 19 **% of First-year Students Receiving Aid:** 36 **% of Students Receiving Grants:** 19 **Average Grant:** $7,000

ADMISSIONS

Admissions Selectivity Rating: 73

# of Applications Received: 70 **% Applicants Accepted:** 94 % **Acceptees Attending:** 88 **GMAT Range (25th to 75th percentile):** 450–570 **Average GMAT:** 510 **Average GPA:** 3.4 **TOEFL Required of Int'l Applicants:** Yes **Minimum TOEFL (paper/computer):** 500/173 **Application Fee:** $30 **International Application Fee:** $30

Regular Application Deadline: rolling **Regular Notification:** rolling **Deferment Available:** Yes **Maximum Length of Deferment:** 1 year **Transfer Students Accepted:** Yes **Non-fall Admissions:** Yes **Need-Blind Admissions:** Yes

EASTERN KENTUCKY UNIVERSITY

ADDRESS: COATES CPO 5-A, 521 LANCASTER AVENUE, RICHMOND, KY 40475
PHONE: (859) 622-1742 • FAX:
E-MAIL: GRADUATESCHOOL@EKU.EDU
WEBSITE: WWW.GRADSCHOOL.EKU.EDU/

GENERAL INFORMATION

Type of School: Public **Academic Calendar:** Semester Schedule:

STUDENTS

Enrollment of Parent Institution: 15,763 **Enrollment of Business School:** 67 **% Male/female:** 50/50 **% Part-time:** 91

ACADEMICS

Student/faculty Ratio: 7:1 **% Female Faculty:** 32 **% Minority Faculty:** 5

Prominent Alumni: Howard Thompson, Dean, College of Business, Eastern KY University; Steve Pence, Lt. Gov., State of Kentucky.

FINANCIAL FACTS

Tuition (in-state/out-of-state): $5,610/$15,910 **Books and Supplies:** $750 **Room & Board:** $5,000

ADMISSIONS

Admissions Selectivity Rating: 69

# of Applications Received: 31 **% Applicants Accepted:** 87 % **Acceptees Attending:** 93 **GMAT Range (25th to 75th percentile):** 450–540 **Average GMAT:** 504 **Average GPA:** 3.3 **TOEFL Required of Int'l Applicants:** Yes **Minimum TOEFL (paper/computer):** 550/213 **Application Fee:** $35 **International Application Fee:** $35

Regular Application Deadline: 7/9 **Deferment Available:** Yes **Maximum Length of Deferment:** 5 years **Transfer Students Accepted:** Yes **Non-fall Admissions:** Yes

EDHEC BUSINESS SCHOOL
THESEUS-EDHEC MBA

ADMISSIONS CONTACT: MAUREEN BYRNE, ADMISSIONS MANAGER
ADDRESS: CAMPUS LILLE, 58 RUE DU PORT, LILLE, 59046 FRANCE
PHONE: 011-33 3 2015 4465 • FAX: 011-33 3 2015 4841
E-MAIL: MAUREEN.BYRNE@EDHEC.EDU
WEBSITE: WWW.THESEUS-MBA.COM

GENERAL INFORMATION
Type of School: Private

STUDENTS
Enrollment of Business School: 17 **% Male/female:** 83/17 **%**
International: 72 **Average Age at Entry:** 34 **Average Years Work**
Experience at Entry: 7

FINANCIAL FACTS
Tuition: $27,000 **Room & Board:** $700

ADMISSIONS
Admissions Selectivity Rating: 68
# of Applications Received: 17 **% Applicants Accepted:** 100 **%**
Acceptees Attending: 100 **Average GMAT:** 600
Regular Application Deadline: 5/31 Application
Deadline/Notification Round 1: Dec./Jan Round 2: Feb./Mar. Round
3: Apr./May Round 4: May/Jun.

EM LYON (FRANCE)
EM LYON

ADMISSIONS CONTACT: CHRISTÈLE FERNAND, HEAD OF DEVELOPMENT &
RECRUITMENT
ADDRESS: 23, AV. GUY DE COLLONGUE, ECULLY, 69134 FRANCE
PHONE: 0033 4 78 33 77 83 • FAX: 0033 4 78 33 61 69
E-MAIL: IMBA@EM-LYON.COM
WEBSITE: WWW.EM-LYON.COM

GENERAL INFORMATION
Type of School: Private

STUDENTS
Enrollment of Parent Institution: 2,800 **Enrollment of Business**
School: 112 **% Male/female:** 70/30 **% Part-time:** 71 **%**
International: 65 **Average Age at Entry:** 33 **Average Years Work**
Experience at Entry: 8

ACADEMICS
Student/faculty Ratio: 3:1 **% Female Faculty:** 28
Joint Degrees: Prominent Alumni: Jean Pascal Tricoire, President,
Schneider Electric; Didier Barret, President Merck Generique;
Christian Seux, CEO, Becton Dickinson.

FINANCIAL FACTS
Tuition: $32,837 **Room & Board:** $10,500

ADMISSIONS
Admissions Selectivity Rating: 85
# of Applications Received: 95 **% Applicants Accepted:** 51 **%**
Acceptees Attending: 67 **Average GMAT:** 610 **TOEFL Required of**
Int'l Applicants: Yes **Minimum TOEFL:** 240 **Application Fee:** $131
International Application Fee: $131
Application Deadline/Notification: Round 1: 01/15, Round 2: 02/19,
Round 3: 04/02, Round 4: 05/07
Deferment Available: Yes **Maximum Length of Deferment:** 1 year
Transfer Students Accepted: Yes **Need-Blind Admissions:** Yes
Applicants Also Look At: HEC School of Management-Paris, IMD,
RSM Erasmus University.

EMPORIA STATE UNIVERSITY
SCHOOL OF BUSINESS

ADMISSIONS CONTACT: MARY SEWELL, GRADUATE ADMISSIONS COORDINATOR
ADDRESS: EMPORIA STATE UNIVERSITY, CAMPUS BOX 4003, 1200
COMMERCIAL STREET, EMPORIA, KS 66801
PHONE: 620-341-5403 • FAX: 620-341-5909
E-MAIL: GRADINFO@EMPORIA.EDU
WEBSITE: WWW.EMPORIA.EDU

GENERAL INFORMATION
Type of School: Public

STUDENTS
Enrollment of Parent Institution: 6,473 **Enrollment of Business**
School: 117 **% Male/female:** 52/48 **% Out-of-state:** 2 **% Part-time:**
22 **% Minorities:** 1 **% International:** 52 **Average Age at Entry:** 26

ACADEMICS
Student/faculty Ratio: 5:1 **% Female Faculty:** 5 **% Minority Faculty:**
19
Prominent Alumni: Donna Jacobs, VP, Nuclear Services, Diablo
Corporation; Shawn Keough, Ph.D., Professor, University of Texas—
Tyler.

FINANCIAL FACTS
Tuition (in-state/out-of-state): $4,554/$12,186 **Fees:** $786 **Books**
and Supplies: $720 **Room & Board:** $6,260 **Average Grant:** $6,887

ADMISSIONS
Admissions Selectivity Rating: 61
# of Applications Received: 24 **% Applicants Accepted:** 183 **%**
Acceptees Attending: 77 **GMAT Range (25th to 75th percentile):**
440–550 **Average GMAT:** 498 **Average GPA:** 3.3 **TOEFL Required of**
Int'l Applicants: Yes **Minimum TOEFL (paper/computer):** 550/213
Application Fee: $40 **International Application Fee:** $75
Regular Application Deadline: Rolling **Deferment Available:** Yes
Maximum Length of Deferment: Contingent **Transfer Students**
Accepted: Yes **Non-fall Admissions:** Yes **Need-Blind Admissions:**
Yes **Applicants Also Look At:** Institute of Undergraduate Business
Studies.

EMPLOYMENT PROFILE

Primary Source of Full-time Job Acceptances

Percent Employed 53

Grads Employed by Industry: ....% avg. salary:

Finance 71

General Management 7

Other..21

Top 5 Employers Hiring Grads: Cabellas, Grant Thornton, Wendling Noe Nelson & Johnson, CPA, Hopkins Manufacturing, CCH.

ESCP-EAP European School of Management
ESCP-EAP Paris London Madrid Berlin Torino

Admissions Contact: Francyne Marcar, UK Marketing Communications Manager
Address: 527, Finchley Road, Hampstead, London, NW3 7BG England
Phone: 011-44-207-443-88-73 • Fax: 011-44-207-443-88-74
E-mail: ukadmission@escp-eap.net
Website: www.escp-eap.net

GENERAL INFORMATION

Type of School: Private **Academic Calendar:** September

STUDENTS

Enrollment of Parent Institution: 3,300 **Enrollment of Business School:** 229 **% Male/female:** 45/55 **% International:** 86 **Average Age at Entry:** 25 **Average Years Work Experience at Entry:** 1

ACADEMICS

Student/faculty Ratio: 20:1 **% Female Faculty:** 25

Joint Degrees: Prominent Alumni: Jean Pierre Raffarin, Former Prime Minister/France; Hei Sturtz, President Cap Gemini Ernst & Young; Ignacio Garcia Alves, President Arhur D.Little; Werner Josef Lübberink, Director Deutsche Bahn; Antoine Riboud, Danone.

FINANCIAL FACTS

Tuition: $15,000 **Books and Supplies:** $1,000 **Room & Board:** $10,000

ADMISSIONS

Admissions Selectivity Rating: 60*

# of Applications Received: 523 **% Applicants Accepted:** 62 **% Acceptees Attending:** 70 **Application Fee:** $200 **International Application Fee:** $200

Application Deadline/Notification: Round 1: 03/01 / 05/01; Round 2: 05/01 / 06/01; Round 3: 06/05 / 07/01.

Deferment Available: Yes **Maximum Length of Deferment:** 1 year **Need-Blind Admissions:** Yes

EMPLOYMENT PROFILE

Primary Source of Full-time Job Acceptances

School-facilitated Activities 45 (20%)

Graduate-facilitated Activities 75 (34%)

Unknown..103 (46%)

Percent Employed 13

Grads Employed by Industry: ....% avg. salary:

Finance 17 $66,000

Marketing 45 $55,000

Consulting......................................19 $60,000

Other..19 $52,000

Top 5 Employers Hiring Grads: L'Oréal, Société Générale, PSA Peugeot Citroën, BNP Pariba, Cap Gemini.

Fairleigh Dickinson University—College at Florham
Silberman College of Business

Admissions Contact: Susan Brooman, Director of Graduate Recruitment & Marketing
Address: 285 Madison Avenue (M-MS1-03), Madison, NJ 07940
Phone: 973-443-8905 • Fax: 973-443-8088
E-mail: grad@fdu.edu
Website: www.fdu.edu

GENERAL INFORMATION

Type of School: Private

STUDENTS

Enrollment of Parent Institution: 12,186 **Enrollment of Business School:** 432 **% Male/female:** 50/50 **% Out-of-state:** 11 **% Part-time:** 76 **% Minorities:** 17 **% International:** 16 **Average Age at Entry:** 29

ACADEMICS

Student/faculty Ratio: 20:1 **% Female Faculty:** 18 **% Minority Faculty:** 25

Joint Degrees: MBA in Management/MA in Corporate and Organizational Communications, 72 credit program. MBA in Human Resource Management/MA in Industrial/Organizational Psychology.

Prominent Alumni: Cheryl Beebe, VP & CFO, Corn Products International, Inc.; Dennis Strigl, President & COO, Verizon Communications; Robert Huth, President & CEO, David's Bridal; Joseph Mahady, President, Wyeth Pharmaceuticals; John Legere, CEO, Global Crossing Ltd.

FINANCIAL FACTS

Tuition: $15,102 **Fees:** $608 **Books and Supplies:** $2,000 **Room & Board:** $13,268 **% of Students Receiving Aid:** 63 **% of Students Receiving Loans:** 33 **% of Students Receiving Grants:** 17 **Average Award Package:** $3,500 **Average Grant:** $3,250

ADMISSIONS

Admissions Selectivity Rating: 75

# of Applications Received: 191 **% Applicants Accepted:** 69 %
Average GMAT: 525 **Average GPA:** 3.5 **TOEFL Required of Int'l
Applicants:** Yes **Minimum TOEFL (paper/computer):** 550/213
Application Fee: $40 **International Application Fee:** $40
Regular Application Deadline: rolling **Regular Notification:** rolling
Deferment Available: Yes **Transfer Students Accepted:** Yes **Non-fall
Admissions:** Yes **Need-Blind Admissions:** Yes

EMPLOYMENT PROFILE

Top 5 Employers Hiring Grads: Verizon, M & M Mars, IBM, Deloitte,
Price Waterhouse

FU JEN CATHOLIC UNIVERSITY
COLLEGE OF MANAGEMENT

ADMISSIONS CONTACT: PEI-GI SHU, ASSOCIATE DEAN
ADDRESS: NO. 510, CHUNG-CHENG RD., HSINGCHUANG, TAIPEI HSIEN, 24205
TAIWAN
PHONE: 011-886-2-2905-2613 • FAX: 011-886-2-2905-2186
E-MAIL: CLARE@MAILS.FJU.EDU.TW
WEBSITE: WWW.MANAGEMENT.FJU.EDU.TW

GENERAL INFORMATION

Type of School: Private **Affiliation:** Roman Catholic/Jesuit

STUDENTS

Enrollment of Business School: 116 **% Male/female:** 60/40 **% Out-
of-state:** 1 **% Part-time:** 40 **% International:** 1 **Average Age at
Entry:** 30 **Average Years Work Experience at Entry:** 2

ACADEMICS

% Female Faculty: 45

Prominent Alumni: Yi-Jeng Peng, V.P./ Bank of Overseas Chinese;
Wan-Li Wang, V.P./ CFSB; Wen-Zong Shu, General Manager/ Home
Box; Ying-Chung Lyu, Senior V.P.; Yen-Mu Chen, President/ Furniture
Company.

FINANCIAL FACTS

Tuition: $4,063 **Books and Supplies:** $625 **% of Students Receiving
Aid:** 25 **% of First-year Students Receiving Aid:** 10 **% of Students
Receiving Grants:** 12

ADMISSIONS

Admissions Selectivity Rating: 99

# of Applications Received: 2,497 **% Applicants Accepted:** 5 %
Acceptees Attending: 98 **Average GPA:** 3 **Application Fee:** $65
Regular Application Deadline: 3/5

EMPLOYMENT PROFILE

Primary Source of Full-time Job Acceptances

Graduate-facilitated Activities 2 (9%)
Unknown..21 (91%)
Average base starting salary $1,180
Percent Employed 85

Grads Employed by Industry:	.... %	avg. salary:
Finance	13	$1,250
Human Resources	9	$1,000
Marketing	48	$1,250
MIS	9	$1,100
General Management	17	$1,100
Other	4	$1,200

GEORGE MASON UNIVERSITY
SCHOOL OF MANAGEMENT

ADMISSIONS CONTACT: ANGEL BURGOS, MBA DIRECTOR
ADDRESS: 4400 UNIVERSITY DRIVE, MSN 5A2, ENTERPRISE HALL, ROOM 28,
FAIRFAX, VA 22030
PHONE: 703-993-2136 • FAX: 703-993-1778
E-MAIL: MBA@GMU.EDU
WEBSITE: WWW.SOM.GMU.EDU

GENERAL INFORMATION

Type of School: Public **Environment:** City **Academic Calendar:**
Semester

STUDENTS

Enrollment of Parent Institution: 30,332 **Enrollment of Business
School:** 319 **% Part-time:** 86 **% International:** 56 **Average Years
Work Experience at Entry:** 7

ACADEMICS

Prominent Alumni: Michael G. Anzilotti, MBA '83, President/CEO
First Virginia Bank; William Page Johnson II, BS Finance '88, The
Commissioner for Revenue, City of Fairfax, VA; Terri Malone,
MBA'05, Washington NatL Opera Singer/Northrop Grumman Exec;
Bill Hey, MBA'76, Natl. Pres/The American Society of Civil Engineers;
Walter Howell, MBA'84, Sr.VP /Computer Associates International,
Inc.

FINANCIAL FACTS

Tuition (in-state/out-of-state): $13,320/$23,640 **Fees:** $0 **Books
and Supplies:** $1,000

ADMISSIONS

Admissions Selectivity Rating: 83

# of Applications Received: 269 **% Applicants Accepted:** 59 %
Acceptees Attending: 65 **Average GMAT:** 588 **Average GPA:** 3.2
TOEFL Required of Int'l Applicants: Yes **Minimum TOEFL
(paper/computer):** 650/250 **Application Fee:** $60
Regular Application Deadline: 4/1 **Regular Notification:** 5/15
Application Deadline/Notification Round 1: 04/01 / 05/15 Round 2:
05/15 / 06/30
Deferment Available: Yes **Maximum Length of Deferment:** 1
semester **Non-fall Admissions:** Yes **Need-Blind Admissions:** Yes

GEORGIA COLLEGE & STATE UNIVERSITY
THE J. WHITNEY BUNTING SCHOOL OF BUSINESS

ADMISSIONS CONTACT: MARYLLIS WOLFGANG, DIRECTOR OF GRADUATE ADMISSIONS
ADDRESS: GC&SU CAMPUS BOX 107, MILLEDGEVILLE, GA 31061
PHONE: 478-445-6289 • FAX: 478-445-1336
E-MAIL: MARYLLIS.WOLFGANG@GCSU.EDU
WEBSITE: WWW.GCSU.EDU

GENERAL INFORMATION
Type of School: Public **Environment:** Town **Academic Calendar:** Semester

STUDENTS
Enrollment of Business School: 135 **Average Age at Entry:** 26

ACADEMICS
Student/faculty Ratio: 17:1 **% Female Faculty:** 36 **% Minority Faculty:** 26
Prominent Alumni: Tony Nicely, GEICO President and CEO; Alex Gregory, YKK Corporation of America President and CEO; Mike Garrett, Georgia Power Company President and CEO.

FINANCIAL FACTS
Tuition (in-state/out-of-state): $5,812/$13,365 **Fees:** $858 **Books and Supplies:** $700 **Room & Board (on/off campus):** $6,282/$6,850 **Average Award Package:** $7,005 **Average Grant:** $2,336

ADMISSIONS
Admissions Selectivity Rating: 79
# of Applications Received: 108 **% Applicants Accepted:** 53 **% Acceptees Attending:** 91 **GMAT Range (25th to 75th percentile):** 430–510 **Average GMAT:** 500 **Average GPA:** 3.3 **TOEFL Required of Int'l Applicants:** Yes **Minimum TOEFL (paper/computer):** 500/173 **Application Fee:** $35 **International Application Fee:** $0
Regular Application Deadline: Rolling **Regular Notification:** Rolling
Deferment Available: Yes **Maximum Length of Deferment:** One year
Transfer Students Accepted: Yes **Non-fall Admissions:** Yes

GRENOBLE ECOLE DE MANAGEMENT (FRANCE)
GRENOBLE GRADUATE SCHOOL OF BUSINESS

ADMISSIONS CONTACT: MS ELIZABETH GORRILLA, MARKETING AND ADMISSIONS MANAGER
ADDRESS: 12 RUE PIERRE SÉMARD, BP 127, GRENOBLE, 38003 FRANCE
PHONE: 011 +33 (0)4 76 70 62 31 • FAX: 011 +33 (0)4 76 70 61 77
E-MAIL: ELIZABETH.GORRILLA@GGSB.COM
WEBSITE: WWW.GGSB.COM

GENERAL INFORMATION
Type of School: Private

STUDENTS
Enrollment of Business School: 26 **% Male/female:** 91/9 **% International:** 82 **Average Age at Entry:** 32 **Average Years Work Experience at Entry:** 9

FINANCIAL FACTS
Fees: $35,820 **Room & Board:** $15,000

ADMISSIONS
Admissions Selectivity Rating: 83
# of Applications Received: 77 **% Applicants Accepted:** 64 **% Acceptees Attending:** 53 **GMAT Range (25th to 75th percentile):** 550–700 **Average GMAT:** 600 **Average GPA:** 3.4 **TOEFL Required of Int'l Applicants:** Yes **Minimum TOEFL (paper/computer):** 587/240 **Application Fee:** $116
Regular Application Deadline: 5/26 **Regular Notification:** 5/26 Application Deadline Round 1: 4/14, Round 2: 4/28, Round 3: 5/12, Round 4: 5/26
Deferment Available: Yes **Maximum Length of Deferment:** 1 year
Transfer Students Accepted: Yes **Non-fall Admissions:** Yes

EMPLOYMENT PROFILE
Primary Source of Full-time Job Acceptances
School-facilitated Activities 22%
Graduate-facilitated Activities 12%
Unknown 66%
Grads Employed by Industry:.......
Finance 2
Human Resources...........................15
Marketing 9
MIS 46
Operations...6
Consulting...7
General Management 9
Other...6

HENDERSON STATE UNIVERSITY
SCHOOL OF BUSINESS ADMINISTRATION

ADMISSIONS CONTACT: MISSIE BELL, GRADUATE SCHOOL ADMINISTRATIVE ASSISTANT
ADDRESS: 1100 HENDERSON STREET, BOX 7802, ARKADELPHIA, AR 71999-0001
PHONE: (870) 230-5126 • FAX: (870) 230-5479
E-MAIL: GRAD@HSU.EDU
WEBSITE: WWW.HSU.EDU/SCHOOLOFBUSINESS

GENERAL INFORMATION
Type of School: Public **Environment:** Rural Academic

STUDENTS
Enrollment of Parent Institution: 3,754 **Enrollment of Business School:** 45 **% Male/female:** 50/50 **% Out-of-state:** 5 **% Part-time:** 25 **% Minorities:** 10 **% International:** 20

ACADEMICS

Student/faculty Ratio: 6:1 **% Female Faculty:** 38

Prominent Alumni: Theresa Brown, Senior Systems Software Analyst; Junious Babbs, Assist. Superintendent of Little Rock School Dist.; Richard Hoover, NASA; Billy Hudson, Professor at Vanderbilt University; Bob Fisher, President of Belmont University.

FINANCIAL FACTS

Tuition (in-state/out-of-state): $2,916/$5,832 **Fees:** $411 **Room & Board:** $3,874

ADMISSIONS

Admissions Selectivity Rating: 61

# of Applications Received: 19 **% Applicants Accepted:** 100 **% Acceptees Attending:** 32 **GMAT Range (25th to 75th percentile):** 390–670 **Average GMAT:** 450 **Average GPA:** 3 **TOEFL Required of Int'l Applicants:** Yes **Minimum TOEFL (paper/computer):** 550/213 **Application Fee:** $0 **International Application Fee:** $40

Regular Application Deadline: Rolling **Regular Notification:** Rolling **Transfer Students Accepted:** Yes **Non-fall Admissions:** Yes **Need-Blind Admissions:** Yes

IDAHO STATE UNIVERSITY
COLLEGE OF BUSINESS

ADMISSIONS CONTACT: GORDON B. BROOKS, SR., ASSISTANT DEAN FOR GRADUATE PROGRAMS
ADDRESS: BOX 8020, POCATELLO, ID 83209
PHONE: 208-282-2504 • FAX: 208-236-4367
E-MAIL: BROOGORD@ISU.EDU
WEBSITE: COB.ISU.EDU

GENERAL INFORMATION

Type of School: Public **Environment:** Town **Academic Calendar:** Semester

STUDENTS

Enrollment of Parent Institution: 13,977 **Enrollment of Business School:** 109 **% Male/female:** 75/25 **% Part-time:** 56 **% Minorities:** 4 **% International:** 10 **Average Age at Entry:** 32

ACADEMICS

Student/faculty Ratio: 23:1 **% Female Faculty:** 20 **% Minority Faculty:** 2

FINANCIAL FACTS

Tuition (in-state/out-of-state): $5,520/$13,220 **Books and Supplies:** $1,000 **Room & Board:** $7,500

ADMISSIONS

Admissions Selectivity Rating: 82

# of Applications Received: 73 **% Applicants Accepted:** 59 **% Acceptees Attending:** 74 **GMAT Range (25th to 75th percentile):** 440–710 **Average GMAT:** 562 **Average GPA:** 3.4 **TOEFL Required of Int'l Applicants:** Yes **Minimum TOEFL (paper/computer):** 550/213 **Application Fee:** $55 **Regular Application Deadline:** 6/1 **Regular Notification:** 6/7

Deferment Available: Yes **Maximum Length of Deferment:** 2 years **Transfer Students Accepted:** Yes **Non-fall Admissions:** Yes

INDIANA UNIVERSITY NORTHWEST
SCHOOL OF BUSINESS AND ECONOMICS

ADMISSIONS CONTACT: JOHN GIBSON, DIRECTOR, UNDERGRADUATE AND GRADUATE PROGRAMS IN BUSINESS
ADDRESS: 3400 BROADWAY, GARY, IN 46408-1197
PHONE: 219-980-6635 • FAX: 219-980-6916
E-MAIL: JAGIBSON@IUN.EDU
WEBSITE: WWW.IUN.EDU/~BUSNW

GENERAL INFORMATION

Type of School: Public **Academic Calendar:** Semester

STUDENTS

Enrollment of Parent Institution: 4,300 **Enrollment of Business School:** 115 **% Male/female:** 100/0 **% Part-time:** 99 **Average Age at Entry:** 35

ACADEMICS

Student/faculty Ratio: 10:1 **% Female Faculty:** 26 **% Minority Faculty:** 37

FINANCIAL FACTS

Tuition (in-state/out-of-state): $3,750/$8,750 **Fees:** $375 **Books and Supplies:** $999 **% of Students Receiving Loans:** 30 **% of Students Receiving Grants:** 1 **Average Grant:** $999

ADMISSIONS

Admissions Selectivity Rating: 65

# of Applications Received: 50 **% Applicants Accepted:** 70 **% Acceptees Attending:** 100 **Average GMAT:** 470 **TOEFL Required of Int'l Applicants:** Yes **Minimum TOEFL:** 550 **Application Fee:** $25 **International Application Fee:** $55

Deferment Available: Yes **Maximum Length of Deferment:** One semester **Transfer Students Accepted:** Yes **Non-fall Admissions:** Yes **Need-Blind Admissions:** Yes **Applicants Also Look At:** Purdue University—Calumet, Valparaiso University.

INDIANA UNIVERSITY—PURDUE UNIVERSITY AT FORT WAYNE
SCHOOL OF BUSINESS AND MANAGEMENT

ADMISSIONS CONTACT: SANDY FRANKE, SECRETARY, MBA PROGRAM
ADDRESS: NEFF 366, 2101 COLISEUM BOULEVARD EAST, FORT WAYNE, IN 46805-1499
PHONE: 260-481-6498 • FAX:
E-MAIL: EMAIL@SCHOOL.EDU
WEBSITE: WWW.IPFW.EDU/BMS/MBA1.HTM

GENERAL INFORMATION

Type of School: Public **Environment:** Village **Academic Calendar:** Semester

STUDENTS

Enrollment of Parent Institution: 10,749 **Enrollment of Business School:** 191 **% Male/female:** 65/35 **% Part-time:** 91 **Average Age at Entry:** 32

ACADEMICS

Student/faculty Ratio: 1:1

FINANCIAL FACTS

ADMISSIONS

Admissions Selectivity Rating: 60*

# of Applications Received: 45 **% Applicants Accepted:** 91 **% Acceptees Attending:** 95 **Application Fee:** $30

Regular Application Deadline: 7/15 **Regular Notification:** 1/1

Deferment Available: Yes **Maximum Length of Deferment:** 1 year **Non-fall Admissions:** Yes

INSTITUTO DE EMPRESA
INSTITUTO DE EMPRESA

ADMISSIONS CONTACT: JULIAN TRIGO, DIRECTOR OF ADMISSIONS
ADDRESS: MARÍA DE MOLINA 11-13-15, MARIA DE MOLINA 11, 13, 15, MADRID, MA 28006 SPAIN
PHONE: 011 34 91 568 9610 • FAX: 011 34 91 568 9710
E-MAIL: ADMISSIONS@IE.EDU
WEBSITE: WWW.IE.EDU

GENERAL INFORMATION

Type of School: Private

STUDENTS

Enrollment of Business School: 286 **% Male/female:** 63/37 **% International:** 89 **Average Years Work Experience at Entry:** 4

ACADEMICS

Student/faculty Ratio: 11:1

Prominent Alumni: Fernando Barnuevo, J.P. Morgan Chase, Head of Global Investment Mgmt; Pilar de Zulueta, Warner Bros. Southern Europe Director; José María Cámara, President of Sony Music, Spain; Juan PableSan Agustín, Vice President, CEMEX; Isabel Aguilera, COO, NH Hoteles.

FINANCIAL FACTS

Tuition: $73,400 **Books and Supplies:** $1,000 **% of Students Receiving Aid:** 45 **% of Students Receiving Loans:** 50 **% of Students Receiving Grants:** 5 **Average Award Package:** $1,377,000

ADMISSIONS

Admissions Selectivity Rating: 98

# of Applications Received: 1,205 **% Applicants Accepted:** 29 **% Acceptees Attending:** 83 **Average GMAT:** 685 **Average GPA:** 3.7 **Application Fee:** $184

Regular Application Deadline: Rolling **Regular Notification:** Rolling

Deferment Available: Yes **Maximum Length of Deferment:** 2 years **Non-fall Admissions:** Yes **Need-Blind Admissions:** Yes **Applicants**

Also Look At: IMD(International Institute for Management Development), INSEAD, London Business School.

EMPLOYMENT PROFILE

Primary Source of Full-time Job Acceptances

Average base starting salary $87,300

Grads Employed by Industry: ...... %

Finance	11
Human Resources	6
Marketing	10
MIS	3
Operations	5
Strategic Planning	4
Consulting	11
Communications	5
Entrepreneurship	10
General Management	19
Global Management	6
Other	4
Internet/New Media	3
Non-profit	2

Top 5 Employers Hiring Grads: KPMG, Johnson & Johnson, Landwel, Ernest & Young, BBVA.

INSTITUTO TECNOLOGICO Y DE ESTUDIOS SUPERIORES DE MONTERREY (ITESM)
EGADE, MONTERREY CAMPUS

ADMISSIONS CONTACT: LIC. OLGA RENÉE DE LA TORRE, ACADEMIC SERVICES DIRECTOR
ADDRESS: AV. FUNDADORES Y RUFINO TAMAYO, COL. VALLE ORIENTE, SAN PEDRO GARZA GARCÍA, NL 66269 MEXICO
PHONE: 011-52-818-625-6204 • FAX: 818-625-6208
E-MAIL: ADMISIONES.EGADE@ITESM.MX
WEBSITE: WWW.EGADE.ITESM.MX

GENERAL INFORMATION

Type of School: Private **Academic Calendar:** Quarter

STUDENTS

Enrollment of Parent Institution: 19,358 **Enrollment of Business School:** 597 **% Male/female:** 79/21 **% Part-time:** 90 **% International:** 66 **Average Age at Entry:** 28 **Average Years Work Experience at Entry:** 5

ACADEMICS

Student/faculty Ratio: 14:1 **% Female Faculty:** 25

Joint Degrees: Double Degree MBA (1 year more than the regular length). **Prominent Alumni:** Eugenio Clariond Reyes-Retana, General Director of IMSA Group; Fernando Canales Clariond, Ministry of

Economic Affairs, Mexico Government; Jose Antonio Rivero Larrea, President of Administration Board, Autlan Group; Jose Antonio Fernandez Carbajal, General Director of FEMSA Group; Luis Sada Gonzalez, General Director of John Deere Mexico.

FINANCIAL FACTS

Tuition: $17,500 **Books and Supplies:** $780 **Room & Board (on/off campus):** $7,800/$6,400 **% of Students Receiving Aid:** 26 **% of First-year Students Receiving Aid:** 24 **% of Students Receiving Loans:** 3 **% of Students Receiving Grants:** 23 **Average Grant:** $11,375

ADMISSIONS

Admissions Selectivity Rating: 60*
# of Applications Received: 199 **% Applicants Accepted:** 73 **% Acceptees Attending:** 74 **Average GMAT:** 615 **Average GPA:** 3.5 **Application Fee:** $115
Regular Application Deadline: 5/1 **Regular Notification:** 6/1
Deferment Available: Yes **Maximum Length of Deferment:** 1 year
Transfer Students Accepted: Yes **Non-fall Admissions:** Yes

EMPLOYMENT PROFILE

Grads Employed by Industry:	%
Finance	38
Marketing	12
Operations	25
Strategic Planning	6
Other	19

IOWA STATE UNIVERSITY
COLLEGE OF BUSINESS

ADMISSIONS CONTACT: AMY HUTTER, DIRECTOR, MBA RECRUITMENT & MARKETING
ADDRESS: 1360 GERDIN BUSINESS BUILDING, AMES, IA 50011
PHONE: 515-294-8118 • FAX: 515-294-2446
E-MAIL: BUSGRAD@IASTATE.EDU
WEBSITE: WWW.BUS.IASTATE.EDU/MBA

GENERAL INFORMATION

Type of School: Public **Environment:** Town **Academic Calendar:** Semester

STUDENTS

Enrollment of Parent Institution: 26,380 **Enrollment of Business School:** 94 **% Male/female:** 62/38 **% Out-of-state:** 8 **% Part-time:** 62 **% International:** 31 **Average Age at Entry:** 26 **Average Years Work Experience at Entry:** 3

ACADEMICS

Student/faculty Ratio: 4:1 **% Female Faculty:** 9 **% Minority Faculty:** 12
Joint Degrees: MBA/MS in Statistics 3 years, MBA/MS in Community and Regional Planning 3 years, MBA/BS in Engineering 5 years.

FINANCIAL FACTS

Tuition (in-state/out-of-state): $7,718/$18,132 **Fees:** $930 **Books and Supplies:** $1,000 **Room & Board:** $10,200 **% of Students Receiving Aid:** 50 **% of First-year Students Receiving Aid:** 50 **Average Award Package:** $8,120 **Average Grant:** $1

ADMISSIONS

Admissions Selectivity Rating: 82
# of Applications Received: 210 **% Applicants Accepted:** 69 **% Acceptees Attending:** 65 **Average GMAT:** 595 **Average GPA:** 3.4 **TOEFL Required of Int'l Applicants:** Yes **Minimum TOEFL (paper/computer):** 600/250 **Application Fee:** $30 **International Application Fee:** $70
Regular Application Deadline: Rolling **Regular Notification:** Rolling
Deferment Available: Yes **Maximum Length of Deferment:** One year
Non-fall Admissions: Yes **Need-Blind Admissions:** Yes **Applicants Also Look At:** Drake University, University of Iowa.

EMPLOYMENT PROFILE

Primary Source of Full-time Job Acceptances

School-facilitated Activities	23 (69%)
Graduate-facilitated Activities	12 (31%)
Unknown	35 (100%)
Average base starting salary	$57,848
Percent Employed	94

Grads Employed by Industry:	%	avg. salary:
Finance	21	$51,800
Human Resources	3	
Marketing	11	$61,667
MIS	12	$74,500
Operations	33	$53,000
Consulting	6	$68,000
General Management	14	$43,500

JACKSON STATE UNIVERSITY
SCHOOL OF BUSINESS

ADMISSIONS CONTACT: JESSE PENNINGTON, DIRECTOR OF GRADUATE PROGRAMS
ADDRESS: PO BOX 18660, JACKSON, MI 39217
PHONE: 601-432-6315 • FAX: 601-987-4380
E-MAIL: GADMAPPL@CCAIX.JSUMS.EDU
WEBSITE: WWW.CCAIX.JSUMS.EDU/BUSINESS

GENERAL INFORMATION

Type of School: Public **Environment:** Metropolis **Academic Calendar:** Semester

STUDENTS

Enrollment of Parent Institution: 6,292 **Enrollment of Business School:** 1,104

ACADEMICS

Student/faculty Ratio: 99:1

FINANCIAL FACTS

Tuition (in-state/out-of-state): $1,920/$2,378 **Books and Supplies:** $9,999 **% of Students Receiving Aid:** 8 **Average Grant:** $9,999

ADMISSIONS

Admissions Selectivity Rating: 60*

# of Applications Received: 160 **% Applicants Accepted:** 77 % **Acceptees Attending:** 89 **TOEFL Required of Int'l Applicants:** Yes **Minimum TOEFL:** 525

Regular Application Deadline: rolling **Regular Notification:** rolling

Deferment Available: Yes

JAMES MADISON UNIVERSITY
COLLEGE OF BUSINESS

ADMISSIONS CONTACT: KRISTA D. DOFFLEMYER, ADMINISTRATIVE ASSISTANT
ADDRESS: ZANE SHOWKER HALL, MSC 0206, ROOM 616, HARRISONBURG, VA 22807
PHONE: 540-568-3253 • FAX: 540-568-3587
E-MAIL: MBA@JMU.EDU
WEBSITE: WWW.JMU.EDU/MBA

GENERAL INFORMATION

Type of School: Public **Environment:** Town **Academic Calendar:** Aug–July

STUDENTS

Enrollment of Parent Institution: 17,918 **Enrollment of Business School:** 116 **% Male/female:** 71/29 **% Out-of-state:** 21 **% Part-time:** 79 **% International:** 8 **Average Age at Entry:** 31 **Average Years Work Experience at Entry:** 4

ACADEMICS

Student/faculty Ratio: 18:1 **% Female Faculty:** 27 **% Minority Faculty:** 14

Prominent Alumni: George Temidas, Director Security Division, IBM; Marcus Cutts, Director Security Division, Federal Reserve.

FINANCIAL FACTS

Tuition (in-state/out-of-state): $6,720/$19,104 **Books and Supplies:** $2,000 **% of Students Receiving Aid:** 68 **% of First-year Students Receiving Aid:** 80 **% of Students Receiving Loans:** 41 **% of Students Receiving Grants:** 40 **Average Award Package:** $9,252 **Average Grant:** $5,166 **Average Student Loan Debt:** $13,100

ADMISSIONS

Admissions Selectivity Rating: 76

# of Applications Received: 32 **% Applicants Accepted:** 84 % **Acceptees Attending:** 81 **GMAT Range (25th to 75th percentile):** 520–670 **Average GMAT:** 575 **Average GPA:** 3.2 **TOEFL Required of Int'l Applicants:** Yes **Minimum TOEFL (paper/computer):** 550/100 **Application Fee:** $55 **International Application Fee:** $55

Regular Application Deadline: 7/1 **Regular Notification:** rolling

Deferment Available: Yes **Maximum Length of Deferment:** 1 year

Transfer Students Accepted: Yes

KANSAS STATE UNIVERSITY
COLLEGE OF BUSINESS ADMINISTRATION

ADMISSIONS CONTACT: LYNN WAUGH, GRADUATE STUDIES ASSISTANT
ADDRESS: 107 CALVIN HALL, MANHATTAN, KS 66506-0501
PHONE: 785-532-7190 • FAX: 785-532-7809
E-MAIL: LWAUGH@KSU.EDU
WEBSITE: WWW.CBA.KSU.EDU

GENERAL INFORMATION

Type of School: Public **Environment:** Village **Academic Calendar:** Semeters

STUDENTS

Enrollment of Parent Institution: Enrollment of Business School: 91 **% Male/female:** 70/30 **% Out-of-state:** 4 **% Part-time:** 18 % **Minorities:** 9 **% International:** 22 **Average Age at Entry:** 24 **Average Years Work Experience at Entry:** 2

ACADEMICS

Student/faculty Ratio: 5:1 **% Female Faculty:** 22 **% Minority Faculty:** 4

FINANCIAL FACTS

Tuition (in-state/out-of-state): $6,855/$19,340 **Fees:** $666 **Books and Supplies:** $1,000 **Room & Board (on/off campus):** $5,000/$6,000 **% of Students Receiving Aid:** 18 **% of First-year Students Receiving Aid:** 12 **Average Grant:** $2,500

ADMISSIONS

Admissions Selectivity Rating: 89

# of Applications Received: 86 **% Applicants Accepted:** 40 % **Acceptees Attending:** 100 **Average GMAT:** 548 **Average GPA:** 3.4 **TOEFL Required of Int'l Applicants:** Yes **Minimum TOEFL (paper/computer):** 550/213 **Application Fee:** $50 **International Application Fee:** $60

Regular Application Deadline: 9/1 **Regular Notification:** 7/15

Deferment Available: Yes **Maximum Length of Deferment:** 1 year **Transfer Students Accepted:** Yes **Need-Blind Admissions:** Yes **Applicants Also Look At:** Oklahoma State University, University of Kansas, University of Nebraska—Lincoln, University of Oklahoma, Wichita State University.

EMPLOYMENT PROFILE

Grads Employed by Industry:	%	avg. salary:
Finance	30	$46,000
Human Resources	8	$52,000
Marketing	8	$42,000
MIS	8	$55,000
Consulting	22	$42,000
Communications	8	$57,000
Entrepreneurship	8	$38,000

King Fahd University of Petroleum and Minerals (Saudi Arabia)
College of Industrial Management

Admissions Contact: Assistant Dean for Graduate Programs, CIM, Assistant Dean for Graduate Programs
Address: P. O. Box: 1570, Dhahran, 31261 Saudi Arabia
Phone: 011-966-3-860-1143 • Fax: 011-966-3-860-3850
E-mail: SGHAMDI@KFUPM.EDU.SA
Website: WWW.KFUPM.EDU.SA/

GENERAL INFORMATION
Type of School: Public **Academic Calendar:** Sept–June

STUDENTS
Enrollment of Business School: 193 **% Out-of-state:** 10 **% Part-time:** 87 **% Minorities:** 23 **% International:** 23 **Average Age at Entry:** 29 **Average Years Work Experience at Entry:** 3.5

ACADEMICS
Student/faculty Ratio: 20:1 **% Minority Faculty:** 60
Prominent Alumni: K. Alfaleh, VP, Aramco; A. Al Khuraimi, VP, SABIC; A. Alothman, VP, Fin-Aramco; T. Batteeri, CEO, Saudi Electric; S. Sheikh, Cheif Economist, NCB.

FINANCIAL FACTS
Tuition: $0 **Fees:** $0 **Books and Supplies:** $0 **Room & Board (on/off campus):** $6,500/$11,000

ADMISSIONS
Admissions Selectivity Rating: 72
# of Applications Received: 108 **% Applicants Accepted:** 62 **% Acceptees Attending:** 100 **GMAT Range (25th to 75th percentile):** 370–560 **Average GMAT:** 450 **Average GPA:** 3.1 **TOEFL Required of Int'l Applicants:** Yes **Minimum TOEFL (paper/computer):** 520/190 **Application Fee:** $0 **International Application Fee:** $0
Regular Application Deadline: 10/31 **Regular Notification:** 11/21 **Deferment Available:** Yes **Maximum Length of Deferment:** none **Transfer Students Accepted:** Yes **Non-fall Admissions:** Yes

EMPLOYMENT PROFILE
Primary Source of Full-time Job Acceptances
School-facilitated Activities 20%
Graduate-facilitated Activities 80%
Grads Employed by Industry: ....%
Finance 15
Human Resources........................8
Marketing 11
MIS 10
Consulting.......................7
General Management 10
Other................................28

Korea Advanced Institute of Science and Technology
College of Business

Admissions Contact: Ms Okjoo Kim, Manager
Address: Admissions Team, 373-1 Guseong-dong, Yuseong-gu, Daejeon, 305-701 South Korea
Phone: 011-82-42-869-2143 • Fax: 011-82-42- 869-2420
E-mail: GOODISLAND@KAIST.AC.KR
Website: WWW.KAIST.AC.KR

GENERAL INFORMATION
Type of School: Public **Academic Calendar:** Feb–Jan

STUDENTS
Enrollment of Parent Institution: 2,383 **Enrollment of Business School:** 295 **% Male/female:** 80/20 **% International:** 2 **Average Age at Entry:** 32 **Average Years Work Experience at Entry:** 5.5

ACADEMICS
Student/faculty Ratio: 14:1 **% Female Faculty:** 12

FINANCIAL FACTS
Tuition: $16,951 **Room & Board (on/off campus):** $1,271/$6,357 **% of Students Receiving Aid:** 19 **% of First-year Students Receiving Aid:** 19 **% of Students Receiving Loans:** 13 **% of Students Receiving Grants:** 19

ADMISSIONS
Admissions Selectivity Rating: 60*
# of Applications Received: 516 **% Applicants Accepted:** 64 **% Acceptees Attending:** 87 **Application Fee:** $105 **International Application Fee:** $105
Regular Application Deadline: 11/2 **Regular Notification:** 9/10 **Non-fall Admissions:** Yes

EMPLOYMENT PROFILE
Percent Employed 98

Kuwait University
College of Business Administration

Admissions Contact: (+965) 498-5322 or 498-5272, Admission officer
Address: Kuwait University-College of Graduate Study-Khaldia-Bulding2, Kuwait P.O box 5969, safat 13060 Kuwait
Phone: (+965) 498-7102 • Fax: (+965) 481-0499
E-mail: GRADADM@KUC01.KUNIV.EDU.KW
Website: WWW.GRADUATE.EDU.KW

GENERAL INFORMATION
Type of School: Public

STUDENTS

Enrollment of Parent Institution: 45 **Enrollment of Business School:** 145 **% Male/female:** 30/70 **% Part-time:** 95 **% International:** 30 **Average Age at Entry:** 25 **Average Years Work Experience at Entry:** 3

ACADEMICS

Student/faculty Ratio: 7:1

FINANCIAL FACTS

Tuition (in-state/out-of-state): $1,060/$0 **Fees (in-state/out-of-state):** $320/$0

ADMISSIONS

Admissions Selectivity Rating: 66

# of Applications Received: 12 **% Applicants Accepted:** 100 **% Acceptees Attending:** 100 **GMAT Range (25th to 75th percentile):** 450–559 **Average GMAT:** 520 **Average GPA:** 3.2 **TOEFL Required of Int'l Applicants:** Yes **Minimum TOEFL (paper/computer):** 550/213 **Application Fee:** $0 **International Application Fee:** $0

Regular Application Deadline: 1/31 **Regular Notification:** 5/15 Application Deadline/Notification Round 1: 01/31 / 05/15 **Deferment Available:** Yes **Maximum Length of Deferment:** one year

LA SALLE UNIVERSITY
SCHOOL OF BUSINESS ADMINISTRATION

ADMISSIONS CONTACT: KATHY BAGNELL, DIRECTOR, MARKETING AND GRADUATE EOLLMENT
ADDRESS: 1900 WEST OLNEY AVENUE, PHILADELPHIA, PA 19141
PHONE: 215-951-1057 • FAX: 215-951-1886
WEBSITE: WWW.LASALLE.EDU/ACADEM/SBA/GRAD/INDEX.SHTML

GENERAL INFORMATION

Type of School: Private **Environment:** Metropolis **Academic Calendar:** Trimester

STUDENTS

Enrollment of Parent Institution: 5,408 **Enrollment of Business School:** 687 **% Male/female:** 59/41 **% Part-time:** 90 **% Minorities:** 12 **% International:** 11 **Average Age at Entry:** 32

FINANCIAL FACTS

Tuition: $12,800 **Fees:** $85

ADMISSIONS

Admissions Selectivity Rating: 60*

# of Applications Received: 142 **% Applicants Accepted:** 85 **% Acceptees Attending:** 89 **TOEFL Required of Int'l Applicants:** Yes **Minimum TOEFL:** 550 **Application Fee:** $35

Regular Application Deadline: 8/14 **Regular Notification:** rolling **Deferment Available:** Yes **Non-fall Admissions:** Yes

LEHIGH UNIVERSITY
COLLEGE OF BUSINESS AND ECONOMICS

ADMISSIONS CONTACT: CORINN MCBRIDE, DIRECTOR OF RECRUITMENT AND ADMISSIONS
ADDRESS: 621 TAYLOR STREET, BETHLEHEM, PA 18015
PHONE: 610-758-3418 • FAX: 610-758-5283
E-MAIL: MBA.ADMISSIONS@LEHIGH.EDU
WEBSITE: WWW.LEHIGH.EDU/MBA

GENERAL INFORMATION

Type of School: Private **Environment:** City **Academic Calendar:** Semester

STUDENTS

Enrollment of Parent Institution: 6,845 **Enrollment of Business School:** 279 **% Male/female:** 65/35 **% Part-time:** 83 **% Minorities:** 4 **% International:** 37 **Average Age at Entry:** 32 **Average Years Work Experience at Entry:** 7

ACADEMICS

Student/faculty Ratio: 6:1 **% Female Faculty:** 20 **% Minority Faculty:** 27

Joint Degrees: MBA & Engineering (MBA & E) 45 Credit Hours MBA & Educational Leadership (MBA/MEd.) 45 Credit Hours.
Prominent Alumni: Dexter Baker, Ret. Chairman & CEO, Air Products & Chemicals; Stephen A. Riordan, Editor, Boston Globe; William H. Glenn, VP. Finance, CFO Dresser Rand Co; E. Joseph Hochreiter, Chairman and CEO M Cubed Technolgies, Inc; John E. McGlade, President & CEO, Air Products and Chemicals.

FINANCIAL FACTS

Tuition: $11,340 **Fees:** $300 **Books and Supplies:** $1,300 **Room & Board:** $10,800 **% of Students Receiving Aid:** 8 **% of First-year Students Receiving Aid:** 15 **Average Award Package:** $24,260 **Average Grant:** $11,000

ADMISSIONS

Admissions Selectivity Rating: 88

# of Applications Received: 253 **% Applicants Accepted:** 61 **% Acceptees Attending:** 77 **GMAT Range (25th to 75th percentile):** 590–670 **Average GMAT:** 633 **Average GPA:** 3.3 **TOEFL Required of Int'l Applicants:** Yes **Minimum TOEFL (paper/computer):** 600/250 **Application Fee:** $65

Regular Application Deadline: 5/1 **Regular Notification:** rolling **Deferment Available:** Yes **Maximum Length of Deferment:** One year **Transfer Students Accepted:** Yes **Non-fall Admissions:** Yes **Need-Blind Admissions:** Yes

EMPLOYMENT PROFILE

Primary Source of Full-time Job Acceptances

School-facilitated Activities 4 (33%)
Graduate-facilitated Activities 2 (17%)
Unknown.......................................6 (50%)
Average base starting salary $76,000
Percent Employed 15

Grads Employed by Industry: ......% avg. salary:

Finance 50 $82,600

Operations...34 $75,666

Consulting 8

Other..8

Top 5 Employers Hiring Grads: BlackRock, Bristol-Myers Squibb, CHEP, Procter & Gamble, MasterFoods

LOUISIANA STATE UNIVERSITY— SHREVEPORT
COLLEGE OF BUSINESS ADMINISTRATION

ADMISSIONS CONTACT: SUSAN WOOD, MBA DIRECTOR
ADDRESS: ONE UNIVERSITY PLACE, SHREVEPORT, LA 71115
PHONE: 318-797-5213 • FAX: 318-797-5017
E-MAIL: SWOOD@PILOT.LSUS.EDU
WEBSITE: WWW.LSUS.EDU/BA/MBA

GENERAL INFORMATION
Type of School: Public **Environment:** City **Academic Calendar:** Semester

STUDENTS
Enrollment of Parent Institution: 4,237 **Enrollment of Business School:** 150 **% Male/female:** 47/53 **% Part-time:** 93 **% Minorities:** 10 **% International:** 5

ACADEMICS
Student/faculty Ratio: 20:1

FINANCIAL FACTS
Tuition (in-state/out-of-state): $3,245/$9,420 **% of Students Receiving Aid:** 60

ADMISSIONS
Admissions Selectivity Rating: 60*
# of Applications Received: 70 **% Applicants Accepted:** 71 **% Acceptees Attending:** 80 **TOEFL Required of Int'l Applicants:** Yes **Minimum TOEFL:** 550 **Application Fee:** $10
Regular Application Deadline: 6/30 **Regular Notification:** rolling **Non-fall Admissions:** Yes

LOUISIANA TECH UNIVERSITY
COLLEGE OF BUSINESS

ADMISSIONS CONTACT: DR. DOUG AMYX, ASSOCIATE DEAN OF GRADUATE STUDIES
ADDRESS: PO BOX 10318, RUSTON, LA 71272
PHONE: 318-257-4528 • FAX: 318-257-4253
E-MAIL: GSCHOOL@CAB.LATECH.EDU
WEBSITE: WWW.CAB.LATECH.EDU

GENERAL INFORMATION
Type of School: Public **Environment:** Rural **Academic Calendar:** Quarter

STUDENTS
Enrollment of Parent Institution: 11,203 **Enrollment of Business School:** 49 **% Male/female:** 54/46 **% Minorities:** 2 **% International:** 15

ACADEMICS
Student/faculty Ratio: 25:1 **% Female Faculty:** 19 **% Minority Faculty:** 24

FINANCIAL FACTS
Tuition (in-state/out-of-state): $3,876/$7,456 **Fees:** $280 **Books and Supplies:** $1,000 **Room & Board:** $6,700

ADMISSIONS
Admissions Selectivity Rating: 83
# of Applications Received: 32 **% Applicants Accepted:** 75 **% Acceptees Attending:** 88 **GMAT Range (25th to 75th percentile):** 450–700 **Average GMAT:** 510 **Average GPA:** 3.2 **TOEFL Required of Int'l Applicants:** Yes **Minimum TOEFL (paper/computer):** 550/213 **Application Fee:** $30 **International Application Fee:** $40
Regular Application Deadline: 8/1
Deferment Available: Yes **Maximum Length of Deferment:** 1 year **Transfer Students Accepted:** Yes **Non-fall Admissions:** Yes

MARSHALL UNIVERSITY
LEWIS COLLEGE OF BUSINESS

ADMISSIONS CONTACT: DR. MICHAEL A. NEWSOME, MBA DIRECTOR
ADDRESS: CORBY HALL 217, 400 HAL GREER BOULEVARD, HUNTINGTON, WV 25755-2305
PHONE: 304-696-2613 • FAX: 304-696-3661
E-MAIL: EMAIL@SCHOOL.EDU
WEBSITE: LCOB.MARSHALL.EDU

GENERAL INFORMATION
Type of School: Public **Environment:** Town **Academic Calendar:** Semesters

STUDENTS
Enrollment of Business School: 80 **% Male/female:** 40/60 **% Minorities:** 15 **% International:** 30 **Average Years Work Experience at Entry:** 2

ACADEMICS
Student/faculty Ratio: 5:1 **% Female Faculty:** 10 **% Minority Faculty:** 10

FINANCIAL FACTS
Tuition (in-state/out-of-state): $2,020/$5,653 **Fees (in-state/out-of-state):** $1,100/$1,250 **Books and Supplies:** $1,000 **Room & Board:** $4,000 **% of Students Receiving Aid:** 50 **% of First-year Students Receiving Aid:** 50

ADMISSIONS
Admissions Selectivity Rating: 74
# of Applications Received: 100 **% Applicants Accepted:** 84 **% Acceptees Attending:** 95 **Average GMAT:** 530 **Average GPA:** 3.5

TOEFL Required of Int'l Applicants: Yes **Minimum TOEFL (paper/computer):** 525/195 **Application Fee:** $30 **International Application Fee:** $25

Regular Application Deadline: Rolling **Regular Notification:** Rolling

Transfer Students Accepted: Yes **Non-fall Admissions:** Yes

EMPLOYMENT PROFILE

Grads Employed by Industry: ......% avg. salary:
Accounting 75

McNeese State University
MBA Program

Admissions Contact: Tammy Pettis, University Admissions
Address: Box 92495, Lake Charles, LA 70609-2495
Phone: 337-475-5145 • Fax: 337-475-5189
E-mail: info@mcneese.edu
Website: www.mcneese.edu/colleges/business/mba

GENERAL INFORMATION

Type of School: Public **Environment:** City **Academic Calendar:** Semester

STUDENTS

Enrollment of Parent Institution: 8,423 **Enrollment of Business School:** 78 **% Male/female:** 68/32 **% Out-of-state:** 3 **% Part-time:** 64 **% Minorities:** 1 **% International:** 36 **Average Age at Entry:** 30

ACADEMICS

Student/faculty Ratio: 16:1 **% Female Faculty:** 1 **% Minority Faculty:** 45

Joint Degrees: None.

FINANCIAL FACTS

Tuition (in-state/out-of-state): $3,054/$9,120 **Books and Supplies:** $1,000 **Room & Board (on/off campus):** $3,200/$3,600

ADMISSIONS

Admissions Selectivity Rating: 63

# of Applications Received: 36 **% Applicants Accepted:** 97 **% Acceptees Attending:** 51 **GMAT Range (25th to 75th percentile):** 250–690 **Average GMAT:** 480 **Average GPA:** 3.6 **TOEFL Required of Int'l Applicants:** Yes **Minimum TOEFL (paper/computer):** 500/173 **Application Fee:** $20 **International Application Fee:** $30

Regular Application Deadline: rolling **Regular Notification:** rolling

Deferment Available: Yes **Maximum Length of Deferment:** 1 year **Transfer Students Accepted:** Yes **Non-fall Admissions:** Yes **Need-Blind Admissions:** Yes

Memorial University of Newfoundland
Faculty of Business Administration

Admissions Contact: Lisa Savage, MBA Program Assistant
Address: Faculty of Business Administration, Memorial University of Newfoundland, St. John's, NL A1B 3X5 Canada
Phone: 709-737-8522 • Fax: 709-737-2467
E-mail: mba@mun.ca
Website: www.business.mun.ca

GENERAL INFORMATION

Type of School: Public

STUDENTS

Enrollment of Parent Institution: 17,800 **Enrollment of Business School:** 124 **% Male/female:** 40/60 **% Part-time:** 62 **% International:** 28 **Average Age at Entry:** 25 **Average Years Work Experience at Entry:** 7

ACADEMICS

Student/faculty Ratio: 15:1 **% Female Faculty:** 35

FINANCIAL FACTS

Tuition: $2,000 **Fees:** $610 **Books and Supplies:** $1,300 **Room & Board (on/off campus):** $3,500/$5,200 **% of Students Receiving Grants:** 6 **Average Grant:** $1,200

ADMISSIONS

Admissions Selectivity Rating: 87

# of Applications Received: 82 **% Applicants Accepted:** 40 **% Acceptees Attending:** 70 **GMAT Range (25th to 75th percentile):** 520–740 **Average GMAT:** 600 **TOEFL Required of Int'l Applicants:** Yes **Minimum TOEFL (paper/computer):** 580/237 **Application Fee:** $40

Regular Application Deadline: 3/15

Deferment Available: Yes **Maximum Length of Deferment:** One year **Transfer Students Accepted:** Yes **Non-fall Admissions:** Yes **Need-Blind Admissions:** Yes

Michigan State University
The Eli Broad Graduate School of Management

Admissions Contact: Jeff McNish, Director, MBA Admissions
Address: Full-Time MBA Program, 215 Eppley Center, East Lansing, MI 48824-1121
Phone: 517-355-7604 • Fax: 517-353-1649
E-mail: mba@msu.edu
Website: mba.msu.edu

GENERAL INFORMATION

Type of School: Public **Environment:** Town **Academic Calendar:** Semester

STUDENTS

Enrollment of Parent Institution: 43,401 **Enrollment of Business School:** 181 **% Male/female:** 69/31 **% Out-of-state:** 67 **% Minorities:** 14 **% International:** 40 **Average Age at Entry:** 28 **Average Years Work Experience at Entry:** 5

ACADEMICS

Student/faculty Ratio: 35:1 **% Female Faculty:** 20 **% Minority Faculty:** 5

Joint Degrees: JD/MBA 4 years, MBA/M-GM (MBA/MA in Global Management) with Thunderbird. **Prominent Alumni:** Matthew Barnhill, SVP, Market Research, BET; Susan Oaks, VP, A.T. Kearney, Inc.; Robert A. Olstein, Chairman, The Olstein Financial Alert Fund; Toichi Takenaka, President & CEO, Takenaka Corp.; Robert A. Chapek, President, Buena Vista Home Entertainment.

FINANCIAL FACTS

Tuition (in-state/out-of-state): $17,750/$24,850 **Fees:** $31 **Books and Supplies:** $1,700 **Room & Board:** $7,752 **% of Students Receiving Aid:** 87 **% of First-year Students Receiving Aid:** 90 **% of Students Receiving Loans:** 49 **% of Students Receiving Grants:** 63 **Average Award Package:** $17,750 **Average Grant:** $6,358 **Average Student Loan Debt:** $36,997

ADMISSIONS

Admissions Selectivity Rating: 92

# of Applications Received: 594 **% Applicants Accepted:** 33 **% Acceptees Attending:** 52 **GMAT Range (25th to 75th percentile):** 580–700 **Average GMAT:** 636 **Average GPA:** 3.3 **TOEFL Required of Int'l Applicants:** Yes **Minimum TOEFL (paper/computer):** 600/250 **Application Fee:** $85

Application Deadline/Notification Round 1: 11/01 / 12/18 Round 2: 01/09 / 02/23 Round 3: 02/20 / 03/30 Round 4: 04/10 / 05/11

Need-Blind Admissions: Yes **Applicants Also Look At:** Arizona State University, Penn State University, Purdue University—West Lafayette, The Ohio State University, University of Michigan, University of Wisconsin—Madison, Vanderbilt University.

EMPLOYMENT PROFILE

Primary Source of Full-time Job Acceptances

School-facilitated Activities 74 (83%)
Graduate-facilitated Activities 15 (17%)
Average base starting salary $83,588
Percent Employed 13

Grads Employed by Industry: ......% avg. salary:

Finance 27 $84,019
Human Resources..........................3 $76,167
Marketing 18 $82,467
MIS 3 $85,333
Operations......................................29 $82,606
Consulting......................................15 $89,815
General Management 5

Top 5 Employers Hiring Grads: Cummins Inc., Ford Mortor Company, Intel Corporation, Johnson & Johnson, Procter & Gamble.

MICHIGAN TECHNOLOGICAL UNIVERSITY
SCHOOL OF BUSINESS AND ECONOMICS

ADMISSIONS CONTACT: CAROL WINGERSON, SR STAFF ASSISTANT, GRADUATE SCHOOL
ADDRESS: GRADUATE SCHOOL, 1400 TOWNSEND DRIVE, HOUGHTON, MI 49931
PHONE: 906-487-2328 • FAX: 906-487-2284
E-MAIL: CTWINGER@MTU.EDU
WEBSITE: WWW.SBE.MTU.EDU

GENERAL INFORMATION

Type of School: Public **Academic Calendar:** Semester

STUDENTS

Enrollment of Business School: 23 **% Male/female:** 43/57

ACADEMICS

Student/faculty Ratio: 1:1 **% Female Faculty:** 25 **% Minority Faculty:** 15

FINANCIAL FACTS

Tuition: $12,840 **Fees:** $800 **Books and Supplies:** $850 **Room & Board:** $8,830

ADMISSIONS

Admissions Selectivity Rating: 80

# of Applications Received: 50 **% Applicants Accepted:** 52 **% Acceptees Attending:** 46 **TOEFL Required of Int'l Applicants:** Yes **Application Fee:** $0 **International Application Fee:** $0 **Regular Application Deadline:** Rolling **Regular Notification:** Rolling **Transfer Students Accepted:** Yes **Non-fall Admissions:** Yes **Need-Blind Admissions:** Yes

MIDDLE TENNESSEE STATE UNIVERSITY
JENNINGS A. JONES COLLEGE OF BUSINESS

ADMISSIONS CONTACT: TROY A. FESTERVAND, DIRECTOR, GRADUATE BUSINESS STUDIES
ADDRESS: PO BOX 290 BAS N222, MURFREESBORO, TN 37132
PHONE: 615-898-2368 • FAX: 615-904-8491
E-MAIL: GBS@MTSU.EDU
WEBSITE: WWW.MTSU.EDU/~GRADUATE/PROGRAMS/BUAD

GENERAL INFORMATION

Type of School: Public **Environment:** Village

STUDENTS

Enrollment of Business School: 396 **% Male/female:** 77/23 **% Minorities:** 12 **Average Age at Entry:** 24

ACADEMICS

Student/faculty Ratio: 20:1

FINANCIAL FACTS

Tuition (in-state/out-of-state): $2,250/$6,100 Fees: $300 Books and Supplies: $1,000 Room & Board: $2,500

ADMISSIONS

Admissions Selectivity Rating: 65

# of Applications Received: 231 % Applicants Accepted: 83 % Acceptees Attending: 105 Average GMAT: 490 Average GPA: 3.2 TOEFL Required of Int'l Applicants: Yes Minimum TOEFL (paper/computer): 525/197 Application Fee: $25 International Application Fee: $30

Regular Application Deadline: 7/1 Regular Notification: 8/1

Deferment Available: Yes Maximum Length of Deferment: varies Transfer Students Accepted: Yes Non-fall Admissions: Yes

MISSISSIPPI STATE UNIVERSITY
COLLEGE OF BUSINESS AND INDUSTRY

ADMISSIONS CONTACT: DR. BARBARA SPENCER, DIRECTOR OF GRADUATE STUDIES IN BUSINESS
ADDRESS: P.O.DRAWER 5288, MISSISSIPPI STATE, MS 39762
PHONE: 662-325-1891 • FAX: 662-325-8161
E-MAIL: GSB@COBILAN.MSSTATE.EDU
WEBSITE: WWW.CBI.MSSTATE.EDU/GSB

GENERAL INFORMATION

Type of School: Public Environment: Town Academic Calendar: Semester

STUDENTS

Enrollment of Parent Institution: 16,206 Enrollment of Business School: 91 % Male/female: 53/47 % Out-of-state: 12 % Part-time: 21 % Minorities: 8 % International: 7 Average Age at Entry: 27

ACADEMICS

Student/faculty Ratio: 3:1 % Female Faculty: 32 % Minority Faculty: 11

Joint Degrees: MBA in Project Management (12 months to 2 years). Prominent Alumni: John Grisham, Best-selling author; Bailey Howell, Hall of Fame basketball player; Hartley Peavey, Founder, Peavey Electronics; Turner Catledge, Former Executive Editor, The New York Times; Pat Spainhour, Retired Chairman & CEO, Ann Taylor Stores.

FINANCIAL FACTS

Tuition (in-state/out-of-state): $6,894/$15,828 Fees: $0 Books and Supplies: $950 Room & Board: $7,760 % of Students Receiving Aid: 68 % of First-year Students Receiving Aid: 73 % of Students Receiving Loans: 31 % of Students Receiving Grants: 35 Average Award Package: $13,333 Average Grant: $2,886

ADMISSIONS

Admissions Selectivity Rating: 76

# of Applications Received: 71 % Applicants Accepted: 70 % Acceptees Attending: 72 GMAT Range (25th to 75th percentile): 475–540 Average GMAT: 498 Average GPA: 3.4 TOEFL Required of

Int'l Applicants: Yes Minimum TOEFL (paper/computer): 575/232 Application Fee: $30

Regular Application Deadline: 7/1 Regular Notification: Rolling

Deferment Available: Yes Maximum Length of Deferment: 1 year Transfer Students Accepted: Yes Non-fall Admissions: Yes Need-Blind Admissions: Yes

EMPLOYMENT PROFILE

Primary Source of Full-time Job Acceptances

School-facilitated Activities	9 (47%)
Graduate-facilitated Activities	10 (53%)
Unknown	4
Percent Employed	67

Grads Employed by Industry: ...... %

Finance	21
Human Resources	4
Marketing	8
MIS	17
Operations	8
Consulting	4
General Management	8
Other	8

MOREHEAD STATE UNIVERSITY
COLLEGE OF BUSINESS

ADMISSIONS CONTACT: JESSICA THOMPSON, ADMISSIONS SPECIALIST
ADDRESS: 701 GINGER HALL, MOREHEAD, KY 40351
PHONE: 606-783-2039 • FAX: 606-783-5061
E-MAIL: GRADUATE@MOREHEADSTATE.EDU
WEBSITE: WWW.MOREHEADSTATE.EDU

GENERAL INFORMATION

Type of School: Public

STUDENTS

Enrollment of Parent Institution: 9,100 Enrollment of Business School: 161 % Male/female: 93/7 % Out-of-state: 19 % Part-time: 91 % International: 3

ACADEMICS

Student/faculty Ratio: 20:1 % Female Faculty: 25 % Minority Faculty: 33

FINANCIAL FACTS

Tuition: $5,730

ADMISSIONS

Admissions Selectivity Rating: 82

# of Applications Received: 250 % Applicants Accepted: 13 % Acceptees Attending: 28 Average GMAT: 498 TOEFL Required of Int'l Applicants: Yes Minimum TOEFL (paper/computer): 525/61 Application Fee: $0

Regular Application Deadline: 8/1

Deferment Available: Yes **Maximum Length of Deferment:** 1 year
Transfer Students Accepted: Yes **Non-fall Admissions:** Yes

MORGAN STATE UNIVERSITY
EARL GRAVES SCHOOL OF BUSINESS AND MANAGEMENT

ADMISSIONS CONTACT: , DIRECTOR OF GRADUATE ADMISSIONS
ADDRESS: 1700 EAST COLD SPRING LANE, BALTIMORE, MD 21251
WEBSITE: WWW.MORGAN.EDU/ACADEMICS/SBM/ACADEMIC/SBM

GENERAL INFORMATION
Type of School: Public **Environment:** City **Academic Calendar:** Semester

STUDENTS
Enrollment of Parent Institution: 5,900 **Enrollment of Business School:** 103 **% Part-time:** 100

ACADEMICS
Student/faculty Ratio: 12:1

FINANCIAL FACTS
Room & Board: $2,990

ADMISSIONS
Admissions Selectivity Rating: 60*
TOEFL Required of Int'l Applicants: Yes **Minimum TOEFL:** 600
Application Fee: $20
Regular Application Deadline: rolling **Regular Notification:** rolling
Deferment Available: Yes

MURRAY STATE UNIVERSITY
COLLEGE OF BUSINESS AND PUBLIC AFFAIRS

ADMISSIONS CONTACT: DR. GERRY NKOMBO MUUKA, ASSISTANT DEAN AND MBA DIRECTOR
ADDRESS: 109 BUSINESS BUILDING, GRADUATE ADMISSIONS OFFICE, SPARKS HALL, MURRAY, KY 42071
PHONE: 270-762-6970 • FAX: 270-762-3482
E-MAIL: CBPA@MURRAYSTATE.EDU
WEBSITE: WWW.MURSUKY.EDU/QACD/CBPA/MBA/INDEX

GENERAL INFORMATION
Type of School: Public **Environment:** Village **Academic Calendar:** Semester

STUDENTS
Enrollment of Parent Institution: 9,000 **Enrollment of Business School:** 160 **% Part-time:** 53 **Average Age at Entry:** 31

ACADEMICS
Student/faculty Ratio: 20:1

FINANCIAL FACTS
Tuition (in-state/out-of-state): $4,185/$11,700 **Room & Board:** $3,800

ADMISSIONS
Admissions Selectivity Rating: 60*
# of Applications Received: 121 **% Applicants Accepted:** 75 %
Acceptees Attending: 52 **TOEFL Required of Int'l Applicants:** Yes
Minimum TOEFL: 525 **Application Fee:** $25
Regular Application Deadline: rolling **Regular Notification:** rolling
Deferment Available: Yes **Transfer Students Accepted:** Yes **Non-fall Admissions:** Yes

NANYANG TECHNOLOGICAL UNIVERSITY
NANYANG BUSINESS SCHOOL

ADMISSIONS CONTACT: ASSOCIATE PROFESSOR OOI LEE LEE, DIRECTOR (MBA)
ADDRESS: THE NANYANG MBA, NANYANG BUSINESS SCHOOL, NANYANG AVENUE, BLK S3, B3A, SINGAPORE, 639798 SINGAPORE
PHONE: 011-65-67906183 • FAX: 011-65-67913561
E-MAIL: NBSMBA@NTU.EDU.SG
WEBSITE: WWW.NANYANGMBA.NTU.EDU.SG

GENERAL INFORMATION
Type of School: Public

STUDENTS
Enrollment of Parent Institution: 28,949 **Enrollment of Business School:** 282 **% Male/female:** 72/28 **% Part-time:** 34 %
International: 81 **Average Age at Entry:** 31 **Average Years Work Experience at Entry:** 7

ACADEMICS
Student/faculty Ratio: 2:1 **% Female Faculty:** 27
Joint Degrees: NTU-Waseda Double MBA 1 year, NTU-St Gallen Double MBA 1.5 years, NTU-ESSEC Double MBA 1.5 years.
Prominent Alumni: Ms. Jill Lee, Senior Executive Vice President & CFO, Siemens Ltd.; Mr. Yeo Tiong Eng, Sr. Reg. Financial Dir., Molex Far East South Mgt. P/L; Ms. Elsie Sim, GM, Sales & Operations, Shell Eastern Petroleum; Mr. Terence Chan, CEO, CAD-IT Consultants (Asia) Pte. Ltd.; Mr. Chew Hong Gian, Executive VP & Head of Operations, Singapore Exchange.

FINANCIAL FACTS
Tuition: $19,000 **Books and Supplies:** $5,000 **Room & Board (on/off campus):** $7,000/$10,000 **% of Students Receiving Grants:** 9 **Average Grant:** $173,000

ADMISSIONS
Admissions Selectivity Rating: 94
# of Applications Received: 904 **% Applicants Accepted:** 30 %
Acceptees Attending: 62 **GMAT Range (25th to 75th percentile):** 610–690 **Average GMAT:** 652 **Average GPA: TOEFL Required of Int'l Applicants:** Yes **Minimum TOEFL (paper/computer):** 600/250
Application Fee: $35
Regular Application Deadline: 3/31 **Regular Notification:** 4/30
Deferment Available: Yes **Maximum Length of Deferment:** 1 year
Transfer Students Accepted: Yes **Non-fall Admissions:** Yes

EMPLOYMENT PROFILE

Primary Source of Full-time Job Acceptances

School-facilitated Activities 45 (76%)

Graduate-facilitated Activities 14 (24%)

Average base starting salary $57,797

Percent Employed 40

Grads Employed by Industry: ......%

Finance 57

Marketing 15

MIS 2

Operations.......................................12

Consulting.......................................6

General Management 4

Other...4

Top 5 Employers Hiring Grads: Cisco Systems, OCBC Bank, PricewaterhouseCoopers, ABN Amro Bank, Bain & Company.

NATIONAL SUN YAT-SEN UNIVERSITY
COLLEGE OF MANAGEMENT

ADMISSIONS CONTACT: COLLEGE OF MANAGEMENT, PROF. PING-YI CHAO
ADDRESS: 70 LIEN-HAI ROAD, KAOHSIUNG, 804-24 TAIWAN
PHONE: -4151 • FAX: -4245
E-MAIL: CHAOPY@MAIL.NSYSU.EDU.TW
WEBSITE: WWW.CM.NSYSU.EDU.TW

GENERAL INFORMATION
Type of School: Public

STUDENTS
Enrollment of Parent Institution: 9,830 **Enrollment of Business School:** 617 **% Male/female:** 52/48 **% Part-time:** 51 **Average Age at Entry:** 25 **Average Years Work Experience at Entry:** 2

ACADEMICS
Student/faculty Ratio: 17:1 **% Female Faculty:** 20

Prominent Alumni: Chu Chen, Kaohsiung Mayor; Bo-Chang Chen, President of Tong Lung Metal Industry Co., Ltd.; Chin-Nan Hsieh, President of Lung Ching Steel Enterprist Co., Ltd.; Chao-Dong Ong, Manager of China Steel Structure Co., Ltd.; Yu -Chang Hu, Cognoscente of CMMI.

FINANCIAL FACTS
Tuition: $3,400 **Fees:** $1,046 **Books and Supplies:** $175 **Room & Board (on/off campus):** $3,000/$4,300 **% of Students Receiving Grants:** 38 **Average Grant:** $1,050

ADMISSIONS
Admissions Selectivity Rating: 60*

# of Applications Received: 5,663 **% Applicants Accepted:** 11 **% Acceptees Attending:** 100 **Application Fee:** $0 **International Application Fee:** $0

Regular Application Deadline: 4/30 **Regular Notification:** 5/30

Applicants Also Look At: National Chengchi University

NEW YORK UNIVERSITY, EMBA
NEW YORK UNIVERSITY STERN EXECUTIVE MBA PROGRAM

ADMISSIONS CONTACT: PETER TODD, ADMISSIONS COORDINATOR
ADDRESS: 44 WEST 4TH STREET, SUITE 10-66, NEW YORK, NY 10012
PHONE: 212-998-0789 • FAX: 212-995-4222
E-MAIL: EXECUTIVE@STERN.NYU.EDU
WEBSITE: WWW.STERN.NYU.EDU/EXECUTIVE/EMBA

GENERAL INFORMATION
Type of School: Private

STUDENTS
Enrollment of Business School: 100 **% Male/female:** 71/29 **% Minorities:** 12 **% International:** 20 **Average Age at Entry:** 33 **Average Years Work Experience at Entry:** 10

ADMISSIONS
Admissions Selectivity Rating: 97

# of Applications Received: 600 **% Applicants Accepted:** 25 **% Acceptees Attending:** 67 **Average GMAT:** 660 **Average GPA:** 3.4 **Application Fee:** $150

Regular Application Deadline: 2/27 **Regular Notification:** Rolling

Deferment Available: Yes **Maximum Length of Deferment:** 1 year

Non-fall Admissions: Yes

NICHOLLS STATE UNIVERSITY
COLLEGE OF BUSINESS ADMINISTRATION

ADMISSIONS CONTACT: BECKY LEBLANC-DUROCHER, DIRECTOR OF ADMISSIONS
ADDRESS: PO BOX 2004, THIBODAUX, LA 70310
PHONE: 877-642-4655 • FAX: 985-448-4929
E-MAIL: ESAI-BL@NICHOLLS.EDU
WEBSITE: WWW.NICHOLLS.EDU

GENERAL INFORMATION
Type of School: Public **Environment:** Village **Academic Calendar:** Semester

STUDENTS
Enrollment of Parent Institution: 7,482 **Enrollment of Business School:** 116 **% Male/female:** 49/51 **% Out-of-state:** 1 **% Part-time:** 59 **% Minorities:** 6 **% International:** 12

ACADEMICS
Student/faculty Ratio: 15:1 **% Female Faculty:** 19

Prominent Alumni: Barry Melancon, President, AICPA; John Weimer, Justice, Louisiana Supreme Court; Billy Tauzin, U.S. Representative.

FINANCIAL FACTS
Tuition (in-state/out-of-state): $3,075/$8,523 **Books and Supplies:**

$2,000 **Room & Board:** $4,584 **% of Students Receiving Aid:** 20 **Average Grant:** $4,000

ADMISSIONS

Admissions Selectivity Rating: 62

# of Applications Received: 70 **% Applicants Accepted:** 99 % **Acceptees Attending:** 57 **Average GMAT:** 486 **Average GPA:** 3.1 **TOEFL Required of Int'l Applicants:** Yes **Minimum TOEFL (paper/computer):** 550/213 **Application Fee:** $20 **International Application Fee:** $30

Regular Application Deadline: 7/1 **Regular Notification:** Rolling **Deferment Available:** Yes **Maximum Length of Deferment:** 1 semester **Transfer Students Accepted:** Yes **Non-fall Admissions:** Yes **Need-Blind Admissions:** Yes

NORTH DAKOTA STATE UNIVERSITY
COLLEGE OF BUSINESS ADMINISTRATION

ADMISSIONS CONTACT: PAUL BROWN, MBA DIRECTOR
ADDRESS: PO BOX 5137, FARGO, ND 58018
E-MAIL: PAUL.BROWN@NDSU.EDUX
WEBSITE: WWW.NDSU.EDU/CBA/

GENERAL INFORMATION

Type of School: Public **Environment:** City

STUDENTS

Enrollment of Business School: 537 **% Male/female:** 60/40 **% Part-time:** 89 **% International:** 8 **Average Age at Entry:** 29

ACADEMICS

Student/faculty Ratio: 19:1
Joint Degrees: MBA/JD 3.5 to 5 years

FINANCIAL FACTS

Tuition (in-state/out-of-state): $4,600/$10,800 **Fees:** $340

ADMISSIONS

Admissions Selectivity Rating: 60*

# of Applications Received: 162 **% Applicants Accepted:** 90 % **Acceptees Attending:** 80 **TOEFL Required of Int'l Applicants:** Yes **Minimum TOEFL:** 550 **Application Fee:** $35

Regular Application Deadline: 7/15 **Regular Notification:** rolling **Deferment Available:** Yes **Non-fall Admissions:** Yes

NORTHERN ILLINOIS UNIVERSITY, COLLEGE OF BUSINESS
MBA PROGRAMS

ADMISSIONS CONTACT: MONA SALMON, ASSISTANT DIRECTOR
ADDRESS: BARSEMA 203, DEKALB, IL 60115
PHONE: 866-648-6221 • FAX: 815-753-1668
E-MAIL: MBA@NIU.EDU
WEBSITE: WWW.COB.NIU.EDU/MBAPROGRAMS

GENERAL INFORMATION

Type of School: Public **Environment:** Rural

STUDENTS

Enrollment of Parent Institution: 25,000 **Enrollment of Business School:** 528 **% Male/female:** 100/0 **% Part-time:** 99 **Average Age at Entry:** 32 **Average Years Work Experience at Entry:** 9

ACADEMICS

Student/faculty Ratio: 24:1 **% Female Faculty:** 19 **% Minority Faculty:** 4

FINANCIAL FACTS

Tuition (in-state/out-of-state): $8,154/$11,538 **Books and Supplies:** $750

ADMISSIONS

Admissions Selectivity Rating: 68

# of Applications Received: 262 **% Applicants Accepted:** 97 % **Acceptees Attending:** 70 **Average GMAT:** 550 **Average GPA:** 3.2 **TOEFL Required of Int'l Applicants:** Yes **Minimum TOEFL (paper/computer):** 550/213 **Application Fee:** $30

Regular Application Deadline: 6/1 **Regular Notification:** Rolling **Deferment Available:** Yes **Maximum Length of Deferment:** 24 months **Transfer Students Accepted:** Yes **Non-fall Admissions:** Yes **Need-Blind Admissions:** Yes

OAKLAND UNIVERSITY
SCHOOL OF BUSINESS ADMINSTRATION

ADMISSIONS CONTACT: PAUL M. TRUMBULL, COORDINATOR OF GRADUATE BUSINESS PROGRAMS
ADDRESS: 432 ELLIOTT HALL, ROCHESTER, MI 48309-4493
PHONE: 248-370-3287 • FAX: 248-370-4964
E-MAIL: GBP@LISTS.OAKLAND.EDU • WEBSITE: WWW.SBA.OAKLAND.EDU

GENERAL INFORMATION

Type of School: Public **Environment:** Town **Academic Calendar:** Semester

STUDENTS

Enrollment of Parent Institution: 17,736 **Enrollment of Business School:** 470 **% Male/female:** 66/34 **% Out-of-state:** 5 **% Part-time:** 95 **% International:** 5 **Average Age at Entry:** 28 **Average Years Work Experience at Entry:** 5

ACADEMICS

Student/faculty Ratio: 19:1 **% Female Faculty:** 19 **% Minority Faculty:** 5

FINANCIAL FACTS

Tuition (in-state/out-of-state): $7,452/$12,902 **Books and Supplies:** $826 **Room & Board:** $7,170 **Average Grant:** $4,500

ADMISSIONS

Admissions Selectivity Rating: 74

# of Applications Received: 116 **% Applicants Accepted:** 84 **% Acceptees Attending:** 90 **Average GMAT:** 535 **Average GPA:** 3.23 **TOEFL Required of Int'l Applicants:** Yes **Minimum TOEFL (paper/computer):** 550/213 **Application Fee:** $50

Regular Application Deadline: 8/1 **Regular Notification:** rolling

Deferment Available: Yes **Maximum Length of Deferment:** 1 year **Transfer Students Accepted:** Yes **Non-fall Admissions:** Yes **Need-Blind Admissions:** Yes **Applicants Also Look At:** Wayne State University.

OHIO UNIVERSITY
COLLEGE OF BUSINESS

ADMISSIONS CONTACT: JAN ROSS, ASSISTANT DEAN, GRADUATE PROGRAM
ADDRESS: 514 COPELAND HALL, ATHENS, OH 45701
PHONE: 740-593-4320 • FAX: 740-593-1388
E-MAIL: ROSSJ@OHIO.EDU
WEBSITE: WWW.COB.OHIOU.EDU/GRAD

GENERAL INFORMATION

Type of School: Public **Environment:** Rural **Academic Calendar:** Quarters

STUDENTS

Enrollment of Parent Institution: 19,000 **Enrollment of Business School:** 112 **% Male/female:** 70/30 **% Out-of-state:** 50 **% Part-time:** 52 **% Minorities:** 16 **% International:** 18 **Average Age at Entry:** 25 **Average Years Work Experience at Entry:** 2

ACADEMICS

Student/faculty Ratio: 4:1 **% Female Faculty:** 25 **% Minority Faculty:** 10

Joint Degrees: MBA/MSp 2 years, MBA/MA International Affairs 2 years, MBA/MHA 2 years.

FINANCIAL FACTS

Tuition (in-state/out-of-state): $12,675/$25,995 **Fees:** $5,000 **Books and Supplies:** $4,000 **Room & Board:** $10,000 **% of Students Receiving Aid:** 70 **% of First-year Students Receiving Aid:** 70 **Average Award Package:** $15,000 **Average Grant:** $8,000

ADMISSIONS

Admissions Selectivity Rating: 87

# of Applications Received: 149 **% Applicants Accepted:** 38 **% Acceptees Attending:** 95 **GMAT Range (25th to 75th percentile):** 470–670 **Average GMAT:** 533 **Average GPA:** 3.3 **TOEFL Required of**

Int'l Applicants: Yes **Minimum TOEFL (paper/computer):** 600/250 **Application Fee:** $50 **International Application Fee:** $55

Regular Application Deadline: 1/15 **Regular Notification:** 4/1

Deferment Available: Yes **Maximum Length of Deferment:** 1 year **Transfer Students Accepted:** Non-fall Admissions: **Need-Blind Admissions:** Yes

OKLAHOMA STATE UNIVERSITY
SPEARS SCHOOL OF BUSINESS

ADMISSIONS CONTACT: JANICE ANALLA, ASSISTANT DIRECTOR, MBA PROGRAM
ADDRESS: OKLAHOMA STATE UNIVERSITY, 102 GUNDERSEN HALL, STILLWATER,
OK 74078-4022
PHONE: 405-744-2951 • FAX: 405-744-7474
E-MAIL: MBA-OSU@OKSTATE.EDU
WEBSITE: SPEARS.OKSTATE.EDU/MBA

GENERAL INFORMATION

Type of School: Public **Environment:** Town **Academic Calendar:** Semester

STUDENTS

Enrollment of Parent Institution: Enrollment of Business School: 319 **% Male/female:** 65/35 **% Part-time:** 72 **% Minorities:** 1 **% International:** 22 **Average Age at Entry:** 24 **Average Years Work Experience at Entry:** 5

ACADEMICS

Student/faculty Ratio: 25:1

Joint Degrees: MBA/MSTM 2.5 years, DO/MBA 1.5 years.

Prominent Alumni: Tiffany Sewell Howard, Chief Operating Officer, The Charles Machine Works; Dennis Reilley, CEO, Praxaire; Charlie Eitel, Chairman & CEO, Simmons Companies; Don Humphries, V.P. & Treasurer, Exxon Mobile.

FINANCIAL FACTS

Tuition (in-state/out-of-state): $3,601/$12,610 **Fees:** $1,754 **Books and Supplies:** $4,460 **Room & Board:** $6,780 **Average Award Package:** $4,000 **Average Grant:** $1,000 **Average Student Loan Debt:** $8,000

ADMISSIONS

Admissions Selectivity Rating: 79

# of Applications Received: 95 **% Applicants Accepted:** 66 **% Acceptees Attending:** 68 **GMAT Range (25th to 75th percentile):** 510–610 **Average GMAT:** 560 **Average GPA:** 3.5 **TOEFL Required of Int'l Applicants:** Yes **Minimum TOEFL (paper/computer):** 575/233 **Application Fee:** $40 **International Application Fee:** $75

Regular Application Deadline: 7/1 **Regular Notification:** rolling

Deferment Available: Yes **Maximum Length of Deferment:** 1 year **Transfer Students Accepted:** Yes **Non-fall Admissions:** Yes **Need-Blind Admissions:** Yes **Applicants Also Look At:** The University of Tulsa, University of Arkansas—Fayetteville, University of Kansas, University of Oklahoma.

EMPLOYMENT PROFILE

Primary Source of Full-time Job Acceptances

School-facilitated Activities 18 (45%)
Graduate-facilitated Activities 23 (55%)
Percent Employed 15

Grads Employed by Industry:.......% avg. salary:

Accounting 3 $43,000
Finance 45 $52,257
Marketing 9 $49,619
MIS 9 $66,000
Operations.....................................9 $49,000
Consulting......................................9 $49,000
General Management 7 $41,500
Other..9 $53,900

OREGON STATE UNIVERSITY
COLLEGE OF BUSINESS

ADMISSIONS CONTACT: ANITA HUGHES, MBA PROGRAM COORDINATOR
ADDRESS: 200 BEXELL HALL, COLLEGE OF BUSINESS, CORVALLIS, OR 97331
PHONE: 541-737-3716 • FAX: 541-737-4890
E-MAIL: OSUMBA@BUS.OREGONSTATE.EDU
WEBSITE: WWW.BUS.OREGONSTATE.EDU

GENERAL INFORMATION

Type of School: Public **Environment:** Town **Academic Calendar:** Quarter

STUDENTS

Enrollment of Parent Institution: 20,100 **Enrollment of Business School:** 80 **% Male/female:** 57/43 **% Out-of-state:** 10 **% Part-time:** 35 **% Minorities:** 10 **% International:** 24 **Average Age at Entry:** 27 **Average Years Work Experience at Entry:** 3

ACADEMICS

Student/faculty Ratio: 3:1 **% Female Faculty:** 15 **% Minority Faculty:** 18

FINANCIAL FACTS

Tuition (in-state/out-of-state): $9,126/$14,796 **Fees:** $2,496 **Books and Supplies:** $1,350 **Room & Board (on/off campus):** $6,336/$6,500

ADMISSIONS

Admissions Selectivity Rating: 84

# of Applications Received: 120 **% Applicants Accepted:** 67 **% Acceptees Attending:** 100 **GMAT Range (25th to 75th percentile):** 530–610 **Average GMAT:** 576 **Average GPA:** 3.27 **TOEFL Required of Int'l Applicants:** Yes **Minimum TOEFL (paper/computer):** 575/233 **Application Fee:** $50

Regular Application Deadline: 3/8 **Regular Notification:** Rolling **Deferment Available:** Yes **Transfer Students Accepted:** Yes **Non-fall Admissions:** Yes **Need-Blind Admissions:** Yes **Applicants Also Look At:** Portland State University, University of Oregon.

EMPLOYMENT PROFILE

Primary Source of Full-time Job Acceptances

Unknown...16 (100%)
Percent Employed 33

Grads Employed by Industry:.......% avg. salary:

Marketing 52 $50,000
MIS 24 $75,000
Operations.....................................12 $60,000
General Management 12 $80,000

PACE UNIVERSITY
LUBIN SCHOOL OF BUSINESS

ADMISSIONS CONTACT: SUSAN FORD-GOLDSCHEIN, ASSOCIATE DIRECTOR OF
GRADUATE ADMISSION
ADDRESS: ONE PACE PLAZA, EXECUTIVE MBA, NEW YORK, NY 10038
PHONE: (212) 346-1531 • FAX: 212-346-1585
E-MAIL: GRADNYC@PACE.EDU
WEBSITE: WWW.PACE.EDU/LUBIN

GENERAL INFORMATION

Type of School: Private **Environment:** Metropolis **Academic Calendar:** Semester

STUDENTS

Enrollment of Parent Institution: 12,912 **Enrollment of Business School:** 773 **% Male/female:** 50/50 **% Out-of-state:** 9 **% Part-time:** 73 **% Minorities:** 5 **% International:** 51 **Average Age at Entry:** 27 **Average Years Work Experience at Entry:** 2

ACADEMICS

Student/faculty Ratio: 21:1 **% Female Faculty:** 13 **% Minority Faculty:** 36

Joint Degrees: MBA/JD. **Prominent Alumni:** Ivan G. Seidenberg, Chairman and CEO Verizon Communications; Joseph R Ficalora, Chairman, President and CEO, NY Community Bancorp; William C. Nelson, Chairman and CEO, Home Box Office; Mel Karmazin, CEO Sirius Satellite Radio Inc.; Marie J. Toulantis, CEO BarnesAndNoble.com.

FINANCIAL FACTS

Books and Supplies: $3,450 **Room & Board (on/off campus):** $10,490/$19,427 **% of Students Receiving Aid:** 77 **% of First-year Students Receiving Aid:** 63 **% of Students Receiving Loans:** 48 **% of Students Receiving Grants:** 26 **Average Award Package:** $21,997 **Average Grant:** $4,981 **Average Student Loan Debt:** $37,347

ADMISSIONS

Admissions Selectivity Rating: 77

# of Applications Received: 826 **% Applicants Accepted:** 56 **% Acceptees Attending:** 40 **GMAT Range (25th to 75th percentile):** 510–580 **Average GMAT:** 540 **Average GPA:** 3.21 **TOEFL Required of Int'l Applicants:** Yes **Minimum TOEFL (paper/computer):** 570/230 **Application Fee:** $65

Regular Application Deadline: 8/1 **Regular Notification:** rolling

Transfer Students Accepted: Yes Non-fall Admissions: Yes Need-Blind Admissions: Yes Applicants Also Look At: Fairleigh Dickinson University, College at Florham, Fordham University, Hofstra University, Iona College, Long Island University—C.W. Post, St. John's University.

EMPLOYMENT PROFILE

Primary Source of Full-time Job Acceptances

School-facilitated Activities 56

Graduate-facilitated Activities 52

Unknown...19

Grads Employed by Industry: ......% avg. salary:

Finance 58 $67,588

Marketing 9 $75,605

MIS 4 $87,500

Operations.......................................4 $84,750

General Management 7 $66,157

Top 5 Employers Hiring Grads: Deloitte Touche, Ernst & Young, JPMorganChase, Grant Thornton, KPMG.

PENNSYLVANIA STATE UNIVERSITY—HARRISBURG
SCHOOL OF BUSINESS ADMINISTRATION

ADMISSIONS CONTACT: DR. THOMAS STREVELER, DIRECTOR OF ENROLLMENT SERVICES
ADDRESS: 777 WEST HARRISBURG PIKE, MIDDLETOWN, PA 17057
PHONE: 717-948-6250 • FAX: 717-948-6325
E-MAIL: HBGADMIT@PSU.EDU
WEBSITE: WWW.HBG.PSU.EDU/SBUS

GENERAL INFORMATION

Type of School: Public **Environment:** Village **Academic Calendar:** Semester

STUDENTS

Enrollment of Parent Institution: 3,239 **Enrollment of Business School:** 207 **% Male/female:** 64/36 **% Out-of-state:** 5 **% Part-time:** 88 **% Minorities:** 7 **% International:** 5 **Average Age at Entry:** 27 **Average Years Work Experience at Entry:** 3

ACADEMICS

Student/faculty Ratio: 12:1

FINANCIAL FACTS

Tuition (in-state/out-of-state): $12,000/$17,592 **Books and Supplies:** $4,170 **Average Grant:** $4,200

ADMISSIONS

Admissions Selectivity Rating: 68

# of Applications Received: 76 **% Applicants Accepted:** 91 **% Acceptees Attending:** 90 **Average GMAT:** 520 **Average GPA:** 3 **TOEFL Required of Int'l Applicants:** Yes **Minimum TOEFL (paper/computer):** 550/213 **Application Fee:** $50

Regular Application Deadline: 7/18 **Regular Notification:** rolling **Deferment Available:** Yes **Maximum Length of Deferment:** 3 years **Transfer Students Accepted:** Yes **Non-fall Admissions:** Yes **Need-Blind Admissions:** Yes

RIDER UNIVERSITY
COLLEGE OF BUSINESS ADMINSTRATION

ADMISSIONS CONTACT: JAMIE MITCHELL, DIRECTOR, GRADUATE ADMISSIONS
ADDRESS: PJ CIAMBELLI HALL, 2083 LAWRENCEVILLE ROAD, LAWRENCEVILLE, NJ 08648-3099
PHONE: 609-896-5036 • FAX: 609-895-5680
E-MAIL: GRADADM@RIDER.EDU
WEBSITE: WWW.RIDER.EDU/CBA

GENERAL INFORMATION

Type of School: Private **Environment:** Village **Academic Calendar:** Semester

STUDENTS

Enrollment of Parent Institution: 5,982 **Enrollment of Business School:** 250 **% Male/female:** 40/60 **% Out-of-state:** 13 **% Part-time:** 83 **% Minorities:** 53 **% International:** 40 **Average Age at Entry:** 27

ACADEMICS

Student/faculty Ratio: 10:1 **% Female Faculty:** 27 **% Minority Faculty:** 15

Joint Degrees: BS/BA/MBA 5 years; BS/BA/MAcc 5 years **Prominent Alumni:** Michael Cardillo, Former President, Aetna US Healthcare; Clare Hart, Chair, Exec. VP, President, Dow Jones & Co. Inc.; Terry McEwen, Director, NJ State Dept. of Banking and Insurance; Donald Noe, Managing Director,Global Head, JPMorgan Chase Bank; Michael S. Spector, Vice President, GlaxoSmithKline.

FINANCIAL FACTS

Books and Supplies: $5,320 **% of Students Receiving Aid:** 34 **% of First-year Students Receiving Aid:** 43 **% of Students Receiving Loans:** 22 **% of Students Receiving Grants:** 15 **Average Award Package:** $11,385 **Average Grant:** $6,143 **Average Student Loan Debt:** $28,796

ADMISSIONS

Admissions Selectivity Rating: 74

# of Applications Received: 97 **% Applicants Accepted:** 64 **% Acceptees Attending:** 66 **GMAT Range (25th to 75th percentile):** 450–560 **Average GMAT:** 503 **Average GPA:** 3.3 **TOEFL Required of Int'l Applicants:** Yes **Minimum TOEFL (paper/computer):** 585/240 **Application Fee:** $50

Regular Application Deadline: 8/1 Application Deadline/Notification Round 1: 08/01 / Round 2: 12/01 / Round 3: 05/01 /

Deferment Available: Yes **Maximum Length of Deferment:** 1 year **Transfer Students Accepted:** Yes **Non-fall Admissions:** Yes **Need-Blind Admissions:** Yes **Applicants Also Look At:** Rowan University, Rutgers, The State University of New Jersey.

Saint Mary's University of Minnesota
School of Graduate & Professional Programs

ADMISSIONS CONTACT: SARAH LANG, DIRECTOR OF ADMISSIONS
ADDRESS: 2500 PARK AVENUE, MINNEAPOLIS, MN 55404-4403
PHONE: 612-728-5100 • FAX: 612-728-5121
E-MAIL: TC-ADMISSION@SMUMN.EDU
WEBSITE: WWW.SMUMN.EDU/GRADPRO

GENERAL INFORMATION
Type of School: Private **Affiliation:** Roman Catholic **Environment:** Rural

STUDENTS
Enrollment of Business School: 134

ACADEMICS
Student/faculty Ratio: 12:1

FINANCIAL FACTS
Tuition: $8,520 **Fees:** $0 **Books and Supplies:** $500 **Average Award Package:** $18,090

ADMISSIONS
Admissions Selectivity Rating: 60*
# of Applications Received: 50 **% Applicants Accepted:** 80 %
TOEFL Required of Int'l Applicants: Yes **Minimum TOEFL (paper/computer):** 550/213 **Application Fee:** $25
Regular Application Deadline: rolling **Regular Notification:** rolling
Transfer Students Accepted: Yes **Non-fall Admissions:** Yes

Saint Mary's University (Canada)
Sobey School of Business

ADMISSIONS CONTACT: LEAH RAY, MANAGING DIRECTOR, MBA PROGRAM
ADDRESS: 923 ROBIE STREET, HALIFAX, NS B3H 3C3 CANADA
PHONE: 902-420-5002 • FAX: 902-420-5119
E-MAIL: MBA@SMU.CA
WEBSITE: WWW.SOBEY.SMU.CA

GENERAL INFORMATION
Type of School: Private **Academic Calendar:** Semester

STUDENTS
Enrollment of Parent Institution: 8,000 **Enrollment of Business School:** 82 **% Male/female:** 40/60 **% Out-of-state:** 60 **% Part-time:** 68 **% International:** 40 **Average Age at Entry:** 28 **Average Years Work Experience at Entry:** 6

ACADEMICS
Student/faculty Ratio: 5:1
Joint Degrees: MBA/CMA 28 months.

FINANCIAL FACTS
Tuition: $9,235 **Fees:** $480 **Books and Supplies:** $1,000 **% of Students Receiving Aid:** 20 **% of First-year Students Receiving Aid:** 10 **% of Students Receiving Grants:** 20 **Average Grant:** $2,500

ADMISSIONS
Admissions Selectivity Rating: 85
# of Applications Received: 114 **% Applicants Accepted:** 64 %
Acceptees Attending: 78 **GMAT Range (25th to 75th percentile):** 550–720 **Average GMAT:** 610 **Average GPA:** 3.3 **TOEFL Required of Int'l Applicants:** Yes **Minimum TOEFL (paper/computer):** 580/237 **Application Fee:** $70
Regular Application Deadline: 5/31 **Regular Notification:** rolling
Early Decision Program: Yes **ED Deadline/notification:** January 31st **Deferment Available:** Yes **Maximum Length of Deferment:** 1 year **Transfer Students Accepted:** Yes **Need-Blind Admissions:** Yes

Salisbury University
Franklin P. Perdue School of Business

ADMISSIONS CONTACT: SHARON HARRINGTON, INTERIM MBA DIRECTOR
ADDRESS: 1101 CAMDEN AVENUE, SALISBURY, MD 21801-6837
PHONE: 410-548-5564 • FAX: 410-548-2908
E-MAIL: SRHARRINGTON@SALISBURY.EDU
WEBSITE: MBA.SALISBURY.EDU

GENERAL INFORMATION
Type of School: Public **Environment:** Town **Academic Calendar:** Semester

STUDENTS
Enrollment of Parent Institution: 7,000 **Enrollment of Business School:** 93 **% Male/female:** 60/40 **% Part-time:** 56 **% Minorities:** 1 **% International:** 12 **Average Age at Entry:** 27 **Average Years Work Experience at Entry:** 2

ACADEMICS
Student/faculty Ratio: 22:1 **% Female Faculty:** 5

FINANCIAL FACTS
Tuition (in-state/out-of-state): $7,800/$16,380 **Fees:** $1,470 **Books and Supplies:** $1,000 **Room & Board:** $8,000 **Average Grant:** $9,680

ADMISSIONS
Admissions Selectivity Rating: 70
# of Applications Received: 58 **% Applicants Accepted:** 91 %
Acceptees Attending: 87 **Average GMAT:** 450 **Average GPA:** 3.25
TOEFL Required of Int'l Applicants: Yes **Minimum TOEFL (paper/computer):** 550/213 **Application Fee:** $45
Regular Application Deadline: 3/1 **Regular Notification:** 4/1
Transfer Students Accepted: Yes **Need-Blind Admissions:** Yes

SAM HOUSTON STATE UNIVERSITY
COLLEGE OF BUSINESS ADMINISTRATION

ADMISSIONS CONTACT: DR. LEROY ASHORN, ASSOCIATE DEAN/COORDINATOR OF GRADUATE STUDIES
ADDRESS: PO BOX 2056, HUNTSVILLE, TX 77341-2056
PHONE: 936-294-1239 • FAX: 936-294-3612
E-MAIL: BUSGRAD@SHSU.EDU
WEBSITE: COBA.SHSU.EDU

GENERAL INFORMATION
Type of School: Public **Environment:** Town **Academic Calendar:** Schedule:

STUDENTS
Enrollment of Business School: 164 **% Male/female:** 49/51 **% Part-time:** 71 **% Minorities:** 7 **% International:** 5

ACADEMICS
Student/faculty Ratio: 0:1

FINANCIAL FACTS
Tuition (in-state/out-of-state): $6,822/$11,466

ADMISSIONS
Admissions Selectivity Rating: 63
# of Applications Received: 108 **% Applicants Accepted:** 71 %
Acceptees Attending: 53 **GMAT Range (25th to 75th percentile):** 460–550 **Average GMAT:** 504 **TOEFL Required of Int'l Applicants:** Yes **Minimum TOEFL (paper/computer):** 550/213 **Application Fee:** $20

Regular Application Deadline: 8/1 **Regular Notification:** rolling
Transfer Students Accepted: Yes **Non-fall Admissions:** Yes **Need-Blind Admissions:** Yes

SAMFORD UNIVERSITY
SAMFORD UNIVERSITY SCHOOL OF BUSINESS

ADMISSIONS CONTACT: MR. LARRON C. HARPER, DIRECTOR OF GRADUATE STUDIES
ADDRESS: DBH 203E, SCHOOL OF BUSINESS, 800 LAKESHORE DR., BIRMINGHAM, AL 35229
PHONE: 205-726-2040 • FAX: 205-726-2464
E-MAIL: LEPHILLI@SAMFORD.EDU
WEBSITE: WWW.SAMFORD.EDU/BUSINESS

GENERAL INFORMATION
Type of School: Private **Affiliation:** Baptist **Environment:** Town

STUDENTS
Enrollment of Parent Institution: 4,440 **Enrollment of Business School:** 136 **% Male/female:** 100/0 **% Part-time:** 100 **Average Age at Entry:** 31 **Average Years Work Experience at Entry:** 7

ACADEMICS
Student/faculty Ratio: 12:1 **% Female Faculty:** 23 **% Minority Faculty:** 10

Joint Degrees: MBA/MAcc 1.5–7 years, MBA/JD 3–7 years MAcc/JD 3–4 years, MBA/MDiv 3–7, MBA/MSN 2–7.

FINANCIAL FACTS
Books and Supplies: $600

ADMISSIONS
Admissions Selectivity Rating: 77
# of Applications Received: 29 **% Applicants Accepted:** 59 %
Acceptees Attending: 335 **Average GMAT:** 520 **Average GPA:** 3.5
Application Fee: $25
Regular Application Deadline: Rolling **Regular Notification:** Rolling
Deferment Available: Yes **Maximum Length of Deferment:** 1 year
Transfer Students Accepted: Yes **Non-fall Admissions:** Yes **Need-Blind Admissions:** Yes **Applicants Also Look At:** University of Alabama—Birmingham.

SOUTHEASTERN LOUISIANA UNIVERSITY
COLLEGE OF BUSINESS

ADMISSIONS CONTACT: SANDRA MEYERS, GRADUATE ADMISSIONS ANALYST
ADDRESS: SLU 10752, HAMMOND, LA 70402
PHONE: 800-222-7358 • FAX: 985-549-5632
E-MAIL: SMEYERS@SELU.EDU
WEBSITE: WWW.SELU.EDU/ACAD_RESEARCH/COLLEGES/BUS

GENERAL INFORMATION
Type of School: Public **Environment:** Village **Academic Calendar:** Semester

STUDENTS
Enrollment of Parent Institution: 14,757 **Enrollment of Business School:** 147 **% Male/female:** 55/45 **% Out-of-state:** 4 **% Part-time:** 20 **% Minorities:** 15 **% International:** 13 **Average Age at Entry:** 26

ACADEMICS
Student/faculty Ratio: 6:1 **% Female Faculty:** 24 **% Minority Faculty:** 20
Prominent Alumni: Robin Roberts, ESPN Sportscaster; Russell Carollo, Pulitzer Prize Winner; Harold Jackson, President (Retired) Sunsweet Products; James J. Brady, Former President, National Democratic Party; Carl Barbier, Federal Judge.

FINANCIAL FACTS
Tuition (in-state/out-of-state): $2,216/$6,716 **Fees:** $1,105 **Books and Supplies:** $1,200 **Room & Board (on/off campus):** $5,990/$7,660 **% of Students Receiving Aid:** 50 **% of First-year Students Receiving Aid:** 73 **% of Students Receiving Loans:** 26 **Average Award Package:** $8,721 **Average Student Loan Debt:** $7,141

ADMISSIONS
Admissions Selectivity Rating: 64
# of Applications Received: 44 **% Applicants Accepted:** 98 %

Acceptees Attending: 84 GMAT Range (25th to 75th percentile): 400–640 Average GMAT: 480 Average GPA: 3.21 TOEFL Required of Int'l Applicants: Yes Minimum TOEFL (paper/computer): 525/195 Application Fee: $20 International Application Fee: $30 Regular Application Deadline: 7/15 Regular Notification: rolling Deferment Available: Yes Maximum Length of Deferment: 1 year Transfer Students Accepted: Yes Non-fall Admissions: Yes Need-Blind Admissions: Yes

SOUTHERN UTAH UNIVERSITY
SCHOOL OF BUSINESS

ADMISSIONS CONTACT: STEVE ALLEN, DIRECTOR OF ADMISSION
ADDRESS: 351 WEST UNIVERSITY BLVD., CEDAR CITY, UT 84720
PHONE: 435-586-7740 • FAX: 435-865-8223
E-MAIL: ADMINFO@SUU.EDU
WEBSITE: WWW.SUU.EDU/BUSINESS

GENERAL INFORMATION
Type of School: Public Academic Calendar: July–June

STUDENTS
Enrollment of Business School: 48 % Male/female: 75/25 % Out-of-state: 6 % Part-time: 33 % Minorities: 2 % International: 4

ACADEMICS
Student/faculty Ratio: 4:1 % Female Faculty: 2

FINANCIAL FACTS
Tuition (in-state/out-of-state): $6,474/$21,364 Fees: $522 Books and Supplies: $800 % of Students Receiving Aid: 10 % of First-year Students Receiving Aid: 10 Average Award Package: $7,170

ADMISSIONS
Admissions Selectivity Rating: 70
# of Applications Received: 59 % Applicants Accepted: 90 % Acceptees Attending: 91 Average GMAT: 522 Average GPA: 3.4 TOEFL Required of Int'l Applicants: Yes Minimum TOEFL (paper/computer): 500/173 Application Fee: $50
Regular Application Deadline: 3/31 Regular Notification: 4/1
Deferment Available: Yes Maximum Length of Deferment: 1 year Transfer Students Accepted: Yes Non-fall Admissions: Yes Need-Blind Admissions: Yes Applicants Also Look At: Utah State University, Weber State University.

EMPLOYMENT PROFILE
Grads Employed by Industry: ....%
Finance 37
Human Resources...........................3
Marketing 10
Operations.......................................7
General Management 20
Other..23

ST. CLOUD STATE UNIVERSITY
HERBERGER COLLEGE OF BUSINESS

ADMISSIONS CONTACT: GRADUATE STUDIES OFFICE, ANNETTE DAY, GRADUATE ADMISSIONS MANAGER
ADDRESS: 720 4TH AVE. SOUTH, AS-121, ST. CLOUD, MN 56301-4498
PHONE: 320-308-2112 • FAX: 320-308-3986
E-MAIL: GRADUATESTUDIES@STCLOUDSTATE.EDU
WEBSITE: WWW.STCLOUDSTATE.EDU/MBA

GENERAL INFORMATION
Type of School: Public Academic Calendar: Semester

STUDENTS
Enrollment of Parent Institution: 16,334 Enrollment of Business School: 166 % Male/female: 71/29 % Out-of-state: 18 % Part-time: 75 % Minorities: 10 % International: 48 Average Age at Entry: 28 Average Years Work Experience at Entry: 5

ACADEMICS
Student/faculty Ratio: 25:1 % Female Faculty: 27 % Minority Faculty: 20

FINANCIAL FACTS
Tuition: $14,292 Fees: $165 Books and Supplies: $1,800

ADMISSIONS
Admissions Selectivity Rating: 80
% Acceptees Attending: 48 GMAT Range (25th to 75th percentile): 470–700 Average GMAT: 525 Average GPA: 3.3 TOEFL Required of Int'l Applicants: Yes Minimum TOEFL (paper/computer): 550/213 Application Fee: $35
Regular Application Deadline: rolling Regular Notification: rolling ED Deadline/notification: 04/15 / 06/15Deferment Available: Yes Maximum Length of Deferment: 2 years Non-fall Admissions: Yes Need-Blind Admissions

ST. JOHN FISHER COLLEGE
RONALD L. BITTNER SCHOOL OF BUSINESS

ADMISSIONS CONTACT: OFFICE OF GRADUATE ADMISSIONS, MBA ADMISSIONS COORDINATOR
ADDRESS: 3690 EAST AVE, OFFICE OF GRADUATE ADMISSIONS, ROCHESTER, NY 14618
PHONE: 585-385-8161 • FAX: 585-385-8344
E-MAIL: GRAD@SJFC.EDU
WEBSITE: WWW.SJFC.EDU/BITTNER

GENERAL INFORMATION
Type of School: Private

STUDENTS
Enrollment of Parent Institution: 3,704 Enrollment of Business School: 88 % Male/female: 38/62 % Part-time: 61 % Minorities: 18 Average Age at Entry: 33

FINANCIAL FACTS

Tuition: $46,000 **Average Award Package:** $29,967

ADMISSIONS

Admissions Selectivity Rating: 76

# of Applications Received: 74 **% Applicants Accepted:** 61 % **Acceptees Attending:** 80 **GMAT Range (25th to 75th percentile):** 460–550 **Average GMAT:** 501 **Average GPA:** 3.3 **TOEFL Required of Int'l Applicants:** Yes **Application Fee:** $30

Regular Application Deadline: 7/1

Deferment Available: Yes **Maximum Length of Deferment:** 1 year **Transfer Students Accepted:** Yes **Non-fall Admissions:** Yes **Need-Blind Admissions:** Yes **Applicants Also Look At:** University of Rochester.

EMPLOYMENT PROFILE

Percent Employed 100

Grads Employed by Industry: ....%

Finance 10

Marketing 10

Operations.......................................30

General Management 40

Other..10

STEPHEN F. AUSTIN STATE UNIVERSITY

NELSON RUSCHE COLLEGE OF BUSINESS

ADMISSIONS CONTACT: MICHAEL D. STROUP, MBA DIRECTOR
ADDRESS: PO BOX 13004, SFA STATION, STEPHEN F. AUSTIN STATE UNIVERSITY, NACOGDOCHES, TX 75962-3004
PHONE: 936-468-3101 • FAX: 936-468-1560
E-MAIL: MBA@SFASU.EDU
WEBSITE: WWW.COB.SFASU.EDU

GENERAL INFORMATION

Type of School: Public **Environment:** Town

STUDENTS

Enrollment of Parent Institution: 10,000 **Enrollment of Business School:** 45 **% Male/female:** 60/40 **% Out-of-state:** 5 **% Part-time:** 50 **% Minorities:** 25 **% International:** 15 **Average Age at Entry:** 25 **Average Years Work Experience at Entry:** 3

ACADEMICS

Student/faculty Ratio: 10:1 **% Female Faculty:** 30 **% Minority Faculty:** 10

Prominent Alumni: Dr. Phil Stetz, Entrepreneurship; Dr. John Lewis, Finance; Dr. Dave Gundersen, Management.

FINANCIAL FACTS

Tuition (in-state/out-of-state): $1,134/$7,236 **Fees (in-state/out-of-state):** $126/$804 **Books and Supplies:** $1,000 **Room & Board (on/off campus):** $5,000/$6,500 **% of Students Receiving Aid:** 15

% of First-year Students Receiving Aid: 5 **% of Students Receiving Loans:** 5 **Average Award Package:** $3,500 **Average Grant:** $3,500

ADMISSIONS

Admissions Selectivity Rating: 60*

# of Applications Received: 60 **GMAT Range (25th to 75th percentile):** 290–660 **Average GMAT:** 510 **Average GPA:** 3.0 **TOEFL Required of Int'l Applicants:** Yes **Minimum TOEFL (paper/computer):** 550/213 **Application Fee:** $25 **International Application Fee:** $50

Regular Application Deadline: 8/1 **Regular Notification:** 8/15

Deferment Available: Yes **Maximum Length of Deferment:** 1 year **Transfer Students Accepted:** Yes **Non-fall Admissions:** Yes **Need-Blind Admissions:** Yes **Applicants Also Look At:** Northwestern University, Sam Houston State University, Texas State Univeristy—San Marcos, University of North Texas.

EMPLOYMENT PROFILE

Grads Employed by Industry: ....% avg. salary:

Finance 15 $65,000

Marketing 25 $45,000

General Management 20 $45,000

TENNESSEE STATE UNIVERSITY

ADMISSIONS CONTACT: LISA SMITH, DIRECTOR OF PUBLIC SERVICE
ADDRESS: 330 10TH AVENUE NORTH, SUITE K, NASHVILLE, TN 37203
PHONE: 615-963-7137 • FAX: 615-963-7139
E-MAIL: LSMITH11@TNSTATE.EDU
WEBSITE: WWW.COB.TNSTATE.EDU

GENERAL INFORMATION

Type of School: Public **Environment:** City

STUDENTS

Enrollment of Business School: 100

ACADEMICS

Student/faculty Ratio: 12:1

Prominent Alumni: Nicole Dunigan, Vice President, First Tennessee Bank; Thelma Harper, Senator, State of Tennessee; Kevin Williams, Vice President, General Motors; Karen Isabel, CEO, Dalmatian Creative Agency, Inc; Darren Johnson, Author, Entrepreneur.

FINANCIAL FACTS

Tuition (in-state/out-of-state): $2,569/$4,847 **Fees (in-state/out-of-state):** $428/$2,937 **Books and Supplies:** $2,000 **Room & Board (on/off campus):** $3,160/$4,000

ADMISSIONS

Admissions Selectivity Rating: 60*

Average GMAT: 510 **Average GPA:** 3.2 **TOEFL Required of Int'l Applicants:** Yes **Minimum TOEFL:** 500 **Application Fee:** $25

Deferment Available: Yes **Transfer Students Accepted:** Yes **Non-fall Admissions:** Yes **Need-Blind Admissions:** Yes

TEXAS A&M UNIVERSITY—COMMERCE

COLLEGE OF BUSINESS AND TECHNOLOGY

ADMISSIONS CONTACT: VICKY TURNER, GRADUATE ADMISSIONS
ADDRESS: P O BOX 3011, COMMERCE, TX 75429
PHONE: 903-886-5167 • FAX: 903-886-5165
E-MAIL: GRADUATE_SCHOOL@TAMU-COMMERCE.EDU
WEBSITE: WWW.TAMU-COMMERCE.EDU/GRADUATEPROGRAMS

GENERAL INFORMATION

Type of School: Public **Academic Calendar:** Semester

STUDENTS

Enrollment of Parent Institution: 7,678 **Enrollment of Business School:** 489 **% Male/female:** 56/44 **% Part-time:** 61 **% Minorities:** 53 **% International:** 23 **Average Age at Entry:** 22

ACADEMICS

Student/faculty Ratio: 27:1 **% Female Faculty:** 10 **% Minority Faculty:** 10

Joint Degrees: BPA/MBA 5 years. **Prominent Alumni:** Sam Rayburn, Speaker of the House; Sheryl Leach, Creator of Barney; Durwood Merril, Baseball Umpire, Texas Baseball Hall of Fame; Duane Allen, Oak Ridge Boys, Lead Singer; Wade Wilson, Dallas Cowboys Quaterback Coach.

FINANCIAL FACTS

Tuition (in-state/out-of-state): $6,800/$15,050 **Books and Supplies:** $700 **Room & Board (on/off campus):** $2,850/$2,170

ADMISSIONS

Admissions Selectivity Rating: 70

# of Applications Received: 1,215 **% Applicants Accepted:** 60 **% Acceptees Attending:** 65 **GMAT Range (25th to 75th percentile):** 380–620 **Average GMAT:** 460 **Average GPA:** 3 **TOEFL Required of Int'l Applicants:** Yes **Minimum TOEFL (paper/computer):** 500/173 **Application Fee:** $35 **International Application Fee:** $50

Regular Application Deadline: 6/1 **Regular Notification:** Rolling

Deferment Available: Yes **Maximum Length of Deferment:** 2 Semesters **Transfer Students Accepted:** Yes **Non-fall Admissions:** Yes **Applicants Also Look At:** Baylor University, Southern Methodist University, Texas Christian University, The University of Texas at Arlington, University of Dallas, University of North Texas, University of Phoenix.

UNION GRADUATE COLLEGE

SCHOOL OF MANAGEMENT

ADMISSIONS CONTACT: RHONDA SHEEHAN, DIRECTOR, GRADUATE ADMISSIONS AND REGISTRAR
ADDRESS: LAMONT HOUSE, 807 UNION ST., SCHENECTADY, NY 12308
PHONE: 518-388-6148 • FAX: 518-388-6686
WEBSITE: WWW.UNIONGRADUATECOLLEGE.EDU

GENERAL INFORMATION

Type of School: Private **Environment:** Town **Academic Calendar:** Trimester

STUDENTS

Enrollment of Parent Institution: 500 **Enrollment of Business School:** 279 **% Male/female:** 67/33 **% Out-of-state:** 4 **% Part-time:** 63 **% Minorities:** 15 **% International:** 14 **Average Age at Entry:** 26 **Average Years Work Experience at Entry:** 3

ACADEMICS

Student/faculty Ratio: 15:1 **% Female Faculty:** 38 **% Minority Faculty:** 9

Joint Degrees: JD/MBA 4 years, BA/BS-MBA 5 years, PharmD/MS or MBA 6 years.

FINANCIAL FACTS

Tuition: $23,000 **Fees:** $125 **Books and Supplies:** $15,000 **Room & Board:** $10,000 **% of First-year Students Receiving Aid:** 70 **Average Award Package:** $18,000 **Average Grant:** $4,000 **Average Student Loan Debt:** $21,000

ADMISSIONS

Admissions Selectivity Rating: 76

# of Applications Received: 139 **% Applicants Accepted:** 73 **% Acceptees Attending:** 77 **GMAT Range (25th to 75th percentile):** 500–630 **Average GMAT:** 550 **Average GPA:** 3.3 **TOEFL Required of Int'l Applicants:** Yes **Minimum TOEFL (paper/computer):** 550/213 **Application Fee:** $60

Deferment Available: Yes **Maximum Length of Deferment:** 1 year **Transfer Students Accepted:** Yes **Non-fall Admissions:** Yes **Need-Blind Admissions:** Yes **Applicants Also Look At:** Albany Law School, Rensselaer Polytechnic Institute.

EMPLOYMENT PROFILE

Percent Employed 20

UNIVERSITE LAVAL
FACULTÉ DES SCIENCES DE L'ADMINISTRATION

ADDRESS: BUREAU DU REGISTRAIRE, PAVILLON JEAN-CHARLES-BONENFANT,
2345, ALLÉE DES BIBLIOTHÈQUES, LOCAL 2440, UNIVERSITÉ LAVAL, QUÉBEC,
QC G1V 0A6 CANADA
PHONE: 418-656-3080 • FAX: 418-656-5216
E-MAIL: REG@REG.ULAVAL.CA
WEBSITE: WWW.FSA.ULAVAL.CA

GENERAL INFORMATION

Type of School: Public **Academic Calendar:** Semester

STUDENTS

Enrollment of Parent Institution: 37,181 **Enrollment of Business School:** 936 **% Male/female:** 60/40 **% Out-of-state:** 36 **% Part-time:** 70 **% International:** 50 **Average Age at Entry:** 28 **Average Years Work Experience at Entry:** 4

ACADEMICS

Student/faculty Ratio: 25:1 **% Female Faculty:** 30

FINANCIAL FACTS

Tuition (in-state/out-of-state): $2,090/$10,488 **Books and Supplies:** $17,307 **Room & Board (on/off campus):** $5,800/$9,200

ADMISSIONS

Admissions Selectivity Rating: 79

# of Applications Received: 1,112 **% Applicants Accepted:** 65 **% Acceptees Attending:** 47 **Average GPA:** 3.0 **TOEFL Required of Int'l Applicants:** Yes **Minimum TOEFL (paper/computer):** 550/213 **Application Fee:** $30

Regular Application Deadline: 2/1 **Regular Notification:** Rolling **Deferment Available:** Yes **Maximum Length of Deferment:** 1 year **Non-fall Admissions:** Yes

EMPLOYMENT PROFILE

Percent Employed 72

Grads Employed by Industry: ......% avg. salary:

Top 5 Employers Hiring Grads: Desjardins, Banque Laurentienne, Ranstad, Canadian government, Université Laval.

UNIVERSITY COLLEGE DUBLIN
UCD MICHAEL SMURFIT GRADUATE BUSINESS SCHOOL

ADMISSIONS CONTACT: ELAINE MCAREE, MBA ADMISSIONS MANAGER
ADDRESS: UCD SMURFIT SCHOOL OF BUSINESS, CARYSFORT AVENUE,
BLACKROCK, CO. DUBLIN, IRELAND
PHONE: 00 353 1 7168862 • FAX: 00 353 1 7168981
E-MAIL: MBA@UCD.IE
WEBSITE: WWW.UCD.IE/SMURFITSCHOOL

GENERAL INFORMATION

Type of School: Public

STUDENTS

Enrollment of Parent Institution: 22,000 **% Male/female:** 69/31 **% International:** 54 **Average Age at Entry:** 30 **Average Years Work Experience at Entry:** 7

ACADEMICS

Student/faculty Ratio: 3:1 **% Female Faculty:** 23

Joint Degrees: CEMS Masters (Community of European Management Schools) 1 year. **Prominent Alumni:** Patrick Haren, Group Chief Executive, Viridian; Cathal McGloin, CEO and Founder, Perform; JP Donnelly, Managing Director, Ogilvy & Mather.

FINANCIAL FACTS

Tuition: $45,942 **Books and Supplies:** $2,000 **Room & Board:** $11,203/$12,000 **% of Students Receiving Aid:** 40 **% of First-year Students Receiving Aid:** 40 **% of Students Receiving Loans:** 8 **% of Students Receiving Grants:** 31 **Average Award Package:** $23,000 **Average Grant:** $18,885 **Average Student Loan Debt:** $56,100

ADMISSIONS

Admissions Selectivity Rating: 60*

# of Applications Received: 162 **% Applicants Accepted:** 22 % **Average GMAT:** 623 **TOEFL Required of Int'l Applicants:** Yes **Minimum TOEFL (paper/computer):** 600/250 **Application Fee:** $35

Application Deadline/Notification Round 1: 02/01, Round 2: 03/28, Round 3: 05/23, Round 4: 07/11.

Deferment Available: Yes **Maximum Length of Deferment:** 1 year **Transfer Students Accepted:** Yes **Need-Blind Admissions:** Yes **Applicants Also Look At:** IESE Business School, INSEAD, RSM Erasmus University, University of Dublin, Trinity College, University of London, University of Oxford, University of Warwick.

EMPLOYMENT PROFILE

Percent Employed 95

Grads Employed by Industry: ......%

Finance 30

Human Resources..........................3

Marketing 25

MIS 6

Operations......................................6

Strategic Planning..........................6

Consulting.....................................15

General Management 9

Top 5 Employers Hiring Grads: McKinsey, Dell, Ulster Bank, Citibank, CRH

UNIVERSITY OF ALABAMA IN HUNTSVILLE
COLLEGE OF BUSINESS ADMINISTRATION

ADMISSIONS CONTACT: DR. J. DANIEL SHERMAN, ASSOCIATE DEAN
ADDRESS: ASB 102, HUNTSVILLE, AL 35899
PHONE: 256-824-6681 • FAX: 256-890-7571
E-MAIL: GRADBIZ@UAH.EDU
WEBSITE: WWW.UAH.EDU

GENERAL INFORMATION
Type of School: Public **Environment:** City **Academic Calendar:** Semester

ACADEMICS
Student/faculty Ratio: 5:1 **% Female Faculty:** 15 **% Minority Faculty:** 29

FINANCIAL FACTS
Tuition (in-state/out-of-state): $5,132/$10,532 **Books and Supplies:** $900

ADMISSIONS
Admissions Selectivity Rating: 71
TOEFL Required of Int'l Applicants: Yes **Minimum TOEFL:** 550 **Application Fee:** $40
Regular Application Deadline: 8/1 **Regular Notification:** 1/1
Transfer Students Accepted: Yes **Non-fall Admissions:** Yes **Need-Blind Admissions:** Yes

UNIVERSITY OF ALASKA ANCHORAGE
COLLEGE OF BUSINESS AND PUBLIC POLICY

ADMISSIONS CONTACT: AL KASTAR, DIRECTOR OF ADMISSIONS
ADDRESS: PO BOX 141629, ANCHORAGE, AK 99514-1629
PHONE: 907-786-1480 • FAX: 907-786-4888
E-MAIL: AYADMIT@UAA.ALASKA.EDU
WEBSITE: WWW.CBPP.UAA.ALASKA.EDU

GENERAL INFORMATION
Type of School: Public **Environment:** City

STUDENTS
Enrollment of Business School: 100 **% Male/female:** 40/60 **% Part-time:** 65 **% Minorities:** 39 **% International:** 25

ACADEMICS
Student/faculty Ratio: 20:1 **% Female Faculty:** 19 **% Minority Faculty:** 35

FINANCIAL FACTS
Tuition (in-state/out-of-state): $5,418/$11,070 **Fees:** $560 **Books and Supplies:** $750 **Room & Board:** $8,350

ADMISSIONS
Admissions Selectivity Rating: 77
# of Applications Received: 64 **% Applicants Accepted:** 70 %
Acceptees Attending: 76: **Average GPA:** 3.2 **TOEFL Required of Int'l Applicants:** Yes **Minimum TOEFL:** 550 **Application Fee:** $60
Regular Application Deadline: Rolling **Regular Notification:** Rolling
Deferment Available: Yes **Maximum Length of Deferment:** One semester **Transfer Students Accepted:** Yes **Non-fall Admissions:** Yes **Need-Blind Admissions:** Yes

UNIVERSITY OF ALASKA— FAIRBANKS
SCHOOL OF MANAGEMENT

ADMISSIONS CONTACT: NANCY DIX, DIRECTOR
ADDRESS: P.O. BOX 757480, FAIRBANKS, AK 99775
PHONE: 907-474-7500 • FAX: 907-474-5379
E-MAIL: ADMISSIONS@UAF.EDU
WEBSITE: WWW.UAFSOM.COM/GPMBA

GENERAL INFORMATION
Type of School: Public **Environment:** City

STUDENTS
Enrollment of Parent Institution: 5,025 **Enrollment of Business School:** 30 **Average Age at Entry:** 32 **Average Years Work Experience at Entry:** 10.3

ACADEMICS
Student/faculty Ratio: 3:1 **% Female Faculty:** 30 **% Minority Faculty:** 20

FINANCIAL FACTS
Tuition (in-state/out-of-state): $4,824/$9,846 **Fees:** $670 **Books and Supplies:** $1,076 **Room & Board (on/off campus):** $6,030/$10,413 **Average Grant:** $16,928 **Average Student Loan Debt:** $12,166

ADMISSIONS
Admissions Selectivity Rating: 90
% Acceptees Attending: 92 GMAT Range **Average GMAT:** 547 **Average GPA:** 3.5 **TOEFL Required of Int'l Applicants:** Yes **Minimum TOEFL (paper/computer):** 550/213 **Application Fee:** $50
Regular Application Deadline: 8/1 **Regular Notification:** 8/1
Deferment Available: Yes **Maximum Length of Deferment:** 1 year **Transfer Students Accepted:** Yes **Non-fall Admissions:** Yes **Need-Blind Admissions:** Yes **Applicants Also Look At:** University of Alaska—Anchorage.

UNIVERSITY OF ARKANSAS— LITTLE ROCK

COLLEGE OF BUSINESS

ADMISSIONS CONTACT: DR. KEN GLACHUS, MBA ADVISOR
ADDRESS: 2801 SOUTH UNIVERSITY AVENUE, LITTLE ROCK, AR 72204
PHONE: 501-569-3356 • FAX: 501-569-8898
WEBSITE: WWW.CBA.UALR.EDU

GENERAL INFORMATION

Type of School: Public **Environment:** City **Academic Calendar:** Semester

STUDENTS

Enrollment of Parent Institution: 9,925 **Enrollment of Business School:** 225 **% Male/female:** 58/42 **% Out-of-state:** 1 **% Part-time:** 87 **% Minorities:** 8 **% International:** 15 **Average Age at Entry:** 29

FINANCIAL FACTS

Tuition: $30,500

ADMISSIONS

Admissions Selectivity Rating: 60*

# of Applications Received: 87 **% Applicants Accepted:** 66 **% Acceptees Attending:** 74 **TOEFL Required of Int'l Applicants:** Yes **Minimum TOEFL:** 550 **Regular Application Deadline:** Rolling **Regular Notification:** Rolling

Deferment Available: Yes **Applicants Also Look At:** Babson College, Indiana University—South Bend, Rensselaer Polytechnic Institute.

UNIVERSITY OF BALTIMORE

MERRICK SCHOOL OF BUSINESS

ADMISSIONS CONTACT: DEAN DREIBELBIS, ASSISTANT DIRECTOR OF ADMISSIONS
ADDRESS: 1420 NORTH CHARLES STREET, BALTIMORE, MD 21201
PHONE: 888-664-0125 • FAX: 410-837-4774
E-MAIL: MBA@TOWSON.UBALT.EDU
WEBSITE: WWW.UBTOWSONMBA.COM

GENERAL INFORMATION

Type of School: Public **Environment:** Metropolis **Academic Calendar:** Semester

STUDENTS

Enrollment of Parent Institution: 5,240 **Enrollment of Business School:** 518 **% Male/female:** 58/42 **% Out-of-state:** 17 **% Part-time:** 77 **% Minorities:** 15 **% International:** 37 **Average Age at Entry:** 30 **Average Years Work Experience at Entry:** 4

ACADEMICS

Student/faculty Ratio: 15:1 **% Female Faculty:** 30 **% Minority Faculty:** 34

Joint Degrees: MBA/JD, MBA/MS in Nursing, MBA/PhD in Nursing, MBA/Pharm.D., MBA/MAJCS in Jewish Communal Studies, MBA/MAJE in Jewish Education. **Prominent Alumni:** William Donald

Schaeffer, Govenor, State of Maryland; Peter Angelos, Owner, Baltimore Orioles; Joseph Curran, Attorney General, State of Maryland; Vernon Wright, Vice Chairman, MBNA America Bank.

FINANCIAL FACTS

Books and Supplies: $900

ADMISSIONS

Admissions Selectivity Rating: 83

# of Applications Received: 434 **% Applicants Accepted:** 44 **% Acceptees Attending:** 81 **GMAT Range (25th to 75th percentile):** 480–535 **Average GMAT:** 525 **Average GPA:** 3.2 **TOEFL Required of Int'l Applicants:** Yes **Minimum TOEFL (paper/computer):** 550/213 **Application Fee:** $30

Regular Application Deadline: rolling **Regular Notification:** rolling **Deferment Available:** Yes **Maximum Length of Deferment:** 1 year **Transfer Students Accepted:** Yes **Non-fall Admissions:** Yes **Need-Blind Admissions:** Yes **Applicants Also Look At:** Loyola College in Maryland, University of Maryland—College Park.

UNIVERSITY OF CENTRAL MISSOURI

HARMON COLLEGE OF BUSINESS ADMINISTRATION

ADMISSIONS CONTACT: LAURIE DELAP, ADMISSIONS EVALUATOR, GRADUATE SCHOOL
ADDRESS: WARD EDWARDS 1800, WARRENSBURG, MO 64093
PHONE: 660-543-4328 • FAX: 660-543-4778
E-MAIL: DELAP@UCMO.EDU
WEBSITE: WWW.UCMO.EDU/GRADUATE

GENERAL INFORMATION

Type of School: Public **Environment:** Rural **Academic Calendar:** Semester

STUDENTS

Enrollment of Parent Institution: 10,711 **Enrollment of Business School:** 53 **% Male/female:** 57/43 **% Out-of-state:** 40 **% Part-time:** 38 **% Minorities:** 8 **Average Age at Entry:** 26 **Average Years Work Experience at Entry:** 3

ACADEMICS

Student/faculty Ratio: 2:1 **% Female Faculty:** 29 **% Minority Faculty:** 2

FINANCIAL FACTS

Tuition (in-state/out-of-state): $5,784/$11,232 **Fees:** $0 **Books and Supplies:** $1,200 **Room & Board:** $5,412 **% of Students Receiving Grants:** 50

ADMISSIONS

Admissions Selectivity Rating: 71

# of Applications Received: 74 **% Applicants Accepted:** 66 **% Acceptees Attending:** 51 **GMAT Range (25th to 75th percentile):** 440–540 **Average GMAT:** 482 **Average GPA:** 3.3 **TOEFL Required of**

Int'l Applicants: Yes **Minimum TOEFL (paper/computer):** 550/213
Application Fee: $30 **International Application Fee:** $50
Regular Application Deadline: Rolling **Regular Notification:** Rolling
Deferment Available: Yes **Maximum Length of Deferment:** 2
semesters **Transfer Students Accepted:** Yes **Non-fall Admissions:**
Yes **Need-Blind Admissions:** Yes **Applicants Also Look At:** Missouri
State University, Southeast Missouri State University, University of
Missouri—Kansas City.

University of Colorado—

Boulder
Leeds School of Business

Admissions Contact: Anne Sandoe, Director of MBA Programs
Address: UCB 419, Boulder, CO 80309
Phone: 303-492-8397 • Fax: 303-492-1727
E-mail: LeedsMBA@colorado.edu
Website: leeds.colorado.edu/mba

GENERAL INFORMATION

Type of School: Public **Environment:** City **Academic Calendar:**
Semester

STUDENTS

Enrollment of Parent Institution: 28,624 **Enrollment of Business
School:** 240 **% Male/female:** 67/33 **% Out-of-state:** 49 **% Part-
time:** 47 **% Minorities:** 8 **% International:** 19 **Average Age at Entry:**
28 **Average Years Work Experience at Entry:** 5

ACADEMICS

Student/faculty Ratio: 4:1 **% Female Faculty:** 12 **% Minority
Faculty:** 6
Joint Degrees: JD/MBA 4 years full time, MBA/MS in
Telecommunications and/or Computer Science, 3–3.5, MBA/MA in
Fine Arts 3 years, MBA/MA in Theatre and Dance 3 years, MBA/MA
Germanic Languages 3 years, MBA/MS Environmental studies 3
years and MBA/MA in Anthropology 3 years. **Prominent Alumni:**
Kevin Burns, Managing Principle, Lazard Technology Partners; John
Puerner, President & CEO, Los Angeles Times; Patrick Tierney, CEO,
Reed Elsevier; Dick Fuld, CEO, Lehman Brothers; Michael Leeds,
Pres & CEO, Flightstar.

FINANCIAL FACTS

Tuition (in-state/out-of-state): $10,487/$24,634 **Fees:** $1,300 **Books
and Supplies:** $3,000 **Room & Board (on/off campus):**
$12,245/$13,000 **% of Students Receiving Aid:** 47 **% of First-year
Students Receiving Aid:** 56 **% of Students Receiving Grants:** 47
Average Award Package: $23,200 **Average Grant:** $4,750 **Average
Student Loan Debt:** $32,000

ADMISSIONS

Admissions Selectivity Rating: 89
# of Applications Received: 282 **% Applicants Accepted:** 51 **%
Acceptees Attending:** 55 **GMAT Range (25th to 75th percentile):**
590–680 **Average GMAT:** 630 **Average GPA:** 3.4 **TOEFL Required of**

Int'l Applicants: Yes **Minimum TOEFL (paper/computer):** 600/250
Application Fee: $70
Regular Application Deadline: 4/1 **Regular Notification:** 6/15
Application Deadline/Notification Round 1: 12/01 / 02/15 Round 2:
02/01 / 04/15 Round 3: 04/01 / 06/15
Early Decision Program: Yes **ED Deadline/notification:** 12/1 / 2/15
Deferment Available: Yes **Maximum Length of Deferment:** 1 year
Need-Blind Admissions: Yes **Applicants Also Look At:** Arizona State
University, Colorado State University, The University of Texas at
Austin, University of California—Berkeley, University of Colorado—
Denver, University of Denver, University of Washington.

EMPLOYMENT PROFILE
Primary Source of Full-time Job Acceptances

School-facilitated Activities	....	41 (87%)
Graduate-facilitated Activities	....	7 (15%)
Unknown	....	1 (2%)
Percent Employed	....	87

Grads Employed by Industry:	**% avg. salary:**
Finance	38 $67,400
Marketing	23 $72,850
Operations	6 $75,500
Consulting	21 $64,500
General Management	6 $65,000
Other	6 $65,000

University of Colorado at

Colorado Springs
Graduate School of Business Administration

Admissions Contact: Tamara McCollough, MBA Admissions Coordinator
Address: 1420 Austin Bluffs Parkway, Colorado Springs, CO 80918
Phone: 719-262-3408 • Fax: 719-262-3100
E-mail: mbacred@uccs.edu
Website: business.uccs.edu/mba

GENERAL INFORMATION

Type of School: Public **Environment:** Metropolis **Academic
Calendar:** Semester

STUDENTS

Enrollment of Parent Institution: 8,520 **Enrollment of Business
School:** 454 **% Male/female:** 100/0 **% Part-time:** 100 **Average Age
at Entry:** 30 **Average Years Work Experience at Entry:** 8

ACADEMICS

Student/faculty Ratio: 8:1 **% Female Faculty:** 16 **% Minority
Faculty:** 5

ADMISSIONS

Admissions Selectivity Rating: 72
# of Applications Received: 98 **% Applicants Accepted:** 92 **%
Acceptees Attending:** 82 **GMAT Range (25th to 75th percentile):**

470–640 **Average GMAT:** 560 **Average GPA:** 3.1 **TOEFL Required of Int'l Applicants:** Yes **Minimum TOEFL (paper/computer):** 550/213 **Application Fee:** $60 **International Application Fee:** $75 **Regular Application Deadline:** 6/1 **Regular Notification:** Rolling **Deferment Available:** Yes **Maximum Length of Deferment:** 1 year **Transfer Students Accepted:** Yes **Non-fall Admissions:** Yes **Need-Blind Admissions:** Yes

UNIVERSITY OF COLORADO— DENVER
BUSINESS SCHOOL

ADMISSIONS CONTACT: SHELLY TOWNLEY, GRADUATE ADMISSIONS COORDINATOR ADDRESS: CAMPUS BOX 165, PO BOX 173364, DENVER, CO 80217-3364 PHONE: 303-556-5900 • FAX: 303-556-5904 E-MAIL: GRAD.BUSINESS@CUDENVER.EDU. WEBSITE: WWW.BUSINESS.CUDENVER.EDU

GENERAL INFORMATION
Type of School: Public **Environment:** Metropolis **Academic Calendar:** Semester

STUDENTS
Enrollment of Parent Institution: 11,050 **Enrollment of Business School:** 1,249 **% Male/female:** 89/11 **% Out-of-state:** 1 **% Part-time:** 71 **% Minorities:** 10 **% International:** 14 **Average Age at Entry:** 25

ACADEMICS
Student/faculty Ratio: 35:1
Joint Degrees: MBA can be combined with any MS degree

FINANCIAL FACTS
Tuition (in-state/out-of-state): $7,844/$18,638 **Fees:** $594 **Books and Supplies:** $1,700 **Room & Board (on/off campus):** $9,950/$8,110 **% of Students Receiving Aid:** 61 **% of First-year Students Receiving Aid:** 24 **% of Students Receiving Loans:** 52 **% of Students Receiving Grants:** 22 **Average Award Package:** $7,380 **Average Grant:** $4,640 **Average Student Loan Debt:** $33,815

ADMISSIONS
Admissions Selectivity Rating: 60*
# of Applications Received: 547 **% Applicants Accepted:** 74 **% Acceptees Attending:** 64 **TOEFL Required of Int'l Applicants:** Yes **Minimum TOEFL (paper/computer):** 525/197 **Application Fee:** $50 **International Application Fee:** $75
Regular Application Deadline: 6/1 **Regular Notification:** rolling **Deferment Available:** Yes **Maximum Length of Deferment:** 1 year **Transfer Students Accepted:** Yes **Non-fall Admissions:** Yes **Need-Blind Admissions:** Yes

UNIVERSITY OF DELAWARE
ALFRED LERNER COLLEGE OF BUSINESS & ECONOMICS

ADMISSIONS CONTACT: DENISE WATERS, DIRECTOR RECRUITMENT & ADMISSIONS ADDRESS: 103 ALFRED LERNER HALL, NEWARK, DE 19716 PHONE: 302-831-2221 • FAX: 302-831-3329 E-MAIL: MBAPROGRAM@UDEL.EDU WEBSITE: WWW.MBA.UDEL.EDU

GENERAL INFORMATION
Type of School: Public **Environment:** Town **Academic Calendar:** Semester

STUDENTS
Enrollment of Parent Institution: 20,000 **Enrollment of Business School:** 395 **% Male/female:** 63/37 **% Out-of-state:** 60 **% Part-time:** 82 **% Minorities:** 7 **% International:** 58 **Average Age at Entry:** 32 **Average Years Work Experience at Entry:** 5

ACADEMICS
% Female Faculty: 15 **% Minority Faculty:** 15
Joint Degrees: MA/MBA, Economics; MBA/MS OEDC; MBA/MS ISTM, MBA/MS, Engineering, MBA/PhD, Biotechnology. **Prominent Alumni:** Thomas R. Carper, U.S. Pfizer Senator, Delaware; Thomas Oliver, CEO, Cool Systems; Kenneth Whitney, Sr. Managing Director, Blackstone Group; David Kerr, Sr. VP, Endo Pharmaceuticals; Dennis Sheehy, CEO, Touch Media.

FINANCIAL FACTS
Tuition (in-state/out-of-state): $9,000/$18,594 **Fees:** $800 **Books and Supplies:** $1,600 **Room & Board (on/off campus):** $9,000/$10,200 **% of Students Receiving Aid:** 11 **% of First-year Students Receiving Aid:** 23

ADMISSIONS
Admissions Selectivity Rating: 78
# of Applications Received: 172 **% Applicants Accepted:** 72 **% Acceptees Attending:** 88 **Average GMAT:** 570 **Average GPA:** 3.1 **TOEFL Required of Int'l Applicants:** Yes **Minimum TOEFL (paper/computer):** 600/260 **Application Fee:** $60
Regular Application Deadline: 5/1 **Regular Notification:** rolling **Deferment Available:** Yes **Maximum Length of Deferment:** 1 year **Transfer Students Accepted:** Yes **Non-fall Admissions:** Yes **Need-Blind Admissions:** Yes **Applicants Also Look At:** Drexel University, Temple University, Villanova University.

EMPLOYMENT PROFILE
Primary Source of Full-time Job Acceptances
School-facilitated Activities 3 (19%)
Graduate-facilitated Activities 3 (19%)
Unknown..10 (62%)

Grads Employed by Industry:.......% avg. salary:

Finance	14 $67,000
Human Resources	3 $70,000
Marketing	11 $59,000
MIS	6 $65,000
Consulting	3 $65,000
Other	8 $75,000

Top 5 Employers Hiring Grads: Pfizer, DuPont, Bank of America, Ernst & Young, AIG.

UNIVERSITY OF DETROIT MERCY
COLLEGE OF BUSINESS ADMINISTRATION

ADMISSIONS CONTACT: TYRA ROUNDS, DIRECTOR OF RECRUITING
ADDRESS: 4001 W. McNICHOLS, DETROIT, MI 48221-3038
PHONE: 313-993-1245 • FAX: 313-993-3326
E-MAIL: ADMISSIONS@UDMERCY.EDU
WEBSITE: WWW.BUSINESS.UDMERCY.EDU

GENERAL INFORMATION

Type of School: Private **Affiliation:** Roman Catholic **Environment:** City **Academic Calendar:** Semester

STUDENTS

Enrollment of Parent Institution: 5,667 **Enrollment of Business School:** 96 **% Male/female:** 92/8 **% Part-time:** 81 **% Minorities:** 2 **% International:** 10 **Average Age at Entry:** 24 **Average Years Work Experience at Entry:** 3

ACADEMICS

Student/faculty Ratio: 30:1 **% Female Faculty:** 17 **% Minority Faculty:** 13

Joint Degrees: JD/MBA 3 years. **Prominent Alumni:** Thomas Angott, Chairman of the Board, C.F. Burger Co.; Thomas Capo, Dollar Thrifty Automotive Group; Armando Cavazos, Pres.& CEO, Credit Union One; James Padilla, Pres. Ford Motor Co.; Emil Simon, Owner, The Rollick Beverage Co.

FINANCIAL FACTS

Tuition (in-state/out-of-state): $16,830/$16,830 **Fees:** $570 **Books and Supplies:** $1,200 **Room & Board:** $3,775 **Average Grant:** $40,000

ADMISSIONS

Admissions Selectivity Rating: 73

# of Applications Received: 56 **% Applicants Accepted:** 89 **% Acceptees Attending:** 62 **GMAT Range (25th to 75th percentile):** 470–670 **Average GMAT:** 570 **Average GPA:** 3.4 **TOEFL Required of Int'l Applicants: Application Fee:** $30 **International Application Fee:** $50

Application Deadline Round 1: 08/15, Round 2: 12/15, Round 3: 04/15, Round 4: 05/15.

Deferment Available: Yes **Maximum Length of Deferment:** 2 years
Transfer Students Accepted: Yes **Non-fall Admissions:** Yes
Applicants Also Look At: Oakland University, University of Michigan—Dearborn, Wayne State University.

EMPLOYMENT PROFILE

Top 5 Employers Hiring Grads: Daimler Chrysler, Ford Motor, Bank One, Comerica.

UNIVERSITY OF HAWAII AT MANOA
SHIDLER COLLEGE OF BUSINESS

ADMISSIONS CONTACT: CHERI HONDA, GRADUATE COORDINATOR
ADDRESS: 2404 MAILE WAY, HONOLULU, HI 96822
PHONE: 808-956-8266 • FAX: 808-956-9890
E-MAIL: MBA@HAWAII.EDU
WEBSITE: WWW.SHIDLER.HAWAII.EDU

GENERAL INFORMATION

Type of School: Public **Environment:** Metropolis **Academic Calendar:** Semester

STUDENTS

Enrollment of Parent Institution: 17,532 **Enrollment of Business School:** 319 **% Male/female:** 61/39 **% Out-of-state:** 8 **% Part-time:** 49 **% Minorities:** 18 **% International:** 21 **Average Age at Entry:** 29 **Average Years Work Experience at Entry:** 4.4

ACADEMICS

Student/faculty Ratio: 25:1 **% Female Faculty:** 5 **% Minority Faculty:** 10

Joint Degrees: MBA/JD 4 years, MBA/Nursing 3 years. **Prominent Alumni:** Robin Campaniano, Pres &CEO/Insurance; Brenda Lei Foster, Presiden & CEO, ULU Group, Inc; Sharon Weiner, VP/DFS Hawaii; C. Dudley Pratt, Jr., Former Trustee/Campbell Estate; David McCoy, Former CEO/Campbell Estate.

FINANCIAL FACTS

Tuition (in-state/out-of-state): $10,896/$16,272 **Fees:** $172 **Books and Supplies:** $900 **Room & Board (on/off campus):** $12,000/$14,000 **Average Award Package:** $12,281 **Average Grant:** $25,000 **Average Student Loan Debt:** $7,644

ADMISSIONS

Admissions Selectivity Rating: 88

# of Applications Received: 313 **% Applicants Accepted:** 39 **% Acceptees Attending:** 55 **GMAT Range (25th to 75th percentile):** 500–710 **Average GMAT:** 575 **Average GPA:** 3.3 **TOEFL Required of Int'l Applicants:** Yes **Minimum TOEFL (paper/computer):** 600/250 **Application Fee:** $50

Regular Application Deadline: 5/7 **Regular Notification:** Rolling
Early Decision Program: Yes **ED Deadline/notification:** Fall, 03/07 / 5/7 **Transfer Students Accepted:** Yes **Non-fall Admissions:** Yes **Need-Blind Admissions:** Yes

EMPLOYMENT PROFILE

Grads Employed by Industry:.......% avg. salary:

Accounting	5	$45,000
Finance	15	$45,000
Human Resources	5	$40,000
Marketing	25	$50,000
MIS	10	$55,000
Consulting	5	$40,000
General Management	10	$55,000
Global Management	25	$55,000

UNIVERSITY OF HOUSTON— CLEAR LAKE
SCHOOL OF BUSINESS

ADMISSIONS CONTACT: KEVIN MCKISSON, REGISTRAR/DIRECTOR, ACADEMIC RECORDS
ADDRESS: 2700 BAY AREA BLVD, HOUSTON, TX 77058-1098
PHONE: 281-283-2500 • FAX: 281-283-2522
E-MAIL: ADMISSIONS@UHCL.EDU
WEBSITE: WWW.UHCL.EDU

GENERAL INFORMATION
Type of School: Public **Environment:** Metropolis **Academic Calendar:** Semester

STUDENTS
Enrollment of Parent Institution: 7,522 **Enrollment of Business School:** 363 **% Male/female:** 61/39 **% Out-of-state:** 12 **% Part-time:** 65 **% Minorities:** 19 **% International:** 23 **Average Age at Entry:** 30 **Average Years Work Experience at Entry:** 5

ACADEMICS
Student/faculty Ratio: 18:1 **% Female Faculty:** 31 **% Minority Faculty:** 19
Joint Degrees: Master of Healthcare Administration/MBA 3 years. Foundation courses may be required in addition to above hours and may lengthen time of program.

FINANCIAL FACTS
Tuition (in-state/out-of-state): $3,600/$13,608 **Fees (in-state/out-of-state):** $9,504/$10,116 **Books and Supplies:** $1,800 **Room & Board:** $12,836 **% of Students Receiving Aid:** 20 **Average Award Package:** $8,300 **Average Grant:** $1,000 **Average Student Loan Debt:** $26,916

ADMISSIONS
Admissions Selectivity Rating: 75
# of Applications Received: 113 **% Applicants Accepted:** 81 **% Acceptees Attending:** 80 **GMAT Range (25th to 75th percentile):** 460–570 **Average GMAT:** 518 **Average GPA:** 3.2 **TOEFL Required of Int'l Applicants:** Yes **Minimum TOEFL (paper/computer):** 550/213 **Application Fee:** $35 **International Application Fee:** $75

Regular Application Deadline: 8/1 **Regular Notification:** rolling **Deferment Available:** Yes **Maximum Length of Deferment:** 1 year **Transfer Students Accepted:** Yes **Non-fall Admissions:** Yes **Need-Blind Admissions:** Yes **Applicants Also Look At:** Houston Baptist University, University of Houston, University of St. Thomas.

UNIVERSITY OF LONDON
LONDON BUSINESS SCHOOL

ADMISSIONS CONTACT: DAVID SIMPSON, ASSOCIATE DIRECTOR, MBA MARKETING & ADMISSIONS
ADDRESS: REGENT'S PARK, LONDON, NW1 4SA ENGLAND
PHONE: 011 44 20 7000 7511 • FAX: 011 44 20 7000 7501
E-MAIL: MBAINFO@LONDON.EDU
WEBSITE: WWW.LONDON.EDU

GENERAL INFORMATION
Type of School: Private

STUDENTS
% Male/female: 100/0 **% International:** 90 **Average Age at Entry:** 28 **Average Years Work Experience at Entry:** 5

ACADEMICS
Student/faculty Ratio: 8:1
Joint Degrees: EMBA-Global.

FINANCIAL FACTS
Tuition: $35,675 **Books and Supplies:** $500 **Room & Board:** $25,500 **% of Students Receiving Loans:** 56 **Average Grant:** $17,980

ADMISSIONS
Admissions Selectivity Rating: 60*
# of Applications Received: 1,849 **GMAT Range (25th to 75th percentile):** 650–710 **Average GMAT:** 680 **Average GPA:** 3.3 **TOEFL Required of Int'l Applicants:** Yes **Application Fee:** $280
Application Deadline/Notification Round 1: 10/19 / 11/16 Round 2: 01/04 / 02/12 Round 3: 02/29 / 04/11 Round 4: 05/02 / 06/04
Deferment Available: Yes **Maximum Length of Deferment:** 1 year **Need-Blind Admissions:** Yes **Applicants Also Look At:** Columbia University, Harvard University, INSEAD, New York University, Northwestern University, Stanford University, University of Pennsylvania.

EMPLOYMENT PROFILE
Grads Employed by Industry:.......% avg. salary:

Finance	38	$97,550
Consulting	30	$110,355
General Management	32	$99,620

UNIVERSITY OF LOUISIANA AT MONROE
COLLEGE OF BUSINESS ADMINSTRATION

ADMISSIONS CONTACT: MIGUEL PEREZ, COORDINATOR OF ASSESSMENT AND INTERNAL AFFAIRS
ADDRESS: 700 UNIVERSITY AVENUE, MONROE, LA 71209-0100
PHONE: 318-342-1100 • FAX: 318-342-1101
E-MAIL: PEREZ@ULM.EDU
WEBSITE: ELE.ULM.EDU/MBA

GENERAL INFORMATION
Type of School: Public **Academic Calendar:** Semester

STUDENTS
Enrollment of Parent Institution: 10,942 **Enrollment of Business School:** 77 **% Male/female:** 60/40 **% Out-of-state:** 11 **% Part-time:** 19 **% Minorities:** 5 **% International:** 40 **Average Age at Entry:** 27

ACADEMICS
Student/faculty Ratio: 2:1 **% Female Faculty:** 30 **% Minority Faculty:** 4

FINANCIAL FACTS
Tuition (in-state/out-of-state): $1,900/$7,858 **Fees:** $382 **Books and Supplies:** $600 **Room & Board:** $2,560 **Average Grant:** $5,000

ADMISSIONS
Admissions Selectivity Rating: 74
# of Applications Received: 77 **% Applicants Accepted:** 58 **% Acceptees Attending:** 78 **GMAT Range (25th to 75th percentile):** 390–710 **Average GMAT:** 480 **Average GPA:** 3 **TOEFL Required of Int'l Applicants:** Yes **Minimum TOEFL (paper/computer):** 480/157 **Application Fee:** $20 **International Application Fee:** $30
Regular Application Deadline: 7/1 **Regular Notification:** 7/15
Deferment Available: Yes **Maximum Length of Deferment:** 1 year
Transfer Students Accepted: Yes **Non-fall Admissions:** Yes

UNIVERSITY OF MAINE
MAINE BUSINESS SCHOOL

ADMISSIONS CONTACT: MAXINE EWANKOW, PROGRAM ASSISTANT, BUSINESS GRADUATE PROGRAMS
ADDRESS: 5723 DP CORBETT BUSINESS BUILDING, ORONO, ME 04469-5723
PHONE: 207-581-1973 • FAX: 207-581-1930
E-MAIL: MBA@MAINE.EDU
WEBSITE: WWW.UMAINE.EDU/BUSINESS

GENERAL INFORMATION
Type of School: Public **Environment:** Village **Academic Calendar:** Semester

STUDENTS
Enrollment of Parent Institution: 11,300 **Enrollment of Business School:** 79 **% Male/female:** 61/39 **% Out-of-state:** 1 **% Part-time:**
37 **% Minorities:** 1 **% International:** 23 **Average Age at Entry:** 27 **Average Years Work Experience at Entry:** 6

ACADEMICS
Student/faculty Ratio: 4:1 **% Female Faculty:** 40
Prominent Alumni: Nick Heymann, Securities Analyst; Bernard Lown, Nobel Peace Prize winner; Steven King, Writer; Olympia Snowe, U.S. Senator; Mike Bordick, Professional baseball.

FINANCIAL FACTS
Tuition (in-state/out-of-state): $5,328/$15,210 **Fees:** $644 **Books and Supplies:** $800 **Room & Board:** $7,150 **Average Grant:** $5,000

ADMISSIONS
Admissions Selectivity Rating: 81
# of Applications Received: 42 **% Applicants Accepted:** 64 **% Acceptees Attending:** 56 **GMAT Range (25th to 75th percentile):** 530–610 **Average GMAT:** 576 **Average GPA:** 3.5 **TOEFL Required of Int'l Applicants:** Yes **Minimum TOEFL (paper/computer):** 550/213 **Application Fee:** $50
Regular Application Deadline: 6/1 **Regular Notification:** 7/1
Deferment Available: Yes **Maximum Length of Deferment:** 1 year **Transfer Students Accepted:** Yes **Non-fall Admissions:** Yes **Need-Blind Admissions:** Yes **Applicants Also Look At:** University of New Hampshire, University of Southern Maine.

UNIVERSITY OF MANCHESTER
MANCHESTER BUSINESS SCHOOL

ADMISSIONS CONTACT: GAER BUCHANAN, ADMISSIONS ADMINISTRATOR
ADDRESS: MBA ADMISSIONS OFFICE, BOOTH STREET WEST, MANCHESTER, M15 6PB ENGLAND
PHONE: 00-44-161-275-6364 • FAX: 00-44-161-275-6556
E-MAIL: GAER.BUCHANAN@MBS.AC.UK • WEBSITE: WWW.MBS.AC.UK/MBA

GENERAL INFORMATION
Type of School: Public

ACADEMICS
Prominent Alumni: Rijkman Groenink, Chairman of the Managing Board, ABN AMRO; Robert H. Herz, BA (Econ), Chairman, US Financial Accounting Standards Board; Sir Terry Leahy, Chief Executive, Tesco; Paul Skinner, Chairman, Rio Tinto; David Varney, Executive Chairman, Her Majesty's Revenue and Cust.

FINANCIAL FACTS
Tuition: $53,100

ADMISSIONS
Admissions Selectivity Rating: 60*
TOEFL Required of Int'l Applicants: Yes **Minimum TOEFL (paper/computer):** 600/250
Regular Application Deadline: 7/9 **Regular Notification:** 7/30 **Application Deadline/Notification Round 1:** 02/26 / 04/30 **Round 2:** 03/26 / 05/14 **Round 3:** 05/28 / 07/30 **Round 4:** 07/09 / 07/30
Deferment Available: Yes **Maximum Length of Deferment:** 1 year

EMPLOYMENT PROFILE

Primary Source of Full-time Job Acceptances

School-facilitated Activities 43%

Graduate-facilitated Activities 57%

Grads Employed by Industry: ......% avg. salary:

Finance 22 $110,240

Marketing 21 $92,100

Operations.....................................12 $93,900

Strategic Planning........................5 $106,950

Consulting......................................26 $91,800

General Management 14 $73,550

UNIVERSITY OF MANITOBA
I.H. ASPER SCHOOL OF BUSINESS

ADMISSIONS CONTACT: EWA MORPHY, GRADUATE PROGRAM MANAGER
ADDRESS: 324 DRAKE CENTER, WINNIPEG, MB R3T 5V4 CANADA
PHONE: 204-474-8448 • FAX: 204-474-7544
E-MAIL: ASPERMBA@UMANITOBA.CA
WEBSITE: WWW.UMANITOBA.CA/ASPER

GENERAL INFORMATION

Type of School: Public **Environment:** City

STUDENTS

Enrollment of Parent Institution: 26,000 **Enrollment of Business School:** 120 **% Male/female:** 60/40 **% Part-time:** 72 **% International:** 9 **Average Age at Entry:** 32 **Average Years Work Experience at Entry:** 10

ACADEMICS

Student/faculty Ratio: 30:1 **% Female Faculty:** 18 **% Minority Faculty:** 32

Prominent Alumni: F. Ross Johnson, Chairman/CEO RJM Group; Robert W. Pollock, Chairman, Drake International; Gerald W. Schwartz, Chair, President and CEO, Onyx Corp.; Martin S. Weinberg, President, CEO Assante Corporation; Bill McCallum, President and CEO, Great-West Life Annuity Insurance.

FINANCIAL FACTS

Tuition: $16,201 **Books and Supplies:** $2,543 **Room & Board (on/off campus):** $5,800/$10,174 **% of First-year Students Receiving Aid:** 10 **Average Grant:** $4,000

ADMISSIONS

Admissions Selectivity Rating: 76

# of Applications Received: 67 **% Applicants Accepted:** 72 **% Acceptees Attending:** 62 **GMAT Range (25th to 75th percentile):** 444–633 **Average GMAT:** 566 **Average GPA:** 3 **TOEFL Required of Int'l Applicants:** Yes **Minimum TOEFL (paper/computer):** 550/213 **Application Fee:** $75 **International Application Fee:** $90 **Regular Application Deadline:** 6/1 **Regular Notification:** rolling **Transfer Students Accepted:** Yes **Non-fall Admissions:** Yes

EMPLOYMENT PROFILE

Primary Source of Full-time Job Acceptances

School-facilitated Activities 4 (15%)

Graduate-facilitated Activities 14 (50%)

Unknown...10 (35%)

Percent Employed 12

Grads Employed by Industry: ......% avg. salary:

Finance 5 $62,500

Marketing 5 $97,500

Communications...........................5 $77,500

General Management 36 $82,143

Quantitative...................................24 $91,250

Other...11 $75,000

Internet/New Media.......................5 $102,500

UNIVERSITY OF MICHIGAN— DEARBORN
SCHOOL OF MANAGEMENT

ADMISSIONS CONTACT: CHRISTINE BRZEZINSKI, GRADUATE ADMISSIONS
COORDINATOR
ADDRESS: SCHOOL OF MANAGEMENT, 19000 HUBBARD DR., DEARBORN, MI
48126-2638
PHONE: 313-593-5460 • FAX: 313-271-9838
E-MAIL: GRADBUSINESS@UMD.UMICH.EDU
WEBSITE: WWW.SOM.UMD.UMICH.EDU

GENERAL INFORMATION

Type of School: Public **Environment:** City **Academic Calendar:** Semester

STUDENTS

Enrollment of Parent Institution: 8,600 **Enrollment of Business School:** 417 **% Male/female:** 61/39 **% Part-time:** 88 **Average Age at Entry:** 28

ACADEMICS

Student/faculty Ratio: 18:1 **% Female Faculty:** 27 **% Minority Faculty:** 30

Joint Degrees: MBA/MA (Finance) 2–5 years, MBA/MSEngineering 4–5 years, Dual MBA & Master of Health Services Administration.

FINANCIAL FACTS

Books and Supplies: $1,200

ADMISSIONS

Admissions Selectivity Rating: 78

# of Applications Received: 112 **% Applicants Accepted:** 63 **% Acceptees Attending:** 76 **Average GMAT:** 535 **Average GPA:** 3.2 **TOEFL Required of Int'l Applicants:** Yes **Minimum TOEFL (paper/computer):** 560/220 **Application Fee:** $60 **Regular Application Deadline:** 8/1 **Regular Notification:** Rolling **Deferment Available:** Yes **Maximum Length of Deferment:** 1 year

Transfer Students Accepted: Yes Non-fall Admissions: Yes Need-Blind Admissions: Yes Applicants Also Look At: Eastern Michigan University, Michigan State University, Oakland University, University of Detroit—Mercy, University of Michigan, Wayne State University.

UNIVERSITY OF MINNESOTA
CARLSON SCHOOL OF MANAGEMENT

ADMISSIONS CONTACT: JEFF BIEGANEK, DIRECTOR OF ADMISSIONS
ADDRESS: 321 NINETEENTH AVENUE SOUTH, SUITE 4-106, MINNEAPOLIS, MN 55455
PHONE: 612-625-5555 • FAX: 612-625-1012
E-MAIL: FTMBA@UMN.EDU
WEBSITE: WWW.CARLSONSCHOOL.UMN.EDU

GENERAL INFORMATION

Type of School: Public Environment: Metropolis Academic Calendar: Semester

STUDENTS

Enrollment of Parent Institution: 50,402 Enrollment of Business School: 1,922 % Male/female: 65/35 % Part-time: 89 % Minorities: 10 % International: 40 Average Age at Entry: 29 Average Years Work Experience at Entry: 5

ACADEMICS

Student/faculty Ratio: 15:1 % Female Faculty: 22 % Minority Faculty: 20
Joint Degrees: JD/MBA 4 years, MHA/MBA 3 years, MD/MBA 5 years. Prominent Alumni: Charles W. Mooty, CEO, International Dairy Queen; William G. Van Dyke, Chairman, President & CEO, Donaldson Company, Inc.; Curtis C. Nelson, President & COO, Carlson Companies; Robert A. Kierlin, Chairman, Fastenal Company; Barbara J. Mowry, President & CEO, TMC Consulting.

FINANCIAL FACTS

Tuition (in-state/out-of-state): $21,300/$30,320 Fees: $2,500 Books and Supplies: $4,000 Room & Board (on/off campus): $13,000/$15,000 % of Students Receiving Aid: 77 % of Students Receiving Loans: 41 % of Students Receiving Grants: 63 Average Award Package: $29,260 Average Grant: $19,200 Average Student Loan Debt: $41,877

ADMISSIONS

Admissions Selectivity Rating: 88
# of Applications Received: 418 % Applicants Accepted: 53 % Acceptees Attending: 56 Average GMAT: 641 Average GPA: 3.3 TOEFL Required of Int'l Applicants: Yes Minimum TOEFL (paper/computer): 580/240 Application Fee: $60 International Application Fee: $90
Regular Application Deadline: 4/15 Regular Notification: 5/15 Application Deadline/Notification Round 1: 12/15 / 02/15 Round 2: 02/15 / 04/15 Round 3: 04/15 / 05/15
Early Decision Program: Yes ED Deadline/notification: 12/15 / 2/15 Deferment Available: Yes Maximum Length of Deferment: 1 year Need-Blind Admissions: Yes

EMPLOYMENT PROFILE

Primary Source of Full-time Job Acceptances
School-facilitated Activities 68 (77%)
Graduate-facilitated Activities 20 (23%)
Average base starting salary $82,436
Percent Employed 97

Grads Employed by Industry:	%	avg. salary:
Finance	24	$78,100
Marketing	33	$80,574
MIS	1	
Operations	7	$75,417
Consulting	12	$93,732
General Management	3	
Other	8	

Top 5 Employers Hiring Grads: Northwest Airlines, Best Buy Co., Inc., Ecolab, Cargill, Deloitte.

UNIVERSITY OF MINNESOTA—DULUTH
LABOVITZ SCHOOL OF BUSINESS AND ECONOMICS

ADMISSIONS CONTACT: CANDY FURO, ASSOCIATE ADMINISTRATOR
ADDRESS: 21 LSBE, 412 LIBRARY DRIVE, DULUTH, MN 55812
PHONE: 218-726-8986 • FAX: 218-726-6789
E-MAIL: GRAD@D.UMN.EDU
WEBSITE: WWW.D.UMN.EDU/SBE/DEGREEPROGS/MBA

GENERAL INFORMATION

Type of School: Public Environment: Village Academic Calendar: Semester

STUDENTS

Enrollment of Parent Institution: 11,184 Enrollment of Business School: 77 % Part-time: 100 Average Age at Entry: 32 Average Years Work Experience at Entry: 8.5

ACADEMICS

Student/faculty Ratio: 20:1 % Female Faculty: 23
Prominent Alumni: Jon Gerlach, CFO; Chris Mahai, President/CEO; Elaine Hansen, Director; Jim Vizanko, CFO.

FINANCIAL FACTS

Books and Supplies: $1,000 Room & Board: $6,000

ADMISSIONS

Admissions Selectivity Rating: 76
# of Applications Received: 21 % Applicants Accepted: 95 % Acceptees Attending: 95 GMAT Range (25th to 75th percentile): 470–660 Average GMAT: 553 Average GPA: 3.4 TOEFL Required of Int'l Applicants: Yes Minimum TOEFL (paper/computer): 550/213 Application Fee: $55 International Application Fee: $75
Regular Application Deadline: 7/15 Regular Notification: 9/1 Application Deadline/Notification Round 1: 07/15 / 08/31 Round 2: 11/01 / 12/31 Round 3: 05/01 / 05/30

Deferment Available: Yes **Maximum Length of Deferment:** 1 year **Transfer Students Accepted:** Yes **Non-fall Admissions:** Yes **Need-Blind Admissions:** Yes **Applicants Also Look At:** St. Cloud State University, University of Minnesota, University of St. Thomas.

THE UNIVERSITY OF MONTANA— MISSOULA
SCHOOL OF BUSINESS ADMINISTRATION

ADMISSIONS CONTACT: KATHLEEN SPRITZER, ADMINISTRATIVE OFFICER
ADDRESS: SCHOOL OF BUSINESS ADMIN., UNIV. OF MONTANA, MISSOULA, MT 59812
PHONE: 406-243-4983 • FAX: 406-243-2086
E-MAIL: KATHLEEN.SPRITZER@BUSINESS.UMT.EDU
WEBSITE: WWW.MBA-MACCT.UMT.EDU

GENERAL INFORMATION
Type of School: Public **Environment:** City **Academic Calendar:** Semester

STUDENTS
Enrollment of Parent Institution: 13,564 **Enrollment of Business School:** 184 **% Male/female:** 46/54 **% Part-time:** 47 **% Minorities:** 5 **% International:** 10 **Average Age at Entry:** 29 **Average Years Work Experience at Entry:** 2.5

ACADEMICS
Student/faculty Ratio: 26:1 **% Female Faculty:** 31 **% Minority Faculty:** 1
Joint Degrees: JD/MBA 3 years, MBA/PharmD 5 years.

FINANCIAL FACTS
Tuition (in-state/out-of-state): $6,150/$14,230 **Books and Supplies:** $1,800 **Room & Board:** $8,750 **% of Students Receiving Aid:** 10 **% of Students Receiving Grants:** 10 **Average Grant:** $9,000

ADMISSIONS
Admissions Selectivity Rating: 60*
# of Applications Received: 146 **% Applicants Accepted:** 75 **% Acceptees Attending:** 88 **GMAT Range (25th to 75th percentile):** 460–710 **Average GMAT:** 566 **Average GPA:** 3.2 **TOEFL Required of Int'l Applicants:** Yes **Minimum TOEFL (paper/computer):** 580/237 **Application Fee:** $45
Regular Application Deadline: 4/15 **Regular Notification:** 5/1
Deferment Available: Yes **Maximum Length of Deferment:** 1 year **Transfer Students Accepted:** Yes **Non-fall Admissions:** Yes **Need-Blind Admissions:** Yes **Applicants Also Look At:** Idaho State University, Montana State University, University of Oregon, University of Washington, Washington State University.

UNIVERSITY OF NEBRASKA— KEARNEY
COLLEGE OF BUSINESS AND TECHNOLOGY

ADMISSIONS CONTACT: LINDA JOHNSON, DIRECTOR, GRADUATE ADMISSIONS & PROGRAMS
ADDRESS: 905 W 25TH ST, FOUNDERS HALL ROOM 2131, KEARNEY, NE 68849
PHONE: 800-717-7881 • FAX: 308-865-8837
E-MAIL: JOHNSONLI@UNK.EDU
WEBSITE: WWW.UNK.EDU/ACAD/MBA

GENERAL INFORMATION
Type of School: Public **Academic Calendar:** Semester

STUDENTS
Enrollment of Parent Institution: 6,478 **Enrollment of Business School:** 65 **% Male/female:** 59/41 **% Out-of-state:** 13 **% Part-time:** 66 **% International:** 11 **Average Age at Entry:** 25 **Average Years Work Experience at Entry:** 2.2

ACADEMICS
Student/faculty Ratio: 2:1 **% Female Faculty:** 38

FINANCIAL FACTS
Tuition (in-state/out-of-state): $3,060/$6,332 **Fees:** $684 **Books and Supplies:** $800 **Room & Board (on/off campus):** $6,800/$8,000

ADMISSIONS
Admissions Selectivity Rating: 73
# of Applications Received: 8 **% Applicants Accepted:** 100 **% Acceptees Attending:** 88 **GMAT Range (25th to 75th percentile):** 440–640 **Average GMAT:** 500 **Average GPA:** 3.4 **TOEFL Required of Int'l Applicants:** Yes **Minimum TOEFL (paper/computer):** 550/213 **Application Fee:** $45
Regular Application Deadline: 5/1 **Regular Notification:** Rolling
Deferment Available: Yes **Maximum Length of Deferment:** 1 year **Transfer Students Accepted:** Yes **Non-fall Admissions:** Yes **Applicants Also Look At:** Creighton University, University of Nebraska at Omaha, University of Nebraska—Lincoln.

UNIVERSITY OF NEBRASKA— LINCOLN
COLLEGE OF BUSINESS ADMINISTRATION

ADMISSIONS CONTACT: JUDY SHUTTS, GRADUATE ADVISER
ADDRESS: CBA 125, LINCOLN, NE 68588-0405
PHONE: 402-472-2338 • FAX: 402-472-5180
E-MAIL: CGRADUATE@UNLNOTES.UNL.EDU
WEBSITE: WWW.CBA.UNL.EDU

GENERAL INFORMATION
Type of School: Public **Environment:** City **Academic Calendar:** Semester

STUDENTS

Enrollment of Parent Institution: 22,973 **Enrollment of Business School:** 133 **% Male/female:** 70/30 **% Out-of-state:** 7 **% Part-time:** 50 **% Minorities:** 2 **% International:** 16 **Average Age at Entry:** 25 **Average Years Work Experience at Entry:** 7

ACADEMICS

Student/faculty Ratio: 6:1 **% Female Faculty:** 17 **% Minority Faculty:** 13

Joint Degrees: MBA/JD 4 years, MBA/Arch 3 years. **Prominent Alumni:** Warren Buffet, Chairman, Berkshire Hathaway; W. Grant Gregory, Former Chrmn. Touche, Ross & Co.; Paul Hogan, Founder and CEO Home Instead Senior Care; Jim Davidson, Founder and Managing Director Silver Lake Partners; John Horner, CEO Arcadia Group.

FINANCIAL FACTS

Tuition (in-state/out-of-state): $5,376/$14,496 **Fees:** $810 **Books and Supplies:** $964 **Room & Board (on/off campus):** $7,497/$7,900 **% of Students Receiving Aid:** 51 **% of First-year Students Receiving Aid:** 69 **% of Students Receiving Loans:** 27 **% of Students Receiving Grants:** 38 **Average Award Package:** $15,000 **Average Grant:** $9,179

ADMISSIONS

Admissions Selectivity Rating: 87

# of Applications Received: 97 **% Applicants Accepted:** 61 **% Acceptees Attending:** 71 **GMAT Range (25th to 75th percentile):** 570–650 **Average GMAT:** 620 **Average GPA:** 3.5 **TOEFL Required of Int'l Applicants:** Yes **Minimum TOEFL (paper/computer):** 550/213 **Application Fee:** $45

Regular Application Deadline: 6/15 **Regular Notification:** rolling **Deferment Available:** Yes **Maximum Length of Deferment:** one semester **Transfer Students Accepted:** Yes **Non-fall Admissions:** Yes **Need-Blind Admissions:** Yes **Applicants Also Look At:** Arizona State University, Creighton University, University of Iowa, University of Kansas, University of Nebraska—Omaha.

EMPLOYMENT PROFILE

Primary Source of Full-time Job Acceptances

School-facilitated Activities	9 (38%)
Graduate-facilitated Activities	14 (58%)
Unknown	1 (4%)
Average base starting salary	$64,150
Percent Employed	90

Grads Employed by Industry: ...... % avg. salary:

Finance	21	$51,440
Marketing	17	$55,500
MIS	8	$50,000
Operations	8	$47,500
Consulting	8	$77,000
General Management	17	$65,500
Other	21	$64,490

Top 5 Employers Hiring Grads: Sandhillls Publishing, First National Bank Omaha, Ameritas, Cisco Systems, Bunge International.

UNIVERSITY OF NEBRASKA— OMAHA

COLLEGE OF BUSINESS ADMINISTRATION

ADMISSIONS CONTACT: LEX KACZMAREK, DIRECTOR, MBA PROGRAM
ADDRESS: 6001 DODGE STREET, OMAHA, NE 68182-0048
PHONE: 402-554-2303 • FAX: 402-554-3747
E-MAIL: MBA@UNOMAHA.EDU
WEBSITE: CBA.UNOMAHA.EDU/MBA

GENERAL INFORMATION

Type of School: Public **Environment:** Metropolis **Academic Calendar:** Semester

STUDENTS

Enrollment of Parent Institution: 14,969 **Enrollment of Business School:** 279 **% Male/female:** 100/0 **% Part-time:** 100 **Average Age at Entry:** 28 **Average Years Work Experience at Entry:** 5

ACADEMICS

Student/faculty Ratio: 16:1 **% Female Faculty:** 42 **% Minority Faculty:** 5

Joint Degrees: MBA/MS-MIS 1.5–10 years. **Prominent Alumni:** James R. Young, Pres. and COO, Union Pacific Railroad; R. Craig Hoenshell, Former CEO, Avis and American Express Internationa; Ronald J. Burns, Former Pres. and CEO, Union Pacific; Bernard R. Reznicek, Former Chairman, Pres. and CEO, Boston Edison Comp; Samuel G. Leftwich, Former Pres., K-Mart Corporation.

FINANCIAL FACTS

Tuition: $0 **Books and Supplies:** $0 **Room & Board (on/off campus):** $6,500/$9,500 **% of Students Receiving Aid:** 6 **% of First-year Students Receiving Aid:** 7 **% of Students Receiving Grants:** 2 **Average Award Package:** $10,525 **Average Grant:** $4,348

ADMISSIONS

Admissions Selectivity Rating: 78

# of Applications Received: 103 **% Applicants Accepted:** 74 **% Acceptees Attending:** 64 **GMAT Range (25th to 75th percentile):** 520–610 **Average GMAT:** 566 **Average GPA:** 3.46 **TOEFL Required of Int'l Applicants:** Yes **Minimum TOEFL (paper/computer):** 550/213 **Application Fee:** $45 **International Application Fee:** $45

Regular Application Deadline: 7/1 **Regular Notification:** rolling **Deferment Available:** Yes **Maximum Length of Deferment:** 1 year **Transfer Students Accepted:** Yes **Non-fall Admissions:** Yes **Need-Blind Admissions:** Yes **Applicants Also Look At:** Creighton University, University of Nebraska—Lincoln.

University of New Mexico
Robert O. Anderson Graduate School of Management

Admissions Contact: Mary Berger, Graduate Programs Advisor
Address: The University of New Mexico, 1924 Las Lomas Blvd.,
Albuquerque, NM 87131
Phone: 505-277-3888 • Fax: 505-277-9356
E-mail: mba@mgt.unm.edu
Website: www.mgt.unm.edu

GENERAL INFORMATION

Type of School: Public **Environment:** Metropolis **Academic Calendar:** Semester

STUDENTS

Enrollment of Parent Institution: 32,347 **Enrollment of Business School:** 368 **% Male/female:** 100/0 **% Part-time:** 100 **Average Age at Entry:** 28 **Average Years Work Experience at Entry:** 3.9

ACADEMICS

Student/faculty Ratio: 26:1 **% Female Faculty:** 31

Joint Degrees: MBA/MA (Latin American Studies) 3–4 years, MBA/JD 4 years. **Prominent Alumni:** Daniel L. Jorndt, CEO, Walgreen's; Ann Rhoades, President, PeopleInk; Judith Rogala, President & CEO, La Petite Academy; Waneta Tuttle, CEO, Exagen Diagnostics; Milton H. Ward, President & CEO, Cyprus Amax Minerals Co. (Ret.).

FINANCIAL FACTS

Tuition (in-state/out-of-state): $3,154/$8,323 **Fees:** $280 **Books and Supplies:** $2,000 **Room & Board (on/off campus):** $16,964/$18,022 **% of Students Receiving Aid:** 55 **% of First-year Students Receiving Aid:** 52 **% of Students Receiving Loans:** 36 **% of Students Receiving Grants:** 30 **Average Award Package:** $5,424 **Average Grant:** $2,849 **Average Student Loan Debt:** $25,134

ADMISSIONS

Admissions Selectivity Rating: 86

# of Applications Received: 253 **% Applicants Accepted:** 53 **% Acceptees Attending:** 88 **GMAT Range (25th to 75th percentile):** 500–600 **Average GMAT:** 559 **Average GPA:** 3.52 **TOEFL Required of Int'l Applicants:** Yes **Minimum TOEFL (paper/computer):** 550/213 **Application Fee:** $50

Regular Application Deadline: 6/1 **Regular Notification:** rolling **Deferment Available:** Yes **Maximum Length of Deferment:** 1 Year **Transfer Students Accepted:** Yes **Non-fall Admissions:** Yes Ne

EMPLOYMENT PROFILE

Primary Source of Full-time Job Acceptances

School-facilitated Activities 20 (54%)
Graduate-facilitated Activities 17 (46%)

Grads Employed by Industry: .... % avg. salary:

Finance 9 $48,000
Human Resources........................4 $56,275
Marketing 3 $51,000
Operations...................................1 $65,000
General Management 2 $44,000
Other...3 $60,667

University of New Orleans
College of Business Administration

Admissions Contact: Roslyn Sheley, Director of Admissions
Address: Admin Bldg Rm 103, New Orleans, LA 70148
Phone: 504-280-6595 • Fax: 504-280-5522
E-mail: admissions@uno.edu
Website: www.uno.edu

GENERAL INFORMATION

Type of School: Public **Environment:** Metropolis **Academic Calendar:** Semester

STUDENTS

Enrollment of Parent Institution: 17,360 **Enrollment of Business School:** 810 **% Male/female:** 51/49 **% Out-of-state:** 30 **% Part-time:** 46 **% Minorities:** 25 **% International:** 26 **Average Age at Entry:** 30

ACADEMICS

Student/faculty Ratio: 24:1

Prominent Alumni: Dr. James Clark, Chairman of the Board, Netscape Communications; Michael Fitzpatrick, CEO, Rohm & Haas; Erving Johnson, Starting Center, Milwaukee Bucks; Mike Ketteing, President & General Manager, Gillett Broadcasting; Dr. Reuben Arminana, President, Sonoma State University.

FINANCIAL FACTS

Tuition (in-state/out-of-state): $3,300/$10,800 **Books and Supplies:** $1,150 **Room & Board:** $4,122 **Average Grant:** $2,697

ADMISSIONS

Admissions Selectivity Rating: 67

# of Applications Received: 575 **% Applicants Accepted:** 67 **% Acceptees Attending:** 62 **GMAT Range (25th to 75th percentile):** 400–510 **Average GMAT:** 459 **Average GPA:** 3 **TOEFL Required of Int'l Applicants:** Yes **Minimum TOEFL (paper/computer):** 550/213 **Application Fee:** $40

Regular Application Deadline: 7/1 **Regular Notification:** 9/1 **Deferment Available:** Yes **Maximum Length of Deferment:** 1 semester **Transfer Students Accepted:** Yes **Non-fall Admissions:** Yes **Need-Blind Admissions:** Yes

THE UNIVERSITY OF NEW SOUTH WALES (UNSW)
AGSM MBA PROGRAMS

ADMISSIONS CONTACT: BRONWYN ALLAN, TEAM LEADER, ADMISSIONS
ADDRESS: AGSM BUILDING, UNSW, SYDNEY NSW, 2052 AUSTRALIA
PHONE: 0061 2 99319490 • FAX: 0061 2 99319205
E-MAIL: ADMISSIONS@AGSM.EDU.AU
WEBSITE: WWW.AGSM.EDU.AU

GENERAL INFORMATION
Type of School: Public

STUDENTS
% Male/female: 81/19 **% International:** 56 **Average Age at Entry:** 29 **Average Years Work Experience at Entry:** 7

ACADEMICS
Student/faculty Ratio: 4:1 **% Female Faculty:** 26

Joint Degrees: MBA/LLM, 2 years. **Prominent Alumni:** Peeyush Gupta, CEO, ipaq Securities; Guy Templeton, Chief Executive, Minter Ellison Lawyers.

FINANCIAL FACTS
Tuition: $48,930 **Books and Supplies:** $3,000 **Room & Board:** $20,000

ADMISSIONS
Admissions Selectivity Rating: 87

# of Applications Received: 171 **% Applicants Accepted:** 63 **% Acceptees Attending:** 58 **GMAT Range (25th to 75th percentile):** 620–700 **Average GMAT:** 656 **Average GPA:** 3.0 TOEFL **Minimum TOEFL (paper/computer):** 600/250 **Application Fee:** $75

Regular Application Deadline: 10/15 Application Deadline Round 1: 09/01, Round 2: 10/15

Deferment Available: Yes **Maximum Length of Deferment:** 1 year **Transfer Students Accepted:** Yes

EMPLOYMENT PROFILE
Grads Employed by Industry:.......% avg. salary:

Finance	17	$92,821
Marketing	9	$104,500
Strategic Planning	22	$85,662
Consulting	35	$109,923
General Management	13	$81,190
Other	4	$78,413

Top 5 Employers Hiring Grads: AT Kearney, Macquarie.

THE UNIVERSITY OF SOUTHERN MISSISSIPPI
COLLEGE OF BUSINESS

ADMISSIONS CONTACT: GABRIEL MCPHEARSON, ASSISTANT TO THE DIRECTOR
ADDRESS: 118 COLLEGE DRIVE #5096, HATTIESBURG, MS 39406-5096
PHONE: 601-266-4653 • FAX: 601-266-5814
E-MAIL: MBA@USM.EDU
WEBSITE: WWW.USM.EDU/MBA

GENERAL INFORMATION
Type of School: Public **Environment:** City **Academic Calendar:** Semester

STUDENTS
Enrollment of Parent Institution: 15,030 **Enrollment of Business School:** 93 **% Male/female:** 58/42 **% Out-of-state:** 24 **% Part-time:** 59 **% Minorities:** 8 **% International:** 8 **Average Age at Entry:** 27

ACADEMICS
Student/faculty Ratio: 30:1 **% Female Faculty:** 25 **% Minority Faculty:** 15

Joint Degrees: MBA/MPH, Master of Public Health) 2–6 years.

FINANCIAL FACTS
Tuition: $4,312 **Fees (in-state/out-of-state):** $0/$5,430 **Books and Supplies:** $1,600 **Room & Board (on/off campus):** $5,800/$7,600 **% of Students Receiving Aid:** 75 **% of Students Receiving Grants:** 25 **Average Grant:** $8,690

ADMISSIONS
Admissions Selectivity Rating: 78

# of Applications Received: 73 **% Applicants Accepted:** 56 **% Acceptees Attending:** 76 **GMAT Range (25th to 75th percentile):** 450–560 **Average GMAT:** 508 **Average GPA:** 3.4 **TOEFL Required of Int'l Applicants:** Yes **Minimum TOEFL (paper/computer):** 550/213 **Application Fee:** $25

Regular Application Deadline: 7/15 **Regular Notification:** rolling

Deferment Available: Yes **Maximum Length of Deferment:** 2 semesters **Transfer Students Accepted:** Yes **Non-fall Admissions:** Yes **Need-Blind Admissions:** Yes

EMPLOYMENT PROFILE
Primary Source of Full-time Job Acceptances

Unknown	13 (100%)

Grads Employed by Industry:.......% avg. salary:

Accounting	7	$35,056
Finance	15	$35,056
Marketing	15	$35,000
Operations	7	$48,600
General Management	23	$37,301
Other	31	$58,375

Top 5 Employers Hiring Grads: Cintas, Frito Lay, Walgreen, Sherman Williams Co., AmSouth Bank

UNIVERSITY OF NORTH TEXAS
COLLEGE OF BUSINESS

ADMISSIONS CONTACT: DENISE GALUBENSKI OR KONNI STUBBLEFIELD, GRADUATE ACADEMIC ADVISORS
ADDRESS: P.O. BOX 311160, DENTON, TX 76203
PHONE: 940-369-8977 • FAX: 940-369-8978
E-MAIL: MBA@COBAF.UNT.EDU
WEBSITE: WWW.COBA.UNT.EDU

GENERAL INFORMATION

Type of School: Public **Environment:** City **Academic Calendar:** Semester

STUDENTS

Enrollment of Parent Institution: 34,500 **Enrollment of Business School:** 639 **% International:** 10 **Average Age at Entry:** 28 **Average Years Work Experience at Entry:** 6

ACADEMICS

Student/faculty Ratio: 45:1 **% Female Faculty:** 22 **% Minority Faculty:** 17

Joint Degrees: MBA/MS (Operations Management, Engineering Technology), MBA/MS (Merchandising), MBA/MS (Hospitality Management). **Prominent Alumni:** Laura Wright, CFO, Southwest Airlines; Noreen Hey, VP of Packaging & Hotels, Travelocity; Brent Ryan, Owner of Ryan & Co.; Mike Bowlin, Former Chairman of the Board, ARCO; J. Russell Crews, CFO, Snelling Personnell Services.

FINANCIAL FACTS

Tuition (in-state/out-of-state): $1,898/$4,400 **Fees:** $639 **Books and Supplies:** $1,000 **Room & Board:** $6,000

ADMISSIONS

Admissions Selectivity Rating: 72

# of Applications Received: 343 **% Applicants Accepted:** 55 **% Acceptees Attending:** GMAT Range (25th to 75th percentile): 410–530 **Average GMAT:** 468 **Average GPA:** 3 **TOEFL Required of Int'l Applicants:** Yes **Minimum TOEFL (paper/computer):** 550/213 **Application Fee:** $50 **International Application Fee:** $75

Regular Application Deadline: 7/15

Deferment Available: Yes **Maximum Length of Deferment:** Three semesters **Transfer Students Accepted:** Yes **Non-fall Admissions:** Yes **Need-Blind Admissions:** Yes

UNIVERSITY OF SAN DIEGO
SCHOOL OF BUSINESS ADMINISTRATION

ADMISSIONS CONTACT: MS. KACY KILNER, ADMISSIONS DIRECTOR, MBA PROGRAMS
ADDRESS: 5998 ALCALA PARK, SAN DIEGO, CA 92110-2492
PHONE: 619-260-4860 • FAX:
E-MAIL: MBA@SANDIEGO.EDU
WEBSITE: WWW.SANDIEGO.EDU/BUSINESS

GENERAL INFORMATION

Type of School: Private **Affiliation:** Roman Catholic **Environment:** Metropolis

STUDENTS

Enrollment of Parent Institution: 7,483 **Enrollment of Business School:** 219 **% Male/female:** 62/38 **% Part-time:** 92 **% Minorities:** 8 **% International:** 18 **Average Age at Entry:** 26 **Average Years Work Experience at Entry:** 4.4

ACADEMICS

% Female Faculty: 25 **% Minority Faculty:** 15

Joint Degrees: MBA/JD 4 years, MBA/MSN 3 years, MBA/MSRE 2.5 years, MBA/MSGL 2.5 years, IMBA/JD 4 years.

FINANCIAL FACTS

Tuition: $35,700 **Fees:** $136 **Books and Supplies:** $1,300 **Room & Board (on/off campus):** $10,960/$8,910 **% of Students Receiving Aid:** 100 **% of First-year Students Receiving Aid:** 100 **% of Students Receiving Loans:** 44 **% of Students Receiving Grants:** 100 **Average Award Package:** $26,845 **Average Grant:** $15,981

ADMISSIONS

Admissions Selectivity Rating: 90

# of Applications Received: 156 **% Applicants Accepted:** 37 **% Acceptees Attending:** 31 **GMAT Range (25th to 75th percentile):** 608–675 **Average GMAT:** 646 **Average GPA:** 3.23 **TOEFL Required of Int'l Applicants:** Yes **Minimum TOEFL (paper/computer):** 580/237 **Application Fee:** $45

Regular Application Deadline: 6/15 **Regular Notification:** rolling

Deferment Available: Yes **Maximum Length of Deferment:** 1 year **Need-Blind Admissions:** Yes

UNIVERSITY OF SAN FRANCISCO
MASAGUNG GRADUATE SCHOOL OF MANAGEMENT

ADDRESS: 2130 FULTON STREET, LONE MOUNTAIN, SAN FRANCISCO, CA 94117-1045
PHONE: 415-422-2089 • FAX: 415-422-2066
E-MAIL: GRADUATE@USFCA.EDU
WEBSITE: WWW.USFCA.EDU/SOBAM

GENERAL INFORMATION

Type of School: Private **Affiliation:** Jesuit **Environment:** Metropolis

STUDENTS

Enrollment of Parent Institution: 8,110 **Enrollment of Business School:** 275 **% Part-time:** 27 **% Minorities:** 28 **% International:** 40 **Average Age at Entry:** 28 **Average Years Work Experience at Entry:** 4

ACADEMICS

Student/faculty Ratio: 3:1 **% Female Faculty:** 20 **% Minority Faculty:** 25

Joint Degrees: JD/MBA; MAPS/MBA (Asian Pacific Studies), MSEM/MBA (Master of Science in Environmental Management), MSFA/MBA. **Prominent Alumni:** Gordon Smith, CEO, PG&E; Lip Bu-Tan, Founder, Walden International Investment Group; Mary Callanan, Retired Treasurer for the County/City of San Fran; Angela Alioto, Attorney, Political Leader; Pierre Salinger, Former Press Secretary to the US President.

FINANCIAL FACTS

Tuition: $24,875 **Fees:** $444 **Books and Supplies:** $1,250 **Room & Board:** $8,830

ADMISSIONS

Admissions Selectivity Rating: 77

# of Applications Received: 373 **% Applicants Accepted:** 67 **% Acceptees Attending:** 42 **GMAT Range (25th to 75th percentile):** 500–680 **Average GMAT:** 573 **Average GPA:** 3.2 **TOEFL Required of Int'l Applicants:** Yes **Minimum TOEFL (paper/computer):** 600/250 **Application Fee:** $55 **International Application Fee:** $65

Regular Application Deadline: Regular Notification: Application Deadline/Notification Round 1: 11/15 / 12/31 Round 2: 01/15 / 2/28 Round 3: 3/15 / 5/31 Round 4: 5/15 / 6/30

Deferment Available: Yes **Maximum Length of Deferment:** 1 year **Transfer Students Accepted:** Yes **Applicants Also Look At:** Pepperdine University, Santa Clara University, University of California—Irvine, University of San Diego.

EMPLOYMENT PROFILE

Grads Employed by Industry:	%	avg. salary:
Finance	14	$72,000
Marketing	39	$70,000
MIS	7	$63,000
Consulting	4	$65,000
General Management	4	$59,000
Other	31	$55,000
Non-profit	1	$52,000

UNIVERSITY OF SOUTH ALABAMA
MITCHELL COLLEGE OF BUSINESS

ADMISSIONS CONTACT: OFFICE OF ADMISSIONS,
ADDRESS: MEISLER HALL SUITE 2500, MOBILE, AL 36688-0002
PHONE: 251-460-6141 • FAX: 251-460-7876
E-MAIL: ADMISS@USOUTHAL.EDU • WEBSITE: MCOB.SOUTHALABAMA.EDU

GENERAL INFORMATION

Type of School: Public

STUDENTS

Enrollment of Parent Institution: 13,500 **Enrollment of Business School:** 135 **% Male/female:** 55/45 **% Minorities:** 55 **% International:** 10 **Average Age at Entry:** 28

ACADEMICS

Student/faculty Ratio: 31:1 **% Female Faculty:** 21 **% Minority Faculty:** 10

FINANCIAL FACTS

Tuition (in-state/out-of-state): $4,008/$8,016 **Fees:** $2,460 **Books and Supplies:** $1,200 **Room & Board (on/off campus):** $4,750/$7,200

ADMISSIONS

Admissions Selectivity Rating: 76

# of Applications Received: 80 **% Applicants Accepted:** 78 **% Acceptees Attending:** 73 **Average GMAT:** 550 **Average GPA:** 3.4 **TOEFL Required of Int'l Applicants:** Yes **Minimum TOEFL:** 525 **Application Fee:** $25

Regular Application Deadline: 7/15 **Regular Notification:** 7/25 **Transfer Students Accepted:** Yes **Need-Blind Admissions:** Yes

UNIVERSITY OF SOUTH FLORIDA
COLLEGE OF BUSINESS

ADMISSIONS CONTACT: WENDY BAKER, ASSISTANT DIRECTOR OF GRADUATE STUDIES
ADDRESS: 4202 E. FOWLER AVE. BSN 3403, LOC BSN 103, TAMPA, FL 33620
PHONE: 813-974-3335 • FAX: 813-974-4518
E-MAIL: MBA@COBA.USF.EDU
WEBSITE: WWW.COBA.USF.EDU

GENERAL INFORMATION

Type of School: Public **Environment:** Metropolis **Academic Calendar:** Semester

STUDENTS

Enrollment of Parent Institution: 45,524 **Enrollment of Business School:** 390 **% Male/female:** 56/44 **% Part-time:** 62 **% Minorities:** 9 **% International:** 23 **Average Age at Entry:** 28 **Average Years Work Experience at Entry:** 3.2

ACADEMICS

Student/faculty Ratio: 4:1 **% Female Faculty:** 25 **% Minority Faculty:** 7

Joint Degrees: MBA/MSM (Management Information Systems) 2–5 years, MSE/MBA (entrepreneurship). **Prominent Alumni:** Rob Carter, Executive VP & CIO, Federal Express Corporation; Joie Chitwood III, President & COO, Indianapolis Motor Speedway; D. Beatty D'Alessandro, Senior Vice President & CFO, Graybar Electric Co.; John Reich, FDIC Dir. of the U.S. Office of Thrift Supervision; Rear

Admiral Adam Robinson, Jr., US Navy Commander & Chief, Nat'l Naval Med. Cntr.

FINANCIAL FACTS

Tuition (in-state/out-of-state): $6,050/$21,530 **Fees:** $37 **Books and Supplies:** $1,300 **Room & Board:** $8,620

ADMISSIONS

Admissions Selectivity Rating: 78

# of Applications Received: 272 **% Applicants Accepted:** 56 % **Acceptees Attending:** 55 **GMAT Range (25th to 75th percentile):** 490–610 **Average GMAT:** 540 **Average GPA:** 3.25 **TOEFL Required of Int'l Applicants:** Yes **Minimum TOEFL (paper/computer):** 550/213 **Application Fee:** $30

Regular Application Deadline: 6/1 **Regular Notification:** 6/1 **Deferment Available:** Yes **Maximum Length of Deferment:** 1 year **Transfer Students Accepted:** Yes **Non-fall Admissions:** Yes **Need-Blind Admissions:** Yes **Applicants Also Look At:** The University of Tampa, University of Florida.

EMPLOYMENT PROFILE

Primary Source of Full-time Job Acceptances

School-facilitated Activities 7 (37%)
Graduate-facilitated Activities 5 (26%)
Unknown...7 (37%)
Average base starting salary $51,000
Percent Employed 73

Grads Employed by Industry: ....% avg. salary:

Finance 42 $48,000
Human Resources..........................5
Marketing 21 $45,000
MIS 5
Operations.....................................5
Consulting 5
General Management 10
Other...5

UNIVERSITY OF SOUTH FLORIDA—ST. PETERSBURG
COLLEGE OF BUSINESS

ADMISSIONS CONTACT: KEVIN COUGHLIN, DIRECTOR OF ADMISSIONS AND RECORDS
ADDRESS: 140 7TH AVENUE SOUTH, BAY 104, ST. PETERSBURG, FL 33701
PHONE: 727-873-4143 • FAX: 727-873-4525
E-MAIL: KEVINC@STPT.USF.EDU
WEBSITE: WWW.STPT.USF.EDU

GENERAL INFORMATION
Type of School: Public

STUDENTS

Enrollment of Business School: 133 **% Part-time:** 100 **Average Age at Entry:** 32 **Average Years Work Experience at Entry:** 4

ACADEMICS

Student/faculty Ratio: 20:1 **% Female Faculty:** 33 **% Minority Faculty:** 7

ADMISSIONS

Admissions Selectivity Rating: 84

# of Applications Received: 93 **% Applicants Accepted:** 62 % **Acceptees Attending:** 88 **GMAT Range (25th to 75th percentile):** 490–580 **Average GMAT:** 565 **Average GPA:** 3.4 **TOEFL Required of Int'l Applicants:** **Minimum TOEFL (paper/computer):** 550/213 **Application Fee:** $30

Regular Application Deadline: 7/1 **Regular Notification:** Rolling **Deferment Available:** Yes **Transfer Students Accepted:** Yes **Non-fall Admissions:** Yes **Applicants Also Look At:** University of Florida, University of South Florida.

UNIVERSITY OF SOUTHERN INDIANA
COLLEGE OF BUSINESS

ADMISSIONS CONTACT: DR. PEGGY HARREL, DIRECTOR OF GRADUATE STUDIES
ADDRESS: 8600 UNIVERSITY BOULVARD, EVANSVILLE, IN 47712
PHONE: 812-465-7015 • FAX: 812-464-1956
E-MAIL: GSSR@USI.EDU
WEBSITE: BUSINESS.USI.EDU

GENERAL INFORMATION

Type of School: Public **Environment:** City **Academic Calendar:** Semester

STUDENTS

Enrollment of Parent Institution: 9,939 **Enrollment of Business School:** 101 **% Male/female:** 33/67 **% Part-time:** 94 % **International:** 50 **Average Age at Entry:** 32 **Average Years Work Experience at Entry:** 7

ACADEMICS

Student/faculty Ratio: 26:1 **% Female Faculty:** 19 **% Minority Faculty:** 19

FINANCIAL FACTS

Tuition (in-state/out-of-state): $4,121/$8,133 **Fees:** $200 **Books and Supplies:** $900 **Room & Board (on/off campus):** $6,542/$8,464 **% of Students Receiving Aid:** 24 **% of First-year Students Receiving Aid:** 4 **% of Students Receiving Loans:** 18 **% of Students Receiving Grants:** 9 **Average Award Package:** $5,522 **Average Grant:** $2,422

ADMISSIONS

Admissions Selectivity Rating: 74

# of Applications Received: 38 **% Applicants Accepted:** 84 % **Acceptees Attending:** 78 **GMAT Range (25th to 75th percentile):**

480–590 **Average GMAT:** 536 **Average GPA:** 3.5 **TOEFL Required of Int'l Applicants:** Yes **Minimum TOEFL (paper/computer):** 550/213 **Application Fee:** $25

Regular Application Deadline: rolling **Regular Notification:** rolling **Transfer Students Accepted:** Yes **Non-fall Admissions:** Yes **Need-Blind Admissions:** Yes

UNIVERSITY OF ST. GALLEN (SWITZERLAND)
MBA-HSG

ADMISSIONS CONTACT: MR. PRASAD OSWAL, PROGRAMME MANAGER
ADDRESS: BLUMENBERGPLATZ 9, ST. GALLEN, 9000 SWITZERLAND
PHONE: 0041-71-224-7355 • FAX: 0041-71-224-2473
E-MAIL: MBA@UNISG.CH
WEBSITE: WWW.MBA.UNISG.CH

GENERAL INFORMATION
Type of School: Public

FINANCIAL FACTS
Tuition: $38,322 **Room & Board:** $14,000

ADMISSIONS
Admissions Selectivity Rating: 60*
Average GMAT: 680 **TOEFL Required of Int'l Applicants:** Yes
Minimum TOEFL: 260 **Application Fee:** $0
Regular Application Deadline: 6/15 Application Deadline Round 1: 01/15, Round 2: 03/30, Round 3: 06/15.
Deferment Available: Yes **Maximum Length of Deferment:** 1 Year
Need-Blind Admissions: Yes

UNIVERSITY OF STRATHCLYDE— GLASGOW
UNIVERSITY OF STRATHCLYDE GRADUATE SCHOOL OF BUSINESS

ADMISSIONS CONTACT: 141-553- 6118, LUCY REYNOLDS
ADDRESS: 199 CATHEDRAL STREET, GLASGOW, G4 0QU SCOTLAND
PHONE: 141-553-6118 • FAX: 141-553-6162
E-MAIL: ADMISSIONS@GSB.STRATH.AC.UK
WEBSITE: WWW.GSB.STRATH.AC.UK

STUDENTS
Enrollment of Parent Institution: Enrollment of Business School: 107 **% Male/female:** 86/14 **% Part-time:** 37 **% Minorities:** 88 **% International:** 84 **Average Age at Entry:** 32 **Average Years Work Experience at Entry:** 9

ACADEMICS
Student/faculty Ratio: 4:1 **% Female Faculty:** 11
Joint Degrees: MBA with a specialism in Leadership Studies, 2.5–3 years.

FINANCIAL FACTS
Tuition: $31,600 **Books and Supplies:** $150 **Room & Board (on/off campus):** $13,500/$15,300

ADMISSIONS
Admissions Selectivity Rating: 70
# of Applications Received: 280 **% Applicants Accepted:** 90 **% Acceptees Attending:** 42 **Average GMAT:** 560 **Average GPA:** 3.4 **TOEFL Required of Int'l Applicants:** Yes **Minimum TOEFL (paper/computer):** 600/250 **Application Fee:** $0 **International Application Fee:** $0
Regular Application Deadline: rolling **Regular Notification:** rolling
Deferment Available: Yes **Maximum Length of Deferment:** 2 years
Non-fall Admissions: Yes

EMPLOYMENT PROFILE

Grads Employed by Industry:	%	avg. salary:
Accounting	2	$130,000
Finance	13	$130,000
Marketing	5	$85,500
Consulting	10	$142,000
Entrepreneurship	10	$0
Other	41	$95,000
Internet/New Media	15	$114,000
Non-profit	4	$66,500

Top 5 Employers Hiring Grads: Mott McDonald, BT, RBoS, Standard Life, Prince and Princess of Wales Hospice.

THE UNIVERSITY OF TEXAS AT EL PASO
COLLEGE OF BUSINESS ADMINISTRATION

ADMISSIONS CONTACT: LAURA URIBARRI, DIRECTOR OF MBA PROGRAMS
ADDRESS: ROOM 103, COLLEGE OF BUSINESS ADMINISTRATION, EL PASO, TX 79968
PHONE: 915-747-5379 • FAX: 915-747-5147
E-MAIL: LMURIBARRI@UTEP.EDU
WEBSITE: MBA.UTEP.EDU

GENERAL INFORMATION
Type of School: Public **Environment:** Metropolis **Academic Calendar:** Semester

STUDENTS
Enrollment of Parent Institution: 19,900 **Enrollment of Business School:** 288 **% Male/female:** 50/50 **% Part-time:** 90 **Average Age at Entry:** 32 **Average Years Work Experience at Entry:** 3.75

ACADEMICS
% Female Faculty: 10 **% Minority Faculty:** 29
Joint Degrees: MBA/ MPA (MBA/Master in Public Administration) 3–6 years.

FINANCIAL FACTS

Books and Supplies: $3,512 **Room & Board:** $10,572

ADMISSIONS

Admissions Selectivity Rating: 67

# of Applications Received: 180 **% Applicants Accepted:** 84 **%
Acceptees Attending:** 93 **Average GMAT:** 480 **Average GPA:** 3
TOEFL Required of Int'l Applicants: Yes **Minimum TOEFL
(paper/computer):** 600/250 **Application Fee:** $30 **International
Application Fee:** $60

Deferment Available: Yes **Maximum Length of Deferment:** 2 years
Applicants **Transfer Students Accepted:** Yes **Non-fall Admissions:**
Yes **Need-Blind Admissions:** Yes

THE UNIVERSITY OF TEXAS AT TYLER

SCHOOL OF BUSINESS ADMINISTRATION

*ADMISSIONS CONTACT: DR. MARY FISCHER, COORDINATOR OF GRADUATE
PROGRAMS IN BUSINESS*
ADDRESS: 3900 UNIVERSITY BOULEVARD, TYLER, TX 75799
PHONE: 903-566-7433 • FAX: 903-566-7372
E-MAIL: MFISCHER@UTTYLER.EDU
WEBSITE: WWW.UTTYLER.EDU/CBT/MBA

GENERAL INFORMATION

Type of School: Public **Environment:** City **Academic Calendar:**
Semester

STUDENTS

Enrollment of Parent Institution: 6,150 **Enrollment of Business
School:** 189 **% Part-time:** 99 **Average Age at Entry:** 3

ACADEMICS

Student/faculty Ratio: 20:1 **% Female Faculty:** 45 **% Minority
Faculty:** 33
Joint Degrees: MSN/MBA 2–6 years, MBA/MEng 2–6 years.

FINANCIAL FACTS

Books and Supplies: *$975*

ADMISSIONS

Admissions Selectivity Rating: 77

# of Applications Received: 110 **% Applicants Accepted:** 76 **%
Acceptees Attending:** 100 **Average GMAT:** 513 **Average GPA:** 3.1
TOEFL Required of Int'l Applicants: Yes **Minimum TOEFL
(paper/computer):** 550/213 **Application Fee:** $25 **International
Application Fee:** $50

Regular Application Deadline: rolling **Regular Notification:** rolling
Deferment Available: Yes **Maximum Length of Deferment:** 1 year
Non-fall Admissions: Yes **Need-Blind Admissions:** Yes

UNIVERSITY OF TORONTO

JOSEPH L. ROTMAN SCHOOL OF MANAGEMENT

*ADMISSIONS CONTACT: CHERYL MILLINGTON, DIRECTOR OF MBA RECRUITING
AND ADMISSIONS*
ADDRESS: 105 ST. GEORGE STREET, TORONTO, ON M5S 3E6 CANADA
PHONE: 416-978-3499 • FAX: 416-978-5812
E-MAIL: MBA@ROTMAN.UTORONTO.CA
WEBSITE: WWW.ROTMAN.UTORONTO.CA

GENERAL INFORMATION

Type of School: Public **Environment:** Metropolis

STUDENTS

Enrollment of Parent Institution: 67,000 **Enrollment of Business
School:** 330 **% Male/female:** 73/27 **% Part-time:** 19 **% Minorities:**
50 **% International:** 40 **Average Age at Entry:** 28 **Average Years
Work Experience at Entry:** 5

ACADEMICS

Student/faculty Ratio: 7:1 **% Female Faculty:** 22
Joint Degrees: JD/MBA 4 years), BASC/MBA 5 years, 8 months
MA/MBA (Russian & Eastern European Studies) 4 years. **Prominent
Alumni:** Joseph L. Rotman, Founder & Chairman, Clairvest Group
Inc.; Ian Locke, General Partner, Jefferson Partners, Toronto; Don
Morrison, COO, Research In Motion, Waterloo, Ont.; John Cassaday,
President & CEO, Corus Entertainment; Richard Nesbitt, CEO, TSX
Group.

FINANCIAL FACTS

Tuition (in-state/out-of-state): $21,800/$29,800 **Books and
Supplies:** $5,000 **Room & Board:** $10,000 **% of Students Receiving
Aid:** 70 **% of First-year Students Receiving Aid:** 70 **% of Students
Receiving Loans:** 70 **% of Students Receiving Grants:** 20 **Average
Grant:** $8,000

ADMISSIONS

Admissions Selectivity Rating: 60*

# of Applications Received: 1,010 **GMAT Range (25th to 75th percentile):** 550–770 **Average GMAT:** 642 **Average GPA:** 3.4 **TOEFL
Required of Int'l Applicants:** Yes **Minimum TOEFL (paper/comput-
er):** 600/250 **Application Fee:** $150

Regular Application Deadline: 4/30 **Regular Notification:** 7/1
Application Deadline/Notification Round 1: 01/15 / 03/15 Round 2:
04/30 / 07/01

Early Decision Program: Yes **ED Deadline/notification:** 01/15 / 3/15
Deferment Available: Yes **Maximum Length of Deferment:** 1 year
Need-Blind Admissions: Yes **Applicants Also Look At:** McGill
University, Queensland University of Technology, University of
Western Ontario, York University.

EMPLOYMENT PROFILE

Primary Source of Full-time Job Acceptances

School-facilitated Activities 53%

Graduate-facilitated Activities 47%

Percent Employed 93

Grads Employed by Industry: ....% avg. salary:

Finance 53 $80,000

Marketing 8 $68,526

Operations.....................................9 $78,633

Consulting.....................................18 $105,500

General Management 8 $89,083

Other...4 $82,560

Top 5 Employers Hiring Grads: CIBC, RBC Financial Group, TD Bank Financial Group, BMO Financial Group, Johnson & Johnson.

UNIVERSITY OF WARWICK
WARWICK BUSINESS SCHOOL

ADMISSIONS CONTACT: HEATHER BROADBENT, MBA MARKETING & RECRUITMENT TEAM
ADDRESS: WARWICK BUSINESS SCHOOL, COVENTRY, CV4 7AL ENGLAND
PHONE: 011-44 (0)24 7652 4100 • FAX: 011-44 (0)24 7657 4400
E-MAIL: WARWICKMBA@WBS.AC.UK
WEBSITE: WWW.WBS.AC.UK

GENERAL INFORMATION

Academic Calendar: Trimester

STUDENTS

Enrollment of Parent Institution: 18,000 **Enrollment of Business School:** 475 **% Male/female:** 68/32 **% Part-time:** 85 **% International:** 82 **Average Age at Entry:** 32 **Average Years Work Experience at Entry:** 8

ACADEMICS

Student/faculty Ratio: 12:1

Prominent Alumni: Svein Stokke, Director, Citigroup; Keith Bedell-Pearce, Chairman, Norwich & Peterborough Building Society; Mike O'Driscoll, President, Aston Martin, Jaguar, Land Rover; Steven Falk, Director of Financial Services, Manchester Utd FC; Roger Lovering, Head of Card Services, HSBC Bank plc.

FINANCIAL FACTS

Tuition: $41,399 **Books and Supplies:** $2,500 **Room & Board:** $12,000 **% of Students Receiving Aid:** 10 **% of Students Receiving Grants:** 10 **Average Award Package:** $20,000 **Average Grant:** $20,000

ADMISSIONS

Admissions Selectivity Rating: 86

# of Applications Received: 224 **% Applicants Accepted:** 61 **% Acceptees Attending:** 53 **GMAT Range (25th to 75th percentile):** 550–680 **Average GMAT:** 610 **Average GPA:** **TOEFL Required of Int'l Applicants:** Yes **Minimum TOEFL (paper/computer):** 620/260 **Application Fee:** $132

Deferment Available: Yes **Maximum Length of Deferment:** 1 year
Applicants Also Look At: Cranfield University, London Business School, University of Cambridge, University of Manchester, University of Oxford.

EMPLOYMENT PROFILE

Primary Source of Full-time Job Acceptances

School-facilitated Activities 40%

Graduate-facilitated Activities 60%

Percent Employed 96

Grads Employed by Industry: ....%

Finance 19

Human Resources...........................2

Marketing 21

MIS 5

Operations.....................................2

Strategic Planning.........................16

Consulting.....................................19

Entrepreneurship...........................2

General Management 10

Other...2

Top 5 Employers Hiring Grads: Deloitte, Cap Gemini, Johnson & Johnson, Pepsico, Proctor & Gamble.

UNIVERSITY OF WEST FLORIDA
COLLEGE OF BUSINESS

ADMISSIONS CONTACT: GRADUATE ADMISSIONS OFFICE, GRADUATE ADMISSIONS OFFICERS
ADDRESS: 11000 UNIVERSITY PKWY, BLDG 18, PENSACOLA, FL 32514
PHONE: 850-474-2230 • FAX: 850-474-3360
E-MAIL: ADMISSIONS@UWF.EDU
WEBSITE: UWF.EDU/MBA

GENERAL INFORMATION

Type of School: Public **Environment:** City

STUDENTS

Enrollment of Parent Institution: Enrollment of Business School: 178 **% Male/female:** 60/40 **% Out-of-state:** 80 **% Part-time:** 90 **% International:** 80 **Average Age at Entry:** 29

ACADEMICS

Student/faculty Ratio: 25:1 **% Female Faculty:** 13 **% Minority Faculty:** 13

Joint Degrees: MBA/MS 20 months.

FINANCIAL FACTS

Tuition (in-state/out-of-state): $8,325/$30,093 **Books and Supplies:** $1,000 **Average Grant:** $1,400

ADMISSIONS

Admissions Selectivity Rating: 84

# of Applications Received: 71 **% Applicants Accepted:** 49 **% Acceptees Attending:** 80 **GMAT Range (25th to 75th percentile):**

460–600 **Average GMAT:** 537 **Average GPA:** 3.4 **TOEFL Required of Int'l Applicants:** Yes **Minimum TOEFL (paper/computer):** 550/213 **Application Fee:** $30

Regular Application Deadline: 6/1 **Regular Notification:** Rolling

Deferment Available: Yes **Maximum Length of Deferment:** 1 year **Transfer Students Accepted:** Yes **Non-fall Admissions:** Yes **Applicants Also Look At:** Florida State University, Troy University, University of Florida.

UNIVERSITY OF WISCONSIN— EAU CLAIRE
SCHOOL OF BUSINESS

ADMISSIONS CONTACT: MS. JAN STEWART, MBA PROGRAM ASSISTANT
ADDRESS: 105 GARFIELD AVENUE, EAU CLAIRE, WI 54702-4004
PHONE: 715-836-4733 • FAX: 715-836-2409
E-MAIL: ADMISSIONS@UWEC.EDU
WEBSITE: WWW.UWEC.EDU/COB/ACADEMICS/MBA

GENERAL INFORMATION

Type of School: Public **Environment:** Town **Academic Calendar:** Semester

STUDENTS

Enrollment of Parent Institution: 10,500 **Enrollment of Business School:** 130 **% Male/female:** 55/45 **% Out-of-state:** 80 **% Part-time:** 90 **% Minorities:** 5 **% International:** 80 **Average Age at Entry:** 28 **Average Years Work Experience at Entry:** 7

ACADEMICS

Student/faculty Ratio: 5:1 **% Female Faculty:** 30

FINANCIAL FACTS

Tuition (in-state/out-of-state): $6,223/$16,833 **Books and Supplies:** $1,000 **Room & Board:** $4,266

ADMISSIONS

Admissions Selectivity Rating: 60*

Average GMAT: 530 **Average GPA:** 3.2 **TOEFL Required of Int'l Applicants:** Yes **Minimum TOEFL (paper/computer):** 550/213 **Application Fee:** $45

Regular Application Deadline: Rolling **Regular Notification:** Rolling

Deferment Available: Yes **Maximum Length of Deferment:** 1 year **Transfer Students Accepted:** Yes **Non-fall Admissions:** Yes

EMPLOYMENT PROFILE

Grads Employed by Industry:.......%
Accounting	20
Marketing	20
MIS	10
Operations	10
Entrepreneurship	10
General Management	30

UNIVERSITY OF WISCONSIN—LA CROSSE
COLLEGE OF BUSINESS ADMINISTRATION

ADMISSIONS CONTACT: KATHY KIEFER, DIRECTOR
ADDRESS: 1725 STATE STREET, LA CROSSE, WI 54601
PHONE: 608-785-8939 • FAX: 608-785-6695
E-MAIL: ADMISSIONS@UWLAX.EDU
WEBSITE: WWW.UWLAX.EDU

GENERAL INFORMATION

Type of School: Public **Academic Calendar:** Semester

STUDENTS

Enrollment of Parent Institution: 9,198 **Enrollment of Business School:** 59 **Average Age at Entry:** 28 **Average Years Work Experience at Entry:** 3

ACADEMICS

Student/faculty Ratio: 25:1 **% Female Faculty:** 28 **% Minority Faculty:** 22

FINANCIAL FACTS

Tuition (in-state/out-of-state): $7,588/$18,200 **Books and Supplies:** $500 **Room & Board:** $5,000

ADMISSIONS

Admissions Selectivity Rating: 72

# of Applications Received: 38 **% Applicants Accepted:** 82 **% Acceptees Attending:** 74 **Average GMAT:** 533 **Average GPA:** 3.25 **TOEFL Required of Int'l Applicants:** Yes **Minimum TOEFL (paper/computer):** 550/213 **Application Fee:** $48

Regular Application Deadline: rolling **Regular Notification:** rolling

Deferment Available: Yes **Maximum Length of Deferment:** rolling **Transfer Students Accepted:** Yes **Non-fall Admissions:** Yes **Need-Blind Admissions:** Yes

UNIVERSITY OF WISCONSIN— OSHKOSH
COLLEGE OF BUSINESS ADMINSTRATION

ADMISSIONS CONTACT: LYNN GRANCORBITZ, MBA PROGRAM ASSISTANT DIRECTOR AND ADVISOR
ADDRESS: 800 ALGOMA BLVD., OSHKOSH, WI 54901
PHONE: 800-633-1430 • FAX: 920-424-7413
E-MAIL: MBA@UWOSH.EDU
WEBSITE: WWW.MBA.UWOSH.EDU

GENERAL INFORMATION

Type of School: Public **Environment:** Village **Academic Calendar:** Semester

STUDENTS

Enrollment of Parent Institution: 10,528 **Enrollment of Business**

School: 525 **% Male/female:** 55/45 **% Out-of-state:** 2 **% Part-time:** 95 **% Minorities:** 2 **% International:** 3 **Average Age at Entry:** 32 **Average Years Work Experience at Entry:** 5

ACADEMICS
Student/faculty Ratio: 11:1 **% Female Faculty:** 15 **% Minority Faculty:** 5

FINANCIAL FACTS
Tuition (in-state/out-of-state): $4,664/$13,622 **% of Students Receiving Aid:** 5 **% of First-year Students Receiving Aid:** 5 **% of Students Receiving Loans:** 5

ADMISSIONS
Admissions Selectivity Rating: 71
# of Applications Received: 115 **% Applicants Accepted:** 90 **% Acceptees Attending:** 93 **GMAT Range (25th to 75th percentile):** 470–610 **Average GMAT:** 540 **Average GPA:** 3.1 **TOEFL Required of Int'l Applicants:** Yes **Minimum TOEFL:** 550 **Application Fee:** $45
Regular Application Deadline: 7/1 **Regular Notification:** rolling
Deferment Available: Yes **Maximum Length of Deferment:** 3 years
Transfer Students Accepted: Yes **Non-fall Admissions:** Yes
Applicants Also Look At: Adolfo Ibañez University (Chile), Marquette University.

EMPLOYMENT PROFILE
Primary Source of Full-time Job Acceptances
Graduate-facilitated Activities 100 (100%)
Percent Employed 50

UNIVERSITY OF WISCONSIN— PARKSIDE
SCHOOL OF BUSINESS AND TECHNOLOGY

ADMISSIONS CONTACT: BRAD PIAZZA, ASSISTANT DEAN
ADDRESS: 900 WOOD ROAD, BOX 2000, KENOSHA, WI 53141-2000
PHONE: 262-595-2046 • FAX: 262-595-2680
E-MAIL: PIAZZA@UWP.EDU
WEBSITE: WWW.UWP.EDU/DEPARTMENTS/BUSINESS

GENERAL INFORMATION
Type of School: Public **Environment:** City **Academic Calendar:** Semester

STUDENTS
Enrollment of Parent Institution: 5,000 **Enrollment of Business School:** 81 **% Male/female:** 60/40 **% Part-time:** 87 **% Minorities:** 16 **% International:** 2 **Average Age at Entry:** 33 **Average Years Work Experience at Entry:** 3

ACADEMICS
Student/faculty Ratio: 6:1 **% Female Faculty:** 35 **% Minority Faculty:** 30

FINANCIAL FACTS
Tuition (in-state/out-of-state): $6,730/$17,500 **Fees:** $277 **Books and Supplies:** $300

ADMISSIONS
Admissions Selectivity Rating: 63
# of Applications Received: 28 **% Applicants Accepted:** 96 **% Acceptees Attending:** 93 **GMAT Range (25th to 75th percentile):** 330–680 **Average GMAT:** 460 **Average GPA:** 3.0 **TOEFL Required of Int'l Applicants:** Yes **Minimum TOEFL (paper/computer):** 550/213 **Application Fee:** $45
Regular Application Deadline: 8/1 **Regular Notification:** rolling
Deferment Available: Yes **Maximum Length of Deferment:** 1 year
Transfer Students Accepted: Yes **Non-fall Admissions:** Yes **Need-Blind Admissions:** Yes

UNIVERSITY OF WYOMING
COLLEGE OF BUSINESS

ADMISSIONS CONTACT: TERRI L. RITTENBURG, DIRECTOR OF MBA PROGRAM
ADDRESS: P.O. BOX 3275, LARAMIE, WY 82071
PHONE: 307-766-2449 • FAX: 307-766-4028
E-MAIL: MBA@UWYO.EDU
WEBSITE: BUSINESS.UWYO.EDU/MBA

GENERAL INFORMATION
Type of School: Public **Environment:** Town **Academic Calendar:** Semester

STUDENTS
Enrollment of Parent Institution: 11,904 **Enrollment of Business School:** 63 **% Male/female:** 64/36 **% Part-time:** 48 **% International:** 18 **Average Age at Entry:** 28

ACADEMICS
Student/faculty Ratio: 3:1

FINANCIAL FACTS
Tuition (in-state/out-of-state): $2,988/$8,676 **Fees (in-state/out-of-state):** $246/$298 **Books and Supplies:** $300 **Room & Board (on/off campus):** $6,212 **% of Students Receiving Loans:** 34

ADMISSIONS
Admissions Selectivity Rating: 60*
Average GMAT: 558 **Average GPA:** 3.2 **TOEFL Required of Int'l Applicants:** Yes **Minimum TOEFL (paper/computer):** 525/197 **Application Fee:** $40 **International Application Fee:** $0
Regular Application Deadline: 2/1 **Regular Notification:** Rolling
Deferment Available: Yes **Maximum Length of Deferment:** 1 year
Transfer Students Accepted: Yes **Need-Blind Admissions:** Yes

UTAH STATE UNIVERSITY
JON M. HUNTSMAN SCHOOL OF BUSINESS

ADMISSIONS CONTACT: SCHOOL OF GRADUATE STUDIES, ADMISSIONS OFFICER
ADDRESS: 0900 OLD MAIN HILL, LOGAN, UT 84322-0900
PHONE: (435) 797-1189 • FAX: (435) 797-1192
E-MAIL: GRADSCH@CC.USU.EDU
WEBSITE: WWW.HUNTSMAN.USU.EDU

GENERAL INFORMATION

Type of School: Public **Environment:** Town **Academic Calendar:** Semester

STUDENTS

Enrollment of Parent Institution: 24,421 **Enrollment of Business School:** 190 **% Male/female:** 67/33 **% Out-of-state:** 21 **% Part-time:** 79 **% Minorities:** 13 **% International:** 10 **Average Age at Entry:** 28 **Average Years Work Experience at Entry:** 7

ACADEMICS

Student/faculty Ratio: 4:1 **% Female Faculty:** 19 **% Minority Faculty:** 10

Joint Degrees: MSEE/MBA (Electrical Engineering) 2 years.
Prominent Alumni: Ron Labrum, Pres & CEO Cardinal Health; Annette Herman, CEO United Healthcare Utah; Kay Toolson, CEO Monaco Coach; Mark James, VP Human Res Honeywell; Michael Kraupp, VP Finance SkyWest Airlines.

FINANCIAL FACTS

Tuition (in-state/out-of-state): $4,265/$14,929 **Fees:** $3,258 **Books and Supplies:** $1,800 **Room & Board:** $4,580 **% of Students Receiving Aid:** 20 **% of First-year Students Receiving Aid:** 20 **% of Students Receiving Grants:** 20 **Average Award Package:** $6,000 **Average Grant:** $2,800 **Average Student Loan Debt:** $8,000

ADMISSIONS

Admissions Selectivity Rating: 82

# of Applications Received: 192 **% Applicants Accepted:** 82 **% Acceptees Attending:** 65 **GMAT Range (25th to 75th percentile):** 410–690 **Average GMAT:** 538 **Average GPA:** 3.6 **TOEFL Required of Int'l Applicants:** Yes **Minimum TOEFL (paper/computer):** 550/213 **Application Fee:** $55

Regular Application Deadline: 2/15 **Regular Notification:** 3/15

Deferment Available: Yes **Maximum Length of Deferment:** 1 year
Transfer Students Accepted: Yes **Need-Blind Admissions:** Yes
Applicants Also Look At: Brigham Young University, University of Utah, Weber State University.

EMPLOYMENT PROFILE

Grads Employed by Industry:.......% avg. salary:

	%	avg. salary
Finance	11	$59,428
Human Resources	1	$50,000
Marketing	4	$112,500
MIS	3	$72,000
Operations	5	$93,333
Entrepreneurship	5	
General Management	8	$67,572

VALDOSTA STATE UNIVERSITY
LANGDALE COLLEGE OF BUSINESS ADMINISTRATION

ADMISSIONS CONTACT: JUDY TOMBERLIN, GRADUATE SCHOOL
ADDRESS: 903 N. PATTERSON STREET, VALDOSTA, GA 31698-0005
PHONE: (229) 333-5696 • FAX: (229) 245-3853
E-MAIL: MBA@VALDOSTA.EDU
WEBSITE: WWW.VALDOSTA.EDU/LCOBA/GRAD

GENERAL INFORMATION

Type of School: Public **Environment:** City **Academic Calendar:** Semester

STUDENTS

Enrollment of Parent Institution: 10,500 **Enrollment of Business School:** 31 **% Male/female:** 50/50 **% Part-time:** 100 **% International:** 8 **Average Age at Entry:** 30 **Average Years Work Experience at Entry:** 8

ACADEMICS

Student/faculty Ratio: 3:1 **% Female Faculty:** 20

FINANCIAL FACTS

Tuition (in-state/out-of-state): $3,766/$12,544 **Fees:** $708 **Books and Supplies:** $800 **Room & Board:** $2,684 **Average Grant:** $1,000

ADMISSIONS

Admissions Selectivity Rating: 82

# of Applications Received: 21 **% Applicants Accepted:** 48 **% Acceptees Attending:** 80 **GMAT Range (25th to 75th percentile):** 500–640 **Average GMAT:** 534 **Average GPA:** 3.3 **TOEFL Required of Int'l Applicants:** Yes **Minimum TOEFL (paper/computer):** 550/213 **Application Fee:** $25

Regular Application Deadline: Rolling **Regular Notification:** Rolling

Deferment Available: Yes **Maximum Length of Deferment:** One semester **Transfer Students Accepted:** Yes **Non-fall Admissions:** Yes **Need-Blind Admissions:** Yes

WESTERN ILLINOIS UNIVERSITY
COLLEGE OF BUSINESS AND TECHNOLOGY

ADMISSIONS CONTACT: , DIRECTOR OF MBA PROGRAM
ADDRESS: 1 UNIVERSITY CIRCLE, 115 SHERMAN HALL, MACOMB, IL 61455
PHONE: 309-298-3157 • FAX: 309-298-3111
E-MAIL: ADMISSIONS@WIU.EDU
WEBSITE: WWW.WIU.EDU/USERS/MICOBTD

GENERAL INFORMATION
Type of School: Public **Environment:** Village **Academic Calendar:** Semester

STUDENTS
Enrollment of Parent Institution: 132 **Enrollment of Business School:** 132 **% Male/female:** 58/42 **% Out-of-state:** 1 **% Part-time:** 37 **% Minorities:** 1 **% International:** 15 **Average Age at Entry:** 24

FINANCIAL FACTS
Tuition (in-state/out-of-state): $3,287/$6,574 **% of Students Receiving Aid:** 34

ADMISSIONS
Admissions Selectivity Rating: 60*
# of Applications Received: 250 **% Applicants Accepted:** 50 %
Acceptees Attending: 60 **TOEFL Required of Int'l Applicants:** Yes
Minimum TOEFL: 550 **Application Fee:** $30
Regular Application Deadline: rolling **Regular Notification:** rolling
Deferment Available: Yes **Maximum Length of Deferment:** 1 year
Non-fall Admissions: Yes

WESTERN KENTUCKY UNIVERSITY
GORDON FORD COLLEGE OF BUSINESS

ADMISSIONS CONTACT: MS. PAULA NEWBY, MBA PROGRAM DIRECTOR OF ADMISSIONS
ADDRESS: 1906 COLLEGE HEIGHTS BLVD #11056, BOWLING GREEN, KY 42101-1056
PHONE: 270-745-5458 • FAX: 270-745-3893
E-MAIL: MBA@WKU.EDU
WEBSITE: WWW.WKU.EDU/MBA

GENERAL INFORMATION
Type of School: Public **Academic Calendar:** Semester

STUDENTS
Enrollment of Parent Institution: 18,664 **Enrollment of Business School:** 124 **% Male/female:** 39/61 **% Out-of-state:** 3 **% Part-time:** 71 **% International:** 78 **Average Age at Entry:** 28

ACADEMICS
% Female Faculty: 12 **% Minority Faculty:** 3

FINANCIAL FACTS
Tuition: $7,014 **Books and Supplies:** $800 **Room & Board (on/off campus):** $5,348/$2,408

ADMISSIONS
Admissions Selectivity Rating: 77
# of Applications Received: 59 **% Applicants Accepted:** 49 %
Acceptees Attending: 41 **GMAT Range (25th to 75th percentile):** 495–580 **Average GMAT:** 519 **Average GPA:** 3.2 **TOEFL Required of Int'l Applicants:** Yes **Minimum TOEFL (paper/computer):** 550/213
Application Fee: $35
Regular Application Deadline: 6/15 **Regular Notification:** Rolling
Transfer Students Accepted: Yes **Non-fall Admissions:** Yes

WESTERN MICHIGAN UNIVERSITY
HAWORTH COLLEGE OF BUSINESS

ADMISSIONS CONTACT: HAL BATES, DIRECTOR, RECRUITING AND RETENTION
ADDRESS: 2110 SCHNEIDER HALL, MS #5411, KALAMAZOO, MI 49008-5411
PHONE: 269-387-5964 • FAX: 269-387-5710
E-MAIL: BUS-ADV-OFFICE@WMICH.EDU
WEBSITE: WWW.HCOB.WMICH.EDU

GENERAL INFORMATION
Type of School: Public **Environment:** City **Academic Calendar:** Semester

STUDENTS
Enrollment of Parent Institution: 24,433 **Enrollment of Business School:** 363 **% Male/female:** 63/37 **% Out-of-state:** 1 **% Part-time:** 42 **% Minorities:** 10 **% International:** 28 **Average Age at Entry:** 28
Average Years Work Experience at Entry: 6

ACADEMICS
Student/faculty Ratio: 13:1 **% Female Faculty:** 6 **% Minority Faculty:** 8

FINANCIAL FACTS
Tuition (in-state/out-of-state): $8,274/$17,524 **Fees:** $690 **Books and Supplies:** $5,111 **Room & Board (on/off campus):** $7,042/$6,994 **Average Award Package:** $11,100 **Average Grant:** $4,100 **Average Student Loan Debt:** $19,000

ADMISSIONS
Admissions Selectivity Rating: 77
# of Applications Received: 219 **% Applicants Accepted:** 57 %
Acceptees Attending: 78 **GMAT Range (25th to 75th percentile):** 470–550 **Average GMAT:** 513 **Average GPA:** 3.1 **TOEFL Required of Int'l Applicants:** Yes **Minimum TOEFL (paper/computer):** 550/213
Application Fee: $40 **International Application Fee:** $100
Regular Application Deadline: 7/1 **Regular Notification:** 8/1
Deferment Available: Yes **Maximum Length of Deferment:** Two Semesters **Transfer Students Accepted:** Yes **Non-fall Admissions:** Yes **Applicants Also Look At:** Michigan State University, University of Michigan, Wayne State University.

WESTERN WASHINGTON UNIVERSITY
COLLEGE OF BUSINESS AND ECONOMICS

ADMISSIONS CONTACT: VACANT, PROGRAM MANAGER
ADDRESS: 516 HIGH ST., PARKS HALL 419, BELLINGHAM, WA 98225-9072
PHONE: 360-650-3898 • FAX: 360-650-4844
E-MAIL: MBA@WWU.EDU
WEBSITE: WWW.CBE.WWU.EDU/MBA

GENERAL INFORMATION
Type of School: Public **Environment:** City

STUDENTS
Enrollment of Business School: 76 **% Male/female:** 57/43 **% Part-time:** 47 **% Minorities:** 2 **% International:** 12 **Average Age at Entry:** 29

FINANCIAL FACTS
Tuition (in-state/out-of-state): $6,608/$16,844

ADMISSIONS
Admissions Selectivity Rating: 60*
# of Applications Received: 78 **Average GMAT:** 545 **TOEFL Required of Int'l Applicants:** Yes **Minimum TOEFL (paper/computer):** 567/227 **Application Fee:** $50
Regular Application Deadline: 5/1 **Regular Notification:** 6/1
Deferment Available: Yes **Maximum Length of Deferment:** 1 year
Non-fall Admissions: Yes

WIDENER UNIVERSITY
SCHOOL OF BUSINESS ADMINISTRATION

ADMISSIONS CONTACT: ANN SELTZER, GRADUATE ENROLLMENT PROCESS ADMINISTRATOR
ADDRESS: 1 UNIVERSITY PLACE, CHESTER, PA 19013
PHONE: 610-499-4305 • FAX: 610-499-4615
E-MAIL: SBAGRADV@MAIL.WIDENER.EDU
WEBSITE: WWW.WIDENER.EDU

GENERAL INFORMATION
Type of School: Private **Environment:** Town **Academic Calendar:** Semester

STUDENTS
Enrollment of Parent Institution: 6,460 **Enrollment of Business School:** 105 **% Male/female:** 40/60 **% Part-time:** 90 **% International:** 10 **Average Age at Entry:** 29 **Average Years Work Experience at Entry:** 7

ACADEMICS
Student/faculty Ratio: 6:1 **% Female Faculty:** 39 **% Minority Faculty:** 5
Joint Degrees: MBA/JD 3–4 years, MBA/MS (Engineering) 2–5

years, MBA/PhD (Clinical Psychology) 5 years, MBA/PhD (Health Care Management/Clinical Psychology) 5 years, MD/MBA.
Prominent Alumni: Leslie C. Quick, founder, Quick & Reilly; H. Edward Hanway, CEO, Cigna Corp.; Paul Biederman, Chairman, Mellon Mid-Atlantic; Tiffany Tomasso, VP, Suise Assisted Living.

FINANCIAL FACTS
Tuition: $21,600 **Fees:** $200 **Books and Supplies:** $850 **Room & Board:** $7,650 **% of Students Receiving Aid:** 9 **% of First-year Students Receiving Aid:** 3 **% of Students Receiving Loans:** 8 **% of Students Receiving Grants:** 5 **Average Award Package:** $19,174 **Average Grant:** $9,660

ADMISSIONS
Admissions Selectivity Rating: 83
# of Applications Received: 130 **% Applicants Accepted:** 45 **% Acceptees Attending:** 85 **GMAT Range (25th to 75th percentile):** 450–540 **Average GMAT:** 533 **Average GPA:** 3.2 **TOEFL Required of Int'l Applicants:** Yes **Minimum TOEFL (paper/computer):** 550/213 **Application Fee:** $25
Regular Application Deadline: 5/1 **Regular Notification:** Rolling
Deferment Available: Yes **Maximum Length of Deferment:** 1 year
Transfer Students Accepted: Yes **Non-fall Admissions:** Yes **Need-Blind Admissions:** Yes **Applicants Also Look At:** Drexel University, La Salle University, Penn State University—Great Valley, Saint Joseph's University, Temple University, University of Delaware, Villanova University.

WINSTON-SALEM STATE UNIVERSITY
SCHOOL OF BUSINESS AND ECONOMICS

ADMISSIONS CONTACT: TOMIKIA LEGRANDE, DIRECTOR OF GRADUAGE ENROLLMENT MANAGEMENT
ADDRESS: GRADUATE SCHOOL, ANDERSON CENTER-WINSTON SALEM STATE UNIVERSITY, WINSTON SALEM, NC 27110
PHONE: 336-750-2021 • FAX: 336-750-2355
E-MAIL: GRADUATE@WSSU.EDU
WEBSITE:
WWW.WSSU.EDU/WSSU/GRADUATESTUDIES/GRADUATE+PROGRAMS/EVENING+MBA/

GENERAL INFORMATION
Type of School: Public **Academic Calendar:** Fall

STUDENTS
Enrollment of Parent Institution: 5,700 **Enrollment of Business School:** 42 **% Male/female:** 50/50 **% Part-time:** 100 **% Minorities:** 48 **% International:** 2 **Average Age at Entry:** 38 **Average Years Work Experience at Entry:** 10

ACADEMICS
Student/faculty Ratio: 15:1 **% Female Faculty:** 22

ADMISSIONS

Admissions Selectivity Rating: 79

% Acceptees Attending: 93 **Average GMAT:** 480 **Average GPA:** 3.0
TOEFL Required of Int'l Applicants: Yes **Minimum TOEFL
(paper/computer):** 550/213 **Application Fee:** $40 **International
Application Fee:** $40

Regular Application Deadline: 7/15

Deferment Available: Yes **Maximum Length of Deferment:** 2 years

Transfer Students Accepted: Yes **Non-fall Admissions:** Yes **Need-
Blind Admissions:** Yes

WINTHROP UNIVERSITY
COLLEGE OF BUSINESS ADMINISTRATION

*ADMISSIONS CONTACT: PEGGY HAGER, DIRECTOR OF GRADUATE PROGRAMS
ADDRESS: 213 THURMOND BUILDING, ROCK HILL, SC 29733
PHONE: 803-323-2409 • FAX: 803-323-2539
E-MAIL: MBAOFFICE@WINTHROP.EDU
WEBSITE: CBA.WINTHROP.EDU*

GENERAL INFORMATION

Type of School: Public **Environment:** Town **Academic Calendar:**
Semester

STUDENTS

Enrollment of Parent Institution: 7,304 **Enrollment of Business
School:** 250 **% Male/female:** 100/0 **% Part-time:** 40 **Average Age
at Entry:** 29 **Average Years Work Experience at Entry:** 5

FINANCIAL FACTS

Tuition (in-state/out-of-state): $4,216/$7,753

ADMISSIONS

Admissions Selectivity Rating: 65

# of Applications Received: 53 **% Applicants Accepted:** 92 **%
Acceptees Attending:** 73 **Average GMAT:** 490 **Average GPA:** 3.3
TOEFL Required of Int'l Applicants: Yes **Minimum TOEFL:** 550
Application Fee: $50

Regular Application Deadline: 7/15 **Regular Notification:** Rolling

Deferment Available: Yes **Maximum Length of Deferment:** 1 year

Transfer Students Accepted: Yes **Non-fall Admissions:** Yes

WRIGHT STATE UNIVERSITY
RAJ SOIN COLLEGE OF BUSINESS

*ADMISSIONS CONTACT: MICHAEL EVANS, DIRECTOR, MBA PROGRAMS
ADDRESS: 100 RIKE HALL, 3640 COLONEL GLENN HIGHWAY, DAYTON, OH
45435-0001
PHONE: 937-775-2437 • FAX: 937-775-3545
E-MAIL: MBA_DIRECTOR@WRIGHT.EDU
WEBSITE: WWW.WRIGHT.EDU/BUSINESS*

GENERAL INFORMATION

Type of School: Public **Environment:** City **Academic Calendar:**
Quarter

STUDENTS

Enrollment of Parent Institution: 16,913 **Enrollment of Business
School:** 459 **% Male/female:** 56/44 **% Out-of-state:** 2 **% Part-time:**
80 **% Minorities:** 1 **Average Age at Entry:** 31 **Average Years Work
Experience at Entry:** 5

ACADEMICS

Student/faculty Ratio: 8:1 **% Female Faculty:** 24 **% Minority
Faculty:** 1

Joint Degrees: MBA/MS (Nursing) 2–5 years, MBA/MS (Economics)
2–5 years, MBA/MD 4 years.

FINANCIAL FACTS

Tuition (in-state/out-of-state): $10,500/$17,796 **Books and
Supplies:** $1,300 **% of Students Receiving Grants:** 35 **Average
Award Package:** $10,500

ADMISSIONS

Admissions Selectivity Rating: 74

# of Applications Received: 550 **% Applicants Accepted:** 64 **%
Acceptees Attending:** 131 **Average GMAT:** 525 **Average GPA:** 3.1
TOEFL Required of Int'l Applicants: Yes **Minimum TOEFL
(paper/computer):** 550/213 **Application Fee:** $25

Regular Application Deadline: 8/1 **Regular Notification:** 8/15

Deferment Available: Yes **Maximum Length of Deferment:** 4 quarters **Transfer Students Accepted:** Yes **Non-fall Admissions:** Yes
Need-Blind Admissions: Yes

SCHOOL SAYS . . .

In this section you'll find schools with extended listings describing Admissions, curriculum, internships, and much more. This is your chance to get in-depth information on programs that interest you. The Princeton Review charges each school a small fee to be listed, and the editorial responsibility is solely that of the university.

AMERICAN UNIVERSITY
Kogod School of Business

AT A GLANCE

American University's Kogod School of Business is among the best business schools in the Washington, DC area and is the school of choice for interdisciplinary business education. The Kogod School of Business was established in 1955 as Washington, DC's first university-level school of business.

Kogod offers graduate business degrees with an unmatched opportunity to integrate business education with other renowned AU disciplines such as international services, law, and politics. Kogod's dual degrees and programs, strong co-curricular programs, endowed scholarships, thought-leading research, and comprehensive career services attract high-quality students and faculty.

FACULTY

Kogod's faculty members are internationally recognized scholars, outstanding lecturers and researchers, and advisors who are committed to the highest standards of teaching. They bring real business challenges into the classroom for you to solve. You will find many faculty members serving as consultants to major corporations and governments, or actively engaged in research.

STUDENTS

At Kogod we believe education should extend beyond the classroom. Hands-on experiences enhance leadership ability, communication skills, and self-confidence. K-LAB (Kogod Leadership and Applied Business) allows students to learn valuable professional skills in real-world settings and includes options to participate in graduate study abroad, the annual case competition, and a variety of advisory boards.

CAREER SERVICES AND PLACEMENT

Preparation for life after graduation begins on your first day at Kogod, and we offer a number of services to help make your employment search as successful as possible. These services include one-on-one career counseling, development workshops, on-campus recruiting, career fairs, and networking events. Career development is also an important part of the MBA year-long "signature" course, Strategic Management in a Global Environment.

LOCATION AND ENVIRONMENT

American University's Kogod School of Business is situated on a beautiful, 84-acre campus in one of the most desirable residential neighborhoods of Northwest Washington, DC. There are 37 buildings on campus, and the Kogod building offers classrooms, student lounges, and a computer lab. Over the next year Kogod is expanding and adding almost 20,000 square feet of learning space, including seven new classrooms, a career-management center, a student lounge, a financial services and information technology lab, two seminar rooms, and three break-out rooms.

MAJORS AND DEGREES OFFERED

MBA (full-time), MBA (part-time), MS in Taxation, MS in Accounting, Graduate Business Certificates, MS in Finance, MS in Finance and Real Estate, LLM/MBA, JD/MBA, MBA/MA in International Studies

ACADEMIC PROGRAMS

The Kogod MBA program is flexible and provides a solid grounding in theory and practice. The program focuses on the managerial aspects of information technology and global business practices.

The Kogod MBA is a 51-credit-hour program, including 25.5 credit hours of required courses and 25.5 credit hours of electives. Students entering the full-time program in the fall semester should complete the curriculum in 21 months. To learn more about the MBA program, visit www.kogod.american.edu/grad.

Kogod offers an extensive set of interdisciplinary programs that include three dual-degree programs: LLM/MBA, JD/MBA, and the MA/MBA. Visit www.kogod.american.edu/dualdegree.

Kogod graduate students may also decide to design their own Career Tracks. Career Tracks may be combined with up to nine credits taken outside of Kogod. Visit www.kogod.american.edu/careertracks.

CAMPUS FACILITIES AND EQUIPMENT

The Kogod School of Business is situated in the center of American University's beautiful 84-acre campus. The Kogod School of Business is expanding. The present Kogod building will be connected to an adjacent existing classroom structure. The existing classroom structure will be completely renovated with an additional story and a new facade. Construction began in the spring of 2007, and the goal is to complete the expansion for the Spring 2009 academic term.

The expansion will include seven new classrooms, a career management center, a student lounge area, a financial services and information technology lab, two seminar rooms and three break-out rooms. For more information, please visit www.kogod.american.edu/expansion.

TUITION, ROOM, BOARD AND FEES
Costs 2007–2008

The tuition fee for the Kogod School of Business of American University is $27,404 per semester for full-time MBA students and $1,048 per credit hour for part-time MBA students.

Tuition

Fewer than 9 credit hours: $1079 per credit hour
12 or more credit hours: $14,113 per semester

Graduate Student Fees

Graduate student fee (all students): $30 per semester
Sports center fee (full-time students): $65 per semester
Sports center fee (part-time students): $30 per semester
Technology fee (full-time) $95 per semester
Technology fee (part-time) $30 per semester

ADMISSIONS PROCESS

The application process for the Kogod School of Business is an electronic process. Complete the online application at www.kogod.american.edu/apply.

Kogod application requirements include the following: a bachelor's degree from a regionally accredited college or university, official GMAT score (international students: TOEFL paper-based score of 600 or computer-based score of 250), an interview, resume, personal statement, two letters of recommendation, and a $75 application fee.

Applicants may also be considered for admission without reference to their undergraduate average if they have maintained a 3.3 cumulative grade point average in a master's program completed at an accredited institution.

American University
Kogod School of Business
Attn: Graduate Admissions
4400 Massachusetts Avenue Northwest
Washington, DC 20016
Telephone: 202-885-1913
Fax: 202-885-1078
E-mail: kogodmba@american.edu
www.kogod.american.edu

ARIZONA STATE UNIVERSITY
W.P Carey School of Business

AT A GLANCE
Success in the job market is the hallmark of the W. P. Carey MBA - Full-time Program at Arizona State University (ASU). Our placement rate after graduation places us among the top ten MBA programs in North America. Consider the Full-time Program if you seek to build broad business skills in conjunction with a functional emphasis in one of many areas of specialization. Delivered over the course of 21 months, the case-based and team-oriented learning format integrates a core business curriculum with an in-depth specialization. Classes are small, with less than 50 students in core courses, allowing you to interact closely with your peers and faculty members. A required internship between the first and second years of the program, together with a career leadership course, set the stage for a successful post-graduate career. Our student-services and career management teams provide you with the personalized service and individual attention you need to achieve academic success, while also focusing on your future.

FACULTY
The W. P. Carey School is home to an internationally recognized faculty who possess deep understanding of the global business environment. In addition to publishing their research in top-tier academic journals, our faculty members consult with more than 300 firms around the globe.

STUDENTS
W. P. Carey MBA Full-time Program students hail from diverse backgrounds. The average student in the fall 2007 entering class was 27 years old, with 4.5 years of professional work experience. The class included 35 percent international students and 10 percent total ethnic minority enrollment. Our 2007 incoming class brought students from around the globe - including Bangladesh, China, Costa Rica, France, India, Mexico, South Korea and other nations.

CAREER SERVICES AND PLACEMENTS
As a W. P. Carey MBA student, you will have access to personalized career development services and lifelong career management skills through our Graduate Career Management Center (CMC). The center is nationally recognized for its expertise in career development and corporate recruiting. Through career assessment and leadership workshops, webinars, resume development assistance and on-campus recruiting events, you will build lifelong connections within the MBA employment market. Post-graduate employment of Full-time Program students is near the top of all U.S. business schools, with 97 percent of students securing employment within three months of graduation.

LOCATION AND ENVIRONMENT
The ASU Tempe campus is located in the Phoenix metro area, which is known for its attractive climate, natural resources and extraordinary business growth. The campus houses a nationally-recognized arboretum, which encompasses the entire campus, and the university is nationally known for its sustainability efforts and programs. Phoenix is home to an international airport, museums, major sports teams and venues, and cultural activities.

OFF-CAMPUS OPPORTUNITIES
W. P. Carey MBA students may choose from a number of off-site electives, with practicum offerings in China, Southeast Asia, Argentina, the Balkans, France and Spain, Germany, and Australia, as well as a business public policy course in Washington, D.C.

MAJORS AND DEGREES OFFERED
The W. P. Carey School of Business offers a master of business administration (MBA) degree and dual-degree programs, as well as undergraduate and doctoral degrees in a number of disciplines.

ACADEMIC PROGRAMS
The W. P. Carey MBA builds and strengthens your knowledge, skills and managerial abilities through a rigorous curriculum, as you engage in technical and analytical skill-building exercises and case studies. During the first year, you will build fundamental knowledge in the disciplines of accounting, marketing, ethics, statistics and management. Integrated courses will teach you how business disciplines relate to one another, and how singular decisions affect company success across functions. In the second year, you will select courses from diverse focus areas that complement the foundational core courses. Your specialization choices include financial information and markets, information management, real estate, sports business, strategic marketing and services leadership, supply chain financial management, and supply chain management. Optional secondary specializations are available in health sector management, international business, and management. The small and cohesive class size provides for individual learning, close faculty interaction and an intense sense of community and commitment to personal and professional development.

CAMPUS FACILITIES AND EQUIPMENT
The W. P. Carey School of Business is housed in two buildings that contain an auditorium, lecture halls, seminar rooms, a graduate suite and a coffeehouse. The business complex is equipped with wireless access ports within its buildings and patio area. The graduate suite offers a student center, technology-equipped team rooms and open study areas.

FINANCIAL AID
W. P. Carey MBA - Full-time Program tuition and fees for the 2008-2009 academic year are $16,228 for Arizona residents and $27,920 for non-residents.

Financial resources - including scholarships, grants, fellowships and assistantships are available annually to full-time applicants, based on the merit of individual applications.

STUDENT ORGANIZATIONS AND ACTIVITIES
Co-curricular activities play a vital role in the W. P. Carey MBA community. Our student clubs and organizations provide activities that complement your academic experience. Among our student organizations are those promoting consulting, entrepreneurship, volunteerism, sports business, finance, supply chain management, sustainability and more.

ADMISSIONS PROCESS
Admission to the W. P. Carey MBA is selective. Most students have three to five years of full-time work experience and have earned a bachelor's degree or the equivalent from a regionally accredited institution. The W. P. Carey MBA Admissions Committee looks for well-rounded individuals with strong leadership skills and academic credentials, managerial experience or potential, and the ability to contribute to the diversity of the class. Transcripts, GMAT scores, TOEFL scores (for international students), work history, essay questions, letters of recommendation and a required interview all influence the admission decision. Qualifying domestic students will be invited for a personal interview through our campus visit program. Many scholarship opportunities are available annually to full-time applicants, based on the merit of individual applications. Early participation in the application process ensures consideration for the most lucrative financial awards. While applications are accepted on a "rolling admissions cycle" basis, with applications accepted throughout the year, admission is to the fall term only.

BABSON COLLEGE
F.W. Olin Graduate School of Business

AT A GLANCE

At the F.W. Olin Graduate School of Business at Babson College, we have a rich tradition of excellence in cultivating entrepreneurial thinking. While some of our graduates pursue start-up ventures, far more of our graduates use their entrepreneurial training to succeed in the corporate environment. Here, entrepreneurship isn't about starting a business; it's a state of mind.

Babson features four unique degree programs that prepare students to become superior managers and to meet the needs of progressive organizations.

Our Two-Year MBA program features Babson's innovative modular approach and emphasizes the practical application of business ideas.

The One-Year MBA Program is an accelerated, full-time MBA program for students with an undergraduate business degree and at least two years of post-graduate work experience. The One-Year program allows qualified students to earn an MBA degree in just 12 months, including an initial summer semester featuring Babson's innovative modular curriculum.

The Babson Evening MBA program offers the flexibility and convenience that working professionals require. And its dynamic curriculum features the same pacesetting modular learning approaches that we use in our full-time programs.

The Fast Track MBA is a part-time program combining traditional classroom instruction with Web-based, distance learning. Students earn a degree in just 24 months-much faster than a traditional part-time MBA. Students attend classes on-campus during intensive, two day sessions approximately every six weeks. Its convenience and flexibility make Fast Track the perfect choice if for those balancing work, long-term career goals, and other demands. Fast Track is now offered in Wellesley, Massachusetts and Portland, Oregon.

FACULTY

Babson's faculty is an internationally and professionally diverse group. The faculty includes seasoned corporate executives, visionary entrepreneurs, and academic thought leaders.

STUDENTS

Students are admitted to the program based on a careful evaluation of academic records, professional qualifications, GMAT scores, and personal attributes. Interviews are required for admission to full-time MBA programs. The current Two Year class's GMAT average is 631, and the average undergraduate GPA is 3.21. International students must submit TOEFL results and official English translations of all academic documents. All candidates should have strong mathematics, computer, economics, and business writing skills.

CAREER SERVICES AND PLACEMENTS

The Center for Career Development's Relationship Management team will work with you in planning a career strategy, including developing your personal marketing communication plan and preparing for networking activities and interviews.

LOCATION AND ENVIRONMENT

Babson College is located in Wellesley, Massachusetts, 12 miles from Boston. Babson's Fast Track MBA is also offered in Portland, Oregon.

OFF-CAMPUS OPPORTUNITIES

The Global Management Program gives MBA students the chance to work as project managers and consultants with more than 250 companies operating in 40 countries. This program is application-based and is available to full-time MBA students and full-time Evening MBA students who have completed 30 credit hours.

Babson fosters the entrepreneurial spirit through a variety of activities and opportunities, including electives, endowed chairs in entrepreneurship, induction of innovative business people into the Academy of Distinguished Entrepreneurs on Founder's Day, the Douglass Foundation Entrepreneurial Prizes, and the Babson Entrepreneurial Exchange, a student-run network of current and future entrepreneurs who exchange information about business development and venture opportunities.

Successful business partnerships have always been a major component of Babson's programs. First-year student teams consult with Boston-area organizations through the year-long Babson Consulting Alliance Program. The Management Consulting Field Experience offers a variety of second-year consulting projects.

MAJORS AND DEGREES OFFERED

Babson offers a Master of Business Administration degree.

ACADEMIC PROGRAMS

All programs emphasize the global aspects of business and the value of the entrepreneurial spirit.

The Two-Year MBA program stresses innovation, creative problem-solving, and the ability to recognize opportunity. The first year takes students through the business development cycle. The second year allows students to focus on their interests with electives.

The One-Year MBA is an accelerated program that allows students with undergraduate business degrees to complete their MBA in three full-time semesters. The One-Year MBA begins with an intensive Summer Program. Students then join second-year students in the Two-Year MBA program to complete their elective coursework in the Fall and Spring semesters.

The Fast Track MBA program makes it possible for working professionals to continue their careers while earning an MBA in 24 months. Fast Track, offered in Wellesley, Massachusetts and Portland, Oregon, features a curriculum that combines in-person and Web-based learning.

The Evening MBA builds on a more compact core of ten courses, four of which feature a cross-disciplinary approach. The Evening MBA provides students the greatest opportunity to adjust their program pace to fit their personal and professional lives.

CAMPUS FACILITIES AND EQUIPMENT

Babson students have access to an extensive business collection through Horn Library, as well as a staff of professionals to help them find the information they need.

Students work individually and in groups using a focused collection of print, audiovisual, and computerized resources. The library subscribes to a browsing collection of 700 periodicals and newspapers; thousands more are available from any computer on campus through Internet subscriptions with Dow Jones Interactive, InfoTrac Web, Lexis/Nexis Universe, ProQuest Direct, FirstSearch, and Primark's Global Access.

Within Horn Library students may access a variety of electronic resources, such as Bloomberg, Reuters, Bridge, Compustat, and Morningstar, for economics, financial information, marketing, accounting, entrepreneurship, etc. Financial resources are also showcased in the Stephen D. Cutler Investment Management Center in the library. Group study rooms linked to Babson's computer network provide space for team meetings and individual study.

BELMONT UNIVERSITY
Jack C. Massey Graduate School of Business

AT A GLANCE
The Jack C. Massey Graduate School of Business was founded in 1986 through a gift from one of the country's most successful entrepreneurs. Mr. Massey remains as the only U.S. businessperson to ever take three different private companies public to the New York Stock Exchange. The School was created to offer graduate business programs to Nashville area working professionals and offers both the MBA and MACC degrees in a weeknight, evening format on the Belmont University campus. Belmont is the only private university in Tennessee to maintain AACSB International accreditation in business and accounting.

FACULTY
Over 90% of graduate faculty are doctorally-qualified and full-time professors, while the remainder are practicing business professionals. Continuing faculty are hired on the basis of their academic and professional preparation, as well as a demonstrated commitment to high-quality graduate instruction.

STUDENTS
The typical Massey MBA student has 6 years of business experience, is 29 years old, and works full-time, while completing the degree program in 2 years. The majority of MACC students are younger, with less business experience and are preparing to sit for the CPA exam. Many are full-time graduate students.

LOCATION AND ENVIRONMENT
As an academic unit within Belmont University, The Massey Graduate School is located in the heart of Nashville, Tennessee, a rare place combining big-city charisma and small-town charm. Known internationally as "music city," Nashville is also a hotbed for entrepreneurship, healthcare, and international trade. Belmont University is located on a 62-acre campus and maintains a total enrollment of over 4,800 students.

MAJORS AND DEGREES OFFERED
The Massey Graduate School offers two degree programs:

The Master of Business Administration (MBA) degree requires 34 credits, with specialty tracks in accounting, entrepreneurship, finance, general business, healthcare management, marketing, and music business. The MBA is offered in a part-time evening format (Monday - Thursday) and designed specifically for working professionals.

The Master of Accountancy (MACC) degree requires 30 credits and is designed to prepare students to meet the 150 hour CPA requirement.

ACADEMIC PROGRAMS
The Massey Graduate School resides within the College of Business Administration, which also includes the Center for Entrepreneurship, the Center for Business Ethics, and the Scarlett Leadership Institute, each of which houses additional learning opportunities for students. A Summer Accounting Institute option for aspiring MACC students offers non-business undergraduates a fast-track summer preparation opportunity to begin their graduate accounting course work.

All graduate students complete a brief study-abroad experience course as part of their degree requirements. Trips are scheduled between terms and typically last 8-10 days. Destination options for 2008-09 include the Czech Republic, Ireland, Denmark, Brazil, Chile, India, and Great Britain.

The curriculum is designed with 2-credit hour courses instead of the traditional 3-credit format. This gives Massey students a greater breadth of curriculum in the core business/accounting offerings, while also assuring a greater number of electives for matching to a particular student career plan. All students also complete a required entrepreneurship course, as well as advanced preparation in business ethics.

CAMPUS FACILITIES AND EQUIPMENT
All classes are held in the Jack C. Massey Business Center, which includes a variety of high-tech classrooms, computer lab space, a finance trading center, and student support offices. Graduate students also have a separate computer lab workspace, as well as a well-equipped study area.

FINANCIAL AID
Tuition charges for 2008-09 are calculated at $2,200 for all MBA students and $1,700 for all MACC students. There are a limited number of scholarship opportunities (e.g., merit, financial need, minority status), as well as graduate assistant opportunities.

ADMISSIONS PROCESS
All MBA applicants are required to complete the GMAT test, submit a personal essay and two recommendations, submit transcripts from all undergraduate coursework, and have completed a minimum of two years of professional business experience. The experience requirement is waived for MACC applicants. A personal interview is required of all graduate applicants prior to an admission decision.

BENTLEY COLLEGE
McCallum Graduate School of Business

AT A GLANCE

Bentley is a national leader in business education, blending the breadth and technological strength of a large university with the values and student focus of a small college. Bentley educates students and generates new knowledge by uniting the rigor, relevance, creativity and intellectual dynamics of business and the liberal arts.

At the McCallum Graduate School, a broad array of offerings, including PhDs in Business and Accountancy, Day and Evening MBA, Master of Science and certificate programs, emphasize the impact of technology on business practice.

We seek distinction by:

• Emphasizing in our curricula and research those fields of knowledge emerging at the intersection of business and the liberal arts (such as business and information technology, ethics and social responsibility, and global commerce and culture)

• Continuing to lead in the integration of information technology into business education;

• Engaging in pedagogy that emphasizes student-centered learning and field-based experiences firmly grounded in theory;

• Developing and supporting a faculty that embraces cross-disciplinary endeavors while immersed in the primary disciplines of business and liberal arts

• Refreshing our curricula and disseminating new knowledge by undertaking leading-edge applied research, often in partnership with external organizations;

• Continuously improving a sophisticated technology and associated support infrastructure;

• Encouraging ethical and socially responsible behavior, and intellectual, social and cultural diversity, in every dimension of institutional life;

• Promoting a culture of engagement, and responsiveness to change, in the worlds of professional, political and social practice, both on and off campus.

The McCallum Graduate School prepares students for careers in services-oriented, information-intensive professions.

We do so by offering:

• A distinctive array of MS programs, each offering the depth, sophistication and orientation to emerging practice necessary to launch and advance careers in the knowledge-based service professions;

• An MBA designed to educate leaders of knowledge-based service professions, emphasizing the impact of IT on business practice, and the integration of business processes across functional disciplines;

• A school-wide emphasis on ethics and social responsibility;

• Extensive opportunities to interact with the business community through field-based coursework, consulting projects, work experiences and career advising.

CAMPUS & LOCATION

Bentley is located in suburban Waltham, Massachusetts just 10 miles from Boston. Getting to Boston from Bentley is easy. The college runs a free shuttle bus to Harvard Square in Cambridge, where you can take public transportation into the heart of the city.

PROGRAMS & CURRICULUM

As a business university, Bentley offers academic programs targeted at the intersection of business and technology. An emphasis on continuous innovation underlies everything we do, from curriculum development to teaching methods to program delivery options.

The graduate programs of Portfolio 360, along with our Day MBA program integrate business, technology, ethics, and global understanding, so that students will be fluent in the principles and practices that drive corporate decision-making.

The breadth of programs-including 17 concentrations in the MBA and a suite of Master of Science degrees-combined with the opportunity to gain deep understanding in these fields, provides a powerful student-centered learning environment. An innovative and extensive curriculum, a faculty of committed teachers and scholars, an array of state-of-the-art facilities, and ongoing input from the corporate community further position students for today's global marketplace.

FACULTY, RESEARCH AND FACILITIES

McCallum Graduate School of Business offers a wealth of "people" resources: nationally recognized faculty and staff advisers whose support and guidance help students reach their full potential. Bentley professors pursue a rigorous agenda of scholarship and applied research. Support from corporations, government organizations, private foundations and individuals helps fuel leading-edge research at Bentley and enables us to build and maintain the technology-rich facilities-including the Design and Usability Center, financial Trading Room, Center for Marketing Technology, Accounting Center for Electronic Learning and Business Measurement, and Center for Languages and International Collaboration-that bolster research and enhance the quality of education at Bentley. Most classes incorporate projects and assignments that make use of the specialized software available in these facilities, allowing students to apply concepts learned in class. The centers and labs - all among the first of their kind in higher education-feature the same high-end hardware and software that businesses use. Many of the labs benefit the corporate community as well, offering consulting and employee education.

CAREER SERVICES & PLACEMENT

The Nathan R. Miller Center for Career Services helps graduate students learn how to leverage a graduate degree in the job market, fine tune personal and professional goals and connect with leading employers in a range of industries. Resources include the Career Management Series, recruitment and internship programs, career fairs, online databases, and more. Armed with up-to-the-minute information about job market trends, career advisors at Bentley work with graduate students to define professional goals, plan job search strategies, and identify networking opportunities.

One-on-one advising with an experienced career counselor can help to sharpen career development goals. An active campus recruiting program links graduate students with top U.S. companies such as Liberty Mutual, Deloitte & Touche, EMC Corporation, and Raytheon.

EXPENCES & FINANCIAL AID

Tuition for the 2008–2009 academic year is $3,150 per three-credit course. Bentley offers several types of financial assistance, including scholarships, assistantships and loans. Some awards are need-based; others recognize academic achievement or merit. The Graduate Financial Assistance staff can answer questions and offer guidance on the programs most appropriate for a student's financial situation.

ADMISSIONS

Required documents include: completed application form and supplements, official transcripts from all prior undergraduate and graduate course work, two written recommendations, resume, results of the Graduate Management Admission Test and, if applicable, score on the Test of English as a Foreign Language. Refer to the Graduate Admissions website regarding application deadlines at: http://www.bentley.edu/graduate/calendar.cfm

CALIFORNIA POLYTECHNIC STATE UNIVERSITY—SAN LUIS OBISPO

AT A GLANCE

The Orfalea College of Business at California Polytechnic State University, San Luis Obispo (Cal Poly) offers one-year MBA programs that follow the educational philosophy of "learn by doing". The programs' in-class experience includes simulations of management decision-making scenarios, case studies, team exercises, extensive interaction with faculty and other students, and personal communication and presentation skills enhancement. The Orfalea College of Business' (OCOB) MBA programs are accredited by the AACSB and admit a limited number of students each year. This select group of graduate students fosters an eclectic student body with a strong sense of community and a culture that emphasizes high quality performance. Students accepted into and enrolled in Cal Poly's OCOB MBA programs may: • Enter the program without an undergraduate business degree and without completing prerequisite business course requirements. • Choose an accelerated option (Track One) that allows full-time students to follow a prescribed course of study and complete the program in less than a yea or a traditional, non-accelerated option (Track Two) • Study relevant, current, challenging, and intellectually stimulating courses. • Enroll in short intensive summer sessions to complete the MBA program and/or follow the accelerated option requirements. • Enroll in a 2-1/2 week business study tour to mainland China • Work with renowned faculty in a friendly and professional academic atmosphere. • Live and study on California's beautiful Central Coast In addition to a general management MBA, Cal Poly offers an MBA with a Specialization in Agribusiness, and an MBA with a specialization in Graphic Communication Document Systems Management, an MS in Accounting - Taxation. Two-year dual-degree options are also available for students wishing to pursue two graduate degrees simultaneously. For example, a formal, joint MBA/MS program in Engineering Management (EMP) and various other informal MBA/MS or MBA/MA dual-degree options are available. Beginning in Fall 2009, a Masters of Science in Economics will be offered.

FACULTY

Outstanding faculty teach in Cal Poly's MBA programs. Each faculty member has a terminal degree in his/her discipline, e.g., PhD or JD. Further, each faculty member is active and engaged in his or her discipline, whether it's their research and publication work, consulting and/or their community and professional service.

STUDENTS

With 300 clubs on campus, MBA students have many opportunities for activities outside the classroom. Offering the ability to demonstrate leadership and collaboration, the GSB Association is a popular choice. This club hosts a variety of fundraising, professional and social events. It organizes a Professional Speaker Series giving students the opportunity to network with industry professionals. Firms also find the Speaker Series to be a valuable recruitment tool.

Cal Poly MBA students have a proud tradition of competition. They participate annually in the International Collegiate Business Strategy Competition; and the MBA Business Ethics Competition. In 2006, they won that competition defeating teams from USC, Loyola Marymount, University of Washington and College of William and Mary and in 2008 they earn 2nd place. There is the Bank of America Low Income Housing Challenge competition, comprised of a multidisciplinary team of City Planners, Architects, Construction and Business Managers. This competition involves developing an affordable housing development proposal. In 2005, Cal Poly's team won that competition, defeating teams from Stanford and UC Berkeley.

CAREER SERVICES AND PLACEMENT

The Cal Poly Career Services office offers extensive career counseling, career employment services, online databases and résumé books, student employment, career exploration and job search preparation workshops, employment-related events such as job fairs and a Career Resource Center.

LOCATION AND ENVIRONMENT

Cal Poly is located in San Luis Obispo, an idyllic city of 45,000 located on the beautiful Central Coast of California, midway between San Francisco and Los Angeles. San Luis Obispo's small-town casual atmosphere makes it an excellent location in which to study and socialize away from the large metropolitan areas; however, close enough for easy interviews and contacts. Cal Poly students can enjoy almost any type of outdoor recreation-at the beaches, along coastal dunes and ridges, mountains, and nearby lakes, ranging from mountain biking, hiking, horseback riding, golf, sailing, kayaking, camping, or just relaxing in an unspoiled natural setting. The Orfalea College of Business occupies a modern building which offers multimedia capabilities and instructional technology in all classrooms. In addition to the largest computer laboratory on campus, the building offers wireless internet, small meeting rooms, and student lounges.

MAJORS AND DEGREES OFFERED

The Cal Poly Orfalea College of Business offers a General Management Masters in Business Administration (MBA), as well as specializations in Agribusiness and Graphic Communication Document Systems Management. Also available, an MBA & MS in Engineering Management (EMP) dual degree, and Masters of Science in Accounting - Taxation, and a Masters in Industrial & Technical Studies (MS in I & TS). In addition, Cal Poly offers a variety of informal dual degree options where a student can link the MBA degree with certain other graduate degree programs on campus. Beginning in Fall 2009, a Masters of Science in Economics will be offered.

ACADEMIC PROGRAMS

The Cal Poly MBA program is a 60-64 unit program that provides students who are willing to commit to a rigorous schedule of prescribed courses the option to complete the program in less than 11 months (Track I). A traditional MBA model (Track II) for those not pursing this accelerated option and/or simultaneously pursuing joint/dual degrees is also offered.

The Cal Poly Orfalea College of Business MBA programs have a distinctly Cal Poly character — coursework emphasizing the fundamentals and consistent with our "learn by doing" philosophy, integrative learning, and the opportunity for international study. Our methods of instruction entail extensive interaction; thus, we limit the number of students admitted to our programs to foster a real sense of community.

We invite you to visit our campus, business school and the San Luis Obispo community to sample what we have to offer.

Special Programs

In addition to a general management MBA, Cal Poly offers an MBA with a Specialization in Agribusiness, an MBA with a specialization in Graphic Communication Document Systems Management, and an MS in Accounting - Taxation. Beginning in Fall 2009, a MS in Economics will be offered.

Two-year dual-degree options are also available for students wishing to pursue two graduate degrees simultaneously. A joint MBA/MS program in Engineering Management (EMP) and various other MBA/MS or MBA/MA dual-degree options are available.

CALIFORNIA STATE UNIVERSITY—FULLERTON

AT A GLANCE
Since 1963, the Mihaylo College of Business and Economics' nationally recognized faculty, award winning student groups, forward-looking curriculum and flexible programs have attracted talented and diverse students from across the globe. These students have made the College the largest accredited business school in California, and the fifth largest in the United States. Additionally, the College is one of two schools in the Los Angeles metro area to hold the prestigious dual accreditation in business administration and accounting from AACSB International, the world wide accrediting body for business schools.

The MBA program provides four electives in the 15 course program, allowing students to select from 11 areas of concentration, tailoring their MBA degree to their professional, personal and educational goals. The Fully-Employed MBA (FEMBA) and MS in Taxation programs are offered at CSUF Irvine Campus. These programs are in an accelerated, cohort format, where students take one course every eight weeks. All MBA Courses are held in the late afternoon or early evening hours, accommodating the needs of working professionals.

FACULTY
One of the strengths of the MBA program is the diversity of its faculty, in terms of education, training and cultural backgrounds. This diversity translates into the ability to prepare our students for the global world. Here, teaching does get equal billing with research. All graduate level courses are taught by our most highly qualified faculty, people who have proven themselves as researchers and instructors - not one or the other alone.

STUDENTS
Each program in the Mihaylo College of Business and Economics attracts students from across the globe. This rich diversity adds to a dynamic classroom experience where students learn from both peers and professors. A challenging curriculum, team projects, and intense field experiences give our students a competitive edge.

Most students attend our MBA program part-time and work full-time. The average student has between 4-6 years of work experience and is 27. About 32% of our students are international and 47% are female.

LOCATION AND ENVIRONMENT
Cal State Fullerton is a comprehensive, regional university with a global outlook. Our expertise and diversity serve as a distinctive resource and catalyst for partnerships with public and private organizations. We strive to be a center of activity essential to the intellectual, cultural, and economic development of our region.

The University is situated amid the vital, flourishing area that includes Orange County, Metropolitan Los Angeles, and the Inland Empire. Orange County is one of the most vibrant, diverse business communities in the nation, with entertainment attractions, performing arts venues and multicultural communities.

MAJORS AND DEGREES OFFERED
MBA (Fullerton Campus)
Fully Employed MBA (Irvine Campus)

MS in Accounting

MS in Taxation (Fullerton or Irvine)

MS in Information Systems

MS in Information Technology (Online)

MA in Economics

ACADEMIC PROGRAMS
The MBA curriculum challenges students academically and encourages them to examine their existing morals, leadership style and goals. The 33-45 unit curriculum is designed to give participants broad, strategic managerial perspectives, while balancing theory with practical application, and strengthening leadership skills. Each MBA course is built on a forward-looking curriculum reflecting the ever-changing needs to today's organizations. Students discuss current issues, learn from past case studies, forecast future trends, and participate in dynamic group discussions. The MBA curriculum consists of ten interdisciplinary courses that provide a thorough foundation in conceptual, quantitative, strategic, analytic, and problem-solving skills. Students may select a concentration area, comprised of four courses, to specialize their degree. Concentrations include: Accounting, Economics, E-commerce, Entrepreneurship, Finance, Information Systems, International Business, Management, Management Science, and Marketing; or earn a broad-based degree with a General concentration.

The culmination of the MBA program is the Business Strategy Capstone which moves students out of the classroom and into the workplace. Students put their knowledge to the test as they become consultants for area businesses. At the end of each semester, student reports are submitted into a national competition, in which the College's teams have placed in the national top ten for the last 18 years.

CAMPUS FACILITIES AND EQUIPMENT
MIHAYLO HALL—The College will move into its new, $87.5 million state-of-the-art facility in August 2008. Nearly 10,000 square feet is dedicated to student study and collaboration.

POLLAK LIBRARY—This facility promotes individual as well as collaborative learning with state-of-the-art equipment and specialized information services.

COMPUTER LABS—A wide range of computer labs are available in the College and throughout the campus.

REC SPORTS—Rec Sports, a program of the Titan Student Union, serves the campus community through a variety of recreational, educational, and fitness programs.

TITAN STUDENT UNION—The Titan Student Union is the campus center for social, cultural, and recreational services.

FINANCIAL AID
Fees for California residents at the Fullerton campus are $1,295 for part-time students (1-6 units) and $2,012 for full-time students (7 or more units). All MBA classes are 3 units each; part-time students take 1-2 classes a semester, while full-time students enroll in 3 or more classes per semester.

Tuition for non-resident students is $339 per unit in addition to resident fees (see above).

Summer 2007 fees were $1126 for part-time students and $1843 for full-time students.

The FEMBA program is only offered at the Irvine Campus and is not subsidized by state tax dollars. Tuition for Irvine Campus programs (FEMBA and MS Taxation) is $1446 per course.

A wide range of scholarships are available to graduate students. Please visit http://business.fullerton.edu/graduateprograms/costs/Scholarships .

Subsidized/Unsubsidized Stafford Loans are available.

ADMISSIONS PROCESS
Prospective students must complete an online graduate application. For complete admissions information, please visit http://business.fullerton.edu/admissions.

CENTRAL MICHIGAN UNIVERSITY
College of Business Administration

AT A GLANCE

The Master of Business Administration at Central Michigan University prepares graduate students for leadership positions in today's global economy. The program is accredited by AACSB International - The Association to Advance Collegiate Schools of Business.

Many courses are taught by Six Sigma Black Belt-certified faculty and SAP Enterprise Software for Management is integrated into the curriculum.

FACULTY

The College of Business Administration faculty are highly renowned and dedicated to the success of our students. Many faculty are practicing and consulting members of the business community and conduct significant research. Several are Six Sigma Black Belt-certified and are well equipped to teach students the specialized concepts and methodologies of data-driven decision-making skills.

STUDENTS

Students in the program come from a wide variety of academic, professional, and personal backgrounds. The diversity of the international and domestic students offers a rewarding learning environment by adding numerous perspectives and insights to teamwork situations.

CAREER SERVICES AND PLACEMENT

CMU provides a variety of career services, including scheduling of on-campus interviews with potential employers. Students can register for e-recruiting services, resumes are

critiqued and mock interviews are provided to help you better prepare for real interviews. Career advising services are provided as well. (www.careers.cmich.edu)

LOCATION AND ENVIRONMENT

Central Michigan University's 480-acre campus is accommodating, friendly, and conveniently located in the heart of a classic college town. CMU faculty, staff, students, and community residents care about each other and feel quite safe to walk on and off campus, to shop, and to attend sporting events or other recreational opportunities.

MAJORS AND DEGREES OFFERED

The College of Business Administration offers three graduate degree programs. The Master of Business Administration (MBA), the Master of Science in Information Systems (MSIS) and the Master of Arts in Economics (M.A. in Economics).

ACADEMIC PROGRAMS

The MBA program requires 30-31 credit hours. The accelerated eight-week courses allow full-time students to complete the program in 12 months. Part-time students can expect to complete the program in two or three years. Individuals who possess an undergraduate degree in business will be most prepared to begin the program; those with other undergraduate degrees and business credits will be asked to meet prerequisite requirements.

Students will specify a primary area of concentration in one of the following areas: accounting, consulting, finance, general business, international business, and management information systems (SAP emphasis).

Students will also complete an applied, integrated project in which skills and competencies are applied to actual business problems.

The MSIS program is also accredited by AACSB International. The program is designed for individuals who do not have previous information systems or computing-related degrees. The program prepares students to enter various information systems positions in business, consulting, gov-

ernment, or nonprofit organizations; to teach computer applications and information systems at community colleges; or to enter doctoral programs in information systems-related areas after graduation. The program requires 30 credit hours and is open to full-time or part-time students.

Students will specify a primary area of concentration in one of the following areas:

Business Processing Engineering, Systems Applications, General Business, and Teaching/Training. SAP Enterprise Software for Management is used in several courses in the Business Processing Engineering Concentration.

The M.A. in Economics is designed for students who wish to gain marketable skills in applied economics and for students who wish to strengthen their preparation in order to continue work toward a doctorate in economics. The program requires 30 credit hours and is open to full-time or part-time students.

SPECIAL PROGRAMS

Housed within CMU's Applied Business Studies Complex, our LaBelle Entrepreneurial Center helps small businesses reorganize and competitively reposition themselves and provides real-world connections between graduate students, corporations, and small businesses.

CAMPUS FACILITIES AND EQUIPMENT

Located at the center of campus, Park Library provides state-of-the-art facilities for students. The adjacent Bovee University Center is a hub of vibrant activity, with auditoriums, restaurant services, and a variety of student service offices and student organizations.

FINANCIAL AID

In-State Tuition: $388.00 per credit hour

Out-of-State Tuition: $719.00 per credit hour

International students must provide proof of funding of $25,000 for an academic year.

Domestic students - estimate for housing, food, utilities, tuition, books and supplies: $20,174

Domestic students and international students may apply for graduate assistantships and fellowships. International students may be eligible for Out-of-State Tuition Merit Awards. For more information, visit: www.grad.cmich.edu

ADMISSIONS PROCESS

The College accepts applications from students who have earned a baccalaureate degree from an accredited university or college. To be admitted to the MBA program, a student must present both an acceptable score on the Graduate Management Admission Test (GMAT) and an acceptable grade point average (GPA). Our College uses a set index formula to determine a candidate's eligibility for admission. Applicants must achieve at least 1,050 points based on this formula: 200 times the undergraduate GPA plus the GMAT score, which must be independently 450 or higher. International students must also submit a score of at least 79 (internet-based test), 213 (computer-based test), or 550 (paper-based test) or higher on the Test of English as a Foreign Language (TOEFL).

All application procedures take place through CMU's College of Graduate Studies (www.grad.cmich.edu). Domestic students should apply for admission at least six weeks prior to the start of the semester of entry. International students should apply at least six months in advance of a semester start date.

CLARK UNIVERSITY
Graduate School of Management

AT A GLANCE

Clark University Graduate School of Management (GSOM) offers the Master of Business Administration (MBA) and the Master of Science in Finance (MSF). As a GSOM student, you will benefit from small class sizes and close interactions with talented faculty who are dedicated researchers, practitioners and educators. As a GSOM graduate, you will join an international alumni network of leaders in multinational corporations, family businesses, and new ventures.

FACULTY

Clark GSOM faculty are dedicated teachers, practitioners and researchers. Our full-time faculty advance their respective fields through unique research, extensive corporate consulting, and active participation in professional associations. Our full-time faculty is supplemented by an accomplished group of adjunct faculty, many who are practicing professionals in the region's technology, biotech, financial services and insurance industries.

STUDENTS

Clark GSOM is proud to welcome a diverse student population who represent the multinational nature of business today. Generally over 70% of full-time students are from outside the U.S. They come to Clark from a wide variety of industry and functional backgrounds, from large multinational corporations and small family-run enterprises, and at different stages in their careers. This multiplicity of experiences and backgrounds benefits our students as they learn first-hand how to manage in a diverse community.

Clark GSOM draws heavily on local industries for their part-time student population including technology, financial services, biotechnology, banking, health care, manufacturing and the non-profit sector.

CAREER SERVICE AND PLACEMENT

What happens when successful corporate recruiters 'cross over' to university career services? Experience the difference at The Stevenish Career Management Center at the Clark University Graduate School of Management (GSOM).

Drawing upon a combined three decades of corporate recruiting and HR expertise, we create successful relationships with employers looking to hire talented, resourceful business professionals-for internships, jobs and to build a pipeline of future employees. Our real-world, real-life approach to career planning and job searching provides students with the optimal skill set to achieve their goals.

We take a business partner approach in working with companies. Employers frequently join us on campus for recruiting and valuable career development activities such as resume critiques, participating in special topic panels and guest lecturing on current career issues. We provide employers with student and alumni candidates who match specific job or internship qualifications as well as the cultural fit.

In the past, Career Services meant career counseling. At Clark's GSOM it means rigorous training in career and job search fundamentals coupled with aggressive career placement activities. Students learn professional strategies that will last a lifetime, bringing immediate value to their careers and the workplace.

LOCATION AND ENVIRONMENT

Clark University is located in the second largest city of New England, just one hour from Boston and three hours from New York City.

Clark's main campus is thoroughly integrated into the surrounding urban neighborhood creating a thriving academic community within the city of Worcester. Facilities on campus include extensive library and research resources, athletic facilities, computing and digital multi-media production space, wireless network capability and a strong on-campus extra-curricular tradition.

Evening classes for part-time students are also held at Clark's Graduate Management Center in Framingham.

MAJORS AND DEGREES OFFERED

Master of Business Administration (MBA)

Master of Science in Finance (MSF)

ACADEMIC PROGRAMS

The Clark MBA provides students with the skills and vision to make strategic business decisions in the global business environment. MBA concentrations: Accounting, Finance, Marketing, Global Business, MIS, and Management.

The Clark MSF develops skills in applied finance theory. The program addresses corporate finance, securities markets, risk management and derivatives markets, statistics and modeling, and global finance.

FINANCIAL AID

Tuition for the 2008-2009 academic year is $3,180 for a full semester course (one unit); $1,590 for a half-semester course (1/2 unit).

MBA program: 16 units, of which 4.5 can be waived with equivalent undergraduate coursework or waiver exams.

MSF program: 10 units

Clark offers merit-based scholarships ranging from 25 to 100% of tuition. Many students also receive graduate assistantships and are compensated with a stipend. All full-time students are considered for scholarships and assistantships.

Full and part-time domestic students are also eligible for a variety of student loan programs. Clark University's Office of Financial Assistance assists MBA and MSF students in identifying and applying for these funds.

ADMISSIONS PROCESS

Clark GSOM seeks individuals who will add diversity and vitality to our program. We encourage applications from candidates with a variety of educational backgrounds including business, liberal arts, sciences and social sciences, and who hold baccalaureate degrees or the equivalent from accredited institutions.

Admission is open to full-time and part-time students. Classes meet once/week and are offered in the daytime and evening.

The MBA program enrolls new students in September and January. The MSF program admits new students in September only.

CLEMSON UNIVERSITY

AT A GLANCE
Clemson University is ranked 27th among the nation's public doctoral-granting universities. The innovative and flexible MBA program - accredited by AACSB International — prepares candidates for senior-level management positions in the global marketplace. An MBA from Clemson will give you the analytical, theoretical, strategic and real-world knowledge to lead businesses. And you will gain expertise in competencies recruiters say they want most - leadership, team development and communication skills. Small, interactive and diverse classes, coupled with individual attention from faculty mentors and coaches, will give you ample opportunity to improve your leadership style and polish communication skills. In fact, we think you'll find that the Clemson MBA environment provides a dynamic, supportive culture that will help you achieve your career goals.

Uniquely, about 50 percent of our full-time MBA candidates are awarded graduate assistantships in which they serve as consultants for area businesses, helping company executives with market assessments, product plans, competitive research, etc. Numerous dual-degree options also are available, as are study abroad programs in Belgium, China and Italy.

FACULTY
The Clemson MBA faculty includes Fulbright Scholars, top researchers, research center directors, innovative entrepreneurs and award-winning teachers and scholars. They have broad work experience and collaborate with industry and government leaders. Over 98 percent of MBA faculty hold a PhD.

STUDENTS
Clemson's MBA students hail from all over the world. Students range in age, backgrounds, levels of work experience and interests. About 40 percent of students have science or engineering undergraduate degrees, with 24 percent from the sciences, 20 percent from the humanities and 16 percent from engineering. About 30 percent of students are women and roughly 20-30 percent of students are international.

CAREER SERVICES AND PLACEMENT
The MBA Career Development Office offers candidates individualized professional coaching along with intern and job search support (resume review, interview preparation, salary negotiation, etc). Companies that have hired recent MBA interns and graduates include Blackbaud, Bausch & Lomb, CapGemini, Colonial Life, Disney, GE, Home Depot, Lockheed Martin, Michelin, Milliken, Nestle, Northwestern Mutual, Resurgent Capital Service, Schneider and Target.

LOCATION AND ENVIRONMENT
Clemson attracts students looking for a strong sense of community, school spirit and a love of winning - in academics, in athletics and in life. Clemson students attend seminars by prominent professionals, view Broadway touring shows, visit art galleries and watch Division I sporting events. More than 250 student organizations appeal to a wide variety of interests and talents.

Clemson University is located on 1,400 wooded acres in the northwestern part of South Carolina at the foot of the Blue Ridge Mountains. Adjacent to Lake Hartwell, the area boasts a beautiful climate perfect for year-round golf, hiking, biking, boating, camping and rafting. Clemson is about an hour from Greenville, South Carolina, and two hours from Atlanta, Georgia or Charlotte, North Carolina.

MAJORS AND DEGREES OFFERED
The Clemson MBA offers both a full-time program and a part-time program for working professionals. Courses are offered afternoons and evenings on campus and evenings in Greenville, South Carolina. MBA students may combine an MBA with another master's degree in a variety of disciplines including Computer Science, Economics, Engineering, Marketing, Professional Communications and others.

ACADEMIC PROGRAMS
The 21-month full-time program (62 hours) offers students a strong, in-depth foundation in graduate-level business topics combined with a choice of specializations, or with the opportunity to design their own specialization if earning a dual master's degree. Designated specializations include Innovation and Entrepreneurial Leadership, Real Estate, Marketing Management and Supply Chain and Information Management.

Clemson's MBA for Working Professionals (33-45 hours) allows individuals to take courses full-time or part-time. Students can maintain their full-time careers, as courses are taught in the evenings. This program requires at least two years of relevant work experience.

The Clemson MBA curriculum incorporates case studies, consulting projects for real companies, field trips, traditional lectures, role-playing, simulations and teamwork. It also features seminars with top industry speakers and professional development activities, such as an annual ethical leadership case competition, taped presentations and mock interviews and workshops on leadership, case interviewing, cross-cultural communication and more.

CAMPUS FACILITIES AND EQUIPMENT
Clemson University offers several top-level facilities and resources. Most MBA classes are taught in "executive" style classrooms (tiered rooms in a U-shape) with integrated computer and audio/video resources. Clemson's main library provides a variety of services and extensive online access to electronic information. The campus is supported by an enterprise-class computing environment.

FINANCIAL AID
Graduate assistantships are awarded on a competitive basis to highly qualified full-time students, regardless of citizenship. Assistantships pay a stipend of $6,000 per year (2 semesters) for 15 hours per week of work AND reduce the student's tuition to a flat fee of $950 per semester ($1,900 per year). This represents an annual savings in tuition of $7,386 (in-state) and $16,610 (out-of-state).

Full-time students (12 credit hours or more) who do not hold assistantships pay tuition and medical fees as follows:

Tuition on Clemson's Campus

South Carolina resident $4,642/semester; Out-of-state-resident $9,255/semester

Tuition at the Greenville University Center

South Carolina resident $535/credit hour; Out-of-State resident $918/credit hour

ADMISSIONS
Acceptance is based on a careful appraisal of students' academic records, GMAT, TOEFL, essay, letters of recommendation, interview and work experience. Students are evaluated on an individual basis. A minimum GPA of 3.0, GMAT score of 600, TOEFL score of 580 on the paper-based test or 237 on the computer-based test, plus a minimum of one-two years of work experience are preferred. Two years of work experience are required for undergraduate business majors. Application deadlines for the full-time program are April 15 for international students and June 15 for domestic students. For the part-time program, deadlines are April 15, July 15 and November 1. Visit our admissions and application Website at www.clemson.edu/business/mba/apply.htm for details.

Clemson MBA Office
124 Sirrine Hall
Clemson, SC 29634-1315
Phone: 864-656-3975
fax: 864-656-0947
Admissions e-mail: mba@clemson.edu
Web address: www.clemson.edu/mba

COLORADO STATE UNIVERSITY

The Distance MBA Program

AT A GLANCE

Colorado State University's flexible and comprehensive Distance MBA Program (AACSB accredited since 1970) offers business professionals one of the nation's oldest and most respected academic programs focused on business application through group collaboration. Students around the world receive the full classroom experience within days of it being delivered in our classrooms.

FACULTY

Students in The Distance MBA Program learn from some of the best minds in business as well from within academia. The MBA faculty are chosen from the best the College of Business has to offer; students are taught by the best in their field and most of the professors bring private sector experience to the classroom, as well.

STUDENTS

The typical student in The Distance MBA Program is 33 years old and has about 12 years of full-time professional experience. Their average undergraduate cumulative GPA was 3.12 and their GMAT score was 580. The typical student does not have an undergraduate degree in business but rather in engineering, science/math or technology.

CAREERS SERVICES AND PLACEMENT

The majority of The Distance MBA Program students are fully employed when they enter the program and do not require career services or counseling; however, the College of Business does off the services of the Career Liaison and the University's Career Services as well as provided opportunity postings from corporations around the world on a regular basis to the students. They may get assistance on resumes, interviewing ideas for use with internal and external opportunities.

LOCATION AND ENVIRONMENT

With more than 25,000 students, Colorado State University serves as a major center for education, business, research and service in Fort Collins and Northern Colorado. Located in an economically and culturally vibrant city of 132, 000 residents; the University is nestled in the foothills of the Rocky Mountains.

MAJORS AND DEGREES OFFERED

The Distance MBA Program offers a comprehensive program that brings the on-campus classroom environment to working professionals around the world via DVD, video streaming, and through networking technology. The Distance MBA Program began in 1967; as the oldest and first accredited distance MBA it is known for its forward thinking as it relates to content delivery and communications applications between students, professors, and staff.

The Distance MBA Program attracts professionals throughout the United States and from around the world to study together in a dynamic learning atmosphere. Students learn from others' diverse work experiences, leading to successful team building and long-term networking. This program focuses on fundamental aspects of advanced business, including domestic and international case studies that highlight issues and concepts with immediate applicability to the workplace.

ACADEMIC PROGRAMS

The Distance MBA Program may be completed in a 2 or 4-year format. With the same academic content and rigor as the on-campus Professional MBA Program, lecture content is delivered to the distance MBA students via mixed-media DVDs that capture the entire lecture to include PowerPoint(r) slides, student questions, discussions, presentations and special speakers. Distance MBA students earn a Master of Business Administration from Colorado State University not an online or distance degree.

The Program offers a comprehensive MBA that provides its students with a solid foundation in Accounting, Finance, Marketing, Management, and Computer Information Systems; this curriculum gives those without the formal business education a solid foundation on which to build and direct their career in a more horizontal manner.

The Distance MBA Program curriculum is the same academic content and rigor as the on-campus Professional MBA Program. Further, students earn an MBA from Colorado State University not a distance or online degree.

SPECIAL PROGRAMS

In 2008, the College of Business introduced a certificate in finance to complement The Distance MBA Program; this certificate may be taken by an MBA alumna or individuals who have already completed the two finance courses from the MBA core. This three class certificate may also be taken by finance professionals in the community; the classes are offered on-campus and at a distance.

CAMPUS FACILITIES AND EQUIPMENT

The Distance MBA Program is recorded at the same time as the on-campus Professional MBA Program is conducted each week. The campus MBA is held in a room with four commercial TV cameras; the full classroom dynamic is captured to include the full lecture, PowerPoint slides, student questions, discussions, presentations and special speakers. This content is burned to DVDs and mailed out to students around the world the next morning. Additionally, this content is available to all students via video streaming.

The Program offers students a personal connection to the campus and to their peers through direct interaction via a unique MBA Intranet that allows threaded and chat room discussions to give the feeling of being connected to the classroom and the campus.

FINANCIAL AID

Tuition for the 2008-09 Academic Year is $620.00 per credit hour for the 36-credit program totals $22,320.00 plus textbooks. There is a minor University technology fee assessed each fall and spring semester of $15.00.

The MBA programs qualify for Federal Financial Aid (FASFA) as well as many other financial aid programs; the Montgomery GI Bill and military tuition assistance is also accepted. All active-duty, reservist, National Guard and veterans may participate in the Tuition Reduction Program as well as federal and state employees.

ADMISSIONS PROCESS

The admissions criteria for The Distance MBA Program is a 3.0 cumulative GPA in undergraduate study, at least 4 years of full time professional experience and an average GMAT score of 580. If an applicant has a 3.0 cumulative GPA or better and at least 8 years of full time professional experience OR a graduate degree then they are encouraged to petition for a waiver to the GMAT requirement. Full admission criteria and all applicable forms may be found at www.admission.CSUmba.com.

Admissions are a scheduled in the fall and spring of each year. The application deadline for fall admissions is July 15 and for the spring admission, the deadline is December 8. While there are classes in the summer, there are no admissions in the summer term.

DRUCKER SCHOOL OF MANAGEMENT

AT A GLANCE

The Drucker School of Management, located in Claremont, California, is dedicated to training effective and ethical leaders and managers in whatever industries they serve. This focus stems from our belief that management is a liberal art, a human enterprise encompassing perspectives from the social and behavioral sciences. Named after one of the most prominent management thinkers of the 20th century, Peter F. Drucker, the Drucker MBA program offers a high-quality, interactive educational experience: small classes averaging 25 students per class and instruction from world renowned professors. Approximately 70% of our classroom instruction is either in discussion or case analysis format, and we incorporate team building in classroom projects and presentations.

FACULTY

Our faculty at the Drucker School set the benchmark for the highest standards of academic excellence. The faculty is committed to creating a rich learning experience for students, while outside the classroom they produce influential publications and guide private, public and non-profit organizations in best practices. Students have access to experts in strategic management, leadership, marketing management, new venture finance, and global markets.

CAREER SERVICES AND PLACEMENT

The career services available to students at the Drucker School are designed to provide the tools needed to successfully navigate into the working world and beyond. The department brings major US corporations on campus to interview-such as GE Capital, Deloitte & Touche, Johnson & Johnson, and Disney. Each year there are career fairs held on campus and a series of workshops and panels aimed at empowering students to embrace the career path of their choice.

LOCATION AND ENVIRONMENT

Nestled in the foothills of the San Gabriel Mountains, the city of Claremont is famous for its tree-lined streets, world-renowned colleges, and charming "old town" restaurants and shops. Located 25 miles east of Los Angeles, Claremont provides the atmosphere of a New England college town within comfortable driving distance of major Southern California attractions and sports stadiums.

MAJORS AND DEGREES OFFERED

Master of Business Administration (MBA)

Master of Arts in Politics Economics and Business (MAPEB)

Master of Arts in Art and Cultural Management (MAACM)

Master of Science in Financial Engineering

Dual Degrees

Executive Management Program

Certificates

PhD in Management

ACADEMIC PROGRAMS

The Drucker School attracts students who exhibit strong leadership skills and achievement. The MBA program emphasizes the importance of social responsibility in the complex, globally-connected economy while focusing on ethical management. Our MBA program is ranked among the nation's TOP 10 in faculty and classroom experience according to the Princeton Review.

CURRICULUM

The MBA curriculum is designed to enable students to simultaneously build knowledge and develop professional skills. Core courses provide candidates with an understanding of the fundamental disciplines of management. Elective courses enable students to specialize in a particular field of interest. Our flexible scheduling allows for both full-time and part-time study. Students are also able to take courses outside of the management program in other disciplines through the various schools at Claremont Graduate University and the Claremont College Consortium.

SPECIAL PROGRAMS

Dual Degree: Dual degrees allow students to obtain two degrees in an accelerated period of time. The dual degrees the Drucker School offers are MBA/MSMIS, MBA/MSFE, MBA/MSHRD, MBA/MS, and MBA/MA.

Joint Degree: The Master of Arts in Politics, Economics and Business (MAPEB) is a joint degree program with curriculum shared between the Drucker School of Management and the School of Politics Economics and Business. The Master of Arts in Arts and Cultural Management (MAACM) is a joint degree from the Drucker School and the School of Arts and Humanities.

In addition to challenging academic programs, students can also participate in a number of special interest clubs designed to further both academic and career interests: the Consulting Club, the Finance Club, the Marketing Club, Women in Leadership, Net Impact, and the Drucker School Student Association among others.

FINANCIAL AID

There are several departmental fellowships available to students, including the Doris Drucker Women in Leadership Fellowship, a new scholarship opportunity intended to honor Doris Drucker, the wife of famed management scholar and social philosopher Peter Drucker. This scholarship rewards exceptional women wishing to further their careers in management and leadership. More information on this and other fellowship opportunities may be viewed at www.cgu.edu/fellowships.

Institutional financial aid is based on the applicant's professional work experience, academic qualifications, and GMAT score. It is applied for as a part of the application process. Government loans (FAFSA-for U.S. citizens and permanent residents) and International Student loans are also available.

ADMISSIONS PROCESS

We do not have minimum requirements for the GMAT and GPA as we attempt to individualize each student's application by evaluating the "whole person."

In addition to a completed application, two letters of recommendation, official transcripts from every college/university attended, a personal statement, current resume, official GMAT scores and the TOEFL (for international students) must also be submitted. There is a $60 application fee and interviews are arranged by invitation.

Applications to the MBA program are accepted for fall, spring and summer on a rolling admission basis, with priority fellowship/financial aid deadlines of February 15th for the fall semester.

ADDITIONAL INFORMATION

www.cgu.edu/discoverdrucker

FAIRFIELD UNIVERSITY
Dolan School of Business

AT A GLANCE

Fairfield University was founded in 1942 by the Jesuits, a Roman Catholic order renowned for its 450-year-old tradition of excellence in education and service to others. This Jesuit tradition inspires a commitment to educating the whole person for a life of leadership in a constantly changing world. Fairfield University welcomes students of all faiths and beliefs who value its mission of scholarship, truth, and justice, and it values the diversity their membership brings to the university community.

Faculty members are in the classroom at all times and are unusually accessible to students as mentors and advisors. The relationship between faculty and students leads to creative collaborations on independent study and hands-on research.

LOCATION AND ENVIRONMENT

Set on 200 acres of woods and rolling lawns with views of the nearby Long Island Sound, Fairfield's campus is a beautiful setting for study and personal growth. Nearby, the beaches of the Sound offer recreation as well as research opportunities for marine biology and environmental science students, while the woods and trails of New England offer hiking, biking and other outdoor activity. Metro North railroad, also in town, takes students to New York City for all the diverse cultural and career opportunities available. Excursions to New York are frequently built into the class curriculum, as well as into social opportunities for students. Fairfield County itself is a Mecca for small and large corporations. With one of the largest concentrations of Fortune 500 companies in the nation.

ACADEMIC PROGRAMS

An MBA program is meant to be a generalist degree which covers all the relevant topical areas and gives a student the opportunity to specialize, but not major, in a functional area of business. The MBA program has three components: core courses, breadth courses, and specialization or concentration courses. The core courses are functional courses; they are designed to provide fundamental tools and functional area competencies for students who either did not major in a business specialty as undergraduates, did not perform well academically as undergraduates, or took only a portion of the functional and tool courses that comprise the MBA core. This is called "leveling," i.e., everyone starts at the same level, or nearly so, before they go on to take advanced coursework. Therefore, the core courses are prerequisites to the breadth of the MBA program.

The full MBA program is comprised of the breadth courses and the specialization courses. The new AACSB accreditation standards require at least 30 semester hours of study beyond the core. The Dolan School of Business will limit the number of options that it offers in both the breadth and specialization courses to strengthen the program.

Core Courses - 18 credits
AC 400	Introduction to Accounting
FI 400	Principles of Finance
MG 400	Organizational Behavior
MK 400	Marketing Management
OM 400	Integrated Business Processes
QA 400	Applied Business Statistics

Breadth Courses - 18 credits
AC 500	Accounting for Decision-Making
FI 500	Shareholders Value
IS 500	Information Systems
MG 500	Managing People for Competitive Advantage
MG 503	Legal and Ethical Environment of Business
MK 500	Customer Value

Concentration Courses - 12 credits

Four concentration courses are required from the following concentrations (Accounting, Finance, Human Resource Management, ISOM, General Management, International Business, Marketing or Taxation).

Elective Course - 3 credits
Any 500 level free elective.
Capstone Course - 3 credits
MG 584   Global Competitive Strategy

The Master of Science in Finance (30 credits)

The Master of Science in Finance provides unique opportunities for individuals who want to enhance their career opportunities in the areas of investments, corporate finance, or banking. The main program consists of ten 3-credit courses (7 required and 3 electives) and is especially useful for those who want to pursue advanced certification, such as the CFA, CFM, CFP. Applicants should hold an undergraduate or an MBA degree and have an adequate background in the areas of microeconomics, macroeconomics, financial accounting, and statistics.

Master of Science in Accounting (30 credits)

The M. S. in Accounting is designed to provide students with a Bachelor of Science degree in Accounting with an opportunity to complete the degree a 12 month period, based on undergraduate coursework, as well as fulfill the 150 hour criterion to sit for the uniform CPA examination, as passed in the State of Connecticut and most other jurisdictions. Students complete their studies over one or two summers and one academic year immediately following undergraduate commencement (May through the following May or August).

The Master of Science in Taxation (30 credits)

The M.S. in Taxation is designed to prepare students for careers in the field of taxation. Students will learn to use a variety of tax authorities (e.g., statutory, judicial, and administrative) and other resources to critically consider and resolve complex tax issues. The program consists of 10 three-credit courses (7 required and 3 electives) and it is especially useful for industry managers and executives, financial services and public accounting professionals, and others seeking a specialized education in taxation. Applicants must have a baccalaureate degree in accounting or finance or equivalent coursework prior to beginning the program. In addition, Federal Income Taxation I and II, or the equivalent are program prerequisites.

Certificate Programs for Advanced Study (15 credits)

The certificate program is designed to provide a complete integration to the theory and practice of contemporary business. The Certificate Programs for Advanced Study are suitable for working professionals who have already earned a graduate degree whose responsibilities are currently or expected to be in a particular specialty, and who desire greater depth of academic preparation in that subject area; or for individuals outside of the area who desire to understand multifunctional thinking in order to compete effectively in the marketplace.

FINANCIAL AID

Student Loan programs available. Merit Scholarships and Graduate Assistantships available.

ADMISSIONS PROCESS

Contact Mrs. Marianne Gumpper.

www.fairfield.edu/gradadmis

FLORIDA INTERNATIONAL UNIVERSITY
Chapman Graduate School of Business

AT A GLANCE

Located in Miami, Florida, The Chapman Graduate School of Business is characterized by its rich active learning environment extending beyond the classroom, into the surrounding community, and across borders. Miami is recognized worldwide as the "Gateway to the Americas"; students enrolled in the Chapman School's programs are completely immersed in this world-class trade and commerce hub. The Chapman School has made significant investments over the past years in the fields of information technology, international business and entrepreneurship, helping it to gain national recognition in those strategic areas. Business Week has consistently ranked the Chapman Graduate School as the leading business school in South Florida.

According to U.S. News & World Report's America's Best Graduate Schools (2008) the Chapman School is ranked #23 among MBA programs with an international specialization. Courses in the International MBA (full-time) program are taught by faculty who are experts in their field and bring a global business perspective to the classroom. The learning experience is further enriched by the fact that 45 percent of the student body is international. The study abroad and internship opportunities provide students with practical international business experience. The curriculum includes a foreign language component, where students choose between Chinese (Mandarin), Spanish, Advanced Business English or Portuguese. Students electing the China Track participate in a semester-long study abroad and take Chinese language courses both during their year at the Chapman Graduate School and for one month in China.

FACULTY

A dynamic force for excellence within Miami's only public, multi-campus research university. The dedicated, multicultural faculty of more than 100 in the College of Business Administration includes seven Eminent Scholars and a cadre of internationally distinguished experts in international business, information systems, operations research, knowledge management, e-commerce, international banking and trade, financial derivatives, consumer marketing and research, global marketing, human resource management, and corporate responsibility. The faculty brings a wealth of corporate and entrepreneur experiences to the classroom, combining practical knowledge with theory. As a result, this creates a dynamic and challenging learning experience for students.

LOCATION AND ENVIRONMENT

The Chapman Graduate School is located on the 344-acre campus of Florida International University, featuring lush tropical landscaping and impressive architecture. Strategically located in Miami, a truly global metropolis, Florida International University has the advantage of being at the center of it all. The Chapman Graduate School brings together people from all over the world with a diversity of backgrounds, experiences, and

cultures to create a unique learning environment. Our tropical weather means students can enjoy year-round sporting and recreation activities from boating and water sports to tennis and golf.

ACADEMIC PROGRAMS

At the Chapman School you'll find a set of innovative programs that provide you with the knowledge and skills to advance your career in today's dynamic global marketplace.

- International MBA - A one-year, full-time, lock-step program with classes being offered during the day.

- Evening MBA - Designed for working professionals with 2 or more years of professional work experience. Classes offered Monday - Thursday evenings.

- Downtown MBA - Designed for working professionals in the downtown Miami area, classes meet two evenings per week at the Downtown Center.

- Professional MBA - A lock-step program offering classes on Saturdays for working professionals with 4 or more years of professional work experience.

- Executive MBA - A lock-step program offering classes on Saturdays tailored to the mid-level executive with eight or more years of work experience.

- MBA for Public Managers - Tailored for city, county, federal, and state employees. Classes meet Friday evenings and Saturday mornings.

- Master of Science in Taxation - Catered to tax professionals and accountants, the program satisfies the requirement for the CPA exam in the state of Florida. It is a lock-step program with classes held on Saturdays except during tax season.

- Master of Accounting - Tailored for students who have an undergraduate degree in accounting, the program satisfies the requirement for the CPA exam in the state of Florida. It is a lock-step program with classes held on Saturdays.

- Master of International Business - Designed for professionals with a business background who wish to further their career in a global business environment. Classes offered Monday - Thursday evenings.

- Master of Science in Finance - Designed for working professionals who wish to broaden their understanding of domestic and global financial services, classes meet Friday evenings and Saturdays in a lock-step format.

- Master of Science in Management Information Systems - A lock-step program offering classes on Saturdays for working IT professionals who wish to advance their knowledge of the latest technological advancements in MIS and management of information technology.

- Master of Science in Human Resource Management - Tailored for those with careers in Human Resources or those who wish to pursue a career in Human Resource Management, classes are offered on Saturdays in a lock-step format.

- Master of Science in International Real Estate - A lock-step program offering classes two evenings per week designed for working professionals who wish to acquire skills necessary in today's international real estate marketplace.

- Doctor of Philosophy in Business Administration

ADMISSIONS PROCESS

Particular program-specific requirements are listed on our program web sites, which are accessible at: http://business.fiu.edu/chapman. To be eligible for admission, prospective student must hold a Bachelor's degree or equivalent from an accredited institution and a minimum undergraduate GPA of 3.0 in upper division courses (last 60 credit hours). Official transcripts from all previously attended institutions are required to be submitted in a sealed university envelope. Applications and more information can be found online at http://gradschool.fiu.edu.

FLORIDA STATE UNIVERSITY

AT A GLANCE

Florida State University's College of Business equips the CEOs of tomorrow with the analytical tools needed to excel in the world's marketplace. FSU's Online MBA, the perfect fit for the top executive on the go, is taught by the same world-renowned scholars who lecture on campus. Online students learn alongside professional peers who bring their own valuable work experiences to the online dialogue. FSU's accelerated Full-time MBA offers a fast track in an atmosphere that fosters creativity and rewards problem-solving. On-campus students may pursue concentrations in finance or marketing.

FACULTY

The College of Business faculty consists of 114 full-time personnel, including one Francis Eppes Professor, seven Endowed Chairs, three University Named Professorships and 27 Endowed Named Professorships.

STUDENTS

FSU has a diverse population representing every county in Florida, all 50 states and more than 137 countries. 25 percent are minority; 57 percent are women.

LOCATION AND ENVIRONMENT

Florida State University is a comprehensive, national graduate research university with more than 41,000 students and more than 300 undergraduate, graduate and professional programs. The university is located in the bustling Southern city of Tallahassee, the state's capital known for its tree-lined canopy roads and beautiful springtime. The College of Business enrolls nearly 400 MBA students, primarily through its growing Online MBA program. Students attending school in Tallahassee will find a wide range of entertainment outside of school, from live music to water sports, from art venues to college sporting events. The city also abounds in family-friendly activities, including hands-on museums and parks.

Take a virtual tour of the Florida State University campus:

http://www.fsutour.org/#

OFF-CAMPUS OPPORTUNITIES

FSU's MBA program offers an international experience in Panama.

MAJORS AND DEGREES OFFERED

Florida State University's College of Business has MBA programs tailored for different student needs:

Online MBA - Designed with the busy, working professional in mind, Online MBA students attend class from anywhere in the world. FSU's high-quality distance-learning structure features the same core courses and professors as the on-campus, face-to-face MBA programs. Students may pursue a general MBA or choose from concentrations in real estate finance and analysis and hospitality administration.

Full-time MBA - Finishing in 12 months' time, FSU's Full-time MBA program is designed for students who are disciplined, organized and welcome fast-paced challenges. Students participate in rigorous and competitive project work with a cohort of high-achieving peers. Students may pursue a general MBA or choose from concentrations in finance or marketing and supply chain management.

Part-time MBA - The Part-time MBA on-campus program is a good fit for those in north Florida who want to change careers, advance on the job or simply develop personally without having to leave the workforce or relocate. The program can be completed in a little more than two years at a pace of two night courses per semester.

Joint Degrees - The College of Business partners with the College of Law and College of Social Work to offer joint graduate degrees for on-campus students.

CAMPUS FACILITIES AND EQUIPMENT

The Charles A. Rovetta Business Building contains approximately 76,000 net square feet of classroom space, faculty and staff offices and support facilities, including a master's student computer lab providing networking and printing services. Nearby Robert Manning Strozier Library provides research help and study areas. On-campus students have access to the Leach Student Recreation Center, which offers more than 20,000 square feet of workout space. Campus recreation also offers exercise classes, intramural sports and outdoor pursuits.

Financial Aid

The cost of the MBA program differs between on-campus and online students and is subject to change each year based on Legislative appropriation. Visit http://cob.fsu.edu/grad/attend_financial.cfm#programcosts for up-to-date information. Tuition assistantships for full-time, on-campus students are available. Scholarships, fellowships and grants also are available from Florida State University and external sources.

ADMISSIONS PROCESS

Interested students may fill out an application online at https://admissions.fsu.edu/gradapp/ The application fee is $30.

GISMA BUSINESS SCHOOL

AT A GLANCE

GISMA Business School in Germany offers two highly international AACSB-accredited MBA programs in cooperation with Purdue University's Krannert School of Management, Indiana, USA.

The full-time program lasts 11 months; the on-the-job Executive program lasts 22 months. Both programs are internationally accredited (AACSB, AMBA) and represented in rankings all over the world, e.g.: Financial Times (rank 11 in the world for GISMA's Executive MBA Program).

GISMA's programs provide a combination of theory and business-related topics moving beyond typical lectures and exams to experiential learning exercises, computer simulations, student consulting projects and off-site trips. Study groups are diverse with regards to first academic degrees, cultural background, and work experience.

FACULTY

A world-class team of instructors are the cornerstones of the academic program at GISMA Business School. In addition to helping students acquire the necessary skills and know-how to become tomorrow's business leaders, they are dedicated to providing a positive learning experience.

Plus a couple of faculty members (in the additional fields provided below the text field):

- Prof. Dr. David Schoorman - GISMA Dean
- Prof. Dr. Jen Tang - Quantitative Methods
- Prof. Dr. Lynda Thoman - Accounting
- Prof. Dr. Nicolas Kfuri - International Marketing
- Dr. Michael Höck - Operations Management

CAREER SERVICES AND PLACEMENT

Besides its top-notch academic program, GISMA Business School also offers extensive career counseling and job-finding services. Right from the start, professional coaches are there to help students target careers which are a close match for their individual wishes, abilities and strengths.

GISMA's 90 percent job placement rate within three months of graduation says a lot about the effectiveness of Career Center support in areas such as potential evaluation, interview coaching and assessment center training.

The Career Center service portfolio at a glance:

- Potential evaluation, resume and interview coaching, assessment center training.
- Frequent in-house presentations and visits to companies for valuable insight into the personnel needs of global enterprises. In-house presentations occur four to five times per module (with the program consisting of five modules), while field visits to companies take place once during each module.
- Participation in the annual MBA Career Fair staged in collaboration with other business schools in Germany. Here students get to know potential employers face-to-face in workshops, presentations and interviews. As a rule, 15 percent of all participating students receive one or more job offers right after the fair.
- Distribution of resumes to key HR contacts at international corporations, both via online portals and in the form of a printed Resume Book.
- Daily updates on job offers and online job portals, recruiting events, and European programs for young professionals.
- Contacts to GISMA alumni working in global enterprises.
- Free phone, fax and videoconferencing services for staying in touch with potential employers and recruiters.

LOCATION AND ENVIRONMENT

The central building of GISMA Business School—commonly referred to as the Rotunda (Rotunde in German) due to its round shape — is located on the outskirts of Hannover in the neighborhood of the Hannover Medical University complex and major firms such as TUI and Hannover Rück.

The Rotunda building—which is open from early in the morning till late at night—provides an ideal atmosphere for classroom learning, communication and individual study.

MAJORS AND DEGREES OFFERED

GISMA's internationally recognized MBA degrees can be pursued either full time (in 11 months) or part time (in 22 months)—the latter program being designed to meet the needs of executives wishing to study without taking a career break.

ACADEMIC PROGRAMS

1. **MBA program (full time)**
   11-month course of study in Hannover for young management professionals from around the world who hold a college degree and have already had some job experience. The average age of GISMA students is 28. With its distinctly "real-world" approach, GISMA's MBA program excels at preparing graduates for the challenges of an increasingly global, highly dynamic marketplace. The learning environment is characterized by a pronounced spirit of teamwork among young people from a great variety of cultural, educational and professional backgrounds.

2. **Executive MBA program (part time)**
   Our "International Master's in Management Program" (IMM) is designed for managerial professionals that have typically worked for an average of ten years, and takes 22 months to complete. Thanks to its concentrated phases of learning, this program is set up in such a way as to enable participants to strike a healthy balance between work, family and study.

FINANCIAL AID

GISMA Business School enables qualified applicants to participate in its full-time MBA program regardless of their financial means. Various forms of financial aid are available to cover tuition (EUR 25,000) and living costs:

GISMA Education Fund:

Candidates can apply to the GISMA Education Fund for student loans. This enables students to finance up to 85 percent of their tuition without the need for parental sponsorship or bank guarantees.

GISMA Foundation scholarships:

The GISMA Foundation makes scholarships available to applicants with exceptional qualifications.

Scholarships by sponsoring firms:

Scholarships are also offered by firms supporting the GISMA cause.

ADMISSIONS PROCESS

Student selection is based on a combination of individual academic performance, work experience, leadership potential, personal traits, international-mindedness and motivation to play an active role in an international student body.

The program is open to all qualified individuals, regardless of their professional or cultural backgrounds. A previous degree in business or economics is not required.

HKUST BUSINESS SCHOOL

AT A GLANCE

Located in Hong Kong, the international business hub and financial center, the HKUST Business School is recognized as one of the youngest and most respected schools in Asia. Established in 1991, we are the first Asian business school to receive dual accreditations from AACSB and EQUIS. Our MBA program has been enjoying global recognitions, with the Economist Intelligence Unit (EIU) ranked us No. 20 in the world and No. 1 in Asia in 2007, and the Financial Times World No. 17 in 2008.

FACULTY

We have 140 faculty members from 15 countries, all PhD qualified. Around 50-60 teach MBA courses. Seasoned business leaders are also invited to serve as Adjunct Professors to provide students with industrial insights.

STUDENTS

Diversity is probably the best word to describe our full-time cohort. We operate in a small class size of 80, with students from 20+ nationalities. 85% of the class comes from outside Hong Kong, with average 5 years of work experience.

CAREER SERVICES AND PLACEMENT

Our dedicated MBA Career Services team offers various resources, career workshops and networking opportunities to support and enhance job search and career management skills of our full-time students.

More information at www.mbacareer.ust.hk

LOCATION AND ENVIRONMENT

The HKUST Business School is housed in the scenic HKUST Clearwater Bay Campus spreading over 60 hectares by the port shelter. Public transport is conveniently available with city center less than 30 minutes away.

http://publish.ust.hk/univ/campusvr/quicktime/a03_piazza.html

MAJORS AND DEGREES OFFERED

HKUST offers full-time, part-time and executive MBA programs to fit executives with different motivations at various stages of career. The full-time program is 16-month incorporating opportunity for internship and international exchange. The 2-year part-time program is offered both in Hong Kong and Shenzhen. The EMBA program jointly organized with Kellogg School of Management is catered for executives at senior management level.

ACADEMIC PROGRAMS

HKUST is known for melding the best elements of western business education with Asian management philosophies. Our full-time program is 16-month incorporating opportunity for internship in summer, and a semester of international exchange with our 51 partner schools in 15 countries. Concentrations on China business, financial services, and information technology management are available.

Candidates with substantial work experience and international exposure may opt for an intensive 12-month study.

CAMPUS FACILITIES AND EQUIPMENT

Students here enjoy all benefits of a full-scale university campus within a relaxing environment. Student housing and amenities such as banks, medical clinics, a supermarket, and catering outlets are conveniently located on campus. Other facilities include a five-story library, computer barns, wireless internet access, language center, swimming pools, fitness center, tennis courts and soccer pitch.

FINANCIAL AID

Program fee for the full-time program is HK$ 320,000 (~US$41,000) for intake 2008. Students are advised to budget at least HK$100,000 for living expenses for 12-month study in Hong Kong. For students on international exchange, tuition fees are included in the program fee; however travel and living expenses vary according to locations thus are not budgeted in the above estimate.

MBA scholarships of HK$25,000 to HK$150,000 are available to full-time students based on merit and financial needs.

ADMISSIONS PROCESS

Applicants are expected to have a bachelor degree, a satisfactory GMAT score, and minimum one-year post-qualification full-time work experience. Candidates need to submit TOEFL/IELTS results if English was not the language of instruction at undergraduate level.

HKUST accepts applications from October to March. Application can be submitted online with an application fee of HK$ 500 (~US$ 64). Shortlisted candidates will be invited for either face-to-face or video interview.

Online application: www.mba.ust.hk/application

HOFSTRA UNIVERSITY
Frank G. Zarb School of Business

AT A GLANCE

At Hofstra University, you'll find a dynamic university with a drive for excellence that matches your own. With an outstanding faculty, expanding academic offerings, and state-of-the-art facilities, Hofstra is recognized nationally as a university on the rise. Yet our average graduate class size is just nine. Hofstra offers a vibrant campus life on a 240-acre campus that is a registered national arboretum.

FACULTY

The Zarb School employs more than 81 full-time, highly credentialed faculty - 90 percent of whom hold the highest degrees in their fields. At the Zarb School every course is taught by a member of the faculty. Students benefit from their teachers' years of experience in business and research and their understanding of the day-to-day challenges of business.

STUDENTS

Students enrolled in the graduate programs at the Zarb School form a dynamic, achievement-oriented community. These students represent 10 states and 23 countries. About 25% are members of minority groups, 24% are international students and 37% are women. Many students in these graduate programs have previous work experience.

CAREER SERVICES AND PLACEMENT

A wide variety of career placement opportunities and resources are available to graduate students at the Zarb School. The Graduate Business Career Services actively assists students with a range of services including internships, part-time employment, recruitment activities and general career counseling. These services are supplemented by the M.B.A./M.S. Resume Book and Web site.

LOCATION AND ENVIRONMENT

Hofstra's distinctive 240-acre campus, a registered arboretum, is located in suburban Long Island, just 25 miles from New York City.

With New York City just a short ride by train or car, students take advantage of the theaters, museums, concerts and professional sports as well as business internships offered by one of the world's greatest cities. Students can also explore Long Island, which offers world-class beaches, museums, shopping, plus many internship and employment opportunities.

MAJORS AND DEGREES OFFERED

M.B.A. in Accounting, Finance, Health Services Management, Information Technology, International Business, Management, Marketing, Quality Management, Sports and Entertainment Management, and Taxation.

Executive Master of Business Administration (E.M.B.A.).

Juris Doctor/Master of Business Administration (J.D./M.B.A.) (with the Hofstra School of Law).

M.S. in Accounting, Finance, Human Resources Management, Information Technology, Marketing, Marketing Research, Quantitative Finance, and Taxation.

Combined B.B.A./M.B.A.

Combined B.B.A./M.S. in Accounting, Human Resources Management, Marketing, Marketing Research and Taxation.

ACADEMIC PROGRAMS

All graduate programs offered by the Frank G. Zarb School of Business are accredited by AACSB International. The school is among just 10 percent of the nation's business schools with dual AACSB accreditations for its pro-

grams in business and accounting. The Zarb School offers a challenging 41-48 credit M.B.A. program that includes a 15-credit concentration in a major discipline. Our unique curriculum focuses on analysis, decision making and management, through which students gain the knowledge they need to succeed in business. The Hofstra M.B.A. program provides students with broad exposure to the functional areas of business, opportunities to gain hands-on experience in a specific field and specialized instruction in the leadership aspects of business. In the fall of 2008, the school will launch a new, full-time day M.B.A. program.

SPECIAL PROGRAMS

The Zarb School of Business offers a number of special programs designed to meet the needs of its students. We recently added M.B.A. programs in Health Services Management, Quality Management, and Sports and Entertainment Management, and an M.S. in Quantitative Finance.

Other innovative programs include a J.D./M.B.A. program, offered in conjunction with the Hofstra Law School; and an Executive M.B.A. program, which features a schedule designed to allow working professionals to complete their degrees.

The school's internship program takes advantage of the proximity of New York City, allowing students to gain on-the-job experience in areas such as finance, business, media, advertising and entertainment.

CAMPUS FACILITIES AND EQUIPMENT

The Hofstra campus houses 112 buildings, including 37 residence halls and libraries that contain 1.2 million print volumes and offer 24/7 electronic access to more than 50,000 journals and electronic books. C.V. Starr Hall, home to the Zarb School of Business, features the Martin B. Greenberg Trading Room, one of the most advanced academic trading rooms in the nations. Additionally, through Hofstra's online library, students have access 24/7 to about 30 business databases.

FINANCIAL AID

Tuition is assessed on a per-credit basis, and is $875 for each credit for 2008-2009, with courses carrying two and three credits each. Hofstra is a private institution, so tuition is the same for residents and nonresidents of New York state. Financial aid is available in the form of fellowships, which provide partial tuition credit, and graduate assistantship positions.

ADMISSIONS PROCESS

Admission is selective. Candidates are required to complete the graduate application and all supporting forms and to submit two letters of recommendation, a résumé, a statement of professional objectives, official transcripts from every college or university attended, and scores obtained on the Graduate Management Admission Test (GMAT).

International students are also required to submit scores obtained on the TOEFL.

For the most recently admitted class, the middle 80 percent range of GMAT scores was from 430 to 640; and the average undergraduate grade point average was 3.2 on a 4.0 scale. All credentials submitted in support of the application for admission are carefully considered in making the admission decision.

Hofstra subscribes to a rolling admissions policy, with suggested filing deadlines of May 1 for fall admission and November 1 for spring admission. Candidates are generally advised of admission decisions no later than four weeks after the application is completed.

INDIANA UNIVERSITY OF PENNSYLVANIA
Eberly College of Business and Information Technology

AT A GLANCE

The Eberly College of Business and Information Technology MBA program (accredited by AACSB International), with its global strategy focus and highly international student and faculty composition, is designed to sharpen students' managerial, analytical, and decision-making skills so that they can compete in today's global environment. The Eberly MBA program has a long tradition of providing cost-effective preparation for a successful career in business. Consumers Digest magazine ranks IUP as number four in the magazine's June 2007 rankings of the "Best Values in Public Colleges and Universities." IUP is the highest-ranked university in Pennsylvania and is ranked at 40 out of 100 colleges and universities selected for Kiplinger's Personal Finance magazine's February 2007 "Best Values in Public Colleges" listing.

FACULTY

Eberly MBA courses are taught by faculty members who have doctoral degrees in their fields of specialization and extensive research and publication track records. Their international backgrounds and/or exposure, experience in industry, and current research projects bring an ideal blend of theory and practice to the MBA courses. Eberly faculty members serve as editors on nine national/international journals.

STUDENTS

Eberly provides students with an opportunity to learn with a diverse group of individuals. More than half the students are from 15 countries other than the U.S., 35 percent have previous business work experience, and 10 percent are currently working full-time in professional careers. Eberly College takes great pride in the activities and initiatives of its College of Business Student Advisory Council and the members of its 14 student organizations. In addition to having the opportunity to serve on university-wide committees, students serve on Eberly College committees for strategic planning, technology, curriculum, outcomes assessment, student services, and programming.

CAREER PLACEMENT AND SERVICES

IUP assists MBA students with job placement through its recruiting programs, computerized job-search database, résumé referrals, individual counseling, workshops, and job fairs. Many major corporations recruit on the IUP campus, and recent MBA graduates have accepted positions with companies such as Accenture, BearingPoint, Citizens Bank, Coca- Cola, Deloitte & Touche, Tohmatsu, Deutsche Bank, Dow Chemical, GE, IBM, Merrill Lynch, MetLife, Novell, Renault, Rockwell International, Siemens, Symantec, Walt Disney, and World Bank. During 2007-2008, the Eberly College held a career fair that attracted more than 25 businesses and governmental agencies. Separately, 55 employers came to campus for one-on-one interviews.

LOCATION AND ENVIRONMENT

Indiana University of Pennsylvania enrolls 14,000 students from across the nation and around the globe. With 30,000 residents in the rolling foothills of the Allegheny Mountains, the community of Indiana has been commended in terms of safety. It is a place of tree-lined streets, pleasant neighborhoods, and friendly shops and restaurants. Pittsburgh is a short drive to the southwest from IUP. A variety of recreational activities are available year-round, such as skiing in the winter and swimming or baseball in the summer.

MAJORS AND DEGREES OFFERED

Eberly College offers a full-time, on-campus MBA program for young professionals and recent college graduates that can be completed in 12 months. In addition, an executive MBA program for experienced working professionals is available at IUP's off-campus sites in the Pittsburgh area. A Master of Education in Business and Workforce Development (M.Ed.) is also offered. The college offers undergraduate bachelor's degrees in accounting, business education, business technology support, entrepreneurship and small business management, finance, general management, human resource management, supply chain management, international business, management information systems, and marketing.

ACADEMIC PROGRAMS

The Eberly MBA is a 36-credit, integrated, general management program with an option to complete concentrations/specializations (nine additional credits) in accounting, finance, management information systems, supply chain management, international business, human resource management, and marketing. The MBA courses focus on business applications and current analytical tools and techniques and strongly emphasize information technology utilization in managerial problem solving. A wide variety of elective courses are available in the concentration areas. Opportunities are available for internships with local, national, and international organizations.

CAMPUS FACILITIES AND EQUIPMENT

A state-of-the-art, $12-million facility houses the MBA classrooms. The Eberly complex is a beautiful, four-story facility that offer a spacious atrium for student interaction and studying, wireless access, a café, a 450-seat auditorium, and a 24-hour computing lab operation. Students of the Eberly College study in one of the most technologically advanced business schools in the country. The Eberly complex houses more than 600 computer workstations; more than 20 file servers; nine computing labs, including a financial trading room; digital production studio; wireless technology; and access to comprehensive online business periodicals and journals databases. The college has a partnership with SAP America, the worldwide leader in ERP (Enterprise Resource Planning) software.

The Financial Trading Room in Eberly offers students databases and related software to conduct financial analysis and learn valuation techniques, arbitrage techniques, and portfolio risk-management strategies.

FINANCIAL AID

Tuition, Pennsylvania residents, 2007-2008; $3,107/semester

Tuition, non-Pennsylvania residents, 2007-2008: $4,972/semester

Miscellaneous fees are approximately $700/semester.

On-campus housing costs: from $1,670/semester (double) to $2,300/semester (single)

More than 30 percent of full-time MBA students receive graduate assistantships on a competitive basis that include a full- or partial-tuition waiver and stipend. International students are eligible to compete for partial-tuition waiver during the first semester of study.

ADMISSIONS PROCESS

Requirements for admission include a completed undergraduate degree in any field with a superior academic track record from an accredited institution, GMAT scores, academic/professional letters of recommendation, and the applicant's career goal statement. The average GMAT score of admitted candidates is 530; the average undergraduate grade point average is 3.1. International applicants must also submit an official TOEFL score report with a minimum score of 61 (iBT Score) and an affidavit of financial support indicating availability of funds to study in the U.S. For information and a complete application packet, visit www.eberly.iup.edu/mba; contact Dr. Krish Krishnan, Eberly College MBA Program, 301 Eberly College of Business and Information Technology, IUP, 664 Pratt Drive, Indiana, PA 15705; or e-mail iup-mba@iup.edu or Krishnan@iup.edu.

LOYOLA UNIVERSITY—NEW ORLEANS

AT A GLANCE

The business environment of today, and surely that of tomorrow, is characterized as one of constant change, uncertainty, and greater connectivity through technology. Our MBA program has been designed to prepare individuals to thrive in this dynamic, global marketplace.

At Loyola University New Orleans, we provide a distinctive mix of faculty excellence and individualized attention to create a superb learning environment in which you can excel. By studying with us, you will enhance your ability to critically analyze business issues, work in a team environment, appropriately apply technology, and effectively communicate your ideas. Equally important is the emphasis we place on providing you the foundation necessary to make ethical decisions in today's complex society.

Loyola's MBA program is composed of 54 credit hours. However, students with an undergraduate degree from an AACSB-accredited business school may waive up to 15 credit hours of the basic core classes. This program is ideal for business undergraduates and working professionals, but also works very well for students with non-business degrees. You decide how quickly you want to complete the program. Whether full-time or part-time, by attending evening classes, you have the opportunity to build your resume during the day through internships or participation in various organizations. Work experience is preferred, but not required, to support your application.

There are three key elements of the program: business ethics, leadership, and entrepreneurship, all taught with a global perspective. The average class size is 13 students, ensuring an interesting, interactive classroom experience.

STUDENTS

Loyola's MBA program is a small evening program that allows the MBA students to develop a close-knit community and group of friends. The main student group is the MBA Association, which provides leadership opportunities to interested students; it also coordinates community-service projects and schedules special events.

CAREER SERVICES AND PLACEMENT

Loyola maintains a Career Development Center to serve all undergraduate and graduate students of the university. Services include self-assessment instruments, career counseling, internship and job placement services, and guidance in resume writing, interviewing, job search, and salary negotiation skills. The office organizes on-campus recruiting events. The MBA Association also contributes by organizing networking events.

In recent years, Loyola MBAs have been placed with Chevron, Emeril's Homebase, Entergy, Ernst & Young, LLP, Harrah's Entertainment, Ochsner Health System, Shell, Target Corporation, and Whitney Bank.

LOCATION AND ENVIRONMENT

Loyola University New Orleans is located in the heart of the old residential section of New Orleans. This gracious southern city is one of the most fascinating in the United States. The fascination with New Orleans has grown stronger since Hurricane Katrina. While many areas of New Orleans were greatly affected by the hurricane, The French Quarter, The Central Business District (CBD), and St. Charles Avenue, where Loyola is located, were spared from the flood. New Orleans is facing a long road to recovery from Hurricane Katrina, but New Orleans is a resilient city that will overcome the challenges that lie ahead.

Often described as more European than American in nature, it is known for its jazz, cuisine, the French Quarter, café au lait, the architecture, streetcars, riverboats, a bustling seaport, the history, the writers, and Mardi Gras. New Orleans offers world-class events and facilities such as the New Orleans Jazz and Heritage Festival, the Crescent City Classic, the Sugar Bowl, the Audubon Zoo, and the Aquarium of the Americas. Music weaves through every aspect of life in the Crescent City, from one of the oldest opera companies in the nation to jazz bands in street parades.

Our school is located five miles, by streetcar, from the Central Business District on a historic avenue in the heart of one of the most beautiful neighborhoods. Across the street you will find Audubon Park, a perfect place to enjoy jogging and picnicking among ancient oak trees or strolling past tranquil lagoons to the Audubon Zoo and the Mississippi River.

MAJORS AND DEGREES OFFERED

Loyola University New Orleans offers a traditional MBA program that can be taken at a full-time or part-time basis. Additionally, we offer a JD/MBA program in coordination with the College of Law.

ACADEMIC PROGRAMS

Loyola's MBA program is an exceptionally flexible program. Students can choose to study part or full time; some students with business undergraduate degrees are able to finish in one calendar year. Students who have heavy outside obligations may want to take only three or four courses a year. You decide how quickly you want to complete the program.

Loyola's MBA Program is composed of 54 credit hours. However, students with an undergraduate degree from an AACSB-accredited business school may waive up to 15 credit hours of the Foundation Courses.

This program is ideal for business undergraduates and working professionals, but also works very well for students with non-business degrees. Whether full time or part time, by attending evening classes, students have the opportunity to build their resumes during the day either through internships or participating in various organizations. Work experience is preferred, but not required, to support this application.

There are three key elements to the program: business ethics, leadership, and entrepreneurship, all taught with a global perspective. Average class size is only 13 students, ensuring an interesting, interactive classroom experience.

Classes begin each fall and spring. Classes are taught in the evening and occasionally on Saturday. This allows you to continue working full-time or it can allow you to participate in internships to add to your MBA experience.

CAMPUS FACILITIES AND EQUIPMENT

The College of Business offers wireless Internet connections throughout the building and has a computer lab dedicated for business students.

Loyola's J. Edgar and Louise S. Monroe Library offers the latest in online technology, as well as traditional book and periodical references. Students and faculty have online computer network access at each table and study carrel, allowing more than 700 simultaneous computer links to millions of resources across the globe. It was named one of the ten best college libraries by Princeton Review in 2008.

FINANCIAL AID

Tuition for the 2008-2009 academic year is $807 per credit hour. For additional information about tuition and financial aid, please visit http://www.business.loyno.edu/mba/tuition.html.

ADMISSIONS PROCESS

Loyola requires the following of applicants to its MBA program: official transcripts for all pas postsecondary academic work; an official score report for the GMAT; two recommendation letters; a 400-word essay; and a resume. International students whose first language is not English must also submit TOEFL scores; all international students must provide an affidavit demonstrating sufficient financial resources to support themselves during their tenure at the university. Work experience, though not required, is strongly recommended.

MERCER UNIVERSITY

AT A GLANCE

Mercer University was founded in 1833. The University has 11 schools and colleges and four regional academic centers across the state of Georgia. Mercer is the only independent university of its size in the country to offer programs in 11 diversified fields of study.

The Eugene W. Stetson School of Business and Economics, established in 1984, provides a balanced curriculum that blends the theoretical with the application so students can put what they learn into practice immediately. Stetson School of Business and Economics is accredited by the Southern Association of Colleges and Schools (SACS) and the prestigious AACSB International— the Association to Advance Collegiate Schools of Business. The School offers a variety of graduate programs on the Atlanta campus.

FACULTY

The largest of Mercer's 10 schools and colleges, the Stetson School of Business and Economics has a faculty of 40 full-time and 20 adjunct members. The School's accomplished faculty members bring real-world business experiences to the classroom as well as educational knowledge from some of the nation's most prestigious institutions of higher education. With a steadfast commitment to students, faculty members place an emphasis on research and writing to ensure that students are taught the newest thoughts and trend, alongside the time-test theories and practices used in business.

STUDENTS

The Atlanta campus caters to adult learners with classes offered in the evenings or on weekends, with 546 students in the Stetson School of Business and Economics.

LOCATION AND ENVIRONMENT

The Cecil B. Day Graduate and Professional Campus of Mercer University is located on a superb tract of approximately 300 beautifully wooded acres in northeast Atlanta. The campus is easily accessed from two interstate highways, I-85 and I-285. Located in one of the major growth corridors of Atlanta, the campus is conveniently close to a rapidly growing business and corporate environment, as well as to an expanding population base. To find more information on the Atlanta campus, please go to

http://www2.mercer.edu/StudentLife/Atlanta/default.htm

MAJORS AND DEGREES OFFERED

- Master of Business Administration (MBA) - The Flexible MBA classes meet once per week for eight weeks in the evenings or on Saturdays. Mercer's MBA program is committed to small class sizes, a highly credentialed teaching faculty, and specializations that meet students' areas of interest through a Personalized Portfolio of Study (PPS). The MBA curriculum includes four foundation courses, seven core courses, four electives in the PPS, and a capstone course for a total of 36 hours.

- Professional Masters of Business Administration (PMBA)- This is a sixteen month cohort program, meeting every other weekend, designed for business professionals with four years or more of experience. The program includes a trip to a major commercial and financial center within the United States; the trip serves as the focal point for much of the team-based activity within the program.

- Executive Masters of Business Administration (EMBA) - The EMBA is a sixteen month cohort program for individuals with at least seven years of significant business experience, including some managerial experience. Classes are held on Friday afternoons from 1:00 - 7:00 pm and all day Saturday from 8:00 am - 6:00 pm every other week. The EMBA has an international focus and the weeklong Best Practices Field Residency is to an international destination.

ACADEMIC PROGRAMS

Study abroad programs for MBA students are offered each year, usually in the summer. The Executive MBA students attend a field residency at an international destination.

SPECIAL PROGRAMS

Mercer University's Executive Forum is Georgia's premier business enrichment program. Founded in 1979, it is an invaluable resource for the business community and professionals by presenting high-quality management and leadership speakers on timely topics. Benefits for members include business networking opportunities, employee development skills and knowledge of current business trends.

CAMPUS FACILITIES AND EQUIPMENT

The Cecil B. Day Graduate and Professional Campus in Atlanta is comprised of eight major academic buildings. Other facilities include the Student Center, the I.M. Sheffield Jr. Physical Education Complex, a cafeteria, copy center, and the Monroe F. Swilley Jr. Library. The Stetson School of Business is housed in a modern building with classrooms, presentation rooms, computer labs, faculty offices, student lounges and study carrels, team breakout rooms, and other facilities specifically designed for working adult students with busy lives.

FINANCIAL AID

Mercer University assesses tuition and fees each term and keeps the cost of education at a reasonable level to help qualified students finance a Mercer education. Many types of financial assistance are available along with payment plans. To inquire about the cost of a specific program please go to http://atlanta.merceraid.com/.

ADMISSIONS PROCESS

Applicants seeking graduate admission must have a bachelor's (undergraduate) degree with an acceptable grade point average from an accredited college or university. The degree may be in any discipline. There are five admission points of entry each year.

The application process is:

- Complete the online application (https://www.mercer.edu/admissions/ SecureForms/atlssbeapply.shtm).
- Submit official GMAT score.
- Submit one official transcript from each college and university attended
- Attend a personal interview with faculty.

Additional requirements for international applicants are listed on the MBA admissions website http://www2.mercer.edu/Business/Admissions/ MBA_Atlanta.htm

MIP

AT A GLANCE

MIP was born out of the partnership between the University Politecnico di Milano, the first technology institution in Italy, and some of the most important Italian and international multinationals. Its International MBA program offers students real business-world experience and international exposure.

FACULTY

The faculty composes of professors from Politecnico di Milano, visiting professors from other universities and consultants from the business world. In 2007/2008 academic year, there are in total 98 professors and 41% of them are visiting professors or speakers from the business world.

CAREER SERVICES AND PLACEMENT

The Career Services provide individual counseling and personal development activities to support our students to get to where they want. They establish contacts with potential recruiters to allow our students to gain access to the available job opportunities.

2007 Placement Statistics

Within three months of graduation, 90% of the 2007 MBA class received job offers in the following sectors: Manufacturing(52%), Financial Services(3%), Consulting Services(21%) and Other Services(21%).

Countries of employment include Italy, Germany, Brazil, Turkey, UK, USA, China, Japan, Belgium, Luxemburg, Switzerland and The Netherlands.

Companies that hire our graduates include ABB, Accenture, Acer, Bain, BCG,

Berloni, Borsa Italiana, Capgemini, Eli Lilly, Ferrari, Fiat Group, Gucci, Indesit,

Italcementi Group, Magneti Marelli, Manulli Rubber, Mediolanum, Procter&Gamble,

Siemens, Sky, Sorgenia, Vodafone and Whirlpool.

LOCATION AND ENVIRONMENT

In 2007/2008, the business school has 830 students pursuing their programs of MBA (International Class & Italian Class and Evening MBA), Executive MBA and Master in Strategic Project management. However, the MBA class places a strong emphasis on small class setting to allow optimal students and professors interaction.

The campus is located at:

Via Garofalo 39
20133 Milan
Italy

MAJORS AND DEGREES OFFERED

The International MBA last for 14 months with concentrations in Design & Luxury Management, Finance, International Business and Management, ICT Management and New Product & Venture Development. At the end of the MBA program, students are required to perform a 3 months project work in a company.

The Dual Degree in MBA & Master in International Business is offered by MIP and The Chapman Graduate School of Business at Florida International University. The program is carried out in Milan and Miami.

ACADEMIC PROGRAMS

The unique parts of our program include Business Plan, Business Game and Project Work.

Students will have a chance to participate in exchange programs abroad in France, Belgium, Greece and India.

CAMPUS FACILITIES AND EQUIPMENT

Internet access, discounted price for gym subscription, etc.

FINANCIAL AID

Tuition Fee is 24,500 euros. (including participation fee, didactic material, internet access in the campus)

The cost of living is around 1000euros every month.

Scholarships are merit-based and need-based.

The following financial aid is available:

- Companies scholarships
- Special partial scholarships offered by the Chamber of Commerce for International students
- MIP contributions covering from 25% to 50% of the tuition fee
- MIP assistantship covering 50% of the tuition fee. (The chosen students will be required to work approximately 8 hours per week inside MIP)
- Italian Cultural Centers. (Students should contact the local Italian institute to find out if it offers special scholarships for students studying in Italy.)

ADMISSIONS PROCESS

The admissions requirements are outlined below:

- University degree or equivalent from an accredited institution
- Official university transcripts
- Good GMAT score ° (The average was 620 for the class 2007)
- Certificate of English Proficiency. We accept TOEFL, IELTS, Toiec, Cambridge Certificate of Advanced English (C1) or Certificate of Proficiency in English (C2).
- 2 letters of reference.

MISSOURI STATE UNIVERSITY

AT A GLANCE
The College of Business Administration (COBA) at Missouri State University is the largest public AACSB accredited College of Business in Missouri and in the Midwest Region, with approximately 4,600 students. Meeting rigorous AACSB International (The Association to Advance Collegiate Schools of Business) accreditation standards means that the College and the University have committed the necessary resources to achieve and maintain a high quality, nationally competitive program. Meeting these criteria also insures that COBA graduate students will be taught by terminally-degreed faculty, who are actively publishing in their disciplines. According to COBA graduate students at Missouri State, educational value is defined by a high quality program, low tuition rates, and low living costs in an attractive, safe environment.

FACULTY
The College of Business employs 118 full-time and 40 part-time faculty. A total of 95 percent of the full-time faculty hold doctorates. Many faculty have received state and national recognition for accomplishments in teaching and research.

STUDENT BODY
As our graduate students come from the ranks of working professionals, traditional students and a significant percentage being international, such diversity offers the opportunity for students to share a broad range of perspectives on global business events. International students make up approximately 30% of the graduate student population and represent 32 countries from around the world.

CAREER SERVICES AND PLACEMENT
Students are assisted in their career search by the Career Services Center located within the College of Business in Glass Hall. Resume preparation assistance, enhancement of interviewing techniques, and internship placement assistance are some of the services provided. Each fall, over 200 firms visit the College of Business during the annual COBA Career Fair and/or recruit on campus.

LOCATION AND ENVIRONMENT
The Missouri State University campus is located in the heart of Springfield, Missouri.

Updated campus amenities include a recently expanded library and the latest in technology access and offerings.

MAJORS AND DEGREES OFFERED
The College of Business at Missouri State includes six academic departments of Accounting, Computer Information Systems, Finance, Industrial Management, Management, and Marketing, offering a total of 25 undergraduate and graduate majors.

COBA has five graduate programs, including the Master of Accountancy, Master of Business Administration, Master of Science in Computer Information Systems, Master of Health Administration and Master of Project Management.

ACADEMIC PROGRAMS
The Master of Accountancy program is designed to fulfill the education needs of professional accountants. The mission of the program is to offer graduate students the opportunity to build upon the foundation of their undergraduate program and to enhance their business common body of knowledge and specialized accounting knowledge beyond the undergraduate level.

The Missouri State MBA program has an important strength — flexibility. Along with integrating a variety of courses offered by six departments in the College of Business Administration, the MBA program allows students the opportunity to tailor their degree to meet their career needs. Apart from the 21 credits of required courses, students may choose an area of concentration (12 credits) to help focus their MBA degree. Most courses used to fulfill area of concentration requirements are business courses, but some individuals find that their specific interests and needs require coursework from other areas of study. This flexibility gives MBA graduates the opportunity to structure an MBA degree to match their interests. If needed, Missouri State's program provides a solid foundation of prerequisite graduate-level courses that prepare students for the advanced topics covered in the core MBA program. Students with appropriate prior academic preparation in business will be able to complete the 33 credit program in one calendar year.

The MS CIS Program is an accelerated course of study leading to a Master of Science in Computer Information Systems degree. Developed exclusively for Information Technology professionals with three or more years of work experience, the program enables students to earn an accredited MS CIS degree in just 23 months without interrupting their careers. Students spend only two weeks each year on campus (one week in July and one week in January). The remainder of the course work is completed via distance learning.

The Master of Health Administration degree includes a number of health management and policy courses contributed by Public Health, Economics & Political Science in addition to courses taught by business faculty. The program is designed for students holding undergraduate degrees who wish to further their careers in the administration of health organizations.

CAMPUS FACILITIES AND ENVIRONMENT
COBA is housed in David D. Glass Hall, an 185,000 square foot state-of-the-art building containing classrooms, four computer classrooms and four computer labs supplied with the latest technological equipment.

The Meyer Library recently underwent a renovation/expansion project which doubled library space. New facilities include a significant area for Special Collections and Archives, electronic classrooms and media labs for student and faculty use. The addition also includes 12 group study rooms, 19 faculty studies, 10 multimedia workrooms for teams of students, and multimedia workstations for individual use.

FINANCIAL AID
Tuition for the 2008-07 is $214 per credit hour for in state students. Out of state resident tuition is $418. Graduate assistantships are available which cover the cost of tuition and also provide a stipend. Such assistantships are awarded on a competitive basis and require the student to work for 20 hours per week.

ADMISSIONS PROCESS
Admission requirements for the various COBA graduate programs vary. For specific admission information for a particular graduate program, visit the website at www.coba.missouristate.edu. Qualified applicants may enter the program at the beginning of any semester, including the summer.

NEW JERSEY INSTITUTE OF TECHNOLOGY

AT A GLANCE
Make the next 12-18 months really count-get an advanced degree from NJIT's top-ranked business school.

NJIT has a flexible schedule-attend classes weekends, nights and online.

The New Jersey Institute of Technology's business school is an outstanding value. Our fast-paced advanced degree programs for working professionals turn out successful entrepreneurs and top-level Fortune 1000 executives alike. Taught by award-winning professors, technology experts and A-list business leaders, the NJIT SOM curriculum is based on the progressive teaching methods of blended learning and directed study. Our degree programs concentrate on leading-edge business strategies and technology management, producing well-rounded executives ready to face the opportunities and challenges of business in the global marketplace.

Students and faculty at the NJIT School of Management enjoy the benefits of being part of a renowned technological research university. In partnership with the College of Computing Sciences, our business school offers specialization areas in management information systems and e-commerce. This gives our students the opportunity to learn the latest management strategies and the newest technological breakthroughs. SOM also collaborates with the Newark College of Engineering, offering students the option to take elective courses in engineering management and manufacturing engineering. Foreign study and foreign study immersion tours are also offered. For undergraduates, SOM offers a Bachelor of Science in Management program with an accelerated 1-year master's degree.

Less than 10% of the world's business schools have achieved the honor of business accreditation from the Association to Advance Collegiate Schools of Business. The AACSB designation insures NJIT's business school students the highest standards and best practices in advanced degree education.

CAMPUS AND LOCATION
Whether you're a current student who needs assistance or you want to learn more about our programs, our office is here to help.

Campus Location: Central Avenue Building, 3rd floor
Office Hours: Monday-Friday, 8:30 am to 4:30 pm
Phone: 973-596-3248
Fax: 973-596-3074
New Jersey Institute of Technology
School of Management
University Heights
Newark, NJ 07102-9938

DEGREES OFFERED
NJIT's School of Management weaves the whys and hows of technology throughout the curriculum. Through rigorous and comprehensive coursework, students learn to solve problems, make effective decisions, and use innovation to get ahead in business.

We offer a BS in Business, an MS in Management, an MBA, an Executive MBA, and Minor in Business.

The MBA Program
Our MBA is a 48-credit program focused on meeting the challenges of an increasingly complex and technologically driven business environment. It is offered as both a full- and part-time program with evening, weekend and online courses.

Our part-time MBA is designed to ensure that students have the flexibility they need to complete the program in a timely manner while meeting their professional responsibilities.

Concentrations are available in: E-commerce, Finance, Marketing, MIS, Operations management

The Executive MBA (EMBA)
Designed for working professionals, our accelerated, 18-month, 48-credit program prepares high potential managers and entrepreneurs for leadership positions.

Our Innovative EMBA Curriculum: Directed Study, Blended Learning and Saturday Classes

The accredited Executive MBA degree prepares students with leading-edge tools and strategies to manage business in a rapid-paced global economy. Renowned as a leader in technology education, NJIT equips MBA candidates with the added capacity to manage technology-a competitive advantage in today's high-tech business environment.

NJIT's business school's innovative curriculum is based on the progressive teaching methods of blended learning and directed study. The emphasis is on putting forward-thinking management strategies to work in traditional corporate settings. Our solution-focused program consists of 10-week learning modules, followed by a faculty-led team challenge that puts students' new-found knowledge and skills to the test in real-world business situations.

PROGRAMS AND CURRICULUM
Get Involved
There are several clubs and organizations for business students. We encourage you to learn more about them and become involved in something that interests you. Faculty advisors to student organizations work with club members to arrange for visits to leading companies in the region, bring in guest speakers from industry, and offer seminars on careers in business and management. These are very valuable experiences that will enhance your time at NJIT and the School of Management.

Get Connected
SOM supports a student run e-community that gives students the opportunity to share ideas, socialize and get to know each other. The community is hosted on the Highlander Pipeline campus portal, and membership is restricted to business students and requires a valid UCID.

Get Going
There are many informal activities on campus that are an important part of student life. Since business students take courses in leadership, strategy, and performance management, they should do better in competitive sports. Why not put this hypothesis to the test and join one of our intramural sports teams?

STUDENTS
NJIT's EMBA candidates are a microcosm of America's business and ethnic diversity, providing the perfect laboratory for cross-industry collaboration and peer-to-peer networking.

Industries served by our MBA students include education, finance, government, health care, internet, manufacturing, non-profits, telecommunications, transportation and more.

ADMISSIONS
Visit us at: http://som.njit.edu/index.php

The School of Management is proud to affirm its commitment to attracting a diverse student body. We believe that diversity enriches the educational process and represents an important advantage to our students. NJIT has one of the most diverse campuses in the United States, ranking among the nation's leading schools for graduating minority students into the management profession.

NORTH CAROLINA STATE UNIVERSITY

AT A GLANCE

At NC State's Jenkins Graduate School of Management, we've created an MBA with focus. The NC State MBA Program will help you develop a keen understanding of general business and management principles. And your concentrated study of a technology-oriented business process or function will give you an edge in the marketplace.

The NC State MBA offers both a full-time program and part-time evening program.

Our focus on outstanding MBA education is illustrated by a reputation for excellence in technology management, an innovative faculty with cutting-edge teaching and research, quality students from diverse backgrounds, and unmatched value in management education.

CAMPUS AND LOCATION

NC State was founded in 1887 as a land-grant institution that has become one of the nation's leading research universities. Located in the Research Triangle, a world-renowned center of research, industry, and technology, the College of Management is housed on the 2,110-acre main campus of NC State, which lies just west of downtown Raleigh, the state capital. NC State comprises eleven colleges and schools, serving a total student population of over 30,000.

DEGREES OFFERED

MBA—Master of Business Administration: Full-time (56 credit hours) and part-time (47 credit hours) programs. Concentrations: BioPharma Management, Entrepreneurship & Technology Commercialization, Financial Management, Marketing Management, Product Innovation Management, Services Management, and Supply Chain Management

ACADEMIC PROGRAMS

The NC State MBA curriculum was designed to prepare students for management careers and to provide unique offerings of technology-oriented courses and concentrations. The curriculum is built around core classes in the basics of management, a specialized concentration and open electives.

Your MBA concentration will give you an opportunity to focus your studies on a specialized technology process or critical business function. Each concentration includes some required courses and a choice among electives in that field, and most require students to complete a semester-long team project by working closely with a corporate client to solve a relevant business problem.

No matter what your background, you will be surrounded by classmates with a wide range of experience. In some of the technical courses, you will work on projects with students from NC State's highly regarded graduate programs in computer science, engineering, design, and the sciences.

FACILITIES

The College of Management is located in Nelson Hall, which houses classrooms, computer labs, and the offices of the faculty members and students. Classrooms have been completely remodeled with tiered seating, laptop connections, and complete multimedia facilities. Nelson Hall is also wireless accessible.

EXPENSES AND FINANCIAL AID

The estimated annual tuition for the 2007-2008 school year is $12,261 for North Carolina residents in the full-time program and $7,674 for North Carolina residents in the part-time program. For non-residents, the estimated annual tuition for the 2007-2008 school year is $24,184 for students in the full-time program and $16,616 for students in the part-time program.

Graduate assistantships are available to full-time students. Graduate assistantships cover tuition, health insurance, and a monthly stipend. Grants and loan programs are available through the Graduate School and the University's Financial Aid Office.

FACULTY

The College of Management has built a faculty rich in technology-related business expertise, management experience and practical research. Our professors also have a passion for teaching and a commitment to working closely with industry to solve real-world problems. Our faculty excel in both traditional scholarly pursuits and practical, corporate-sponsored research. We are home to a number of extensively published scholars, and editors and editorial board members of prestigious research journals.

STUDENTS

Almost all MBA students have professional work experience, many in high-technology industries, such as telecommunications or software and others in industries, such as health care or financial services. A technical background is not essential for the MBA, but all students must be willing to learn about technology and the management challenges it creates.

The average full-time MBA student has four years of work experience. The age range of students is between 22 and 45. Women comprise approximately 26 percent of each entering class; members of minority groups, approximately 12 percent; and international students, 29 percent.

ADMISSIONS

Admission to the MBA program is highly competitive. Applicants need to demonstrate the following personal accomplishments and attributes:

1. Strong intellectual performance and academic promise, evidenced by previous undergraduate and graduate work as well as GMAT scores

2. An employment history demonstrating management potential

3. Leadership skills, maturity, creativity, initiative and teamwork orientation

4. A desire and willingness to learn about technology and the management challenges it creates

MBA students must have a baccalaureate degree from an accredited college or university. Admissions decisions are based on previous academic performance, GMAT scores (610 average), essays, letters of reference, and previous work experience. Applicants whose native language is other than English, regardless of citizenship, must also submit TOEFL scores of at least 250 (computer-based test). Interviews are required for applicants for both the full-time and part-time MBA programs.

SPECIAL PROGRAMS

The NC State MBA Program now offers a joint masters degrees in Microbial Biotechnology, Veterinary Medicine, and Accounting.

CAREER SERVICES AND PLACEMENT

MBA students have access to a wide range of programs and services to enhance their marketability, including career counseling and workshops on resume writing, cover letters, interviewing, and job search strategies. In addition to on-campus recruiting for permanent jobs and internships, the Career Resource Center maintains an online resume referral and job posting service, hosts job fairs, and maintains a library of information about career opportunities with specific companies.

NOVA SOUTHEASTERN UNIVERSITY

AT A GLANCE

Located on a beautiful 300-acre campus in Fort Lauderdale, Nova Southeastern University has more than 26,000 students. It is the largest independent institution of higher education in the Southeast, and it is the 6th largest independent institution nationally. NSU's H. Wayne Huizenga School of Business and Entrepreneurship is the only school in the nation with entrepreneurship in its name, which says a lot about who we are. In addition to being the largest MBA program in Florida, the Huizenga School offers bachelor's, master's and doctoral degrees to more than 7,000 students.

FACULTY

The Huizenga School has more than 50 full-time faculty members. Criteria for the selection of the full-time faculty members include teaching effectiveness, field experience, and research and publication. The faculty members at NSU's business school are both academically and practically experienced, bringing a real-world education to each classroom.

CAREER SERVICES AND PLACEMENT

Career Services provides services to all students from the time they enter the university throughout their career. Contact NSU Career Services at www.nova.edu/career for information on programs, accessing your career consultant, job leads, the Career Track model, eRecruiting, choosing a career, and much more.

LOCATION AND ENVIRONMENT

Near, far, wherever you are...It is our belief that every student with the desire to take advantage of the innovative programs offered at NSU's Huizenga School should be able to do so. In this spirit, we have established more than 30 locations worldwide where students can participate in the unique educational opportunities we have available. In addition, we offer online programs for those who prefer them.

MAJORS AND DEGREES OFFERED

At the Huizenga School, we've created an environment where tomorrow's leaders and entrepreneurs can gain the skills and confidence that will change the landscape of business. The Huizenga School's flexible programs are designed for working professionals. We offer part-time or full-time classes, during the day, evenings, or weekends. Classes are available on campus, corporate sites or online. Online program formats include chat rooms, e-mail, bulletin board, and etc.

Bachelor's Programs: Accounting, Business Administration, Economics, Finance, Management, Marketing, Sport and Recreation Management

MBA Programs: Entrepreneurship, Finance, Real Estate Development

Master's Programs: Accounting, Business Administration, Human Resource Management, International Business Administration, Public Administration, Taxation, Leadership

Doctoral Programs: Business Administration

SPECIAL PROGRAMS

The Hudson Institute of Entrepreneurship and Executive Education at Nova Southeastern University offers executive education programs that help organizations become more effective in the 21st century. To us, executive education equals practical concepts, strategies, and competencies that can be applied to relevant business challenges and enhanced professional development. Our programs emphasize superior organizational performance by analyzing the root cause of problems, assessing change, and providing unique training instruction and content that impact shifting strategic directions and influence managerial advancement.

FINANCIAL AID

Nova Southeastern University offers a comprehensive program of financial aid to assist students in meeting educational expenses. In order to qualify and remain eligible for financial aid, students must be fully admitted into a university program; eligible for continued enrollment; a United States citizen, national, or permanent resident; and making satisfactory academic progress toward a stated educational objective in accordance with the university's policy on satisfactory progress for financial aid recipients. For information on sources of financial aid and for application forms, please call free: (800) 806-3680.

ADMISSIONS PROCESS

Master's Admissions: Applications for our Master's degree programs are individually reviewed and admission is offered to those applicants who meet both qualitative and quantitative criteria. All required documentation must be received before an admission decision can be offered.

Required documentation:

1. Completed Master's Application for Admission and non-refundable $50 application fee.

2. Evidence of conferral of baccalaureate degree from a regionally accredited institution.

3. Overall undergraduate GPA of 2.50 or greater on a 4.00 scale as reflected on official, final transcripts of all undergraduate institutions attended. Applicants will be considered eligible for admission if their undergraduate GPA in the final 60 hours of their enrollment is a 2.50 or greater on a 4.00 scale.

4. GMAT (Graduate Management Admission Test) or GRE (Graduate Record Examination) scores are required of all applicants who have earned a 2.25-2.49 cumulative undergraduate GPA or who have earned a GPA of 2.25-2.49 in the last 60 hours of their undergraduate program. The minimum acceptable GMAT score is 450. The minimum accepted GRE score is 1,000.

NYENRODE BUSINESS UNIVERSITEIT

AT A GLANCE

Situated just 20 minutes south of Amsterdam in the grounds of a 13th century castle, Nyenrode Business Universiteit was created by business for business. Founded in 1946, the university has a wide portfolio of business education programs, and has extensive links with the Dutch and international business communities. Its teaching philosophy is geared towards developing globally minded business leaders and managers, fostering leadership and true entrepreneurial spirit within rigorous and demanding academic programs.

Nyenrode Business Universiteit also offers a range of English-and Dutch-taught management education programs, ranging from in-company to open programs,

STUDENTS

Nyenrode graduates have a reputation for entrepreneurial prowess. We look for evidence of lateral thinking, self-discipline, and emotional intelligence. The student needs to demonstrate that you set high standards for yourself, think outside the box, and work well with those around you.

Our International MBA class typically counts between 20 and 40 students per year, and 90% of our student body is International. The average age is 30 and students have approximately 5 years of working experience before starting the program.

Students also come from a variety of professional backgrounds, we currently have students coming from the music industry, consultancy, IT, engineering, or telecommunications.

Once they graduate, our students become part of our global alumni network, which consists of over 15.000 professionals worldwide.

CAREER SERVICES AND PLACEMENT

The Nyenrode Career Services is designed to act as a link between students and alumni and companies. The team aims to enable Nyenrode students with the skills needed for lifelong career management and provide the corporate base both national and international, the opportunities to get in contact with our students.

Provided services for students: Careers fair, company presentations , job opportunities , one-to-one counseling, workshops

Provided services for companies: Careers fair, company presentations, CV's online, Interview possibilities, job platform, projects/Thesis

LOCATION AND ENVIRONMENT

The Nyenrode estate radiates a unique atmosphere. Nestled in a typically Dutch landscape, it combines the allure of olden times - with its Castle and long tradition of education - with a modern and leading role in education and entrepreneurship. The deer park, maze, rose garden, walking and jogging routes through the woods, an avenue with age-old chestnut trees - these are just a few of the features that make the campus so exceptional in the Netherlands.

MAJORS AND DEGREES OFFERED

Nyenrode offers graduate level programs in the fields of general management, as well as accountancy and controlling:

The Master of Science in Management

Combining theory, practice and personal development, the MSc in Management takes 16 months to complete and starts every August.

The International MBA

Including an international module at the Kellogg School of Management, the International MBA takes 13 months to complete and starts every October.

Part-time MBA

The Part-time MBA helps you gain the internationally respected MBA title while combining work and study in just 21 months. It includes international modules in the US and South Africa. Starts every April

ACADEMIC PROGRAMS

The International MBA is a general management MBA that takes 13 months to complete. Combining theory and practice, the program also features an international module at the Kellogg School of Management, USA.

CAMPUS FACILITIES AND EQUIPMENT

Apart from the Nyenrode castle, the campus has a library, campus housing, sporting facilities (tennis courts, rugby field, on-campus gym, jogging tracks) but also has 2 restaurants, 1 hotel and the Plesman building which has an Executive room, a bar, lounge and a reading cellar. The Plesman pavilion also has cozy rooms for overnight stay.

Also, the Nyenrode Start-up Accelerator facilitates and stimulates the creation of new companies set up by Nyenrode graduates and faculty members.

FINANCIAL AID

Loan opportunities

An exclusive study financing package is offered by ABN AMRO Bank to international applicants for our International MBA. The financial package can be used to cover not only tuition fees, but also accommodation and general expenses.

Scholarships

Through the contributions of Nyenrode Business Universiteit, Nyenrode alumni, and companies, the university is in a position to offer a significant number of scholarships for the 2008/2009 IMBA program.

Nyenrode Scholarships are awarded on the basis of the student's application as well as an additional essay competition. In addition to the scholarship, each winner will be assigned an experienced business manager as a personal coach during the course of the program.

ADMISSIONS PROCESS

In order to apply for the International MBA program, you will need to fulfill the following requirements:

• A minimum of three (3) years of work experience

• A university degree (or equivalent) with an excellent academic record

• A thorough command of written and spoken English

• Acceptable score on the Graduate Management Admission Test (GMAT)

• Acceptable score on either the TOEFL or the IELTS tests for non-native English speakers

• An application package, including 5 written essays and 2 letters of recommendation

• A selection interview, which takes place after the complete application package has been reviewed by our Admissions Committee.

The application deadline for students requiring a visa is July 1, and for students not requiring a visa is August 31.

The application deadline for scholarships is May 31.

PACIFIC LUTHERAN UNIVERSITY
School of Business

AT A GLANCE

Pacific Lutheran University has a long tradition of providing excellent undergraduate (BBA) and graduate (MBA) business education. The School of Business has been accredited by AACSB International since 1976 and enjoys a strong reputation among businesses locally and globally.

The MBA program is distinct in approach and design to meet the needs of working professionals, including convenient evening classes. The program takes 20-22 months to complete (or 16 months for those students who are looking for an accelerated program) and students have the option of tailoring their coursework to earn a general management MBA, or an MBA with an emphasis in Technology & Innovation Management, Entrepreneurship & Closely Held Business, or Health Care Management.

The dynamic curriculum focuses on four cornerstones: (1) global perspective and appreciation for diversity, (2) an ethical decision and responsible approach to decisions, (3) effective leadership, and 4) a predisposition for innovation and change. The 10 day international experience is included in tuition.

The BBA program combines a rigorous upper division curriculum with a strong liberal arts foundation. Students tailor their degree with one of the four concentrations: Finance, Management and Human Resources, Marketing, and Professional Accounting. The BBA program takes a hands-on approach to education emphasizing internships and international study away programs.

CAMPUS AND LOCATION

Pacific Lutheran University is located in Tacoma, Washington, one hour south of Seattle. It is a port city along the Puget Sound and enjoys a maritime climate. Residents of Washington enjoy the natural beauty of the Pacific Northwest and easy access to outdoor activities— skiing, biking, hiking, kayaking, and sailing. Tacoma also hosts thriving theatre and arts communities.

DEGREES OFFERED

Bachelor of Business Administration (BBA)

Master of Business Administration (MBA)

Dual Degree in MBA/MSN (Master of Business Administration and Master of Science in Nursing)

FACILITIES

The Morken Center for Learning and Technology is home to the School of Business. The $21 million facility, completed in 2006, is LEED Certified Gold by the U.S. Green Building Council for environmental friendliness and conservation. Morken has wireless access, lab classrooms, research labs, project workrooms, a multimedia lab, electronics lab, lounge areas, a café, and a public events room.

EXPENSES AND FINANCIAL AID

PLU offers academically rigorous classes, a supportive campus community unlike any other, and preparation for success in the world – your time and money will be well spent.

2008–09: Undergraduate tuition is $26,800 per year. The MBA program charges a per-course tuition rate of $2,727, which is guaranteed for six consecutive enrolled semesters. Based on a 15 course curriculum, the total MBA program tuition is $40,905

FACULTY

All School of Business faculty are doctorally qualified, with the exception of the Executive in Residence, and have significant industry and international experience. This means that students are engaging with real business leaders with global experience every day in the classroom. Faculty members are both leading researchers and publishers in their fields and dedicated teachers, always accessible to students. All PLU classes are taught by professors—there are no teaching assistants.

STUDENTS

PLU is a selective university. The average incoming undergraduate GPA is 3.60, and graduate GPA is 3.30. It is recommended that applicants to the MBA program have at least two years of work experience, creating a population of peers with a wealth of experience to share in the classroom. The average age in the MBA program is 31.

ADMISSIONS

Undergraduate: PLU welcomes applications from students who exhibit capacities for success at the university level. We look for students who:

- Demonstrate success in a challenging college preparatory curriculum
- Desire academic and personal challenges
- Communicate clearly
- Serve in their community, church or school
- Will share unique or special talents

Each application is reviewed based on grade point average, class rank, transcript patterns, standardized test scores, personal essay, and an academic recommendation. Applications for admission are evaluated without regard to race, color, national origin, creed, religion, age, gender, sexual orientation, disabling conditions, financial resources or any other status protected by law. Please visit www.plu.edu/external/admission/home.php for application information.

Graduate: Admission to the MBA program is competitive and selection is based on several criteria including a holistic assessment of the merits of each applicant. We look for students who:

- Have demonstrated success in a challenging undergraduate or master's level program
- Desire academic, personal and career challenges
- Communicate clearly and demonstrate leadership capability in a variety of settings
- Serve in their community, workplace, church or school
- Will bring a unique perspective to the classroom environment

For application information please visit www.plu.edu/mba/admission.html.

SPECIAL PROGRAMS

The MBA program, with the generous support of State Farm, the PLU Business Network Alumni Association and the Dwight Zulauf Fund, sponsors the annual MBA Executive Leadership Series bringing in business executives to share their insights and stories with MBA students and the business community. This is a networking opportunity and an invaluable experience for students to hear first hand about current trends in industry.

CAREER SERVICES AND PLACEMENT

The School of Business partners with the Career Development & Student Employment Office to mentor students in the job search. The School of Business also has a mentorship program that matches alumni with students. The PLU Business Network Alumni Association sponsors networking events and career planning workshops.

For more information please contact us at School of Business, Pacific Lutheran University, Tacoma, Washington, 98447, business@plu.edu, or 253-535-7244, www.plu.edu/busa.

PITTSBURG STATE UNIVERSITY
Gladys A. Kelce School of Business

AT A GLANCE

Pittsburg State University, located in Pittsburg, Kansas, is a comprehensive public university established in 1903. The Graduate School was established in 1929, and has grown to include more than 50 programs in 30 majors within four colleges. The Graduate School grants degrees on two levels: the master's degree and the Specialist in Education. Evening courses, off-campus locations for many programs, and a variety of online courses are offered.

The Kelce College of Business, accredited by the AACSB-International Association for Management Education, recognizes the importance of preparing students to meet the challenges of the global workplace. The Master of Business Administration degree (MBA) is a professional program designed to prepare future business executives to join the corporate ranks or start their own business. Pittsburg State University offers an MBA degree with concentrations in accounting, general administration, or international business. The MBA is designed to accommodate students from diverse educational backgrounds and interests. Approximately 40% of the students admitted to the MBA program do not have undergraduate degrees in business administration.

FACULTY

The College of Business has a dedicated faculty whose hard work helped PSU achieve AACSB accreditation. There are 28 full-time faculty members in the College of Business, all with doctoral degrees.

STUDENTS

Graduate students number approximately 1,200 at PSU. MBA students total approximately 120 each semester.

LOCATION AND ENVIRONMENT

Pittsburg State University (PSU) is a safe and beautiful campus located on 484 acres in southeast Kansas. Pittsburg, Kansas, is a college town whose 20,000 residents are happy to have the University at its center.

There is campus-wide wireless Internet access and state-of-the-art facilities with mediated classrooms.

PSU is constructing and renovating several buildings, increasing parking spaces, and doing everything possible to make student life easier. At Pitt State, students come first!

ACADEMIC PROGRAMS

Master of Business Administration Degree with a Major in Accounting, General Administration, or International Business.

For additional information, visit: www.pittstate.edu/kelce

For information regarding the more than 50 programs in 30 majors at PSU visit: www.pittstate.edu/cgs

CAMPUS FACILITIES AND EQUIPMENT

PSU is a wireless campus of 484 acres and has state-of-the-art mediated classrooms.

Graduate students may live in any of the residence halls. Crimson Village apartments are available to all full-time PSU students with families who meet HUD income requirements.

Library holdings of 1 million items.

PSU is constructing and renovating campus buildings and increasing parking.

FINANCIAL AID

For current tuition and fees visit: www.pittstate.edu/registrar/fees.html

ADMISSIONS PROCESS

For admission requirements visit: www.pittstate.edu/cgs/ProspectiveStudents/AdmissionRequirements.html

RENSSELAER POLYTECHNIC INSTITUTE
Lally School of Management

AT A GLANCE

The Lally School of Management and Technology was founded in 1963 as an integral part of Rensselaer Polytechnic Institute. Building on Rensselaer's heritage of more than 175 years of leadership in science and engineering, the Lally School develops technologically-savvy, entrepreneurial business leaders who can initiate and guide innovation for commercial success. All programs enable the next generation of business leaders to combine their passion for technology with the management ability to succeed in today's challenging global marketplace.

FACULTY

Working in a highly collegial setting, Lally's faculty are scholars of significant standing and deep experience in a wide range of business contexts.

Our research-oriented faculty focus on advancing business through using the basic disciplines of economics, behavioral science, and analytical methods.

Our clinical faculty strive to exploit their experience and professional expertise to turn theory into practice. They bring real world business experiences into the Lally learning environment.

Members of our research-oriented and clinical faculty work very closely with students to share and benefit from an undeniably innovative spirit within a diverse, cross-functional setting.

CAREER SERVICES AND PLACEMENT

The Lally School Career Resource Center provides extensive career resources including workshops, mock interview sessions, and career counseling. Industry partnerships are an integral design characteristic of all Lally programs. Our industry partners work with us to influence curriculum to meet the most current demands in an ever-changing workplace; provide meaningful internship and co-op experiences for students; and create industry programs that become the platform for cutting-edge faculty research. Through the strong ties with Lally's industry partners, students can stretch themselves to reach their career goals, especially in business contexts with pronounced technology influences.

LOCATION AND ENVIRONMENT

Rensselaer's 275-acre campus is a blend of modern style and classic design. Built into a hillside, it overlooks the historic city of Troy and the Hudson River.

The area offers a relaxed lifestyle with many cultural and recreational opportunities, with easy access to both the high-energy metropolitan centers of the Northeast-such as Boston, New York City, and Montreal, Canada-and the quiet beauty of the neighboring Adirondack Mountains.

Rensselaer is committed to a campus culture and engaging student experience, where students can learn and grow in an environment that encourages discovery, creativity, innovation, and diversity.

MAJORS AND DEGREES OFFERED

MBA; 3-year Pathfinder MBA, for graduating seniors in engineering, science, or math; Executive MBA; MS Management, can have a focus on technology commercialization and entrepreneurship or financial modeling and analytics; PhD research program

ACADEMIC PROGRAMS

The Lally M.B.A. program prepares business leaders with the skills and thinking that are essential for meeting the day-to-day, real-world challenges of running a business within the evolving dynamics of the global economy. Through experiential hands-on instruction, students acquire an overall understanding of the new sources of value creation brought about by the convergence of globalization and the information technology (IT) revolution.

The curriculum is built on streams of knowledge, enabling students to gain critical expertise in launching, running, and growing a successful business: creating and managing an enterprise; value creation, managing networks, and driving innovation; developing innovative products and services; formulating and executing competitive business strategies; and managing the business implications of emerging technologies. These streams of knowledge focus on critical business issues in today's global marketplace and integrate all discrete business functions, from finance and operations to global marketing and supply chain management, within the dynamics of each course experience.

Key modules complement the streams of knowledge. Modules include global business, decision models, social responsibility and business ethics, and succeeding in knowledge-intensive organizations.

Students in the Pathfinder MBA program attend MBA classes the first year; get paid experience during the second year at a Co-op in the U.S. or abroad; and, in the third year, return to campus to complete the MBA program.

Special Programs: Pathfinder MBA, Focused MS in Management

CAMPUS FACILITIES AND EQUIPMENT

The Lally School of Management and Technology is located in one of Rensselaer's most historic buildings. A 1998 renovation transformed the Pittsburgh Building into a technology-intensive center for teaching and research.

The facility features four large classrooms with facilities that are computer-interactive, and set up for videoconferencing and distance education. The building also includes fully networked faculty and staff offices, wireless access, a computer study hall, student and faculty lounges, a fifth-floor outdoor terrace, a centrally located student services suite, and a food service concession.

FINANCIAL AID

Full-time graduate tuition for the 2008-09 academic year is $36,950. Other costs (estimated living expenses, insurance, etc.) are projected to be about $12,605. Therefore, the cost of attendance for full-time graduate study is approximately $49,555 per year. Part-time study and cohort programs are priced separately.

Upon application to the Lally School, you are automatically considered for financial aid. MS Students or Evening MBA students are not eligible for fellowships. Fellowships are competitive and are granted based on merit.

ADMISSIONS PROCESS

The Lally School of Management & Technology attracts candidates who can clearly articulate and act on their personal and professional goals. Accepted candidates share a strong entrepreneurial spirit and are confident about their analytical and quantitative skills. Required items include completion of the online Rensselaer graduate application, essay questions, resume, transcripts, 2 letters of recommendation, and a GMAT score.

RICE UNIVERSITY

AT A GLANCE

Rice University aspires to path-breaking research, excellence in teaching and contributions to the enhancement of our world. As the university's business school, The Jesse H. Jones Graduate School of Management adheres to those same values to cultivate a diverse community of learning and discovery.

More specifically, the Jones School develops principled, innovative thought leaders in global communities. Through a combination of rigorous curriculum, elite faculty and impressive facilities, students receive an outstanding business school experience. The result is innovative leadership that engages the entrepreneurial spirit and impacts business on a global level.

The Jones School is one of the world's best teaching and research universities, offering Full-Time MBA, MBA for Executives, and MBA for Professionals programs. A Ph.D. program in Management will debut in the fall of 2009 and recently-introduced business concentrations highlight the school's strengths while allowing full-time MBA students to focus on areas of interest.

FACULTY

The Jones School's faculty is consistently recognized for their knowledge, research, teaching ability, and student focus. Each member of the Jones faculty maintains a balance between teaching and research, ensuring that students receive the most current, leading-edge education.

STUDENTS

The Jones School attracts students both nationally and internationally. In fact, 29 percent of first year students hail from outside the United States and another 26 percent are from outside of Texas. A variety of student organizations are available and many sponsor guest speakers, visit area businesses, and take on special projects. In addition, weekly corporate-sponsored "partios"-parties on the Jones School patio-provide relaxation and opportunities to network and bond with fellow students.

CAREER SERVICES

The Career Management Center (CMC) is housed within the Jones School building and works only with Rice MBA students and alumni. The CMC serves to support each student's development of a career plan throughout their two years at the Jones School. From day one of immersion to graduation, the CMC works individually with students to ensure they develop the strategy, job search skills, and networking opportunities that will help them succeed in the MBA job market.

Additional information is available through our website at www.jonesgsm.rice.edu.

LOCATION AND ENVIRONMENT

Rice University is located on a beautiful wooded 300-acre campus in central Houston, minutes from the downtown business district and the city's world-class theater district. The campus is located across the street from the renowned Texas Medical Center and within walking distance to the museum district, Houston Zoological Gardens, and Hermann Park.

MAJORS AND DEGREES OFFERED

The Jones School focuses all of its energy on graduate business education. A Rice MBA is available via full-time, evening (MBA for Professionals), or weekend (MBA for Executives) programs designed to accommodate students at every stage of their career. Also available are an MBA/Masters in Engineering in conjunction with the George R. Brown College of Engineering at Rice, and an MBA/MD in conjunction with Baylor College of Medicine. Beginning in 2009, the Jones School will offer a Ph.D. in Management to develop business school faculty.

ACADEMIC PROGRAMS

Every course offers unparalleled opportunity to work one-on-one with an accessible, involved, and energetic faculty. The Jones School faculty maintains an important balance between teaching and research, believing that current industry knowledge is as critical as textbooks to your education.

A comprehensive core curriculum focuses on managerial and leadership skills, ethics, information technology, and communication skills in addition to the functional areas. An Action Learning Project in first year gives students the opportunity to learn how to integrate disciplines and turn knowledge into action. Students take at least 28.25 elective credit hours, which allow them to custom design their curriculum to suit career goals.

FACILITIES AND EQUIPMENT

McNair Hall is the 167,000-square-foot home of the Jones School. It offers a state-of-the-El Paso finance center; the Business Information Center (BIC); tiered classrooms; behavior research and observation room for marketing research and interviews; a 450-seat auditorium; and a career planning center. Fully loaded laptops are provided to all students, and the Jones School is equipped to make sophisticated use of electronic access.

FINANCIAL AID

Application fee: $100

Tuition: $36,000 for the 2008–2009 year. Laptop computer, hardware, and software are included in this price.

Total estimated expenses: approximately $57,000 per year

Financial Aid: Approximately 75 percent of students attending the Jones School receive some form of financial aid and/or merit-based scholarships. Rice University's Office of Student Financial Services also administers a variety of federally and privately funded loan programs.

ADMISSIONS PROCESS

The Jones School considers each aspect of the application when making admissions decision. The application requirements include: GMAT (GRE or MCAT for join candidates); TOEFL for international applicants; transcripts from educational institutions; resume; confidential evaluations; essays; interview (invitation only); completed application form and application fee.

Academic Background: A four-year undergraduate degree from an accredited college or university is required for U.S. applicants. International applicants must have an undergraduate degree equivalent to a four-year U.S. degree. Those with a three-year Bachelor of Commerce (BCom) degree must also have a two-year Master of Commerce (MCom) degree. Undergraduate and graduate GPAs, GMAT scores (GRE or MCAT for joint candidates), choice of major, electives, course load, and grade patterns are all considered.

Leadership Potential: Demonstrated leadership and management experiences, both on the job and through extracurricular activities, will help us assess leadership potential. We look for individuals with at least 2 years of professional work experience.

Confidential Evaluations: Evaluations from employers provide perspective on potential student capabilities, enabling us to assess your qualifications more accurately.

Essays: Three essays articulating career goals, work experience, and reasons for choosing Rice University's Jones School are a crucial component of the application process. These essays are designed to convey intangibles such as reasons for pursuing an MBA; benefits of academic, professional and personal opportunities; and personal expectations of the Jones School experience.

SAN FRANCISCO STATE UNIVERSITY
College of Business

FACULTY
The MBA Program is broadly-based and highly-structured, offering a balanced preparation for managerial careers. Management is studied as a function which coordinates people, materials and information to meet selected objectives. The MBA prepares students for responsible positions in a rapidly changing world, heightens intellectual curiosity for life-long learning, and assists the student to develop initiative, imagination and creativity. In both the public and private sectors, the MBA is a widely-recognized degree.

After acceptance to the MBA Program, students will need to demonstrate basic competencies in mathematics, statistics and written English. Students will also need to take or waive the 9 foundation courses. These courses will prepare the student for the program's advanced requirements.

CAMPUS AND LOCATION
San Francisco State University

College of Business

Graduate Programs

835 Market Street, Suite 550

San Francisco, CA 94103-1901

The College of Business at San Francisco State University is one of the largest business schools in the US, located in one of the world's most dynamic and exciting business environments, San Francisco and the Bay area. The College of Business, Graduate Programs is conveniently located in downtown San Francisco, nearby to many fortune 500 companies in the Bay Area.

DEGREES OFFERED
Masters of Business Administration (MBA)

Masters of Science in Business Administration (MSBA)

Executive Masters of Business Administration (EMBA)

PROGRAMS AND CURRICULUM
The curriculum balances the art and science of management; not only understand theoretical issues, but also apply theory in diverse management situations. Courses are designed to give a comprehensive and relevant understanding of today's management environment. Case studies of business situations and guest speakers with specialized expertise are essential part of the curriculum.

FACILITIES
10 Class Rooms (each rooms with their own projectors)

1 Computer Lab (31 computers)

5 Breakout Rooms

2 Conference Rooms

EXPENSES AND FINANCIAL AID
Fees as of Fall 2007

Per Semester:	Part-Time (0-6 units)	Full-Time (more than 6 units)
California Residents:	$2,032	$3,249
Non-residents:	$2,032	$3,249
	+ $339 per unit	+ $339 per unit

FINANCIAL AID
For information regarding to Financial Aid, please visit San Francisco State University's Financial Aid Office- SSB- 302 | (415) 338-7000 | http://www.sfsu.edu/~finaid/ | e-mail: finaid@sfsu.edu

FAFSA: In addition, please check Free Application for Federal Student Aid | 1-800-4-FED-AID (1-800-433-3243) |http://www.fafsa.ed.gov/

FACULTY
There are seventy two faculty members who teach in the eight functional areas at San Francisco State, College of Business Graduate Programs from Accounting to Sustainable Business. All sixty four full-time faculty members hold a doctorate degree. Our faculty is extremely diverse with eleven female members and thirty two international faculty members.

STUDENT BODY
The GBA: The Graduate Business Association (GBA) is a not-for-profit, volunteer student organization which supports graduate business students at San Francisco State University in their academic endeavors (MBA/MSBA).

The association is an active part of the College of Business. It sponsors events, brings speakers to campus, and provides a forum for networking, exchanging ideas and socializing. The GBA is open to all SFSU business graduate students.

You can contact us at gba@sfsu.edu. There is also a Yahoo! Usergroup and mailing list at: http://groups.yahoo.com/group/SFSU_GBA/

Recognizing that approximately 70% of the participants in the graduate business program consist of part-time students, our goal is to develop networking events that offer students the opportunity to meet peers, alumni and business professionals. The Graduate Business Association provides its members with current information and updates regarding the graduate program, professional events and workshops that take place throughout the school year.

ADMISSIONS
The Division of Graduate Studies

San Francisco State University

1600 Holloway Avenue, ADM 250

San Francisco, CA 94132

Students are required to complete or submit the following:

Graduate Admissions Application—complete online via "CSU Mentor"

Application Fee—$55.00 payable to SFSU.

Official Transcripts—Send official transcripts from all colleges, universities, and community colleges attended.

GMAT Test Scores—The GMAT Exam is required for admissions by all applicants.

Statement of Purpose—State reason for pursuing a graduate business degree at SFSU, past accomplishment that would indicate potential as a successful candidate, and projections for the future.

TOEFL Test Scores—TOELF is required for applicants who have earned an undergraduate degree from a country where English is not the official language.

Letters of Recommendation and Resume (Optional- highly recommended)

ST. JOHN'S UNIVERSITY
Tobin College of Business

AT A GLANCE
For nearly 80 years, The Peter J. Tobin College of Business has offered future business leaders a strong foundation in management education. Our flexible curriculum, network of over 35,000 alumni worldwide, talented and dedicated faculty, outstanding resources and commitment to a values-based business education all make the college unique in providing business leadership skills for life.

FACULTY
The faculty at the Tobin College of Business is drawn from leading institutions all over the world. They are complemented by business practitioners who regularly serve as adjunct instructors or co-teachers. Ninety percent of the faculty members hold the highest terminal degree in their fields and six members are internationally recognized Fulbright Scholars; numerous others are frequent consultants to business and the business news media.

STUDENTS
The Tobin College has succeeded in launching the careers of more than 35,000 business leaders worldwide. Special opportunities exist for students to network with alumni of the college for the purposes of career information, development and internships.

CAREER SERVICES AND PLACEMENT
These services and resources include career advisement, on-campus interviews, full- and part-time employment opportunities, a career resource library, resume preparation and interview techniques. We have a high rate of job placement for M.B.A. students within three months of graduation.

LOCATION AND ENVIRONMENT
Tobin College has three residential campuses in exciting New York City as well as a campus in Rome, Italy.

Queens Campus
8000 Utopia Parkway
Queens, NY 11439

Staten Island Campus
300 Howard Avenue
Staten Island, NY 10301

Manhattan Campus
101 Murray Street
New York, NY 10007

Rome Campus
Rome Graduate Center
Via Marcantonio Colonna, 21
Rome, Italy 00192

MAJORS AND DEGREES OFFERED
The M.B.A. degree is offered with specializations in accounting, taxation, decision sciences, executive management, finance, financial services, international business, international finance, marketing management, insurance, actuarial sciences, risk management, and computer information systems for managers. Successful completion requires a minimum of 36-credit hours - additional credits may be required, depending on previous business and economics course work. The degree can be completed on either a part- or full-time basis. The Master of Science (M.S.) degree is offered in taxation, accounting and in risk and insurance. Advanced Professional Certificates (APCs) are available to individuals who have completed the M.B.A. degree and are interested in accruing additional skills. Eighteen credits are required for completion of the APC.

ACADEMIC PROGRAMS
St. John's recognized early on the importance of globalization for future business leaders and as a result is one of the first American business schools to establish a presence internationally in Rome, Italy. Today, it is a thriving center for students interested in the intersection of business and international markets.

The M.B.A. curriculum offers enhanced flexibility for students to design a program that best meets their own professional and personal objectives. Courses in social responsibility, managing in today's complex environment, and the ethics of management are required of all students and serve as its foundation.

The Tobin College is fully accredited by AACSB International - The Association to Advance Collegiate Schools of Business.

SPECIAL PROGRAMS
In addition to study abroad programs, selected students can participate in the Executive-in-Residence program, which provides special opportunities to serve as consultants in partnership with senior corporate executives in solving business challenges.

An alumni-funded Student Investment Fund also enables students to obtain hands-on investing experience under the guidance of seasoned faculty members and alumni with vast Wall Street experience.

CAMPUS FACILITIES AND EQUIPMENT
The Main Library of the University is on the Queens campus. Together with the collections of the Loretto Memorial Library on the Staten Island campus, the Law School Library, the Oakdale Campus Library, the Kathryn and Shelby Cullom Davis Library in Manhattan and the Rome campus library, the total University library collection numbers 1.7 million volumes and includes more than 6,000 periodic subscriptions.

The Financial Information Lab, opened in September of 2007 on the Queens campus, enhances the education provided to our students through the establishment of a learning environment that brings real-time news, market information, financial data and analysis to our students and faculty. This type of facility enables our students to learn about and live in financial markets and business environments and situations throughout the world.

Students will benefit from the most contemporary learning technology and tools of analysis that are available in the marketplace today.

FINANCIAL AID
Tuition in 2008-2009 is $880 per credit. An additional $150 general fee per term is due at the time of registration. A limited number of graduate assistantships are awarded, based on academic merit.

ADMISSIONS PROCESS
All applicants must possess a baccalaureate from an accredited institution or the international equivalent. Candidates are encouraged to begin the application process early and should submit, in addition to the $40 nonrefundable application fee, official transcripts from all undergraduate, graduate, and professional schools attended. In addition, results of the GMAT taken within the last five years, a resume, letters of recommendation and a personal statement should also be submitted. Details of these requirements are available at the Office of Admissions or from the University's Web site. Applicants whose native language is not English must also submit the results of the TOEFL.

CONTACT US
Are you St. John's? Contact us at 877-STJ-5550, Ext. T1345A or www.stjohns.edu/learnmore/01404.stj to find out!

SYRACUSE UNIVERSITY
Whitman School of Management

AT A GLANCE

Whitman is thriving! Business Week regards Whitman as one of the cream of the crop in its inclusion of MBA programs considered for their ranking. Our Entrepreneurship Program is ranked #1 in the nation by Entrepreneurship Magazine and The Princeton Review in 2006 and top ten by U.S. News & World Report and Fortune Small Business in August 2007. And Princeton Review ranks the Whitman among the "Best Business Schools." From opening our new Real Estate Center to launching the Orange Value Fund to our most recent grant to create a Women's Business Center, Whitman is thriving! The Whitman School is proud to nurture graduates who want to develop as entrepreneurial managers who will become leaders in an era of global competitiveness and technological advancements. We do this in an environment that promotes firsthand experiences where students can hone their communication and interpersonal skills as well as their analytic and problem solving capabilities, giving our students a dynamic and relevant business education.

FACULTY

Faculty in the Whitman School are committed to discovering and disseminating relevant knowledge, contributing perspectives on frontline business issues, and advancing the theory and practice of management. Faculty research spans a diverse range of topics and methodologies and all faculty strive to reach the highest level of excellence.

STUDENTS

International students comprise 55 percent of the student body at the Whitman School. The Office of International Students (OIS) offers services ranging from immigration advice to personal counseling. OIS is housed in its own building and is a friendly place for all students to visit, relax, read a newspaper, and talk with staff. The office organizes many social and cultural events to promote on-campus diversity.

LOCATION AND ENVIRONMENT

Founded in 1870, Syracuse University is a private, nonsectarian research institution consisting of 13 colleges offering over 250 programs of study. One of the oldest schools in the state of New York, SU is also one of only 62 research universities in the U.S. to be elected to the prestigious Association of American Universities (AAU). SU offers a remarkable combination of academic excellence and a relaxed lifestyle amid the splendor of upstate New York.

The 220-acre campus rests on a hill overlooking the city of Syracuse, providing an ideal blend of urban and peaceful environments. SU consists of 170 buildings surrounding a historic central quadrangle. The University has more than 19,000 students; over 70 percent live in the 13 residence halls on campus. The student/faculty ratio is 12:1.

SU is a 20-minute walk from downtown Syracuse, a medium-sized city with many recreational and cultural options, including parks, museums, art galleries, and a symphony orchestra. Located in the geographical center of New York State, Syracuse enjoys four distinct seasons and is only a four-hour drive from the largest city in the U.S., New York City. SU is also within easy driving distance of Boston, Montreal, Toronto, Niagara Falls, Buffalo, Philadelphia, Washington DC, Pittsburgh, Cleveland, and Providence.

MAJORS AND DEGREES OFFERED

Master of Business Administration: Full-Time Two-Year Traditional, Full-Time Accelerated MBA, Independent Study MBA (iMBA. **MS in Accounting:** Full-Time One-Year MS in Accounting, Independent Study MS in Accounting (iMS in Accounting). **MS in Finance:** Full-Time One-Year MS in Finance. **MS in Media Management:** Full-Time One-Year MS in Media Management. **PhD:** Full-Time PhD.

ACADEMIC PROGRAMS

Full-Time MBA: The program offers students a rigorous and experiential two-year program that prepares them to become strategic thinkers and innovators in an ever-changing global economy. Students generally complete an internship in the summer between the first and second. **Full-Time Accelerated MBA:** Students with four or more years of full-time work experience and an undergraduate degree in business from an AACSB International-accredited institution are eligible for the one-year 36-credit accelerated program. **Independent Study MBA (iMBA):** The iMBA is a limited-residency distance learning MBA program for executives that follows a unique flexible format combining in-person residency and online learning. A minimum of five years of full-time professional work experience is required for admission. **MS in Accounting:** The MS in Accounting program produces graduates with the educational requirements needed to take the CPA exam in New York. An undergraduate degree in accounting is required for this one-year program. **Independent Study MS in Accounting (iMS):** The iMS program offers full-time accounting professionals a distance-learning program that prepares them to qualify for the CPA exam in New York. The program follows a unique flexible format combining in-person residency and online learning. An undergraduate degree in accounting is required for admission. **MS in Finance:** Students in the MS in Finance program graduate from the rigorous, one-year curriculum prepared to manage the risks associated with operating in a global marketplace. An undergraduate degree in finance or economics is required for admission. **MS in Media Management:** Syracuse University's Newhouse School of Public Communications and Whitman teamed up to offer this program. **PhD:** The program emphasizes independent study and close collaboration with Whitman faculty.

CAMPUS FACILITIES AND EQUIPMENT

Classrooms facilitate creative use of educational technologies. Quality spaces for public events and informal interactions include a state-of-the-art auditorium, a Grand Hall, a cafe, plentiful team breakout rooms, and comfortable conversation areas throughout the entirely wireless-access building. A lounge and a computer cluster specifically for graduate students builds identity and cohesion.

FINANCIAL AID

Approximately 65 to 75 percent of incoming full-time MBA students are awarded financial aid based on merit through a scholarship or fellowship.

The estimated total cost (including tuition, books, fees, and living expenses) for attending the Whitman School full-time for the 2007-2008 academic year is US$48,655 for a single graduate student.

ADMISSIONS PROCESS

Admission to the Whitman School MBA and MS programs is highly selective. We seek candidates who can contribute to the school and who aim to assume leadership roles in organizations around the world—individuals who have displayed the drive, the leadership potential, and the intellectual capacity to achieve their goals.

The Admissions Committee uses several criteria in their admissions decisions, including the applicant's academic achievement, communication skills, previous work history, and standardized test scores. A completed application form must be accompanied by two letters of recommendation preferably from past supervisors, a current resume, all academic transcripts, a GMAT score, essays, and a $65 application fee. Since the admissions decision involves several criteria, there are no set minimums for the GMAT or GPA average. The 2007 entering class had an average GPA of 3.3 (on a 4.0 scale) and an average GMAT of 615.

TEMPLE UNIVERSITY
Fox School of Business

AT A GLANCE
With more than 6,000 students and 150 full-time faculty, The Fox School is the largest, most comprehensive business school in the region and among the largest in the world. Established in 1918, the school has a long history of innovation in education, introducing new curriculum and programs in advance of current business trends.

With over 45,000 graduates, two-thirds of whom live and work in the Philadelphia metropolitan area, The Fox School is the primary source of management talent in the region. This important network of business associates continues to connect with The Fox School by mentoring and advising students; speaking at events; introducing employers to the school, resulting in internship, recruitment and hands-on learning opportunities; and providing financial support.

FACULTY
On all of our campuses, the Temple faculty includes instructors who are distinguished and active members in their fields. Professors bring the critical perspective of scholars and the practical knowledge of their discipline to their classrooms.

STUDENTS
Fox MBA Class Profile for 2007

Applicants: 310

Applicants enrolled: 68

Percent male/female: 71/29

Percent U.S. citizens: 64

Percent international: 36

Percent minority (U.S. origin): 4

Average age: 27

Average work experience: 5 years

Average GMAT: 642

LOCATION AND ENVIRONMENT
The city of Philadelphia is the cornerstone of life at Temple. One of the largest cities on the East Coast, Philadelphia is home to a variety of forward-looking businesses, progressive work in technology and science, and thriving artistic output. While the city is the product of a rich history, it is also a center for twenty-first-century innovation and culture.

Beginning January 2009, Temple will deliver its full-time MBA program from its brand new state-of-the-art facility on its main campus. Alter Hall can be described as groundbreaking. This new building will reflect the school's globally recognized quality and its emphasis on technology.

The part-time Professional MBA program is conducted at Temple University's Center City facility and the Fort Washington campus. Classes at Center City are held during the day and in the evening, while only evening classes are offered in Fort Washington.

MAJORS AND DEGREES OFFERED
MBA, PhD: Business Administration

MS: Actuarial Sciences, Accounting and Financial Management

MA, PhD: Economics

MS: Finance, Financial Engineering, Healthcare Finance, Human Resource Management, Management Information Systems, Marketing

MS, PhD: Statistics

ACADEMIC PROGRAMS
The Fox School of Business offers 11 areas of concentration to a mix of both full-time and part-time students. With programs in accounting, business administration, economics, finance, general and strategic management, healthcare management, human resource management, international business administration, international business (tri-continent), management information systems, and risk management and insurance, Fox gives graduate students an unusually wide array of choices.

The Fox MBA is a full-time, two-year cohort program, and The Fox Professional MBA provides management education to working professionals on a part-time basis. Both programs prepare individuals to assume leadership roles in corporations, as well as in governmental and nongovernmental organizations which also require business management skills.

The Fox School also offers specialized master's degrees which provide an educational experience with a more concentrated scope in a specific business discipline.

CAMPUS FACILITIES AND EQUIPMENT
Temple University's facilities are on the cutting edge of technology and expose today's students to tomorrow's innovation. The brand new Alter Hall (opening January 2009) will incorporate innovation in smart classroom design, one of the longest stock tickers in the United States, a trading room/business simulation center, and other technology for teaching and learning designed to prepare students by mirroring a business environment. To encourage the teamwork intrinsic to the corporate world, the building will include breakout and interview rooms, recruiting offices, conference centers, and MBA commons, a special lounge specifically for the MBA student population.

FINANCIAL AID
At current rates, in-state students can expect to pay about $41,200 USD in tuition and fees for a full-time Fox MBA degree, while out-of-state and international students can expect to pay $60,300 USD in tuition and fees for the entire degree program. Tuition for full-time specialized master's degree programs can range from $23,600 to $36,800 USD for Pennsylvania residents and $31,200 to $53,800 USD for non-Pennsylvania residents, depending upon the number of prerequisite courses needed to complete the program.

Temple University's Office of Student Financial Services assists eligible MBA students in obtaining State and Federal Government grants and guaranteed loans. Students may begin to file the FAFSA for 2008—2009 during the application process, and can file for loans with lenders after being offered admission to the MBA.

The Fox School of Business has a limited number of scholarships for full-time students with high academic grades and test scores. Scholarships are offered at the time of acceptance into The Fox School. The Fox School also has a limited number of graduate externships for assignments in academic and administrative departments.

ADMISSIONS PROCESS
Application Deadlines for MBA, MA, or MS Applicants

Full-time, fall semester only: June 1 (March 15 if you possess international credentials requiring evaluation)

Part time MBA/MS, fall semester: June 1

Part time MBA, Full time MA/MS spring semester: September 30

JD/MBA MD/MBA applicants: April 1

TEXAS CHRISTIAN UNIVERSITY
The Neeley School of Business

AT A GLANCE
At the Neeley School, we bring together highly motivated professionals and exceptional faculty in a personalized, interactive environment. Neeley is one of an elite group of accredited business schools to offer a 12-Month Accelerated MBA degree along with the two-year Full-Time MBA. Learning here goes beyond the classroom, to hands-on experiences that impact the bottom line. Our students stay on top of the quickly changing business environment through frequent and meaningful interaction with business leaders. Our commitment to you is an experience that is personal, connected, and real.

FACULTY
At the Neeley School, our faculty is comprised of talented individuals who are leading experts in their respective fields. They are frequently published in leading business journals and as textbook authors. Many are sought-after business consultants, sit on corporate boards, have owned their own businesses, or have themselves held influential positions with leading companies. They maintain close ties with top professionals in their fields of expertise. Most importantly, our faculty members are top-notch teachers.

With the program's relatively small size, Neeley faculty members come to know students personally, taking time to challenge, engage and inspire each class member. As trusted mentors, Neeley faculty provide the behind-the-scenes guidance and encouragement that can make a real difference in your career.

STUDENTS
Neeley MBA students are in good company, interacting with other highly motivated, rising professionals who have a variety of academic and career successes under their belts. Purposefully selected to create a broad cross-section of industry experience, academic credentials and geographic backgrounds, Neeley's rich mix of students invariably produces a lively give-and-take in the classroom and the opportunity for students to evaluate issues from many different perspectives.

You will find that Neeley students challenge yet support one another. Progressing through the curriculum as a cohort group, our students quickly develop close working relationships that often lead to lifelong friendships and extremely valuable long-term professional networks.

LOCATION AND ENVIRONMENT
Texas Christian University (TCU) is located in the heart of Fort Worth, the 17th-largest city in the United States is consistently cited as one of the best places to live and work.

Fort Worth is home to the world headquarters of American Airlines, BNSF Railway, Bell Helicopter Textron, Pier 1, Alcon Laboratories, DFW International Airport and other cutting-edge corporations that share close ties with TCU.

The entire Dallas/Fort Worth Metroplex features include some of the nation's best entertainment, dining, shopping and sports.

MAJORS AND DEGREES OFFERED
TCU/Neeley awards a Masters of Business Administration Degree.

ACADEMIC PROGRAMS
Full-time MBA—21 months to complete

Accelerated Full-time MBA—12 months to complete

Evening Professional MBA—24–33 months to complete

Executive MBA —16 months to complete

CAMPUS FACILITIES AND EQUIPMENT
Neeley School students praised the state-of-the-art facilities in The Princeton Review's 2007 survey, ranking the Neeley School of Business #9 for Best Campus Facilities out of 282 national business schools.

Smith Hall, built in 2003, is a three-floor, 50,000-square-foot student-centered learning environment.

Tandy Hall, built in 1989, is a three-story, 46,000-square-foot building designed to resemble a corporate headquarters. .

Rogers Hall—the elder statesmen of the Neeley School building, Dan Rogers Hall was built in 1957 and has undergone renovations to keep it up to date with 21st century business.

FINANCIAL AID
Tuition and Fees for the 2008–200909 academic year:

Tuition: $935 per semester hour

MBA Fee (Full-Time MBA): $1,995 per semester (estimated)

MBA Fee (Professional MBA): $650 per semester (estimated)

Full-Time MBA (on an annual basis)

Tuition: $25,245

Fees: $3,990

Total: $29,235   For one academic year

Books and materials, estimated: $1,600

Accelerated MBA (for full 12-month program)

Tuition: $33,660

Fees: $5,985

Total : $39,645 For full 12-month MBA

Book and materials, estimated: $1,900

Professional MBA (on an annual basis, assuming 18 semester hours)

Tuition: $16,830

Fees: $1,950

Total: $18,780 For one academic year

Books and materials, estimated: $900

Scholarships and Graduate Assistant Awards for Full-Time Students

The Neeley School offers merit-based awards to help students in the transition back to the classroom. Typically, 75% of Neeley MBA students receive scholarships and/or graduate assistant awards. Last year, awards ranged from $2,000 to $38,000 with an average of $18,000 per year.

ADMISSIONS PROCESS
TCU seeks to bring together highly motivated and academically talented students from a broad range of backgrounds who are dedicated to success.

An application will not be reviewed for admission until all of the materials listed below are received. It is not necessary to collect all materials to send as a single package.

Admission Checklist: Application Form , Application Essays, Application fee of $75, Official transcripts from each college or university previously attended, Official GMAT scores, Three Letters of Recommendation, Admission Interview (by invitation only), **For International Candidates:** Official TOEFL scores (non-native English speakers only), International Student/Scholar Form, Financial Statement.

THE UNIVERSITY OF ARIZONA
Eller College of Management

AT A GLANCE

The University of Arizona's Eller College of Management offers an AACSB-accredited MBA designed around your goals. Small class sizes allow the Eller MBA staff and faculty to spend time understanding your objectives, then tailoring meaningful projects, internships, and independent study around those goals, ultimately facilitating the transition into your desired career path. The program's 5:1 student-faculty ratio allows you to create a personalized experience.

The Eller MBA is a recognized leader in management information systems and tops national rankings in entrepreneurship through its McGuire Center for Entrepreneurship.

CAMPUS AND LOCATION

The University of Arizona's Eller College of Management is situated in the heart of Tucson, Arizona, with a population just over one million. Surrounded by mountains rising to 9,000 feet, with an average high/low temperature of 82/54° F and roughly 350 days of sunshine each year, Tucson offers an ideal climate for year-round outdoor activities.

DEGREES OFFERED

As an Eller MBA, you may concentrate in accounting, entrepreneurship, finance, management information systems, or marketing.

The Eller MBA offers accelerated dual-degree options in science and technology, allowing students to complete two master's degrees in as little as two years. Additional dual MBA-master's degrees include medicine, law, pharmacy, finance, international management, management information systems, or optical sciences.

The Eller College also offers an accelerated, 18-month Evening MBA for working professionals and a 14-month Executive MBA for managers with significant experience.

PROGRAMS AND CURRICULUM

The Eller MBA is built around a progressive series of real-world programs and activities, designed to test the skills you build in core classes through practical application. You'll kick off your experience with a multi-day "MBA Boot Camp," as well as a two-credit graduate-level course on teams and leadership. Then you'll spend your first semester building your analytic framework and developing soft skills in business communication, and your second completing your core curriculum while undertaking a business consulting project in your area of interest. These lessons will come to bear on a summer internship or international field project. In your second year of the program, you'll have the opportunity to customize your experience through varied elective offerings. With an international class trip, study abroad and exchange programs, and a variety of courses related to international business, the Eller MBA offers its students opportunities to manage the challenges and seize the opportunities of a global and connected marketplace.

FACILITIES

Since 1992, the Eller College of Management has been housed in the four-story, 180,000-square-foot McClelland Hall. The $19-million building is built around an open-air, sunlit courtyard and houses classrooms, student activity areas, computer laboratories, centers for corporate research, public and community spaces, and faculty and administrative offices. The College has Wi-Fi throughout, paid parking at garages and surface lots in the immediate vicinity, and is a short walk from restaurants, coffee houses, and convenience stores.

EXPENSES AND FINANCIAL AID

Total estimated costs for the Eller MBA program for 2008-2009 are $29,032 for Arizona residents and $41,669 for non-residents and international students. These estimates do not include the costs of the international trip, health insurance, or a one-time enrollment fee.

The Eller MBA program offers merit-based scholarships, including graduate assistantships, for qualified in-state and out-of-state students. The college works with The University of Arizona Office of Student Financial Aid on coordinating federal and private loans.

FACULTY

The Eller MBA's 5:1 student-faculty ratio ensures that you'll have the opportunity to develop close working relationships with our top faculty. These leaders bring their experience in research and corporate consulting into the classroom to enrich academic work with real-world application. Our faculty publish in top-tier journals, win industry awards, and collaborate with other faculty from around the country on topics ranging from why U.S. firms are holding such high reserves of cash to the effect of online customer reviews on corporate strategy.

STUDENTS

While the Eller MBA program is relatively small, The University of Arizona is home to more than 37,000 students, so you will receive the benefits of a large institution while taking classes in an intimate setting. At the Eller MBA program, underrepresented minorities make up on average 18 percent of programs, the male-female ratio averages 70:30, and international students make up nearly 35 percent of the class, representing ten or more countries.

ADMISSIONS

The Eller College will work closely with you throughout admissions to ensure that your application process is personal, simple, and successful. We are interested in applicants with an academic background demonstrating strong intellectual capacity; professional experience including challenging assignments, career progression, carefully considered goals, and a strong work ethic; and personal qualities demonstrating leadership potential, initiative, involvement, and integrity.

Admissions packets must include transcripts, GMAT scores, references, essay questions, and professional resume, as well as TOEFL scores for international applicants. An interview is also required. The Eller MBA program processes admissions for fall in three rounds with rolling admissions; deadlines are November 15, February 15 (final international deadline), and April 15.

CAREER SERVICES AND PLACEMENT

In 2007, 75 percent of Eller MBAs had accepted jobs by graduation, and 85 percent had accepted jobs within three months of graduation. At the Eller MBA program, your own career search begins during orientation week and continues throughout your two years in the program. Whether you have committed to a clear career path, or you plan to consider a variety of career options before selecting a particular field, function, or industry, the Office of Career Development helps guide your process-from internship through full-time recruiting.

UNIVERSITY OF CALIFORNIA—LOS ANGELES
Anderson School of Management

AT A GLANCE
Established in 1935, UCLA Anderson School of Management annually educates more than 1,600 students enrolled in MBA and doctoral programs, and some 2,000 executives and managers participating in executive education programs. UCLA Anderson's academic programs and departments are perennially ranked among the best in the world. Award-winning faculty, renowned for their research and teaching, combine with rigorous academic programs, successful alumni and world-class facilities to provide an unmatched learning environment.

FACULTY
The mainstay of UCLA Anderson's high-quality management education programs is its esteemed faculty. Each year, UCLA Anderson faculty members demonstrate the caliber of their intellectual abilities by publishing groundbreaking research in leading scholarly journals. Time and again, they are rated highly for their research productivity, as evidenced by the awards they receive and by key business school rankings and citation studies.

STUDENTS
UCLA Anderson attracts exceptional students who are selected both for their overall abilities and for the contributions they can make to the school experience. UCLA Anderson offers a collegial environment unique among schools of business and management with a close-knit community of diverse, high-potential peers. International students representing approximately 53 countries bring a global perspective to classroom discussions and other activities.

CAREER SERVICES AND PLACEMENT
John E. Parker Career Management Center (Parker CMC) assists UCLA Anderson MBA students and alumni in creating personal career development strategies and connecting to employment opportunities worldwide by leveraging a powerful global network of professional business executives. The Parker CMC also partners with MBA recruiters and their firms throughout the world to ensure they receive the timely services and guidance needed to fill important positions within their organizations.

LOCATION AND ENVIRONMENT
Located in the heart of Southern California's vibrant economy, UCLA Anderson is at the epicenter of international business activity as measured by new business starts, venture capital availability, technological innovation and new product introduction. All are local influences that impact the day-to-day academic and practical experiences of UCLA Anderson faculty and students.

Provide a URL to a page on your website where a prospective student can watch video of your campus: http://www.anderson.ucla.edu/x9488.xml

MAJORS AND DEGREES OFFERED
MBA: Designed for exceptionally capable, highly motivated students who seek deep immersion in management education and academic life, the MBA program emphasizes analytical and problem-solving skills, as well as team and individual-based decision-making competencies within a global perspective.

Fully Employed MBA: Designed for working professionals, FEMBA is a three-year program that prepares emerging managers to take on increased levels of responsibility and expanded management roles within their organizations.

Executive MBA: Catering to mid-career professionals, the two-year EMBA program seeks to develop broad-based management skills, and emphasizes an integrated, cross-functional approach to management proficiency in analytical problem-solving skills and development of strategic leadership skills.

UCLA-NUS Global Executive MBA: This dual-degree program is designed to train top executives for the global marketplace. Students enter two of the world's leading graduate management education programs: UCLA Anderson and National University of Singapore Business School.

Master of Financial Engineering: This one-year program provides a depth of study in finance that is more quantitatively oriented than in traditional MBA programs, while also emphasizing the development of key leadership skills.

Doctoral Management : This research-oriented program leads to the Doctor of Philosophy (Ph.D.) degree and emphasizes independent inquiry, research methodology and publication of research results, preparing students for research and teaching careers in academia, industry and government.

ACADEMIC PROGRAMS
Applied Management Research (AMR) program is a critical part of the MBA curriculum. Teams comprising second-year MBA students work closely with a faculty advisor to serve as strategic consultants to major companies, confronting organizational and competitive problems and providing recommendations for action.

Global Access Program (GAP) provides FEMBA students the opportunity to gain international field study experience by helping start-up companies from abroad research and develop "investment grade" business plans. GAP, which encompasses a challenging six-month course, enables students to glean valuable consulting and entrepreneurial experience.

John Wooden Global Leadership Program (JWGLP): Inspired by legendary coach, author and speaker, John Wooden, the JWGLP is dedicated to motivating individuals to achieve their highest potential in the realms of business, management and leadership. The JWGLP includes: The John Wooden Leadership Colloquia, The John Wooden Leadership Scholarships, The John Wooden Executive in Residence, and The John Wooden Global Leadership Award.

CAMPUS FACILITIES AND EQUIPMENT
Eugene and Maxine Rosenfeld Library is the information partner of UCLA Anderson and an integral part of Anderson Computing & Information Services. One of the 13 UCLA libraries, it is ranked as a leading academic business library in the College and University Business Libraries Statistics.

FINANCIAL AID
MBA Tuition and Fees (estimated for 2008-09)

$31,760 per year = California Residents

$39,050 per year = Non-Residents

All admitted full-time students who are U.S. citizens or permanent residents may apply for need-based financial aid. We have partnered with MBA LOANS and Sallie Mae to provide loan funding to admitted international students, including students who cannot secure a co-borrower. A limited number of research assistant and teaching assistant positions are available, as well as fellowship support.

ADMISSIONS PROCESS
The Admissions Committee seeks to create a community of students who bring unique contributions from their diverse backgrounds and experiences and who will collectively enrich the educational experience. Committee members carefully consider biographical and academic background information, GMAT score and (for most international applicants) TOEFL score, achievements, awards and honors, employment history, letters of recommendation, and college and community involvement, especially where candidates have served in leadership capacities.

UNIVERSITY OF CALIFORNIA—RIVERSIDE

AT A GLANCE
The A. Gary Anderson Graduate School of Management (AGSM) is all about growth. We are the program of choice for students, recruiters, and faculty members who wish to focus on how to identify and evaluate growth opportunities, how to launch and develop, as well as manage and sustain those opportunities. AGSM faces the important growth markets of the future along the Pacific Rim, in Asia , and in South America. All of the growth industries of the future are in our backyard: biotechnology, nanotechnology, information, technology, communications, and health care services. AGSM is also about personal growth; we challenge our students to grow as individuals, as leaders, as managers, and as contributors to community. We invite you to come grow with us.

FACULTY
The A. Gary Anderson Graduate School of Management has a renowned, multi-cultural faculty, representing excellence in their respective areas. Faculty members have doctorates from world-class universities and publish research in top journals in their fields. Faculty members also have industry and consulting experience and teach in executive programs and workshops.

STUDENTS
Diverse backgrounds and experiences are characteristic of students in the AGSM M.B.A. program. The average age of students is 27. Approximately 50 percent are women , and 10 percent are members of minority groups. Approximately 70 percent of AGSM's M.B.A. students are international students. The International Services Center provides special assistance to international students and their dependants. The diverse student population helps create a dynamic learning experience which enhances the overall M.B.A experience and the intellectual environment at AGSM.

CAREER SERVICES AND PLACEMENT
A full range of internship and career planning services is offered through the M.B.A. Career Center. The center is staffed by professional counselors to address the specific career needs of graduate business students. Services available include on-campus interviews, career seminars and resume writing workshops, mock interviews, and individual counseling.

LOCATION AND ENVIRONMENT
The 1,200-acre Riverside campus of the University of California is conveniently located some 50 miles east of Los Angeles, within easy driving distance of most of the major cultural and recreational offerings in southern California. Enrollment at UCR is approximately 13,000, nearly 10% graduate students. The campus, with modern classroom buildings, beautiful commons, and 161-foot Carillon Tower, is designed to support the academic and research programs as part of its assigned mission in the University of California system. A city of 250,000, Riverside has several major shopping malls, a symphony orchestra, an opera association, two community theaters, an art center, and many restaurants in proximity to the campus.

ACADEMIC PROGRAMS
The M.B.A. curriculum balances the art and science of management, with an emphasis on managing through information, and recognizes the global context of management. The program stresses the essential interdependencies that exist across functional areas, emphasizing the development of superior management skills as well as theoretical foundations.

The curriculum includes six major components including core courses, electives, internship, and a capstone course. Electives are offered in several areas including accounting, finance, supply chain management, marketing and international management. Significant emphasis is placed on teamwork, which is accomplished through study groups and team projects.

The program is designed to accommodate the unique requirements of both career professionals and full-time students. Courses are offered in the evenings to permit career professionals to complete the M.B.A. on a part-time basis. In this way, full-time and part-time students take classes together, enriching the educational experience of both.

Special Programs

Global Focus

Most AGSM required courses include a global perspective, with recognition of the international issues that affect each functional area. In addition, electives in many of the functional areas provide opportunities for in-depth studies of international topics.

CAMPUS FACILITIES AND EQUIPMENT
The University library is the focal point of research and study at UCR. The collection includes more than 1.8 million bound volumes, 13,316 serial subscriptions, and 1.6 million microforms.

The M.B.A. program is housed in Anderson Hall. M.B.A. students have access to the latest computing equipment, including PC platforms and powerful UNIX workstations.

FINANCIAL AID
Several kinds of financial assistance are available. These include fellowships, teaching assistantships, and research assistantships. Applicants indicate interest in support on the application form. Student loans may be applied for through the UCR Financial Aid office.

ADMISSIONS PROCESS
Admission is open to eligible students from all undergraduate majors. Admission is based on several criteria, including the quality of previous academic work as measured by GPA for the last two years of undergraduate work, scores on the Graduate Management Admission Test (GMAT), letters of recommendation, and potential for success in the program.

A course in quantitative methods is a prerequisite to the program. Students may be admitted without this course but must meet this requirement during their first two quarters in residence.

Applications are accepted for the fall quarter, only. The application deadline for International students is February 1, and for domestic students, May 1.

For further information, go to http://www.agsm.ucr.edu

UNIVERSITY OF COLORADO AT BOULDER
Leeds School of Business

AT A GLANCE

At the Leeds School of Business, innovation and creativity are based on a strong foundation in business theory and practice that is applied in new ways and made relevant in competitive local, national, and international markets. Leeds has built a national reputation for its strength in core business disciplines and specialty programs in Entrepreneurship and Real Estate. Leeds offers full-time MBA, part-time MBA, and Executive MBA programs.

Recent Leeds highlights include the dedication and opening of the Koelbel Building, multiple faculty research recognitions, the appointment of a faculty chair in Growth Management and Sustainability, and a team win at the 2007 International Business Case Masters competition in Germany.

FACULTY

Leeds faculty are leading scholars and business practitioners and integrate their research into the curriculum and their teaching. The faculty actively partner with local entrepreneurs and CEOs to generate hands-on learning experiences and challenge students to develop new problem-solving skills.

STUDENTS

Students come to Leeds from a wide variety of professional backgrounds, undergraduate institutions and majors, and from different parts of the country. They choose Leeds for the high level of interaction with faculty, rigorous academic program, exposure to entrepreneurship and innovation, involvement in emerging industries, life-style proposition, and return on investment.

CAREER SERVICES AND PLACEMENT

Leeds' Career Connections takes a proactive role in preparing incoming MBA students to strategize short and long term goals that lead to summer internships and permanent placement. Leeds' Centers of Excellence in Entrepreneurship and Real Estate also play a significant part in the networking process for students interested in smaller companies and start-up ventures, or real estate development.

LOCATION AND ENVIRONMENT

Leeds offers a highly individualized academic experience with approximately 240 MBA students in its full-time and part-time programs. The University of Colorado at Boulder, as a premiere research university, provides broad resources with the latest in engineering and technology innovation and a beautiful campus setting with breathtaking mountain views. The Boulder-Denver business corridor is an epicenter for start-up and venture activity, new and emerging industries, and is a national hub for telecommunications, high tech, and bio tech companies.

MAJORS AND DEGREES OFFERED

Leeds' MBA program offers a general management foundation with the ability to customize with a functional area of expertise in marketing, finance, management, or systems. Students may combine this breadth and depth of study with one of Leeds' nationally recognized specialties in Entrepreneurship or Real Estate.

ACADEMIC PROGRAMS

Leeds has formed dual degree programs with eight other graduate departments at the University of Colorado at Boulder (See Form J). Aside from dual degree options, students may take up to four graduate school electives outside of the MBA curriculum. Three full-semester exchange opportunities with ITESM-Monterrey Tec in Monterrey, Mexico and with Instituto de Empressa in Madrid, Spain and the Indian Institude of Management, Calcutta are available for study abroad.

SPECIAL PROGRAMS

(See Form D) Eight dual degree options are available through the Leeds School of Business: JD/MBA, MBA/MS in Telecommunications, MBA/MS in Computer Science, MBA/MS in Environmental Studies, MBA/MA or MFA in Fine Arts, MBA/MA in Theatre and Dance, MBA/MA in Germanic and Slavic Languages, MBA/MA in Anthropology.

CAMPUS FACILITIES AND EQUIPMENT

Recently expanded and renovated, Leeds' Koelbel Building is a showcase of environmental stewardship and state-of-the-art classroom technology. The Koelbel Building offers spacious classrooms, an information commons, team rooms, corporate interviewing suites, community space, and breathtaking mountain views.

FINANCIAL AID

As a public institution, the University of Colorado offers comparatively low tuition rates. US citizens and permanent residents who are not Colorado residents can establish residency during the first year of the program and qualify for in-state tuition for the second year of the program. In addition, merit fellowships are awarded to outstanding candidates admitted to the full-time MBA program. Need-based awards are available and require applicants to file a Free Application for Federal Student Aid (FAFSA) form.

ADMISSIONS PROCESS

The admissions process, while selective, is designed to be personal and holistic. Applications are viewed with a number of criteria in mind including educational background, GMAT, professional work experience, letters of recommendation, interviews, essays, and an optional creativity challenge.

UNIVERSITY OF CONNECTICUT
School of Business

AT A GLANCE
Educating leaders for more than 125 years, the University of Connecticut (UConn) is ranked among the top 5% of business schools worldwide according to Business Week, U.S. News & World Report, The Wall Street Journal and The Princeton Review. UConn's highly regarded MBA Program is known for its innovative curriculum design that incorporates distinctive learning accelerators to leverage traditional academic instruction with high-profile corporate partnering in solving practical, real-time challenges. Working alongside research faculty and corporate executives to develop solutions to real industry problems, these unique experience-based opportunities allow students to acquire a business education like no other. Ultimately, UConn MBA graduates have it all: the fundamental knowledge, skills, and practical experience necessary to compete in business today.

The UConn School of Business is nationally accredited by AACSB International - The Association to Advance Collegiate Schools of Business, and is a member of the Graduate Management Admissions Council (GMAC) and the European Foundation for Management Development (EFMD). UConn is also accredited by the New England Association of Schools & Colleges (NEASC).

FACULTY
UConn's faculty offer a wealth of academic and business experience to students. Over 96% of them have earned a PhD or the highest degree in their field. Most are actively involved in scholarly activities that enable them to stay current in and contribute to their fields of knowledge, as well as to bring a balanced perspective between theory and practice into the classroom.

STUDENTS
UConn MBA students come from a wide variety of undergraduate institutions, both domestic and international. Their undergraduate degrees represent majors in many diverse areas - from engineering and English, sciences and fine arts, to business to economics. In a typical class of students, 40 percent are women, the average age is 28, and approximately 35 percent are international students. Friendliness and informality characterize student life at the main campus. Social and professional organizations, including the Graduate Business Association (GBA), offer a variety of activities to satisfy the needs of students.

CAREER SERVICES AND PLACEMENT
UConn's career planning activities begin during orientation and continue throughout the MBA program. Primary recruiters include General Electric, CIGNA, Aetna, IBM, United Technologies Corp., Wachovia, Hartford Financial Services, PricewaterhouseCoopers, Gerber Technologies, ESPN, and UBS Warburg. For the class of 2007, the median salary was $75,000 and went as high as $145,000 plus bonus.

LOCATION AND ENVIRONMENT
UConn has grown in recent years from a strong regional school to a prominent national academic institution with over 28,000 students, 170,000 alumni, and 120 major buildings on 3,100 acres at the main campus in Storrs. The state capital and metropolitan area of Hartford is 30 minutes away, Boston is a 90 minute drive, and New York City is a 3-hour drive.

MAJORS AND DEGREES OFFERED
UConn offers MBA and MS (Accounting) degrees, as well as a variety of dual-degree programs including: MBA/JD, MBA/MD, MBA/MA in international studies, MBA/MSW, MBA/MS in nursing, and MBA/MA of international management (MIM). A post graduate Advance Business Certificate is also offered in various business concentrations.

ACADEMIC PROGRAMS
UConn offers MBA and MS (Accounting) degrees, as well as a variety of dual-degree programs including: MBA/JD, MBA/MD, MBA/MA in international studies, MBA/MSW, MBA/MS in nursing, and MBA/MA of international management (MIM). A post graduate Advance Business Certificate is also offered in various business concentrations.

SPECIAL PROGRAMS
UConn's experiential learning accelerators are what distinguish it from other top-quality MBA programs. These dynamic multi-partner initiatives create a dynamic environment that significantly leverages the learning process, allowing students to acquire a business education like no other. Learning accelerators include the aforementioned MBA Integration Project; GE edgelab; SS&C Technologies Financial Accelerator; Innovation Accelerator; $2 million Student Managed Fund; and Corporate MBA Assistantship.

CAMPUS FACILITIES AND EQUIPMENT
UConn students study in state-of-the-art research and learning facilities. Classrooms and meeting spaces are outfitted with broad multimedia capability reflecting the School's commitment to meet the demands of the information era.

FINANCIAL AID
2007-2008 tuition and fees for the full-time MBA program for the academic year (two semesters) are $10,594 for Connecticut residents and $24,814 for non-residents. Housing and living costs vary among candidates, but are approximately $5,788 for graduate resident housing and $4,210 for meals. Additional costs including required health insurance, textbooks, mobile computer, laundry and incidentals, bring the total yearly cost of attending the MBA program to approximately $27,000 for Connecticut residents and $41,000 for non-residents.

Financial aid is available in the form of loans, scholarships, and graduate assistantships. Most financial aid is awarded on the basis of established need, primarily determined through an analysis of an applicant's Free Application for Federal Student Aid (FAFSA). For further information, students may also contact the University of Connecticut's Financial Aid Office at 860-486-2819 or via the web at www.financialaid.uconn.edu.

ADMISSIONS PROCESS
Admission to UConn's MBA Program is very competitive. The minimum requirements for admission include two years of postgraduate professional work experience; a minimum 3.0 GPA on a 4.0 scale, or the equivalent, from a four-year accredited institution; and a total GMAT score of at least 560. For international students whose native language is not English, a TOEFL score of at least 233 (computer-based) is required. The application deadline for international applicants is February 1 and for domestic applicants, April 15.

UNIVERSITY OF HAWAII—MANOA
Shidler College of Business

AT A GLANCE

A leader among U.S. business schools in its focus on the Asia-Pacific region, the Shidler College of Business at the University of Hawaii—Manoa provides students with an in-depth understanding of the best business practices, an awareness of languages and cultures, and a solid comprehension of emerging technologies within today's complex global economic environment. Founded in 1949, the college offers students a wide selection of degree, certificate and high-impact executive programs in a unique multicultural learning environment enhanced by collaborative learning, research projects, international speakers, internships, study abroad opportunities, and career services. In the past several years, U.S. News & World Report has ranked the college among the top 25 U.S. graduate business schools for international business.

The business program offers an integrated curriculum in five major fields: accounting, finance, marketing, management, and information technology to accentuate the practical application of business theories. The curriculum incorporates the latest technology, offers specific concentration fields such as the recently added Entrepreneurship and Innovation courses and is designed with an Asia-Pacific perspective to respond to the changing economic conditions.

For more information, call 808-956-8266 or visit www.shidler.hawaii.edu.

FACULTY

The Shidler College of Business faculty is a diverse group of internationally accomplished researchers and highly recognized teachers, holding doctoral degrees from Columbia, Carnegie-Mellon, MIT, Stanford, Purdue, Harvard, and other major universities. Our faculty's international experience and business research in the Asia-Pacific region provide an exceptional learning experience for students.

STUDENTS

Total enrollment in all MBA programs ranges from 322 to 400, with approximately 45 Full-Time MBA/China International MBA/Japan-focused MBA per cohort and 200 Part-Time MBA students. More than a third of these students are women, and 30 percent are international students. The average MBA student is 29 years old with four years of work experience beyond the bachelor's degree. The Executive MBA program generally draws 35—40 students; the typical Executive MBA student is 36 years old with 12 years' work experience.

ALUMNI

An extensive network of alumni—from the 50-plus years of the college's existence—spans the globe and provides a helpful link to international opportunities. There are over 24,000 Shidler alumni worldwide.

CAREER SERVICES AND PLACEMENT

The College houses a full-service Internship and Career Development Center offering internships in Hawaii, the US Mainland and abroad, full-time employment placement, on-campus interviews, career fairs and workshops on resume building, interview skills, negotiating salary, business etiquette and dressing for success.

LOCATION AND ENVIRONMENT

The Shidler College of Business at the University of Hawaii—Manoa is located in Honolulu on the Island of Oahu. Nestled in beautiful Manoa Valley, the college is just minutes away from Waikiki, downtown Honolulu, and most major cultural centers.

MAJORS AND DEGREES OFFERED

Bachelor of Business Administration, Master of Business Administration (Full-Time or Part-Time), Japan-focused MBA, China-International MBA, US International MBA, Executive MBA, Executive MBA—Vietnam, Neighbor Island MBA, Joint Juris-Doctorate/MBA, Joint MS in Nursing Admin/MBA, Master of Accounting, Master of Human Resource Management, PhD in International Management.

ACADEMIC PROGRAMS

The Shidler College of Business at the University of Hawaii—Manoa offers the only AACSB International—accredited graduate programs in the state.

The Full-Time MBA (21 months) and the Part-Time MBA (36 months) only admit in the fall. Both are 48-credit-hour programs with an optional summer internship.

The China International MBA is a 21-month cohort program that provides intensive study in the language, culture, and business practices of China.

The Japan-focused MBA is a 21-month cohort program that provides intensive study in the language, culture, and business practices of Japan.

The Executive MBA program is an intensive cohort experience that allows working professionals the opportunity to complete their degree within 22 months in Hawaii, attending class one night a week and every other Saturday.

The Executive MBA in Vietnam, which is held in Hanoi and Ho Chi Minh City, is a 24 month program open to U.S., Vietnamese, and international applicants.

The Master of Accounting program is a 30-credit-hour program that is designed to prepare students for careers in professional accounting. Completion time takes 18 to 24 months.

The PhD program in international management offers specializations in Asian finance, international accounting, international marketing, global information technology management, and international organization and strategy. Completion time takes 4 - 5 years.

Financial Aid

Full-Time MBA tuition (2008-2010) is $27,840 for state residents and $42,960 for non-residents. Part-Time MBA tuition (2008 - 2011) is $29,352 for residents and $45,444 for non-residents. China International MBA tuition (2008 - 2010) is $35,850. Japan-focused MBA tuition (2008 - 2010) is $35,032. The Master of Accounting tuition for 2008—2009 is $538 per credit for residents and $826 for non-residents. The total cost for the Executive MBA program (2007 - 2009) is $33,000, which includes tuition, fees, books, parking and meals.

Over 1 million dollars in merit-based scholarship aid is available to all qualified applicants.

ADMISSIONS PROCESS

The ideal student entering the program has a solid academic record, high test scores, strong motivation, and well-thought-out career goals. Admission requirements include a minimum grade point average of 3.0 or higher (on a 4.0 scale) in the last 60 credits of undergraduate or graduate course work. Applicants whose native language is not English must submit official TOEFL scores. Work experience of at least two years is required for the MBA programs, and four years is required for the Executive MBA; no work experience is required for the MAcc. All applicants are required to submit official GMAT scores, statement of objectives, resume, and 2 letters of recommendation. Interviews are by invitation only.

THE UNIVERSITY OF IOWA
Tippie School of Business

AT A GLANCE

The University of Iowa's Henry B. Tippie School of Management offers a Master of Business Administration (MBA) degree consistently ranked in the top 50 MBA programs in the world. Many characteristics contribute to the quality of the Tippie MBA, including a flexible curriculum and great placement results. Here are a few of the attributes that set Tippie apart from other programs.

A Personal Touch: Or students are never just a face in the crowd. They form relationships with classmates, faculty, and staff that continue long after the formal program is complete. In fact, our students are on a first-name basis with the dean. By limiting class size, we provide a program that meets individual needs.

Reputation: The Tippie School of Management attracts the best and brightest students from around the world, making the program one of the most reputable programs in the world. While at Tippie, students enhance their knowledge of business fundamentals, develop leadership experience, and further their professional development. We produce graduates that go on to business success across the country and the world.

The Tippie MBA is one-of-a-kind. Taught by world-class faculty in a dynamic, Big Ten town, the Tippie MBA is an outstanding value.

STUDENTS

Tippie MBAs are active players in determining the type of MBA experience delivered. Student organizations offer an opportunity to develop their leadership potential and team building skills. Student clubs organize professional development events, career networking opportunities, social events, and many other activities that enhance the Tippie MBA experience.

The entering class in the fulltime MBA Program averages approximately three years of work experience, an average GPA of 3.36 (4.0 scale), and a GMAT score of 652.

LOCATION AND ENVIRONMENT

Iowa City is a diverse, highly cosmopolitan community of 60,000 set in the natural scenic beauty of Iowa's rolling hills and woods. It was selected the number-one place to live in the nation by Editor & Publisher magazine, named one of the 10 most enlightened towns in the country by Utne Reader, and listed in the book The 100 Best Small Art Towns in America.

The University of Iowa campus is seamlessly integrated with the Iowa City community. The 1,900-acre campus is located along both sides of the Iowa River. The campus community provides a rich variety of activities and resources for students.

ACADEMIC PROGRAMS

The Tippie MBA Program emphasizes applied business learning in a collaborative, team-based environment. The curriculum is founded on a core of courses that includes key functional areas of finance, marketing, accounting, statistics, organizational behavior, operations management, economics, and strategic management. Students select a concentration from one of the following areas: accounting, entrepreneurship, finance, strategic management and consulting, management information systems, marketing or operations management. An individually designed concentration is also an option for those with more specific interests.

CAMPUS FACILITIES AND EQUIPMENT

The state-of-the-art facilities of the John Pappajohn Business Building provide a comfortable arena for learning. The Internet conferencing system allows students to work in real-time on a project.

Some building highlights:

• The Marvin A. Pomerantz Business Library provides a 30,000-volume resource area with electronic access to libraries around the world

• Laptop computers are available for checkout from the library for use throughout the building

• A wireless LAN provides Internet access to any student with a network-enabled laptop

• Our Instructional Technology Center features 100 computer workstations (the largest on campus), two 32-seat computer classrooms, and a computerized operations/behavioral laboratory

FINANCIAL AID

The Tippie MBA provides one of the best returns on investment available. This nationally accredited program provides a top-notch education that can help students take their career to the next level.

2008–2009 Academic Year Tuition and Fees
Annual Tuition

Iowa residents: $13,584, Nonresidents: $24,914, Computer fees: $245, Health fees: $210, Student Union, activities, and service fees: $229, Building fee: $119

Merit-based Financial Aid

Merit-based financial aid is offered to outstanding candidates each year. The criteria for these awards mirror those for admission—academic record, work history, leadership experience, test scores—those with the highest qualifications receive offers for aid. Both domestic and international applicants are eligible for awards. Awards may consist of a scholarship, a graduate assistantship, or both. Most scholarships average approximately $5000. Graduate assistantships provide a salary of approximately $8,000, a contribution toward health insurance costs, and resident tuition status for non-Iowa residents.

ADMISSIONS PROCESS

The Tippie MBA seeks candidates demonstrating the ability to complete a rigorous academic program and the potential for success.

Academic Background: In addition to GPA, we consider the difficulty of the major completed and the reputation of the institution. We do not require a specific minimum GPA. However, last year's class average was 3.36.

Standardized Tests: GMAT: All candidates must submit a GMAT score. We do not require a specific minimum score, however, the class average is approximately 652.

TOEFL: Candidates from countries where English is not the native language must submit a TOEFL score. The minimum acceptable score is 250 (computer test), 600 (paper test), or 100 (internet.

A minimum of two years of full-time work experience after completion of the bachelor's degree is recommended. Successful applicants typically have three to five years of work experience.

Evidence of leadership ability is important in demonstrating the candidate's potential for contributing to the learning environment. Ideal candidates have clear records of leadership in school, work, and the community.

An interview is required before an admission offer is made. An admission interview is included in your campus visit. For those who are not able to visit Iowa City, an alternate format, usually a telephone interview, is arranged. Interviews are also available with Tippie representatives who may be traveling to your city.

UNIVERSITY OF MASSACHUSETTS—BOSTON

AT A GLANCE

The University of Massachusetts (UMass) Boston boasts over 13,000 commuting students in its undergraduate, graduate, and continuing education programs, making it the second-largest campus of the University of Massachusetts system. UMass Boston is a community of scholars who take pride in academic excellence, diversity, research, and service. The fabric of academic research and scholarship is tightly woven into the public and community service needs of Boston and the modern metropolitan center.

The UMass Boston College of Management offers Master's degrees in Business Administration (MBA), Accounting (MSA), Finance (MSF), International Management (MSIM) and Information Technology (MSIT). Drawing students from greater Boston and around the world, our Master's programs bring together a diverse group of highly talented young professionals from the healthcare, financial services, manufacturing, IT, consulting and education industries, among others.

STUDENTS

Our students in the UMass Boston graduate business programs are a diverse mix of professionals from a wide range of professional, geographic and cultural backgrounds. Hailing from some 31 states and 57 countries, graduate students in the College of Management are accomplished managers, accountants, educators, healthcare providers, researchers and consultants who seek the knowledge and credentials needed to enhance and advance their careers. They come to us with an average of nearly 6 years of professional experience.

CAREER SERVICES AND PLACEMENT

All part- and full-time graduate students in the College of Management have full access to a wide range of career assistance from the University Career Services Office and the College's own Career Center. Our graduates have enjoyed great success in obtaining professional employment in a number of fields, including financial services, IT, manufacturing, health care, education, and government/nonprofit management. Over 200 employers regularly recruit students on campus, including Ernst & Young, Fidelity Investments, Raytheon, Biogen Idec, PricewaterhouseCoopers, Bank of America, Massachusetts General Hospital, Gillette/Proctor & Gamble, and EMC. The College also has exclusive, innovative internship programs with a number of area firms, including Genzyme and State Street Corporation.

MAJORS AND DEGREES OFFERED

Master of Business Administration (MBA), Master of Science in Accounting (MSA), Master of Science in Finance (MSF), Master of Science in Information Technology (MSIT), Master of Science in International Management (MSIM).

The College of Management is fully accredited by the Association to Advance Collegiate Schools of Business (AACSB), the New England Association of Schools and Colleges (NEASC) and the International Association for Management Education.

Part-time study and evening class options are available. Students with undergraduate or prior graduate coursework are able to waive up to 21 credits (7 courses) of the MBA core, or up to 15 credits of the core of one of the specialized Master's programs.

We offer specializations in the following areas: Accounting, Environmental Management, Finance, Fundraising and Nonprofit Management, Healthcare Management, Human Resource Management, Information Systems, International Management, Internet Marketing, Marketing, Operations Management.

ACADEMIC PROGRAMS

The graduate programs in the UMass Boston College of Management combine strategically focused management curricula with optional specializations that prepare students for specific management responsibilities. Classes are typically taught by experienced, full-time faculty with both academic and professional qualifications. Small class size creates an active learning environment with a great deal of faculty-student interaction. Both course work and student resources help students develop the communications, presentation and analytical skills required of contemporary managers. The College of Management graduate program is committed to the success of all its students, and to providing the individual attention and support that will turn their academic accomplishments into professional reality.

Special Programs

A number of research centers are associated with the UMass Boston College of Management:

- The Center for Collaborative Leadership
- The Venture Development Center
- The Greater Boston Manufacturing Partnership
- The Minority & Small Business Development Center
- The Financial Services Forum

More information is available about individual centers at http://www.management.umb.edu/businesscenter/business_index.php.

FINANCIAL AID

Full-time annual tuition & fees: $10,180 (in-state), $20,700 (out-of-state)

Part-time tuition & fees: $425/credit (in-state), $860/credit (out-of-state)

Roughly 40% of UMB students receive some form of aid; about 20% receive scholarship or grant assistance.

Average scholarship/grant: $15,000

Average debt upon graduation: $16,500

ADMISSIONS PROCESS

Admissions is highly competitive The Office of Graduate Admissions accepts and processes applications for all graduate programs at the University; all supporting documents should be sent to the Office of Graduate Admissions, University of Massachusetts Boston, 100 Morrissey Blvd., Boston, MA 02125-3393. Applications can be completed on-line at https://www.umassadmin.net/isis/application/weba_index1.asp?inst=umbos&career=grad&center=grad.

Admission to our graduate programs is based on prior academic performance, professional experience and accomplishments, GMAT scores, essays, interviews, and recommendations. The process is selective and produces one of the best-qualified groups of graduate student cohorts in the Greater Boston area.

UNIVERSITY OF MIAMI
School of Business Administration

AT A GLANCE

The University Of Miami School of Business Administration is a comprehensive business school, offering undergraduate business, full-time MBA, Executive MBA, PhD and non-degree executive education programs.

FACULTY

Educated at some of the world's finest academic institutions, the School of Business Administration faculty are world-renowned and prestigious. In addition to teaching and conducting leading-edge business research, the school's distinguished faculty members are active in management consulting and serve on corporate boards across the globe.

LOCATION AND ENVIRONMENT

The School is located in a major hub of international trade and commerce and acclaimed for the global orientation and diversity of its faculty, students and curriculum. Coral Gables, Florida infuses Old World ambiance with New World technology.

OFF-CAMPUS OPPORTUNITIES

Off-campus Executive MBA programs are offered at locations across Florida—Tampa, Orlando, and Delray Beach; and abroad — Nassau, Bahamas. Visit our website at www.bus.miami.edu/grad for program schedule, curriculum, and information sessions.

MAJORS AND DEGREES OFFERED

The University of Miami, School of Business Administration, offers a full-time, Two-Year MBA Program (48 credits). JD/MBA and MD/MBA degrees can be earned, requiring admission to both the law or medical school and the MBA program. Executives and professionals may earn an MBA degree by attending Saturday or Saturday/Monday evening classes and specialize in one of the following areas: Health Sector Management and Policy, International Business, Management, or MBA/Master of Science in Industrial Engineering (MBA/MSIE). The School also offers a Spanish language Masters program for Executives and Professionals that live or conduct business in Latin America, Master of Science in Professional Management (Maestria en Ciencias de Gerencia Profesional). For more information please visit us at www.bus.miami.edu/grad.

ACADEMIC PROGRAMS

At the School of Business Administration, the curriculum provides a decidedly flexible framework for learning. A variety of teaching methods are utilized: lecture, discussion, case method, and team projects. Classes are small in order to encourage exchange of ideas between teacher and student, and among students.

CAMPUS FACILITIES AND EQUIPMENT

Classes are held in a 24 million dollar, award-winning complex that was built for the exclusive use of graduate business students. The facility features a virtual library, high tech classrooms with executive seating, a graduate student lounge, break-out rooms, and a computer lab. The Ziff Graduate Career Services Center is exclusively dedicated to helping graduate business students find employment opportunities, obtain internships, and prepare them to compete for top job positions.

TUITION, ROOM, BOARD AND FEES

Graduate tuition for the 2008-2009 academic year is $1,424 per credit hour.

FINANCIAL AID

A limited number of graduate assistantships, offered to outstanding applicants in the fall semester, usually include both a tuition scholarship and a monthly stipend. The Graduate Assistantship may cover up to 75 percent of the tuition cost. Graduate students are eligible to apply for student loans and work-study assistance through the University's Office of Financial Assistance Services.

STUDENT ORGANIZATIONS AND ACTIVITIES

The University of Miami values its multicultural community and student organizations. There are a number of student-run, professional and social organizations that encourage and support career goals. There are also interest-based MBA Clubs which allow students with similar interests to network with industry professionals. MBA students may also participate in the MBA Consultants Program and offer business expertise to local non-profit organizations. In addition, the Graduate Career Services Center encourages/awards students to attend national career conferences and events such as Wall Street Week, Wall Street Forums, Global MBA/Masters Employment Conference, National Association of Women MBA, Nationals

ADMISSIONS PROCESS

The Graduate Business Admissions Committee welcomes applications from individuals whose undergraduate degrees are from accredited colleges or universities. Student applications are reviewed on an individual basis to determine the applicant's potential for success in the MBA Program. Applicants are encouraged to submit their application in advance of the set deadline for each round. A competitive GMAT score, GPA, and work experience are essential to be considered for admission. Other factors considered by the Admissions Committee include an essay, letters of recommendation, and community involvement. Students applying to the MBA Programs for Executives and Professionals are required to have a minimum of three years of professional work experience, and may be required to take the GMAT.

UNIVERSITY OF MISSOURI—ST. LOUIS

AT A GLANCE

As the premiere public research institution in St. Louis, UM-St. Louis offers more than 49 undergraduate, 30 master's and 13 doctoral programs. Not only do we provide quality academics, but UM-St. Louis provides many social, athletic and extracurricular opportunities in which our students become involved.

Our programs reflect our mission as a public metropolitan research university: our faculty members' and students' scholarship advances understanding of their disciplines in rapidly changing local, regional, and global contexts.

CAMPUS AND LOCATION

Student enrollment has grown from 600 in 1963 to more than 15,500. Faculty and students are still most concerned with the education of new talent, which is the basis for the future social, intellectual, and economic health of Missouri's largest metropolitan area. From its beginning on what was once the site of a country club with a single building, UM-St. Louis has grown to a large modern campus of more than 320 acres with more than 60 buildings used to support academic and other University activities.

DEGREES OFFERED

There are six graduate degree programs and four graduate certificate programs offered through the College of Business Administration.

Degree Programs:

Doctor of Philosophy in Business

Master of Business Administration (evening program)

Professional MBA (blended weekend/online program)

International MBA (offers overseas experience)

Master of Science in Information Systems

Master of Accounting

Certificates:

Business Administration

Human Resource Management

Logistics and Supply Chain Management

Marketing Management

PROGRAMS AND CURRICULUM

The Professional MBA program is a 23-month (48-credit hour) program that meets one weekend per month (Friday-Saturday). Approximately half of the course is in a lecture format, and the remainder of the course relies on the various communication methods available on the Internet.

The International MBA program is unique as it is the only two-year/two-degree program in the nation that involves multiple partnerships. The unique format of the program allows participants to enroll in two graduate business programs simultaneously-UM-St. Louis and one of our global partner institutions in Austria, China, Japan, India, Mexico or France. Students complete the first year at one of partner institutions and the second year at UM-St. Louis. All students complete a foreign internship.

FACILITIES

The Millennium Student Center is a 165,000-square foot facility that includes a four-story rotunda, a third-floor gallery with clerestory windows, and a climate-controlled pedestrian bridge leading to the academic quadrangle. In addition, there is a fireside social lounge, a quiet study lounge, a student art gallery, a large tiered meeting chamber, an expanse of first-class conference areas, twin television lounges, a game room and a cyber lab.

Virtually all student services and functions are under one roof. The following departments are conveniently located in the Millennium Student Center: Center for Student Success, Student Activities, Student Government, Student Organizations, Admissions, Registration, Financial Aid, Cashiers, Degree Audit, Career Services, Counseling Services, Women's Center, Multi-Cultural Relations, Health Services, Accessibilities Services, Food Services, Bookstore, Convenience Store and a full service bank.

EXPENSES AND FINANCIAL AID

Information concerning the fees for both resident and non-resident students is available at: http://www.umsl.edu/services/finance/general_fees.htm

Awards and assistantships are generally only awarded to students who have completed several courses in one of the degree programs. Several monetary awards based on performance in one of the graduate business programs are available on an annual basis. Graduate assistants can earn reduced tuition, the amount of reduction based on the number of hours the student is employed by the College of Business.

FACULTY

Our faculty are highly-qualified teachers and researchers who hold terminal degrees from some of the world's most prestigious academic institutions. They are actively engaged in cutting-edge academic research and real-world consulting.

STUDENTS

UM-Saint Louis is considered one of the most culturally and ethnically diverse campuses in the state. With a strong unity of purpose, we are committed to creating an engaging and harmonious climate where talents of diverse faculty, staff and students flourish.

ADMISSIONS

Consideration is given to a candidate's academic record, scores on the Graduate Management Admissions Test (GMAT), work and leadership experience, a personal narrative on the application form, and recommendations.

Information about the applicant process is available at: http://www.umsl.edu/admission/apply/preappinfo.htm

CAREER SERVICES AND PLACEMENT

Career Services works in partnership with employers and the campus community by assisting students and alumni to develop, implement, and evaluate job search strategies.

THE UNIVERSITY OF NEW SOUTH WALES
AGSM MBA Program

AT A GLANCE

The AGSM MBA Program provides a world-class business education and extensive business networking opportunities that will help you achieve your career and personal goals. You'll also find extensive opportunities for personal development in one of the most livable cities in the world - Sydney, Australia.

The AGSM MBA is ranked in the top 20 outside the US (Financial Times, 2008), and was the first in Australia to be granted AACBS Accreditation. The MBA course commences with the innovative "Foundations of Management", a three-week intensive overview of general management, in which you'll pick up skills that will be invaluable during your MBA and into the executive world beyond. This is followed by a rigorous grounding in Organisational Behaviour, Economics, Accounting, Data Analysis & Decision Making under Uncertainty, Finance, Marketing Management, Operations Management and Strategy. The last two sessions are where you can choose from a wide selection of Electives, or, as so many of the AGSM MBA students choose to do, go on International Exchange at a top business school such as Wharton or London Business School.

The community of faculty, students and industry networks, together with the design of the MBA Program produce a learning experience that will prepare you for the rigors of senior management, and lay the foundation for you to achieve your career goals. With over 200 faculty members at the Australian School of Business at the University of New South Wales, and a typical cohort of students representing over 25 countries and a multitude of industries, the AGSM MBA Program is truly diverse. Collaboration within an intellectually stimulating environment at the cutting edge of management thought promotes the confidence you will need to tackle emerging issues at the highest level.

The AGSM MBA is the most prestigious MBA in Australia, with an enviable reputation amongst employers of MBA graduates. The Career Management Program provides you with the tools you will need to find that ideal job. Over 20 top companies actively recruit from AGSM MBA Programs, and the network provided by current students, alumni, faculty and through the many events held on campus will give you the connections to explore employment and entrepreneurial options.

You will be studying in Sydney, one of the most exciting cities in the world. The campus is located in Sydney's Eastern Suburbs, close to some of the world's most beautiful beaches. Many students live nearby in the suburbs of Coogee, Bondi, Centennial Park, Randwick, Kingsford and Maroubra, and enjoy the multicultural, outdoor lifestyle that Sydney has to offer.

All in all, you'll find that an AGSM MBA will mean new opportunities both professionally and in terms of your personal development.

FACULTY

Rigour and diversity are the hallmark qualities of the research undertaken by the faculty teaching on AGSM programs. Their work, which is published in world-class academic, business and practitioner journals, has made seminal contributions to management practice. Faculty teaching on AGSM programs have been recognised by a number of prestigious awards and prizes, and some of these faculty have been identified in international surveys as the leading figures worldwide in their academic fields, based on their career publications.

Faculty are selected to teach on AGSM programs from the wider group of academics working in the Australian School of Business. Their research is international, with classic work undertaken in the major discipline areas such as finance, organisational behaviour, statistics and marketing, as well as cross-discipline research in general management, strategy, corporate governance, and management decision making.

The unique combination of an active research agenda, a wealth of industry experience and impressive teaching abilities, enables faculty teaching on AGSM courses to offer fresh perspectives to business and deliver challenging, research-driven education with powerful new ideas to students and managers.

STUDENTS

"Having made the decision to return to Sydney to undertake my MBA, the AGSM was an obvious choice due to its reputation and ranking. What surprised me about the AGSM was the diversity of students in the full time program, both in terms of their professional background and their country of origin. This mix contributed to widely different perspectives on business challenges that were both enlightening and refreshing. Before embarking on the MBA I could not have imagined how life changing the experience would be," Fiona Macrae, Class of 2008.

"I treated the opportunity to travel from the US to Sydney in pursuit of an MBA as an adventure, and the experience did not disappoint. Over the past 18 months I've received a world class education that has helped me to grow on a number of levels, both personally and professionally. I'll be leaving the program supremely satisfied in an experience that helped me to rapidly accelerate my career as well as develop a network of friends spanning the globe. If you're looking for an MBA that represents the total package, look no further than the AGSM," Danny Van Clief, Class of 2008.

CAREER SERVICES AND PLACEMENT

The Careers Centre provides students with the opportunity to develop career management skills and is specifically designed to give students the tools to facilitate their job search and manage their career. You will also be able to leverage off the global business and alumni network of 10,000 members spread across 68 countries.

MAJORS AND DEGREES OFFERED

MBA (Full-time)

MBA (Executive - Part Time)

Graduate Certificate in Change Management

FINANCIAL AID

The fees for the full-time MBA for 2009 entry are set at AUD$57,120.

ADMISSIONS PROCESS

The AGSM MBA Admissions staff are always available to help prospective students with the completion of their application. The AGSM MBA Programs website provides a detailed description of what is required.

UNIVERSITY OF NOTRE DAME
Mendoza College of Business

AT A GLANCE

Mendoza places an emphasis on providing an excellent business education that puts priority on ethics and values. MBA students learn leadership skills so that they can solve some of the toughest problems in business, and do so with a consciousness of how their actions impact the larger community. The curriculum provides a balanced mastery of all functional areas of business-finance, accounting, marketing and management. Signature courses in Problem-Solving and Innovation gives students the tools to diagnose problems, understand the critical issues and frame innovative solutions.

Further, students are exposed to the complexities of global business through a series of engagements with leaders worldwide. Immersions in Asia, Latin America and Europe provide opportunities to experience other cultures first-hand. Signature lecture series, such as Ten Years Hence, bring in internationally renowned experts to discuss some of the most vital trends and issues facing the current age. Students also have the opportunity to broaden their problem-solving and entrepreneurial skills by participating in service projects in locations ranging from Jamaica, South Africa, Mexico, to here in the Midwest.

In the classroom, "live case" experiences allow MBA students to analyze, investigate and offer solutions for real-life problems presented by executives from some of the largest global organizations, including GE, Hewlett-Packard, Starbucks, Nestle, Walgreens and OfficeMax.

The Mendoza College graduate degrees include: Master of Business Administration (MBA), Master of Science in Accountancy (MSA) and a Master of Nonprofit Administration (MNA). The College also offers an Executive MBA in Chicago and on the Notre Dame campus, as well as additional non-degree and custom executive education courses. Joint-degree programs are available in science, engineering and juris doctor.

Building a strong social network is important to the MBA program as well. There are club activities relating to careers in technology, investments, marketing, entrepreneurship or other timely interests. Students participate in a wide variety of competitive and non-competitive sports, including all-night soccer matches and Notre Dame's annual Bookstore Basketball tournament. The Notre Dame MBA graduate becomes part of the most extensive network of alumni clubs in higher education, with more than 120,000 members in 281 chapters-59 of which are international. Long after graduation, Mendoza alumni turn to each other for career counseling, professional networking and trusted friendships.

CAREER SERVICES AND PLACEMENT

At the University of Notre Dame, the number one priority of the MBA Career Development office is our students. Students drive our process as we consistently provide individualized career counseling and advising. Our function-specific approach means your career coach has deep experience in the field of interest to you. Our coaches come from successful consulting, marketing and finance careers.

The Notre Dame MBA Career CatalystTM, our comprehensive career development process, helps you identify and secure a meaningful and successful career. The process consists of five phases that are essential for success.

LOCATION AND ENVIRONMENT

The University of Notre Dame is an independent, national Catholic university located in Notre Dame, Indiana. Located adjacent to the city of South Bend and approximately 90 miles southeast of Chicago, Notre Dame offers students the best of both worlds: a small, Midwestern town and large metropolitan city within close proximity. Notre Dame's campus, considered one of the most beautiful in the country, contains 1,250 acres, two lakes, and many renowned structures including the Basilica of the Sacred Heart, a designated national monument; our Lady of Lourdes Grotto; the Hesburgh Library, home to the Word of Life mural, a.k.a. "Touchdown Jesus," and, of course, the famous golden dome atop our Main Building.

The Mendoza College of Business has several renowned centers of thought.

- The Gigot Center for Entrepreneurial Studies fosters innovation among current and aspiring entrepreneurs. Through a unique curriculum, business plan competitions, and mentoring opportunities with Notre Dame alumni, students gain vital experience and the skills necessary to build successful businesses.

- The Fanning Center for Business Communication provides course work in all facets of human communication, from writing and speaking to listening and group interaction. In addition to classroom success, Fanning Center faculty have also earned an international reputation for their research and publications.

- The Institute for Ethical Business Worldwide seeks to promote positive illustrations of ethical and socially responsible business conduct throughout the world. We stress the importance of ethical leadership as a cornerstone to building a stronger sense of integrity and values into all business firms.

- The Center for Ethics and Religious Values seeks to strengthen ethical foundations in business and public policy decisions by fostering dialogue among academic and corporate leaders, as well as by research and publications. The center's ethics curriculum is integrated throughout Notre Dame's business course work.

ACADEMIC PROGRAMS

With more than 100 elective courses, seven concentration tracks and two formats, the Notre Dame MBA program provides students with a challenging and flexible educational experience.

The One-Year MBA program is designed for students who have an undergraduate degree in business. This program enables students to begin study in May and graduate the following May. Beginning with a 10-week summer semester, students attend intensive sessions in the core disciplines that normally are explored during the first year of the Two-Year program. After the summer semester, students move directly into the second year of the Two-Year program. Students are required to complete 46 credit hours.

In the Two-Year MBA program, students attend classes for four semesters. Each semester consists of two seven-week modules, which gives students greater flexibility in choosing courses to suit individual interests, more opportunity to study abroad, and more professional development. An Interterm in every semester allows students to enroll in one-week courses to deepen or broaden their expertise or, when coupled with break week, enables students to study in China, Belgium or India. Students are required to complete 63 credit hours of work over four semesters.

UNIVERSITY OF NORTH CAROLINA AT CHARLOTTE

AT A GLANCE

The MBA Program at UNC Charlotte offers students the opportunity to invest in themselves and their careers by earning a highly respected MBA. As an MBA student at the Belk College of Business, you will learn more than management, finance and marketing. Our program is distinguished by its full and engaging curriculum, taught by our outstanding resident faculty. It is designed to teach you to think strategically, to communicate effectively and to work productively as part of a team - giving you the tools to succeed in today's complex, fast paced business environment.

The MBA is offered in both a full-time and flexible evening format. The full-time MBA is a highly selective 17-month program. Students enter this program as a cohort following a set schedule that begins in August and concludes the following December. Core courses are offered at the UNC Charlotte campus during the day with concentration courses taken at UNC Charlotte Uptown in the evening. Students are also extended the opportunity to participate in professional internships or study-abroad programs during the summer term. The Flexible MBA is self-paced evening program, allowing students the option of completing the degree in as few as 18 months although students with full-time careers generally take 24-36 months to finish All Flexible MBA courses meet one evening per week, allowing students seeking a balance between work, graduate school, family and other commitments maximum flexibility.

You may concentrate your MBA in one of nine defined academic areas (business finance, information & technology management, international business, management, marketing, economics, real estate finance and development, financial institutions / commercial banking, supply chain management) as well as the option to define your own. These choices allow you to customize your MBA to help you achieve your individual career goals and develop additional depth in an area of particular interest.

The MBA program at UNC Charlotte is fully accredited by AACSB International, the premier accrediting agency for programs in business administration and accounting. This prestigious distinction is achieved as a result of the world-class faculty and highest caliber students that make up the Belk College of Business.

FACULTY

All of our faculty have earned a PhD, JD or DBA and are academically qualified by AACSB Standards. Belk College faculty combine academic research excellence with real-world work and consulting experience.

CAREER SERVICES AND PLACEMENT

The UNC Charlotte MBA approaches career services as a personal development process. You will work one-on-one with a career advisor to develop an individualized plan based on your personal career goals. Recent surveys indicate a 100% placement of our graduates within 6 months.

LOCATION AND ENVIRONMENT

The University of North Carolina at Charlotte is located in one of the largest financial centers of the United States. In addition, many of the nations leading service, manufacturing, retail and nonprofit corporations are headquartered in the area. The area is rapidly growing and expanding, as is UNC Charlotte.

The main campus (9201 University City Blvd) sits on more than 1000 acres in northern Charlotte. The University also has an Uptown Charlotte location (220 N. Tryon) where about 50 percent of the MBA courses are delivered.

MAJORS AND DEGREES OFFERED

Full-Time Master of Business Administration (MBA)

Flexible MBA

MBA in Sports Marketing/Management

Master of Accountancy

Master of Science in Economics

Master of Science in Math Finance

Ph.D. in Business Administration

ACADEMIC PROGRAMS

The MBA is a 37 credit hour program begins with developing a comprehensive understanding of the functions of an organization then builds upon this foundation to develop effective strategic management. Selecting elective courses in an academic concentration allows candidates to specialize their degree to further individual goals. Additional course work may be required of students in a preparatory component based on academic preparation and experience.

FINANCIAL AID

Scholarship, Fellowship and Assistantship information can be found at www.mba.uncc.edu.

ADMISSIONS PROCESS

Admission to the UNC Charlotte MBA program is selective. We seek candidates who are motivated and aim to assume leadership roles in organizations locally and around the world. Candidates must have obtained the equivalent of a U.S. bachelor's degree from a fully accredited university to be eligible for admission to the UNC Charlotte MBA.

Previous study of business is not required, as the program offers a 13 credit preparatory component that provides non-business majors the background they need to be successful in the rest of the program. These preparatory courses are waived for candidates with sufficient undergraduate preparation.

Admissions decisions are based on several criteria, including the applicant's academic achievement, previous work history, and standardized test scores. A completed application form must be accompanied by three letters of recommendation, a current resume, all academic transcripts, a GMAT score, statement of purpose, and a $55 application fee.

Work experience is not required for admission to the MBA program, however it is strongly recommended. The average student in the UNC Charlotte Flexible (evening) MBA has more than 7 years of professional work experience. Since the admissions decision involves several criteria, there are no set minimums for the GMAT or GPA average. The fall 2007 entering class had an average undergraduate GPA of 3.3 (on a 4.0 scale) and an average GMAT score of 591.

In addition to the above, international students must also submit an official financial statement verifying sufficient resources to cover education and living expenses. International students are also required to provide TOEFL scores (557 on paper-based test or 220 on the computer-based test).

Applications to the Flexible MBA are accepted for fall, spring and summer entry on a rolling admissions basis. The Sports MBA and Full-Time MBA begin each fall.

UNIVERSITY OF RHODE ISLAND

College of Business Administration

AT A GLANCE

Since its inception in 1961, the Master of Business Administration programs at the University of Rhode Island match the needs of participants from all degrees and career paths! Choose from a variety of

MBA programs including: One Year (full-time day) MBA, Evening (part-time) MBA program, 4+1 IME/MBA, PharmD/MBA, Dual Degree MBA/MO (Master of Oceanography) First of it's kind in the world!

All MBA programs offer you: AACSB accreditation, Strong reputation worldwide, Nationally and internationally recognized faculty, Updated facilities and technology including wireless classrooms, trading room, and computer lab, Career opportunities after graduation, Value, Great learning environment.

MAJORS AND DEGREES OFFERED

One Year Full Time MBA, Evening Part Time MBA, MBA/PharmD dual degree, 4+1 IME/MBA, MBA/Master of Oceanography 16 month dual degree, Master of Science in Accounting, Ph.D. in Business.

ACADEMIC PROGRAMS

The One Year MBA at URI integrates course work, career planning and development, and work experience within a one calendar year period, at our main campus in Kingston, RI. The program starts in August and continues over the Fall and Spring semesters. During the Summer, you will be taking two evening courses as well as participating in a 6-credit internship or taking two electives instead. There is a total of 15 courses, or 45 credits, in this program. Only 25 students are accepted each year.

The Evening MBA Program prepares you for careers as effective leaders and managers. The program is designed to emphasize conceptual, analytical, technical, and interpersonal skills. Material for this non-thesis program is presented through lectures, discussions, case studies, and both individual and group projects. The MBA program does not require previous instruction in business administration. The program consists of 15 courses (36 to 45 credits, depending upon your undergraduate major). Included in the 45 credits are 9 credit hours of electives that enable you to specialize in a particular area of study. The classes are held at the URI Feinstein Providence campus, 80 Washington Street, downtown Providence, RI.

The 4+1 IME/MBA allows students currently enrolled in the IME program at URI to apply early to the One Year MBA program, and waive some entry level courses because of equivalent undergraduate courses.

MBA/PharmD—allows students currently enrolled in the PharmD program at URI to apply early to the One Year MBA program, or Evening MBA program and take classes after reaching 120 credits in their PharmD program. We are allowed to use the PharmD classes as electives in the MBA program.

MBA/Master of Oceanography—the new one of a kind program allows a student to combine the two degrees in just 16 months!

One Year MBA Program: Ballentine Hall is the home to the College of Business Administration in Kingston. A complete transformation to the building was completed in the summer of 2003. The new building houses a dedicated MBA classroom, live trading room, wired classrooms with state of the art video equipment, computer lab, and student lounge.

Evening MBA Program: The Providence Evening MBA Program at URI is structured to meet your needs by scheduling classes one night per week, Monday through Thursday evenings (times of 6:00 - 8:45 p.m., 6:30 - 9:15p.m., or 7:00 -9:45 p.m.) at URI's Feinstein Providence Campus at the Shepard Building located on 80 Washington Street in downtown Providence, Rhode Island. Evening courses are periodically available in Kingston as well. Some intensive weekend electives, Saturday and distance learning courses are also available. Classes are offered in the Fall (Sept-Dec) and Spring (Jan-May)

semesters. We also offer two Summer sessions (May-June and June-July) in which classes meet twice a week for five weeks from 6:00-9:45pm.

Special Programs: MBA-MO

TUITION, ROOM, BOARD AND FEES

One Year MBA Program Fees

Listed below are the estimated costs for full-time tuition for the entire program in the 2007/2008 academic year. Tuition for the entire one year program (two full semesters plus both summer sessions) is as follows:

In-state residents (living in RI for one year): $ 12,711

Out-state residents: $34,914

Additional fees for in/out state per semester: $1508 (for Fall and Spring which includes health, registration, and student services fees); $200/year on campus or $125/year commuter parking fee; one time $35 transcript and $45 graduation fees.

Evening MBA Program Fees

Students registered for 8 credits or less per semester are charged the following Part-Time Fees in 2007/2008:

Rhode Island Residents: $385/credit hour

Non-residents: $1058/credit hour

New Regional Rate for Eligible MA Residents starting 2008

FINANCIAL AID

Financial Assistance is available to the MBA student through several sources:

Payment plans are available.

Low interest, government guaranteed loans through the William D. Ford Direct Student Loan Program. Inquiries concerning the Loan Program should be addressed to:

Student Financial Aid Office
Green Hall
Kingston, RI 02881
(401) 874-2314

Graduate assistantships are available to a limited number of full-time MBA students. Recipients work either 10 hours per week and get 1/2 tuition free for the fall and spring plus a stipend ; or work up to 20 hours of research or administrative support and you will get full tuition for the fall and spring as well as a stipend. It is also possible to obtain a graduate assistantship through other University departments. Interested students should contact the Graduate Programs Office.

For international students and US citizens who do not qualify for the William D. Ford loan, private loans are available through MBALOANS run by the Graduate Management Admission Council. Call them at 1-888-440-4622 and talk with a customer representative to initiate a loan application for the Tuition Loan Program (TLP).

ADMISSIONS PROCESS

The application can be started online at http://www.uri.edu/gsadmis/

UNIVERSITY OF ROCHESTER
William E. Simon Graduate School of Business

AT A GLANCE
The William E. Simon Graduate School of Business Administration at the University of Rochester in Rochester, New York offers an integrated, cross-functional approach to management, which uses economics as both the framework and common language of business, and the skills to become an effective leader. Programs offered are full-time MBA and MS programs, Executive MBA and Part-Time MBA and MS programs.

The school is accredited by the AACSB—The International Association for Management Education since 1966. Simon: where thinkers become leaders.

CAMPUS AND LOCATION
The Simon School is situated on the River Campus of the University of Rochester, near the banks of the Genesee River, and three miles from downtown Rochester, New York. The Simon School is one of seven schools and colleges within the University of Rochester.

DEGREES OFFERED
Full-Time Study: The MBA degree requires 67 hours of study and a 3.0 grade-point average. There are two entrance dates, September or January. The degree requirements for the January entrance are the same as those for fall entry.

Part-Time Study: Applicants to the Part-Time MBA Program may matriculate in any quarter. They may also take up to four classes before matriculating to the program. The part-time MBA degree requires 64 hours of study and a 3.0 grade-point average.

Executive MBA Programs: Offers candidates a fully accredited MBA degree without career interruption. Classes meet every other Friday/Saturday for two academic years in Rochester, New York; and Bern, Switzerland. (22 months).

MS Programs: Nine Master of Science in Business Administration programs are offered: Accountancy, Marketing, General Management, Medical Management, Manufacturing Management, Service Management, Information Systems Management, Technology Transfer and Commercialization and Finance.

Each M.S. degree is offered on a full-time or part-time basis. Certificate Programs are offered in five areas of study.

ACADEMIC PROGRAMS
The Simon School's MBA programs are designed to train individuals to solve management problems as team members in a study-team structure. It is a place where thinkers become leaders. The curriculum emphasizes learning the principles of economics and effective decision making through a mix of lecture, case study, and project courses. Nine core courses are required. A three-credit course over two quarters in business communications is required of all full-time students. Eleven elective courses are required.

FACILITIES
Schlegel Hall is a four-story classroom and student-services building. The building contains nine case-style classrooms, which seat 35 to 100 students, and 21 rooms for group study. Classrooms are equipped with state-of-the-art audio and visual technology.

Carol G. Simon Hall houses the school's administration, faculty and PhD students. Carol G. Simon Hall is linked to Schlegel and Gleason Halls by the Florescue-von Manstein Plaza and is also connected to it by a tunnel. The building contains more than 75 offices, several conference rooms, and a variety of lounge spaces for Faculty and staff.

James S. Gleason Hall is the 38,000-square-foot classroom building linked to Schlegel Hall. Gleason Hall houses five new classrooms, up to 16 study rooms, and a significantly expanded Career Management Center suite, including eight dedicated interview rooms.

EXPENSES AND FINANCIAL AID
In addition to the $125 application fee, tuition is $1,228 per credit hour, or $36,840 per year, for 2007–2008. The cost of books and supplies averages $1,500 a year, and living expenses (rent, food supplies, personal expenses, and health insurance) were estimated at less than $10,000 for the 2007–2008 academic year. Both U.S. and international applicants are eligible for merit awards.

STUDENT BODY
Each September approximately 120 students enter the Simon community. Another 50 students join their classmates in January. September entrants complete the first-year core courses during the fall, winter, and spring quarters; the majority of January entrants complete core courses during the winter, spring, and summer quarters. Within each cohort, students are assigned to a study team of 4 or 5 members. Each team always includes representatives from at least three countries.

In the class of 2007, 17 countries are represented. Prior full-time work experience averages 4.1 years, and the average age is 27. Women comprise 30 percent of the class. Thirty-eight percent of Simon students are members of American minority groups.

ADMISSIONS
A Simon School Admissions Committee reads each application individually and evaluates recommendations, teamwork and communication skills, the nature and scope of prior work experience, the undergraduate academic record, GMAT scores. All undergraduate majors are represented in the program.

SPECIAL PROGRAMS
During the two-week Orientation Program, students participate in self-assessment exercises, personal selling and communication skills instruction, corporate leadership training, and one-on-one career counseling. In addition, students participate in several VISION (the student-managed portion of a Simon MBA) modules designed to enhance leadership skills in the areas of team building, training in diversity issues, ethical decision making, and social responsibility.

ADDITIONAL INFORMATION
Year after year, the Simon School consistently ranks high on the lists of top b-school programs. These rankings include: *BusinessWeek*, *U.S. News & World Report*, *Financial Times of London*, *Forbes*, and *The Wall Street Journal*.

CAREER SERVICES AND PLACEMENT
The Career Management Center team works diligently to develop new and enhance existing corporate partnerships to provide a wide range of career opportunities for both summer internships and full-time career positions.

The Career Management Center's Counseling and Education staff offers targeted, personalized counseling to assist students in identifying, initiating, and implementing highly effective career plans.

UNIVERSITY OF SOUTH CAROLINA
Moore School of Business

AT A GLANCE

Moore School of Business is known for its expertise and experience in international business. Top-ranked in national and international surveys, Moore School's undergraduate and graduate programs offer students opportunities to learn and work in a global business environment. Moore School's International MBA has been the top-ranked international business program at a U.S. public university since 1989, according to U.S. News & World Report. The Wall Street Journal ranks the Moore School seventh in the world for international business. The Financial Times MBA 2007 report ranks the Moore School first among all schools worldwide on "international experience." Moore is the only U.S. school ranked in the top ten for "international experience" by its alumni.

The University of South Carolina's international business faculty has been rated #1 in research productivity by the Journal of International Business Studies. Many other programs and departments, such as entrepreneurship, insurance, and management science, also receive high marks. The Moore School of Business is accredited by AACSB International-The Association to Advance Collegiate Schools of Business. In 1998, the university named its business school after South Carolina native and New York businesswoman Darla Moore, becoming the first comprehensive university to name its business school after a woman.

FACULTY

Virtually all 100 have terminal degrees, and all full-time faculty are academically and professionally qualified. Their involvement in research and publishing has brought them recognition from peer institutions. Many of our faculty serve on the editorial boards of leading academic journals; many also serve as editors of top publications. Corporate support and endowed chairs attract and reward permanent faculty as well as visiting professors, adjunct professors, and distinguished lecturers. Most of our adjunct professors come to the Moore School after spending years in the business world.

STUDENT BODY

The students in the IMBA program come from a wide variety of backgrounds. Enrollment in the IMBA for summer II in 2007 was 107 students. Women represent 35 percent of this student population, international students make up 25 percent and members of minority groups represent 10 percent. The typical entering student is 27 years old and has approximately 3½ years of work experience. IMBA students have an average GMAT score of 640 and an average GPA of 3.33.

CAREER SERVICES AND PLACEMENT

Moore School of Business Office of Career Management partners with students to achieve their career goals. A highly structured Career Development Curriculum prepares students for their job search soon after they come to campus. The Office of Career Management (OCM) uses the Birkman Method as an assessment instrument to advise students on programs of study, internship opportunities, and job search plans. The OCM also partners with a leader executive outplacement firm, Lee Hecht Harrison, who coach second year students in their job search. More than 150 companies come to USC to recruit each year. Top recruiters include Citigroup, General Motors, BB&T, CHEP, BMW, Deloitte & Touche, ExxonMobil, Bank of America, Pricewaterhouse Coopers, and BellSouth. Students use online resume services and video conference facilities for contacts and interviews worldwide.

LOCATION AND ENVIRONMENT

Moore School of Business has an urban campus with green space and gardens, historic buildings, and easy access to recreation and cultural events. With its location in the heart of Columbia, the capital of South Carolina, students can take advantage of water sports on the nearby rivers and lakes, hiking and skiing in the mountains, and fishing and sailing on the Atlantic Coast. In town, the Columbia Museum of Art provides traveling exhibitions and a substantial permanent collection. The Town Theatre, the Workshop Theatre, and the Koger Center are among the many venues offering theater beyond the very active University performances. Columbia is home to the world-class Riverbanks Zoo and Botanical Garden and the historic State Museum. Nightlife abounds around campus, with live bands performing rock, jazz, and blues, and the area is the origin of popular groups such as Hootie and the Blowfish. The gentle southern climate makes outdoor sports and recreation a year-round pursuit.

MAJORS AND DEGREES OFFERED

Bachelor of Science in Business Administration, International Master of Business Administration, Master of Business Administration, Master of Human Resources, Master of Accountancy, Master of Arts in Economics, Doctor of Philosophy in Business Administration, Doctor of Philosophy in Economics.

ACADEMIC PROGRAMS

The Moore School is best know for its International Master of Business Administration (IMBA) degree with two program options: the Language Track and the Global Track. Regardless of the option chosen, all students study the same internationalized core of course work. The core courses emphasize the global aspects of the various functional areas, consistent with the program's mission to provide students with an expertise in the international dimensions of business.

Special Programs: Moore School of Business offers specialized master's degrees in accounting (Master of Accountancy, economics (MA in Economics), and human resources (Master of Human Resources). Also offered is an MBA for working professionals, the Professional MBA, distributed by satellite to 23+ receiving locations throughout South Carolina and now in Charlotte, NC. This program has been on-going for more than 30 years and features professors teaching by live television with interactive audio. Flexibility of start date, class time, curriculum, and location, attracts working professionals in business, engineering, and accounting, who want to enhance their careers by earning an MBA from an accredited university.

CAMPUS FACILITIES AND EQUIPMENT

Moore School of Business at the University of South Carolina is housed in a nine-story building with offices and classrooms in close proximity to foster interaction between students and faculty. Facilities include the Elliott White Springs Business Library, Japan Business Library, Center for Entrepreneurship, James C. Self Computer Lab, Center for Business Communication, auditoriums, media classrooms, tv studio classrooms, meeting rooms, and teleconference facilities.

FINANCIAL AID

Moore School of Business has been rated a "best buy" and a fast "ROI" at various times by Forbes and BusinessWeek.

A set program fee for each program in lieu of tuition and strong merit-based financial aid packages and work grants make Moore attractive to talented students. IMBA Language and Global Track program fees are $35,000 for SC residents, and $52,000 for non-resident students.

ADMISSIONS PROCESS

GMAT scores, undergraduate GPA, work experience, and essays are the most important elements of a graduate application portfolio. Depending on the competitiveness of the program to which the student is applying, the GMAT should be between 570 and 680, the TOEFL has a minimum requirement of 600 (250 CAT, 100 IB), and the undergraduate GPA should be about 3.3 or higher. Most graduate programs prefer students with two or more years work experience. The application deadlines for the IMBA are November 15 (round I) and February 15 (round II) for best consideration and financial aid.

UNIVERSITY OF SOUTHERN CALIFORNIA
Marshall School of Business

AT A GLANCE
The Marshall School of Business IBEAR MBA Program is an intensive 12-month, full-time program in international management, which gives tomorrow's business leaders the tools to excel in a fast-paced global environment. Designed for mid-career managers, it is a challenging program rooted in practical skills with many unique features not found in more conventional MBA programs.

Join a select, diverse group of mid-career managers
The IBEAR MBA attracts an extremely international and highly accomplished group of participants. Coming from as many as 16 countries and with an average of 10 years work experience, the diversity and professional achievements of the class make for lively and informed classroom discussions.

Learn from an outstanding, internationally oriented faculty in a truly internationalized MBA
The IBEAR MBA develops tools for success in global business competition. The first half of the program consists of MBA core courses similar to those found in the first year of two-year MBA programs. These core courses are taught with a strong international emphasis. During the second half of the program, IBEAR participants take globally focused electives in each critical functional area. Participants apply skills learned in these classes to a five-month international consulting project.

IBEAR courses and program enhancements emphasize business in and between Asia, North America and South America. This does not, however, exclude other regions of the world.

CAMPUS AND LOCATION
Study in the heart of Southern California's dynamic new economy and great weather. IBEAR participants benefit from USC's location in the heart of one of the world's most dynamic regional economies. Southern California and Los Angeles benefit more each year from their huge population and landmass, temperate climate, massive ports, and proximity to Asia and Latin America. Sectors of long-time strength and trade, entertainment, manufacturing, defense, aerospace, sports, fashion and product design, financial services, leisure and tourism, entrepreneurial small business are being joined by emerging new economy sectors such as multimedia, ecommerce, venture capital, biotechnology, health care, telecommunications and software development.

IBEAR MBA Admissions
3415 South Figueroa Street, DCC 115
Los Angeles, CA 90089-0872
Tel: 213-740-7140
Fax: 213-740-7559
Email: ibearmba@marshall.usc.edu

DEGREES OFFERED
Key Features of the IBEAR MBA Program include:

• One intensive year at USC in the heart of L.A.'s business, sports and cultural center. Nineteen internationalized core courses and international business electives. Learn from the Marshall School's practical international business savvy faculty.

• Earn the USC MBA degree. Ranked 9th in international business by U.S. News and World Report.

• Study with 60 select, experienced, mid-career international business focused participants with diverse backgrounds.

• Self-sponsored participants supported by Marshall's outstanding Career Resource Center, ranked in the Top 10 by Businessweek.

• Join the large, well-organized, vital USC Trojan and IBEAR family throughout the world. Life-long, world-wide.

• Experience Southern California's dynamic international business environment and great year-round weather.

PROGRAMS AND CURRICULUM
The IBEAR Transition Program emphasizes team-building and persuasive presentation skills. Participants improve their presentation graphics skills for the many professional presentations they will make during the year. Special accounting and business math workshops are required of those who need supplemental preparation. Self-sponsored participants attend career development workshops. Social activities, including a night at the Hollywood Bowl and a beach party, help participants and their families become familiar with each other.

Take advantage of the program's many special features:
• A unique, "hands-on" international business consulting project which often includes international travel for research

• Frequent luncheon roundtables with guest executives

• An action-learning team development retreat

• Enrollment in IBEAR's annual Asia/Pacific Business Outlook conference

• Optional language training in Chinese, Japanese and Spanish

• Career search support from both IBEAR and the Marshall Career Resource Center

FACILITIES
Instruction takes place in Popovich Hall, one of the most technologically advanced MBA facilities in North America. IBEAR's own state-of-art multimedia case room supports its emphasis on team-based, case-based and project-based learning. Popovich Hall's career services center includes a large research center for student use and 14 interview rooms.

EXPENSES AND FINANCIAL AID
IBEAR awards several scholarships of $10,000-$30,000 to high-potential self-sponsored applicants, both international and domestic. Hanjin Endowed Scholarship of $15,000-$25,000 is available to high-potential Korean American applicant by the Hanjin Group of Korea. In addition, a Honjo International Scholarship is awarded to an international applicant.

ADMISSIONS
Admission decisions are based on the applicant's work experience, academic background, GMAT and TOEFL test results, letters of recommendation and leadership potential as reflected in the application essays. Applicants must have completed a minimum of five years of full-time work experience prior to the start of the program. Applicants must submit proof of a four-year bachelor's degree or its equivalent from an accredited college or university. GMAT and TOEFL results are evaluated in the context of the experience, background and accomplishments of the applicant. Potential applicants are encouraged to visit the IBEAR MBA program office and also to meet with IBEAR alumni.

Applications are accepted on a rolling basis. Applicants are encouraged to open their application file early by submitting the application form and essays. Applicants should not wait for test results before they send us the application form. In accordance with our need to comply with new national visa procedures, it is strongly recommended that international applicants apply early. IBEAR communicates with applicants by e-mail, phone, fax, and air courier to ensure a swift, service oriented process.

UNIVERSITY OF TAMPA
John H. Sykes College of Business

AT A GLANCE
The John H. Sykes College of Business is accredited by AACSB International—The Association to Advance Collegiate Schools of Business. The university is also accredited by Southern Association of Colleges and Schools to award associate's, baccalaureate, and master's degrees. The university was founded in 1931 by visionary community leaders who wanted to provide the best possible educational opportunity for their community. The graduate business programs at The University of Tampa prepare students for leadership responsibilities in a technically sophisticated, diverse global environment where change rules.

FACULTY
All graduate faculty members have PhDs. More than half of our graduate faculty have won awards for teaching and professional excellence. Many of our faculty have owned their own businesses, have helped lead and build major companies, or are engaged in consulting at the highest leadership levels.

STUDENT BODY
Total number of students: 412, Percent part-time: 66, Percent full-time: 33, Percent male/female: 64/36, Percent international: 47, Average GMAT: 529, Average work experience: 5 years.

CAREER SERVICES AND PLACEMENT
The Career Services Center provides graduate students individualized attention and services including HIRE-UT Job Listing System and Resume Database, resume critique, design and referral, personal career advising, interview skills refreshers, internships, on-campus company interview opportunities, and informational interviews.

LOCATION AND ENVIRONMENT
The 100-acre University of Tampa campus offers a full-service educational setting that includes a comprehensive library, a broad range of technology and support, an active Career Services and Placement Center, and many student programs.

There is much more to Tampa's location than beautiful beaches and pleasant year-round temperatures. Tampa Bay is one of the fastest-growing areas in the U.S. and a great place to be for career building. Tampa is Florida's West Coast center for the arts, banking, real estate, law, transportation, international business, education, communications, health care, and scientific research.

MAJORS AND DEGREES OFFERED
MBA: part-time, full-time, and Saturday formats, Master of Science in Accounting (MSA), Master of Science in Finance (MS-FIN), Master of Science in Marketing (MS-MKT), Master of Science in Technology and Innovation Management (MS-TIM).

ACADEMIC PROGRAMS
MBA program elements include: Fast Start Workshop, Leadership Development Program, Integrated Core, MBA Concentrations offered in accounting, economics, entrepreneurship, finance (with a track in Investment Analysis and CFA), international business, management, management information systems, marketing and nonprofit management and innovation, Capstone Experience

Special Programs: Interaction with local community leaders and organizations is part of UT's graduate business education. The university is woven into the Tampa Bay community through internships, experiential learning opportunities, community forums, advisory boards, business outreach programs, and several centers and institutes. Among the discussion and speaker groups that meet regularly on campus are the Fellows Forum and the Business Network Symposium.

CAMPUS FACILITIES AND EQUIPMENT
The John H. Sykes College of Business is an 80,000-square-foot facility with more than 30 classrooms and faculty offices. The Macdonald-Kielce Library offers UTOPIA, an online catalog that provides Web access to library holdings and links to e-books and several databases. The Vaughn Center has multi-cuisine dining facility, Campus Store, cybercafe, game rooms, and computer labs. Housing is available for graduate students in Straz Hall and Kennedy Place.

FINANCIAL AID
Tuition for 2008-2009 is $472 per credit hour (Saturday MBA tuition is $595 per credit hour.) In addition, a $35 student services fee is required each term. The cost of books, supplies, health insurance, parking, and personal expenses is additional.

Graduate Assistantships are available each academic year to qualified full-time graduate business students. Assistantships provide tuition waiver for up to six classes per year plus a $3,000 stipend. Recipients must be full-time students and work 20 hours per week. The university offers a variety of financial aid programs. Graduate students who are not currently employed may apply for a noncredit internship with a local business.

ADMISSIONS PROCESS
Admission to UT's graduate business programs is competitive and is based on a number of factors. Application deadlines are:

Fall semester
Domestic applicants: June 1 for priority deadline or July 15 for final admission
International applicants: June 1 for final admission

Spring semester
Domestic applicants: Nov. 1 for priority deadline or Dec. 15 for final admission
International applicants: Nov. 1 for final admission

All students admitted must have earned four-year undergraduate degrees from a regionally accredited college or university. A specific undergraduate degree is not required.

The Graduate Management Admissions Test (GMAT) is required for all programs but may be waived for the Saturday MBA, MS in Finance, MS in Marketing and MS in Technology and Innovation Management programs based on a minimum GPA from an AACSB accredited four-year institution, relevant coursework and required work experience.

To be considered for graduate admissions, applicants must submit the following information: Completed application, $40 application fee, Official transcripts of all previous college work received directly from each institution, Graduate Management Admissions Test (GMAT) score report. Two professional reference forms completed by individuals that attest to the applicant's professional background and academic potential, Resume, Personal Statement , Individual interviews are recommended but required for the Saturday MBA and MS-TIM programs. International applicants only: Test of English as a Foreign Language (TOEFL) or International English Language Testing System (IELTS) score report

Applicants should submit materials to:
The University of Tampa, Graduate Studies
Box O
401 West Kennedy Boulevard
Tampa, FL 33606-1490
Telephone: 813-258-7409
Fax: 813-259-5403
E-mail: utgrad@ut.edu
Website: www.ut.edu/graduate

UNIVERSITY OF TOLEDO
College of Business Administration

AT A GLANCE

One of the best in the Midwest, the MBA program at The University of Toledo features affordability and flexibility that help you expand your skills and opportunities without interrupting your career. The college's history of excellence in practical, relevant education based on cutting-edge research and business engagement will take your career to the next level. The UT MBA curriculum is designed to equip future leaders with relevant, real-world knowledge about the workings of every level of the enterprise: employees, customers, the firm itself, and all levels of the economy.

CAREER SERVICES AND PLACEMENT

The MBA program features special opportunities and resources to enhance your education and career. Through Corporate Graduate Assistantships, highly qualified students work 15-20 hours a week at a local company while pursuing an MBA full-time. MBA students can also utilize the resources of the Business Career Programs Office, which organizes on-campus recruiting, resume reviews, walk-in advising, mock interviews, and the biannual Business Career Fair, which attracts more than 90 companies.

LOCATION AND ENVIRONMENT

The University of Toledo was established in 1872, became a member of the state university system in 1967, and merged with the former Medical University of Ohio in 2006. UT is a community built around 11 academic colleges and professional programs matched only by a handful of public universities nationwide. UT's main campus, located along the banks of the Ottawa River in a residential section of the city, includes historic buildings, modern facilities and abundant green space. The university's campus was also named one of the 100 most beautifully landscaped university campuses in the country. The College of Business has also embarked on a $13 million dollar expansion, which is slated to open in the fall of 2009.

MAJORS AND DEGREES OFFERED

The College of Business Administration offers the following degrees: BBA (12 different fields), MBA (full-time and part-time), JD/MBA Dual Degree, Executive MBA, Master of Science in Accountancy (MSA), PhD in Manufacturing and Technology Management, Post-Doctoral Bridge to Business Program

MBA Specializations are available in: Administration, Finance, Human Resources, Information Systems, International Business, Leadership, Marketing (3 tracks): CRM and Marketing Intelligence; Marketing Management; Professional Sales, Operations and Supply Chain Management, Technological Entrepreneurship.

ACADEMIC PROGRAMS

You can earn an MBA program at UT in as little as one calendar year by completing 12 courses. Since we offer all of our core courses in the fall, spring, and summer, you will find that the UT MBA program is designed specifically for your busy schedule, allowing you to take the courses you need when you want to take them. Every UT MBA student is able to customize their MBA by taking their 9 credits of electives in one specific specialization.

The Executive MBA program is designed specifically for working professionals with three to five years of experience in a managerial role. EMBA students work in a cohort and complete the program in only 15 months working in weekend residencies on Friday nights and Saturdays.

The Master of Science in Accountancy (MSA) degree program is designed to meet the needs of the professional in accounting and to qualify candidates to sit for the CPA examination in Ohio. The UT MSA degree is a 30-semester-hour program and typically includes 21 semester hours of account-

ing classes and nine semester hours of diversification electives. Every MSA applicant's background is evaluated and an individualized plan of study is developed with the program director.

We also offer a joint JD/MBA degree program in conjunction with the College of Law, consistently ranked in the top 100 programs in the country by U.S. News & World Report.

All of The University of Toledo's business degree programs can be completed without career interruption.

CAMPUS FACILITIES AND EQUIPMENT

The College of Business Administration is fully equipped to instruct students in a cutting-edge learning environment that integrates technology into the curriculum. Over 100 laptop computers are available for students to check out on a daily basis. All of our laptops have integrated wireless network access, which allows students to get online in Stranahan Hall, the college's main building. The John Neff Stock Trading Floor is one of only 30 such facilities in the country and gives students real- and delayed-access to feeds from stock exchanges around the world. The college is also breaking ground in the fall of 2007 on the $12 million Savage and Associates Complex for Business Learning and Engagement expansion.

TUITION, ROOM, BOARD AND FEES

2007—2008 Academic Year Tuition and Fees (approximate, based on 6 credits per term)

Ohio residents: $5,000

Nonresidents: $10,000

Please visit the Bursar's Office webpage at http://bursarsoffice.utoledo.edu for the most current information on tuition and fees. Merit-based scholarships, Federal Stafford Loans, and private educational loans and graduate assistantships are available to eligible students.

Graduate students who are regularly admitted to a degree program from Hillsdale, Lenawee, Macomb, Monroe, Oakland, Washtenaw, and Wayne Counties in Michigan are eligible for the Michigan In-State Tuition Initiative, which allows students with permanent residency in those counties to attend UT at the in-state tuition rate.

ADMISSIONS PROCESS

Admission to the MBA and MSA programs takes place in all three semesters: fall (August), spring (January), and summer (May).

We encourage prospective students to apply online. The Admissions Committee requires the following documents in order to evaluate an application:

- Application for admission
- Application fee
- Three letters of recommendation
- One official transcript from each university attended
- Official GMAT results
- Official TOEFL results (if necessary)

Applicants are encouraged to apply as early as possible to ensure that their applications are processed and that they can be admitted for the term they want.

Since the Executive MBA is a cohort-based program, applicants can only enter the program in August of each calendar year. Applications are considered on a space-available basis.

UNIVERSITY OF TORONTO
The Rotman School

AT A GLANCE

The Rotman School has set out to redesign business education for the 21st century and become one of the world's top-tier business schools. The School is developing an innovative curriculum built around Integrative ThinkingTM and Business DesignTM.

Earning an MBA gives you the opportunity to compete for jobs at the highest level, in a wide range of industries. Rotman is proud to say:

93% of students seeking employment where employed within 3 months after graduation.

92% of students seeking employment had jobs in the summer of 2007.

FACULTY

The Rotman faculty - 67 per cent of which is international — is currently ranked #18 in the world by the Financial Times for its research output. Our Finance department is ranked #6 in the world.

STUDENTS

The Rotman School deliberately seeks out students who have done interesting things with their lives since completing their undergraduate education. They have worked in the real world for an average of five years, traveled, and sought out experiences that make for an incredibly dynamic class.

LOCATION AND ENVIRONMENT

The Rotman School has the distinct advantage of being located in the heart of downtown Toronto, North America's third-largest financial centre.

105 St. George St.
Toronto, ON
M5S 3E6

OFF-CAMPUS OPPORTUNITIES

The Rotman School presents its students with many opportunities to maximize the international dimension of their MBA education. In their second year, students have the opportunity to participate in the MBA International Exchange Program for one full term.

Study Tours: The International Study Tours are designed to provide students with the opportunity to understand the opportunities and risks associated with the emergence of important markets in the world economy.

International Exchange Program: The International Exchange Program at the Rotman School provides a unique opportunity for MBA students to immerse themselves in a new academic and social culture, and to enhance their ability to think and learn in a multicultural and international business environment.

MAJORS AND DEGREES OFFERED

The Rotman School offers a suite of world-class management programs:

The Rotman MBA is available in two-year and three-year formats:

One-Year MBA for Executives: Master of Finance, Omnium Global Executive MBA, Rotman PhD

The Rotman School also offers combined MBA degrees with The Faculty of Law (JD/MBA), and The Faculty of Applied Science and Engineering (Jeffrey Skoll BASc/MBA)

ACADEMIC PROGRAMS

In the competitive field of MBA education, we provide you with a solid grounding in the business fundamentals, including marketing, strategy, finance, accounting and organizational behaviour, but we also teach you to go beyond these traditional 'silos' to see how they interrelate to form the big picture

Two-Year MBA: Before you are immersed in our intense program, we provide you with some introductory information and learning. The Pre-MBA Program, which features pre-courses and workshops. The complete program includes: international student orientation, a welcome event, pre-courses in Accounting, Finance and Quantitative Methods, and professional skills workshops.

The first year is divided into four quarters, lasting seven weeks. Working in a small study group of four or five students, you will be exposed to a new way of thinking about management and business, and develop your knowledge, your critical faculties and your practical skills.

Second year is divided into three terms: fall, winter intensive, and spring. In order to complete the two-year MBA program, you must complete ten elective-year courses in total (five per term).

Three-Year Morning MBA: The majority of the core courses are offered on Tuesday and Thursday mornings, from 7 to 8:59 am. Students are also required to complete three one-week-long sessions at various points in the first two years of study. Electives, offered in the second and third year, may be taken in the morning or any time in the afternoon and evening (depending on availability).

Three-Year Evening MBA: You will take a combination of required courses and electives in the Three-Year Evening MBA program, which comprises nine terms. Courses usually take place two nights per week, for nine successive terms. Students must own a laptop computer that meets Rotman specifications.

Master of Finance: The Master of Finance program provides students with the best theoretical and applied finance training currently available in the world. The program offers a mix of theoretical and applied courses at the highest academic and professional levels, with content that goes significantly deeper and broader than that offered by an undergraduate commerce degree, a CFA, or any other professional program.

MFin classes are scheduled one evening per week plus every other Saturday. The program lasts for 20 months, with no classes in August or over the School's two-week December break.

FINANCIAL AID

Each year, the Rotman School grants approximately $3.7 million in entrance scholarships, fellowships and awards to about 15 per cent of our students. These are offered on the basis of exceptional merit.

Financial Aid Options: Scotia Professional Student Plan (SPSP, Rotman Interest Subsidy Program (RISP), Employment Opportunities, Teaching and Research Assistantships, Rotman Scholar Awards

Summer Employment: Over 90 per cent of Rotman students find employment during the summer, with internships usually running from May to August, midway through the two-year MBA program.

ADMISSIONS PROCESS

The following criteria are used in assessing application. Your application file should include:

- The formal application form
- The application fee of $150 CAD
- Original transcripts of all post-secondary academic programs attended
- Completed essays
- Original GMAT score report
- Two professional reference letters
- English facility test score reports, if applicable
- Interview in person or by telephone by invitation of the Admissions Committee

VANDERBILT UNIVERSITY
Owen Graduate School of Management

AT A GLANCE

The Vanderbilt MBA is a rigorous, yet intimate and collaborative educational experience, in which all members of the community are encouraged and empowered to fulfill their potential.

- With an average of 175-200 students in each class and a faculty-to-student ratio of 10:1, students have opportunity to interact and engage with each other and with faculty.

- Approximately 25% of Owen students come from outside of the United States, with domestic students coming from the West Coast, New England and all points in between.

- The Vanderbilt MBA program is noted for its academic rigor and has recognized strengths in Finance, Health Care, Human and Organizational Performance and Marketing.

- The Leadership Development Program provides all students with an opportunity to examine and explore their unique leadership capabilities. The first year of the program includes a personal assessment, peer feedback and coaching.

- The quality of life is excellent at Vanderbilt. The faculties are well-designed and tech-savvy, set on Vanderbilt's beautiful, historic campus in Nashville-a vibrant, friendly city that was named the nation's #1 Smartest Place to Live by Kiplingers.

FACULTY

Owen faculty is comprised of the finest scholars, researchers, teachers and practitioners. They infused the classroom with academic research and professional experience to create a cutting-edge and relevant educational experience.

STUDENTS

Recruiters love Owen graduates. In addition to academic qualifications, they bring to the table the desire to make an impact, the drive to work hard, and the ability to both lead and be a strong contributor to a team. While here, students are empowered and encouraged to improve the community and the Owen experience for those who follow. Student-driven initiatives include the founding of owenbloggers.com, the hosting of the national Net Impact conference, Project Pyramid and the Human Capital Case Competition.

CAREER SERVICES AND PLACEMENT

Throughout the Owen experience, the Career Management Center (CMC) acts as a personal team of career coaches. They offer a weekly newsletter, one-on-one counseling sessions, career skills workshops, industry-related seminars, company information sessions, on-campus interviews, recruiter feedback, networking trips and off-campus career consortia. Students receive individual assistance in defining career goals, executing career search strategies and negotiating job offers.

LOCATION AND ENVIRONMENT

Recently selected by Newsweek as a "New Ivy League" school, Vanderbilt has a strong faculty of more than 1,800 full-time members and a diverse student body of about 10,000. The 330-acre campus is less than two miles from Nashville's downtown business district, combining the advantages of an urban location with a peaceful, park-like setting of broad lawns, shaded paths, and quiet plazas.

MAJORS AND DEGREES OFFERED

Vanderbilt offers several degree and non-degree programs, including an MBA, a health care MBA and an Executive MBA, a MS Finance and a Master of Accountancy. There are also dual-degree programs, the most common being a JD/MBA and an MD/MBA.

ACADEMIC PROGRAMS

The Vanderbilt MBA is constructed around a robust foundation of general management skills and market-driven Specializations, Concentrations and Emphases. The seven-week "mod"-modular— calendar promotes accelerated learning and opportunities for unique immersion experiences.

- Current career Specializations include Health Care, Corporate Finance, Investment Management, Brand Management, , Human Capital, and Operations;

- Concentrations include Accounting, Finance, General Management, Human and Organizational Performance, Information Technology, Marketing, Operations and Strategy;

- Emphases include Real Estate Finance and Entrepreneurship.

In addition, Owen students have the opportunity to take classes for credit at Vanderbilt's other top-ranked professional schools such as Divinity, Education, Engineering, Nursing and Law.

In addition to a highly-regarded Leadership Development Program, the program requires and encourages study in ethics, the global perspective and community service.

CAMPUS FACILITIES AND EQUIPMENT

All incoming students are required to have a laptop computer with wireless capabilities. The computer network, including extensive electronic resources in the school's award-winning Walker Management Library, is accessible throughout the building, in the courtyard and from the Starbuck across the street.

FINANCIAL AID

All admitted applicants are considered for merit-based scholarships, which range from $4,000 per year to full tuition and the prestigious Dean's Scholar award that includes an additional $5,000 per year stipend.

ADMISSIONS PROCESS

The Admissions Committee evaluates applicants on the basis of academic ability, professional experience, personal qualities, and leadership potential. In recent years, applicants offered admission to the Vanderbilt MBA program average a 3.3 GPA, 650 GMAT, 630 TOEFL and five years of post-baccalaureate work experience.

Prospective students who are visiting campus may schedule either an informative or evaluative interview with an admissions officer regardless of their status in the admissions process. Otherwise, candidates must submit a completed application before being invited to schedule an interview, which may be conducted in person or by telephone. Both options are given equal consideration in the evaluation process, but a campus visit is strongly recommended whenever possible.

Demonstrated achievement in academic, professional and community activities; well-defined career goals; interpersonal skills; professional presence; maturity and sound judgment; critical thinking and analytical skills; initiative and motivation; team skills; knowledge of and interest in the Vanderbilt MBA program.

Appropriate business attire is recommended, unless specified otherwise. Please bring a copy of your current resume to the interview.

http://mba.vanderbilt.edu/admissions

VIRGINIA COMMONWEALTH UNIVERSITY
School of Business

AT A GLANCE

Located on two downtown campuses in Richmond, Virginia, Virginia Commonwealth University ranks among the top 100 universities in the country in sponsored research and enrolls 30,000 students in more than 195 certificate, undergraduate, graduate, professional, and doctoral programs in 15 schools and one liberal arts college. The School of Business is located on VCU's main academic campus in Richmond's historic Fan District. It employs 100 full-time faulty and enrolls more than 2,100 undergraduate and 480 graduate students. Students receive instruction primarily from graduate faculty, over 95 percent of whom hold a doctorate or equivalent professional degree. The School of Business is accredited by the AACSB—The International Association for Management Education. The VCU School of Business is an integral part of the Richmond business community. Students regularly participate in local internships and workshops, and are heavily recruited by local companies.

FACULTY

The School of Business has 102 full-time faculty members. Many faculty have been recognized nationally for their teaching effectiveness, research contributions, and service to professional organizations. Faculty members are best known for their contributions in information systems, organizational behavior, financial research, global marketing management, and international business activities.

STUDENT BODY

Approximately 500 students are currently enrolled in the master's and doctoral programs of VCU's School of Business. Seventy-two percent of our master's students are fully employed in the greater Richmond area and study on a part-time basis. Women make up 40 percent of the graduate student population, and students have an average of six years of work experience beyond their undergraduate degrees.

CAREER SERVICES AND PLACEMENT

Students have access to a career counselor throughout their program. The Career Center maintains an active job bank and assists students in resume and interview preparation

LOCATION AND ENVIRONMENT

Richmond, the capital of Virginia, is a diverse cultural city, surrounded by historic neighborhoods, parks, and a thriving James River. The city consistently ranks among "Best Places to Live and Work in America" in several national publications.

MAJORS AND DEGREES OFFERED

Master of Business Administration

Master of Science in Business with the following concentrations: Finance, Decision Sciences, Global Marketing Management, Human Resource Management and Industrial Relations, Real Estate Valuation, Master of Accountancy, Master of Arts in Economics, Master of Science in Information Systems, Master of Taxation, Dual Degrees, MBA/PharmD, MBA/MSIS

Doctor of Philosophy in Business with the following concentrations: Information Systems, Accounting, Management

ACADEMIC PROGRAMS

The Master of Business Administration (MBA) focuses on the development of functions and techniques of management, as well as an understanding of environmental and economic forces that influence administration and decision making. Students may choose to concentration in a particular area or complete a general concentration.

The Master of Science in Business programs focus on a particular discipline. Most require four foundation courses and ten advanced courses.

The Master of Accountancy degree was revised in the spring of 2000 to address a requirement that future candidates for the CPA exam must have completed at least 150 credit hours of college study to be eligible to sit for the examination. Most undergraduates complete 120 credit hours, so students intending to take the CPA examination are encouraged to consider earning the additional credit hours of study in the integrated Master of Accountancy program.

The Master of Taxation program includes a comprehensive study of tax laws and regulations, administrative practice and procedure, and tax research fundamentals, and is designed to develop both technical knowledge and conceptual understanding within the field of taxation. Ethical considerations are stressed within the framework of individual courses.

The Master of Science program in Information Systems is designed to prepare students for specialized roles in information systems. The MS program is offered in both the traditional semester format, and in an executive (alternate weekend) format. The executive program (Fast Track Executive MS in IS) focuses on Information Technology Management and is designed for students with six or more years professional experience.

Graduates of the Master of Arts in Economics will have the knowledge and experience to qualify for a wide and rapidly expanding range of analyst positions in the private or public sectors.

SPECIAL PROGRAMS

The School of Business boasts a very active advisory board of more than 65 senior executive officers of national and international companies; many of them based in Richmond, Virginia. Members of the Business Council serve as advisors on curricula and other school activities. Relationships developed through the Business Council serve as a pathway to business by providing more than 150 internship opportunities annually to students in School of Business programs.

The Alumni Council, the leadership group for the school's 14,000 alumni, provides advice and assistance for various activities throughout the year. The Alumni Council sponsors special events, education series, and recruitment activities for School of Business students annually.

CAMPUS FACILITIES AND EQUIPMENT

The School of Business is currently housed in the VCU Business Building, a facility that offers state-of-the-art technology classrooms, computer facilities, and team meeting rooms. University Library Services administers the James Branch Cabell and Tompkins-McCaw research libraries on both campuses and provides numerous electronic resources, federal and state documents, patents, and a wide variety of microform and media resources.

TUITION, ROOM, BOARD AND FEES

For the 2006–2007 academic year, in-state tuition and fees for full-time students were $4,170.50 per semester. Out-of-state tuition and fees for full-time students totaled $8,791 per semester. In-state tuition rates for part-time students were set at $435.35 per credit hour. Out-of-state part-time students paid $947.50 per credit hour. A limited number of master's assistantships are available through the Graduate Studies in Business office for full-time master's-level students with exemplary academic credentials. Endowed scholarships are also available through GSIB on an annual basis.

ADMISSIONS PROCESS

Applicants to graduate programs in the VCU School of Business must submit the following: Application for admission and fee, Two copies of official transcripts from each university or college attended, Three letters of recommendation, A current resume, A personal statement, A current GMAT score (except MA in Economics which requires the GRE)

Application procedures vary slightly by degree program.

WILLAMETTE UNIVERSITY
Atkinson Graduate School of Management

AT A GLANCE

Willamette offers a selection of MBA programs designed to meet your goals. Programs include the Early Career MBA for students seeking their first professional position or career change, and the MBA for Professionals for experienced working individuals.

All Willamette MBA programs emphasize hands-on learning and develop the knowledge, professional resume and interpersonal skills sought by employers. In addition, all Willamette MBA programs are accredited by AACSB International - the global hallmark of excellence in business education.

The Early Career MBA:

As a leader in early career MBA education, Willamette's full-time Early Career MBA is specifically designed to prepare students for their first professional position or career change. In just 21 months, students learn the core principles of management, refine their career interests, develop an in-depth understanding of one or more areas of interest, and build the portfolio needed to succeed in a competitive job market.

Elective areas of interest include accounting, finance, general management, human resources, information systems, international management, marketing, organizational analysis, public management, and quantitative analysis/management science.

The distinct design of Willamette's Early Career MBA makes it an excellent choice for students seeking an MBA directly after completion of their bachelor degree or after one or more years of work experience.

The MBA for Professionals:

Willamette's MBA for Professionals provides individuals with three or more years of work experience the opportunity to complete their MBA while employed. The program offers the rare combination of a quality AACSB International accredited MBA, experiential learning and convenient evening classes.

The MBA for Professionals can be completed in 24 months of evening study. The program is cohort based and taught in Portland and Salem.

FACULTY

Faculty are excellent teachers who are committed to their students and to the educational model of "learning by doing." They are easily accessible to students and alumni. They are also leaders of community and professional organizations; award winning teachers and researchers; authors of books, articles, and software; editors and reviewers of professional journals; entrepreneurs; and consultants. They make Willamette an exciting place to learn.

STUDENTS

Student Body - Early Career MBA

Early Career M.B.A. students are full-time students who come from around the world and across the U.S. to prepare for their first professional position or career change. The average student is 25 years of age and has zero to three years of full-time work experience. Words used to describe our students by their references include: energetic, creative, ethical, exceptional, friendly, mature, hard working, insightful, professional, reliable, respected, team players and leaders.

Student Body - MBA for Professionals

MBA for Professionals students have three or more years of work experience and are preparing for career advancement and enhancement. The average student is 33 years of age and employed while completing their MBA. Students represent a wide variety of organizations from the Port-

land and Salem metropolitan areas (business, consulting, entrepreneurial ventures, government, not-for-profits).

CAREER SERVICES AND PLACEMENT

Career services include an organized program of the best practices of career management, workshops, internship programs, on-campus interviews, employment postings, databases, individual counseling, mentoring programs, career/networking fairs, peer advisors and student professional organizations.

89% of Early Career students who graduated in 2007 received a job offer within three months of graduation. Typical employers includes Nautilus, IBM, Mentor Graphics, KPMG, Hewlett Packard Company, Key Bank, Intel Corporation, Tektronix and Providence Health Systems.

Nearly 100% of Early Career students participate in an internship. A sample of internship employers includes Columbia Sportswear, ESCO, Flir Systems, Hewlett Packard, Merrill Lynch, Microsoft, Morgan Stanley, Nike, Oregon Zoo, Saber Consulting, T-Mobile, Tektronix, U.S. State Department and State of Oregon.

LOCATION AND ENVIRONMENT

Willamette University is located in Salem, Oregon and has a Portland Center in the Pearl District of Portland, Oregon. Our location offers an excellent quality of life, friendly people, mild climate and the recreational resources of the beautiful Pacific Northwest. Professionally, the Portland-Salem area provides convenient access to a multitude of businesses (including Northwest legends Nike, Intel, and Tektronix) and hosts a variety of government and not-for-profit organizations.

MAJORS AND DEGREES OFFERED

Willamette offers a Master of Business Administration degree accredited by AACSB International. Degree formats include 1) the full-time Early Career MBA for students seeking their first professional position or career change, and 2) the evening MBA for Professionals program for working individuals with three or more years of work experience.

ACADEMIC PROGRAMS

• Early Career MBA - 21 month full-time program that builds the knowledge and experience needed for career entry or career change. Areas of interest include: Accounting, Finance, Human Resources, International Management, Marketing, Organizational Analysis, Public Management, and Quantitative Analysis.

• Accelerated MBA: 12 to 15 month program for students seeking career change or advancement who have strong knowledge of business and professional experience. Accelerated students focus their studies in the elective courses of the Early Career MBA program.

• MBA/JD: four year joint degree that combines Willamette's Early Career MBA and Doctor of Jurisprudence programs.

• MBA for Professionals: 24 month program for working individuals with three or more years of experience who want to complete their MBA while employed. Students develop an enterprise wide view of management and immediately apply what they learn to their work place.

SPECIAL PROGRAMS

The Early Career MBA includes features that powerfully enhance the professional experience of students. These programs include: PACE Consulting and Business Plan, Career Roadmap, Oregon Ethics in Business Awards, Integrated Knowledge Exercise Weeks, New Ventures to Market, Student Investment Fund, Atkinson Management Today, and international exchange programs with Bordeaux Business School and Copenhagen Business School.

WRIGHT STATE UNIVERSITY
Raj Soin College of Business

AT A GLANCE
With an enrollment of over 450 graduate students and 1,200 undergraduate students, we offer the benefits of a comprehensive business program and diverse student body. At the same time our small class sizes and highly engaged faculty offer the mentoring and leadership development MBA students need to advance their careers.

FACULTY
Because the College of Business is accredited by AACSB International, our faculty meet the highest standards in teaching, research and professional qualifications. The College prides itself in using only professionally qualified full-time and part-time faculty. None of our classes are taught by teaching assistants. 76 full-time faculty. Average class size of 35 students. Meet our faculty at www.wright.edu/business/facstaff/

Our MBA advising staff is available by phone, email or in-person at your convenience at 937-775-2437 or rscob-admin@wright.edu

CAREER SERVICES AND PLACEMENT
Comprehensive Career Services include internship programs, career development, networking events, recruiting and hiring services for students, alumni and employers. Customized to your personal career goals and employers' talent acquisition needs www.wright.edu/business/careers/

LOCATION AND ENVIRONMENT
An exciting community of nearly 17,000 students, Wright State University is located near Dayton, Ohio and Wright Patterson Air Force Base. In addition, the College of Business offers its weekend MBA program in south Dayton and northern Cincinnati and at the Lake Campus in Celina, Ohio.

MAJORS AND DEGREES OFFERED
Our MBA offers an integrated and in-depth curriculum that develops each student's strategic decision-making, analytical thinking and leadership skills. Because every student is at a different stage in their careers and personal life, we offer three convenient options for completing your MBA degree: part-time evenings, part-time weekends or full-time day classes.

Regardless of which location or time you chose, you will experience the same high quality faculty and curriculum. The MBA curriculum consists of (1) Strategic Cost Management (2) Analysis of Global Economic Conditions (3) Financial Analysis and Decision Making (4) Legal and Ethical Decision Making (5) Leading Teams and Organizations (6) Marketing Strategy (7) Information Technology and Business Transformation (8) Supply Chain Management (9) a capstone course, Developing and Implementing Competitive Strategies. Students also chose three electives from concentrations in Finance; International Business; Management Innovation and Change; Marketing; Project Management or Interdisciplinary Business.

Additionally for students who do not have an undergraduate degree in business or need to refresh their coursework, four foundation courses are offered including Survey of Accounting, Survey of Economics, Survey of Finance, Survey of Quantitative Business Analysis.

Chose the location and time most convenient for you:

- Evening program on Main Campus Apply any quarter. Complete the program at your own pace.

- Weekends in south Dayton or northern Cincinnati. Meet Friday evenings and Saturday mornings. Complete the program in eight quarters with the same group. Apply three months in advance.

- Full-time program. Day and evening classes on Main Campus. Apply by March 31. Begin each fall.

The College also offers joint MBA degrees in medicine and nursing plus a health care certificate leading to an MBA. Four additional masters degrees in accountancy, information systems, logistics and economics are also offered www.wright.edu/coba/grad/

ACADEMIC PROGRAMS
Study Abroad - Students can pursue both long and short term study abroad courses in over 30 countries. Faculty regularly lead two or three week study abroad courses in a variety of countries.

SPECIAL PROGRAMS
The College of Business is known for its strong linkages with the business community. See examples of how our teaching and research missions are enhanced www.wright.edu/business/biscom/

CAMPUS FACILITIES AND EQUIPMENT
Main Campus courses are offered in Rike Hall, a newly renovated building which offers state-of-the-art wireless technology, computer labs, electronic classrooms. Our Soin Trading Center has been recognized as one of the top ten academic financial trading centers in the nation by BusinessWeek Online.

Computer labs and wireless access are available campus-wide. A full-range of business and government resources and databases can be accessed online through the The Paul Lawrence Dunbar Library with more than 140 research databases, 5,700 electronic journals, and 22,000 e-books.

TUITION, ROOM, BOARD AND FEES
Tuition: In-state $310 per credit. Out-of-state $527 per credit hour. MBA required credits range from 48 hours with an undergraduate degree in busines to 64 credit hours if the MBA student does not have prior undergraduate courses in business. See www.wright.edu/admissions/fees3.html.

Raj Soin College of Business awards tuition scholarships and graduate assistantships. Apply by March 31 for the following fall term. Each academic department also awards annual scholarships. Apply by March 1. A listing is on line at www.wright.edu/rscob/about/scholarship_project.htm

In addition, the Office of Financial Aid http://www.wright.edu/admissions/finaid/ and Office of Veterans Affairs http://www.wright.edu/admissions/va/ offer financial aid to students.

ADMISSIONS PROCESS
Admission to the MBA program is based on a combination of the candidate's undergraduate GPA and their GMAT score. Details at www.wright.edu/coba/grad/

DECODING DEGREES

Many business programs offer a number of degrees, including joint- or combined-degree programs with other departments (or with other schools) that you can earn along with your MBA. You'll find the abbreviations for these degrees in the individual school profiles, but we thought we'd give you a little help in figuring out exactly what they are.

AGSIM	American Graduate School of International Management Social Service Administration		MA	Master of Arts
			MAB	Master of Agribusiness
APC	Advanced Professional Certificate		MAcc	Master of Accountancy (or Accounting)
BA	Bachelor of Arts		MAAE	Master of Arts in Applied Economics
BASC	Bachelor in Engineering		MAEcon	Master of Arts in Economics
BBA	Bachelor of Business Administration		MAg	Master of Agriculture
BPA	Bachelor of Public Affairs		MAIB	Master of Arts in International Business
BS	Bachelor of Science		MAIS	Master of Accounting and Information Systems
BSB	Bachelor of Science in Business			
BSBA	Bachelor of Science in Business Administration		MALL	Master of Arts in Language Learning
			MAPS	Master of Asian Pacific Studies
CIS	Computer Information Systems (or Sciences)		MAR	Master of Arts in Religion
			MArch	Master of Architecture
DBA	Doctor of Business Administration		MAS	Master of Actuarial Science
DDS	Doctor of Dental Surgery		MBA	Master of Business Administration
DMD	Doctor of Dental Medicine		MBE	Master of Business Education
DO	Doctor of Osteopathic Medicine		MBI	Master of Business Informatics
DPS	Doctor of Professional Studies		MBS	Master of Business Studies
EdD	Doctor of Education		MD	Doctor of Medicine
EDM	Executive Doctor of Management		MDIV	Master of Divinity
EMBA	Executive MBA		ME	Master of Engineering
EMIB	Executive Master of International Business		MECOM	Master of Electronic Commerce
EMPA	Executive Master of Public Administration		MEd	Master of Educational Leadership/ Master of Education
EMS	Executive Master of Science			
EMSM	Executive Master of Science in Management		MEM	Master of Engineering and Management
			MEng	Master of Engineering
EMSMOT	Executive Master of Science in Management of Technology		MF	Master of Forestry
			MFA	Master of Fine Arts
EMST	Executive Master of Science in Taxation		MHA	Master of Health Administration
GDPA	Graduate Diploma in Accounting		MHR	Master of Human Resources
GEMBA	Global Executive Master of Business Administration		MHRM	Master of Human Resources Management
HRIM	Hotel, Restaurants and Institutional Management		MIA	Master of International Affairs
			MIAS	Master of International and Area Studies
IAMBA	Information Age Master of Business Administration		MIB	Master of International Business
			MIE	Master of Industrial Engineering
IMBA	International MBA		MILR	Master of Industrial and Labor Relations
IPD	Interdisciplinary Product Development		MIM	Master of International Management
JD	Juris Doctorate		MIS	Management Information Systems
LLB	Bachelor of Law			

MISM	Master of Information Systems Management
MLAS	Master of Liberal Arts and Science
MMIS	Master of Management Information Systems
MMR	Master of Marketing Research
MMS	Master of Management Science
MNO	Master of Nonprofit Organizations
MOD	Master of Science in Organizational Development
MPA	Master of Public Administration
MPAcc	Master of Professional Accounting
MPH	Master of Public Health
MPIA Affairs	Master of Public and International
MPL	Master of Planning
MPP	Master of Public Policy
MRED	Master of Real Estate Development
MS	Master of Science
MSA	Master of Science in Accountancy (or Accounting)
MSAIS	Master of Science in Accounting Information Systems
MSAT	Master of Science in Accountancy, Taxation
MSB	Master of Science in Business
MSBA	Master of Science in Business Administration
MSE	Master of Science in Engineering
MSEC	Master of Science in Electronic Commerce
MSF	Master of Science in Finance
MSFA	Master of Science in Financial Analysis
MSFS	Master of Science in Foreign Services
MSG	Master of Science in Gerontology
MSGFA	Master of Science in Global Financial Analysis
MSHA	Master of Science in Health Administration
MSHFID	Master of Science in Human Factors in Information Design
MSIAM	Master of Science in Information Age Marketing
MSIB Business	Master of Science in International
MSIE	Master of Science in Industrial Engineering
MSIM	Master of Science in Industrial Management
MSIMC	Master of Science in Integrated Marketing Communications
MSIR	Master of Science in Industrial Relations
MSIS	Master of Science in Information Systems
MSISE	Master of Science in Industrial and Systems Engineering
MSISM	Master of Science in Information Systems Management
MSIT	Master of Science in Information Technology
MSITM	Master of Science in Information Technology Management
MSM	Master of Science in Management
MSMIS	Master of Science in Management Information Systems
MSMOT	Master of Science in Management of Technology
MSN	Master of Science in Nursing
MSOD	Master of Science in Organization Development
MSpAd	Master of Sports Administration
MSRE	Master of Science in Real Estate
MSS	Master of Social Science
MSSA	Master of Science in Social Administration
MST	Master of Science in Taxation
MSTM	Master of Science in Telecommunications Management
MSW	Master of Social Work
MTAX	Master of Taxation
MTLM	Master of Transportation and Logistics Management
NEMBA	National Executive Master of Business Administration
PharmD	Doctor of Pharmacy
PhD	Doctor of Philosophy
SM	Master of Science
TSM	Telecommunications Systems Management
VMD	Doctor of Veterinary Medicine

INDEX

ALPHABETICAL INDEX

W

X

Y

INDEX BY LOCATION

INDEX BY COST

ABOUT THE AUTHOR

Nedda Gilbert is a graduate of the University of Pennsylvania and holds a master's degree from Columbia University. She has worked for The Princeton Review since 1985. In 1987, she created The Princeton Review corporate test preparation service, which provides Wall Street firms and premier companies tailored educational programs for their employees. She currently resides in New Jersey.

NOTES

NOTES

NOTES

NOTES

Paying For Graduate School 101

You've been to college. You've got the degree (and the student loans) to show for it. So you might be thinking, "Hey, I did this once, do I really need to go over it all again?" In a word, yes.

You're not going to grad school to study the exact same things you've already spent four years learning, are you? So why assume that you don't need to learn anything new about paying for grad school?

While you might understand the basics about how federal loans work and how scholarships, grants, and fellowships can reduce the final bill, there are lesser-known and fairly new options out there. After all, laying down $100,000—possibly more—in loans, cash, and other funds in exchange for a top-notch education requires just as much research and planning as deciding which school gets all that dough!

The good news is that you still have a little time before you have to really worry about signing on the dotted line for any type of financial assistance. Take a moment right now and let us show you what it takes to afford an excellent postgraduate education.

YOU'RE NOT AN UNDERGRAD ANYMORE...

Graduate school is not College 2.0. Not only are you not going to be studying the same things this time around, but your circumstances aren't the same either. Maybe you're coming back to school after a few years in the professional world, maybe you've got a family now, maybe you want a higher degree to give you an edge over others in your field. Whatever the changes, you're going to have to take them into account when considering how to pay for school and when applying for financial aid.

One important difference to keep in mind is that this time, at least with respect to government-sponsored loans, you'll be considered independent. Lenders will not take into account your parents' income and assets—just yours. Your credit history will also be important. When you started college as an undergrad, you probably had little or no credit history to speak of. By now, however, you've no doubt accumulated some, most likely through your undergraduate student loans and/or some high-interest credit card debt. If your credit history is less than positive, lenders may require you to have a co-signer.

More Grad School Tips from The Princeton Review
Graduate School Companion

If you have no credit history or a creditworthy co-borrower, you should consider Preprime™: an underwriting methodology pioneered by MyRichUncle. It takes into account your academic performance and student behavior to see if you will be a responsible borrower. www.myrichuncle.com/ PreprimeLoans.aspx